W9-AMP-401

Characters in YOUNG ADULT LITERATURE

Characters in YOUNG ADULT LITERATURE

WITHDRAWN
FROM THE
CARL B. YLVISAKER LIBRARY
Concordia College, Moorhead, MN

John T. Gillespie • Corinne J. Naden

DETROIT • NEW YORK • TORONTO • LONDON

CURR PROF 809.3 G478c
Gillespie, John Thomas
Characters in young adult
literature

Gale Research Staff

Kevin S. Hile, *Senior Editor*
Joyce Nakamura, *Managing Editor*

Copyeditors: Diane Andreassi, Laurie Hillstrom, Marijke Rijsberman, Doug Smith, and Michaela Swart Wilson
Proofreaders: Sharon R. Gunton, Janet L. Hile, Melissa Hill, Motoko Fujishiro Huthwaite, and Crystal Towns

Mary Beth Trimper, *Production Director*
Evi Seoud, *Assistant Production Manager*
Shanna Heilveil, *Production Assistant*
Susan M. Trosky, *Permissions Manager*
Maria L. Franklin, *Permissions Specialist*
Michele Lonoconus, *Permissions Associate*
Cynthia Baldwin, *Product Design Manager*
Tracey Rowens, *Senior Art Director*
Randy Bassett, *Image Database Supervisor*
Mikal Ansari and Robert Duncan, *Imaging Specialists*

This publication is a creative work copyrighted by Gale Research and fully protected by all applicable copyright laws, as well as by misappropriation, trade secret, unfair competition, and other applicable laws. The author and editor of this work have added value to the underlying factual material herein through one or more of the following: unique and original selection, coordination, expression, arrangement, and classification of the information.

All rights to this publication will be vigorously defended.

Copyright ©1997
Gale Research
645 Griswold St.
835 Penobscot Bldg.
Detroit, MI 48226-4094

All rights reserved, including the right of reproduction in whole or in part in any form.

∞™ This book is printed on acid-free paper that meets the minimum requirements of American National Standard for Information Services—Permanence Paper for Printed Library Materials, ANSI Z39.48-1984.

Library of Congress Cataloging-in-Publication Data

Gillespie, John Thomas. 1928-
Characters in young adult literature / John T. Gillespie, Corinne J. Naden
p. cm.
Includes bibliographical references and index.
ISBN 0-7876-0401-1 (alk. paper)
1. Young adult literature—Stories, plots, etc. 2. Characters and characteristics in literature. 3. Young adult literature—Book reviews. 4. Youth—Books and reading. I. Naden, Corinne J. II. Title.
Z1037.A1G47 1997
[PN1009.A1]
809.3'00835—dc21 97-4998
CIP

#36246090

10 9 8 7 6 5 4 3 2 1
Printed in the United States of America

Contents

Preface

Introduction

In the lengthy history of publishing, the emergence of a distinctive body of literature suitable for adolescents is a relatively recent development. It was only after World War II that educators, parents, and publishers began to realize that readers from roughly twelve to eighteen years of age had distinctive needs and tastes in literature. Young adults required their own unique literary genre.

With the publication of such ground-breaking books as S. E. Hinton's *The Outsiders* and Paul Zindel's *The Pigman* in the late 1960s, the development of this new literary form gained momentum. Although young adults continued to read both the classics and other books originally intended for adults, they gravitated to this new literary form that addressed their individual reading needs.

It is the purpose of this book to survey the entire field of young adult literature by outlining the plots and delineating the important characters in a representative group of novels that are significant in the development of literature suitable for young adults. *Characters in Young Adult Literature* (*CYAL*) is intended for use by both professionals and students alike. It has therefore been written with both of these audiences in mind.

Scope of This Work

CYAL is aimed primarily at teachers and librarians who work with young adults, as well as at teenage audiences themselves. It includes discussions of over 2,000 characters from 232 literary works for children by 148 authors. The authors represented here are primarily from English-speaking nations, although some authors from other countries whose books have been translated into English are also contained within these pages. Over 70 illustrations from books and film adaptations have also been included in *CYAL*.

Literary works to be included in *CYAL* were selected without regard for dates of publication. Thus, this book represents a broad history of the genre, from Daniel Defoe's *Robinson Crusoe* to Francesca Lia Block's *Baby Be-Bop*. After the initial selection list was compiled, the books were then ranked by an advisory board according to four categories: 1. Quality (excellence in writing), 2. Significance (books of historical importance), 3. Suitability (appropriateness in age and interest levels, and 4. Popularity. Although popularity was considered an important criterion, the first three categories were weighed somewhat more heavily so that the final list would not be filled with books of passing importance. The lists were then tabulated, and the top books selected to provide a balance of 50% young adult books, 25% literary classics, and 25% adult books often read by teenage audiences.

Advisory Board

The final list of authors and works for *CYAL* was compiled with the indispensable advice of a national advisory board, the members of which are listed below. Their understanding of the needs of scholars, librarians, and teachers, as well as those of the ultimate beneficiaries of any understanding of young adult books, the readers themselves, ensured that the entries would be most relevant to this book's intended audience.

Raymond W. Barber, Director of Libraries, William Penn Charter School, Philadelphia, Pennsylvania

Michael Cart, contributor of columns concerning young adult literature to *Booklist;*

lecturer, consultant, and author of books, including *From Romance to Realism: Fifty Years of Growth and Change in Young Adult Literature*

Judy Druse, Librarian at Mabee Library, Washburn University of Topeka, Topeka, Kansas

Marilee Fogelsong, Coordinator of Young Adult Services, New York Public Library, New York, New York

Bonnie Kunzel, Young Adult Librarian, New Brunswick Free Public Library, New Brunswick, New Jersey

Susan B. Madden, Literary and Young Adult Service Coordinator, King County Library System, Seattle, Washington

Amy Spaulding, Associate Professor, C. W. Post Center, Long Island University, Brookville, New York

Pam Spencer, Library Program Specialist, Chapel Square Media Center, Annandale, Virginia; author of *What Do Young Adults Read Next?*

Organization

The entries are arranged alphabetically by author. Each entry begins with the author's name, birth and death dates, nationality, and principal occupations. Authors are listed according to the names by which they are best known to readers. If an author writes under a pseudonym, his or her legal name (or other variant name) is also provided for reference purposes. When an author entry contains more than one title, these titles are arranged chronologically. (Works in a series are arranged chronologically under the series heading and the series heading is placed according to the date of the first published title in that series.) Title headings include the full title (including a foreign-language title where required), the genre, and the date of publication. When a book has been written by two co-authors, both of these names have been listed in the header, along with each author's respective birth/death dates and vocations.

The essay on each title begins with a brief plot synopsis and analysis of themes so that readers will have a context for understanding the characters, who establish their identities through action. Subsequent parts of the essay analyze major characters in some depth and minor characters at a length commensurate with their importance. (For ease of use, character names appear in boldface the first time they are mentioned in the text.) These character discussions are critical: they explicate characters' contributions to conflicts and themes, evaluate their effectiveness in communicating themes, and occasionally evaluate their aesthetic contributions.

The essay concludes with a list of works for further reading. This list is highly selective, focusing on standard reference works, such as those published by Gale Research (including *Something about the Author, Children's Literature Review, Dictionary of Literary Biography, Contemporary Authors, Something about the Author Autobiography Series, Twentieth-Century Young Adult Authors, Contemporary Literary Criticism,* and *Twentieth-Century Literary Criticism.*), or on titles of wide appeal that can be found in any large metropolitan library. These secondary works contain further bibliographic information so that readers can locate the scholarly articles and books that have shaped the authors' understanding of young adult literature over the years. (Dashes at the beginning of citations indicate a repetition of author information.)

Sequels, Series, Trilogies, and Other Related Works

In the world of young adult literature, many characters reappear in sequels, series, and trilogies. In order to avoid duplication of discussions in the character essays, these works have been organized in the following manner:

For Sequels:

In cases where all the major characters in a book appear in one or more sequels that are given equal coverage, a single character essay has been written to avoid duplication of information. Each plot summary concludes with the line "See below for character descriptions" to notify the user that there is no separate character essay for that particular book.

For Series, Trilogies, and Tetralogies:

Some series in young adult literature, such as the "Hardy Boys" books, contain too many books to be covered adequately within *CYAL*. In these cases, a representative title has been selected to help illustrate the major characters in the series, and a general discussion of the series is provided.

Trilogies and tetralogies are very popular in young adult literature, especially in the genres of fantasy and science fiction. In some cases, such as Isaac Asimov's "Foundation Trilogy," only one book has been selected as representative of the entire series as per recommendations from the advisory board. However, in instances where all the books in a trilogy or tetralogy are discussed, the books have been grouped together under one title (for example, Tolkien's "The Lord of the Rings"). For ease of reference, each title in the series is set in boldface within the combined plot summary.

For Other Related Works:

There are a number of instances in which characters appearing in one book are featured in other works not discussed in detail in *CYAL*, either because the characters do not change significantly in subsequent books by the author or because the book in which they are discussed has been deemed to be the most important work in the series. For reference purposes, however, the authors, when necessary, have added at the end of each plot summary a list of titles in which the characters also appear.

Character and Title Index

Characters in Young Adult Literature (*CYAL*) has been released simultaneously with its companion book, *Characters in Children's Literature* (*CCL*). Because these books together cover a broad spectrum of children's and young adult literature, two genres which are closely related though not identical, characters and titles from both *CYAL* and *CCL* have been indexed together here. Fewer than five percent of the characters appear in both books.

It was the goal of the authors and editor to index character names in such a way as to make them easily accessible to users of this book. For this reason, characters have been indexed alphabetically by their first names. Thus, the narrator in Theodore Taylor's *The Cay* is listed as "Phillip Enright" not "Enright, Phillip." Also, if a character is known by more than one name—for example, "Jayfox" is also "Jerome Foxworthy" in Bruce Brooks' *The Moves Make the Man*—both names are boldfaced in the characters discussion and both are included in the index. Characters who are commonly known by a rank or other title (for example, Mr., Ms., Captain, or Reverend) are listed alphabetically by that title. Mrs. March in *Little Women*, for example, is thus indexed under "Mrs." In young adult literature, many characters are also given generic names, such as "mother" or "narrator." In these instances, the title of the novel in which they appear is provided in parentheses after the character's name. For example, a narrator might be indexed as "narrator (*The Time Machine*)." Characters who appear in unrelated stories (for example, King Arthur appears in several books by different authors), or who are identified by only a common first name, such as Mary or John, will be treated similarly in instances where a neglect to do so might cause confusion.

Acknowledgments

The authors would particularly like to thank their editor, Kevin S. Hile, for his patience and help, as well as the eight consultants for their efforts and expertise. We hope that the result is a book that will be of both interest and value.

We Welcome Your Suggestions

To offer comments or suggestions about *Characters in Young Adult Literature*, write to: The Editor, *Characters in Young Adult Literature*, Gale Research, 835 Penobscot Bldg., 645 Griswold St., Detroit, MI 48226-4094.

Acknowledgments

Page 7—Cover of *Watership Down,* by Richard Adams. Avon, 1975. Copyright © 1972 by Rex Collings, Ltd. Reproduced by permission of Avon Books, New York. **Page 14**—Zelinsky, Paul O., illustrator. From a jacket of *The Remarkable Journey of Prince Jen,* by Lloyd Alexander. Dutton Children's Books, 1991. Jacket illustration © Paul O. Zelinsky, 1991. Used by permission of the publisher, E. P. Dutton, an imprint of New American Library, a division of Penguin USA. **Page 19**—Barkley, James, illustrator. From a jacket of *Sounder,* by William H. Armstrong. HarperCollins, 1969. Illustrations copyright © 1969 by James Barkley. Reproduced by permission of HarperCollins Publishers, Inc. **Page 25**—Greer Garson and Laurence Olivier in a scene from *Pride and Prejudice,* photograph. The Kobal Collection. Reproduced by permission. **Page 30**—Jacket of *Nothing but the Truth: A Documentary Novel,* by Avi. Orchard Books, 1991. Copyright © 1991 by Peter Catalanotto. All rights reserved. Reproduced by permission of Orchard Books, New York. **Page 53**—Bralds, Braldt, illustrator. From a cover of *The Mists of Avalon,* by Marion Z. Bradley. Ballantine Books, 1982. Reproduced by permission of Ballantine Books, a division of Random House, Inc. **Page 57**—Ribes, Frederika, illustrator. From a cover of *Notes for Another Life,* by Sue Ellen Bridgers. Bantam Books, 1989. Cover art copyright © 1989 by Frederika Ribes. Reproduced by permission of Bantam Books, a division of Bantam Doubleday Dell Publishing Group, Inc. **Page 61**—Joan Fontaine and Orson Welles in a scene from *Jane Eyre,* photograph. Archive Photos. Reproduced by permission. **Page 66**—Winfield, Wayne, illustrator. From a jacket of *The Moves Make the Man,* by Bruce Brooks. Harper & Row, Publishers, 1984. Jacket art © 1984 by Wayne Winfield. Jacket © 1984 by HarperCollins Publishers, Inc. Reproduced by permission of HarperCollins Publishers, Inc. **Page 72**—Luise Rainer and Paul Muni in a scene from *The Good Earth,* photograph. The Kobal Collection. Reproduced by permission. **Page 81**—Collier, John, illustrator. From a cover of *My Antonia,* by Willa Cather. Cover illustration © John Collier. Reproduced by permission of Houghton Mifflin Company. **Page 86**—Cover of *Rainbow Jordan,* by Alice Childress. Avon, 1982. Copyright © 1981 by Alice Childress. All rights reserved. Reproduced by permission of Avon Books, New York. **Page 95**—Norman, Elaine, illustrator. From a cover of *Celine,* by Brock Cole. Aerial Fiction, 1993. Cover art © 1993 by Elaine Norman. Reproduced by permission of Aerial Fiction, a division of Farrar, Straus and Giroux. **Page 97**—Cesare, Di, illustrator. From a cover of *My Brother Sam Is Dead,* by James Lincoln Collier and Christopher Collier. Scholastic Inc., 1974. Copyright © 1974 by James Lincoln Collier and Christopher Collier. All rights reserved. Reproduced by permission. **Page 100**—Sivavec, Diane, illustrator. From a cover of *Prairie Songs,* by Pam Conrad. HarperTrophy, 1993. Cover art © 1993 by Diane Sivavec. Cover © 1993 by HarperCollins Publishers. Reproduced by permission of HarperCollins Publishers, Inc. **Page 104**—Accornero, Franco, illustrator. From a cover of *The Lords of Discipline,* by Pat Conroy. Bantam Books, 1987. Cover art copyright © 1987 by Franco Accornero. All rights reserved. Reproduced by permission of Bantam Books, a division of Bantam Doubleday Dell Publishing Group, Inc. **Page 109**—Illustration by N. C. Wyeth. From *The Last of the Mohicans,* by James Fenimore Cooper. Charles Scribner's Sons, 1919. **Page 127**—Illustration from *Robinson Crusoe,* by Daniel Defoe. David McKay,

Publisher, n.d. Reproduced by permission of Random House, Inc. **Page 135**—Illustration by Frederic W. Pailthorpe. From *Great Expectations,* by Charles Dickens. Dodd, Mead & Company, 1942. **Page 143**—Illustration from *The Adventures of Sherlock Holmes,* by A. Conan Doyle. A & W Visual Library, 1975. Copyright © 1975 by A & W Publishers, Inc. **Page 145**—Illustration by Norman Price and E. C. Van Swearingen. From *The Three Musketeers,* by Alexandre Dumas. Grosset & Dunlap Publishers, 1953. Copyright © 1953, by Grosset & Dunlap, Inc. All rights reserved. **Page 157**—Robert Redford and Mia Farrow in a scene from *The Great Gatsby,* photograph. The Kobal Collection. Reproduced by permission. **Page 162**—Cover of *Johnny Tremain,* by Esther Forbes. Dell Publishing, 1969. Reproduced by permission of Bantam Books, a division of Bantam Doubleday Dell Publishing Group, Inc. **Page 165**—Illustration by Eros Keith. From *The Slave Dancer,* by Paula Fox. Simon & Schuster Books for Young Readers, 1973. Copyright © 1973 by Paula Fox. Reproduced by permission of Simon & Schuster Books for Young Readers, a division of Simon & Schuster, Inc. **Page 174**—Cicely Tyson in a scene from *The Autobiography of Miss Jane Pittman,* photograph. Archive Photos. Reproduced by permission. **Page 179**—Illustration by John Schoenherr. From *Julie of the Wolves,* by Jean Craighead George. Illustrations copyright © 1972 by John Schoenherr. All rights reserved. Reproduced by permission of HarperCollins Publishers, Inc. **Page 182**—Hugh Edwards and Tom Chapin in a scene from *Lord of the Flies,* photograph. Archive Photos. Reproduced by permission. **Page 187**—Kristy McNichol and Bruce Davison in a scene from *Summer of My German Soldier,* photograph. AP/Wide World Photos. Reproduced by permission. **Page 189**—Timothy Hutton and Dinah Manoff in a scene from *Ordinary People,* photograph. The Kobal Collection. Reproduced by permission. **Page 203**—Cover of *Mr. and Mrs. Bo Jo Jones,* by Ann Head. Signet Books, 1968. Copyright © 1967 by Ann Head. All rights reserved. Used by permission of the publisher, Signet Books, a division of Penguin USA. **Page 205**—Sweet, Darrell K., illustrator. From a cover of *Tunnel in the Sky,* by Robert A. Heinlein. Ballantine Books, 1977. Reproduced by permission of Ballantine Books, a division of Random House, Inc. **Page 210**—Jon Voight and Alan Arkin in a scene from *Catch 22,* photograph. The Kobal Collection. Reproduced by permission. **Page 215**—Sting and Kyle MacLachlan in the 1983 motion picture *Dune,* photograph. The Kobal Collection. Reproduced by permission. **Page 224**—Nick Stahl and Mel Gibson in a scene from *The Man without a Face,* photograph by Joel Warren. The Kobal Collection. Reproduced by permission. **Page 229**—Howell, Troy, illustrator. From a jacket of *Redwall,* by Brian Jacques. Philomel Books, 1986. Jacket illustration © 1986 by Troy Howell. Reproduced by permission of Philomel Books. **Page 231**—Patrick, Pamela, illustrator. From a cover of *Dogsbody,* by Diana Wynne Jones. Bullseye Books, 1990. Cover art © 1990 by Pamela Patrick. Reproduced by permission of Alfred A. Knopf, Inc. **Page 235**—Tandy, R. H., illustrator. From *The Secret of the Old Clock,* by Carolyn Keene. Grosset & Dunlap Publishers, 1930. Copyright © 1930, by Grosset & Dunlap, Inc. Renewed 1957 by Harriet Adams and Edna Squier Children. All rights reserved. Reproduced by permission. **Page 244**—Jack Nicholson in a scene from *One Flew Over the Cuckoo's Nest,* photograph. The Kobal Collection. Reproduced by permission. **Page 247**—Sissy Spacek and William Katt in a scene from *Carrie,* photograph. Archive Photos/United Artists. Reproduced by permission. **Page 254**—Gregory Peck in a scene from *To Kill a Mockingbird,* photograph. The Kobal Collection. Reproduced by permission. **Page 265**—Acuna, Ed, illustrator. From a cover of *The Brave,* by Robert Lipsyte. Charlotte Zolotow Books, 1991. Jacket art © 1991 by Ed Acuna. Jacket © 1991 by HarperCollins Publishers, Inc. Reproduced by permission of HarperCollins Publishers, Inc. **Page 271**—Illustration by Kyuzo Tsugami. From *The Call of the Wild and Other Stories,* by Jack London. Grosset & Dunlap Publishers, 1965. Copyright ©, 1965, by Grosset & Dunlap, Inc. All rights reserved. Reproduced by permission. **Page 273**— Lowry, Lois, photographer. From a cover of *The Giver,* by Lois Lowry. Houghton Mifflin Company, 1993. Jacket photograph © 1993 by Lois Lowry. Reproduced by permission of Houghton Mifflin Company. **Page 277**—Cover of *The Tricksters,* by Margaret Mahy.

Scholastic Inc., 1988. Copyright © 1986 by Margaret Mahy. All rights reserved. Reproduced by permission. **Page 291**—Clark Gable and Vivien Leigh in a scene from *Gone with the Wind,* photograph. The Kobal Collection. Reproduced by permission. **Page 297**—Cover of *Hoops,* by Walter Dean Myers. Bantam Doubleday Dell Books for Young Readers, 1983. Reproduced by permission of Bantam Doubleday Dell Books for Young Readers, a division of Bantam Doubleday Dell Publishing Group, Inc. **Page 307**—Cover of *The Kidnapping of Christina Lattimore,* by Joan Lowery Nixon. Dell Publishing, 1992. Copyright © 1979 by Joan Lowery Nixon. All rights reserved. Reproduced by permission of Bantam Doubleday Dell Publishing Group, Inc. **Page 309**—Weiman, Jon, illustrator. From a cover of *Z for Zachariah,* by Robert C. O'Brien. Collier Books, 1987. Copyright © 1974 by Sally Conly. All rights reserved. Reproduced by permission of the illustrator. **Page 311**—From a cover of *Island of the Blue Dolphins,* by Scott O'Dell. Dell Publishing, 1987. Copyright © 1960 by Scott O'Dell. All rights reserved. Reproduced by permission of Bantam Doubleday Dell Publishing Group, Inc. **Page 337**—Engraving by Fritz Eichenberg. From *Tales of Edgar Allan Poe,* by Edgar Allan Poe. Random House, 1944. Copyright © 1944, renewed 1971 by Random House, Inc. Reproduced by permission. **Page 340**—John Wayne and Kim Darby in a scene from *True Grit,* photograph. Archive Photos/Paramount. Reproduced by permission. **Page 343**—Benson, Linda, illustrator. From a cover of *The Ruby in the Smoke,* by Philip Pullman. Random House Sprinters, 1987. Cover art © 1987 by Linda Benson. All rights reserved. Reproduced by permission of Random House, Inc. **Page 349**—Richard Thomas in a scene from *All Quiet on the Western Front,* photograph. The Kobal Collection. Reproduced by permission. **Page 355**—Tom Cruise in a scene from *Interview with the Vampire,* photograph. Archive Photos, Inc. Reproduced by permission. **Page 357**—Cover of *Wolf by the Ears,* by Ann Rinaldi. Scholastic Inc., 1991. Text copyright © 1991 by Ann Rinaldi. All rights reserved. Reproduced by permission. **Page 359**—Cover of *A Fine White Dust,* by Cynthia Rylant. Dell Publishing, 1987. Copyright © 1986 by Cynthia Rylant. All rights reserved. Reproduced by permission of Bantam Doubleday Dell Publishing Group, Inc. **Page 365**—Cover of *Words by Heart,* by Ouida Sebestyen. Bantam Books, 1981. Cover art copyright © 1981 by Bantam Books. Reproduced by permission of Bantam Books, a division of Bantam Doubleday Dell Publishing Group, Inc. **Page 367**—Boris Karloff and Mae Clarke in a scene from *Frankenstein,* photograph. The Kobal Collection. Reproduced by permission. **Page 377**—Marcus, Barry, illustrator. From a cover of *A Tree Grows in Brooklyn,* by Betty Smith. HarperPerennial, 1992. Cover illustration © 1992 by Barry Marcus. Reproduced by permission of HarperCollins Publishers, Inc. **Page 381**—Cover of *The Bronze Bow,* by Elizabeth George Speare. Houghton Mifflin Company, 1961. Copyright © 1961, renewed 1989 by Elizabeth George Speare. All rights reserved. Reproduced by permission of Houghton Mifflin Company. **Page 397**—Illustration by James Daugherty. From *Uncle Tom's Cabin,* by Harriet Beecher Stowe. Coward, McCann & Geoghegan, Inc., 1929. Copyright © 1929, by Coward-McCann, Inc. All rights reserved. **Page 399**—Mikolaycak, Charles, illustrator. From a cover of *The Eagle of the Ninth,* by Rosemary Sutcliff. Sunburst Books, 1993. Cover art © 1993 by Charles Mikolaycak. Reproduced by permission of Sunburst Books, a division of Farrar, Straus and Giroux, Inc. **Page 402**—Billy Mumy, with other cast members, in a scene from *Bless the Beasts and Children,* photograph. The Kobal Collection. Reproduced by permission. **Page 404**—Kieu Chin, with other cast members, in a scene from *The Joy Luck Club,* photograph. The Kobal Collection. Reproduced by permission. **Page 411**—Cover of *The Cay,* by Theodore Taylor. Avon, 1970. Copyright © 1969 by Theodore Taylor. Reproduced by permission of Avon Books, New York. **Page 423**—Illustration by Steven Kellogg. From *The Adventures of Huckleberry Finn,* by Mark Twain. William Morrow, 1994. Illustrations copyright © 1994 by Steven Kellogg. All rights reserved. Reproduced by permission of William Morrow and Company, Inc. **Page 429**—Illustration by Barry Moser. From *Around the World in Eighty Days,* by Jules Verne. Translated by George Makepeace Towle. William Morrow, 1988. Illustrations copyright © 1988 by Pennyroyal Press. All rights reserved. Reproduced by permission of William Morrow and Company, Inc. **Page 439**—Whoopi Goldberg and Margaret Avery in a scene from *The Color Purple,* photograph. Archive Photos/Warner Bros. Reproduced by permission. **Page 442**—Gabel, Matt, illustrator. From a cover of *The Time Machine,* by H. G. Wells. Worthington Press, 1995. Illustrations © 1995 by Worthington Press. Reproduced by permission of the publisher. **Page 448**—Zudeck, Darryl, illustrator. From a cover of *The Machine Gunners,* by Robert Westall. Borzoi Sprinters, 1990. Cover art copyright © 1990 by Darryl Zudeck. All rights reserved. Reproduced by permission of Alfred A. Knopf, Inc. **Page 469**—Knabel, Lonnie, illustrator. From a cover of *The Devil's Arithmetic,* by Jane Yolen. Puffin Books, 1990. Cover illustration copyright © Lonnie Knabel, 1990. Used by permissions of Puffin Books, a division of Penguin Books USA Inc. **Page 471**—Thompson, John, illustrator. From a cover of *The Pigman,* by Paul Zindel. Bantam Books, 1983. Cover art copyright © 1983 by John Thompson. All rights reserved. Reproduced by permission of Bantam Books, a division of Bantam Doubleday Dell Publishing Group, Inc.

Characters in YOUNG ADULT LITERATURE

Douglas Adams

1952-, English novelist

The Hitchhiker Series

(science fiction, 1979-1992)

PLOT: In the opening book of this series, ***The Hitchhiker's Guide to the Galaxy*** (1979), Arthur Dent, an average English suburbanite, is warned by his friend Ford Prefect (who is actually a space alien doing research in England for the massive electronic tome *The Hitchhiker's Guide to the Galaxy*) that a Vogon spaceship commanded by Prostetnic Vogon Jeltz is approaching Earth with orders to destroy it to create a celestial bypass. Ford and Arthur escape to the spaceship operated by the odious Vogons only seconds before the Earth is destroyed. After being ejected into empty space by the inhospitable Vogons, they are rescued by a passing state-of-the-art spaceship, *Heart of Gold,* commanded by Zaphod Beeblebrox, the President of the Imperial Galactic Government and wheeler-dealer supreme who, with the help of the spaceship he has just stolen, hopes to find wealth on the planet Magrathea. Also on the spaceship with the two-headed Zaphod are his girlfriend and Earthling, Trillian, a gloomy robot named Marvin, and the ever-cheerful shipboard computer, Eddie.

On Magrathea, Zaphod, Trillian, and Ford enter the planet's inner caverns. While Arthur and Marvin are guarding the spaceship, they are approached by an elderly man named Slartibartfast who spirits Arthur away in his aircar into the heart of the planet. He tells Arthur that millions of years ago the Earth was built on this planet with the help of the supercomputer, Deep Thought, that had also calculated the answer to Life, the Universe and Everything as "42." After a series of adventures, the galactic wanderers—Arthur, Ford, Trillian, and Zaphod Beeblebrox—are reunited.

In ***The Restaurant at the End of the Universe*** (1980) Gag Halfrunt, a prominent galactic psychiatrist, hires the Vogon spaceship commanded by Captain Vogon Jeltz to destroy Arthur and Trillian because they know that the answer to the secret of the universe is 42. Powerless to combat the Vogon ship, Zaphod calls on his deceased great-grandfather, Zaphod Beeblebrox the Fourth, to help. He does so by miniaturizing *Heart of Gold* and putting it in Zaphod's pocket while commissioning his great-grandson to embark on a quest to find the Ruler of the Universe. During this quest Zaphod meets Zarniwoop, who also wants to find the Ruler of the Universe and, on the desolate planet Frogstar World B, meet Pizpot Gargravarr, who serves as guide to the Total Perspective Vortex. Eventually, Zaphod is reunited with his friend and spaceship. They travel through time to the restaurant at the end of the Universe, where the clientele can nightly view the destruction of the universe under the guidance of the overly genial master of ceremonies, Max Quordlepheen.

In the restaurant, Ford meets his old pal, rock musician Hotback Desiato, but, anxious to get on with his quest, Zaphod demands that his friends leave before witnessing the great cataclysm. During the flight, the friends are once more separated. Zaphod, along with Zarniwoop and Trillian, finds the Ruler of the Universe, who appears to be unaware of his powers, while Arthur and Ford become stowaways on a spaceship filled with frozen bodies which are are being sent to colonize a new planet. When they land they discover that, through the mysteries of time and space, they are actually colonists on prehistoric Earth.

In ***Life, the Universe and Everything*** (1982) help comes to Arthur and Ford in the form of a large sofa they find in a field. It transports them to England, where Slartibartfast transports them out of the Earth's atmosphere by spaceship shortly before the planet's destruction. Through the miracle of Informational Illusions, Slartibartfast recreates the history of the aggressive planet, Krikkit. Krikkit was defeated in a mammoth war and encased in a spacial envelope which requires a key made up of several components to unlock. Slartibartfast reveals that Krikkit robots have escaped the planet and are now successfully collecting the components to unlock the bellicose planet. Coincidentally, the last of these components, the Golden Bail, is aboard the *Heart of Gold,* the spaceship which Zaphod and Trillian still inhabit. When the bail is stolen by the Krikkit robots, Zaphod and Trillian join forces with Arthur, Ford, and Slartibartfast to foil the Krikkiter's plot.

Arthur has become homesick for Earth in ***So Long, and Thanks for All the Fish*** (1985), so he hitches a ride to England on a friendly spacecraft. He gets a ride from a car driven by a man named Russell and his attractive sister, Fenchurch with whom Arthur falls in love. Arthur finds that, some months before, when the Vogons destroyed the Earth in a parallel existence, all the world's dolphins disappeared. He and Fenchurch share idyllic moments and venture to California to talk with John Watson, alias Wonko the Sane, who claims to maintain contact with the dolphins, whose superior intelligence had warned them of the Earth's fate. Wonko the Sane's prize possession is a parting gift from them: a fishbowl with the inscription "So long, and thanks for all the fish." Ford Prefect arrives on a giant spacecraft. Now deeply attached to one another, Arthur and Fenchurch beg Ford to take them with him when he returns to outer space, which he does.

Tricia McMillan and her counterpart, Trillian, are living in parallel universes in ***Mostly Harmless*** (1992). Tricia is an English television personality, and her other half is cavorting somewhere in the universe after leaving the Earth seventeen year ago with the two-headed Zaphod Beeblebrox. Each identity is oblivious to the other's existence. Tricia is abducted by space aliens and taken to the newly discovered tenth planet, Persephone, which is nicknamed Rupert.

Elsewhere in the galaxy, Ford Prefect is displeased with Vann Harl, his new boss at the editorial office of *The Hitchhiker's Guide to the Galaxy.* With the help of Colin, a robot whom Ford has made friendly by playing with his circuits, Ford steals Vann's credit and identity cards.

Arthur Dent, still recovering from Fenchurch's leaving him, lives on the remote planet Lamuella with a tribe whose leader is named Old Thrashberg. His peaceful retreat is disrupted with the arrival of Trillian and her teenage daughter, Random, who was conceived by Trillian using sperm Arthur had sold to a sperm bank. When Trillian leaves, Arthur finds himself left with an unpleasant, maladjusted youngster for whom he must play the role of father. Random travels back to Earth, where she knows her parents originated, and Arthur, accompanied by Ford, also heads for Earth. At the same time, both Tricia and Trillian arrive on Earth, too, and there is a monumental confrontation during which Random accuses both her real mother and Tricia of abandonment. This melodrama is interrupted suddenly and fatefully, when the Vogon ship, whose captain is Prostetnic Vogon Jeltz, enters the Earth's atmosphere and, once again, accomplishes its mission of destroying Earth.

CHARACTERS: Arthur Dent is an average, ordinary man. Lacking any deep emotional convictions, he accepts whatever comes his way without complaint or comprehension. For example, he doesn't mourn the end of the Earth but has temporary qualms about a life without such institutions as a McDonald's hamburger or Nelson's Column. Although once very fond of Trillian, he tolerates her running off with Zaphod with only slight disappointment. Arthur wears a perpetually worried look which hides the fact that he doesn't comprehend what's really going on. He is justifiably confused by the intricate workings of outer space and often shows an amazing lack of logic or intelligence. Sometimes in his naivete, however, he stumbles accidentally upon simple solutions to complex problems which have baffled those around him. Like many an Englishman before him, his major concern is the tea supply and its maintenance. This space-age Candide is described as about thirty years of age, tall, and dark-haired. At school he was unpopular and inept at sports and now is happiest when he can live in peace without fuss or bother. When his relative prosperity on Lamuella is interrupted by the arrival of Random, Arthur displays buried feelings and tenderness when he tries to calm and understand his new-found daughter. His attempts at paternal affection are both unusual for him and touching in their sincerity. Through the course of these novels Arthur shows some character development: he sometimes is able to control his own affairs, starts making independent decisions, and increasingly displays courage and a desire to fight oppression.

Though he appears to be an Earthling, **Ford Prefect** was actually born six hundred light years away on a small planet. While doing research for the galactic encyclopedia, *The Hitchhiker's Guide to the Galaxy,* he came to Earth, where he pretended to be an out-of-work actor, although perceptive Earthlings noticed that he smiles too broadly, never blinks, and often stares longingly at the sky. His friendship with Arthur leads to saving his life when they both escape Earth's destruction. Ford has wiry, ginger-colored hair and a delightful sense of humor. He is eccentric, clever, fast-talking, and intelligent, as well as enterprising, imaginative, and a loyal friend to Arthur. Ford magnanimously accepts whatever new misfortunes Fate has dealt him, but is resourceful and imaginative in seeking solutions. He is essentially a pragmatist, rather than allowing himself to be led by some vague idealism. While not above stealing on occasion, he is generally a moral man with decent intentions. Occasionally, his practicality fails him and he is motivated by more lofty emotions. He loves alcohol, good times, and parties, and he wears a leather satchel around his neck that contains many amazing objects, including a copy of his beloved *Hitchhiker's Guide.*

The title of President of the Imperial Galaxy belongs to two-headed **Zaphod Beeblebrox**, who has spent two of his ten presidential years in prison for fraud. But there is no real power connected to his position. In fact, Zaphod believes that his major responsibility is to attract attention away from his office. He has been described as an "adventurer, ex-hippie, good-timer (crook? quite possible), manic self-promoter, terribly bad at personal relationships, often thought to be completely out to lunch." He is now two hundred years old, though he often acts like an adolescent. He loves creating effects and is considered by many, including Trillian, to be a terrible show-off. He was once physically normal (except, of course, for his two heads) but, to create an impression, he has undergone surgery to have a third arm attached just beneath the right one. He has tousled hair, is always unshaven, and uses such archaic expressions as "cool" and "froody." Zaphod is known for his dash, conceit, and bravado. He is a thorough extrovert, imaginative, irresponsible, and foolhardy. Although inept mechanically, he deceives everyone with his facade of knowledge. His shrink, Gag Halfrunt, describes him as "one of my profitable patients. He has personality problems beyond the dreams of analysts." Self-preservation and personal aggrandizement often outweigh Zaphod's feelings of loyalty or devotion to friends. However, though rarely seen, Zaphod has a tiny conscience. An ex-confidence man who is often untrustworthy and manic, he is also fascinating and appealing in his dash and inventiveness.

Trillian was born **Tricia McMillan** on Earth, but when she ditched Arthur and ran off into outer space with Zaphod, she became Trillian. She is described as "slim, darkish, humanoid, with long waves of black hair, a full mouth, an odd little knob of a nose and ridiculously brown eyes." She is intelligent and logical in her thinking, possessing both good taste and common sense. Trillian has college degrees in math and astrophysics and is a good judge of character. For example, she is aware of Zaphod's weaknesses (she calls him "a terrible show-off") but finds that his endurance and boldness are compensating qualities. She also shows courage, daring, and clear thinking in times of trouble and is always loyal to her friends. In an amazing display of fearlessness, imagination, and intelligence, she helps confound the plans of the warlike Krikkiters. Her other self, living in a parallel universe, is the ambitious, efficient Tricia, a prominent British television news anchor. Her hold on reality becomes tenuous, particularly after being confronted by an hysterical Random who says Tricia is her mother. Tricia is basically a lonely person, torn between her life of glamour and distinction and becoming a wife and mother.

The Vogons are one of the most unpleasant races in the Galaxy. They are ugly, reptilian, and thoroughly odious. To see **Prostetnic Vogon Jeltz**, the captain of their prize starship, is not a pleasant experience. He possesses a high-domed nose, small pig-like forehead, and dark-green, rubbery skin. He has trouble smiling because he has forgotten how it is done. Though thoroughly vile, Jeltz is not completely evil or scheming, although he is not above corruption and graft. He is ill-tempered, bossy, officious, and, worst of all, the writer of dreadful poetry, which he inflicts upon unfortunate audiences. Jeltz unquestioningly and tirelessly obeys commands, even when it involves exterminating innocent people or repeating assignments already accomplished, such as the destruction of Earth.

Nicknamed the Paranoid Android, **Marvin** is a sorry example of robotry. With a low voice that connotes hopelessness, he hates humans and other robots and believes the galaxy is out to get him. He lives in a private, rather unpleasant world of his own. Self-pitying, depressed, and self-deprecating, he is prone to lament: "No one can help me . . . not that anyone tries." Marvin thrives in his relationship with his master Zaphod in which he is the masochist reveling in Zaphod's deliberate sadism. With a complete lack of confidence in himself and his abilities, Marvin constantly complains, is hyper-sensitive, and is a hypochondriac. Yet in his own muttering, grumbling way, he often delivers the travelers from danger.

Eddie is the endlessly cheery shipboard computer on *Heart of Gold.* In spite of Zaphod's brusqueness and occasional verbal abuse from others, Eddie remains buoyant and jovial. He tries always to be helpful and supportive, using expressions like "Good luck, guys" to encourage the travelers. In times of great stress when annihilation seems imminent, Eddie provides reassurance and help by singing "You'll Never Walk Alone," an inspirational song from the Broadway musical *Carousel.* Eddie has another, more matriarchal voice, which he uses when he feels the group needs more forceful treatment and perhaps a little hectoring.

Slartibartfast is the tallish, elderly gentleman whom the group meets on Magrathea. He takes pride in his part in the creation of the original Earth (he got an award for Norway) and looks forward to being in charge of Africa in the construction of a new one. He is a wise, kindly man who takes Arthur into the administrative core of the planet. He shows great integrity and self-sacrifice in his devotion to saving the universe from the War Lords of Krikkit. A man whose broad knowledge and wisdom encompasses the entire universe, Slartibartfast is willing to renounce his own identity and existence to save others. This decency, honor, and courage are displayed in his loyalty toward his friends and his allegiance to higher causes.

Gag Halfrunt is one of the Galaxy's most prominent and successful psychiatrists. He is so devoted to his profession, the mumbo-jumbo he proclaims, and the rich lifestyle it has brought him, that he will resort to murder to preserve them. Thus he orders the destruction of *Heart of Gold,* fearful that should the secret to the meaning of life be found it would ruin his business. Totally friendless, he has never had the knack of taking the advice he so readily gives to his patients.

Zaphod's great-grandfather is **Zaphod Beeblebrox the Fourth** (the Beeblebroxes count backwards, so our hero is Zaphod Beeblebrox the First). When he is recalled from the dead, he appears as a small, bent, gaunt figure with two wispy-haired heads, one lolling in sleep. He is a stern, unforgiving man with a voice like fingernails across a blackboard. Opinionated, grouchy, and reluctant to help his no-good progeny, he can neither forget nor pardon the absence of flowers from his great-grandson at his funeral. Given to pontificating about the past, he is keenly disappointed that Zaphod has not accomplished more, and therefore, as payment for saving his life, he commits his great-grandson to a quest to find the Ruler of the Universe. Another reason for this seemingly generous act is that he doesn't want to be bothered with Zaphod I in the afterlife.

Ford's friend from his days as a wild youth is **Hotblack Desiato**, the platinum-suited leader of the Disaster Area, the biggest, loudest, richest rock band in history. Unfortunately, when Ford sees Hotblack at the restaurant and tries to elicit memories of their former days of living high and pub crawling, his very fat, unhealthy looking friend is silent and unresponsive. His comatose state is the result of a decision to spend a year dead for tax purposes.

Max Quordlepheen is the master of ceremonies at Milliways, the restaurant at the end of the universe. Smooth-talking, insincere, and artificial, he epitomizes the shallow, superficial show-biz host. Cunning and diabolical, his actions before the show are described as those of "a mantis contemplating an evening's preying." He knows how to appeal to an audience's basic instincts and targets its weaknesses for exploitation. His face is described as "too long for a start, the eyes too sunken and hooded, the cheeks too hollow, his lips too thin and too long."

On Frogstar World B, Zaphod encounters only the voice of **Pizpot Gargravarr**. His voice and body are mismatched and have agreed on a trial separation which, one gets the impression, will lead to a divorce. Pizpot does not like his work directing hapless victims into the Total Perspective Vortex, where they are so awed by the glimpse of the whole universe and their infinitesimal role in it that their minds perish. Because he dislikes his job, he has a mournful, unhappy demeanor and a fatalistic attitude toward life. Though always polite and solicitous, he has learned to be stern and demanding.

Zaphod is sometimes a pawn in the plans of **Zarniwoop**, a mysterious individual who is the creator of a substitute, artificial universe to which he retreats when necessary. He and Zaphod become involved in the quest for the **Ruler of the Universe**. When Zarniwoop and Zaphod meet the Ruler, however, they are disappointed. He is a tall, shambling man, with rough, straw-colored hair; he lives in a shack with a leaky corrugated roof. Dressed in shabby clothes, he is completely unaware of his powers and disinterested in learning about them. He neither knows his own name nor anything about the world outside his shack. For a moment, when the old man makes reference to the Lord, they feel they are making progress, only to find that this is the name of his cat to whom he is devoted.

The great love in Arthur's life is **Fenchurch,** a woman who is described as "heart-thumping beautiful.... [S]he was tallish with dark hair which fell in waves around a pale and serious face. When she smiled, warmth and life flooded into her face and impossibly graceful movement into her body." Fenchurch possesses a rare sensitivity and a cosmic intelligence which makes her attractive to Arthur. She exudes a magnetic allure and an unconventional way of looking at the world. Her cosmic awareness troubles her because she does not understand this other-worldly aspect of her character which makes her aware of extraterrestrial phenomena. Attractive both physically and mentally, she is, at times, kittenish and playful and, at others, confused and vulnerable.

John Watson, also known as **Wonko the Sane** lives on the southern Pacific coast with his wife in an inside-out house, where all of the rooms and furniture are outdoors. In keeping with his house, he is an unorthodox oddball out of step with the culture around him, yet, in his own creative, ingenious way, he represents a logic and wisdom that modern man has overlooked. When his beloved dolphins, with whom he felt a unique kinship, disappear, he experiences an overpowering sense of loss.

When **Colin**, the little robot who was a security guard at the *Hitchhiker's Guide* office, has his responsibility chip removed by Ford, he is transformed into a docile, perpetually happy, and totally contented mechanism. Always cheery and bright, he becomes attached to Ford and shows his loyalty by warning him of danger, protecting him, and helping Ford make an escape after his attack on his new editor-in-chief, **Vann Harl**. Harl is an employee of InfiniDim Enterprises, which has taken over the

Guide. He is a smooth-faced, officious, meddlesome young man who wants to turn the publication into something Ford abhors—that is, the product of a structured, well-managed, efficient organization. Harl is a glib, slippery individual who is overbearing and patronizing toward others.

Trillian's mixed-up daughter is **Random**, the product of Trillian being impregnated with sperm sold by Arthur to a sperm bank. Random is an exceedingly unpleasant, demanding girl who is petulant and given to fits of anger, weeping, and stone throwing. As the author explains, "It wasn't that she wanted to be difficult, as such, it was just that she didn't know how or what else to be." An explanation for this repulsive, perverse behavior could be that her life has been one of constant galaxy hopping and time traveling with her mother. Confused about her origins and parentage, Random defies her father and travels to Earth, seeking answers to her questions.

Further Reading

Authors and Artists for Young Adults. Vol. 4. Detroit: Gale Research, 1990.

Brucolli, Mary, and Jean W. Ross, eds. *Dictionary of Literary Biography Yearbook: 1983.* Detroit: Gale Research, 1984.

Contemporary Literary Criticism. Vols. 27, 60. Detroit: Gale Research, 1984, 1990.

Kroph, Carl R. "Douglas Adam's 'Hitchhiker' Novels as Mock Science Fiction." *Science Fiction Studies* 15 (March 1988).

Watson, Noelle, and Paul E. Schellinger, eds. *Twentieth-Century Science Fiction Writers.* 3rd ed. Chicago: St. James, 1991.

Richard Adams

1920-, English novelist

Watership Down

(animal fantasy, 1972)

PLOT: Fiver, one of a large group of wild rabbits who live in a comfortable warren called Sandleford, warns his brother, Hazel, of impending doom. Fiver has had a vision that their hillside home will be covered with blood, but when he and Hazel tell the Chief Rabbit, their message of doom is not believed. Unfortunately for Sandleford and its rabbits, Fiver's prediction comes true: the hillside where the warren is located is slated for a housing development, and all the rabbits are killed with poison gas. Fiver, Hazel, and a small band of other rabbits, including Dandelion, Pipkin, Hawkbit, Blackberry, Speedwell, Bigwig, and Silver, escape this fate and set off courageously to find a new and safe place to live.

So begins their perilous journey of adventure. Along the way, they run into Cowslip who invites them to join his warren. It seems like an idyllic spot, where plenty of lettuce and carrots are readily available for food. But Fiver starts to get nervous and says they must move on. His fear is proved justified when Bigwig is injured in a snare, and it becomes clear that the rabbits in Cowslip's warren are being fattened up for humans to eat. The Sandleford rabbits set off again for the hills. This time the quarreling that had occurred between the members of the group has abated, for the experience with the snares has shown them the dangers they face and that their survival depends on the strength of their group.

Hazel then leads the rabbits to Watership Down, which seems to be a suitable enough spot, but there is one problem: they still have no does. Hazel decides that they will need to scout the area and finds help in an unlikely ally named Kehaar, whom he rescues when they find the seabird with an injured wing. After nursing Kehaar back to health, the bird agrees to help them out. Serving as reconnaissance, Kehaar locates a farm where some rabbits are being kept in hutches, as well as a big warren of wild rabbits to the south. Hazel leads the others on a raid on Nuthanger farm, where they manage to release two does, but this is clearly not enough for their new warren, so Hazel decides they must journey to the warren in the south.

The warren turns out to be a place called Efrafa. The rabbits there are led by General Woundwort, a tyrant who has organized his warren into a totalitarian state. Under Woundwort's rule, the Efrafans have lost all personal liberties and live in constant fear of the "Owslafa," the warren's secret police. Driven by their need to find does, Hazel sends Bigwig to infiltrate Efrafa's ranks and free as many of the rabbits as possible. Against all odds, a daring escape is made culminating in a fight between Bigwig and General Woundwort and then Woundwort's lethal confrontation with a fierce dog.

At last, with Hazel and Fiver's prodding, the rabbits establish a new warren on Watership Down. With the does they rescued from Efrafa and, in a raid led by Hazel, from nearby Nuthanger Farm, there are now enough rabbits to establish a new warren. Along the way, Hazel, Fiver, and the others have had many strange experiences and made unusual friends, including a mouse and the large seabird named Kehaar. In the last dramatic episode of the novel, Hazel makes the most unusual friend of all when he is attacked by the cat at Nuthanger farm. Injured but alive, he is rescued by a little girl whose father nurses him back to health and releases Hazel back into the wild. At the novel's conclusion, Hazel, who has become the leader of Watership Down, has helped to create a new and happy home. His work well done, he is taken into heaven by the mystical Rabbit of Inlé to receive his final reward.

CHARACTERS: *Watership Down,* Adams's first novel and the winner of the 1973 Carnegie Medal, was an instant success when it was published in England as a juvenile title. The novel had such broad appeal, however, that its American publisher released it as an adult title. Today, the novel is read by people of all ages, although it is popular chiefly with children in upper elementary and junior high schools. In this allegorical novel, a maverick band of wild rabbits sets off on a quest for a better home and a better society. They remain wild rabbits at all times, obeying the laws of nature, but Adams gives each a distinct and unforgettable personality.

Hazel becomes chief rabbit of the maverick band. At first, he is the only one to believe his brother, Fiver, that a terrible tragedy is coming to their warren. Hazel is strong-willed, cautious, and intelligent. A born leader, he is wise enough to listen to other rabbits in their small band when they have

Watership Down, ***Adams's first novel, was originally published as a juvenile book, but it has since been read by millions of people of all ages.***

ideas that will better the group's chances of survival and happiness. For example, he listens patiently when Blackberry comes up with the unconventional idea of having the buck rabbits dig holes for shelter (a task customarily performed by does) to help them survive in winter. Hazel is quick to understand that, if they are to escape the mistakes of the past, change is necessary. He leads his small but growing band with patience and benevolence, and only after he has lived many, many summers longer than wild rabbits usually do, does the Black Rabbit of Inlé take him from the world of the living. Feeling young and healthy once again, Hazel joins the Black Rabbit in a delightful romp through the wood, where the first primroses are just starting to bloom.

Hazel's brother, **Fiver**, received his name because he was the fifth and smallest in his litter. Though he is weaker and more timid than the other rabbits, he possesses a supernatural power of precognition, which allows him to warn the Sandleford rabbits of their impending destruction. This is not Fiver's only contribution to the group's safety, however, for his acute sense of impending trouble often saves the unwary rabbits from danger and eventually leads them to safety on Watership Down.

Another vital ally for Hazel is **Bigwig**, a big and strong rabbit who at the beginning of the story is a member of the Sandleford Warren "Owsla," the lapin police. Bigwig is the first rabbit that Hazel and Fiver are able to convince that the warren is in genuine danger and that they should leave immediately. Bigwig soon becomes the muscle of the group to complement Hazel's brains and leadership, becoming a valuable ally. But he is more than just brawn, for Bigwig proves himself to be very courageous, accepting the dangerous assignment of infiltrating Efrafa to rescue the rabbits there so that they could join Hazel's group. Toward the end, he faces the terrifying General Woundwort, a much larger and fiercer rabbit than Bigwig, in a bloody battle that only ends when Kehaar manages to chase the General away.

The tyrant, **General Woundwort**, has organized his warren into a totalitarian state devoid of personal liberties. The strongest of his litter of five, the General had been born some three years earlier and had learned to survive on his own while still a kitten after his parents were killed. Becoming wild and savage, he developed into a terrifyingly ruthless and brave fighter. In order to become even more powerful, he surrounded himself with rabbits like **Captain Holly** who were willing to follow his commands and thus became the leader of his own warren, Efrafa, which, in his paranoia to remain in control, he has turned into a totalitarian state. After Bigwig makes his daring raid on Efrafa to free the does under Woundwort's control, the General gives chase and meets his end when he decides to attack a dog rather than run from it as the other Efrafan rabbits do. Whether or not he survives the encounter is left open to speculation, and he becomes a kind of sinister legend to the rabbit kittens at Watership Down, whose mothers tell them to behave or else the General will get them.

The novel abounds with other rabbit characters, each with different strengths. Some of the rabbits, including **Buckthorn**, **Hawkbit**, **Speedwell**, and **Strawberry**, do not have much to individuate them from the group, but other rabbits have more character. **Blackberry**, for example, is quite clever and is the one who figures out that the rabbits can float across streams on a wooden board, a trick that later proves helpful in their escape from the Efrafans. **Dandelion** is the storyteller of the little band, a talent that proves useful in comforting the others whenever they are frightened. He tells them stories of their folk hero, El-ahrairah, as well as other tales that provide the reader with insights into the lapin culture Adams created. **Silver** is a hefty but quiet fellow who has not yet found his standing among the other rabbits, though he proves himself to be courageous when rats attack the warren. **Pipkin**, a small rabbit like Fiver, is rather timid but finds inspiration from Hazel, whom he admires, and he later volunteers to accompany Hazel on the dangerous mission to Efrafa.

Other characters outside Hazel's rabbit followers serve important roles as well. **Cowslip**, whom the Watership Down rabbits meet at the warren where a man is fattening up the residents for his dinner plate, shows what can happen to an animal when it's taken out of its natural environment. Cowslip, as well as the others in his warren, does not act like a typical rabbit. His fear of death from the snares—a reality he refuses to admit out loud—causes him to speak in a strange, clouded manner. He is philosophical and fascinated by unusual diversions like poetry and art, which only serve to distract his attentions from the inevitable. Finally, there is **Kehaar**, who becomes a friend to the Watership Down rabbits, though he is a seagull. Kehaar proves useful as a plot device when he quickly locates places where the rabbits can find does. When the rabbits first find him, Kehaar is very aggressive and doesn't trust them, but Hazel's kindness to him soon wins him over, and he proves himself to be a loyal and important ally.

Further Reading

Authors and Artists for Young Adults. Vol. 16. Detroit: Gale Research, 1995.

Adams, Richard. *The Day Gone By: An Autobiography.* New York: Knopf, 1991.

———. "Some Ingredients of *Watership Down:* The Thorny Paradise." In *Writers on Writing for Children.* Edited by Edward Blishen. Carmel Valley, CA: Kestral, 1975.

Berger, Laura Standley, ed. *Twentieth-Century Young Adult Writers.* 1st ed. Detroit: St. James, 1994.

Children's Literature Review. Vol. 20. Detroit: Gale Research, 1990.

Contemporary Literary Criticism. Vols. 4, 5, 18. Detroit: Gale Research, 1975, 1976, 1981.

Gilman, Richard. "The Rabbit's Iliad and Odyssey." *New York Times Book Review* (March 24, 1974).

Green, T. "Richard Adams' Long Journey from Watership Down." *Smithsonian* 10 (July 1979).

Henderson, Lesley, ed. *Contemporary Novelists.* 5th ed. Chicago: St. James, 1991.

Hunt, Peter. "The Good, the Bad and the Indifferent: Quality and Value in Three Contemporary Children's Books." In *The Signal Approach to Children's Books: A Collection.* Edited by Nancy Chambers. Metuchen, NJ: Scarecrow Press, 1988.

Inglis, Fred. "Cult and Culture: A Political Psychological Excursion." In *The Promise of Happiness: Value and Meaning in Children's Fiction.* Cambridge: Cambridge University Press, 1981.

Something about the Author. Vol. 69. Detroit: Gale Research, 1992.

Louisa May Alcott

1832-1888, American author

Little Women; or, Meg, Jo, Beth and Amy

(novel, 1868)

PLOT: Set in Massachusetts in the mid-1800s, this is the story of the March family. Mr. March, the father, is away at war serving as a chaplain; Mrs. March, whom the girls call "Marmee," is their beloved mother and keeper of their warm and nurturing family life. The Marches have four girls. The eldest, at 16, is Margaret, or Meg, who is pretty and somewhat plump. Next is Jo. She is 15, tall and coltish, irrepressible and funny, and already set on becoming a writer. Her one vanity is her beautiful dark and thick hair. Elizabeth, or Beth, is everybody's darling. At 13, she is shy, timid, and sweet. She is so peaceful about life in general that her father calls her "Little Tranquillity." The baby is Amy, with blue eyes and blonde hair and a somewhat high opinion of herself.

With Mr. March off at war tending to his duties as a chaplain, Christmas finds the family lonely and short on money, though never short on love and dreams. Feeling fortunate for each other's company, they talk about the marvelous presents they would have if they could afford them, and they delight in what few gifts they actually can give. Ready to eat their festive, if meager, dinner, they decide to take what food they have to share with a poor immigrant family. The day is made more merry when the March girls stage one of their dramatic presentations, written and directed by Jo.

Meg and Jo are invited to a New Year's dance at Mrs. Gardiner's. Meg is delighted, but Jo, who hates such displays, attends only reluctantly. However, once there she meets another hesitant guest named Laurie. His full name is Theodore Lawrence. A sixteen-year-old who lives with his grandfather, he happens to be the March family's wealthy neighbor, James Laurence. Laurie and the March girls become fast friends. After some debate, he is even allowed to become the sole male in their theater presentations.

Later in the year, Marmee receives a telegram saying her husband is very ill. She must go to Washington, D.C., to take care of him. The money for the trip must be borrowed, of course, for the Marches have none. Irritable but wealthy Aunt March answers Marmee's request for help. Jo, who mysteriously disappears while her mother is preparing for the journey, suddenly comes home with twenty-five dollars to help defray expenses for the trip. When asked where the money came from, Jo takes off her bonnet, revealing that she has sold her beautiful hair. Laurie's grandfather also aids the March family by kindly offering the services of his employee, John Brooke. Brooke will accompany Marmee to Washington, while Laurence keeps an eye on the girls at home.

While their mother is away, Beth comes down with a raging fever. Always frail, she nearly dies and

Marmee must be summoned back from Washington. Beth recovers, although her health is never again fully restored. Mr. March also recovers and at last returns home. The war ends and the years pass. Laurie goes to college at his grandfather's request, and Meg marries John Brooke. Amy travels to Rome as the companion of wealthy Aunt March. Unhappy as she is to leave her family, Jo feels that she must try her wings as a journalist in New York. There, she meets a poor professor, Friedrich Bhaer, and falls in love. Sadness overcomes the whole family when Beth, whose heart has been damaged from the fever, dies. Eventually, Jo and Friedrich and Laurie and Amy marry, and all the families grow and flourish in happiness.

CHARACTERS: This children's classic was Alcott's first novel and an instant success. It is based on her childhood recollections of her life in Boston and Concord, Massachusetts. Jo is the author's alter ego, and her real-life sisters were Anna, Elizabeth, and May. Alcott's other novels include *An Old-Fashioned Girl* (1870), the six-volume work, *Aunt Jo's Scrap Bag* (1872-82), *Little Men* (1871), *Eight Cousins* (1875), and *Jo's Boys* (1886). A volunteer nurse during the Civil War, Alcott contacted typhoid and, like Beth, never fully recovered from her illness.

The most memorable of the girls in *Little Women* is **Jo March**, a bright, witty young girl who resists all attempts to turn her into a feminine beauty. She is, instead, tall, energetic, and full of boundless enthusiasm for life and people. She bosses her sisters around, including Meg, the eldest, saying that their father told her to be the man of the family while he is away. Under Jo's excitable exterior, however, is a warm, sensitive, and loving heart. When Beth is left in poor health after the fever, it is Jo who looks after her. And when wealthy Aunt March announces that she needs a companion on her European trip, it is Jo who would dearly love to go, for she longs to see the world and become a writer. But Jo and her brisk, domineering aunt do not mix well, so Jo reluctantly but graciously sees young Amy off on the trip she so desperately wished to take.

For a time, Jo is in love with Laurie, but she resigns herself to the fact that he has stronger feelings for Amy. Later, when she falls in love with a professor and they marry, she settles down with her husband at a school called Plumfield. They will never be rich, Jo knows, but the school becomes a happy home for all those who need "teaching, care, and kindness." Add to that mix Jo's own rambunctious boys and life is spirited in the new household. As she tells her mother at the end of the novel, "There's no need for me to say it, for every one can see that I'm far happier than I deserve. We never shall be rich ... but I have nothing to complain of and never was so jolly in my life."

Jo's sister, **Meg March**, is a pretty young woman who takes her position as the eldest daughter quite seriously, even though she cannot quite stand up to Jo and often ends up laughing at her. However, Meg shows her backbone clearly when she does stand up to bossy Aunt March, who scolds her for intending to marry John Brooke. When Aunt March tells her she should have more sense than to marry someone without money or position, Meg retorts, "I couldn't do better if I waited half my life!"

The two youngest girls offer interesting contrasts to their sisters. Shy, timid **Beth March** seems to live in a secure world of her own, a peaceful world where she is rarely disturbed, except by those she loves. She is most significant as the character whose sad end brings a sense of tragedy to the otherwise happy family. When Jo returns home one spring, Beth confesses that she knows she has not long to live. In a moving scene, she tells her beloved sister, "I'm not afraid, but it seems as if I should be homesick for you even in heaven." **Amy March**, of all the girls, has the highest opinion of herself, which is partially the result of her being the youngest. A pale, slender lass, she is always mindful of her manners. This delights aristocratic, brusque Aunt March, who takes a fancy to the girl and invites her to Europe as her companion. Petulant and arrogant, Amy has years of growing up to do before her marriage to Laurie brings strength and devotion to her character. Their daughter, born frail and small, reminds them both of Beth, and this shadow on their lives changes Amy into a more compassionate, sweeter young woman. She says to her mother, "In spite of my one cross [meaning her frail daughter], I can say with Meg, 'Thank God, I'm a happy woman.'"

Laurie Laurence, who serves as the most significant love interest in the story, is a fun-loving, friendly young man who is delighted when the lively March family enters his somewhat staid life with his wealthy grandfather. When he goes off to college to please his grandfather, he becomes a dandy, flirting and haphazardly throwing his life away. It takes his marriage to Amy and the birth of their daughter for him to realize that pain and loss can come to anyone. Laurie changes from an irresponsible man-about-town to a stronger and more serious young man by the end of the novel.

There are a number of notable minor characters in *Little Women*. **John Brooke**, who is employed by the elder Laurence, is a quiet, serious, gentle, and loving man who wins Meg's heart. Laurie's grandfather, **James Laurence**, is a refined, elderly gentleman whose austere appearance and manners cover up a kind soul that is welcomed with affection into the March family. Jo's husband, **Friedrich Bhaer**, is a foreign-born professor with a fine mind and a quiet manner. Older than Jo and not physically attractive, he is shy and hesitant at first in showing his obvious affection for her. **Mrs. March**, called **Marmee**, and **Mr. March** are loving parents who adore their children and constantly give them models of strength and honor to follow. At the novel's conclusion, when all the families are gathered around their matriarch, Mrs. March tells her daughters, "Oh, my girls, however long you may live, I never can wish you a greater happiness than this!"

Further Reading

Burke, Kathleen. *Louisa May Alcott.* New York: Chelsea House, 1988.

Children's Literature Review. Vol. 1. Detroit: Gale Research, 1976.

Bruccoli, Matthew J., and Richard Layman, eds. *Realism, Naturalism, and Local Color, 1865-1888.* Vol. 2 of *Concise Dictionary of American Literary Biography.* Detroit: Gale Research, 1987.

Elbert, Sarah. *A Hunger for Home: Louisa May Alcott and* Little Women. Philadelphia: Temple University Press, 1984.

Estes, Glenn E., ed. *American Writers for Children before 1900.* Vol. 42 of *Dictionary of Literary Biography.* Detroit: Gale Research, 1985.

Janeway, Elizabeth. "Meg, Jo, Beth, Amy, and Louisa." *New York Times Book Review* (19 September 1968).

Johnston, Norma. *Louisa May: The World and Works of Louisa May Alcott.* New York: Macmillan, 1991.

Keyser, Elizabeth. *Whispers in the Dark: The Fiction of Louisa May Alcott.* Knoxville: University of Tennessee Press, 1993.

MacDonald, Ruth K. *Louisa May Alcott.* Boston: Twayne, 1983.

Myerson, Joel, ed. *The American Renaissance in New England.* Vol. 1 of *Dictionary of Literary Biography.* Detroit: Gale Research, 1978.

Nineteenth-Century Literature Criticism. Vol. 6. Detroit: Gale Research, 1984.

Santrey, Laurence. *Louisa May Alcott: Young Writer.* Mahwah, NJ: Troll, 1986.

Stern, Madeleine B. *Critical Essays on Louisa May Alcott.* Boston: G. K. Hall, 1984.

———. *Louisa May Alcott.* Norman, OK: University of Oklahoma Press, 1985.

Yesterday's Authors of Books for Children. Vol. 1. Detroit: Gale Research, 1977.

Lloyd Alexander

1924-, American young adult fantasy novelist

Westmark

(young adult novel, 1981)

PLOT: In this first book of the Westmark trilogy, which the author says is not a fantasy but is "no less fantastic," King Augustine and Queen Caroline are still grieving for their daughter, who disappeared six years earlier. The power of the medieval kingdom of Westmark now lies mainly in the hands of the chief minister, the villainous Cabbarus.

Cabbarus requires all publications in the kingdom to get government permission before going to print. Thinking he will get the permission in the morning, a printer's devil, Theo, accepts a commission from the dwarf Musket on behalf of his master, Dr. Absalam. But the press is raided and Theo flees. He reluctantly joins up with Musket and Dr. Absalam, who is actually Count Las Bombas, a charlatan. They soon meet a young urchin named Mickle, who is a talented ventriloquist. Being without a family, she joins them. Theo is attracted to her, but when Las Bombas sets up a phony clairvoyant act involving the girl, Theo leaves them. Next, he joins a group of students led by the charismatic Florian, who refers to all of them as his children. Later, Theo learns the phony act of Las Bombas has been uncovered and that Las Bombas, Musket, and Mickle are in jail.

After Theo rescues them from prison, Las Bombas meets his old enemy, Skeit, who realizes that Cabbarus might be interested in clairvoyance to keep the king and queen in line. Skeit brings Mickle, Theo, Musket, and Las Bombas to meet Cabbarus in an old torture chamber in the palace basement. Mickle acts strangely and falls into a trance. When she awakens, she has recovered her lost memory. She recalls wandering into the chamber and falling into a well. Instead of rescuing her, Cabbarus had made sure she fell down the well, but she survived and has been wandering the streets without her memory ever since. Mickle, who is actually the long-lost Princess Augusta, is reunited with her parents. The life of the evil Cabbarus is spared by Theo, who asks that he be banished from the kingdom instead. Theo then becomes the king's adviser.

In books two and three of the trilogy, Theo changes from a peace-loving figure to the falcon-like Kestrel when he repels an invasion of the kingdom in The Kestrel *(1982). In* The Beggar Queen *(1984) Mickle has ascended the throne and, along with Theo, is forced into hiding when Cabbarus returns. But good triumphs; Mickle and Theo marry and give up the throne so that Westmark can become a democracy.*

CHARACTERS: The first of three picaresque novels of high adventure, *Westmark* breathes new life into the usual stereotypes of lost princess, modest but valiant hero, and hateful villain. The central theme is expressed in the dedication: "For those who regret their many imperfections, but know it would be worse having none at all." The central character is a printer's apprentice named **Theo**. Despite his poor background, he has learned to read and is apprenticed to the good master Anton. Theo is a fine craftsman who loves virtue and hates violence of any kind. It is with great reluctance that he takes up with the likes of Musket and Las Bombas after the raid on the print shop that kills his master. Nonetheless, Theo is immediately aware that Las Bombas is a fraud and a charlatan. However, he stays with him because he is immediately drawn to the pitiful street urchin, Mickle. Drab as a sparrow with a narrow face and beak-like nose, she has pale blue eyes. Theo is enchanted. He is, however, disturbed by the recurring and frightening dreams that plague Mickle. After learning of the phony act performed by Las Bombas and involving Mickle to cheat people out of their money, Theo is torn between wanting to stay with her and his desire to distance himself from this chicanery. In the end he leaves, knowing he has done the right thing, but miserable nonetheless.

When the evil Cabbarus's deceptions have finally been uncovered, Theo admits that he hates the man but he can't have someone's death on his conscience. So he begs that his life be spared and that Cabbarus be banished instead. Later, when Theo questions himself about his decision, he is handed a scrap of paper from the court physician, Dr. Torrens. It is from Florian and says only, "My Child, you did well. Perhaps you even did right."

The frightened waif **Mickle** has a recurring, terrifying dream in which she is drowning. Sometimes, however, she also has a dream in which her mother and father are playing with her. This puzzles Theo because Mickle has told him that she never knew her parents. When she eventually recovers her memory, she recalls that she is actually **Princess Augusta** and has been a victim of Cabbarus's treachery.

Florian is a charismatic firebrand who leads a group of children, although he is but a few years older than Theo. In time, Theo earns the highest honor Florian can bestow—to be called one of his children. For all his charm and charisma, Florian is a serious man whose intention is to overthrow the evil government of Cabbarus and establish a democracy. Later, it is ascertained that Florian is actually a member of the royal family.

The evil **Cabbarus**, the chief minister, has usurped the power of the kingdom by preying on the grief of the king and queen over the disappearance of their only child. Of course, it is actually he who is the true source of their sorrow, for, with murderous intentions, he caused their child to fall into the well six years earlier. One of the methods by which Cabbarus keeps power in the kingdom is to make sure that everything that is printed has his approval. He will stop at nothing to maintain control over others, including urging the king to try to communicate with the voice of his supposedly dead daughter. When the court physician, the good **Dr. Torrens**, objects, Cabbarus urges the king to banish him, which he does over the objections of the queen. Torrens falls into a river but is rescued and joins Florian's revolutionary group. When the corruption of the evil Cabbarus is uncovered, Torrens returns. He advises Theo to travel around Westmark to see for himself what the kingdom is like, then he will be able to find out what the people want and so help the kingdom to be ruled for the benefit of all.

Theo first meets the dwarf **Musket**, who stands no higher than the middle button of Theo's jacket, when he appears at the print shop with a printing commission. When the militiamen arrive, Theo takes refuge in Musket's coach, and in this way is introduced to the charming fraud known as Count Las Bombas. **Las Bombas** is an out-and-out swindler, but an engaging one. When Theo first meets him, he goes by the name of **Dr. Absalam**. Theo soon learns that Las Bombas assumes whatever identity best serves the occasion. This charlatan, scoundrel though he may be, is nothing if not resourceful, and Theo soon grows to like him despite himself. Las Bombas's appealing nature is one reason why Theo decides to accompany him and Musket on their journey. At the end of the novel, when the treachery of Cabbarus has been uncovered, Las Bombas has no qualms about requesting a reward from the king. When Theo says he ought to be ashamed, Las Bombas admits he is, but he is more ashamed of being penniless. Thus armed with money, he sets off with a light heart to find adventure—and a gullible public—once again.

The Remarkable Journey of Prince Jen

(young adult novel, 1991)

PLOT: Prince Jen, the well-meaning but naive son of King T'ai, monarch of the T'ang Kingdom, volunteers to represent his father on a journey to T'ien-kuo, a land where all people enjoy harmony and happiness. King T'ai wants to see how this is accomplished but is too ill to make the journey himself. With his servant Mafoo, who is not happy about the trip, Prince Jen sets out for T'ien-kuo. Following instructions from Master Wu, he carries six gifts with him: an iron sword, a leather saddle, a wooden flute, a bronze bowl, a sandalwood paint box, and a kite. Though humble in appearance, in reality the gifts are magical.

Jen immediately proves his ineptness by losing the saddle, but this loss is compensated for by the appearance of Voyaging Moon, a beautiful flute player who joins the travelers. Jen gives her the wooden flute that he carries because she plays it so beautifully. He warns her, however, that it is just a loan, since it is intended for the leader of T'ien-kuo. In turn, Voyaging Moon warns Jen and Mafoo about a bandit named Natha Yellow Scarf. Indeed, they soon run into the bandit, but luckily for Prince Jen, Natha accepts the sword instead of killing them. The magic weapon is capable of slicing in two anything that it touches.

Prince Jen and his companions have many adventures. Moxa, the Mad Robber, is next to join them. After an episode in which a magistrate named Fat-choy beats up the prince, the group meets an old man, Master Shu, who wears a wooden collar around his neck. Under the threat of death, it is forbidden for anyone to remove the collar. But Jen is only too happy to remove it because the collar was put on Master Shu by Fat-choy. When the party tries to

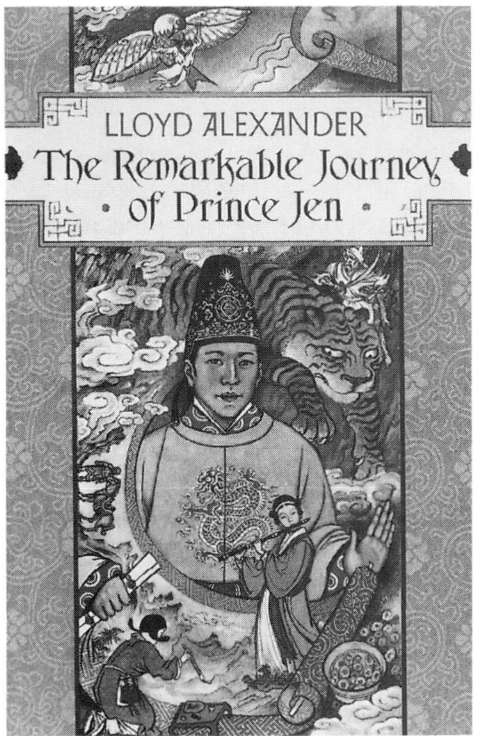

Prince Jen learns about true happiness as he journeys to the fabled kingdom of T'ien-kuo.

cross the River Lo, their boat is capsized and Jen is separated from the others. This is especially distressing to Jen because by this time he is in love with Voyaging Moon. While Jen searches for the others, Voyaging Moon plays the flute at an inn to earn money. In one way or another, Jen manages to lose or give away the remaining gifts and decides to give up his journey to T'ien-kuo. But he runs into trouble with Fat-choy and is forced to wear a wooden collar. All winter long, Jen tries unsuccessfully to free himself. Finally, he meets Mafoo and Moxa once again and is freed from the collar.

Prince Jen learns that his father has died, making him the new king of T'ang. But he has lost his identification that proves he is the late king's son. Jen is reunited with Voyaging Moon only to discover that Natha has taken over the capital of T'ang and made himself king. He also has made a bargain with Voyaging Moon to marry him. Jen goes to the village to confront Natha, but a great eagle sweeps out of the sky and destroys the dreaded bandit. The eagle turns out to be a young girl to whom Jen gave the magic kite when she was in need.

After all the gifts are returned, King Jen and Voyaging Moon are married and live happily ever after. When they set out once again to fulfill Jen's promise to his father to journey to T'ien-kuo, they are told by Jen's teacher, Master Hu, that they should not seek what they have already found, for their happiness and harmony can be found right at home.

CHARACTERS: Prince Jen is an engaging but naive young man who knows little about responsibility or maturity but finds both on his journey to the kingdom of T'ien-kuo. He is well-meaning as he sets out on the journey for his father, but he has little comprehension of the pitfalls that lie ahead. With his long hair bound under his tall, stiff cap and his royal robes wrapped around him, Jen tries to maintain an air of calm dignity, but it is difficult for him to do. His good intentions constantly get him into trouble, such as when the travelers come upon the old man drowning in the river. Jen tries to help him but succeeds only in nearly drowning himself. Jen is constantly astonished by the events that befall him, becoming sure of only one thing: his growing love for Voyaging Moon. In the end, it is this love for her that prompts him to take on the dreaded bandit Natha. Jen is often bewildered by how he is rescued, not realizing that it is his own goodness and kindness to others that provides its own reward.

Prince Jen's faithful if irreverent servant, **Mafoo**, is round-faced and bandy-legged. He is very unwilling to make the journey to the kingdom of T'ien-kuo and doesn't mind saying so. Throughout the entire trip, Mafoo is disparaging of their intentions and fearful of the outcome. About the only time the feisty servant becomes calm and respectful is when he must sadly inform his charge after the old king's death that he is no longer the young lord prince but is instead King of T'ang.

Prince Jen is charmed by the appearance of **Voyaging Moon**, although her high cheekbones and long, black hair, which hangs loosely over her shoulders, do not make her beautiful in the traditional sense. Rather than becoming impressed with the presence of the prince, she immediately points out that she would be useful on their journey, since she was born and raised in the district and knows the country well. After she is reunited with the prince, who learns that Natha is now king, she admits to Jen that she made a bargain with the bandit. In exchange for a few hours with the prince, she has agreed to marry Natha. Of course, Prince Jen can't allow this to happen, and with courage and conviction he goes into the bandit's den. When the couple is reunited and Master Hu asks Jen why he wants to travel to T'ien-kuo looking for something he has already found, it is Voyaging Moon who first grasps the old man's meaning. "Come home," she says to her husband. "If, that is, we ever truly left it."

Master Hu is Jen's beloved old teacher who instructed him in the art of princely virtues. He stops the prince and Voyaging Moon from attempting once again the journey to the kingdom of T'ien-kuo, telling them they need only to look at themselves and their own kingdom to locate the happiness they seek. **Master Wu** is the wise man who sends Jen and Mafoo on the journey with the six seemingly humble, but actually magical, gifts. These items prove their usefulness and, in the end, save the life of Jen and his beloved. On his journey Prince Jen also meets **Master Shu**, a strange old man with long, white hair and a frail build. When Jen first sees him, the old man is wearing a heavy wooden yoke called a Cangue—a Collar of Punishment. When Jen attempts to free him, Master Shu warns that the collar bears the seal of the magistrate and to remove it would mean a certain death sentence. Prince Jen ignores this danger and proclaims that he will free him by royal command anyway.

There are also two villains whom Jen and the others meet: the bandit **Natha Yellow Scarf** and the magistrate Fat-choy. Natha is tall and fierce-looking, his face chalked a deathly white and streaked with crimson. From the moment he sees Voyaging Moon, he is determined to have her and strikes a bargain with her in return for a few hours with Jen. But goodness wins out and Natha is destroyed by the gifts of Master Wu and by the love and caring of the remarkable Prince Jen. Official of the First Rank **Fat-choy** is obese and bald as a lemon. Never has there been such an oily magistrate as this one, and he relishes the opportunity to clap the naive prince into a wooden collar. Another seedy character, **Moxa**, is not as villainous as his reputation as the Mad Robber would have him be. Lanky and thin, he looks more poverty-stricken than mad. He offers Jen such sage advice as "never rob someone who has already been robbed," since that only makes them feel worse, and "never rob the poor," because that only adds to their misery.

Further Reading

Alexander, Lloyd. "The Fortune-Tellers." *Horn Book* 70 (January/February 1994): 46-47.

———. "1986 Regina Medal Recipient." *Catholic Library World* 58 (July/August 1986): 14-15.

Authors and Artists for Young Adults. Vol. 1. Detroit: Gale Research, 1989.

Berger, Laura Standley. *Twentieth-Century Children's Writers.* 4th ed. Detroit: St. James, 1995.

———. *Twentieth-Century Young Adult Writers.* 1st ed. Detroit: St. James, 1994.

Contemporary Literary Criticism. Vol. 35. Detroit: Gale Research, 1985.

May, Jill P. *Lloyd Alexander.* Boston: Twayne, 1991.

Something about the Author. Vols. 3, 49, 81. Detroit: Gale Research, 1972, 1988, 1995.

Something about the Author Autobiography Series. Vol. 19. Detroit: Gale Research, 1995.

Anonymous

American diarist

Go Ask Alice

(diary, 1971)

PLOT: The entries in this diary, kept by an anonymous young girl, begin four days before her fifteenth birthday and end about two years later. Anonymous is the oldest child of two loving, attentive parents. Her father is a university professor and her mother manages the household, which includes a younger son and daughter, Tim and Alexandria (Alex, for short). When Dad accepts a new university position, the resulting move creates an emotional upheaval for Anonymous, particularly over leaving her beloved Gran and Gramps and her boyfriend, Roger. With the exception of Anonymous, the family members soon adapt to their new surroundings, but she eventually finds a friend in another loner, Beth Baum.

At a party one day, Anonymous is given a soda laced with LSD. She is perplexed but intrigued with the results and later repeats the experience, during which she deliberately loses her virginity to a teenager named Bill Thompson. With another girlfriend and fellow drug user, Chris, Anonymous begins using a greater variety of drugs. She grows more distant from her mother and father, whom she considers domineering and unapproachable. Chris and Anonymous begin selling drugs for their two boyfriends, Richie and Ted, who the girls discover are gay. Feeling angry and betrayed, they turn the two young men in to the police and run away to San Francisco, where they take a variety of poor-paying jobs and continue to be exploited by people like Sheila, the owner of a boutique where Chris gets a job.

After two months, they contact their parents and return to their homes. A contrite and remorseful Anonymous tries to reform, but Chris again supplies her with drugs and she runs off to Oregon to live a promiscuous hippie life with such commune inhabitants as the pathetic Doris. Anonymous again comes home, beaten and repentant. After she is forced by circumstances to inform on Jan, a classmate whose drug use is out of control, she is persecuted by Jan and her friends who seek revenge. The only bright spot in Anonymous's life is the loving relationship she has with a college student named Joel Reems.

Anonymous almost dies after eating some acid-laced candy supposedly planted by the vengeful Jan. After a hospital stay, she is sent to a mental institution, where she meets a pathetic young girl, Babbie. Her father engineers a release, and Anonymous makes great progress in going straight, but three weeks after her last diary entry she is found dead of an overdose. The mystery remains whether it was an accidental or premeditated death.

CHARACTERS: When **Anonymous** first introduces herself through her diary entries she appears to be an average adolescent: worried about her personal appearance (she is on a strict diet to loose weight), devastated when her boyfriend Roger temporarily strays, worried about her social standing among her peers, and anxious to please her parents and friends. She is devoted to her family, works hard to maintain good grades, and tries to be a dutiful, responsible daughter. Also in typical teenage fashion, she is beginning to rebel against parental authority and develops the attitude that adults just don't understand her. A series of unfortunate occurrences, such as a move to a new environment where she has no friends and the death of her grandparents, bring instability into her life and make her particularly vulnerable to any escape route that promises to ease her pain and confusion. When she begins taking drugs, these feelings grow and the "Mr. Hyde" aspect of her personality emerges. The diary entries become increasingly filled with sex, profanity, and obscenities. She sinks lower and lower until she loses all sense of values and dignity. However, her basic decency, respectability, and love of family always bring her back to her senses eventually. Like the prodigal son, she begs forgiveness after returning to her family. Unfortunately, despite her firm resolve, she is unable to escape her past and her drug connections. Anonymous is a pathetic figure, well-meaning, susceptible, courageous, and ultimately tragic.

Dad and **Mom** are devoted, loving parents who try to furnish an environment where their children can grow and reach full potential. Intellectual (Dad is the Head of the Political Science Department at a college) but not unapproachable, they are caring and forgiving toward their daughter; they try to understand and appreciate her problems. Perhaps their major flaw is not comprehending the gravity of the situation and taking more drastic steps, including sending her someplace where she could escape the influence of her drug-dependent friends.

Anonymous has two siblings and grandparents of whom she is very fond. Her brother Tim, an eighth grader, is a pleasant, mature youngster who loves his sister and sympathizes with her problems. Anonymous says he "has a clear, decent, honorable outlook on life" and "tries to see things from his parents point of view." Young sister **Alex** (short for **Alexandria**), is a grade schooler who is an affable child devoted to the other members of her family. Anonymous's grandparents, **Gran** and **Gramps**, are also caring and understanding people. Gramps is a wise, discerning man who was once involved in politics. Loyal and concerned about his granddaughter, he tells her that the greatest difficulty she faces after her return from San Francisco is forgiving herself. After Gramp's death, Gran, who has devoted her life to her husband, slips into ill health and also dies.

Anonymous's first friend after the family move is the young Jewish girl, **Beth Baum**, the daughter of a local doctor. A shy, reclusive girl who loves reading, she and Anonymous form an instant close friendship that is broken when Beth goes to summer camp and later joins a different social clique. The switch proves not to be a wise choice for Anonymous. At the party where she is first introduced to drugs, **Bill Thompson** takes care of her and nurses her through the experience. Later, during another drug trip, Anonymous loses her virginity by having sex with him.

Anonymous first meets **Chris** at the boutique where Chris works part-time. Chris is a year older than Anonymous and instantly ingratiates herself by sharing beauty secrets and fashion tips with the younger girl. Alienated from her separated parents and rebelling against authority, Chris uses a variety of drugs and initiates Anonymous into their use. She persuades Anonymous to sell drugs and later to run away to San Francisco. When the two return defeated and chastened, Chris is the first to return to drug use and start Anonymous back on the road to self-destruction. Though basically decent and not intentionally immoral, she is weak and unable to break the destructive cycle of her drug habit.

Two of the friends with whom Chris and Anonymous take drugs are the attractive, young pre-med students, **Richie** and **Ted**, with whom Anonymous first smokes pot. The two secretly gay lovers take advantage of the young, naive girls, who have fallen in love with them. They exploit them and force them to become pushers to feed their habits. Before running off to San Francisco, Chris and Anonymous inform on them.

In San Francisco, the two girls meet and are impressed by **Sheila**, the glamorous, charming owner of a fashionable boutique. Though Sheila is outwardly solicitous and concerned about the girls, during one of her drug parties she and a male companion rape and physically abuse Chris and Anonymous, ending their friendship.

Jan is the spiteful, malicious classmate of Anonymous who conspires to force Anonymous back into the drug scene after her repentant return from San Francisco. When Anonymous is forced to call Jan's parents after the girl begins behaving wildly because of an overdose, Jan sets out to destroy Anonymous by every foul method possible. She succeeds by feeding her candies laced with acid.

During her drug-related travels, Anonymous meets two pathetic victims of the drug culture, **Doris** and **Babbie**. Doris, who has had four different stepfathers by age ten, was forced to have sex with stepfather number five when she was eleven. Later, in a foster home, she is introduced to drugs and a lesbian relationship. When Anonymous meets her in a commune in Oregon, Doris is still only a child, but already one without hope or a future. Babbie, an inmate in the mental institution where Anonymous is admitted, has a similar background. At thirteen, she has been on drugs for two years, feeding her habit by becoming a "BP," or baby prostitute. She also appears to be completely crushed and filled with despair.

William Armstrong

1914-, American young adult novelist

Sounder

(young adult novel, 1969)

PLOT: This winner of the 1970 Newbery Award takes place in the southern United States during the late nineteenth century. The story centers on a young black boy, his mother and father, and three siblings. None of the family can read or write, although the boy once tried to get an education by walking eight miles to school. He had to give this up, however, when the severe winter weather made the daily trip too difficult. An important member of the family is Sounder, a stray hunting dog his father found wandering in the fields one day. The dog is part bulldog and part Georgia redbone hound. He follows the father home and becomes one of the family. The boy, who is the oldest child, becomes especially attached to Sounder.

One winter day, while the family is starving because of the severe weather, the white sheriff and his deputies arrive to arrest the father for stealing food from a local smokehouse. Sounder is shot while trying to protect his master. Wounded, the dog runs away and disappears. Sometime later Sounder returns, badly injured in body and spirit, but the boy is overjoyed to see him. The family learns that the father will be sent to a labor camp, so the boy must do the field work when summer comes. Though he wanders from town to town in search of his father, the years pass without any sign of him. One day, the boy finds a book in a trash can and also meets a schoolmaster who takes pity on him. The schoolmaster offers to teach him to read the book if the boy will help with chores.

In time, the boy learns to read and teaches his younger brothers and sisters. At last, the father returns, a man broken in body and spirit just like Sounder. Upon seeing the father return, Sounder barks for the first time since he was injured. Within a short time, both the father and Sounder die. The boy chooses to remember both of them walking together, tall and proud.

CHARACTERS: This is a tale of great pain, cruelty, and tragedy. It is also a tale of the dignity of the human spirit, as expressed in the determination of the **boy**. When he is a young lad, he is determined to learn to read and write. For two years he tries to walk the eight miles daily to the school, but during the harsh winter weather he is forced to give up his chance at an education. The boy is deeply attached to **Sounder**, the dog that follows his father home one day.

Although the boy sees much of the cruelty of life around him, he says little about it. When he sees his mother frying sausages one cold November morning, he knows that something is wrong because the winter so far has been bitterly cold and the crops lean. Only possum and raccoon pelts have kept the family alive. Although he is grateful for the good meals that the sausage provides, he is concerned as to where the food came from. His worries prove justified when the white sheriff and his deputies come to their cabin to take away his father for stealing from the local smokehouse. The boy watches in silence as his father is handcuffed and thrown into the back of a wagon. His father will not return home again for many years, and by then the strong man he once knew will have disappeared, just as the once strong Sounder returns a changed animal after nursing his wounds. After Sounder is shot, the boy finds the dog's ear in the road and puts it under his pillow that night, wishing fervently for Sounder to be alive.

Stoically, the boy endures the cruelty of others, such as when he visits his father at Christmastime before he is sent to a labor camp. The homes in town are bright with Christmas ornaments. The boy has only a cake, which his mother has made to deliver to his father, but the cruel jailkeeper destroys the cake while looking for a saw or file. Through all this brutality and hardship, the boy's determination remains, and one day it is rewarded when he finds a book by Montaigne. At long last, he has found someone—the schoolmaster—who will unlock the secrets of reading and bring joy into his life.

Both mother and father endure the hardships of their lives with silence and strength. When the boy visits his **father** in jail, the older man tells him not to grieve for his plight. He assures his son that he will get word to him after the court hearing. But of course he can't, and it is years before the father is able to return to the family. By then, he is a different man than the one who left. While he had the strength to live until he was able to return home, his body finally gives out after his return, and he dies a short time later. He has accepted his pain and the tragedy of his life with dignity and endurance.

The **mother**, despite the harshness of her life, understands her son's great desire for an education. When the schoolmaster offers to house and feed the boy, letting him attend school in exchange for chores, she accepts, although the loss of her son will mean further hardship for her at home. She realizes that the boy's new knowledge will bring hope that life will one day be better for the family.

The minor, mainly white characters in this story have been called somewhat stereotyped: the **jailkeeper** is cruel and has a frightening appearance, while the white **sheriff** and his deputies are completely heartless. The only minor character who shows compassion is the **schoolmaster**. He sees how the boy clings to the treasured book he has found and recognizes his great desire to learn.

Further Reading

Berger, Laura Standley, ed. *Twentieth-Century Young Adult Writers*. 1st ed. Detroit: St. James, 1994.

Chevalier, Tracy, ed. *Twentieth-Century Children's Writers*. 3rd ed. Detroit: St. James, 1989.

Children's Literature Review. Vol. 1. Detroit: Gale Research, 1976.

Collier, Laurie, and Joyce Nakamura, eds. *Major Authors and Illustrators for Children and Young Adults*. Detroit: Gale Research, 1993.

Contemporary Authors New Revision Series. Vol. 9. Detroit: Gale Research, 1983.

De Montreville, Doris, and Doon Hill, eds. *Third Book of Junior Authors*. New York: H. W. Wilson, 1972.

Something about the Author Autobiography Series. Vol. 7. Detroit: Gale, 1989.

Ward, Martha, ed. *Authors of Books for Young People*. 3rd ed. Metuchen, NJ: Scarecrow, 1990.

A boy and his faithful dog, Sounder, suffer from hunger and racism in the American South in Armstrong's 1969 Newbery Medal-winning novel.

Isaac Asimov

1920-1992, American novelist

Foundation

(science fiction, 1951)

PLOT: Set in the distant future, this science fiction classic, the first in a trilogy, tells of the Foundation, a project intended to save humanity from an aeons-long period of barbarism. The planet Trantor, located near the center of the Milky Way galaxy, is the hub of the twelve-thousand-year-old Galactic Empire. About forty billion people live on Trantor, making it the densest clot of humanity ever seen, as well as the most advanced planet in the Empire.

Trantor is actually a single city that covers the planet's surface, and its enormous population is almost entirely devoted to administrating the Empire. It depends on trade from the outer worlds to provide it with all its necessary supplies.

Hari Seldon, born in the 11,988th year of the Galactic Era, is the legendary mathematician of Trantor. When Gaal Dornick arrives from faraway Synnax to work with Seldon, he soon learns that the famed mathematician is out of favor with the authorities of the Imperial Government. Using mathematical models, Seldon can see into the future and has prophesied that the Empire is dying, the end of Trantor is near, and nothing can prevent its destruction.

The entire Galactic Empire will decline and fall, declares Seldon, who is brought to trial by the Commission of Public Safety. What will follow is a period of ignorance, barbarism, and darkness that will last thirty thousand years. Although nothing will save the Empire, Seldon says that he can at least save future generations from thousands and thousands of years of misery by completing the *Encyclopedia Galactica.* By the time the Empire collapses, the project will be completed, and it will contain all the knowledge that has been acquired through the centuries. In this way, the human race will not have to rebuild civilization from scratch. Far from being willing to listen to Seldon's reasoning, however, the Commission banishes him and his thirty-thousand-man project staff to the planet Terminus at the edge of the galaxy. They are told that they can finish their work in peace there if they wish to.

Some fifty years pass. One day, Seldon, now in a wheelchair, appears in front of the mayor of Terminus City, Salvor Hardin. Seldon explains to an astonished Hardin and his board of trustees that the entire encyclopedia project was a fake. In fact, he wanted to be banished by the Commission to Terminus, for it is here, on this small planet, that the seeds of a new empire are to be sown. It will be the start of the Second Galactic Empire, for the original Galactic Empire is indeed dying. However, Seldon cautions that the Empire, although weakened, is still strong enough to cause trouble and must be overcome. So begins the slow formation and growth of the Foundation as it comes to dominate kingdoms on the outskirts of the Galaxy.

The other two books in the "Foundation Trilogy" are Foundation and Empire *(1952), which explains how the Foundation grows strong enough to defeat the First Empire, and* Second Foundation *(1953), which involves the period after the First Empire's defeat. Years later, Asimov supplemented his trilogy with* Foundation's Edge *(1982),* Foundation and Earth *(1986), the prequel* Prelude to Foundation *(1988), and* Forward the Foundation *(1993).*

CHARACTERS: Asimov's Galactic Empire can be likened to ancient Rome and its collapse and fall. The author also points out aspects of American society in decline, such as its failure to pick up garbage or polluting pure drinking water, which are indications of a modern society in the initial stages of collapse. **Hari Seldon**, the principal character in *Foundation,* is a somewhat mysterious genius who is aware of these small signs of decay, whereas others—certainly the central government—choose to ignore them.

Seldon was born in the 11,988th year of the Galactic Era and dies in 12,069. More commonly, these dates are given in terms of the current Foundational Era: 1 to 79 F.E. Born to middle-class parents living on Helicon in the Arcturus sector, Seldon is the son of a grower of hydroponically raised tobacco plants. Although not all facts about Seldon's early life are known with certainty, it is said that at a very early age he demonstrated an amazing mathematical ability. As an adult he became recognized as the master mathematician of the Empire.

Basically a decent man, Seldon is increasingly torn by his feelings of responsibility for saving humankind from the coming calamity. He knows that the Empire will be destroyed from within, just as ancient Rome was. Nothing, not even his own abilities as a genius, can stop this decay and fall. Yet the Empire must be saved, and Seldon sees a way to do so. Initially, he creates the science of psychohistory, which allows him to predict events and even shape them long after his death. When he predicts the end of the Empire, he uses his new science to help speed up the creation of the Second Empire, which he regards as humanity's only hope for salvation.

More and more Seldon becomes obsessed with his dream, turning into a lonely and melancholy man in the process. He loses friends and family members because of his obsession, and the erosion of his family parallels the Empire's decline. By the end of the novel, when Seldon has survived his own destruction and has seemingly succeeded in his plans, the Emperor **Cleon II** is killed—vaporized beyond recognition. The emperor's assassin is a distraught man named **Mandell Gruber**, who commits the crime for no other reason than because he did not want to be the Empire's First Gardener. Seldon's psychohistory had been proven correct. The Empire would be saved, but the Emperor had been killed for the most trivial of reasons.

Gaal Dornick is an Empire "country boy." He has spent his life on Synnax, a star system at the edges of the Blue Drift. A mathematics scholar himself, he has come to Trantor to work with the famed Seldon. Although Dornick has never been on Trantor before, he has seen it on hypervideo and sometimes in three-dimensional newscasts that cover such things as Imperial coronations and Galactic Council sessions. He is quite familiar with the capital. No star system, no matter how far away, is ever cut off from civilization in the Empire, which includes some twenty-five million inhabited planets. All of them owe some allegiance to the seat of power.

Dornick meets Seldon two years before the legend's death and becomes the leading authority on the details of Seldon's life and his theory of psychohistory. Dornick, using concepts other than math, defines psychohistory as a branch of mathematics that deals with how human groups react to fixed social and economic stimuli. Dornick eventually learns that Seldon's banishment to Terminus at the end of the galaxy is what the mathematician had planned in order to plant the seeds for the Foundation.

Salvor Hardin and others in *Foundation* are like satellites revolving around the mysterious and melancholy Seldon and the events leading to the fall of the Galactic Empire and the creation of the Second Empire. Hardin is the mayor of Terminus, a lone planet circling an isolated sun located on the fringe of the Empire. It is poor in resources and has little economic value. In fact, Terminus remained largely unsettled for some five centuries after its discovery, until the coming of Seldon and his encyclopedists. When Hardin meets the famed mathematician, Seldon is in a wheelchair, but that is the least of the surprises. Seldon explains to Hardin that the entire idea of creating the *Encyclopedia Galactica* to save the Empire is a fraud and has always been a fraud. The fall can't be stopped, but it can be shortened to a thousand years, he tells Hardin. Terminus is to become part of the seeds of the Second Empire's foundation. In this way, a strange new society is forced upon the astonished mayor of Terminus.

Further Reading

Asimov, Isaac. *In Memory Yet Green: The Autobiography of Isaac Asimov, 1920-1954.* New York: Doubleday, 1979.

Asimov, Isaac. *In Joy Still Felt: The Autobiography of Isaac Asimov, 1954-1979.* New York: Doubleday, 1980.

Authors and Artists for Young Adults. Vol. 13. Detroit: Gale Research, 1994.

Berger, Laura Standley, ed. *Twentieth-Century Young Adult Writers.* 1st ed. Detroit: St. James, 1994.

Bleiler, E. F. *Science Fiction Writers.* New York: Scribner's, 1982.

Bloom, Harold. *Twentieth-Century American Literature.* Vol. 1 of *The Chelsea House Library of Literary Criticism.* New York: Chelsea House, 1986.

Children's Literature Review. Vol. 12. Detroit: Gale Research, 1987.

Contemporary Literary Criticism. Vols. 1, 3, 9, 19, 26. Detroit: Gale Research, 1973, 1975, 1978, 1981, 1983.

Cowart, David, and Thomas L. Wymer, eds. *Twentieth-Century American Science-Fiction Writers.* Vol. 8 of *Dictionary of Literary Biography.* Detroit: Gale Research, 1981.

Erlanger, Ellen. *Isaac Asimov: Scientist and Storyteller.* Minneapolis: Lerner Publications, 1986.

Fiedler, Jean, and Jim Mele. *Isaac Asimov.* New York: Ungar, 1982.

Grigsby, John L. "Asimov's Foundation Trilogy and Herbert's Dune Trilogy: A Vision Reversed," *Science Fiction Studies* 8 (July 1981).

Gunn, James. *Isaac Asimov: The Foundations of Science Fiction.* New York: Oxford, 1982.

Hassler, Donald M. *Isaac Asimov.* San Bernardino, CA: Borgo, 1991.

Henderson, Lesley. *Contemporary Novelists.* Detroit: St. James, 1991.

Ingersoll, Earl G., ed. "A Conversation with Isaac Asimov," *Science Fiction Studies* 14 (March 1987).

Olander, Joseph D., and Martin Harry Greenberg, eds. *Isaac Asimov.* New York: Taplinger, 1977.

Patrouch, Joseph F. *The Science Fiction of Isaac Asimov.* New York: Doubleday, 1974.

Slusser, George E. *Isaac Asimov: The Foundations of His Science Fiction.* San Bernardino, CA: Borgo, 1979.

Something about the Author. Vols. 26, 74. Detroit: Gale Research, 1982, 1993.

Toupence, William F. *Isaac Asimov.* New York: Twayne, 1991.

Wakeman, John, ed. *World Authors, 1950-1970.* New York: H. W. Wilson, 1975.

Watson, Noelle, and Paul E. Schellinger, eds. *Twentieth-Century Science Fiction Writers.* 3rd ed. Detroit: St. James, 1991.

Margaret Atwood

1939-, Canadian novelist

The Handmaid's Tale

(science fiction, 1986)

PLOT: In the year 2195, the keynote speaker at the Twelfth Symposium on Gileadean Studies devotes his time to a discussion of the authenticity of certain tapes that describe what life was like for a handmaid known as Offred. Offred lived in the Republic of Gilead, a monotheocracy, in what was once the United States of America. Some time past the twentieth century, Gilead reacted to a sharply declining worldwide birthrate by instilling a society more repressive than the strict mores of the original Puritans. Those women who demonstrate reproductive fitness by having produced one or two healthy children are designated handmaids. As childbearer, they are protected and wear great flowing red capes with white winged headgear to set them apart from other women. Offred (a name that simply designates that she is part of the household of a certain commander—in this case, "of Fred") keeps a forbidden record of her life, her feelings, her fears, and her dreams.

The agency that keeps the handmaids under control is known as the Aunts. The authorities have cleverly deduced that the easiest way to keep the handmaids in line is to have other women controlling them. Childless, infertile, or older women clamor for inclusion in the Aunts because membership affords them at least some power in this male-dominated society. But the Aunts are not the only way the handmaids are kept down. Each handmaid is assigned another handmaid for a partner, a setup that is designed to encourage each woman to spy on the other. In Offred's case, her partner is Ofglen. Offred does not know whether Ofglen is a real believer in the system, but she can't take the chance of confiding in her.

Life begins to change for Offred when the Commander begins calling her to him for pastimes other than sexual intercourse. This is unheard of in this tightly controlled society. Offred is not completely certain what he wants with her, but she enjoys the discussions about language and other matters in which he is interested. Despite this, Offred remains unhappy with her life of enslavement.

As in all repressive societies, there are rumors of subversive groups striving to break free of the chains of control. In Gilead, this takes the form of the elusive Mayday underground, a shadowy organization that is said to have some connection to the so-called Underground Femaleroad (a system reminiscent of the Underground Railroad of the pre-Civil War era).

In the end, was it the Commander who was responsible for her freedom? After all, in a sense he has been harboring a fugitive, not adhering to the strict rules. His own life could have been in danger, too. And so, when Nick appears at Offred's door and tells her to go with the strangers who are standing there, telling her they belong to Mayday, she does so. Although she is suspicious of a possible trap, she goes. As she leaves, she sees the Commander and his wife, Serena Joy, standing in the hallway. Serena Joy asks what she has done to be taken away by the guards, but they will not say. As Offred steps into the waiting van with the guards on either side, she has no way of knowing whether she is stepping into a new life or into total blackness.

From the record found in 2195, the possibility exists that Offred was able to escape to freedom, possibly even to England, since Canada was hesitant to antagonize its powerful neighbor to the south. It appears that Nick, a man who wears the uniform of a Guardian but with whom Offred had formed a forbidden relationship, engineered her departure. But the people of the twenty-second century never learn whether she managed to escape her handmaid existence, was sent to the dreaded Colonies, or was caught and executed.

CHARACTERS: The handmaid **Offred** can't accept her passive, imprisoned existence, though she pretends to for the benefit of appearances. She still has memories of her daughter and the smells and sounds of her former life. Although she leads a pampered existence and has been told that she is a national treasure and should feel privileged, she longs to be free. But Offred is too afraid to run away. When the Commander begins calling for her, she is surprised to find that he is seeking her companionship, not just a sexual interlude. He takes her to a forbidden room where the two of them play a game of Scrabble. Of course, such activities are forbidden between a man and his handmaid. The Commander is married, and his association with Offred is supposed to be solely for procreation. Offred finds it exciting to do forbidden things with the Commander. The Commander also requests that she kiss him goodnight as if she meant it, and he gives her a present: an old copy of *Vogue* magazine, which is also taboo.

The **Commander** obviously knows that he is breaking the strict societal rules of Gilead when he begins his relationship with Offred. Why does he take such a chance? The answer is probably that, in his exalted position, he believes himself above the law. As a director of the Eyes, he does not pay much attention to what he considers to be minor infractions of the rules. However, when Offred is taken away by the guards, the Commander stands behind her, already distancing himself. If she talks too much he will undoubtedly be considered a security risk and executed.

Serena Joy, the Commander's wife, is white with fear when Offred is taken away. She is in a strange position in this society. As the Commander's wife, she has certain status, which she takes advantage of by traveling and making speeches about how wonderful it is for women to stay at home (something she, of course, does not do). Although she is incapable of bearing children, she participates while the Commander and Offred make love. Offred wonders whether it is she or the Commander's wife who is worse off.

Nick is a shadowy figure dressed in the uniform of the Guardians. These men are not true soldiers but are responsible for taking care of routine policing or menial tasks. They are usually either very young or very old or stupid. Some Guardians, however, are actually part of the true policing authority known as the Eyes. Offred is not sure what to make of Nick, except that she is drawn to him. If Nick is indeed able to engineer her escape, then he could be a member of the shadowy Mayday underground. If so, in his position he is probably also a member of the dreaded Eyes. Personal servants, as Nick is to the Commander, often carried out this role incognito. However, even his status as one of the Eyes will not necessarily protect him if the truth about his unauthorized sexual relationship with a handmaid is uncovered. The penalties for such behavior are severe.

Offred's current handmaid partner is **Ofglen**. She acts demurely and Offred can't be sure whether or not she believes in the social order. Both women know that if either of them escapes the other will be held responsible. It is a precarious situation for both handmaids to be in. Ofglen has connections with the underground Mayday association. When this secret is uncovered, it puts both her and Nick in grave danger.

The Aunt assigned to protect—actually control—Offred is **Lydia.** It is uncertain whether she truly believes in what are known in Gilead as "traditional values," or whether she simply likes being part of the control group that gives her some measure of power in an otherwise male-dominated world. There is, however, an even better reason for becoming one of the Aunts. Older, infertile, or childless women like Lydia are considered "redundant" and are in danger of being exiled to the dreaded Colonies. Usually those sent to the Colonies become toxic cleanup personnel. If they are lucky, they are sent to harvest fruit or pick cotton. Aunt Lydia is fond of sayings. When Offred wonders why all handmaid rooms are decorated the same, Aunt Lydia says, "Think of it as being in the army." When Offred wonders about her society, Aunt Lydia says, "The Republic of Gilead knows no bounds. Gilead is within you." Of Offred's own imprisoned life, Aunt Lydia comments, "This may not seem ordinary to you now, but after a time it will. It will become ordinary."

Further Reading

Authors and Artists for Young Adults. Vol. 12. Detroit: Gale Research, 1994.

Berger, Laura Standley, ed. *Twentieth-Century Young Adult Writers.* 1st ed. Detroit: St. James, 1995.

Bloom, Harold, ed. *Twentieth-Century American Literature.* Vol. 1 of *The Chelsea House Library of Literary Criticism.* New York: Chelsea House, 1986.

Critical Survey of Long Fiction. Vol. 1. Englewood Cliffs, NJ: Salem, 1983.

Davidson, Arnold E., and Cathy N. Davison, eds. *The Art of Margaret Atwood: Essays in Criticism.* Toronto: Anansi, 1981.

McCombs, Judith, ed. *Critical Essays on Margaret Atwood.* Boston: Hall, 1988.

Nicholson, Colin. *Margaret Atwood: Writing and Subjectivity.* New York: St. Martin's, 1994.

Rosenberg, Jerome H. *Margaret Atwood.* Boston: Twayne, 1984.

Something about the Author. Vol. 50. Detroit: Gale Research, 1988.

Toye, William, ed. *Oxford Companion to Canadian Literature.* New York: Oxford University Press, 1983.

Van Spanckeren, Kathryn, and Jan Garde Castro. *Margaret Atwood: Vision and Forms.* Carbondale: Southern Illinois University Press, 1988.

Jane Austen

1775-1817, English novelist

Pride and Prejudice

(novel, 1813)

PLOT: Set in the English countryside during the early nineteenth century, this novel chronicles the path to matrimony of three of the five Bennet sisters. The Bennet family consists of Mr. Bennet, the intelligent, long-suffering husband of Mrs. Bennet, who is a silly chatterbox intent only on marriage for her daughters: Jane, the oldest, Elizabeth, Mary, Kitty, and Lydia.

The Bennet children range in age from fifteen to the early twenties and are therefore all eligible for marriage, according to the customs of that time. News reaches the Bennets at their home in Hertfordshire that the neighboring estate of Netherfield Park has been rented by a rich bachelor, Charles Bingley. He is soon welcomed into the local polite society, along with his sister, Caroline, and his best friend, Fitzwilliam Darcy. Bingley, who is immediately attracted to Jane, creates a favorable impression with his easygoing charm, but Darcy, an arrogant, prideful person, is disliked by all, including Elizabeth. Her prejudice against this man increases when she learns from Mr. Wickham, an attractive army officer stationed nearby, that Darcy was guilty of cheating him out of his inheritance.

Later, a distant relative of the Bennets, a pompous, self-important clergyman named Mr. Collins, arrives at the Bennet household intent on marriage. When his proposal is refused by Elizabeth, he is immediately accepted by Charlotte Lucas, Elizabeth's best friend. In spite of Bingley's growing attention to Jane, he and his party suddenly leave the area and return to town. While visiting the newly married Charlotte and Mr. Collins at their home in Kent, Elizabeth meets the grande dame of the area, the dictatorial Lady Catherine de Bourgh, and her sickly daughter, Anne. Elizabeth once again encounters Darcy, who turns out to be Lady Catherine's nephew. After several meetings, Darcy unexpectedly proposes marriage to Elizabeth, who refuses him partly because of his treatment of Wickham. In an explanatory note after the rejection, Darcy explains that it was Wickham who was the villain. He had attempted an elopement with Darcy's young sister, Georgiana, to secure her fortune and Darcy's intervention caused this rift.

Elizabeth and Darcy meet again when Elizabeth is the guest of Mr. Gardiner, Mrs. Bennet's brother, and his wife, who live close to Pemberly, Mr. Darcy's luxurious estate. She is beginning to think much more kindly toward him when her visit is cut short by the news that her youngest sister, the silly, impetuous Lydia, has run off with Mr. Wickham. When the couple is finally located, a wedding is hastily arranged. Later, Elizabeth learns from Mrs. Gardiner that it was Darcy who located the couple in London and financed the marriage, paying off Wickham's substantial debts and giving him a handsome income. When Mr. Bingley and Darcy return to Netherfield Park, further reconciliations take place. Jane and Mr. Bingley become engaged, which pleases Mrs. Bennet. Hoping that her daughter, Anne, will one day marry Darcy, Lady Catherine visits the Bennets and demands that Elizabeth renounce any plans that involve Darcy. Elizabeth refuses. When Darcy hears of this conversation, he proposes and is happily accepted by Elizabeth, proving that both prejudice and pride can be overcome.

CHARACTERS: This classic novel was originally titled *First Impressions,* referring to the often erroneous opinions one can form after an initial meeting. It is dominated by two strong characters who have such an experience, **Elizabeth Bennet** and Fitzwilliam Darcy. Elizabeth is an attractive girl, who is also high-spirited, intelligent, willful, and outspoken. Although never rude or impertinent, she speaks her mind freely and acts honestly and independently, even though it might displease others. For example, she refuses Mr. Collins's proposal, although it incurs the anger of her mother, and she later refuses a similar proposal from the wealthy, desirable Darcy, because, at the time, she dislikes his temperament.

Greer Garson and Laurence Olivier portrayed Elizabeth Bennet and Fitzwilliam Darcy in the 1940 film version of **Pride and Prejudice,** *a classic story of love and mistaken first impressions.*

Contrary to the times, Elizabeth is determined that if she cannot find a husband that she can both love and respect, she will not marry. This feeling of self-worth, along with her ability to think independently, are two of her most endearing qualities. Her strength of character is revealed in several episodes in the story. For example, she courageously stands up to the domineering Lady Catherine and refuses to compromise. She is a loyal, steadfast member of her household who is always aware of other people's feelings and sensibilities.

An obedient daughter (except in extreme circumstances), she is particularly devoted to her father and elder sister, Jane, whom she protects and defends even though it causes her inconveniences and jeopardizes friendships. Her bouts of verbal sparring with Darcy show her wit, delightful sense of humor, and intelligence. Except in the case of Darcy, Elizabeth is a wise judge of character. An important step toward maturity and self-knowledge occurs when she realizes that she is not infallible in making judgments and that her own character can change and improve.

Fitzwilliam Darcy is described as a "fine, tall person, with handsome features and noble mien." The security that his wealth and position have provided has led him to be disdainful of the common and artificial. This is shown in behavior that appears arrogant, haughty, and aloof. To protect himself from the foolishness and vulgarity that surround him, he has developed a superior, often condescending attitude toward others. He has a "forbidding, disagreeable countenance," and his fastidious, overcritical behavior gives the impression of extreme vanity and conceit. These external qualities disguise a man of extreme intelligence, discernment, and reserve. Challenged by Elizabeth's charm, quick wit, and sparkling conversation, he suddenly comes to life and realizes he has met someone worthy of himself. Although anxious to hide the more compassionate side of his nature, his generosity and good works, when revealed, show him to be a man of conscience and high moral feelings. Like Elizabeth, Darcy changes over the course of the novel. His initial rejection by Elizabeth forces him to examine his prideful nature and temper his actions with greater consideration for others.

Lady Catherine de Bourgh, Darcy's aunt, is a haughty, ill-mannered autocrat. Class-conscious and conceited, she is determined that her sickly daughter Anne will marry Darcy and resorts to every method, including shameless bullying of Elizabeth, to get her way. Her authoritative manner, coupled with a nosy, opinionated personality, makes her both disagreeable and comic. She thrives on the flattery that Mr. Collins and others feed her. Another relative of Darcy's to appear in the story is his sixteen-year-old sister, **Georgiana Darcy**. Georgiana is a sweet, gentle person, but because she is shy and reserved, gives the impression of being aloof and excessively proud.

Elizabeth's parents provide a study in contrasts. **Mrs. Bennet** is a silly, gossipy woman whose sole purpose in life is to marry off her daughters. She is described as "a woman of mean understanding, little information and uncertain temper." Her meddling, vulgar behavior is an embarrassment to Elizabeth and the principal reason for Darcy's initial disdain of the Bennets. Her tactless, thoughtless prattling often results in humorous situations and inexcusable social gaffes. When thwarted, however, she can become spiteful and mean-spirited. Forever scheming, she is prone to imaginary nervous attacks to get attention and pity. She is a poor judge of character and totally unable to probe beyond surface appearances. This lack of understanding and superficiality lead to a number of bad decisions involving her family. Because of all these flaws, she emerges as one of the great comic figures in literature.

Her husband, the long-suffering **Mr. Bennet**, is "an odd mixture of quick parts, sarcastic humor, reserve, and caprice." Although he often escapes his silly wife by retreating to the quiet of his library, he cares particularly about his two eldest daughters. His attitude toward the other children and his wife usually is one of scorn or indifference. His pithy remarks about his wife and the foibles of others around him add sarcastic wit to the novel, but his failure to provide proper direction and guidance to his household is reprehensible and ultimately the cause of some of the family's problems. He supports Elizabeth, his favorite, in such situations as her rejection of Mr. Collins and encourages her independent behavior, but in spite of his understanding, Elizabeth gradually realizes that her beloved father is flawed by his inability to accept responsibility within the family and his indolent behavior.

Jane Bennet, Mr. Bennet's other favored daughter, has a sweet, gentle disposition that prevents her ever thinking ill of others. Her innate goodness and trusting nature border on the naive. She is exceptionally pretty and talented; however, being a modest, reserved girl, she often is not aggressive enough socially. This leads Mr. Bingley to think she is indifferent to his advances. She is a great confidante and supporter of Elizabeth, and because of her placid, tranquil nature, she acts as a quieting influence.

The other Bennet girls play less significant parts in the story. **Lydia Bennet**, the youngest of the children, is a high-spirited foolish girl who, under her mother's influence, has become man-crazy. Given to "amusement and vanity," she is an easy target for Wickham's blandishments. **Mary Bennet** is a plain, ill-mannered young woman given to excessive moralizing and agonizing music-making at parties, and **Kitty Bennet** is a frivolous girl who, like her sister, Lydia, is a scatterbrained flirt.

Charles Bingley, "a singular man of large fortune," is "wonderfully handsome and extremely agreeable." He is well-liked, unaffected, good humored, and outgoing. He is sensible and popular with all who meet him. At ease in society, his open nature and warmth impress Jane Bennet. His only fault is to be overly influenced by others' opinions. His sister, **Caroline Bingley,** is quite different. Outwardly pleasant and solicitous, she is actually a proud, conceited snob. She feigns concern over Jane, while actually turning her brother against her. Sly, vindictive, and cunning, she secretly hopes to marry Darcy, which makes her so jealous of Elizabeth that she spreads false rumors to break up their relationship.

The rejected suitor in the story is **Reverend William Collins**, whom Elizabeth accurately describes as "a conceited, pompous, narrow-minded, silly man." Easily impressed by wealth and position and always anxious to please, he is excessively polite and given to inconsequential chatter. He is often disagreeable and irksome and completely dominated by his patroness Lady Catherine. His obnoxious self-importance is balanced by the sensible intelligence of his new wife, the former **Charlotte Lucas.** At age twenty-seven, Charlotte was fearful of remaining an old maid and consented to this alliance.

The villain of the novel is **George Wickham**. At first he is presented as an outwardly charming commissioned officer whose handsome features and pleasant manners easily attract women, but gradually one learns he is an unprincipled rogue who has squandered his small inheritance and is now out to gain a fortune through marriage. Without scruples, he shamelessly maligns Darcy who has been his benefactor, seduces Lydia, and accepts cash to marry her.

Further Reading

Amis, Martin. "Miss Jane's Prime." *Atlantic Monthly* 265 (February 1990).

Bloom, Harold. *Jane Austen.* New York: Chelsea House, 1986.

Bruccoli, Matthew J., and Richard Layman, eds. *Writers of the Romantic Period, 1789-1832.* Vol. 3 of *Concise Dictionary of British Literary Biography.* Detroit: Gale Research, 1992.

Craik, W. A. *Jane Austen: The Six Novels.* London: Methuen, 1965.

Fergus, Jan S. *Jane Austen: A Literary Life.* London: Macmillan, 1991.

Handley, Graham. *Jane Austen: A Guide through the Critical Maze.* New York: St. Martin's, 1992.

Honan, Park. *Jane Austen: Her Life.* New York: St. Martin's, 1987.

Magill, Frank N. *Critical Survey of Long Fiction: English Language Series: Authors.* Vol. 1. Englewood Cliffs, NJ: Prentice-Hall, 1983.

Morgan, Susan. *In the Meantime: Character and Perception in Jane Austen's Fiction.* Chicago: University of Chicago Press, 1980.

Mudge, Bradford K., ed. *British Romantic Novelists, 1789-1892.* Vol. 116 of *Dictionary of Literary Biography.* Detroit: Gale Research, 1992.

Nineteenth-Century Literature Criticism. Vols. 1, 13, 19. Detroit: Gale Research, 1981, 1986, 1988.

Paris, Bernard J. *Character and Conflict in Jane Austen's Novels: A Psychological Approach.* Detroit: Wayne State University Press, 1978.

Avi

(pen name for Avi Wortis)

1937-, American young adult novelist

The True Confessions of Charlotte Doyle

(historical novel, 1990)

PLOT: In 1832, after almost eight years in England, Mr. Doyle is suddenly recalled to the head office of his shipping firm in Providence, Rhode Island. To complete her school year without interruption, his daughter, thirteen-year-old Charlotte, remains behind and books passage later as the sole passenger on a brig called the *Seahawk.*

At the Liverpool docks, when Charlotte mentions the name of the ship's captain, Jaggery, stevedores refuse to handle her luggage. This is only one of the disturbing portents of things to come. Before sailing, she meets the unpleasant second mate, Mr. Keetch, and an ordinary sailor, Barlow, who begs her to leave the ship. A kindly old black man, Zachariah, the ship's cook, visits her tiny roach-infested cabin and shows a genuine concern for her safety. He gives her a small dagger, which she reluctantly accepts.

At first Charlotte can't understand the crew's hostile attitude toward Captain Jaggery, who appears to be a perfect gentleman. Jaggery asks her to report to him any mutinous activity within the crew. Later she discovers that he is actually a sadistic, cunning man whose crew is rightfully planning a mutiny to avenge his cruelty during the ship's previous voyage to England. Because of her informing, a sailor named Cranick is killed by Jaggery, and her friend Zachariah is flogged into unconsciousness.

Charlotte is given to believe that he has died of his wounds. Filled with remorse and guilt, Charlotte switches sides and, though at first the crew is suspicious of her, she is gradually accepted as an ally. To rid himself of this pesky girl, Jaggery secretly murders the first mate, Hollybrass, with the dagger he has stolen from Charlotte and accuses her of committing the crime. Zachariah, who has been secretly nursed back to health below ship by the crew, frees Charlotte from the brig before she is scheduled to be hanged. On deck, she is confronted by a pistol-brandishing Jaggery and, in the ensuing chase, the captain loses his balance and drowns in the ocean.

Upon arriving in Providence, Charlotte, unable to adjust to the rigid confines of her father's stern jurisdiction, puts on her sailor's clothes one evening and creeps off to join the crew, including Zachariah, aboard what has become her real home, the *Seahawk*.

CHARACTERS: This Newbery Honor book, a rousing sea adventure told in the first person, contains authentic details about the days of trans-Atlantic sailing ships, including appended material on understanding ship's time and well-labeled diagrams of the parts of a brig.

The central character and narrator is the plucky heroine, **Charlotte Doyle**. Over the course of the novel, she is transformed from a proper, staid young lady into a self-reliant, courageous woman who is willing to risk life and limb in the pursuit of justice. In the opening scenes of the novel, she appears as a prim, somewhat prissy person described as an "ordinary girl of parents in good standing." She is used to being protected and supervised by her elders and is easily impressed with the outward appearance of gentility as displayed at first by Captain Jaggery. Without question she has adopted the values of her parents, including a belief in class distinction and the overriding importance of propriety.

However, when the truth of Jaggery's villainy is revealed, these superficial values are discarded and Charlotte develops a new set of standards in which truth, loyalty to friends, and the importance of fighting unjust cruelty and misuse of power become paramount. Also, hidden qualities of courage, resourcefulness, and dependability are revealed when she rejects the authority and safety offered by Jaggery and instead chooses the more dangerous course of action by allying herself with the crew, even though at first they distrust her motives. Her friendship with Zachariah, the lowly black cook, and the devotion she later feels toward him, also demonstrates these internal changes. The final rejection of her old self and the lifestyle she once represented occurs when Charlotte rebels against the repressive, confining conventions of her stern, unyielding father in favor of the simple, honest life of an ordinary seaman. Symbolically, she dons the sailor's coarse blouse and trousers, clothes that only a few months before she had rejected when Zachariah had offered them to her.

The villain of the novel is **Captain Andrew Jaggery**. At first he presents himself to Charlotte as a gracious and cultivated gentleman who is solicitous of her well-being, even though he does nothing to change her wretched living conditions. She is deceived by the elegance of his quarters, his compliments, and his apparent concern for his family at home, including a daughter of whom, he claims, Charlotte reminds him. Only later does Charlotte realize that Jaggery's appearances, oily charm, and feigned interest are tools to worm his way into her confidence so that he can use her as a spy. When she realizes the truth and tries to help Zachariah, whom Jaggery has unmercifully flogged, the captain turns on her with the same savagery that he has used on the crew. Realizing that she can testify against him when they reach port, he plans her death, first by exposing her to incredible dangers during a hurricane and then by accusing her of committing a murder for which he was actually guilty. With true poetic justice, this evil monster is drowned while trying to kill the only person aboard ship who once respected and admired him.

Zachariah, the old, illiterate, black sailor, who describes himself as a "cook, surgeon, carpenter, and preacher," is always dressed in rags, has a wizened face, and his mouth is missing half its teeth. Beneath this almost frightening exterior, however, there is a man of great kindness, jovial disposition, and courage, who knows more than most men about human nature, as well as seamanship. Throughout the novel he consistently displays high moral values and a nobility of spirit. In spite of Charlotte's initial disdain and verbal abuse, he continues to show her kindness and concern, first by giving her a dagger for protection and nursing her through a terrible bout of seasickness, and later by defending her life even though it places his own in danger. These fine qualities lead Charlotte to love and respect him above all others on the ship. Understandably, it is Zachariah whom she misses most when she reaches Providence. The loss of his friendship and genuine goodness is one of the reasons she decides to return to the *Seahawk.*

Charlotte's father, **Mr. Doyle**, is portrayed as a martinet who is more concerned with outward gentility than the well being of his daughter. When he discovers a diary Charlotte has kept during the voyage, he is so shocked that he burns the document and chastises his daughter for having an overactive imagination. His stern discipline and lack of understanding are two factors that drive Charlotte away from her home.

Some of the other crew members of the *Seahawk* are **Mr. Keetch,** the second mate who, though first presented as a disagreeable, dour man whose movements seem ferret-like to Charlotte, later realizes the wickedness of Captain Jaggery and casts in his lot with the mutineers to the point of helping Charlotte escape from Jaggery. The first mate, **Mr. Hollybrass**, is a conscientious, obedient crewman who believes in doing his duty and obeying his captain. However, even he eventually finds Jaggery's villainy impossible to tolerate any more. At this point, Jaggery murders him in a plot to implicate Charlotte. Two other crew members are **Mr. Cranick** and **Barlow.** Cranick is a seaman who had been so physically abused by Jaggery on the previous voyage that he has lost an arm. Seeking revenge, he stows away on the *Seahawk* to lead the mutiny. After his discovery, he is shot by Jaggery. Barlow, an ordinary seaman, is the first to warn Charlotte of the dangers she faces aboard the *Seahawk.*

Nothing But the Truth: A Documentary Novel

(young adult novel, 1991)

PLOT: Fourteen-year-old Philip Malloy, a freshman at Harrison High School, is annoyed when he is transferred at midterm to the homeroom of his English teacher, Miss Margaret Narwin. Philip, though charming and well-liked, is inclined to laziness and self- indulgence, except for anything connected with track and his efforts to make the school team.

When Philip's smart-alecky attitude and abysmal academic work result in a "D" in English, he is told by Coach Jamison that this grade automatically disqualifies him from the track team. Philip vows to get out of Miss Narwin's homeroom and her English class. His strategy is to hum in homeroom during the national anthem, although school rules require a "respectful silence." After three days of this confrontational behavior and repeated warnings, Philip is suspended from school for two days.

His parents appeal to their neighbor, Ted Griffen, who is seeking a campaign theme in the upcoming school board election in which he is a candidate. In turn, Griffen notifies a local newspaper reporter, Jennifer Stewart, whose slanted and inaccurate story on the incident appears under the heading, "Suspended for Patriotism." The story is released nationally and even featured by the scandal-seeking talk show host Jake Barlow. Soon the Molloy household is flooded with telegrams and letters supporting the gallant young man who has stood up for his rights

Philip Malloy's plan to get kicked out of English class backfires when he becomes a pawn to politicians and the media in Avi's insightful look at American society.

and love of country. Similarly, Miss Narwin also receives letters, all critical, many demanding her resignation.

Ironically, the two protagonists, both more miserable with each new development, are now pawns in a larger power struggle involving the sensation-hungry news media and the school administration—represented by the school superintendent, Dr. Albert Seymour and the high school principal, Dr. Gertrude Doane—a pending budget vote, and a scheduled school board election. Sickened and ashamed, Philip transfers to another school while Miss Narwin, forced to take a leave of absence, contemplates resigning from teaching. Ted Griffin, meanwhile, wins the school board election.

CHARACTERS: This novel, which takes place over a period of four weeks, is told entirely through documents: memos, letters, diary entries, conversations, and transcripts. Characters are developed through reported actions, writings, and speeches, but not by direct exposition or descriptions by the author.

There are two central characters in the story: **Philip Malloy** and Margaret Narwin. Through comments from teachers and fellow students, Philip is first introduced as a likable, intelligent, good-looking young man, an average student with an abiding love of track. However, there soon emerges a deeper, less attractive side to his character. He is academically lazy, particularly with subjects he finds dull, and has an exaggerated sense of his own abilities. He has developed a wise-cracking, nonchalant personality, which he calls the "Malloy Magic." He uses this to evade difficult situations and impress those around him, particularly girls, and he invents excuses to justify his own self-indulgence and laziness. For example, Philip shifts the blame onto Miss Narwin for his track team disqualification, rather than accepting responsibility for his failure and applying himself to improving his grade. At home, he never tells his parents the real reason for his not being part of the track team. Although Philip never overtly lies, he doesn't tell the truth either.

Philip selfishly creates the national anthem controversy solely as a wheeler-dealer maneuver to find a facile way out of a problem for which he himself is responsible. Not foreseeing the far-reaching, harmful consequences of his actions, he tries in vain to contain the crisis. When things get out of control, he realizes how irresponsibly he has acted. In the final scene of the novel, which takes place at his new school, Philip sobs when asked to lead in the singing of the national anthem, indicating that he now realizes how foolishly he has behaved and how much this has cost himself and others. This lesson brings him one step closer to achieving maturity.

Philip's teacher, **Margaret Narwin**, is a dedicated professional who applies standards of excellence in her class. After twenty-one years in the classroom, she has mastered her job and achieved a reputation for being a fine teacher. She has a deep concern for her pupils, including Philip, and is always seeking new ways to reach them and make her subject interesting. Insightful enough to admit that she is somewhat old-fashioned in her approach to teaching, Miss Narwin even volunteers to take a summer course on new teaching methods, a request that is not funded by the administration. She applies high standards to herself and her professional obligations, and she expects similar attitudes from her students. In spite of her efforts to understand and help Philip and an appeal not to have him suspended, she becomes the innocent victim in a controversy that he has created for selfish reasons. She protects her school district by maintaining a discreet silence on the crisis, only to find that, one by one, her colleagues desert her and make her a convenient scapegoat. Understandably, she feels betrayed and abandoned. Unfortunately, when she becomes sufficiently aroused to tell her side of the story, the media have lost interest. She emerges as a tragic figure whose life and career have been ruined by the irresponsible and callous actions of others.

Philip's parents are portrayed as well-meaning but somewhat gullible. They accept their son's word without proper investigation. Ironically, **Mr. Malloy**, while insisting that his son stand up for his rights, is portrayed as accepting criticism unquestioningly in his workplace and in taking swift action to correct his mistakes.

The ideas that patriotism is the last refuge of scoundrels and truth is often sacrificed in times of stress motivate many of the remaining characters. **Dr. Albert Seymour**, the school superintendent, and **Dr. Gertrude Doane**, the high school principal, have good intentions but are willing to sacrifice Miss Narwin in order to keep peace in the district and insure that the next school budget is passed. **Ted Griffen**, a school board candidate and opportunist, irresponsibly instigates a crisis supposedly involving an individual's right to be patriotic in order to insure his election. The two principal news media personnel portrayed—**Jennifer Stewart**, a local reporter, and **Jake Barlow**, a rabble-rousing radio talk show host—are more interested in producing a sensational story than in accurate, objective reporting. Barlow, with his emotional, judgmental rhetoric, is particularly offensive.

Other minor characters include Philip's classmates and faculty members, including **Coach Jamison**, who at one point admonishes Philip for "doing a number" on Miss Narwin and wisely tells him, "A rule is a rule—to get along you have to play along."

Further Reading

Avi. "The True Confessions of Charlotte Doyle: Acceptance Speech." *Horn Book* 68 (January/February 1992).

Berger, Laura Standley, ed. *Twentieth-Century Young Adult Writers.* 1st ed. Detroit: St. James, 1994.

Children's Literature Review. Vol. 24. Detroit: Gale Research, 1991.

Collier, Laurie, and Joyce Nakamura, eds. *Major Authors and Illustrators for Children and Young Adults.* Detroit: Gale Research, 1993.

Gallo, Donald R. *Speaking for Ourselves: Autobiographical Sketches by Notable Authors of Books for Young Adults.* Urbana, IL: National Council of Teachers of English, 1990.

Marinak, Barbara Ann. "Author Profile: Avi." *Book Report* 10 (March/April 1992).

Rochman, Hazel. "A Conversation with Avi." *Booklist* 88 (15 January 1992).

Something about the Author. Vol. 71. Detroit: Gale Research, 1993.

James Baldwin

1924-1987, American novelist

Go Tell It on the Mountain

(novel, 1953)

PLOT: Hailed as a milestone in the development of American literature upon its 1953 publication, *Go Tell It on the Mountain* is Baldwin's first novel, a story that features African Americans described from a nonracial point of view. The story covers one day in the life of members of a fundamentalist church in Harlem. The central figure is fourteen-year-old John, whom everyone has predicted will become a preacher like his father one day. But John is at an age when he is confused about what he wants for his future: he seems to want salvation and damnation almost equally. On the morning of his birthday, he wakes up feeling that he has made a decision. He resolves not to be like his father or his father's fathers.

The story is told in three sections. Part One is "The Seventh Day," which deals with John's religious awakening. It describes the young man's confusion about his spiritual calling and future. Part Two, "The Prayers of the Saints," uses flashbacks to show important events in the lives of three other principal characters: Gabriel Grimes, John's often violent and hypocritical father; Elizabeth Grimes, the young man's mother, who has a tender but silent relationship with her son; and Florence Grimes, Gabriel's sister and a woman of strong character. Part Three is "The Threshing Floor," which describes the young boy's ultimate salvation with poetic intensity. John descends into the hell of confusion and doubt, agonizing over his struggle between self-denial and his image of a holy man. When the inward storm is over, John is ready to act on his new sense of convictions about his future, even though conflict may well lie ahead.

CHARACTERS: *Go Tell It on the Mountain* contains many autobiographical elements. For example, Baldwin, like young John, was the illegitimate son of a tyrannical storefront preacher. The book also contains themes that can be found in Baldwin's later novels, such as the place of religion in the lives of African Americans, attitudes toward white people, troubled family relationships, and the nature of suffering. **John Grimes** is the focus of all the action in the novel, as he struggles to come to terms with his sense of salvation and future calling. His decision over whether or not to become a holy man holds the book together. He also represents the struggle all maturing people endure while overcoming fears, doubts, and the harsh realities of life around them. As religious awakening stirs within him, John responds to ever more conflicting feelings. He participates in the same world of religious ecstacy that others in the congregation enjoy, but he does not share their belief or inner strength and is strangely unmoved by the experience. His confusion about his religious feelings is magnified by his growing awareness of how much self-denial plays a part in this religious world. His father confuses him as well. The good preacher that John sees in church often stands in sharp contrast to the violent, brutal figure he encounters at home. And although his father contends that white people are wicked and to be shunned, John knows that not all of them can be bad. Ultimately, John must descend into despair in order to find his own personal path to salvation.

Gabriel Grimes is a violent man. He typifies the fanatic evangelism of some preachers who are determined to dominate other people. Gabriel is often brutal at home, needing to assert his authority over the often matriarchal society in the black community. In this way, he gains some control in a world ruled by whites that leaves him feeling impotent. He can't find compassion within himself to help others or recognize the sins in his own heart, so he seeks a leading role in the church, which he pursues with hypocritical cunning and determination. His harsh personality is contrasted by that of his wife. Hardworking and gentle **Elizabeth Grimes** loves her son, but remains meekly silent about her brutal husband's abuse. Her religion is based upon her fear of Gabriel and her feelings of guilt about the past. John, it is revealed, is not the son of Gabriel but rather of a man named Richard, whom Elizabeth had loved and planned to marry until he committed suicide after being falsely accused and arrested by white men. Ever since that time, Elizabeth has endured her guilt and loneliness silently.

Florence Grimes is aware of the troubles in Elizabeth's life. Consumed by hatred for her brother Gabriel, she contrasts the violent drunkenness of his youth with the piety he now feigns. Florence is very afraid of death, especially imminent death. Despite her fear and her need for God's saving grace, she can't help but desire revenge against her brother. Throughout the novel, however, Florence attains a good deal of self-awareness and growth.

Minor characters flesh out the realities—some good, some bad—of John's world and contribute to his confusion and eventual self-realization. Florence's husband, **Frank**, a somewhat irresponsible but charming man, will never fulfill her dreams of a good marriage; **Brother Elisha** serves as a model for what John might become as he matures. Elisha has already wrestled with sexuality versus his religious feelings. The spiritual world has won him over, but, as he cautions John, there is a price to pay: one must be willing to give up all selfish pursuits to find salvation and stay away from the devil. There is also **Deborah**, the girl next door who is filled with the somberness of religion, and sensual **Esther**, who is not bothered by any feelings of guilt. When Gabriel, in his righteousness, says that she has served Satan all her days, Esther tells him what she thinks of religion: "I just don't feel it *here*," she protests. "Don't you know I'm a woman grown and I ain't fixing to change?" She adds, "I ain't done nothing I'm ashamed of."

If Beale Street Could Talk

(novel, 1974)

PLOT: Fonny is twenty-two years old. Tish is nineteen. They are black, poor, and surrounded by the hardships of life and racial prejudice in the big city. But they are far from beaten, as long as they have each other. Friends for a long time, Fonny and Tish have only recently realized they are in love and want to get married. They both work, but at night Fonny pursues his love of carving forms from wood and stone. He longs to be a sculptor, and as the young couple makes plans for their marriage, they hope to be able to rent a loft in which to live so that Fonny will be able to continue his work. Tish's family is pleased with the news of the coming marriage, but the reaction in Fonny's family is not so cordial. Although his father, Frank, seems happy over the news, his mother and sisters are not. Fonny suspects they do not like Tish.

It seems like a miracle when they discover a suitable place to live. Their happiness is tempered, however, by the fact that their new home is in a neighborhood patrolled by the bigoted Officer Bell. One night, Bell very nearly carts Fonny off to jail for defending Tish against a menacing street punk. When a witness tells Bell that the two young people are telling the truth about the incident, he lets them go, but Fonny suspects the policeman is out to get him. Sometime later, Fonny is picked out of a lineup and charged with rape, though he is innocent. He has never been in trouble with the law and has never taken drugs. But a woman charges that she was raped by a dark-skinned man. Fonny is dark-skinned, while the three others in the lineup all have light skin. Fonny is accused and sent to jail, and it is there that he learns that Tish is pregnant.

Tish, her family, and Fonny's father hire a white lawyer to defend the innocent young man. The attorney discovers that the woman who accused Fonny of the rape, Mrs. Rogers, has gone to Puerto Rico. Fonny's father and Tish's family, including her mother, Sharon, and father, Joseph, work extra jobs to earn more money toward Fonny's defense. Tish herself tries to keep on working as the time for the baby's birth nears. She also tries to keep up Fonny's spirits while he languishes in jail. Tish's mother, Sharon, decides to go to Puerto Rico to get Mrs. Rogers to change her testimony. She finds the women living with a man named Pietro Alvarez. Though Alvarez will not help her, Sharon finds the woman, who refuses to change her testimony.

Once back in New York, Sharon learns that Mrs. Rogers has lost the baby that was a result of the rape and has been taken to an asylum. Obviously, there is now no chance at all that she will change her testimony. Fonny's trial is postponed. This news so devastates his father that sometime later Frank is found in his car with the doors locked and the motor running. When Tish's father brings her the terrible news about Frank's death, she thinks immediately that she must tell Fonny. Before she can tell him, however, she goes into labor.

CHARACTERS: Tish is a survivor in a harsh world. Although frightened by society's brutality and worried about her baby's future and of what will happen to Fonny, whom she deeply loves, Tish nevertheless retains her sense of pride. She may bend, but she will not break. There is a natural, inborn dignity to Tish as she tries to stand up against the cruelest of circumstances. She gains strength from the closeness and caring of her parents, who stand up for her and for Fonny in their times of stress. In turn, Tish gives that strength and love to Fonny, who often despairs while waiting in jail. When she sees him in prison, she often remarks to herself that he does not look well. But she always tries to lift his spirits, even when sometimes it is difficult to keep up her own.

Fonny is a good young man who is never in trouble with the law and doesn't do drugs. However, bigoted **Officer Bell**, who is dedicated to getting the "punks" off the street, considers Fonny to be just another criminal. A dreamer, perhaps, but a worker, too, Fonny holds down a job while he nurtures the impossible dream of being able to continue what he really loves to do: create stone and wood carvings. He is desperately lonely in jail and often afraid, although he does not admit this. Fonny realizes that he is at everyone's mercy while in jail and the thought terrifies him. He also worries that he will grow old in prison. The dreamer in Fonny is perhaps best described by the way in which he tries to tell Tish of his love for her and for his carving. He tells her that he will never give her a hard time chasing other women, and that she is his only love—except for his wood and stone art. Sometimes she might think that he ignores her because he is so busy, so wrapped up in his carving, but he wants her to understand that no matter where his work and his dream world takes him, he will always come back to her.

Tish considers her mother, **Sharon**, to be a beautiful woman. In her youth she wanted to be a singer and ran off with a traveling band. She met Tish's father, **Joseph**, in a bus stop in Albany. He was kind to her and carried her bags. He helped her get settled in a rooming house when they got to New York City. In a week, they were married, and have been ever since. Both parents realize how much Tish and Fonny love each other, and they are happy for the young couple. When she sees no other way, Sharon goes to Puerto Rico to help find evidence that will clear Fonny. But her determination and courage, even her pleading, will not change the story of the woman who claimed that it was Fonny who raped her.

Frank is the only one of Fonny's family who is genuinely delighted by his son's marriage plans. When it is clear that the families must come up with extra money to try to gain evidence that will free Fonny, Frank systematically begins to steal from the garment center where he works. He sells the hot goods in Brooklyn and Harlem. He does not say this to Tish or to Fonny, but Tish knows, just as she knows that her own father is doing the same thing at the docks where he works. She also knows that her father and Frank would gladly go to jail if it would free Fonny and allow their grandchild to be born into a whole family.

Further Reading

Authors and Artists for Young Adults. Vol. 4. Detroit: Gale Research, 1990.

Berger, Laura Standley, ed. *Twentieth-Century Young Adult Writers.* 1st ed. Detroit: St. James, 1984.

Bloom, Harold, ed. *James Baldwin.* New York: Chelsea House, 1986.

———. *Twentieth-Century American Literature.* Vol. 1 of *The Chelsea House Library of Literary Criticism.* New York: Chelsea House, 1986.

Bruccoli, Matthew J., and Richard Layman, eds. *Concise Dictionary of American Literary Biography: The New Consciousness 1941-1968.* Detroit: Gale Research, 1987.

Campbell, James. *Talking at the Gates: A Life of James Baldwin.* New York: Viking, 1991.

Contemporary Literary Criticism. Vols. 1, 2, 3, 4, 5, 8, 13, 15, 17, 42, 50. Detroit: Gale Research, 1973, 1974, 1975, 1975, 1976, 1978, 1980, 1980, 1981, 1987, 1988.

Critical Survey of Long Fiction. Vol. 1. Englewood Cliffs, NJ: Salem Press, 1983.

Davis, Thadious M., and Trudier Harris, eds. *Afro-American Fiction Writers after 1955.* Vol. 33 of *Dictionary of Literary Biography.* Detroit: Gale Research, 1984.

Gounard, Jean-Francois. *The Racial Problem in the Works of Richard Wright and James Baldwin.* Westport, CT: Greenwood Press, 1992.

Helterman, Jeffrey, ed. *American Novelists since World War II.* Vol. 2 of *Dictionary of Literary Biography.* Detroit: Gale Research, 1978.

Kenan, Randall. *James Baldwin.* New York: Chelsea House, 1994.

King, Malcolm. *Baldwin: Three Interviews.* Middletown, CT: Wesleyan University Press, 1985.

Kinnamon, Kenneth. *James Baldwin: A Collection of Critical Essays.* Englewood Cliffs, NJ: Prentice Hall, 1974.

Lee, A. Robert. *James Baldwin: Climbing to the Light.* New York: St. Martin, 1991.

Macebuh, Stanley. *James Baldwin: A Critical Study.* New York: Joseph Okpaku, 1973.

MacNicholas, John, ed. *Twentieth-Century American Dramatists.* Vol. 7 of *Dictionary of Literary Biography.* Detroit: Gale Research, 1981.

McCarthy, Mary. "A Memory of James Baldwin." *New York Review of Books* 36 (27 April, 1989).

O'Daniel, Thurman B., ed. *James Baldwin: A Critical Evaluation.* Washington, DC: Howard University Press, 1981.

Porter, Horace A. *Stealing the Fire: The Art and Protest of James Baldwin.* Middletown, CT: Wesleyan University Press, 1989.

Pratt, Louis H. *James Baldwin.* New York: Twayne, 1978.

Rosset, Lisa. *James Baldwin.* New York: Chelsea House, 1989.

Standley, Fred L., and Nancy V. Burt. *Critical Essays on James Baldwin.* Boston: G. K. Hall, 1988.

———, and Louis H. Pratt, eds. *Conversations with James Baldwin.* Jackson: University Press of Mississippi, 1989.

———, and Nancy V. Standley. *James Baldwin: A Reference Guide.* Boston: Hall, 1980.

Sylvander, Carolyn Wedin. *James Baldwin.* New York: Ungar, 1980.

Troupe, Quincy, ed. *James Baldwin: The Legacy.* New York: Simon, 1989.

Wakeman, John, ed. *World Authors 1950-1970.* New York: H. W. Wilson, 1975.

Weatherby, W. J. *James Baldwin: Artist on Fire.* New York: Fine, 1989.

Jay Bennett

1912-, American novelist

Deathman, Do Not Follow Me

(young adult novel, 1968)

PLOT: The first of Jay Bennett's many popular suspense novels for teens, this novel is set in contemporary Brooklyn, the author's home community. The story begins when high school senior Danny Morgan is not paying attention in class, so his strict but caring teacher, Mr. Warfield, gives him a special assignment to report on the Van Gogh exhibit that is currently at the Brooklyn Museum. Since his father's death, Danny, the quarterback on the school's football team, has earned a reputation for being a loner, although he does have one close friend, George Cheever, and an attentive girlfriend, Carol. He is also a thoughtful, obedient son who loves and supports his working mother.

At the Museum, Danny is particularly impressed with the gallery's newest Van Gogh acquisition. The painting becomes more meaningful after it is explained to him by another museum visitor, the elderly, effete Mr. Collingwood, who is accompanied by his younger, attractive wife. When Danny forgets his report at home, an irate Mr. Warfield sends him back to the museum. To verify his visit, Danny must have a note signed by one of the guards, Alfred Cobb, Mr. Warfield's wartime buddy. Danny again approaches the painting and realizes that it is not the painting he saw days before—it is a fake. In shock, he tells Cobb, who denies the accusation and mysteriously tells Danny not to "rock the boat." Disturbed and not fully trusting his own judgment, Danny tells no one, but that night he receives a mysterious phone call from a stranger who repeats Cobb's warning. Later, Mr. Collingwood visits Danny and tells him that he and his accomplices, including Cobb, have stolen the painting and asks him to remain silent until the painting can be smuggled out of the country. Before Danny can decide on a course of action, Mrs. Collingwood contacts him and, at a secret meeting, tells him that to protect her husband from his murderous partners she has taken the painting. After telling Danny its location, she leaves, only to be killed by a truck while trying to escape a limousine in which her husband is a passenger. Before he can reach the police, Danny is taken prisoner. He is offered bribes and then tortured, but he refuses to divulge the whereabouts of the stolen canvas. Alerted by his suspicions concerning Cobb and fearful of Danny's well-being, Mr. Warfield traces Danny's whereabouts and, with the help of the police, rescues the boy and captures the culprits.

CHARACTERS: The hero of this exciting mystery is **Danny Morgan**, a tall, lean senior in high school with quiet eyes and a reputation for being a loner. Danny has already planned his future life: first, a football scholarship to a college like U.C.L.A., then a few years of professional ball with a team like the Giants or the Rams, and finally a peaceful life teaching in a college in upstate New York. He is anxious to proceed with his dream and becomes impatient when teachers like Mr. Warfield put what he considers petty obstacles in his way. He bristles at being thought of as a loner, though this label accurately describes his behavior. As Mr. Warfield says, "You're a strange kid. You go out for a sport. You make good at it. And yet you're always alone even when you're a vital part of a team." Crushed by the untimely death of his beloved father and living a frugal, almost spartan existence with his hard-working, caring mother, he has become a withdrawn and private person. He is an obedient, dutiful son who complies with his mother's requests, such as not accepting an after-school job, even though he knows she is being old-fashioned and overly protective. Danny worries about living up to responsibilities and expectations and agonizes internally over wrong football calls to the point of losing sleep. This sensitivity is also shown in his behavior toward his girlfriend, Carol. He loves her deeply but is unable to tell her his true feelings.

Danny has a disquieting ability to sense oncoming trouble and to forecast imminent tragedy. Years before, he predicted a fatal accident involving acrobats. The Van Gogh assignment aroused the same feelings, one symptom being a haunting song he remembers that begins, "Deathman, do not follow me." In his isolation he seems to lack strong moral convictions or obligations to the outside world, but he faces danger and possible death to fight for justice and defeat the robbers. He resists handsome bribes and suffers extreme pain without revealing the whereabouts of the stolen painting. This courage and gallantry demonstrate that Danny really cares about other people and is less a loner than people think. After his ordeal, Danny emerges a stronger person who is more aware of his inner strengths.

Danny's teacher, **Mr. Warfield**, a stocky man with a rugged, leathery face and chiselled features, is better liked as a man than as a teacher. He is a strict disciplinarian and often uses sarcasm with his students. A veteran of World War II, during which he killed several men, he was a prisoner of the Japanese and survived the Bataan Death March. Troubled by these violent experiences, life has become very precious to him, and he overreacts when he feels his students are wasting time or losing opportunities. Danny, an independent spirit who is often lost in his own thoughts, feels that Mr. Warfield particularly resents this and has singled him out for harsh treatment. Actually, Mr. Warfield is impressed with Danny's potential but is alarmed by his solitary ways. In his own brusque way, he is trying to reach out to Danny. When this concern results in his dramatic rescue, Danny finally realizes that Mr. Warfield is a true friend who is anxious to help him.

With his expensive clothing, handsome features, white silky hair and graceful movements, **Mr. Collingwood** impresses Danny as a distinguished, cultivated gentleman. His encyclopedic knowledge of art and keen sensitivity also show that he is a man of rare discernment and taste. Unfortunately, his obsessive love of art has led to a life of crime. Unable to afford the art works he so loves, he has resorted to stealing pictures, either to build his own collection or to sell to collectors to maintain his luxurious lifestyle. Under this veneer of good breeding and fine manners, there is also a streak of cruelty. His wife mentions this to Danny and points to a scar on her face as proof. Danny also experiences this man's brutality firsthand while being questioned. Obviously a gifted and accomplished man, Mr. Collingwood has destroyed his life to pursue a deadly fixation. His wife, **Marion Collingwood**, is easily twenty years younger than her husband. Pert and youthful, she is a handsome woman who dresses attractively. She is totally devoted to her husband and worships him completely, in spite of being a victim of his cruelty. To save him from being harmed by his accomplices, she hides the stolen painting, and, unfortunately, is accidently killed while avoiding capture.

Danny's mother, **Mrs. Morgan**, is a tall, quiet woman with dark hair and small features who has supported her family by working as a public librarian since her husband's death. Although often exhausted from her work and responsibilities, she always has time for the son she adores. An attentive, caring mother, she worries about her son to the point of being overprotective. Proud and old-fashioned, she wants nothing to interfere with Danny's school career and therefore asks him not to work after school. Understandably, Danny is devoted to his tender, loving mother. Danny's father, **Mr. Morgan**, is already dead at the beginning of the novel, but his presence is felt by the terrible void that Danny feels over this loss. He was a handsome, tall man with blond hair and quiet, gentle ways. An attentive, loving father, he sacrificed his ambition of becoming a lawyer to take a job in the post office to support his family.

Carol, Danny's girlfriend, is a tall, beautiful girl with long honey-blonde hair. Though independent and filled with self-confidence, she likes being with this reserved, sometimes distracted young man, who often puzzles her with his remoteness. Astute in her observations, she tells Danny that "there's something locked away in you." She is a charming girl with a splendid sense of humor. Like Mr. Warfield, she is genuinely fond of Danny and has a sincere desire to reach out to him.

Two minor characters are **George Cheever**, Danny's pleasant, affable teammate and devoted friend and **Alfred Cobb**, the little, bald guard at the Museum who had served in the army with Mr. Warfield. For unexplained reasons, he has become a criminal and part of Mr. Collingwood's scheme to steal the Van Gogh painting.

Say Hello to the Hit Man

(young adult novel, 1976)

PLOT: Since his mother's death three years ago, Fred Morgan has tried to erase every connection he had with his father, big-time New York racketeer Eddie Corell, even to the point of adopting his mother's maiden name. Convinced that his father's criminal activities led to his mother's death from worry and anxiety, both Fred and his uncle, Arthur Morgan, hate the wealthy mobster they consider to be a murderer. After his mother's funeral, Fred stayed briefly with his uncle, but at the age of nineteen he moved to his own apartment in the East Village. He attends New York University, where he is the particular favorite of his English professor, Dr. Elwood. Fred has a girlfriend, Teresa Rizzo, and is leading a modest, comfortable life when his peace of mind is shattered by a late-night phone call from "the Hit Man," who tells Fred that he has been marked for death.

Thinking his father's rivals are behind this, Fred visits Corell, who is devastated to think that his only child, whom he loves dearly, is in danger. He begs Fred to come to the safety of his home and, after Fred's stubborn refusal, assigns some of his henchmen, including John Heller, to protect his son. The harassment continues, but fortunately Fred is diverted from his worries by meeting a young girl, Callie Ross, with whom he falls in love. After Heller is murdered and the phone calls continue, Fred is convinced nothing can save him. Through his father's sleuthing, Fred learns that his uncle, who is dying of cancer, had engineered the plot to have him killed in order to get even with Corell. The hit man is actually Callie, who has been hired to murder him. In spite of Fred's pleading, his father shoots Callie. Bitter and disillusioned, Fred turns his father in to the police.

CHARACTERS: Professor Elwood correctly says that **Fred Morgan** is a "gifted and hurt" young man. Unable and unwilling to unburden himself to others, he carries with him his grief over his beloved mother's early death, as well as hatred for the man he considers responsible. Eager to cleanse himself of the corruption and crime that surrounds his father, Fred has tried to start life afresh and to erase all traces of his past. Fred is a stubborn, independent person who refuses help from anyone, particularly his father. A handsome, intelligent young man, he is a fine student with a strong interest in the arts and literature, but because of his pervading bitterness and melancholy, he has become known as a loner and has few friends. Seeking a simple life in which he can live in decency and peace, he is vulnerable to Callie's advances and her feigned sincerity and idealism. Fred has a peace-loving, non-violent nature. Therefore, thoughts of killing and brutality particularly repel him; he easily becomes a victim of paralyzing fear when he believes his death is inevitable. Before she is shot, Callie praises Fred for his tenderness and basic decency. This decency and high moral sense compel him to bring his father to justice.

Fred's father, **Eddie Corell**, is the tough mastermind behind New York's crime syndicate. Though outwardly living a life of culture and style, he is the "polished facade" covering corrupt labor unions, political graft, and an underworld of prostitution, gambling, and drugs. Fred says that under the veneer of culture he is only "a common hood." In his early fifties, Corell is rangy and tall, with handsome features and thick black hair. Capable of great charm, he truly adored his wife but was unable to change his way of life in spite of her entreaties. This love has been transferred to his son, whose alienation has caused him heartbreak and agony. He is sincere in wanting only the best for Fred and will stop at nothing to protect him, in spite of Fred's withering scorn and sarcasm. In his daily life, Corell is a shrewd, ruthless, and cruel criminal who deals with evil and death daily and commits murder without regret. Corell doesn't realize that the noble act of saving Fred will compel his son to turn him in to the authorities.

The character of Fred's dead mother, **Jessie Morgan**, is revealed through the memories of other people in the story. A woman of great beauty and personality, she genuinely loved and respected her husband, until she found out about his connections with criminal figures. Fred says to his father, "She hated your values, your crimes," and after she was unable to change him, she sank into fits of depression and anxiety that eventually led to her death. Nevertheless, she never spoke ill of her husband. Fred adored his loving mother and has not come to terms with her untimely death.

Fred's uncle, **Arthur Morgan**, also blames Corell for his sister's death. A slight man with delicate features, he is in his late sixties. A gentle, pleasant person, he is crushed when Fred leaves his home to seek a more independent life. Morgan is a wealthy art lover who is unmarried and solitary. He broods after learning that he has incurable cancer. After he believes he has been rebuffed by Fred, he becomes more obsessed with his hatred of Corell and desires revenge. At this point, he decides to destroy Corell's most beloved possession: his son. He hires Callie and begins his mad plot for vengeance. When Arthur's scheme is discovered, Corell shoots him.

At first Fred believes that meeting **Callie Ross** is one of the few fortunate occurrences in his life. She is a bright, observant girl who appears to have an intuitive knowledge of his interests and problems. Waif-like and a loner, she instills in Fred an immediate need to protect and shelter her. Callie appears to have a great deal in common with Fred: both are only children who are bitter and alienated from their parents. Callie tells Fred that she has been on her own since her early teens but now wants to be a painter and take classes at Fred's university. Callie offers him compassion and affection and, in his confused, vulnerable state, Fred responds by falling deeply in love with her. Callie is described as twenty-two, tall, and lithe, with attractive features and gleaming blonde hair. Secretly, she has been hired by Arthur Morgan to kill Fred for forty thousand dollars, and she lures John Heller to his death as part of the bargain. Confronted with her crimes by Corell, she begs Fred to save her and tells him that in spite of her terrible actions, she really does love and admire him. Whether this declaration is true or not is never proved because Corell shoots her.

The thug assigned by Corell to protect Fred is **John Heller**. Tough and rugged, Heller is only in his early thirties, though his hair has already gone gray. His eyes are also as gray and cold as two small stones. A hired killer, he strong-arms Fred's congenial neighbors into vacating their apartment so he can tail Fred more effectively. Ruthless and without pity, his life is devoted to being Corell's enforcer. Heller is particularly attentive to guarding Fred because he knows that if he fails to save Fred, Corell will have him killed. Callie, following Arthur's instructions, shoots Heller in a dark alley and leaves his body to be discovered by Fred.

At New York University, Fred has two friends. The first is **Professor Elwood**, his English teacher. Elwood is aware of Fred's talents and intelligence but also knows that the boy has a troubled personal life. When Fred becomes distracted and misses classes because of the phone threats, Elwood offers his help, but Fred finds it impossible to confide in this gentle and considerate man. Fred also can't reveal his problems to his girlfriend, the sweet, caring **Teresa Rizzo**. When the young man mistakenly believes that Teresa's family has connections with the underworld, he momentarily thinks that these connections might be responsible for his harassing phone calls. In his confusion and desperation, Fred turns against her. Hurt and perplexed, Teresa tries to regain his confidence, but, realizing that he is deeply troubled, withdraws, leaving the vacuum that is later filled by Callie.

Further Reading

Authors and Artists for Young Adults. Vol. 10. Detroit: Gale Research, 1993.

Berger, Laura Standley, ed. *Twentieth-Century Young Adult Writers.* 1st ed. Detroit: St. James, 1995.

Contemporary Literary Criticism. Vol. 35. Detroit: Gale Research, 1985.

Holtze, Sally Holmes, ed. *Sixth Book of Junior Authors and Illustrators.* New York: H. W. Wilson, 1989.

Something about the Author. Vols. 41, 87. Detroit: Gale Research, 1985, 1996.

Something about the Author Autobiography Series. Vol. 4. Detroit: Gale Research, 1987.

Ward, Martha, ed. *Authors of Books for Young People.* 3rd ed. Metuchen, NJ: Scarecrow, 1990.

Francesca Lia Block

1962-, American novelist

Weetzie Bat

(young adult novel, 1989)

PLOT: Weetzie is still in high school in Los Angeles (which she calls Shangri-L.A.) when she meets Dirk McDonald, the best looking boy at school. In their psychedelic fantasy world, they like to spend time going "duck hunting" together—that is, looking for boyfriends: one for Weetzie and another for Dirk, who is gay. Weetzie's father, Charlie Bat, visits from New York, and Weetzie hopes in vain for a reconciliation between him and her mother, Brandy-Lynn. One day, Weetzie receives a magic lamp from Dirk's Grandma Fifi that contains a genie able to grant three wishes. Weetzie's wishes all come true: a lover named Duck Drake for Dirk, one called My Secret Agent Lover Man for herself, and a house (inherited from Grandma Fifi) where they can all live together peacefully. Weetzie's circle of friends also includes a Rastafarian man named Valentine Jah-Love, his Chinese wife, Ping Chong, and their baby, Raphael.

Because My Secret Agent Lover Man doesn't want to have children, Duck and Dirk volunteer to help Weetzie, who later gives birth to Cherokee Bat. About the same time, My Secret Agent Lover Man is bewitched by Vixanne Wigg, who bears him a child named Witch Baby, who comes to live with Weetzie and company. The death of Charlie Bat as a result of drugs, coupled with the news of the death of so many of Duck's gay friends, produces such sadness in Duck one day that he leaves home. Frantically, Dirk searches for him and eventually finds him in San Francisco. Dirk convinces Duck to return, and Weetzie and her family have a joyous reunion.

See below for character descriptions.

Witch Baby

(young adult novel, 1991)

PLOT: Years have passed since the events in the first novel, and Weetzie and My Secret Agent Lover Man have become successful filmmakers, along with their extended family. The only unhappy one in the group is Witch Baby, who is growing up lonely and confused. She is now completely out of control and delights in causing mayhem and disorder. Although she secretly supplies My Secret Agent Lover Man with inspiration for new movies, no one recognizes her contributions. She has two secret passions: the first is drum playing and the second is Raphael. When Raphael shows an interest in learning the drums, Witch Baby is encouraged but later learns the boy only wishes to impress his own secret love, the beautiful Cherokee Bat. Learning the truth, Witch Baby flies into another destructive rage. Later, she alienates Coyote, My Secret Agent Lover Man's best friend, by stealing his sacred Joshua tree seeds and planting them in a vacant school yard. She also hurts her friend Duck Drake by blurting out to his mother, Darlene, that her son is gay.

Witch Baby then falls in love with a young movie actor, Angel Juan Perez. But when he and his family, who are all illegal immigrants, are forced to return to Mexico, Witch Baby's heart is again broken. Puzzled about the identity of her real parents, Witch Baby learns from My Secret Agent Lover Man that he is her real father and that her mother is a witch named Vixanne Wigg. Determined to find out where she really belongs, the youngster runs away from home and locates Vixanne, the leader of a coven of witches who are also Jayne Mansfield worshippers. During her indoctrination sessions, Witch Baby suddenly realizes how much she misses Weetzie and her real family. She returns and is joyfully reunited with all her friends. In her absence, each has realized how much they love this unusual creature and, during the shower of attention and love she receives when she comes back, Witch Baby knows she has both a home and a family who care about her.

See below for character descriptions.

Cherokee Bat and the Goat Boys

(young adult novel, 1992)

PLOT: While Weetzie and the other adults in the household are in South America filming a movie, Cherokee Bat, Witch Baby, and Raphael are left alone in their Beachwood Canyon home in Los Angeles. Feeling lonely and depressed, Witch Baby reverts to her earlier, troubled ways and immerses herself in a mud bath, refusing to leave except to eat small meals. In desperation, Cherokee goes to Coyote Dream Song for advice. With his help, she fashions a magical pair of wings for her near-sister. This gift, plus the sudden return of Which Baby's former boyfriend, Angel Juan, effects a cure. Soon all four friends, under the name the "Goat Boys," are making great music together: Witch Baby on drums, Raphael on vocals and guitar, Angel Juan on bass, and Cherokee dancing and beating the tambourine. When Raphael begins to lose confidence in the group after a disastrous opening night at Zombo's Rockin' Coffin night club, Coyote helps Cherokee make haunches of braided goat hair for Raphael to wear. The trinkets magically revive his spirits. Later, Witch Baby steals from Coyote a pair of enchanted goat horns for Angel Juan to wear, and Cherokee dons a pair of strange boots shaped like goat hooves. Although the act is successful with each of these additions to their costumes, their actions and values begin to change. They skip school, begin drinking heavily, take drugs, and become sexually promiscuous. Through Coyote's intervention, Cherokee narrowly escapes death while trying to fly by jumping off the top of a tall building. This near tragedy brings the group back to their senses. Under Coyote's guidance, they discard their enchanted keepsakes, and the four friends return to their former spontaneous and unaffected ways, looking forward to the return of Weetzie and family.

See below for character descriptions.

Missing Angel Juan

(young adult novel, 1993)

PLOT: Witch Baby is devastated when her lover, Angel Juan, leaves for New York, where he hopes to build a career in music. After receiving several postcards from him, Witch Baby realizes Angel Juan still has no home. She worries about him and decides to try and locate him in New York. Once there, she moves into the empty Greenwich Village apartment where Weetzie's dead father, Charlie Bat, once lived. At the apartment, she is greeted by Charlie's ghost, who begins to show her around New York in the same way he had years before with his daughter, Weetzie. Together they tour the Village, Central Park, the Metropolitan Museum, and Brooklyn, where Witch Baby relives, with Charlie, scenes from his childhood. In each place, Witch Baby sees a mysterious ghoul-like man dressed in white.

Alone, she traces Angel Juan to the meat packing district in Manhattan, and there, in the window of a diner called Cake's Shakin' Palace, she sees a life-size statue of Angel Juan. The proprietor, Mr. Cake, is the same man who has followed her around Manhattan. On investigating the basement of the diner, she finds many other life-like statues and realizes that Mr. Cake kidnaps runaways and turns them into mannequins. Fortunately, she finds Angel Juan still alive. As they flee the diner, Cake turns into a mannequin. Realizing that this experience is about leaving and letting go, Witch Baby returns to L.A., happy with the knowledge that Angel Juan is safely ensconced in Charlie Bat's old apartment.

See below for character descriptions.

Baby Be-Bop

(young adult novel, 1995)

PLOT: Dirk McDonald always knew he was gay but has kept his sexual identity a secret, afraid of revealing himself to his family and friends. When he is almost sixteen, he meets and falls in love with Pup Lambert, a boy who shares many of Dirk's interests. When Pup deserts Dirk to form a steady attachment with Tracey Stace, Dirk is so hurt that he tries to tell Pup how he feels about him. Rebuffed, Dirk changes his lifestyle. Filled with guilt and self-loathing, he begins to hang out in tough leather bars. One night he is severely beaten by a gang of skinheads who call him a "faggot." Though he finds his way home, Dirk sinks into a coma. In his coma he is visited by a sad-eyed woman who introduces herself as Gazelle Sunday and tells Dirk her life story. Raised by a cruel aunt who trained her as a seamstress and kept her a prisoner in their apartment, she is visited one day by a mysterious stranger who orders a dress to be made and holds her in his arms. Later she realizes that she is pregnant and, after her aunt's death, raises her daughter, Fifi. Dirk realizes that he is hearing the story of his family and that Fifi is actually his beloved grandmother. Fifi has incredible dancing ability and joins the show business act of Martin and Merlin. Later in the story, Dirk sees his grandfather, the sickly magician Derwood McDonald, who dies shortly after the birth of Dirby, their only child. Dirby then introduces himself and tells how his amazing gift of writing poetry gained him the name Be-Bop Bo-Peep. Dirk also meets his mother, Just Silver, and hears about the nickname they gave him, Baby Be-Bop. Both his parents die in a car accident when Dirk is only a child and he moves in with his grandmother.

A genie, the same stranger who visited his grandmother years before, appears before Dirk. He gives Dirk an indication of his future by showing him the Drake household and pointing out Duck, a young man who, like Dirk, is gay, unhappy, and unfulfilled. Moving to Los Angeles, Drake learns about the gay lifestyle from Bam-Bam during their platonic relationship. In the last episode of the vision, Duck is alone waiting to meet his future love, Dirk. When he awakens in a hospital, Dirk is recovering from his wounds and is filled with an inner peace and acceptance of himself that gives him the strength to move on.

CHARACTERS: While she was in high school in Los Angeles, Francesca Lia Block saw a teenager hitchhiking in a prom dress and cowboy boots. Later, she saw another girl with pink sunglasses driving a pink car with a license plate that read "Weetzie." These two incidents were the inspiration for the creation of an L.A. punk kid with an insatiable need to give and receive love and affection. **Weetzie Bat** is not an average American kid. Block describes her as "a skinny girl with a bleach-blonde flat-top. Under the pink Harlequin sunglasses, strawberry lipstick, earrings dangling charms, and sugar-frosted eyeshadow, she was really almost beautiful." Her behavior is as unconventional as her looks. She enjoys cruising around L.A. looking for the man of her dreams, and after she finds him she thinks that having a baby by her two gay friends, Dirk and Duck, is perfectly acceptable. Weetzie finds a hidden beauty in all the sleazy glitz of Los Angeles that most people find repulsive and cheap. She is attracted to the bizarre, the incongruous, and the inappropriate. Weetzie is a cheerful, outgoing, and generous girl who hates cruelty and phoniness. A child of nature, she is loyal to her friends, unselfish in her motives, and naive in her childlike desire to bring peace and happiness to her friends. This independent spirit possesses a forgiving, ingenuous nature, unfettered by social conventions or rules concerning propriety. With the arrival of Cherokee Bat and Witch Baby, Weetzie matures and becomes an attentive mother. While not abandoning her delightfully unorthodox view of life, she simply extends the love with which she is filled to encompass more people.

Weetzie's dear friend is the best-looking guy at school, **Dirk McDonald**. He wears his hair in a shoe-polish-black Mohawk and drives a red '55 Pontiac named Jerry. "With his black leather and Mohawk and armloads of chain and his dark-smudged eyes, Dirk was the coolest," thinks Weetzie. Like Weetzie, he enjoys hedonistic pursuits and all the tawdry razzle-dazzle of the big city. But beneath all this restless, nervous activity, Dirk is looking for the man of his dreams, and when he meets Duck he settles down and becomes faithful. His love for Duck is so deep and lasting that he gives up everything to search for his lover when Duck becomes despondent and leaves home. Dirk is a loyal friend who delights in the happiness of others, particularly his friend Weetzie. At times, he ruminates about life and reaches such mystifying conclusions as "Love is a dangerous angel." In his early teens, Dirk had great difficulty accepting his homosexuality. He is hurt and confused when his best friend, **Pup Lambert**, rejects him after his confession of love. Pup is a daring, bold, good-looking boy who delights in using other people's swimming pools without permission and engaging in petty thievery to satisfy his needs. Dirk adores him, but Pup is basically straight and drops Dirk when an attractive girl begins paying attention to him. Unsure and frightened by his sexual feelings, he later confesses, "I Love You, Dirk, but I can't handle it." Though saddened and further confused, Dirk rebounds when the mystical experience recounted in *Baby Be-Bop* changes his attitudes about himself and his sexuality. Through his vision he learns that all love is good and should be cherished. He emerges from this experience confident and unashamed, eager to give and receive love.

During his coma, Dirk meets his great-grandmother, **Gazelle Sunday**, an amazing woman who survived cruelty and abuse from her sadistic aunt and emerged a strong, loving woman capable of raising a family and supporting herself. She loves all the things of which she was once deprived, including art and dance, and she is determined to foster any artistic talents in her child. When young and trusting, her innocence is taken from her, but, far from feeling self-pity or guilt, she exults in the precious gift that has been given her: a child. **Fifi**, her daughter, grows up experiencing all the freedom that was denied her mother. She, too, has natural talents and a love of life and living. She has an idyllic romance with the gentle, fragile **Derwood McDonald**, who is able to enchant insects so that they obey his every wish. This considerate, sensitive man was born with a weak heart and realizes his life will be short. During their short time together, the two share a wonderful if brief love.

During her show business career, Fifi works with two partners she adores, **Martin** and **Merlin**. They are gay men who love one another, but like so many of their generation, they have to hide their love when they are with other people. Each "dates" Fifi at times to keep up appearances. Although Dirk likes them as friends, he can't accept this deceit and hypocrisy and, instead, wants truth and honesty in his life. Fifi is already an older woman when we meet her in *Weetzie Bat*, but she is still bursting with the exuberance she has always had. Full of love for others, she exudes a perpetual spirit of joy, exhilaration, and love of life. She is described as "a sweet, powdery old lady who baked tiny, white, sugar-coated pastries for them, and played them tunes on a music box with a little dancing monkey on top." Fifi loves her grandson deeply and, in spite of her age, accepts and approves of his curious habits and routines. A generous, understanding woman, upon her death she leaves her house to Dirk and Weetzie, and they move into the cottage with its "fairy-tale roof," roses, lemon trees, and an interior "filled with plaster Jesus statues, glass butterfly ashtrays, and paintings of clowns."

In his delirium, Dirk also meets the parents he scarcely knew before their sudden deaths, **Dirby** and **Just Silver McDonald**. Dirby inherited the same other-worldly, mystical qualities of his father, but his talents were shown in the amazing poetry he wrote while still a teenager. First known as Bo-Peep in the bars where he wrote, this was later changed to **Be-Bop Bo-Peep** when people realized the quality of his work. He met and fell in love at first sight with his future wife, Just Silver, a stunningly beautiful model and actress who has renounced her family name. In his dream, Dirk confesses his homosexuality to his family. His father's response typifies their beliefs: "I know you are, buddy. . . . I want you to be different, Dirk. I want you to fight. I love you, buddy. I want you not to be afraid."

Dirk's lover, **Duck Drake**, is described as "a small blond surfer" with freckles on his nose and hair cut in a flat-top. A surfing fanatic, "Sometimes he slept on picnic tables at the beach so he could be up at dawn for the most radical waves." He, too, is transformed by love and proves to be Dirk's loyal, unselfish lover. Before moving in with Dirk, Duck also had to come to terms with his sexuality. His guilt and isolation drove him from his home in Santa Cruz to find companionship and self-discovery in Los Angeles. He is taught the ropes by a bar-hopping, irresponsible young gay man named **Bam-Bam**. Duck falls in love with this charming, carefree youngster. Though their love is not physically consummated, Duck learns about gay life from him, as well as gaining a greater acceptance of himself. Duck knows he has found true love when he meets and moves in with Dirk, but because he is a sensitive, impressionable man, Duck becomes despondent at the constant reminders around him of death from AIDS. Not wanting to inflict his bad moods and depression on others, he leaves but is later both touched and grateful when Dirk finds him and brings him home.

Duck is haunted by the memory of his adored father who was killed in a surfing accident. He also loves his mother, **Darlene**, and is disappointed and hurt when she initially is unable to accept that he is gay. When she later comes to him in an accepting and loving mood, Duck's wounds are healed and he feels wanted again. Since her husband's death, Darlene, a caring, generous woman, also feels the loneliness and isolation caused by her husband's death and the tremendous responsibility of raising Duck's eight brothers and sisters. When Duck visits, he disapproves of her new live-in boyfriend, an affable, kind man, mainly because Duck feels no one can replace his father. At first Darlene is taken aback when Witch Baby tells her that Duck is gay, but after the initial surprise, this unselfish woman realizes that love knows no bounds and that her son's happiness is what is most important.

Weetzie's father is **Charlie Bat**, a handsome, charming man who loves his daughter dearly and worries about her welfare, though he never interferes with her chosen lifestyle. A screenwriter who grew to hate everything about L.A. that Weetzie now loves, he returned to New York after the breakup of his marriage, hoping to write "real quality stuff" because the "Hollywood trash is bullshit." His marriage was destroyed by his womanizing and drinking, and he never achieved his writing goals. Instead, his health continued to decline, concluding with his early death from an overdose of drugs. Weetzie adores her father and is unsuccessful in her many attempts to save and rehabilitate him. Later, when Witch Baby visits New York, Charlie, who appears as a ghost, showers the same care and love he showed Weetzie on his near-granddaughter. Through revisiting his haunts and reliving scenes from his childhood, the sadness and goodness in his life are revealed.

Charlie's ex-wife is **Brandy-Lynn**, Weetzie's mother, who is a somewhat pathetic figure. Once a promising starlet, she gave up her career when she married, and though she never stopped loving her husband, she could not tolerate his indulgence in women and booze. She continues to miss him even after his death and gains solace by sharing in Weetzie's life. She dislikes being alone and sometimes turns to alcohol for relief.

While Weetzie is working as a waitress, she meets her dream lover, **My Secret Agent Lover Man**. A movie director, he "wore a slouchy hat and a trench coat, was unshaven and had the greenest eyes Weetzie had ever seen." Though accepting of her friends and lifestyle, Lover Man has a more conventional nature than Weetzie and can't endorse her unorthodox way of becoming pregnant. When he strays and has an affair with the practicing witch **Vixanne Wigg**, the wickedly beautiful, diabolical mistress of a witch coven that is also a Jayne Mansfield fan club, he begs forgiveness and asks to return to the woman he adores. Later, he finds it difficult to accept Witch Baby, partly because of her destructive, spiteful ways and partly because of his own guilt in fathering her. In time, the power of love triumphs and he and Witch Baby form a close father-daughter relationship.

With her dark, tangled hair, tilted purple eyes, and curly toes, **Witch Baby** has a name that suits her appearance. Growing up an outsider without any sense of identity or belonging, she gains attention by being destructive and nasty. Her pain and agony has turned her into a rebellious, contrary person who is fixated on evil and suffering. She dwells on the negative side of life. For example, Los Angeles is, for her, not the city of angels, but Devil City, Los Diablos. Her bedroom walls are covered with clippings about murders, disasters, and world calamities, and most of her actions cause other people harm. Unfortunately, whenever Witch Baby tries to reach out to others these actions are ignored, misinterpreted, or rebuffed. For example, she loses the two loves in her life, Raphael and Angel Juan, and Coyote scolds her when she tries to beautify the neighborhood by planting his tree seeds. Finally, the pain becomes too great for her to bear and she runs away. This action triggers a new beginning in her life. Others realize how much she has meant to them, and she discovers her own worth and the power of belonging. Through this transformation she also finds that pain is a natural and universal part of life and that she is not unique in experiencing it. For the first time in her life, Witch Baby allows herself to cry. Later, she learns other valuable lessons through her loving relationship with Angel Juan. Her magical experiences in New York searching for her lost love educate Witch Baby about the bitter nature of loss and letting go. When she returns to Los Angeles after these experiences, she is a wiser, more mature person, capable of accepting life's painful realities.

Witch Baby's near-sister is the beautiful blonde, **Cherokee Bat**, Weetzie's daughter. Proud of the fact that she has three fathers—Duck, Dirk and My Secret Agent Lover Man—Cherokee is the delight of her family. Outgoing, generous, and loving, she provides an unfortunate contrast to the difficult Witch Baby. Cherokee is not spoiled by the attention and adoration showered on her. Instead, she reciprocates by showing kindness and consideration to others. She is the driving force behind the formation of the Goat Boys group and, in a misguided attempt to help each of them, she inadvertently precipitates their decline into loose living. However, her strength and endurance also bring about their redemption and reformation. The one true love of Cherokee's life is Raphael, whom she honestly adores. Weetzie's friends include a family that consists of a Rastafarian from Jamaica named **Valentine Jah-Love**, his Chinese girlfriend, **Ping Chong**, and their child, **Raphael Chong Jah-Love**. Valentine and Ping met while Ping, a fashion designer, was working in Jamaica. They are both madly in love, though their relationship has been attacked by bigots. Both work for My Secret Agent Lover Man behind the scenes of his movies. Their only child is the handsome Raphael, with whom both Witch Baby and Cherokee have fallen in love. With his almond eyes and dreadlocks, Raphael is an extremely attractive young man. As part of the Goat Boys, he succumbs to the temptations of fame, including booze, women, and drugs, but his love for Cherokee brings him back to reality.

Another family friend is **Coyote Dream Song**, a misplaced Westerner and dreamy mystic who longs for the natural life away from the big city and modern technology. A Native American, Coyote has immersed himself in the lore, magic, and wisdom of his people and their tragic history. He realizes the power of nature and its supernatural energy. He warns Cherokee and the goat boys that they must be wary of unleashing evil forces when they assume new identities by wearing horns, wings, etc. A caring, wise man, he continually tries to help those around Weetzie. Through his knowledge and loving care, he restores Cherokee and her friends to their normal life.

Angel Juan, one of the five children of Gabriela and Marquez Perez, is a gentle, talented young man who instinctively senses both Witch Baby's inner pain and her hidden beauty. Their tender relationship ends suddenly when he and his parents are deported to Mexico. After his return, he resumes his relationship with Witch Baby and they become lovers. With his innate wisdom and charm, he is able to tame and transform the difficult Witch Baby. However, in time he longs for independence and growth. Always a restless seeker of self-knowledge and fulfillment, he courageously travels alone to New York to seek his fortune. There he is saved from tragedy by the intervention of Witch Baby, with whom he learns the unhappy but liberating aspects of parting and moving on.

Angel Juan's nemesis is **Mr. Cake**, the proprietor of Cake's Shakin' Palace, a diner in Manhattan's meat packing area. A tall, white-haired man who dresses completely in white and has almost transparent white skin, Witch Baby says he is "probably the most gorgeous human being I have ever seen and the most nasty-looking." Using his mesmerizing manners, the diabolical Cake abducts innocent runaways that he follows around the city and, after capturing them, turns them into mummy-like mannequins. He has followed Witch Baby, hoping she will be his next victim. but fortunately she and Angel Juan escape. When Witch Baby shoots him with her camera, he is changed into a dummy like his victims.

Further Reading

Authors and Artists for Young Adults. Vol. 13. Detroit: Gale Research, 1994.

Berger, Laura Standley, ed. *Twentieth Century Young Adult Writers.* 1st ed. Detroit: St. James, 1995.

Campbell, Patricia J. *Horn Book* 69 (January/February 1993): 57-63.

Children's Literature Review. Vol. 33. Detroit: Gale Research, 1994.

Jones Patrick. *Horn Book* 68 (November/December 1992): 697-701.

Something about the Author. Vol. 80. Detroit: Gale Research, 1995.

Something about the Author Autobiography Series. Vol. 21. Detroit: Gale Research, 1996.

Judy Blume

1938-, American novelist

Forever

(young adult novel, 1975)

PLOT: On New Year's Eve, Katherine Danzinger and her friend, Erica, go to Sybil Davison's party. Katherine is a high school senior waiting to hear whether Michigan, Penn State, or Denver has accepted her college application. At the party, she meets fellow senior Michael Wagner, an avid skier with reddish-blonde hair and glasses. It is practically love at first sight. A short time later, Michael calls Katherine and the two begin dating. She has had dates before and once even thought she might be in love with Tommy Aronson. But, as she tells her younger sister, Jamie, she realizes now that what she felt for Tommy was just infatuation. Tommy was only interested in sex, which was why Katherine broke up with him. She is still a virgin.

Little by little, the physical relationship between Katherine and Michael intensifies. Then they make love one night. After that, Katherine decides to behave responsibly, so she goes to a clinic to get a birth control pill prescription. As graduation nears, they plan to spend the summer together before going to college. Katherine will go to Denver and Michael will spend the winters there so they can be together (he plans to make up the credits during the summer so he will graduate on time). Katherine's parents like Michael, and they are aware of the increasing intensity of his romance with their daughter, but they are not thrilled with this plan. Katherine is equally upset when her parents arrange for her to teach tennis at Jamie's summer camp in New Hampshire. Then she finds out that Michael has to work for the summer in North Carolina anyway. Despite this separation, they pledge their devotion to each other. For her birthday, Michael gives Katherine a small silver disk. On the back it is engraved, "Forever ... Michael."

But although they write to each other during the summer, Katherine and Michael begin to drift apart. Other thoughts begin to preoccupy Katherine, including the devastation she feels over the death of her beloved grandfather. Despite herself, she is also drawn to another counselor at the camp named Theo. When Michael, disturbed by her sudden lack of correspondence, arrives, Katherine has to tell him that she has changed. She doesn't understand why, but she is attracted to another boy. Michael can't comprehend her change of heart and is hurt and angry. Perhaps if they had met ten years later, Katherine thinks, the relationship would have ended differently, but she knows that for now she is not ready for a lifetime commitment.

CHARACTERS: Falling in love for the first time is a wonderful experience, and **Katherine Danzinger** is thrilled with her relationship with Michael. A serious and responsible young woman, she begins taking birth control once she makes the commitment to a physical relationship with him. Katherine has good, caring parents, and although she is unhappy when they practically force her into taking the job at her sister's camp for the summer, she understands their concerns about her and Michael. Katherine's sister, **Jamie**, who is in the seventh grade, is a talented artist who adores Michael, too. But she doesn't believe she will ever understand the ups and downs of first love.

At the beginning of her time at camp, Katherine writes letters to Michael about how she can't wait for the day when they will be together again. All of her letters are signed "love forever." In time, however, she begins to notice that another counselor, Theo, is paying attention to her. Later, she wonders how it is possible to love one person and be attracted to another. She kisses each letter that arrives from Michael to show that she is not the least bit interested in Theo, but she is still upset about her slight attraction to him. When she receives the news of her beloved grandfather's death, Katherine is comforted by Theo and she kisses him. At first he kisses her back, but then he pushes her away, saying, "Not like this ... not with death for an excuse." Slowly, Katherine realizes that as wonderful as first love is, she is simply not ready for a long-term commitment.

Michael Wagner is a likeable teenaged boy, enjoying the wonder of a first love and a serious sexual relationship. He is nearly as inexperienced as Katherine when their affair begins. His feelings for her are genuine, though, and like Katherine he believes love can last forever. When she confronts him with the fact that her feelings have changed, he feels betrayed. He tells her that it doesn't matter anyway because he has been sleeping with girls all around North Carolina during the summer. But Katherine knows he is not telling the truth. "You'll never know, will you?" he screams back at her in his hurt and confusion.

Theo is Katherine's friend at the camp and her other love interest. Although she begins to notice that he watches her a lot, he remains a friend and keeps his distance until the day she is shaken by her grandfather's death. Katherine clings to him, but Theo gently pushes her away and wisely says that people often use sex to take their minds off of tragedies. Katherine is at first offended. She realizes, however, that she is attracted to Theo, even though it is hard to understand how this could happen when she loves Michael. After Katherine sees Michael for the last time and is feeling somewhat depressed, her mother tells her that she has a phone call from Theo.

Some of Katherine's friends have relationships that serve as contrasts to what happens between her and Michael. Katherine has been friends with **Erica** since the ninth grade. Erica, who is only four feet, ten inches tall, is outspoken and uninhibited. She begins dating **Artie Lewin**, a friend of Michael's. Artie is a talented actor, which turns out to be more important to him than Erica. Erica gets nowhere with Artie and it begins to concern her. When she tries to urge him toward a closer relationship, he unexpectedly threatens to kill himself. She then decides not to see him any longer. Although Artie says he understands, he later carries out his threat with an unsuccessful attempt at suicide.

Katherine is disturbed to learn that **Sybil Davison** is pregnant. Overweight Sybil decided not to say anything until it was too late for an abortion. She knew if her parents found out, they would insist on the abortion. The child is born prematurely and is adopted. When Katherine visits Sybil almost immediately afterwards, Sybil says that she has decided to take off fifty pounds and go to Smith College. She won't get pregnant again, but she is not giving up sex, vowing that if she ever has another child she will keep it.

Katherine's parents, **Mr.** and **Mrs. Danzinger**, are portrayed as loving and caring people. They obviously are worried about what their daughter is going through, but they just as clearly trust her and believe she will act responsibly. In a stereotypical example of fatherly behavior, Mr. Danzinger resents the relationship between Michael and Katherine more than his wife does, but they both share a closeness with their daughter that is built on love and respect for her growing independence.

Tiger Eyes

(young adult novel, 1981)

PLOT: Often called the author's finest work, *Tiger Eyes* is a story of death, violence, fear, and adjustment. Fifteen-year-old Davis "Davey" Wexler lives with her family in Atlantic City, New Jersey, in an apartment above her father's 7-Eleven store. The time is the early 1980s. Davey's family includes her mother, Gwendolyn, her seven-year-old brother, Jason, and her cat, Minka. Her best friends are a tall, skinny black girl named Lanaya and a boy named Hugh. The story opens on a very sad note. Davey and her family are about to attend the funeral of her father, Adam Wexler, who was killed during a robbery at his store. The pain of the loss is compounded by the senselessness of the crime, which brings home feelings of insecurity and fear in a world that can easily destroy the fabric of our lives.

Time passes, and Davey, Jason, and her mother try to adjust to this total disruption of their lives. It is overwhelmingly difficult for them. Only young Jason seems to adjust to the terrible loss. As the months pass and Davey and her mother seem unable to go on with their lives, the decision is made to go to Los Alamos, New Mexico, for a change of scene. In the Southwest, the family stays with Davey's aunt and uncle, Elizabeth, called Bitsy, and Walter Kronick. Having left an environment in which they no longer felt secure, they have a new kind of adjustment to face in New Mexico. Perhaps because the Kronicks live in what is called "Atomic City," or perhaps because Walter works in the weapons lab, Davey's aunt and uncle are almost pathologically concerned about accidents and everyone's safety.

Davey attends Los Alamos High and takes a job as a candy striper at the local medical center. As she begins to explore the canyons around the area, she meets Wolf, a young man in whom she finds a kindred spirit. He is suffering as she is because his father is dying. She also becomes friends with Jane, a bright girl with no self-confidence and a drinking problem.

Davey's mother has been seeing a family counselor, Miriam Olnick, to help overcome her depression. When she sees that her daughter is still having trouble adjusting, she convinces Davey to see the counselor as well. Reluctant at first, in time Davey is able to discuss her father's death and the details of that terrible night. At the novel's end, the family returns to Atlantic City with plans to sell the store and perhaps find a place on the beach. For the time being, it is enough to know that they are together and home once more.

CHARACTERS: Davey Wexler is a smart and likeable fifteen-year-old with brown hair and eyes like a cat. Although assertive, she is not afraid to show her emotions or her sense of humor. At the outset of the novel, Davey is experiencing feelings of great loss over her father's death. By the story's conclusion, she has gone through the normal emotions of denial, fear, grief, anger, guilt, and finally acceptance. She is still sad and lonely without him, but she is stronger and can face life anew as well. Davey is aided in this spiritual growth by her work at the local medical center.

The novel also addresses the theme of racial prejudice, especially concerning various ethnic groups in New Mexico. Davey, whose best friend back home is a black girl named **Lanaya**, is shown as more mature in her attitudes than the adults around her. At school, she befriends people who seem somewhat outside the mainstream, such as Jane, a girl from a wealthy family who lacks self-confidence and finally acknowledges a drinking problem. Davey also refuses to stereotype people on the basis of ethnic background. She becomes friendly with **Wolf**, a bright young Hispanic who works in the lab. She discredits the belief she hears from others that this "typical" Hispanic is just out to rape white girls. Instead, she and Wolf become close as they share his pain over the approaching death of his father, **Willie Ortiz**, who has cancer. When Mr. Ortiz passes away, Davey must confront her emotions, which also helps her to face her own father's death.

Tied in with the theme of death in this novel is the theme of love, presented in all forms in this story. At the end, Davey begins to understand that she can still love her father even though he is gone from her and she must adjust to life without him. **Gwendolyn Wexler**, Davey's mother, is portrayed as a woman who has great difficulty coming to terms with her beloved husband's murder. But she seeks help from a counselor and persuades her daughter to do the same. By the novel's end, she begins to recover enough from her depression to become friendly with a man, whom Davey regards as a nerd. Mostly because of his age, Davey's brother, **Jason**, is the family member whose adjustment to his father's death is the easiest. He provides much of the comic relief in the book.

The themes of security and fear in the wake of a senseless murder are enhanced by Davey's aunt and uncle, **Bitsy** and **Walter Kronick**. These two are preoccupied by their concern for everyone's safety. They have reserved space for all their family members in a bomb shelter. They don't want Davey to take driver's education because they consider driving a car too dangerous. Their overprotection and need to control everyone's lives finally begin to wear on Davey and her mother. By the end of the novel, Gwen realizes that she can't let safety and security become the focus of her life, despite what has happened to her husband.

Davey's friends help to illustrate other points in the novel. The character of **Jane** demonstrates a secondary theme: the problem of teenage drinking. An insecure rich girl, Jane turns to alcohol for courage and can't admit that she has a drinking problem. Through Davey's friendship and encouragement, Jane is persuaded to seek help from a counselor. The importance of good counseling is also shown through the minor but important character, **Miriam Olnick**, Gwen's counselor and eventually Davey's as well. With Miriam, Davey is at last able to voice her deep and conflicting emotions about her father's death.

Just as Long as We're Together

(young adult novel, 1987)

PLOT: It's wonderful to be nearly thirteen years old and starting the seventh grade, especially when you have two best friends like Stephanie Hirsch's. One is *very* smart and longtime pal Rachel, and the other is Alison, who was adopted from Vietnam and has recently moved to Connecticut from California. Alison's mother is a famous television personality.

Stephanie's home life goes abruptly sour one year. When her father returns from a trip, she learns that he and her mother are planning a trial separation. This is extremely upsetting for Stephanie, doubly so because they have kept it from her until now. Her younger brother, Bruce, seems more wrapped up in his fear of nuclear war and his nightmares than their parents' problems. To add to the mess, Rachel keeps secret the fact that she has been put into an advanced math class. Although Rachel explains that she didn't want to tell Stephanie for fear of hurting her, Stephanie *is* hurt and begins to overeat and gain weight.

Christmas turns out to be horrible. Stephanie and Bruce visit their father and his "friend," Iris. Stephanie quickly sizes up the situation and behaves badly. Back home at school, her friend Eric Macaulay introduces her to the new boy, Max Wilson, as "El Chunko." This is followed by a fight with Rachel, who claims that Stephanie won't face reality and lives in a fantasy world. The one bright spot is that Bruce is invited to the White House to meet the president as a reward for his second place in a "kids for peace" contest.

Stephanie's thirteenth birthday arrives and she still isn't speaking to Rachel. Her mother tries to tell her that she should not take out her anger over her father on her best friend, but Stephanie is stubborn. When her father calls to announce that his friendship with Iris is over and he will be moving to New York, Stephanie has hopes for a reconciliation. Her mother says that's not likely, however, which makes Stephanie angry all over again.

In March, Alison comes down with the flu and confesses to Stephanie that her parents are having their own child, and she is terrified that they won't love her as much anymore. This prompts a talk between Stephanie and her mother and a promise that they will say just what they feel. Soon Alison has adjusted to the prospect of a new arrival and helps to pick out the baby's name.

An accidental meeting with Rachel sparks a quiet conversation between the two. As they talk about their feelings and the hurt they suffered from each other, they agree to see each other the next day. Maybe the old friendship can be restored.

CHARACTERS: This is, above all, a novel of friendship and the ups and downs of the teenage years. **Stephanie Hirsch** is a likeable young girl with all the insecurities and highs and lows of someone nearing the age of thirteen. She is secure with her life at home and school and has two best friends. When she learns of her parents' breakup, she is shocked and angry that they kept it a secret for so long. When she overhears her parents discussing the separation, she blurts out, "I suppose now you think I'm gullible. Well, I'm not. I can't be easily tricked by you or by anyone else."

Stephanie's anguish over her parents affects her relationships with others. She fights with her mother and, most of all, with Rachel. Stephanie's secure world is falling apart, and she finds it easier to put the blame elsewhere than to face her own fears and insecurities. Rachel tells her this frankly, but it is not something that Stephanie wants to hear. Closing in on all these difficulties are Stephanie's thirteenth birthday and her growing interest in boys such as **Eric** and **Max**. There is also the problem of overeating, and her realization that the nickname "El Chunko" must mean it's time to do something about it.

After Alison confesses her fears about the new baby to Stephanie, she has a talk with her mother. Stephanie admits that sometimes she pretends everything is okay when it's not. She and her mother admit that they are both optimists. After a meeting with Rachel, a conversation, and a casual promise to see each other the next day, Stephanie starts back on the road to security and moves a little closer toward maturity. She wonders what Alison will say when she tells her that she and Rachel are speaking again. Stephanie decides that she'll probably be glad.

Stephanie has been friends with **Rachel** for a long time. She has always known that Rachel is very smart, but it has never interfered with their friendship before. Learning that Rachel has been put into an advanced math class is bad enough, but perhaps Stephanie would have taken it more calmly had not the trouble in her own household cropped up. Rachel's explanation—which is reminiscent of the one Stephanie's parents gave—that she kept the advancement a secret because she did not want to hurt her best friend does not soothe Stephanie. However, by the novel's end there is a promise that the two girls are seeing their cautious way back to the friendship they once had.

If any teenager might be labeled insecure, it would be **Alison.** Although she seems to be a well-adjusted young girl who is secure with her adoptive family, underlying fears come to the surface when her parents announce they are having their own biological child. At first she is terrified that they will no longer love her and want her as they did. She announces to Stephanie that she will go to Paris and find her real mother. But when Alison recovers from the flu, she feels a little better about the situation—and a little more secure. After all, she says, she can always go to Paris later.

Mr. and Mrs. Hirsch are two loving parents caught in a personal tragedy. It is Stephanie's father who wants the separation because he "feels bored with his life." Although her mother tries to put the best face on the situation, she indicates that a reunion is unlikely. Both parents, however, remain deeply concerned about their children. For a ten-year-old, Stephanie's brother, **Bruce**, is extraordinarily concerned about the possibility of a nuclear war. On the other hand, he takes the separation a little more calmly than does his sister.

Further Reading

Authors and Artists for Young Adults. Vol. 3. Detroit: Gale Research, 1990.

Berger, Laura Standley, ed. *Twentieth-Century Young Adult Writers.* 1st ed. Detroit: St. James, 1994.

Berger, Laura Standley, ed. *Twentieth-Century Children's Writers.* 4th ed. Detroit: St. James, 1995.

Children's Literature Review. Vol. 2. Detroit: Gale Research, 1976.

Contemporary Literary Criticism. Vols. 12, 30. Detroit: Gale Research, 1980, 1984.

De Montreville, Doris, and Elizabeth D. Crawford, eds. *Fourth Book of Junior Authors and Illustrators.* New York: H. W. Wilson, 1978.

Estes, Glenn E., ed., *American Writers for Children since 1960: Fiction.* Vol. 52 of *Dictionary of Literary Biography.* Detroit: Gale Research, 1986.

Lee, Betsey, *Judy Blume's Story.* New York: Dillon, 1989.

Something about the Author. Vols. 2, 31, 79. Detroit: Gale Research, 1971, 1983, 1995.

Ward, Martha, ed. *Authors of Books for Young People.* 3rd ed. Metuchen, NJ: Scarecrow Press, 1990.

Weidt, Maryann. *Presenting Judy Blume.* Boston: Twayne, 1989.

Ray Bradbury

1920-, American novelist

Fahrenheit 451

(science fiction, 1953)

PLOT: This surreal science fiction classic takes place in an American city over a period of a few days in the not-too-distant future. In the culture that has evolved, thinking is considered an unhealthy activity that threatens the new social order. All intellectual activity has, therefore, been forbidden, including the possession and reading of books.

Into this setting, Bradbury introduces Guy Montag, a "fireman" whose job is to find the remaining owners of books, arrest them, and burn both their books and their homes. Guy is becoming more uneasy with his job, particularly after he meets a teenage neighbor, Clarisse McClellan, whose questioning nonconformism upsets him. He is also disturbed when, during a book raid led by his boss, Captain Beatty, the elderly lady they were targeting prefers self-immolation over living without her books.

At home, Guy's wife, Mildred, offers no support. She has become a thoughtless automaton who obeys and seemingly enjoys the mind-dulling pleasures of multi-screened, participatory television. Her life is so dull and meaningless that after Guy saves her from an apparent suicide attempt she doesn't remember the incident. As Guy continues to question the values of his society, he becomes more daring in his actions. He steals a book during a raid and both Mildred and Captain Beatty see it in his possession. In a moment of candor, he shows Mildred other books that he has saved and begs her to read them. When he learns that Clarisse has been killed for her unconventional ways, he seeks help from a sympathetic old professor named Faber. Together they concoct a wild scheme to build a printing press and plant copies of books in each of the fire houses so they will have to be destroyed. Faber recommends that Guy show more caution with his co-workers. With suitable apologies, Guy returns the book that

Captain Beatty has seen but feels that his boss no longer trusts him.

When Mildred invites two of her dull friends, Mrs. Phelps and Mrs. Bowles, home to watch television, Guy is so appalled by their insensitive, stupid behavior that he recklessly brings out some of his books and frightens them off by reading to them. After returning to the firehouse, he and Captain Beatty respond to an alarm. With horror, Guy realizes it is his address. Mildred has informed on him and he must not only witness, but also participate, in the destruction of his own home.

When Captain Beatty tries to arrest him, Guy kills him with his flamethrower and destroys the firehouse's massive Mechanical Hound, a killing machine that uses its odor sensitive components to search out and destroy its prey. Though wounded, Guy manages to reach Faber's home. They take elaborate precautions to destroy Guy's scent because another Hound is on his trail. At the same time that the authorities are tracking Guy, television news reports confirm the outbreak of another world war. Faber and Guy separate and flee the city.

To further confuse the Hound, Guy crosses a river and finds that he is in a rural area. Here he is sheltered by a group of outcasts, led by a man named Granger, who reveal themselves as vagrant writers, professors, and other intellectuals. This band and others like them around the country are dedicated to preserving books through the only safe process available: memorization. As bombers destroy the city he has just left, Guy joins the group and pledges loyalty to their cause. They hope that in the world that emerges from the war, humankind will heed the truth and wisdom that they are preserving.

CHARACTERS: The title of this ground-breaking novel comes from the temperature at which paper burns, a symbol of the malevolent social order that keeps people powerless by reducing their need and ability to question and think. Bradbury explores themes here that reoccur in his other books: the importance of individual freedom, the necessity of remembering the lessons of the past, and the dangers of relying too much on technology. **Guy Montag** represents the nobility and courage that can be aroused in common people when confronted with such injustice and oppression. Guy realizes that a life deprived of thought is an empty life, and he questions the purpose of existence when individuality is destroyed and personal growth denied. The mindless recreations offered people, such as sports, tinkering with machines, and brain-numbing television, sicken him, as does the conditioning process that produces living robots devoid of any social conscience.

His final transformation into an active rebel against the system occurs after he discovers that Clarisse has been murdered solely because she innocently challenges the rationale behind current practices like burning books. Witnessing an old woman destroy herself for her beliefs becomes another turning point for Guy. Once aroused, he realizes the importance of his crusade, even risking his life for the cause. Guy is also a loyal, caring husband who tries to bring some spiritual values into Mildred's life. Even though this results in her reporting him to the authorities, he mourns her death when he realizes she has been killed during the destruction of his home city. Though not a born hero, Guy grows in stature and nobility with each challenge he confronts.

Outwardly, **Mildred Montag** appears to be the perfectly conditioned model of social correctness. She unquestioningly conforms in every way, particularly in filling her time watching senseless television. Although she rejects Guy's attempts to make her more aware and understanding, it is apparent that there is an emptiness in her life of which she is not aware. Another character who has been conditioned by society to oppose Guy is **Captain Beatty**, who, like Mildred, is also unaware of the emptiness in his life. He is presented as a rabid book burner, willing to murder and pillage to prevent challenges to the social order. He appears to revel in his work and gain satisfaction from preserving the present social system. He is also cunning and evil, particularly when he plays a cat-and-mouse game to trap Guy. However, Guy notes that in their final struggle he does nothing to protect himself, as though he welcomes death to fill the same unnamed inner void in his life that troubled Mildred.

Guy takes a gamble that pays off when he seeks help in contacting **Faber**, an acquaintance from years before. More cautious and fearful than the somewhat headstrong Guy, Faber is also a believer in the cause and has been secretly finding ways to sabotage the system. He courageously risks his life to help Guy, first in Guy's plans to hamper the activities of the firemen and later by hiding him and aiding in his escape. Another proponent of the cause is **Granger**, the leader of the band of outcasts who are trying to help preserve the remnants of civilization and humanism by memorizing important books so they can be passed on to future generations. His caring attitude toward Guy and his optimistic belief that the struggle will eventually lead to victory and a better life inspire Guy to join forces with him.

Guy's first stirrings of dissatisfaction are inspired by his contact with **Clarisse McClellan**. Though she appears only briefly in the novel, she acts as an important catalyst in producing Guy's rejection of the existing social order. She is seventeen years old and appears, like many teenagers, to have both a healthy questioning attitude about conditions and a trusting, open personality. Unfortunately, in Clarisse's society these are considered dangerous qualities that must be rooted out before they spread to others. She disappears suddenly and later is reported dead.

Mildred's two friends are **Mrs. Phelps** and **Mrs. Bowles**. With their enameled faces and superficial attitudes, they are typical products of this diseased society. Mrs. Bowles, for example, has had several husbands, dozens of abortions, and two children by Caesarian section (she refused to subject herself to the discomfort of regular childbirth). As with other children born in this society, they were removed immediately to state-run nursery centers. To Mrs. Bowles, this is a relief. The inconvenience of raising children would interfere with her social life and ardent television watching. Mrs. Bowles becomes hysterical when Guy flourishes a book and reads to them, but Mrs. Phelps reacts differently. Listening to Guy read the poem, "Dover Beach," touches her psyche so profoundly that she sobs quietly, moved by its message. It appears that Mrs. Phelps has retained a shred of humanity after all.

Further Reading

Berger, Laura Standley, ed. *Twentieth-Century Young Adult Writers.* 1st ed. Detroit: St. James, 1994.

Contemporary Literary Criticism. Vols. 1, 3, 10, 15, 42. Detroit: Gale Research, 1973, 1975, 1979, 1980, 1987.

Cowart, David, and Thomas L. Wymer, eds. *Twentieth-Century American Science Fiction Writers, Part 1: A-L.* Vol. 8 of *Dictionary of Literary Biography.* Detroit: Gale Research, 1981.

Helterman, Jeffrey, and Richard Layman, eds. *American Novelists since World War II.* Vol. 2 of *Dictionary of Literary Biography.* Detroit: Gale Research, 1978.

Henderson, Lesley, ed. *Contemporary Novelists.* 5th ed. Chicago: St. James, 1991.

Mogan, David. *Ray Bradbury.* Boston: Twayne, 1982.

Nolan, William F. *The Ray Bradbury Companion.* Detroit: Bruccoli/Gale Research, 1975.

Platt, Charles. *Dream Makers: Science Fiction and Fantasy Writers at Work.* New York: Ungar, 1987.

Ryan, Bryan, ed. *Major Twentieth-Century Writers: A Selection of Sketches from Contemporary Authors.* Detroit: Gale Research, 1991.

Something about the Author. Vol. 64. Detroit: Gale, 1991.

Susset, George E. *The Bradbury Chronicler.* San Bernardino, CA: Borgo, 1977.

Watt, Donald. *Ray Bradbury.* New York: Taplinger, 1980.

Marion Zimmer Bradley

1930-, American novelist

The Mists of Avalon

(fantasy, 1982)

PLOT: This vast, complex, and lengthy fantasy covers approximately sixty-years, beginning slightly before the birth of King Arthur and ending a few years after his death. Told primarily from the viewpoint of the women who surround this legendary king, the story also deals with the power conflict between the emerging Christian Church and the established pagan religion led by Druid priests and priestesses who worship the Goddess and have their central religious community on the misty island of Avalon. Ingraine is one of the many daughters of Taliesin the Merlin, a wizard of the pagans. She is married to Duke Gorlois of Cornwall and lives in his castle in Tintagel with her younger sister, Morgause, and baby daughter, Morgaine, later known as Morgan le Fay. Ingraine heeds a command from her half sister, Viviane, the chief priestess of Avalon, to abandon her husband and have an affair with the High King of Britain, Uther Pendragon. After Gorlois's death in battle, Ingraine marries Uther, moves to his palace at Caerleon, and bears him a son, Arthur, whom Viviane hopes will establish the supremacy of paganism over Christianity after he becomes king. Morgaine becomes a maiden neophyte at Avalon, where she meets Viviane's son, the handsome Lancelet, and the beautiful Gwenhwyfar, who is being raised in a nearby convent.

Years later in Avalon, Arthur participates in a mysterious coming-of-age ritual in which he must sleep with an innocent virgin. Through Viviane's trickery, the virtuous young man deflowers his own half sister, Morgaine, who is so horrified at what has happened that she leaves Avalon and seeks shelter in Lothian, where her aunt, Morgause, is now married to King Lot. There, she secretly bears a child, first called Gwydion and later Modred, who is reared by Morgause along with her sons, Gawaine and Gareth. In the meantime, Arthur, unaware that he has an heir, marries the fair Gwenhwyfar, moves his capital to Camelot, and assembles a group of knights around him, including Caius, Arthur's foster brother; two brothers named Balan and Balin; and Lancelet, who secretly loves Gwenhwyfar.

Morgaine becomes a lady-in-waiting at the court and jealously detects the innocent attraction that Gwen and Lancelet share. Through trickery she forces Lance to marry another lady-in-waiting, Elaine. In time Elaine bears him two children, a son, Galahad, and a daughter, Nimue, who, at Morgaine's dictate, is sent to Avalon. Elaine dies in childbirth, leaving Lancelet free once more to court Gwen.

In this version of the King Arthur legend, Bradley offers a unique twist by telling the story from the perspective of its women characters.

In her pursuit of power in the name of the Goddess and to insure that her son, Modred, will become king, Morgaine hatches many diabolical schemes. After marrying the aged King Uriens of Northern Wales, she becomes the lover of his son, Accolon, and devises an aborted ambush to murder Arthur during which Accolon is killed. Convinced that the new Merlin, Kevin, has become a Christian pawn, she sends Nimue to seduce him and bring him back to Avalon, where he is murdered. Modred is also scheming to gain power. After trying unsuccessfully to discredit Lancelet's reputation at the court, he reveals to all the now-consummated affair between Gwen and Lancelet, forcing the two lovers to flee Camelot.

As the glory days of Camelot draw to a close, the knights disperse to seek the Holy Grail, and young Galahad dies during this quest. Gwen enters a nunnery, and Modred leads a revolt against Arthur during which both Modred and the king are killed.

Lancelot becomes a priest, and Morgaine, now forced to admit the ascendancy of Christianity, retreats into the mists of Avalon.

Bradley's The Forest House *(1994) and* Lady of Avalon *(1997) are set during the years before King Arthur's birth.*

CHARACTERS: The focal point of the action and the many intrigues present in the novel is the guileless, honorable **King Arthur**. Born of Uther Pendragon and Ingraine, Arthur was schooled in the pagan faith. However, under the influence of his wife, Gwenhwyfar, Arthur gravitates toward Christianity, which causes the Druids to become concerned and leads to Morgaine's treason. Arthur is a handsome man with blond, curly hair, attractive features, and a fair complexion. He is trusting and often naive in his relations with others. A man of the highest moral principles, he refuses to believe that others could wish him harm, but when treachery and intrigue are uncovered, he exhibits a forgiving, compassionate nature. His noble, virtuous character is a model for others at court and inspires extreme loyalty and devotion in his knights and followers. Arthur is a valiant warrior, excellent ruler, and devoted husband. He successfully defeats the Saxons and, leading by example, introduces an era of peace and prosperity in Britain that is characterized by the king's benevolence and fine statesmanship. While others wish to banish Queen Gwen because she is unable to bear a son, Arthur continues to shower love and devotion on his wife, never blaming her or violating his wedding vows.

Arthur's high moral standards and sensitive nature often cause him to be overly critical of his own actions. He frequently blames himself when wrongs are committed, though he is innocent of them. For example, when he learns that he has unknowingly committed incest with his half sister, the pain and self-condemnation he experiences are agonizing for him. Arthur's display of love and obligation toward his knights, particularly Lancelet, is touching and sincere. He is also tolerant and open-minded enough to allow both the pagan and Christian faiths to coexist in his kingdom. The king's trusting and ethical nature eventually leads to his downfall when unscrupulous forces betray his confidence and cause his death.

Arthur's half sister, **Morgaine**, later known a **Morgan le Fay**, is obsessed with preserving the pagan worship of the Goddess. While still a child, she is sent by her mother, Ingraine, to be raised by the priestesses on the isle of Avalon. Since that time, she has become fanatical in her desire to perpetuate the faith and preserve the king's allegiance to it. A small, delicate, black-haired woman, Morgaine's dark, serious eyes and heavy eyebrows lend her an elf-like appearance. Even her mother calls her a changeling. Morgaine's intense, passionate nature and manic devotion to her cause brings unhappiness to herself and those around her. Her sensuous, lusty inner nature, which she tries to suppress, often explodes in illicit love affairs that also bring disaster and tragedy. Seemingly without conscience, she relentlessly pursues a lost cause, leaving behind her a trail of death and destruction. She abandons her child, Gwydion, later named Modred, until she finds he can be manipulated to seize power from Arthur; she feigns love and devotion to Gwenhwyfar only to betray her; she tricks Lancelet, whom she secretly loves, into sleeping with Elaine and forcing him into an unwanted marriage; and she commits adultery with her husband's son to secure his allegiance in a plot against Arthur. As Morgaine's monstrous schemes grow in audacity and daring, her unhappiness and desperation also increase until, with her cause defeated and her world in tatters, she winds up a broken, pathetic figure whose lifelong pursuits will remain forever unfulfilled.

Morgaine's mentor is her aunt, **Viviane**, the high priestess in Avalon who is also known as the Lady of the Lake. Described as "small, dark and glowing," she is considered a fairy woman who, like others in her family, has the gift of the Sight, the ability to see into the future. Viviane is a strong woman, dedicated to her mission in life: the preservation and strengthening of the cult of the Goddess. She sacrifices, schemes, and plots, manipulating and controlling others while firmly believing that the end justifies the means. She tricks Morgaine into having sex with Arthur, her half brother, hoping that the fruit of the union will be the next ruler of Britain. By Christian standards Viviane's actions seem unprincipled and depraved, yet she feels they are justified, righteous, and condoned by her faith. Viviane is a role model for Morgaine, who in time reveres her aunt and seeks to emulate her. The mother of Arthur's beloved knight, Lancelet, Viviane is murdered by Balin, another of Arthur's knights, who believes that she was responsible for his mother's death.

Morgause, Morgaine's other aunt, is a cool, calculating woman who is ambitious and cunning. After marrying Lot, the King of Orkney, she moves to his palace in Lothian, where she raises a family of sons, all of whom she sends to Camelot to gain elevated positions at the court. She is a woman with an insatiable sexual appetite, having a series of younger lovers even before the death of her equally promiscuous husband. After his death, she flaunts her sexual exploits openly, causing particular embarrassment to Morgaine. Motherhood makes Morgause a more loving, understanding person, and she accepts Morgaine's child, Gwydion, into her household and raises him as her own son.

Like other women at King Arthur's court, Morgaine falls in love with **Lancelet**. Darkly handsome, with an aquiline face and slender build, he possesses such natural grace and beauty that every one envies and loves him. A shy, modest man, he is known for his sweet, gentle disposition. Lancelet is a completely honorable man who is governed by his high principles and lofty ideals. His adoration and love for Arthur is so great that, in moments of extreme introspection, he wonders whether there is a sexual element involved. A fearless fighter for justice, Lancelet endures hardship and adversity without complaint to serve his king and his ideals. He is compassionate towards others less fortunate than himself and is always willing to sacrifice himself for the welfare of others. For years Lancelet agonizes over his secret passion for Gwenhwyfar and resists consummating the affair. After his wife, Elaine, dies and he and Gwen sleep together, the pangs of remorse and guilt continue to haunt him. When their affair is discovered, he enters a Christian monastery. Shortly after being ordained into the priesthood, he dies.

Lancelot's son, **Galahad**, is like his father in both appearance and nature. Incredibly handsome, he also believes in lofty ideals and high principles. Though chosen by Arthur to be his successor, Galahad deserts the court to engage in a quest for the Holy Grail. When he is successful, the spiritual encounter is so overpowering that the sensitive young man dies during the ecstasy of the experience.

Morgaine's mother is **Ingraine**, an independent, petulant woman who is stubborn and unconstrained. She is married to an older man, the honorable Christian, **Gorlois**, Duke of Cornwall, and has given him one daughter. She obeys the order from Avalon to have an adulterous affair with the pagan High King, **Uther Pendragon**, a fierce warrior and passionate lover, in order to give birth to an heir that will secure a future ruler born into their religion. Consumed with righteous outrage and despairing over the loss of the woman he adored, Gorlois withdraws his allegiance to Uther and is killed in battle by his rival. Uther becomes a faithful husband to Ingraine and a loving father to his son, Arthur. A strong-willed, powerful man, he is an outstanding administrator and leaves Arthur a legacy of strength. After Ingraine has succeeded in her purpose, she, like her son, begins a gradual conversion to Christianity, ending her days as a serene, docile old lady in a convent.

Ingraine's father is **Taliesin the Merlin**, the wise man and prophet of the pagans. Though a Druid priest and wedded to the rituals and beliefs of his religion, he tolerates Christianity and, like Arthur, believes they can coexist. During his life his wisdom and gentleness lend moderation and temperance to the cult. After his death, the new Merlin is the crippled **Kevin the Bard**. As a result of childhood accidents, Kevin has become an ugly, grotesque creature referred to as a "misshapen toad." An excellent harpist and troubadour, he is continually in demand as an entertainer at Arthur's court, where he radiates such gentleness and grace that people accept his physical deformity and grow to respect and admire him. Morgaine becomes so enthralled with his charm and innocence that she accepts him as a lover. When she discovers that he has relinquished some of the pagan holy objects to Christian use, she plots successfully to have him return to Avalon, where he is murdered. Morgaine uses as a decoy the young daughter of Lancelet, **Nimue**, who as a child was taken to Avalon to become a priestess. Brainwashed by Morgaine, the innocent Nimue is sent to Camelot to entice Kevin, through her beauty and flattery, to return with her to Avalon. During the seduction, she genuinely falls in love with Kevin, and after his murder she is so conscience-stricken that she commits suicide.

The fair **Gwenhwyfar** (also called **Gwen**) is described as "dazzlingly pretty: she seems all white and gold, her skin pale as ivory, her eyes palest sky-blue, her hair long and pale and shining like living gold." Raised in a convent, she comes to wed Arthur as a timid, shy, modest young girl of only seventeen. She is virtuous, beautiful, naive, and totally unprepared for her queenly role. Her charming, gracious personality gradually wins her many friends and admirers. Though she tries to be faithful to Arthur, whom she adores, her secret passion for Lancelet gnaws at her, filling her with guilt and shame. Her feelings of inadequacy grow when it becomes apparent that she will never bear children. Increasingly, she retreats into the solace of the Church and the confessional and soon believes that her mission on earth is to make Arthur a total Christian and renounce any affiliation with his pagan lineage. After years of denial, she allows Lancelet to make love to her, but they are discovered through Modred's treachery. Gwen flees Camelot and ends her days in the same convent where she spent her childhood.

In addition to Lancelet, other knights that gather around King Arthur's fabled Round Table include two of Morgause's sons, **Gawaine** and **Gareth**. Gawaine is a bull-like man—big, tall, and powerfully built, he is also hot-headed and quarrelsome. His fiery temper and volatile disposition stands in sharp contrast to the sweet, gentle nature of his younger brother, Gareth, a popular, loyal knight whose good looks have earned him the nickname "Handsome." Arthur's childhood friend, **Caius**, is also a member of the brotherhood. Described as "big, dark and Roman to the core," he is crippled by wounds received in his first battle serving Arthur. A gentle, deferential man, he becomes a faithful advisor to Arthur and chief administrator of the household at Camelot. **Balan**, Viviane's other son and brother to Lancelet, also becomes a knight at Arthur's court. Unlike his handsome foster brother, Balin, Balan is big, coarse and outgoing. **Balin** is a crude, stupid, narrow-minded young man. Believing that Viviane has been responsible for his mother's death, Balin axes her to death in front of Arthur and his court. Balan later avenges Viviane's death and kills Balin.

One of the last additions to Arthur's court and chief cause of the fall of Camelot is **Gwydion**, who is later called **Modred**. Arthur's son by an incestuous relationship with Morgaine, Modred is raised by his aunt Morgause. Modred, a bright, attractive boy, is eager to learn and anxious to please. He also is cold and calculating in his relationships with others. Aware of his parentage and stigmatized by incest and illegitimacy, Modred grows into manhood obsessed with claiming his birthright: the monarchy. Cunning and shrewd, he hides his true motives under a facade of charm and obedience. He is successful in his scheme to have Gwenhwyfar's infidelity discovered so that Lancelet, whom he admires but distrusts, must flee Camelot. Later, he allies himself with the mutinous Saxons and leads a revolt against Arthur during which both he and his father are killed.

Further Reading

Arbur, Rosemarie. *Marion Zimmer Bradley.* Mercer Island, WA: Starmont, 1985.

———. *Twentieth-Century Science Fiction Writers.* 2nd ed. Chicago: St. James, 1986.

Authors and Artists for Young Adults. Vol. 9. Detroit: Gale Research, 1992.

Berger, Laura Standley, ed. *Twentieth-Century Young Adult Writers.* 1st ed. Chicago: St. James, 1994.

Contemporary Literary Criticism. Vol. 30. Detroit: Gale Research, 1984.

Cowart, David, and Thomas L. Wymer, eds. *Twentieth-Century American Science-Fiction Writers.* Vol. 8 of *Dictionary of Literary Biography.* Detroit: Gale Research, 1981.

Watson, Noelle, ed. *Twentieth-Century Science Fiction Writers.* 3rd ed. Chicago: St. James, 1991.

Sue Ellen Bridgers

1942-, American novelist

Notes for Another Life

(young adult novel, 1981)

PLOT: Normal family life for thirteen-year-old Wren Jackson and her sixteen-year-old brother, Kevin, has been severely disrupted because their father, Tom, has been institutionalized for depression. Their mother, Karen, has had to go to work in Atlanta, so Wren and Kevin have spent the past six years living with their devoted grandparents, Bliss and Bill, in a small southern town. Even though their home life is happy and loving, both children long for the reunion of their family, or at least they hope they can join their mother in Atlanta.

However, during a visit, Karen reveals that she is planning to move to a job in far-off Chicago. She is obviously torn between her love for the children and her wish to lead an independent life. She later writes to Bliss that she is planning to divorce her husband. When Bliss tells Wren and Kevin this news, Kevin takes it particularly hard. In the hospital, Kevin mentions this to his father because he mistakenly believes that Tom already knows. When Tom shows visible signs of anxiety, Kevin is sorry he said anything.

But things begin to look better when Tom, whose condition has improved thanks to a new drug, is allowed to come home for a visit. At first he appears normal, but then the old depression shows signs of returning. Both children are deeply affected by this setback. But Wren, who is a talented musician, has her piano music and her boyfriend, Sam Holland, to fall back on. Kevin, who already worries that he will inherit his father's mental illness, has more problems coping. His difficulties are compounded when he breaks his wrist in a tennis match and loses his girlfriend, Melanie.

After his father's condition worsens and his mother returns for a farewell visit before moving to Chicago, Kevin takes an overdose of Seconal. Bliss finds him in time and Kevin is saved. Although he is quick to recover physically, his psychological recovery takes more time. The young pastor at the local Baptist church, Jack Kensley, helps Kevin to face his fears and talk about his problems. By the novel's conclusion, Wren gets ready for high school and Kevin goes back to tennis and his girlfriend. Life, for the time being, resumes its normal routine.

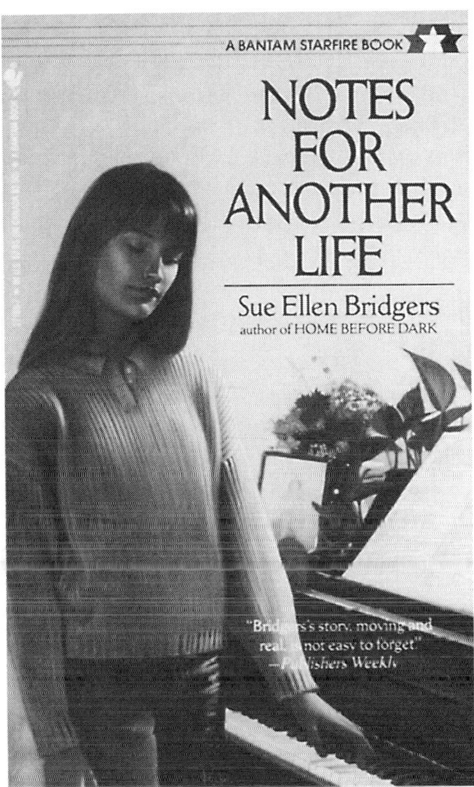

Young Wren Jackson must learn to cope with an institutionalized father in Bridgers's sensitive look at mental illness.

CHARACTERS: Wren Jackson is a lively, loving teenager who shares a close and warm relationship with her older brother. Although she is distressed by the breakup of her family, she enjoys the security and love of her grandparents, as well as friends and a talent for playing the piano. When she meets **Sam Holland**, who shows a definite interest in her, she is at first embarrassed and shy. Gradually, however, she grows to care about and admire this young man and his loving family. Wren is better equipped to survive the blows to family security caused by her mother's move to Chicago and her father's obviously deteriorating condition. The security of her relationship with Sam and her interest in her music help her through the periods of stress as she adjusts to a family life that seemingly will never return to what it once was. But Wren is as distressed as Kevin when they visit the hospital and find their father's condition has not improved and might even be worsening.

Kevin Jackson, who is three years older than his sister, fears that he will inherit his father's mental illness. Not as good a student as his sister, with whom he shares a close relationship, he clings to his love for tennis and for **Melanie**. When he momentarily loses both, he cracks under the stress and takes a drug overdose. As his physical recovery continues, Kevin, with the help of the young pastor, **Jack Kensley**, is able to voice his fears about the possibility of mental illness. His return to tennis once his wrist is healed and his reunion with Melanie also help to bring stability back into his troubled young life. By the novel's end, Kevin has progressed enough to feel comfortable talking to his mother about his problems.

Karen Jackson is clearly torn between a desire for a life of her own and her role as a mother and wife. She finds it difficult to confront her children with the impending divorce, leaving that task to their grandmother. When she returns home once more before moving to Chicago, where she has accepted a job promotion, she does not realize that this makes Kevin feel rejected. This, coupled with his father's further deterioration, is too much for the teenager to handle.

Bliss is an especially loving and caring grandparent to Wren and Kevin. As their paternal grandmother, she understands the torment Wren and Kevin are enduring and tries to dispel their concerns over the "craziness myths" in the Jackson family. Although she knows there is no good time to tell the children of the impending divorce, she tells Wren first on a ride home from the hospital. She does so in a quiet, conventional manner. Then, understanding the difference between the two children, she says that she'd like to find a way to tell Kevin that wouldn't be too painful, so she and Wren decide to tell him together.

Permanent Connections

(young adult novel, 1987)

PLOT: About six miles from Tyler Mills, North Carolina, in the southern Appalachians, is the old farmstead of Rob Dickson's family. This is where the sullen seventeen-year-old finds himself—under protest—after he has been sent from his home in Montclair, New Jersey, to care for his Uncle Fairlee, agoraphobic Aunt Coralee, and half-senile Grandpa. Rob knows his parents are not unhappy to have him out of their way. Rebelling against his family, he has become secretive, has done poorly in school, and has experimented with drugs. Rob's relatives, including Coralee's sister, Rosalee, and Rob's cousin, Leanna, are too cantankerous to find help for him.

In this beautiful, rural setting, which Rob hates, he meets Ellery Collier, another unhappy, transplanted person who longs to return to her friends back home. A classical musician, the beautiful Ellery is living in this remote region because her mother, Ginny, left Ellery's father and their home in Charlotte to pursue her interest in weaving. Rob falls for Ellery and wants a casual sexual relationship with her, which she refuses. Depressed by this rejection, Rob turns once again to drugs, leading to his arrest on marijuana charges. Prodded by Deputy Sheriff Gatewood, Rob very nearly implicates his friend Travis, his cousin Leanna's boyfriend, for helping him to get the marijuana. Travis's brothers grow the plants on their remote tree farm. Rob becomes sick with dread that, under the influence of the drug, he has caused legal problems for Travis, who has been such a good friend to him, and to his family, even though what they are doing is illegal. Racked with guilt, Rob takes his first steps on the road to responsibility and changes his outlook on life. He goes to trial on the marijuana charge, but the charges are dismissed for lack of substantial evidence. The judge gives Rob a stern warning.

Rob has reached a turning point in his life and his relationship with Ellery, who later tells him she has decided not to move away. Rob tells her in turn that his father will let him stay if he wishes. For the first time in his young life, Rob feels that he knows where he is going.

CHARACTERS: Rob Dickson is a teenage boy alienated from his family and bristling with inner hostility. Throughout the book, flashbacks to earlier times convey that the tenderness he feels for his family is masked by his own unhappiness. He feels vaguely unworthy, having little faith in himself and his abilities, which accounts for his sullenness and why he sometimes resorts to drugs. When he is faced with the possibility of causing great harm to his friend Travis, however, he finds solace with the help of an Episcopalian priest, who tells him that "you would do well to forgive yourself," pointing out that Rob's enemy is his own fear that he is his family's worst failure.

Travis has more faith in Rob than Rob has in himself. His concern that he has brought harm to Travis and his family is what makes Rob finally acknowledge his responsibility for himself and his own actions. He realizes that, without intending to, he could very well have deeply hurt the people that he cares about. This revelation leads to Rob's gradual change and a more hopeful view of the future.

Ellery Collier is far more disciplined than Rob, but she, too, is an unhappy outsider in this remote region. Her decision not to let Rob use her sexually to alleviate his own misery causes him to return to marijuana for comfort. Ellery is upset with her mother and constantly argues with her because she blames her mother for tearing their family apart. In the end, Ellery matures enough to accept other people's feelings more readily. She opts to stay in the country and indicates that she would like a closer relationship with Rob.

Rob's cousin, **Leanna**, wants to escape her home and go to college. She is less successful at getting away from her boyfriend, Travis, whom she loves but feels is forcing her into a commitment she is not sure she wants. She has a good relationship with Travis, but she can't help feeling that somehow she has mortgaged her future too early. **Travis**, Rob's good-natured friend, doesn't want to wait to marry Leanna. He wants to share an apartment while they go to college and pictures a happy-ever-after future with her.

Rob's **Aunt Coralee** suffers from a fear of the outdoors—agoraphobia—and will not leave the house. Ellery's mother, **Ginny**, is drawn to Coralee because Ginny sees that she has been victimized by other people's expectations just as she has been. As Ginny says, "I didn't make a decision all my own until I was almost forty." Finally, Ginny is able to induce Coralee to walk out on the porch. From there, she helps the older woman to make more decisions and go more places. This makes **Rosalee**, Coralee's sister and Leanna's mother, jealous. Rosalee sees her place in the family as taking care of every aspect of family life. Yet in reality Rosalee is anything but the nurturer. She drives away family members, including her own daughter, through her criticism and efforts to control them, such as when she tries to keep Leanna at home while she goes to college. She fails to see that Ginny was able to get Coralee out of the house by being reassuring and loving, not by telling the woman she is crazy as Rosalee does. With all her cooking and caring and constant harping, Rosalee may look like the traditional mother figure watching out for her family, but she is far from an ideal parent.

Other minor characters in the story include **Uncle Fairlee**, whose injury is what causes Rob to go the country. A bachelor who has never married, he remains outside of the frictions that infiltrate the rest of the family and maintains a good perspective about everybody. **Gatewood**, the deputy sheriff, can be considered the real villain in this story, even though Travis's relatives are breaking the law by growing marijuana. In his seemingly genial manner, Gatewood reminds Rob again and again that the one way he can avoid prison is to squeal on his friends.

Further Reading

Authors and Artists for Young Adults. Vol. 8. Detroit: Gale Research, 1992.

Berger, Laura Standley, ed. *Twentieth-Century Young Adults Writers.* 1st ed. Detroit: St. James, 1994.

Children's Literature Review. Vol. 18. Detroit: Gale Research, 1989.

Contemporary Literary Criticism. Vol. 26. Detroit: Gale Research, 1983.

Estes, Glenn E., ed. *American Writers for Children since 1960: Fiction.* Vol. 52 of *Dictionary of Literary Biography.* Detroit: Gale Research, 1984.

Hipple, Ted. *Presenting Sue Ellen Bridgers.* New York: Twayne, 1990.

Holtze, Sally Holmes, ed. *Fifth Book of Junior Authors and Illustrators.* New York: H. W. Wilson, 1983.

Something about the Author. Vol. 22. Detroit: Gale Research, 1981.

Something about the Author Autobiography Series. Vol. 1. Detroit: Gale Research, 1986.

Charlotte Brontë

1816-1855, English novelist

Jane Eyre

(novel, 1847)

PLOT: Jane Eyre, an orphan, has an unhappy life at Gateshead Hall, the home of her aunt, Sarah Reed, and her bullying cousins, John, Eliza, and Georgiana. A plain, lonely girl, Jane takes refuge in reading. When she is ten years old, she leaves Gateshead for Lowood School, some fifty miles away, after being interviewed by the overbearing minister and treasurer of the school, Mr. Brocklehurst. The only one sad to see her go is Bessie Lee, the maid.

At Lowood, which is in terrible disrepair, Jane makes friends with another motherless student, the sickly and pious Helen Burns, who later dies in Jane's arms, and the school superintendent, Miss Temple. Jane survives six years at the school and becomes a teacher there for two years. When Miss Temple marries and leaves, Jane no longer wishes to remain at Lowood, so she advertises for a teaching position.

Jane receives only one reply, which is from a Mrs. Fairfax who manages the house known as Thornfield at Millcote and who is related to its owner, Edward Fairfax Rochester. Jane is to teach Adele Varens, Rochester's foster child. Rochester, who is away from Thornfield much of the time, is a brooding, unattractive man in his late thirties, but Jane finds him fascinating, and his attitude toward Adele reveals a kind heart beneath his gruff exterior. While Jane is falling in love with him, some strange happenings occur at Thornfield, such as a mysterious fire. This is blamed on one of the servants, Grace Poole. Rochester also begins courting a local woman.

One day Jane visits her aunt, who is dying but still rejects her. Before her death, she tells Jane that her uncle, John Eyre, has been trying to locate her. When Jane returns to Thornfield, Rochester suddenly proposes marriage. She is startled but accepts, sending a letter to her uncle about the forthcoming marriage. The wedding is stopped, however, when a solicitor, Mr. Briggs, arrives to announce that Rochester is already married. Indeed, Rochester takes them to the third floor of Thornfield where his insane wife, Bertha Mason Rochester, is guarded by Grace Poole. Briggs learned of this from Bertha's brother, Richard Mason, who is the business partner of Jane's uncle.

Jane runs away from Thornfield to Whitcross and, after some penniless times, is befriended by the Rivers family, Diana and Mary and their stern minister brother, St. John. Jane becomes head mistress at a local girls school. Later, she learns she has inherited money from her uncle and that she is related to the Rivers family. She shares her inheritance with them but rejects St. John's marriage proposals.

Still in love with Rochester, Jane returns to Thornfield only to discover it has burned down to a shell. She learns that Bertha set the fire and died despite Rochester's attempts to save her. He was blinded in the fire and mangled a hand that later had to be amputated. Jane goes to Ferndean, where Rochester is now living. When she tells him that she refused St. John Rivers's offer of marriage, Rochester realizes she still wants to marry him. They marry and settle at Ferndean, where, ten years later, they are content with married life. Jane continues her friendship with the Rivers family, including St. John, who is now in India. Adele visits from boarding school, and Rochester, who has recovered his vision in one eye, is able to see their newborn son.

CHARACTERS: The story of **Jane Eyre** is the story of one young girl's evolution into a woman. Even while she endures the misery of her life with the Reeds, she demonstrates a need to be herself and to take responsibility for her own actions. Although she suffers the unkindness of her aunt and cousins, she finally confronts her aunt, refusing to allow herself to be taken advantage of any more. Once at Lowood, Jane is again faced with conditions that tax her endurance. Her friend Helen Burns accuses her of caring too much about human relationships, but Jane can't retreat into a life of submission. Life is to be lived and enjoyed, she believes. Unlike Helen, she can't put up with the bad meals and surly teachers at Lowood.

Once at Thornfield, Jane is proud of her independence, although she still feels quite alone in the world. However, she faces the challenges of her new job with strength and overcomes her fears. At first, she will not admit her feelings for Rochester, even to herself, but slowly a mutual admiration for and trust in each other develops. Yet even as their relationship grows closer and Rochester proposes marriage, Jane is not yet secure enough in her own worth to accept her place as his wife and lady of the manor. It is only after she has secured her relationship with the Rivers family and received an inheritance from her uncle, making her financially well off, that she evolves into a complete and independent woman. When Jane finds the strength to leave her relationship with St. John and return to Rochester, she is ready to assume her new role with confidence and security. Totally in control of her life, she is able to marry the man she loves.

Evident throughout the novel are the Victorian mores of the time. Mrs. Fairfax, for instance, disapproves of Jane's impending marriage to Rochester

Jane Eyre and Rochester (portrayed here by Joan Fontaine and Orson Welles in a 1944 film version of Jane Eyre*) find happiness at last after enduring many travails.*

because of the difference in their ages; St. John Rivers rejects Jane's offer to travel with him unless they are married; and Jane flees Thornfield after learning of the existence of Rochester's wife because she fears she will be forced to become his mistress. Later, at Ferndean, she learns that this was not to be the case.

Edward Fairfax Rochester, with his grim features and decisive nature, has felt cheated in life after long years spent married to a madwoman. His marriage was prearranged, and he has paid the penalty, so he wanders across Europe searching for the love and companionship for which he yearns. Although his exterior is gruff and cantankerous, Rochester has a kind heart. Jane recognizes this by the way he cares for his foster child, Adele Varens, even though he does not believe that he is truly her father. His essential goodness is further evidenced by his attempts to save his wife from the fire at Thornfield, even though her death would mean, and does mean, his freedom. At the same time that he longs to be rid of this madwoman he does not love, he castigates himself for the dissipated, loveless life he leads. His inward battle causes him to swing from acting affectionately and protectively toward Jane to bitter outbursts. His love for her and his overwhelming need for a meaningful life nearly lead him to committing the crime of bigamy. However, when Bertha dies in the fire despite his attempts to save her, he is able to look forward to a life with Jane. His new happiness is further enhanced by the fact that enough vision is restored in one eye to enable him to see their infant son.

Bertha Mason Rochester is Rochester's mad wife, the daughter of a wealthy planter. The insanity that runs in the family is concealed from Rochester at their marriage. After four years of worsening behavior, Rochester can no longer endure these conditions and he takes his wife to England and Thornfield, where he sequesters her in the top floor under the supposedly careful ministrations of the servant, **Grace Poole**. But when Bertha can escape from her keeper, who tends to drink too much gin, she causes mischief and damage. Aware that her husband wishes to marry Jane Eyre, she sets fire to Jane's bed during one of these escapades and then jumps from the roof and dies despite Rochester's attempts to save her.

The life of Rochester's foster child, **Adele Varens**, is considerably brightened by the addition of Jane Eyre to the household. Although she is cared for by Rochester, who refuses to acknowledge that she might be his daughter, she is neglected and without warm loving care until Jane arrives. Jane's invitation to Thornfield comes from **Mrs. Alice Fairfax**, a motherly sort and relative of Rochester's who discourages Jane's pending marriage because of the difference in their ages. Her character stands in sharp contrast to the kind of woman Jane has known in her childhood.

Jane's early years are spent with her aunt, **Sarah Reed**, a mean-spirited woman who spoils her own three children and resents her promise to care for Jane. She dies alone and unloved by her own children, rejecting Jane's attempts at reconciliation. Sarah Reed's children, **John**, **Eliza**, and **Georgiana Reed** are spoiled bullies who are overindulged by their mother and who intimidate Jane at every opportunity. They grow up to spurn their mother; in fact, when his mother refuses to give Gateshead to him, John threatens to kill her and himself. He dies a violent death at age twenty-one. **Bessie Lee**, a maid, is the only member of the household at Gateshead Hall who shows any kindness to Jane. At one point, she even visits the young girl at Lowood and gives her encouragement.

At Lowood School, Jane is interviewed by **Mr. Brocklehurst**, the straight-as-an-arrow, narrow-minded minister who is the school's manager and treasurer. The school improves greatly when he leaves. The superintendent of Lowood, **Miss Maria Temple**, is a graceful, self-confident woman whom Jane comes to idolize. She befriends both Jane and her friend Helen and encourages their progress. When she marries, Jane realizes that the school no longer holds any joy for her. Jane's pious friend at Lowood is sickly fourteen-year-old **Helen Burns** who is overly religious. On her deathbed in Jane's arms, she anticipates her meeting with God.

In contrast to Jane Eyre, **St. John Rivers** is not a whole person. He lives a narrow life and pursues a narrow philosophy. However, he is still important to Jane, not only because he helped her when she was destitute after leaving Thornfield, but also because he is a charismatic man. He denies his humanity and devotes his energies to the church. At the novel's end, Jane recognizes that St. John has become a religious zealot and that he will probably die in the service of God. His sisters, **Diana** and **Mary**, are gentle people who befriend Jane and welcome her into their family. Eventually, both sisters marry and settle down to happy lives.

Further Reading

Allott, Miriam, ed. *The Brontës: The Critical Heritage.* London: Routledge, 1974.

Authors and Artists for Young Adults. Vol. 17. Detroit: Gale Research, 1996.

Blom, Margaret. *Charlotte Brontë.* New York: Twayne, 1977.

Bloom, Harold. *The Brontës.* New York: Chelsea, 1987.

Boumelha, Penny. *Charlotte Brontë.* Bloomington: Indiana University Press, 1990.

Critical Survey of Long Fiction. Vol. 1. Englewood Cliffs, NJ: Prentice-Hall, 1983.

Evans, Barbara, and Gareth Lloyd Evans. *The Scribner Companion to the Brontës.* New York: Scribner's 1982.

Fraser, Rebecca. *The Brontës: Charlotte Brontë and Her Family.* New York: Crown, 1988.

Gaskell, Elizabeth C. *The Life of Charlotte Brontë.* New York: Penguin, 1985.

Gates, Barbara T., ed. *Critical Essays on Charlotte Brontë.* New York: Twayne, 1989.

Gerin, Winifred. *Charlotte Brontë: The Evolution of Genius.* Oxford: Oxford University Press, 1991.

Gordon, Lyndall. *Charlotte Brontë: A Passionate Life.* New York: Norton, 1994.

Hoeveler, Diana. *Approaches to Teaching Brontë's Jane Eyre.* New York: Modern Language, 1993.

Knies, Earl A. *The Art of Charlotte Brontë.* Columbus: Ohio State University Press, 1969.

Nadel, Ira B., and William E. Fredeman, eds. *Victorian Novelists before 1885.* Vol. 21 of *Dictionary of Literary Biography.* Detroit: Gale Research, 1983.

Nestor, Pauline. *Charlotte Brontë's "Jane Eyre."* New York: St. Martin's, 1992.

The New Moulton's Pre-Twentieth-Century Criticism of British and American Literature. Vol. 8 of *The Chelsea House of Literary Criticism.* New York: Chelsea, 1989.

Nineteenth-Century Literature Criticism. Vols. 3, 8, 33. Detroit: Gale Research, 1983, 1985, 1992.

Tayler, Irene. *Holy Ghosts: The Male Muses of Emily and Charlotte Brontë.* New York: Columbia University Press, 1992.

Wheat, Patricia H. *The Adytum of the Heart: The Literary Criticism of Charlotte Brontë.* Cranbury, NJ: Fairleigh Dickinson University Press, 1992.

Winnifrith, Tom. *A New Life of Charlotte Brontë.* New York: St. Martin's, 1988.

Emily Brontë

1818-1848, English novelist

Wuthering Heights

(novel, 1847)

PLOT: Most of the action of this novel takes place on the wild English moors around the beginning of the nineteenth century. The story centers around the menacing old house called Wuthering Heights and is told mainly in flashbacks by Mr. Lockwood, who has rented Thrushcross Grange in the village, and Nelly Dean, the Grange's devoted servant.

Although Mr. Lockwood begins his tale in 1801, the story actually begins years before when Mr. Earnshaw, a kindly Yorkshire farmer who owns Wuthering Heights, brings a homeless waif from Liverpool into his family. The uncouth boy, who is given the name Heathcliff, joins Mrs. Earnshaw, who is not fond of him; daughter Catherine, who loves him; and son Hindley, who strongly resents the father's obvious affection for the newcomer. After the death of his parents, Hindley becomes master of Wuthering Heights and is cruel to Heathcliff, and as a result Heathcliff begins to develop a sullen, morose character.

When Hindley's wife, Frances, dies after the birth of their son, Hareton, Hindley sinks deeper into cruelty and dissipation. Catherine, meanwhile, has grown into a haughty and arrogant woman. Despite the love between her and Heathcliff, she often derides him for his lack of breeding and manners and willfully encourages the attention of gentlemanly Edgar Linton, who lives at the Grange. When Catherine and Edgar marry, Heathcliff leaves Wuthering Heights, returning later with all the appearances of having become a rich gentleman himself.

The love between Heathcliff and Catherine is obvious to Edgar, who grows increasingly jealous. But after giving birth to Edgar's child, Cathy, Catherine dies. Heathcliff is determined to exact revenge on the two men he hates: Hindley Earnshaw and Edgar Linton. To wreak his vengeance, he accepts Hindley's invitation to return to live at the Heights, where he proceeds to turn the weaker man into a drunkard and gambler, eventually gaining all of his property, including Wuthering Heights. Hindley dies about six months after Catherine's death. Hindley's son, Hareton, whom Heathcliff raises as part of his plan to punish the Earnshaws, is now a pauper. Meanwhile, Heathcliff has married Isabella, Edgar Linton's sister. But when she learns of her husband's true nature, she runs off to London, where she gives birth to their son, Linton, a sickly, weak boy, whom Heathcliff does not see until Isabella dies many years later.

Thinking to exact the last measure of revenge on Edgar Linton, now ill and near death, Heathcliff decoys Edgar's beloved daughter Cathy to Wuthering Heights. He vows to return her to her father only if she marries Linton. Cathy agrees if Heathcliff will allow her to see her father. This is done, and after Edgar's death, Cathy and Linton marry and live with Heathcliff at Wuthering Heights. When Linton dies, Heathcliff seems to have extracted his total revenge of power and money over those he hated.

But that is not to be. Seeing the love develop between Cathy, Catherine's daughter, and Hareton, Hindley Earnshaw's son, Heathcliff seems to have lost the will to punish his supposed enemies. Perhaps it is because he sees in Hareton's eyes his own lost youth and the young man's startling resemblance to Catherine, his aunt. After Heathcliff dies, Cathy and Hareton marry and inherit Wuthering Heights, where love has at last defeated hatred.

CHARACTERS: Sometimes cited as the finest novel in the English language, *Wuthering Heights* is a passionate, brooding story of love, hate, and revenge set on the wild moors of Yorkshire, England, the author's home. "Wuthering" is a Yorkshire word for weathering, an apt description of the crumbling but rugged and menacing old house that is the site of most of the drama. The story covers three generations of characters who inhabit the Grange and Wuthering Heights.

The character of **Heathcliff**, which serves as his only name, is the heart of this brooding novel, which revolves around his all-engrossing passion for Catherine Earnshaw. A sullen, vengeful, and often cruel man, his life is spent in spiritual torment after her death. Although readers might feel some sense of understanding and pity for Heathcliff in his early years because of his treatment by Hindley, who constantly makes him feel like an outsider, and because of Catherine's seemingly heartless decision to spurn his devotion, Heathcliff's unrelenting bent toward revenge against those who have wronged him later makes him an unsympathetic character. He is a man torn between love and hate, both of which he passionately feels. Whatever good there is in Heathcliff turns to evil as he exacts his full measure of revenge over the passage of some seventeen years. Yet in the end, even this passion for revenge is drained as, despite himself, he begins to love the son of his old enemy.

Catherine Earnshaw, the heroine who dies halfway through the book, is a wild and impetuous girl whose arrogance causes her to push aside any and all who would stand in her way. She loves Heathcliff as she loves the moors, with an abiding passion, yet she heartlessly casts him aside to marry Edgar Linton. Part of her, however, does so in the hope that her action will wake Heathcliff from the dominance that Hindley exerts over him after the death of her father. She dies angry at her husband for not understanding the love between herself and Heathcliff and angry at Heathcliff for not understanding why she married Edgar. Catherine's brother, **Hindley Earnshaw**, is a man who acts in cruel ways, although his bitterness is made somewhat understandable by the lack of his father's affection and by the intrusion of Heathcliff. Of an artistic temperament, he is no match for Heathcliff's vengefulness or his sister Catherine's wild spirit.

In the neighboring house to Wuthering Heights, called the Grange, live the Lintons. **Edgar Linton** is portrayed as a tender, gentle man, a typical hero of a Victorian novel, who is far overshadowed by the dominating nature of Catherine, his spirited wife. **Isabella Linton**, Edgar's sister, is an immature woman who persuades herself that Heathcliff loves her, even in the face of his obvious actions to the contrary. Despite warnings from her brother and from Catherine, she marries him. Her one act of strength and independence is to run off to London after an altercation during which she speaks against Catherine, and Heathcliff strikes her.

Once in London, Isabella gives birth to **Linton Heathcliff**, an effeminate boy with many of his mother's characteristics. However, he does have his father's cruel streak, which he exhibits to those who thwart him. His one redeeming quality is his love for Catherine and Edgar's daughter, **Cathy Linton**, which she recognizes and to some extent returns. Cathy has some of her mother's free spirit and independence, although not Catherine's strength of character and fascination of spirit. She does, however, have strong qualities of loyalty and sympathy for those she loves, including **Hareton Earnshaw**, Hindley's son. Hareton is reared for much of his young life by Heathcliff, who tries to turn him into a brute. But despite his uncouth manner, the boy instead grows up to be very much like his Aunt Catherine, exhibiting a strong capacity for love, which he shows to Cathy Linton.

The list of minor characters includes **Mr. Earnshaw**, a stalwart Yorkshire farmer who has little time for his weakling son, and **Mrs. Earnshaw**, who loves her son and rebuffs Heathcliff. Hindley's wife, **Frances Earnshaw**, is a delicate young woman who is not strong enough to survive the birth of her son, Hareton. The two narrators of the story are **Mr. Lockwood**, the first narrator whose citified ways often reveal a superior attitude toward the people of the moors, and **Nelly Dean**, a servant at the Grange and lively storyteller of the second part of the novel.

Further Reading

Allott, Miriam, ed. *The Brontës: The Critical Heritage.* London: Routledge & Kegan Paul, 1974.

Benvenuto, Richard. *Emily Brontë.* Boston: Twayne, 1982.

Bloom, Harold, ed. *The Brontës.* New York: Chelsea House, 1987.

Bruccoli, Matthew J., and Richard Layman, eds. *Victorian Writers, 1832-1890.* Vol. 4 of *Concise Dictionary of British Literary Biography.* Detroit: Gale Research, 1991.

Frank, Katherine. *A Chainless Soul: A Life of Emily Brontë.* Boston: Houghton, 1990.

Gerin, Winifred. *Emily Brontë: A Biography.* Oxford: Clarendon, 1971.

Magill, Frank N. *Critical Survey of Long Fiction: English Language Series: Authors.* Vol. 1. Englewood Cliffs, NJ: Prentice-Hall, 1983.

Martin, C. *The Brontës.* Vero Beach, FL: Rourke, 1989.

Nineteenth-Century Literature Criticism. Vol. 16. Detroit. Gale Research, 1987.

Pinion, F. B. *A Brontë Companion: Literary Assessment, Background, and Reference.* New York: Barnes & Noble, 1975.

Bruce Brooks

1950-, American young adult novelist

The Moves Make the Man

(young adult novel, 1984)

PLOT: There is absolutely nothing that Jerome Foxworthy—known as Jayfox—can't do with a basketball. The seventh-grader can dribble, pass, triple pump, reverse jump, and stutter step with the best of them. He has the moves; he also has the grades. Jayfox has tested second-highest among all seventh-graders in Wilmington, North Carolina.

Jayfox is about to take a big change in his life. The Supreme Court has desegregated the nation's schools, and now, all by himself, he is going to integrate Chestnut Junior High in Wilmington, the town's biggest all-white school. Jayfox is not too bothered by becoming the school's first black student, though. With his mother's encouragement, he knows he can get along anywhere.

One day, Jayfox notices another superior athlete named Braxton Rivers III (Bix, for short). He is white and plays shortstop like no one Jayfox has ever seen. Jayfox also notices a beautiful woman watching Bix play. She acts weird, jumping up and down and calling his name at odd times, and Jayfox learns that she is Bix's mother. The two boys meet in economics class and gradually become friends. As they come to know one another, Jayfox discovers that Bix will never tell a lie—not even a small white lie to spare someone's feelings. Consequently, when Jayfox tries to teach him all his basketball moves, including how to "fake," or fool the opponent, Bix outright refuses to learn this technique. In fact, he gets angry about it and stalks off the court. When they meet again, Bix says that his mother has tried to commit suicide and

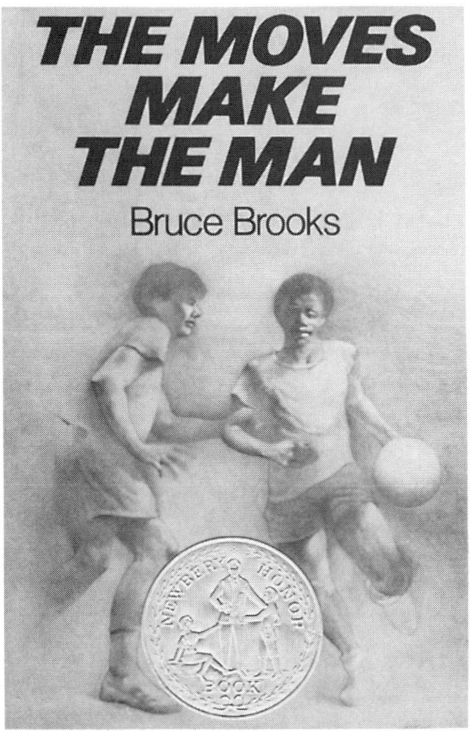

Jayfox has all the right basketball moves, but will that count when he tries to be the first African American at Chestnut Junior High?

is now in a mental institution. Bix's stepfather will not let him visit her because he blames Bix for the suicide attempt, which occurred after his mother walked into his room naked and carrying a knife. When she asked whether he loved her, Bix didn't at that moment so he said so. The frank reply led her to attempt suicide.

In order to win the right to see his own mother, Bix bets his stepfather, a former basketball star, that he can beat him one-on-one on the court. Jayfox acts as referee for this strange game. The stepfather looks like a winner until, finally, Bix uses the fakes that Jayfox taught him. He wins, but the visit with his mother is a disaster. She does not even recognize him, and Bix rushes from the hospital. After that, Bix disappears and no one can find him. Months later Jayfox gets a card postmarked Washington, D.C. Although there is no message, Jayfox knows it is from his friend. For the first time since Bix left, Jayfox decides to go out and play some basketball to see if the moves are still there.

CHARACTERS: This first novel by Bruce Brooks was hailed for its humor, its realistic characters, and its exciting portrayal of sports. It was a Newbery Honor Book and winner of the *Boston Globe-Horn Book* Award.

Jerome Foxworthy, who is usually called **Jayfox** in the story, is a delightful and somewhat irreverent youngster with a sense of humor and a good measure of self-esteem. His mother has taught him to know who he is and be proud of it, but he is neither boastful nor conceited. A good student and basketball player, he is somewhat apprehensive about becoming the first black player at his new school, but he is confident enough to overcome any difficulties. Jayfox likes Bix immediately, although he feels that his new friend carries his passion for the truth to an extreme. For example, he is surprised when Bix stalks off the court and refuses to learn Jayfox's "fake" moves. Although Jayfox is happy when Bix finally uses the fakes to win the bet with his stepfather, he is greatly saddened by the scene at the hospital. Since Bix asks Jayfox to go with him, Jayfox sees his friend nearly destroyed when his mother does not recognize him. The shock is so great that Jayfox gives up his beloved basketball until he knows that Bix is alive and well.

Braxton Rivers III—Bix, for short—is a troubled young man who is put under great emotional stress by the increasing mental instability of his mother. Usually friendly and easygoing, Bix's personality changes when confronted with untruths in his life. Jayfox is especially startled one day in a cooking class when Bix becomes enraged because the other students pretend that the mock apple pie they are making is real. Bix's extreme reactions against any deviation from the truth become more evident when Jayfox tries to teach his friend his best basketball fakes. Again, Bix becomes enraged and stalks off. It is only when Bix is faced with the prospect of not seeing his mother that he uses fakery to win the bet with his stepfather and thus be allowed to visit the hospital. On the way to the hospital, Bix, his stepfather, and Jayfox stop at a restaurant run by a friend Bix has known for a long time. When the friend will not serve Jayfox, Bix receives another emotional shock. The last straw that finally breaks Bix's fragile emotions comes when his mother does not know him and asks whose boy he is. This causes Bix to run far from the truth.

Midnight Hour Encores

(young adult novel, 1986)

PLOT: Sibilance T. Spooner is a sixteen-year-old musical prodigy who lives in Washington, D.C., with her father, Taxi, who is a newspaperman. They have been together since Sib was a day old and Taxi took her away from California and her hippie mother, Connie. Sib and Taxi have an unusually adult relationship. A recognized genius on the cello and mature beyond her years, Sib is also a tall, bossy, lonely teenager given to sarcastic bantering with her father, who lets her do pretty much as she pleases.

Each year Taxi asks Sib if she wants to meet her mother. Sib has always declined in the past, but this year she says yes. So Taxi fixes up a vintage 1960s Volkswagen bus, and the two set out for California with Sib's cello and some old records. On the way, they compose a tone poem they call "The Peace and Love Shuffle." It is about life during the "Age of Aquarius," the hippie period of the 1960s when Connie let her husband and child leave so that she could "find herself." The trip also gives Sib an opportunity to learn things she did not know before about her father. For instance, in the early years he took her along on his job when he could not afford a baby-sitter.

Sib meets her mother and is immediately drawn to her. They spend several days together, during which Connie explains that she was not ready to be a mother sixteen years ago. Now she has a successful career in real estate. Sib realizes that her father has arranged the trip fully expecting that she will decide to stay and live with Connie. But before Taxi leaves, he attends Sib's audition for a musical scholarship. She has never played better. However, Connie is annoyed after the performance because, for an encore, Sib plays the tone poem she and Taxi composed on the trip across the country. For that, she nearly loses the scholarship.

When Taxi is ready to begin his trip home, he can't find Sib to say goodbye. He leaves in the Volkswagen bus, but only after making Connie promise that Sib will call if she needs him. After some minutes on the highway, however, he hears a cello. Sib is in the back of the van, playing for the start of their journey.

CHARACTERS: This offbeat story tells of a young girl's search for identity and self-discovery. It contrasts a sophisticated teenager of the 1980s with the hippie culture of the 1960s. The novel is especially interesting for its use of the world of classical music as a backdrop, for the unusual relationship between father and daughter, and for the details of life during the Age of Aquarius.

Indicative of the mature relationship between **Sibilance T. Spooner** and her father is the fact that Taxi let her change her name when she was eight years old. (Her mother had named her Esalen Starness Blue.) Sib is a smart, self-assured young girl who loves her music and is determined to be the best at it. Mature beyond her years, she exudes a sort of world-weary demeanor and is much given to sarcasm. This helps to deflect the loneliness she feels, for her talent sets her apart from other teenagers, and she has no friends except for Taxi. Although she is apprehensive about meeting her mother and is not immediately convinced by Connie's explanations about why she abandoned her family, Sib is fascinated despite herself. In truth, she is eager for the love she never experienced from this woman. She begins to envision a life together with the mother she never knew.

During her audition for the scholarship in San Francisco, Sib knows she has never played better. Part of her wants the scholarship, since music is her life. But she also notices Taxi sitting in the very last row, just as he has always done at her recitals. She then realizes that he is her life, too. On the cross-country trip, Sib begins to see beneath the banter and discover what a loving, caring parent he has always been. Unlike her mother, he has always been there for her. Sib decides that, although she needs her music in her life, she needs her father, too. This decision leads her—at the risk of embarrassing her mother and losing the scholarship—to play the tone poem about the 1960s she and her father composed on their cross-country trip.

Taxi Spooner is an unusual man and unconventional father. The sarcastic banter that characterizes his relationship with Sib sometimes conceals the deep love and pride he feels for her. Convinced that Sib has the right to know her mother, he asks whether she wants to visit Connie every year. When Sib finally says yes, he decides to help her learn about the culture of the time when she was born, reasoning that perhaps then she will be able to understand the woman who let her go. He fixes up the Volkswagen bus—a relic from the sixties—and starts off on a journey of instruction with his daughter. He never criticizes Connie's actions, but instead tries to explain to Sib the mood of the time. At one point on the trip, they stop to visit an old friend of Taxi's. She too had abandoned her child years before, and Sib begins to wonder if any of the hippies wanted their children. After his preparations lead to a successful meeting between Sib and Connie, Taxi fully expects that Sib will stay with her mother. At the end of the novel, his joy at hearing the strains of the cello in the back of the bus is obvious.

Connie, a small woman with bright-blue eyes, is smart, opinionated, and unapologetic. She does not try to excuse her actions in leaving her family, but merely explains to Sib the way she had been sixteen years before. She obviously feels something for her daughter, and she seems to be interested in having Sib stay with her. After the scholarship recital, however, she asks Taxi, "You mean you were going back to Washington and leaving her with me?" Taxi answers, "I assumed you two had arranged that." Rather than genuine warmth, Connie's feelings for her daughter seem to be on a more practical level. Now that Connie is a successful businesswoman and on the board of the institute offering the scholarship, it seems only fitting that her daughter should be the winner. Since Connie wants others to be impressed with her talented daughter, she is annoyed when Sib jeopardizes her chances by playing the tone poem. In fact, Sib leaves the hall before knowing that she has indeed won the scholarship. It no longer matters.

Further Reading

Berger, Laura Standley, ed. *Twentieth-Century Young Adult Writers.* 1st ed., Detroit: St. James, 1994.

Children's Literature Review. Vol. 25. Detroit: Gale Research, 1991.

Gallo, Donald R., ed. *Speaking for Ourselves: Autobiographical Sketches by Notable Authors of Books for Young Adults.* Urbana, IL: National Council of Teachers of English, 1990.

Something about the Author. Vol. 72. Detroit: Gale Research, 1993.

Terry Brooks

1944-, American fantasy writer

The Sword of Shannara

(fantasy, 1977)

PLOT: Many years ago in a mythical land, a Druid named Breman forged a sword for the royal family of Shannara to combat the evil power of the exiled Druid, Brona, known as the Warlock Lord. Eons later, Brona, in an alliance with the gnomes, sets out on a renewed plan of conquest. To combat him, the giant Druid, Allanon, contacts the sole remaining member of the Shannara family, young Shea Ohmsford, who, unaware of his birthright, has been living with his stepfather, Curzad Ohmsford, and stepbrother, Flick Ohmsford, who are innkeepers in Shady Vale. Allanon gives Shea magical Elfstones which can be used to escape from any supernatural beings he encounters. In their quest to retrieve the magical sword and fight the power of darkness, Shea, Flick, and Allanon are joined by a friend of Shea's, Menion Leah. Others who join the party are Balinor, the Prince of Callahorn; the gallant dwarf, Hendel; and two young elves, Durin and Dayel.

The eight intrepid wayfarers experience many fantastic adventures on their dangerous journey north to the Skull Kingdom of the Warlock Lord, where the Sword is housed. Following an earthquake, Shea becomes separated from the rest of the party, is captured by gnomes, and is later rescued by two robbers, Panamon Creel and a gigantic, mute rock troll named Keltset. Together the three continue the quest which leads them into Skull Castle, where they find that a malevolent gnome, Orl Fane, has possession of the sword. In the meantime, the rest of the company disbands to recruit forces to fight the enormous gnome legions who are marching south to battle under the direction of Brona's henchmen, the Skull Bearers. To collect his forces, Prince Balinor must first unseat his brother, Palance Buckhannah, who has usurped his father's throne with the help of his wicked advisor, Stenmin. Balinor is successful and is later joined by Flick, who has secured the help of Eventine Elessedil, king of the elves.

Menion Leah and his new girlfriend, Shirl Ravenlock, along with Hendel, Durin, and Dayel, join the defenders in a great battle at the city of Tyrsis, Callahorn's capital. The gnomes are defeated, although Hendel is killed. In the north, Shea gains possession of the sword, confronts the Warlock Lord, and successfully destroys him and his power. In time, the crusaders are reunited in victory, after which they return to their respective homes. It takes many months for Shea and Flick to resume the quiet life of being the sons of an innkeeper after all the incredible adventures they have experienced.

Other books in the Shannara series include The Elfstones of Shannara *(1982),* The Wishsong of Shannara *(1985),* The Scions of Shannara, *(1990),* The Druid of Shannara *(1991),* The Elf Queen of Shannara *(1992), and* The Talismans of Shannara *(1993).*

CHARACTERS: The quest for the Sword of Shannara and the dangerous pursuit of Brona, the Warlock Lord, are missions that are thrust on the reluctant, naive **Shea Ohmsford**, the last surviving member of the Shannara family. He is an average young man who is filled with doubts about how he will react when confronted by challenging dangers; he wonders whether he has the necessary bravery and fortitude to survive under arduous conditions. At first Shea disbelieves the story of his origins and refuses to acknowledge any obligations he might have to his people. In spite of these doubts, Shea shows he is worthy of his charge. Fiercely loyal to his brother, Flick, Shea is resourceful, imaginative, and dependable. Though living with humans, Shea has many elfin physical characteristics, including fine features and a hint of pointed ears. He is slim and lithe with a face that reveals his basic honesty and intelligence. Conservative in his attitudes, he nevertheless adapts quickly to the harsh, often life-threatening situations he faces. When Shea, with sword in hand, faces Brona, he discovers that the sword's only power is to produce self-awareness. He first sees himself with all his deficiencies and weaknesses, but then beholds the side of his character that is now emerging: a mature, heroic fighter for truth and justice.

The leader of the quest is the wise Druid historian and philosopher, **Allanon**. A massive man standing over seven feet tall, he has a long, deeply lined face, craggy features, a long flat nose, and a short black beard. This wandering mystic and scholar presents a huge and forbidding exterior and astounds others with his undefinable powers and immense strength. Allanon is, at times, short-tempered and impatient, particularly when he perceives stupidity, but with his friends he also displays kindness and understanding. A man of incredible courage and endurance, he survives misfortunes that would defeat most other men. Balinor says of Allanon, "The man possesses a greater knowledge of the races and the threat that faces them than anyone else. Allanon's power is beyond anything we have ever seen." Allanon is unswerving in his dedication to defeat Brona, partly because—as he reveals at the end of the novel—he is the son of **Breman**, the noble Druid who was the highly esteemed leader of the Druid Council. Breman foresaw the continuing threat of Brona and conceived the idea of the Sword, a weapon with the power to defeat him. In memory of his father, Allanon continues this epic struggle.

Allanon's adversary is a former Druid, the evil **Brona**, also known as the **Warlock King**, **Skull King**, and **Lord of Darkness**. During his studies as a Druid, Brona uncovered the deepest secrets of sorcery and mastered them. In the process he lost his own identity and eventually his soul in an obsessive need to extend his power and dominate the races. Allied with the gnomes, he is driven by a craving to control his universe and destroy the only adversary that could challenge him, Shea. Brona is synonymous with all that is diabolic and sinful in the world. Ruthless and devoid of mercy, he is the embodiment of evil. When Shea thrusts the Sword into him, Brona is given a glimpse of his inner satanic soul, and dies from the revelation. Brona's minions are the **Skull Bearers**: huge, terrible, bat-like, creatures with crooked legs and claws that can cut through stone. Traveling by night, their eyes emit a reddish glow and their mouths a deathlike cry. Although one falls to his death in the fires at Druid's Keep in a struggle with Allanon and another is destroyed by Shea's use of the Elfstones, others survive to lead the attack on Tyrsis. However, they are destroyed during the battle.

Shea's stepbrother is **Flick Ohmsford**, son of the honest, hard-working innkeeper of Shady Vale, **Curzad Ohmsford**. Flick is a stocky young man with shaggy eyebrows and grizzled brown hair. Beneath his calm facade, he has a restless nature and longs for action and adventure. He is pragmatic in his thinking and given to being a pessimist. A courageous warrior with great endurance and spirit, Flick, like Shea, also changes during the quest: "He developed an inner strength and maturity and a confidence in himself he had never before and . . . had passed a supreme test of raw courage and perseverance that even a seasoned fighter would have found frightening." Flick's constant devotion to his brother is one of his most endearing characteristics.

Although people call him "the biggest wastrel in the entire Southland," **Menion, Prince of Leah** also proves to be a staunch, responsible colleague of Shea's. A handsome, flashy adventurer, Menion's life prior to the quest was one wild escapade after another. Flip, brash, and spunky, Menion is considered the best bowman and tracker in the Southland. An audacious, brilliant tactician, he will only kill in self-defense. With his lithe body, attractive features, and graceful movements, he is the picture of a dashing, devil-may-care prince. Generous and loyal, Menion rightly predicts that the crusade for the Sword will bring new meaning and purpose to his life. During one of his adventures, Menion rescues the lovely **Shirl Ravenlock**, princess of the city of Kern. A striking beauty, she is a slim, graceful damsel with long, titian-colored hair. Shirl is a sensitive, independent girl with good intentions and high spirits, and she and Menion fall madly in love.

The most noble of all the Shea's companions is **Balinor, Prince of Callahorn**, son of King Ruhn Buckhannah. Remarkable for his courage, wisdom, and sacrifice, Balinor has rugged, strong features that hide an inner gentleness. Earnest, virtuous, and trustworthy, he commands respect and admiration from others. Durin the elf correctly calls Balinor the most remarkable man he has ever met. Balinor has a long, ugly scar on his right cheek that he received from his jealous, unstable younger brother, **Palance Buckhannah**, who envies Balinor's position and wants to bypass him to become king. Erratic and consumed by hatred, Palance has taken as an advisor the unscrupulous mystic, **Stenmin**, who is using drugs and evil powers on Palance to increase his paranoia and dementia. Stenmin, who is secretly in the employ of the Warlock Lord, mortally wounds Palance after he is unmasked as being a wicked, self-serving traitor.

Three other members of the crusade against Brona are **Hendel the Dwarf** and the two elves, **Durin** and **Dayel**. Hendel is a powerfully built dwarf, slightly over five feet tall, who carries an arsenal of weapons around his broad waist. Irascible, independent, and grouchy, Hendel is also noted for being tight-mouthed and abrupt. However, he is an experienced woodsman and, perhaps, the most gallant member of the band. Fearless as a lion, he single-handedly takes on scores of the enemy and accepts dangerous assignments that would dismay others. He dies valiantly during the siege of Trysis. The elf brothers, like Hendel, are also noted for their courage and fortitude. The older, Durin, has been recently married but has obeyed his king's request to go on this special mission. Dayel, who is not yet twenty, is a shy, likable young man whose boyish charm endears him to the others. The brothers are devoted to each other and to the cause they serve. Their king is **Eventine Elessedil**, the most beloved and respected king of the Elves.

When separated from the group, Shea is saved from a band of gnomes by two robbers, **Panamon Creel** and the rock troll, Keltset. Panamon is a lovable rogue whose occupation is thievery and skullduggery. Arrogant, overconfident, and audacious, he dresses flamboyantly in scarlet. With a wide, friendly mouth, youthful manner, and small moustache, he cuts a dashing figure, even though Shea figures he is over forty. At first eager to exploit Shea and his situation, Panamon in time becomes a faithful, if not completely trustworthy, ally. His companion of two months is **Keltset**, a huge, dark, mute giant who has bark-like skin the color of well-done meat. A creature of incredible power and strength, he comes from an old and honored family. His parents were killed by Brona, and Keltset wants both to avenge his family and aid Shea in his quest. He provides enormous help in locating the Sword and is later killed before leaving Skull Kingdom.

The disgusting, contemptible gnome who has possession of the Sword is **Orl Fane**. An army deserter and battleground scavenger, he gained possession of the Sword after it was lost during a battle between the elves and gnomes. Miserable, even by gnome standards, he is hated and despised by his fellows and has become an outcast. Half-mad and susceptible to hallucinations, Orl is killed by Shea, who wields the Sword that the gnome tried to hide.

Further Reading

Authors and Artists for Young Adults. Vol. 18. Detroit: Gale Research, 1996.

Berger, Laura Standley, ed. *Twentieth-Century Young Adult Writers.* 1st. ed. Chicago: St. James, 1994.

Contemporary Authors. Vols. 77-80. Detroit: Gale Research, 1979.

Contemporary Authors New Revision Series. Vol. 14. Detroit: Gale Research, 1985.

Something about the Author. Vol. 60. Detroit: Gale Research, 1990.

Pearl S. Buck

1892-1973, American novelist

The Good Earth

(historical novel, 1931)

PLOT: This novel is set primarily in nineteenth-century rural China and covers a period of over fifty years in the life of Wang Lung, a peasant who eventually becomes a wealthy landowner. While still a young man, he enters the opulent House of Hwang—the palace of the area's richest family—to claim as his bride O-Lan, a plain but hardworking slave he has purchased. Together they work long, backbreaking hours cultivating Wang Lung's small piece of land. O-Lan frugally manages the humble family home, where Wang Lung's father also lives. Soon the family begins to grow: O-Lan gives birth to sons Nung En and Nung Wen, and a docile, simple-minded daughter whom they call the Fool. Wang Lung prospers and buys more land from the Hwang family—whose fortunes are in decline—but when a severe drought parches the land, his family, now close to starvation, flees south to the big city. Once there Wang Lung becomes a rickshaw driver and O-Lan and the others collect a few coppers by begging. A puny, feeble baby is born, and O-Lan kills it as an act of mercy and expedience.

Swept up in a revolt of peasants, Wang Lung and O-Lan are present when a rich man's home is plundered. By accident, they acquire enough silver and jewels to return home and buy more land. Wang Lung is able to expand their house and hire men to help him, including his faithful friend, Ching. O-Lan gives birth to twins, but Wang Lung grows increasingly dissatisfied with his homely, docile wife. In a tea house in town run by Cuckoo—a former mistress of the House of Hwang's Old Lord—he finds the fragile, kittenish Lotus Blossom. She becomes his concubine and moves with Cuckoo into a new wing of Wang Lung's house. This breaks O-Lan's heart, although she never speaks of this stranger in her home. The household is further increased when Wang Lung is forced to give food and shelter to an indigent uncle—who is a member of a gang of local

Poor farmer Wang Lung becomes a wealthy landowner in Buck's Pulitzer Prize-winning saga of nineteenth-century China, The Good Earth *(scene from the Metro-Goldwyn-Mayer 1937 film).*

bandits—his wife, and their licentious son. O-Lan is stricken with a fatal form of cancer, and a contrite Wang Lung cares for her. Before her death, she gains satisfaction from being present at her eldest son's marriage to the daughter of a prosperous grain merchant. O-Lan, and later Wang Lung's father, are buried on a hillock on the family's large land holding.

Because family tensions are growing, Nung En, who revels in displays of the family's wealth, persuades Wang Lung to buy the deserted House of Hwang and renovate it. The family, including the newly married Nung Wen and his wife, move to their luxurious new quarters. The uncle and his family, now conveniently hooked on opium to make them harmless, are left behind. The parents soon die from their drug habit and the wastrel son joins the army, leaving the family home vacant. As his own death approaches, Wang Lung, now nearing seventy, moves back to his land, accompanied by a faithful slave named Pear Blossom and a few servants. One day while strolling the land with his sons, Wang Lung overhears their plans to eventually sell off the property. He protests because this land has been both his livelihood and his salvation. They reassure him, but glance at each other and smile knowingly.

CHARACTERS: This story, told in a simple, objective writing style, won a Pulitzer Prize in 1932. It describes the cycle of life and its relation to the forces of nature as seen through the experiences of a Chinese family, and it does so in a passive, nonjudgmental manner. In some ways the central character of the novel is the good earth of China—the land that has the power to give life or take it away. It is the force that controls the destiny of those who rely upon it for their livelihood, and in the end it supplies them with an eternal resting place.

Wang Lung is first portrayed as an eager, ambitious young man who is excited by the prospect of a new wife and a family. He is obsessively hardworking and eager to succeed, but he is also aware of the traditions and obligations imposed by his culture. In spite of his preoccupation with gaining wealth through the ownership of land, his family is always uppermost in his thoughts. He makes many sacrifices to insure the well-being of his children, and he dutifully respects and cares for his father. In spite of the inconvenience and hardship, he also offers a place in his home to an ungrateful uncle and his lecherous family. At times, Wang Lung must go hungry himself to feed his family. He is also a faithful friend who believes in repaying kindnesses, as witnessed by his solicitous treatment of his land manager, Ching, who once gave food to Wang Lung though he was near starvation himself.

There are weaknesses in Wang Lung's character, however. He is prone to act rashly and impetuously, although he usually returns to more rational behavior with reflection and a good night's sleep. His callous treatment of O-Lan, the woman who sacrificed all for him, as well as his obsession with the beautiful Lotus Blossom, are the sins of a thoughtless middle-aged man looking for the sensuous love he never had. His eventual regret and remorse for these cruelties come too late for him to make amends. But the abiding passion in Wang Lung's life is the land—the good earth—which is the source of life and prosperity for him. Throughout his life, he continually returns to it for its purifying, regenerative powers.

Wang Lung's wife, **O-Lan**, is a stoically submissive, uncomplaining tower of strength. Unfortunately, she has a very plain appearance, possessing a common, large-featured face, coarse skin, a dull, plodding demeanor, and huge, spreading feet that had not been bound when she was a child, as was often the custom in China to make women's feet petite. Aware of these physical shortcomings, she tries to remain as inconspicuous as possible and never draws attention to herself. She sacrifices all for her husband and refuses any show of finery and wealth even when this becomes possible. She is always the realist, carefully thinking through the consequences of each decision and courageously acting in the way that is best for her husband. This often results in her making painful decisions, such as killing her sickly newborn so that her starving family can continue to survive. O-Lan believes that a wife must slavishly obey her husband's wishes, and her compliance to this creed is touchingly portrayed, particularly during the time when Wang Lung betrays her. She shows a remarkable ability to sustain both physical and emotional pain. For example, she takes only a few hours to give birth before returning to work in the fields. Ever humble and quiet, she endures her husband's indifference, lack of gratitude, and infidelity. O-Lan lashes out only when her kitchen is invaded by Cuckoo, Lotus Blossom's servant and a woman who treated O-Lan cruelly when she was a slave in the House of Hwang. Ironically, O-Lan does not live to see her family move to this great palace, although she is able, through her strength and willpower, to live to see her eldest son married.

Neither of Wang Lung's two eldest sons can match the strength and energy of their parents. Though known at home simply as Elder and Younger, their schoolteacher names them **Nung En** and **Nung Wen**, signifying different sons of a prosperous farmer. Nung En is often rebellious and ashamed of his parents' humble origins. He uses his father's ignorance to his own advantage and is happiest when spending Wang Lung's money to buy valuable objects to impress others. He is the one who persuades his father to buy the Hwang palace and refurbish it at enormous expense. Nung Wen is more like his mother in both appearance and temperament. He is a born businessman, shrewd and calculating. He is penurious to the point of becoming a miser, and he deliberately marries a simple farm girl beneath his station in order to avoid expense and acquire an obedient, undemanding wife.

Of Wang Lung's twins, the boy, suffering from the unrequited love for a servant named **Pear Blossom**, leaves home to join the army, and the girl marries the son of a wealthy businessman. Pear Blossom is a young, pretty slave owned by Wang Lung's family when they move to the House of Hwang. Innocent and fearful, she gives herself to an aged Wang Lung because she likes older men who show her kindness. Although this affair is short-lived, she stays on as his servant and moves with him to the original family home. The demented daughter known as the **Fool** is an object of pity. She is a docile, harmless creature who is unable to speak and instead smiles continuously. Wang Lung wonders if the terrible periods of starvation caused this brain damage. Despite her condition, both parents love and tend to this pathetic creature.

When Wang Lung first meets his mistress, **Lotus Blossom**, she is described as small and slender with a "body light as bamboo" and a little pointed face like a kitten's. An experienced courtesan, she knows how to manipulate men, particularly those like Wang Lung, who have never experienced true physical gratification. When ensconced in Wang Lung's household, she becomes a demanding, whining problem child, forever requiring attention, expensive presents, and exotic foods. As she grows old and fat, Wang Lung ceases to be interested in her sexually, but he dutifully continues to submit to her whims and costly requests. Her chaperone and caretaker is **Cuckoo**, a former courtesan and madame. She too is avaricious, always plotting new schemes to make money and get expensive presents from Wang Lung.

Wang Lung's faithful, honest friend is **Ching**, the generous man who shared food with Wang Lung when both were starving. When Wang Lung returns from the city with his loot, he hires Ching to help oversee his lands. Ching proves to be a loyal, trustworthy employee, noted for his hard work and reliability. When he dies as an old man, he is still faithfully trying to do the physical work of a much younger man. Wang Lung holds him in such high regard that he wants to bury him as part of the family, and he plans to do so until Nung En, always aware of correct protocol, objects.

Further Reading

Buck, Pearl S. *My Several Worlds.* Cutchogue, NY: Buccaneer, 1992.

Contemporary Literary Criticism. Vols. 7, 11, 18. Detroit: Gale Research, 1977, 1979, 1981.

Doyle, Paul A. *Pearl S. Buck.* Boston: Twayne, 1980.

Kimbel, Bobby Ellen, ed. *American Short Story Writers, 1910-1945, Second Series.* Vol. 102 of *Dictionary of Literary Biography.* Detroit: Gale Research, 1991.

LaFarge, Ann. *Pearl Buck.* New York: Chelsea House, 1988.

Magill, Frank N. *Critical Survey of Long Fiction: English Language Series: Authors.* Vol. 1. Englewood Cliffs, NJ: Prentice-Hall, 1983.

Martine, James J., ed. *American Novelists, 1910-1945.* Vol. 9 of *Dictionary of Literary Biography.* Detroit: Gale Research, 1981.

Mitchell, Barbara. *Between Two Worlds: A Story about Pearl Buck.* Minneapolis, MN: Carolrhoda, 1988.

Something about the Author. Vol. 25. Detroit: Gale Research, 1981.

Olive Ann Burns

1924-1990, American novelist

Cold Sassy Tree

(novel, 1984)

PLOT: Cold Sassy, Georgia, is a small town where news spreads fast by word of mouth. So when Grandpa E. Rucker Blakeslee announces one July morning in 1906 that he is marrying Miss Love Simpson, the milliner down at Grandpa's store, everyone soon knows about it. The scandal is that Grandpa Blakeslee is fifty-nine years old, while Miss Love is a very young woman. Even more shocking to the citizens of Cold Sassy, and especially the Blakeslee family, is that Granny Blakeslee has only been dead three weeks when Grandpa Blakeslee announces his engagement.

The only member of the Blakeslee family who is not upset is Grandpa's favorite grandson, Will Tweedy, who narrates the story eight years after the described events occur. Fourteen years old when the main story takes place, Will also has a summer that is about as eventful as his Grandpa's. Daydreaming one afternoon while sitting on a railroad trestle, Will is almost killed when the train comes through. He has no choice but to lay as flat as he can between the rails and let the train run over him. Although he gets blisters from the heat and loses his straw hat, Will survives, and the story is all over town in minutes. Will's other big adventure is his first real kiss. He kisses a "mill girl" named Lightfoot McLendon. Unfortunately, they are spotted by Miss Alice Ann, and Will figures he is going to get the devil when Mama finds out. Still, it was worth it, for he will remember his first kiss for a long time.

Much of the story, however, focuses on Will's grandfather. The Blakeslee family and the townspeople are outraged when Grandpa and Love Simpson quickly elope. Will's mama and his Aunt Loma even consider running Miss Love Simpson right out of town for what she has done. But Will discreetly discovers that Grandpa and Miss Love actually have "an arrangement." As it turns out, theirs is a marriage of convenience. Miss Love has agreed to tend the house for Grandpa, and in return she will inherit the house after his death. Grandpa needs some help, and Miss Love, who has no family, has always wanted a home of her own. They sleep in separate bedrooms.

But Grandpa and Miss Love surprise even themselves when they grow to genuinely care about one another. Grandpa falls in love, and the May-December marriage becomes a romance. Unfortunately, Grandpa gets pneumonia and dies, but not before he learns that he is going to be a father again. The town gives Grandpa a marvelous send-off, and Miss Love decides that she will remain in Cold Sassy with the only family she and her child have.

The world has changed since that time in 1906, Will reflects. Cold Sassy's name is now Progressive

City, a name he feels is not nearly as interesting. But Will, who at twenty-two now has a college diploma, will cherish his memories of his childhood there.

CHARACTERS: Will Tweedy, the narrator and a main character in the story, tells about his fourteenth summer in retrospect as a twenty-two-year-old college graduate. As a teenager, Will is a curious, respectful young man who adores his grandpa and who regards his entire family with amusement and affection. Sometimes mischievous, he gets into trouble in the episodes where he almost gets hit by a train and when he kisses Lightfoot McLendon. Will confesses inwardly to a bit of jealousy concerning Grandpa's affections toward Miss Love, and he is rather intrigued by the May-December match, observing the couple with increasing interest. Because Will is his Grandpa's favorite and because he is naturally curious, he is more privy to the actual marriage arrangements between the two.

Grandpa E. Rucker Blakeslee can only be described as a character. He certainly flaunts convention when he announces his decision to marry the young Miss Love Simpson. No one in town, except Will Tweedy, knows that it is only a marriage of convenience. But in time, Miss Love and Will learn the truth about Grandpa. He has always had "a cravin'" for Miss Love. In fact, Granny Blakeslee knew about it, and it was Granny and Grandpa who had the marriage of convenience. Having another child would have killed her, the doctor said, so the two lived more as brother and sister. But Granny tells him before she dies, that if he finds another wife, she would take it as a compliment. After her death, he thinks that the only way he can win Miss Love as his wife is to offer her the house and an arrangement.

After Grandpa's death, practically the whole town turns out for the funeral party, which is all according to Grandpa's plans. Will Tweedy is not too pleased, however, when the will is read. Grandpa has left him four hundred dollars for his education, provided that he comes into Grandpa's store regularly for a period of at least ten years after leaving college. This had been a sore point between the two of them.

Young **Miss Love Simpson** certainly surprises the small town of Cold Sassy when she accepts Grandpa's offer of marriage. Although Grandpa finally tells Love of his true feelings for her, Love has decided that she will never marry, which is why she accepted Grandpa's arrangement in the first place. When he said he just wanted a housekeeper, that is all she expected to be. But her initial reason for not marrying Grandpa in the true sense is not because she does not love him. She has a dark secret: when she was a child her stepfather raped her. Since then Miss Love has felt that she has been defiled and therefore could never be worthy of marriage.

But true love wins, even in a May-December romance. When Grandpa later becomes sick with pneumonia, Love is worried that he will not learn that he is to be a father again. Will is tactful enough to go downstairs when he hears Love about to tell Grandpa the news. He never learns Grandpa's reaction, however, for soon Miss Love's scream wakes Will up, and he knows Grandpa has died.

Will's **mama** is usually the mildest of persons, but she really gets herself riled up over Grandpa's marriage plans. A plain, no-nonsense woman, she fears what the town will say. Actually, she is a bit afraid of Grandpa, since she is not sure whether he has forgiven her for being a girl (she thinks he wanted a son) and for marrying a Presbyterian, although as far as Will can tell, Grandpa has never shown anything but approval of his father. In fact, according to the story, when Mama announced her intention to marry Will's dad, the deacons of the Baptist church turned her right out of communion. Grandpa was furious, and he stood up for her against all of them. Will can't quite understand why Mama doesn't return the favor by defending his marriage.

Will understands **Aunt Loma**'s reaction a little better. Besides Will's mama, she is the only child of Grandpa and Granny to live more than a few years. She is spoiled and becomes very upset when she doesn't get her own way. In Cold Sassy, people say that Aunt Loma was behind the door when they passed out tact. Will is not fond of his aunt. She is only six years older than he is, yet she bosses him around all the time. Will feels a little sorry for Miss Love Simpson, who has to contend with the willful Loma. As it turns out, however, Miss Love proves to be a pretty good match for Will's red-haired and spoiled relative.

Lightfoot McLendon, the "mill" girl, is the recipient of Will Tweedy's first real kiss. Will may never forget it, but Lightfoot seems to. She announces that she is going to get married to Hosie Roach, now that Grandpa has given him a job at the store. But she promises she will never forget Will.

Further Reading

Berger, Laura Standley, ed. *Twentieth-Century Young Adult Writers.* 1st ed. Detroit: St. James, 1995.

Burns, Olive Ann. "Boy, Howdy, Ma'am, You Have Sent Us a Fine Book." *English Journal* 78, no. 8 (December 1989): 16-20.

Contemporary Authors New Revision Series. Vol. 41. Detroit: Gale Research, 1993.

Something about the Author. Vol. 65. Detroit: Gale Research, 1991.

Orson Scott Card

1951-, American novelist

Ender's Game

(science fiction, 1985)

PLOT: Andrew Wiggin, nicknamed Ender, is the third super-intelligent child born to the Wiggin family, at some unspecified time far in the future. Both his brother Peter, who is four years his senior, and his sister Valentine, who is two years older, have already been scouted as candidates for the elite Battle School. The Battle School is a training institution designed to produce leaders for the inevitable third war with the buggers, a race of intelligent grasshopper-like beings who have lost their first two attempts to conquer Earth and its planetary colonies. Ender's siblings were ultimately found to be unsuitable because Peter is too cruel and hateful to work with others, while Valentine is the opposite—too pacifistic and conciliatory. Ender is carefully monitored from an early age as well. Colonel Graff, the principal of the Battle School, is convinced of Ender's potential when, at age six, Ender courageously faces a group of older bullies at school and (unknowingly) fatally wounds their ringleader. Then Graff decides to take Ender away for training in hopes of making him the next commander of world federation forces, following in the footsteps of Mazer Rackham, who led the world to victory during the last invasion sixty years before.

Ender is taken on a space flight to the school, where he becomes a "Launchie," or beginning student. Graff deliberately arranges a number of grueling experiences that will test the boy's endurance and ability to act alone. These include alienating him from other trainees, placing him in a position of ridicule with students older than himself, and forcing him to think and make difficult decisions. He passes every test, but not without damage to the sensitive side of his nature. In time, he gains the respect of his fellow Launchies and assumes a leadership role among the students. He gradually makes a circle of friends and admirers with such unusual names as Shen, Alai, Dink Mecker, and Petra Arkanian—the only girl in his original training group. He also makes some enemies, principally Bonitio De Madrid, nicknamed Bonzo, an older boy who resents Ender's growing power.

Ender becomes the commander of one of the student armies and leads them to victory in mock battles despite unbelievable odds. He also wins a showdown fight that Bonzo stages, although news of Bonzo's subsequent death from his wounds is kept from Ender to prevent feelings of remorse. In the meantime, Peter and Valentine secretly gain access to the adult communication network on Earth and begin writing influential political polemics under the pen names of Locke and Demosthenes. Peter, however, is still not able to disguise his frightening desire for power.

After four years in Battle College, where he has succeeded beyond all expectations, Ender, now only ten, is sent to Commander School on the planet Eros. Here, his only teacher is the legendary Mazer

Rackham. Ender is reunited with his Battle School colleagues via an electronic simulation, and under his leadership they engage in a series of major mock battles in space against the buggers. After their final victory, it is revealed that the war was real and Ender has saved the Earth and virtually wiped out the alien race. Sickened by all the death and destruction he has caused, Ender decides to accept Valentine's invitation to become a colonist on a planet that once belonged to the buggers. Ender, now barely a teenager, will be its first governor.

Card continues the Ender books with the sequels Speaker for the Dead *(1986) and* Xenocide *(1991).*

CHARACTERS: This novel is the first of the Ender series, which continues with *Speaker for the Dead* and *Xenocide.* Some of its major themes include childhood and the methods and consequences of psychological manipulation.

The hero of the novel is **Ender Wiggin**, a most unusual child whose great intelligence and original thinking make him a born leader. At first Graff is afraid that Ender is "too malleable" and "too willing to submerge himself in someone else's will" to become an effective military leader. Through all the ordeals he faces, however, Ender preserves his own identity while becoming a shrewd strategist and commander. Although he sometimes feels lonely and persecuted, Ender hardens himself physically and psychologically to achieve an almost superhuman position of influence and power. Through intense conditioning, he learns to show only the tough, resolute, sometimes heartless side of his personality. Outwardly he shows a killer instinct, while inwardly his gentle nature never leaves him. He loves his sister and is sickened by unnecessary death. That he is responsible for the deaths of two of his tormentors is deliberately kept from him by adults who fear that his conscience will cause him to drop out of the training program. In the end, he has been manipulated so thoroughly by Graff, Rackham, and others that he becomes suspicious of everyone's motives and feels he can trust no one. His disillusionment exhausts him, but he finally overcomes it. Since he is basically a survivor and an idealist, Ender becomes a colonist, hoping one day to bring the forces of the Earth and the buggers together in a lasting peace.

Ender's two siblings, **Peter** and **Valentine Wiggin**, are opposites in every way except for the amazing intelligence they share. Peter is cunning and diabolically cruel. He enjoys torturing animals and is so filled with jealousy for his younger brother that he contemplates killing him. Graff accurately calls him "one of the most ruthless and unreliable of human beings" and "a husbandman of pain." He is also devious and can present an appearance of friendship and goodness that disguises his inner nature: he believes that "the power to cause pain is the only power." Although Peter possesses "the soul of a jackal," and his ultimate goal is power, he is able to funnel his energy into writing anonymous political statements on computer networks.

Whereas Peter exploits others' fears and weaknesses for his own gain, Valentine influences people by using praise and her innate good nature. She has a great sense of adventure and is an active partner with her brother in the Locke-Demosthenes hoax, an enterprise that also displays her great writing talent. She is aware of Peter's wickedness but manages to deflect it from herself. Her overriding concern is for Ender. She acts as a stabilizing influence in his life, and ultimately it is her love that prevents him from returning to Earth after the war, where he would fall under the evil manipulations of Peter.

Colonel Hyrum Graff, the director of primary training at the Battle School, says that his mission in life is "to produce the best soldiers in the world." His dedication to this ideal, particularly in Ender's case, is fanatical and obsessive. In order to turn Ender into an efficient fighting machine, he forces the boy to endure such emotional and physical pain that Ender almost cracks. This fanaticism prevents Graff from intervening in the Ender-Bonzo confrontation, even though he knows it will lead to the death of one of the boys. Although he goes to trial for his actions, he is later acquitted. Ironically, Graff's radical and seemingly inhuman schemes are successful. Ender emerges from his grueling ordeals to become the world's savior.

Bonitio De Madrid—or **Bonzo** for short—is a tall, slender, aristocratic young man with a strong sense of Spanish honor. He is also Ender's nemesis. When new to the school, Ender is placed under Bonzo's command. At first Bonzo is contemptuous of the six-year-old and does not allow Ender to participate in the war games. When Ender later disobeys and wins honors, Bonzo can no longer tolerate the rivalry and has Ender transferred to another group. When Ender eventually bests Bonzo in the war games, the resulting shame and loss of respect lead Bonzo to provoke the fight in which he is killed. The other powerful influence in Ender's training is **Mazer Rackham**, the legendary commander who led the Earth's forces to victory in previous wars. Like Graff, he is totally dedicated to his mission: preventing a bugger victory at any cost. He employs ruthless, harsh, and cruel tactics to train Ender, and rationalizes their use by pointing to the sacrifices he himself has made to help train new leaders.

Ender's friends include **Dink Mecker**, who is quite wise and knows how to play the power game. At first he believes that the bugger scare is a hoax, but in Ender's time of crisis he is a staunch supporter. **Shen**, a small, ambitious Launchie, becomes one of Ender's first friends. **Alai**, who is Arabic, is at first one of Ender's rivals, but gradually the two develop a friendship based on mutual respect and admiration. Ender's only female friend at school is **Petra Arkanian**, a tough, aggressive fighter who takes no abuse from the boys and dishes out her share of insults.

Further Reading

Authors and Artists for Young Adults. Vol. 11. Detroit: Gale Research, 1993.

Berger, Laura Standley, ed. *Twentieth-Century Young Adult Writers.* 1st ed. Detroit: St. James, 1994.

Contemporary Authors New Revision Series. Vol. 27. Detroit: Gale Research, 1989.

Contemporary Literary Criticism. Vols. 44, 47, 50. Detroit: Gale Research, 1987, 1988, 1988.

Fletcher, Marilyn P., ed. *Reader's Guide to Twentieth-Century Science Fiction.* Chicago: American Library Association, 1991.

Ryan, Bryan, ed. *Major Twentieth-Century Writers: A Selection of Sketches from Contemporary Authors.* Detroit: Gale Research, 1991.

Schellinger, Paul E., and Noelle Watson, eds. *Twentieth-Century Science Fiction Writers.* 3rd ed. Chicago: St. James, 1992.

Alden R. Carter

1947-, American young adult novelist

Up Country

(young adult novel, 1989)

PLOT: Sixteen-year-old Carl Staggers has problems. His mother, Veronica, is an alcoholic and often brings strange men home at night. Carl also has several stolen car stereos at home that he is working on. Handy with electronics, he plans to sell the stereos and save his money so he can escape Milwaukee and his mother. Carl wants to continue his education and get an engineering degree. Toward this end, his friend Steve steals stereos from cars and gives them to Carl to fix. Then they split the money they get from selling them.

At Christmas time, his mother is picked up for drunk driving and sent to a rehabilitation center. Carl, despite his protests, is sent to northern Wisconsin to live with his Uncle Glen and Aunt June, whom he barely remembers, and their son, Bob. Although life is boring for Carl at first in Blind River, he is gradually drawn into the family and community life. He develops a friendship with a girl named Signa, yet he is determined to get back to Milwaukee and his plan.

More and more, as Carl realizes that his mother is not responding to treatment, he feels responsible for her. For the first time, he begins to doubt the feasibility of his plan. Then he is called back to

Milwaukee by the police, who have picked up Steve and learned about the stolen stereos. Carl faces reform school. Even if he can avoid this fate, he feels he must return to his mother. Either way, his dream plan is lost.

But a social worker named Mullan fixes things so that Carl will not go to reform school. Instead, he must work to return the three thousand dollars he owes from the stolen stereos. Given a choice as to what to do next, he decides to return to his mother to help her. But after a judge warns him that he will be severely punished if he breaks the law again, Carl sees what his future must be. He realizes that he can't help his mother and that he must live his own life. Carl's aunt and uncle are given custody over him, and he looks forward to a promise of a new life up country.

CHARACTERS: Carl Staggers is a boy trying to maintain some sense of balance in a life that is off-kilter. He is aware that his mother, Veronica, has a serious drinking problem, and he is aware of her frequent relationships with strange men. He is also well aware that what he and his friend Steve are doing with stolen stereos is illegal and dangerous. But Carl rationalizes that his plan somehow makes it all right, and that this is his only way out of the hopeless maze of despair and unhappiness in which he finds himself.

Carl has no one to turn to but himself. Rather than looking to his mother for guidance, he feels he must guide her. He has only a vague recollection of his father and that is from a snapshot. When he is sent to Blind River in northern Wisconsin, Carl is prepared to be bored in the small community with relatives he barely knows. Even though he admits to himself that his aunt and uncle are kind people and that even his cousin Bob is tolerable, Carl will not let himself become involved in family life or community; he also resists the beginning of what could be a romance with a schoolmate named Signa.

When Carl is called back to Milwaukee, he begins to doubt the possibility of his dream. He also begins to look at the truth of what he has been doing concerning stolen property. When he is given the choice of a foster home or returning up country, he chooses his aunt and uncle.

The school principal in Blind River, Mr. Dowdy, tells Carl that he is not responsible for his mother's drinking, but he will not listen. Carl can't accept the fact that he has to relinquish responsibility for his mother. It is only after the social worker Mullan tries to tell him that he has to think about his own needs, too, that Carl finally begins to mature and take charge of his own life. Sadly, he realizes that he can't go back to his former life. If his mother is to change, she is must do it on her own. Carl tells his mother that he will not be coming back, something his mother has already foreseen.

Carl's mother, **Veronica**, is an alcoholic and a prostitute. She promises her son time and again that she will straighten out, but when she goes to the rehabilitation home after her drunk driving charge, she does not respond well to treatment. It is then that Carl begins to feel that his place is with her back in Milwaukee, as if his presence there will somehow rehabilitate her. At the end of the novel when Carl tells his mother that he must move on, the reader is left with the feeling that Veronica knows full well that she has lost both herself and her son.

Uncle Glen and **Aunt June** are kind people who accept the troubled Carl into their home without judging him for his past. Although they try to involve him in their home life, they are met with resistance and apathy. Nonetheless, when Carl is given the choice of a foster home or returning to them, they accept him with open arms. But when Aunt June tries to get Carl to talk about his problems in Milwaukee, he refuses to talk to her. Carl's cousin **Bob** is a likeable youngster of about Carl's age, though he seems much younger to the street-smart Carl.

Carl meets **Signa Amundsen** in school and is obviously drawn to her. She shares his interests and offers him her friendship and the possibility of romance. But Carl is too caught up with his problems to open up to anyone. At first he regards life in the small town as boring. But little by little the friendship and kindness of Signa and his family begin to chip away at the emotional walls he has built.

Two people who help Carl mature are **Mr. Dowdy**, the school principal in Blind River, and **Mullan**, the social worker. They help him to see that his mother's drinking is a problem she must face and conquer and that he can't do it for her. They enable Carl to see that he can still love his mother and live his own life. She can't be allowed to ruin his dreams and his chances for happiness.

Further Reading

Authors and Artists for Young Adults. Vol. 17. Detroit: Gale Research, 1996.

Berger, Laura Standley, ed. *Twentieth-Century Young Adult Writers.* 1st ed. Detroit: St. James, 1995.

Cagle, Katherine R. "Love, Life and Potato Salad: An Interview with Alden Carter." *North Carolina Libraries* 49 (1991): 212-13.

Children's Literature Review. Vol. 22. Detroit: Gale Research, 1991.

Gallo, Donald R., ed. *Speaking for Ourselves, Too: More Autobiographical Sketches by Notable Authors for Young Adults.* Champaign-Urbana, IL: National Council of Teachers of English, 1993.

Something about the Author. Vol. 67. Detroit: Gale Research, 1992.

Something about the Author Autobiography Series. Vol. 18. Detroit: Gale Research, 1994.

Willa Cather

1876-1947, American novelist

My Ántonia

(novel, 1918)

PLOT: This novel, set almost entirely in rural Nebraska, spans a period of over thirty years in the late nineteenth and early twentieth centuries. Orphaned at age ten, Jim Burdon, the narrator, is sent with laborer Jake Marpole from Virginia to live with his grandparents on their farm near the town of Black Hawk, Nebraska. Their neighbors—Mr. and Mrs. Shimerda; their sons, nineteen-year-old Ambrosch and simple-minded Marek; and their daughters, Ántonia, a pretty fourteen-year-old, and her younger sister, Yulka—are poor immigrants recently arrived from Bohemia who live primitively in a dugout. The Shimerdas share their crowded household with Peter Krajiek, a conniving fellow Bohemian who takes advantage of the family.

As Jim adjusts to his new surroundings, he becomes attached to his loving grandparents, their farmhand Otto Fuchs, and especially to young Ántonia, an alert, friendly girl of independent spirit. At Mr. Shimerda's request, Jim begins teaching Ántonia to speak English. Through the Shimerdas, he also meets two lonely Russian immigrants, Peter and Pavel. Jim's first winter on the prairie is particularly severe. Mr. Shimerda becomes so despondent at the conditions under which his family is living that he kills himself. But with the help of friends, particularly the Burdons, the resourceful Shimerdas manage to survive the winter. Both Ambrosch and Ántonia find work as farm laborers, and eventually the family moves into a proper house.

In time, Jim and his grandparents relocate to Black Hawk, where Jim attends high school. Many farm girls, including Ántonia, move to town to work as domestics. Ántonia initially works for Jim's neighbors, the Harlings, who treat her as part of the family. But when she innocently visits a local dance palace after work and begins attracting young men, Mr. Harling fires her after she refuses to change her ways. She then goes to work for a licentious money lender, Wick Cutter, and eventually Jim must save her from being raped by him. Ántonia then finds work at a local hotel. After high school, Jim attends college in Lincoln and there renews his acquaintance with another hired girl from Black Hawk, Lena Lingard, who has become a successful dressmaker. Lena tells Jim that Ántonia has a serious boyfriend, Larry Donovan, who is a railway conductor.

Jim transfers to Harvard University and does not return to Black Hawk for several years. When he visits, he learns that Ántonia was jilted by Larry in Denver, where they were to be married, and returned in shame to the family farm to have a child. He goes to see her and finds a quieter, sadder Ántonia than the girl he remembers, but with the same trusting and indomitable nature. Twenty more years pass before Jim, who by this time is a successful New York lawyer trapped in a loveless marriage, again travels west. This time he learns that Ántonia has married Anton Cusak, and he makes a detour to visit the Cusak family on their farm. When he arrives, he is surrounded by a swarm of happy youngsters of various ages, all Ántonia's children. She has at last found fulfillment on the land she loves with a man who adores her. Jim is welcomed into the household. When he reluctantly leaves after a wonderful visit lasting several days, he is filled with memories of Ántonia, her family, and their struggles. Most of all he is struck by the fact that Ántonia, though battered and oppressed, never lost her passion for life.

CHARACTERS: Told in simple, moving prose, this tribute to America's pioneer women is widely considered to be Willa Cather's finest novel. Dominating the work is the character of **Ántonia Shimerda**, who overcomes many obstacles and tragedies to finally reach fulfillment with a loving family on the land that is her heritage. Ántonia is introduced as a lively, friendly young girl who is also shrewd and intelligent. When Jim meets Ántonia, she is pretty, with big, warm eyes and brown curly hair, as well as being quick, eager to learn, and hardworking. She is also deeply devoted to her family, her Bohemian roots, and the father she adores. Her only fault is that she can sometimes be too trusting and kind. An enthusiastic and outgoing woman, Ántonia approaches cooking, farming, and learning the English language with equal zeal.

Though Ántonia is proud and independent, she is also deeply bound by family tradition. For example, she unquestioningly defers to her older brother after her father dies and sacrifices her own life by working first as a farm laborer and later as a domestic to help her family. In matters involving her

The life and struggles of young Ántonia, an immigrant girl from Bohemia, have a dramatic impact on the idealistic Jim Burdon in Cather's 1918 novel.

own destiny, however, she proves to be a strong-willed person who refuses to be dominated unfairly. Among other instances, this is shown when she leaves the security and love of the Harling household when she believes that Mr. Harling is imposing unfair restrictions on her personal life. Ántonia is also fun-loving and vivacious, with a profound belief in the goodness of other people. At one point she says, "I never could believe harm of anyone I loved." This belief leads to betrayal, but not defeat. At the end of the novel she emerges like a true earth-mother, battered but not diminished.

The book's narrator, **Jim Burdon**, possesses a "natural romantic and ardent disposition." He is a dreamer who approaches life with great excitement and forms strong friendships. Jim is also a great lover of nature who marvels at the awesome beauty of the Nebraska farmlands, the abundant flora and fauna, and the wonder of seasonal changes. He believes in truth and honesty, so he rejects the affected and artificial behavior of his peers in favor of the genuine, sincere friendships he forms at the local dance palace, including those with Ántonia and Lena Lingard. He is also a devoted, loving, and obedient grandson. When his grandmother objects to his mixing with the "riffraff" at the dance house, for example, he stays away to give his grandparents peace of mind. Jim is loyal, sympathetic, and solicitous of the welfare of others. Unfortunately, his trusting and pliant nature leads him into a marriage that produces wealth but not happiness.

Jim's grandparents are of hardy pioneer stock. **Grandfather Burdon** is a dignified, religious man who shows tolerance and understanding toward all people regardless of their background and culture. Though he is sometimes undemonstrative, his careful deliberation in thought and action lends stability to the household. Like his wife, he believes in the Christian tradition of helping one's neighbors, and so he gives unselfishly to the unfortunate Shimerda family. **Grandmother Burdon** is a tall woman with a loving disposition. She is intelligent, alert, hardworking, and an excellent housekeeper. She is also conscious of decorum and correct behavior and tries to instill these qualities in young Jim.

The Burdons' two hired hands are **Otto Fuchs** and **Jake Marpole**. Otto, an immigrant from Austria, possesses a colorful, magnetic personality. A former cowboy, stage-driver, bartender, and miner, he is full of wonderful stories and songs. Jim loves this man, who looks like a desperado with his curly mustache and sombrero. Otto teaches Jim many practical skills, including horsemanship. On the other hand, Jake Marpole, a Virginia mountain boy, is somewhat slow-witted and given to violent fits of temper, which are followed by periods of great remorse and contrition. Jake is well-meaning, trusting, and somewhat naive. The Burdons worry about the fate of this illiterate, vulnerable man when he and Otto leave the farm after the Burdons move to Black Hawk.

The head of Ántonia's family at the novel's beginning is **Mr. Shimerda**, who has arrived in Nebraska already old and frail. He knows nothing about farming, having been forced to emigrate from his comfortable, respectable life as a weaver in Bohemia by his ambitious wife, who wanted new opportunities for her family. He is ill-equipped to cope in this environment and is easily exploited by **Peter Krajiek**, their unwanted boarder. Peter cheated the family when he sold them the dugout and their initial provisions, and he continues to control them by acting as their interpreter and link with the outside world. Mr. Shimerda is a pathetic, tragic figure. He begins the story as a tall, proud gentleman who loves the finer things in life, especially music, and is punctilious in his old world dress and manners. But he soon becomes depressed by the terrible living conditions his family endures. Realizing that he is unable to change the situation, he gradually falls into fits of melancholy. Losing hope and the will to live, this dignified, loving man commits suicide by shooting himself.

Mrs. Shimerda is totally unlike her husband. She is basically a mean-spirited woman who is overly ambitious for her family. Always complaining and dour, she plays on the sympathy of others to get her way and is envious of those more fortunate than herself. When she feels outsiders are unduly interfering, she shows a conceited, boastful, and demanding nature. Jim's grandparents tolerate her and show sympathy, but young Jim actively dislikes her. The Shimerda's oldest son, **Ambrosch Shimerda**, is a short, broad-backed, peasant-like man who, after his father's death, rules the Shimerda household, including Ántonia. He is sly and untrusting and is disliked by most people. Nevertheless, he is a genuinely religious man who works hard and makes great sacrifices to help his family. **Pavel**, a sickly farmhand, and his friend, **Peter**, are two industrious, taciturn Russians who live together in a log house and work for the Shimerdas. In their homeland, they sacrificed a young bride by throwing her out of their sleigh when it was attacked by wolves. As a result, they were ostracized and forced to emigrate to the new world. After Pavel's death from consumption, Peter moves on.

Other residents of Black Hawk include the middle-class Harling family, who take in Ántonia.

Mrs. Harling is an energetic, bright, twinkling woman who genuinely loves Ántonia and is unhappy when she leaves. **Wick Cutter**, Ántonia's employer after the Harlings, is a villainous hypocrite who gives outward signs of respectability while planning his seduction of Ántonia. His hatred of his wife leads him to murder her and then commit suicide. **Lena Lingard**, a devoted friend to Jim, is the daughter of humble Norwegian parents who overcomes her background through sheer determination to become a leading dressmaker in Lincoln. **Larry Donovan**, a dishonest passenger conductor on the railway, leads Ántonia on with promises of marriage. When his crimes are discovered, however, he flees, leaving her unmarried and pregnant.

Further Reading

Arnold, Marilyn, ed. *A Reader's Companion to the Fiction of Willa Cather.* Westport, CT: Greenwood Press, 1993.

Baechler, Lea, ed. *Modern American Women Writers.* New York: Collier, 1993.

Bennett, Mildred. *The World of Willa Cather.* Lincoln: University of Nebraska Press, 1961.

Bloom, Edward A., and Lillian D. Bloom. *Willa Cather's Gift of Sympathy.* Carbondale: Southern Illinois University Press, 1962.

Bloom, Harold. *Ántonia.* New York: Chelsea House, 1991.

Brown, E. K., and Leon Edel. *Willa Cather: A Critical Biography.* New York: Knopf, 1953.

Bruccoli, Matthew J., and Richard Layman, eds. *Realism, Naturalism and Local Color, 1865-1917.* Vol. 3 of *Concise Dictionary of American Literary Biography.* Detroit: Gale Research, 1988.

Daiches, David. *Willa Cather: A Critical Introduction.* Boston: Twayne, 1975.

Martine, James J., ed. *American Novelists, 1910-1945.* Vol. 9 of *Dictionary of Literary Biography.* Detroit: Gale Research, 1981.

Gerber, Philip. *Willa Cather.* Boston: Twayne, 1975.

Keene, Ann T. *Willa Cather.* New York: Messner, 1995.

Lee, Hermione. *Willa Cather: Double Lives.* New York: Pantheon, 1990.

Magill, Frank N., ed. *Critical Survey of Long Fiction: English Language Series,* Vol. 2. Englewood Cliffs, NJ: Prentice-Hall, 1983.

O'Brien, Sharon. *Willa Cather.* New York: Chelsea House, 1995.

Randall, John H. III. *The Landscape and the Looking Glass: Willa Cather's Search for Value.* Boston: Houghton, 1960.

Rosowski, Susan J. *The Voyage Perilous: Willa Cather's Romanticism.* Lincoln: University of Nebraska Press, 1986.

Schroeder, James, ed. *Willa Cather and Her Critics.* Ithaca, NY: Cornell University Press, 1967.

Slote, Bernice, and Virginia Faulkner, eds. *The Art of Willa Cather.* Lincoln: University of Nebraska Press, 1974.

Something about the Author. Vol. 30. Detroit: Gale Research, 1983.

Twentieth Century Literary Criticism. Vols. 1, 11, 31. Detroit: Gale Research, 1978, 1983, 1989.

Alice Childress

1920-, American young adult novelist

A Hero Ain't Nothin' but a Sandwich

(young adult novel, 1973)

PLOT: Benjie Johnson, a thirteen-year-old African American boy, lives in a squalid Harlem tenement apartment with his hardworking, devoted mother, Rose, his aging grandmother, Mrs. Ransom Bell, and Rose's common-law husband of four years, the quiet, responsible Butler Craig. Rose's husband had abandoned the family many years before, but now Rose has found fulfillment in her loving relationship with Butler. Benjie is a likable, friendly youngster whose drug use begins quietly with a few marijuana joints shared with friends like Jimmy-Lee Powell. Soon Benjie moves to harder stuff like heroin and is unable to control his escalating habit. He becomes distant and defensive with his family and gradually loses the friendship of Jimmy-Lee, who can no longer communicate with him.

Nigeria Greene, a black nationalist and seventh-grade teacher at Benjie's junior high school, notices telltale signs of drug abuse, such as Benjie's nodding off to sleep in class. He reports this to Bernard Cohen, Benjie's English teacher and one of the few white teachers at the school. As a result, Benjie spends a week in a detoxification center. Back home everyone tries to give him advice and support, but feelings of stress and tension persist. When Benjie steals some of Butler's clothes to get money for a fix, Butler decides that his presence in the apartment is adding to the boy's problems and moves downstairs to a vacant room. Unhappy over Butler's absence, Rose tries everything in her power to help rehabilitate Benjie, even to the point of visiting a spiritualist who sells her a fake cure-all.

Eventually, Butler catches Benjie stealing a toaster from a neighbor's kitchen and chases him to the roof of their building. When Benjie loses his footing, Butler grabs him. Dangling six stories above the street, Benjie begs Butler to drop him because he wants to die. Instead, Butler drags him to safety and holds him in his arms. This episode helps convince Benjie that Butler really loves him. Later, when he is suffering from withdrawal pains, Benjie writes over and over again, "Butler is my father." Benjie appears to reach a turning point when he attends the funeral of a fellow junkie who has died of an overdose. At the end of the novel, there are other encouraging signs that he might be able to kick the habit: he faithfully visits his parole officer; he becomes trustworthy with money; he resumes his friendship with Jimmy-Lee; and, best of all, he begins calling Butler "Dad."

CHARACTERS: Several people act as narrators in this novel, including Benjie, his family members, his teachers, and his friends. Besides providing a variety of points of view on Benjie's story, this narrative technique also brings to life a gallery of interesting characters who represent different attitudes and backgrounds.

Since Benjie's birth and her husband's departure, **Rose Johnson** has had the sole responsibility of supporting herself, her mother, and her young son. To accomplish this, she works two jobs—full-time in a factory and, on weekends, part-time for a catering service. She adores Benjie and is heartsick when he slips into a life of drugs. On the one hand, she welcomes Butler's love and attention, but on the other she finds it difficult to deal with the resentment and hostility that this brings out in Benjie. Though she is filled with tenderness and compassion for her son, Rose often finds it impossible to express these feelings to him directly.

Butler Craig, Benjie's more-or-less stepfather, is in a difficult position. He wants to counsel and help Benjie, but he can't break through the barriers of the boy's resentment. Butler is a stable, hardworking man who shoulders many of Rose's household responsibilities without complaint. Strong, unselfish, dependable, and a perfect role model for Benjie, he is devoted to Rose and her family. Although he now works as a maintenance man (Benjie calls him a plain janitor) in a downtown building, he had once hoped to become a great jazz saxophonist. The need for a steady income forced him to shelve those dreams, however.

Benjie's grandmother, **Mrs. Ransom Bell**, has become fearful and despondent in her old age. Afraid to leave the apartment because she was recently robbed and beaten outside her church, she sits indoors and broods. As the daughter of Mississippi sharecroppers, she has led a tough life. She even spent some time dancing in speakeasies during prohibition in the 1920s. Her devoted husband died when Rose was young, and since then Mrs. Bell has found increasing solace in her religion. Like her daughter, she is distraught over Benjie's drug problem.

At the center of the novel is **Benjie Johnson**, a well-liked, friendly, good-hearted youngster who is fatherless and unhappy about the terrible environment in which he lives. He feels trapped in his tight family circle, and he thinks that Butler has stolen the love intended for him. Benjie also lacks a sense of identity and belonging, which he perceives as a gap in his life. He finds school to be a drag and sees no future for himself growing up in Harlem. He voices this inner despair and disillusionment when he states that "a hero ain't nothin' but a sandwich." When he first begins to take out his frustrations by using drugs, he vehemently denies his dependency and rebels against anyone who tries to warn him about his growing habit. Later, he rationalizes by claiming that he is experimenting with drugs in order to prepare for a career as a social worker. Finally, his innate honesty and intelligence make him face reality and try to kick the habit. His friends and family hope it is not too late.

Benjie's dearest friend is **Jimmy-Lee Powell**, a trusting, loyal buddy who feels guilty for giving Benjie his first joint. Jimmy-Lee stops after their one experiment with pot, and he tries everything he can think of to prevent Benjie's descent into addiction, but his efforts are rebuffed. As Jimmy-Lee wisely says, "Friendship begins to split when one is caught in the habit and the other is not." Although Jimmy-Lee's home life is not ideal—his father, a former freedom-rider, has become a street-corner preacher, while his mother works full-time to sustain the household—the boy is hopeful about his future and happy to welcome Benjie back as his friend.

The two junior-high teachers who show a special interest in and affection for Benjie present a study in contrasts. The first, **Bernard Cohen**, is a caring, white, Jewish teacher who is subjected to reverse discrimination in his practically all-black school. He feels stigmatized by his whiteness and resents the humiliating comments of many of his students. He is also sickened by the drug scene and by the many classroom interruptions that prevent him from teaching effectively. Though he would like to transfer, he believes that white teachers can make important contributions in ghetto schools. At heart, he is a middle-class liberal who believes in racial integration. Though a dedicated and effective teacher, he senses increasing hostility from his colleagues, particularly the black militant **Nigeria Greene**, another popular seventh-grade teacher. Nigeria, "built like an oversized football player," is bitter about his country's racist history. He instills feelings of black pride in his students at every opportunity and encourages them to stand up for their rights. Though he is often accused of fomenting tension and hostility, he believes that extreme measures must be taken to right society's wrongs. When he attends testimonials and similar functions for black causes, he has the uneasy feeling that perhaps he is adopting some of the white man's values he professes to reject.

Rainbow Jordan

(young adult novel, 1981)

PLOT: When Rainbow Jordan was born, her mother and father, Kathie and Leroy, were only fifteen and sixteen. Although they got married, neither was prepared for the responsibilities of raising a family. They soon separated, and Leroy moved to Detroit. Since then, Rainbow's life has been played out in a series of rooming houses and foster homes. Without bankable skills, Kathie makes her living as a go-go dancer. At the time the story begins, she is out of town on a gig with her current manager-lover, Burke. Rainbow, now fourteen and mature for her age, is being sent back to the home of an "interim guardian" where she has stayed before.

The guardian is Josephine Lamont, a dressmaker. She dotes on her accountant husband, Hal Lamont, even though she knows he has roving eyes and takes unfair advantage of her. When Rainbow arrives, Hal is absent, supposedly visiting a relative. Miss Josie is a good-hearted soul who believes in the sanctity of middle-class values and in keeping up appearances regardless of the circumstances. Rainbow is also living in a dream world, believing that one day Kathie, whom she adores, will return and provide her with a stable and secure home life. At school, Rainbow is secretive about her real situation, even maintaining that Miss Josie is her aunt.

Rainbow's boyfriend is Eljay, an attractive, fast-talking kid who pressures her to have sex with him. Other friends are Buster and his girlfriend Beryl, an undisciplined girl who later finds that Buster has made her pregnant. Because Rainbow is afraid that she will lose Eljay if she continues to hold out, she arranges a tryst at her mother's vacant apartment. When Eljay arrives, however, he has a new girlfriend with him. Rainbow, again rejected and humiliated, angrily sends them both away. In the meantime, Josie discovers that the apartment key is missing and goes to the apartment, where Rainbow provides a pathetically honest description of what happened.

Back at the Lamont apartment, Rainbow discovers that Hal has left Josie for a much younger

Despite a life of abuse and poverty, Rainbow Jordan remains hopeful, trusting, and, in the end, triumphant.

woman. The two women talk about their respective problems and realize that they need more honesty in their lives. Josie must lower her defenses and accept the realities of life, and Rainbow must realize that her mother does not love her as much as she believes. The next day is parent conference day at school. Though Rainbow has begged her mother to be there, she does not appear. Josie volunteers to attend as her "aunt," but Rainbow says, "Let's do it right. I'm tellin' them you my friend who take care of me cause my mother is away."

CHARACTERS: The novel, often told in the strong street language of Harlem, is narrated by three different protagonists: Kathie Jordan, her daughter, Rainbow, and Miss Josie Lamont. This technique adds depth to the story and gives it a layered effect.

Rainbow's mother, **Kathie Jordan**, is basically well-meaning, but because she is very attractive and was raised as a street kid, she gravitates toward the fast life and has a series of boyfriends. Although she loves her daughter, she rebels against the confines and restrictions of having to care for her. Her frustration leads her to lash out both verbally and physically against Rainbow, but afterward, filled with remorse and guilt, she assuages her conscience by giving her expensive gifts. Kathie is fearful of growing old without the security of a husband, and therefore is often exploited by violent men who take advantage of her.

In spite of the mistreatment **Rainbow Jordan** has endured in her brief life, she is a remarkably open and trusting girl. In her continual search for love and security, she often leaves herself vulnerable to being hurt. For example, she adores and forgives her mother, even though Kathie has subjected her to years of abuse. Rainbow is often exploited emotionally, which brings her periods of sorrow and heartbreak. At one point she says, "My soul is hurtin'," but being a resourceful girl without feelings of self-pity, she bounces back to try again. Rainbow is proud and at times defiant, but usually this bravura simply hides her inner loneliness and confusion. She is also conscientious in fulfilling her responsibilities, and honest and candid in her relationships. In the end, this inner strength allows her to triumph over the many humiliations, betrayals, and rejections she has suffered. By the end of the novel, readers are confident that Rainbow will continue to cope in the face of continuing troubles.

Josephine Lamont, or **Miss Josie**, supplies short-term care to youngsters supported by welfare authorities—partly because she and her husband can't have children of their own, and partly for the money. She is a responsible, kindly person who possesses sound values and a caring nature, but her reverence for bourgeois values and her pursuit of a life of decorum produce an atmosphere of affectation and artificiality in her household. For example, dresses are called garments, and dinner is always served by candlelight. She also tries desperately to avoid facing the reality that she is growing old. She lies about her age and uses hair dye and complexion lighteners to hide the aging process. Finally, she deceives herself about her husband's behavior. She is deeply devoted to him, but he continually cheats on her and eventually leaves her for a younger woman. Only when he writes asking for a divorce does she acknowledge that much of her life has been a sham. Miss Josie shows a genuine love for Rainbow and basically has a good heart. The various difficulties she experiences during the novel lead her to continue her search for love and security with greater honesty and truth.

Josie's husband, **Hal Lamont**, is a good-natured, cheerful accountant who longs for more adventure in his life than his well-meaning wife can give him. Though she showers love and attention on him, his roving eye leads him to find satisfaction elsewhere. He does have the decency to accept blame for the breakup of his marriage, however, and he promises to continue providing financial help to Josie.

Rainbow's friends include **Eljay**, a strutting show-off who carries a blaring boombox and attracts girls like flies. His attractive demeanor and brash ways capture Rainbow's heart to such an extent that she decides to give in to his persistent entreaties and have sex with him. Although he talks about birth control, he gives her no assurances that precautions will be taken. Fortunately for her, Rainbow waits too long and the fickle Eljay finds someone else to satisfy him. Rainbow's chum, **Beryl**, is given too much freedom and not enough guidance from her parents. As a result, she shoplifts and accepts money for quick feels from older men to buy the luxuries she wants. Eventually, she is impregnated by **Buster**, a pot-smoking young man who is not prepared for fatherhood.

Another unsavory character is Kathie's current escort, **Burke**. He is a smooth-talking, heavy-set, six-foot-tall man who, when he is drunk, becomes prone to fits of jealousy and terrible physical violence. Although he is attentive and pleasant when sober, Kathie is frightened of him but unable to escape his presence.

Further Reading

Collier, Laurie, and Joyce Nakamura, eds. *Major Authors and Illustrators for Children and Young Adults.* Detroit: Gale Research, 1993.

Contemporary Literary Criticism. Vols. 12, 15. Detroit: Gale Research, 1980, 1980.

Gallo, Donald R. *Speaking for Ourselves: Autobiographical Sketches by Notable Authors of Books for Young Adults.* Urbana, IL: National Council of Teachers of English, 1990.

Jordan, Shirley M. *Broken Silences: Interviews with Black and White Women Writers.* New Brunswick, NJ: Rutgers University Press, 1993.

Smith, Jessie Carney, ed. *Notable Black American Women.* Detroit: Gale Research, 1992.

Something about the Author. Vol. 48. Detroit: Gale Research, 1987.

Arthur C. Clarke

1917-, English science fiction novelist

Childhood's End

(science fiction, 1953)

PLOT: In this grim novel, Clarke takes his readers into a future in which Earth is ruled by an alien race of Overlords. The Overlords have positioned their ships over all of the planet's major cities. Six days after his race's arrival, the alien Karellen broadcasted a message to the human race, declaring himself to be Supervisor of Earth. Humans will be allowed to govern themselves, except in international affairs which will now be controlled by the Overlords. Their superior powers make all resistance futile. This is proven when Earth fires an atomic missile at one of the spaceships and it disappears without any effect.

Over the next fifty years, humanity learns not to disobey the Overlords, even though they do not understand precisely what their purpose is. These brilliant creatures from outer space, in a short span of time, eliminate all ignorance, poverty, disease, and fear from Earth, but at the price of complete domination.

No one, not even United Nations Secretary General Stormgren, who has been inside one of the spaceships for conferences, can fathom the Overlords' purpose. Stormgren knows that underground movements are afoot to overtake and defeat the Overlords, and he tries to convince the rebellious leaders that such efforts are futile. When Stormgren is kidnapped by rebels who wish to prove they are a threat to the Overlords, he is freed by Karellen. Karellen inflicts a kind of paralysis upon the kidnappers by slowing time for them so that Stormgren has a chance to escape, but only after Karellen has learned who the opposition leaders are.

The mystery of the Overlords intrigues Jan Rodricks, a young man studying for his doctorate in engineering, with a minor in astronomy, at the University of Cape Town. Through an accident stemming from a game played at a party, Jan stumbles upon some information that leads him to discover the small and insignificant star that must be the home of the Overlords. With the help of Professor Sullivan, he plans to stow away on a spaceship and make the journey to the Overlords' home world.

So begins a wondrous and fantastic space journey. When Jan returns, he has been gone for eighty years. He is met by Karellen, who finally reveals the unbelievable secret behind the appearance of the Overlords. Karellen explains that the Overlords are themselves controlled by what is called the Overmind. The Overmind—for reasons unknown to the Overlords—has been absorbing races from all over the universe, just as it is doing with the people of Earth. The Overmind has decided that because humans have been investigating the strange forces of telepathy and precognition, and coming too close to answers that might destroy the universe, that this is to be the last generation of humans on Earth.

As the only man to survive, Jan watches as the last atoms of Earth are simply leached away into space. Sitting in front of a darkened screen beyond the planet Pluto, Karellen watches in silence as the human race is wiped from his sight. As for his own race of creatures, Karellen does not know what fate awaits. They are at the mercy of the Overmind.

CHARACTERS: The character of **Karellen**, Supervisor for Earth, whom humans regard as the chief of the Overlords, is depicted as calm, all-knowing, and all-powerful. Yet, when the human race is about to disappear into nothingness, he reveals to Jan his own powerlessness. Karellen explains that a century ago the Overlords came to earth to save humankind from its own destruction. They eliminated disease, ignorance, and poverty. In all this time, humans have feared the Overlords, but Karellen notes that the true danger came from a more powerful source, one far greater than the Overlords and one that the Overlords must obey. Even the Overlords do not understand what this force, called the **Overmind**, is. However, the Overmind grew alarmed when earth scientists began to experiment with concepts such as telepathy and precognition. Fearing that humans might open a Pandora's box that would cause the eventual destruction of the universe, the Overlords were sent to control humanity, but especially to stop all work on paranormal psychology. The Overmind, says Karellen, is trying to extend its power. This transformation of mind, which has already absorbed many races, must now absorb the human race. And so, this will be the last generation of homo sapiens.

Engineering student **Jan Rodricks** begins his space odyssey with the accidental discovery of what he believes to be the home star of the Overlords. When he returns from his eighty-year journey, he finds that he will be the last of his kind. At the climax of history, he watches with almost detached interest as the stars grow dimmer and a great haze seems to take over Earth. In this utterly incredible moment, Jan experiences no fear or panic. Jan is portrayed as a calm and collected scientist who, like Karellen, accepts his fate when it becomes clear resistance is futile.

Stormgren, Secretary General of the United Nations, has more contact with Karellen than any human. An intelligent, dedicated man, he is the only one to experience the fantastic journey to the heart of the Supervisor's ship, some fifty kilometers above the earth. But Stormgren never sees Karellen during these visits; he can only hear him and sense the alien's presence. Stormgren respects Karellen, though he tries in various, mostly futile ways to extract more information from Karellen about the Overlords' mission.

2001: A Space Odyssey

(science fiction, 1968)

PLOT: Space navigators David Bowman and Frank Poole, along with three frozen hibernauts and a talkative computer named Hal, are aboard the spaceship *Discovery* on a mission to Saturn. They have been told that the purpose of the mission is to enter and explore the atmosphere of the planet. Trouble arises, however, when Hal announces that the computer's Fault Prediction Center indicates failure of one of the units within seventy-two hours. Although the faulty part is fixed, that is not the end of the astronauts' problems. Hal still insists there is trouble ahead. Faced with an increasingly frustrating and odd behaving Hal, Bowman threatens to turn the computer off. Before long, navigator Poole, working outside the ship, is disconnected from his safety lines and drifts off into space. The sleeping hibernauts are also disconnected from the pods that maintain their bodies and die. Bowman is left alone with Hal. Realizing that the computer killed the others to protect itself, Bowman disconnects all of Hal's circuits and is truly alone in space.

Dr. Heywood Floyd, communicating with the spaceship from Earth, finally tells Bowman the true reason for the mission. A monolith of hard, black material has been found on the Moon near the crater Tycho and its origins traced to the eighth satellite of Saturn, Japetus. It is evidence of a civilization some three million years ahead of humankind. Floyd believes that when the monolith was unearthed it triggered some kind of signal that will alert the alien civilization that built it that humanity has begun to venture out into space. Whether or not the aliens will be friends or foes, Floyd can't be sure.

Bowman sails on alone toward Japetus on an incredible mission into the unknown. As he approaches Japetus, he makes a startling discovery. On the moon's surface is a mile-high vertical slab—the big brother of the monolith found on Earth's moon. As Bowman nears this so-called Eye of Japetus, it is as though it blinks a signal and allows the *Discovery* to enter. Bowman calls back to Earth, "The thing's hollow—it goes on forever—and—oh my God!—it's *full of stars!*"

Bowman enters the monolith and voyages through time. When he returns, he has metamorphosed into a new being. He realizes he has awakened some awesome, unfathomable energy, and that he is now master of the Earth. Like a newborn infant, he doesn't understand who he is or what lies ahead, but he will learn.

Clarke has written three sequels to this novel: 2010: Odyssey Two *(1982),* 2061: Odyssey Three *(1988), and* 3001: The Final Odyssey *(1997).*

CHARACTERS: David Bowman is presented as an intelligent, nervy, highly trained technician. A consummate professional, he is able to endure the seven-year voyage to Saturn with great patience; and when Hal begins to threaten the mission, he coolly and decisively determines to disconnect the computer. Unfortunately, this leads to Poole and the three hibernauts' murders. Alone in deep space with only radio contact with Earth, Bowman shows great courage as he continues his new mission to discover the nature of the monolith on Japetus. He is able to adapt to his solitary existence. Filled with scientific curiosity and a need for adventure, Bowman has a thoroughly human reaction as he enters the Eye of Japetus. He allows his excitement to take over and exclaims with wonder that the monolith is "full of stars." Like his counterpart, **Frank Poole** is a highly trained and methodical worker, perfect for this mission. He goes about his chores with deliberate slowness, allowing for no error. Poole volunteers to go on a spacewalk to fix the faulty unit. He thus falls into the computer's trap when Hal directs the spacepod to hit Poole and drag his body out into space.

Perhaps the most interesting character of *2001* is not human at all. The highly advanced **Hal 9000** computer ("Hal" stands for Heuristically ALgorithmic computer) is the brain and nervous system of *Discovery.* Hal is a masterwork of the third computer breakthrough. The first breakthrough in the science appeared in the 1940s with the vacuum tube, which was replaced in the 1960s by solid-state microelectronics. In the 1980s, Clarke speculated at the time he wrote the book, neural networks similar to the human brain would be created, making Hal possible.

Hal's paranoid and eventually homicidal behavior is a hazard that results from his programming. Created to have an innocent view of the world, Hal does not understand the human practice of deception. When he is programmed by Dr. Floyd to conceal the true nature of the *Discovery*'s mission (which was also known to the hibernauts), the conflicting commands wreak havoc on the computer's circuitry and cause Hal to act erratically. Thus, when Bowman threatens to disconnect Hal, the computer reacts violently and kills Poole and the hibernauts.

Dr. Heywood Floyd had been called to the space station on the Moon—some two years before the *Discovery* sets out on its mission to Saturn—to see the monolith and speculate on its origins and purpose. He is put in charge of organizing the mission to Saturn, and it is also Dr. Floyd who is responsible for concealing the nature of the mission from Bowman and Poole. He did not know, however, that Hal would react so adversely to its conflicting orders. After the deaths of the other astronauts, Floyd tells Bowman, "At the moment, we do not know whether to hope or fear. We do not know if, out on the moons of Saturn, you will meet with good or with evil—or only with ruins a thousand times older than Troy."

Further Reading

Authors and Artists for Young Adults. Vol. 4. Detroit: Gale Research, 1990.

Berger, Laura Standley, ed. *Twentieth-Century Young Adult Writers.* 1st ed. Detroit: St. James, 1994.

Bleilor, E. F. *Science Fiction Writers.* New York: Scribner's, 1982.

Contemporary Literary Criticism. Vols. 1, 4, 13, 18, 35. Detroit: Gale Research, 1973, 1975, 1980, 1981, 1985.

De Montreville, Doris, and Elizabeth D. Crawford, eds. *Fourth Book of Junior Authors and Illustrators.* New York: H. W. Wilson, 1978.

Hollow, John. *The Science Fiction of Arthur C. Clarke.* Athens: Ohio University Press, 1987.

Moskowitz, Sam. *Seekers of Tomorrow: Masters of Modern Science Fiction.* New York: World, 1966.

Olander, Joseph D., and Martin H. Greenberg, eds. *Arthur C. Clarke.* New York: Taplinger, 1977.

Rabkin, Eric S. *Arthur C. Clarke.* Rev. ed. Mercer Island, WA: Starmont, 1980.

Samuelson, David N. *Arthur C. Clarke: A Primary and Secondary Bibliography.* Boston: Hall, 1981.

Slusser, George E. *The Space Odysseys of Arthur C. Clarke.* San Bernardino, CA: Borgo, 1978.

Smith, Curtis C., ed. *Twentieth-Century Science-Fiction Writers.* 2nd ed. Chicago: St. James, 1986.

Something about the Author. Vols. 13, 70. Detroit: Gale Research, 1978, 1993.

Ward, Martha, ed. *Authors of Books for Young People.* 3rd ed. Metuchen, NJ: Scarecrow, 1990.

Watson, Noelle. *Twentieth-Century Science Fiction Writers.* 3rd ed. Chicago: St. James, 1991.

Bill Cleaver

1920-1981, American novelist

Vera Cleaver

1919-1992, American novelist

Where the Lilies Bloom

(novel, 1969)

PLOT: In rural North Carolina, the Luther family is grubbing out a living in a ramshackle house on the edge of property owned by "all cheat and sneak" Kiser Pease. The family consists of an ailing father, Roy Luther, his fourteen-year-old daughter Mary Call, her older, simple-minded sister Devola, ten-year-old Romey, and five-year-old Irma Dean. Apart from a bit of gardening and sharecropping for Kiser, the Luthers earn a living by gathering witch hazel leaves and selling them to Mr. Connell, the local grocery store owner who has a nosy and interfering wife.

When Roy Luther suffers a massive, debilitating stoke, Mary Call assumes leadership of the family and resolves to keep the group together without asking for charity. Through a book that belonged to her dead mother, she educates herself and the children in the practice of wildcrafting, or gathering of wild medicinal plants to sell. Kiser, who in his mindless way is infatuated with Devola, catches pneumonia and, as payment for nursing him back to health, Mary Call has him deed their house and land to her family. Roy Luther dies and, according to his wishes, Mary Call and Romey bury him on the side of their mountain. Fearing that news of his death will mean separation and foster homes, Mary Call swears the youngsters to secrecy and begins an elaborate subterfuge to keep his death quiet.

The hardest person to discourage is Kiser Pease, who is intent on seeing Roy Luther to get permission to marry Devola. Mary Call eventually runs out of excuses, but a fortuitous car accident sends Kiser to the hospital, giving the family a reprieve.

The winter brings many misfortunes to the Luthers. The living room roof collapses, and Kiser's sister, Goldie, arrives, claiming that the Luther property is rightfully hers and that the family must vacate the house. When Kiser buys their property from his sister and gives it to the Luthers as a gift, Mary Call relents and allows him to marry Devola. After the marriage, Kiser becomes the children's legal guardian. By the time spring arrives in their valley, Devola has moved in with her husband, and the rest of the family is safe and secure in their own home.

CHARACTERS: Mary Call Luther, is the narrator and driving force in keeping her family together. Though only fourteen, she is more enterprising and courageous than most adults. Fiercely determined to fight adversity and dedicated to maintaining her family at any cost, she exhibits amazing strength of character and courage. She is practical, hard-working, and industrious. With amazing resourcefulness, she is able to counter every hardship and tribulation with tenacity and determination. Whether it be practicing wildcrafting or blackmailing Kiser to get a deed to their property, Mary Call is a warring crusader with an unerring belief in the righteousness of her cause. She devises ingenious solutions to her problems, only some of which work, but when they don't she picks up the pieces and starts over. When faced with Goldie's eviction notice, she says in true Scarlett O'Hara fashion, "My name is Mary Call Luther and someday I'm going to be a big shot. I've got the guts to be one. I'm not going to let this beat me. If it does, everything else will for the rest of my life."

Mary Call sacrifices herself to the point of not allowing herself to grieve over her father's death or giving herself time for personal grooming. The result is a wild, untamed look that matches her temperament. Intensely proud, she refuses to beg for help because, "Charity is one of the worst things there is. It does terrible things to people." Mary Call is crafty and cunning in handling others, but she is always the realist. Her fanatical sense of purpose and love of family, coupled with the great sacrifices she is forced to make for their well-being, often make her impatient with them, particularly when they seem to lack her grit and stick-to-it-iveness. At such times, she is apt to be overbearing and irritable. She forgets that they are children and lashes out, sometimes unreasonably, against them, especially when they don't obey her orders absolutely. At these times, she is also prone to bouts of self-pity that are understandable, considering the stress and responsibility she bears. Through these hardships, she gains self-knowledge, maturity, and a more accepting nature. Her resourcefulness, courage, and fortitude remain an inspiration; she shows that dignity and strength can exist in spite of poverty and the most adverse conditions. As she says, "Guts. It's what it takes to get along in this world."

Mary Call's father is **Roy Luther**, an honorable, highly principled man who has been worn down by poverty, the death of his wife, and the responsibility of four children. He has tried to instill in them sound moral values, an abhorrence of charity, and a belief in the importance of family. He rejects modern conventions to the point of insisting that, upon his death, there be neither a preacher nor undertaker but only a simple homemade burial. He is a loving, caring father and, when he dies, Mary Call wants to obey his wishes. She inherits from him his practical, unpretentious attitudes and distrust of strangers.

Mary Call is intensely protective toward her siblings, particularly the vulnerable **Devola**. At eighteen, she is stunningly beautiful with long, golden hair and exquisite features. Unfortunately, she is, in Mary Call's words, "cloudy-headed." Slow to learn and understand, she is, nevertheless, always cheerful and agreeable. A free, innocent spirit who is filled with goodness, love, and sympathy, Devola enjoys performing household chores like cooking and baking. Fearful that her simplicity and purity can be exploited, Mary Call is overly protective, particularly when it comes to Kiser, but, as Devola shows greater independence and confidence (for example, she is the only one who knows how to drive a car), Mary Call relents.

Like Mary Call, her ten-year-old brother **Romey** is mature beyond his years. A bright, sensitive youngster, he is anxious to share family responsibilities with his older sister. He is a slight, fine-boned boy who would rather read a book than play baseball. When Romey begins to feel that he is the man of the family, this macho pose causes some conflict with Mary Call, who at times can be bossy and overbearing. However, Romey can also be a compassionate, hard-working, understanding boy who is Mary Call's chief source of help and comfort. Like his sister, Romey matures as he copes with adversity. His youngest sister is five-year-old **Irma Dean**. She has a sweet disposition and is well-behaved and uncomplaining. Always good-natured, she is a resourceful little girl who bravely endures hardships. Her older siblings are devoted to her and her well-being.

The family's landlord is **Kiser Pease**, an ignorant, well-meaning farmer who is also their neighbor. Because Roy Luther worked for Kiser, Mary Call has a low opinion of the man—"He's mean and he's stingy and he's a bully," she declares. This evaluation is partly correct, but Kiser is transformed by his innocent and pure love for Devola. He suddenly becomes generous and unselfish toward the Luthers, showering them with presents, including livestock, food, and, ultimately, their house. Like a love-sick puppy, he becomes putty in Mary Call's hands. Kiser is superstitious (he even has a keyhole opening near the top of his chimney to provide an exit for witches), uneducated, and dense. In his simplicity and openness, Kiser often appears as a pathetic oaf whose genuine love for Devola causes him agony. He is far from handsome, especially due to his ugly, discolored teeth, and looks as if he is forty, though he is actually around thirty. Despite all his faults, plain, uncomplicated Kiser will make Devola a good husband.

Kiser's sister is the unsympathetic, hostile **Miss Goldie Pease**. Described as squat with blue, waffled hair and a long, humorless mouth, she is totally without compassion or charity. Tough as nails, she is unyielding in her plan to evict the Luthers. A crafty, uneducated woman, Goldie has delusions of grandeur and a mean spirit that brings difficult challenges to Mary Call.

The owner of the local general store five miles from the Luther home is kindly **Mr. Connell**. Always helpful and understanding, he often makes little gifts of food and supplies to Mary Call when his wife isn't looking. Described as short, meaty, and melancholy, Mr. Connell is dominated by his tall, stingy wife, who Mary Call says has a dishonest smile. **Mrs. Connell** is a nosy, interfering woman who, under the pretense of being a do-gooder, meddles in other people's business. She is a gossip who is determined to find out the truth about Roy Luther's health and thus causes many problems for Mary Call. Romey finally frightens her off their property one night by donning a bear skin that scares Mrs. Connell away.

Further Reading

Authors and Artists for Young Adults. Vol. 12. Detroit: Gale Research, 1994.

Berger, Laura Standley, ed. *Twentieth-Century Young Adult Writers.* 1st ed. Detroit: St. James, 1994.

Chevalier, Tracy, ed. *Twentieth-Century Children's Writers.* 3rd ed. Detroit: St. James, 1989.

Children's Literature Review. Vol. 6. Detroit: Gale Research, 1984.

De Montreville, Doris, and Doon Hill, eds. *Third Book of Junior Authors.* New York: H. W. Wilson, 1972.

Something about the Author. Vols. 22, 76. Detroit: Gale Research, 1981, 1994.

Ward, Martha, ed. *Authors of Books for Young People.* 3rd ed. Metuchen, NJ: Scarecrow, 1990.

Brock Cole

1938-, American novelist

The Goats

(young adult novel, 1987)

PLOT: An evening excursion from summer camp to Goat Island becomes a nightmare for young, vulnerable Howie. The target of a cruel joke, he is stripped of his clothes by fellow campers and left behind. But he finds a girl named Laura on the island who has suffered a similar fate. They realize that they are this year's designated goats—the social misfits who are the victims of the other campers' cruelty. Finding a log on the beach and clinging to it, they paddle to the mainland, where they break into a boarded-up summer cottage and find some clothes and provisions. The next day, they head for the public beach, take money from a parked car, and phone Laura's mother, busy businesswoman Maddy Golden, for help. (Howie's parents are archaeologists in Turkey and unavailable.)

But Maddy misunderstands the immediacy of her daughter's problem and promises to come for visitor's weekend, which is two days off. At a gas station, the two mingle with some inner-city kids, who are headed for a different camp. With the help of two of them, Tiwanda and Calvin, they stow away on a school bus and spend the night hidden in the camp's dormitories. They are surprised and gratified at the kindness they receive from these new friends, except for a sullen teenager named Pardoe.

Maddy is contacted by the authorities at camp about her daughter's absence. She sets out for the camp, where the situation is explained to her by the camp manager, Mr. Wells, and his assistant, counselor Margo Cutter. Meanwhile, with a five dollar loan from Tiwanda, the two runaways leave their hideout, but they are forced to spend most of the money on tampons because Laura is beginning her period. Through a clever ruse, Laura tricks a motel clerk into believing that they are the children of vacationers who have just checked out and now want to spend an extra night because of car trouble. The cleaning lady sees the youngsters in bed together (Howie is innocently helping Laura fight an attack of the shivers), suspects the worst, and reports them to an already-suspicious management.

After setting off a fire alarm, the two youngsters manage to escape. Back at the camp, Laura is able to speak to her mother. She explains how much she and Howie now mean to each other and that they can't be separated until his parents return. Maddy promises that Howie can stay with them, but he is so afraid of being returned to camp that he runs into the woods. Laura chases after him and reassures him. When Maddy arrives, the two walk to her car hand in hand.

CHARACTERS: Described by his camp counselors as "kind of wimpy" and "little and klutzy," **Howie Mitchell** is a bespectacled, pre-pubescent who is bookish and interested chiefly in science and learning, rather than sports or social popularity. A sensitive, friendless youngster, he is the son of two respected archaeologists who had him late in their lives. Although they love their son and want the best for him, they are at a loss as to what to do with him. Howie soon senses this and spends most of his time at home trying to be invisible. At camp he is easily labeled a social misfit, immature for his years and a perfect target for his peers' cruel joke. Howie has led a sheltered life and, when confronted with senseless brutality, he can neither comprehend nor cope with it. He is innocent and ill-prepared for his ordeal, but he is able to muster untapped inner resources. Though he is miserable, he comforts and protects Laura, refusing to feel sorry for himself, and even devises a scheme to get off the island. With his newfound sense of independence, he finds that he likes adventure and thrives on challenge and trials. At first Howie is more assertive than Laura and becomes the leader of the pair, but in time this situation changes and they share responsibilities. Howie blossoms when he realizes that a person his own age depends on him, trusts him, and even loves him. Resourceful, inventive, and still sexually innocent, he has a fanciful imagination and loves the unknown, the mysterious, and the unexplained. He is so honest and without guile that he worries about reimbursing everyone for the items they had to steal to survive. Through his experiences with Laura, Howie discovers a sense of self-worth. For the first time in his life, he is glad to be alive.

Thirteen-year-old **Laura Golden** has been classified by her campmates as "a real dog," the lowest category in their rating scale. She is skinny to the point of being gaunt, with shoulder blades that stick out and a face dominated by thick designer glasses. A counselor calls her "a little fox with glasses." Laura calls herself "socially retarded for my age." She is lonely, fearful, and completely dependent upon her mother. As she says, "I need somebody to take care of me!" Although she has begged her mother to take her home from camp, Laura is unaware of her unpopularity and not prepared for the terrible cruelty inflicted on her. She is crushed and devastated by the actions of her fellow campers. In agony she cries out to Howie, "I thought they liked me."

Adversity produces an amazing transformation in Laura. She learns to stand up for her rights, make decisions, lie when necessary, and take the initiative. Suddenly she ceases being a follower and gradually assumes a leadership role. She also responds to the love and attention others show her. She is touched by the kindness and concern of Tiwanda and the other inner-city kids who are so much poorer than she is. She finds that she can return Howie's care and solicitude with equal love and affection. With these changes comes a joy in being independent. After hatching the motel scheme, she suddenly says, "I'm brilliant, don't you think?" Laura demonstrates her new confidence and security in many ways: by assuming responsibility for Howie after their rescue, by learning to laugh and be tender toward others, and by calling herself by her real first name, Shadow, not Laura. In short, she has discovered that she has the strength never to be a goat again.

Laura's mother, **Maddy Golden**, is an ex-flower child whose husband has been institutionalized after a drug overdose. In a full reversal, she has become an independent, forceful businesswoman who has successfully risen to an important position in her office. She is a direct, dynamic woman who has unconsciously intimidated Laura and unknowingly made her overly dependent. Maddy genuinely loves her daughter and hopes that sending her to a summer camp will make her more relaxed and confident. Ironically, these goals are achieved in a way she didn't plan. Maddy's busy schedule has unfortunately made her remote from, and impatient with, her daughter. She expects too much of Laura and gives too little of herself. When the truth of Laura's harrowing experiences are revealed, she is sickened and realizes that she is partly to blame for Laura's problems and hopes to makes amends in the future.

During their ordeal, Howie and Laura get help from two black, inner-city kids from another camp. **Tiwanda** is a tall, heavy girl who has maintained a loving, caring attitude toward others in spite of growing up in a tough neighborhood. She is realistic and streetwise—a fact reflected in her language when she refers to whites as "the Man"—but also protective and giving. Without hope of recompense, she befriends the pathetic Laura, shares her possessions with her, and gives her five dollars when she leaves. Her compassion is not reserved only for those in need, however. For example, she refuses to pass judgement on Pardoe, whom the other campers hate and want punished. Because she has learned from her own adversity, she has come to accept life and its unfairness, while trying in her own small way to ease the pain of others. Her male counterpart is **Calvin**, the tall, black teenager who cares for and protects Howie during the youngster's night at the public camp. He, too, is streetwise and knows when and when not to play by the rules.

Pardoe, is a creepy, morbid camper with a pale, unhealthy complexion and fair hair. His voice is described as "soft and dark like a bruise." He comes from a terrible family background where Tiwanda says he was "hurt bad." He lives by his wits and by masterminding one scam after another. Unstable and warped by his past experiences, Pardoe is attracted to Laura, and at one point he tries to lure her away from the others, but Howie intervenes.

Two of the camp officials that Maddy meets are **Mr. Wells** and **Margo Cutter**. Mr. Wells, also known at the camp as Mr. Bob, is a fat, outwardly jolly man who nods, smiles, and uses every trick possible to ingratiate himself to the parents. He underestimates the intelligence and concern of Maddy, however, and deliberately covers up the truth behind Laura's disappearance. When discovered, he tries to make excuses to cover his inefficiency and lack of supervision. Margo Cutter, a camp counselor, shows more genuine feeling toward Maddy, but she uses so much social work jargon that her advice proves ineffectual. For example, she does not think that Laura and Howie should remain together after their rescue because this would "develop a dependency which would interfere with their resocialization later." She is, however, some help in reuniting mother and daughter.

Celine

(young adult novel, 1989)

PLOT: During her junior year in high school, sixteen-year-old Celine Morienval is living with her twenty-two-year-old stepmother, Catherine, while her father is on an extended lecture tour in Europe. Having promised her father that she would "show a little maturity," Celine hopes that if she proves herself she might be able to take a summer trip to Italy to see her friend and study art. Secretly, Celine, who is unhappy with her home life, makes plans not to return home should she be allowed to go. She and her stepmother have an odd kind of relationship. Though Catherine is officially the parent, she and Celine are not that different in age, and they have other things in common, too: they are both separated from their fathers, and neither one cares much for house cleaning.

One day when Celine returns home from school, she runs into the kid across the hall, Jake Barker. His mother isn't home yet, so Celine takes him in and they get acquainted. Pretty soon, Celine finds she can't get rid of Jake. A few days later, he invites her to go on a trip with him and his father. Celine agrees to tag along because Mr. Barker is an artist and she thinks he might be interesting. But to her surprise, he makes a pass at her.

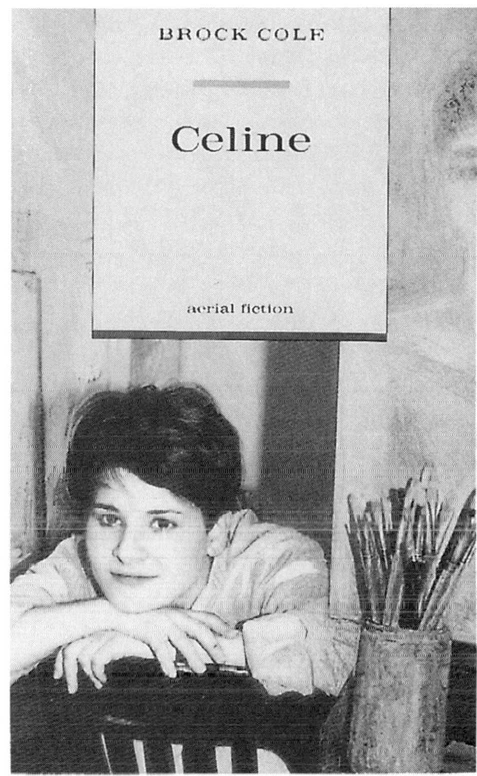

Celine Morienval learns to accept her life and her young mother-in-law in this coming-of-age novel.

Back at school, for a painting assignment in art class one day, Celine decides to paint fellow student Lucile, who agrees to pose if Celine will go to a party with her because Lucile's mother won't let her go with a boy. This works out for Celine as well, since Catherine probably wouldn't let her go with her nerdy boyfriend Dermot anyway. The party, however, is a complete disaster as far as Celine is concerned, and Lucile gets drunk and throws up. Celine rescues her and takes her home. Naturally, Lucile's mother finds out and tells Catherine, and Catherine gets upset and tells Celine she isn't demonstrating the maturity expected of her.

Meanwhile, Jake is having a particularly bad time because his parents are splitting up. Celine is quite startled to run into Mr. Barker again with his latest love, who turns out to be Celine's art teacher, Miss Denver. Catherine goes off on a trip, leaving Celine alone for a few days. She calls Celine later to say she might come home early and that she has talked to Celine's father. He's coming home and wants the three of them to go camping and talk about how this family is going to work. Though she has her doubts, Celine agrees to this plan. For the rest of the weekend, however, she and Jake are stuck with only each other. Jake asks her if she still wants to move to Italy, to which Celine replies that maybe just now isn't the time to go.

CHARACTERS: **Celine Morienval** is a charming, unconventional teenager, in some ways older than her years, in others silly and childlike. Living with a stepmother who is only a few years older than herself, the two are more like roommates than mother and daughter. Celine is a television addict, as well as an artist, a fact that entrances young **Jake Barker**, whose mother across the hall doesn't have a television and doesn't approve of Celine—not at first, anyway. But Jake soon comes to adore her, and despite herself, Celine is drawn to the unhappy little boy who is suffering because of the breakup of his parents' marriage. Celine relates to Jake the happy years of her life when she and her mother lived together. But then another man came into her mother's life, and now her mother is in South America and Celine doesn't see her anymore. Later, Celine learns from her art teacher, **Miss Denver**, who confides in her somewhat, that the teacher is having an affair with a married professor from the Art Institute. The professor turns out to be none other than Jake's father.

Celine slowly comes to an understanding with her stepmother, **Catherine**. This, combined with her growing fondness for young Jake, gives Celine some reason to reevaluate her feelings about her current life. Although Celine at first resents her stepmother, she eventually finds that they have many things in common. Not only are they about the same age, but they have similar tastes for the unconventional. Catherine's concern for her stepdaughter is genuine, and Celine realizes that Catherine has offered her an olive branch of friendship when she calls the girl's father in Europe and a trip is planned for the three of them.

A couple of minor characters in the story affect Celine's emotional growth. Celine feels strangely drawn to nerdy **Dermot**, but his affection for her is so intense that she feels guilty her feelings for him aren't that great. When she goes to the party with her friend **Lucile**, whom Celine considers to be a beautiful young girl going through a boy-crazy phase, Dermot is there, too, but she doesn't see much of him because she is too busy rescuing Lucile from the mess she gets into by throwing up all over herself. Neither Dermot nor Lucile provide good examples for Celine as to how to act more maturely.

Further Reading

Authors and Artists for Young Adults. Vol. 15. Detroit: Gale Research, 1995.

Berger, Laura Standley, ed. *Twentieth-Century Young Adult Writers.* 1st ed. Detroit: St. James, 1994.

Children's Literature Review. Vol 18. Detroit: Gale Research, 1989.

Holtze, Sally Holmes, ed. *Sixth Book of Junior Authors and Illustrators.* New York: H. W. Wilson, 1989.

McDonnell, Christine. "New Voices: New Visions: Brock Cole." *Horn Book* 68 (September-October 1989).

Something about the Author. Vol. 72, Detroit: Gale Research, 1995.

Christopher Collier

1930-, American historian

James Lincoln Collier

1928-, American novelist

My Brother Sam Is Dead

(historical novel, 1974)

PLOT: This novel, written by two brothers, covers the first four years of the American Revolution (1775-1778) and its effects upon the Meeker family of Redding in southern Connecticut. In addition to Eliphalet (nicknamed "Life") Meeker, the local tavern keeper, and his wife Susannah, the family consists of eleven-year-old Tim and his older brother Sam, who is sixteen. In April, 1775, Sam returns home from his first year of college at Yale wearing the uniform of the Rebels. He and his father, a staunch Tory and pacifist, quarrel, and Tim sees his family torn apart when Sam angrily leaves home after stealing the family's musket, Brown Bess. The next day, after a church service led by Mr. Beach, the Anglican minister, Tim and Sam's girlfriend, Betsy Read, granddaughter of the patriot, Colonel Read, visit Sam, who is hiding in the tepee of the only Indian in town, Tom Warrups. Sam leaves to rejoin his unit and, as the revolution escalates, the townspeople experience increasing fear, distrust, and suspicion. Alternately, the Loyalists and Rebels occupy the town, each committing atrocities. Mr. Heron, a respected resident, tries to conscript Tim as a messenger, but Tim fails to deliver the message he is given and never knows which side would have benefitted from his services.

In the fall of 1776, Life Meeker and his son Tim set out to trade cattle and pigs in Verplanks Point, a port on the Hudson River in New York. On the return trip, Life is taken prisoner by a band of marauders and Tim, narrowly escaping capture himself, returns home alone with the provisions. In the spring, the family learns that Mr. Meeker has died of cholera on a prison ship. Sam's regiment is sent to Redding for winter encampment. When Sam intercepts two Patriot soldiers intent on stealing the Meeker cattle, the soldiers take Sam prisoner and accuse him of being the cattle thief. He is sentenced to death. In spite of appeals to General Putnam, no reprieve is granted and Tim witnesses his brother's execution.

Years later, Tim has become a successful merchant. He looks back at the tragic events that destroyed his family and wonders if there might have been another way instead of war to achieve freedom.

CHARACTERS: The narrator and central character is young **Tim Meeker**, whose own inner turmoil creates a battleground similar to that reflected in the Revolution. Anxious to be an obedient son to the father he admires and respects, he feels ties to the Tory side; yet he idolizes his older, brilliant brother, Sam, and sympathizes with his ardent belief in justice and freedom. Torn by these conflicting loyalties, the boy's life becomes an agony of indecision and personal confusion. Tim is a brave youngster who courageously protects and defends his family. After Sam leaves and his father dies, Tim assumes massive responsibilities and obligations, becoming the man of the family though he is not yet a teenager. He sacrifices his schooling and opportunities for a future career to help the family. Tim is an ethical, honorable boy who hates dishonesty and wrong-doing. Quick-thinking and bright, he outwits and escapes the marauders who have taken his father prisoner. With each adversity and crisis Tim faces, he shows amazing inner resources and endurance. This is evident in his futile last-minute rescue

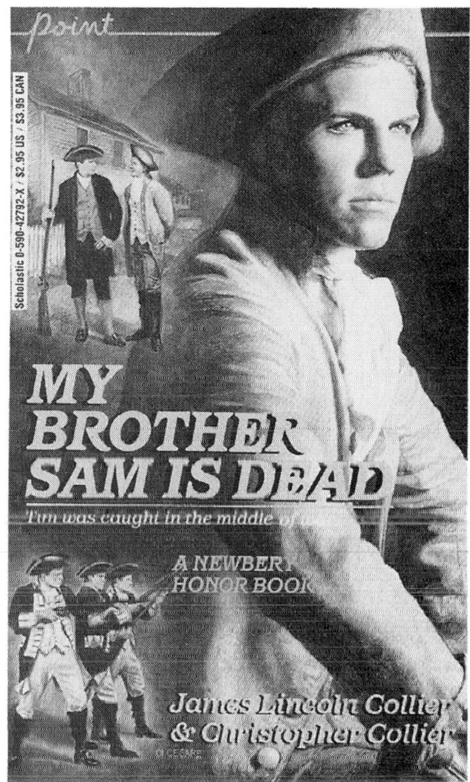

Set during the American Revolution, this story shows the impact of war on a family whose loyalties are torn between two countries.

attempt in which he plans to kill if necessary to save his brother's life. Over the course of the novel, Tim is able to sort out his personal conflicts and mature quickly. In spite of self-doubts and uncertainties, he develops into a solid, sensible young man who is gradually able to see the war and his losses from an adult perspective. At first, he is obsessed with pleasing and gaining the approval of Sam, whom he adores. Although he continues to love his brother and risks his life to save him, Tim gradually is able to evaluate Sam's actions objectively as an equal. Unlike Sam, who still glorifies the heroics of war, Tim eventually sees it as an abomination that "turns people into animals." In commenting on Tim's sudden transformation from boy to man, his mother says, "He had to grow up fast. He didn't have much choice."

Tim's father, **Life Meeker** (his given name is Eliphalet) is an industrious, hard-working tavern and general store owner who earns his living honestly and honorably. Scarred by the frontier battles he has experienced, he loathes war and supports the status quo as represented by the reign of George III. Aware that there are injustices in the present regime, he believes they can be corrected by peaceful means. Always a realist, he tells Sam, "What's the use of principles if you have to be dead to keep them?" A God-fearing man who unfailingly fulfills his duties as the family's chief provider, Mr. Meeker is also proud and courageous. Regardless of the odds, he fearlessly stands up for his personal beliefs in truth and justice and loses his life while trying to assure the well-being of his family. Mr. Meeker also has a stubborn, authoritarian side to his character, however. He is unyielding in his opposition to Sam's desire to join the Rebels and believes that, simply because he is the boy's father, he must be obeyed. As he says, "I'm his father. I don't have to be questioned on my behavior." When this attitude causes an irreparable rift between father and son, Mr. Meeker shows his gentler side when, caught off-guard, he weeps over the loss of Sam.

Mr. Meeker's wife, **Susannah Meeker**, is first presented as a passive, obedient woman who does not contradict her husband (even when she knows he is wrong), but instead behaves like a woman who has been taught to "love, honor and obey." When Mr. Meeker is adamant about not communicating with Sam after he leaves home, the first signs of independence and rebellion appear and, after her husband's death, Mrs. Meeker emerges as a plucky, courageous woman. She gallantly endures hardships and efficiently assumes many managerial responsibilities. Without the opinions of her husband, she sees the Revolution only in personal terms. "Patriotism has got my husband in prison and one of my children likely to be dead any minute," she says at one point. A kindly, religious person and a loving mother, Mrs. Meeker turns to alcohol as a means of escape, but, in time, her inner strength returns and she accepts her adversities like a true survivor.

Sam Meeker is only sixteen when he leaves school to join the patriots' cause. A brilliant student and great debater at Yale, his emotions are fired by the idealism of the Revolution, and he is willing to die for his principles. An independent spirit, he longs for both personal and national freedom and inspires his younger brother, Tim, with his bold, energetic conduct. Inclined to be opinionated and impulsive, his rash, impetuous behavior often gets him into trouble. Like his father, Sam is both brave and pigheaded, though he shows great devotion to his brother, even when Tim opposes some of his actions. A utopian romantic, Sam learns the painful realities of war and, ironically, dies at the hands of an American firing squad.

Sam's girlfriend is **Betsy Read**, a pretty, young woman who also believes fervently in the patriots' cause. Her love for Sam is both innocent and intense, and she risks her well-being several times to help him. In spite of her devotion to Sam, naive, trusting Betsy, in time, realizes the futility of war. Before Sam's death she says, "I don't care who wins anymore. I just want it to be over." Betsy's grandfather, **Colonel Read**, is a compassionate soldier who, although he believes in the patriots' cause, quits the army because he doesn't approve of the war. He is a comforting influence on the Meekers during their troubles.

Three other neighbors and friends of the Meekers are Mr. Heron, Tom Warrups, and Mr. Beach. **Mr. Beach** is the elderly Anglican minister. A quiet, peace-loving man, he is certain that rational behavior will prevail and a revolution will not happen. An ardent Tory, he preaches sermons against the Rebels and prays for the well-being of King George. **Tom Warrups** is the only Indian in town. The grandson of a famous Indian chief, he has become thoroughly Americanized and now lives quietly in a tepee-like hut behind the Read property. A friend to all, he hides Sam after the boy leaves his family and gives him a place to sleep when he returns to town. Though well-liked, Tom must behave deferentially toward others to be accepted. For example, when he visits the Meeker tavern "he didn't sit because he was only an Indian." **Mr. Heron** is an affluent, well-educated townsman who has made his fortune as a surveyor. Though outwardly a Tory, he is a man of mystery who might be a double agent. He is very fond of Tim and, after Sam's death, teaches him the skills of surveying without charge.

The army officer who orders Sam's death is **General Putnam**. A great patriot, and an honest, admirable man, he has a reputation of being tough as nails and inflexible. Obsessed with keeping stern discipline in the ranks, he sacrifices Sam to keep the troops in line. As one of his officers says, "He's thinking that if he executes someone, he'll shorten the war and save more lives." Sam becomes the scapegoat to fulfill this uncompromising soldier's plans for the future.

Further Reading

Authors and Artists for Young Adults. Vol. 13. Detroit: Gale Research, 1994.

Berger, Laura Standley, ed. *Twentieth-Century Young Adult Writers.* 1st ed. Detroit: St. James, 1994.

Chevalier, Tracy, ed. *Twentieth-Century Children's Writers.* 3rd ed. Detroit: St. James, 1989.

Collier, Laurie, and Joyce Nakamura, eds. *Major Authors and Illustrators for Children and Young Adults.* Detroit: Gale Research, 1993.

Contemporary Authors New Revision Series. Vol. 33. Detroit: Gale Research, 1991.

Contemporary Literary Criticism. Vol. 30. Detroit: Gale Research, 1984.

Holtze, Sally Holmes, ed. *Fifth Book of Junior Authors and Illustrators.* New York: H. W. Wilson, 1983.

Something about the Author. Vols. 8, 16, 70. Detroit: Gale Research, 1976, 1979, 1993.

Ward, Martha, ed. *Authors of Books for Young People.* 3rd ed. Metuchen, NJ: Scarecrow, 1990.

Pam Conrad

1947-, American young adult novelist

Prairie Songs

(young adult novel, 1985)

PLOT: The beauty, harshness, and loneliness of the prairie come to life in this sensitive, thoughtful story of young Louisa Downing, who lives in rural Nebraska at the turn of the century. Louisa loves this land, the only home she has ever known, even though she recognizes its isolation. Her younger brother, Lester, loves it too, although sometimes it's hard to tell because he is so shy. He will speak only to Louisa and their parents. One day, a different kind of beauty comes to the Nebraska prairie when Mrs. Emmeline Berryman and her physician husband, William, move "next door"—just three miles across the flatlands. Emmeline, who is pregnant, is the most beautiful creature Louisa has ever seen, and both she and Lester are spellbound by this fragile woman with her magnificent violet dress and pink parasol. But Emmeline is really too fragile in mind, body, and spirit for this harsh land, which is so different from her former home in New York City.

Louisa could not be happier when Emmeline is persuaded to teach at her and Lester's school. Under Emmeline's tutoring, Louisa's love for poetry grows, and Lester responds to her, too, showing signs of coming out of his shell. But Emmeline does not blossom. The fear of her strange surroundings never leaves her, and Emmeline retreats ever more into a private despair that is made worse when her baby dies.

Despite everything the Downings do to comfort and cheer her, Emmeline does not respond and sinks more and more into depression. During one bitterly cold period when her husband is away,

The beauty and terrible harshness of the American prairie comes to life in Conrad's 1985 novel.

Emmeline is alone at their sod home. Louisa's mother understands her fears and tries to get her to come to the Downing home, but Emmeline refuses. In fear for her well-being, Momma, Louisa, and Lester walk the three miles in the bitter cold to the Berryman's to check on the frightened woman, but it is too late. They find Emmeline Berryman out in the snow, frozen to death.

CHARACTERS: Louisa Downing is an inquisitive, sensitive, and practical young girl who loves her Nebraska prairie home. Surrounded by miles of flat grasslands as far as the eye can see, she appreciates its beauty, while acknowledging its lonely isolation. When she hears that they are to have neighbors just three miles across the prairie, she is thrilled, and when she sees the fragile, lovely Emmeline Berryman, she is even happier. Never has Louisa seen such a delicate creature, who makes her own tough mother look like a dried walnut in comparison. Louisa is even more fascinated when she sees all the books that Emmeline has brought to the prairie from New York City.

But it doesn't take Louisa long to realize that Emmeline is unsuited to the rigors of prairie life. When Louisa looks out of her prairie sod home, she sees the comfort of the flat prairie, which is "like a blank wall without too many things on it." But she recognizes that Emmeline sees the same view from a different perspective. For the older woman, the lonely prairie is frightening, full of dangers from animals and Indian attacks. And as Louisa matures during the months after the Berrymans enter her life, she begins to see how differently people react to the same situations. When she overhears a conversation between her mother and father in which her father speaks harshly about not wanting to argue over the loneliness of prairie life, Louisa suddenly questions the feelings of her own mother. Could she be lonely out here? It had never occurred to Louisa before. Louisa is happy beyond measure when Emmeline agrees to tutor both her and her brother, Lester. After the Berryman baby dies, however, the lessons stop, although Emmeline later says she wants to resume them.

Months after Emmeline Berryman's death, Louisa and the family go to Central City for the Fourth of July celebrations. She is especially proud of how her mother looks in her best gingham dress. Doc Berryman had given her all of Emmeline's fine clothes, but Momma will not wear them. Instead, she uses the fine bits of cloth for quilts. Suddenly, Louisa sees that her mother does not look like a dried walnut at all. Although not beautiful in the same way that Emmeline Berryman was, she is nevertheless attractive in a way that makes Louisa feel very good inside.

Emmeline Berryman is a lovely and fragile creature who is completely unsuited to the harshness of prairie life at the turn of the century. Completely lost in this environment, her obvious fears are evident in a conversation with Louisa's mother. Momma explains to Emmeline that sometimes—rarely—some Indians will come to the prairie, but they have never caused any trouble. Emmeline is immediately stricken with fear to the point that she later allows Momma to teach her how to shoot a rifle. Emmeline is incapable of adjusting to her new life. When she is asked why she and her husband came to Nebraska in the first place, Emmeline merely fusses with the hem of her apron and answers, "William."

Any chance of her adjustment to this harsh life dies when the cradle that Emmeline has been waiting for is broken before it can be delivered. She loses control of herself over the news, as if this were some omen of the impending tragedy that would manifest itself in the death of the Berryman baby. After that, Emmeline slowly retreats into madness. No longer able to cope and no longer willing to try, she dies alone on the alien prairie.

In poignant contrast to Emmeline is **Momma Downing**. She is a woman who accepts reality and comes to grips with her responsibilities and problems. That she, too, has moments of great loneliness is evident in a conversation with her husband, which is overheard by Louisa, but Momma has learned to overcome her fears. She tells Emmeline that she must not fear the return of Indians. She admits that at first she herself was afraid, but, though she remains cautious, she is not as scared as she once was. For Momma, a kind of "hope and acceptance" has replaced her fear. Momma has great hopes for her children, but she worries about Lester because of his shyness. She recognizes that he needs more attention in order to flower than does the more resilient Louisa. Momma Downing is the strength of the prairie, the almost stereotyped indomitable spirit of the pioneer. Her inner goodness and caring shine through so that her daughter realizes in time what true beauty really is.

The character of **Poppa Downing** remains mainly in the background. He is the epitome of the hardworking plainsman who has a strong sense of his responsibility and place in the world. He does his job, protects his family, and complains little, although he is obviously uncomfortable with the notion that at times his wife might be lonely herself.

Young **Lester Downing** is shy to the point that his mother worries about him ever coming out of his shell. But even Lester responds to the loveliness of the fragile Emmeline, and although he shudders initially at the thought of going to school, he responds to her teaching just as Louisa does. In the end, Louisa comes to realize that Lester will take his own time to grow and mature. "You'll do something in time," she says. "When you're ready. No use forcing a sunflower to bloom."

The reasons for **William Berryman**'s decision to practice medicine out on the prairie and away from the clamor of New York City are never clear. He is solicitous of his wife, but he obviously knows she is frail, as is evident when he returns home with the cherished cradle, which he knows has been broken in transit. He tries to forestall her distress, but to no avail. He is determined that his wife should adjust to these strange surroundings. When she admits to Momma that at home she grew up with servants and a cook, her husband comments that she had cooked for them for a year before they came here and "did quite well."

What I Did for Roman

(young adult novel, 1987)

PLOT: Sixteen-year-old Darcie is reluctantly spending the summer with her Aunt May and Uncle Ed because her mother is traveling in Europe with her new husband. Darcie doesn't particularly like her gruff uncle, who is her mother's older brother, but at least she has the chance to talk to Aunt May about a subject no one seems to want to discuss: Darcie's father. Darcie has never seen him and doesn't even know what he looks like. She only knows that he and her mother never married and that her mother was only seventeen when Darcie was born. Through Aunt May's photographs, Darcie learns that her father was Paul Brigadier, but she finds out little more than that because her uncle flies into a rage when he learns that she is asking questions.

Darcie's aunt and uncle run a restaurant at a large city zoo where Darcie meets and is immediately fascinated by the seal and bird keeper, a handsome young man named Roman. She develops a crush on this strange person who often speaks in riddles; she tells him of her desire to find out more about her father. Roman warns her of the dangers of such a quest, but he says that if she tracks him down somewhere in the city he will go with her.

Darcie locates a man named Brigadier who turns out to be her grandfather. Through confrontations with this man, as well as arguments and conversations with her aunt and uncle, Darcie finally learns the truth. Her father is dead, killed in a military accident when he was overseas. After finding out that his sister was pregnant, Darcie's uncle offered Paul Brigadier money to join the army and go away. Paul returned the money but joined the army anyway and said he would return after two years to marry Darcie's mother and claim his child. However, Paul gave the money to Aunt May, who never told Uncle Ed about it. She was afraid it would make him more upset, and when Paul was killed there seemed to be little point in telling anyone.

In her grief, Darcie goes to Roman. She finds him crying over a dead seal. Too upset with problems of her own, she does not notice that Roman's strange behavior has taken him over the edge. He vows to stand up to death and to do so by spending the night in the lion's den. He asks Darcie to join him, and, as if in a spell, she says there is nothing she would not do for Roman. Once inside, Darcie realizes that Roman is sick. When she calls for help, the guard comes and Darcie barely escapes, but Roman does not.

When her mother returns, they are able to talk. Darcie even tells her about Roman. She realizes that her desperate need for love made her blind to his problems, but she still thinks of him once in a while—perhaps not in the way that he was, but the way she *thought* he was.

CHARACTERS: Darcie is a sixteen-year-old obsessed with the desire to learn more about the man who is her father. She has been so cut off from him that she learns what he looks like only from photos in Aunt May's album. Darcie has no idea whether he is alive or dead when she decides to seek him out despite her aunt and uncle's objections.

Caught up by her need to be loved, Darcie becomes fascinated with the mysterious Roman. She quickly develops a crush on this handsome, charming young man who often speaks in riddles and appears to be totally devoted to the animals he cares for. She is so wrapped up in her own needs, however, that she doesn't notice his strange behavior or his tendency to overreact whenever his animals are threatened. At one point in their relationship, Darcie blurts out that she loves Roman. He tells her he is too old for her—he is twenty-five—but he offers her friendship and something more. He agrees to accompany her on her trip to see the man named Brigadier, whom she mistakenly believes to be her father. Instead, he turns out to be her grandfather.

By the novel's end, Darcie realizes that her grief over her father has blinded her to Roman's flaws. She understands, too, that her mother did not know that Ed had offered Darcie's father money to go away. She also realizes that her mother has found love with her new husband and a new life, and Darcie begins to feel somewhat secure in their new home.

Uncle Ed is a gruff, rather unlikable man with strict ideas about behavior and morality. But he truly loves his younger sister, Darcie's mother, and wanted to save her from what he thought would be more unhappiness by trying to buy off Paul Brigadier. Part of Uncle Ed's gruffness toward Darcie is the result of his bitterness over his sister's illegitimate child, and Darcie learns from her aunt that it was some time before the baby was even admitted into his home. Darcie will perhaps never learn to love her uncle, but she understands him a little better when she learns the truth about her own background.

All her life, **Aunt May** has been trying to keep peace in her marriage and her family. Her husband is a difficult man, and she placates him constantly. When Darcie confronts her with the fact that she knows about the four thousand dollars that her father returned, Aunt May admits that she took the money but never told her husband or Darcie's mother about it. Aunt May explains that she bought things for Darcie with the money through the years, but she never told her husband because she knew it would upset him if he thought Paul Brigadier had returned the money. Aunt May just wanted to keep the peace. Then, when she learned of Paul's death in the military accident, there didn't seem to be a reason to tell the truth.

Roman Sandman is a mysterious charmer. When Darcie first sees him, the sun is shining like a halo through his dark, curly hair. She is fascinated and instantly smitten. When a thief attempts to take Uncle Ed's money outside the restaurant one day, Roman intervenes and foils the holdup. Darcie is impressed because he seemed to disregard the danger so easily. This is just one of the signs of Roman's sickness that Darcie doesn't notice, so blinded is she by her need to have him care for her. Roman's attachment to his animals is almost mystical, and his reaction when one of them dies or is threatened is extreme. In the end, Roman's illness leads to his death and almost kills Darcie as well. When Darcie comes to her senses in the lion cage and urges Roman to leave, he says that this is merely a test. Darcie realizes that Roman is trying to prove that he is fated to die. At that point, she also realizes that she must escape—both from the lion's cage and from the spell Roman holds on her.

Darcie's **mom** never becomes an active character in the novel. She communicates with her daughter through postcards as she travels with her new husband in Europe. However, her love for her daughter is genuine and, in fact, she returns early from her honeymoon to be with Darcie.

Further Reading

Berger, Laura Standley, ed. *Twentieth-Century Young Adult Writers.* 1st ed. Detroit: St. James, 1994.

Children's Literature Review. Vol. 18. Detroit: Gale Research, 1989.

Conrad, Pam. "The Last Book: Thoughts on the Immortality of Children's Authors." *Horn Book* 68 (May/June 1992): 309-10.

Holtze, Sally Holmes, ed. *Sixth Book of Junior Authors and Illustrators.* New York: H. W. Wilson, 1989.

Rinn, Miriam. "Author Profile: Pam Conrad." *Horn Book* 12 (May/June 1993): 28-30.

Something about the Author Autobiography Series. Vol. 19. Detroit: Gale Research, 1995.

Pat Conroy

1945-, American novelist

The Lords of Discipline

(novel, 1980)

PLOT: Will McLean begins his senior year at Carolina Military Institute—a thinly disguised replica of The Citadel in Charleston, South Carolina—as the United States is becoming increasingly involved in Vietnam. Sardonic Will claims to be anti-military, yet he is proud to "wear the ring." The ring is a symbol that means he has survived the sometimes sadistic rituals that students must endure to prove their manhood at the Institute.

The commandant of cadets, Colonel Thomas Berrineau, also known as the Bear, secretly asks Will to watch over Pearce, the Institute's first black cadet. There has been talk that some cadets are out to get him. Will mentions "The Ten"—a mysterious underground group of cadets that is rumored to be deadly—but the Bear says he does not know whether the group really exists. Will tells only his roommates about his agreement with the Bear to keep an eye on Pearce. His roommates are Tradd St. Croix—a well-bred, sensitive young man from a prominent Charleston family whose father, Commerce, was an Institute man—and Mark Santoro and Dante "Pig" Pignetti, whom Will loves like brothers. The four cadets are closer than family.

The story then turns back to Will's first three years as a cadet and chronicles his growing disgust with Institute discipline, which he sees turning decent young men into sadistic bullies. Particularly vicious is Hell Night, when first-year cadets are

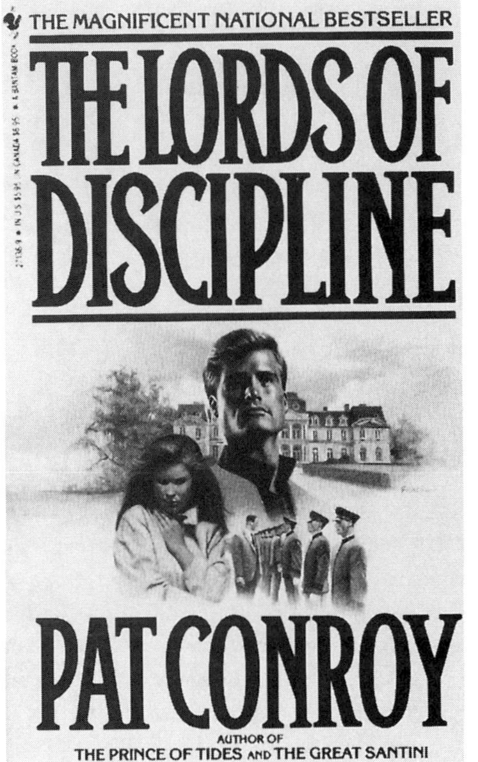

Conroy's fictional military academy is a thinly disguised attack on The Citadel in Charleston, South Carolina, and its hypocritical practices.

subjected to physical and emotional abuse at the hands of older students. During his cadet years, Will falls in love with Annie Kate Gervais, a young woman who is pregnant. He befriends her and sees her through this difficult time, though he does not know the father's identity. When the child is born and dies, Annie leaves.

As a senior, Will learns more about the evil work of The Ten. By tracking down an ex-cadet who mysteriously left the Institute, he finally gathers facts about this deadly group. When Cadet Pearce disappears, Will and his roommates find The Ten's hideout and witness Pearce being tortured. More detective work discloses the identify of The Ten and the organization's link to the four-star general who is the Institute's president. This victory is overshadowed by the shocking suicide of fun-loving Pig. Threatened with expulsion for a rule infraction, Pig prefers death to disgrace. Presumably, with The Ten's identities and deadly tactics out in the open, the nightmare at the Institute will end. But it will never end for Will, who learns that one of The Ten is none other than Tradd, his closest friend. Will also finds out that Tradd was the father of Annie's child and that Tradd's mother, Abigail, set up the meeting between Annie and Will.

Graduation day is bittersweet. Though he was threatened with expulsion himself, Will stood up to the Institute. In the process, however, he lost his two closest friends—one through death, and the other through treachery. He says goodbye to the third of his beloved roommates without realizing that he will soon lose Mark too—to the war in Vietnam. In a sense, not one of the four blood brothers survives their brutal transition into manhood at the Institute.

CHARACTERS: Beneath his witty and sardonic demeanor, **Will McLean** is a young man of honor and sensitivity. He is caring and intelligent, but he tries to cover up his feelings with sarcasm and biting humor. He is at odds with himself as he grows to manhood. Essentially anti-military, he is determined to succeed at the Institute, mostly to disprove his late father's doubts about his strength and abilities. Yet part of him responds with fierce pride to the sight of hundreds of cadets marching in tight formation across a parade ground where so many of America's heroes have marched, and he is immensely proud to wear the ring that identifies him as an Institute man. He is brought to tears by the strong bonds of love and friendship he feels for his roommates, Tradd, Mark, and Pig. Yet he is also horrified by what he sees as sadistic, brutal behavior sanctioned by some at the Institute under the pretense of military discipline.

Will has always felt awkward with young women. In fact, his roommates once wondered whether he and Tradd were gay. But Will feels at ease with Annie and finally admits to himself that he loves her. He is deeply hurt by her rejection and departure, and suffers even more when he learns that Tradd is the father of Annie's child. However, the deepest hurt that Will endures—outside of Pig's suicide—is Tradd's betrayal. He knows he will always love Tradd, but he also knows he can never forgive him. Will McLean leaves the Institute no longer a boy. Though he will be an Institute man all his life, the ring has come to symbolize only his pride in himself.

Tradd St. Croix bears the heavy responsibility of being the last son of an aristocratic Southern family steeped in history and tradition. He knows he will never be able to please his father. **Commerce St. Croix**, Tradd's father and an Institute man himself, wanted an athlete for a son, but instead he got slim, brilliant Tradd, who loves poetry and architecture. Tradd tries to explain to Will that he became a member of The Ten because he needed respect. With The Ten, he says, he felt manly for the first time. He later discovers that he was admitted to The Ten only because his father had been a member long ago. Tradd swears that he never realized how far the group would go and begs Will's forgiveness, but Will is unable to forgive him for what he did to their friendship.

Will chose his other roommates, **Mark Santoro** and **Dante (Pig) Pignetti**, because they were strong, invincible physical specimens. In his early days at the Institute, Will figured it would be a smart move to surround himself with the strongest men possible. Through the years, however, a strong bond of love and friendship has grown between the roommates. Both Mark and Pig are deeply proud of their admission to the Institute and determined to bring honor not only to themselves but to their families, who have sacrificed in order for them to attend military school. Their feelings of family honor are so strong that Pig—even though he is defended by his roommates—takes his own life rather than face disappointing his family over his expulsion for breaking minor rules.

The sarcastic bantering that characterizes the relationship between Will and Colonel **Thomas (Bear) Berrineau** covers up their deep respect for each other. The Bear is a gruff-looking hulk with a pulpy nose, white-thatched hair, and a cigar forever stuck in his mouth. He talks tough—and he is—but every cadet soon learns that if there is trouble, the Bear is the man to see. He is an Institute man to the core. He does not want to see the school integrated any more than The Ten does, but he is an honorable man and willing to abide by rules of decency and fair play, no matter what the cost. Although the Bear does not admit it to Will, he has always known of The Ten's existence. For a short time after Will finds The Ten's secret meeting house, he falsely believes the Bear to be one of them. After graduation, however, Will asks the Bear to sign his diploma over the president's signature so that there will be at least one respectable name on the certificate. The Bear points to Will's own name and says, "There already is, Bubba."

Annie Kate Gervais is a minor character, but one with a profound effect on Will. She is a strange figure in that her motivations are never fully explored. She keeps the identity of her baby's father a secret, as well as the reason she goes through with the pregnancy. She obviously welcomes Will's attention, and even allows him to make love to her, but then she disappears from his life easily and seemingly without a thought as to what effect it will have on him. Will receives one letter from her from California, after Annie learns from Abigail St. Croix that Will knows the truth about her baby's father. She says she is not sure if she loved Will, but that a part of her did. She also asks him to never answer her letter.

Will regards **Abigail St. Croix**, Tradd's mother, as the epitome of gracious, cultured, aristocratic Southern womanhood. He is enchanted by her and grateful that she has included him as part of the family. She even gives him a key to the elegant St. Croix residence in Charleston. His bitterness and pain upon learning that Tradd is the father of Annie's child thus becomes even more profound when he discovers that Abigail deliberately set up a meeting between Will and Annie. She tells Will, "I didn't care for the girl and I would never have given my approval for Tradd to marry her." But she knew that Will would feel sorry for Annie and would take care of her. The careless manner in which Abigail uses him provides Will with a bitter lesson on friendship, honor, and family.

The Prince of Tides

(novel, 1986)

PLOT: Savannah Wingo, a young and gifted poet, has attempted suicide once again. Although she is expected to live, as the novel begins she can't speak. Her new psychiatrist, Susan Lowenstein, asks Savannah's twin, Tom Wingo, to come to New York City in the hope that he might be able to shed light on his sister's history of mental illness.

Tom lives in the low country of South Carolina, where the Wingo children were born and raised. He is a teacher and a high school football coach. Like Savannah, Tom is a troubled drifter—his career is lackluster, and his marriage is falling apart. But he loves Savannah and agrees to try to help her. Once he settles into his sister's Greenwich Village apartment, he reluctantly begins to talk with Susan Lowenstein about his sister's deep troubles. These sessions become increasingly painful for Tom as he shares some of the Wingo family's troubled past. He talks about the island off the Carolina coast where he, Savannah, and their brother, Luke, grew up. He tells stories about their father, Henry Wingo, a troubled, violent, and often cruel man who once kept a Bengal tiger named Caesar in the backyard. He also tells Susan about his mother, Lila Wingo, who hides her own unhappiness by pretending that her dysfunctional family is close, serene, and respected in the community.

But Tom is holding something back, and Susan Lowenstein knows it. Only when he speaks of the low country, of his great love and almost mystical passion for his island home, does he become whole. When the psychiatrist tries to prod him into revealing whatever secrets he is keeping, he retreats into humor and sarcasm. Slowly, however, Tom and Susan draw closer. In their desire to help Savannah, they begin to help each other. After Tom learns of Susan's own failing marriage, he finally unburdens himself of the Wingo family's dark secrets.

Tom describes the terrible, violent tragedy that forever haunts his life and is surely behind Savannah's retreat from reality. One night, three convicts broke into their home on the island and raped his mother, his sister, and himself. Luke, unable to prevent the crimes, untied Caesar instead, and the tiger killed all three men. Then their mother presided over a grim cleanup of the house and disposal of the bodies. Tom tells Susan that his mother would not allow any of the children to seek medical or psychological help after that night because she feared it might damage "the family's position in the town." As an added tragedy, Luke later dies when he stubbornly defends his island from government officials who say they want to preserve it.

Now that Susan is aware of the terrible pain that Savannah has been concealing, perhaps she can find a way to help her; now that Tom has released his own feelings about the past, perhaps he too can heal. This difficult period brings Tom and Susan together in a way they never imagined. For a short time they enjoy the love that has grown between them, but they both realize that it will, and must, end. Susan Lowenstein will always be a part of him, just as he will always be haunted by his past. But Tom Wingo is stronger and determined to start over, so he returns to the low country and the family he loves.

CHARACTERS: Tom Wingo is a sensitive, introspective man with a deep love for the low country of South Carolina. He becomes lyrical when he speaks of his island home and the love he shared with his siblings—his twin sister Savannah and his quiet brother Luke. But Tom has kept the dark and violent secret of the rape of his family hidden for too long. He does not speak of it to anyone—except Susan Lowenstein—even though it is ruining his life. He is drifting aimlessly through life, and his marriage is in trouble. Although he is deeply wounded to learn of his wife's interest in another man at the beginning of the novel, he also knows that it is his own fault. He seems to be going through the motions of living, hiding his pain and unhappiness behind sarcasm and indifferent humor.

Tom has long seen the signs of his sister's illness, but he could not help her any more than he could help himself. It is only when he goes to New

York to help Susan Lowenstein piece together events leading up to Savannah's suicide attempt that Tom begins to find his own salvation. Through this cleansing process, Tom's life takes on new meaning. He can never erase the terrible pain of that horrible night nor the tragedy of Luke's death, but as he tells Susan on their last night together, "You've changed my life. I've felt like a whole man again. . . . You've made me face it all and you made me think I was doing it to help my sister."

As much as he loves Susan, Tom knows that he must return to South Carolina because that's where he belongs. About a year after his return, with his marriage becoming more stable and his sister home and healing, he acknowledges that he has learned some things about himself that will serve him well. For example, he knows that this land and this family are his real life and his destiny, and he prays it will always be enough. However, sometimes when he's driving toward his Southern home on a crisp autumn night he'll whisper, "Lowenstein, Lowenstein."

Susan Lowenstein is an attractive, intelligent New York psychiatrist. She is cool and blunt, pulls no punches in her dealings with Tom Wingo, and is every bit his match. She genuinely wants to help Savannah and doggedly pursues the truth that she believes Tom is hiding. She also realizes well before Tom does that by helping Savannah, he is cleansing himself as well. When she falls in love with Tom, it is very real for her. Although she knows he must return to the South and to his family, part of her wants him to stay regardless of the consequences. Yet, like the Wingos, Susan Lowenstein is a survivor.

Except for the end of the novel, **Savannah Wingo** is a character seen only in flashbacks from childhood through the eyes of her twin. Tom and Savannah share a deep love and closeness. Much like her twin in temperament and wit, Savannah is unlike him in that the low country so beloved by Tom became a prison for her, and she made her escape at an early age. Just as she knew she must write poetry, she also knew she must live in New York. In some ways, Savannah seems tougher than Tom, more independent, and more able to pursue her own destiny. But she is also more vulnerable, for their dark secret is ruining not only her life but her sanity as well. She will always be damaged and vulnerable, and Tom will always fear for her. But she, too, is a survivor. She tells Tom that during her illness something came apart inside her, something that cannot be fixed. But he replies that her own art can fix it. She can write beautiful poems, and with her words she can bring Luke back to life for them both.

Luke Wingo does not have the wit or genius of his twin siblings. Quiet, fun-loving, and loyal, he shares with them a passionate love of their sea island home. Neither Tom nor Savannah realize the depth of his attachment to the land. Not even their love can prevent him from defending it to the death. Savannah describes her feelings for the low country in words, and Tom feels it passionately in his heart, but Luke's attachment is an integral part of his being.

The children's mother, **Lila Wingo**, has spent a lifetime deluding herself about her family. In her later years, the transition becomes complete, and she refuses to recognize what is really happening to all of them. After Savannah's latest suicide attempt, Lila asks Tom why Savannah is doing this to *her*. "Haven't I suffered enough?" she asks. Tom can't forgive his mother for her pretentiousness. Throughout the novel, Lila is an often humorous and sometimes pitiable figure, as she doggedly tries to pull the Wingos up to some imagined level of social respectability. However, Lila's strange sense of decorum is the reason she refuses to acknowledge the tragic events of her family's past. Tom can never forgive his mother for this because it nearly causes the destruction of the whole family.

The family patriarch, **Henry Wingo**, is a sad, often cruel man who takes out his own failure to achieve his dreams on his wife and children. Like his wife, he has hopes of glory that never materialize. He is incapable of showing warmth and love for his children. Tom's hatred for Henry grows with each act of cruelty, and he longs for the day when he will be big enough and strong enough to inflict punishment on his father. In the end, after Tom and Savannah have made progress toward cleansing themselves, they have a sort of reconciliation with their father, when the damaged Wingo family tries to find a measure of peace and happiness.

Further Reading

Childress, M. "Pat Conroy Writes His Life." *Southern Living* 16 (March 1981).

Contemporary Authors. Vols. 85-88. Detroit: Gale Research, 1980.

Contemporary Literary Criticism. Vol. 30. Detroit: Gale Research, 1974.

Flora, Joseph M. *Contemporary Fiction Writers of the South.* Westport, CT: Greenwood Press, 1993.

Ryan, Bryan, ed. *Major Twentieth-Century Authors: A Selection of Sketches from Contemporary Authors.* Detroit: Gale Research, 1991.

Stagg, S. "PW Interviews Pat Conroy." *Publishers Weekly* 230 (5 September, 1988).

Toolan, D. "The Unfinished Boy and His Pain." *Commonweal* 118 (22 February, 1991).

Welsh, William J. *Speak So I Shall Know Thee: Interviews with Southern Writers.* Ashboro, NC: Down Home Press, 1993.

James Fenimore Cooper

1789-1851, American novelist

The Last of the Mohicans

(historical novel, 1826)

PLOT: In 1757, during a time of war between England and France, four people are traveling through the wilderness of the colony of New York near Lake George. Major Duncan Heyward, a young British officer, David Gamut, a religious psalm singer, and Alice and Cora Munro, the beautiful daughters of Colonel Munro, are on their way to meet the Colonel at Fort William Henry. Cora, it is later learned, is part black. Their guide is named Magua, a villainous Huron Indian who intends to lead the party into an ambush. But Magua's plans are thwarted when the travellers are joined by Hawkeye—a white man whose real name is Nathaniel Bumppo, though he is also called "Natty"—and his Delaware Indian friends, Chingachgook and Uncas, whom Hawkeye regards as a son. Magua, however, manages to escape into the woods.

The next day the group is attacked by Indians. Hawkeye and his friends flee to find help. The others are captured and led to Magua. Magua proposes marriage to Cora, but she refuses. Hawkeye returns with help and all the Indians are killed except Magua, who escapes once more. The group finally reaches the fort and Colonel Munro. Heyward then leaves for a battle with the French.

When Munro learns that no reinforcements are coming to the beleaguered fort, he agrees to a surrender. But during the withdrawal, the garrison is attacked by Indians and most of the women and children are massacred. Magua takes Alice and is pursued by Cora and David Gamut. These four are soon followed by Hawkeye, his two Indian friends, Munro, and Heyward. In trying to rescue Alice, Uncas is captured. Aided by cunning and disguise, Hawkeye and Heyward rescue Alice, and all, including Uncas and David, escape and head for the Delaware camp, where Cora is held captive. But Magua has reached the camp first and taken Cora away with him. When Hawkeye and the others arrive, Uncas speaks to Tamenund, patriarch of the Delawares, revealing himself to be a descendent of a great chief who was once Tamenund's friend. With the help of the Delawares, they go in search of Magua and Cora.

In the ensuing battle, Cora is fatally stabbed, Uncas is killed by Magua, and Magua is shot by Hawkeye. Cora and Uncas, who loved one another, are buried side by side. The others leave, except for Hawkeye and Chingachgook. When his Indian friend laments that he is now all alone in the world, Hawkeye declares that this is not so. The two friends will go on together without Uncas, the last of the Mohicans.

CHARACTERS: Also known as **Leatherstocking** or **Natty Bumppo**, **Hawkeye** is a "weatherbeaten scout," a lean and lank man with "nervous eyes." He is a solitary figure, representing the best of civilization and the most noble traits of the "savage." Although he is somewhat idealized, he is also portrayed as human, humble, modest, sometimes fussy and garrulous. He is proud of his marksmanship and has the manners of a gentleman, wanting to protect so-called helpless women from harm. Hawkeye is often suspicious of people, but he is essentially an honest and upright man, consistently just in his dealings with others. He is the ideal, rugged individualist. If he has a flaw, it is that he is almost too proud of his white blood, claiming never to have turned native and lived completely as an Indian. Despite his minor flaws, Hawkeye is the ideal mythic hero, a man of imagination and cleverness, fair play and honesty, a man to be counted on both as protector and as friend.

Uncas is the title character, the last of the Mohicans. With his tragic death dies the entire Mohican tribe. He is a graceful man with "terrible and calm" eyes. His proud carriage and fearless demeanor liken him to the noble Greek. He is, in a sense, the adopted child of Hawkeye. Like most of the characters in this novel, Uncas is a relatively static figure. His character does not develop through the novel but rather is revealed through his words and actions. The change that is perceived in him is more a result of his growing love for Cora than any refinement of his character. Uncas's father, **Chingachgook** is portrayed as the noble Mohican woodsman. Though he has lost his son, at the novel's end he looks forward to a future with Hawkeye.

The antagonist of this novel is **Magua**, who appears as a "dark and savage" man. Thoroughly the villain, his complex motivations make him an interesting character beyond his evil intent. After he captures Cora, Magua tells her of his disgrace at her father's hands: he was whipped for drinking. He wants her to marry him to disgrace her father, but she refuses. As he sees it, he has no alternative but to kill her, although he can't bring himself to do so, indicating his feelings for Cora are more genuine than he realizes. However, he whips the other warriors into a frenzy of killing. Evil and treacherous, he is nevertheless a figure of complex emotions, allowing the reader a glimpse of what he might have been under other circumstances.

Of the two daughters of Colonel Munro, **Alice Munro**, the younger, is the least interesting. A sentimental heroine, she is a pale and "tender blossom." She refers to Cora as "my more than sister, my mother." When Cora suggests that if she submits to Magua she might be able to save the younger woman, Alice has the courage to say no to the idea. **Cora Munro** is actually Alice's half-sister, her mother being from the West Indies. Her eyes are dark and thoughtful; Heyward refers to her as noble minded. Her sometimes brooding nature stems from what is described as the tragedy of her mixed race. Beloved of Uncas, she is knifed by one of Magua's warriors, and David Gamut sings an "anthem" over her grave.

An illustration by N. C. Wyeth showing Hawkeye successfully ignoring the religious songs of David Gamut in **Last of the Mohicans.**

The father of Cora and Alice, **Colonel Munro** is the stalwart commander of Fort William Henry who goes into decline after its fall. At one point in the novel, he tells his life story to Duncan, revealing that Cora's mother is from the West Indies. This fact causes Munro much anger when Duncan later proposes to Alice because he feels that the young man is scorning his older daughter due to her mixed blood.

Major Duncan Heyward is the sentimental hero who has feelings for the lovely Alice. A stereotype of the traditional hero in a novel of this type, he is active and brave, although his characterization is limited beyond that. His sterling qualities are obvious, even though, in comparison to Hawkeye or the

Delawares, he is far less knowledgeable of the frontier. He is, however, a man to be depended upon.

David Gamut might be described as the novel's comic relief. Carrying his religious psalms book into the wilderness, he is able to report on the whereabouts of the captive women because the Indians tolerate him in their camp, believing he is feeble-minded because of his habit of bursting into song at any opportunity. When Hawkeye and Uncas don disguises to rescue Alice, David helps them by disguising himself as Uncas. He adds humor to the story in several instances, such as when Hawkeye can't help but be amused by David's appearance after his body is painted and his head is shaved, leaving just a tuft of hair.

The patriarch of the Delawares, **Tamenund**, appears only briefly near the end of the novel. It is left to him to comment sadly upon the worsening plight of the American Indians and the grim fate of the noble Mohicans.

Further Reading

Critical Survey of Long Fiction. Englewood, NJ: Salem Press, 1983.

Darnell, Donald. *James Fenimore Cooper: Novelist of Manners.* Newark, DE: University of Delaware Press, 1993.

Dekker, George, and John P. McWilliams. *Fenimore Cooper: The Critical Heritage.* London: Routledge, 1973.

Fielder, Leslie A. *Love and Death in the American Novel.* New York: Stein & Day, 1966.

Franklin, Wayne. *The New World of James Fenimore Cooper.* Chicago: University of Chicago Press, 1982.

Fussell, Edwin. *Frontier: American Literature and the American West.* Princeton, NJ: Princeton University Press, 1965.

Grossman, James. *James Fenimore Cooper.* Stanford, CA: Stanford University Press, 1949.

Lawrence, D. H. *Studies in Classic American Literature.* New York: Doubleday, 1961.

McWilliams, John. *Last of the Mohicans: Civil Savagery and Savage Civility.* New York: Twayne, 1994.

Myerson, Joel, ed. *Antebellum Writers in New York and the South.* Vol. 3 of *Dictionary of Literary Biography.* Detroit: Gale Research, 1979.

Nineteenth-Century Literature Criticism. Vols. 1, 27. Detroit: Gale Research, 1981, 1990.

Peck, H. Daniel. *New Essays on "The Last of the Mohicans."* New York: Cambridge, 1992.

Rans, Geoffrey. *Cooper's Leather Stocking: A Secular Reading.* Chapel Hill: University of North Carolina Press, 1991.

Ringe, Donald A. *James Fenimore Cooper.* New York: Twayne, 1961.

Walker, Warren S. *James Fenimore Cooper.* New York: Barnes & Noble, 1962.

Robert Cormier

1925-, American novelist

The Chocolate War

(young adult novel, 1974)

PLOT: The two elements representing power at Trinity School, a Massachusetts parochial boy's day school, are the Assistant—now Acting—Headmaster, evil Brother Leon, and the Vigils, a secret student association. The leaders of the Vigils are Carter, the president, Obie, the secretary, and Archie Costello, the cynical, diabolical Assigner, the officer who conceives and administers the tasks of hazing to unfortunate students. Into this environment is thrust a new boy, Jerry Renault, a spunky loner who is still recovering from the recent death of his mother and is unable to communicate with his dispirited father. His only friend at Trinity is another new boy, Roland Goubert, nicknamed Goober.

Brother Leon's future depends on the success of the annual chocolate sale. This year he has overextended his commitment and is desperately seeking the support of every student. Goober's first assignment from Archie is to loosen every screw in Brother Eugene's classroom with the result that all the furniture collapses when the teacher enters his room one morning. To teach Brother Leon a lesson, Archie next gives Jerry the assignment of publicly refusing to accept his quota of chocolates to sell. Brother Leon becomes desperate when sales plummet but is assured, through secret negotiations with Archie, that the assignment is only temporary. However, after being commanded by Archie to begin selling the chocolates, Jerry continues to refuse. In his locker, Jerry has a poster with the words, "Do I dare disturb the universe?' on it. Without thinking of the consequences, Jerry has answered, "Yes." Archie, realizing that his authority, as well as that of Brother Leon, is being challenged, applies sterner measures. A program of harassment is organized—Jerry's locker is ransacked, assignments are stolen, and he receives nightly anonymous phone calls. The campaign of terror culminates in a severe beating by a group of neighborhood thugs led by Emile Janza, the school's "goon." Archie fiendishly promises Jerry a fair fight to avenge himself on Janza on the school's athletic grounds, but, unknown to Jerry, he organizes a raffle in which each ticket allows the purchaser to call a punch for either Janza or Renault. The situation gets out of hand and Janza beats Jerry unmercifully while Brother Leon, watching from a hilltop, does nothing to stop it. Fortunately, another Brother intervenes, but Jerry is so badly beaten he must be taken to a hospital. In the ambulance with Goober, Jerry tells his friend that, no matter what the poster says, it is better to conform than to disturb the universe.

CHARACTERS: Jerry Renault is neither an intrepid hero nor a fearless reformer, but merely a vulnerable young man who decides to take a small stand on behalf of his rights. He is a lonely boy who is still adjusting to the recent death of his beloved mother and a move to a new school. Not able to communicate with his father, whom he inwardly ceases to respect, and without any real friends, he hopes, in spite of his small stature, to make the freshman football team so that he can feel part of something and give some meaning to his empty life. When Archie first sees Jerry on the football field, he accurately describes him as "tough and stubborn," two characteristics that are displayed when he begins the chocolate war. A reluctant hero and always a little bewildered, Jerry shows amazing courage and inner strength in his solitary crusade, even though he often agonizes over his decision. Disgusted with the misuse of power by both Brother Leon and Archie, his conscience and moral sense will not allow him to participate in a scheme from which both will profit. Though he often agonizes over the wisdom of his decision, he steadfastly and courageously endures pain, loneliness, and isolation for his beliefs. Though he exhibits unusual grit and resolution, he emerges defeated having learned a terrible, negative lesson: that one can't fight the system and it is safer to conform, even if this means compromising one's ideals.

Jerry's only ally is **Roland Goubert**. Also known as **Goober**, he is a tall, lanky freshman who "has the look of a loser." Content to be left to his football and track, he was once a happy-go-lucky, cheerful boy, but under the reign of terror of Brother Leon and the Vigils he has become fretful and insecure. Terrified at carrying out Archie's assignments yet feeling powerless to oppose him, he is also sickened by Brother Leon and his cruelty. Ultimately, he becomes discouraged and despondent, gives up sports, and becomes reclusive. He admires Jerry and worries that his posture will lead to tragedy. Though intimidated, he remains supportive of Jerry. The only other person who might help Jerry is his father, **Mr. Renault**, a pharmacist who works long irregular hours. Though a caring parent, he is a drab, accepting, uninteresting man who can't communicate meaningfully with his son. Crushed by the death of his wife, he has become a boring, lethargic individual, who is no help to Jerry when he needs him.

Archie Costello is handsome, blond, intelligent, quick-witted and articulate. He is also a brutal, heartless cynic who enjoys humiliating and inflicting pain on others. Although he prefers mental cruelty over physical violence, when the latter is necessary he does not hesitate to send out his enforcer, Emile. His personal rule for survival is to never admit anything, never apologize, and always deny. A charmer when necessary, Archie is always mentally two steps ahead of those around him. With these gifts, he commands respect and obedience from others like Obie and Emile. He is insolent, irreligious, and in love with power. Believing that Jerry's rebellion is a threat to his position, he is ruthless in crushing it. A supreme strategist and manipulator, he believes that everyone is greedy and cruel and has a weakness or a price that can be exploited. His statement that "Life is shit" summarizes his perverted credo.

On the surface, **Brother Leon** seems pale and ingratiating, with behavior not unlike a henpecked husband. But beneath this deceptive exterior is a power-driven, religious hypocrite who seeks to gain complete control of Trinity School. In the classroom he rules like a petty tyrant, using his pointer as a sword, humiliating weak students, and intimidating others through sarcasm and other bullying tactics. He stoops to changing grades to assert his power. Though he feels contempt for the students, he shamelessly appeals to their school spirit to help accomplish his own goals. Given to uncontrollable rages when thwarted, he is so vindictive toward Jerry that he condones the cruel, unwarranted punishment given him by the Vigils. A man who has sold his soul to achieve his ambitions, Brother Leon succeeds through corruption and misuse of power.

The secretary of the Vigils, **Obie**, is actually Archie's errand boy whom he manipulates shamelessly. As a result, Obie's attitude toward Archie is a combination of admiration, fear, and hatred. With his thin, sharp face and a permanent worried look, Obie is frequently torn between obeying Archie, whom he knows is evil, and listening to his conscience. Though he suffers pangs of guilt, he is too weak to withstand peer pressure and the need to maintain his position of power. Ultimately, he continues to participate in acts that he knows are wrong. **Carter**, the president of the Vigils, is the school jock. A football player, he sees things in terms of violence and physical action. Whereas Archie is more cerebral, Carter prefers administering physical punishment. Archie is sometimes grudgingly forced to capitulate under Carter's brute strength.

Emile Janza, the football tackle and Archie's enforcer, is a savage, cruel brute whose only joy is inflicting pain on others. With his small, piggy eyes, hulking figure, and sickening giggle, he is evil personified. Blackmailed into submission by Archie, he nevertheless respects and admires Archie, hoping one day to be more like him. Never playing by the rules, he steals, lies, and revels in his sadism.

I Am the Cheese

(young adult novel, 1977)

PLOT: This complex, bleak novel contains three separate narratives, each running concurrently. In the first, a young man named Adam Farmer tells of his nightmarish, seventy-mile bicycle ride from Monument, Massachusetts, to Rutterburg, Vermont, where he intends to deliver a package to his father. During the journey, Adam experiences multiple misfortunes, including being attacked by a ferocious dog and forced into the ditch by thugs, having his bike stolen, and retrieving it in a narrow escape from the thief. The reader realizes that this journey is really a fantasy, similar to an anxiety dream, taking place in the mind of an extremely disturbed, fearful Adam.

The second plot takes place in an institution where Adam is being interrogated by a man called Brint. Brint, who is called "T" in the transcripts of the interrogation, is drilling Adam to find out what he knows about his parents' past. These sessions produce the third narrative in which Adam reconstructs his past life. In the eighth grade, Adam begins to realize that his loving parents are shielding him from a frightening secret. Gradually, the truth emerges. When Adam was a baby, his father, a newspaperman, testified in Washington against powerful subversive elements. To protect him and his wife and son from reprisals, they were placed in a Witness Relocation Program, given completely new identities, and relocated to Monument, Massachusetts. Their son, born Paul Belmonte, became Adam Farmer. The Farmers are periodically visited and receive instructions from an agent named Grey, who also uses the alias Thompson. Burdened by the knowledge of his precarious existence, Adam, like his parents, begins living a life of anxiety, always fearful of the future. His only release comes during the times he spends with his girlfriend, the vivacious Amy Hertz.

One day when Adam is fourteen, Grey warns the family that they must move. During their flight, both parents are killed by unknown assailants in an engineered car crash in which Grey appears to be implicated. Traumatized by these experiences, Adam suffers great psychological stress and is institutionalized for three years. In periodic flights of fancy, he rides his bicycle around the hospital grounds, recreating the nightmarish journey from Monument to Rutterburg, the site of the hospital, seeking his dead father. By the story's conclusion, Brink completes his interrogation, the purpose of which was to determine how much Adam knows about the criminal elements his father fought. Satisfied that the young man knows nothing, Brint files a report, recommending that Adam be "terminated," or, failing this, remain at the institution indefinitely.

CHARACTERS: Adam Farmer, or **Paul Belmonte**, is the pathetic pawn in a confusing, ambiguous battle against an unknown organization that could be masterminded by the government, crime bosses, or both. He is introduced as a quiet, shy boy who prefers the world of books and jazz records to being with people or playing sports. Adam is extremely dependent on his parents, whom he loves and admires. His narrow, secure world is shattered when, after learning the truth, he becomes fearful, suspicious, and withdrawn. Now more reliant on his parents than ever before, he comments that "fear had forged love." Though bashful and timid, he forms a touching relationship with outgoing Amy, who thrills him with his first kiss. Later, in the institution, Adam relies on drugs that alternately help him remember or forget. Without a family and drug dependent, his sanity collapses and he loses touch with reality. At first he feels that Brint might help him, but he later realizes that he is merely using him to obtain information. Isolated, dislocated, and without hope, he sings the nursery rhyme his parents once sang to him, "Farmer in the Dell." When he reaches the end and the line "The Cheese Stands Alone," he realizes that he is the cheese.

Adam's father, **David Farmer**—originally **Anthony Belmonte**—is a loving, gentle parent who, because of his belief in truth and justice, has been forced to exchange his exciting life as a newspaperman for the less interesting one of an insurance agent. Although bored with his job and always fearful of the future, he does not complain or regret his decision. He is a fair and honest man who dislikes withholding the truth from his son about his origins, but he knows that ignorance will make Adam safer. When he must later tell Adam the truth, he is frank and straightforward. Like his son, he is bookish and a jazz lover, but he also enjoys sports. David Farmer is a courageous, virtuous man who has risked his life for his ideals.

Louise Farmer is proud of her husband and supports him completely. However, the duplicity in their lives has taken its toll. Once high-spirited and joyful, she has become fearful and withdrawn. Now pale and subdued, she rarely leaves the house and often stays alone in her room. She confesses to always being afraid and suspicious, a victim of what she calls the "Never Knows," as in "one never knows if tomorrow will bring exposure." With Adam she is always loving, sweet, and sympathetic. However, she resents her new identity and longs for some personal freedom. She is also more defiant than her husband: she has disregarded instructions and kept some mementos of their former life, allows herself bouts of anger, and resents the constant intrusion of Mr. Grey into their lives. In spite of these passing moods, she remains a loyal, devoted wife and a caring mother.

Adam's girlfriend, **Amy Hertz**, dislikes physical exercise but loves playing innocent pranks, which she calls "Numbers." For example, she enjoys doing a Number in a supermarket by filling shopping baskets full of groceries and leaving them behind, blocking the aisles. She is talkative, fun-loving, vivacious, and, in many ways, the opposite of Adam, whom she calls Ace. Adam genuinely loves this self-assured, spunky girl who dares to be unconventional and succeeds in being different. She is Adam's first love, and he hates not being able to tell her the truth. In the institution, he continually looks back wistfully at the good times they shared and longs to recapture them.

Mr. Grey, also known as **Mr. Thompson**, is a sinister man who acts as a liaison between the Farmers and the relocation agency. Adam thinks he is appropriately named because he usually dresses in grey, has grey hair, and has a drab, bland personality. During the relocation, he acts like a god, intruding into the Farmer's lives by making decisions about their identity, occupation, religion, and location. Mrs. Farmer distrusts him, but the family is at his mercy. Though Adam believes that Grey betrayed his parents and was responsible for their deaths, Brint, in his final report, exonerates him and requests his reinstatement in the agency. Grey's true function and nature are left a mystery.

Brint, referred to as **"T"** in the tape transcriptions, is likewise an enigma. Adam first thinks he is a doctor sent to help him. Later, he realizes that Brint cares nothing about his well-being. His malevolent purpose is to use any means possible, including feigned interest in Adam, to find out how much Adam knows about his father's investigation. Brint is cold, distant, merciless, and efficient. At one point, his reptilian expression makes Adam think that he is "one of those men who had been his father's enemy." Brint's true identity is never revealed.

After the First Death

(young adult novel, 1979)

PLOT: By coincidence, the day that attractive teenager Kate Forrester takes her ailing uncle's place driving sixteen preschoolers to their summer day camp is the same day that foreign terrorists strike. They are four in number: their leader, Artkin, sixteen-year-old Miro Shantas, the brutish Antibbe, and Stoll, their black van driver. The men hope that through their acts of terrorism they will help secure freedom for their unidentified foreign homeland. Hijacking the bus, they tranquilize the children with candy laced with drugs and drive both van and bus onto an abandoned railway bridge, where, using powerful radio equipment, they make contact with a nearby army base, Fort Delta. For the release of their hostages they make several demands, including dismantling a powerful, secret international operation known as Inner Delta. The demands are received by the leader of this operation, General Rufus L. Briggs, the code name for General Mark Marchand, a noted behavioral scientist. One child dies from the drugged candy and, therefore, instead of killing the driver, Kate, as planned, the terrorists allow her to live to take care of the children. Kate finds she has an extra ignition key, but when she makes a brave effort to drive the bus to safety, the engine dies. Armed forces surround the bus, and when a trigger-happy soldier accidently kills Antibbe, Artkin retaliates by taking one of the children, Benjamin, and performing a public execution. The army seizes the terrorist's ringleader in Boston, but the hijackers refuse to believe the news and demand a neutral, unarmed person to deliver proof of the capture. General Marchand thinks of his son, the sensitive, trusting teenager, Ben. Before sending him to the bus, General Marchand gives the boy a series of incorrect clues about a proposed attack, knowing that the boy will crack under interrogation and reveal the false information. This is, indeed, exactly what happens, and the terrorists are caught off guard when the real attack occurs. During the assault, Artkin is killed, Ben is wounded, and Miro escapes, using Kate as a shield. The two hide in the woods, and when Kate tries to awaken some feelings of humanity in the boy by suggesting that Artkin was really his father, Miro shoots her. Ben survives his wound but is emotionally traumatized by his father's betrayal. He attempts suicide by taking sleeping pills but survives. Later, he enrolls in the military academy where his father was a student. Ben's mother visits him, and later, General Marchand, hoping for reconciliation and forgiveness, also goes to see him. During the first brief meeting, Marchand is unable to express his true feelings and leaves the room to collect his thoughts. When he returns some hours later, it is too late—Ben's second suicide attempt has been successful.

CHARACTERS: The substitute bus driver is **Kate Forrester**, an extremely attractive teenager with long, blond hair and a slender, lithe body. Before the nightmarish events after the hijacking, Kate was a very popular, well-liked girl, a cheerleader, prom queen, and captain of the girl's swimming team. Suddenly, her well-ordered, sheltered existence changes when her life is threatened by diabolical strangers. She tries to remain outwardly calm, but the terror of the situation is too much for her to control her weak bladder, and she is embarrassed when she begins dribbling urine. Nevertheless, before dwelling on her own problems she always thinks first of the children's needs and is their stalwart advocate. Though inwardly afraid, she conceals her panic and repeats to herself, "I will not cry." Eventually, she summons the inner strength and courage she never knew she had and defies the hijackers in a futile escape attempt; later, she proves her bravery again by taking Ben's place before he is killed. However, she always realizes that her enemies are more cunning and crafty than she is and that her efforts are doomed to failure. Innocent and inexperienced, she employs the only strategy she has found to be successful: manipulating men with her feminine charm and sensuality. However, this ploy doesn't work and, as she predicted, Miro murders her.

The youngest of the terrorists is the sixteen-year-old boy who uses the alias **Miro Shantas**. Without a father or mother, he has lived a pathetic life of begging and stealing to survive in a refugee camp and has committed himself to freeing a native land that he has never seen. A bright, clever boy with a gift for languages and learning, he and his brother Aniel were chosen by Artkin for special training in terrorism. With his deep-brown, penetrating eyes, Miro reveals a passionate heart. He has learned to master his emotions, as well as his physical reactions, so that neither can betray him. Never having had a real childhood, he can't understand feelings of love and tenderness; he doesn't know the purpose of a toy and can feel no empathy for the children. He believes that killing someone will make his life meaningful and feels cheated when he is at first denied his right to kill Kate. Concerned only that he will not do a professional job, Miro is not afraid of killing. On the other hand, he shows touching loyalty and trust toward first his brother, Aniel, who was killed in a shootout, and then toward Artkin. He basks in Artkin's infrequent compliments and longs for his approval.

Kate sometimes thinks that Miro is a "strange, pathetic boy," but his vulnerability and his miserable background have produced a monster, a doomed victim who has been manipulated by others and who is destined for the violent death he expects. Like a feral cat, he can't respond to love or kindness, both of which he regards as weaknesses. For one moment he feels love for Kate, but when she attempts an escape he again feels betrayed and abandoned. His only motivation for living comes from loyalty to his comrades and the cause they represent. When Miro escapes with Kate as a hostage and she suggests that the dead Artkin was his father, Miro, knowing he was partly responsible for Artkin's death, howls like a trapped animal and reacts in the only way he knows—with violence. Holding her close to him, he shoots Kate in the heart.

Another major victim of the kidnapping is also a teenager, **Ben Marchand**. A sensitive, intelligent boy who has a quiet, studious nature, he looks up to his father, Mark, with the same admiration and loyalty that Miro feels toward Artkin. Although he loves his mother, Ben can't communicate with her. Overly emotional and impressionable, Ben recently suffered the agony of rejection when a girl he loved spurned him. He is therefore particularly vulnerable when approached by his father to act as the go-between with the hijackers. At first flattered and honored by his father's trust, he is shattered to learn that his father has manipulated and betrayed him by feeding him incorrect information, knowing he would crack under torture and become an informer. Guilt-ridden and feeling worthless and rejected, Ben is sure his father thinks of him only as a weakling and a coward. After the experience, he says, "I am a skeleton rattling my bones, a ghost laughing hollow up the sleeves of my shroud." Deceived by his father, emotionally shattered, and knowing the world regards him as a weakling, Ben commits suicide.

Ben's father, **Brigadier General Markus L. Marchand**—code name **Rufus L. Briggs**—was a distinguished research psychologist in the area of behavior intervention and a candidate for a Nobel prize when he was tapped by the army to head secret projects that now include Inner Delta. A Pacific-area veteran of World War II, Mark is devoted to his country and his current undertaking. When a showdown approaches with the terrorists, his allegiance and commitment to his country and work are such that he is willing to sacrifice his son for them. Patriotism triumphs over humanity and trust. From the inner knowledge he has of his son, he exploits the boy's weaknesses to defeat his enemies. At first, he isn't able to comprehended the magnitude of his duplicity and betrayal, until his son's attempted suicide makes him realize the flaw in his fanaticism and his failure as a father. Now guilt-ridden and haggard from sleepless nights and tranquilizers, he seeks his son's forgiveness. By the time he has mustered the courage to speak, however, it is too late. Ben's second suicide attempt is successful. Ben's mother, **Mrs. Marchand**, is a kind, witty, stylish woman, who is a loving wife and mother. Unfortunately, she has only a slight influence on her husband and little profound contact with her son.

The leader of the terrorists is **Artkin**, a dark, brooding man who is a master at manipulating others. Abrasive one moment and gentle the next, he is usually emotionless and machine-like in his actions. Cold and brutal, he enjoys baiting people and taking advantage of their weaknesses. Fanatically devoted to his cause, he feeds on danger and conspiracy. He has already lost part of a hand to the crusade and knows that one day it will cost him his life. With nothing to loose and everything to gain, he has become a ruthless killing machine, sparing no one including his comrades. Miro reveres Artkin and tries to emulate him and gain his approval.

Stroll, another terrorist, is a silent, sullen black man who is capable of remaining motionless for hours. He is the group's driver and technician, being adept at maneuvering the van and building explosive devices. The last of the hijackers is **Antibbe**, a heavyset, lumbering man with a "grimace like thunder and a frown like an earthquake." He is a hulking brute, who, unlike the others, is a mercenary.

We All Fall Down

(young adult novel, 1991)

PLOT: Four reckless high school students from the town of Vickburg in eastern Massachusetts become high on alcohol and decide to trash a house in the upper-middle-class section of Burnside, a neighboring town. Their leader, the senior Harry Flowers, has secretly obtained a key. The other three hellraisers are Harry's stooges, Marty Sanders and Randy Pierce, who are also seniors, and Buddy Walker, a sensitive junior. Buddy has turned to alcohol and bad company as a result of his confusion over his parents imminent divorce. The four teens' victims are the Jerome family: mother, father, sixteen-year-old Jane, fourteen-year-old Karen, and their young brother, Artie. Harry and his followers not only vandalize the Jerome home but also urinate on the walls and defecate on the floor. Their wild rampage is interrupted by the arrival of Karen, who is pushed down the basement stairs and falls into a coma. All of this has been secretly observed by the Avenger, a demented, unidentified individual who recalls at age eleven killing a school bully and later murdering his suspicious grandfather to keep him quiet.

The Jeromes, particularly Jane, are stunned by this senseless violence and distraught at Karen's unconscious state. All the neighbors express regret and concern, including the retarded handyman, Mickey Stallings, cruelly nicknamed Mickey Looney. Although the automobile used in the crime is traced to Harry Flowers, his parents' money helps him escape arrest and avoid incriminating his friends. Buddy, whose family situation is also affecting his younger sister, Addy, becomes more conscience-stricken. Out of guilt and pity, he befriends Jane without revealing that he was one of Harry's gang. They fall in love and soon are inseparable. The Avenger, seeing them kiss, believes that Jane knows Buddy's true identity and that she is betraying her family. When he kidnaps her, intent on murder, the identity of the Avenger is revealed. He is actually Mickey Stallings, the demented handyman. Jane is able to break through his crazed state and appeal to his better nature. After telling her about Buddy's part in the vandalism, Mickey kills himself. Though Karen recovers and life seemingly returns to normal, Jane can't forgive Buddy for his actions and duplicity. In spite of Buddy's protests, she refuses to see him again.

CHARACTERS: The two protagonists in the novel are **Jane Jerome** and Buddy Walker. Sixteen-year-old Jane is an attractive girl with small features, high cheekbones, and shoulder-length, dark hair. At first, she is presented as an innocent teenager with a happy home life and several good friends. She is a sensitive, loving daughter who is concerned for the well-being of her family and friends. Her unusual ability to empathize with others is shown in her kind behavior toward the simple-minded Mickey Stallings and her love for Buddy. The senseless destruction and violence, however, leave telltale scars. She becomes anxious, is less trusting and more suspicious of others, and has bouts of insecurity. Her inner fortitude gradually emerges, however, particularly when she courageously confronts and outwits the murderous Mickey. Her growing maturity is also shown in her decision to leave Buddy, the boy whom she loves but can no longer trust.

Buddy Walker is a tragic figure. Devastated by his parents' oncoming divorce and separated from the father he idolizes, he becomes morose and melancholy. Unable to cope with these setbacks, he turns to alcohol, which he uses as a crutch. In his lost, dazed state he becomes easy prey for Harry. Sickened by his behavior in the Jerome house, he seeks absolution and forgiveness through his friendship with Jane. When this relationship turns to love, he feels reborn, needed, and able to confront his problems without drinking. But when this world crumbles around him, too, he lacks the inner strength to cope with Jane's final rejection and returns to his pathetic, aimless, alcohol-dependent existence.

The dark interior of **Harry Flowers** is contradicted by his blonde hair, handsome looks, and meticulous dress that emphasizes the color white. The spoiled son of a prominent architect, he is a malevolent, evil character who delights in destruction and abuse. Machiavellian in his plots, he is ruthless and without scruples. Through his wit and audacity, he dominates his two cronies, **Marty Sanders** and **Randy Pierce**, both of whom lack Harry's diabolical intelligence and, therefore, follow him like puppy dogs seeking guidance and approbation. Buddy compares them to Abbott and Costello, Marty being the wisecracking, agitated, Abbott and Randy, an overweight, bewildered, buffoon like Costello.

Mr. and **Mrs. Jerome** are ideal parents in the support, care, and affection that they shower on their children. Mr. Jerome, the business manager for the local telephone company, is an attentive, church-going gentleman whose one passion is golf. He and his wife, though distraught at their daughter's coma and the mindless destruction of their home, still find time to bolster the sagging spirits and growing uneasiness of both Jane and Artie. Their trust and confidence in Jane and her ability to make decisions show their wisdom and maturity in handling their children. **Artie**, Jane's younger brother, is a typical youngster who is Nintendo-mad. However, the vandalism and its consequences also affect him. He becomes sulky and distant, unable to comprehend or assimilate these events. Again the concern and support of his parents help him and, when Karen recovers, he returns to his joystick. **Karen Jerome** is first portrayed as perky, vivacious, and inclined to annoy Jane by continually borrowing her clothes without permission. The degree of love the family feels for her is shown by their concern when she lies helpless in a hospital bed.

Buddy's parents are also portrayed sympathetically, though the dissolution of their marriage is causing havoc in their children's lives. **Mrs. Walker**, a successful businesswoman, tries gallantly to maintain appearances after her husband leaves her for another woman, but inwardly she feels her resources dwindling and her defenses collapsing. This problem becomes so acute that she plans to attend a retreat to get help. **Mr. Walker** shares his son's character traits. Like Buddy, he can't face the consequences of his actions. Unhappy with leaving his family, he is unable to correct the error or adjust properly to his new situation. In his frustration and confusion, he turns to alcohol, just like his son.

Mickey Stallings, also known as **Mickey Looney**, is the half-witted handyman who works in the Jerome's neighborhood. Though somewhat frightening in appearance with his bloated stomach, bulging eyes, and completely bald head, outwardly he is a quiet, docile man who loves dogs and other animals. This mild exterior hides a psychopathic personality that has already caused him to commit two murders. He becomes fixated on Jane, who is always kind and gentle to him. This perverted love turns to obsession, and his voyeurism leads to witnessing the destruction of the Jerome household. When he sees Jane kissing one of the vandals, he feels she has betrayed both him and her family. Instead of killing her as planned, he cuts his wrists and dies after Jane makes him realize the enormity of his crime.

Further Reading

Authors and Artists for Young Adults. Vol. 3. Detroit: Gale Research, 1990.

Berger, Laura Standley, ed. *Twentieth-Century Young Adult Writers.* 1st ed. Detroit: St. James, 1994.

Campbell, Patricia J. *Presenting Robert Cormier.* New York: Twayne, 1985.

Contemporary Literary Criticism. Vols. 12, 30. Detroit: Gale Research, 1980, 1985.

Estes, Glenn E., ed. *American Writers for Children since 1960: Fiction.* Vol. 52 of *Dictionary of Literary Biography.* Detroit: Gale Research, 1986.

Holtze, Sally Holmes, ed. *Fifth Book of Junior Authors and Illustrators.* New York: H. W. Wilson, 1983.

Something about the Author. Vols. 10, 45. Detroit: Gale Research, 1976, 1986.

Stephen Crane

1871-1900, American novelist

The Red Badge of Courage

(historical novel, 1895)

PLOT: Filled with heroic dreams of triumphs on the battlefield, young Henry Fleming enlists in the Union Army during the Civil War and leaves his mother and the farm on which he has spent his entire life. Disillusionment comes early, however, when he has to endure the boredom of army training and the endless marches and delays before reaching the front. He becomes acquainted with two other privates known as the Tall Soldier, Jim Conklin, and the Loud Soldier, Wilson. When battle action is imminent, Henry is fearful of how he will act under fire and receives little consolation from either Jim or Wilson. He survives the first skirmish without problems, but when the Confederates stage a surprise attack, Henry, along with some others of his regiment, flees in disarray.

Ashamed and guilt-ridden, Henry joins a retreating column of wounded men, one of whom (Jim, the tall soldier) dies before his eyes. Another soldier, a tattered man also near death, tries to talk to Henry, who callously ignores him, fearful that someone will discover he ran from the enemy. Later, he encounters another group of retreating Union soldiers, one of whom, half-crazed by the battle, hits him on the head with the butt of his rifle. Stunned but now possessing a wound—the red badge of courage—Henry finds his way back to his regiment, where he is greeted as a hero by Wilson. Pretending that his injury is a bullet wound, Henry's conscience is troubled by the deception.

In the next battle, Henry acts like a man possessed, holding his position and firing his rifle continuously even after the enemy flees. During a later attack, when the flag bearer is killed, Henry takes up the flag and again distinguishes himself with Wilson by his side. In the next skirmish, Henry once more exhibits great bravery by leading a charge against the Confederates. He has now become a veteran, a hardened soldier who, through harrowing trials, has gained maturity and proven to himself and to others that he is a good, dependable soldier capable of conquering his fears and performing acts of courage and endurance.

CHARACTERS: Written some thirty years after the Civil War, *The Red Badge of Courage* describes events that occurred six years before the author's birth. The sense of terror, honor, and courage it conveys, however, has all the immediacy of a soldier's narrative, justifying its position as a timeless anti-war novel. This short novel is told in the third person from the viewpoint of the young, callow recruit, **Henry Fleming**, who is called "the youth" throughout the novel. Henry undergoes an amazing transformation during the course of the novel, particularly in the few days in which he sees battle. He is first introduced as a naive, idealistic farm boy who regards warfare as a noble pursuit and soldiering as a heroic profession. "He had dreamed of battles all his life.... He had read of marches, sieges, conflicts, and he had longed to see it all." Henry experiences a disenchanting training period, but when real battle approaches he suddenly feels the first pangs of fear and doubts his own inner strength and ability to remain steadfast under gunfire. When he panics during the first enemy attack, shamelessly dropping his rifle and running from the battlefield in terror, Henry is unable to admit to his cowardice. Trying to justify his actions, Henry blames others, including his officers. Inwardly, though, he feels guilt, self-loathing, and a paralyzing fear that he will be found out.

When Henry receives his "red badge" and returns a respected hero to his regiment, the fear of discovery gradually diminishes. Though still living a lie, he now becomes arrogant, condescending toward others, and unusually self-assertive. Filled with a consuming hatred for the enemy that exposed his weakness, he behaves like a madman in the skirmishes that follow. Like one possessed, he becomes frenzied and performs reckless feats of daring and heroism to prove to himself and others that he is a man and not a coward. His ego bolstered, Henry is able to take his rightful, honored place among his comrades. Having proven himself, he is also one more step closer to maturity. Conquering his demons of self-doubt and insecurity, he gains a feeling of confidence and inner peace. "He felt a quiet manhood, nonassertive but of sturdy and strong blood. He knew that he would no more quail before his guides wherever they should point. He was a man."

Henry's closest companion is another private, **Wilson**, referred to as the **Loud Soldier** and later as **Friend**. Like Henry, Wilson also experiences a transformation under the stress of battle. At first he is presented as a scrappy, sarcastic, loud-mouth who complains about everything. A know-it-all, he is also often grumpy. Pictured as an energetic, belligerent braggart, Wilson is impatient to get into the fight and is scornful of the thought that he might lose his courage in battle. However, before the first important skirmish, Wilson betrays his fears and misgivings by entrusting Henry with a packet of his personal letters in case he dies in battle. When Henry returns wounded, Wilson, now a battle veteran, has changed. For the first time he shows generosity and compassion. He binds Henry's wound, allows him to use his blanket, and shares his canteen with him. He admires Henry's supposed courage and fortitude and regards him as both a hero and leader. When Henry exhibits the same bombastic, petulant behavior that he was once guilty of, Wilson responds with understanding and tolerance. Now subdued and filled with an inner confidence, Wilson has a new, more mature perspective on life, a "quiet belief in his purposes and his abilities." Henry, who had once viewed Wilson as "a swaggering babe ... filled with tinsel courage," thinks Wilson has "now climbed a peak of wisdom from which he could perceive himself as a very wee thing." This new perspective allows Wilson to accept the war and its consequences, as well as giving him courage in battle based on principles rather than bravado. He now feels the spirit of brotherhood with his fellow soldier and, in short, has become a wiser man than Henry.

Henry's other friend is another private, **Jim Conklin,** also known as the **Tall Soldier**. Jim has a practical, realistic nature and is not given to the outbursts of Wilson. He is cool, composed, and accepting of his fate. Jim has a philosophical, mature view of the war and tells Henry that he probably would run from battle if everyone else around him did, otherwise he would stay and fight. He is in many ways an average man, decent, caring and accepting of life. When he is mortally wounded and one side of his body is ripped to shreds, he still shows incredible physical strength and courage. Delirious from his wounds, he performs a macabre dance before falling dead to the ground. His demise and suffering greatly affect Henry.

Henry meets another severely wounded soldier during his desertion, the **Tattered Man**. Though he is losing touch with reality and becoming delirious because of a severe head wound, this man tries to help Jim before his death and extends his friendship to Henry, thinking that the boy is also wounded. His inquiries about Henry's health stir up feelings of guilt and shame, and the boy, in an act of callous cruelty, flees from the scene leaving the wounded soldier alone and helpless in a field. Later, this image haunts Henry.

Henry's **mother** appears briefly at the beginning of the novel. She is a religious, hard-working women who is opposed to Henry's enlistment, but later she accepts her son's decision. She disappoints Henry by being austere and cold in her farewell but shows genuine concern for her son by giving him sound, practical advice, as well as eight pairs of socks so that her boy will be "jest as warm and comf'able as anybody in the army."

Further Reading

Bassan, M., ed. *Stephen Crane: A Collection of Critical Essays.* Englewood Cliffs, NJ: Prentice-Hall, 1967.

Benfey, Christopher. *The Double Life of Stephen Crane.* New York: Knopf, 1992.

Berryman, John. *Stephen Crane.* New York: Sloane, 1950.

Bloom, Harold. *Stephen Crane's The Red Badge of Courage.* New York: Chelsea, 1987.

Cady, Edwin H. *Stephen Crane.* Rev. ed. Boston: Twayne, 1980.

Cazemajon, Jean. *Stephen Crane.* Minneapolis: University of Minnesota Press, 1969.

Colvert, James B. *Stephen Crane.* San Diego: Harcourt, 1984.

Critical Survey of Long Fiction. Vol. 2. Englewood Cliffs, NJ: Prentice-Hall, 1983.

Gibson, Donald B. *The Fiction of Stephen Crane.* Carbondale: Southern Illinois University Press, 1968.

———. *The Red Badge of Courage: Redefining the Hero.* Boston: Twayne, 1985.

Halliburton, David. *The Color of the Sky: A Study of Stephen Crane.* New York: Cambridge, 1989.

Holton, Milne. *Cylinder of Vision: The Fiction and Journalistic Writing of Stephen Crane.* Syracuse: Syracuse University Press, 1958.

Kimbel, Bobby Ellen, and William E. Grant, eds. *American Short-Story Writers, 1880-1910.* Vol. 78 of *Dictionary of Literary Biography.* Detroit: Gale Research, 1988.

Knapp, Bettina L. *Stephen Crane.* New York: Ungar, 1987.

Mitchell, Lee Clark, ed. *New Essays on The Red Badge of Courage. The American Novel Series.* Cambridge: Cambridge University Press, 1986.

Nagel, James. *Stephen Crane and Literary Impressionism.* University Park: Pennsylvania State University Press, 1980.

The New Molton's Pre-Twentieth-Century Criticism of British and American Literature. Vol 10 of *Chelsea History Library of Literary Criticism.* New York: Chelsea, 1989.

Pizer, Donald, and Earl N. Harbert, eds. *American Realists and Naturalists.* Vol. 12 of *Dictionary of Literary Biography.* Detroit: Gale Research, 1982.

Pizer, Donald, ed. *Critical Essays on Stephen Crane's The Red Badge of Courage.* Boston: G. K. Hall, 1990.

———. *The Red Badge of Courage.* New York: Norton, 1993.

Quartermain, Peter, ed. *American Poets, 1880-1945: Third Series.* Vol. 54 of *Dictionary of Literary Biography.* Detroit: Gale Research, 1987.

Twentieth-Century Literary Criticism. Vols. 11, 17, 32. Detroit: Gale Research, 1983, 1985, 1989.

Chris Crutcher

1946-, American novelist

Running Loose

(young adult novel, 1983)

PLOT: For seventeen-year-old Louie Banks, senior year at a small high school in Trout, Idaho, is an exciting and harrowing one. Louie is growing up in a typical middle-class family. He has a kid sister, Tracy, a mother, Brenda, who is a housekeeper, and a father, Norman, who runs a gas station where Louie works part-time. Louie is an enterprising young man who also works as a custodian at a local bar, the Buckhorn, run by one-armed Dakota, and he also plays on his championship high school eight-man football team. Two of his teammates are his best friend, Carter Sampson, and nemesis, Boomer Cowans. The brightest spot in Louie's life is his girlfriend, Becky Sanders, a young woman who he feels is perfect in every way.

Before a crucial game one day, Coach Lednecky suggests that his team should play dirty if necessary to get their rival's star, a new black player named Kevin Washington, out of the game. When Boomer creams Washington, Louie is so incensed that he leaves the game in disgust and is suspended for insubordination by Principal Jasper. After a week, he is reinstated through the intervention of his father, the school board chairman, but he is unofficially banned from all sports.

Louie's loving relationship with Becky is brought to a tragic end when she is killed in an automobile accident. At the funeral, Louie becomes so enraged when the visiting minister gives a eulogy full of artificial sentiments that he interrupts the service and must be escorted out. His life is at an all-time low, when the assistant coach, Mr. Madison, interests Louie in trying out for track. After being threatened with a lawsuit by Becky's father, Fred Sanders, if they don't comply, Jasper and Lednecky grudgingly allow Louie to run "unofficially" on the track team. At the most important track meet, Louie meets his chief competitor, Washington, in the two-mile race and manages to break the tape just before him.

Louie is happy to learn that a tree will be planted on the school grounds honoring Becky. However, he finds that the words on the accompanying plaque are really an ego trip for Principal Jasper. Outraged once more, Louie one night knocks the plaque off its concrete base and throws it into the river. Principal Jasper isn't fooled. He confronts Louie, who tells a boldfaced lie and denies defacing the memorial. He has decided that, when necessary, you must fight dishonesty by being dishonest. At graduation, when his father tells Louie how proud he is of him, Louie is moved to tears. Later, when Principal Jasper replaces the missing plaque with an identical one, Louie knows he has another job on his hands.

CHARACTERS: The narrator and protagonist of the novel is **Louie Banks**, a likable, hard-working young man who is so unassuming about his virtues and talents that he becomes, at times, self-deprecating. He knows he will never be a distinguished football star like his friend Carter, and he has become resigned to a modest 2.46 grade point average. However, he hopes that with hard work and perseverance he can get through college and lead a productive, normal life. A compassionate and humane person, Louie has never made love to a girl for fear she would be ashamed and "feel crappy" afterwards; he is also particularly kind to the younger, weaker players during football practice. For these admirable sentiments, Boomer brands him a wimp and coward. Apart from the tender, positive feelings he has for Becky, Louie is content to go through life as an average person hoping not to "screw things up," but he underestimates his own courage and endurance. When his sense of honor and fair play are affronted by Coach Lednecky, Louie takes a stand and accepts punishment rather than back down. His courageous fight against prejudice and unsportsmanlike behavior displays a unique and previously untapped strength of character. He again demonstrates this independent, gallant facet of his personality when, grief-stricken by Becky's death, he interrupts the funeral to object to the pompous, phony words of the minister, and then later destroys Mr. Jasper's plaque. Being a loner is difficult for him, even though he has the support of those who count: his parents, Dakota, and Carter. Louie is amazed that so little in life is straightforward and understandable. Through these experiences, Louie matures and learns a lot about life. He now knows about the true nature of friendship, love, and loss, and he has found that "there's no use being honorable with dishonorable men." He has also learned to accept himself and recognize his own virtues, and, most of all, that it is everybody's job to fight for fairness and decency because "you are responsible for every damn thing you do."

Louie calls his father and mother by their first names, **Norm** and **Brenda**, an indication of the equality and closeness of their relationship. Norm is a service station owner, a respected community member, and chairman of the local board of education. A calm, shrewd man, he respects his son and, although he offers occasional bits of advice, allows Louie to make his own decisions and work out his own destiny. He is objective and nonjudgmental toward his family, but he shows great pride in Louie's fight for justice and helps him face the consequences. He tells Louie that he "must do what you have to do." A good negotiator, he is careful and judicious in his relations with others. Louie considers himself lucky to have such a wise, understanding parent. Brenda is more emotional than her husband but equally supportive of her son, though she tends to worry more about the less important aspects of her son's well-being—like the condition of his underwear—than the broader issues.

The love of Louie's life is **Becky Sanders**. So popular and attractive she could have any boy she wanted, she chooses Louie, much to his surprise. Becky is five-foot-nine, with long, dark brown hair, green eyes, and a charming smile. She is bright, self-assured, and mature for her years. It is she, and not the bashful Louie, who initiates their relationship by asking for the first date. Later, when they have fallen in love, she refuses the gift of his letter sweater, claiming that they don't need exterior tokens as proof that they like each other. Having spent her childhood in a big city with a neurotic mother, she is more experienced and sophisticated than Louie. Her independence and honesty are matched by the devotion she shows Louie, even volunteering to quit cheerleading as a sign of support. She is also a realist and, after telling Louie that he was right to protest the unsportsmanlike conduct on his team, claims he should now get on with his life. More sexually experienced than Louie, Becky engineers their first opportunity to sleep together. When Louie's innocence and timidity prevent a consummation, she is understanding and respectful. She is a steadying influence on Louie, who is devastated by her senseless death. Equally affected is Becky's understanding father, **Fred Sanders**, a brilliant lawyer who sympathizes with Louie and understands his outburst at the funeral. He also backs Louie in his fight against Jasper and Lednecky.

Carter Sampson, Louie's best friend, is a better athlete and more pragmatic than Louie. Described as "big, strong, fast and smart," he has an enviable football record and works hard through exercise and practice to maintain it. Since his father abandoned the family years before, Carter has become a realist about life and its difficulties. He knows Coach Lednecky is wrong and calls him a "lowlife," but he shrugs it off, neither condoning nor condemning him publicly because Carter's future college career depends on getting a football scholarship and Lednecky controls the strings. He plays it cool, but he is always a loyal friend to Louie, trying to negotiate a truce between his friend and the coach and warning Boomer of the consequences if he continues to bully Louie. Carter tries to be ethical and honorable, but circumstances force him to work within the system, even if it means a temporary compromise of his ideals.

The running back of the football team is big, strong, and dumb **Boomer Cowans**, Louie's sworn enemy. He enjoys bullying people and seeing others suffer; he brags about his considerable, but actually nonexistent, love life and tries to impress everyone with his feats on and off the football field. Because Louie continually calls his bluff, Boomer, who can't take criticism, tries to strong-arm him. He is an ignorant ("you'd have to add three points to his grade point average to bring it up to an F") bigot who feeds off Coach Lednecky's remarks about black athletes and translates them into disgusting racial slurs and flagrant prejudice. Easily swayed and without self-control, he commits a blatant act of violence against Washington and, when Louie objects, calls him a "nigger lover."

With his brush cut, tough manners, and bearlike appearance, **Coach Lednecky** is the picture of a high school athletic coach. With him, winning is everything, and he has the three-year winning streak of his football team to prove his tactics work. Though outwardly a gentleman, he is racially prejudiced and unprincipled. He advises his team to play dirty to win and condones Boomer's racial slurs by keeping silent. When later confronted by Louie, he self-righteously denies any wrongdoing and demands that the boy be punished. Ironically, this cowardly, contemptible person teaches a course in U.S. government and civics at the high school. **Principal Jasper** is a carbon copy of Lednecky. A former coach who is described as a "hardass," he is a tough disciplinarian and egotist who allows injustice to flourish, provided his reputation remains untarnished. Conservative and obstinate, he still believes girls are not emotionally equipped for competitive athletics.

Lednecky's assistant is a recent college graduate, **Coach Madison**, who is spending his first year at Trout High. Though he knows his job is on the line, he secretly comes to Louie's defense and helps him get on the school's track team. He feels particularly sympathetic toward Louie because his own girlfriend was also killed in an accident. He shares Louie's belief in the importance of integrity and fair play. Coach Madison's assistance, courage, and commitment help restore Louie's faith in others. Another of Louie's supporters is **Dakota**, a one-armed man who sports a hook instead of a hand. He runs the Buckhorn bar where Louie works and is a strong supporter of Louie, who describes him as "a rugged-looking old fart" who "never finished fourth grade but is real decent and smart as hell."

Stotan!

(young adult novel, 1986)

PLOT: Now in their senior year of high school, the four members of Spokane's Frost High School swimming team and their "den mother," Elaine, remain close buddies as they have for years. Walker Dupree is the team captain, and his colleagues are Jeff Hawkins, a bright, outgoing joker, Lion (short for Lionel) Serbousek, an intelligent but eccentric boy, and Nortie Wheeler, who is the best swimmer but also quiet and withdrawn, principally because of a deplorable home situation in which he is physically abused by his neurotic father. Elaine Ferral, the fifth member of the group, is an intelligent, independent girl whom all the boys regard as their best friend. They also respect and admire their tough coach, Max Il Song, a Korean American who often acts as their surrogate father. Max announces that the first week of their Christmas vacation will be devoted to especially tough drills and workouts called Stotan week, a term whose structure and meaning combines the words stoic and spartan. No one is prepared for the backbreaking exertion and deadening fatigue it involves, but the four endure it and emerge triumphant and pleased by their success.

In addition to physical trials, there are also personal problems to overcome. Nortie is so battered by his father that to ease the pain he is given illegal drugs by Walker's older junkie brother, Long John. Walker is so upset when he finds out that he punches his brother and, with the help of his teammates, moves Nortie to his house. The gang also fights a group of school bigots, led by Marty O'Brian, who are spreading racial hate materials and target Nortie as their victim because he has a black girlfriend, Milika. Walker's love life also troubles him. He finds after all these years that he really is attracted to Elaine but is reluctant to hurt his present girlfriend, Devnee. In Havre, Montana, where the team participates in a meet, Jeff suddenly collapses and, after tests are made, discovers that he is suffering from terminal leukemia. The news is devastating. The three remaining members enter the state swimming meet in Seattle and do well. In spite of the judge's objections, they enter the four-man relay event, but there is no one to complete their fourth lap: the water remains still as a silent tribute to Jeff.

As his senior year ends, Walker muses that it has produced more questions than answers, but it has also brought him a greater spirit of acceptance. Perhaps that is part of being a Stotan.

CHARACTERS: The narrator and captain of the swim team is **Walker Dupree**, an extremely likable, honest eighteen-year-old. He has five major concerns: the welfare of the team, getting along with his elderly parents with whom he has little in common, coping with his diminishing ardor for his steady girlfriend, Devnee, keeping his secret love for Elaine in check, and caring for his drugged-out older brother, Long John. Walker was born when his Dad was fifty-five and, although his mother and father are good, caring parents, they are unable to get involved in his interests, with the result that Walker has been left to grow up by himself. This explains his special attachment to Coach Max, whom he regards as a second father. Under Max's guidance and with a strenuous workout program, Walker has become "a big, fast, sleek piece of work." Walker tries to develop his other talents and, though he will probably go to college on a sports scholarship, his main ambition is to pursue his considerable writing skills. Walker is attuned to other people's feelings. He agonizes over Nortie's wretched home life and tries to instill confidence and self-reliance in him through counseling. Eventually, he provides a room for Nortie in his own home.

Walker is fearful of hurting Devnee's feelings and therefore postpones a breakup, and he feels responsible for his older brother and tries to protect him. These are heavy responsibilities for a high school student, but he handles them competently and without complaint. As well as being a loyal, compassionate friend, he believes in fighting for principles like fair play and respect for others. Walker actively opposes Marty O'Brian and his gospel of hate and intolerance, but he sees his role in life more as an observer than a crusader. From his distressing senior year experiences, he has "learned that asking 'why' is more often than not a waste of time; that it is more important just to know what is so." With this new-found acceptance of life, he has come to appreciate the truly important aspects in life like friendship and courage.

The most talented swimmer in the group is pathetic **Nortie Wheeler**. He is a worried, anxious boy burdened by an abusive, vicious father who beats up both him and his mother. His father drove Nortie's older brother to suicide but, in spite of this, Nortie still tries to love and please his father and earn his respect. His fear of becoming a child abuser like his father, however, forces him to drop his job in a day care center and his ambition of becoming a social worker or teacher. Instead, he becomes intrigued with the vagaries of human behavior and decides to aim for a career in psychology. At present, he is a follower rather than a leader, a young man who looks to his friends for the guidance and affection he lacks at home. He has an accepting nature, never complaining or self-pitying. Nortie is so vulnerable and trusting that his buddies rally to protect him, first from his father and then from the bullying Marty O'Brian. Nortie's girlfriend, **Milika**, is a black girl who has learned through experience to be tough and independent. She is domineering, decisive, and sure of herself—all the things that Nortie is not.

Lion (Lionel) Serbousek is the multi-talented oddball of the group. Orphaned when he was fourteen, he lives alone in two rooms in a condemned building. His living quarters contain a bed, hotplate, a sink that empties into the alley, and a toilet equipped with a seat belt. He is a very talented artist, but with his zany, off-beat attitudes, dress, and possessions, he has gained the reputation of being outrageous and shocking. He is, nevertheless, a devoted friend and a dedicated athlete. Lion loves to explore all sides of an issue and has a reputation for changing his opinions and allegiances. He is, however, loyal to his friends and his belief in justice and respect for others. Lion risks possible suspension because he was on school property when he burned the hate literature that Marty distributed. A true individual, Lion is beyond conformity and the need to please others. He is truly a free, indomitable person and a unique presence in the lives of his friends.

The fourth member of the team is wise-cracking, bright **Jeff Hawkins**. A brash, barrel-chested redhead, he is witty and articulate. Interested in world affairs and research, he loves impressing people with his erudition. He, too, is a loyal friend and fighter against injustice. A born leader, he has imagination, charm, and, as with the others, an unswerving loyalty to his friends. Though dangerously ill, he leaves his house to direct the attack against the racial prejudice of Marty and his gang. Jeff's inner strength and courage are shown when he is told that he has leukemia. He accepts it stoically without self-pity or protest, proving that he is a master Stotan.

Elaine Ferral is part mascot, part mother confessor, and good buddy to the four friends. Also a master athlete, she has "burned out" on sports and has moved on to other interests like astronomy, spiritual values, and a nontraditional education. Wise and mature beyond her years, Elaine has already moved from adolescence to womanhood.

She is tough, independent, and mature in her manner and attitudes; she publicly humiliates a boy who claims to have slept with her and challenges the principal's right to question her dating a student teacher. A loyal friend, she thinks of Walker only as a dear companion and nothing more.

The boys' respected teacher and coach is **Max Il Song**, a pint-sized powerhouse who wants to convey to his team members the importance of endurance, strength, and discipline. Though quiet and succinct in speech, he wields tremendous influence over the team and never abuses their trust. He accurately says of himself, "I try to be straight and I think I'm pretty decent." Max is a perfect model for the self-control and hard work he preaches. A courageous man, he confronts Marty and his bullying tactics and threatens him with reprisals, even though he knows Marty is a student and could cause problems for him with the administration. Max shows great wisdom and insight. He knows that sometimes it is not appropriate to take a stand on an issue and that one must be responsible for one's own life and actions. As he tells Walker, "Life doesn't forgive you because you're young and ignorant. Life has to be true to itself." By contrast, Max's personal life is not as orderly or successful as he would like: he is divorced and has lost custody of the little daughter he adores.

Marty O'Brian, the baseball team representative on the school's athletic council, is an opinionated, arrogant bully who hides his own insecurities and ignorance by preaching bigotry and racial hatred. He spreads malicious literature that preaches racial intolerance and hides behind his constitutional rights when challenged. Unfair and unethical, he targets the susceptible and defenseless Nortie for special harassment but finally gets his deserved comeuppance when the team members and Max take action.

A couple of other minor characters are important in Walker's life. His brother, **Long John Dupree**, is fifteen years older than Walker. An ex-flower child and Vietnam War veteran, he is hopelessly hooked on booze and drugs. Walker is amazed that he stays out of jail and tries unsuccessfully to salvage this wasted life. Long John is frequently humiliated and harassed by the bikers who supply him drugs on credit. When he gives drugs to under-age Nortie, Walker, for once, loses patience and lashes out against him. Walker's girlfriend is the attractive, innocent **Devnee**. She is an agreeable, pretty girl with short, almost black hair and lovely green eyes. She has a sweet affectionate disposition and is devoted to Walker, a fact that makes him feel guilty about his desire to break off their relationship because of his infatuation with Elaine.

Further Reading

Authors and Artists for Young Adults. Vol. 9. Detroit: Gale Research, 1992.

Berger, Laura Standley, ed. *Twentieth-Century Young Adult Writers.* 4th ed. Detroit: St. James, 1994.

Children's Literature Review. Vol. 28. Detroit: Gale Research, 1992.

Jenkinson, Dave. "Portraits: Chris Crutcher." *Emergency Librarian* 18 (January-February 1991).

McDonnell, Christine. "New Voices; New Visions: Chris Crutcher." *Horn Book* 69 (May-June 1988).

Something about the Author. Vol. 52. Detroit: Gale Research, 1988.

Spencer, Patricia. "Young Adult Novels in the AP Classroom: Crutcher Meets Camus." *English Journal* 78 (November 1989).

Maureen Daly

1921-, American novelist

Seventeenth Summer

(young adult novel, 1942)

PLOT: The ultimate romance novel for every teenaged girl when it was published in the 1940s, *Seventeenth Summer* is the story of the wonder of first love. Although its sweetness and innocence may be somewhat dated, it remains a lovely, gentle tale of a young girl's awakening.

Angie Morrow lives in the small town of Fond du Lac, Wisconsin, with her parents, younger sister, Kitty, and older sister, Margaret. Another older sister, Lorraine, is away at college. Angie meets Jack Duluth right after she graduates from high school at the all-girls Academy just outside of town. He went to the public school, where he was a star basketball player. Her hands are deep in garden dirt when he comes up the path with the bakery goods he is delivering and asks her if she would like to go sailing with him. Angie can't imagine that her mother will let her go, but she does. So begins Angie Morrow's wonderful seventeenth summer, a time of drugstore cokes, movies, and rides in Jack's old car. It also becomes a time of jealousy when an old girlfriend of Jack's appears, and a time of parental disapproval when Angie's father begins to think she is seeing too much of this boy who is, after all, not headed for college as Angie is. But most of all it is a time for falling in love.

This bittersweet seventeenth summer ends for Angie when she boards the train for college in the fall. She dutifully says goodbye to her parents and looks forward to her new life. But as the train pulls out of the station and she sees Jack standing there with his hands jammed in his pockets and his basketball sweater knotted around his neck, Angie knows that life has changed for her forever. She knows she will never again have a summer like this one.

CHARACTERS: Angie Morrow is bright, shy, and innocent. Obedient to her parents, she would never think of breaking the rules of conduct they have taught her, although she is not above bending them to a slight degree. She is well aware of the changing feelings within her and of her growing love for Jack Duluth. Nowhere is the innocence of *Seventeenth Summer* captured so well as in the scene at the country club dance where Angie gets her first real kiss. "In the movies they always shut their eyes," she says, "but I didn't. . . . In the loveliness of the next moment I think I grew up. . . . Sitting on the cool grass in my new sprigged dimity with the little blue and white bachelor's buttons pinned in my hair, Jack kissed me and his lips were as smooth and baby-soft as a new raspberry." Later in the summer, when Jack confesses that he is in love with her, Angie's hands tremble and she is speechless. No boy had ever said this to her before.

Despite her love for Jack, Angie is not the type of person who would defy her parents and change her plans for Jack. One night near the time for her departure, Jack asks her to stay and marry him. For a moment, she hesitates, but she turns him down. First love is never easy. For Angie Morrow it is beautiful beyond description, yet tinged with sadness and an ache in her heart that will never quite be forgotten.

Angie's first love, star basketball player **Jack Duluth**, is a handsome young man, easygoing and friendly. Although far more self-assured than Angie, he, too, is in many ways an innocent teenager experiencing the real wonder of first love. Unlike Angie, Jack has had dates before and knows he is attractive to young ladies. But falling in love is just as much of a revelation for him as it is for her. One night he confesses to Angie that he has had a little experience with girls and even went steady for a while, but his past relationships were never like this one. He can't get Angie Morrow off his mind, and so he tells her that he's in love with her. Sometime later, the two of them are dismayed when Jack's family decides that they will all be moving back to Oklahoma. Like Angie, Jack is bound by the 1940s conventions that are followed by his family, so he doesn't press Angie when she turns down his proposal.

Swede Vincent is Jack's best friend, a decent young man who is overweight and has blonde, kinky hair and an easygoing manner. Swede is popular with the girls and a little out of his league with shy and proper Angie Morrow, but he really likes her and understands the growing love between her and his friend.

Angie's two older sisters are Margaret and Lorraine. **Margaret** is a working girl engaged to a young man from Milwaukee who looks like a giant baby panda. **Lorraine** is home from college for the summer and considers herself to be quite sophisticated. When Angie first asks her mother if she can go on a sailing date with Jack, Lorraine is the one who encourages her when Mrs. Morrow hesitates. But later in the summer, when Jack is invited to dinner with the family, it is Lorraine who embarrasses him by her show of superior knowledge, which emphasizes that Jack is a poor student who is not college material. Much later, Lorraine admits to

Angie that she treated Jack badly because she was upset over breaking up with her own boyfriend, Martin. Angie's third sister, **Kitty**, is ten years old, still loves to play with toys, and adores Jack.

Angie's parents are typical adults of the time. They love their children and show them great affection and care, but they also expect certain rules to be followed without question. **Mrs. Morrow** likes Jack and understands what her daughter is feeling, but she can't help but ask Angie questions about his future plans and the kind of family he comes from. **Mr. Morrow** is less straightforward, although he does question Angie in a mild way about her seeing so much of this young man. Without their saying so, Angie knows in her heart that both of her parents feel that Jack Duluth is not quite up to their standards, no matter how nice he is.

Further Reading

Authors and Artists for Young Adults. Vol. 5. Detroit: Gale Research, 1990.

Berger, Laura Standley, ed. *Twentieth-Century Young Adult Writers.* 1st ed. Chicago: St. James, 1995.

Contemporary Literary Criticism. Vol. 17. Detroit: Gale Research, 1981.

Fuller, Muriel, ed. *More Junior Authors.* New York: H. W. Wilson, 1963.

Kirkpatrick, D. L., ed. *Twentieth-Century Children's Writers.* 2nd ed. New York: St. Martin's, 1983.

Something about the Author. Vol. 2. Detroit: Gale Research, 1971.

Something about the Author Autobiography Series. Vol. 1. Detroit: Gale Research, 1986.

Daniel Defoe

1661-1731, English novelist

Robinson Crusoe

(adventure novel, 1719)

PLOT: Although his father hoped that his son Robinson would find a livelihood in business, the young Crusoe was attracted to the sea. His first voyage ended with a bout of terrible seasickness during a violent storm that forced his vessel back to shore. Undeterred, he set out again on a trader bound for Africa. Captured by pirates and sold into slavery, he eventually made his escape and was taken on a Portuguese freighter to Brazil, where he bought a small plantation. On a voyage to Africa to secure slaves, the ship broke apart on a reef close to an uninhabited Caribbean island.

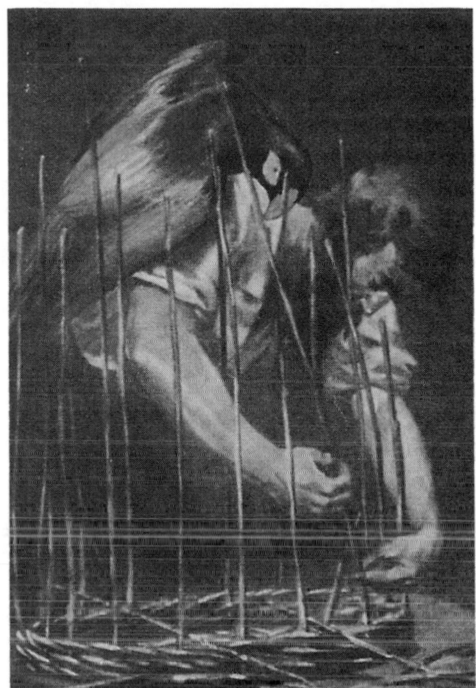

The ingenious and resourceful Robinson Crusoe builds a cage for his parrot in the 1719 novel that would become the model for many later survival stories.

Washed ashore during a high tide, Robinson discovers that he is the sole survivor of the wreck. Before the vessel breaks up, he constructs a crude raft and transports food, ammunition, and supplies from the sinking ship. Slowly, he begins to create a home for himself on this tropical island. He builds two crude shelters on opposite sides of the island, constructs furniture and primitive canoes from local timber, and, in time, grows his own crops of corn and barley. Later, he domesticates enough wild sheep that after several years he owns a sizable herd. As the years pass, Robinson gradually grows to cherish and appreciate his solitary life and his closeness to God.

After twenty years on the island, Robinson becomes aware that natives from the mainland occasionally bring captives to the island's shores and engage in ritualistic feasts. Robinson is appalled and sickened by the gruesome remains of their cannibalistic orgies. Some years later, he is able to rescue a captive that the natives had brought to the island to eat. Robinson names him Friday, after the day of his rescue. The young native soon learns English and becomes Robinson's faithful servant and friend.

The two are making plans to sail to the mainland and get help from Friday's tribe when, unexpectedly, an English ship sets anchor near the island's shore. After overcoming several mutinous crew members, Robinson and Friday restore power to the ship's captain and sail for Europe. A virtual stranger, but wealthy from accumulated plantation earnings, Robinson returns to England after an absence of thirty-five years. Several years later, he returns to his island, where he finds a small colony composed of families of mutineers and native women brought from the mainland. They are thriving and still utilizing many of the innovations and improvements that Robinson had developed.

CHARACTERS: The narrator and hero of this novel, the full title of which is *The Life and Strange Surprising Adventures of Robinson Crusoe,* is its title character. **Robinson Crusoe** is a courageous, enterprising young man who is able to accept adversity and profit from its lessons. He refuses to be intimidated or discouraged by hardships or disasters, instead finding ingenious solutions to his problems. Through a gradual hit-or-miss process, he learns how to become self-sufficient on his castaway island and masters the basics of horticulture, woodworking, and animal husbandry. Over the years, more sophisticated skills are added to his repertoire, including pottery making. His inventive, creative nature is tempered by a great love of living things and compassion for others. Robinson's belief in justice leads him to risk his life to rescue Friday as well as save the surviving crew members from the mutineers. At first he regards Friday as a mere servant, but in time the bond of friendship and love between the two is so strong that Robinson becomes jealous when he thinks Friday wants to leave him and return to his tribe.

Robinson is a devout Protestant whose faith is a source of strength and support. Accepting of God's word and believing that everything in life has a divine purpose, he reads his Bible regularly and takes each of its lessons to heart. He believes in a personal God, one who is merciful and will provide. Never given to self-pity, Robinson seeks to understand why God has singled him out for these predicaments, and in time, when he discovers the delights of his accomplishments and the inner peace that his solitary life has brought him, he says, "I gave humble and hearty thanks that God had been pleased to discover to me, even that it was possible I might be more happy in this solitary condition that I should have been in a liberty of society and in all the pleasures of the world."

Robinson's loyal servant and friend is **Friday,** the hapless native whom Robinson rescues before he can be eaten by his enemies. He is described as "a comely, handsome fellow, perfectly well made, with straight strong limbs, tall and about twenty-six years of age. His face was round and plump; his nose small, a very good mouth, thin lips, and his fine teeth well set, and white as ivory." Eternally thankful for being saved by Robinson from a gruesome death, Friday becomes the embodiment of a loyal, trusting servant. His allegiance and devotion to Robinson is so great that he would willingly die to save his master's life. Beyond the master-servant relationship is a friendship built on mutual respect and love. Without hesitation, Friday gives up the chance to return to his tribe in order to accompany Robinson to England and a totally unknown environment. Friday is a courageous and daring young man whose exploits in dangerous situations continually amaze and astound Robinson. Good-natured and obliging, Friday is also extremely bright and intelligent. He learns English quickly and easily grasps the ways of a cultivated Englishman. He astutely learns to help Robinson in his daily chores and suggests methods of improving their way of life. As Robinson states, "Never man has a more faithful, loving, sincere servant than Friday was to me; without passions, sullenness, or designs, perfectly obliged and engaged; his very affections were tied to me, like those of a child to a father."

Further Reading

Alkon, Paul K. *Defoe and Fictional Time.* Athens: University of Georgia Press, 1979.

Battestin, Martin C. ed. *British Novelists, 1660-1800.* Vol. 39 of *Dictionary of Literary Biography.* Detroit: Gale Research, 1985.

Bloom, Harold. *Daniel Defoe.* New York: Chelsea, 1987.

———. *Daniel Defoe's Robinson Crusoe.* New York: Chelsea, 1988.

Critical Survey of Long Fiction. Vol. 2. Englewood Cliffs, NJ: Salem, 1983.

Daniel Defoe: A Collection of Critical Essays. Englewood Cliffs, NJ: Prentice-Hall, 1976.

Ellis, Frank H., ed. *Twentieth Century Interpretations of Robinson Crusoe.* Englewood Cliffs, NJ: Prentice-Hall, 1969.

Green, Martin. *The Robinson Crusoe Story.* University Park: Pennsylvania State University Press, 1991.

Literary Criticism from 1400 to 1800. Vol. 1. Detroit: Gale Research, 1984.

The New Moulton's Pre-Twentieth Century Criticism of British and American Literature. Vol. 5 of *Chelsea House Library of Literary Criticism.* New York: Chelsea House, 1987.

Ross, John Frederic. *Swift and Defoe: A Study in Relationships.* Philadelphia: R. West, 1977.

Siebert, Donald T., ed. *British Prose Writers, 1660-1800: First Series.* Vol. 101 of *Dictionary of Literary Biography.* Detroit: Gale Research, 1991.

Sitter, John, ed. *Eighteenth-Century British Poets: First Series.* Vol. 95 of *Dictionary of Literary Biography.* Detroit: Gale Research, 1990.

Something about the Author. Vol. 22. Detroit: Gale Research, 1981.

Sutherland, James R. *Daniel Defoe: A Critical Study.* Cambridge: Harvard University Press, 1971.

Watson, Francis. *Daniel Defoe.* New York: Longmans, 1952.

Charles Dickens

1812-1870, English novelist

David Copperfield

(novel, 1850)

PLOT: David Copperfield was born in rural Suffolk six months after his father's death. Spurned at birth by his eccentric great-aunt, Miss Betsey Trotwood, who wanted a niece, he nevertheless enjoyed a happy childhood with his mother, Clara. This included spending time at Yarmouth visiting the family of their servant, loyal Peggotty, whose brother, Daniel Peggotty, had converted a boat into a home to take care of Little Em'ly and Ham, a young niece and nephew from two different families. When David's mother remarries, their household is taken over by her new husband, the cruel Mr. Murdstone and his equally unpleasant sister, Miss Jane Murdstone.

David is packed off to Salem House school near London, where the headmaster is the brutal Mr. Creakle. Here he is befriended by the affable Tommy Traddles and aristocratic, handsome James Steerforth. When David is ten years old, his mother dies and Peggotty marries the local coach driver, Barkis. David is sent to work in an export warehouse and, while there, lodges with the family of Wilkins Micawber, a good-hearted man always on the verge of bankruptcy, and his wife, Emma. David seeks help from his aunt, Miss Betsey Trotwood, in Dover. She accepts the advice of a dull-witted, amiable man, Richard Babley, known as Mr. Dick, with whom she shares her house. She also decides to finance David's education at Mr. Strong's school in nearby Canterbury. While there, David, now nicknamed Trotwood, lodges with Miss Betsey's lawyer, Mr. Wickfield, and his loving daughter, Agnes. David also becomes acquainted with Uriah Heep, whose oily manner and clammy handshake disgust the young boy.

After finishing school, David takes Steerforth with him to visit the Peggottys and finds that Little Em'ly is attracted to his friend, though she is engaged to Ham. When David is articled to the law firm of Spendlow and Jorkins, he falls madly in love with his employer's daughter, the immature Dora Spenlow. Two upheavals change his stable existence. Steerforth runs off with Little Em'ly and Miss Trotwood loses her fortune. David takes a job with Mr. Strong at his former school and later becomes a court reporter. After Mr. Spendlow dies, David, now twenty-one, marries the impractical Dora, who is unable to run their household. Micawber has become Uriah Heep's secretary, and, to ease his conscience, reveals that Heep has been cheating Mr. Wickfield for years and that he was also responsible for Miss Trotwood's financial losses.

Micawber decides to start a new life for himself and his family in Australia, leaving with Daniel Peggotty and Little Em'ly, who has been deserted by the unfaithful Steerforth. When Dora's health declines, the loyal Agnes nurses her, but David's fragile doll-wife dies and a grieving David decides to forget his sorrows by journeying abroad. Before he leaves, he visits Yarmouth to give Ham a letter from Little Em'ly. During a violent storm at sea, Ham ventures out to save a stranger in distress, but they both drown. When the bodies are washed ashore, the stranger is identified as Steerforth.

David stays in Europe for three years. When he returns, he realizes that his heart really belongs to his adoring friend, Agnes. To bring the two together, Miss Trotwood craftily makes up a lie and hints that Agnes is about to get married. David visits Agnes to extend his best wishes and the two confess their true love for each other. After their marriage, David is free to begin his career as a novelist with the woman he adores.

CHARACTERS: *David Copperfield* is regarded by many as Dickens's best novel; the author himself called it his "favourite child." Adding to its appeal is the immediacy of a first person narrative and the fact that many of the early scenes are autobiographical. The narrator and hero of the novel is **David Copperfield**. As a small boy he displays the intelligence, trust and affability that will characterize his adulthood. He thrives on affection from family and friends, but when it is withdrawn he suffers from fear and loneliness. His sensitive heart is easily bruised, and he has trouble adjusting to the suffering he sees around him. David shows increasing strength of character and inner resources during the course of the novel. For example, as a youngster, he courageously seeks the help of the unknown Betsey Trotwood and later meets his financial reverses with industry and perseverance by finding work and mastering the skills of court reporting. He also shows intellectual maturity with his success as a writer. David is a loyal and trusting friend, always willing to help others and to accept responsibilities. He survives poverty, oppressive work, a disappointing marriage, and the death of his friends. In the end, he emerges a strong, affectionate, sensitive man who is both self-sufficient and aware that he requires the moral support of loving friends.

David's mother, **Clara Copperfield**, is a pretty and caring woman who is also impractical and overly dependent on others. Her vulnerable, sensitive, and somewhat vain nature makes her easy prey for the attentions of **Mr. Murdstone**, a handsome, controlling man with a sadistic nature. Outwardly, he adheres to the codes of Victorian morality, while delighting in harming others and breaking their spirits. He is described as "fiendishly self-righteous and diabolically pleased with himself." He is perfectly matched with his cruel, manipulative sister, **Jane Murdstone**, another believer in "firmness." She is a gloomy-looking lady with dark eyebrows, who, characteristically, keeps her money in a hard steel purse stored "in a very jail of a bag, which hung upon her arm by a heavy chain."

David's loving nurse and his mother's housekeeper is **Clara Peggotty**, whom he describes as the "best, truest, most devoted and self-denying friend." Her plain, ruddy exterior, hides her beautiful, selfless inner nature. Peggotty is wooed by the taciturn, bashful stagecoach driver, **Mr. Barkis**, a simple, thrifty man whose marriage proposal consists of three words, "Barkis is willin'." At his death, Peggotty, her family, and David profit from Barkis's frugality and prudence.

Daniel Peggotty, Peggotty's brother who is a fisherman and seafood dealer, lives in Yarmouth. He is strong in both body and character, though poor and uneducated. Unselfish, kind, and dependable, he plays the role of benevolent and devoted father to his two charges with quiet dignity. The first is his pretty, intelligent, and affectionate niece, **Little Em'ly**, who is David's first love. She desires to elevate her station in life and has therefore adopted artificial airs. Her ambition leads to her infatuation with the aristocratic but heartless Steerforth. Conscience-stricken after being abandoned, she is too ashamed to go home. Later, she emigrates to Australia and remains a spinster. Daniel's second charge is **Ham Peggotty**, a fisherman and later a boat builder. Ham is a huge man, "broad in proportion, with a simpering boy's face and curly light hair." He is quiet, unselfish, and considerate. Though crude and simple in manners, he repeatedly shows great strength of character and nobility. This sincere, humble man is drowned while trying to save Steerforth's life.

At Salem House school, David encounters the ferocious headmaster, **Mr. Creakle**. Sadistic and cunning, his chief delight is flogging and bullying the boys in his school. David retains two of his classmates as friends. **Tommy Traddles** is a likable, loyal friend who was "the merriest and most miserable of all the boys." He became a shy, steady, amiable man, first as a barrister and later as a highly respected judge. His good nature and faithfulness endear him to David, whose other school acquaintance is the complex **James Steerforth**. Extremely attractive, wealthy, and sophisticated, James presents a dashing exterior but is inwardly heartless, self-centered, and arrogant. Spoiled by his doting mother, his contempt for the lower classes and his dissolute lifestyle leads to his callous seduction of Em'ly.

David's landlord while at the warehouse is **Wilkins Micawber**, the eternally optimistic but always impoverished gentleman described as "a stoutish middle aged person ... with no more hair on his head (which was a large one and very shining) than there is upon an egg." He is a good-hearted, happy-go-lucky man given to flowery language in both speech and writing. Exceedingly impractical and financially naive, Micawber and his family live in poverty and are continually on the verge of being sent to debtor's prison. He has an emotionally volatile nature that leads to violent mood swings and behavior characterized by bouts of sobbing, followed by euphoria, after receiving any bit of good news. He is usually a cheery, lovable, comic figure whose positive attitude is epitomized in his often-used phrase, that he is "waiting for something to turn up." His sense of honesty and justice lead him to unmask Uriah Heep. He later prospers in Australia. His wife, **Emma Micawber**, is loyal and devoted to her husband, and, though born to a higher class and the victim of her husband's impracticality, swears never to leave him.

David's great aunt, **Betsey Trotwood**, is a strong-willed, well-to-do, eccentric woman who hides an understanding, sympathetic nature under a harsh, formidable exterior. "There was inflexibility in her face, in her voice, in her gait ... but her features were handsome though unbending and austere." She proves to be David's financial salvation and, though abrupt and sharp-tongued, is a loyal, dedicated friend. Her companion, **Richard Babley,** better known as **Mr. Dick**, is a harmless, crazed fugitive from a lunatic asylum who wants to spread his ideas across the land by writing them on a kite. He is genial, kind and, according to Miss Trotwood, an infallible judge of character.

Mr. Wickfield is Betsey Trotwood's lawyer, who has succumbed to immoderate drinking after the death of his wife. His vice allows Uriah Heep to take advantage of this highly principled, compassionate man. His devoted daughter, **Agnes Wickfield**, is a saintly, self-effacing, ideal woman. She is sensible, unassuming, loyal, steadfast, and sacrificing. Agnes unselfishly cares for her father without reproach, uncomplainingly nurses Dora during her last illness, and, at last, receives her reward by becoming David's loyal, devoted wife.

Mr. Wickfield's clerk is the infamous **Uriah Heep**. Given to false modesty and claims of being humble, he is actually an unscrupulous hater of members of the upper class and is intent on rewarding himself by cheating them. He has a scheming, sly, malignant disposition masked by hypocritic fawning. In line with his character, he possesses a cadaverous face, clammy handshake, and closely cropped hair with hardly any eyebrows and no lashes. His plotting and forgeries are finally exposed by Mr. Micawber, and he is sent to prison.

David's first wife is **Dora Spenlow**, a pampered, protected girl who is unable and unwilling to face life's realities. She is a beautiful doll-like creature, with a delightful little voice and coquettish ways. Impractical and childish, she neither knows nor cares to know about running a household. David's loving, dainty, silly "child-wife," eventually becomes a hinderance to him. After a year or two of marriage, her health declines and she dies, thus making way for Agnes and David's happy marriage.

A Tale of Two Cities

(historical novel, 1859)

PLOT: This novel takes place in Paris and London over an eighteen year period before and during the French Revolution. Lucie Manette travels to France with a family friend, Mr. Jarvis Lorry, an agent of the banking house, Tellson and Co. She is on a mission to retrieve her father, Dr. Alexander Manette, recently freed after eighteen years in the Bastille and now living in a squalid room above the wine shop of Ernest and Madame Defarge, two pro-Revolutionaries. Five years later, the Manettes testify at Old Bailey in a case where Charles Darnay, whom they met on their passage to England, is accused by a secret agent, John Barsad, of spying for the French. The case is dismissed when Stryver, Darnay's lawyer, points out that physical identification can be incorrect by using the uncanny resemblance of his associate, Sidney Carton, to the accused as an example. Carton, an alcoholic, directionless man who brilliantly prepares the legal cases of the cunning Mr. Stryver, suddenly finds a purpose in life when he becomes attracted to Lucie.

Soon, Darnay, Carton, and Stryver, all seekers of Lucie's hand in marriage, become frequent guests of the Manette household that is governed efficiently by the fiery Miss Pross. Other visitors include Mr. Lorry and his porter, Jerry Cruncher. Unknown to the others, Darnay is actually a French aristocrat, the nephew of the hated Monseigneur, the Marquis of St. Evremonde. Darnay left France hoping to sever connections with his corrupt despotic family, but intrigues often draw him back, particularly when his uncle kills a peasant child and is, in turn, murdered in his bed. Lucie, the soul of gentleness and kindness, marries Darnay and they have a child, also named Lucie.

Six years later, in 1789, the Revolution escalates and the Bastille is stormed. Defarge recovers documents hidden there by Dr. Manette in his cell. When Darnay returns to France to save a faithful servant from the Revolutionists, he is accompanied by Mr. Lorry. When his identity is discovered he is arrested, and Lucie and her father come to help. Dr. Manette's sympathetic testimony at Darnay's trial succeeds and he is set free on the condition that he remain in France. Shortly afterwards, however, he is once again arrested, accused of crimes against the people by Defarge and an unknown party. Anxious to help, Carton, Miss Pross, and Jerry Crutcher also appear in Paris. One day in the street, Miss Pross recognizes her no-good brother, Solomon Pross, who is actually the informer Barsad, now working as a spy for the French. At Darnay's trial, Defarge testifies against him and names the other accuser as Dr. Manette, using as evidence the Bastille papers, in which the doctor chronicled the crimes of the St. Evremonde family and showed they were responsible for his imprisonment. Darnay is found guilty and sentenced to death.

By blackmailing Barsad, Carton gains access to Darnay's cell, drugs Darnay and, after having him carried from the cell, assumes his identity. The Manettes and Darnay escape to England, but Madame Lafarge tries to stop their departure and is accidently shot and killed in a struggle with Miss Pross. The housekeeper, now completely deafened by the gun blast, also escapes with Mr. Cruncher. Carton dies on the guillotine, sacrificing his life for the lives of the friends he loved.

CHARACTERS: Dickens was fascinated by the French Revolution. He once stated that he had read Thomas

Carlyle's weighty history of the revolution "five hundred times." From this absorbing interest came a lively story filled with memorable characters. When we first meet **Lucie Manette** she is only seventeen and described as "a short, slight pretty figure, with a quantity of golden hair and a pair of blue eyes." Lucie is quiet, gentle, and completely devoted to her newfound father to the point of stating she would never marry if it would interfere with his well-being. This same unselfish devotion is shown toward her husband when she risks her life by going to Paris for his trial. Her ability to love others around her, including those less fortunate, inspires an amazing adoration. For example, Carton is reborn with the aid of the simplicity and beauty of her love; her father regains his spiritual and physical health under her care; Mr. Lorry regards her as a daughter; and Miss Pross would face death to help her "Ladybird." Even the vulgar Stryver is captivated by her charms. Lucie is also the quintessential Victorian heroine, fainting under stress and being essentially passive and submissive.

Her father, **Dr. Alexander Manette**, is more complex but no less sympathetic than his daughter. When first introduced, he has recently been released from prison and is described as white-haired, stooped, and of faint voice. Broken in spirit and body by eighteen years in prison, his mind retains the scars that this solitude and loneliness have produced. Under stress, he reverts to repeating his cell number, "One hundred and five, North Tower," and he earns money by making shoes, the occupation he learned in prison. Gradually, the love and attention he receives from his daughter help rebuild his mental stability. His amazing nobility and strength of character are demonstrated by his steadfast silence concerning atrocities inflicted by Darnay's family. He knows that to divulge these would harm both Darnay and his daughter. A strong believer in truth and justice, he was sent to prison for his convictions and continues after liberation to risk his well-being to fight for a just cause, the freedom of his son-in-law.

Charles Darnay, born **Charles St. Evremonde**, is noble in birth and principles. His shame at the atrocities inflicted on others by his family has lead him to renounce his birthright and seek anonymity in England. He is always aware of the suffering of others. At his trial in England, he shows concern over the well-being of Lucie, who has been asked to testify, and he returns to France, innocently believing that he can face the mob and save his faithful servant. He is unselfish in his love for Lucie, and his passion for truth leads him to tell Dr. Manette of his family origins. These good intentions and his naivete often lead to misfortunes from which he needs help from others. Though virtuous and admirable in character, Darnay needs others to achieve his goals.

By contrast, **Sydney Carton** has a seriously flawed character, but one that is more interesting—and ultimately more admirable—than his look-alike Darnay's. Carton is an extremely intelligent, well-born man of ability who has fallen into a directionless disillusionment that leads to debauchery and alcoholism. He is a self-described jackal for his exploiting employer, Mr. Stryver. A man who has always helped others but never himself, his world-weary attitude and disagreeable demeanor are transformed when he encounters Lucie and suddenly has something to live for. Through her love, he begins to reform and seek redemption. His sacrifice to save his friends ultimately brings meaning to his life.

The counsel for the defense at Darnay's trial in England is the well-named **Mr. Stryver**, a glib, unscrupulous, ambitious man of the kind that gives lawyers a bad name. Pompous and conceited, he is the lion to Carton's jackal. He exploits the latter's weaknesses and takes credit for his brilliant research.

The two revolutionaries, **Ernest** and **Madame Defarge**, operate a wine shop in Paris. Whereas Monsieur Defarge seems motivated by genuine love of humanity and believes that the revolution will ultimately correct society's inequities, Madame Defarge is more bloodthirsty and eager for revenge. She is a stout, bull-like woman with heavily ringed hands and steady, strong features. Vindictive and unforgiving, she conscientiously incorporates the names of her proposed victims into her ever-present knitting, and during the time of execution she takes a prominent place near the guillotine. Bloodthirsty and crazed with the idea of destroying all but the peasant class, she is willing to sacrifice even innocent people like Lucie to satisfy her hatred. Although her husband calls her "a great woman, a strong woman," her major weakness is a consuming malevolence. Monsieur Defarge, Dr. Manette's former servant, generally follows his wife's leadership and, although he shows some sympathy towards Dr. Manette, generally allows the Revolution to take precedence over any feelings of compassion toward others.

Jarvis Lorry, the confidential clerk employed at the banking company of Tellson and Co., is a loyal and mild-mannered friend to the Manettes. For example, he brings Lucie to her father in Paris, helps in their return to England, supports Dr. Manette during his spells of derangement, and participates in carrying out the scheme to save Darnay. A confirmed bachelor, he is very orderly and methodical in his appearance and habits. In addition to fine attire, he sports a strange little crisp, flaxen wig. His assistant, **Jerry Cruncher**, is an odd-job man, part porter, part messenger at Tellson's. Sometimes abusive toward his wife and loutish son, Mr. Cruncher leads a double life: respectable bank worker by day and grave robber by night (he describes himself as a "resurrection man"). His comments and unusual behavior add some humor to the story.

Miss Pross, a wild red-haired woman, is so masculine in movement and appearance that many, at first, take her to be a man. She is Lucy's nurse, guardian, and housekeeper, who is a fine cook of both English and French cuisines. She is prone to a nervous disorder that produces "a fit of the jerks." Inside her gruff, blunt exterior beats a devoted, loving heart that would cheerfully stop beating for her darling Lucie. Indeed, she almost has that opportunity. Even though she always tries to find the best in everyone—even her no-good brother Solomon—she instinctively recognizes the evil in Madame Defarge, and risks her life in a struggle with the gun-wielding harridan.

Darnay's uncle, the **Marquis St. Evremonde**, represents the worst in French aristocracy. Insensitive, cynical, and cruel, he cares only for his own well-being and pleasures. A handsome man with polished manners and an impeccable wardrobe, he is the arch villain of the novel. **John Barsad**, originally **Solomon Pross**, is another villain who changes his allegiances and victims according to whomever pays him the most. Carton blackmails him into helping Darnay escape.

Great Expectations

(novel, 1861)

PLOT: Young Pip, short for Philip Pirrip, an orphan, is being raised in a small English coastal town by his strict, unfeeling elder sister and her husband, Joe Gargery, a kind, guileless blacksmith. Such townspeople as the pompous corn dealer, Uncle Pumblechook and the would-be actor, Mr. Wopsle, are family friends. One day in the marshes, Pip is accosted by a manacled escaped convict who demands help from the frightened child. Pip manages to steal food and a file for the man, and, while delivering them, notices a second convict skulking in the distance. The man Pip has aided is caught by the police, but before being led away he promises to repay the boy for his help.

Pip is invited to play at the mansion of an eccentric old lady, Miss Haversham, who lives in seclusion with her adopted daughter, the enchanting, aloof Estella, who is about Pip's age. Time has stopped for Miss Haversham ever since she was jilted on her wedding day. She still often wears her wedding dress and maintains a deserted room where her moldy wedding cake is now a home for spiders. Miss Haversham gives Joe the necessary indenture money for Pip to be an apprentice blacksmith. Therefore, some time later, when Miss Haversham's lawyer, Mr. Jaggers, informs Pip that an unknown benefactor has given money for him to relocate to London and live the life of a gentleman, Pip believes it is a gift from Miss Haversham.

In London, Pip rooms with a pleasant young man, Herbert Pocket, while also spending time at the home of his tutor, Herbert's father, Matthew Pocket. There he meets another student, the disagreeable Bentley Drummle. Pip also makes friends with Mr. Jagger's clerk, John Wemmick and, at Mr. Jaggers's home, meets his servant, a sullen woman named

Molly. Under Miss Haversham's direction, Estella moves to London, where she destroys Pip's hopes of romance by marrying Bentley. On his twenty-third birthday, Pip meets his real benefactor, Abel Magwitch, the escaped convict of years before who has illegally returned to England after making a fortune in Australia. Using the assumed name of Mr. Provis, he has risked his life to see the young man he turned into a gentleman.

Further disclosures reveal that the second convict is the villainous enemy of Magwitch, Arthur Compeyson, the man who betrayed Miss Haversham. It is also learned that Molly, an acquitted murderess, and Magwitch are Estella's real parents. Pip's world suddenly collapses about him. Miss Haversham dies in a fire that also destroys part of her house; and Joe's wife dies as a result of a vengeful attack by a former employee, Dorge Orlick, who is later caught. Also, the attempt by Pip and Herbert to smuggle Magwitch out of the country is foiled. Unfortunately, during the flight Magwitch saw his enemy, Compeyson, and in the ensuing struggle, Compeyson is killed and Magwitch is caught by the police. Magwitch later dies in prison. Because the convict's fortune is declared public property, Pip is once again, as he was when a child, poor and without expectations. He falls ill and is nursed back to health by Joe and his new wife, the Gargery's former housekeeper, faithful Biddy. Later, Pip joins Herbert in his successful export business in London. Eleven years pass and Pip, recently returned from a year abroad, goes to his childhood home. On a visit to Miss Haversham's deserted home, he discovers that Estella is a widow. Through her adversity, she has become a warmer, more compassionate person. The two childhood friends take each other's hand and walk away together.

Pip introduces Joe to Miss Havisham in a scene from* Great Expectations, *illustrated by Frederic W. Pailthorpe.

CHARACTERS: The plot of *Great Expectations* is essentially the journey of the narrator, **Philip Pirrip**, or **Pip**, from childhood to manhood and maturity, during which he must reject false values based on wealth and position for those involving love, respect, and generosity. When Pip is introduced, he is a frightened, lonely orphan whose life under the fearful tyranny of his older sister is moderated only by the kindness of her uneducated husband, Joe, who is a model of unselfishness and honesty. Pip is depicted as good-natured, bright, and friendly. However, when he encounters wealthy Miss Haversham and later sees the lifestyles of London society, his values change. He becomes an indolent, selfish, profligate ashamed of his roots and the homespun values of his family. Although his conscience nags him, he exchanges Joe's friendship and trust for a hopeless quest for the icy Estella and undesirable associates like Bentley Drummle. Only after his dismay at learning that his benefactor is a crude, wretched convict does Pip begin to change and realize that his snobbish behavior was built on false assumptions and aspirations. Through the friendship that developed with Magwitch, the loss of his fortune, and the threat of debtor's prison, Pip's superficial values crumble. But with the help of Joe, Biddy, and Herbert, he discovers the importance of human relationships and virtues like honesty, dignity, and hard work. These experiences have molded a stronger character, but one tinged with sadness and disenchantment.

The gentle, unselfish blacksmith, **Joe Gargery**, represents all the virtues of the common working man. Pip accurately calls him "a mild, good-natured, sweet-tempered, easy going, foolish, dear fellow" and "that gently, Christian man." He is also patient, generous and forgiving. Though shunned by Pip because of his crude, uneducated ways, he nurses the young man through his illness and gives Pip a new meaning for the word "gentleman." Though outwardly simple, Joe is a wise man whose positive values involving faith and hope have been learned through difficult experiences, including his saintly patience and forbearance with his difficult first wife.

The life of the half-mad **Miss Haversham** ended at twenty minutes to nine when, on her intended wedding day, she received a letter of rejection from Compeyson. Since then, she has been motivated only by self-pity and revenge. Miss Haversham's abnormal obsession with the past is illustrated by her insistence on wearing her tattered and yellowing wedding dress. Her revenge surfaces when she raises Estella to be a breaker of mens' hearts who is incapable of love. Miss Haversham is outwardly kind to Pip, but nevertheless pursues her twisted mission in life by intentionally misleading him into believing that she is his benefactor and by giving him false hope in his pursuit of Estella. Though she dwells in an imaginary world nursing her shame and anguish, she is sufficiently in touch with reality to selfishly manipulate those around her in order to assuage her own wounded pride. She began life as a beautiful, spoiled daughter of a rich businessman, but has become the white-haired, gaunt, wild-eyed, lonely woman whom, ultimately, Pip can only pity. On her deathbed after the fire, she pathetically asks for forgiveness, but it is too late to undo the harm that she has caused.

Miss Haversham's ward, **Estella**, is the cold, aloof, incredibly beautiful girl who was raised to be the instrument of Miss Haversham's revenge against men. As she states, "I stole her heart away and put ice in its place." Herbert Pocket says Estella is "hard, haughty and capricious to the last degree." She is often arrogant and unfeeling toward Pip, yet she exhibits an honesty and forthrightness that is admirable. Because she attracts men but is unable to return their love, her personality is both intriguing and pitiful. She is a social snob and disdainful of Pip's lowly origins (ironically, her own, of which she is never aware, are much humbler). But her disastrous marriage to Bentley Drummle and the decreasing influence of Miss Haversham produce changes in Estella. At the end of the novel, the reader encounters a more mature woman who is capable of love and compassion.

Mr. Jaggers, the cold, efficient, shrewd lawyer who represents both Miss Haversham and Abel Magwitch, is a study in contrasts. Physically, he is a burly, dark-complexioned man with a bald head, bushy eyebrows, and suspicious eyes. A secretive, unemotional man, he always maintains a cold business-like demeanor in his relations with others. He is overly cautious and often unscrupulous and ruthless with his clients; his frequent contacts with criminals have given him a knowledge of human nature and a cynical attitude. Yet a softer side occasionally appears: he successfully defends Molly on a murder charge and employs her as his maid, and he often shows Pip an uncharacteristic thoughtfulness. Mr. Jaggers's clerk, **John Wimmick**, leads a double life. At work, he is a cold, wooden, precise man whose mouth reminds Pip of a mail slot, but at home he is a gentle, relaxed, quite delightful man, devoted to his aged parent and his fiancee.

Pip's benefactor, **Abel Magwitch**, also known as **Mr. Provis**, is first introduced as a ferocious escaped convict. When he reappears later, he is still coarse in speech and manner, but he has become a wealthy sheep rancher. Obsessed with the concept of what constitutes a gentleman and a desire to repay Pip's kindness, he decides to create his own gentleman. At first, Pip is revolted by this uncouth man, but during Magwitch's final illness he realizes that the convict is an admirable person, one of high principles who is capable of tenderness and affection.

Herbert Pocket is Pip's first roommate in London. He unselfishly introduces Pip to London life and, in an affable way, corrects his manners.

Always cheerful and loyal, he is a man of high character who never stoops to Pip's snobbish ways and is always the model of a true gentleman. **Matthew Pocket**, Herbert's father, is Pip's tutor.

Some minor characters include: **Mrs. Joe Gargery**, Pip's mean-spirited, shallow, self-pitying older sister, who dies as a result of a head blow from **Dorge Orlick**, the villainous former employee who is motivated by hatred and jealousy; **Mr. Pumblechook** is a pompous, untruthful humbug who pretends, for his own edification, to be Pip's benefactor; and **Biddy** is the bright, trustworthy, loving girl who becomes the second Mrs. Joe Gargery. **Mr. Wopsle**, the parish clerk, supplies comic relief with his histrionics and theatrical aspirations. Two of the novel's villains are **Bentley Drummle**, the "idle, proud, niggardly, reserved and suspicious" man who later marries and abuses Estella, and **Arthur Compeyson**, Miss Haversham's suitor who took her money, jilted her, and later lives a life of crime. He incurs Magwitch's enmity by betraying him and falsely accusing him of corrupting his character.

Further Reading

Ackroyd, Peter. *Dickens.* New York: Harper, 1990.

Adrian, Arthur A. "David Copperfield: A Century of Critical and Popular Acclaim." *Modern Language Review* 11 (spring 1950).

Benstock, Bernard, and Thomas F. Staley, eds. *British Mystery Writers, 1860-1919.* Vol. 70 of *Dictionary of Literary Biography.* Detroit: Gale Research, 1988.

Bloom, Harold, ed. *Charles Dickens.* New York: Chelsea House, 1987.

———. *David Copperfield.* New York: Chelsea House, 1992.

———. *Charles Dickens' "Great Expectations."* New York: Chelsea House, 1994.

———. *Charles Dickens' "A Tale of Two Cities."* New York: Chelsea House, 1996.

Bradbury, Nicole. *Charles Dickens' Great Expectations.* New York: St. Martin's, 1991.

Collins, Philip. *Charles Dickens.* London: Routledge, 1987.

Colsell, Michael. *Critical Essays on Charles Dickens' "Great Expectations."* Boston: G. K. Hall, 1990.

Critical Survey of Long Fiction. Vol. 2. Englewood Cliffs, NJ: Salem, 1983.

Cruikshank, Robert J. *Charles Dickens and Early Victorian England.* London: Pitman, 1949.

Davis, Earle Roscoe. *The Flint and the Flame: The Artistry of Charles Dickens.* Columbia: University of Missouri, 1963.

Dexter, Walter. *Charles Dickens: The Writer and His Work.* Philadelphia: Ayer, 1977.

Fielding, K. J. *Charles Dickens: A Critical Introduction.* New York: Longmans, 1958.

Ford, George H. *Dickens and His Readers.* Princeton, NJ: Princeton University Press, 1955.

Fredeman, William E., and Ira B. Nadel, eds. *Victorian Novelists before 1885.* Vol. 21 of *Dictionary of Literary Biography.* Detroit: Gale Research, 1983.

Hobsbaum, Philip. *A Reader's Guide to Charles Dickens.* New York: Farrar, Straus, 1972.

Hornback, Bert G. *Great Expectations: A Novel of Friendship.* New York: Macmillan, 1987.

Johnson, Edgar. *Charles Dickens: His Tragedy and His Triumph.* New York: Simon & Schuster, 1952.

Lucas, John. *Charles Dickens: The Major Novels.* New York: Penguin, 1993.

Martin, Christopher. *Dickens.* Vero Beach, FL: Rouke, 1990.

Miller, J. Hillis. *Charles Dickens: The World of His Novels.* Cambridge, MA: Harvard University Press, 1958.

Murray, Brian. *Charles Dickens.* New York: Continuum, 1994.

Nelson, Harland S. *Charles Dickens.* New York: Twayne, 1981.

Nineteenth-Century Literature Criticism. Vols. 3, 8, 18, 26. Detroit: Gale Research, 1983, 1985, 1988, 1990.

Pearson, Hesketh. *Dickens, His Character, Comedy and Career.* New York: Harper, 1949.

Sell, Roger D. *Great Expectations.* New York: St. Martin's, 1994.

Stanley, Diane, and Peter Vennema. *Charles Dickens: The Man Who Had Great Expectations.* New York: Morrow: 1993.

Storey, Graham. *David Copperfield.* New York: Twayne, 1991.

Symons, Julian. *Charles Dickens.* New York: Roy, 1951.

Thesing, William B., ed. *Victorian Prose Writers before 1867.* Vol. 55 of *Dictionary of Literary Biography.* Detroit: Gale Research, 1987.

Wilson, Angus. *The World of Charles Dickens.* Chicago: Academy Chicago, 1985.

Peter Dickinson

1927-, English novelist

Eva

(science fiction, 1988)

PLOT: This novel, set in the unspecified future, covers a two-year period, with a brief epilogue set twenty years later. After a terrible accident, Eva Adamson, who is almost fourteen-years-old, awakens to discover that to save her life her brain has been placed in the body of Kelly, a young female chimp who lived in the International Chimpanzee Pool managed by Dr. Dan Adamson, Eva's father. After the initial shock, Eva adjusts relatively quickly to her new body with the help of her parents and Dr. Joan Pradesh, the person who is in charge of this innovative medical procedure. Also useful to Eva is her prior knowledge of the habits and language of chimps that she has absorbed through watching them at the Pool, where they have been kept for observation and experimentation. Eva's operation and medical expenses are paid for by a "shaper" network called SMI (an ultra-sophisticated form of television) and a fruit juice company called World Fruit. To pay for this financial help, she is forced to appear in commercials and on talk shows. After one demeaning interview, Eva gets revenge by planting a loud chimpanzee kiss on the show's host, Dirk Ellan. Only Grog (Giorgio) Kennedy, son of a volatile shaper director, seems to understand her misery and loneliness.

In spite of parental objections, Eva visits the Pool alone and becomes friends with a number of the chimps, including a male named Sniff. For the first time in months, she is at peace with herself. Grog hatches a plan to help Eva. He persuades SMI and World Fruit to photograph commercials involving the chimps and Eva on a deserted tropical island, St. Hilaire. During a violent typhoon, Eva and several chimps escape, and under her leadership they elude capture. After calling a truce, Eva negotiates an agreement whereby the chimps, including herself, will be allowed to live on the island in peace, except for the occasional filming of commercials. Twenty years later, Eva lies dying. Surrounded by her chimpanzee family and friends, she is grateful that she and her group have escaped the artificiality and hollowness of a technological society so that they could live a natural life.

CHARACTERS: Peter Dickinson is at home writing for both young people and adults. He has explored a wide variety of genres, ranging from mystery and horror to historical adventure and science fiction. *Eva,* a science fiction novel, paints a bleak picture of a future filled with dehumanizing technology. Through an amazing medical breakthrough, **Eva Adamson** has had her life torn in two. Though living in a chimpanzee's body, she is able to think as a human and speak through the use of a typewriter-like keyboard that produces human words and can change emphasis and expression upon command. She lives in a world where humans have no respect for nature, having destroyed the environment and many forms of animal life to the point where most people's knowledge of nature comes from viewing video recordings. In contrast, Eva enjoys the primal, natural emotions exhibited by the chimpanzees and appreciates their simple feelings of familial love and guileless rivalries. Though she has a human brain, her instincts and unconscious feelings are those of a chimp. Within her there is "an interface, a borderland where human ends and chimp begins." She begins living a double life—not really belonging to one species or the other. When finally forced to decide on her true identity, she realizes that she feels more at home in the natural world of the chimps. In so doing, Eva rebels against the tawdry materialism she sees around her, the commercial exploitation of animals, and the future destruction of the chimps.

Once an open and trusting daughter, Eva is now forced to plot secretly. Though scarcely in her teens, she shows great courage in defying unjust authority and manipulative commercial interests. She becomes outspoken and dauntless in fighting for her cause and develops amazing leadership qualities. When she makes the extremely difficult decision to leave her parents, she shows great fortitude and belief in her ideals. Eva also shows compassion and sensitivity towards others and is ingenious in findings solutions for each of her problems. When she achieves her goal of freedom on the island, "She could not imagine that she would ever by so happy again, so filled with tingling, sparking peace." Before her death, she is told that humans can't cope with the rampant nihilism in the world and are committing suicide. Once again, she realizes that her defiance and sacrifice have not been in vain.

Eva's father, the bearded, attractive zoologist, **Dan Adamson**, is a brilliant scientist and loving father. Fearful that his projects involving observation of chimpanzee behaviors will collapse for lack of financial support, he sometimes compromises his values and sells surplus animals to laboratories, believing that the end justifies the means. He is devoted to his project, sometimes allowing his scientific curiosity to outweigh his better instincts, and enjoys the notoriety of having a celebrity daughter. But he is always concerned about Eva's happiness and well-being. He understands Eva's situation and sympathizes with the choice she has to make. After she decides to remain on the island with her charges, he is supportive and reassuring. Though distraught over losing a daughter, he realizes that this choice is what she wants.

Eva's mother, **Lil Adamson**, is also an understanding, devoted parent but has more difficulty than her husband adjusting to Eva's chimpanzee ways. When Eva begins walking in a knuckling fashion and swinging from objects, Mrs. Adamson sometimes has difficulty disguising her shock. For this reason, she wants Eva to be isolated from the chimps at the Pool and to associate only with humans. This conflict causes problems for both mother and daughter. Eventually, Eva's instinctive behavior prevails, and her mother, in another display of empathy and tenderness, gives in to her daughter's wishes. She, too, is devastated when Eva remains on the island with her chimpanzees.

The leader of the project that saved Eva's brain is **Dr. Joan Pradesh**, a pioneer in the field of neuron memory. She is an astute, extremely intelligent woman who is highly regarded in her field. She despises the sensation-seeking media and their exploitation of Eva and tries to shelter her patient from this kind of exposure. However, her belief that the destruction of animals is justified when it saves human lives eventually produces conflicts between herself and Eva, whose conscience is troubled when see has to publicly oppose the woman who saved her life.

Among Eva's supporters in the animal rights groups, the most passionate and fervent is **Giorgio Kennedy**, better known as **Grog**. Usually a pleasant, easygoing, relaxed young man, he becomes fiercely intense and inflexible when discussing the use of animals in scientific experimentation. A nonconformist and born crusader, he gives Eva the direction and backing she needs to fulfil her dreams. He organizes the expedition to St. Hilaire and helps arrange her escape with the chimps. When the scheme is successful, Grog is left behind in an uncaring, human world where materialism is increasing. Unable to cope, he gradually sinks into insanity.

Eva's interviewer on a shaper pseudoscience show is **Dirk Ellan**. On camera he gives the impression of being relaxed, friendly, trustworthy, and understanding, but this is only a show-business veneer to hide a calculating insincerity and large ego. His condescending hypocrisy so offends Eva that she decides to embarrass him by giving him a big slobbery kiss on camera. Though he feigns laughter, Eva sees fright and fury in his eyes. She has given Ellan a suitable come-uppance.

Of all of Eva's chimpanzee friends, **Sniff** is her favorite. He is an odd-looking chimp with a shorter, squarer face than most and large, pale ears. More intelligent than the others, he follows Eva about the Pool, learning new skills and solutions to problems. On St. Hilaire, he is the first to trust and obey Eva and allow her to lead him from the compound into the jungle. When the chimpanzees gain their freedom, he becomes Eva's mate.

Further Reading

Authors and Artists for Young Adults. Vol. 9. Detroit: Gale Research, 1992.

Benstock, Bernard, and Thomas F. Staley, eds. *British Mystery and Thriller Writers since 1940, First*

Series. Vol. 87 of *Dictionary of Literary Biography.* Detroit: Gale Research, 1989.

Berger, Laura Standley, ed. *Twentieth-Century Young Adult Writers.* 1st ed. Chicago: St. James, 1994.

Contemporary Literary Criticism. Vols. 12, 35. Detroit: Gale Research, 1980, 1985.

De Montreville, Doris, and Elizabeth D. Crawford, eds. *Fourth Book of Junior Authors and Illustrators.* New York: H. W. Wilson, 1978.

Dickinson, Peter. "Fantasy: The Need for Realism in Children's Literature." *Education* (spring 1986): 39-51.

Henderson, Lesley, ed. *Twentieth-Century Crime and Mystery Writers.* 3rd ed. Chicago: St. James, 1991.

Hunt, Caroline, ed. *British Children's Writers since 1960, First Series.* Vol. 161 of *Dictionary of Literary Biography.* Detroit: Gale Research, 1996.

Something about the Author. Vols. 5, 62. Detroit: Gale Research, 1973, 1991.

Townsend, John Rowe. *A Sounding of Storytellers.* New York: Lippincott, 1979.

Ward, Martha, ed. *Authors of Books for Young People.* 3rd ed. Metuchen, NJ: Scarecrow, 1990.

Watson, Noelle, ed. *Twentieth-Century Science Fiction Writers.* 3rd ed. Chicago: St. James, 1991.

Franklin W. Dixon

(house pseudonym used by the Edward Stratemeyer Syndicate)

"The Hardy Boys"

(young adult mysteries, 1927-)

PLOT: The "Hardy Boys" series was created by the Edward Stratemeyer Syndicate of East Orange, New Jersey. A virtual book factory dedicated to creating popular stories for young readers, the Stratemeyer syndicate has produced many top-selling series, of which the Hardy Boys is one of the most successful. To create these series, several writers work on different books published under a single pseudonym: Franklin W. Dixon, in the case of the Hardy Boys mysteries. The first author to write Hardy Boys mysteries, however, was Leslie McFarlane. Beginning in 1986, the "Hardy Boys Case Files" series was also launched.

The two brothers who are the heroes of the books, tall, dark-haired Frank Hardy and his year-younger brother, blonde and blue-eyed Joe, are the sons of renowned sleuth Fenton Hardy. Along with their parents, they live in Bayport, a town on the Atlantic Ocean that is a short plane ride from New York City. Students at Bayport High, the boys have followed in their father's footsteps to become amateur sleuths. With intelligence, humor, and just the right amount of daring, they have solved countless crimes over the decades and have become heroes to generations of young boys and girls. Although their characters have been updated over the years, many of their adventures may still seem dated to today's readers. Still, the reliably successful formula of these mysteries keeps young audiences coming back for more.

In *Blood Money: Case Files No. 32* (1989), Frank and Joe travel to Brooklyn, New York, with their father, who has been called to a reading of the will of Josh Moran, whom Fenton Hardy helped send to jail some twenty years earlier. The will leaves ten million dollars to be divided equally among seven men, Fenton included. The catch is that the money will be divided at the end of three months to whomever is still alive. It isn't long before one of the seven—Daniel Carew, a suspected member of the mob and longtime associate of Moran's—is killed. The suspect is also one of the seven: former football hero Thomas Poletti, who is planning to marry Moran's daughter, Emily.

But the Hardy boys and their father don't believe that Poletti is guilty, and they set out to find the real murderer. With some clever sleuthing, and a little help from Dad, Frank and Joe Hardy uncover the truth. The guilty party is Ned Nolan, son of Hugh Nolan, one of the seven named in the will. Hugh was a former detective who lost his job because he was suspected of taking bribe money from Moran. All his life, Ned fumed over what he believed to be false charges only to discover that his father was guilty of taking the money after all.

In *The Tower Treasure* (1992), Frank and Joe Hardy are nearly run down on their motorcycles by a speeding driver. They see him once again that day and barely escape a second time. They notice that the driver has red hair. Soon after, they learn that the car of their friend Chet Morton has been stolen. Chet's bright-yellow jalopy, known as the Queen, is his life, and the Hardy boys want to help him recover it. When they report the theft, they learn that someone attempted a robbery of the ferryboat office and then there was a successful robbery of jewels and securities at Tower Mansion, Bayport's showplace which is owned by the Applegates. The suspect is the caretaker, Henry Robinson, who is the father of Perry, nicknamed Slim, one of the Hardy boys' good friends.

Naturally, Joe and Frank Hardy don't believe Mr. Robinson is the thief, and they set out to prove his innocence. Chet's jalopy is found, and so is a discarded red wig. Slim hears that a strange man had been lurking around the Tower Mansion a few days before the robbery. Some sleuthing turns up the name of John Jackley, known as Red in prison because he had been caught wearing a red wig. Jackley turns up unconscious in the hospital. Before Jackley dies, the Hardy boys hear the words "old tower" and think the money is hidden in the Tower Mansion. Later, the two boys, eating lunch near the railroad tracks, both glance up at two old water tanks. Frank and Joe have the same idea. It leads them to suspect that the stolen treasure is hidden in the old water tower, not the tower of the Tower Mansion. The boys are right and uncover the treasure, but they must first take it away from Hobo Johnny. When the treasure is recovered, Hurd Applegate and his sister, Adelia, apologize to Mr. Robinson, who is cleared of suspicion, and the Hardy boys get a reward.

CHARACTERS: Frank and **Joe Hardy** are typical teenage boys. At eighteen and seventeen respectively, they are intelligent and earnest boys with an interest in being amateur detectives and trying to emulate their famous detective father. The Hardy boys play football, ride motorcycles, study hard in school, date their teenage classmates, and have a good relationship with their parents. Although the brothers are highly idealized, they remain engaging characters nonetheless.

The mysteries in the "Hardy Boys" books are never very complicated. The Hardy boys are not reckless in their pursuit of suspects, but they are not afraid to take some chances, which sometimes leads to dangerous situations for them. In all cases, they use their wits—with perhaps a little bit of luck—to escape any serious trouble. Their adventures bring out the brothers' good character traits, such as loyalty to their friends. In *The Tower Treasure,* for instance, Frank and Joe know immediately that Mr. Robinson would not steal the treasure, even though he is in need of money; and in *Blood Money* the boys refuse to believe that Tommy Poletti, football hero, is a killer. In both cases, the Hardy boys prove to be good judges of character.

Fenton Hardy is the father of the Hardy boys. A famous private detective who was once on the police force, Mr. Hardy is indulgent of his precocious sons, allowing them to accompany him on his cases when the danger does not appear to be too great. He encourages their inquisitiveness and eagerness to solve a mystery, although he always expects the boys to use common sense and obey his orders. Sometimes, Frank and Joe come close to bringing parental disapproval down on their heads, but they always manage to come through. Mr. Hardy is sometimes stern but always loving and caring, and his pride in his sons is obvious. In the early books, **Mrs. Hardy** is a stereotypical mother of an earlier day. Pretty and petite, she is usually at home serving as the anchor of the family, while husband and children run around solving crimes. Although she does not engage in sleuthing herself, Mrs. Hardy is unfailingly supportive and can be counted on to back up her boys in whatever they do. Her presence in these mysteries is usually peripheral. Also making small appearances in the series is another minor character, **Callie Shaw.** Frank sometimes dates Callie, a high school classmate. Their relationship is more friendship than romantic, although Frank likes her better than any girl in school.

Further Reading

Billman, Carol. *The Secret of the Stratemeyer Syndicate: Nancy Drew, the Hardy Boys, and the Million Dollar Fiction Factory.* New York: Ungar, 1986.

Johnson, Deidre, ed. *Stratemeyer Pseudonyms and Series Books: An Annotated Checklist of Stratemeyer and Stratemeyer Syndicate Publications.* Westport, CT: Greenwood, 1982.

Mason, Bobbie Ann. *The Unembarrassed Muse: The Popular Arts in America.* New York: Dial, 1970.

McFarlane, Leslie. *Ghost of the Hardy Boys.* New York: Two Continents, 1976.

Prager, Arthur. *Rascals at Large; or, The Clue in the Old Nostalgia.* New York: Doubleday, 1971.

Something about the Author. Vols. 1, 67. Detroit: Gale Research, 1971, 1992.

Zuckerman, Ed. "The Great Hardy Boys Whodunit." *Rolling Stone* (September 9, 1976).

Arthur Conan Doyle

1859-1938, English novelist

The Hound of the Baskervilles

(mystery novel, 1902)

PLOT: On a fine October morning in 1889, amateur detective Sherlock Holmes and his friend, Dr. John H. Watson, are at the breakfast table in their flat at 221B Baker St., London. Holmes is using his uncanny powers of observation to determine the nature of last night's caller, who left his walking stick behind. These musings are interrupted by the arrival of the man himself, Dr. Mortimer, a country doctor who has come to ask for help. The doctor first reads from a 1742 document that tells of the origin of the curse of the wealthy Baskerville family of Baskerville Hall, which is close to the moors of Dartmoor in Devon. The curse involves a massive ghost hound that rips out the throats of the descendants of the profligate Hugo Baskerville, who, generations earlier, had wickedly abducted an innocent peasant girl. This spectral dog supposedly still roams the moors and, only three months ago, the body of Sir Charles Baskerville, surrounded by large paw marks, was found outside his mansion.

The new heir, Sir Henry Baskerville, a nephew of the deceased, has arrived from Canada, and Dr. Mortimer, a concerned neighbor of the Baskervilles, wants advice. Holmes discovers that the young man has received a note warning him not to go to the moors, that he is being followed by a sinister stranger, and that one of the young man's boots has been stolen from the hotel. Watson is sent by Holmes to Devon with Sir Henry to investigate the situation. He meets several of the neighbors, including naturalist Jack Stapleton and his beautiful, fascinating sister, Beryl, as well as the eccentric Mr. Frankland and his daughter, Mrs. Laura Lyons.

At their first meeting, Beryl, mistaking Watson for Sir Henry, mysteriously begs him to return to London. There are frequent reports by the residents of seeing a giant dog in the area, and Watson notes the strange behavior of the Baskervilles' butler, Barrymore, and his wife. He and Sir Henry later discover that the Barrymores are secretly supplying food and clothing to Mrs. Barrymore's depraved brother, Selden, who has escaped from nearby Princetown prison and is now living on the moors.

Watson explores an abandoned hovel and finds Sherlock Holmes living there, collecting evidence. Holmes has found that Stapleton is really the son of a ne'er-do-well younger brother of Sir Charles Baskerville, and at the death of Sir Charles and Sir Henry, he is in line to inherit Baskerville Hall. Holmes is convinced that Stapleton, capitalizing on the family legend, is really Sir Charles's murderer. When Selden is found dead on the moors wearing Sir Henry's cast-off clothing, Holmes realizes that he must move fast. While Sir Henry dines alone with Stapleton in the naturalist's home, Holmes and Watson wait outside. On his way home, Sir Henry is attacked by a huge dog that is shot by Holmes. Inside, they discover Beryl bound and gagged in an upstairs room and, after following Stapleton into the moor, they find evidence that he lost his footing in the deadly bog and met his end there.

The next day in the moor, a lair is discovered where Stapleton kept the fearsome beast he had trained to attack on command. Later, Holmes gives further explanations. Stapleton had tailed Sir Henry in London, where he stole the boot to give the hound the necessary scent for the attack on the young man.

Beryl, who was actually Stapleton's wife and not his sister, was so sickened by her husband's action that she followed him to London, where she wrote the note warning Sir Henry. To recover his equilibrium, Sir Henry embarks on an ocean voyage with Dr. Mortimer while Holmes and Watson are satisfied that another criminal has been brought to justice.

Sherlock Holmes also appears in the novels A Study in Scarlet (1888), *The Sign of Four* (1890), and *The Valley of Fear* (1915), and in the short story collections *The Adventures of Sherlock Holmes* (1892), *The Memoirs of Sherlock Holmes* (1893), *The Return of Sherlock Holmes* (1905), *His Last Bow: Some Reminiscences of Sherlock Holmes* (1917), and *The Case-Book of Sherlock Holmes* (1927).

An Illustration by Sidney Paget of super-sleuth Sherlock Holmes contemplating one of his famous cases.

CHARACTERS: Sherlock Holmes and Dr. Watson first appeared in the novel *A Study in Scarlet*, published in 1887. *The Hound of the Baskervilles* first appeared in nine installments (August, 1901 through April, 1902) in the popular *Strand Magazine* and was published in book form in 1902.

Sherlock Holmes, one of the most colorful creations in all of English literature, was inspired by two people—one real, the other fictional. The primary one was Dr. Joseph Bell, Doyle's teacher at medical school in Edinburgh, and the second was C. Auguste Dupin, the detective Edgar Allan Poe created for his mystery stories. Both men, like Holmes, were great observers of seemingly insignificant details, with keen analytic powers and consuming interests in mental processes. Holmes was named after Oliver Wendell Holmes, a distinguished scientist and empiricist who, like Holmes, was an authority on tobacco. Holmes's most salient characteristics are his keen powers of observation, including amazing eyesight and hearing, brilliant deductive powers, and capabilities as a scientist, especially in chemistry. In his sleuthing, he scrupulously applies rules of logic and the scientific method. Unlike **Inspector Lestrode**, who is introduced only briefly at the end of this story but who plays somewhat larger roles in other Doyle tales, Holmes never jumps to conclusions or writes off a clue, no matter how small or apparently insignificant. Holmes is persistent and analyzes a problem until a solution is found; he is also a tireless fighter for justice—a modern Galahad fighting against evil. A man of great physical strength and endurance, Holmes is exceptionally courageous, a quality he demonstrates throughout the story.

Although he enjoys good company, Holmes is essentially a loner who requires solitude to apply his phenomenal powers. He is a chivalrous man, a gentleman—particularly towards women—who never subjects clients or friends to dangers that he would not endure himself. Holmes is also a very cultivated, well-read person, and a fastidious dabbler in the arts who loves the finer things in life, including music and rare violins. On the negative side, Holmes is inclined to be something of a snob; his need to control and dominate situations betrays a certain insecurity on his part. Sometimes he is inclined to pretentiousness, while in other instances he is overly cautious and too secretive of his methods. He also appears to be addicted to tobacco (the two objects most closely associated with Holmes are his magnifying glass and his pipe). These, however, are minor flaws for the man who elevated the role of detective to that of hero. Physically, he has been described as tall, thin to the point of emaciation, hook-nosed, pale, and clean-shaven.

The character of **Dr. John H. Watson** evidently came primarily from the imagination of the author. In some adaptations of the Holmes stories, he is portrayed as a dull buffoon. This is far from the author's intent. Doyle confessed to both admiring and respecting the character of Watson. In many ways, Watson is the perfect foil for Holmes because he represents a typical middle-class Englishman. He is a good listener, and he is unquestioningly loyal to the man he so admires, an admiration that extends to frequently trying to gain the approval of Holmes. Watson does not question the sleuth's often strange behavior and is indulgent concerning Holmes's frequently erratic behavior. Instead, he continually shows a deep understanding and respect for his friend. Although inclined to slow-wittedness and mediocre thinking, his good humor and naivete are endearing characteristics. He is modest, level-headed, mature, and always a complete gentleman. He can easily match Holmes in bravery and courage. As the recorder of Holmes's adventures, he acts as a fine intermediary between the story and the audience. Watson reports the facts as the reader would see them and is both literate and articulate. Physically, he is pictured as a handsome man, slim, mustachioed, and well-groomed.

Young **Sir Henry Baskerville** is a typical hero—handsome in appearance and dashing in demeanor. Though he sometimes shows a fiery temper, he is a man of great courage who has a trusting nature. By contrast, **Jack Stapleton** is the epitome of the arch-villain. He will stop at nothing, even murder, to get his way. He feigns friendship with Sir Henry while plotting to kill him, and keeps his wife a virtual prisoner, submitting her to cruelties and indignities to further his scheme. Though a lover of nature, he trains a dog to be an instrument of death.

Stapleton's wife, **Beryl**, is a "damsel in distress." Though subjected to inhuman treatment, including being forced to assume a false identity, she shows extreme courage and bravely faces danger in trying to warn Sir Henry. Another helpful character is **John Barrymore**, the handsome butler, who is known for his loyalty and trustworthiness. He is so upset at betraying his master by secretly aiding his wife's brother that he tenders his notice and plans to leave Baskerville Hall. Fortunately, Sir Henry keeps him in his employ.

Some of the Baskervilles' neighbors also appear in the story, including **Dr. James Mortimer**, a tall, very thin man whose loyalty and concern for his friend leads him to request Holmes's assistance on the case. He is a man of goodwill and honor, willing to forfeit his own comfort to help others. His interest in phrenology—and, in particular, Holmes's skull—adds a certain comic relief to the novel. Two other neighbors also play minor roles. **Mr. Frankland** is an elderly, surly landlord whose passion for British law has led him into litigation for the mere pleasure of fighting. His daughter, the long-suffering **Laura Lyons**, is dominated by her penurious father.

Further Reading

Carr, John D. *The Life of Sir Arthur Conan Doyle.* New York: Carroll & Graf, 1987

Costello, Peter. *The Real World of Sherlock Holmes.* New York: Carroll & Graf, 1991.

Edwards, Owen Dudley. *The Quest for Sherlock Holmes: A Biographical Study of the Early Life of Sir Arthur Conan Doyle.* New York: Barnes & Noble, 1983.

Hardwick, Michael. *The Complete Guide to Sherlock Holmes.* New York: St. Martin's Press, 1987.

Higham, Charles. *The Adventures of Conan Doyle.* New York: Norton, 1987.

Jaffe, Jacqueline A. *Arthur Conan Doyle.* New York: Twayne/Macmillan, 1987.

Lellenberg, Jon L., ed. *The Quest for Doyle: Thirteen Biographers in Search of a Life.* Carbondale, IL: Southern Illinois University Press, 1987.

Pearson, Hesketh. *Conan Doyle.* New York: Walker, 1961.

Poynter, Michael. *Pictorial History of Sherlock Holmes.* New York: BDD Promo Books, 1991.

Schaefer, Bradley E. "The Astronomical Sherlock Holmes." *Mercury* 22 (January-February 1993): 9.

Shreffler, Philip A. *The Baker Street Reader: Cornerstone Writings about Sherlock Holmes.* Westport, CT: Greenwood Press, 1984.

Starrett, V. *The Private Life of Sherlock Holmes.* New York: AMS Press, 1960.

Symons, Julian. *Conan Doyle: Portrait of an Artist.* New York: Mysterious Press, 1988.

Twentieth-Century Literary Criticism. Vol. 7. Detroit: Gale Research, 1982.

Alexandre Dumas

1802-1870, French novelist

The Three Musketeers

(historical adventure novel, 1844; English translation, 1853; published in France as Les trois mousquetaires*)*

PLOT: D'Artagnon's deepest desire is to become a Musketeer, one of the elite group of personal bodyguards to Louis XIII, a weak king. The young man travels to Paris in 1625 to serve an apprenticeship toward entering the guards. There he meets and becomes fast friends with the best of these swordsmen, Athos, Porthos, and Aramis.

The Musketeers are engaged in a fierce rivalry with the guards of Cardinal Richelieu, who represents the real power in the government. Richelieu develops a plot to embarrass the king with the help of his two favorite spies, the Count de Rochefort and Milady de Winter. The queen has sent a gift of twelve diamond studs to her lover, the Duke of Buckingham, in London. Richelieu tells Lady de Winter, who is in London at the time, to steal two of the studs. Then he suggests to the king that he give a ball and ask his wife to wear the diamond studs.

D'Artagnon learns of Richelieu's plan from Constance Bonancieux, seamstress to the queen, and leaves for London with the other Musketeers to recover the diamonds. D'Artagnon is successful in his mission, and the queen is grateful. The three Musketeers are wounded, however, and Constance is imprisoned by the Count de Rochefort—a man D'Artagnon had met on his original trip to Paris.

D'Artagnon meets Lady de Winter through her brother-in-law, his friend Lord de Winter, and falls in love with her. D'Artagnon deceives the lady one night, and she gives him a sapphire ring, believing him to be the man she truly loves. When he shows Athos the ring, the Musketeer recognizes it as one he had given his wife, whom he believed to be dead. Later, D'Artagnon sees a brand on Lady de Winter's shoulder, marking her as a criminal and proving that

The three Musketeers fend off fiends in an illustration by E. C. Van Swearingen.

she is the wife of Athos. The lady swears revenge on D'Artagnon.

War heats up between England and France. The Musketeers learn that Richelieu has given Lady de Winter a writ of safe conduct and sent her to London to tell Buckingham to end the war or risk having his affair with the queen exposed. In return, de Winter will get her wish: both Constance and D'Artagnon will be killed. But Athos apprehends Lady de Winter, takes the safe-conduct writ, and orders her to leave France at once.

For their part in the fighting, the Musketeers are singled out by Richelieu, who learns that D'Artagnon is not yet one of the elite guards. The cardinal orders that he be made a Musketeer. In the meantime, Lady de Winter arrives in London, where she is imprisoned by her brother-in-law. But she convinces a young jailer of her innocence and he helps her escape. Later, the young man stabs Buckingham to avenge her. Lord de Winter learns of the escape but is too late to help Buckingham, who dies. Lady de Winter flees to France, where she locates the convent where Constance is imprisoned and poisons her. The four Musketeers and Lord de Winter pursue and capture her. A trial is held and Lady de Winter is executed for her deeds.

Upon their return to Paris, D'Artagnon is arrested by the Count de Rochefort, the man who imprisoned Constance. D'Artagnon is taken before Cardinal Richelieu and charged with treason. But the Musketeer recounts Lady de Winter's list of crimes, tells Richelieu of her death, and produces the writ of safe passage that Athos had taken from her. Since he has this writ, D'Artagnon claims he must go free. Richelieu is so impressed with his cleverness that instead of sentencing D'Artagnon to death, he offers the young man a commission in the Musketeers. D'Artagnon gallantly offers the commission to his friends, who just as gallantly decline. The three Musketeers then go their separate ways: Athos returns to his home, Porthos marries a wealthy woman, and Aramis joins a monastery. D'Artagnon makes a friend of his old enemy, de Rochefort, and becomes a lieutenant in the elite Musketeers.

CHARACTERS: The hero of the novel is **D'Artagnon**, the brash young adventurer from Gascony. Impressed with his bravery, the three Musketeers take him into their close bond of comradeship. D'Artagnon has his share of flaws—he is a rash and ambitious character whose conduct is not always of the highest order. For instance, he is supposedly in love with Constance when he falls in love with Lady de Winter and admires the lady's maid as well. But this romantic novel, with touches of the Gothic and historical, is meant to be read in the spirit of the times. Characters are larger than life and generally heroic, adventures are nonstop, strangers come and go with little explanation, people are constantly subjected to the dungeon with seemingly little cause, ladies are always in distress, and Musketeers are always there to rescue them.

D'Artagnon is the embodiment of the idealistic youth of the time who longs to defend noble causes. He will defend his country and his friends with his life, if need be. However, D'Artagnon does not emerge from his adventures as the same idealistic youth who set out on the road to Paris. He is a wiser man than before, after witnessing the foibles of the rich and powerful. Yet his courage and determination grant him success in the dream of his life, for he has become a lieutenant in the Musketeers.

The three Musketeers are courageous and resourceful, energetic to the point of impossibility, and possess their own particular code of ethics. **Athos**, whose real name is Count de la Fere, is a man of obvious nobility. He is brilliant and honorable but given to silences that hide the dark secret of his past: he was married to the Lady de Winter, a criminal whom he believed to have died. **Porthos** is the powerful Musketeer. Not as bright as the others, he is a friendly, courageous sort who ends up marrying a wealthy widow. The elegant **Aramis**, actually Chevalier d'Herblay, is always clothed in black and ends up entering a monastery.

Beautiful **Milady de Winter**, also called **Lady de Winter**, is a marvelous villain, a mysterious figure who will stop at nothing to obtain her goals. Her past is filled with evil deeds. She had an affair with a priest before marrying Athos and is a thief and a murderer, as well as a spy for Cardinal Richelieu. She obtained her title by marrying an English aristocrat, brother of **Lord de Winter**, and then killing him. But even given all of her wicked acts and how much she deserves her fate, the Musketeers' judgment in conducting their own trial and executing her is a bit questionable.

Cardinal Richelieu is a shrewd and cunning man, although not an evil one. The Musketeers do not like him, but they must respect him. Opposed by the weak, stupid, and fearful **King Louis XIII**, Richelieu pursues his own ends by means that are not quite in keeping with the church. He is the real power in the country. **Chevalier de Rochefort**, who eventually becomes a friend to D'Artagnon, is a loyal and trusted spy in the service of Richelieu. The English nobleman, the **Duke of Buckingham**, is based on a real-life historical figure who was romantically involved with the French queen. The story of the diamond studs was apparently true, and his death occurred much in the manner portrayed in the novel. The charming **Constance Bonancieux** is loyal to her mistress, the queen, and serves as a fine contrast to the evil Milady de Winter.

Further Reading

Brosman, Catharine Savage, ed. *Nineteenth-Century French Fiction Writers: Romanticism and Realism, 1800-1860.* Vol. 119 of *Dictionary of Literary Biography.* Detroit: Gale Research, 1992.

European Writers: The Romantic Century. Vol. 6. New York: Scribner's, 1985.

Hemmings, F. W. J. *Alexandre Dumas: The King of Romance.* New York: Scribner's, 1979.

Kunitz, Stanley J., and Vinete Colby. *European Authors, 1000-1900.* New York: H. W. Wilson, 1967.

Levi, Anthony. *Guide to French Literature: 1789 to the Present.* Chicago: St. James, 1992.

Maurois, Andre. *Alexandre Dumas: A Great Life in Brief.* New York: Knopf, 1955.

Nineteenth-Century Literature Criticism. Vol. 11. Detroit: Gale Research, 1984.

Schopp, Claude. *Alexandre Dumas: Genius of Life.* New York: F. Watts, 1988.

Spur, H. A. *Life and Writings of Alexandre Dumas.* New York: Haskell, 1972.

Daphne du Maurier

1907-1989, English novelist

Rebecca

(gothic novel, 1938)

PLOT: While in Monte Carlo, a young shy girl who is employed by an obnoxious and vulgar American, Mrs. Van Hopper, meets a mysterious, brooding, aristocratic, and wealthy Englishman, the widower Maxim de Winter. The poor and awkward young woman falls hopelessly in love with de Winter. Despite their obvious differences, a friendly relationship develops. The young woman is delighted, though surprised, when this aristocratic and fascinating man seems to be interested in her, and she is even more amazed at her luck when he proposes marriage. The wedding is held in Venice, and the second Mrs. de Winter, which is the only name she is given throughout the novel, looks forward to their return to England, where they will live at her husband's grand English country estate of Manderley.

The second Mrs. de Winter is many years younger than her handsome husband. She not only looks up to him but is completely in love with him, and she is thrilled and eager to begin their new life together at Manderley. The young woman's happiness, however, is soon tempered by the constant reminders of her husband's first wife, Rebecca. In every room, even in the smell of flowers in the garden, the presence of Rebecca remains. The dead woman's beauty, an image enhanced by a magnificent ball gown, haunts the second Mrs. de Winter with every step she takes inside the mansion.

Manderley's housekeeper, the ghoulish Mrs. Danvers, keeps the second Mrs. de Winter informed about Rebecca's sophistication and charm, which the young girl feels she desperately lacks. Mrs. Danvers spares no feelings as she describes the attributes of the late Rebecca. The new Mrs. de Winter learns that Rebecca died a year earlier in a boating accident. Her husband identified her body after it was found months later. This tragedy caused him to take a long absence from Manderley, during which he met his new wife.

Although the second Mrs. de Winter tries to make her husband forget Rebecca, she finds it is not an easy task, and she begins to fear that the beautiful woman's memory will forever haunt him. She must also contend with Mrs. Danvers, who makes no secret of the fact that she feels Rebecca will forever be mistress at Manderley and that the newcomer can never replace her.

During Rebecca's life at Manderley, the de Winters gave a great ball each year to which the surrounding country folk were invited. Maxim is now urged to renew the practice, and, surprisingly, he agrees. Anxious to please him, the second Mrs. de Winter dresses in a replica of the gown worn by Rebecca in the portrait. Mrs. Danvers is most helpful with this suggestion. But Maxim is furious when the second Mrs. de Winter, wearing the white gown of Rebecca's portrait as well as a dark wig to match her hair, descends the staircase. He rushes from the house, thinking his new wife meant to embarrass him. When he returns, he learns that a boat has been found with Rebecca's body in it.

The truth now comes out when Maxim de Winter admits that he murdered his first wife. Far from loving her, he hated her for her selfishness and constant affairs with other men. When she confronted him down at the boathouse with her pregnancy, flaunting the fact that the child was not his, he killed her and set her body adrift in the boat. Later, he identified another body as Rebecca's. It is also learned from a Dr. Baker that Rebecca de Winter had cancer and would have died soon anyway. Favell, Rebecca's cousin and one of her lovers, vows revenge on Maxim for what he has done. Maxim and his wife return to Manderley only to discover that Mrs. Danvers has fled and the mansion is on fire. The de Winters leave England and spend the rest of their lives wandering from city to city. Though they have each other, they remain homeless and forever troubled by the memory of Rebecca and Manderley.

CHARACTERS: The **second Mrs. de Winter** is never given a name. In a sense, this is the story of her progression from a helpless naive young girl into a mature woman who comes into her own after the truth about Rebecca is discovered. Initially, it is her innocence that attracts Maxim, even though she is described as "devastatingly plain." Her adoration for her husband does not diminish, even after learning he murdered Rebecca. Although the second Mrs. de Winter triumphs in the end over the memory of her rival, Rebecca, and emerges as a strong, forceful character, she is doomed along with her husband. Having lost Manderley, they are left to travel the world with only each other and their memories. The fact that the image of Manderley constantly returns to their thoughts suggests that Rebecca will live forever, unbidden, in their hearts.

Rebecca de Winter is dead before the novel opens but is a central figure nonetheless. The force of her beauty and sophistication is so strongly felt throughout the novel that she seems as alive to the reader as she does to Maxim and the second Mrs. de Winter. But, in truth, the beautiful Rebecca turns out to have been a demon, taunting her husband with her affairs and then flaunting her pregnancy, which in reality was cancer. Although she is murdered for her wickedness, she is victorious in the sense that both Maxim and the second Mrs. Winter will be forever haunted by her memory.

A fine example of the tortured hero of the Gothic novel is **Maxim de Winter**. Brooding, handsome, and mysterious, he leads the reader early in the novel to believe that he can't forget his first wife, Rebecca, because he loves her still. In truth, his feelings of guilt for murdering her are eating away at him, even though he felt justified in his actions. Maxim has successfully hidden her murder from the rest of the world, but he can't overcome his guilt, even though he does love the young girl who has become the second Mrs. de Winter. Maxim's great obsession is Manderley, the mansion and estate he deeply loves and would do anything to protect. It is ironic that in the end, even though he is absolved of the murder of Rebecca, he loses Manderley forever and, with his wife, must spend the rest of his days in contemplation of his crime and the loss of his beloved home. Critics have noted a certain paternal feeling in Maxim for his second wife, who is many years younger than he. Above all, he was attracted to her innocence and, in fact, often treats her as though she were a child. Interestingly, it is the second Mrs. de Winter who grows in stature and character throughout the novel.

The black-draped figure of the housekeeper, **Mrs. Danvers**, permeates the halls of Manderley and frightens the young and naive new Mrs. de Winter. Mrs. Danvers adored the dead Rebecca and never passes up the chance to show off her beauty and sophistication to the young, naive girl who has come to Manderley as Maxim's second wife. To Mrs. Danvers, Rebecca was a free, courageous woman who lived life to the fullest. She has no intention of allowing the second Mrs. de Winter to assume control of Manderley. To that end, Mrs. Danvers does everything in her power to discredit her. She is the one who convinces the young girl that Maxim would be pleased if she showed up at the ball in a dress imitating the one worn in Rebecca's portrait, and she is pleased with the result when Maxim leaves the mansion in a rage. So hypnotic is her power over the young girl that she very nearly succeeds in persuading the second Mrs. de Winter to jump out a window in her despair. It is thought that Mrs. Danvers had a relationship with Rebecca's former lover, Jack Favell, and leaves with him after she burns Manderley to the ground.

Other characters include: the evil **Jack Favell**, former lover and cousin of Rebecca, who threatens Maxim de Winter with blackmail when the truth about Rebecca's death is uncovered, and the vulgar American, **Mrs. Van Hopper**, who employs the second Mrs. de Winter at the start of the novel. Some critics say that Mrs. Van Hopper's unpleasant personality is the result of du Maurier's dislike of Americans.

Further Reading

Contemporary Literary Criticism. Vols. 6, 11, 59. Detroit: Gale Research, 1976, 1979, 1990.

Cook, Judith A. *Daphne: A Portrait of Daphne du Maurier*. Guilford, CT: Ulverscroft, 1992.

Henderson, Lesley. *Twentieth Century Romance and Historical Writers*. 2nd ed. Chicago: St. James, 1990.

Kelly, Richard Michael. *Daphne du Maurier*. Boston: Twayne, 1987.

Shallcross, Martyn. *The Private World of Daphne du Maurier*. London: Robson, 1991.

Something about the Author. Vol. 27. Detroit: Gale Research, 1982.

Lois Duncan

1934-, American young adult novelist

Killing Mr. Griffin

(young adult novel, 1978)

PLOT: Students in Mr. Brian Griffin's English classes at Del Norte Senior High School have good reason to dislike him. He is demanding, sarcastic, humorless, and dictatorial. Mark Kinney, a secretive, but charismatic senior, has an additional reason. Caught cheating on an English assignment, he was publicly humiliated by Mr. Griffin and has been forced to repeat the course. Kinney devises a clever scheme to get even and persuades his two friends, Betsy Cline, a popular cheerleader, and ace basketball player Jeff Garrett, to join him. Later, David Ruggles, the handsome president of the senior class, enters into the conspiracy, and plain, mousy Susan McConnell, who has a crush on David, is added to act as a decoy. At first the plan runs smoothly. Susan detains Mr. Griffin after school for a conference and then escorts him to his car on the deserted school parking lot. There, Mark, Jeff, and David, wearing masks, tie him up and blindfold him. They drive him in his car to a remote wooded area and leave him to spend the night alone. They plan to return in the morning, again disguised, to free him. After the kidnapping, Betsy picks the boys up in Jeff's car.

Unfortunately, they do not realize that Mr. Griffin suffers from a severe heart condition and must take nitroglycerin tablets. That night, Susan has such pangs of conscience that she persuades David to take her to check on Mr. Griffin's condition. They find him dead of a heart attack. Mark hatches another scheme to cover up the crime. While the three boys bury the body, David secretly removes a school ring from Mr. Griffin's finger as a grim reminder of this terrible incident. The car is left at the airport to suggest that Mr. Griffin has left town.

Slowly, this tangled web begins to unravel. Fearing discovery, they move the car to Jeff's garage for repainting. Mr. Griffin's devoted wife, Kathy, enters the investigation and soon realizes that the pathetic Susan is lying when she states, under Mark's coaching, that she saw a woman in the parking lot waiting for Mr. Griffin in his car. In the woods, hikers find a medicine bottle with prescription data, dropped by Mr. Griffin during a scuffle, and soon the body is unearthed. David's senile grandmother, Irma Ruggles, finds the telltale ring, and in a staged robbery to retrieve it, Mark is responsible for her death. Overcome with remorse and guilt, Susan plans a full confession. To prevent this, Mark visits her home when she is alone, ties her up, and sets the house on fire. Fortunately, she is rescued by Kathy and Detective Baca, who have come to ask her more questions. When the truth is revealed, the onus falls on Mark, who is shown to have a psychopathic personality, but the other four will also suffer punishment for perpetrating a seemingly harmless prank that left two innocent people dead.

CHARACTERS: When it was first published in 1978, this novel created a stir—and it has since been censored in a number of schools—because of its graphic portrayal of teenagers plotting revenge against a hated teacher and their diabolical efforts to cover up their crime. The author has stated that Mark is based on her oldest daughter's first boyfriend, whose charming outward behavior concealed a disturbed inner psyche. The title character of the book, **Mr. (Brian) Griffin**, is a teacher who is disliked by his students because of his stiff, formal, and dignified personality and appearance. Dressed in a navy blue suit with white shirt and tie, he creates a forbidding presence. He is a well-organized, methodical, and hard-working teacher, who has left a successful college teaching career to create self-disciplined, thinking high school students who will be properly prepared for college. Unfortunately, his methods are too harsh. Never praising students, he uses sarcasm liberally and often humiliates individuals publicly. His standards are so high that students feel they are unattainable. He realizes his faults when he confesses to his wife, "I have an abrasive personality." At home, he reveals a different, more human side. He shows great affection for his pregnant wife and is a tender, loving husband.

Sixteen-year-old **Susan McConnell** is a pathetic creature who, because of her innocence and the unrequited love she feels for David, is easily persuaded to join in the conspiracy. Betsy describes her as the "little creep with glasses." She is the ugly duckling of the English class, out of her element both socially and academically. She is an extremely bright junior, surrounded by older, less caring seniors. Logically, in the class study of *Hamlet,* she identifies with Ophelia who, like her, is alienated, lonely, and sickened by a hopeless love. This homely, unhappy girl is easy prey for Mark, but eventually it is her sense of justice, coupled with her growing feelings of guilt, that lead to the novel's climax.

The gang's ringleader and chief instigator is **Mark Kinney**, a heavy-lidded, expressionless, intelligent young man who, because of his distant, enigmatic personality, is able to wield great influence over others. Gradually, as details of his early life are revealed, one realizes that he possesses a pathological personality. As a youngster, he was responsible for the death of his father, although it was considered an accident. At times he gives the appearance of a charming, sincere friend, but inwardly he is a cold, calculating mental case who resorts to murder to protect himself and further his plans.

David Ruggles is the handsome, popular president of the senior class who, without a father, goes home faithfully after school to care for his elderly, confused grandmother, while his mother is away working. He is a well-meaning, conscientious young man who regrets being cajoled into joining Mark in his scheme, but he seems unable to extricate himself. Like Susan, he is a sensitive, serious student who shares with her great feelings of guilt over the death of Mr. Griffin.

The two other participants are **Jeff Garrett** and **Betsy Cline**. Jeff is a tall, easy-going, impressionable basketball player who has been under the influence of Mark since they met in the seventh grade. Although naturally cautious and initially against Mark's plan to kidnap Mr. Griffin, his resentment at receiving an unfair "F" for his English assignments, plus Mark's persuasive powers, change his mind. Betsy is a round-faced, snub-nosed cheerleader who is Jeff's girlfriend. Although not pretty, she possesses a cheerful, outgoing personality that makes her extremely popular. At first, she considers the plot an innocent prank that will teach Mr. Griffin a well-deserved lesson. When it backfires, she panics and follows Mark slavishly in his efforts to produce a cover-up.

Mr. Griffin's wife, **Kathy Griffin**, is devoted to her husband. She sees a tender, loving side to his nature that he hides from others. She sympathizes with the sacrifices he has made for his profession and the enormous amount of time he spends on his work, but she is aware of his classroom reputation and frequently begs him to be less severe and more understanding of his pupils. After his death, she is suspicious of the explanations presented by Mark and his friends and begins an investigation that eventually leads to the unraveling of Mark's plot.

Stranger with My Face

(young adult novel, 1981)

PLOT: Seventeen-year-old Laurie Stratton has emerged from gangly, gawky adolescence into an attractive and desirable member of the "in" crowd, which includes being the girlfriend of handsome, affable Gordon Ahearn. Laurie lives in Cliff House on the tip of an accessible New England island with her artist mother, Shelly, sci-fi writer father, Jim, and two talented siblings, brother Neal, age eleven, and sister Megan, eight. All three youngsters, as well as Laurie's friends, commute to school on the mainland by ferry.

Laurie's peace of mind is shattered when she senses the presence of a malevolent spirit around her, and several friends, as well as Megan, claim to have seen Laurie outdoors when she has actually been at home. As these occurrences multiply, Laurie is visited at night by a look-alike girl named Lia, who seems sinister and forbidding. Unable to tell anyone for fear of ridicule, Laurie changes under the stress of these mysterious visitations. Gradually she loses her friends, including Gordon, and gravitates to two outsiders in the school, newcomer Helen Tuttle, who has grown up on a Navaho reservation in Arizona, and Jeff Rankin, a loner who has become embittered after an accident that left him with terrible facial scars. From Helen, Laurie learns about astral projection, a spiritual phenomenon involving out-of-body experiences that Helen claims is practiced by the Navahos.

Convinced that Lia is actually her twin, Laurie questions her parent about her origins. Reluctantly, they tell her that she was one of a set of identical twins who was adopted while her parents lived in the Midwest. Laurie's mother was a Navaho and her father, who abandoned his family, was a white man. No one knows what happened to the sister, although Laurie's mother claims that she too would have been adopted except that the family felt a sinister aura about her even as a child. When near-fatal accidents occur to both Helen and Jeff, Laurie is convinced that Lia somehow is trying to isolate her from her friends and ultimately possess her body. Through massive willpower, Laurie is able to elicit her own astral powers and, in spirit form, track down Lia. She discovers her in a mental institution in Albuquerque, where she has been confined after committing vicious crimes in each of her foster homes.

Following one of her out of body experiences, Laurie returns to find that, in her absence, the evil Lia has inhabited her body. Unable to intervene, she watches helplessly as the paranoid Lia plots further destruction. Finally, in a climatic scene, Megan, who senses that this is not her real sister, exorcises the evil spirit by using a Navaho eagle talisman that Helen had given Laurie. Laurie returns to her body and later learns that Lia has died and her body was cremated. But Laurie wonders whether her spirit will truly rest forever.

CHARACTERS: Laurie Stratton emerges from her harrowing, supernatural experiences as an emotionally mature young woman. At first, she is pictured as a typical teenager, overly self-conscious of her appearance and her position within the fashionable crowd while basking in the attention she receives from her attractive boyfriend. As she tries to cope with Lia's unwanted interference in her life, Laurie realizes that friendships built on understanding, loyalty, and trust are more important than senior proms and weekend parties. She appreciates the loneliness and isolation that both gawky Helen and the horribly scarred Jeff are experiencing, as well as the support and affection that they give her in spite of their own problems. Also she is able to assimilate the devastating news that she has been adopted and, without rancor, realize that more important than blood relationships in keeping families together are bonds of love and compassion. Through the tender feelings she shares with Jeff, she learns that inner beauty is more important than external appearances. Laurie shows great courage, bravery, and resourcefulness in exploring the fringes of human experiences to solve the mystery concerning Lia and help her endangered friends and family.

Lia Abbott (who goes by the surname of her last adoptive family) is characterized as a thoroughly bad seed. Because of her destructive behavior, she has been shunted from one foster home to another. With each new family, her sense of insecurity, bitterness, and paranoia increases until, while in the Abbott household, she is so jealous of Kathy, the Abbott's natural daughter, that she arranges her death in a horse riding "accident." This incident precipitates her incarceration in a mental institution, where Laurie eventually finds her. Endowed with the powers of astral projection, she visits her sister and vows to isolate Laurie from her friends, possess her body and spirit, and eventually replace her in the household Lia believes is rightfully hers. She is a devious, manipulative, and cunning person who will kill to achieve her wicked goals.

Laurie's two dearest friends are **Helen Tuttle** and **Jeff Rankin**. Helen is an unattractive, quiet redhead whose family has recently moved from the Southwest. Ignored by her fellow students, she maintains her cheerful, self-reliant nature in spite of her obvious isolation and loneliness. She is a spiritual person who introduces Laurie to the concept of astral projection. Helen is Laurie's loyal, supportive friend, but because of Lia's malicious behavior, she suffers a head injury so severe that her parents take her south for special medical treatments. Laurie treasures Helen's gift of an Indian eagle fetish, and in time this saves Laurie's life. Jeff, once a wild, handsome, outgoing kid, has been transformed into a bitter, abrasive, unpopular loner since a can of lighter fluid exploded, leaving half his face badly scarred. Because of Laurie's attention, he regains some of his old cocky confidence. He is Laurie's loyal friend and rescuer even when other friends desert her. The child of divorced parents, he lives alone with his father, a shop owner on the island. At the end, Mr. and Mrs. Stratton show their love and concern for Jeff by financing corrective plastic surgery for him.

Gordon Ahearn, is a lean, well-muscled, attractive teenager with a strong face and sea-green eyes. He is considered a catch by all the girls, and Laurie is flattered by the attention he pays her. Unfortunately, through a series of misunderstandings resulting from Lia's appearances, their relationship disintegrates in spite of Gordon's attempts at reconciliation and understanding. Laurie, under the stress of the situation, is unable to clarify the problems and breaks off their friendship.

Jim and **Shelly Stratton**, Laurie's parents, are an ideal husband and wife team. Successful at their professions, they are understanding, generous, and loving toward each other and their family. Although unable to comprehend the crises Laurie is experiencing, they remain supportive and sympathetic. **Neal Stratton** is like his mother, a natural-born artist. He, too, shows concern over Laurie's problems, as does her insightful young sister, **Megan**, a budding writer like her father. Megan intuitively senses the evil presence that Lia exudes, and it is she who bravely confronts Lia with the Navajo fetish and drives her evil spirit out of Laurie's body.

Further Reading

Authors and Artists for Young Adults. Vol. 4. Detroit: Gale, 1990.

Berger, Laura Standley, ed. *Twentieth-Century Young Adult Writers,* 1st ed. Detroit: St. James, 1994.

Contemporary Literary Criticism. Vol. 26. Detroit: Gale Research, 1983.

Duncan, Lois. *Chapters: My Growth as a Writer.* Boston: Little, Brown, 1982.

———. "1992 Margaret A. Edwards Award Acceptance Speech." *Journal of Youth Services and Libraries* 6 (winter 1993).

Gallo, Donald R. *Speaking for Ourselves: Autobiographical Sketches by Notable Authors of Books for Young Adults.* Urbana, IL: National Council of Teachers of English, 1990.

Kies, Cosette. *Presenting Lois Duncan.* Boston: Twayne, 1994.

Something about the Author. Vol. 36. Detroit: Gale Research, 1984.

Something about the Author Autobiography Series. Vol. 2. Detroit: Gale Research, 1986.

Sutton, Roger. "A Conversation with Lois Duncan." *School Library Journal* 38 (June 1992).

Ralph Ellison

1914-, American novelist

Invisible Man

(novel, 1952)

PLOT: The protagonist remains unnamed throughout this novel. Because he gradually realizes that he has no identity in a white man's world, he is, as in the title, the Invisible Man, or I. M. In his southern high school, I. M. achieves scholastic honors and is invited to repeat his stirring graduation speech to a group of white businessmen at a formal dinner. Mistakenly, he is grouped with some other black boys who are blindfolded and forced to box with each other. Bloodied and humiliated, he finally delivers his speech and is awarded a scholarship.

During his junior year at an all-black college, he is entrusted with the task of chaperoning one of the white trustees, Mr. Norton, during Founder's Day weekend. To kill time, I. M. drives Mr. Norton out of town to sightsee. They stop at the slave quarters of an old plantation, where Mr. Norton meets Jim Trueblood, a poor sharecropper who tells Mr. Norton about his incestuous experience with his daughter. In a state of shock, Mr. Norton has a fainting spell. I. M. takes him to a nearby tavern, where the white man is further accosted by a group of black patients on an outing from their asylum. Back at school, the president, Dr. Bledsoe, hears about these incidents and expels the innocent I. M., but also gives him seven letters of introduction to prominent businessmen in New York.

I. M. travels north and begins presenting the letters, hoping for a job. At his last interview, with Mr. Emerson, I. M. realizes that he has been betrayed and that these are not letters of recommendation, but of condemnation. I. M. next gets a job at the Liberty Paint Factory, where, as he soon discovers, he is hired only to undermine the position of the white workers, who are organizing for better working conditions. After a run-in with one foreman, Mr. Kimbro, I. M. is assigned to assist Lucius Brockway, the supervisor of the vats of boiling paint. Brockway, who is fiercely anti-union, suspects that I. M. wants to join the union at the plant and attacks the young man. During the scuffle, they forget about the vats of paint, one of which explodes with I. M. right next to it. At the factory hospital, he receives electric shock therapy and is then sent on his way, ill and unemployed, his mind in a daze from the shock treatment and his sense of identity and purpose badly undermined.

In Harlem, I. M. is taken in by a kindly woman, Mary Rambo, who gives him room and board. One day, I. M. passes a pathetic scene of old people being evicted from their tenement. His eloquent speech to onlookers brings I. M. to the attention of the Brotherhood (a thinly disguised Communist group). He meets a white man, Brother Jack, who hires him as an organizer and orator in Harlem. He is given a new name and identity, as well as instructions in proper doctrine and policies, by another white man, Brother Hambro. Later, he becomes friendly with two comrades, the charismatic Brother Tod Clifton and Brother Tarp. The brothers believe in racial unity, and this often leads to clashes with their arch-rival in Harlem, Ras the Exhorter, a black nationalist who preaches violence and separation. I. M. innocently makes decisions that are interpreted as going against the party line and is temporarily ostracized. He now realizes that, again, he is only a tool used to fulfill someone else's plans.

After Brother Clifton is shot and killed by a white policeman, I. M. delivers a moving eulogy, which, however, is criticized by the Brotherhood. Ras takes advantage of the situation and through his oratory incites a race riot. By impersonating a con man named Rinehart, I. M. escapes from Ras's men. In the confusion and looting, I. M. is forced to take shelter in an underground hideout. Here, in isolation and despair, he assumes the identity that society wished on him—invisibility.

CHARACTERS: Invisible Man—or **I. M.**—is a twentieth-century Candide, the eponymous hero of Voltaire's satire criticizing society and human nature. Like his prototype, I. M. begins as an innocent, naive young man. A series of harrowing experiences, however, soon rob him of all illusion and hope of being able to find his niche in a society doomed by racism. He eventually discovers that in a white man's world he is a nonentity, a cipher. He begins full of hope, trying to prosper through humility and hard work, and ends in despair and self-imposed exile. One by one, his expectations and best intentions are shattered through no fault of his own. He is degraded by being forced to fight blindfolded at a dinner intended to honor his scholastic achievement. His honest desire to please Mr. Norton leads to an unfair expulsion. At the paint factory, his desire to accommodate and learn brings further hardships and humiliation, and after his accident he is treated like an animal at the factory hospital. When he is taken in by the Brotherhood and given a sense of purpose and importance at last, this illusion is shattered, too, when he gradually comes to realize that he is only an expendable pawn in their ruthless plan for power. With each disillusionment, he retreats deeper into a state of nonidentity. Unwilling to accept the only remaining alternative, the negative philosophy of hatred as preached by Ras, he withdraws both physically and mentally into an underground life.

I. M.'s fortunes take their first turn for the worse when he meets **Mr. Norton**, one of the trustees of I. M.'s southern college. Mr. Norton is a well-intentioned, liberal, white northern businessman, whose goal is to help provide young African Americans with an education. However, his self-congratulatory complacency results in a condescending attitude toward I. M. Ignorant of how many poor blacks live, when Mr. Norton is confronted with this reality in his meeting with **Jim Trueblood**, he is stunned and collapses. Jim Trueblood is a black sharecropper who has "brought disgrace to the black community" by fathering a child with his daughter. His retelling of the details of his fall from grace, his plea for understanding, and Mr. Norton's reactions make for one of the most colorful and humorous episodes in the novel.

Although Mr. Norton tells the black president of I. M.'s college, **Dr. Bledsoe**, that I. M. was blameless, he is indirectly responsible for his expulsion. Dr. Bledsoe professes love for his race, but he is completely selfish in his motives. He uses his race to further personal goals of power and prosperity and is unscrupulous in his efforts to achieve them. Humble before his white benefactors, he is inwardly scornful of them and their motives. Although his life is a mask of hypocrisy, his true nature is revealed in his treatment of I. M. He ruthlessly expels him, fearful that I. M. will become a threat in the future. The bogus letters of recommendation show the extremes of his vindictiveness when his position is threatened. In his desire to advance and maintain his position in a white man's world, he has renounced his conscience.

In his search for a job after his expulsion, I. M. meets **Mr. Emerson**, the son of one of the businessmen for whom I. M. has a letter of introduction. He takes pity on I. M. and, in a patronizing way, confides that he has black acquaintances and a fondness for jazz. He reveals the contents of the supposed letter of recommendation from Dr. Bledsoe and suggests I. M. look for work at the ironically named Liberty Paint Factory. I. M.'s brief and disastrous interlude at the paint factory brings him into contact with **Mr. Kimbro** and **Lucius Brockway**. In their different ways, both bring further misfortunes to I. M. Kimbro is a short-tempered, tyrannical man, who, failing to disguise his contempt for blacks, gives I. M. inadequate directions and then tries to have him fired when he makes mistakes. The vat manager, Brockway, is a black man who is willing to do anything to hang on to his job. It becomes clear that he owes his job tenure in part to his vicious union-busting attitude. He becomes crazed when he mistakenly thinks I. M. is a union man. In the ensuing fight, gauges are not read and an explosion sends I. M. to the hospital.

I. M.'s mentor in the Brotherhood is **Brother Jack**, a short insignificant-looking man with red hair who lives for the organization. Under his plain exterior, Brother Jack hides an iron-willed, sharp-witted personality. To further the ends of the organization, he ruthlessly sacrifices people and uses members mercilessly. He believes in complete obedience to party policy, regardless of the consequences. Through his inflexible, stern leadership, he creates an atmosphere of fear and suspicion among the members. His methods of intimidation run the gamut from withholding praise to removing his glass eye. When he deliberately allows a race riot to occur in Harlem so that the Brotherhood can gain power, I. M. loses the last shred of respect he had for Brother Jack.

I. M. learns party dogma from another white man, **Brother Hambro**. Though not as inflexible as Brother Jack, he, too, believes in total adherence to the party line. His approach, however, is intellectual and abstract. Essentially, he is isolated from the realities of the class struggle by his comfortable upper-middle-class lifestyle.

I. M.'s two black friends in the movement are **Brother Tarp** and **Tod Clifton.** Tarp, an older man, has learned about suffering and racial inequality through bitter experience. Nineteen years on the chain gang have left him with grim memories, a limp, and a desire to help his fellow blacks. His faith in I. M. is shown when he gives him the iron anklet he wore for years. Tod Clifton, a handsome young man, arouses admiration and respect in all who know him. A tireless worker for the Brotherhood, he is a disciplined believer who fights courageously for the cause, even when forced to face Ras and his gang singlehandedly. He suddenly disappears and I. M. sees him on 42nd Street denying his race by selling dancing Sambo dolls. Mystified by this change in behavior, I. M. later realizes that Tod has become so disillusioned by the party and the way the leadership manipulated him that he lost his focus in life. The party's callous reaction to Tod's later death and its leaders' willingness to exploit the situation precipitate a reaction in I. M. similar to Tod's.

Opposed to the Brotherhood is **Ras,** also known as **Ras the Exhorter**, a fanatic black nationalist who, through his inflammatory speeches, has created a large and violent following in Harlem. He regards any communication with whites as a form of Uncle Tomism and therefore finds the multiracial Brotherhood an abomination that should be destroyed.

Although he appears only briefly in the novel, **Rinehart** is a fascinating character. During the riot, street people mistakenly think I. M. is Rinehart, and through these encounters I. M. learns about this man, the ultimate entrepreneur. A leader in the numbers racket, he is also the minister of a street-front church. At various times, I. M. describes him as Rine the runner, Rine the gambler, Rine the briber, Rine the lover, and Rine the Reverend, but above all, Rine the rascal.

Further Reading

Baker, Houston A., Jr. "A Forgotten Prototype: *The Autobiography of an Ex-Colored Man* and *Invisible Man.*" *Virginia Quarterly Review* 49 (summer 1973).

Bishop, Jack. *Ralph Ellison.* New York: Chelsea House, 1988.

Black Literary Criticism. Vol. 1. Detroit: Gale Research, 1992.

Bruccoli, Matthew J., and Richard Layman, eds. *The New Consciousness, 1941-1968.* Vol. 5 of *Concise Dictionary of American Literary Biography.* Detroit: Gale Research, 1987.

Christian, Barbara. "Ralph Ellison: A Critical Study." In *Black Expression.* Edited by Addison Gayle, Jr. New York: Weybright, 1969.

Contemporary Literary Criticism. Vols. 1, 3, 11. Detroit: Gale Research, 1973, 1975, 1979.

Ellison, Ralph. *Going to the Territory.* New York: Random House, 1986.

———. "Interview." *Iowa Review* 19 (fall 1989).

Helterman, Jeffrey, and Richard Layman, eds. *American Novelists since World War II.* Vol. 2 of *Dictionary of Literary Biography.* Detroit: Gale Research, 1987.

Henderson, Lesley, ed. *Contemporary Novelists.* 5th ed. Detroit: St. James, 1991.

Magill, Frank N. *Critical Survey of Long Fiction: English Language Series: Authors.* Vol. 3. Englewood Cliffs, N.J.: Prentice-Hall, 1983.

McSweeney, Kerry. *"Invisible Man": Race and Identity.* Boston: Twayne, 1988.

Nadel, Alan. *Invisible Criticism: Ralph Ellison and the American Canon.* Iowa City: University of Iowa Press, 1988.

O'Meally, Robert G. *The Craft of Ralph Ellison.* Cambridge, MA: Harvard University Press, 1980.

Reilly, John M., ed. *Twentieth-Century Interpretations of Invisible Man: A Collection of Essays.* Englewood Cliffs, N.J.: Prentice-Hall, 1972.

Ryan, Bryan, ed. *Major Twentieth-Century Writers: A Selection of Sketches from Contemporary Authors.* Detroit: Gale Research, 1991.

Smith, Valerie. *African American Writers.* New York: Scribner's, 1991.

Trimmer, Joseph F., ed. *A Casebook on Ralph Ellison's Invisible Man.* New York: Crowell, 1972.

F. Scott Fitzgerald

1896-1940, American novelist

The Great Gatsby

(novel, 1925)

PLOT: Narrator Nick Carraway, fresh from his middle-class Midwest home, moves to West Egg, New York, where he has purchased a small house. A bond salesman, he becomes involved with the wealthy and sophisticated upper-class folk of East and West Egg on Long Island. Nick immediately falls victim to their charm and reckless way of life. Some, like Jay Gatsby, a racketeer and romantic, have made huge fortunes but lack the traditions of inherited wealth. Gatsby, for instance, owns a pretentious mansion. Others, like Daisy Fay Buchanan, a distant cousin to Nick, and her husband, Tom, come from established wealth but have been corrupted by their purposeless existence.

One night at a dinner party, Nick meets the impulsive and attractive Jordan Baker and is reunited with Daisy. He also learns that Tom has a mistress, Myrtle Wilson. She is a married woman so concerned with escaping her social status that she has become involved with Tom, primarily because he wears patent leather shoes.

Nick becomes fascinated by the shadowy, mysterious Gatsby, himself a transplanted Midwesterner who loves to throw lavish parties. Gatsby is in love with Daisy. Although she returns his love, she married the financially secure Tom because Gatsby, at the time, was poor. He acquired his ill-gotten wealth solely to fit in with her sophisticated society.

A crisis interrupts this lavish world when Myrtle is killed in a hit-and-run accident. Daisy and Gatsby were in the car at the time, and Nick learns that it was Daisy, not Gatsby as he supposed, who was driving. Tom, who knows that Gatsby is his rival for Daisy's affections, gives his address to Myrtle's husband, George Wilson, a poor auto repairman, who ironically believes that Gatsby was his wife's lover.

Some time later, Gatsby is murdered in his own home. Wilson then takes his own life. Nick is shaken by the two deaths and by all of their responsibility in this senseless tragedy. Disgusted with the meaninglessness of this sophisticated society, he vows to return to his roots and ponder the fallacy of the American Dream.

CHARACTERS: Jay Gatsby is the pivotal figure of this American classic. A romantic dreamer, he believes that beauty and youth can be held forever if one only has enough money. Therefore, he amasses great wealth as a racketeer and spends it lavishly. Gatsby stands as a symbol for the American dream of wealth and happiness, but a dream that has become corrupted by its adherence to false values. When materialism is adopted as the means to the dream, the dream itself dies in a vast, vulgar "universe of ineffable gaudiness." Gatsby is Fitzgerald's symbol foretelling the end of an era: the Jazz Age generation whose pursuit of happiness amid the most spectacular of backgrounds was the sole meaning of life. Gatsby's tragic and senseless end precedes the disillusionment that would set in with the Great Depression, when gross materialism would prove to be a fruitless pursuit. Gatsby is a sad but fascinating and attractive figure who at an early age created a vision for himself and spends his entire life in its pursuit, never growing or even stopping to live his life along the way. Gatsby leaves the novel as he enters it, with his dream still intact, for he is awaiting

Robert Redford and Mia Farrow portray Gatsby and Daisy in The Great Gatsby, *Fitzgerald's portrayal of flawed values during the Roaring Twenties.*

a phone call from Daisy when he is murdered, a phone call that, whether he lived or died, was highly improbable.

First-person narrator **Nick Carraway** is second in importance only to the character of Gatsby. He opens and closes the work and is closely involved with the plot. Nick can be said to be the only person who undergoes any character development throughout the novel. He is a sensitive and fundamentally decent person who nonetheless becomes attracted by the false values of this wealthy society. Because of his personal development and sense of morality, he is able to perceive the problem with Gatsby's dream, even as he is able to understand that Gatsby's flaws make him a better person than the vacuous Daisy and Tom Buchanan. Nick's own sense of responsibility is a good contrast with the total irresponsibility of the Buchanans, who, even before the murder of Gatsby, depart for New York City, leaving the resulting chaos of their actions to be straightened out by others. Nick's conviction at the end of the novel that Gatsby "is worth the whole damn bunch put together" shows his growth and understanding of this amoral society. Nick sees that, despite Gatsby's self-delusion—and even vulgarity—he possessed a strength and unselfishness the others lack. Before Nick returns to the Midwest, he does what the others can't do: he lives up to a sense of personal responsibility. It is Nick who sees to the details of Gatsby's funeral when no one else will. Nick now feels a kinship with and a caring for this man.

Daisy Buchanan is more weak than evil, more irresponsible than vicious, more overprotected than senseless. She is portrayed as typical of the women of her social class and status of the period. Behind the beautiful face and enchanting body is nothing—Daisy is a hollow woman, an empty character. Those around her are unreal to her except as symbols. She treats her own little girl as something to be paraded about and admired; there is no real feeling for the child. Daisy is without the power, will, or reasoning to stand up for her beliefs, for she has none. She loves Gatsby, or is at least drawn to him, but she could never leave Tom, with his established, secure wealth, for a man like Gatsby. While Gatsby's dream is therefore built upon illusion, Daisy herself is an illusion. She has no inner resources to direct her life and is thus tossed about by outside influences. Having no concept of how immoral her own irresponsibility is in the tragedy of Myrtle's death and Gatsby's murder, she does not tell Tom the truth about who was driving on the night of the accident, and she never will. She and Tom go off to New York without a thought to the havoc they have left behind and no concern for those who are left to deal with it. The character of Daisy is also associated with the color white, which is the color she always wears, suggesting someone insubstantial, ethereal. One of the ironies of this novel is that the very focus of Jay Gatsby's enduring dream, the love of Daisy Buchanan, is that Daisy is unworthy of his vision.

Daisy's husband, **Tom Buchanan**, is a brutal, uncaring man devoid of all sense of decency and responsibility. He has no real love for his wife and is, in fact, almost openly unfaithful. It is only when Daisy declares her love for Gatsby that Tom takes notice, and then only because "his possessions are threatened." He is incensed with this threat to his marriage, hypocritically decrying the breakdown of the American family, all the while carrying on a shabby affair with Myrtle. Tom sees no conflict between these feelings. After Myrtle's death, Tom reacts with self-pity because he has lost a mistress. He never for a moment laments that he sent Wilson to murder Gatsby, nor does he give a moment's thought to Wilson's own feelings about the death of his wife. In fact, he treats Wilson with open contempt, considering such a man to be far beneath him. Yet, of course, Wilson has far more character than Tom. He grieves for his undeserving wife with a show of love that would be beyond Tom's capacity to comprehend. All actions and all feelings from Tom are directed toward himself. He lives in a moral wasteland and is totally unaware of it.

Myrtle Wilson portrays a different sense of shallowness than Daisy Buchanan. She is a ludicrous character who lives only to rise above the constraints of her own social class, which is why she enters into an affair with Tom. She married her husband, George, because she thought he was better off than she, only to find that on their wedding day he wore a borrowed suit. She is obsessed with her appearance and has no concept of values, traits that produce some light and amusing moments in the novel. She is a pathetic woman who is much like Tom Buchanan in her single-minded and selfish pursuits. Myrtle often speaks harshly of those who come from the "lower orders," apparently forgetting that the "lower orders" are her background as well. Myrtle's husband, **George Wilson**, is a struggling auto repairman who blames himself for the infidelity, and even the death, of his beloved but undeserving wife. He is a sad character who, nonetheless, deserves a measure of respect for his genuine love for his wife.

Jordan Baker has a short-lived romance with Nick. Mainly a way of drawing Nick into the plot, Jordan exhibits much of the qualities—irresponsibility and carelessness—of Daisy. However, unlike the devoted Gatsby, Nick is able to grow beyond his attraction for Jordan, see her as she is, and reject her, which he does at the Buchanans' home. It is this insight that protects Nick, and the lack of it that brings about the destruction of Jay Gatsby.

Further Reading

Berman, Ronald. The Great Gatsby *and Modern Times.* Champaign: University of Illinois Press, 1994.

Bloom, Harold, ed. *F. Scott Fitzgerald.* New York: Chelsea, 1995.

———. *F. Scott Fitzgerald's "The Great Gatsby."* New York: Chelsea, 1995.

Bruccoli, Matthew J., ed. *F. Scott Fitzgerald in His Own Time: A Miscellany.* Kent, OH: Kent State University Press, 1971.

———. *F. Scott Fitzgerald.* New York: Harcourt, 1981.

———. *New Essays on* The Great Gatsby. Cambridge: Cambridge University Press, 1985.

Cowley, Malcolm. *Fitzgerald and the Jazz Age.* New York: Scribner's, 1966.

Critical Survey of Long Fiction. Vol. 3. Englewood Cliffs, NJ: Prentice-Hall, 1983.

Donaldson, Scott. *Fool for Love: F. Scott Fitzgerald.* New York: Congdon & Weed, 1983.

Eble, Kenneth Eugene. *F. Scott Fitzgerald.* New York: Twayne, 1963.

Fahey, William A. *F. Scott Fitzgerald and the American Dream.* New York: Crowell, 1973.

Graham, Sheilah. *Beloved Infidel.* New York: Bantam, 1959.

Hindus, Milton. *F. Scott Fitzgerald: An Introduction and Interpretation.* New York: Holt, 1968.

Hoffman, Frederick J., ed. *"The Great Gatsby": A Study.* New York: Scribner's, 1962.

Kazin, Alfred. *F. Scott Fitzgerald: The Man and His Work.* Cleveland: World, 1951.

Kimbel, Bobby Ellen, ed. *American Short-Story Writers, 1910-1945, First Series.* Vol. 86 of *Dictionary of Literary Biography.* Detroit: Gale Research, 1989.

Lehan, Richard D. *F. Scott Fitzgerald and the Craft of Fiction.* Carbondale: Southern Illinois University Press, 1969.

LeVot, Andre. *F. Scott Fitzgerald: A Biography.* New York: Doubleday, 1983.

Lockridge, Ernest, ed. *Twentieth-Century Interpretations of* The Great Gatsby. Englewood Cliffs, NJ: Prentice-Hall, 1968.

Martine, James J., ed. *American Novelists, 1910-1945.* Vol. 9 of *Dictionary of Literary Biography.* Detroit: Gale Research, 1981.

Mellow, James R. *Invented Lives: F. Scott and Zelda Fitzgerald.* Boston: Houghton Mifflin, 1984.

Meyers, Jeffrey. *Scott Fitzgerald: A Biography.* New York: Harper Collins, 1994.

Miller, James E., Jr. *F. Scott Fitzgerald: His Art and His Technique.* New York: New York University Press, 1964.

Mizener, Arthur. *The Far Side of Paradise: A Biography of F. Scott Fitzgerald.* Boston: Houghton Mifflin, 1965.

———. *Scott Fitzgerald and His World.* New York: Putnam, 1972.

Piper, Henry Dan. *F. Scott Fitzgerald: A Critical Portrait.* New York: Holt, 1965.

———. *Fitzgerald's* The Great Gatsby. New York: Scribner's, 1970.

Rood, Karen Lane, ed. *American Writers in Paris, 1920-1939.* Vol. 4 of *Dictionary of Literary Biography.* Detroit: Gale Research, 1980.

Turnbull, Andrew. *Scott Fitzgerald.* New York: Scribner's, 1962.

Twentieth-Century American Literature. Vol. 3 of *Chelsea House Library of Literary Criticism.* New York: Chelsea, 1986.

Twentieth-Century Literary Criticism. Vols. 1, 6, 14, 28, 55. Detroit: Gale Research, 1978, 1982, 1984, 1988, 1995.

Paul Fleischman

1952-, American novelist

The Borning Room

(historical novel, 1991)

PLOT: Born in 1851, Georgina Lott is growing up in rural Ohio with a loving family that includes her mother and father, grandfather, and four older siblings. Their New England-style home, built by Grandfather, includes a simple borning room off the kitchen—a place that is used for giving birth, for dying, and for caring for the sick. It is there that Georgina was born. Her mother, Emmaline, was under the care of the trusted midwife Mrs. Radtke.

Though Ohio is a free state, it is considered a crime to harbor an escaped slave. Georgina is eight when, while wandering in the woods one day, she happens on a sick slave named Cora. Not wishing to get her family involved, Georgina secretly begins taking care of Cora in the barn. However, when Georgina's mother is in a difficult labor and Mrs. Radtke has not yet arrived, Georgina turns to Cora for help. The baby's placement is wrong, and through massage Cora is able to turn the baby around and young Zeb is safely delivered. Cora is helped by the family until arrangements are made with some Quakers to smuggle her to Canada.

Later, Georgina's beloved Grandfather, a freethinker, suffers a serious stroke and dies. It is the first great loss that Georgina will have to suffer. By 1865, other members of the household have married and left. But the family welcomes into their home Aunt Erna, a severe authoritarian who has been widowed. Expecting another baby, Mother is taken into the borning room. Instead of the midwife, Dr. Roop is summoned. Unfortunately, both mother and baby die. But a second child, whom they name Ellsworth, is born alive.

As the years pass, Georgina's brother Zeb's new teacher, Clement Bock, enters the family circle. A charming man, he soon becomes a favorite. Both Ellsworth and Zeb are later stricken during a diphtheria epidemic. Ellsworth recovers, but Zeb grows worse until Mr. Bock saves him by using ground eggshells to break the throat membrane that is suffocating him. In the spring of 1869, Georgina and Clement marry. A year and a half later, an ancient Mrs. Radtke helps deliver their first child, Emmaline Bellflower Bock. The cycle of births and deaths continues in the borning room until one day, in 1918, an old and frail Georgina enters it for the last time.

CHARACTERS: This short novel, scarcely one hundred pages long, is constructed of six vignettes, each involving the borning room. They are all told by the narrator, **Georgina Caroline Lott**, who was born on January 11, 1851, in this tiny but significant room off the kitchen. A pretty girl with honey-colored hair kept in braids, Georgina shows at an early age the same spunk and spirit that have characterized many of those in the Lott family. Brought up to hate slavery, she hides Cora without consulting anyone to insure that only she would be fined or imprisoned if caught. Though sick with apprehension and anxiety, she proceeds independently to help this forlorn creature. This daring act of courage and independence is typical of the young girl, who accepts household responsibilities far beyond her years. She is an obedient daughter, filled with love and compassion for her friends and family. Open-minded, she accepts differences in others and believes in the freedom of choice concerning religion and individual beliefs. Her dislike of insincerity and prejudice and her courage to speak her mind help make her Grandfather's favorite. A talented and bright girl, Georgina is adept at self-education and easily absorbs and appreciates fine literature and the rudiments of music, though she drops out of school early to help her mother at home. She is an enterprising, hard-working person who is demure and reserved when she is with others, but she can be assertive and forceful when necessary. For example, she is polite but firm in countering Aunt Erna's attempts to dominate the household. Like her mother before her, Georgina becomes an exemplary wife and mother, asking little of life and giving much.

As a child, the two greatest influences on Georgina, are **Grandfather Lott** and her parents. Grandfather represents all the strength, dignity, and courage of the early pioneers. He bravely brought his wife and baby by wagon from New Hampshire to Ohio, and by a huge maple on his property he built a sturdy, New England-type house for his family to live in in peace and harmony. A deeply religious man of high principles, he never goes to church but instead finds God in the wonders and glory of nature and life on earth. Every Sunday, when the rest of the family is attending services, he wanders through the woods savoring the beauties and marvels of creation. On his deathbed and unable to speak, he maintains his fierce independence and resists the entreaties of ministers to recant and accept Christianity. As he faced life, he faces death—courageously, firm in his belief in mankind and the sanctity of all forms of life. Grandfather is a free thinker who believes in human dignity and the sacred right of freedom. He is an ardent abolitionist who would rather follow high principles and maintain a clear conscience than obey unjust man-made laws. Usually quiet, he becomes aroused when involved in a fight for fairness and equality. After Grandfather's death, Georgina's father builds a coffin and he is buried on his property next to Grandmother. As the body is lowered into the earth, Georgina thinks about this remarkable, unique man and "how he'd tried to teach me to savor everything I encountered—every sight, every scent, every sound, every taste."

Georgina has two loving parents. Particularly significant in her life is **Emmaline Lott**, her mother. A hard-working, tireless woman, she generously sacrifices herself and her needs for her family. For instance, she carries the churn into the borning room and continues her chores though enduring severe labor pains before Georgina's birth. Uncomplaining, she is always there to guide, support, and instruct. She instills in her children a love of the arts. A violinist, she arranges family musicales after chores are done and promotes the love of good literature by conducting read-aloud sessions of the works of such writers as Charles Dickens. An amazing woman with positive, warm instincts and a belief in the power of love, she "filled any room she was in with light." After her mother dies in childbirth, Georgina tries to emulate Emmaline and take her place in the household.

Georgina's father is **Joseph Lott**. A quiet, God-fearing man, he is an untiring bread-winner and sacrificing parent. Patient and industrious, he becomes a model for his children. Like his father, Joseph is a firm believer in individual freedom. He, too, hates slavery and will disobey the law, if necessary, in the name of human freedom. When Emmaline dies, he is outwardly strong but inwardly inconsolable. His sense of loss and guilt motivate him to try to contact his beloved wife with the help of a spiritualist.

Two non-family members are associated with the birth of children in the Lott household. **Mrs. Radtke** is a German midwife who, though filled with superstitions and only a primitive knowledge of medicine, is expert in delivering babies. A permanent figure in the community, she and her mare, Frieda, are familiar sights. In addition to midwifery, Mrs. Radtke, with her knowledge of the area's demographics, has become the resident matchmaker. In her old age, Mrs. Radtke is bent and slow, and her work is usually performed by medical doctors. Georgina, however, uses her at the birth of her first child. **Dr. Roop** is brought in by Georgina's father to apply modern procedures, including the use of chloroform, in delivering a baby. Unfortunately, through incompetence or unforeseen complications, both mother and baby die. Through Aunt Erna's last-minute intervention, a second child is born unharmed.

After her husband and two sons die, **Aunt Erna** comes to live with the Lotts. A demanding, opinionated woman, she and Georgina clash over control of the household after Emmaline's death. Rigid, sarcastic, and absurdly puritanical, she is described as "tall and thin as a cornstalk, dressed always in her mourning black." Fortunately for Georgina, a debilitating case of arthritis later causes Aunt Erna to be confined to her room.

The escaped slave **Cora** is a short, scrawny woman with graying hair who is covered with scratches, swellings, and scars when Georgina finds her. A pathetic figure, she had been used as a breeder on various plantations. Forced to sleep with different men and heartsick over having each of her children taken from her, she has resorted to self-inflicted abortions and to frantically finding a way to escape. At one point in the story, her knowledge of midwifery saves the life of Georgina's mother.

Mr. Clement Bock, one of the local school teachers, is a cheery, candid, and sincere young man who is refreshingly honest and direct. An eloquent man with a fine sense of humor, he, like Georgina, loves literature and music. An accomplished artist, he soon realizes Georgina's sterling qualities. After he ingeniously saves the life of Georgina's young brother Zeb during a diphtheria epidemic, a short courtship begins resulting in the happy marriage of Clement and Georgina.

Further Reading

Authors and Artists for Young Adults. Vol. 11. Detroit: Gale Research, 1993.

Berger, Laura Standley, ed. *Twentieth-Century Young Adult Writers.* 1st ed. Chicago: St. James, 1994.

Chevalier, Tracy, ed. *Twentieth-Century Children's Writers.* 3rd ed. Chicago: St. James, 1989.

Holtze, Sally Holmes, ed. *Fifth Book of Junior Authors and Illustrators.* New York: H. W. Wilson, 1983.

Something about the Author. Vols. 39, 72. Detroit: Gale Research, 1985, 1993.

Ward, Martha, ed. *Authors of Books for Young People.* 3rd ed. Metuchen, NJ: Scarecrow, 1990.

Esther Forbes

1891-1967, American historical novelist

Johnny Tremain

(young adult historical novel, 1943)

PLOT: Called by some critics the best American historical novel ever written for young readers, *Johnny Tremain* is the only work in this genre by its Pulitzer Prize-winning author. Set in Boston in the late eighteenth century, the story focuses on

His career as a silversmith ruined, young Johnny Tremain takes up the cause of liberty in Forbes's 1943 tale of the American Revolution.

fourteen-year-old Johnny Tremain, an apprentice to a silversmith. A bright and talented boy, Johnny is inclined to be somewhat arrogant and bossy. He is proud of both his talents and his position as unofficial manager of the shop. The owner, Mr. Lapham, is inclined to let Johnny do pretty much as he pleases; Johnny's favored status is enhanced because Mr. Lapham's daughter-in-law also likes him.

Johnny's life changes abruptly, however, after patriot John Hancock orders a silver piece from the Lapham shop. As Johnny rushes to finish it, he is given a defective cup to work with by one of the other apprentices, Dove, who dislikes the arrogant young man. The cup breaks and Johnny's hand is burned so badly that the scarring prevents him from moving his fingers properly. His promising career as a silversmith is ruined, and he is reduced to working as an errand boy.

Remembering his dead mother's words about a wealthy relative, Jonathan Lyte, Johnny hopes to get help from the merchant by showing him a silver cup with a special crest given to him by his mother. Lyte, however, rejects all suggestions that they are related and calls Johnny a thief for having the cup. However, the boy is proven innocent by Lyte's granddaughter, Lavinia, and Johnny's friend, Rab Silsbee, who works for the *Boston Observer* newspaper.

Johnny joins Rab as an employee of the newspaper, which supports independence from England. He moves into Rab's attic room, where such patriots as Paul Revere and Sam Adams sometimes hold secret meetings. As tensions grow between England and the colonies, Johnny becomes more involved with the patriots. He even takes part in the Boston Tea Party by joining other boys dressed as Indians to dump tea into Boston Harbor. This act, in retaliation for what the colonists regard as unfair taxation, spurs the two sides closer to war.

Johnny becomes the eyes and ears of the colonists as he wanders about the city, gathering information. When he hears of British plans concerning Lexington and Concord, he tells Paul Revere, who warns the colonists of the planned attack. War erupts at Lexington, where Rab has gone to help defend his hometown. Johnny goes to Lexington, too, and finds his friend fatally wounded. Before he dies, Rab gives Johnny his musket, which Johnny accepts, although his crippled hand will not allow him to fire it. However, Doctor Warren assures Johnny that, even though Johnny will never be a silversmith, the scar tissue can be cut away so that he can use it to shoot. Johnny takes his place among the patriots in their fight for freedom. He also learns from Lavinia that he is indeed her father's great-nephew.

CHARACTERS: Gifted and clever, **Johnny Tremain**, a skinny lad of fourteen, is inclined to be bossy and self-important. He is disliked by most of the other apprentices because he orders them around and practically runs the Lapham silver shop himself. However, he is favored by Mr. Lapham for his hard work and skill, as well as by Mr. Lapham's daughter-in-law, who gives Johnny special treatment because she likes him.

Johnny's future seems assured. He will grow up to be a great and talented silversmith who will marry his employer's daughter and inherit the shop. But when his hand is severely burned and scarred, his world changes. The once frivolous boy begins a slow change from an arrogant youngster to a young patriot caught up in the revolution.

At first, Johnny is filled with hatred for Dove, the apprentice who caused the accident by giving him a defective cup. As the weeks wear on, he grows more and more sorry for himself as his once exalted status in the silversmith shop is reduced to that of an errand boy. He is dealt another blow to his pride when he is rejected by wealthy relative Jonathan Lyte, from whom he seeks help. Johnny begins his transformation to patriot when he moves into the attic room of Rab Silsbee. As such men as Paul Revere and John Hancock hold secret meetings in the attic hideaway, Johnny is caught up in a cause that transcends his own misfortune. With growing bravery, he becomes the eyes and ears of the patriots as he travels about Boston's streets, gathering information that will help the colonies. After the battle at Lexington, Johnny is confronted with Rab's death. As he shoulders Rab's musket and is given assurances from Doctor Warren that the scar tissue can be cut away so that he can hold the gun, Johnny is ready to take his place among his fellow patriots.

Mr. Lapham, the owner of the silver shop where Johnny works, is a dignified, peaceful, but remote old man with little interest in running his own business. More and more, he relies on the diligence and genius of Johnny Tremain. But when Johnny is injured so severely that he can no longer serve the old man, Lapham has little use for him. One of Mr. Lapham's apprentices, **Dove**, dislikes Johnny because he is favored at the shop, even though Dove is older and has been working there longer. He resents Johnny's skill with silver. This leads him to hand Johnny a defective silver cup, which brings about the accident that ends Johnny's plans to be a silversmith.

The merchant **Jonathan Lyte**, who is pompous, overbearing, and impressed with his own wealth and status, is little disposed to welcome the young man who claims to be his relative. Far from being receptive, he is incensed when the boy introduces himself as Johnny Lyte Tremain and shows him a silver cup that bears the family's distinctive crest. Rather than admit to any relationship with this wretched lad, he throws the boy out and accuses him of stealing the cup. In the end, when the Lytes are fleeing the colonies for England at the outbreak of the war, **Lavinia Lyte** admits to Johnny that he is truly her father's great-nephew.

From **Rab Silsbee**, who is a few years older than Johnny, the boy learns the meaning of patriotic fervor. Friendly and sympathetic to Johnny's plight after his accident, Rab invites him to share his attic room. In doing so, he shares with Johnny his growing excitement for the coming revolution. Learning by Rab's example rather than his words, Johnny becomes more and more involved in colonial affairs. Rab's enthusiasm and belief in the cause extend far beyond his work at the *Boston Observer* or his meetings with the leaders of the colonists. When fighting is about to break out, Rab must return to his hometown of Lexington to help in its defense. Sorry that he never had a chance to fire his musket before he is shot, Rab gives his gun to Johnny. He knows Johnny will bring it honor.

Doctor Warren is a kindly man who takes part in the revolution by tending to the sick and wounded. After examining Johnny's crippled hand, he brings hope to the boy by telling him that he will be able to cut away the scar tissue. This will free his thumb enough so that Johnny can fire Rab's musket.

Further Reading

Berger, Laura Standley, ed. *Twentieth-Century Young Adult Writers.* 4th ed. Detroit: St. James, 1994.

Brown, Muriel W., and Rita S. Foudray. *Newbery and Caldecott Medalists and Honor Book Winners: Bibliographic and Resource*

Material through 1990. 2nd ed. Chicago: Neal-Schuman, 1992.

Children's Literature Review. Vol. 27. Detroit: Gale Research, 1992.

Chevalier, Tracy, ed. *Twentieth-Century Children's Writers.* 3rd ed. Chicago: St. James, 1989.

Contemporary Authors Permanent Series. Vol. 1. Detroit: Gale Research, 1975.

Czech, John, ed. *American Writers for Children, 1990-1960.* Vol. 22 of *Dictionary of Literary Biography.* Detroit: Gale Research, 1983.

Something about the Author. Vol. 2. Detroit: Gale Research, 1971.

Ward, Martha, ed. *Authors of Books for Young People.* 3rd ed. Metuchen, NJ: Scarecrow, 1990.

Paula Fox

1923-, American novelist

The Slave Dancer

(historical novel, 1973)

PLOT: The year is 1840 and slavery is still legal in the United States. However odious the practice is on land, no American ship is allowed to engage in it legally. Thirteen-year-old Jessie Bollier, the novel's narrator, lives in New Orleans with his widowed mother, who is a seamstress, and his nine-year-old sister, Betty. They exist in the direst poverty in what is now called the French Quarter. Jessie helps his family by earning a few pennies each day by playing his fife for the amusement of the sailors and others on the docks.

One evening his mother sends him to Aunt Agatha's to borrow some candles so she can continue her sewing. Before he can complete his errand, however, Jessie is kidnapped by two men who throw a canvas bag over him and take him by raft to a small sailboat. When the bag is removed, Jessie recognizes the two kidnappers as Claudius and Purvis, sailors who were in the group listening to him play his fife on the docks that afternoon. They then take him to a ship called the *The Moonlight.* The master of the vessel is Captain Cawthorne, a cruel man who nicknames Jessie "Bollweevil." Most of the thirteen crew members are as sadistic and cruel as the captain, including mate Nicholas Spark and the calculating Ben Stout.

Jessie quickly learns that he has been imprisoned aboard a slave ship setting out on a four-month voyage to Bight of Benin in Africa. The intended cargo is slaves, who will later be sold in Cuba. At first, Jessie can't understand why he has been kidnapped and what his function will be. Life becomes even more grim when the ship arrives at its destination and takes on the slave cargo. Shackled and terrified, they are loaded into the hold, packed in like animals. To his horror, Jessie now discovers why he is on board. The prisoners must be taken to the deck each day for exercise, or they will die, and Jessie must provide the fife music to prod the slaves into a dance to keep their muscles strong. Jessie soon takes note of a young, wide-eyed boy in the slave cargo named Ras (though Jessie doesn't learn the boy's name until much later). When the cruel Sparks throws Jessie's fife into the mass of slaves and makes him go and find it, it is Ras who retrieves the instrument for him.

On the last night before they are to unload the slaves in Cuba, a macabre dance is enacted. The slaves are fed rum and dressed in odd bits of costume to provide fun for the sailors. Both slaves and sailors become drunk, but panic breaks out when an American naval ship is spotted on the horizon. Before the ship can reach them, a terrible storm breaks out. Jessie and Ras hide in the hold while the storm batters and destroys the ship. The boys crawl out to find the ship listing badly and the crew and slaves gone.

Jessie and Ras escape and manage to reach the shore of Mississippi, where an escaped slave, Daniel, helps them. He is able to send Ras north via the Underground Railroad and instructs Jessie how to find his way back to his home in New Orleans. Jessie explains in his narration that he returns home and later travels north, where he becomes an apothecary in Rhode Island. He serves in the Civil War and survives an ordeal in the infamous Andersonville prison. But even with all the horrors of war, the greater horror remains his memories of that terrible slave ship and its helpless and terrified human cargo.

CHARACTERS: In this grim, realistic story of the horrors that humans can inflict upon one another, **Jessie Bollier** learns a harsh lesson and develops character and self-knowledge in the process. The

Fox portrays the cruelties of the slave trade in this story about a white boy who is kidnapped to work aboard a slave ship.

reader suffers with him as he goes through both physical and mental agonies while on *The Midnight.* Well portrayed is Jessie's growing dislike of the slaves simply because their plight so devastates him. Cut off from family and friends, alone and afraid, Jessie finds himself at first adopting some of the sailors' attitudes as a defense mechanism against the inhumanity he witnesses. But as he grows physically and morally, he resists conforming to the outlook of the older men and is therefore able to survive his ordeal while they do not. The novel presents a vivid picture of how the institution of slavery diminishes the oppressors as well as the oppressed.

When Jessie returns home, he is surprised not only by how quickly he slips back into his own life at first, but also how changed his **mother**, his sister, **Betty**, and **Aunt Agatha** seem toward him, as though they somehow understand his ordeal. When he tells his mother of what he has seen and suffered, she cries, "I can't hear it! I can't bear it!" Betty speaks to him more softly now and Aunt Agatha no longer calls him a bayou lout. In a sense, Jessie does not survive this experience. He eventually escapes from his poverty-stricken home to go north and learn a trade, but this is a hard-won victory for the young man. He is tormented for the remainder of his days by the cruelty and alienation he has witnessed, and by the injustice of the deaths of nearly all the slaves aboard *The Midnight.* Jessie reveals to the reader that he will no longer be able to listen to music, especially to the sound of his fife. As for Ras, he lives forever in Jessie's memory.

None of the slave characters, except **Ras,** are developed or given a name in this novel. Ras can't speak to Jessie, of course, and it is only when the two boys come ashore and meet Daniel that Jessie learns his name. In the short time they have together before Ras is shipped north to safety on the Underground Railroad, he and Jessie begin to communicate by learning a few words of each other's language. When the two must part, they face each other and Ras touches Jessie's nose. "Nose," he says with a smile. Then he touches his front teeth. "Teef," he said. "Teeth," Jessie corrects. Then Ras is gone. Jessie feels a great hollowness, which, in a sense, he will always feel.

The only other black character to be portrayed with any depth is **Daniel**, a kindly old man and escaped slave who lives in a cabin near the Mississippi shore and agrees to help Jessie and Ras. When Jessie tells his horrible story, Daniel replies only, "That's the way it was." He cautions Jessie when he leaves that if he tells his people about Daniel, surely someone will come and get him. Jessie swears he will not tell. With sadness, Jessie leaves the home of the man who saved his life.

The crew of *The Midnight* is filled with disreputable characters. The chief of this brutish crowd is the sadistic **Captain Cawthorne**. He cares nothing for his cargo, his crew, or Jessie. After Jessie sees some of the slaves who are pitched overboard, he refuses to play his fife. Under the captain's orders, he is beaten into submission. The mate **Nicholas Spark** is no better than the captain. He enjoys tormenting and abusing the slaves. After one incident in which a slave rebels, Spark shoots him in the back. The captain throws Spark overboard for this, not because what he did was wrong but because he destroyed valuable property. **Claudius** and **Purvis** are two loutish sailors who claim not to approve of stealing small boys off the docks but only do so to obey the captain's orders. However, Jessie finds that Purvis is the only one aboard ship whom he can talk to.

One-Eyed Cat

(historical novel, 1984)

PLOT: This novel is set in upstate New York during the Depression year of 1935 and tells of young, sensitive Ned Wallis. Ned is growing up in a loving family that consists of his saint-like father, James Wallis, the local congregational minister, and an attentive mother, Martha, who is often confined to a wheelchair because of her severe arthritis. On the eve of Ned's eleventh birthday, his mother's urbane brother, Uncle Hilary, arrives and gives him a present of a Daisy air rifle. Ned's father, a nonviolent man, decides to put the gun in the attic until Ned is older. That night, Ned secretly takes the gun outdoors and shoots at a grey shadow he sees by the barn. He is certain someone saw him from the attic window and thinks it might be their demanding housekeeper, Mrs. Scallop. On a visit to Mr. Scully, an eighty-year-old man for whom Ned works after school, the boy sees a gray feral cat with one eye. They begin feeding him, but Ned, who is convinced that the cat was his victim, feels great pangs of guilt. Although his feelings of shame increase each time he sees the cat, he tells no one, including his family, about his disobedient act. Ned becomes preoccupied with caring for the cat, and, when Mr. Scully suffers a stroke and is sent to a nursing home, Ned secretly continues the feeding. Mr. Scully's daughter, an unfeeling woman named Doris, arrives and clears out the house. Before Mr. Scully dies, Will confesses to him that he believes he was responsible for the cat's injury. The old man, now without the power of speech, simply holds the boy's hand in a gesture of forgiveness. Ned's mother responds to a new treatment and, one night, slips out of the house for a walk. Ned follows her and, while they are talking, they see in the distance the one-eyed cat accompanied by two kittens. Ned confesses to his mother about the air rifle incident, and she tells him it was she who witnessed the scene but had wisely remained silent. She also tells him that she understands Ned's problem of feeling unable to live up to his father's perfection and goodness. Her own feelings of inadequacy caused her to leave her husband once when Ned was young, but love for him and her child made her return. They walk back home, where they are welcomed back by Mr. Wallis, who was worried about their absence.

CHARACTERS: This novel is told from the point of view of **Ned Wallis**, an eleven-year-old sixth-grader. Ned is a quiet, introspective young boy who is deeply attached to his mother and father. He is sensitive about being a minister's son and the responsibilities and obligations that this involves. Because he is shy and quiet, he feels uncomfortable when he must accompany his family to parishioners' homes for dinner. He feels these occasions are like taking charity. He respects and loves his father but is intimidated by his inherent goodness and charity. Although Ned never voices complaints or tries to rebel, he suffers under the stifling restrictions that this life has forced on him. Ned continually faces a inner struggle between being a normal boy, with an urge to cut loose and have fun, and trying to emulate his father, whom he regards as a paragon of virtue. As a result, whenever he fails to live up to his father's high standards Ned suffers exceptional pangs of guilt and inner torment.

Ned is obedient and deferential toward both parents. Though deeply disappointed by his father's edict concerning the gun, he acquiesces without complaint but, in an understandable act of defiance and disobedience, he retrieves the gun for a trial shot. Subsequently, his life becomes dominated by two conflicting courses of action: whether to confess or conceal his deed. He first chooses the latter, but, with each lie he tells to hide his secret, he feels more remorse and shame. Being secretive and dishonest with his parents causes him great mental anguish. Ned feels he has a special relationship with his mother because of her openness and understanding, and he prefers that others do not share their special bond. Therefore, he feels slight pangs of jealousy when he notices that his mother and her brother, Uncle Hilary, have a special and private rapport. Ned shows a rare compassion toward others. He is sick with anxiety over the fate of the one-eyed cat. To his friends, he shows loyalty and sympathy. His love and devotion to Mr. Scully is touching and sincere and, in spite of her erratic ways, he is polite and considerate in his dealings with their housekeeper, Mrs. Scallop. During the course of the novel, Ned learns a great deal about life and death, the meaning of family love, and the expiation of guilt.

Ned's father, the **Reverend James Wallis**, is a tender, caring man whose virtuous nature can prove intimidating to some people, including both his wife and his son. A model of patience and endurance, he is always polite and well-mannered and tries to think of what is best for everyone. Though without material wealth and living under the strain of caring for a sickly wife, he never complains or reveals any anger or stress. He is a forgiving man who shows great affection and concern for both his wife and Ned. Always available for comforting words and guidance, he epitomizes the unselfish, altruistic way of life and is content to live a simple, plain life, gratefully accepting what blessings have been bestowed upon him and his family. A man of peace, he hates violence and therefore takes Ned's gun from him until the boy is old enough to decide whether he really wants it. He has a generous and giving nature, even sharing his meager resources with others. Far from being sanctimonious, he has a gentle sense of humor and a forgiving but realistic view of people's weaknesses and foibles. The fact that he is unaware of his saintliness makes his goodness and perfection all the more impressive. Ned is particularly proud of his father on Sundays when he appears before his congregation with "an amethyst tie pin in his black silk tie, black trousers with the satin stripe down each side and the cutaway jacket."

Ned's mother, **Martha Wallis**, is perhaps less saintly than her husband but equally gentle and loving toward her family. She suffers incredible, debilitating pain from rheumatoid arthritis, and is usually confined either to bed or a wheelchair. She was once a fun-loving, carefree, independent person, who loved a life of action, parties, and horseback riding. Her brother's presence and conversation rekindle her freedom-loving spirit and the life of sophistication she once led. Uncomplaining, she not only fights her pain but also the enervating feelings of helplessness she experiences sometimes. Though completely without self-pity, she misses the adventure she once had in her life. For example, during a severe thunderstorm, she longs to be out in it to feel the violence and power of nature again. Mrs. Wallis had problems adjusting to living the exposed, public life of the wife of a clergyman, particularly with a husband whose virtues were so great. Ashamed of not being as "good" as him, and afraid that she would one day disappoint him, she once left her husband, but the bonds of love for him and her child brought her back. Like Mr. Wallis, she consciously tries not to dominate or stifle her son's development, however their innate goodness and compassion do create burdens of conscience in the boy of which she is more aware than her husband. Mrs. Wallis is wise and understanding. For instance, though she has witnessed the incident with the air rifle, she remains silent, waiting for the appropriate moment when her son can unburden himself and seek forgiveness.

Mrs. Wallis's tall, thin, handsome brother, **Uncle Hilary**, is an affectionate, sophisticated man who lives in New York City but travels widely. He possesses a bubbling, cheerful disposition and exudes an urbane, cultured aura without ever being condescending or superior. He is a generous, outgoing, spirited man, with a zest for living and a genuine love for his nephew whose experience and horizons he would like to expand. He frequently sends Ned gifts from foreign lands and offers to take him on trips. Uncle Hilary graciously accepts the fact that his gift of the air rifle is considered inappropriate by his brother-in-law and feels no resentment. Understandably, Ned has a special place in his heart for Uncle Hilary.

Ned does chores for the Wallis's eighty-year-old neighbor, **Mr. Scully**, who lives alone in a dilapidated house. He is a small, stooped man who is devoted to his absent daughter, Doris. Old-fashioned (he refuses to use the newfangled refrigerator his daughter bought him), he continues to mend his own socks and cook for himself. Worried about the future and being taken to an old folks home, Mr. Scully prepares for death and begins sorting through all his memorabilia and, while doing this, fascinates Ned with stories of his childhood. Ned and he strike up a mutually loving relationship: Ned enjoys Mr. Scully's company and attention, and the old man gains a new interest in life, particularly when they begin caring for the stray one-eyed cat that comes for food. Nearing his death and now almost completely paralyzed, he squeezes Ned's hand in a parting show of forgiveness, understanding, and love when Ned confesses that he injured the cat.

One of the more unpleasant characters in the novel is **Doris**, Mr. Scully's neglectful and inconsiderate daughter. She seldom writes to him, only sending infrequent postcards. When she arrives at her father's home to settle his affairs, she proves to be insensitive and brusque. Even the ever-charitable Reverend Wallis confesses that "she did her duty, but only in a grudging way." Equally disagreeable is the Wallis's housekeeper, **Mrs. Scallop,** a giant of a woman with a sharp, grinding voice and a changeable temperament—one day affectionate and the next, inexplicably difficult and sullen. Whereas the Bible has only ten commandments, she has hundreds that she applies erratically to the family, particularly Ned. Although she feigns being humble and self-effacing, she is actually vindictive and mean-spirited. Mrs. Wallis has playfully nicknamed her **Mrs. Snort-and-Bellow**. But when Mrs. Scallop's behavior becomes too trying (for example, she tells the already guilt-ridden Ned that he is responsible for his mother's illness), even the compassionate Reverend Wallis agrees that she must go. In his usual benevolent way, he waits until he finds another position for her before he tactfully suggests that she leave.

The Moonlight Man

(young adult novel, 1986)

PLOT: Since fifteen-year-old Catherine Ames's parents divorced several years ago, she has seen little of her father, Harry Ames, who is an author. Both of her parents have since remarried, and she has just completed her first year away from her mother at a Montreal private boarding school as the story opens. While her mother and stepfather are celebrating a belated honeymoon in Europe, Catherine is sent to her father's to spend the summer. After staying at her school three weeks after classes have ended and running out of excuses for the school administrators, she receives a somewhat apologetic call from her father, who was supposed to have picked her up when school let out. This is the inauspicious beginning of a five week summer visit that takes her to a rented cottage close to the Atlantic coastline in rural Nova Scotia, where her father is staying alone while his second wife is visiting relatives. Mr. Ames is an appealing, erudite man, eager to impress and charm everyone he meets, including the impressionable Catherine. But within two days she discovers a hidden side to her father's personality: his addiction to alcohol. One day he invites two locals, Farmer Glimm and Mr. Conklin, to their house, and the three get so roaring drunk that Catherine, furious and disillusioned, must drive the guests home at 5:00 a.m., while her father lies unconscious in the back seat of their station wagon.

The next morning her father is so apologetic that he wins Catherine's forgiveness. Gradually, their lives become more routine, and Catherine meets other neighbors, including the cleaning woman, Mrs. Conklin, and a loquacious minister, Reverend Ross. Catherine grows to love and then to pity her enigmatic, immature father, who craves attention and admiration. A few days before she has to leave for school, a young off-duty Mountie, Officer Alistair Macbeth, takes Mr. Ames and a reluctant Catherine on a tour of local bootleggers. Her father drinks so much that, when they return to the cottage, he becomes violently ill, and Catherine has to ask Reverend Ross for help. The next day, there is a violent scene when her surly, unrepentant father grabs her and demands forgiveness. By the time Catherine is scheduled to leave, their relationship has become amicable once again, but when Catherine says goodbye and "See you," her father replies with a kiss and says, "Not if I see you first."

CHARACTERS: This exploration of a changing relationship between a father and daughter is told from the viewpoint of **Catherine Ames**, an enterprising, intelligent girl who is mature beyond her fifteen years. Though now with two sets of parents, she has developed a healthy degree of independence and self-sufficiency and is unwilling to follow the easy course of playing one parent against the other. She scarcely knows her father but looks forward to a summer with the dashing, bon vivant who had two novels published before he was twenty-six. Though upset by his three weeks of silence when he didn't pick her up from school, Catherine is so anxious to love this artistic, charming man whom she has admired from afar that she makes excuses for him and forgives his tardiness without bitterness. Like everyone else, she immediately succumbs to his wit and charismatic behavior.

Though fascinated with her father's stories and imaginative comments, in time, Catherine's awe for her father disintegrates, and she is able to match his witty repartee with equally perceptive and scintillating quips. Her quick wit and alert intelligence often surface when she has to face a father who is trying to smooth-talk his way out of mortifying situations. Instead of being intimidated by him as she was initially, Catherine realizes that allowing herself to be blindly impressed by her father's cleverness would ultimately destroy her own identity. She is frightened and disgusted by his drinking, but forgives him nevertheless, hoping that he will keep his promises of abstinence—as she says at one point, "his words fed a hope always at risk of fading."

Catherine is a level-headed realist. She wants to believe her father when he promises to take her to Italy, but she knows this will never actually happen. She is also outspoken and honest in her relationships. Although she knows it will cause rancor and bitterness, she fearlessly confronts her father about his drinking. By the time she leaves, Catherine's attitude toward her father has changed. Instead of a man to admire unconditionally, he has become in her eyes a somewhat pathetic has-been, getting by on charm with little substance. Although her love is now tinged with pity, she is still devoted to him in spite of his flaws. Catherine has learned the painful lesson that idols have feet of clay, and one must accept people on their own terms.

Catherine's father, **Harry Ames**, is a man who enjoys impressing others with his charm, erudition, and good taste. He is an original, a "midnight man," an enigma who defies categorization. Believing that it somehow makes him more attractive to others, he takes pride in his iconoclastic viewpoints and his unconventional and unorthodox behavior, which includes being thrown out of two colleges for "riotous behavior." Once considered a precocious literary talent of great promise, Harry Ames's promise of a bright future did not materialize because of his dilettantism and lack of self-discipline. Instead, he has become a hack writer of travel books. He is also emotionally immature and spoiled. Erratic and changeable, he lacks the willpower and perseverance to control and develop his massive talents, settling instead for second best. As Catherine's mother says, "he thrived on chaos." Unable to come to terms with himself and find inner peace, he has lived a restless life, never settling in one place, always unsatisfied and seeking escape. He craves attention and needs to be loved and admired, even by the locals for whom he has little respect. He can't face the reality of his unfulfilled promise, and so he drinks to escape reality and his obligations.

Mr. Ames gets testy when challenged and becomes defensive when questioned about his drinking. He suffers from dramatic mood swings that change him from being nonchalant and relaxed to depressed and sullen. After drinking bouts, he experiences what he calls his "humblies" when he has regrets and wants reassurance and encouragement. At these times he relies on his own charm and the forgiving nature of others to win back trust after he has misbehaved. Catherine muses that "she had never seen anyone so talented with emotion and ideas," and she compares him to Scheherazade because of his ability to weave stories and be a brilliant conversationalist. He genuinely loves literature—particularly fine poetry—and can hold an audience spellbound with his readings. Age (he is now fifty) and liquor, have taken their toll on Mr. Ames, however. Though once attractive, he now has a protruding belly, blotchy complexion, sunken eyes, and oyster-colored skin. After a bout of drinking, his hands tremble so much that he can't hold a cup and, at one point, must be shaved by Catherine because he can't handle a razor. His experiences with Catherine during her four-week visit make him face the painful reality of his weaknesses and failure, an experience he doesn't want to repeat. And so, though he knows it will trouble and upset her, he cruelly insinuates at their parting that he doesn't want to see her again.

Two of Mr. Ames's drinking partners are the local bus driver, middle-aged **Mr. Conklin**, who is tall, frail-looking and, in Catherine's opinion, silly, and a local farmer, **Mr. Glimm**, a short, melancholy man who is also middle-aged. Neither share Mr. Ames's interests, except they are attracted by his clever wit and bohemian ways and are flattered in having such a distinguished drinking partner.

Mrs. Landy, Mr. Ames's housekeeper, lives in a hamlet several miles to the east of his home. Thin as a hairpin and with a little twist of mouse hair on her head, she is a fine cleaner but a terrible cook. Though she is taciturn and always businesslike, Mr. Ames delights in charming her and she, in turn, basks in his attention and flattery. She often talks about her son, "little Jackie," who Mr. Ames and Catherine surmise is a child. After they buy little Jackie a tricycle as a farewell present, they discover Mrs. Landy's son is a grown man, though small in stature, who works at the local restaurant.

Mr. Ames refers to the **Reverend Ross** as a 'ferocious prig,' but because Ross is an ardent fisherman and Mr. Ames wants to cultivate his skill in the sport, a casual friendship has been formed between them. Reverend Ross is straight-laced, puritanical, and dour. He is a non-stop talker who does not succumb to Mr. Ames's charms and therefore has the effect of making the author impatient and petulant. When Catherine's father becomes ill after a drinking bout, she is forced to seek the reverend's aid. Though still distant and detached, Reverend Ross shows sympathy and understanding and admits candidly that he too once suffered from alcoholism.

Catherine's mother, **Beatrice**, is introduced briefly in the novel. She is a copyeditor in a publishing house and is now married to an academician, **Carter Beade**, Catherine's stepfather. She loves her daughter dearly and, in contrast to her former husband, Beatrice is a "daylight woman," a level-headed, practical, neat, and orderly person. Unable to cope with Harry's drinking and instability, she divorced him when Catherine was a child.

Further Reading

Authors and Artists for Young Adults. Vol. 3. Detroit: Gale Research, 1990.

Berger, Laura Standley, ed. *Twentieth-Century Young Adult Writers.* 1st ed. Detroit: Gale Research, 1994.

Children's Literature Review. Vol. 1. Detroit: Gale Research, 1976.

Contemporary Literary Criticism. Vols. 2, 8. Detroit, Gale Research, 1974, 1978.

De Montreville, Doris, and Elilzabeth D. Crawford, eds. *Fourth Book of Junior Authors and Illustrators.* New York: H. W. Wilson, 1978.

Estes, Glenn E., ed. *American Writers for Children since 1960.* Vol. 52 of *Dictionary of Literary Biography.* Detroit: Gale Research, 1986.

Something about the Author. Vols. 17, 60. Detroit: Gale Research, 1979, 1990.

Ward, Martha. *Authors of Books for Young People.* 3rd ed. Metuchen, NJ: Scarecrow, 1990.

Anne Frank

1929-1945, German diarist

The Diary of a Young Girl

(war memoir, 1947; English translation, 1952; originally published in the Netherlands as Het achterhuis*)*

PLOT: "It's a wonder I haven't abandoned all my ideals, they seem so absurd and impractical. Yet I cling to them because I still believe, in spite of everything, that people are truly good at heart." This is just one of the extraordinarily mature statements recorded by a German-Jewish girl living in Holland while hiding from Nazi persecution during World War II. Anne Frank was thirteen years old when she made her first diary entry and fifteen when she wrote the final one. The entries in between are neither the work of a professional writer nor the scribblings of a teenage girl. They are, instead, a document of World War II and a testimony to the strength and nobility of the human spirit—even when confronted with the most evil of evils.

Anne, her sister, Margot, and their parents, Mr. and Mrs. Otto Frank, moved from Germany to Holland when Anne was four years old. Her father was a successful businessman, and the Frank family made many friends in their new home. After the outbreak of war in Europe, it soon became apparent that Jews were to be treated differently from other citizens. In 1940, Anne was transferred from the school she attended in Amsterdam to a Jewish lyceum. That May, Germany invaded the Netherlands and crushed all outward Dutch resistance.

Day by day, life became more dangerous for the Jews in Holland. A special law required them to wear a yellow, six-pointed Star of David on their clothing, labeling them as a persecuted group. Mr. Frank began to formulate plans for the family to leave the country, but by the summer of 1942, the Gestapo—Hitler's police force—began raiding apartments looking for Jews to send to concentration camps. In July of that year, the Franks went into hiding with another family—Mr. and Mrs. Van Daan (their real family name was Van Pels, but Anne changed it in the diary) and their son, Peter—on the third floor of a secret apartment, where they spent the next two years in self-imposed exile.

These two years are detailed in Anne's diary, in which she recorded not only the daily happenings in her life but also her own philosophy as it evolved against a background of unspeakable horror. Anne reveals an astonishing awareness of human nature and of her own abilities in her entries. Despite the horror and fear that each day brought her, she was able to keep alive her spirit and determination. In her diary, she reveals her thoughts to an imaginary friend she called Kitty, a name she got from a Dutch novel for girls that was popular at the time.

The apartment hideout was discovered by the Germans on August 4, 1944. Both families were arrested and deported to concentration camps. Of them all, only Otto Frank survived. The Franks' two friends who served as links to the outside world during their two years of exile were also sent to concentration camps, but they survived. Anne and her sister died in March, 1945, at Bergen-Belsen camp, two months before the Allies liberated Holland and two months before her sixteenth birthday.

Although her papers spilled out onto the floor when the Nazis raided the apartment, Anne's writing survived because the soldiers considered it to be of no importance. Friends of the Franks found the diary papers and gave them to Otto Frank after he returned from the camps. The first edition of the diary was published in 1947, and there have been a number of editions afterward, including the most authoritative to date: *The Diary of a Young Girl: The Definitive Edition,* published in 1995.

CHARACTERS: The central character is, of course, **Anne Frank** herself. She is in many ways a typical teenager of the time—temperamental and moody, tactless and stubborn. She dotes on her father, is critical of her mother, and feels that her older sister does not have time for her. She is also intelligent (though her schoolwork is only average), honest, and courageous. Anne's first diary entries are filled with self-criticism and self-analysis. Because she is cut off from friends and all the normal activities of teenage life, her feelings are forced inward. Since she is emotionally and intellectually sensitive, Anne finds it difficult to adapt to living in such close quarters with others, especially in the first few months, and she longs for her own independence.

Although Anne is critical of those around her, she is smart enough to realize her own shortcomings as well. As the months of self-imposed exile drag on, she comes to a kind of maturity far beyond her years. She sees her parents in a new light, becoming less critical of her mother and more rational in her feelings toward her father. She even begins to look upon her older sister as a person who might have feelings as well.

By the end of the first year, Anne's great realization about herself is that she is extremely lonely. In order to assuage her loneliness, she develops an affection for Peter Van Daan, son of the family who shares the Franks' hiding place. Their relationship is more friendship than anything else, but it helps to fill a need within the maturing Anne. As her need for love is at least partially fulfilled, she begins to feel more compassion toward the others who share her cramped and fear-filled prison.

Perhaps the most extraordinary aspect of Anne's diary is her ability to look beyond her own horror at the actions of human beings under extreme duress. She is brave enough to question the motivations of people, and strong enough to endure as she gropes for answers. Each day of her life during those two years is filled with horror, fear, and humiliation, yet her spirit finds the strength to look ahead. Anne died of typhus in a concentration camp, unaware that the diary of her ordeal would become a famous work of literature.

Otto Frank is a cultured, well-to-do businessman of courage and foresight. He anticipated the Nazi persecution and planned in advance how to protect his family. Others look to him for comfort and direction. Otto rarely reveals his suffering or his true feelings, but he willingly becomes a peacemaker and confidante to those who need his help. He is somewhat overindulgent with Anne because he feels that she needs more attention, although at times it might have been better for him to let her handle situations on her own. He also sometimes dominates others too much. Otto Frank was the only member of the two families in exile to survive the war. In 1957, he was interviewed by producer George Stevens in preparation for turning Anne Frank's story into a motion picture. Stevens especially wanted to find out how the diary could have escaped destruction by the Nazis. Ironically, it seems that the Gestapo just thought that the papers in a cloth-covered book looked worthless.

Anne's mother is a cultured and refined woman who is accustomed to the good life. **Mrs. Frank** is aware that her younger daughter regards her as a rival for her husband's affection, but Anne often rebuffs her attempts to bring them closer together. As a result, Mrs. Frank turns to her older daughter for comfort and companionship. She is dependent upon her husband, who tries to shield her from unpleasantness. She endures the ordeal of self-imposed exile with calm silence. **Margot Frank** is a reserved young girl on the brink of womanhood. She is intelligent but less outspoken than Anne. She is aware of her younger sister's often hostile attitude toward her, but she deals with it by ignoring Anne rather than confronting her. Margot is much like her father in that she endures much and complains very little. She understands Anne better than her sister gives her credit for, since they share the same feelings of fear and loneliness, but Margot bears the ordeal in reserved and gracious silence. Near the end of their period of isolation, Margot tries to become closer to Anne, but she does not force the issue when the younger girl draws back.

The vain and petty **Mrs. Van Daan** is more capable of handling domestic chores in their cramped quarters than is Mrs. Frank. Not particularly intelligent, she can be warm and generous at times, although she often becomes hysterical in her fear about the war and their future. Mrs. Van Daan disagrees with the Franks' rather liberal attitude toward child rearing and tends to cause problems on that score. Although she is often the only one with whom Anne can discuss some topics openly, Mrs. Van Daan is somewhat jealous of the young girl because of her close relationship with her son. **Peter Van Daan** is a shy and withdrawn young man, but he is also gentle, intelligent, and courageous. Although well-mannered and friendly, he is limited in his ability to express affection, except to his cats. Peter resents being born a Jew and having to endure the threat of Nazi persecution. He keeps to himself as much as possible and is more dependent upon Anne in their relationship than she is on him. Peter's father, **Mr. Van Daan**, is a stern but loving parent. An opinionated man, he seems to thrive on bickering with his wife. He is reasonably competent and intelligent and willingly performs whatever chores are asked of him, although he complains openly when he is not feeling well.

Further Reading

Amdur, Richard. *Anne Frank.* New York: Chelsea House, 1993.

Authors and Artists for Young Adults. Vol. 12. Detroit: Gale Research, 1994.

Berger, Laura Standley, ed. *Twentieth-Century Young Adult Writers.* 1st ed. Detroit: St. James, 1994.

Gies, Miep, and Alison L. Gold. *Anne Frank Remembered.* New York: Simon, 1988.

Schnabel, Ernst. *Anne Frank: A Portrait in Courage.* New York: Harcourt, 1958.

Something about the Author. Vols. 42, 87. Detroit: Gale Research, 1986, 1996.

Steenmeijer, Anne G., and Otto Frank. *A Tribute to Anne Frank.* New York: Doubleday, 1971.

Tames, Richard. *Anne Frank.* New York: Watts, 1991.

Twentieth-Century Literary Criticism. Vol. 17. Detroit: Gale Research, 1985.

Verhaevan, Rian, and Ruud Van Des Rol. *Anne Frank: Beyond the Diary.* New York: Viking, 1993.

Wilson, Cara. *Love Otto: The Legacy of Anne Frank.* Kansas City: Andrews & McMeel, 1995.

Ernest J. Gaines

1933-, American novelist

The Autobiography of Miss Jane Pittman

(novel, 1971)

PLOT: The story of the invincible Jane Pittman, who lives to be 110, begins in the closing year of the Civil War, when she is about ten years old. At that time she is then a savagely abused slave known as Ticey. When some Yankee soldiers advance through her master's plantation, a young soldier from Ohio, Corporal Brown, spots the tattered waif and renames her Jane in honor of the girl he left behind. When the war ends and Ticey receives her freedom, she begins her new life with a new name, Jane Brown. She joins a group of recently freed slaves who are heading north. But the band is attacked by a murderous group of southern veterans, and many are killed. Jane finds herself alone with a two-year-old orphan named Ben. The two wander for days, relying on the kindness and handouts of strangers, some white, some black. Eventually, they are taken in by Mr. Bone, the owner of a large plantation, where Jane works in the fields while Ben attends school.

When the land is reclaimed by a southerner, Colonel Eugene Dye, he becomes Jane's new boss. Teenaged Ben's activities to secure greater rights for the downtrodden workers force him to flee the plantation or be killed by the Ku Klux Klan. Jane accepts a marriage proposal from the hard-working Joe Pittman, who loves her in spite of the fact that she can't have children because of injuries she suffered when she was a slave. In time, the two leave Dye's plantation and move to a ranch where Joe becomes famous for his ability to break wild horses.

Cicely Tyson portrays Jane Pittman in the 1974 adaptation of Gaines's novel about an extraordinary woman who lived from the Civil War to the Civil Rights Movement.

After ten years of happiness, Jane's recurring premonitions about Joe's violent death come true: he is killed by one of the wild stallions. In time, Jane moves again and becomes a laundress.

In 1898, Ben, now a discharged army officer and a veteran of the Spanish-American War, returns and builds a school to educate young black children. Because he teaches a doctrine of fairness and equality for all, the white locals conspire to silence him. Ben is murdered by a paid assassin, Albert Cluveau, and Jane, heartbroken and weary, moves to a plantation known as Samson. The Samson family consists of the patriarch, Paul, his son Robert, Robert's wife Miss Amma Dean, and their son, Tee Bob. Robert also has another son, Timmy, by a black mistress. In time, Timmy's presence becomes an embarrassment, and the boy is sent away. During her years at Samson, Jane witnesses the maturation of Tee Bob. While the boy is in college, he becomes infatuated with the plantation's new school teacher, Mary Agnes LeFabre, a gentle, attractive, light-skinned creole. When Mary Agnes rejects his love, Tee Bob commits suicide, and it is only through the efforts of Jules Raynard that Mary Agnes escapes being lynched and is sent back to her home in New Orleans.

Among Miss Jane's neighbors, many years later, is Jim, a young boy so Christ-like in action and demeanor that some people think he might be a new savior. However, when he grows up he rejects a life in the church to become a freedom fighter and follower of Dr. Martin Luther King, Jr. Jim organizes a demonstration in the nearby town of Bayonne to integrate the public water fountain and toilets. Jane fears for his life, and the night before the demonstration her anxieties are proven justified when Jim is murdered. In spite of Robert Samson's warnings that he will evict her, Jane Pittman, now 109 years old, joins a few stalwart friends, and together they go to Bayonne to continue the crusade of the martyred Jim.

CHARACTERS: This inspiring, heroic story is dominated by the narrator, **Miss Jane Pittman**, through whose eyes the reader witnesses the history of black oppression and servitude from the Civil War to the civil rights movement of the early 1960s. Jane Pittman is the embodiment of the spirit of survival. Continually persecuted and deprived of her basic rights, she nevertheless remains defiant, though never arrogant. Although her heart is broken many times, she is always able to pick up the pieces and try again.

Her story is a chronicle of loss. Two young men, both of whom she loves like they were her own sons, are killed because they believe in the equality and dignity of people, regardless of race. Also, her husband, the man who gives her love and security, dies an early and violent death. Jane accepts these tragedies stoically and without self-pity and moves on, hoping that some day the hate and prejudice will lessen. Her devotion to the people for whom she works and her years of grinding poverty, abuse, and arduous manual labor without reward except a bare subsistence are touchingly portrayed. In the end, even Jane—wise, understanding, and accepting—must take a stand and risk all for the cause Jim believed in. She emerges a woman of great dignity, strength, and endurance. The injustices and unpunished crimes of which she is a victim, and the strength and fortitude with which she faces her problems, produce a sense of admiration and respect for her indomitable spirit.

Ben, who later in life adopts the name **Ben Frederick Douglass** in honor of his hero, is the young man Jane raised after his mother was killed in a raid by patrollers in the aftermath of the Civil War. A bright young man and a distinguished veteran of the Spanish-American War, he devotes his life to educating his people and giving them a sense of self-worth so that they can take an equal place in society. Knowing that these actions can endanger his life, this gentle, gallant man nevertheless persists in his crusade until he is killed by a paid assassin.

Ben's killer, **Albert Cluveau**, is a strange, half-demented man totally devoid of conscience or sense of guilt. He matter-of-factly tells Jane, who is his friend and fishing partner, of the people he has killed. When word is spread that a contract is out on Ben's life, Jane can't believe that Albert would betray her and kill Ben. When he does, Jane confronts him, not for revenge, but to warn him that God's wrath will destroy him, a prophesy that eventually comes true.

Jane's common-law husband, **Joe Pittman**, is a symbol of strength and honesty. His love for Jane is touching and enduring. Joe is Colonel Dye's most valuable worker, and to prevent him from leaving his employ, Dye fraudulently demands that Joe repay huge trumped-up debts. Joe complies, although raising the money places him in virtual bondage for a year. He is a tireless worker, a master of his trade, and a good provider for Jane. His conscientiousness, pride, and insistence on meeting work obligations often place his life at risk and ultimately cause his death.

Another person of great importance to Jane is the young, idealistic **Jim**. Raised by Jane and a group of her friends in the Samsom compound, Jim, like Ben before him, heeds a call to help his people. Courageously and unselfishly, he joins the fight for civil rights led by Dr. King, and like his mentor he becomes a martyr for the cause.

The plantation on which Jane meets Joe is owned first by **Mr. Bone** and later by **Colonel Eugene Dye**. Bone took over the abandoned plantation and, in his austere, business-like manner, exploits his workers to make a profit. His successor, Dye, is more diabolical and devious in his methods. Allied to the repressive white supremacists, he rules with an iron fist, using every method, legal and otherwise, to retain his power and his workers. A mean-minded, cunning man, he tries to thwart Joe's plans to leave the plantation with Jane. When foiled, he disowns them both in a vindictive fit of rage.

Robert Samson, Jane's last "master," represents the typical twentieth-century racist. More refined, less outwardly cruel, and more secretive, he nevertheless stands for white supremacy and will fight viciously to maintain his power, position, and wealth. He refuses to accept his half-black son, Timmy, and eventually banishes him. When confronted with Jim's freedom demonstration, he heartlessly tries to squelch participation by any of his people by firing and evicting suspected supporters. Even Jane, his loyal servant for years, is not spared.

Samson's wife, **Miss Amma Dean**, like a faded, old-fashioned southern belle of the past, remains silent even though she is aware of her husband's hypocrisy and philandering. She lives for her beloved son, **Tee Bob**, and when he kills himself she becomes even more pathetic and reclusive. As a youngster, Tee Bob was spoiled. An only child, he was pampered by both his mother and father and given all the attention and love typically lavished on a young southern gentleman. With **Miss Mary Agnes LeFabre**, the beautiful, dignified new school teacher on the plantation, he begins a gentle courtship that appears to go unnoticed except by Miss Amma. Mary Agnes is unaware of the boy's growing ardor and maintains her polite, somewhat aloof demeanor when they are together. This only increases Tee Bob's obsession, and he keeps pursuing her, even though he knows Mary Agnes is part black. When his proposal of marriage is graciously but firmly refused, Tee Bob is unprepared to accept rejection and commits suicide. Mary Agnes, who has consistently acted maturely and realistically in her friendship with Tee Bob, now faces the wrath of whites who, in their search for a scapegoat, accuse her of entrapment. She is saved by the intervention of **Jules Raynard**, a wise, white-haired man who has befriended Jane and shared many conversations with her through the years. With his firm, commonsense manner, he makes the Samsons realize that it is society and its taboos that have really caused Tee Bob's death.

The most significant of the minor characters is **Corporal Brown**, the young northern soldier who took pity on a pathetic young slave he met one day on a southern plantation. Naming her Jane, he encouraged her to find her path to freedom and so set off her colorful and heroic odyssey.

Further Reading

African-American Writers. New York: Scribner's, 1991.

Berger, Laura Standley, ed. *Twentieth-Century Young Adult Writers.* 1st ed. Detroit: St. James, 1994.

Bruccoli, Matthew J., and Richard Layman, eds. *Broadening Views, 1968-1988.* Vol. 6 of *Concise Dictionary of American Literary Biography.* Detroit: Gale Research, 1988.

Bryant, Jerry H. "From Death to Life: The Fiction of Ernest J. Gaines." *Iowa Review* 3 (winter 1972).

Callahan, John F. "A Movable Form." In *The African-American Grain: The Pursuit of Voice in Twentieth-Century Black Fiction.* Urbana, IL: University of Illinois Press, 1988.

Draper, James P., ed. *Black Literature Criticism.* Vol. 2. Detroit: Gale Research, 1992.

Davis, Thadius M., and Trudier Harris, eds. *Afro-American Fiction Writers after 1955.* Vol. 33 of *Dictionary of Literary Biography.* Detroit: Gale Research, 1984.

Gaines, Ernest J. "Interview." *MELUS* 11 (summer 1984).

Henderson, Leslie, ed. *Contemporary Novelists.* 5th ed. Detroit: St. James, 1991.

Hicks, Jack. "To Make These Bones Live: History and Community in Ernest Gaines's Fiction." *Black American Literature Forum* (spring 1977).

Magill, Frank N. *Critical Survey of Long Fiction: English-Language Series: Authors.* Vol. 3. Englewood Cliffs, NJ: Prentice-Hall, 1983.

Powell, Charles H. "The Quarters: Ernest J. Gaines and the Sense of Place." *Southern Review* (summer 1985).

Ryan, Bryan. *Major Twentieth-Century Writers: A Selection of Sketches from Contemporary Authors.* Detroit: Gale Research, 1991.

Shelton, Frank W. *Fifty Southern Writers after 1900.* Westport, CT: Greenwood, 1987.

Smith, Valerie, ed. *African-American Writers.* New York: Collier, 1993.

Nancy Garden

1938-, American novelist

Annie on My Mind

(young adult novel, 1982)

PLOT: When the story opens, Liza Winthrop, a freshman at the Massachusetts Institute of Technology, is writing a letter she may never send to Annie Kenyon back at school in Berkeley, California.

Liza thinks back to their meeting about a year ago in the Metropolitan Museum of Art in New York City. Their attraction to each other then was instantaneous and, to Liza, more than a little confusing. In a flashback, the friendship and attraction grows little by little between the two girls, even though their backgrounds are so different. Liza lives in Brooklyn Heights with her parents and brother, Chad, attends the private school Foster Academy, and will enter M.I.T. when she graduates. Annie is from a poorer background and attends a public school with security guards. She has a beautiful singing voice and plans to study in California.

After Liza and Annie engage in a more than friendly kiss one day, they realize that their feelings for each other are not what are considered to be the norm. Confused and unsure about "being gay," they restrain their actions until one day when they are alone in the home of two teachers from the Foster Academy, Ms. Widmer and Ms. Stevenson. Liza has offered to feed their cats while they are on spring vacation. During one of the feeding visits when Annie accompanies Liza to the teachers' home, the girls discover that the older women are also gay. Freed from restraint and alone in the house, the girls make love in the upstairs bedroom. However, they are "discovered" by one of Liza's classmates and a teacher who were worried when Liza did not show up for a school meeting she had forgotten about.

Liza is forced to tell her parents about how she and Annie were caught, but denies she is a lesbian to protect their feelings. Annie does not tell her parents because, as she says, they would not understand. Ms. Widmer and Ms. Stevenson are fired from the Academy, which causes Liza to feel guilty. But Ms. Widmer tells her not to punish herself "for people's ignorant reactions to what we all are." Ms. Stevenson adds, "Don't let ignorance win. Let love."

The girls part company when Annie goes to California and Liza moves to Boston. Annie sends letters to Liza, but they go unanswered as confusion and guilt cloud Liza's mind and heart. However, as Christmas vacation nears and Liza tries once again to write to Annie, her mind suddenly is made up. She phones Annie at school, and Annie promises to fly to Boston for a few days before they both return to New York. Liza tells Annie that Ms. Widmer was right. The truth has made her free to love Annie.

CHARACTERS: Liza Winthrop has wanted to be an architect for as long as she can remember. She spends a lot of time alone in museums, so she is somewhat surprised at herself when she not only meets and talks to Annie Kenyon but enjoys walking through the museum with her. Liza realizes that her growing feelings for Annie are somewhat different than anything she has yet experienced, but she can't put into words what she is feeling. When they kiss, Liza's confusion grows along with her attraction to Annie. Frightened by what she is feeling, Liza pulls back from a physical relationship until the opportunity presents itself in the home of the teachers. Suddenly, Liza feels liberated and happy, and she admits to herself that her love for Annie is real.

However, when Liza is confronted with the reality of what the world thinks about a lesbian relationship, and it results in the dismissal of the two teachers from Foster Academy, she is overcome by guilt and confusion. It takes time and soul-searching for Liza to understand herself and to come to terms with the fact that she loves another woman.

Although neither of the girls has experienced a full-blown lesbian affair, **Annie Kenyon** is the more knowledgeable of the two in that she has long suspected that she is gay. However, she is careful not to force her own feelings on Liza, often drawing back lest she harm someone she loves. In terms of the physical act of lovemaking, Annie is every bit as hesitant as Liza, but once she commits herself she is more sure of her actions and her role. When the two split up after the teachers are dismissed and the girls go off to school, it is Annie who writes letters to Liza. When Liza finally decides how she feels about their affair and about herself, Annie responds with joy and love.

Ms. Stevenson is one of the teachers dismissed from the Foster Academy after the truth of her relationship with Ms. Widmer is uncovered. In a meeting with Liza and Annie before the two women leave the school for retirement, she tries to ease the girls' sense of guilt. **Ms. Widmer** advises the girls that truth is what will make them free.

Liza's parents, **Mr.** and **Mrs. Winthrop**, try to be supportive when they are confronted with their daughter's relationship. However, even though they stand up for her when she is threatened with expulsion from school, Liza knows that to tell them about her feelings for Annie would only hurt and confuse them. So, in the end, Liza denies she is a lesbian, allowing her mother especially to dismiss the incident as foolishness between adolescent girls.

Liza and her younger brother, **Chad**, have always had a close and easy relationship. He is confused, hurt, and bewildered at first when the truth about Liza and Annie is uncovered. Liza fears that their relationship has been forever jeopardized. But when she returns to school after the incident she tells Chad that it's okay if he doesn't want to walk in with her. But Chad refuses, and, although still confused about his sister's relationship, he says, "Yell if you need me. I've got a left jab that packs quite a wallop." Liza rewards him with a hug.

Further Reading

Authors and Artists for Young Adults. Vol. 18. Detroit: Gale Research, 1996.

Berger, Laura Standley, ed. *Twentieth-Century Young Adult Writers.* 1st ed. Chicago: St. James, 1994.

Holtze, Sally Holmes, ed. *Fifth Book of Junior Authors and Illustrators.* New York: H. W. Wilson, 1983.

Something about the Author. Vols. 12, 77. Detroit: Gale Research, 1977, 1994.

Something about the Author Autobiography Series. Vol. 8. Detroit: Gale Research, 1989.

Jean Craighead George

1919-, American young adult novelist

Julie of the Wolves

(young adult novel, 1972)

PLOT: This classic nature and survival story won the 1973 Newbery Award for best children's book. George collected a vast amount of data on wolf lore when she was sent to Alaska for a research article on arctic wolves, and from that came the idea for this young adult novel. *Julie of the Wolves* is also a story of the clash between two cultures—the primitive life of the Eskimo and the modern Western world. The novel is a three-part story that describes the life and amazing journey of Julie, or Miyax, as she is called in her native Eskimo language. Parts one and three tell of her solo trek across the frozen tundra of Alaska. The middle part details her early years, beginning with her birth on Nunivak Island in the Eskimo settlement of Mekoryak.

After her mother's death, Julie and her father, Kapugen, head north to an isolated seal camp, where he wants her to forget white civilization and learn the ways of his people. Kapugen teaches his daughter to love all nature, including wolves, who, he says, will love her if she talks to them. At age nine, Julie's Aunt Martha insists that the girl return to Mekoryak for schooling. Kapugen, saddened over his daughter's departure, goes on a seal hunt and does not return. Meanwhile, Julie becomes pen pals with Amy Pollack, who lives in San Francisco, and invites her new friend for a visit.

At age thirteen, Julie returns to Barrow because she has been pledged to marry David, the son of Naka, her father's hunting partner. Married in name only and forced to work like a slave, Julie escapes and begins a three-hundred-mile trek to the coast. From there she plans to work her way down to San Francisco and to Amy. Instead, she becomes lost on the tundra. When she meets a wolf pack, she remembers what her father taught her. She lives with the wolves through the arctic summer and grows to love them. One day, human hunters kill and wound some of the wolves, and Julie decides not to return to civilization after all. Instead, she builds a snow house and lives alone until a passing Eskimo family brings news of her father, who is alive and living in the village of Kangik. Julie and Kapugen are reunited, but she is dismayed to see that her father, although overjoyed to see her, has become civilized by white culture and has married a white woman. Dejected and unhappy, Julie returns to her ice home. Over time, however, she realizes that the days of the old culture are changing. "The hour of the wolf" has passed, and she must go home.

See below for character descriptions.

***Miyax tries to help her friend, Kapu, after the wolf is shot in a scene from George's* Julie of the Wolves.**

Julie

(young adult novel, 1994)

PLOT: This successful, acclaimed sequel to *Julie and the Wolves,* written more than twenty years after Julie's first adventures were published, captures the same spirit of wilderness and adventure. It presents a vivid, challenging picture of the problems of co-existing cultures and traditions. After a time of living alone in the Alaskan wilderness and returning to the culture of her native Eskimo people, Julie goes to the village of Kangik to live with her father, whom she had long thought to be dead. But Kapugen is no longer the man of the north she remembered. Now used to a telephone and radio, things Julie feels would be scorned by a true Eskimo, Kapugen is married to Ellen, a white woman from Minnesota. They soon have a son, named Amaroq, which means wolf leader. Julie is dismayed to learn that her father was the hunter who shot her wolf-father when she was alone in the wilderness. He explains that he had to do so because the wolf pack was killing the musk oxen herd that his villagers tend and depend on for a living. Worse still, Julie knows that more wolves might be killed. They usually feed on caribou, but no caribou have come near the village this year. The wolves, led by Kapu, are on the outskirts of the village because they know Julie is there. If they are hungry, they will kill the oxen, and then they will be shot. This is the new law that her father lives by, which he calls the Minnesota law of his wife's people. Although Julie loves Ellen, she knows that Ellen's culture does not understand what the Eskimo know: people and animals coexist for the welfare of both.

Meanwhile, Julie has met and fallen in love with a Siberian Eskimo named Peter Sugluk. He's going to the University of Alaska in Fairbanks and wants Julie to marry him and go to school also. The idea is tempting because she has decided to become a teacher, but she feels that her place is in the village, where she can protect the wolves. When the wolves threaten the herd and her father prepares to kill them, Julie tells her stepmother a story. It is her own story of becoming lost in the wilderness and being saved by a pack of wolves. Ellen concedes that the Minnesota law perhaps does not work in this place. Julie goes out to follow her father as he hunts, only to discover that the musk oxen herd has broken free. For reasons unknown, the wolves do not attack. Julie realizes that her father has set the herd free. The Eskimo will once again have a wild herd, he says, as they did long ago. Julie thinks that perhaps now she can go off to school, at least when the caribou return. Soon she hears Kapu, the wolf leader, howl in the night. Kapugen tells her, "They are saying that the caribou are coming." And indeed they are. The village and wolves are saved. Julie will go to school, and, as she says, "I will marry Peter when I am all grown up."

CHARACTERS: The title character in both books, **Julie**, or **Miyax**, is a young girl of amazing courage and resiliency who survives under conditions of great adversity. Most interesting is her slow resolution of the conflict she feels between modern civilization and the primitive life of her people. When she first begins to correspond with her friend in San Francisco, Julie grows envious of Amy Pollack's seemingly prosperous and easy life, which Julie wishes to join. But her meeting with the wolf pack entirely changes her values. She is adopted as a member of the pack and grows to love these courageous animals, giving them names to recognize their individual personalities. When the hunters kill the leader, whom Julie has named Amaroq—Eskimo for wolf leader—the white culture becomes for her a hated civilization that only destroys. She turns her back on that culture and vows to live alone by following the ways of her ancestors. Although she is overjoyed when she learns that her father is alive, Julie is deeply dismayed to see that he, too, has abandoned the ways of their people and has even married a white woman. Her pain drives her back to the tundra and isolation. It is a sign of true maturity, however, that Julie is eventually able to face reality. Though she still regards modern civilization with distrust, she comes to realize that she must make compromises as times change. Reluctantly, she leaves her secluded home to find a new life once again with her father.

In the sequel, Julie is much the same girl of strength and courage as she was in *Julie of the Wolves*. She is more mature and understanding of the ways of others, but no less determined to save her beloved wolves. Here she experiences her first awakening to love, although she recognizes that with all the schooling she has ahead of her it will be a long time before she and Peter will marry.

Kapugen is a kindly man and loving father, who, in the beginning, believes that it is best for Julie to be raised in the traditional way of her people. He loves nature and teaches his daughter to respect wild animals, especially the wolves of the north, whose intelligence and courage he much admires. Kapugen is despondent when his daughter leaves for school. He arranges a marriage for Julie at age thirteen because that is part of the Eskimo culture, but he is not aware of the cruelty of his partner Naka or the incompetence of Naka's son, David. In time even Kapugen, the hunter and lover of wild nature, accepts the inevitability of change and rejoins white society. Throughout most of this sequel, Kapugen is much changed from the man of the tundra that Julie once knew. He has adopted much of the white culture, from radios to telephones, and, of course, he has married Ellen, a white woman. But in the end, even though it seems that Kapugen has forgotten the laws of the wild, he reaches back to life according to the teachings of his Eskimo heritage, thereby saving Julie's beloved wolves.

Naka, a hunter and Kapugen's partner in *Julie of the Wolves*, is a cruel man, especially when he is drunk, which he frequently is. Julie's life in Barrow grows increasingly desperate, and the physical abuse Naka inflicts upon his wife gives Julie intimations of worse things to come. Naka forces her to work under conditions that come closer and closer to slavery as she spends day after day sewing parkas and other items for tourists. Julie is forced to marry Naka's son, **David**, who, it turns out, is mentally retarded. Their marriage is a union in name only, until the day that David attacks her sexually. This act gives Julie the impetus she needs to escape from her intolerable drudgery and to head for what she envisions will be a life of prosperity and joy in San Francisco.

The wolves Julie meets on her journey in the first book come alive as real characters in this novel. They are named by Julie and play an important part in the story of her survival and growth. The author explores relationships in the wolf family, which have many parallels to human society. Each animal has a distinctive personality. **Amaroq**, the wise leader, becomes Julie's wolf-father and is later killed by the hunters. **Jello**, the pack outcast, tries to harm Julie to the extent of destroying her camp and is killed by Amaroq. Julie names the liveliest of the pups **Kapu,** after her father. He is wounded by the hunters, but Julie nurses him back to health. He becomes the new leader of the pack after Amaroq's death.

The new person in Julie's life in *Julie* is **Peter Sugluk**, a modern Eskimo whose foster parents are among Kangik's villagers. When he explains that men in Siberia know immediately when they are in love, Julie is flattered but wary because of her disastrous first marriage to David. Although Peter is clearly part of the modern world and plans to attend the university in Fairbanks, he has a great understanding and respect for the ways of the culture to which he belongs. Understanding Julie's reluctance to leave her beloved wolf pack in danger, he promises to return for her when the time is right.

Julie's stepmother, **Ellen**, who appears in the sequel, comes from an entirely different culture than that of her husband. She has great difficulty breaking through to Julie, who at first pretends she doesn't understand English so that Ellen can't talk to her. But Ellen truly loves her husband and new stepdaughter, and she tries hard to understand their ways. However, it is not until Julie tells her story that the two cultures become truly joined in her heart and mind.

Further Reading

Berger, Laura Standley, ed. *Twentieth-Century Young Adult Writers.* 1st ed. Detroit: St. James, 1994.

Children's Literature Review. Vol. 1. Detroit: Gale Research, 1976.

Collier, Laurie, and Joyce Nakamura, eds. *Major Authors and Illustrators for Children & Young Adults.* Detroit: Gale Research, 1993.

Contemporary Literary Criticism. Vol. 35. Detroit: Gale, 1985.

Estes, Glenn E., ed. *American Writers for Children since 1960: Fiction.* Vol. 52 of *Dictionary of Literary Biography.* Detroit: Gale Research, 1986.

Gallo, Donald R. *Speaking for Ourselves: Autobiographical Sketches by Notable Authors of Books for Young Adults.* Urbana, IL: National Council of Teachers of English, 1990.

Melvin, Helen. "Jean Craighead George." *Horn Book* 49 (August 1973).

Something about the Author. Vol. 68. Detroit: Gale Research, 1992.

William Golding

1911-1993, English novelist and academic

Lord of the Flies

(novel, 1954)

PLOT: This story tells how a group of civilized English schoolboys revert to savagery when they are marooned on a lush tropical island after the plane that was carrying them away from an atomic war crashes, killing all the adults on board. The first characters introduced are Ralph, a friendly, decent boy, and Piggy, a near-sighted, overweight youngster. By blowing on a conch, Ralph convenes the remaining group of survivors, a large group of boys who range in ages from about six to twelve. Among them are Jack, who is the leader of the black-robed choirboys, including Roger, a cruel, sullen boy, Simon, a dreamy, other-worldly loner, and the identical twins, Sam and Eric. At first, under the elected leadership of Ralph, plans are made to organize the group into various work parties and to light a signal fire on the island's only mountain, using Piggy's glasses and the sun's hot rays. Jack's choirboys become the designated hunters of the wild pigs on the island.

Gradually, in spite of the efforts of Ralph and Piggy, the sense of order and responsibility break down. Fear grips the boys, particularly the younger ones, and there is talk of a beast that roams the island at night. As their savagery increases, Jack usurps Ralph's leadership role and, capitalizing on

Hugh Edwards and Tom Chapin portray Piggy and Ralph in a 1963 adaptation of **Lord of the Flies.**

the boys' fears and baser instincts, sets up a rival group at Castle Rock led by himself and his obedient hunters. Only a few remain faithful to Ralph. One night during an electric storm, Jack's group engages in an orgiastic dance around the head of a pig they have killed, the lord of the flies, and, mistaking shadows in the bushes for their imagined beast, they attack it with sharpened spears, accidentally murdering the gentle Simon. In a raid on Ralph's encampment, Jack and his henchmen steal Piggy's glasses to make their own fire. Ralph's group, which now includes only Piggy, the twins, and a few of the youngest children, confronts Jack at Castle Rock and asks for the glasses and a reconciliation. Jack orders that the twins be taken prisoner, and he and Ralph fight. Roger dislodges a huge rock that kills Piggy and throws his body into the sea. Only Ralph escapes into the jungle, where he is pursued by Jack and his chanting, blood-thirsty gang. As they close in for the kill, a British ship arrives, attracted by the smoke of a forest fire accidently started during the chase. Seeing the gang of near-naked youngsters smeared with war paint, wearing feathers, and carrying spears, a British officer says he is disappointed that a group of British boys couldn't have "put up a better show." In an afterward to the novel, the author says that the novel is "an attempt to trace the defects of society back to the defects of human nature" and that the "shape of a society must depend on the ethical nature of the individual."

CHARACTERS: Though it was initially rejected by twenty-one publishers and received mixed reviews in the United States and the author's native England, *Lord of the Flies* has gained a wide readership, especially among college students. It has sold over seven million copies and is still in print today. The novel's protagonist is **Ralph**, a golden-haired, athletic, well-adjusted boy of slightly more than twelve years of age. He is a born leader and one who instantly instills confidence in others. Fair-minded and decent, he represents the democratic, optimistic side of human nature. Being "all-boy," he revels in the spirit of fun and adventure that being marooned on a desert island promises, but he also realizes that responsibilities must be shouldered and that their first priorities should be facilitating a rescue and taking care of the younger, weaker members of the group. He is sensitive to others' feelings. For example, he apologizes to Piggy for revealing to the others his hated nickname, and, in a spirit of fairness, appoints Jack leader of the hunters to compensate for Jack's loss of the election to become group leader. When the boys succumb to laziness, suspicion, and savagery, Ralph continues to fight for the principles of equality, cooperation, and shared accountability, in spite of his disillusionment and growing apprehension. Though outnumbered, he confronts Jack to secure Piggy's glasses and, in spite of ostracism and rejection, he thinks of the common good and almost single-handedly keeps the rescue fire going. Ralph possesses common sense, clearsightedness, and an intelligence that is lacking in most of the other boys. He is loyal to his friends, including the often obnoxious Piggy. However, he is not without flaws. Ralph sometimes commits foolish acts and even becomes a part of the frenzy that leads to Simon's death. As his problems increase and he becomes a hunted animal, his belief in mankind's innate decency dissolves, and he realizes that evil and cruelty are natural components of life. Through his traumatic experiences, he has gained a kind of fearful maturity.

The leader of the choirboys is **Jack Merridew**, who is described as tall, thin, and bony. Red-haired and almost ugly in appearance, he is introduced as a bullying, ill-tempered, power-hungry youngster. If Ralph symbolizes the spirit of democracy in human nature, Jack represents dictatorship and the abuse of power. He is the first to shed all aspects of civilized behavior, and, as leader of the hunters, he runs naked through the wood, paints his body with dabs of clay and charcoal, and emits blood-curdling screams as he reverts to the life of the unrestrained savage. He becomes obsessed with killing, blood, power, and destruction. Jack is bossy, cruel, and domineering, and he intimidates others with his abusive remarks and appeals to both their baser cravings and their hitherto suppressed savage qualities. Like all dictators, he also capitalizes on fears and apprehensions, obeying rules only at his own convenience. He worships power and strength, and is scornful of the needs of the younger, more vulnerable boys. Jack loathes Piggy for his weakness and his common sense and, though he at first admires Ralph, he turns on him viciously when Ralph becomes a threat to his growing power. Jack is impetuous, careless, insecure, and insanely jealous of Ralph's authority. Though sometimes displaying bravery and resourcefulness, his cruelty and vicious behavior far outweigh these virtues. Jack represents the triumph of disorder and violence over intellect and reason.

Piggy is an object of pity and derision. He is fat, unathletic, asthmatic, and shortsighted. Also, judging by his grammar and vocabulary, he comes from a social class lower than the rest of the boys. Since his mother's death, he has been raised by an overly protective aunt who has turned him into a whining, dependent sissy. He dislikes the island and, unlike the others, feels no sense of adventure or challenge in his situation. He arouses contempt in the other boys because of his physical weakness, unattractive appearance, and his constant complaining. Piggy is a coward who relies on Ralph to fight his battles and as a result is taunted, beaten, robbed of his glasses, and eventually killed by Roger at Jack's instigation. Piggy, however, has an overriding positive characteristic—he is wise beyond his years. A realist who understands the evil in human nature, he believes in science and therefore rejects the superstitious idea that a beast lives on the island. His useful suggestions concerning building the fire, constructing shelters, and organizing the group often fall on deaf ears, though they represent a rational, practical course of action. His "intellectual daring" leads to Jack's enmity and scorn of him, but Ralph realizes the boy's potential, saying that Piggy "talks sense." Being a budding intellectual, Piggy is considered an outsider and is eventually marked for extinction in Jack's primitive society.

Among Jack's choirboys is a quiet aesthete named **Simon**. A "skinny vivid little boy," he is given to dream-like trances and solitary walks in the jungle, where he feels at one with the wildness of nature. Even Ralph confesses about Simon, "He's queer. He's funny." A dreamer and visionary, Simon is almost saint-like in his unselfishness and his desire to help others and share with them his food and possessions. Unable to communicate with the other boys, he is at home in the spiritual world. After talk of a wild beast living on the island, Simon realizes through his meditations that people create these beasts from within themselves and that they exist in all of us. His gentleness and isolation leave him vulnerable to the violent impulses in the boys' society so that, like a sacrificial lamb, Simon is murdered.

If Jack represents lust for power, **Roger**, Jack's henchman and enforcer, epitomizes senseless destruction and cruelty. He delights in terrorizing and torturing those who are weak and defenseless. Described as a slight, furtive boy whom no one really knows, he keeps to himself "with an inner intensity of avoidance and secrecy." He delights in death and inflicting pain and is without fear or conscience. In the boys' tiny world, he becomes the epitome of evil. Roger enjoys tormenting the little ones and torturing the twins after they have been captured by Jack. It is Roger who dislodges the rock that kills Piggy.

The identical twins **Sam** and **Eric** are so inseparable and completely alike that they become known collectively as **Samneric.** Their thought patterns are so uncannily similar that they often complete each other's sentences. Good-natured, helpful, and cooperative, they represent the best characteristics of the younger members of the group. They remain loyal to Ralph but, in time, are captured by Jack and Roger, who make them serve as hunters and betray the ideals Ralph represents.

Further Reading

Authors and Artists for Young Adults. Vol. 5. Detroit: Gale Research, 1991.

Babb, Howard. *The Novels of William Golding.* Columbus, OH: Ohio State University Press, 1970.

Baker, James R. *Critical Essays on William Golding.* Boston: G. K. Hall, 1988.

Berger, Laura Standley, ed. *Twentieth Century Young Adult Writers.* 1st ed. Detroit: St. James, 1995.

Beum, Robert, ed. *Modern British Essayists, Second Series.* Vol. 100 of *Dictionary of Literary Biography.* Detroit: Gale Research, 1990.

Biles, Jack I., and Robert O. Evans, eds. *William Golding: Some Critical Considerations.* Lexington: University Press of Kentucky, 1979.

Carey, John, ed. *William Golding: The Man and His Books.* New York: Farrar, Straus, & Giroux, 1986.

Contemporary Authors New Revision Series. Vol. 33. Detroit: Gale Research, 1991.

Contemporary Literary Criticism. Vols. 1, 2, 3, 8, 10, 17, 27, 58, 81. Detroit: Gale Research, 1973, 1974, 1975, 1978, 1979, 1981, 1984, 1990, 1994.

Critical Survey of Long Fiction. Vol. 3. Englewood Cliffs, NJ: Salem, 1983.

Dick, Bernard F. *William Golding.* New York: Twayne, 1987.

Friedman, Lawrence S. *William Golding.* New York: Continuum, 1993.

Gindin, James Jack. *William Golding.* New York: St. Martin's, 1988.

Hodson, Leighton. *William Golding.* New York: Capricorn, 1969.

Hynes, Samuel L. *William Golding.* New York: Columbia University Press, 1964.

Johnston, Arnold. *Of Earth and Darkness: The Novels of William Golding.* Columbia: University of Missouri Press, 1980.

Kinkead-Weekes, Mark. *William Golding: A Critical Study.* Boston: Faber, 1984.

Nelson, F.William. *William Golding's Lord of the Flies: A Source Book.* New York: Odyssey, 1963.

Oldsey, Bernard S. *The Art of William Golding.* New York: Harcourt, 1965.

———, ed. *British Novelists, 1930-1959.* Vol. 15 of *Dictionary of Literary Biography.* Detroit: Gale Research, 1983.

Reilly, Patrick. *Lord of the Flies: Fathers and Sons.* New York: Twayne, 1992.

Twentieth-Century American Literature. Vol. 3 of *Chelsea House Library of Literary Criticism.* New York: Chelsea House, 1986.

Whitley, John S. *Golding: Lord of the Flies.* London: Arnold, 1970.

Joanne Greenberg

1932-, American novelist

I Never Promised You a Rose Garden

(novel, 1964; originally published under the pen name Hannah Green)

PLOT: Deborah can't bear to live in the real world, which she considers too brutal and uncaring, so she escapes into a fantasy place of her own making. A place of lush green fields and bright golden gods and goddesses, this special world for Deborah is called the Kingdom of Yr. When she is there, especially when she has reached a kind of neutral place known as the Fourth Level, which is attained only by accident, she is able to forget about the real world around her.

With great reluctance, sadness, guilt, and a little shame, Deborah's parents have brought her to a mental hospital. It is here that Deborah must begin her slow and painful road back to mental health. Her sympathetic but honest psychiatrist, Dr. Fried, doesn't promise her a rose garden, but she does help Deborah leave the world she has invented and reenter the often harsh and uncaring world she so fears.

Deborah spends four years at the hospital, traveling between the Kingdom of Yr and the real world. At first afraid and resistant to therapy, she sometimes mutilates herself. But, little by little, she learns to trust herself. Faced with the daunting prospect of trying to make up for the four years of high school she lost, Deborah begins to travel between the hospital and tutorial school. Her pride and self-confidence grow as she stubbornly fights to take back her life.

CHARACTERS: The author based this novel on her personal experiences with schizophrenia, originally publishing the work under a pseudonym to protect her family. Later, as her family came to understand more about her past, Greenberg allowed the story to be reprinted under her real name. The author's firsthand knowledge of mental illness makes her portrayal of **Deborah Blau** especially poignant. Deborah is a sixteen-year-old schizophrenic who is admitted to a mental institution by her parents on the advice of doctors. Although she is intelligent and can carry a conversation, sometimes her reasoning becomes illogical and she laughs at inappropriate times. Deborah's problems began when she was five. After the traumatic experience of having a tumor in her urethra removed, the skies seemed to darken for her, a darkness that Deborah felt certain would last for the rest of her life. The next great change in her life occurred at age nine when she was at a camp and two girls refused to walk with her because she was Jewish. Whenever life became too cruel for Deborah to bear, she would begin to retreat into her own special Kingdom of Yr. At the age of sixteen she attempted suicide, which is what led her parents to take her to the institution.

Dr. Fried decides to take Deborah's case in the beginning based mainly on the girl's young age. Sixteen is younger than any patient the doctor has had before. The doctor, who has painful memories of Nazi Germany and can therefore understand Deborah's fears about the cruel realities of life, is herself somewhat of a stranger in this institution. One of Dr. Fried's first tasks is to interview Deborah's mother, **Esther Blau**, to find out whether the woman will be a hindrance or a help in her daughter's treatment. Immediately, the doctor senses the tug of wills between mother and daughter that has existed over the years.

Esther feels that she knows her daughter far better than her husband does, although she does not want to hurt him by saying so. Unlike her husband, she knows that Deborah's wrist-cutting attempt at suicide is not the real reason for placing their daughter in the mental hospital. Esther knows that the suicide was only a manifestation of a deep and penetrating sickness in her daughter. It is Esther who constructs the story of what they "tell the family." Their younger daughter, Suzy, will be fed a story about anemia and Deborah's need for a special rest place; the grandparents will be told much the same thing.

Esther relates the family history to Dr. Fried, telling her how both sides of Deborah's family are immigrants and how, according to her side of the family, Esther had married beneath her social status. When Deborah was born, a fair-skinned, lovely blonde baby, their pride was tremendous. But when, at the age of five, the child had developed a tumor that caused incontinence, their perfect daughter became flawed. And even when the tumor was long cured, Esther admitted that there were certain indications that Deborah was a "disturbed" child. Through the years, Esther tried to look the other way when manifestations of Deborah's strange behavior began to show themselves. But when her daughter slit her wrists in a clumsy attempt at suicide, Esther could look away no longer. Dr. Fried recognizes that Esther's love for her daughter is genuine and so is her pain. She tells the woman not to blame herself or her husband, or even Deborah. "She needs your support, not your self-recrimination," says Dr. Fried.

When Deborah's mother speaks of her daughter's experience at the age of nine, almost willing pain upon herself, the doctor tells her of a man she once treated in Germany. He inflicted the most horrible tortures upon himself. When she asked him why, he explained that the world inflicts horrible tortures upon people, but if he does them to himself, at least he is the master of his own destruction. Dr. Fried warns, "You can never make the world over to protect the ones you love so much. But you do not have to defend your having tried."

Deborah's father is **Jacob Blau**, an accountant whose family emigrated from Poland. Not a man capable of opening his heart, he loves his daughters but can't tell them so. He and his wife are very concerned about how to tell their younger daughter, **Suzy**, about Deborah's illness. Finally, on Esther's insistence, they confront the twelve year old with the truth. Showing little emotion at the news beyond saying "It all fits now. It makes sense," Suzy goes back to her piano lessons. But she soon returns to ask, "It's not like she's Napoleon or something . . . is it?" Assured that is not the case, Suzy returns to her music once again, commenting, "I hope she comes home soon—sometimes I miss her a lot."

Among the many inmates she meets in the hospital, Deborah forms a friendship with **Carla**. Carla is very matter-of-fact about her illness. "My mother shot me and my brother and herself," Carla says. "They died; I lived. My father married again, and I went crazy." With that harsh story, Deborah learns that starkness and crudity are important privileges to those in the mental hospital, and they are used to the fullest.

Further Reading

Authors and Artists for Young Adults. Vol. 12. Detroit: Gale Research, 1994.

Berger, Laura Standley, ed. *Twentieth-Century Young Adult Writers.* 1st ed. Detroit: St. James, 1995.

Contemporary Authors New Revision Series. Vol. 32. Detroit: Gale Research, 1991.

Contemporary Literary Criticism. Vols. 7, 30. Detroit: Gale Research, 1977, 1984.

Something about the Author. Vol. 25. Detroit: Gale Research, 1981.

Bette Greene

1934-, American novelist

Summer of My German Soldier

(historical novel, 1973)

PLOT: Set in the small town of Jenkinsville, Arkansas, during World War II, the central character of this novel is twelve-year-old Patty Bergen. Patty, the daughter of Jewish parents who own the local department store, is a thin, nervous child, awkward, lonely, and unable to please her parents. Retreating into a world of make-believe, her active imagination gets her into trouble, especially with her father, who has a bad temper and often beats her. Patty's only real friend is her six-year-old sister, Sharon, who tries to protect her. Patty finds some companionship in Ruth, the family's black maid, and with her Grandpa and Grandma Fried, who live in Memphis and whom Patty adores. But she seldom gets to see them.

Life changes for Patty, however, after a trainload of German prisoners arrive at a newly completed camp just outside of town. One day while working in the family store, Patty waits on one of the German prisoners, who has been brought into town with the others to do some shopping. The charming man's name is Anton Reiker, the son of an English-born mother and a university professor. Reiker buys pencils and paper and some cheap pieces of ladies jewelry. Sometime later Patty once again meets Reiker after he has escaped by bribing a guard with supposedly expensive jewelry. Winning her over with his charm, he convinces Patty to conceal him in her secret hideaway over her family's garage. She supplies him with food and often has long talks with him, during which she learns that Reiker actually hates Hitler. For the first time in her life, Patty feels that someone has taken an interest in her. This warm, caring man gives some meaning to her life.

When Patty's father beats her one day, Reiker leaves his hiding place to help her. When the beating stops before he can come to her aid, he returns to the garage, but Ruth has already seen him. She agrees to help Patty protect him. However, Patty realizes that Reiker must leave before he is inevitably discovered and decides to go with him. Reiker gently tells her she must stay, giving her his great-grandfather's gold ring, his only personal possession, as a remembrance.

Foolishly, Patty later shows the ring to her father, claiming she got it from a tramp. Her father calls in the sheriff, thinking the tramp could be a child molester, but fortunately nothing else comes of this. That fall Patty is questioned by FBI agents about the ring, and she learns that Reiker was shot in New York City while resisting arrest. She admits the truth about how she aided the escaped soldier, but she does not implicate Ruth. Charged with delinquency, Patty is given four to six months in the state reformatory. Her only visitor is Ruth, who has been fired by Mr. Bergen for defending Patty.

CHARACTERS: Twelve-year-old **Patty Bergen** feels isolated and worthless. She has no friends except her younger sister and often feels alienated from her schoolmates because she is Jewish. She is able to endure her lonely life by escaping into a world of make-believe. Yet her fantasies often bring her more trouble when she lets her imagination get the best of her, irritating her parents.

When Patty first sees **Anton Reiker** and the other German soldiers, she is amazed that they do not look at all like the terrible murderers she expected. In fact, they look much like American soldiers. Reiker has black hair and green eyes and speaks fluent English. Patty learns that his mother was English and his father was a German university professor. His easygoing, charming manner intrigues Patty, and later, when she discovers he has escaped, she hides him in the unused servants' quarters over the garage. She brings Reiker food and some of her father's clothes. In return, this kind man takes an interest in Patty and gives her her first sense of self-worth. In their many conversations, Patty learns of his hatred of Hitler and his pretense of loyalty to the Nazis to avoid extermination. When it is time for Reiker to leave, Patty wants to go with him, but Reiker gently turns her down. "You know what you are asking is impossible," he says, "but if you're saying that you love me . . . then know this, Patty, it's not completely one-sided. I love you too, and in my own way I'll miss you." Later, Patty learns that Reiker was shot in New York City.

Besides her younger sister, **Sharon**, about the only person Patty talks to is the family's black maid, **Ruth**, who tries to induce a little self-confidence in Patty. For example, when Patty goes to work at the store, Ruth tells her to take off her faded shorts and put on a pretty dress to show others she takes pride in her appearance. When Ruth discovers that Patty is hiding the soldier in the quarters over the garage, she confronts Patty and demands the truth. Patty

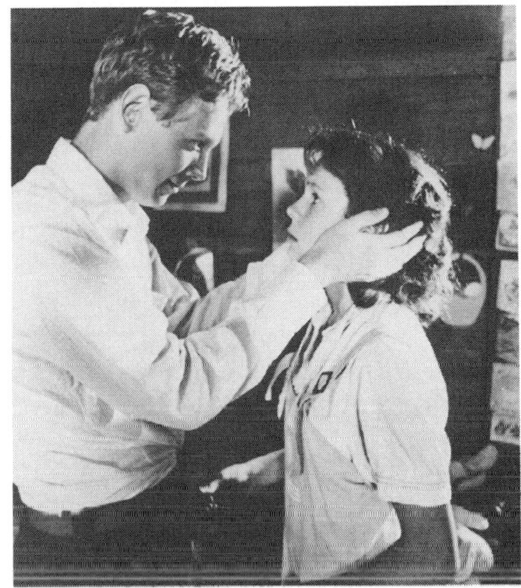

Kristy McNichol plays Patty in the 1978 film version of **Summer of My German Soldier.**

admits that she is shielding Reiker and convinces Ruth to aid her in her deception. For her part, when Patty is questioned by the FBI, she shields Ruth from any charges of complicity in the crime. When Patty is sent to the state reformatory for sheltering the German soldier, Ruth is her only visitor. "Be strong," she tells Patty, "and don't let them folks get you down 'cause better times a-coming for you. I feels it in my bones." When she walks away, looking frail and old, Patty laments that she has nothing to give her. Ruth replies, "You got love to give Honey Babe, ain't nothing better'n that."

Patty's parents are unsympathetic characters who are unsupportive and even abusive toward their daughter. Patty believes she appears plain compared to her beautiful mother, whom she can never seem to please. In Patty's eyes **Mrs. Bergen** is an artist's vision of sensitivity, intelligence, and love. Yet she shows no kindness toward her daughter. Instead, Mrs. Bergen either ignores Patty or nags her for the slightest reasons. Nagging, however, is preferable to the treatment Patty receives from her father. **Mr. Bergen** is a man with a violent temper. One day when Patty is caught throwing tiny stones at hubcaps of passing cars, Patty's father beats her with his fists.

Patty finds it hard to understand why her father dislikes **Grandpa** and **Grandma Fried**, although she suspects that it started when Grandpa didn't give her father a job in his real estate business. To Patty, they are the only loving people in her life. She loves visiting them in their twelve-year-old Victorian house in Memphis. Patty's grandmother conspires with her by planning special trips and giving her money, all of which is kept secret form Patty's mother. The older woman understands how difficult family life is for Patty. When she leaves her grandparents' house, Patty always feels as if she is leaving her true home.

Further Reading

Authors and Artists for Young Adults. Vol. 7. Detroit: Gale Research, 1991.

Berger, Laura Standley, ed. *Twentieth-Century Young Adult Writers.* 1st ed. Detroit: St. James, 1994.

Children's Literature Review. Vol. 2. Detroit: Gale Research, 1976.

Contemporary Literary Criticism. Vol. 30. Detroit: Gale Research, 1984.

Holtze, Sally Holmes, ed. *Fifth Book of Junior Authors and Illustrators.* New York: H. W. Wilson, 1983.

Something about the Author. Vol. 8. Detroit: Gale Research, 1976.

Something about the Author Autobiography Series. Vol. 16. Detroit: Gale Research, 1993.

Judith Guest

1936-, American novelist

Ordinary People

(novel, 1976)

PLOT: Seventeen-year-old Conrad Jarrett is back in high school after spending several months in a mental institution. Although he has physically recovered from a suicide attempt after the accidental drowning of his older and beloved brother, Buck, he still finds it difficult to return to the old routines of his life. He has returned to the school swim team, his old buddies, and his middle-class Illinois home with his mother, Beth, and his father, Calvin, but he doesn't feel connected to them or his life anymore. Conrad senses that his parents are floundering in their attempts to come to grips with the disasters that have overtaken their once-happy family. He is also painfully aware that Buck was his mother's favorite.

Reluctantly, Conrad begins seeing psychiatrist Tyrone C. Berger. Initially uncommunicative and uncooperative, Conrad nonetheless begins to feel drawn to the casual, bear-like man. He starts to talk about his grief, his loss, and his feelings of estrangement from his mother. He also has a meeting with Karen Aldrich, who shared his months in the mental institution. He comes away from the meeting more unsettled than before because she tells him that they must choose their friends and associates carefully. They are both on shaky ground and cannot afford to spend time with people (like themselves) who unsettle them. Conrad's relationships with family and friends grow steadily worse. He senses that his presence is causing a rift between his parents and that his mother can't forgive him for being the son who lived. He feels estranged from his friends and doesn't even get along with Jeannine Pratt, a girl from his choir practice who really seems to like him.

While his parents are vacationing down south and Conrad is staying with his grandparents, he sees a newspaper article reporting his friend Karen's suicide. In total despair, he rushes to Dr. Berger, and in a dramatic session he is able to face the truth. He must forgive himself for being the brother that lived after the boating accident. He was the stronger one, not Buck. He held onto the boat when Buck could not. Conrad returns home to give his life another try but finds that his family's future is uncertain. His mother has gone away for an indefinite period, but his father awkwardly tries to express his love. The novel ends with Conrad's realization that love can get him through the hard times.

CHARACTERS: Conrad Jarrett is a sensitive adolescent whose confidence in himself has been badly shaken with the accidental drowning of his older brother, whom he adored. Unable to come to grips with his own survival in the face of what he senses to

Conrad (Timothy Hutton) confides in Jeannine (Dinah Manoff) about his emotions over his brother's death in the 1977 film version of Ordinary People.

be his mother's unhappiness, he sought to end his own life and now finds it difficult to live with the reminder of what he attempted. Awkward, self-deprecating, and lonely, he uses caustic humor to disguise his feelings. He is easily turned away by what he perceives as rejection, particularly from his mother, but from others like Karen as well. He desperately wants his life to return to normal, but he knows that can never be. After the shock of Karen's suicide, he comes to grips with his true fears, learning that punishing himself for his feelings of guilt is not the answer. He realizes that he will survive if he lets himself feel pain and that, if he doesn't allow himself to feel pain, he won't feel anything else either. He learns that love will provide him with the strength that will make all else bearable. Conrad knows he loves his father and that he is not responsible for his mother's inability to accept the tragedy that has befallen the family. In the end, Conrad is ready to accept life as it is.

Conrad's mother, however, never comes to terms with her older son's death. To make the situation worse, **Beth Jarrett** can't cope with her grief—and shame—over her younger son's suicide attempt. She is embarrassed by Conrad's need to see a psychiatrist, wanting him to be strong enough to heal himself. Her embarrassment makes her lash out at her husband after a party, where he has mentioned to friends that Conrad is consulting Dr. Berger. This is "dirty linen" that must be kept within the family. Displays of emotion or improper behavior embarrass her because they disrupt the image of the perfect middle-class American family that the Jarretts have always presented to the world. She is angry that her family has been changed and disturbed that she is unable to return to the way things were. But her inability to express her emotions is her most devastating flaw. During a terrible fight with her husband over Conrad, she is unable to answer him directly when he asks, "Do you love me, Beth?" Instead she says, "I feel the same way about you that I have always felt." Realizing that a rift has grown between them, Beth leaves Calvin for an "extended vacation."

Calvin Jarrett is a well-meaning, sensitive, but unseeing man. Until he can no longer ignore the unhappiness and despair of his only remaining child, he spends his time trying to placate his rigid wife and smooth over a family life that he knows (but will not admit) is falling apart. He accepts Beth's accusations that he gives in too much to Conrad, saying he just wants to "make things right." Eventually, he accepts the fact that he can't change what has happened and that he can't ignore it either. In the last scene of the book, he also comes to terms with his feelings about his sons, telling Conrad why he never yelled at him as much as he did at Buck. Conrad might have felt ignored because of it, but to Calvin, Conrad was the good kid, the one that didn't need yelling at, the one that was easy to raise. He tells Conrad, "You were the one I never worried about. That was the problem. I should have been worrying. I wasn't even listening."

Conrad's therapist, **Dr. Tyrone C. Berger**, is portrayed as a scruffy but wise psychiatrist with a casual manner. With infinite patience and a fine sense of humor, he leads Conrad toward a realization of his true feelings about Buck's death and his own survival. It is Berger who shows Conrad that some things can't be foreseen or solved, but merely endured. He helps the boy to come to grips with his own pain and sense of guilt over his brother, to face the inadequacies of his relationship with his mother, and, most of all, to forgive himself for surviving.

A number of minor characters help to fill in the social setting that the Jarrett family suddenly finds itself at odds with. **Jeannine Pratt** is a pretty teenager who is drawn to Conrad, sensing the loneliness behind his often awkward demeanor. **Karen Aldrich** emerges from her months in a mental hospital determined to show the world, including Conrad, that she can make it by denying her problems, only to end up taking her own life.

Further Reading

Authors and Artists for Young Adults. Vol. 7. Detroit: Gale Research, 1991.

Bannon, B. A. "Story behind the Book *Ordinary People.*" *Publishers Weekly* 209 (April 19, 1976).

Contemporary Authors New Revision Series. Vol. 15. Detroit: Gale Research, 1985.

Contemporary Literary Criticism. Vols. 8, 30. Detroit: Gale Research, 1978, 1984.

Janeczko, P. "Interview with Judith Guest." *English Journal* 67 (March 1978).

Ryan, Bryan, ed. *Major Twentieth-Century Writers: A Selection of Sketches from Contemporary Authors.* Detroit: Gale Research, 1991.

Rosa Guy

1928-, American novelist

The Friends

(young adult novel, 1973)

PLOT: Fourteen-year-old Phyllisia Cathy has recently left her West Indian home with her mother, Ramona, and older sister, Ruby, to live with their father, Calvin, a restaurant owner, in an apartment in Harlem. At school, she is cruelly teased for her accent and being the pet of their teacher, the sarcastic Miss Lass. After being beaten up by the school bully, Beulah, Phyllisia accepts the friendship and protection of the class loner, a feisty, destitute waif named Edith Jackson. Though Phyllisia is ashamed of Edith's appearance, the two form a friendship. Edith brings Phyl to her home, a dilapidated rat's nest, where she meets the Jackson family: Edith's four younger sisters, older brother, and a father who sits silently in the corner of the living room. Since Mrs. Jackson's death three years before, Edith has been the head of the family. When Calvin, a strict, unreasonable man, forbids Phyllisia to see this "ragamuffin," their friendship languishes and Phyllisia does little to revive it. Edith drops out of school and Phyllisia learns that Mr. Jackson has abandoned his family and that Edith and her older brother must work full time to support themselves and the family. With Edith gone, Phyllisia cultivates a brief friendship with the snooty Marion Robbins.

Phyllisia has family problems of her own when her mother, Ramona, develops cancer and, in spite of the tender care she receives from her daughters, becomes depressed, loses hope, and wastes away. When she dies, the only element that held the family together disappears. Calvin becomes more violent and overbearing with the two girls and forbids them to leave the apartment except for school-related activities. Although Ruby acquiesces, Phyllisia rebels. She skips school, loses all interest in life, and begins seeing a Puerto Rican man she met in a park. The more detached and defiant her behavior, the more abusive and unreasonable Calvin becomes. Through the intervention of two family friends, cousin Frank Cathy and Mr. Charles, a truce is declared and arrangements are made to send the two sisters back to the islands. Before leaving, Phyllisia visits Edith for the first time in several months and learns that her older brother and youngest sister are dead and that social workers are placing the remaining family members, including Edith, in an orphanage. Edith is defeated and broken in spirit. Phyllisia realizes the great love she has for her friend and, by appealing to her father, manages to change his mind about sending the girls away. With this reprieve, Phyllisia, who has learned from these trials, creates an opportunity for herself to help Edith and begin a new life with her father.

CHARACTERS: The central character and narrator is **Phyllisia Cathy**. At fourteen, she is plain, overly tall, and still has a girlish figure. Conscious of her ordinary appearance, she resents the beauty and popularity of her sixteen-year-old sister, Ruby. Phyllisia has a serious, proud nature and rejects the superficial interests of her classmates. She is a sensitive, contemplative girl, deeply devoted to her mother and anxious to do well in school. She also longs for some recognition and appreciation. When her mother dies, she loses the only person who trusts and loves her; she also loses all desire to live and begins starving herself. Her father, with his "operation foodstrap," saves her life by forcing her to either eat or be whipped. Fiercely proud yet helpless, she becomes rebellious and does everything possible to spite her father. With her stubborn defiance, she ruins her own life in order to get revenge. When she honestly realizes that her overriding snobbishness and pride are the reasons that she can't accept either the poverty and shabbiness of Edith or the personality of her father, she gains both self-knowledge and maturity. Edith's triumphant spirit teaches Phyllisia a lesson in humility and gives her a new perspective on life in which values are based on actions not social position. During the year-long span of the plot, Phyllisia matures both physically and emotionally.

Phyllisia's savior is **Edith Jackson**. Described as coming to school "with clothes unpressed, her stockings bagging about her legs with big holes, which she tried to hide by pulling them into her shoes," Edith has a square little face and tiny, wiry body. She looks like a gnome but could be pretty if she had the time or money to care for herself. Though shabby in appearance, Edith exudes a wealth of goodness and decency. She is the epitome of kindness and compassion. Cheerful and bright, she exudes confidence even though her troubles and responsibilities are crushing. She has a kindly, generous nature and gives what she can to others even though it deprives her of basic comforts. A feisty fighter for justice, she stands up to wrongdoing with courage and strength. She is considerate of others' needs and feelings and is ready with a suitable compliment or comforting gesture. Never self-pitying or complaining, she endures each hardship with an inner strength and hope for the future. By the novel's end, Phyllisia is able to see Edith's inner beauty and resolves to maintain their friendship.

Unlike her sister, Phyllisia, **Ruby Cathy** is more frivolous and flexible. A beautiful girl with haunting eyes and thick hair, she receives the attention and concern that Phyllisia longs for. She is referred to as the "coolest chick around." Popular with the boys, her interests are primarily social and superficial. But Ruby also has a caring, sacrificing nature. She tends to both her mother and sister during their illnesses without complaint and has a sweet disposition that makes her popular with others. She lacks the spunk and spirit of her younger sister, however, and accepts her father's cruel and unreasonable behavior because of her basic submissive nature and fear of his physical abuse. Ruby is a passive person who tries to keep peace in the family at all costs, including forfeiting her own identity and rights.

The girls' father, **Calvin Cathy**, is a complex individual who, with his friends, is a jolly, ebullient fellow but at home is a harsh taskmaster who easily resorts to physical violence if his wishes are not obeyed. A hard-working man who runs a hole-in-the-wall eatery in Harlem, he has no time for his children and is impatient when their needs get in his way. Believing in Victorian standards of female modesty, he is overly protective, inflexible, and authoritarian, and his big, broad, and handsome appearance helps him command respect. Inclined to being a braggart and a bully, he has forgotten his roots and behaves in a snobbish, condescending way to those he feels are his inferiors. For example, he forbids Phyllisia to see the ragged, unkempt Edith. However, he shows a softer side when he is genuinely shattered by the death of his wife, the only person who understood and loved him.

Calvin's wife is the gentle, wise **Ramona Cathy**. Known for her great beauty and charm, Ramona changed when she left the freedom and calm of her island home for an unpleasant, confining life in a Harlem apartment. Once a high-spirited, happy woman, she became increasingly secretive and withdrawn. After a cancer operation, in which a breast was removed, she feels ugly and undesirable. As her illness progresses, she becomes an invalid who relies on her daughters' care. But, throughout all of this, she remains a loving, understanding mother who is able to hold her husband in check and still give guidance and courage to her family.

Minor characters include the family friends **Frank Cathy** and **Mr. Henry**. Like his cousin, Calvin, Frank is inclined to be hot-tempered and impatient, whereas Mr. Henry is a calm, reasonable man who is steady and dependable. Both are aware of Calvin's boasting and bad temper. Because of their fondness for Phyllisia and Ruby, they intervene when the girls are held as virtual prisoners in the apartment and persuade Calvin to send them back to the islands. **Miss Lass** is Phyllisia's white teacher. Frightened and intimidated by her students, she turns to sarcasm and ridicule to maintain order in her classroom. Hated by her pupils, she, in turn, suffers their derision and scorn. One of her students is the class bully, big-breasted **Beulah**, who terrorizes Phyllisia, makes fun of her accent, and picks fights with her. Edith intervenes and gives Beulah her comeuppance. At first Phyllisia is impressed with **Marion Robbins**'s beauty and finery. The daughter of a lawyer, she comes from an upper middle-class family, and Phyllisia is flattered to be chosen as a friend. In time, Marion's frivolous interests and shallow values bore Phyllisia and she looks for someone more substantial to be her friend.

The Disappearance

(young adult novel, 1979)

PLOT: Though he was innocent, sixteen-year-old Imamu has just spent a month in jail because he witnessed a murder that his friend Iggy committed. He returns to his squalid Harlem apartment where his alcoholic mother lives with her occasional boyfriends. Disgusted by the filth and his mother's slovenly life, Imamu decides to accept an offer made by a kind woman he met at the courthouse, Mrs. Ann Aimsley, to become her foster son. He relocates to Brooklyn and moves in with the Aimsley family: Ann, her husband, Peter, who owns a garage, and their two children, Gail, an attractive, college-age girl, and her eight-year-old sister, the outspoken Perk. He also meets the Aimsley's lodger, Mr. Elder, and the family's long-standing friend, Dora Belle, a bewitching, promiscuous West Indian woman who has accumulated a fair amount of money, many boyfriends, and three houses. In spite of everyone's best intentions, Imamu has problems in adjusting to his new middle-class surroundings, particularly after he accidentally breaks one of Ann's finest crystal glasses and is caught in a cover-up.

One day, Perk doesn't return from school, and the family calls the police. By a series of coincidences, Imamu falls under suspicion and is taken to the police station, where he is brutally interrogated by two police officers, Sullivan and Otis. Freed for lack of evidence, Imamu returns to the Aimsleys, hoping to prove his innocence. He and Gail join forces and begin to question the neighbors. Gail mistakenly believes that Mr. Elder is involved in the disappearance and, in an embarrassing confrontation, he proves his innocence. Clues then lead Imamu to a fresh piece of concrete in the basement of one of Dora Belle's houses. Part of the concrete is removed, revealing Perk's decomposing body. It turns out that during an argument, Dora Belle had accidently caused Perk's death and tried to hide the body to escape blame. Although the Aimsleys want to welcome Imamu back to their home, he decides to retain their friendship but return to Harlem, where he hopes to rehabilitate his mother.

CHARACTERS: Though still a boy, sixteen-year-old **Imamu**, whose real name is **John Jones**, has already learned many of life's harshest realities. When his father was killed in Vietnam and his mother turned to alcohol, he was forced to fend for himself on the streets of Harlem. In spite of temptations, however, he has avoided both drugs and crime. Though he pretends indifference, Imamu inwardly seeks the comfort and security of a home and therefore accepts Ann Aimsley's offer to join her family. Quiet and sensitive, he hides his vulnerability and loneliness with a mask of silence and aloofness. He has a practical, understanding nature and is tolerant of others and aware of their feelings; however, he refuses to grovel to gain acceptance or favor. This pride and independence are sometimes misinterpreted as arrogance, but Imamu is actually a humble innocent who only seeks recognition and love. Hardships have made him suspicious of others, but he has a compassionate, trusting nature. Imamu is an intelligent young man whose street smarts and logical thinking help solve the mystery of Peck's disappearance. He is also aware of his own developing sexuality and is strongly attracted to both Gail and Dora Belle. He, too, is physically attractive. In Gail's words, he is "tall, slim, good-looking, with large sleepy eyes, the look of the poet." When Imamu returns to Harlem with the blessing of the Aimsleys, he reaffirms his basic idealism and belief in others. He once again proves his strength of character, maturity, and the fact that, above all, he is a survivor.

Imamu's mother, **Mrs. Jones**, is a tragic figure. Once a loving mother and wife, she is remembered by Imamu for her tenderness and frailty. Her life was destroyed with the news of her husband's death. Now hopelessly addicted to alcohol, she has become a vituperative, unfeeling woman filled with despair and bitterness. Occasionally, remnants of her old, caring self reappear when, for example, she travels to Brooklyn to see her son after Imamu is questioned by the police. These few incidents give Imamu hope that somehow this pathetic, weak woman can be saved.

Imamu sees **Mrs. Ann Aimsley** as a combination guardian angel and savior because she realizes the boy's worth and helplessness and has invited him to become part of her family. A practical, well-intentioned person with a firm belief in others, she is described as slim, short, and attractive. Though grey-haired, she is youthful looking. As Imamu says, "she had class and was a great lady." She is dedicated to helping those less fortunate than herself. A fine housekeeper and loving mother, her serene benevolence, unfortunately, fails her when she realizes Imamu might be responsible for Perk's disappearance. Then she becomes hysterical, loses faith in Imamu, and blames herself for bringing him into her home. In a bout of self-pity, she says, "I was only trying to do good." When his idol deserts him, Imamu feels betrayed and abandoned, although Ann tries to make amends when the truth is revealed. A native West Indian, she has become thoroughly Americanized and has embraced both the material and spiritual values of the liberal middle-class. Well-meaning, likable, and understanding, Ann has not had an easy life, but she has learned to cope with several problems, including her husband's infidelity, and find solace in her spotless home and comforting family.

Ann's attractive elder daughter is **Gail Aimsley**, an intelligent, with-it young college student who sports an Afro and up-to-the-minute social ideas about women's equality. In spite of herself, she is attracted to Imamu. During the crisis involving Perk, she shows more maturity and clearer thinking than other members of the family. For her age, she exhibits great wisdom, compassion, and courage and stands up to her parents to defend Imamu. She alone has faith in him, and with a show of independence and nerve she pursues a logical, truth-seeking campaign to find Perk.

Perk, Ann's eight-year-old daughter who becomes the murder victim, is irresistible with her gummy smile, round face, and long curls down to her shoulders. Perk is spoiled but lovable. An endless talker, her gossipy chatter and tactless questions often cause trouble, but her beguiling ways always bring quick forgiveness.

Peter Aimsley is a self-made man who has worked hard to become the owner of a garage. He believes in old-fashioned values and objects to his wife's good works, which he believes are only interfering in other people's lives. He is, therefore, tentative in his acceptance of Imamu. Preferring to be in control of situations, this authoritarian, somewhat inflexible man causes some conflict in the household, particularly with his progressive daughter Gail. Nevertheless, his generous nature and hard-working diligence endear him to all.

Imamu calls **Mr. Elder**, the Aimsley's lodger, "a weird-looking dude," but Ann, in her charitable way, says he is "a lovely man." A solitary figure who once helped Peter get started in business, Mr. Elder has no family and, when he pathetically reaches out for affection, his actions are misinterpreted by Gail, who thinks he might be a child molester. This causes him to become a suspect, but he later proves to Gail that he is innocent.

When Imamu first meets the femme fatale **Dora Belle**, he exclaims that she is "the finest woman he had ever seen." Though actually forty-five, she looks thirty. Straight-backed, tall, and full-figured, she is more than pretty, she is beautiful. Peter, one of her many lovers, calls her a "beautiful buxom beauty" and says, "She's one fine woman and has got bread, too." The owner of three homes, Dora Belle is a tough taskmaster who is outspoken and sharp-tongued when not playing the role of the sexy seductress. A native West Indian, she has lost neither her colorful accent nor her native dialect. A vain woman and a brazen flirt, she prides herself on her many conquests, which include Peter Aimsley, Mr. Elder, other locals, and nearly Imamu. She never married because she never met anyone she felt was worthy of her. Shrewd, tricky, and cunning, she uses her beauty to manipulate others. Noted for her tight-fisted business dealings, her violent temper causes her to accidentally kill Perk.

The two plainclothes men who interrogate Imamu about Perk's disappearance are **Sullivan**, a case-hardened, ruthless man, and his partner, **Otis Brown**, a younger man and sharp dresser who sports a high Afro. Taking advantage of Imamu's age and defenseless position, the two shamelessly humiliate him and use physical force in an attempt to force a confession. Frustrated by his continued insistence of innocence, the two bullies are eventually forced to release him.

Further Reading

Authors and Artists for Young Adults. Vol. 4. Detroit: Gale Research, 1990.

Berger, Laura Standley, ed. *Twentieth-Century Children's Writers.* 4th ed. Detroit: St. James, 1995.

Children's Literature Review. Vol. 13. Detroit: Gale Research, 1987.

Contemporary Literary Criticism. Vol. 26. Detroit: Gale Research, 1983.

Cudjoe-Sewlyn, R., ed. *Caribbean Women Writers: Essays from the First International Conference.* Wellesley, MA: Calaloux, 1990.

Davis, Thadious M., and Trudier Harris, eds. *Afro-American Fiction Writers after 1955.* Vol. 33 of *Dictionary of Literary Biography.* Detroit: Gale Research, 1984.

Norris, Jerrie. *Presenting Rosa Guy.* New York: Twayne, 1988.

Something about the Author. Vols. 14, 62. Detroit: Gale Research, 1978, 1991.

Virginia Hamilton

1936-, American novelist

Sweet Whispers, Brother Rush

(fantasy, 1982)

PLOT: Fourteen-year-old Teresa Pratt, nicknamed Tree, has many responsibilities for one her age. Often left alone for days by her mother, Vy, a practical nurse, Tree has the burden of caring for her handsome but retarded eighteen-year-old brother, Dab, to whom Tree is devoted. Though outwardly independent and self-reliant, Tree is actually still a child who has many fears and longs for love and security. Before going on a job assignment, Vy always leaves a modest amount of housekeeping money and makes arrangements for visits by an inept cleaning woman, Miss Pritcherd.

On her way home from school one day, Tree becomes aware of an attractive, impeccably dressed stranger gazing at her. Later, when Tree looks into the surface of a table in her private walk-in closet, this man once more appears. In time, she realizes that he is actually her uncle, Brother Rush, the ghost of Vy's deceased brother. He begins taking Tree back to witness scenes of her childhood that reveal Vy's cruelty towards Dab when he was a child. Tree also encounters another stranger and discovers that he is her father, Ken, a man with a reputation for gambling. In later visions she sees Brother Rush caring for her and Dab, and she witnesses his physical decline from a painful illness. His death in an automobile accident, she later realizes, might have been a suicide.

After a lengthy absence, Vy returns and tells of plans to start a catering business with her new boyfriend, Silversmith. Dab becomes violently ill, and Tree learns from Vy that, like Brother Rush, he suffers from a hereditary disease called porphyria. Dab dies and Tree, in a violent confrontational scene, blames Vy and her neglect for Dab's death. Tree decides that, after the funeral, she will leave home to search for her father, Ken. In one last encounter with Brother Rush, she sees him and Dab enjoying themselves together. By the time of the funeral, Tree has become more reconciled to her brother's death, particularly after she gets special attention and sympathy from Silversmith's charming teenage son, Don. Vy announces that after their business is established she and Silversmith will marry and create a proper home for Tree. Tree changes her mind and decides to stay. Working things out will be difficult, but Tree is used to challenges.

CHARACTERS: Teresa Pratt, nicknamed **Tree**, believes that her great mission in life is to care for her mentally handicapped brother. She refuses to call him retarded, but instead thinks of him only as being slower and a little different from others. She showers Dab with all the affection and attention that she has been denied in her usually parentless home. Tree is a spunky, enterprising girl who, in addition to her schoolwork, must cook, shop, care for Dab, and manage the family apartment when her mother is away. Though she gives the impression of self-assurance and independence, Tree pathetically longs for love and security. She worships her mother and secretly is afraid that her mother will leave when she remarries. Tree is honest and truthful, both with herself and others, and able to endure disappointment and overcome adversity with amazing resourcefulness, resilience, and courage. However, when her small world collapses around her through Brother Rush's revelations about her family, the sudden appearance of Silversmith, and the devastating loss of her brother, Tree feels lost and unneeded. She becomes angry and releases all the pent up resentment and bitterness she feels towards her mother, blaming her for Dab's death. Cleansed by the grieving process, Tree again becomes a dependable, practical daughter, still searching for the appreciation and love she deserves. At one point, Tree wonders why she can see Brother Rush when others can't, and Silversmith rightfully says that it is because she is still pure, innocent, and without shame.

Tree emerges from her ordeals with all these qualities intact, as well as being a stronger, wiser, and more mature person. Tree's mother is **Viola**, or **Vy**, a big, good-looking woman whom Tree calls a "black beauty." In order to keep her household together, she must spend long periods away from home on nursing assignments. It is a hard life but one which she endures without complaint and without losing hope. She loves her children and, as a working single parent, makes enormous sacrifices for them. She realizes how much Tree forfeits to manage the household in her absence and tries through praise and her devotion to make up for these sacrifices. Ambitious and hard-working, she aspires to a better life for herself and family. Vy has endured great tragedies in her life. All her brothers were afflicted with porphyria and died, and she was abandoned by a husband who was a compulsive gambler. Although she has endured and found the strength to survive and continue, Vy is haunted by a guilt that surfaces upon Dab's death. Years before, she mistreated the boy because she could not accept his handicap or endure her own loneliness. Later, she denied the possibility that Dab might also have porphyria and did not have him tested. Though filled with sorrow and remorse at his death, she is, nevertheless, savagely attacked by Tree. Again Vy shows her great strength of character and compassion by enduring these assaults and continuing to show love and concern for Tree in spite of her vindictive behavior. Vy is a realist and a good businesswoman, but above all she is a loving, wise mother. She expects little from life but is always hopeful of a better future.

Tree's brother is seventeen-year-old **Dab**, short for **Dabney**. A sweet, gentle boy, Dab is liked by everyone and has no enemies. Childlike and helpless, he attends school and never gets into trouble, but he also never brings home a report card. Easily confused and slow, some unkind strangers call him a "loony tune." He is, however, extremely handsome. Girls are attracted by his good looks and innocence. Unaware of conventional morality, he shamelessly brings several of them home to his bed. Dab is not a great talker, but one of his frequently used expressions, "every-thang gone be okey," is typical of his docile, guileless attitude toward life. Having a sensitive nature, he is upset when people laugh at him and he is fiercely attached to Tree, whom he adores. Dab endures great pain from headaches and often spends an entire day making soft crying sounds. To ease his pain, Dab secretly begins using barbiturates and other drugs, not realizing that they will trigger his porphyria. By the time Vy discovers the truth, it is too late and he dies.

The ghost of Vy's dead young brother, **Brother Rush**, first appears to Tree as an attractive eighteen-year-old who watches her when she comes from school. He is a handsome man dressed impeccably from his pinstripe suit to his patent leather shoes. His refined features, full lips, and piercing eyes make Brother Rush very attractive to Tree. Although he never speaks, Tree gets to know him through a series of flashbacks she experiences later via the shiny surface of her closet table. Brother Rush was a numbers runner who made money illegally but generously used it to buy gifts for others. He loved his young niece and nephew, often interceding when Vy mistreated young Dab. An unselfish, fun-loving man, he appears to Tree to give her a sense of her unknown past and to prepare her for the eventual loss of Dab.

Vy realizes that she has a true gem in **Sylvester Smith**, who is also called **Silversmith**. A born gentleman, he genuinely loves and admires Vy and displays amazing kindness and understanding towards Tree, whom he treats as if she was his own daughter. He is thoughtful, wise, compassionate, and very supportive of Vy. Even though Tree hurls insults at him after Dab's death, Silversmith responds with tenderness, offering astute advice on subjects such as how to accept being black. His son, nineteen-year-old **Don Smith**, shares many of his qualities. Also a gentleman, Don is sympathetic to other people's feelings and, like his father, is able to put people immediately at ease. He is friendly to Tree, pretends to flirt with her, and makes her feel important. After the funeral, Don shows he understands Tree's problems by telling her about himself and how he tried to run away from home after his mother's death. With his pleasing, infectious laugh and outgoing manner, Don captivates Tree and gives her the distraction she needs.

Vy's part-time housekeeper is toothless, frizzy-haired **Miss Cenithia Pritcherd**. Though not much of a worker, she accepts directions uncomplainingly. She has had a terribly hard life and appreciates any kindness shown her. Her description of life on the streets helps persuade Tree to remain home instead of running away to seek her father.

A White Romance

(young adult novel, 1987)

PLOT: When Talley Barbour's ghetto school, Colonel Glenn High, is chosen to be a Magnet school, white kids suddenly form a sizable part of the school's population. Talley, a lonely, innocent girl who keeps house for her janitor father, Poppy, welcomes the friendship of a beautiful white girl, Didi Adair, who shares Talley's passion for running. Soon Talley becomes involved with Didi, her divorced mother, Mrs. Vera Adair, and Didi's drug-addicted boyfriend, Roady Dean Lewis, who is financed by a wealthy father and lives in a squalid apartment. Talley becomes captivated by the excitement and mystery of Didi and Roady's love affair, living vicariously through their experiences. She refers to it as "A White Romance," or AWR.

Talley becomes the object of attention of two schoolmates, each intent on giving Talley a romance of her own. Her first admirer is Victor Davis, an honest, upright, black boy she has known for years; the second is the charming, handsome white teenager, David Emory. In spite of Didi's warning, Talley ignores Victor and succumbs easily to the smooth, flattering enticements of David and his display of affluence and independence. Becoming completely infatuated with David, Tally sleeps with him. Their relationship reaches a turning point, however, when Talley ruins a heavy metal rock concert they have eagerly anticipated by becoming sick so that they have to leave before it's over. As David's love for Talley wanes, she becomes more miserable and desperate. Even when she discovers that David's money comes from drug dealing and that he has a reputation for being fickle and heartless, she continues to long for his dwindling love and attention. Her friends, Didi and Roady, offer her consolation and reassurance and, at her lowest point, Talley receives help and another chance from Victor. Slowly, she picks up the pieces and moves on.

CHARACTERS: Innocent, naive **Talley Barbour** is in love with love. A petite, lean, attractive girl, she glorifies and revels in Didi's affair with Roady. In her shy, idealistic way, she wishes "A White Romance" could happen to her. Talley is a conscientious student at school and a helpful, supportive daughter to her father, whom she both fears and idolizes. She has placed her father on a pedestal and feels betrayed when she learns he is having an affair. Talley is a trusting friend who is loyal and understanding. Growing up without a mother and having a father who works evenings, she reaches out to others to ease her loneliness. In this vulnerable, unprotected state, she is an easy prey for the attentions of experienced, suave David. Talley immediately becomes infatuated with him and basks in his attention and flattery. She feels some guilt about having sex with him, however. After he abuses her verbally, she knows she should drop him, but she doesn't have the strength. Talley forgives David's insults, hoping that he will not reject her. When the inevitable split occurs, Talley maintains her pride and dignity, and through the help of her friends she bounces back, wiser and less gullible for the experience. Talley loves the freedom and exhilaration that she experiences while running. Though she has a sensitive nature, she is a born survivor who is able to endure pain and rebuffs and still emerge a stronger, more resilient person.

Talley's best friend is **Didi Adair**, a bright, sympathetic girl who, like Talley, is growing up in a single parent home in a poor neighborhood. Didi is more experienced than Talley. Though not promiscuous, she is more sexually active and has survived an affair with David. She is an independent, straightforward person who shows remarkable understanding and loyalty towards her friends. She tries to warn and protect Talley from David, while also nursing and sustaining Roady. Didi attempts to instill in others the same pride and self-assurance that she feels about herself. Didi is blond and beautiful (Talley says she "Could've been a movie star") yet never vain or egotistical. She appreciates sincerity and honesty in others and possesses these qualities herself. With a keen intelligence, she does well in school without a great deal of effort. Like Talley, Didi loves the freedom and elation that running brings. Didi's two most prominent characteristics are her no-nonsense, realistic attitude towards life and her caring, sacrificing nature. She has the rare capability of being able to assist and empathize with others, including Talley, through their difficult periods.

Didi's boyfriend is the pathetic, fragile, but bright **Roady Dean Lewis**, whose drug use has given him "scrambled brains." Into heavy metal music and electronic equipment, he "knew everything and cared about nothing but music and Didi." Roady has been rejected and disowned by his wealthy, uncaring father, who gives him money to maintain himself and his shabby apartment with the stipulation that he doesn't come home. Big and gangly, Roady lives an unhealthy existence, drinking alcohol, doing drugs, and only occasionally attending school. He is David's best and steadiest customer. A quiet, gentle person, Roady has a childlike, trusting nature. He has been irreparably hurt by his father's rejection and now has turned to Didi for her love and attention. Roady possesses a "special sweetness" that makes everyone want to care for him. Generous to the point of extravagance, Roady is loved by everybody because of his unselfish, innocent nature and amiable disposition. His devotion and tenderness towards Didi inspires Talley into creating the concept of A White Romance. Gradually, Roady realizes that being hooked on drugs eventually results in death. He decides that for himself and his caring friends, particularly Didi, he must change. "I been strung out too long," he says, resolving to cut back on his use.

Clad entirely in leather and sporting a cool haircut with brown hair that is short and spiky on top and long at the sides, **David Emory** succeeds in giving the impression of being a smooth operator and "a cool dude." Incredibly handsome, he has a fantastic smile and a deep voice and exudes charm, wit, and confidence. Even his movements, "all motion and energy like a cat, a panther," reveal self-assurance and arrogance. David likes to control people, using them as puppets and discarding them when they become burdensome or are no longer amusing. Devious and cunning, he is an experienced drug pusher who is able to escape arrest through shrewd, guarded tactics. Completely self-controlled and exceptionally manipulative, he is also a master seducer and wheeler-dealer who attends school only to make contacts for his drug deals. Although he takes advantage of the weakness and good nature of others, particularly the vulnerable Talley, David occasionally shows some redeeming qualities. For example, he shows some concern and fondness for Roady. Generally, however, Victor is right when he says David is "real bad news."

Victor Davis is a decent, honest young man who genuinely cares for Talley, whom he has known all his life and wants to help and protect. He comes from a fine, upstanding family with solid values. Victor is the best athlete in school; he is also on the student council and is a member of the National Honor Society. Ambitious and hard-working, he regards being black as an additional reason to try harder to achieve in a white world. Tough and good-looking, he is gentle and kind towards Talley without being meddlesome. Talley, who is more attracted to the flamboyant David, treats Victor like "an old worn shoe. Something comfortable to wear when you were tired, aching all over." Gradually she realizes the importance of reliability and the old-fashioned dependable virtues that Victor represents.

Talley calls her father **Poppy** and he calls her "young lady." Poppy's real name is **Hale William Barbour**. He is an honorable man who works hard and is extremely attentive to Talley's needs and concerns. Although he is permanently on the afternoon shift and is absent when Talley comes home from school, he tries to protect and safeguard her with his practical advice. He believes that socializing with whites will cause trouble for Talley and frowns on her friendship with Didi. Talley, therefore, hides her relationship with David from her father, fearful of his disapproval and anger. Anxious to present a pure, righteous image to his daughter, Poppy doesn't tell her about his girlfriend. When Talley finds out, she is at first incredulous and then disillusioned to realize that her adored father is only human. Didi's mother is the twice-divorced **Vera Adair.** A plump woman who wears tiny rectangular glasses, Mrs. Adair is an affectionate, caring mother and, for Talley, a dear, understanding friend. She trusts her daughter and provides her with a secure environment and a pleasant, though humble, home.

Further Reading

Apseloff, Marilyn. *Virginia Hamilton.* Columbus: State Library of Ohio, 1979.

Authors and Artists for Young Adults. Vol. 2. Detroit: Gale Research, 1989.

Berger, Laura Standley, ed. *Twentieth-Century Children's Writers.* 4th ed. Chicago: St. James, 1994.

Children's Literary Review. Vols. 1, 11. Detroit: Gale, 1976, 1986.

Contemporary Literary Criticism. Vol. 26. Detroit: Gale Research, 1983.

Davis, Thadious M., and Trudier Harris, eds., *Afro-American Fiction Writers after 1955.* Vol. 33 of *Dictionary of Literary Biography.* Detroit: Gale Research, 1984.

De Montreville, Doris, and Elizabeth Crawford, eds. *Fourth Book of Junior Authors and Illustrators.* New York: H. W. Wilson, 1978.

Estes, Glenn E., ed. *American Writers for Children since 1960,* Vol. 52 of *Dictionary of Literary Biography.* Detroit: Gale Research, 1986.

Kirkpatrick, D. L., ed. *Twentieth-Century Children's Writers.* 2nd ed. New York: St. Martin's, 1983.

Townsend, John Rowe. *A Sounding of Storytellers.* New York: Lippincott, 1979.

Nathaniel Hawthorne

1804-1864, American novelist

The Scarlet Letter

(historical novel, 1850)

PLOT: The story opens in the town of Boston in 1642. A young woman named Hester Prynne is being punished by being forced to stand on a scaffold with a scarlet letter A attached to the front of her dress. She has committed the sin of adultery. For this crime, the women of the Puritan community would have preferred a branding or execution, but because of her beauty and hitherto good deportment, she has been given a lighter sentence.

As Hester looks over the scornful crowd, she spies a small, elderly, deformed man whom she recognizes as the husband she has not seen for two years. At that time she had arrived in Boston ahead of her husband, who had remained in Amsterdam. She was to wait for him there, but she never saw him again until this day. It was generally assumed he had been lost at sea. When she sees him, she cries out and clutches her illegitimate child, whose father she refuses to name. A stranger in the crowd declares that the father of the child should be punished along with Hester.

Back in her cell, Hester is so upset that the jailer, Master Brackett, brings in an old physician to aid her. He is actually Hester's husband, but he is going by the name Roger Chillingworth. He gets Hester to agree never to reveal his true identity because of the shame it would bring him. If she does, he threatens to seek out the child's father and destroy him.

The years pass and Hester raises her child, whom she names Pearl, by taking on sewing jobs. Pearl becomes an unruly child, fascinated with the A on her mother's dress. The townspeople say she is a "demon offspring" and suggest she be taken from Hester's care. Hester appeals to Governor Bellingham in the presence of two guests, John Wilson, a minister, and Reverend Arthur Dimmesdale, who is the father of Pearl. When the Governor seems about to take the child, Dimmesdale intercedes.

All this is observed by Chillingworth, who suspects Dimmesdale's sin. Tormented by guilt, Dimmesdale goes to the square where Hester was punished. Hester and Pearl arrive and Dimmesdale acknowledges his guilt to them. Little Pearl sees Chillingworth watching them. Dimmesdale's health deteriorates. Hester tells him of Chillingworth's identity, removes the scarlet A from her dress, and the two make plans to sail to England with Pearl. But the child will not agree to go until Hester replaces the scarlet letter on her dress. Terrified by his own irrational desires and strange behavior, Dimmesdale prepares to deliver a sermon the next day for the new governor. He takes no notice of Hester and Pearl in the crowd, and Hester begins to realize there is no future for her with him.

After Dimmesdale's inspired sermon, he walks as if in a trance to the scaffold. Chillingworth tries to stop him, but Hester helps him up on the scaffold where he stands with her and Pearl and confesses that he is Pearl's father. He tears off his minister's garb and collapses. Witnesses later swear they saw a scarlet A on his bare chest. Chillingworth also dies shortly after and leaves a good deal of money to Pearl. Hester leaves for England but returns to Boston years later. Upon her death, she is buried near Dimmesdale's grave.

CHARACTERS: To understand the character of **Hester Prynne** and the significance of her misfortune, one must remember that adultery was often punishable by death in seventeenth-century Puritan Massachusetts. Although Hawthorne does not condone adultery in this novel, it is obvious that he finds it far less a crime than the sins of Dimmesdale and Chillingworth. Hester is portrayed as a comely lady whose pride sustains her through her punishment and for all the years of her life. Her upbringing in England helps her face her tribulations with great fortitude.

Hester is the victim in this tragedy. She is a victim of the age in which she lives which forced her into a marriage with a man far older than she and whom she does not love; she is a victim of Chillingworth's foolish decision to send her on alone to America and not to send any message of his welfare; and she is a victim of Dimmesdale's selfishness in allowing an affair when he knew he could neither marry her nor acknowledge responsibility for the child.

Hester acknowledges her sin, wearing the scarlet A long after she could have removed it. She chooses instead to display it to the world as proof of her passion and love. She did not plan to commit adultery or hurt anyone, but she obviously loves Dimmesdale. As she takes the punishment meted to her with dignity, she gains inner strength, which sustains her throughout her life. When she returns to Boston after years in England, she becomes a woman in the community to whom others turn in times of trouble. She has gained respect and she has found happiness from the inner peace that her strength has brought her.

Arthur Dimmesdale is a delicate fellow, well-educated, and modest with a refreshing childlike quality. His sin, however, is that he does not have the courage to acknowledge that he is the father of Hester's child, Pearl. It is this inability to admit his adultery that makes his sin worse than Hester's and ultimately brings about his destruction. While he urges his congregation to admit their sins and be forthright, he himself is hiding a grave sin. The paradox is his undoing.

Dimmesdale offers some reasons in the novel for his refusal to acknowledge his responsibility. One of them is that he could not continue his work for God were he to disclose the fact that Pearl is his child. Yet inwardly he realizes he is merely rationalizing his actions. The guilt finally drives him to madness and death. He is, after all, an imperfect man who longs to be perfect, a weak man who longs to be strong. Even when it is clear that Dimmesdale is destroying himself with his internal conflict, he can't admit his trespasses. Ironically, on the day of his greatest work as a minister when he delivers his finest sermon, he also confesses his greatest sin.

Hester's husband is Roger Prynne, who calls himself **Roger Chillingworth** so as not to be shamed publicly by his wife's adultery. But Chillingworth is far more culpable than he at first appears to be. A small, elderly, deformed, scholarly man, he selfishly takes a lovely young woman for his bride, knowing she does not love him and that he is not the man to share a happy marriage with her. Although he knows he was wrong to marry Hester, instead of accepting his responsibility in the affair he willingly judges Dimmesdale and tries to destroy the man's sanity. In other words, he tries to play God, and in so doing becomes the devil. Although Hester accepts the penalty for her adultery and Dimmesdale is consumed by guilt over it, Chillingworth's desire for revenge while accepting no responsibility in the end brings about his own torturous death.

The child, **Pearl**, is described as a rich beauty. By the novel's end, she is seven years old. She is an intelligent but strange child, and she serves as the obvious symbol of the affair between Hester and Dimmesdale. As she grows older and becomes increasingly curious about the scarlet letter, she adds to her mother's sense of pain and becomes the living embodiment of Dimmesdale's own personal torment. Later in the novel, Pearl's curiosity about the letter on her mother's breast reaches a point where Hester can no longer deny the whole truth to the child. Pearl is the living proof that Dimmesdale is denying his own flesh and blood. A mixture of baffling moods with unusual behavior, she is referred to as "elf-child" or "imp," but sometimes in a more sinister fashion as "demon offspring." At the end of the novel, she is said to have married a member of the nobility in Europe.

Richard Bellingham is the governor whom Hester goes to see to request that Pearl not be taken from her. One of three actual historical figures in this novel, he was governor in 1641, 1654, and 1665 to 1672. Another historical figure is **John Wilson**, who is with Bellingham when Hester requests an audience with him. He was a minister who arrived in Boston from England in 1630. When at the beginning of the novel Hester refuses to reveal the name of her child's father, Wilson delivers a long sermon on the sin of adultery to the witnessing crowd. Early in the story, he also, ironically, convinces Dimmesdale to try to get the truth from Hester. The third historical figure is **Mistress Ann Hibbins**. In the novel she is described as the "bitter-tempered" sister of Bellingham. Supposedly, she is a witch with otherworldly powers who has insight into the transgressions of Dimmesdale and Hester. She was, in fact, executed in 1656 for practicing witchcraft.

Further Reading

Baym, Nina. *The Scarlet Letter: A Reading.* Boston: G. K. Hall, 1986.

Bloom, Harold. *Hester Prynne.* New York: Chelsea House, 1990.

———. *Nathaniel Hawthorne.* New York: Chelsea House, 1986.

———. *Nathaniel Hawthorne's The Scarlet Letter.* New York: Chelsea, 1986.

Cameron, Kenneth Walter. *Hawthorne among His Contemporaries.* Hartford, CT: Transcendental Books, 1969.

Cantwell, Robert. *Nathaniel Hawthorne: The American Years.* New York: Rinehart, 1948.

Colacureio, Michael Jed. *New Essays on The Scarlet Letter.* Cambridge: Cambridge University Press, 1985.

Conway, Moncure D. *Life of Nathaniel Hawthorne.* New York: Haskell, 1968.

Critical Survey of Long Fiction. Vol. 4. Englewood Cliffs, NJ: Prentice-Hall, 1983.

Dauber, Kenneth. *Rediscovering Hawthorne.* Princeton: Princeton University Press, 1977.

Hawthorne, Julian. *Nathaniel Hawthorne and His Wife.* Boston: Houghton Mifflin, 1884.

James, Henry. *Hawthorne.* New York: St. Martin's, 1967.

Kesterson, David B., ed. *Critical Essays on Hawthorne's The Scarlet Letter.* Boston: G. K. Hall, 1988.

Kimbel, Bobby Ellen, and William E. Grant, eds. *American Short-Story Writers before 1880.* Vol. 74 of *Dictionary of Literary Biography.* Detroit: Gale Research, 1988.

Lathrop, Rose Hawthorne. *Memories of Hawthorne.* New York: AMS, 1969.

Lee, A. Robert, ed. *Nathaniel Hawthorne: New Critical Essays.* London: Vision Press, 1982.

Martin, Terence. *Nathaniel Hawthorne.* New York: Twayne, 1983.

Mellow, James R. *Nathaniel Hawthorne in His Time.* Boston: Houghton Mifflin, 1980.

Miller, Edwin H. *Salem Is My Dwelling Place: A Life of Nathaniel Hawthorne.* Iowa City: University of Iowa Press, 1991.

Myerson, Joel, ed. *The American Renaissance in New England.* Vol. 1 of *Dictionary of Literary Biography.* Detroit: Gale Research, 1978.

The New Molton's Pre-Twentieth Century Criticism of British and American Literature. Vol. 8 of *Chelsea House Library of Literary Criticism.* New York: Chelsea House, 1985.

Nineteenth Century Literature Criticism. Vols. 2, 10, 17, 23. Detroit: Gale Research, 1982, 1985, 1988, 1989.

Normand, Jean. *Nathaniel Hawthorne.* Cleveland: Press of Case Western Reserve University, 1970.

Van Doren, Mark. *Nathaniel Hawthorne.* New York: Viking, 1949.

Wagenknecht, Edward. *Nathaniel Hawthorne: The Man, His Tales and Romances.* New York: Continuum, 1989.

Ann Head

(pen name for Anne Christensen Morse)

1915-, American novelist

Mr. and Mrs. Bo Jo Jones

(novel, 1967)

PLOT: July Greher is sixteen and a junior at Trilby High School in a small southern town close to Savannah, Georgia. She comes from an upper-middle-class family, consisting of her banker father, her mother, younger sister, Grace, and twelve-year-old brother, Gregory. July's best pal is Mary Ann Simmons, and her boyfriend of several months is Bo Jo (short for Boswell Johnston) Jones, the seventeen-year-old only son of working-class parents. One night after a party, July and Bo Jo make love, and within a few weeks July discovers that she is pregnant. Unknown to their families, the two sneak across state lines and get married. Breaking the news to the Joneses and the Grehers, which includes starchy Grandmother Greher, is difficult; but the families, who have nothing in common, reluctantly decide to make the best of it. To mollify the Grehers, a hasty church wedding is performed, which is boycotted by Mr. and Mrs. Jones, who resent the interference of July's parents.

Woefully unprepared for parenthood, both youngsters drop out of school and move to a small but comfortable apartment over a friend's garage. Bo Jo takes a job at Mr. Greher's bank, but July's days are lonely and depressing. She spends some time with an aspiring young singer, Louella Consuela, who is also a child bride and who married a horse trainer named Nick, a much older man. July also carries on a secret correspondence with an attractive young man she met briefly named Horace Clark. Anxieties caused by family tensions and the sudden unexpected changes in their lives result in frequent, bitter quarrels during the couple's first months together.

While in the seventh month of her pregnancy, July hemorrhages. In the hospital, she gives birth to a son, Jonathan, who dies two days later. Both families see this as an opportunity to dissolve the marriage and let each of the youngsters return to their former lives. July and Bo Jo consent in silence, but when they return to their little apartment filled with both bitter and pleasant memories, the two realize they have grown to love each other and they decide to stay together.

CHARACTERS: The narrator is **July Greher**, so named by her patriotic parents because she was born on July 4. She is a small, attractive girl with red hair and green eyes who, according to the high school annual, is "spirited." Pampered, but not spoiled, July is serious, sometimes moody, and has refined tastes. For example, she relaxes by listening to Beethoven on the phonograph and has exemplary taste in furnishings and clothes. Well-liked and respected, she is an ideal daughter of whom her parents are extremely proud. July is a clever, intelligent girl who is reflective, self-possessed and independent. Nevertheless, at sixteen she is completely unprepared for the sudden responsibilities and changes thrust upon her. She knows nothing about keeping house or preparing meals, yet with forbearance and gumption, she manages, though at a terrible cost to her emotional stability. Always well-intentioned and accommodating, she tries gallantly but unsuccessfully to bring the two disparate families together, while showing remarkable restraint in handling the difficult Mr. and Mrs. Jones. Often confused when coping with the unforeseen adult problems she faces, July sometimes loses control. However, for her age and experience she generally behaves with remarkable judgment and aplomb. July is a likable, sympathetic girl who matures remarkably fast as a result of her ordeal. As she candidly says, "You can't go back to being a teenager when you've been a woman for a while."

July's boyfriend, **Bo Jo Jones**, is also an amiable, reliable youngster. He is not only Trilby High's star halfback, he is also active in track and the student council. A fine student, he has a part-time job and plans to attend college on a sports scholarship. Like July, he has a practical and serious nature and is capable of accepting responsibility. He is noted for his determination and perseverance in overcoming problems. A dutiful son, he loves and obeys his parents but also never questions his obligations to July, though this may hurt his family. His sense of honor, integrity, and respect for others makes Bo Jo an admirable, sympathetic person. An attractive young man who has a good physique, short hair, a stubby nose, and bright-blue eyes, Bo Jo is, like July, ill-equipped to contend with the problems and changes that have suddenly been thrust upon him. He has not mastered the social graces and conventions that are important to the Grehers and he justifiably resents trading his bright future for a dull bank job. His ordeal strengthens Bo Jo, hastens a maturation, and teaches him the meaning of sacrifice and love.

Bo Jo's parents are **Mr.** and **Mrs. Carson Jones**. Mr. Jones's job is "contract engineer," a fancy name for being a construction foreman in charge of carpenters and bricklayers. He has a working man's interest in solid middle-class values. A hard worker and good provider, he controls his household, makes the decisions, and, when thwarted, shows a violent temper. He is devastated when hopes for Bo Jo's college education are dashed by the premature marriage. Outspoken and blunt, he inwardly blames July for his son's predicament and resents the interference of the Grehers and their position of wealth. His wife also dislikes the Grehers and is hostile to July's supposedly "uppity" ways. She is a meticulous housewife who dutifully obeys her husband and submits to his wishes. The custodian of the family's prefab ranch-style house, she tries to provide a household that reflects "class" and good taste. To her, this means lace doilies and pot roast every Sunday.

By contrast, **Paul** and **Agnes Greher** represent good breeding, culture, and refinement. They live in a large home surrounded by prosperity and comfort. Mr. Greher is a handsome, reserved man who is president of the Greher Guaranty and Trust. He adores his family, particularly July, and painfully

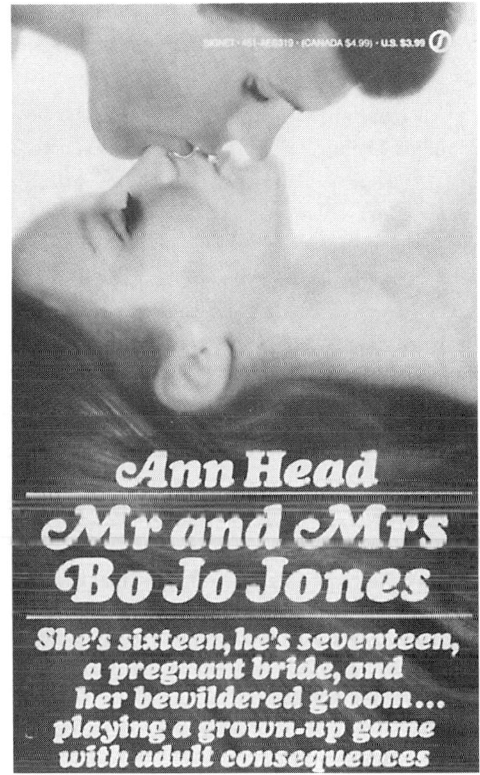

Head tackles the issues of teen pregnancy and social class differences in her 1967 novel.

tries to adapt to her situation. Though well-meaning and considerate, he has problems communicating with Bo Jo, who "feels invisible" in his presence. Mrs. Greher is also quiet and well-bred. Tall and slender, she exudes grace and refinement. She is an understanding and accommodating woman who adores July but, nevertheless, has some trouble accepting her situation and adjusting to the working-class Jones family. Always tactful and discreet, she and her husband support and never censure their daughter.

Like many early adolescents, July's fourteen-year-old sister, **Grace Greher**, places an emphasis on social position and family propriety. She is therefore ashamed of her sister's forced marriage, but she gradually comes to accept and understand the situation. **Gory**, a nickname for **Gregory**, July's bright, twelve-year-old brother, also has trouble comprehending and accepting his beloved elder sister's position. He hates Bo Jo for taking his sister away for him.

Grandmother Greher, whose full name is **Louisa Conduit Greher**, lives in affluence and isolation as the grande dame of the family. Fiercely independent and opinionated, she is an amazing judge of character. July respects and admires her Grandmother, who "never explains anything or makes excuses." In spite of her forbidding exterior and sometimes unapproachable manner, she has an amazing ability to get strangers to relax and talk about themselves. She is the only Greher who genuinely likes and understands Bo Jo, a feeling that is welcomed and reciprocated.

Seventeen-year-old **Louella (Lou) Consuela** serves as a foil for July. She is a talented songwriter and performer who married her husband, the much older, handsome horse trainer **Nick Consuela**, primarily so he would not stray. She is a vivacious girl who hates being a housewife and conceals her loneliness by going to weddings and funerals. When she becomes pregnant, she has an abortion rather than be trapped by raising a family. When Nick finds out, he reacts violently and beats her up, causing Lou to leave him and courageously try for success in show business by herself.

July's dearest friend is **Mary Ann Simmons**, the daughter of a father who has married and divorced several times. Mary Ann is a typical teenager whose chief interests include social affairs and boys. When July's life takes an abrupt turn because of her marriage, Mary Ann is not able to comprehend these changes, and the two grow apart. July finds escape from her lonely life in her little apartment by writing to **Horace Clark**, a handsome, blonde-haired family friend who is a sophomore at Stanford University. He is witty, charming, and, unlike Bo Jo, shares July's interests in literature and music. In time, July realizes that she is deceiving both herself and Bo Jo in continuing this correspondence and breaks off the relationship by telling him of her marriage.

Further Reading

Berger, Laura Standley, ed. *Twentieth-Century Young Adult Writers.* 1st ed. Detroit: St. James, 1995.

Contemporary Authors. Vols. 1-4. Detroit: Gale Research, 1967.

Robert A. Heinlein

1907-1988, American science fiction writer

Tunnel in the Sky

(science fiction, 1955)

PLOT: In the far-distant future, Rod Walker is a senior at Patrick Henry High School on Terra. He learns one day that members of his Advanced Survival class, taught by tough Dr. Matson, are scheduled for their final examination. It will be an endurance test on an unknown planet and will last an unspecified length of time. Rod gets valuable preparation tips from his parents and his sister Helen, an army assault captain of the Amazons. He hopes to team up with his wisecracking buddy, Jimmy Throxton. But when he passes through the space tunnel that takes him instantaneously to his destination, he is separated from Jimmy. Rod finds himself alone in a strange land overrun with tropical vegetation and hostile animal life.

After several harrowing days and nights coping with blood-thirsty beasts, Rod encounters a slightly built, sinewy co-survivor named Jack. (But Rod eventually discovers that Jack is actually a girl named Jacqueline Daudet.) Later, he is also reunited with Jimmy. They are next joined by more students from other endurance courses, including a Zulu named Caroline Mshiyeni, Bob Baxter, Carmen Garcia, and Roy Kilroy. There are also several older students from Teller University: Jock and Bruce, the fractious McGowan brothers, and the intellectual Grant Cowper. As more students, all between ages sixteen and twenty-two, join the group, two things become obvious. First, the devices to take them back to Terra are malfunctioning; second, they must organize into a commune.

Though Rod loses the election to Grant, he retains a position of importance. Rod and Roy scout for a secure living area and discover some abandoned cave dwellings. However, the group, now about seventy-five in number, do not heed Rod's warnings concerning their exposed position and decide to remain in their more comfortable quarters. But the commune lies in the direct path of stampeding animals fleeing an attack of vicious beasts called stobors. The attack is repulsed, but not without casualties, including the death of Grant. Shortly after Rod is elected mayor, rescue parties arrive. Rod does not want to leave his newfound tropical home, but he is persuaded to do so by his sister and the thought of being reunited with his family. Within months, however, Rod is leading his own band of colonists to one of the distant planets.

CHARACTERS: At the beginning of the novel, teenager **Rod Walker** is described by his advisor, Dr. Matson, as being a romantic, "too emotional, too sentimental to be a real survivor type." As a result of his experiences on the tropical planet, however, Rod changes into a mature, self-sufficient, practical young man who becomes an accomplished, efficient leader. Rod is an idealist with old-fashioned attitudes concerning the position of women in society and macho superiority. These beliefs fortunately change through contact with such strong women as Caroline. At first, Rod wants to be the group leader but is inclined to be bossy, impatient, and overly sensitive to criticism. He also has a tendency to jump to conclusions. Rod is touchy about his position in the group and feels disgraced and rejected when Grant wins the first election to be leader. Later, Rod learns to trust others and to live with the will of the majority. He becomes more thoughtful, considerate, and unselfish.

Rod is an inventive, enterprising young man who has a great talent for organizing others and respecting their rights. He is a good strategist and is able to predict future needs of the group. However, his warnings about the vulnerability of the colony and the necessity of moving go unheeded, with disastrous results. Rod is able to instill discipline and respect in others, mainly because he sets an example of bravery and sacrifice. When he becomes mayor after Grant's death, he is conscientious and prudent

A group of young men and women learn to survive in an alien world in this science fiction coming-of-age story.

in fulfilling his duties and completely devoted to making the colony safe and prosperous. He again feels destroyed and rebuffed, however, when his colleagues decide to return to Terra. Nevertheless, he now knows that his future lies in leading other groups to form interstellar colonies.

Rod's teacher in the survival course is **Doctor Matson**, nicknamed the **Deacon**. Tough and uncompromising, Matson is cynical, difficult, and stern. Jimmy calls him "a cold-hearted fish" who "would eat his own grandmother . . . without salt." He is a short, spare man with "a leathery face, a patch over one eye, and most of three fingers missing." Through many bitter experiences, he has learned the qualities necessary for endurance and survival. A firm disciplinarian and complete realist, he gives good counsel to Rod. The Deacon is so impressed by the wisdom of Helen's advice to Rod that he courts her as tenaciously as he browbeats his students. Realizing that he was becoming a cranky old bachelor, he eventually marries Helen and begins a new life as a farmer.

Rod's sister, **Helen Walker**, is an Assault Captain in the army. Ten years older than Rod, she is a tough, practical go-getter with a proven record for leadership and fortitude. Helen is used to handling difficult situations and is proud of getting straight A's in emotional logic and military administration. She is skilled in the use of her knife, Lady Macbeth, which she later gives to Rod. Rugged and sturdy, she is also a dutiful daughter to her parents and an attentive sister to Rod. Helen gives excellent advice to Rod concerning survival needs and later proves to be a suitable marital match for the Deacon.

Rod's best friend is **Jimmy Throxton**, a wisecracking, good-natured young man who is always joking and easing difficult situations with his humor. When found in the jungle by Rod and Jackie, he is near death. After being nursed back to health, he shows his gratitude by being a loyal friend and staunch ally to both of them. More practical and cautious than Rod, he has a generous, unselfish nature and an ability to place people at ease. At one point Jackie says, "Someday I am going to make you take life seriously." She does so by marrying Jimmy and later presenting him with their first child.

The first person Rod encounters on the alien planet is **Jackie Daudet**, who he at first thinks is a boy because of her lithe, firm body and powerful movements. Not wishing to be pampered because of her sex, Jackie goes along with the misconception until Jimmy discovers the truth. She is a skilled woodsman and adept hunter and proves to be more observant about their environment than Rod. A logical thinker and good judge of situations, Jackie is capable of assuming responsibilities and giving expert advice.

The first elected leader of the group is **Grant Cowper**, a handsome college student with a curly, short beard. A government studies major, he impresses everyone with his knowledge, eloquence, and confidence. A bright, intelligent young man, he soon realizes that the theories he has mastered are difficult to put into practice. He over-organizes the colony and is inclined to play favorites. Grant, however, is willing to listen and change and, in time, develops into a highly respected and admired leader. Gradually, Rod loses his feelings of jealousy and becomes Grant's best friend and most trusted advisor. This loved and respected leader is killed during the battle to save the colony from rampaging animals.

There are a number of other interesting members of the commune. The Zulu named **Caroline Mshiyeni** is as "strong as an ox and absolutely fearless." At first, she is fiercely independent, but she learns to cooperate with Rod, whom she adores. Dependable and trustworthy, she also has a wonderful sense of humor and amazing abilities as a hunter. **Bob Baxter** is a Quaker boy who has a gentle, benevolent disposition. He falls in love with and marries **Carmen Garcia**, a practical but emotional girl. Carmen and Bob are faithful, dependable friends and supporters of Rod. In the midst of the animal attack, Carmen gives birth to a girl, the first born in the colony. **Roy Kilroy**, another of the college students, is a decent, understanding, courageous young man who braves the unknown to accompany Rod on the expedition to find better living quarters. When his position of power in the colony as deputy mayor is later given by Grant to Rod, Roy accepts his demotion without complaint or rancor. The two troublemakers in the colony are the lazy, fractious brothers **Jock** and **Bruce McGowan**. Rebellious and insolent, they refuse to cooperate in any of the colony's projects. Jock later dies after being expelled from the colony, and Bruce is beaten into submission by an angry mob tired of his impudence and indolence.

Stranger in a Strange Land

(science fiction, 1973)

PLOT: The spacecraft *Champion* arrives on our planet Terra from an expedition to Mars, bringing with it Valentine Michael Smith. He is the son of two of the original colonists who had been on the first Mars expedition twenty-five years earlier. After all the humans died, Mike, who is also called the Man from Mars, was raised by Martians and mastered their unusual mental powers, including their ability to "grok." To grok is to comprehend and absorb the essences of ideas, situations, or people. Mike has also developed an astonishing capacity to love other beings.

Mike is taken to Bethesda Medical Center, but he is far from safe. Crack newspaper reporter Ben Caxton is suspicious and fearful that Mike, who can claim possession of Mars through an obscure international agreement, might be the target of the Federation. The Federation is an international union of states led by Secretary General Joseph Douglas. Ben contacts his girlfriend, Gillian "Jill" Boardman, a nurse at the hospital, and they uncover a plot to dispose of Mike. After Ben mysteriously disappears, Jill flees with Mike to the home of Ben's friend, Jubal Harshaw, a curmudgeon and genius who lives on an estate in the Poconos. Jubal has three attractive secretaries, Dorcus, Anne, and Miriam, and a valuable handyman, Duke.

At the estate, Mike slowly adjusts to Terran ways. His newfound friends marvel at his amazing powers and his angelic innocence. Jubal contacts Douglas through Madame Becky Vesant, the astrologer of Douglas's wife, Agnes, and an agreement is reached. Mike gives up his claim to Mars (but keeps the accumulated wealth of the original expedition's participants), Ben is released, and Douglas becomes Mike's financial advisor.

Mike learns about Terran religion when he visits the Archangel Foster Tabernacle and meets Bishop Digby and a true believer, Dawn Ardent. Mike decides he wants to travel the world, and with Jill, who is now his lover, he becomes the circus magician Dr. Apollo. They are joined by Patty Paiwonski, a tattooed lady stripper. Failing in show business, Mike realizes that his true mission is to guide humans in the ways of the Martians. He founds a study and meditation center, which includes living quarters, called "the Nest" for his inner circle of friends. But his purposes are misunderstood by the general public, and Mike is attacked by a mob. Although he could save himself, Mike instead becomes a martyr for his cause. Knowing that Mike's soul will continue to guide them from above, his followers disperse to spread his teachings.

CHARACTERS: When he arrives from Mars, the innocent, angelic **Valentine Michael Smith**, also known as **the Man from Mars**, knows no English, has never seen a woman, and doesn't know about sex (Martians are three-legged unisexuals). However, he is endowed with unusual mental powers, such as teleportation (the ability to use the mind to travel to different places while the body remains stationary), telekinesis (the ability to move objects with thought) and telepathy (the ability to enter another's mind). He is also able to make objects or people disappear and control his own metabolism. None of these powers are ever misused or abused by this gentle, saintly man. With his babyish features, sunny, childlike smile, and well-developed body, Mike reminds Jubal of Michelangelo's David. Mike has difficulty in grasping human concepts like evil and sex. Even the difference between fiction and nonfiction confuses him, but towering above the misunderstandings caused by his inexperience is the purity and virtue that he represents. He is a brilliant student and an astute observer of behavior. For example, Mike applies the lessons learned working in the circus when addressing crowds of followers. In time, he wields a messianic appeal. But although he is adored by others, he continues to live a simple, compassionate, and unselfishness life. Mike believes that there is a part of God in each of us and that our purpose in life is to love each other—physically and spiritually—as freely as possible. The last words of this Christ-like figure before the angry mob are "thou are god."

Mike's purity is nicely contrasted with the cynicism of **Jubal Harshaw**, the aging, successful writer and accomplished doctor and lawyer. A rugged individualist who would (and does) take on the entire Federation, Jubal is fearless and daring, but he is also pessimistic. He has cynical but discerning attitudes towards such institutions as organized religion, marriage, and politics. Glib, eloquent, witty, erudite, and irreverent, Jubal dominates all situations and conversations. Jubal is a devoted agnostic and sybarite, describing himself as "an almost extinct breed, an old-fashioned gentleman—which means I can be a cast-iron son of a bitch when it suits me." An older man with grey thatch on his chest but none on his head, Jubal was once a family man and had four daughters. Now he is content to live a secluded life of lazy luxury. Jubal is the first to realize the natural goodness and nobility of Mike and, in spite of his antisocial attitudes, grows to believe in Mike's message of love. On a visit to the Nest, he succumbs to the free love principle and is seduced by the voluptuous Dawn. Mike's death does not, as expected, reinforce Jubal's cynicism. Instead, it makes him a more staunch disciple. He allows his home to be the new headquarters of Mike's followers.

Jubal's three attractive female secretaries are Anne, Miriam, and Dorcus. **Anne** is blonde, pleasantly plump, efficient, and has total recall. In crises, she is the most calm and composed of the three. In spite of her Valkyrie appearance, she is always soft and gentle towards Mike. **Miriam**, a redhead of average size and weight, is also Jubal's attentive, devoted assistant. Dark and slender, **Dorcus** is more emotional than the others and tends to cry under stress. She is noted for her needlepoint. All three are excellent cooks and later become Mike's converts. **Pete** is Jubal's chief handyman and mechanical wizard. A man of very ordinary tastes and attitudes, he rejects Mike because Mike adheres to the Martian practice of eating the dead. Later, he reconciles these differences and leaves Jubal's employ to be a deacon in the Nest, hoping one day to be a priest.

Gillian (Jill) Boardman is a competent nurse and a very attractive woman whose "hobby is men." High-principled and ethical, she believes in fair play and justice. These are the qualities that steer her into helping Mike get out of the hospital, though in doing so she risks her career and even her life. She is inclined to be sentimental and emotional and is somewhat puritanical and prudish about sex. However, under the influence of Mike, Jill loses her inhibitions, practices free love, and becomes a High Priestess of Mike's sect. Though Mike offers to marry her, Jill says that in marriage they "wouldn't be any closer."

Jill's former boyfriend is **Ben Caxton**, an enterprising, tenacious newspaperman noted for his muckraking column, "The Crow's Nest." A persistent, aggressive fighter for justice, he is highly regarded for his decency and honesty. He takes risks and "skates close to the edge; that's how he made his reputation." At first, Ben is mortified by the orgies and free love practiced by Mike and his followers, but, after becoming more closely acquainted with the essence of their beliefs (which includes a night with Dawn) he changes his mind and becomes a supporter. The Secretary General of the Federation of Free Nations is His Excellency the Honorable **Joseph Edgerton Douglas**. Despite the title, Douglas is far from honorable. He is a willful, determined, unscrupulous politician who will resort to kidnapping and perhaps murder to protect and preserve his shaky administration. Jubal capitalizes on Douglas's lust for power and prestige by negotiating a contract with him to be the custodian of Mike's affairs. Behind Joe's bluster is his domineering, shrewd wife, **Agnes Douglas**, the "power behind the throne." She is an impatient, demanding, forceful woman who takes charge in times of crises and makes decisions for her husband. Knowledgeable about foreign affairs and the use of effective strategies, she also has an influential advisor, **Madame Alexandra (Allie) Vesant**. Allie is a plump astrologer who has many distinguished clients and a "talent for the right answers." She is a dear friend of Jubal and plays an instrumental part in effecting a settlement of Mike's financial affairs with Douglas. Like so many others, Allie falls under the spell of Mike and his teachings and becomes a member of the Nest.

Two of Mike's most devoted followers are Dawn and Patty. **Dawn Ardent**, "the highest paid peeler in all Baja California," is devoted to both the art of striptease and her spiritual health. Mike first meets

Dawn while she is a member of the Archangel Foster Tabernacle of the Church of the New Revelation. Later, this cheerful, direct, good-hearted woman becomes a High Priestess in Mike's sect. Mike and Jill first meet **Mrs. Patty Paiwonski** as fellow circus performers. Patty is a completely tattooed lady who performs nude using only her pet twelve-foot boa constrictor, Honey Bun, to cover her body. Her late lamented husband, George, was the artist who covered every inch of her body with scenes from the Bible and other inspirational texts. "A living comic strip" now pushing fifty, Patty is a good-natured, generous, little butterball. She is adored by her friends, including Mike, who eagerly admits this unselfish, caring, earthy woman into his inner circle.

Further Reading

Authors and Artists for Young Adults. Vol. 17. Detroit: Gale Research, 1995.

Berger, Laura Standley, ed. *Twentieth-Century Young Adult Writers.* 1st ed. Detroit: St. James, 1994.

Chevalier, Tracy, ed. *Twentieth-Century Children's Writers.* 3rd ed. Chicago: St. James, 1989.

Contemporary Literary Criticism. Vols. 1, 3, 8, 14, 26, 55. Detroit: Gale Research, 1973, 1975, 1978, 1980, 1983, 1989.

Franklin, H. Bruce. *Robert A. Heinlein: America as Science Fiction.* New York: Oxford University Press, 1980.

Greenberg, Martin H. *Robert A. Heinlein.* New York: Taplinger, 1978.

Kirkpatrick, D. L., ed. *Twentieth-Century Children's Writers.* 2nd ed. New York: St. Martin's, 1983.

Olander, Joseph D., and Martin Harry Greenberg, eds. *Robert A. Heinlein.* New York: Taplinger, 1978.

Rose, Lois, and Stephen Rose. *The Shattered Ring: Science Fiction and the Quest for Meaning.* Louisville: John Knox, 1970.

Slusser, George Edgar. *Robert A. Heinlein: Stranger in His Own Land.* San Bernardino, CA: Borgo, 1976.

———. *The Classic Years of Robert A. Heinlein.* San Bernardino, CA: Borgo, 1977.

Something about the Author. Vols. 9, 69. Detroit: Gale Research, 1976, 1992.

Stover, Leon E. *Robert A. Heinlein.* Boston: Twayne, 1987.

Ward, Martha, ed. *Authors of Books for Young People.* 3rd ed. Metuchen, NJ: Scarecrow, 1990.

Watson, Noelle, ed. *Twentieth-Century Science Fiction Writers.* 3rd ed. Chicago: St. James, 1991.

Joseph Heller

1923-, American novelist

Catch-22

(novel, 1961)

PLOT: Originally called *Catch-18,* the title of Heller's novel was changed to avoid confusion with *Mila 18* by Leon Uris, author of *Exodus. Catch-22* has no plot in the conventional sense, but is rather a pattern of interrelated themes that combine to form an artistic statement on the human condition. It is an intricately designed work with a complex structure and a legion of characters. The use of irony, wit, satire, and sarcasm exposes human follies, all made more palatable by humor. As Heller once explained, "I wanted people to laugh and then look back with horror at what they were laughing at."

Some of the themes tendered in the novel include: the absurdity and immorality of war; the fact that war favors only those who are power-mad and exploitative; the tendency for war to further alienate and depersonalize modern society; the hypocritical nature of what society claims to want in war and peace; the fact that people are alienated from each other, their feelings, and their nature; and the breakdown of communications on all societal levels. The setting for the novel is the fictitious island of Pianosa in the Mediterranean. Two places in particular—Yossarian's tent and a hospital—provide the focus and home base for the men, who are enduring war on this small island. On Pianosa they escape the absurdities and incredible horrors experienced in Europe during the mid-1940s.

Rather than describing the experience of World War II through the eyes of a main character, the author uses many devices to introduce his ideas and themes concerning the absurdity of war. In this way, such characters as Colonel Cathcart, Hungry Joe, Major Major Major Major, Captain Black, Milo

Alan Arkin (left) as Yossarian in the 1970 adaptation of Heller's anti-war novel, Catch-22.

Minderbinder, Aardvark, Appleby, Cargill, Clevinger, Chaplain, and Nurse Duckett—among many others—permeate the story. Essentially, however, the story centers around Yossarian—the antihero and everyman—pausing now and again to look in on another character.

CHARACTERS: Yossarian, a captain and a man who loves culture and travel, is one of the great "dropouts" in American literature. He rejects the system, finding himself in total opposition to all the powers that be. He enters the war with courage—but no particular illusions—and soon finds that he can't live within the establishment's rules because it treats people as mere objects, using war more as a means to regulate others than to establish an objective.

Although he is given no physical description, Yossarian describes himself as a "Supra-man"—a stronger and more powerful version of ordinary people. He has the ability to question the values and mores he sees around him. When society turns against human values, Yossarian remembers that there is a higher law than that of the state. He comes to believe that perhaps in history there are times when a new kind of hero is needed. Yossarian takes a long time to comprehend that he must reject the system around him. He is slow to realize that a person who is sensitive to injustice and inhumanity can't endure the wartime predicament in which he finds himself. But this long delay in self-realization allows the reader to survey—through the actions of numerous characters and the terrible absurdities of battle—the prevailing system responsible for the chaos and inhumanity that Yossarian rejects. As an idealist, Yossarian must come to the painful conclusion that it is impossible to reach a compromise with an oppressive authority without losing one's identity.

Three particularly offensive characters—Colonel Cathcart, Captain Black, and Milo Minderbinder—are poignant examples of what is wrong in society. **Colonel Cathcart** is the arch-villain who puts a premium on conformity. Increasing risks for the men who fly combat missions in order to make himself look good, he is the epitome of the leader who uses other people to advance his own interests. The men are led to believe that they will be rotated to noncombat duties after flying a certain number of missions. But Cathcart keeps raising the number—so much so that some of the men nearly go insane and others plot to kill him. Cathcart embodies the idea of a system that thrives on petty rivalries and insecurity. Another authoritative figure is **Captain Black**, an intelligence officer. He enjoys watching the struggles of those who must endure combat while he sits comfortably out of the line of fire. Captain Black serves to represent the politics of the postwar world, when it became "fashionable" to discredit and embarrass political opponents. Perhaps the most frightening character in the novel, however, is mess officer **Milo Minderbinder**, who is the picture of amoral avarice. He is not above making a profit out of war and, what is worse, sees nothing wrong with anything he does. When Milo bombs his own squadron, his books show that he made an enormous profit, which makes his deed justifiable to his mind.

Other characters in the story, while not overtly evil, have serious flaws. Veteran combat flier **Hungry Joe** believes sex is dirty and feels guilty if he indulges in it. His guilt and repressed sexual behavior cause him to accept undue hardships in war. He has been thoroughly conditioned to fear freedom and self-expression, which are what he wants most. **Major Major Major Major** is the squadron commander. The story of his life dramatizes the breakdown of communication in society and the corruption of long-held American institutions. His self-righteous father could think of nothing more self-aggrandizing than to give his son the family surname for his first and middle names, too, and when he achieved the rank of major, his name became even more redundant. **Aardvark**, or "**Aarfy**," is a bombardier whose name means "earth-pig." He is one of Yossarian's pet antagonists, preoccupied with grinning at other people's feelings. Since he pays more attention to what others are doing than to his own responsibilities, he manages to get the squadron lost when he serves as lead bombardier. Aarfy denies his dependence on other people by disparaging them. **Appleby** is an air force officer who accepts any answer given by authority. He is an all-American boy, undisturbed by the big issues such as religion or social law. Yossarian's intelligence and antiestablishment views place Appleby in constant trouble.

Colonel Cargill of Special Services exposes the absurdity in military life. He is known for his ability to run even the most prosperous business into the ground, which is not easy, as Heller points out, because the government helps businesses in every possible way. When the troops rebel against having even their entertainment selected for them, Cargill is sent to "force" them to enjoy the prescribed shows. **Clevinger** is an air force officer who takes language at its face value, earnestly defending commonly held positions. This allows Yossarian to demonstrate his own sensitive perception of life. **Nurse Duckett** is a character in conflict who vacillates between what she truly wants and what she feels she should want due to external considerations. When Yossarian makes a pass at her, she reports him, but she eventually enjoys a happy relationship with him. Later she marries a doctor so she can be financially secure. Perhaps the only other really admirable character in the novel is **Chaplain**, who, like Yossarian, develops as a person through the course of the novel and in many ways becomes its most thoroughly developed character. He tries to give some broader meaning to his own life by reaching other people, though he realizes that the men resent his efforts to improve their morale.

Further Reading

Aldridge, John W. "*Catch-22*: Twenty-Five Years Later." *Michigan Quarterly Review* 26 (spring 1987).

Bloom, Harold. *Twentieth-Century American Literature.* Vol. 3. New York: Chelsea House, 1986.

Contemporary Literary Criticism. Vols. 1, 3, 5, 8, 11, 36. Detroit: Gale Research, 1973, 1975, 1976, 1978, 1979, 1986.

Helterman, Jeffrey, and Richard Layman, eds. *American Novelists since World War II.* Vol. 2 of *Dictionary of Literary Biography.* Detroit: Gale Research, 1978.

Henderson, Lesley, ed. *Contemporary Novelists.* 5th ed. Detroit: St. James, 1991.

Kostelanetz, Richard, ed. *American Writing Today.* Troy, NY: Whitston, 1991.

Merrill, Robert. *Joseph Heller.* New York: Twayne, 1987.

———. "The Structure and Meaning of *Catch-22.*" *Studies in American Fiction* 14 (autumn 1986).

Pinsker, Sanford. *Understanding Joseph Heller.* Columbia: University of South Carolina, 1991.

Rood, Karen L., Jean W. Ross, and Richard Ziegfield, eds. *Dictionary of Literary Biography Yearbook: 1980.* Detroit: Gale Research, 1981.

Ruderman, Judith. *Joseph Heller.* New York: Continuum, 1991.

Sorkin, Adam J., ed. *Conversations with Joseph Heller.* Jackson: University Press of Mississippi, 1993.

Walden, Daniel, ed. *Twentieth-Century American-Jewish Fiction Writers.* Vol. 28 of *Dictionary of Literary Biography.* Detroit: Gale Research, 1984.

Ernest Hemingway

1899-1961, American novelist

The Old Man and the Sea

(novel, 1952)

PLOT: For the past eighty-four days, the old man Santiago, who fishes off the coast of Cuba close to Havana, has not caught a single fish. His luck is so bad that Manolin, the young boy who usually accompanies him, has been ordered by his father to go fishing with more fortunate fishermen. The next morning, believing that his luck will change, Santiago rows out alone in his battered skiff far into the gulf, where, as he had hoped, he hooks a huge marlin, the largest the old man has ever encountered. For the next three days, there is a monumental battle between man and fish that tests the strength of both to the breaking point. Never letting go of the line, Santiago grabs a few mouthfuls of raw fish he has caught and maintains his spirits and determination by talking to himself about life's problems and the need for tenacity and steadfastness.

Finally, the fish, which proves to be two feet longer than the skiff, surfaces and is harpooned to death by Santiago, who has grown to love and respect his adversary. After strapping the monster to his boat, Santiago heads for port, but the scent of the marlin's blood attracts sharks. With incredible force and determination, he fights off each attack, but the sharks overwhelm him and devour the fish leaving only the head, tail, and a bare skeleton. On the morning of the fourth day, he returns to his village defeated and exhausted, but he is also the object of admiration of the other fisherman. Manolin nurses him, brings him food, and vows to rejoin his friend as his helper. The next day, the indomitable old man, now accompanied by Manolin, again carries the mast down to his boat ready to try his luck again.

CHARACTERS: Santiago, the old but far from senile hero of this short novel, is described as "thin and gaunt with deep wrinkles in the back of his neck." His face is covered with the brown blotches of skin cancer and his hands are scarred from rope burns caused by handling heavy fish. The author says, "Everything about him was old except his eyes and they were cheerful and undefeated." Though living in abject poverty in a tiny shack with scarcely any possessions, he has maintained his dignity and hope. Santiago is an amazing man, gentle in his relationship with the young boy, but not weak; he is proud without being boastful, and is always optimistic in spite of crushing reverses. Though he loves Manolin, he is fearful of becoming a burden to him and, therefore, rejects his offers of help and food. He is resigned to his life, accepting its tribulations and hardships without being submissive or surrendering.

Santiago is a simple man with few needs or desires. He is without bitterness or resentment, although he has suffered greatly throughout the years and has endured great loneliness and suffering. The loss of his wife is still so painful a memory that he has hidden her picture. In his past, while he was in Africa, there were moments of triumph: in one case he was given the name "Champion" because of his physical prowess. Never self-pitying, Santiago accepts his lot in life and bears each adversity with dignity and the will to continue. His pride forbids him to accept charity or borrow money, even though he is destitute. He feigns lack of hunger rather than accept a gift of food.

Santiago is a man of incredible strength and endurance. Determined to land the marlin, he exists for three days on only a little raw fish, a little water, and a few catnaps. His courage and fortitude are almost superhuman. Though in great physical pain from cramped, mutilated hands and back muscles that ache unbearably, he never gives in and instead says, "Fish, I'll stay with you until I am dead." Santiago is an expert fisherman and navigator, who knows the ocean, marine life, and the intricacies of playing the line and landing fish. He possesses a fine native intelligence, as well as impressive acquired skills. Most noteworthy is Santiago's relationship to nature and the creatures of the sea. He loves and respects the fish he is fated to kill and feels sorrow at inflicting pain on this noble creature. He talks to the fish, calls it "my brother," and regards him as more noble and more able than many humans. In his feelings about the oneness of all creatures, Santiago personifies the interrelationship between mankind and the natural world.

Santiago's best friend is the boy, **Manolin.** "The old man had taught the boy to fish and the boy loved him." Since Santiago took the boy out fishing when he was only five, there has developed a delicate, tender friendship between the two. Manolin respects and pities the old man but, though always anxious to help him, is careful not to insult his dignity and pride. His devotion is touching and responsive. When the old man is cold, he wraps him in his only blanket; he runs errands for him and, in spite of objections, brings Santiago beer and food. Manolin admits that he would steal if it would benefit the old man. The boy wants to be with this man whom he idolizes and reveres, but he unwillingly bows to his father's wishes to go out with other fisherman when Santiago's luck appears to have run out.

Manolin shares the old man's interest in American baseball. With rapt attention, the boy enjoys listening to Santiago's stories and opinions about the sport. He respects and heeds Santiago's evaluations of such teams as the "Indians of Cleveland" and shares his profound admiration of Joe DiMaggio. When Santiago returns defeated and injured, Manolin cries openly at the sight of the old man's wounded hands. Manolin readily admits the extent of his love for and devotion to Santiago. At one point he says, "There are many good fishermen and some great ones. But there is only you."

The **marlin** that becomes Santiago's powerful adversary is a majestic specimen that inspires both awe and love in the heart of the old man. "He was eighteen feet from nose to tail" and the largest fish caught in the Gulf waters. When he surfaces, Santiago sees that "He was bright in the sun and his head and back were dark purple and in the sun the stripes on his sides showed wide and a light lavender. His sword was as long as a baseball bat." During the three-day struggle, the fish arouses such admiration in Santiago that he calls him his brother and sympathizes with the suffering that the fish is enduring. Later, when he is killed and lashed to the side of the skiff, Santiago watches as his prize is ingloriously eaten by scavenging sharks. At this point he wishes that he had given the fish his freedom and allowed him to remain magnificent in his strength and splendor.

Further Reading

Baker, Carlos. *Hemingway and His Critics.* New York: Hill & Wang, 1961.

———. *Ernest Hemingway: A Life Story.* New York: Scribner's, 1969.

———. *Hemingway: The Writer as Artist.* 4th ed. Princeton: Princeton University Press, 1972.

Baker, Sheridan. *Ernest Hemingway: An Introduction and Interpretation.* New York: Holt, 1967.

Bloom, Harold, ed. *Ernest Hemingway.* New York: Chelsea House, 1985.

Brenner, Gary. *"The Old Man & the Sea": Story of a Common Man.* New York: Twayne, 1991.

Burgess, Anthony. *Ernest Hemingway and His World.* New York: Simon & Schuster, 1985.

Contemporary Literary Criticism. Vols. 1, 3, 6, 8, 10, 13, 19, 30, 34, 39, 41, 44, 50, 61, 80. Detroit: Gale Research, 1973, 1975, 1976, 1978, 1979, 1980, 1981, 1084, 1985, 1986, 1987, 1987, 1988, 1990, 1994.

Critical Survey of Long Fiction. Vol. 4. Englewood Cliffs, NJ: Prentice-Hall, 1983.

Croft, Steven. "Karl Jasper's Ideas on Tragedy and Hemingway's *The Old Man and the Sea.*" *Notes on Contemporary Literature* 25 (May 1995).

Daiches, David. *The Novel and the Modern World.* Chicago: University of Chicago Press, 1960.

Dictionary of Literary Biography Yearbook: 1981. Detroit: Gale Research, 1982.

Fenton, Charles A. *The Apprenticeship of Ernest Hemingway.* New York: Viking, 1958.

Gurko, Leo. *Ernest Hemingway and the Pursuit of Heroism.* New York: Crowell, 1968.

Hurley, C. Harold, ed. *Hemingway's Debt to Baseball in* The Old Man and the Sea. New York: Mellen, 1992.

Jobes, Katharine T., ed. *Twentieth-Century Interpretations of "The Old Man and the Sea": A Collection of Critical Essays.* Englewood Cliffs, NJ: Prentice-Hall, 1968.

Kimbel, Bobby Ellen, ed. *American Short-Story Writers, 1910-1945, Second Series.* Vol. 102 of *Dictionary of Literary Biography.* Detroit: Gale Research, 1991.

Lee, A. Robert, ed. *Ernest Hemingway: New Critical Essays.* Totowa, NJ: Barnes & Noble, 1983.

Martine, James J., ed. *American Novelists, 1910-1945.* Vol. 9 of *Dictionary of Literary Biography.* Detroit: Gale Research, 1981.

McCaffery, John K., ed. *Ernest Hemingway: The Man and His Work.* New York: Avon, 1950.

Mellow, James R. *Hemingway: A Life without Consequences.* Boston: Houghton Mifflin, 1992.

Messent, Peter. *Ernest Hemingway.* New York. St. Martin's, 1992.

Meyers, Jeffrey, ed. *Hemingway: A Biography.* New York: Harper, 1985.

———. *Hemingway: The Critical Years.* London: Routledge, 1982.

Morgan, Kathleen. "Santiago in *The Old Man and the Sea:* A Homeric Hero." *Hemingway Review* 12, no. 1 (fall 1992): 35-51.

Rood, Karen Lane, ed. *American Writers in Paris, 1920-1039.* Vol. 4 of *Dictionary of Literary Biography.* Detroit: Gale Research, 1980.

Twentieth-Century American Literature. Vol. 3 of *Chelsea House Library of Literary Criticism.* New York: Chelsea House, 1986.

Waldhorn, Arthur. *A Reader's Guide to Ernest Hemingway.* New York: Farrar, Straus, 1972.

Weeks, Robert P., ed. *Hemingway: A Collection of Critical Essays.* Englewood Cliffs, NJ: Prentice-Hall, 1962.

Young, Philip. *Ernest Hemingway: A Reconsideration.* University Park: Pennsylvania State University Press, 1966.

Frank Herbert

1920-1986, American science fiction writer

Dune

(science fiction, 1965)

PLOT: Translated into fourteen languages, *Dune* is one of the most popular science fiction novels ever published. Inspired by the environmental concerns that began to interest the public in the mid-1960s, most of the novel takes place on Arrakis, a desert planet also known as Dune. Its principal inhabitants are a militaristic people known as the Fremen and awesome sandworms so huge that they can swallow a person in one gulp.

Paul Atreides is the son and heir of an exiled royal family. As the story opens, he and his family are getting ready to depart for Arrakis, where they will take over as the ruling power. The novel centers on Paul's growth, both as a man and as a ruler. The Emperor has made a miscalculation by sending the Atreides family to the sand- and rock-filled planet Dune. It was intended as a place of exile and hardship, for even to cross the sand on Dune means encountering violent sandstorms that engulf travelers, or, worse still, the gigantic worms that burrow beneath the sand and suddenly burst forth to gulp down unwary victims.

But the Emperor does not count on Paul, son of Leto Atreides, known as the Red Duke, and Lady Jessica, the boy's mother. Paul thrives in the inhospitable atmosphere of Dune. Instead of fearing the warlike Fremen of the planet, he admires them for their courage and faithfulness. After his father is killed by the Atreides' rivals, the Harkonnens, Paul marshals the Fremen into a formidable fighting force. They are fanatical warriors who begin to look upon Paul as the man who was foretold to lead them to greatness. This gives Paul the military might that he needs, unmatched by any other in the entire empire. In addition, the Fremen have mastered the art of riding the awesome sandworms through the desert, a practice that Paul learns to perfection. Adding to his growing military power, Paul gains

Paul Atreides (Kyle MacLachlan) battles one of the evil Harkonnens (Sting) in the 1983 adaptation of **Dune.**

economic strength by controlling trade in melange, a spice produced by the gigantic worms that is essential for use in space navigation but is also highly addictive.

The novel centers on Paul's spiritual and physical growth as a leader of his people, as he tries to defeat the Harkonnens who have come to occupy Dune, seek revenge for his father's assassination, and bring peace and harmony to his adopted people. It is a constant tug-of-war as he wrestles with his conscience on the issues of power and truth. In the end, however, Paul proves to be a good man and a dedicated leader, defeating the Harkonnens.

Herbert wrote three sequels to Dune: Dune Messiah *(1970),* Children of Dune *(1976), and* God, Emperor of Dune *(1981).*

CHARACTERS: Paul Atreides is an intelligent, inquisitive boy who grows into a charismatic leader on the planet Arrakis. Known as the "one who points the way," he becomes the spiritual leader of the fanatical Fremen. He himself is the result of a breeding process that is run by the mysterious Bene Gesserit women, who have long been trying to breed a person who will be deemed capable of shaping the future. The result of this effort is Paul, a composite of a long line of ancestors who have come alive in him. As such, he struggles against Bene Gesserit control as he seeks to lead his people. At times he is forced to choose between personal sacrifice and tragedy for his followers. The choice is made more difficult by Paul's inconsistency with his visions of the future. The visions, which suggest possible courses of action but do not provide direct answers, come about as an effect of the melange spice to which he has become addicted. Paul therefore can't always foresee what will happen, which sometimes causes him to make wrong or uncertain choices.

Paul is an allegorical figure in the novel. Although he himself is a good man, his efforts to help his followers lead to chaos. When the independent Fremen eventually surrender their freedom to him because they consider Paul to be a prophet, they upset the balance of nature on Arrakis. When the balance of nature is upset, the entire ecosystem begins to come apart. It is this struggle to balance nature that is the recurring theme of the novel.

Leto Atreides, Paul's father, is frequently referred to as the Red Duke. He is a distant cousin of the Emperor, and his family is a rival of the Harkonnens. Unfortunately, the Atreides are on the losing side of the feud, and Leto is captured by the Harkonnens and killed. His death fuels Paul's desire to fight the Harkonnens on Dune. Paul's mother, **Lady Jessica**, is a former concubine of Leto Atreides. According to the Bene Gesserit breeding program, she was ordered to produce a daughter, but for reasons not explained, she defied the orders and produced a son. This should have been a warning to the Bene Gesserits that there might be some danger in regarding Paul as the ultimate product of their breeding program.

Vladimir Harkonnen, commonly referred to as the Baron, is a direct descendent of Bashar Abulurd Harkonnen, who was once banished for cowardice. Before Paul's birth, the Bene Gesserits had planned to breed the daughter from a union between Lady Jessica and Vladimir's nephew. Vladimir is a ruthless tyrant who will do anything to exterminate Paul's family. He is eventually killed by his own granddaughter.

The **Fremen** of Dune are a collection of free tribes on Arrakis, remnants of the Zensunni Wanderers, or Sand Pirates. They are warriors whom Paul admires for their courage and faithfulness. Tough and fanatical in a fight, they are unmatched by any other military group in the Empire.

Further Reading

Berger, Laura Standley, ed. *Twentieth-Century Young Adult Writers.* 1st ed. Detroit: St. James, 1994.

Bleiler, E. F. *Science Fiction Writers.* New York: Scribner's, 1982.

Contemporary Literary Criticism. Vols. 12, 23, 35, 44, 85. Detroit: Gale Research, 1980, 1983, 1985, 1987, 1995.

McNelly, Willis E. *The Dune Encyclopedia.* New York: Putnam, 1984.

O'Reilly, Timothy. *Frank Herbert.* New York: Ungar, 1981.

Something about the Author. Vols. 9, 37. Detroit: Gale Research, 1976, 1985.

Touponce, William F. *Frank Herbert.* Boston: Twayne, 1988.

Watson, Noelle, ed. *Twentieth-Century Science Fiction Writers.* 3rd ed. Chicago: St. James, 1991.

Hermann Hesse

1877-1962, German novelist

Siddhartha

(novel, 1922)

PLOT: Siddhartha, whose name means "he who is on the right road," is born into a Brahmin family and has a tranquil and innocent childhood. Even so, the young man is unable to find inner peace and has recurring disquieting dreams. No one can lead him to the discovery of Self, and so Siddhartha searches for Atman, the individual spirit or Self that is within him. Siddhartha comes to believe that his father is not experiencing Self and so, at some unspecified time, he decides to leave his father's home and join the Samanas. His friend and confidant, Govinda, goes with him. The Samanas are emaciated ascetics who practice meditation and extreme self-denial. They believe that life is but an illusion. Siddhartha remains with them for three years.

Siddhartha attempts to gain salvation through asceticism but finds himself far from knowledge and wisdom. He decides to leave the Samanas, feeling once again that he is learning about life secondhand. Then Gotama Buddha arrives. "Buddha" means "to know," and he has attained Nirvana, which means he has found perfection and no longer needs to struggle through endless cycles of reincarnation. Siddhartha and Govinda go to hear the teachings of Buddha, who describes the Four Noble Truths of Buddhism: the existence of pain, the cause of pain being desire or attachment, enduring pain by suppressing desire, and the Eightfold Path to salvation, including right faith, right life, right language, right purpose, right practice, right effort, right thinking, and right meditation. Govinda will become the Buddha's disciple, but Siddhartha must find his own way to salvation.

Alone now, Siddhartha experiences an awakening in which he sheds his old self. With this awakening, he crosses into the sensual world. It is the ferryman, Vasudeva, who takes Siddhartha across the river into the city where he meets the beautiful Kamala. Because he can read and write, he becomes the partner of the merchant Kamaswami. The years pass, and Kamala is expecting a child. After some twenty years in the city, Siddhartha returns to the river where he will learn from it and the ferryman by going through a kind of psychoanalysis. More time passes and Siddhartha's son is now grown. He knows that the son, just as the father, will have to go away and learn about himself on his own. When the boy leaves, the father experiences the pain of love directly.

Govinda now meets Siddhartha, an old man, at the river. Siddhartha tries to explain to his old friend how he has attained inner peace from the river and the ferryman. Govinda kisses his friend on the forehead and feels that he has touched eternity. Govinda, like Siddhartha, has attained Nirvana.

CHARACTERS: Siddhartha, a Hindu, grows from the impatience of youth to young adulthood and finally to the wisdom of old age. Although he disagrees with his father on how to achieve Nirvana, that is his goal, just as it is his father's. The son's life is filled with different stages that he must endure in order to reach the desired state. His search, as he learns, can't be completed through teachings but only through experiencing life firsthand. It is through the river that Siddhartha is able to find the revelations that lead to wisdom and the depth of his ancestral soul.

Siddhartha's friend and confidant, **Govinda**, will also attain Nirvana, but he is slower to do so. At first, unlike Siddhartha, he believes that he can reach Nirvana through years of learning and study. With time, however, he comes to realize what his friend seems to know instinctively: that the goal can be reached only through direct, firsthand experience. Govinda reaches this state when he is reunited with Siddhartha at the river. Although Govinda functions as Siddhartha's shadow throughout the novel, he is able to reach Nirvana on his own, not as a disciple of his friend.

Kamala symbolizes the expression of Hindu love. She is the opposite of the attainment of Nirvana, functioning as the key to sensual desire. However, like Siddhartha she realizes that love can't be given out indirectly but must be experienced firsthand. In the novel, she is transformed and becomes a follower of Buddhism.

The ferryman, the enlightened **Vasudeva**, shows Siddhartha that the river can be a teacher. First, he takes Siddhartha across the river to the city. Once there, Siddhartha works for the wealthy merchant **Kamaswami**, whose name means "master of the material world." Siddhartha then returns to the river for his final enlightenment. The ferryman symbolizes Krishna, the teacher and human incarnation of the Hindu deity Vishnu.

The supreme god of Buddhism is **Gotama Buddha**, meaning the "enlightened" or "illustrious." He has reached Nirvana, which is the supreme goal for Buddhism. It is a kind of salvation attained through the process of rebirth and by stamping out personal desires. What the Buddhist is seeking is to extinguish all desires and thus end the cycle of life, death, and rebirth, which is associated with evil because it prevents humans from finding their souls. When the cycle has been broken, a person attains Being. Both meditation and thought are the highest processes of human existence, which is why the Buddha is usually depicted in a posture of meditation, signifying that he has reached Nirvana.

Further Reading

Bardine, Byran A. *Hermann Hesse's* Siddhartha *as Divine Comedy*. Dayton, OH: University of Dayton Review, 1993-94.

Boulby, Mark. *Hermann Hesse: His Mind and Art.* Ithaca, NY: Cornell University Press, 1967.

Casebeer, Edwin F. *Hermann Hesse.* New York: Crowell, 1972.

Contemporary Literary Criticism. Vols. 1, 2, 3, 6, 11, 17, 25, 69. Detroit: Gale Research, 1973, 1974, 1975, 1976, 1979, 1981, 1983, 1992.

Field, George W. *Hermann Hesse.* New York: Twayne, 1970.

Freedman, Ralph. *The Lyrical Novel: Studies in Hermann Hesse, Andre Gide, and Virginia Woolf.* Princeton: Princeton University Press, 1963.

Mileck, Joseph. *Hermann Hesse: Life and Art.* Berkeley: University of California Press, 1978.

Something about the Author. Vol. 50. Detroit: Gale Research, 1988.

Zeller, B. *Portrait of Hesse: An Illustrative Biography.* New York: McGraw-Hill, 1971.

Ziolkowski, Theodora. *The Novels of Hermann Hesse.* Princeton: Princeton University Press, 1965.

———. *Hesse: A Collection of Critical Essays.* Englewood Cliffs, NJ: Prentice-Hall, 1973.

S. E. Hinton

1950-, American young adult novelist

The Outsiders

(young adult novel, 1967)

PLOT: While returning home one evening, fourteen-year-old Ponyboy Curtis narrowly escapes being mugged by members of the Socials—or Socs—street gang, well-off kids who drive around in expensive cars. Ponyboy and his brothers are members of the rival gang, the Greasers, hoods from poor neighborhoods who sport long hair and wear leather. Since his parents' death in a car accident, Ponyboy has been living with his two older brothers, twenty-year-old Darren—who prefers to be called Darry—a sullen, moody, intelligent young man who works in construction, and carefree, outgoing Sodapop, a sixteen-year-old school dropout who works in a garage. Other members of the Greasers include Dally Winston, a dangerous brawler, and Johnny Cade, or Johnnycake, a pathetic loner who is unwanted at home but finds a sense of family with the Greasers.

At a drive-in movie, Ponyboy and Johnny have a pleasant time with two Soc girls, Cherry Valance and her friend, Marcia. But later in the evening the boys are attacked by Socs. In order to save Ponyboy, Johnny pulls a switchblade and kills the Soc leader, Bob Sheldon. The boys panic and seek out Dally, who gives them money and directions to a town nearby where they can hide in an abandoned church. After a week, Dally shows up to check on them. When a fire breaks out in the church, all three risk their lives to save some entrapped children, but Johnny is critically injured when a flaming timber falls on him, breaking his back. The three return as celebrities. Darry's emotional greeting convinces Ponyboy, who always thought Darry didn't like him, that his brother really does care.

The Socs stage a rumble to avenge their leader's death but are defeated by the Greasers. However, after Johnny's death in the hospital, Dally goes berserk and robs a store at gun-point. The gang sees him shot down in the street by policemen. Sickened by the fighting that has left three dead, Ponyboy and some other gang members talk of stopping the senseless violence. A court inquiry is held, and Ponyboy is cleared of manslaughter charges for the death of Bob Sheldon. He is not sent to a foster home as he had feared. From this terrible ordeal, stronger bonds of love and loyalty have developed among the three brothers.

CHARACTERS: This novel, with its exploration of the causes and consequences of gang mentality, caused a stir when it was first published, both for its realism and the fact that it was written by a seventeen-year-old girl. It is based on actual events that occurred at her Tulsa, Oklahoma, high school. The novel's narrator is **Ponyboy Curtis**, a quiet, sensitive boy who hides his true feelings under a tough exterior. Proud of his long hair, jeans, leather jacket, and manly demeanor, he really longs to read, watch sunsets, and enjoy peaceful times. He is thoughtful, insightful, and intelligent. However, the macho image he is forced to adopt in his peer group, together with the absence of parental guidance and the constant threat of violence from the Socs, have forced him to accept and participate in the violent world of street gangs. He is courageous and fiercely loyal to both his brothers and his friends. On the other hand, his gentler nature is shown in the tender, caring relationship he has with his friend,

Johnny, his love of poetry, and the way he enjoys quiet moments with Cherry. For all his bravado, Ponyboy is often just a scared kid looking for security, direction, and love.

Now almost seventeen, **Sodapop Curtis** is Ponyboy's favorite brother. He is movie-star handsome, with fine features and a sensitive face. What endears him most to Ponyboy is his understanding and solicitous attitude. Unlike Darry, Sodapop always shows warmth and affection toward his younger brother. He also possesses an endearing, outgoing personality; he is charming, up-beat, and happy-go-lucky—a born teaser who loves company. Ponyboy says that Sodapop "gets drunk on just plain living." Sodapop's problem is that he has too much energy and channels some of his high spirits into street fighting. Beneath his exuberance and perpetual grin, Sodapop hides a sensitive nature. When his girlfriend, whom he loves dearly, breaks up with him, he is genuinely hurt and abandons his carefree, easygoing facade, if only for a short time. True to form, Sodapop eventually lands back on his feet.

Brother **Darry Curtis** is the hard-working, serious member of the family. Now age twenty, he shouldered the responsibility of keeping the family together after his parents' deaths. A bright, popular student and captain of the football team, he was compelled to give up plans to attend college to care for his brothers by taking a job as a roofer with a construction company. Tall, muscular, and handsome, Darry is a natural leader who is able to make difficult decisions tempered by a wisdom beyond his years. Ponyboy describes him as cool, smart, and hard, with a personality to match the iciness of his eyes; he initially considers Darry to be a dominating tyrant who is overly critical and unfeeling. Gradually, however, Ponyboy realizes that Darry is actually just being protective. He eventually acknowledges that Darry was demanding and harsh "because he cared; he was trying to make something of me." One of the most touching scenes in the novel takes place when Ponyboy returns home safely after the fire, and Darry, weeping for joy and relief, holds his brother in his arms.

Ponyboy's best friend is sixteen-year-old **Johnny Cade**, also known as **Johnnycake**. He is a pathetic, frightened outcast who finds love and attention by belonging to the Greasers. Growing up in a home where his father beats him unmercifully and his mother ignores him, he has found a new life as a member of a street gang. Like an abused puppy, he seeks someone to give him a sense of worth and direction. His idol becomes the violent, independent gang member Dally Winston, who is the incarnation of strength and manliness to Johnny. Although he is always self-deprecating, Johnny has many virtues: he is faithful and loyal to his friends, he kills in order to save his buddy Ponyboy, and at the fire he courageously sacrifices his own life to save children whom he says have more reason to live than he does. His conscience stricken by the death he has caused and sick of the life of violence on the streets, Johnnycake at one point says, "I can't take much more.... I'll kill myself." In some respects, his death provides him with an honorable way out of problems that are too much for him.

The fiercest Greaser is **Dally Winston**, a tough, proud hood who learned survival skills on the streets of New York and was first arrested at age ten. Accustomed to cheating, stealing, and even mugging small children, he is a symbol of fear even among the Greasers. His elfin face and pointy chin hide a wild, cunning nature that finds fulfillment only in violence and breaking the law. He partially redeems himself, however, by his gallant actions in saving the children during the fire and by his devotion to Johnny. Unable to express himself except through brute force, he is so upset at Johnny's death that he runs amuck and is killed. This is the culmination of an unfortunate life unconsciously bent on self-destruction.

Ponyboy is attracted to a bright young cheerleader, **Cherry Valance**, whom he first meets at a drive-in theater. Sharp, quick-witted, and independent, Cherry realizes the futility of gang warfare and expresses these feelings to Ponyboy. Unfortunately, she comes from the right side of the tracks and has allegiances with the Socs. When the violence escalates, she tries unsuccessfully to help bring peace. Throughout the novel, she articulates the social problems that cause gang formation and makes a plea for the fighting to end.

Rumble Fish

(young adult novel, 1975)

PLOT: In an unnamed coastal city where he moved after getting out of reform school, Rusty-James meets his old buddy Steve Hays, who is now attending college. The sight of Steve rekindles memories of events five years ago, when Rusty-James was fourteen. The rest of *Rumble Fish* is told in retrospect.

In the flashback, the gang—Steve, B. J. Jackson, Smokey Bennett, and Rusty-James—are hanging out at Benny's pool hall when news comes that Biff Wilcox plans to fight Rusty-James because of insults they traded at school. After making a fast visit to his girlfriend Patty's house, Rusty-James gathers up some friends and meets Biff and his crowd in a deserted parking lot. Even though Biff is two years older and carries a knife, Rusty-James knocks him to the ground. But Biff manages to grab his knife again and slashes Rusty-James in the back. The fight is stopped by Rusty-James's brother, seventeen-year-old Motorcycle Boy, a laconic, handsome loner who was once a respected gang leader but turned distant and moody some time before the main action of the novel takes place. Perhaps because of his many head injuries from gang fights, he suffers bouts of deafness and vision problems. Rusty-James adores his brother. His great ambition in life is to be just like him one day. At the time of the fight with Biff, Motorcycle Boy has just returned from a two-week trip on a stolen motorcycle, but, as usual, he is silent about details except to say he was in California. Under questioning he later admits that he has had the disillusioning experience of visiting their mother, the mistress of a Hollywood celebrity. At the time, Rusty-James and his brother are living with their father, a drunken ex-lawyer. Since his wife left him when the boys were children, their father has sunk into alcoholism and has started drawing welfare.

Events quickly turn against Rusty-James. He is temporarily expelled from school, and Patty's jealousy leads to a split in their relationship. One evening while trying to forget his woes, Rusty-James, along with Steve and Motorcycle Boy, visits the wild part of town. Steve, who doesn't ordinarily drink, becomes tipsy on cheap wine. After the three attend a pornographic film, Motorcycle Boy wanders off on his own, while the other two crash a party. In the early hours of the morning, they are waylaid by two hoodlums. Rusty-James is beaten, but Motorcycle Boy miraculously appears and saves them again. Because of this carousing, Steve is whipped and grounded by his father.

Rusty-James becomes increasingly worried about Motorcycle Boy's erratic antisocial behavior and begins following him. He finds that Motorcycle Boy spends hours at Mr. Dogson's pet store, looking at the caged animals and at the bowls containing Siamese fighting fish, which he calls rumble fish because they fight to the death when placed together. As feared, one night Motorcycle Boy loses his grip on reality. He breaks into the pet shop, frees the animals, and prepares to take the fish to the river. While Rusty-James is pleading for him to stop, the police arrive. But when Motorcycle Boy doesn't hear their commands he is shot. After Motorcycle Boy's death, Rusty-James is sent to a reform school. He emerges emotionless and sullen. Ironically, his wish to be just like his brother has been granted.

CHARACTERS: The narrator and protagonist of this novel is teenager **Rusty-James**. Because his mother abandoned the family when he was two years old and his father is now a helpless drunk, the boy has grown up without direction or guidance. He is basically a good kid with decent instincts, but he is so confused that his sense of values is distorted. He steals, drinks his father's booze, and skips school, where he is always in the "dumb" class. Status in his peer group is of paramount importance to him. He is number one in his gang, and he maintains this position through physical strength and bravado. Fighting to him is a stimulant that produces a drug-like high, yet there is still an emptiness in his life. As friend Steve says, "You're like a ball in a pinball machine. Getting slammed back and forth; and you never think about anything, about where you're going or how you're going to get there." Rusty-James's only anchor and model in life is his brother,

Motorcycle Boy, whom he worships. He comments at one point, "I wanted to be tough like him, and stay calm and laughing when things got dangerous." Unfortunately, his brother is even more mixed up than Rusty-James. When his idol is killed, Rusty-James is powerless to help himself and instead is fated to continue the same purposeless existence without hope or aspiration.

Motorcycle Boy is a complex, tragic figure. More than Rusty-James, he has felt the loneliness of being abandoned and neglected by his parents. At one time, he too was the leader of the gang, with a reputation for his fearless daring during rumbles. He has now given up the gang life, claiming it is no longer "fun." Instead he has become a loner—brooding, keeping to himself, rarely talking, yet still commanding the respect of those around him. This independent, self-reliant attitude makes him particularly attractive to Rusty-James. Motorcycle Boy, named because of his great interest in motorcycles, is tall and ruggedly handsome, with a shock of deep red hair and classic features. His father says of him, "He would have made a perfect knight in a different century.... He was born in the wrong era, on the wrong side of the river." Unlike the knights of old, however, Motorcycle Boy has no purpose or quest to which he can dedicate himself. He is a mixed-up rebel without a cause, who has good intentions but lacks the inner convictions and sense of purpose to turn his life around.

Though the two are completely different, Rusty-James's best friend is **Steve Hays**. Steve is a well-adjusted, studious young man, who comes from a respected, stable family with traditional middle-class values. A good and loyal friend, he repeatedly tries to help Rusty-James straighten out his life. Instead he finds that the association with this friend whom he loves is having the opposite effect and that he is gradually sinking into the same destructive habits (like drinking and stealing) that characterize Rusty-James's life. Realizing that this destructive behavior is a dead end, Steve breaks off their friendship. When the two meet years later, Steve is attending college and bound for a career in teaching.

Rusty-James's **father** is a failed lawyer whose life unraveled when his wife left him. Now a hopeless drunk on welfare, he is a pathetic individual. Although he is passive and harmless, Rusty-James finds it impossible to respect him because of his weak character and wishes he could love his father more.

Rusty-James's friends include **Patty**, his attractive blonde girlfriend, who becomes so tired of his erratic ways and his lack of a responsible attitude towards their relationship that she leaves him for **Smokey Bennett**. Named for the peculiar color of his eyes, Smokey is number two man in the gang. Less impulsive and more calculating than Rusty-James, he realizes the futility of fighting as a method of solving problems.

Tex

(young adult novel, 1979)

PLOT: Fourteen-year-old Tex McCormick and his seventeen-year-old brother, Mason—Mace for short—live together in a modest house some twenty miles from a large Oklahoma city. Their mother died when Tex was only three, and their father, a drifter who earns a living as a rodeo rider, is absent most of the time. Mace, who is a conscientious student and the star of his high school basketball team, hopes for a college sports scholarship to get away from this no-win situation. Tex, lacking direction, is an indifferent ninth-grade student who prefers making mischief over hitting the books. Mace conscientiously and efficiently manages the household, but because they haven't heard from their father for months their financial situation becomes so desperate that one day, while Tex is away, Mace sells their two horses to pay the gas bill. Tex is so devastated when he learns that his beloved Negrito is gone that he runs berserk in the house, and Mace has to resort to punching him to subdue his brother. In time the brothers make up, but Tex feels his brother only tolerates him.

The two brothers have friends in the neighboring Collins family. Mace's best friend was Lem Peters, but after Lem married his girlfriend, Connie, moved to the city, and began dealing drugs, Mace began hanging out with Bob Collins. Tex's closest pal is his classmate Johnny Collins, Bob's brother. Tex is also increasingly attracted to Johnny's younger sister, Jamie, a seventh-grader. After a doctor's appointment during which Mace learns that he has an ulcer, the boys offer a ride in their truck to a hitchhiker who pulls a gun on them. Through Tex's quick thinking, the young man, actually an escaped convict, is forced out of the truck and is later killed by the police. For a short time, the boys become local heroes. Several days later an apologetic Mr. McCormick appears and promises to reform.

When Tex pulls a seemingly harmless prank at school that ends disastrously, he is threatened with expulsion. Both his father and Mace are called to the school. During the ensuing confrontation, Mace, caught up in his emotions, blurts out that Tex is not really Mr. McCormick's son and that their mother had an affair while McCormick was serving time in prison. Dazed and uncomprehending, Tex rushes out into the streets, where he meets Lem Peters, who is on his way to a drug drop. Tex accompanies Lem, but the client, Mr. Kelly, becomes violent and pulls a gun. Although Tex is able to seize the gun, he is shot during the struggle. At the hospital and near death, Tex is touched by his brother's concern and attention. When the crisis is over, he knows he has a real brother who genuinely cares for him.

CHARACTERS: The narrator and protagonist of this novel is **Tex McCormick**, a feisty, courageous teenager who is making the painful journey to sexual and emotional maturity. He scarcely understands the way he feels about the attractive Jamie Collins, but in his fumbling, tentative way, he realizes he is feeling the first pangs of love. Like other things in his life, he deals with this new emotion honestly and directly, confessing to Jamie how he feels, even though her response is not as positive as he had expected. Tex is generally easygoing to the point of thoughtlessness. He doesn't understand his brother's constant complaining about their financial situation and their deadbeat father, whom Tex adores, even though his father has always favored Mace. Tex has never assumed any of the burdensome responsibilities that Mace has and indeed seems detached from their often desperate situation.

In the course of the novel, this guileless, honest innocent learns the power of love and hate. He grows to accept the ugly truth about the man he thought of as his father and to realize that the brother, who often appeared to be only a cranky faultfinder, is in fact a caring individual who only wants the best for him. Tex is also courageous and gutsy. Without hesitation, he risks his own life to save his brother from the gun-wielding hitchhiker and later rescues Lem from the murderous Mr. Greene. He is also a loyal friend, who uncomplainingly accepts punishments that should be shared by Johnny Collins.

Mason McCormick is Tex's complex and at times enigmatic brother. Though only seventeen, he has had to shoulder the responsibilities of running a household and making difficult decisions like selling Tex's beloved horse to pay the bills. He is a proud and sensitive young man whose main ambition is to lead an honest, respectable life. He wants desperately to make something of himself and works hard at both his school work and his basketball game to get the scholarship he deserves. He realizes that his father is undependable and untrustworthy and that he will have to make his own future. Outwardly stern and unyielding, he silently endures inner stress and conflict until he develops an ulcer. Unable to express the real love and concern he feels for his brother, his manner is often that of a grumpy complainer. His love and devotion for his brother emerge only when he is afraid Tex might die. He sobs uncontrollably and promises that he will turn down his scholarship to remain behind and continue to care for Tex.

The boys' father, **Mr. McCormick**, is a good-natured failure, drifting from one job to another without goals or direction. He neglects the welfare of his family, using forgetfulness as an excuse. When he reappears after being away for months, he promises to change and be a better father, but the inherent weaknesses in his character make this reformation unlikely. Although he is a former alcoholic and convict, Tex nevertheless admires and defends him because he thinks the man is his father. When the truth is revealed, Tex is greatly disillusioned.

Johnny Collins is Tex's best friend. Coming from a more affluent family, he has many of the material advantages that Tex lacks, including his own motorcycle. He unselfishly shares all his possessions with Tex and even gives him money when necessary. Less sexually aware than Tex, he can't understand why at times Tex prefers the company of his sister Jamie to his own, and as a result sometimes feels hurt and jealous. His brother, **Bob Collins**, is equally loyal in his friendship with Mace. When their parents criticize Tex and Mace and their way of life, the Collins brothers come to their friends' defense.

Though only in the seventh grade, **Jamie Collins** is mature beyond her years. She is genuinely fond of Tex to the point of loving him, but she wisely refuses to give herself physically to him knowing that their youth, inexperience, and class difference will ultimately separate them. She is, however, sensitive and attentive to Tex and his problems. Always honest and perceptive, she frankly admits to Tex, while he is recovering in the hospital, that she doubts their relationship can last. She says, "I love you though. But I don't think love solves anything."

The fate of **Lem Peters** illustrates Jamie's concerns about young love. While still a teenager, and in spite of parental objections, he married his sweetheart, Connie, and moved to the big city where, lacking skills, he took a low-paying job in a garage. When Connie became pregnant and was unable to work, Lem turned to drug dealing for quick cash. Although Tex is able to clear him of responsibility in the death of Mr. Greene, Lem's future looks grim.

Further Reading

Berger, Laura Standley, ed. *Twentieth-Century Young Adult Writers.* 1st ed. Detroit: St. James, 1994.

Children's Literature Review. Vols. 3, 23. Detroit: Gale Research, 1978, 1991.

Collier, Laurie, and Joyce Nakamura, eds. *Major Authors and Illustrators for Children & Young Adults.* Detroit: Gale Research, 1993.

Contemporary Literary Criticism. Vol. 30. Detroit: Gale Research, 1984.

Daly, Jay. *Presenting S. E. Hinton.* Boston: Twayne, 1989.

Gallo, Donald R. *Speaking for Ourselves: Autobiographical Sketches by Notable Authors of Books for Young Adults.* Urbana, IL: National Council of Teachers of English, 1990.

Isabelle Holland

1920-, American novelist

The Man without a Face

(young adult novel, 1972)

PLOT: Fourteen-year-old Charles (Chuck) Norstadt is spending the summer at his family's summer cottage in an Atlantic coastal community not too far from their year-round New York City apartment. Chuck is with his mother and his two half-sisters: domineering, self-centered Gloria, who is almost seventeen, and Meg, an agreeable eleven-year-old. No one seems prepared or willing to tell Chuck about his absent father, Eric. When Chuck learns that Gloria, whom he despises, will not be leaving home to attend school in the fall, he becomes determined to escape his suffocating home environment by studying during the summer so he can pass the tests necessary to enter St. Matthew's private school in the fall. He seeks help from a former school teacher, the reclusive, withdrawn Justin McLeod, who is known as "the man without a face" because half of his face is horribly disfigured with scars. Reluctantly, Justin takes on Chuck as a pupil.

In spite of Justin's autocratic, curt manner, Chuck grows to admire and respect this man and reaches out to him for the love that has been denied him at home. As their friendship grows, Chuck learns more about Justin. Using a pseudonym, Justin has become a famous writer of fantasy novels. Before his writing career, he had taught at St. Matthew's, until he crashed his automobile while he was drunk, killing a young student who was in the car and causing his disfigurement.

Chuck's mother, who is preoccupied with preparations for her marriage to her fifth husband—their lawyer neighbor, Barry Rumbolt—leaves with her fiance to go apartment hunting in New York. One evening during her absence, Gloria's boyfriend, Percy, kicks Chuck's cat, Moxie, so brutally that Moxie dies in Chuck's arms. After burying the cat, a confused and emotional Chuck spends the night with Justin and they are physically intimate. In the

Justin McLeod (Mel Gibson) finds companionship with a young boy, Chuck Norstadt (Nick Stahl), in the 1993 film version of **The Man without a Face.**

morning, Chuck, ashamed and stunned by the experience, leaves Justin without saying goodbye. Later, after he has passed the entrance exam and is in school, he reflects on what happened and is filled with regrets. He rushes back to Justin's cliff house only to find it deserted. Chuck learns from Barry, Justin's lawyer, that while traveling in Scotland Justin suffered a heart attack and died. As though foretelling the future, Justin left Chuck a comforting letter of reassurance at the house, as well as specifying in his will that Chuck be his sole beneficiary.

CHARACTERS: The narrator of the novel is fourteen-year-old **Charles (Chuck) Norstadt**, a good-looking, affable young man who is also confused and lonely. Described as an attractive blonde youngster with green eyes, Chuck has been growing up with a succession of stepfathers and his mother's boyfriends. What he really needs is a father figure to whom he can relate and who can help him through adolescence. Surrounded by women, including a domineering older sister, he longs for escape and independence. Appropriately, Chuck loves the freedom and exhilaration that flying brings and plans to join the Air Force when he turns seventeen. He has been wounded emotionally so often that he has developed a distant, detached exterior that hides an inner loneliness and emptiness. Without confidence or friends, he mistakenly believes that he lacks intelligence and ability. Chuck seeks someone who will accept him and give him the love he needs. Then he meets Justin, an accomplished and sophisticated writer who evokes both admiration and respect in the vulnerable youngster. As Chuck says, "I'd never had a friend, and he was my friend; I'd never had a father, and he was my father."

At first, Chuck attributes Justin's coldness and haughtiness to dislike, but as the relationship matures, he realizes that Justin inwardly understands and cares. Unable to express or grasp the concept of platonic love, he reaches out (literally) to hold the object of his adoration and, when he initiates the physical intimacy between them, he again retreats, shocked and confused. However, the two months with Justin have matured Chuck and given him valuable insights into himself. Eventually, he is able to assimilate these experiences, appreciate the value of Justin's friendship, and realize that what happened to him was rare and beautiful.

To the people in Chuck's beach community, **Justin McLeod** is a reclusive grouch. Distant and aloof, he has become a completely private person who shuns all social contacts. He has ignored the possibility of corrective plastic surgery and, instead, wears the terrible scars on his face as a badge of guilt that he displays as a form of penitence. The scars are described as "glazed raw beef all over most of one side and flowing across his nose to the other." In many ways, Justin is like Chuck. Rebuffed and hurt, he also has retreated into a shell where he is both afraid and unable to display love or affection. Justin, however, achieves gratification and communication by writing his very successful fantasy novels. Though not stated in the novel, it appears that he is gay and is denying himself any outlet for his feelings because of a former relationship he had while he was teaching. That relationship ended when his drunk driving caused the automobile crash that killed one person and sent Justin to prison for two years.

Now scarred both physically and emotionally, Justin has withdrawn into a life of safety and solitude in which he redirects his feelings of love toward his horse and dog, both of whom were also treated badly in the past. Justin tries to hide his sympathetic, caring nature under a gruff exterior. Fearful of the consequences, he rebuffs every display of affection that Chuck shows and represses his growing feelings of affection, yet he nevertheless supplies the direction and attention that the boy so desperately needs. When the inevitable occurs and Chuck mindlessly rejects him, Justin's guilt and torment are reawakened, and this tragic figure whom Chuck has come to admire and love dies alone, still a prisoner of his emotions.

Chuck's **mother** is described as a pretty woman with curly brown hair, brown eyes, and a triangular face. Though she drinks too much and is inclined to self-pity, she is portrayed as a vulnerable, well-meaning person who is continually searching for a man to provide her with the security and strength that she lacks. She unfortunately tries too hard to placate her eldest, Gloria, with the result that her other two children feel neglected. Although she tries to be a good mother, her guilt over the failure of her marriages and the magnitude of her worries have made her preoccupied and remote. Chuck realizes that she is pathetic and lonely. He would like to communicate with her but finds it impossible. However, it appears that in **Barry Rumbolt**, soon to be husband number five, she has made a very good choice. A widowed lawyer, he is a keen judge of human nature. Nicknamed "Rumble Seat" by the kids, Barry is aware of Gloria's manipulative ways and has grown to understand Chuck's problems and needs. In addition, young Meg adores him and thoroughly approves of the match. He has known Justin for many years and shows a keen understanding of the man and his problems.

Gloria, Chuck's seventeen-year-old half-sister, has few, if any saving graces. She is preoccupied with herself and intent on satisfying her own wishes regardless of others' feelings. As a child she was filled with jealousy over the attention her younger brother, Chuck, received and since then has behaved viciously toward him. Always deprecating and insulting, she delights in making his life miserable. She heaps sarcasm and insults on him and revels in belittling him at every opportunity. Bright, boy-crazy, beautiful, and preoccupied with her looks, she attracts boys easily, but, in time, also repels them with her selfish, manipulative ways. At the end of the summer, Gloria and boyfriend Percy marry in what Barry feels will be "the first of a series of marriages for her."

Chuck's other sister, eleven-year-old **Meg**, is the opposite of Gloria, her half-sister. Short, fat, and wearing braces, she takes out her frustrations and loneliness by over-indulging in food. She is extremely bright and observant and worships her brother whom she often protects from Gloria's vindictiveness. She has a wise and compassionate nature far beyond her years but, like Chuck, suffers from the instability in her household. She adores Barry and thoroughly approves of her mother's choice. With Barry's help, she is even learning to control her appetite.

Although he doesn't appear in the novel, Chuck's absent father, **Eric**, plays an important role in the boy's life. Rarely spoken of, Chuck knows only that he was an average, middle-class, likable man whose job as an engineer often kept him away from home. Chuck has created a heroic image of him but, when the boy accidentally interrupts Gloria's love-making with Percy the night the cat dies, she vindictively reveals that Chuck's father died an alcoholic on a skid row in an unnamed Australian city. This information and how it has been conveyed help drive Chuck to Justin's the night that he sleeps with him.

Further Reading

Authors and Artists for Young Adults. Vol. 11. Detroit, Gale Research, 1993.

Berger, Laura Standley, ed. *Twentieth-Century Children's Writers.* 4th ed. Detroit: St. James, 1995.

Chevalier, Tracy, ed. *Twentieth-Century Children's Writers.* 3rd ed. Detroit: St. James, 1989.

Collier, Laurie, and Joyce Nakamura, eds. *Major Authors and Illustrators for Children and Young Adults.* Detroit: Gale Research, 1993.

Contemporary Authors New Revision Series. Vol. 47. Detroit: Gale Research, 1995.

Contemporary Literature Review. Vol. 21. Detroit: Gale Research, 1990.

Something about the Author. Vols. 8, 70. Detroit: Gale Research, 1976, 1993.

Ward, Martha, ed. *Authors of Books for Young People.* 3rd ed. Metuchen, NJ: Scarecrow, 1990.

Aldous Huxley

1894-1963, English novelist

Brave New World

(science fiction, 1932)

PLOT: A terrible war has left civilization utterly exhausted and completely changed from what it once was. It is now the year 632 A.F. (meaning after the birth of Henry Ford), the deity of Utopia. Stability has returned to civilization after the so-called Nine Years' War, but at the price of many personal freedoms. The government regulates everything, from food supplies to the number of people who are born. But it is not only the *number* of people who are controlled but also what *kind* of people will be born. There are five different castes: the lower castes are bred to be unintelligent so that they will be content with their menial labor, while the more privileged castes are smarter and enjoy all the best that society offers. This is accomplished by fertilizing eggs in test tubes and adding or denying chemicals, nutrients, hormones, and stimuli to the embryos to ensure the resulting children will have certain traits.

But the influence of the state does not end with the test tube. The state motto is "Community, Identity, Stability," ideals that are maintained by conditioning the young to all think alike and by supplying the old with a tranquilizer called soma. Governmental power rests in the hands of ten World Controllers and supplemented by numerous petty officials. The government sponsors diversions in the form of sports and entertainment to keep the populace from thinking too much.

As the story opens, Lenina Crowne has agreed to vacation at a Savage Reservation in New Mexico with Bernard Marx, a rather small and ugly but intelligent fellow who is a member of the Psychology Bureau at the Central London Hatchery. Lenina has recently begun dating Bernard after being nagged by her friend Fanny because she had been dating Henry Foster, a statistics genius, too regularly. Too much dating with the same person is frowned upon.

Lenina and Bernard meet John, the Savage, and his mother, Linda, at the Savage Reservation, which is a preserve where people who are deemed unworthy of following Utopian ways are confined. John has been born outside of Utopia. Bernard himself is critical of Utopian ways and has been threatened by Tomakin, the Director of Hatcheries who also happens to be John's father, with exile if he does not shape up. For Linda's indiscretion in giving birth to this unplanned-for child, she was left behind on the Savage Reservation and forbidden to return to Utopia.

Bernard enlists the aid of Mustapha Mond, a World Controller, to allow John and Linda to return to Utopia. When they do so, Bernard learns he is indeed about to be exiled, but he confronts the Director with John and Lenina, whereupon the Director resigns in disgrace. John's presence in Utopia interests the citizenry and makes Bernard a sort of hero for having brought him there. Along with Helmholtz Watson, Bernard tries to introduce his new friend to Utopian ways, but John grows more disgusted with each passing day. He rejects Lenina's sexual advances on him. Unnerved by the death of his mother from an overdose of soma, John tries to lecture Utopians on their way of life and a riot breaks out. Mustapha Mond exiles Bernard and Helmholtz as the ones responsible for bringing John to Utopia, but John is forced to stay. In desperation, he flees to a place outside of London, but he can't escape the people who come to watch him as if he were a zoo animal. Driven almost frantic by his need to escape and by his recurring sexual desire for Lenina, he begins to beat himself, a desperate act of contrition that is encouraged by the onlooking crowd. Finally, he succumbs to what the crowd wants and takes part in an orgy of soma and sex. When it is over and he comes to his senses, John realizes that he can't long resist this society, and so he kills himself.

CHARACTERS: John the Savage, born outside of Utopia and brought forcibly into it, is a symbol of the artist, a great man seeking to liberate himself. He condemns himself because of the circumstances of his birth and looks forward to his arrival in Utopia so that he can explore the depths of this brave new world. Yet with each passing day he grows more and more disgusted by this crude society and its stifling nature. At first he is merely morose, then he becomes temperamental, and finally independent. He will not listen to Bernard's instructions, telling him at one point that he will no longer be the subject of scrutiny by the members of this society. He also refuses to take soma. John represents the solitary artist in a hostile, materialistic world, brought down to that inferior level by his own physical needs and doubts. He tries desperately to cling to his own high standards, such as refusing the advances of Lenina, but in the end he succumbs to them and realizes that he can't win the struggle. Convinced that there is nothing worth living for in this world, he commits suicide.

A melancholy antihero, **Bernard Marx** is a social outcast. A small and ugly man who wishes to be as attractive as he is intelligent, he has many ideas but seldom acts upon them. Bernard enjoys the power that he gets from being John's protector and mentor. At one point he becomes so upset by John's increasing hostility and refusal to follow his wishes that he must take soma. Although his ideas are anti-Utopian, they stem from his bitterness over his own fate rather than from any deep conviction of ideals on his part. Because his role in bringing John into the Utopian society has given him so much attention and glory, Bernard resents any intrusion upon it and so becomes jealous over the developing friendship between John and Helmholtz Watson. In the end, when Marx is once again threatened with exile from the society he ridicules, he grovels before Mond, begging for mercy and blaming his predicament on John and Helmholtz.

To World Controller **Mustapha Mond** happiness is all relative. He believes that conformity is necessary but never stoops to physical violence to achieve it, always maintaining the manners of a perfect gentleman. Mond rules with an iron hand and is a worthy adversary to John, but a frightening authority figure to Bernard. A somewhat sinister man who has found his own comfortable niche in this ordered society, Mond serves as the mouthpiece for this society, voicing justifications for the status quo. Mond does not care about the flaws of Utopia because he feels he would be powerless to change them anyway. His own ideas do not always conform with those of society—he even agrees with some of John's lofty ideals—but he keeps any thoughts that might conflict with the standard ideology to himself. The system is just attractive enough for Mond to be willing to give up on a good deal of his own freedoms for it.

The **Director of Hatcheries and Conditioning, Tomakin**, is a self-centered, rather prim figure who is quite impressed with his position and aspires to the role of World Controller. When confronted with his indiscretion concerning his relationship with Linda and the birth of his son, John, he must resign in disgrace, his world and future shattered. **Linda**, John's mother, is an outcast for failing to adhere to the rigid rules of the society in which she lives. Her death in the "galloping Senility ward" totally unnerves her son. She dies in an atmosphere of amusement and opiates. Her death also serves as an object lesson to the Utopian children, who are brought by their teachers to the ward so they can be conditioned to view death objectively and without emotion. Death in Utopia does not involve pain, just a sudden onset of senility. John finds this whole experience inhuman and dehumanizing.

Some more minor characters in the novel are given roles to help illustrate the morals and standards of Utopian society. **Lenina Crowne** is an honest young woman whose life revolves around sex and other frivolous amusements. Not particularly intelligent, she persists in wanting to go steady with young men who interest her, even though this is frowned upon by society. When John is introduced to Utopia, Lenina finds her thoughts constantly turning to a possible affair with him. **Helmholtz Watson**, who befriends John, is handsome and clever and mistrusted by officials for just that reason. He symbolizes how ineffectual reasoning is in this civilization, for he is smart enough to realize that what he says amounts to nothing. Lenina's friend, **Fanny**, works in the bottling room at the Hatchery and constantly lectures Lenina on doing the right thing according to the state. **Henry Foster**, whom Lenina dated before Bernard, is a conformist. He is an eager worker with a head for statistics and a complete absence of genuine emotion.

Further Reading

Authors and Artists for Young Adults. Vol. 11. Detroit: Gale Research, 1993.

Atkins, John Alfred. *Aldous Huxley: A Literary Study.* London: J. Calder, 1956.

Berger, Laura Standley, ed. *Twentieth Century Young Adult Writers.* Detroit: St. James, 1995.

Critical Survey of Long Fiction. Vol. 4. Englewood Cliffs, NJ: Prentice-Hall, 1983.

Huxley, Aldous. *Brave New World Revisited.* New York: Harper, 1958.

Rabkin, Eric S. *No Place Else: Explorations in Utopian and Dystopian Fiction.* Carbondale: Southern Illinois University Press, 1983.

Something about the Author. Vol. 63. Detroit: Gale Research, 1991.

Twentieth-Century British Literature. Vol. 3 of *Chelsea House Library of Literary Criticism.* New York: Chelsea House, 1986.

Watts, Harold H. *Aldous Huxley.* New York: Twayne, 1969.

Brian Jacques

1939-, English novelist, radio personality, and storyteller

Redwall

(animal fantasy, 1986)

PLOT: This is the first of a series of animal fantasies that center on the mice of Redwall Abbey, an ancient edifice currently under the direction of a beatific, gentle mouse, the elderly Abbot Mortimer. Among the members of the Order are Methuselah, an ancient scribe, and a young, eager novice named Matthias. To celebrate Mortimer's Golden Jubilee, the woodland creatures gather at the abbey; the party includes Constance the badger, Ambrose Spike the hedgehog, and the Fieldmouse family with their attractive daughter, Cornflower. Meanwhile, a murderous group of bilge rats under the leadership of Cluny the Scourge ride into town, intent on pillaging and plundering. They lay siege to the abbey. Shadow, one of Cluny's henchmen, slips into the abbey and steals part of the tapestry in which the legendary hero of Redwall, Martin, is portrayed.

To protect the abbey from Cluny, Matthias believes that he must search for the stolen piece of tapestry and find the lost sword of Martin. The sword is considered to have magical powers that will help its wielder defend the abbey. During his quest he encounters an eccentric rabbit, Basil Stag Hare, and the squirrel Jess, both of whom join the abbey's defenders. Matthias also meets a group of hostile sparrows who live under the roof of the abbey, including Warbeak, her mother, Dunwing, and the vicious King Bull Sparra. Matthias's journey ends in the underground lair of a giant adder, Asmodeus Poisonteeth, keeper of the sword. Here, with the help of the sparrows and a group of quarrelsome shrews, he gallantly confronts the monster, kills him, and regains possession of the enchanted weapon. In the meantime, Basil and Jess have brazenly raided Cluny's encampment and retrieved the stolen tapestry.

Cluny tries a variety of tactics to capture Redwall, including tunneling underground, using a battering ram, and building a wheeled siege tower. The intrepid band repulses each new assault, but Cluny eventually succeeds by using a traitor to secretly open the abbey's gates. Just as he is about to execute his prisoners, Matthias arrives with an army of sparrows and shrews. In a final confrontation, Matthias kills Cluny by cutting the rope that holds the abbey bell, which falls on the bilge rat. The enemy vanquished, Matthias marries the fair Cornflower, and peace and security once again reign at Redwall Abbey.

Other books in the Redwall *series include* Mossflower *(1988),* Mattimeo *(1989),* Mariel of Redwall *(1991),* Salamandastron *(1992),* Martin the Warrior *(1993),* The Bellmaker *(1994),* Outcast of Redwall *(1995), and* Pearls of Lutra *(1997).*

This book is the first in the very popular "Redwall" series about anthropomorphized animals waging war in a medieval world.

CHARACTERS: The hero of this epic saga is the dauntless little mouse **Matthias**. At first portrayed as an inept but zealous novice who trips on his oversized sandals, Matthias is pictured as lacking dignity and being something of a buffoon. He is transformed by Cluny's menace and the threat to his beloved abbey. A new Matthias emerges, embodying the qualities of the romantic knight: purity, a strong sense of honor, devotion to duty and a worthy cause, and unwavering courage. Along with these qualities, however, he also retains elements of the innocent, brash, headstrong youth he once was. Matthias develops great leadership qualities and quickly becomes an outstanding administrator and tactician. A quick and clever thinker, he is able to talk himself out of dangerous situations, solve enigmatic riddles, accurately judge people's characters, and weigh situations precisely. Above all, he is brave, self-sacrificing, and modest. Although he risks his life innumerable times to save his friends and followers, he feels only embarrassment and discomfort when his deeds are praised. Matthias loves Cornflower with the same purity and wholesomeness that he displays fighting for a worthy cause. As a reward for his unselfish and dauntless service to Redwall, Abbot Mortimer dubs Matthias the Warrior Mouse of Redwall. He leaves the holy order to become the champion of the abbey and raise a family with Cornflower.

Evil incarnate is personified in the bilge rat, **Cluny the Scourge**, leader of a scurvy band of villains consisting of other water and sewer rats, and assorted ferrets, weasels, and stoats. Described as the biggest, fiercest, most savage rat that ever jumped from ship to shore, Cluny is black with pink scars all over his vermin-invested body, including his enormous, whip-like tail, which has a poisonous barb at its tip. He wears a patch over one of his yellow-slitted eyes. With his ragged coat made of bat wings and his immense war helmet, Cluny strikes fear in everyone who sees him. Knowing neither pity nor mercy, he kills without conscience. A crafty, cunning general, Cluny rules his motley crew with an iron fist, sacrificing lives for expediency and double-crossing his most loyal followers. Driven by greed and an insatiable need for power, the bilge rat rules by fear and intimidation. He is given to violent, unpredictable fits of temper during which he often kills without reason. A sly, canny manipulator, Cluny devises elaborate, seemingly foolproof schemes to capture Redwall. However, through either the bungling of his subordinates or the adroitness of abbey dwellers, his plans are usually botched. During hand-to-hand combat with Matthias after the siege has been lifted, Cluny is killed when the massive abbey bell falls on him.

The kindly, gentle leader of Redwood Abbey is elderly **Abbot Mortimer**. He extends the hand of charity to anyone who happens by, dispensing medical aid, food, shelter, and good advice to the needy. This generous mouse is a model for all at Redwall, including Matthias, who regards him as a surrogate father. A pacifist at heart, Mortimer finds it difficult to summon the malevolence necessary to combat Cluny; therefore, he surrenders many of his powers to the War Council led by Matthias and Constance during the siege. However, after Cluny captures the abbey and threatens to kill members of the parish, Mortimer, usually dignified and forgiving, is so outraged that he courageously attacks Cluny single-handedly and without a weapon. Cluny lashes him with his poison-barbed tail and, hours later, the saintly Abbot dies.

Matthias's other mentor at the abbey is the aptly named monk, **Methuselah**, the ancient brother who has kept the abbey records for as long as anyone can remember. The official chronicler of Redwall, he is also a compassionate, sympathetic mouse who understands the speech of all creatures, including birds. This learned historian whom the Abbot calls "the gentlest mouse I ever knew" also acts as mediator and councilor. He takes a special interest in Matthias, gives him special fatherly advice, and helps him overcome the obstacles and solve the riddles that enable Matthias to become Martin's successor. Methuselah is killed during the siege.

At Mortimer's Silver Jubilee, Matthias meets **Cornflower Fieldmouse**, "a decent mouse from a good family," who is very pretty and has the longest eyelashes and softest fur that Matthias had ever seen. She is usually quiet and humble, but during the siege she becomes a model of calm, businesslike efficiency, dispensing food and supplies to the defenders on the ramparts at all hours. Never complaining, she proves herself thoughtful, kind, and capable. Quick-thinking and brave, she repulses an attack of invading rats by pouring hot soup on them. Cornflower is particularly tender and encouraging towards Matthias, whom she grows to love.

Among the defenders of the abbey, one of the bravest and most powerful is the big badger **Constance**. Gruff, slow-thinking, but fearless, she becomes a leader of the group. Cluny regards her as the most hated and feared of the defenders of Redwall. Her courage, sturdy body, incredible endurance, and practical approach to planning battle tactics make her an invaluable team member. Although barbarously insulting to her enemies, she is fiercely loyal and gentle to her friends.

Constance's great friend and ally is **Ambrose Spike** the hedgehog. An amateur magician and sometime ruffian and reprobate, he has a weakness for ale. Stalwart and true, Ambrose is a great help in defending the abbey, as is the eccentric rabbit, **Basil Stag Hare**, a caricature of the "stiff upper lip" English military man of times past. Garrulous, gluttonous, but generous, Basil gives the impression of being archaic with his courtly, old-fashioned manners, use of a swagger stick, and a vocabulary peppered with expressions like "bounder," "old bean," and "blighter." Behind this humorous exterior, however, there is a seasoned campaigner, brilliant tactician, and outrageously daring fighter. Another important helper is **Mrs. Squirrel**, who is nicknamed **Jess**. With her incredible climbing ability, fast reflexes, and dauntless spirit, she performs many brave acts, including saving Matthias's life and, with Basil, rescuing the stolen tapestry.

During his search for Martin's sword, Matthias is captured by an unusual flock of sparrows who live in the abbey's bell tower. Their leader is the mad **King Bull Sparra**, a cruel, unpredictable tyrant who is given to lunatic rages. A moody, dangerous, sly bird, he wants to keep Matthias as a pet but is killed when he tries to prevent Matthias's escape. **Warbeak** is a wild little hooligan who at first dislikes and tries to harm Matthias. Gradually, they become friends, and with the help of her mother, **Dunwing**, Warbeak engineers a plan for Matthias to escape from the sparrow kingdom. After Bull Sparra's death, Warbeak becomes queen of the sparrows and helps liberate Redwall from Cluny.

The thief of Martin's sword is the evil giant adder, **Asmodeus Poisonteeth**. A merciless predator, he kills by using his strong coils, hypnotic eyes, and poisonous fangs. With his sinister blunt head, flickering forked tongue, and round, jet-black eyes, he is a dreaded monster of the woods whom all fear and despise. By using shrewd daring tactics, Matthias is able to trap him in tree roots and cut off his head using the sword that the serpent so jealously guarded.

Further Reading

Authors and Artists for Young Adults. Vol. 20. Detroit: Gale Research, 1997.

Berger, Laura Standley, ed. *Twentieth-Century Children's Writers*. 4th ed. Detroit: St. James, 1994.

Contemporary Authors. Vol. 127. Detroit: Gale Research, 1989.

De Montreville, Doris, and Donna Hill, eds. *Third Book of Junior Authors*. New York: H. W. Wilson, 1972.

Something about the Author. Vol. 62. Detroit: Gale Research, 1991.

Diana Wynne Jones

1934-, English fantasy writer

Dogsbody

(fantasy, 1977)

PLOT: In this fanciful tale, Jones imagines that the stars in the heavens are a race of gods. One of the gods, the Dog Star, Sirius, unfortunately has a bad

A dog named Leo, who is actually the proud star god Sirius, learns about love and kindness from young Kathleen in Jones's 1977 fantasy.

temper, which gets him into trouble when he is accused of murdering one of the other gods. Sirius pleads before the Judgment Seats, saying that the death was an accident. Because of Sirius's high position and faithful service in the past, the Judgment Seats are merciful. Instead of sentencing Sirius to death, they banish him to Earth, where he is sent to find the powerful Zoi that was lost during his crime. On Earth, however, Sirius has been born as a puppy, and he must find the Zoi before his natural lifespan as a dog ends. If he succeeds, he will be reinstated at the Court; if not, he will die as a dog.

So begins the life of Sirius on Earth as a weak little puppy named Leo. He is rescued by a girl named Kathleen who takes him to her home. Although Kathleen loves Leo, her family dislikes the dog. Kathleen's mother is dead, so she lives with her aunt, uncle, and cousins, Basil and Robin. Both Leo and Kathleen are mistreated by the family. Basil dislikes Leo immediately, and Robin thinks the dog looks like a rat.

In time, Sirius learns to talk to cats and other creatures, but his quest for the fallen Zoi is fruitless. It takes the coming together of Sol, Moon, and Earth to help him. Sol, the Denizen of Sirius's luminary, appears as a tiny figure of light. He grew annoyed when he heard the sentence given out to Sirius, and so he came to help. He doesn't know what a Zoi is, but he does know that the one Sirius lost fell to Earth. With Sol's help, Sirius discovers a wide clearing full of rubble where he gets a tingling feeling and is sure the Zoi is nearby. But the search goes on for weeks. Sirius is horrified when he overhears a conversation between Basil and his friend Clive. He learns that the boys are looking for the Zoi, too, even though they don't know what it is.

Sirius must go through many trials as he tries to find the missing Zoi. With the help of Moon on a clear night, he bounds to the clearing place to discover that all sorts of dogs are there to aid him. Sirius finds himself in the midst of a great hunt. After the savage hunt, he recognizes that the Zoi is breathing life into him. He is confronted by the Master of the hunt, who points to the Zoi, which has taken the shape of a pine cone. The Master asks Sirius what it is, and Sirius replies that a Zoi is the stuff of life. It can make or change anything, give life or take it away.

When Kathleen, Basil, and Robin appear, Kathleen knows she has lost her dog forever, but she can't communicate with Sirius to be comforted by him. To make Kathleen happy, Sirius decides he would like to turn back to a dog again. He asks Sol to use the Zoi to transform him, but Sol answers that he can't. A saddened Sirius must leave Earth and return to his own world, but he goes back a changed being. He no longer has the temper he once did. He also has no interest in finding a companion among the gods because he hopes that someday he can be reunited with Kathleen.

CHARACTERS: Sirius, with his glaring, green eyes, is a proud star god with a very bad temper. When he is sentenced to go to Earth to find the Zoi, however, he is quickly humbled. As a dog named **Leo** he is subjected to various mortal canine hazards such as fleas. Sirius is even dismayed to discover that he has amorous feelings for Patchie, a dog with fox-red ears. But the most profound change in Sirius can be seen in his feelings for Kathleen. Even though the girl comes to love him as the puppy Leo, Sirius develops a serious emotional attachment. When his quest for the Zoi has ended, he tells Sol that he wants to be turned back into a dog so he can be with Kathleen. When this proves impossible, Sirius returns to the heavens, refusing to seek a companion there in the hope that he and Kathleen might someday be reunited.

Kathleen is the first person to be kind to Sirius in his puppy form. Orphaned and mistreated by her mother's relatives, she finds comfort in loving Leo, whom she nurtures and protects from harm. The loving bond they form is very strong, and Sirius hopes it will lead to their meeting again someday. Sirius, as Leo, protects Kathleen from the disagreeable **Basil**. Basil doesn't really hate Kathleen, but he treats her badly because that's what the rest of his family does. As Leo grows bigger and stronger, all he has to do is glare at Basil to get the boy to stop picking on Kathleen.

Sol the luminary is a bright, tiny figure of light who heard of Sirius's banishment to Earth and feels it is unjust. He helps Sirius, even though he has no idea what a Zoi is or how to find it. In the end, when Sirius has recovered the Zoi, Sol suggests that he return to his own sphere, forget Kathleen, and start looking for a companion among his own kind.

Howl's Moving Castle

(fantasy, 1986)

PLOT: The land of Ingary is a place with two big problems. One is the Witch of the Waste. Most people in Ingary—and certainly in the town of Market Chipping where spunky Sophie Hatter and her two sisters, Lettie and Martha, live—are frightened silly by the witch. And with good reason.

Although she has remained quiet of late, the witch has threatened the king's daughter, apparently killed the Wizard Suliman, and terrorized the country folk. The other problem in Ingary is the castle that belongs to the Wizard Howl. With its four turrets and puffing, dark smoke, it hovers about the countryside, keeping people on edge. The good folk believe that the Wizard Howl preys on the souls of young girls. To be on the safe side, Sophie, her sisters, and all the other young ladies of the town of Market Chipping are warned never, ever to venture out alone.

Although Sophie has a pleasant, comfortable life (her father owns a hat shop), she is rather bored by her humdrum existence. After her father dies and her stepmother takes over the shop, she puts Sophie and her sisters to work. Sophie is more bored than ever. Unfortunately for her, she exhibits her ill temper one day when none other than the Witch of the Waste walks in. Annoyed at Sophie for this display of bad manners, the witch turns her into an old woman.

Not at all pleased with her misfortune, Sophie leaves the shop in a huff and, seeing Howl's castle hovering above her, she orders it to stop. Sophie enters and meets the wizard's apprentice, Michael, and a fire demon, Calcifer, who is bound by an unspecified contract with the wizard. Sophie and Calcifer decide to help each other. He will break her enchantment if she will break his contract with Wizard Howl. Posing as a cleaning woman, Sophie waits in the castle for the wizard's return. Although he does not prey on the souls of young girls as was rumored, he does steal their hearts rather easily when they fall in love with him. Sophie learns that the wizard is himself under the spell of the Witch of the Waste.

One day, the king of Ingary asks the wizard to find his missing son, Prince Justin. The wizard doesn't have time for this, so he asks Sophie to disguise herself as his mother and go tell the king how unfit Howl is for such a job. But Sophie does more than that. She learns that Calcifer was once a falling star who was afraid of dying. His contract with the wizard is that Howl will keep Calcifer alive. She also learns that the Witch of the Waste is actually trying to create a new person out of parts from the Wizard Suliman, who is not dead after all, and the missing Prince Justin. To complete this new person, the witch wants the head of Wizard Howl. Then the resulting man will become the new king of Ingary, and the witch will be his queen.

It takes a lot of wizardry, and a lot of work on Sophie's part, but the witch's spell is broken and Prince Justin and Wizard Suliman are freed. By the story's end, Sophie and Wizard Howl have become quite taken with each other. As for Calcifer, although he is now free and can go where he wants, he decides to remain at the castle, flickering about the fireplace.

In the sequel to this story, Castle in the Air *(1990), the characters Sophie, Calcifer, and Howl reappear in disguise.*

CHARACTERS: Nothing much fazes the plucky heroine, **Sophie Hatter**, who takes even enchantments in stride. She is the most studious of the three Hatter girls and the most easily bored. But nothing daunts her, not even her first trip into the frightening moving castle. Refusing to be intimidated by anyone, she chides Michael the apprentice for being exploited by the wizard and even stands up to Calcifer the fire demon. (When the demon challenges her, Sophie declares her intention to pour water on him.) Of course, Sophie is actually tenderhearted. When she learns of the witch's spell and how the wizard and Calcifer are involved, she decides to set things right. She is successful and, in the process, falls in love with Wizard Howl.

Wizard Howl is a bit of a dandy and quite a ladies' man, dressing in flashy tunics of scarlet and gold. His fair hair is brushed back and he has curious, glass-green eyes. Although his apprentice, Michael, declares that the wizard is not wicked, Howl asserts that he is. At their first meeting, he is a bit annoyed at Sophie for her outspokenness. He declares that he has reached the stage in his life when everyone is impressed with his power and wickedness, and it won't do for her to contradict him. Sophie pays little attention. When Sophie is able to break the spell that holds Howl and Calcifer, the wizard falls down on the floor. Sophie finds a black lump next to him that is actually his heart. She puts it on his chest, and, carefully pushing, replaces his heart. The wizard revives, complaining only of a hangover. When he is sufficiently recovered to be able to speak properly, he declares that he and Sophie will be able to live happily ever after together.

Besides the wizard, there are two other important characters in the castle. **Michael**, Howl's apprentice, is younger than Sophie but stands a head taller than she. He is quite polite to Sophie when she barges into the castle. Staunchly loyal to his master, he and Sophie constantly argue because she says the Wizard Howl is exploiting him. **Calcifer** the fire demon was once a shooting star who had a fear of dying. Transformed into a demon by the wizard, he is able to live, though with his blue face, purple teeth, and orange eyes he is a frightening sight. Calcifer makes a deal with Sophie that he will break her spell if she does likewise for him. But when Sophie frees Calcifer he decides to stay in the castle.

The Witch of the Waste is a frightening creature with streaming red hair who dresses in a flame-colored robe. Though her appearance is terrifying, it is her magical power that really scares people. When Sophie learns that the witch wants Howl's head as part of the king she is going to construct to rule by her side, Sophie works against the plot to break the dreadful spell placed on Howl.

Sophie's sister **Lettie** is said to be the most beautiful of the Hatter sisters. She is not about to take second best and declares that she will marry a prince. She constantly fights with her youngest sister, **Martha**, and Sophie must take charge and pull them apart when they argue. Never would they be as bold as their older sister Sophie to venture out on the streets alone. They are both much more proper and demure in the shop than Sophie.

Further Reading

Authors and Artists for Young Adults. Vol. 12. Detroit: Gale Research, 1994.

Berger, Laura Standley, ed. *Twentieth-Century Young Adult Writers*. 1st ed. Detroit: St. James, 1994.

Chevalier, Tracy, ed. *Twentieth-Century Children's Writers*. 3rd ed. Chicago: St. James, 1989.

Contemporary Literary Criticism. Vol. 26. Detroit: Gale Research, 1983.

Holze, Sally Holmes, ed. *Fifth Book of Junior Authors and Illustrators*. New York: H. W. Wilson, 1983.

Hunt, Caroline, ed. *British Children Writers since 1960: First Series*. Vol. 161 of *Dictionary of Literary Biography*. Detroit: Gale Research, 1996.

Something about the Author. Vols. 9, 70. Detroit: Gale Research, 1976, 1993.

Carolyn Keene

(house pseudonym used by the Edward Stratemeyer Syndicate)

"Nancy Drew"

(young adult mysteries, 1930-)

PLOT: As successful as the Hardy Boys mysteries, the Nancy Drew series has been one of the most popular creations of the Edward Stratemeyer Syndicate. The series has been written by a variety of authors over the years—most notably, Stratemeyer's daughter, Harriet Stratemeyer Adams (1892-1982) and Mildred Augustine Wirt Benson (1905-)—but it all began with *The Secret of the Old Clock* (1930; revised, 1959). Since her mother's death years before, eighteen-year-old Nancy Drew has lived with her father, the successful lawyer Carson Drew, and housekeeper, Hannah Gruen, in a large house in River Heights. Through a series of encounters with a number of dear friends of the recently deceased Josiah Cowley, a wealthy eccentric, Nancy becomes convinced that, before his death, the old man had written a new will leaving some of his money to these friends and not the entire amount to his distant relatives, the avaricious Topham family. By piecing together a series of clues, Nancy cleverly deduces that there indeed is a new will and its location can be found in notes hidden in an old mantle clock. Unfortunately, before she can secure the clock, it is stolen by a gang of robbers. After several exciting adventures and narrow escapes, Nancy is responsible for capturing the robbers and locating the new will that makes handsome provisions for Josiah's deserving friends.

Beginning in 1986, another series featuring Nancy was begun called "The Nancy Drew Files." In one installment of this series, *Never Say Die* ("The Nancy Drew Files," Case 16, 1987), Nancy demonstrates her usual skills as a sleuth. During an international bicycle racing contest known as the Classic, Nancy Drew's close friend and competition entrant, George (short for Georgia) Fayne, falls victim to a series of almost fatal accidents, including being lured into a tent on the fairgrounds that is set on fire. Convinced that these incidents are part of a plot to prevent George from winning, Nancy, along with her steady boyfriend, Ned Nickerson, begins collecting dossiers on a number of possible culprits. Complications occur when George's sponsor, Stephen Lloyd, a successful computer entrepreneur, reports the theft of a valuable newly developed program and receives demands for one million dollars in ransom money. Through ingenious sleuthing, Nancy connects these crimes and, in a deadly confrontation, captures the thief, Mr. Lloyd's assistant, who had hidden the program disc in one of the wheels of George's bike and had begun a campaign of harassment to force her out of the competition and gain access to her bicycle.

For more information on the Stratemeyer Syndicate, please see the Hardy Boys entry under Franklin W. Dixon.

CHARACTERS: Nancy Drew, the clever, attractive, amateur sleuth, first appears in a series of mysteries begun in 1929. To renew the series' popularity and update the language and attitudes, revisions of the old titles began in the late 1950s. To these were added two other series, *The Nancy Drew Files*, begun in 1986, and two years later a group of books that combined the talents of Nancy and her male counterparts, the Hardy Boys, in the *Supermysteries* series. Although Nancy's somewhat old-fashioned ideas and small-town perspectives have developed into more sophisticated attitudes and the plots involve contemporary situations and more mature love interests, her character remains basically the same. She is an intelligent, appealing young woman who is mature beyond her years. Unwavering in purpose and faithful to her friends regardless of the danger and sacrifice involved, she is courageous and persevering. Nancy is confident and poised in any social situation and possesses any number of skills and proficiencies that help her get out of tight spots. Affluent and independent, neither financial worries nor family obligations ever prevent Nancy from being free to help others or solve another mystery.

In her first adventure,* The Secret of the Old Clock, *Nancy discovers clues to the location of a will concealed within a mantel clock.

Though self-sufficient and without oppressive parental supervision, Nancy is unselfish, unspoiled, and dependable. Other girls at the age of eighteen with personal possessions like a dark blue convertible (later a Mustang GT convertible), might have become self-centered and arrogant, but not Nancy, who is instead modest and unassuming. She is a fierce fighter for justice and a believer in fair play. A loyal, loving daughter, Nancy requires little guidance or discipline. Like other fine detectives, she possesses amazing deductive abilities and has keen powers of observation. With her reddish-gold hair and trim figure, Nancy also presents an attractive appearance that is the envy of others.

Nancy's father is River Heights's best-known and most respected lawyer, **Carson Drew**. Mr. Drew has such confidence in his daughter's innate sense of responsibility that he regards her as an equal who occasionally might profit from his council but rarely needs supervision. His confidence in Nancy's maturity and discernment has produced a healthy, loving relationship and a trusting, permissive attitude toward his daughter that has never been violated or taken advantage of. When necessary, he is always available for advice or help, but otherwise he realizes that his exceptional offspring requires freedom and independence to develop.

The Drew's trusty housekeeper, **Hannah Gruen**, is another of Nancy's great supporters and defenders. Although she often shows concern about the risks that Nancy takes, she is always there to bolster spirits and offer encouragement. In addition to being one of Nancy's friends, Hannah is also a prize cook and excellent housekeeper. Nancy also has a strong ally in her devoted, dependable boyfriend, **Ned Nickerson**. Always attentive and undemanding, Ned respects Nancy's purity. At times he is alarmed at the dangerous situations in which she places herself, but he is always available to save and back the courageous girl he adores.

Further Reading

Bargainnier, Earl F., ed. *Ten Women of Mystery.* Bowling Green, OH: Bowling Green University Popular Press, 1981.

Billman, Carol. *The Secret of the Stratemeyer Syndicate: Nancy Drew, the Hardy Boys, and the Million Dollar Fiction Factory.* New York: Ungar, 1986.

Johnson, Deidre, ed. *Stratemeyer Pseudonyms and Series Books: An Annotated Checklist of Stratemeyer and Stratemeyer Syndicate Publications.* Westport, CT: Greenwood, 1982.

Mason, Bobbie Ann. *The Unembarrassed Muse: The Popular Arts in America.* New York: Dial, 1970.

Prager, Arthur. *Rascals at Large; or, The Clue in the Old Nostalgia.* New York: Doubleday, 1971.

Something about the Author. Vol. 65. Detroit: Gale Research, 1991.

M. E. Kerr

(pen name for Marijane Meaker)

1935-, American young adult novelist

Dinky Hocker Shoots Smack!

(young adult novel, 1972)

PLOT: Set in Brooklyn, New York, *Dinky Hocker Shoots Smack!* is the story of a teenager's struggle to defeat her problems with overeating and to convince her parents to recognize her needs as an individual. Susan Dinky Hocker eats all the time, which is why at five-foot-four she weighs about 165 pounds. Her cat, Nader, eats all the time, too. Dinky's friend, Tucker Wolff, who gave her Nader, tries to tell Dinky that she should not inflict her problems with overeating on the cat. When Dinky's cousin Natalia Line comes to stay with her, Tucker begins to visit Dinky more often. Tucker asks Natalia to a school dance, but Natalia only agrees providing he finds a date for Dinky. Tucker considers this impossible until he remembers P. John Knight, who also has a weight problem.

From the first time they are introduced, P. John insists on calling Dinky by her real name, Susan. The two of them are immediately interested in each other, and their friendship develops into a romantic relationship. Before long, the two of them go on a diet together. At Christmas time, Dinky buys P. John a watch, but her mother makes her return it. He gives her a copy of the *Weight Watchers' Cookbook.* But when P. John objects to the chocolate cake that Mrs. Hocker offers her daughter, he is banished from the house. Soon after, he has an argument with his father and is sent to Maine to live with his aunt.

The friendship between Tucker and Natalia continues, although Natalia has emotional problems stemming from her father's suicide. P. John tries to reach Dinky by sending letters through Tucker, but she ignores them. Off her diet again, Dinky grows fatter than ever. Her difficulties with her self-image and her weight reach a crisis point when P. John returns from Maine, slim and tall. Unthinkingly,

Tucker takes him to visit Dinky, and when she sees him her humiliation is complete. On the night her mother is being honored for her work with drug addicts in the community, Dinky goes around their neighborhood painting on the sidewalks and the sides of buildings: "Dinky Hocker Shoots Smack!"

It takes this incident for her parents to see how they have been neglecting their daughter. Mrs. Hocker quits her work with the drug group, and she and her husband take Dinky on a family vacation to Europe. They vow to try to help her lose weight and to show her how much they really love her.

CHARACTERS: *Dinky Hocker Shoots Smack* grew out of the author's experiences as a creative writing teacher at Manhattan's Center High. Though its central plot concerns the frustrations of an overweight high school girl, it is also about the various forms of escapism people incorporate into their lives. **Susan Dinky Hocker** is irrepressible, funny, and irreverent. She is also a sensitive young teenager who overeats out of a sense of unworthiness. Her parents are so engrossed in their own lives—especially her mother, who runs groups for community drug addicts—that they don't notice their daughter's problem. Dinky allows her parents to prescribe diet after diet for her, yet she knows they never really see her as she is and rarely try to understand what she is feeling. Her veneer of wisecracking humor begins to break down after she meets P. John and realizes he really cares about her. The embarrassment of seeing him so thin after he comes back from Maine, while she has gained weight, is finally too much for her to bear. But at least her relationship with her parents is strong enough that, after Dinky paints graffiti all over the neighborhood, they finally show some genuine concern for her.

Dinky's friend, **Tucker Wolff**, is a bright and amusing young man suffering from the pangs of first love for Natalia. After the sign-painting incident, he tries to explain to Dinky's father how they have been ignoring their daughter. When Tucker mentions P. John, Mr. Hocker says that his wife never really took the relationship that seriously. Tucker tells him, "If it wasn't much, it was all Susan ever had." Tucker is also beginning to look at his own parents more closely. He begins to understand why his mother wants to go back to school, and why she feels there should be more for her to do than being a wife and mother. At the end of the novel, Tucker decides he will wait until fall to see how things work out between Natalia and himself. **Natalia Line** is an emotionally troubled young girl trying to reconstruct her life after the suicide of her father. Whenever she is nervous, she talks in riddles, but she responds to Tucker's caring manner and his genuine feelings for her.

Even more than Tucker, **P. John Knight** seems to understand and sympathize with Dinky best, but this does not prevent him from hurting her feelings. Mature for his years, he genuinely cares for Dinky and sees what her parents' treatment is doing to her. Though he wants to help, he does not realize how he humiliates Dinky by arriving on her doorstep after shedding so much weight. Dinky's mother also fails her. Committed to helping drug addicts recover, **Mrs. Hocker** is so caught up helping those around her that she forgets to pay attention to her own troubled daughter. She does not see that her indulgent attitude toward Dinky is actually careless, even neglectful. This is what P. John realizes when he watches Mrs. Hocker encourage Dinky to take a piece of chocolate cake so she won't hurt the feelings of a recovering drug addict.

Gentlehands

(young adult novel, 1978)

PLOT: Buddy Boyle's sixteenth summer begins promisingly when he meets Skye Pennington at the Sweet Mouth Soda Shoppe, where he waits on tables. She is the attractive daughter of the millionaire head of Penn Industries and a summer resident, along with her mother and father, at the family mansion, Beauregard, in the resort town of Seaville on Long Island. Skye takes a playful interest in Buddy. Though infatuated with her, Buddy is painfully conscious of the differences between them. He is ashamed of both his middle-class background and his own social naivete. His father is a sergeant on the local police force, his mother is an ordinary housewife, and his five-year old brother, Streaker, is an average, somewhat pesky kid. In an effort to impress Skye, he takes her to visit his grandfather, Frank Trenker. Mr. Trenker is a recluse whom Buddy scarcely knows because his grandfather has spent most of his life in Germany. As Buddy expected, Skye is captivated by this cultivated and cultured man who loves fine music, wine, and animals.

Because his parents object to Buddy socializing outside of his class, the boy conceals his meetings with Skye from them. Among the many guests Buddy meets at Beauregard is Nick DeLucca, an investigative reporter pursuing a war criminal. The fugitive is a sadistic concentration camp guard called "Gentlehands," who got his nickname because he liked to play opera recordings—including the "Gentle Hands" aria from *Tosca*—while his victims went to their deaths. One of his victims was Mr. DeLucca's niece.

Although Buddy is at first incredulous, evidence gradually accumulates that Trenker, the man whom Buddy has grown to love and respect, is actually the infamous Gentlehands. Before making a hurried departure from his home, Trenker asks a tearful Buddy to phone a contact in New York City about the arrival of "a package." After Buddy finally accepts the truth about his grandfather, he realizes that "the package" was actually Trenker himself. He tells the authorities, but his grandfather has already escaped. The Penningtons leave Seaville at the end of summer, and Skye prepares to start college at Bryn Mawr. Buddy knows he probably will never see her again. For Buddy, it has been a summer of misplaced love and shattering loss.

CHARACTERS: Buddy Boyle is not only the central character but also the narrator of the novel. He is a bright, amusing, attractive young man who is also easily impressed by wealth. He is flattered by the attention Skye pays him and becomes infatuated with both her glib sophistication and her displays of affluence. This infatuation leads him to deceive his parents and betray his younger brother's trust in him. His search for an identity outside of his background also leads him to be overly impressed by the suave, cultured style of his grandfather. His impressionable nature—a desire to be someone he really is not—leads to disastrous relations with his family. However, when events reveal his social aspirations to be a sham, Buddy is able to profit from the experience. He finds the courage to repudiate both Skye and his grandfather. Symbolically, Buddy rejects them both when he deliberately leaves behind in his grandfather's house the expensive sweater Skye bought him. By reporting the story about "the package" and his suspicions about his grandfather's whereabouts to the police, he acknowledges that Trenker, in spite of his sophistication, was an evil man. In the end, Buddy must cope with disillusionment and loss, but through these painful experiences he has matured.

Buddy's grandfather, **Frank Trenker**, is a complex character. Though outwardly a person of culture and a man who faithfully feeds wild birds and is distressed when a raccoon is caught in a trap, he has also committed gruesome crimes against humanity. His sadistic personality might be the result of his oppressive childhood at the hands of a fanatical father. Trenker is described as a tall, thin, distinguished-looking gentleman with thick white hair and impeccable manners. Because of his frequent displays of erudition, his love of the arts, and his cultivated lifestyle, Buddy's parents regard him as a snob. Mrs. Boyle also can't forgive him for abandoning her mother years before. On the other hand, Buddy's grandfather becomes his role model, showing genuine concern for his personal problems. Trenker's stern, unbending character is indicated in advice to Buddy such as this: "You can be anything you want to be. It's a matter of authority. Whatever a man's confidence, that's his capacity." Trenker's true nature is revealed not only in the revelations about his past but also in how he uses Buddy to help him escape.

Nick DeLucca, the journalist who is investigating the Gentlehands case, is out of his element in the

Pennington household, but he is not overawed by their wealth. In this artificial world of luxury, he maintains his values and honest, straightforward attitude. Although somewhat vulgar in dress and manners, he represents decency and a belief in justice.

Smart, sophisticated **Skye Pennington** is a beauty with long black hair and big blue eyes. Although she is in many ways a spoiled rich girl, she shows a sensitivity toward others' feelings. For example, when her friends make fun of Buddy's cheap sweater, she comes to his defense. Later, after telling an anti-Semitic joke in front of Nick DeLucca, she is ashamed to discover he is Jewish. It does become apparent, however, that Buddy is merely her summer amusement, a toy she can discard whenever she wishes. She is much more loyal to her parents, being tolerant of her scatterbrained mother and obedient to the dictates of her father.

Buddy's father, **Bill Boyle**, is a realist who believes that his son should stay with his own kind. He is hostile toward both the Penningtons' show of wealth and the culture represented by Grandfather Trenker. He maintains that these lifestyles are foreign to his way of life and is thus unable to handle his son's rebellion or understand Buddy's attraction to the refinement and wealth that his own home does not offer. Being stubborn and inflexible, as well as inarticulate, he resorts to physical force, the form of communication he knows best as a police officer. **Inge Boyle**, Buddy's mother, is more understanding toward her son's problems, and she even lies to protect him, but she is dominated by her husband and agrees with his ideas on class differences. Their other son, **Streaker**, is a somewhat demanding five-year-old who adores his older brother.

Night Kites

(novel, 1986)

PLOT: Set in the beach community of Seaville, New York, near the southern tip of Long Island, *Night Kites* is narrated by Erick Rudd, a high school senior who discovers his adored older brother is a homosexual dying from AIDS. The title is from Erick's memory of how once, when he was five, his brother made him a "night kite," with little battery-powered lights on it. To Erick, Pete Rudd has always been like that kite in the night sky—solitary, independent, and unafraid. But the novel is not only about their relationship and the burden of living with someone who has a terminal illness, it is also about how Erick discovers for himself the responsibilities of adult sexuality.

Erick lives at home with his father, a successful, hard-working, New York City investment banker, and his kindly, understanding mother. His older brother, who is 27, lives alone in Greenwich Village, where he teaches and writes science fiction. Erick's girlfriend is the popular, dependable Dill, short for Marion Dilberto, and his best friend is Jack Case, a star athlete who is infatuated with a fast-living loner named Nicki Marr.

The crux of the novel occurs during a weekend the four friends, Erick, Dill, Jack, and Nicki, spend in New York, where they attend a Bruce Springsteen concert. It is during this weekend that both Erick and his father learn that Pete is gay and that the lingering illness from which he suffers is AIDS. Pete talks to Erick about being homosexual and how, except for telling his mother, he has kept this a secret from the family. Also during this weekend, Nicki openly flirts with Erick, who is strongly attracted to her despite his guilt about both Dill and Jack. Back in Seaville, Erick visits Nicki at the hotel her father manages. She seduces him, and they make love in her bedroom. Although Erick tries lying to them, Dill and Jack find out about the affair and he loses both friends. When Erick tries to apologize, Jack punches him out, almost breaking his nose.

Because of his weakening condition, Pete is forced to move to his parents' home, and soon the community discovers the nature of his illness. Many, including Nicki, are openly hostile to Pete. When Nicki breaks off her relationship with Erick, he is left without any of his former friends, but he remains determined to face the challenge ahead of caring for his beloved brother.

CHARACTERS: Erick Rudd is a decent teenager who has, in general, a strong moral character and dedication to his family. Although he sometimes disagrees with his conventional, puritanical father, he tries to be an obedient son. Erick is somewhat afraid of his emotions and unprepared to deal with them, particularly with love. When he betrays both his best friend and trusting girlfriend, he feels terrible pangs of conscience and tries, without success, to make amends. His love and respect for his brother continues after discovering Pete's homosexuality, something Erick accepts but doesn't really understand. By the end of the novel, Erick is isolated, having lost his dearest friends and facing the loss of his brother. Yet he manages to accept these tragedies, and he gallantly turns to face an uncertain future.

Erick's older brother, **Pete Rudd**, is affable, independent, caring, and idealistic. He is not afraid to be different or to stand up for unpopular causes he believes are just. Although these attitudes often cause conflicts with his father, Pete remains loyal to his convictions and refuses to be bullied or intimidated. Because he believed in his writing, he dropped out of a Ph.D. program that promised a secure future. Pete encourages Erick to be daring and independent as well. He tries to show Erick the importance of keeping faith in his convictions and taking control of his destiny. Pete also has strong family loyalties. Rather than cause family discord, he kept his homosexuality a secret from them until his commitment to honesty made him tell his mother. Pete is a courageous figure who faces death without self-pity or resentment.

Arthur Rudd, Erick's father, is a cautious, well-intentioned, self-made man who wants his children to adhere to the traditional values and self-discipline that made him successful. He is a good provider who loves his family, but he has trouble communicating with his sons, particularly Pete, whom he regards as something of a failure. When put to the test, however, love and responsibility are more important to him than his conventional middle-class values: he is unable to understand or condone his son's homosexuality, yet he welcomes Pete back when he becomes seriously ill.

Mrs. Rudd is less conventional than her husband. Born into an environment of wealth and culture, she is interested in the arts and shows a good sense of taste that still eludes Mr. Rudd. She is a loyal and loving wife who defends her husband when she feels her sons are being unfairly critical. Because of her understanding and tolerance, she is closer to her children than her husband is. Pete, for example, tells her and not his father that he is gay. Though he thinks that she has reacted positively to this revelation, Mrs. Rudd later confesses to Erick that she neither comprehends nor accepts what her son has told her. Because of her love for Pete, she continues to support him, but her exterior strength often masks an inner frailty and bewilderment. Her great love for her family is shown when she brings Pete home to die and courageously faces public hostility.

Much of the story also involves Erick's growing sexual awareness, which leads to his relationship with **Nicki Marr**. Described as being "17 going on 25," Nicki is independent and trendy. Though scorned by some of her peers, this blond, green-eyed seductress has many boyfriends. She has an encyclopedic knowledge of rock stars and their music, and her wild, flirty behavior is mirrored in her funky clothes, tacky dresses, wrist chains, and heavy perfume. Her sexual attraction to Erick is more from a sense of challenge than any emotion resembling love. Part of her strange behavior arises from her unconventional background: her dead mother was the local psychic, and her father, a vulgar man who runs a seedy hotel complex, has a weakness for both liquor and girls. Despite her unconventionality, Nicki has accepted many of her father's prejudices, including homophobia and ignorance about AIDS.

Erick's attraction to Nicki results in his hurting two of his other friends. **Jack Case** is a star athlete and a loyal companion. Good-natured Jack suffers the pangs of unrequited love for Nicki. When he feels betrayed by Erick, he strikes out violently against the boy whom he once trusted and ends a friendship that had been one of the most important elements in his life. **Marion Dilberto**, known as **Dill**, is popular, pretty, and dependable, as well as being a good student and a "pompon girl" at her high school. Still sexually innocent, she is genuinely in love with Erick and becomes justifiably hurt and resentful when he betrays her.

Deliver Us from Evie

(young adult novel, 1994)

PLOT: *Deliver Us from Evie* is the story of conflicts between members of the Burrman family, who live on a 150-acre farm in rural Missouri. These conflicts center around the family's adolescent children, particularly their choices about their careers and their discoveries about sexuality.

Almost sixteen years old, Parr Burrman is the youngest of three children and the only one in the family who does not want to be a farmer. But at the beginning of the novel, twenty-year-old Doug, who is away at college, still intends to farm, and so does eighteen-year-old Evie, who lives at home. It is Evie who causes the most painful divisions in the family. Evie dresses in men's work clothes and can fix any machinery on the farm. Although Mrs. Burrman is always trying to get her to wear feminine outfits and pay attention to Cord Whittle, Evie doesn't want the clothes or Cord.

Trouble starts when Evie meets rich and beautiful Patsy Duff, the seventeen-year-old daughter of the man who owns the bank that holds the mortgage on the Burrman's farm. Patsy goes back to boarding school, but Evie visits her at Christmastime. Soon there is talk about Evie and Patsy being lesbians. Mr. Duff tells Mr. Burrman that Evie had better stay away from his daughter, delivering this warning just when the Burrmans need a farm loan.

The family gets the loan, but Cord, who is stung by all the talk and who still hopes for a future with Evie, hangs up a sign in town that says "Evie Loves Patsy." He tells Parr his plan: he expects Patsy's father to be so angry when he sees the sign that he'll send Patsy east to school and out of Evie's way. Then all the gossip will die down. Parr, preoccupied with his new love for pretty Angel Kidder, considers this a good idea. Cord's sign, however, only strengthens the bond between Evie and Patsy. With their relationship out in the open, it is Evie, not Patsy, who leaves first. After a trip to France, the two of them settle together in New York. Their relationship is one that those who love Evie must face and understand.

CHARACTERS: Parr Burrman is a likeable, generally sensible teenager, who is comfortable with everyone in his family, including his sister, Evie. He acknowledges that she is somehow different from other girls her age and simply accepts her as she is. Parr is far more intrigued with Angel Kidder than he is over any talk about the relationship between Evie and Patsy. However, he is ashamed of his part in Cord's decision to hang up the sign in town, and this incident teaches him a lesson in responsibility. Parr does not pretend to understand his sister or the life she has chosen, but he accepts her decision simply because he loves her. When she returns home for a quick visit before moving to New York, there are tears in his eyes when she leaves. As the car pulls away, he shouts, "Tell Patsy hi!"

Evie Burrman is mannish and independent, and she is not distracted by all the gossip about her. The reader never learns when Evie first realizes her sexual feelings or even how she feels about people's reactions to her, but there is little doubt that Evie is uncompromising about her sexuality. She does not apologize for or try to explain her feelings for Patsy, even to her mother. At one point, her mother brings up the subject of lesbianism. "Is that what you claim you are?" she asks. Evie replies, "It's not what I claim I am. It's what I am." If she must leave her family and the farm she loves to live her life as she wishes, this is what she will do. Before leaving for New York, however, she tells her father that she will come back "as long as I'm welcome."

Mrs. Burrman constantly tries to change her daughter. She is well aware of how Evie looks and acts and what people think, but in subtle ways she tries to get Evie to dress "in a more feminine way" and pay more attention to Cord Whipple. Mrs. Burrman knows her daughter will not conform, but she never really accepts her sexuality. In a conversation with Parr, Mrs. Burrman says of her daughter: "It's bad enough to look that way, but it's awful to look it and actually be it. . . . Then you're a stereotype. You're what everybody's always thought one of those women was like." Mrs. Burrman worries not only because of who her daughter is but because she looks like who she is. Even so, when Evie leaves her mother calls after her and Patsy, "Don't you two be strangers!"

Patsy Duff, in contrast to Evie, does not look like the stereotype of a lesbian. She is beautiful and feminine, yet she shares Evie's feelings. Evie's mother acknowledges that for Patsy living life as a lesbian will not be as difficult as it will be for Evie. In a conversation with Parr, Cord Whipple says that Patsy's feelings about Evie won't last because "a girl like Patsy is going to want a man." But at the novel's end, Patsy does indeed leave for New York with Evie to find an apartment and begin a new life.

Mr. Burrman loves his daughter and is quite aware of how she looks and acts. He laughs at his wife's attempts to make Evie more feminine and is quite proud of her extraordinary ability with machinery. At the same time, however, he calls Cousin Joe, a distant relative, "funny" because he is a homosexual. After the sign goes up in town, Dad grows strangely quiet. Parr realizes that his father is embarrassed because the truth about Evie is now public. It is not the morality of the relationship that concerns Mr. Burrman, it is the embarrassment.

Cord Whipple is a simple young man who cannot see beyond the future he imagines with Evie. He tells Parr that Evie's mannish ways are due to farm work and nothing else. She knows machinery because it's in her blood. His views about homosexuality are equally simplistic: two women in love is kid stuff; two men in love is sinful because it says so in the Bible. For Cord, the whole problem is that Patsy is going to a boarding school, so she does not know about men, and that is why she has turned Evie's head.

Angel Kidder is a pretty teenager in love for the first time. This is both her and Parr's first love affair, but she is still more sophisticated than he is. She is actually somewhat manipulative and unfair. When she is late coming home with Parr from a dance, her father is furious. She blames Parr, even though they are late partly because of a bad storm and partly because she herself insisted on parking for a while. She tells Parr that he should have been more responsible; he acknowledges this and then walks away, but her eyes are already on another young man.

Doug Burrman has always wanted to be a farmer, but during the course of this story he changes his mind. He decides he wants to become a veterinarian. Parr thinks this change of mind might have something to do with his latest love, a sorority girl from college named **Bella Hanna**. She has never been on a farm and does not exactly seem fit for that kind of life. When Doug first brings her home, the family secretly whispers to each other, "Don't let her be the one."

Further Reading

Berger, Laura Standley, ed. *Twentieth-Century Young Adult Writers.* 1st ed. Detroit: St. James, 1994.

Collier, Laurie, and Joyce Nakamura, eds. *Major Authors and Illustrators for Children and Young Adults.* Detroit: Gale Research, 1993.

Contemporary Literary Criticism. Vols. 12, 35. Detroit: Gale Research, 1980, 1985.

Gallo, Donald R. *Speaking for Ourselves: Autobiographical Sketches by Notable Authors of Books for Young Adults.* Urbana, IL: National Council of Teachers of English, 1990.

Graham, Joyce L. "An Interview with M. E. Kerr." *Journal of Youth Services in Libraries* 7 (fall 1993).

Gray, B. Allison. "Her, Her, Her: An Interview with M. E. Kerr." *Voice of Youth Advocates* 13 (February 1991).

Kerr, M. E. "Margaret A. Edwards Award Acceptance Speech." *Journal of Youth Services in Libraries* 7 (fall 1993).

———. *Me Me Me Me Me.* New York: Harper, 1983.

Roginski, Jim. *Behind the Covers Volume II.* Englewood, CO: Libraries Unlimited, 1989.

Ryan, Bryan, ed. *Major Twentieth-Century Writers: A Selection of Sketches from Contemporary Authors.* Detroit: Gale Research, 1991.

Something about the Author. Vols. 20, 61. Detroit: Gale Research, 1980, 1990

Something about the Author Autobiography Series. Vol. 1. Detroit: Gale Research, 1986.

Sutton, Roger. "A Conversation with M. E. Kerr." *School Library Journal* 36 (June 1993).

Ward, Martha, ed. *Authors of Books for Young People.* Metuchen, NJ: Scarecrow, 1990.

Ken Kesey

1935-, American novelist

One Flew Over the Cuckoo's Nest

(novel, 1962)

PLOT: Published in the late 1960s, the central theme of *One Flew Over the Cuckoo's Nest* is the conflict between individualism and the rigid rules of a repressive society. The novel takes place in a mental institution in Oregon, where the main characters are either inmates or employees. The narrator is Chief Bromden, a paranoid schizophrenic and Native American who pretends to be a deaf-mute. Life on the ward is strictly regulated by Nurse Ratched, who is known as "Big Nurse." The action of the novel is centered on her struggle with a new inmate, Randle P. McMurphy, for control of the ward. Nurse Ratched and McMurphy are symbols, respectively, of repressive authority and individual freedom.

Far from insane, McMurphy is an uninhibited gambler and confidence man who has committed himself to the mental hospital to escape a six-month sentence at a prison farm. He immediately challenges the authority of Nurse Ratched: McMurphy organizes gambling, including card games, and wins over the other inmates by demanding permission to watch the World Series on television. When McMurphy learns that no one gets out of the ward without Nurse Ratched's okay, he sees the wisdom of conforming, but by now the inmates look to him for leadership. He begins to teach them to be themselves, and they join him in small acts of rebellion. Meanwhile, Nurse Ratched bides her time. She reminds the other patients that McMurphy is a cheating gambler who is only out for himself, and she waits for him to make a mistake.

McMurphy organizes a fishing trip for the inmates, and they are joined on the outing by a prostitute named Candy Starr. After the men return, McMurphy makes the mistake Big Nurse has been waiting for. Chief Bromden is a huge, powerful man, yet he thinks of himself as small and weak. Unknown to the inmates, he has realized his strength and is now able to lift the heavy control panel on the ward. McMurphy bets the others that Chief Bromden can lift the panel, and when they bet against him and lose, they realize McMurphy already knew he could do it. Now they begin to believe what Nurse Ratched has been saying about McMurphy conning them.

After McMurphy and Chief Bromden get into a fight defending an inmate named Big George, they are sent to the ward for the disturbed. When McMurphy refuses to apologize to Nurse Ratched, she sends them both to electro-shock therapy. Chief Bromden returns to the ward and speaks to the inmates for the first time in years. McMurphy also returns a changed man: as the people around him improve, he becomes mentally unstable.

The inmates attempt to escape, but the plan is discovered and McMurphy is blamed. When Nurse Ratched confronts one inmate, Billy Bibbit, about the escape plan, she learns some personal secrets about Billy that drive him to kill himself. Enraged over his death, McMurphy attacks Nurse Ratched, exposing her breasts and undermining at least the appearance of her authority. Yet she has the power to send McMurphy to be lobotomized, and he returns to the ward a vegetable. Nurse Ratched plans to use him to demonstrate her restored authority. To prevent this, Chief Bromden smothers McMurphy.

Patient Scanlon sees the murder and helps Chief Bromden escape, which he does by hurling the control panel through a window. Scanlon promises to tell the authorities that McMurphy was alive after Chief Bromden left. Although it is not certain, the

In the 1975 film version of* One Flew Over the Cuckoo's Nest, *Jack Nicholson plays McMurphy, who loses the battle for human dignity in a mental hospital.

reader is left with the impression that the Chief escapes to a new and fulfilling life and that his freedom is McMurphy's victory after all.

CHARACTERS: Randle P. McMurphy, a confidence man with a genuine affection for people, is crude but likeable. His free manner of self-expression quickly earns him a respected status in the ward among the other inmates, who have until then been dominated by Nurse Ratched. McMurphy is, however, preoccupied with satisfying his personal needs. When he first enters the mental hospital, he is concerned only with making his own life more comfortable, which is why he wanted to avoid working on a prison farm in the first place. But he becomes gradually more involved in helping the others with their struggle against Nurse Ratched. When he realizes he can't leave the ward unless Nurse Ratched says so, it is in a sense too late, for the other patients now look to him for leadership. Yet, as McMurphy helps them gain their freedom, he begins to lose his; as he helps to make them well, his own sanity ebbs away.

In some ways, McMurphy remains the same man he was when he entered the hospital. His big mistake occurs because he can't resist being the con man after all, tricking the others into betting that Chief Bromden can't lift the heavy control panel by himself. A rugged, uncivilized individualist, McMurphy does bear some responsibility for his own downfall. But when he attacks Nurse Ratched—the act that sends him to be lobotomized—he is doing so for the whole group of inmates who want her punished for the death of Billy Bibbit. After he returns to the ward, McMurphy is no longer himself; Chief Bromden recognizes this, so he smothers him without any pangs of conscience. For all practical purposes, McMurphy is already dead.

The villain of the novel is **Nurse Ratched**, a large, gray-haired woman and former army nurse. Throughout the novel, she seems more a symbol than an actual person. Her rigid commitment to control is contrasted with McMurphy's free and uninhibited spirit. Nurse Ratched runs a tightly administered ward. If her patients remain weak, it is easier to control and mold them, and so she promotes fear and suspicion among both inmates and employees. She even controls the ward doctor through his addiction to morphine, blackmailing him for whatever she wants. Nurse Ratched, critics have observed, is a symbol for Kesey of the modern woman intent on destroying the masculinity of men. In Chief Bromden's narration, she is part evil and part machine. She never emerges as more than a symbol, never appearing as a flesh and blood woman with motivations, desires, or dreams.

Chief Bromden, the narrator, has been in the ward since the end of World War II, longer than any other patient. Although six feet seven inches tall, he sees himself as small and weak, and though totally capable of hearing and speaking, he pretends to be a deaf-mute. He believes his white mother turned his Native American father into an alcoholic, which is why he takes his mother's name, as if he were the one to bear the shame. Through his association with McMurphy, Chief Bromden finds the strength to struggle against both his paranoia and his schizophrenia, illnesses that date to his childhood. He begins to speak and act in a sane fashion. By the novel's end, he has taken responsibility for ending McMurphy's life, and he sets out to build a new life for himself outside the mental ward.

There are several other important patients in the story. **Dale Harding** is ashamed of being an effeminate man, but he is probably the strongest of the inmates psychologically. The leader of the Patient's Council and the first to follow McMurphy, he is able to assume leadership when the con man is sent to the disturbed ward. Eventually cured, Harding returns home. **Lifeguard** is a former football player and the one who tells McMurphy that Nurse Ratched must sign his release from the ward. **Big George** is terrified of dirt; his refusal to have an enema sparks the fight that sends McMurphy and Chief Bromden to the disturbed ward. **Billy Bibbit** is a shy thirty-one-year-old who acts like an adolescent and is totally dominated by his mother. Nurse Ratched finds out that he was going to lose his virginity to Candy Starr the night of the escape. When she threatens to tell his mother this, Billy cuts his own throat. **Scanlon** is the last of McMurphy's followers left on the ward at the novel's end. He is the one who helps Chief Bromden escape.

Further Reading

Billingsley, Ronald G. *The Artistry of Ken Kesey.* Eugene, OR: University of Oregon Press, 1991.

Bruccoli, Matthew J., and Richard Layman, eds. *Broadening Views, 1968-1988.* Vol. 6 of *Concise Dictionary of American Literary Biography.* Detroit: Gale Research, 1989.

Charters, Ann, ed. *The Beats: Literary Bohemians in Postwar America.* Vol. 16 of *Dictionary of Literary Biography.* Detroit: Gale Research, 1983.

Contemporary Literary Criticism. Vols. 1, 3, 6, 11, 46, 64. Detroit: Gale Research, 1973, 1975, 1976, 1979, 1988, 1991.

DeLeon, David. *Leaders from the 1960s.* Westport, CT: Greenwood Press, 1994.

Faggen, R. "The Great American Hollow." *Harper's* 289 (August 1994).

Foster, John Wilson. "Hustling to Some Purpose: Kesey's *One Flew Over the Cuckoo's Nest.*" *Western American Literature* 9 (August 1974).

Helterman, Jeffrey, and Richard Layman, eds. *American Novelists since World War II.* Vol. 2 of *Dictionary of Literary Biography.* Detroit: Gale Research, 1978.

Leeds, Barry H. *Ken Kesey.* New York: Ungar, 1981.

Malin, Irving. "Ken Kesey: *One Flew Over the Cuckoo's Nest.*" *Critique: Studies in Modern Fiction* 5 (fall 1962).

Porter, M. Gilbert. *The Art of Grit: Ken Kesey's Fiction.* Columbia, MO: University of Missouri Press, 1982.

Pratt, John Clark, ed. *One Flew Over the Cuckoo's Nest: Text and Criticism.* New York: Viking, 1973.

Ryan, Bryan, ed. *Major Twentieth-Century Authors: A Selection of Sketches from Contemporary Authors.* Detroit: Gale Research, 1991.

Safer, Elaine B. *The Contemporary American Comic Epic: The Novels of Barth, Pynchon, Gaddis, and Kesey.* Columbus, OH: Wayne State University Press, 1990.

Searles, George J., ed. *A Casebook on Ken Kesey's One Flew Over the Cuckoo's Nest.* Albuquerque, NM: University of New Mexico Press, 1992.

Sherwood, Terry G. "*One Flew Over the Cuckoo's Nest* and the Comic Strip." *Critique: Studies in Modern Fiction* 13 (summer 1971).

Something about the Author. Vol. 66, Detroit: Gale Research, 1991.

Stelow, Michael. *Kesey.* Eugene, OR: Northwest Review Books, 1977.

Tanner, Steven L. *Ken Kesey.* Boston, MA: Twayne, 1990.

Stephen King

1947-, American novelist, short story writer, and screenwriter

Carrie

(horror novel, 1974)

PLOT: Set in a small Maine town, *Carrie* is the story of a lonely, friendless, seventeen-year-old girl who possesses a terrifying supernatural power called telekinesis. Carrie knows in a naive way that she is able to make small objects move at will, but her domineering, zealously religious mother stresses over and over that it is a sin to use such a secret tool. Carrie's otherworldly power begins to stir in her one day after she is unbearably humiliated by schoolmates. Because of her part in Carrie's disgrace, Sue Snell feels so guilty that she persuades her steady beau, popular Tommy Ross, into asking Carrie to the prom. Carrie accepts, outwardly defying her mother for the first time.

However, another schoolmate, Christine Hargensen, who is barred from the dance, vows revenge with the help of her roughneck boyfriend Billy Nolan. Her plan involves dropping pig's blood from the gym rafters on the night of the prom to bring about the ultimate disgrace of Carrie White. But when the buckets of blood drop and cover her and others, Carrie gains full control of her strange and terrifying power. The town is nearly destroyed and more than four hundred—mostly teenagers—are killed, including Tommy Ross. Christine and Billy die later that night when their car, which suddenly seems possessed by a strange power, will not stop, and crashes. Carrie also dies, stabbed by her mother just before she successfully wills the older woman's heart to stop. In the aftermath, Sue Snell finds Carrie's body.

CHARACTERS: Carrie White, innocent schoolgirl and vengeful demon, alternates between being a sympathetic and a frustrating character. She generates sympathy as the lonely outcast, the target of cruel taunts, yet her inability to stand up to her deranged mother shows a frustrating lack of backbone. Carrie's humiliation by her schoolmates begins to make a difference, although a small one at first. A growing awareness of her own strange power starts to take over. For instance, she begins to realize that her mother is actually afraid of her forbidden power and a glimmer of defiance creeps to the surface.

Later, at the prom and at ease with Tommy, who seems to like her, Carrie gains self-confidence. A different person shows signs of emerging: a young girl learning for the first time what it is like to be on the inside of a social circle, not the object of disdain. If not completely accepted by Tommy's friends, she at least feels tolerated, respected, perhaps even a trifle feared. It is a heady, intoxicating sensation, and were it not for the horror of the falling blood, the feeling might have gone on to influence and change the life and personality of a young misfit.

But the blood does drop and splatter, and the humiliation is so great this time that the genie can't be put back into the bottle. There is no going back for Carrie now. To go back would be to admit that her mother had been right all along. There is only retaliation, a way out of the horrendous pain she is enduring. For Carrie, the retaliation means unleashing the restraints of her full and terrible power.

Margaret White, Carrie's mother, is so obviously without redeeming qualities that it is difficult to excuse her personality flaws as the result of her mental illness alone. Despite her depressing background, it is hard to sympathize with a mother who seems to loathe her daughter for merely being alive. But as Carrie gains confidence, her mother's power over her recedes. It becomes more and more evident that the mother is aware of—and deeply afraid of—Carrie's telekinetic power. She tries to maintain control over her daughter by isolating her from the outside world, but in doing so Carrie's mother becomes as ignorant of life on the outside as her daughter. Unable to cope with the situation, Margaret suppresses any evidence of Carrie's power from her mind until, for her, it does not exist. In the end, however, it is this very power that kills her.

Sue Snell is more or less a typical teenager. A popular girl, her sense of security and status within her high school community is, not unusually, of utmost importance to her. But after the humiliation of Carrie, she begins to feel a guilt that culminates in her proposal to Tommy that he take Carrie to the prom. Part of her gesture is atonement for a wrong she knows she has committed and part of her hopes that such a gesture will indeed bring Carrie out of her shell. Perhaps more than anyone in the town, Sue Snell realizes that her life will never be the same.

Christine Hargensen is more of a rebel, less sensitive, less caring, less understanding. She becomes the catalyst of the unformed plan to "get Carrie." She discovers that old man Henty has some pigs out on his farm and gives this information to **Billy Nolan** so that he and his gang of toughs can slaughter the pigs and gather the blood that will turn Carrie's first prom into a nightmare. Although not really sure why she has taken up with such a low-life character as Billy or why she has concocted such a terrible plan, Chris finds the excitement that comes when she actually pulls the rope that drops the blood on Carrie and the others is almost too unbearable—and funny.

An important minor character in the plot is **Rita Desjardin**, the gym teacher. Feeling both pity and shame after Carrie's humiliation, she asks the school principal, **Henry Grayle**, to punish the girls who participated in the unbearable taunting that day. From this stems Sue's plan to have Tommy take Carrie to the dance and Chris's horrible scheme of revenge, and ultimately the destruction of the school and nearly the entire town.

Tommy Ross is popular, a jock, and a good student who shows almost surprisingly mature understanding when Sue confides her feelings of shame and guilt about the treatment of Carrie White. Whatever his reasons for doing as Sue asks, Tommy

Carrie (Sissy Spacek) and Tommy (William Katt) just before the climax in the 1976 movie version of King's Carrie.

acts with good grace and ease as Carrie's escort to the dance. He dies quickly and without pain when one of the buckets of blood strikes him squarely on top of the head.

Cujo

(horror novel, 1981)

PLOT: As with many of King's novels, this story is set in the little Maine town of Castle Rock. It is about five years after a cop named Frank Dodd, who had some mental and sexual problems, killed several women in the town and then committed suicide. Parents still threaten their children with stories about Dodd crawling out of his grave to get them if they don't behave. With Dodd safely buried, the townspeople think they are safe. But a new danger is brewing in Castle Rock at the home of the Cambers. Joe, Charity, and their son, Brett live up at the end of the hill with their two-hundred-pound, friendly St.

Bernard, Cujo. One night the dog comes upon Gary Pervier, who is drunk, and uncharacteristically bites him. Other people begin to notice things about Cujo, who seems to be getting meaner and less like himself. Brett Camber notices this change, but when he mentions it to his mother, she dismisses his worries and tells him not to say anything to his father.

When Charity Camber takes Brett to her sister's place in Connecticut for a week, Joe plans a guy's trip to Boston with his friend, Gary, planning to see a Red Sox game and maybe get into a little trouble. But when Joe drives over to Gary's place before the trip, he finds his friend lying dead in a pool of blood. His throat has been ripped open. When he sees a pile of dog droppings, Joe figures Cujo has gone rabid. Before Joe can call for help, however, Cujo reappears and comes after Joe.

Soon after, four-year-old Tad Trenton and his mother, Donna, are driving home in their old Pinto, which is having engine trouble. They see Cujo, covered with blood, come out of the Cambers' garage. Cujo hurls himself at the car, and Donna and Tad are trapped in their stalled car. Even when Cujo disappears, they know he is lurking nearby, just waiting for them to step out of the car. Long hours pass and Donna and Tad's disappearance is noticed, but no one knows where they are. Donna's husband, Vic, at first doesn't bother to go looking for them because his wife's earlier infidelity leads him to think that she is out with another man. Only after they have been gone a long time does Vic overcome his jealousy and become concerned. The police begin a search, and officer George Bannerman finally spots the car. When he steps out to investigate, he, too, is attacked.

Finally, after many hours in the car, Donna realizes her son is dying from lack of air and water. When she spies a baseball bat on the lawn, she gets out of the car. Cujo comes for her and she fights the ferocious dog with the bat. Although he bites her, she kills Cujo. By the time they are rescued, however, Tad is dead. Donna can't believe it. The headlines read that a rabid dog killed four people in a three-day reign of terror. Cujo's remains are cremated. The small cave into which the dog had chased a rabbit some time before the killings is never discovered.

CHARACTERS: The unwilling monster of the story is **Cujo**, a two-hundred-pound St. Bernard who belongs to the Camber family. Cujo is ordinarily a good-natured dog, licking kids' faces with slobbery swipes. But strange feelings begin to enter his mind sometime after he chases a rabbit down a cave. Cujo can't understand it himself; he just becomes meaner and meaner.

King foreshadows the fate of four-year-old **Tad Trenton** when the boy insists toward the beginning of the book that there is a monster in his closet waiting to eat him. His parents, of course, don't believe him, but in the end the boy's fears prove prophetic. Cujo doesn't eat him, but the dog's attack on the family car does lead to his death.

Tad's mother, **Donna Trenton**, is a woman preoccupied by troubles with her marriage, which is falling apart. She has admitted to her husband, Vic, that she had an affair with Steve Kemp some time ago. Though the affair didn't mean anything, it is about to ruin her marriage. She soon has more desperate problems on her hands, however, when Cujo attacks the car. When she realizes that her son is dying, Donna gathers all her courage to save him. She is savagely attacked but is able to kill Cujo to save her son. She nearly loses her mind when she learns he is dead. After four weeks in the hospital, she returns home a shattered woman. But she and her husband decide to try to put their lives and their marriage back together.

Vic Trenton suffers his own personal hell when he is told of his wife's infidelity. He is so certain that she is with Steve Kemp when she disappears that he does not go out to look for her. He later wonders whether Tad would still be alive if he had looked for them sooner. In the end, however, the terrible tragedy of his son's death has made Vic realize that he loves his wife and that he wants their marriage to survive. He knows Donna will suffer for a long time because of her inability to save her son, but he also comes to realize that nothing could have saved him under the circumstances.

Steve Kemp is an unsavory character who refuses to accept Donna's decision to end their affair. When no one is home at the Trenton house, he breaks in and leaves a scrawled message about how he slept with Donna that she and Vic will be sure to see. After that, he feels a little guilty, but by the time he is on the highway and heading toward New York, he has convinced himself that what he did was really an act of courage.

Joe and **Charity Camber** are having problems with their marriage, too. Charity holds a lottery ticket in her hands and dreams of getting away. Their lovable dog, Cujo, finds a grisly means of ridding her of Joe in a way she had certainly never intended. Their son, **Brett Camber**, is one of the first to see the changes slowly occurring in Cujo, but he is told by his mother not to bother his father about it. Some six months after the horrible tragedy of the killings and Cujo's death, Brett's mother gets him a new puppy—a terrier they name Willie.

Gary Pervier is a mean old cuss, a wounded war veteran who doesn't care much about anything, except his three friends—Joe Camber, Brett, and their dog, Cujo. No matter how mean he feels on a particular day, the sight of that big Cujo sitting up and begging for food really tickles him. So he is really surprised on the day Cujo attacks him. His first thought when Cujo bites him is that he has rabies. Although he fights savagely against the animal, Gary dies with the realization that he is drowning in his own blood.

Pet Sematary

(horror novel, 1983)

PLOT: Dr. Louis Creed has taken a position at the University of Maine, and he and his family—wife Rachel, daughter Ellie, infant son Gage, and a cat named Winston Churchill—are delighted to move into what seems a perfect find, the big old house in the town of Ludlow. Across the street live an elderly couple, Jud and Norma Crandall, with whom they become fast friends. Jud introduces them to the rather eerie pet cemetery on their property.

Louis's first taste of uneasiness occurs when a young man, Victor Pascow, dies at the college infirmary. Before he dies from a hole in his head, he says to Louis, "Pet sematary." Sometime later, while the family was away, Louis discovers that Church has died. Jud takes him to an isolated part of the cemetery, where they bury the cat. Before long, Church returns. He seems alive, but he looks different, more aggressive, meaner. Jud tells him of the supposedly strange powers of the cemetery, relating the story of Timmy Baterman, who was dead but returned. Louis is wary of the cat's appearance and manner, but he does not tell his wife about the cemetery. Ellie seems to accept Church as before, except that she says he smells funny.

Tragedy strikes the family when Gage is killed running on the highway. After the funeral, Louis sends Rachel and Ellie back with his in-laws for a few days, promising to join them. Jud senses what he has in mind and tries to stop him, but Louis is determined. In the night he exhumes his son's body and buries him in the old pet cemetery.

When Louis is not at home, Jud is awakened by a hideous mewing. It is Church. He is followed by Gage, dressed in his burial suit. After screaming at the old man about what a whore his wife was, Gage uses a scalpel on Jud.

In the meantime, Rachel, urged on by the premonition of her daughter, who has become hysterical and starts shouting "Paxcow says it's too late," decides to return to Ludlow. She, too, is confronted by her son and is murdered. Louis returns and sees the figure of Gage. Before his eyes, the face of his son changes, becoming first Jud's face, then the ruined face of Victor Pascow. Louis manages to get a hypodermic needle into Gage's arm. Before the boy dies again, Louis sees the real face of his son once more. Louis gently wraps his wife's body in a bedsheet and then sets fire to the Crandall house. When a colleague, Steve Masterton, finds him, Louis's hair has turned white and he holds his wife wrapped in a bloody sheet. Steve follows Louis into the pet cemetery and then runs away in terror.

Later, the police ask Louis about the fire and he answers their questions satisfactorily. That night, alone in his house, he waits until he hears footsteps and feels a cold hand on his shoulder. Rachel's voice, full of dirt, says, "Darling."

CHARACTERS: Louis Creed begins to get uneasy soon after their arrival in Ludlow and the first visit to the "pet sematary." His uneasiness increases when the young Victor Pascow dies at the college infirmary from a hole in his head. Before he dies, he croaks out the words "in the pet sematary." Louis can't believe he heard correctly. After Norma Crandall has a near-fatal heart attack, Louis becomes even more anxious. This is compounded by the death of Church, his burial in the pet cemetery, and his return as a somehow changed and dangerous animal.

The horror for Louis only increases, culminating in the tragic death of his young son on the highway. As though helpless to stop himself, despite the warnings of Jud Crandall, Louis is compelled to return to the cemetery with the body of his buried son. By now, Louis has succumbed to the evil madness of the pet sematary and is helpless to stop the progression of events. His hair turned white, he is lost in his own horror. When he is confronted by Gage with what he has done he kills him with a hypodermic needle. Now he is left with the body of his wife. In order to return her to him, he must go back once more to the pet sematary.

The elderly **Jud Crandall** explains to Louis that the Micmac Indian tribe once laid claim to this area and believed the "pet sematary" to be a magic place where they buried their dead. But later on they claimed that the land had "gone sour." After Church is buried, Jud tells Louis about the experience he had many years ago with his own dog. Later, Louis asks Jud if any humans had ever been buried there recently. Jud tells him the story of Timmy Baterman, whose body was returned after he was killed in World War II in Italy. Sometime after the funeral, he was seen in town. Jud actually saw him, too, and said he "looked damned." Sometime after that, the Baterman house burned down.

Ellie is a perceptive child who senses a change in her cat Church when he returns from the pet cemetery, although she does not know of his death and burial. But she tells her father that Church "smells bad." Following the death of her infant brother, Gage, when she and her mother are with her mother's parents for a few days, Ellie has a series of bad dreams and becomes so hysterical that she must be taken to the hospital. When her grandfather, **Irwin Goldman**, calls Louis to tell him to come, he also says that all he could make out from Ellie's babbling is "Paxcow says it's too late." Paxcow is how Ellie mispronounced the name of the university student who died, **Victor Pascow**. Louis regards those words as "a funeral bell against the wall of his heart."

Steve Masterton, Louis's university colleague, follows him into the pet sematary as he carries the sheet-covered body of his dead wife, Rachel. When Steve calls to him, Louis replies that he must bury Rachel and asks for some help in doing so. In horror, Steve flees from this evil place and later barely remembers having gone to Ludlow to check on Louis at all. It is only sometimes in his dreams that the scene returns to him and he awakens shrieking. Steve never goes into the town of Ludlow again after that night and the next year he takes a job halfway across the country.

Rachel Creed is devastated by the loss of her infant son and returns to her parents' home with Ellie. But after her daughter's hysterical outbursts, Rachel senses that something evil has occurred back in Ludlow and rushes to her husband. Instead, she is confronted by the horror of her son, who has returned from the dead, and she is killed. Buried by her husband in the pet sematary, she, too, returns to her husband from the dead.

Further Reading

Authors and Artists for Young Adults. Vols. 1, 17. Detroit: Gale Research, 1989, 1996.

Beahm, George, ed. *The Stephen King Companion.* Kansas City: Andrews & McMeel, 1989.

Contemporary Literary Criticism. Vols. 12, 26, 37. Detroit: Gale Research, 1980, 1983, 1986.

Daris, Jonathan P. *Stephen King's America.* Bowling Green, OH: Bowling Green State University Press, 1994.

Magistracle, Tony. *Stephen King: The Second Decade.* New York: Twayne, 1992.

Reino, Joseph. *Stephen King: The First Decade, Carrie to Pet Sematary.* Boston: Twayne, 1988.

Saidman, Anne. *Stephen King: Master of Horror.* Minneapolis: Lerner, 1992.

Schweitzer, Darrell, ed. *Discovering Stephen King.* Mercer Island, WA: Starmount House, 1985.

Underwood, Tim, and Chuck Miller. *Fear Itself: The Horror Fiction of Stephen King.* Lancaster, PA: Underwood-Miller, 1982.

———. *Kingdom of Fear: The World of Stephen King.* New York: New American Library, 1987.

Winter, Douglas E. *Stephen King: The Art of Darkness.* New York: New American Library, 1984.

John Knowles

1925-, American novelist

A Separate Peace

(young adult novel, 1960)

PLOT: Fifteen years after leaving Devon, a prep school in New Hampshire, Gene Forrester reflects upon both a summer session and the school year of 1942-43. Against the backdrop of World War II, Gene describes his close friendship with a most unusual boy, Phineas, who is nicknamed Finny. Finny, who was nearing seventeen at the time, has a magnetic personality and is respected as the best athlete in the school, whereas Gene, who is the same age, is more introspective and intellectual. They are roommates and best friends.

During a walk around the campus, Finny dares Gene to join him in a dangerous adventure—jumping from a high tree into the river below. They both succeed and repeat this act, though Gene never loses his fear of jumping. Although the two boys have other friends on campus—like the pathetic Edwin "Leper" Lepellier, the brilliant Chet Douglas, and the witty, well-organized Brinker Hadley—they remain inseparable.

Gene, however, has trouble accepting Finny's perfection and mistakenly begins to believe that his friend is really a covert enemy trying to sabotage his good academic record. One evening, Finny suggests that the two jump from the tree together. On an impulse, Gene jiggles the limb on which Finny is standing and the boy falls to the river bank below, shattering his leg. Overcome with remorse, Gene tries to tell his friend what he has done, but Finny, refusing to believe Gene could so betray him, stubbornly maintains that he only lost his balance.

The autumn term begins without Phineas, who is at home in Boston with a cast on his leg. Gene copes with faculty members, such as the dormitory master, Mr. Ludsbury, and survives a fight with Cliff Quackenbush, the oafish manager of the crew team, but he is overjoyed when Phineas reappears in his dorm room. Though the students talk only of the war in which they soon will be involved, Phineas, now walking with a limp, rejects the war and becomes intent on training Gene to be an Olympic-caliber athlete. Under the leadership of Brinker Hadley, the students become intrigued with what really caused Phineas's fall from the tree. All the boys are summoned to a hearing in the big assembly room, where Leper, who has witnessed the "accident," testifies. Phineas still proclaims his friend's innocence, but he is finally forced to face the truth. He staggers out of the room, stumbles on some slippery stairs, and again breaks his leg.

Gene visits Phineas in the infirmary and—under questioning by his tearful friend—confesses his misdeed, attributing it to some incomprehensible impulse. During a routine setting of Phineas's leg, some bone marrow is released and lodges in his heart, killing him instantly. Gene is too numb to cry, feeling that the loss of Phineas is really like his own death. That June, Gene, now an enlistee in the Navy, watches as the Army Air Corps begins taking over the campus. Although he knows he will soon be part of a global war, Gene realizes that he has already fought his own private war and killed the person he mistakenly believed was his enemy.

CHARACTERS: The narrator, **Gene Forrester**, is so objective in retelling the story that he leaves many of his inner feelings and motivations hidden. On the surface, he is the opposite of Phineas: conventional and reserved, passive and thoughtful, always a follower rather than a leader. Though not an outstanding athlete, Gene is a better-than-average student. He is cautious and guarded in his actions, unwilling to question rules or stand up to authority. Easily swayed by the magnetic Phineas, Gene manages to break these behavior patterns when he shines under the reflected glory of Phineas's nonconformity.

Gene is modest and unassuming to the point that he is unable to believe that Phineas has chosen him as his best friend. He has difficulty expressing his emotions directly and is so restrained that he can't return Finny's displays of affection. When Gene does not respond sympathetically to Leper's problems, Leper accuses him of being a "savage underneath." Though this is an extreme evaluation of Gene—who is basically a well-liked, popular student—there is a core of truth to the assertion. Gene's youth and inexperience make him ill-equipped to deal with situations that require maturity, and therefore his responses in difficult situations can be impulsive and brutal.

In part because of his own hidden internal conflicts and repressed feelings, Gene is attracted to Phineas and establishes him as his role model. But when he can no longer cope with the kind of perfection that Phineas represents, he searches for imperfections that don't exist and begins to doubt his friend's loyalty. At first jealous and then resentful of imagined plots against him, Gene seeks a way to topple his idol. He does this literally by jiggling the tree branch. Later, his guilt makes him overly solicitous toward Phineas. Through these experiences, Gene realizes that he must develop as an individual and not by measuring himself against the abilities of another person. By the end of the novel, Gene observes that wars are made by people "ignorant in the Human heart." In his relationship with Phineas, Gene has fought his own private war.

Phineas, or **Finny**, is a golden boy, an ideal young man. With eye-catching good looks and the grace of a Greek god, he captivates everyone who meets him. He radiates appeal and warmth. An outstanding athlete, Finny revels in action-sports and daring activities. Though he is popular with both faculty and students and always the center of attention, he remains modest and unassuming. As Gene comments, "He didn't know he was unique." Finny is also articulate and imaginative and delights in making up stories and creating outlandish situations.

Phineas also has an independent streak and often acts without thinking. Gene calls him "a model boy who was most comfortable in the truant's corner." Each difficulty that he produces provides another challenge for his charm, imagination, and eloquence. Finny is also deeply trusting; he candidly reveals his emotions and can't understand others who bottle-up their inner feelings. Always his own person, he is unwilling to use his aptitudes and talents solely to impress others or garner praise. Though he easily breaks the school's swimming record while with friends, his self-assurance leads him to refuse to repeat this feat publicly.

Finny has many noble qualities and selflessly gives of himself to others. Although he is not an outstanding student, he accepts this limitation without difficulty. He seems incapable of being cruel or nasty and—with his great love of life and joy in living—can't comprehend negative emotions like jealousy and envy. He is therefore unable to accept Gene's responsibility for the accident. When Finny learns that his accident will prevent him from enlisting in the military and participating in athletics, he simply refuses to accept these limitations, without self-pity or rancor. He dismisses the importance of the war and begins to train Gene to achieve the athletic prominence he has been denied. He is described as a noble individual who "possessed an extra vigor, a heightened confidence in himself, a serene capacity for affection."

One of Gene's other friends at school is **Edwin Lepellier**, nicknamed **Leper**, a pathetic loner who seems to exist on his own planet. With his pinched face and distracted look, he is the butt of jokes and the object of scorn. He lives in his own private world, where butterflies and beaver dams are more important than the war. His interest in skiing and becoming part of a ski patrol leads him to enlist in the army, where he is miserable. Unprepared for basic training, he soon cracks under the severe conditions. Afraid of being discharged as a "psycho," he goes AWOL and returns home. Leper is disappointed when he summons Gene for help and receives only rejection. Though Leper witnessed Phineas's fall, he keeps silent about it, and when he is called to testify at the investigation, his answers are so ambiguous that they confuse the tribunal. For Phineas, however, they are precise enough to convince him that Gene intentionally caused the incident. **Chet Douglas**, another of Gene's friends, is the brightest kid in the senior class. Slim and fair-skinned, he has two obsessions: tennis and his trumpet. A vulnerable, accommodating youngster, he is described as "too obliging and considerate to be popular."

In the interest of clearing up the rumors about Phineas's accident, **Brinker Hadley** organizes the formal student investigation. A clever boy, Brinker is well-liked, a born organizer and a tireless worker in student affairs. He is efficient, dependable, and conscious of political events. When Brinker realizes that he will soon be in the armed forces, however, he sees the futility of involvement in school activities and loses interest. Though he outwardly claims that he wants to see combat, at enlistment time Brinker disappoints his bellicose father by joining the Coast Guard.

Another student is **Cliff Quackenbush**, the unpleasant senior crew leader. He is officious and insulting to Gene, who has volunteered to be his assistant. Quackenbush is an unimaginative slogger and an underachiever who is disliked by the other students. Humiliated by his position in the school, he mistakenly believes he can dominate Gene while Phineas is recovering at home. The boys fight and both fall into a polluted river. This incident ends Gene's involvement with the crew team.

Mr. Ludsbury, the British faculty member in charge of the dormitory, is stern and moralistic. He is noted for his sarcasm and an Adam's apple that bobs rapidly up and down as he speaks. His exaggerated responses to minor school infractions contrast tellingly with the horrifying conditions that the war has produced in the outside world.

Further Reading

Authors and Artists for Young Adults. Vol. 10. Detroit: Gale Research, 1993.

Berger, Laura Standley, ed. *Twentieth-Century Young Adult Writers*. 1st ed. Detroit: St. James, 1994.

Bloom, Harold. *Twentieth-Century American Literature*. Vol. 4. New York: Chelsea House, 1986.

Contemporary Literary Criticism. Vols. 1, 4, 10, 26. Detroit: Gale Research, 1973, 1975, 1979, 1983.

Ellis, James. "*A Separate Peace:* The Fall from Innocence." *English Journal* 53 (May 1965).

Henderson, Lesley, and Noelle Watson, eds. *Contemporary Novelists*. 5th ed. Chicago: St. James, 1991.

Kibler, James E. Jr., ed. *American Novelists since World War II*. Vol. 6 of *Dictionary of Literary Biography*. Vol. 6. Detroit: Gale Research, 1980.

Reed, W. Michael. "*A Separate Peace:* A Novel Worth Teaching." *Virginia English Bulletin* 36 (winter 1986).

Something about the Author. Vols. 8, 89. Detroit: Gale Research, 1976, 1997.

Weber, Ronald. "Narrative Method in *A Separate Peace.*" *Studies in Short Fiction* 3 (fall 1965).

Wolfe, Peter. "The Impact of Knowles's *A Separate Peace.*" *University Review* 36 (March 1970).

Harper Lee

1926-, American novelist

To Kill a Mockingbird

(novel, 1960)

PLOT: This poignant story of growing up in the South of the 1930s—an environment of racial bigotry and injustice—takes place over a two-year period in the small town of Maycomb, Alabama. It is narrated by Jean Louise Finch (nicknamed "Scout"), now an adult, who is a six-year-old about to start school when the novel begins. Spunky and independent, Scout lives with her brother, ten-year-old Jem, and her father, Atticus Finch, a respected attorney. The children's mother died when Scout was two

Atticus Finch (Gregory Peck) argues his case in the 1962 movie adaptation of **To Kill a Mockingbird.**

years old, and the family is cared for under the loving but stern discipline of Calpurnia, who is black.

When the novel begins, it is summer and the Finch children's seven-year-old friend, Dill, has come to stay with his aunt, who lives next door. Imaginative Dill joins Scout and Jem in their everyday adventures. This year their attention focuses on the Radley place just down the street, a source of much excitement and fear for the children. According to the town legend, the Radleys' son, Arthur, known as Boo, got into some minor trouble as a teenager and was forced to stay at home for the next fifteen years. When he was thirty-three, he supposedly stabbed his father in the leg with a pair of scissors. Now the mysterious Boo lives in total isolation in the old house. Despite orders to the contrary from their father, Jem, Scout, and Dill dare each other to peek in the window of the Radley house for a look at Boo. Soon after, they begin to find little objects hidden in a tree near the Radley place. Jem slowly realizes that they are gifts for the children from Boo.

In the meantime, a black man named Tom Robinson is accused of raping a white woman, Mayella Ewell. Mayella is the daughter of Bob Ewell, a shiftless, brutal bigot and the villain of the novel. Atticus agrees to defend Tom and stands firm against a mob that comes to the jail to lynch the prisoner. Despite the fact that Atticus proves Tom could not be the rapist—he has a crippled left arm and could not have attacked Mayella as she describes—the black man is convicted in this town, where racial segregation and bigotry are a way of life. Robinson later takes his own life.

The trial has deeply shaken this small southern town, as the people must face their own feelings of prejudice and injustice. In an act of vengeance against Atticus for defending a black man, Bob Ewell tries to kill Jem and Scout in the woods one evening.

But he himself is killed, and Jem's arm is broken in the fight. Jem is carried home by Boo, and the children and Atticus slowly realize who killed Ewell in the woods that night. Although Atticus's first inclination is to explain the incident to the authorities, he is persuaded to do otherwise. Boo has saved and protected his children and should be allowed to live in peace.

The title of the novel comes from the statement by Atticus Finch to his children that it is a sin to kill a mockingbird. As Miss Maudie Atkinson, who lives across the street, explains to Scout, "Mockingbirds don't do one thing but make music for us to enjoy. They don't eat up people's gardens, don't nest in corncribs, they don't do one thing but sing out their hearts for us. That's why it's a sin to kill a mockingbird."

CHARACTERS: Atticus Finch, at nearly fifty, is older than most parents with children the ages of Scout and Jem. Perhaps that is why he speaks to them in a straightforward manner and treats them almost as adults. They call him Atticus. A fair and honest man who respects the feelings, rights, and opinions of others, he is portrayed as unique in this small southern town, where bigotry and racial discrimination are accepted without thought or reason. Although his character is highly moral, he remains believable and is softened by his wry sense of humor. Despite his innate goodness, Atticus shows the normal human emotions of fear—such as when a mob arrives at the courthouse to lynch Tom Robinson—and self-doubt about his ability to rear his motherless children properly. To help maintain discipline and order in the Finch household, Atticus's stern but loving housekeeper, **Calpurnia**, serves as another parent figure for the children. Her feelings for Jem and Scout are obvious and are returned in kind. Calpurnia helps the children to both understand and respect the black community.

Precocious and outspoken **Scout Finch** (her given name is **Jean Louise Finch**) behaves with dignity and compassion far beyond her years. She is her father's daughter, credited by him with the intelligence to understand the lessons he teaches her. Atticus expects her to judge people on character and not on stereotypes, and she does. Scout has inherited her father's love of books and reading. Each night she shares a few precious moments with him as he reads to her. On the down side, Scout has a quick temper that often gets her into trouble at school as well as at home. She has a tendency to blurt out what she sees and dislikes, regardless of whose feelings are hurt. She is disciplined both by Calpurnia at home and by her first-grade teacher. Through the novel, however, Scout gradually learns to control her quick temper and develops a greater sensitivity for the feelings of others.

Jem is Scout's protector, and their love for each other is obvious. A bright ten-year-old, Jem matures through the novel, becoming moodier and more affected by the ugliness and bigotry he sees about him. It is Jem who first begins to understand that the objects left in the tree are Boo's gestures of friendship. By following Jem's moods, readers can see the loss of childhood innocence and the beginning of awareness of what the real world is like. At first Jem takes for granted the goodness of people; but by the novel's end, this is no longer so. "Why can't they get along with each other?" he says to Scout.

Charles Baker Harris, known as **Dill Harris**, is the highly eccentric friend and playmate of Scout and Jem. He is a bright, imaginative seven-year-old who wears glasses and "linen shorts buttoned to his shirt." Feeling unloved at home, Dill is given to instigating dramatic games. For example, he is responsible for the interest that begins the children's association with Boo. Some say that the character of Dill is based upon a young Truman Capote, who was a childhood friend of Harper Lee.

Boo Radley is a figure who elicits great compassion. As the story unfolds, it becomes obvious that rather than a monster to be feared, he is a sympathetic person who has been cruelly deprived of a normal life. Through his first tentative interactions with the children, Boo's feelings of loneliness and deprivation slowly come to the surface. In his quiet, handicapped way, he comes to feel a sense of love and protection toward Scout and Jem. By the climax of the novel, the reader understands that Boo has to stop Ewell when he tries to harm the children he loves.

Bob Ewell is a brutal, shiftless man without one redeeming quality. He is a loathsome figure who is an example of how ignorance and prejudice can wither the soul. Although Tom Robinson is found guilty of assaulting his daughter, Ewell still seeks revenge for Atticus's handling of the case in court. He tries to kill the Finch children but instead is killed by Boo. His daughter, **Mayella**, is a pitiful character who seeks the friendship of a black man as solace for the physical abuse she receives from her father. When her overtures toward Tom Robinson come to light, she accuses him of rape to cover her shame. Although he is a central figure to the plot, **Tom Robinson** is a one-dimensional character—presented as little more than a good-hearted, almost-too-humble victim.

Further Reading

American Women Writers. Vol. 7. New York: Ungar, 1980.

Authors and Artists for Young Adults. Vol. 13. Detroit: Gale Research, 1994.

Berger, Laura Standley, ed. *Twentieth-Century Young Adult Writers.* 1st ed. Detroit: St. James, 1994.

Bruccoli, Matthew J., and Richard Layman, eds. *The Consciousness, 1941-1968.* Vol. 1 of *Concise Dictionary of American Literary Biography.* Detroit: Gale Research, 1988.

Contemporary Literary Criticism. Vols. 12, 60. Detroit: Gale Research, 1980, 1990.

Erisman, Fred. "The Romantic Regionalism of Harper Lee." *Alabama Review* 26 (April 1973).

Johnson, Claudia. "The Secret Courts of Men's Hearts: Code and Law in Harper Lee's *To Kill a Mockingbird.*" *Studies in American Fiction* 19 (autumn 1991).

———. To Kill a Mockingbird: *Threatening Boundaries.* New York: Twayne, 1995.

———. *Understanding* To Kill a Mockingbird: *A Student Casebook to Issues, Sources, and Historical Documents.* Westport, CT: Greenwood, 1994.

Kibler, James E. Jr. *American Novelists since World War II, Second Series.* Vol. 6 of *Dictionary of Literary Biography.* Detroit: Gale Research, 1980.

Ryan, Brian, ed. *Major Twentieth-Century Writers: A Selection of Sketches from Contemporary Authors.* Detroit: Gale Research, 1991.

Something about the Author. Vol. 11. Detroit: Gale Research, 1977.

Wakeman, John, ed. *World Authors, 1950-1970.* New York: H. W. Wilson, 1975.

Ursula K. Le Guin

1929-, American science fiction and fantasy writer

A Wizard of Earthsea

(fantasy, 1968)

PLOT: Thirteen-year-old Ged's extraordinary powers have long been recognized in his town of Ten Alders on the island of Gont. But his magical abilities don't change his life until after he saves the town from an attack by the pirate Kargs. Falling into a coma after this feat, he is awakened by a wizard named Ogion, who gets the permission of Ged's father to take the boy away for special tutelage.

After a few months with Ogion, Ged is sent to the school of wizardry on Roke, the Isle of the Wise. There he meets two older students, friendly Vetch and the unpleasant Jasper, as well as the head of the school, Archmage Nemmerle. Ged learns all sorts of sorcery, including how to change wind and weather, and how to change himself into other forms. One night, in an angry response to Jasper's goading, Ged is reckless with his powers and calls up a terrible black shadow that attacks Ged, who is badly scarred. The shadow then disappears.

Years later, at age eighteen, Ged is ready for his first assignment: ridding the island of Pendor of a family of dragons. He is able to subdue the chief dragon, even though he feels the presence of the terrible shadow that he once unleashed. On his way to the Court of Terrenon to find weapons to confront the mysterious shadow, the shadow attacks him. Powerless against the shadow, Ged narrowly escapes death. The shadow has somehow learned Ged's name, giving it power over the young wizard. Taking the form of a hawk, Ged flies to Gont and the hut of Ogion.

After a good rest, Ged sails to the isle of Iffish and meets Vetch, now a beloved mage. The two decide to pursue the shadow and sail to the outmost reaches of Earthsea. This time, having gained insights from Ogion, Ged is well prepared for his meeting with the shadow. Ged calls out his own name and his body absorbs the shadow, for Ged has realized that the shadow is his own dark side. Now that he is a whole man, he is once more his own master.

The other books in the "Earthsea" series are The Tombs of Atuan *(1971),* The Farthest Shore *(1972), and* Tehanu: The Last Book of Earthsea *(1990).*

CHARACTERS: In Gont, a land famous for its wizards, the extraordinary powers of young **Ged** have long been recognized. When he is only seven, the boy could shout a rhyme to the goats and they would come to him. From that time on, his powers become more extraordinary. Ged is presented as a good-hearted boy who wants to become a good man. Although he is gifted, his talents don't save him from the problems of growing up, and his struggle with the shadow represents the inner conflict between good and evil that everyone must endure at some point in life. By recognizing and facing up to his dark side, Ged obtains a self-awareness that allows him to mature.

When Ged saves his town from the Karg pirates by engulfing them in a fog, he attracts the attention of the wizard **Ogion the Silent**, who takes it upon himself to teach Ged. But Ged proves to be an impatient student. Extremely bright, gifted, and anxious to learn, Ged grows bored with the quiet tutoring he receives from Ogion, who eventually feels that the boy would be better served at the school of wizardry on the island of Roke. Here he meets **Archmage Nemmerle**, the master teacher and warder of Roke. Nemmerle is older than any living man, his voice quavery as a bird's. Ged learns quickly, but his impatience and lack of self-control cause him to unleash the horrible **shadow** that attacks and scars him. To defeat the shadow, Ged must understand himself better. When he at last accepts that the shadow is his own dark side, Ged is able to name it and, thus, gain power over it and destroy it. This hard-won victory marks Ged's passage into adulthood.

On the island of Roke, Ged meets two very different students, both older than he. **Jasper** is an unlikable person who always goads Ged to show "his style." Jasper treats Ged as inferior, and so when he challenges Ged to summon a spirit from the dead, Ged becomes angry and takes the bet, despite the warnings of others. But the hatred Jasper inspires in Ged causes his enchantment to unleash the evil within him, creating the shadow.

The other student whom Ged meets, **Vetch**, is the opposite of Jasper. Heavy-set, plain-looking, and with unpolished manners, Vetch is a very amiable sort who helps Ged in his pursuit of the shadow. Vetch shows his friendship for Ged when he reveals his true name—Estarriol—to the younger boy. He also goes with Ged to the far reaches of Earthsea, but he proves to be not as courageous as Ged when they confront the shadow and Vetch becomes frozen with terror.

The Left Hand of Darkness

(science fiction, 1969)

PLOT: This complex science fiction novel is set on an alien and cold planet, Gethen, in a future time when humans are far different from the way they are today. On Gethen the people are androgenous: most of the time their gender is neuter, but once a month they become either male or female. During this time—called "kemmer"—a chemical interaction between sexual partners causes each person to select a gender that does not depend on the sex he or she was before. People who were males during the last kemmer can become female and vice versa. Each Gethenian begins on an equal plane. There is no double standard because there is no second sex; there is no burden attached to motherhood, since any individual could become a mother at some time; and there is no sense of mistrust between the sexes.

The tale is mostly told through the eyes of Genly Ai, a black Earthman on a diplomatic mission to the nation of Karhide on the planet Gethen. He has been trying for two years without success to persuade the Gethenians to join the Ekumen, a confederation of eighty or so worlds. So far, Genly has spent two unprofitable years on Gethen. While he waits impatiently for the king to hear his pleas, Genly's spaceship continues to circle the planet.

Genly's Gethenian friend, Estraven, is exiled by the mad king of Karhide, Argaven, and sent to Orgoreyn, the rival nation of Karhide. In danger from those who do not want Gethen to join the Ekumen, Genly is reunited with his friend and together they make a tortuous journey across the notorious ice sheet to North Karhide. Estraven believes that once the king learns of Genly's presence in North Karhide, he will become sympathetic to his mission and allow him to call down his starship, which has been circling the planet all this time. Although Estraven, branded a traitor, is shot while attempting to cross the border back into Orgoreyn, everything else goes as planned and Gethen joins the Ekumen. At the novel's end, Genly, grieving for his friend, goes to Estraven's family to speak of his loss.

CHARACTERS: Genly Ai narrates much of the story, which is frequently interrupted by retellings of the myths and legends of Gethen. He is a young black man from Earth, and a rather conservative sort. When Estraven is exiled because of his dispute with Gethen's leaders over Genly's mission, the Earthman feels betrayed at first. Genly then goes to the neighboring nation of Orgoreyn and is surprised not only to be placed in a forced labor camp, but to be rescued by Estraven. It is only when the two embark on their dangerous and torturous journey over the ice that trust grows between them. Although sometimes, in kemmer, Estraven changes into a woman and love grows between them, both feel that it would be inappropriate to express that love in a sexual manner.

Genly's safe journey across the perilous ice, with the help of Estraven, induces the Gethen leadership to accept Genly's mission and to join the Ekumen. However, his success comes at the price of Estraven's death. The loss is felt very deeply by Genly, and at the end of the novel he visits Estraven's family to speak about the loss of his dear and trusted friend. Thus, *The Left Hand of Darkness* is mainly a tale of trust, betrayal, and love.

Patterns of ancient Chinese thought are also evident in the characters, such as during the journey across the ice when Genly draws the ancient Chinese symbol of a double curve inside a circle—one half is white and the other black. The white side represents the Chinese principle of yang, which is light, masculine, and active. The dark side in the yin principle: dark, feminine, and receptive. The two sides together represent the conciliation of opposites to form perfect harmony. A main theme of the novel, then, is the importance of equality between the sexes.

The other main character of this novel is the Gethen named **Estraven**. An admirable person, Estraven is able to perform great feats of strength and endurance. Possessing great willpower, the Gethen remains true to personal beliefs and values no matter the cost. When Estraven asserts that it is worth conceding some territory to Orgoreyn in a border dispute, the Gethen is labeled a traitor and exiled.

But Estraven has committed other crimes against his people for the sake of higher moral reasons. For example, he steals food—a deplorable crime among the Gethen—in order to keep Genly and himself alive during their journey across the ice. He also has an incestuous relationship with his sibling, and together they have a child. While sex between siblings is permissible on Gethen, it is not allowed for the mother and father to stay together after the child is born. Estraven and his sibling broke this taboo by leaving their clanhome after the child's birth in order to preserve their relationship. For this, they were shunned, and Estraven's sibling dies, presumably by suicide.

The king, **Argaven**, first appeared in Le Guin's short story entitled "Winter's King" in which the permanently frozen planet of Gethen is introduced. The king is a short, pot-bellied figure who grants Genly an audience to listen to his mission. Fearing liars and tricksters, Argaven is not convinced by Genly's arguments to join the Ekumen. By sending Genly away, the king sets the novel's ultimately tragic events in motion.

Further Reading

Authors and Artists for Young Adults. Vol. 9. Detroit: Gale Research, 1992.

Berger, Laura Standley, ed. *Twentieth-Century Children's Writers.* 4th ed. Detroit: St. James, 1994.

Bitter, James. *Approaches to the Fiction of Ursula Le Guin.* Ann Arbor, MI: UMI Research Press, 1984.

Bleiler, E. F., ed. *Science Fiction Writers.* New York: Scribner's, 1982.

Bucknall, Barbara J. *Ursula K. Le Guin.* New York: Ungar, 1981.

Children's Literature Review. Vol. 3. Detroit: Gale Research, 1978.

Contemporary Literary Criticism. Vols. 8, 13, 22, 45, 71. Detroit: Gale Research, 1978, 1980, 1982, 1987, 1993.

Cowart, David, and Thomas L. Wymer, eds. *Twentieth-Century American Science-Fiction Writers.* Vol. 8 of *Dictionary of Literary Biography.* Detroit: Gale Research, 1981.

Cumming, Elizabeth. *Understanding Ursula K. Le Guin.* Columbia, SC: University of South Carolina Press, 1990.

De Bolt, Joseph W. *Ursula K. Le Guin.* Port Washington, NY: Kennikat, 1979.

De Montreville, Doris, and Elizabeth D. Crawford, eds. *Fourth Book of Junior Authors and Illustrators.* New York: H. W. Wilson, 1978.

Estes, Glenn E., ed. *American Writers for Children since 1960: Fiction.* Vol. 52 of *Dictionary of Literary Biography.* Detroit: Gale Research, 1986.

Olander, Joseph D. *Ursula Le Guin.* New York: Taplinger, 1979.

Slusser, George Edgar. *The Farthest Shores of Ursula Le Guin.* San Bernardino, CA: Borgo, 1976.

Something about the Author. Vols. 4, 52. Detroit: Gale Research, 1973, 1989.

Spivak, Charlotte. *Ursula K. Le Guin.* Boston: Twayne, 1984.

Watson, Noelle, ed. *Twentieth-Century Science Fiction Writers.* 3rd ed. Chicago: St. James, 1991.

Madeleine L'Engle

1918-, American novelist

A Wrinkle in Time

(science fiction, 1962)

PLOT: Although essentially a science fiction novel, this unusual, Newbery Medal-winning book is concerned with the powers of the mind and explores such themes as love, the nature of good and evil, and the need for respecting the differences in others and recognizing one's own individuality. The story centers on the Murry family, especially twelve-year-old Meg. Besides Meg's mother, a research scientist who tries to promote a sense of independence and individuality in her children, and her father, a physicist, the family includes ten-year-old twins Sandy and Dennys and the intelligent, gifted Charles Wallace, age five. Charles Wallace is Meg's favorite.

One morning Meg and Charles Wallace pay a visit to Mrs. Whatsit. Ever since this rather unusual woman visited them while seeking shelter from a storm, the two children have been fascinated by her. Mrs. Whatsit lives near the Murry home in a "haunted" house. Meg's school chum, fourteen-year-old Calvin O'Keefe, joins them, and they are welcomed by Mrs. Whatsit and her two companions, Mrs. Who and Mrs. Which. Mrs. Who speaks several languages, but only in terse concise statements; Mrs. Which's voice sounds as if she is talking from inside an echo chamber. All three woman seem to have supernatural powers, and they promise to help Meg and Charles Wallace in the search for their father, who mysteriously disappeared a year ago while he was engaged in a secret space mission. The three ladies explain that in order to find the missing physicist, the children have to travel to outer space. They do so by using the tesseract. By creating a "wrinkle in time," the tesseract shortens the distance between two points via the fifth dimension.

The tesseract takes Meg, Charles Wallace, and Calvin to a friendly planet. They learn that Mr. Murry is being held prisoner on the planet of Camazotz, which is under the influence of a giant black cloud known as the Power of Darkness. Another "tesser" takes them to Camazotz, where the people live like robots, their lives completed dominated by a giant brain called IT. Charles Wallace is hypnotized and turned into a robotlike creature. With the use of Mrs. Who's magic eyeglasses, Meg is able to free her father, who is trapped behind a glasslike wall, but she nearly falls under the spell of IT. Mr. Murry is able to tesser to get Meg, Calvin, and himself to a friendly planet, but Charles Wallace is left behind.

Once again, the three ladies come to Meg's aid. They tell her that she is the only one with the power to free her brother from Camazotz. Although Meg does not understand what they mean, she returns to the planet to face IT and save Charles Wallace. Finally understanding the power she has, Meg says the words "I love you" over and over again until Charles Wallace is freed from the Power of Darkness. Reunited, the family returns home.

Other books in the "Time Fantasy" series are A Wind in the Door *(1973),* A Swiftly Tilting Planet *(1978),* A House Like a Lotus *(1984),* Many Waters *(1986) and* An Acceptable Time *(1989).*

CHARACTERS: The daughter of two scientists, **Meg Murry** is a highly intelligent twelve-year-old. She does poorly in school, however, because the lessons bore her. When her father disappears, it becomes even more difficult for Meg to concentrate on school. Her only solace is her five-year-old brother, Charles Wallace, whom she adores. Meg becomes intrigued with the strange Mrs. Whatsit and her equally strange companions, Mrs. Who and Mrs. Which. Her first tesser trip to cross a "wrinkle in time" is both frightening and exhilarating. Meg is often confused by her surroundings and the strange happenings, but she shows both courage and resourcefulness in her attempts to release her father from his imprisonment on Camazotz. When they are forced to leave Charles Wallace behind, she is distraught. But she is comforted on a friendly planet by one of its faceless inhabitants, whom she calls Aunt Beast. To free her beloved brother, Meg must face her sternest test. She realizes that she is the only one who can save Charles Wallace, whose superior intelligence Meg best understands. Confronting the horrifying IT back on Camazotz, Meg resists its attempts to brainwash her into becoming another automaton like her brother. She then saves Charles Wallace by repeatedly declaring that she loves him.

Charles Wallace Murry, Meg's five-year-old brother, is precociously intelligent and possesses clairvoyant powers. But because he rarely speaks, other children call him Meg's "dumb baby brother." Meg defends her brother by fighting those who make fun of him. When Meg tells her father she is worried about Charles Wallace, Mr. Murry reassures her that everyone develops at his or her own pace. Just as he predicted, when Charles Wallace is ready, he begins to talk in complete sentences.

Charles Wallace also has an uncanny way of understanding Meg. If she walks into the kitchen seeking some warm milk, for example, he is already there warming it up. But Charles Wallace, despite his super intelligence, runs into trouble on the faraway planet. When he meets the Prime Coordinator in the huge Central Intelligence Building, he falls under his hypnotic spell and is turned into another of the robotlike creatures that inhabit the planet Camazotz. It is only through his special bond with Meg that he is saved.

Meg's friend from school is **Calvin O'Keefe**. At fourteen, he is tall, skinny, and smart. His trousers are too short, his orange hair needs cutting, and his eyes are a very bright blue. When he first meets Charles Wallace, he asks whether the little boy is a moron. This enrages Meg, but Charles Wallace doesn't seem to mind. In fact, the two boys hit it off splendidly. The third child of eleven kids, Calvin considers himself very knowledgeable about the opposite sex.

Although Meg has a rather plain appearance, her mother, **Mrs. Murry**, is a beauty with flame-red hair and violet eyes. She is also a research scientist who has very strong ideas about children being allowed to grow and cultivate their own individuality. When Meg finally sees her physicist father, she is shocked at the appearance of **Mr. Murry**. His silky brown hair, which has grown long, is streaked with gray and he has grown a beard. He looks for all the world like a shipwrecked sailor or someone from another century.

The three mysterious women who help the Murry children find their father are Mrs. Whatsit, Mrs. Who, and Mrs. Which. **Mrs. Whatsit** is the Murry's eccentric neighbor. Her face looks a little like an autumn apple, but her eyes are bright, and she proves most helpful in leading the children on their search. **Mrs. Who** wears giant spectacles, which Meg later learns are magical. The plump little woman has a rather strange manner of speaking.

Although she is fluent in many languages, what she says comes out in sometimes mystifying statements, such as "The heart has its reasons, whereof reason knows nothing." The third of the eccentric ladies is **Mrs. Which.** Her manner of speaking is also odd since she sounds as if she were talking from inside an echo chamber.

A House Like a Lotus

(young adult novel, 1984)

PLOT: In this novel, which explores degrees of love and friendship, sixteen-year-old Polly O'Keefe is on her way to Athens, Greece, where she will spend three weeks as a "gofor" at a conference in the village of Osia Theola. The trip was arranged by her friend Maximiliana (Max) Horne, a wealthy artist who lives on Beene Seed Island in South Carolina, the current home of Polly and her scientist parents. The oldest of seven children, Polly and her family have lived in many exotic places as they followed her father's work as a marine biologist. Intelligent, tall, and slow to make friends, Polly adores Max, whom she considers a second mother. However, on this trip to Athens, Polly feels confused and betrayed, for she has learned that her beloved Max, now fatally ill with a rare virus, and Max's longtime companion, Dr. Ursula Heschel, have been lovers for years. To make matters worse, one evening when Max has been drinking to ease her pain, she makes a sexual advance toward Polly, who then runs away. Polly turns to her friend Renny and they make love, later realizing that they will not do so again.

In Athens, while waiting for her aunt and uncle to meet her, Polly meets Zachary, a young man who is travelling around Europe, whose romantic overtures she rejects. At the conference, however, she becomes attracted to Omio, who is from the island of Baki, sensing that he cares for her, too. Later, she and Zach are nearly drowned when their kayak overturns, but Omio saves them. As she recovers, Polly has time to think about what her uncle told her about elevating her friend Max to a godlike status rather than letting her be human.

Polly is shocked once again when she finds out that Omio is married and has a child. Soon, however, she realizes that what he offered her was nothing more than genuine friendship. It was she who was searching for something else. She also realizes that she does not love Zach. Polly is beginning to understand how complicated relationships can be. She thinks back on her wonderful friendship with Max and all that the older woman has meant to her. She asks herself, would she have never wanted to have met Max? Deciding that Max is too important to lose, Polly telephones her and says "I love you." When Max asks her forgiveness for the night when she drank too much, Polly asks to be forgiven in return for the way she behaved.

CHARACTERS: Polly O'Keefe is a sensitive, intelligent teenager who has difficulty making friends with those her own age. When she meets the brilliant and wealthy artist, Maximiliana Horne, the older woman gives her encouragement and a new self-confidence. At first, Polly idolizes Max, but then she feels betrayed when she learns of the older woman's longtime romantic attachment to her friend and companion, Ursula Heschel. She becomes even more upset when the drunk Max makes advances toward her. Through the days that follow in Greece, Polly learns to look at relationships in a new way, learning that there are different degrees of love and friendship. Her own step toward a new maturity occurs when she places a telephone call to Max and tells her that she loves her.

Maximiliana Horne, called **Max** for short, is a new experience for Polly and she soon comes to adore the older woman. Max opens up Polly's eyes to things she had never noticed, including the relationship between her own parents. Polly has always assumed that her parents' marriage was fine, but Max points out that Polly's mother feels restless, though she still loves her husband. The girl's mother has a brilliant scientific mind, but she never gets the chance to use it to its fullest because her own career dreams have been sacrificed for her husband's important work and for the children. This is a revelation to Polly. When Polly shies away from seeing her parents as human beings with needs and wants of their own, Max tells her that she tends to put people on pedestals. This inevitably leads to disappointment, Max warns. It is through Max's eyes that Polly begins to look at life around her in a way she has never done before.

Dr. Ursula Heschel, a short, stocky woman with gray-brown hair, is Max's longtime companion and lover. When Polly first meets her, she thinks the rather nondescript figure is some sort of housekeeper for the wealthy Max. She soon learns that Ursula is a neurosurgeon. When Max and Ursula meet Polly's parents, it is Ursula who truly understands and is fascinated by her father's work. Ursula and Polly's father hit it off so well that Polly wonders if her own mother shouldn't be jealous. Instead, Mrs. O'Keefe asks the two women to dinner.

Soon after arriving in Athens, Polly meets **Zachary Gray** from California. A tall, handsome young man with dark hair and eyes, Zach is travelling around Europe. Polly is obviously intrigued by this wealthy free spirit and flattered by his obvious attraction to her. She begins to feel mature and grown up in his company, even though she rather resents his frank talk about sex. But as Polly matures and begins to question her relationships, she sees that although she may be flattered by Zach's attentions, she does not love him, and there should be more to a relationship than physical attraction.

Polly is next attracted to **Omio**, whom she meets at the conference. When he comes to see her after he has saved her and Zach from the overturned kayak, Polly senses a deepening of her feeling for him. She is shocked when she sees a picture of his wife and son. "Why does that make a difference?" Omio asks. When Polly replies that it doesn't, Omio tells her, "I am married to one wife, and I will be true to her. But that does not mean that no one else can touch my soul." When Polly is unresponsive to that message, Omio agrees that to "deny friendship is unlove."

Polly puts her lovemaking with friend **Renny** into perspective after they talk about it. They acknowledge that it was special between them but that they are young and have a good deal of living to do before making any special commitments. But Renny is concerned that Polly "will make a habit of throwing herself at guys." She tells him to stop worrying.

Polly mother, **Mrs. O'Keefe**, talks with her daughter about relationships after Polly brings up the subject of whether Max and Ursula are lesbians. If so, she wonders, wouldn't her mother be worried about Polly's association with them? Her mother replies that Polly's parents trust her, and they trust Max and Ursula not to do or say anything that would harm their daughter. "Trusting people is risky," says Mrs. O'Keefe. "But when I think of Max and Ursula, I don't feel particularly curious about their sex lives, one way or another. They're opening a world of ideas for you."

Further Reading

Authors and Artists for Young Adults. Vol. 1. Detroit: Gale Research, 1989.

Berger, Laura Standley, ed. *Twentieth-Century Children's Writers.* 4th ed. Detroit: St. James, 1995.

Children's Literature Review. Vols. 1, 14. Detroit: Gale Research, 1976, 1988.

Contemporary Literary Criticism. Vol. 12. Detroit: Gale Research, 1980.

Estes, Glenn E., ed. *American Writers for Children since 1960,* Vol. 52 of *Dictionary of Literary Biography.* Detroit: Gale Research, 1986.

Fuller, Muriel, ed. *More Junior Authors.* New York: H. W. Wilson, 1963.

Something about the Author. Vols. 1, 27, 75. Detroit: Gale Research, 1971, 1982, 1994.

Something about the Author Autobiography Series. Vol. 15. Detroit: Gale Research, 1993.

Ward, Martha, ed. *Authors of Books for Young People.* 3rd ed. Metuchen, NJ: Scarecrow, 1990.

Myron Levoy

1930-, American young adult novelist

Alan and Naomi

(young adult novel, 1977)

PLOT: Set in New York City in 1944, this novel illustrates the debilitating psychological effects of war on young minds. Alan Silverman is an eighth-grader whose favorite pastime is playing stickball in the street, especially with his best friend, Shaun Kelly. One day, Alan returns to his apartment to find that Naomi Kirshenbaum, the girl who has a reputation in the neighborhood of being crazy, has moved in with her relatives upstairs. Naomi, who is about his own age, has been through some horrifying war experiences in France and doesn't talk to anyone. Alan's parents ask him to help Naomi, to spend a little of his after-school time trying to break through her silence. Alan resists at first before giving in. He doesn't want his stickball pals, especially Shaun, to know that he's spending time with the crazy girl, so he tells everyone that he is taking care of a family matter.

At first, helping Naomi seems hopeless, but eventually, with Alan's wonderful use of a puppet he calls Charlie, he gets Naomi to respond, even though she pretends she is a puppet known as Yvette. Little by little they become friends through the puppets, and Alan really begins to like Naomi. He learns that she was present when her father was killed by the Nazis and that she blames herself for his death. However, he knows that unless she responds to him as Alan, not Charlie, they can never truly be friends and Naomi will never emerge from her defensive shell.

With extraordinary patience and kindness, Alan coaxes the fragile Naomi into accepting him for who he is, and they become friends. Eventually, she is able to return to school, where she is in his class. Things begin to look up for Naomi, and Alan is happy too because he truly cares about her. The only fly in the ointment is that Shaun, who has found out what the "family matter" was, is hurt that Alan did not confide in him and will no longer speak to him. Alan knows that it was wrong not to be honest with Shaun and he misses him terribly.

One day on the way to school with Naomi, Alan runs into Joe Condello who shouts some racial slurs about Jews at both of them. Joe and Alan fight, with Alan getting the worst of it, until Shaun appears and rescues Alan. In the meantime, Naomi watches the bloody fight and begins screaming about the Gestapo. After the fight, Alan notices that Naomi has disappeared. He and Shaun later discover her hiding in a coal pile. She will not speak, not even to Alan. Some time later, Alan visits Naomi in a home where she is recuperating, but she still will not speak. Alan's father tells him that he has done all he could and that eventually Naomi will be herself again, but Alan doesn't believe it. He thinks that Naomi has retreated so deeply into herself that she will never come out again.

CHARACTERS: Alan Silverman is a bright youngster who loves stickball and making friends on his block. He really does not want to get involved in trying to help Naomi Kirshenbaum. For one reason, he is certain that his friends, especially Shaun, will think he is a sissy for hanging out with that "crazy-acting girl." Alan, however, is soft-hearted and eventually agrees to try. With wonderful inventiveness, he brings a puppet he calls Charlie upstairs to visit Naomi. At first, she is unimpressed, but Alan is patient and persistent. Eventually, she does respond and begins to trust him. Alan finds that he enjoys her friendship, that he likes Naomi and her lively mind. Soon they begin to share homework and their feelings. Although Alan misses the world of his friends, especially Shaun, he is happy in his new friendship with Naomi.

Alan's fumbling attempts to draw Naomi out of her shell are tender and sometimes funny. He is willing to admit his mistakes, too, especially when he realizes how much he has hurt his friend Shaun by not confiding in him. After the fight with Joe, from which Shaun rescues him, Alan is delighted to have his friend back again. He later realizes, though, that he has lost Naomi, and he fears that the loss is permanent.

The sad face and haunted eyes of **Naomi Kirshenbaum** tell of the mental suffering of this World War II victim. Although she resists any attempts by Alan to break through her shell, eventually she responds to his warm and genuine friendship, confiding in him that she believes herself to be the cause of her father's bloody death. Her father had told her to tear up the maps that he was making so the Nazis would not find them. Naomi does so, but the Nazis find them anyway and beat her father to death. If only she had torn them up enough, Naomi believes, he would still be alive. Alan assures her this is not so, and another crisis is averted. But when Naomi is forced to watch Alan being beaten until Shaun rescues him, she is reminded of her father's death and retreats from the world once more.

Shaun Kelly and Alan Silverman act like typical teenage boys who are embarrassed to express their deep friendship for each other. After stickball games, they hide behind insulting banter: "Goodnight, Jew. Goodnight, Catholic. Screwball. Jerk." Shaun is genuinely hurt when he discovers that Alan did not trust him enough to reveal his secret about Naomi. Nevertheless, Shaun is still a friend, which he proves when he saves Alan in the fight with Joe, and again when he helps Alan find Naomi.

Mr. and **Mrs. Silverman** have a close and easy relationship with their young son. They persuade Alan to help Naomi, and when Naomi retreats into silence after Alan's fight with Joe, Mr. Silverman comforts Alan. He tells his son that he has done his very best for Naomi, as much as anyone could ask of him. He also tries to cheer Alan up by saying Naomi will eventually recover again, but Alan doesn't believe it.

Further Reading

Berger, Laura Standley, ed. *Twentieth-Century Young Adult Writers.* 1st ed. Detroit: St. James, 1994.

Holtze, Sally Holmes, ed. *Fifth Book of Junior Authors and Illustrators.* New York: H. W. Wilson, 1983.

Something about the Author. Vol. 49. Detroit: Gale Research, 1987.

Robert Lipsyte

1938-, American young adult novelist

The Contender

(young adult novel, 1967)

PLOT: *The Contender* is the first novel in Robert Lipsyte's series about the psychological stresses of poverty, the lure of drugs and crime, and the discipline of boxing. The central character in this novel, Alfred Brooks, is a seventeen-year-old African American who has dropped out of high school. He lives with his Aunt Pearl Conway and her three daughters in a Harlem tenement building surrounded by filth, roaches, rats, and drug addicts. Working as a stockboy in a grocery store, Alfred tries to resist the temptations around him. James Mosely, his best friend, is another dropout who hangs out with three unsavory characters: Sonny, Major, and Hollis. When Alfred inadvertently supplies them with confidential information, James and his friends decide to break into the store where he works. But when the robbery is bungled and James is caught, the gang blames Alfred and beats him severely.

At this critical juncture in his life, Alfred is persuaded by Henry Johnson, the crippled janitor at Donatelli's gym, to try boxing. At the gym, Alfred meets Mr. Donatelli and Bill Witherspoon—nicknamed Spoon—a former boxer who is now a schoolteacher. Alfred goes into training, and as his boxing career progresses James's life continues on its downward slide. After being released from jail, James develops a heroin habit and engages in criminal activity to support it.

Alfred is successful in his first fights, but Donatelli realizes that he lacks the "killer instinct" necessary to become a champion, so he advises him not to pursue a career in boxing. The experience, however, has changed Alfred's life. The discipline of athletic training and the people he has met have helped him imagine a different future for himself. Spoon, who is a particularly important role model, persuades him to complete his high school diploma by taking classes at night.

Meanwhile, to feed his heroin habit, James attempts another robbery at the same grocery store where Alfred once worked. Alfred finds him afterwards in the local park, hiding in a cave they used to play in as children. James is bleeding profusely from cuts he received while escaping. In a poignant scene, Alfred persuades him to give himself up and promises to dedicate himself to his recovery.

See below for character descriptions.

The Brave

(young adult novel, 1991)

PLOT: Although Alfred Brooks plays an important role in this second novel in Lipsyte's series, the central character is a different young man torn between the demands of the inner city and the rigors of a boxing career. George Harrison Bayer is also seventeen years old when *The Brave* opens. Half Native American and half white, he lives with his trainer, Uncle Jake Stump, on the Moscondaga Reservation in upstate New York. Sonny's father, a white man, was killed in Vietnam; his mother, Honey Dear, pursues a life in the fast lane, moving often and living with various men, while trying to promote her line of Indian crafts and jewelry.

After being cheated out of a boxing victory and a purse of two hundred dollars, Sonny leaves for New York City to track down his mother and get her permission to join the army. But once he reaches the city—before even leaving the bus terminal—he falls into bad company: Stick, an African American drug dealer, and his girlfriend, Doll, a pathetic, street-wise teenager for whom Sonny feels an immediate attraction. His first experiences on tough 42nd Street (nicknamed the "Deuce") are disastrous. First, he is robbed, and then Stick sets him up as a decoy in a drug bust.

Sonny is arrested, but as a result of this he meets a New York City cop and former boxer named Alfred Brooks. After Alfred's friend, James, died of an overdose, he dedicated his life to fighting drugs on the streets. Alfred sees both Sonny's personal and athletic potential. Despite Sonny's stubborn reluctance, he convinces him he has real potential as a fighter and persuades him to start training at Donatelli's gym in Harlem, which is now owned by Henry Johnson. Under the influence of Alfred, Henry, and the other people he meets there, including Bill Witherspoon, who is now a school principal, Sonny's life begins to change for the better.

Sonny wins several amateur fights and becomes particularly friendly with Spoon's son, Martin, who trains at the gym to please his father, though he

In the second of Lipsyte's three boxing books, Alfred Brooks convinces a troubled young man to turn his life around.

lacks athletic ability. But then Sonny suddenly faces a series of crises. Someone informs the boxing commission that he once fought for money and he loses his amateur status. Then Alfred gets shot during a drug raid and is paralyzed from the waist down. Believing that Stick is behind both these incidents, Sonny returns to the Deuce, where he confronts and disarms Stick, then he takes him to the police despite Doll's pleadings.

At the end of the novel, Sonny is preparing himself for a fight and struggling to keep these events from affecting his concentration. He is fighting at the bottom rung of the professional circuit, but he is still distracted by thoughts about Stick and his upcoming trial, where he will have to testify, and his grief and anxiety over Alfred, who is still in the hospital. His reunion with his mother—who now wants him to come live with her—has also left him feeling confused and ambivalent. But finally Sonny realizes that he must think only of winning his next match. And he does win—a knockout in the third minute of the third round. By the story's conclusion, it is clear that Sonny Bear is heading straight for the title.

See below for character descriptions.

The Chief

(science fiction, 1993)

PLOT: When the third novel in this series begins, it has been two years since Sonny Bear became a professional boxer under the supervision of his Native American trainer, Uncle Jake Stump, and former New York City cop, Alfred Brooks. Sonny is now nineteen, and Alfred, confined to a wheelchair by a bullet wound, has left the force. The novel is narrated by Martin Witherspoon, son of Bill Witherspoon, Alfred's old mentor and a former boxer himself. Sonny's best fried, Martin, has a deep interest both in boxing and Sonny's career, even though he himself is unathletic. Instead of fighting, Martin is studying creative writing at college.

When Sonny becomes so discouraged with his prospects in boxing that he is about to quit, a savvy, young television producer named Robin Bell suggests a new strategy. She convinces him that he can gain some media coverage by challenging the most prominent fighter on the professional circuit, Elston Hubbard, Jr. Hubbard is currently in Las Vegas, training for a fight with an older fighter named John L. Solomon. To pursue her plan, Sonny and Martin travel together to Las Vegas.

With Martin's guidance and good judgment, the scheme works well. It works so well, in fact, that Sonny is invited to join the older fighter and his trainer, Richie, at their camp. John L. Solomon gives him a place in the four-round preliminary fight that precedes the big match. Sonny wins his fight easily, but whatever this might have done for his boxing career is cancelled out by what happens once the main event begins. Elston Hubbard, Jr., beats Sonny's new friend badly, and in a desperate effort to stop the fight and save John from any more brain-damaging blows, Sonny punches out both Elston and his father, Elston Hubbard, Sr. As a result the boxing commission suspends him from the sport.

But this incident does bring him celebrity, though of a different sort than he had imagined. Hollywood promises a television series, and Sonny falls into a luxurious life of parties, alcohol, and women. He is rescued once again by Martin, who brings him back East to help resolve an emerging crisis on the Moscondaga Reservation in upstate New York. This is where Sonny was raised by Jake. The tribe is bitterly divided over the building of a casino on the reservation, and Jake has been shot by one of the extremists. Sonny gallantly confronts the two warring factions and brings peace to his nation. Wishing to profit from Sonny's fame, Elston Hubbard, Sr., forgives the incident in Las Vegas and persuades the boxing commission to lift Sonny's suspension. Hubbard negotiates a contract for Sonny to fight the heavyweight champion, Floyd Hall. Sonny, now at peace with himself and his heritage, is hopeful of another victory in the ring.

CHARACTERS: Alfred Brooks (*The Contender, The Brave, The Chief*) is both a heroic and tragic figure. When he first appears as the central character in *The Contender,* he is a seventeen-year-old high school dropout, street smart but vulnerable to the temptations surrounding him. An African American who is tired of being subservient to his white bosses at the grocery store and sick of the squalor surrounding him in Harlem, Alfred at one point proclaims, "I'm gonna be somebody." He realizes that crime and drugs are not lasting solutions to his problems. Despite the apparent hopelessness of his situation, he is determined and pursues his ambitions in an honest, honorable way. This drive, in addition to his need to protect himself in his rough neighborhood, leads him to boxing. By the time he discovers that he lacks the talent to succeed in this sport, however, he has already gained sufficient inner strength to turn his life around.

Alfred has fine basic instincts. He is helpful to his Aunt Pearl and sympathetic to her problems with raising three daughters. He attends church, is respectful of other people, and is above all a loyal friend. Racked by a guilty conscience when he inadvertently causes the arrest of his friend, James, he tries many times to lead him toward rehabilitation. When this proves impossible, he risks losing James's friendship, rather than following his path of self-destruction. He refuses to compromise his ideals, even when this involves physical harm at the hands of James's hoodlum companions.

In the twenty years that intervene between *The Contender* and *The Brave,* Alfred succeeds in pursuing another profession, raises a fine family, and still maintains the ideals and decency that distinguished him as a teenager. A veteran of the Vietnam War, he is now a respected and admired sergeant in the New York City Police Department. The tragedy of being unable to prevent the death of James from drugs has scarred Alfred and made him more dedicated to fighting the drug trade and its consequences. He identifies with Sonny Bear, who faces choices similar to those he faced years before, and is determined to save him.

Though his years on the force have made him somewhat cynical, they have also given Alfred increased inner strength and the ability to fight against seemingly impossible odds. In the final book, *The Chief,* his inner strength is brought to the ultimate test. Confined to a wheelchair, having lost control of many of his bodily functions, Alfred could easily have become a bitter, disillusioned man. Instead, he maintains his same caring attitude and refuses to retreat into self-pity and remorse. He is still available to help others, particularly Sonny, whom he regards now as a surrogate son.

Unlike Alfred, his friend **James Mosely** (*The Contender*) lacks the fortitude to resist the temptations and unsavory influences of the Harlem streets. Also a dropout, James is unemployed and slips easily into crime and a drug habit that eventually proves fatal. Although he is basically a decent person who wants to live a productive life, he is not able to resist the negative pressures of his environment. Like Alfred, he serves in Vietnam, but after the war his life once again becomes dominated by heroin. His life and tragic death from a drug overdose inspire Alfred to try to save others as vulnerable as James.

Henry Johnson (*The Contender, The Brave, The Chief*), a man with a perpetual grin and a left leg crippled by polio, is the good-natured, caring friend who rescues Alfred after he is beaten up by gang members. Henry is a boxing nut and his infectious enthusiasm inspires Alfred to try his luck at the sport himself. He introduces Alfred to the people at Donatelli's gym, where Henry works as a janitor. After Henry learns the techniques of training by following Alfred's regimen, he is promoted to coaching boxing hopefuls. Later, Henry becomes the owner of Donatelli's, and in *The Brave* he gives Sonny Bear the same support and devotion that he once did to Alfred.

The original owner of the gym is **Mr. Donatelli** (*The Contender*), an honest, tough, boxing enthusiast who encourages Alfred and gives him a job at the gym to pay for his training. He is forthright and truthful in his dealings with others and often acts as an inspiration to Alfred. Although strongly supportive of him, it is Donatelli who eventually realizes that Alfred does not have the inner qualities to make a great fighter. He tells Alfred bluntly, "You don't have the killer instinct . . . the coldness to beat a man into the ground when you sense his weakness." To protect Alfred from possible physical injury, he recommends that the young man "retire"—he won't use the word "quit." His sensitivity to the feelings of others is shown in the way he handles this situation: he saves the boy's self-esteem and dignity by assuring him that other fields of human endeavor need contenders just as much as boxing.

Another positive role model for Alfred is **Bill Witherspoon** (nicknamed **Spoon**, he appears in *The Contender, The Brave, The Chief*). Like Alfred, Spoon had hoped to leave Harlem by using his boxing skills, but he lacked the ability, too. Instead, he became a schoolteacher and later a principal. However, his interest in boxing remains and he continues to work out at the gym. Through his good example and common-sense advice, he helps Alfred to turn his life around and explore other avenues besides boxing. He persuades Alfred to complete his high school education at night and to set his sights on another profession. Later in the series, when Spoon's son, Martin, begins coming reluctantly to the gym and meets Sonny Bear, Spoon also acts as advisor and confidant to him. Spoon tries to help others achieve what he has through hard work, self-discipline, and perseverance. Spoon's comfortable, middle-class attitudes and consuming interest in boxing contrast amusingly with those of his son, who prefers writing and a somewhat bohemian lifestyle.

Aunt Pearl Conway (*The Contender*) is Alfred's hard-working guardian; at the start of *The Contender,* her husband has been dead for several years. She is a religious woman who supports herself and her three daughters by doing domestic work. Despite her protests, Alfred has left school and taken a job to help her make ends meet. Aunt Pearl's love and devotion are important influences that help Alfred achieve success.

Sonny Bear, the protagonist of *The Brave* and *The Chief,* is courageous, intelligent, and a loyal friend who is able to both give and receive affection. He wants to be close to his mother but rejects her way of life and her exploitation of Indian culture. He believes in justice and fair play and is rightfully angered at racial slurs and the stereotyping of minority groups. At first, he is suspicious and resentful of the authority Alfred represents, but in time he realizes that he can benefit from listening to others. Although victories in the ring are important to Sonny, during the two-year period covered by these novels he wins a higher victory by taking two important steps toward maturity.

The first step Sonny takes is learning to control the monster within him—the rage that frequently rises up with such intensity that he lashes out with his fists regardless of the consequences. Alfred calls this condition a passive-aggressive personality, and Uncle Jake says simply that Sonny is possessed by an evil spirit. Cultural differences aside, the two older men help Sonny gain control of his emotions. The crucial test of his new self-discipline comes when Sonny confronts the drug-dealing Stick after Alfred has been wounded. Although enraged and desperate to kill Stick himself, Sonny instead controls his emotions and turns him over to the police.

The second step that Sonny takes toward maturity comes when he accepts his Native American heritage. At first Sonny makes fun of Uncle Jake's frequent references to Indian lore. Uncle Jake often tells stories about the heroism of the Running Braves—a group of courageous young men Sonny's ancestors belonged to—and he often mentions the "Hawk," or inner spirit, within every person that, when understood, can lead individuals to their true destinies. Gradually, Sonny realizes the wisdom in the old man's stories, and he sees how they apply to his own life. When he gathers his people together to negotiate peace, Sonny shows he is indeed worthy of the status of a Running Brave. He has acquired the understanding and control to free the Hawk within himself and gain inner peace.

Sonny's friend and would-be biographer is **Martin Malcolm Witherspoon**, (*The Brave, The Chief*) who is described as a "big fat black kid with round glasses that make him look like an owl." The same age as Sonny, Martin is first presented as an inquisitive nerd who is more pest than friend. Although not interested in boxing, he trains at Donatelli's gym because his father hopes for the impossible: that he will turn into an athlete. Martin does, however, become a valuable training partner for Sonny, learning how to call punches skillfully. Although he realizes that he is something of a disappointment to his father, Martin accepts their differences without rancor. Through most of his friendship with Sonny, Martin seems to empathize with Indian culture and problems more than Sonny does. He is witty, talented, and above all a true friend and supporter who always has Sonny's best interests at heart. He successfully stages the Las Vegas promotional stunt that gains Sonny recognition, and when his friend's career founders in Hollywood, Martin rescues him. His inner strength is shown when he courageously risks his own life in helping get Stick arrested.

Uncle Jake Stump (*The Brave, The Chief*), the old Native American who runs a junkyard on the reservation, is Sonny's wise guardian and conscience. Uncle Jake is devoted to his nephew and is also a fine boxing trainer. As Sonny's surrogate father, he tries to teach him the traditional ways of truth, moderation, and self-knowledge. Steeped in Native American folklore and customs, Uncle Jake is appalled by how the white man and some members of his own tribe have exploited his people. His fight for justice within the tribe makes him enemies, and in an effort to silence him they attempt to murder him. A man of stoic heroism and learning, he is a positive influence on Sonny.

Stick (*The Brave*) is a fourteen-year-old African American who operates a drug ring out of his headquarters in a 42nd Street building in New York City. He got his nickname because he carries a walking stick with an ivory snake's head on the top that hides a shotgun. His charming, smooth-talking exterior hides a ruthless, cunning nature that will resort to murder to protect the profits of his business. Without scruples, he sells drugs to children to build his clientele and deliberately uses Sonny, an innocent acquaintance, as a decoy, indifferent to whether his participation results in the young man's death or imprisonment. He is the leader of a murderous gang known as the X-Men, whose power extends into the prison system.

Stick's companion is **Doll** (*The Brave*), a pathetic, frail teenager whose real name is **Heather**. Her mask of heavy makeup hides a sweet, freckled face. Though only about fourteen, she already has a daughter, who is cared for by others. Sonny is attracted to this waif who seems unable to escape from Stick and the depravity he represents.

The aging fighter Sonny trains with in Las Vegas is **John L. Solomon** (*The Chief*)—a larger-than-life character who is intensely proud of his Jewish heritage. Unlike Sonny, who tends to bury his racial roots, John L. celebrates his Jewish background, making it part of his public persona. Now out of shape and over the hill, he is a somewhat pathetic figure trying for an impossible comeback. Despite his loud, often vulgar bravado in public, in private he is actually a sensitive, sentimental man who responds to kindness and is justifiably afraid of his upcoming fight with Elston Hubbard. He believes in justice and fair play and abhors prejudice of any kind. He likes and protects Sonny, who grows to admire and love him.

John L.'s trainer and manager is **Richie** (*The Chief*), a scrappy, fat runt who "looks like something out of an old gangster movie." With his raspy voice and tough exterior, he hides a slavish devotion to John L. Though he knows John L.'s fight will lead to disaster, he supports him because, as he confides to Sonny, "he needs somebody who cares about him." At first Richie is suspicious of Sonny, but when he realizes that the boy cares for John L., he befriends him and helps promote his career.

Sonny's mother, **Honey Bear**, is an attractive woman with thick black braids. She cares for her son but seems unable to settle down and provide a home for him. Her ambition is to collect enough capital from one of her boyfriends to open a series of boutiques in luxury hotels that would sell jewelry and fake artifacts modeled on Native American designs and patterns. Uncle Jake, who is openly critical of Honey Bear's lifestyle, objects to this flagrant exploitation of the arts and crafts of his people.

Elston Hubbard, Sr. (*The Chief*) is a fight entrepreneur who manages his son's career. More a showman than a sportsman, he uses any trick possible to publicize a fight and create headlines. Although Sonny disagrees with these tactics, he realizes that he must cooperate if he is to succeed in a business where publicity is one of the most important elements for success.

Robin Bell (*The Chief*) is a director and producer who specializes in creating documentaries of sports figures for public television. She is twenty-three, attractive (particularly to Martin), hard-working, and self-assured. She is aware of the struggle women face to get ahead in television and has honed her work habits and her personal style to overcome this additional hurdle. Although ambitious and competitive, she still retains her principles and professionalism.

Further Reading

Authors and Artists for Young Adults. Vol. 7. Detroit: Gale Research, 1992.

Berger, Laura Standley, ed. *Twentieth-Century Young Adult Writers.* 1st ed. Detroit: St. James, 1994.

Collier, Laurie, and Joyce Nakamura, eds. *Major Authors and Illustrators for Children and Young Adults.* Detroit: Gale Research, 1993.

Contemporary Literary Criticism. Vol. 21. Detroit: Gale Research, 1982.

Gallo, Donald R. *Speaking for Ourselves: Autobiographical Sketches by Notable Authors of Books for Young Adults.* Urbana, IL: National Council of Teachers of English, 1990.

Something about the Author. Vol. 68. Detroit: Gale Research, 1992.

Jack London

1876-1916, American novelist

The Call of the Wild

(novel, 1902)

PLOT: Two of Jack London's nineteen novels, *The Call of the Wild* and *White Fang* (1904), are companion pieces. Both feature dogs as the central characters, but while *White Fang* is the story of a dog's evolution from wild animal to domesticated companion, *The Call of the Wild* narrates a dog's progression from civilization back to the wilderness. *The Call of the Wild* is probably his most famous work, though many critics consider *Sea Wolf* (1904) to be a better novel.

The novel begins with four-year-old Buck, a half-Saint Bernard, half-Scottish Shepherd dog, living in California at the home of Judge Miller. As the most prized animal in the house, Buck has little to do but protect the judge's daughters, Molly and Alice, when they go on long walks—a task he performs easily because of his unusually large size.

But Buck's comfortable life abruptly ends when gold is discovered in the Far North. One of Judge Miller's servants leaves to seek out his fortune, and he steals Buck because large dogs are valuable in the north for hauling heavy sleds in the deep snow. Sold for this kind of work, Buck encounters cruelty from his new master—referred to as the Man in the Red Sweater—who teaches Buck that a human with a club must be obeyed. Overworked, hungry, and in constant pain, Buck learns to endure in this uncivilized place. When he defeats the lead dog of his sled team in a fight, Buck takes over that position. This wins him the admiration of his new masters, Frenchmen Perrault and Francois. When these two leave the area, he is sold to a man known only as Scotch Half-Breed, who delivers mail in the harsh North Country. Although not intentionally cruel, the man overworks his team so that many of the dogs die.

Buck survives, however, and is next sold to three adventurers from the south: Charles, a middle-aged man; his wife, Mercedes, who acts as though they are on a camping trip; and her brother, Hal, a cruel young man who carries a whip, a knife, and a gun. These three are ignorant of how to drive a dog team in the wilderness; when they run out of food for the animals and many grow too weak to work, Hal's solution is to beat those who can still stand, including Buck. Charles and his group stumble upon the camp of John Thornton. When they are ready to leave, Buck refuses to move. Hal beats him until Thornton interferes, freeing Buck from his harness. Charles and the others leave and soon die when they fall through the ice and drown in the waters below.

With Thornton, Buck finds love and compassion once again. Thornton nurses him back to health, and man and dog discover a great and lasting admiration for each other. Twice Buck saves Thornton's life. He kills Black Burton, a drunken miner who attacks Thornton. Later, Buck rescues Thornton when he is caught in river rapids and almost drowns. Buck also helps him financially. Thornton makes a bet that his dog can pull a sled that carries a thousand pounds, and Buck actually moves the sled a hundred yards. With the money won from the bet, Thornton, his partners, and Buck head into the deep wilderness to search for a lost gold mine. While the men pan for gold, Buck often goes off by himself, sometimes staying away for days. Upon his return from one of these forays, he discovers that Thornton and his partners have been killed by Indians. Fearlessly, Buck attacks the Indians, killing some and driving away the rest.

There will be no new masters for Buck; he now joins a wild wolf pack. It is said that he became the leader of a new breed, roaming free through the cold darkness of the northlands.

Buck performs a miraculous feat of strength in a scene from The Call of the Wild, *illustrated by Kyuzo Tsugami.*

CHARACTERS: The main character is **Buck**, and the central theme of the novel is his evolution from a life of domesticated ease to survival in the harsh northern wild. For London, Buck represents the idea that within every human is a more primitive version of the individual that can emerge in life-threatening situations or periods of extreme stress. Buck symbolizes the Darwinian idea of "survival of the fittest"—only the strongest and most adaptable will survive. This symbolism is carried further by Buck's exhibiting many human traits, including loyalty, love, and revenge. From his first cruel master, the Man in the Red Sweater, he learns that a single dog is no match for a human with a club. It is a harsh and painful lesson, but it serves him well. Buck knows instinctively that the inept adventurers, Charles, Mercedes, and Hal, will meet with disaster: The wilderness will not forgive their mistakes. It is for this reason, among others, that he refuses to go with them after they reach Thornton's camp just before the trio drowns under the ice.

From Thornton, Buck learns loyalty and love. In return for rescuing him from Hal, Buck twice saves Thornton's life and exerts himself to pull a heavy sled. Yet however close man and dog become, Buck continues to be driven by the primitive urges the wilderness has awakened in him. The dog often longs to go free, but his bond to Thornton always brings him back. But when Thornton is killed and Buck has avenged his friend's death, he leaves his ties to humanity behind. He joins a wolf pack and becomes its leader, a civilized animal that has answered the call of the wild.

There are two people in the story who are the kindest to Buck. At the novel's beginning, Buck's master is gentle, kindly **Judge Miller**, who symbolizes the civilized world, where people live according to law and custom. After being stolen from the Miller home and suffering many abuses and hardships, Buck finally encounters **John Thornton**, an adventurer who also symbolizes the survival of the fittest. He shows great compassion for the dogs who work hard pulling sleds, but none for the stupidity of the three people who venture into the harsh north country with neither the necessary knowledge nor the patience to learn about the wilderness. Thornton shows Buck loyalty and admiration, which he demonstrates when Thornton is offered a thousand dollars for Buck but he refuses.

The men and women who neglect and abuse Buck are many. **Black Burton** is an evil-tempered, malicious bully. When Thornton tries to stop him from tormenting a newcomer to the territory, Burton attacks him and Buck tears the man's throat open. All agree that the dog had sufficient cause to protect his master's life. In contrast to Thornton, the

Man in the Red Sweater is also a cruel figure, but his maliciousness teaches Buck an important lesson: a man with a club must be obeyed. Buck is never broken by this sadistic master, but he learns how to survive under his domination. Less sadistic are the Frenchmen **Perrault** and **Francois**, who may be harsh, but Buck recognizes that they administer justice impartially and fairly, traits he can understand and respect. Likewise, Buck does not resent the **Scotch Half-Breed**. He may overwork the dogs, but he does so because of the many demands that are made on him.

Newcomers to the north country are **Charles**, **Mercedes**, and **Hal**, who represent those least adapted for survival. They die because they fail to understand how to live in the wild. Inept and unprepared to deal with the realities of the north country, they cope with adversity by quarreling with each other and lashing out at the animals. For instance, before they stumble upon Thornton's camp, they discover that they do not have enough food for the dogs. Lack of food causes the animals to grow weak, but instead of recognizing this distress and trying to alleviate it, Mercedes insists on riding in the sled, thereby increasing the dogs' burden. In the end, their incompetence leads them to travel over ice too thin to support their weight, causing them to drown in the freezing waters.

Further Reading

Bains, Rae. *Jack London: A Life of Adventure.* Mahway, NJ: Troll, 1992.

Baltrop, Robert. *Jack London: The Man, the Writer, the Rebel.* London: Pluto, 1976.

Bruccoli, Matthew J., and Richard Layman, eds. *Realism, Naturalism, and Local Color, 1865-1917.* Vol. 2 of *Concise Dictionary of American Literary Biography.* Detroit: Gale Research, 1988.

Cowart, David, and Thomas L. Wymer, eds. *Twentieth-Century American Science Fiction Writers.* Vol. 8 of *Dictionary of Literary Biography.* Detroit: Gale Research, 1981.

Harbert, Earl N., and Donald Pizer, eds. *American Realists and Naturalists.* Vol. 12 of *Dictionary of Literary Biography.* Detroit: Gale Research, 1982.

Hedrick, Joan D. *Solitary Comrade: Jack London and His Work.* Chapel Hill: University of North Carolina Press, 1982.

Hendricks, King. *Jack London: Master Craftsman of the Short Story.* Logan, UT: Utah State University Press, 1966.

Kimbel, Bobby Ellen, ed. *American Short Story Writers, 1880-1910.* Vol. 78 of *Dictionary of Literary Biography.* Detroit: Gale Research, 1989.

Labor, Earl. *Jack London.* Boston: Twayne, 1977.

Magill, Frank J. *Critical Survey of Long Fiction: English-Language Series: Authors.* Vol. 24. Englewood Cliffs, NJ: Prentice-Hall, 1983.

Owenbey, Ray Wilson, ed. *Jack London: Essays in Criticism.* Santa Barbara, CA: Peregrine, 1978.

Powell, John. *Jack London.* Vero Beach, FL: Rourke, 1993.

Schroeder, Alan. *Jack London.* New York: Chelsea House, 1992.

Something about the Author. Vol. 18. Detroit: Gale Research, 1980.

Tavernier-Courbin, Jacqueline. *Critical Essays on Jack London.* Boston: G. K. Hall, 1983.

Twentieth-Century Literary Criticism. Vols. 9, 15, 39. Detroit: Gale Research, 1983, 1985, 1991.

Watson, Charles N., Jr. *The Novels of Jack London: A Reappraisal.* Madison: University of Wisconsin Press, 1983.

Wilson, Ray, ed. *Jack London: Essays in Criticism.* Santa Barbara, CA: Peregrine, 1978.

Lois Lowry

1937-, American young adult novelist

The Giver

(young adult novel, 1993)

PLOT: In this thought-provoking novel, which won the 1994 Newbery Medal, Jonas, who is almost twelve years old, lives in a nearly perfect society. There is no pain or injustice, no poverty or divorce, no disease or war, and no family problems. In this "ideal" world, people are assigned to families, rather than born into them. Jonas's mother, father, and sister, Lily, are not actually related to him. Birth mothers bear the children and adults put in applications if they wish to form a family unit, which can include no more than two children: one boy, one girl.

As Jonas nears his twelfth birthday, he anticipates being given his designated life assignment at the all-important Ceremony of Twelve held each December. At that time, the future jobs of all twelve-year-olds is determined for them. The assignments are made by the Elders, who consider each child's potential and rarely make mistakes. Jonas's father, for instance, is a Nurturer, meaning that he oversees newborns during their first year to make sure they are suitable to be given to a family unit. Jonas's happy-go-lucky friend, Asher, is told he will become an Assistant Director of Recreation; his friend Fiona is to be a Caretaker of the Old. But Jonas is to become the Receiver, a great honor since there is only one in the community and the current Receiver is now very old.

Jonas begins training under the current Receiver, whom he calls the Giver. It is the Giver's responsibility to transfer all the memories of the past to Jonas, as well as the emotions of happiness, sorrow, joy, and pain, which the others in the community will never experience. Society has protected itself by eliminating all memories and experiences that might cause the community harm, but although life is now safe, it is very dull and routine. This controlled world has also made people unimaginative, which in itself is a danger. The Receiver's job, therefore, is to serve as an advisor to the Elders in case an unexpected situation arises. The Receiver is called upon to draw on his memories and offer solutions based on what has occurred in the past. The assignment of Receiver is an honor, but it can be a painful one. Slowly, the Giver transfers memories to Jonas, who is then the only person who can remember them. Jonas begins to experience things he never knew existed. For example, he begins to see colors for the first time (all other people in this world can only see in black and white), and is given the memory of snow, which he has never seen in this weather-controlled world.

These experiences give Jonas a new awareness of the world, and he begins to understand for the first time how emotionally and morally bankrupt the society he lives in truly is. The deciding factor for

This 1994 Newbery Medal winner depicts a society in which all dangers—and everything that makes people human—have been removed.

Jonas comes when he sees his father perform a "releasing ceremony" in which a newborn child who is considered unsuitable is injected with a lethal drug and tossed down a garbage chute. The Giver explains to Jonas that his father can feel no emotions over what he has done.

Jonas decides he can no longer live in this "perfect" society. With one of the newborns called Gabriel, who is sure to be "released," he leaves the community and escapes into the night. Lowry, though, ends the story ambiguously so that the reader is never certain whether or not Jonas and Gabriel find a new home and life.

CHARACTERS: Jonas approaches the Ceremony of Twelve with a mixture of anticipation and apprehension. He is stunned when he discovers that he is selected to be the next Receiver. Although everyone

else is thrilled, Jonas is worried and cautious. He suddenly feels different and somewhat alienated from his friends and family. When he begins the wondrous process of receiving all the memories of society, one of the first gifts Jonas receives is the memory of snow, which no one else in the community knows about since all weather is controlled. As the process continues, Jonas becomes aware that he is receiving more than the physical memory of snow; he is also receiving all the sorrow and pain, joy and happiness of the world.

As Jonas takes in the world's memories, he begins to understand what people in his society have lost for the sake of having a safe and perfect world. When he witnesses with horror that this has made his father so emotionless that he can kill an infant without a second thought, Jonas knows that he must leave forever.

Asher is Jonas's best friend. Unlike Jonas, Asher is a happy-go-lucky boy who scrambles words and phrases, always seems to talk too fast, and is often very funny. He makes the more serious, sedate Jonas smile a lot. Jonas sometimes worries about the future of his friend because he never takes himself seriously. But Jonas's father assures him that the Elders never make mistakes and they will prescribe the correct future for Asher. Indeed, after the Ceremony of Twelve it does seem that the Elders once again are correct, for they give Asher the perfect assignment of Assistant Director of Recreation. Another of Jonas's friends is **Fiona**. She is a quiet girl with a sense of humor and an even greater sense of purpose. She has a gift for taking care of elderly people with great kindness, so it is of little surprise to Jonas when she is named Caretaker of the Old.

Jonas's sister, **Lily**, is only seven, but she already knows the importance of the Ceremony of Twelve. She understands that when she reaches that year, the Elders' decision will dictate her entire life. But since she is only a seven, she sometimes forgets the rules, as when she wishes aloud that perhaps they could bring the troubled child Gabriel into their family unit. Her mother chides her gently, reminding her that there are only two children assigned to each family.

Mother holds a prominent position at the Department of Justice. After the evening meal, during which each family member must share his or her feelings, mother often talks about the offenders who are brought before her for justice. She is especially saddened when a second-time offender appears because she feels she has not done her job right and has failed him. She is also sad because in this society she knows there is no third chance. The man will be "released." No one talks about people who are released. The disgrace is unspeakable. Jonas's **father** is a Nurturer. His very important job entails being responsible for all the physical and emotional needs of every new child during its first year. On many occasions, Jonas has heard his father discuss the child currently in his care, Gabriel, who doesn't quite measure up and is in danger of being released.

Jonas has been singled out for special training from the man he calls the **Giver**. This old man, who is also called the **Receiver**, serves as the receptacle of all society's past experiences, including joy, pain, and physical sensations. The Giver is able to rid himself of painful memories when he transfers these memories into Jonas. The Giver selected Jonas because of his serious nature and inquisitive mind. But the very qualities that make Jonas an excellent candidate for Receiver—wisdom, sensitivity, and intelligence—actually lead to his abandonment of the job and the society that created it.

Further Reading

Authors and Artists for Young Adults. Vol. 5. Detroit: Gale Research, 1990.

Berger, Laura Standley, ed. *Twentieth-Century Young Adult Writers.* 1st ed. Detroit: St. James, 1995.

Children's Literature Review. Vol. 6. Detroit: Gale Research, 1984.

Estes, Glenn E., ed. *American Writers for Children since 1960: Fiction.* Vol. 52 of *Dictionary of Literary Biography.* Detroit: Gale Research, 1985.

Holtze, Sally Holmes, ed. *Fifth Book of Junior Authors and Illustrators.* New York: H. W. Wilson, 1983.

Something about the Author. Vols. 23, 70. Detroit: Gale Research, 1981, 1993.

Something about the Author Autobiography Series. Vol. 3. Detroit: Gale Research, 1987.

Ward, Martha, ed. *Authors of Books for Young People.* 3rd ed. Metuchen, NJ: Scarecrow, 1990.

Margaret Mahy

1936-, New Zealand novelist

The Changeover: A Supernatural Romance

(fantasy, 1984)

PLOT: Fourteen-year-old Laura Chant lives in a suburban New Zealand neighborhood with her divorced mother, Kate, and younger brother, three-year-old Jacko (short for Jonathan). Laura is aware that she has psychic powers, particularly when she looks deeply into the penetrating eyes of an older schoolmate, eighteen-year-old Sorensen "Sorry" Carlisle, whom Laura is convinced is a witch. One day after school, she and Jacko visit a new curiosity shop run by a cadaverous-looking man named Carmody Braque. As a supposed gesture of kindness, he stamps Jacko's hand with a rubber stamp depicting Braque's face. Almost immediately the young boy begins to sicken. Kate, who has recently become friendly with Chris Holly, a likable Canadian, becomes increasingly alarmed when Jacko does not respond to medical treatment and has to be sent to the hospital.

Laura is convinced that Jacko is under a wicked enchantment and visits Sorry at his palatial home, where she encounters his mother, Miryam, and grandmother, Winter. All three admit to being witches and inform Laura that Braque is a lemure, a wicked spirit of the dead. To save Jacko, a witch must place her mark of possession on him. When Jacko's condition worsens, Laura's father, Stephen, is sent for. In this time of crisis, Kate turns increasingly to Chris for help, and Laura becomes more dependent on the Carlisles. Miryam and Winter suggest that she undergo a supernatural process called a changeover to become a witch and use her stamp on the unsuspecting Braque. Sorry, who has become fascinated with Laura, warns that the process is irreversible and that life for an abnormal being can be difficult. Laura consents to the harrowing series of rites and emerges as a witch with her own stamping device. The next day, she goes with Sorry to confront Braque, and places her stamp on his hand. Immediately, Jacko begins to improve. A cringing Braque visits Laura, begging for mercy, but, in an act of great courage to save others like her brother, she lets him perish. Chris and Kate decide to marry. Sorry, who is graduating from high school, enrolls in a four-year wildlife training program. He asks Laura to wait for him and she consents. After all, they now have a great deal in common.

CHARACTERS: Fourteen-year-old **Laura Chant** is a sensitive, clever girl who has an amazing insight into her own and other's feelings. She continues to feel resentment and a sense of abandonment over her parents' divorce three years earlier and "mourns over a vanished father." Laura is emerging from the upheavals of puberty with a body that is "blatantly female" and a need to assume the responsibility of being sexually mature. She also realizes that she has been given a special gift: the ability to foretell disasters before they strike. In spite of all these unnerving circumstances, Laura is able to have a normal teenage life. She is a helpful, obedient daughter to Kate, whom she adores, and is a loving, caring sister to her delightful brother. Laura is a bright, articulate girl who has a cheerful disposition and is mature beyond her years. However, she feels an inner sense of loneliness and emptiness. The events surrounding Jacko's illness produce several emotional crises for Laura from which she emerges a stronger, more self-sufficient young woman.

At first she feels indignant about her mother's affair with Chris and behaves in a belligerent, unpleasant way, but she later realizes that this hostility is the result of jealousy and a groundless fear that she will lose Kate's affection. Later, Laura confronts and overcomes these feelings, realizing that her mother deserves a life of her own. Similarly, as she explores the true nature of love, Laura is able to accept and forgive her father and respond to her deep feelings for Sorry. Laura shows enormous courage and sacrifice in consenting to become a witch to save her brother, especially since she knows this process can't be reversed. Frightened and vulnerable, she later confronts and vanquishes the evil Braque. Laura's physical appearance is a throwback to a distant Polynesian ancestor. She has woolly, brown hair, dark eyes, and olive skin. Laura is an amazing person, vulnerable yet strong, dauntless but fragile. Her sacrifice is a triumph of love over evil.

Laura's mother is thirty-five-year old **Kate**. Though not a model housekeeper, she is a resourceful, hard-working mother who has a full-time job. Although she must scrounge for every penny to support the family, she is able to shower attention and love on her two children. Kate deprives herself of small comforts to feed and clothe Laura and Jacko, but she never complains about the sacrifices she makes. She shows an amazing maturity and lack of bitterness in accepting her husband's infidelity, the subsequent divorce, and her present strained circumstances. Kate is an optimistic, witty, and resourceful person who treats her children, particularly Laura, like valuable partners who deserve respect and understanding. She exudes an aura of nobility and integrity. But under this bright, good-natured, accepting exterior, Kate is still a person who needs support and love. When she finds this in Chris, she responds without shame or regret. An attractive blonde, and still a young woman, Kate deserves a second chance at love. Kate's son is three-year-old **Jacko**, short for **Jonathan**. He is a blond, curly-haired youngster who is well-behaved, imaginative, and affable. To him, "life is always lovely." His tragic illness and near-death experience are extremely poignant because he is such an endearing, lovable, and defenseless child.

At school, Laura is attracted to eighteen-year-old **Sorensen Carlisle**, nicknamed **Sorry**, particularly because of his grey "tricky, looking-glass eyes with quicksilver surfaces." To his teachers and classmates, Sorry is a clever, charming, somewhat passive student given to occasional audacious remarks. He is considered scholastically bright and is known to be interested in wildlife and photography, but otherwise he is a loner without many friends. Privately, however, Sorry is a witch. Sophisticated, intelligent, and witty, he has at his disposal amazing supernatural powers, though he shows great restraint and caution in their use. Like Laura, Sorry is also vulnerable. His feelings of parental rejection have produced a stammer, which he tries to control, and a sardonic, often caustic attitude which is intensified when he discovers that Laura's initial visit is for help not sex. After he recovers from this further rejection, Sorry reveals a tender, caring nature in his treatment of Laura. He shows self-control and consideration towards her, respecting her virginity and not taking advantage of her susceptibility. He comforts her, courageously accompanying her when she goes to confront Braque, and he teaches her how to control her new powers. Sorry is a dependable, loving son, but he is aware that his mother and grandmother can be manipulative and, at times, devious. Though a little eccentric in his tastes and manners, Sorry proves to be an honorable, decent man worthy of Laura's love.

Sorry's immediate family consists of his reclusive mother, **Miryam Carlisle**, and grandmother, **Winter**, who live in seclusion with Sorry in a large isolated mansion. Cool, calm Miryam is tall and good-looking. She is particularly striking because her hair is completely white, though she is not yet forty. Both she and her mother, whose head resembles that of an elegant tortoise, show great kindness and consideration towards Laura. Both are devoted witches, faithful to their principles and powers. This dedication has caused them to make some decisions they regret. The first was to allow Miryam to become pregnant so (they hoped) there would be another female witch in the family to create a magical circle of three. The second occurred when they rejected Sorry after his birth and placed him in a foster home, from which he later escaped.

The wicked spirit of the dead who feeds off the body of Jacko is **Carmody Braque**. Completely evil, he deprives children of their lives so he can exist and spread death and destruction wherever he goes. Without compassion or mercy, he rejects Laura's pleas to take her body and restore her brother to health. With his large teeth and thin rubbery lips, he looks like a grinning puppet. After being stamped by Laura, however, he becomes a sniveling monstrosity pleading for his life. Realizing that he is essentially cruel and heartless, Laura banishes him to his grave.

Apart from her family, Kate has two loves in her life. The first is her former husband, **Stephen Chant**, a charming, shallow man who survives on his charisma and wit. Though genuinely fond of his children, he was unfaithful to his wife and since the divorce has been neglectful and distant. The other is **Chris Holly**, originally from Canada, who is a newly appointed librarian in the district. Balding and without distinctive features, Chris is an amusing, clever, cheerful person who is genuinely fond of Kate. He is reliable, polite, and outgoing. Also a divorcee, Chris, who has a degree in philosophy, shows great tact, patience, and understanding particularly with Laura whom he knows resents his presence. Kate accurately describes him as "a man of taste and judgement."

The Tricksters

(fantasy, 1986)

PLOT: Jack and Naomi Hamilton have gathered their family and guests together to celebrate an old-fashioned Christmas of sunning and swimming at their coastal New Zealand cottage. The ninety-year-old beach house, Carnival's Hide, is permeated with the memory of Teddy Carnival, son of the owner, Edward. After Teddy drowned at the age of twenty, Edward Carnival and his daughter Minerva returned to England and the house was sold. The Hamiltons have five children: their oldest son, Charlie, twenty-one-year-old Christo (or Christobel), seventeen-year-old daughter Harry (whose real name is Ariadne), Serena, and Benny, who is seven. Their guests are Robert Huxley, a friend of Charlie's; a visiting English forester named Anthony Heskett; and Emma Forbes, an unmarried mother, and her daughter, Tibby, both of whom have become a part of the Hamilton household. Harry is the most imaginative and private of the Hamilton children. She is secretly writing a medieval romance involving knights and villains. While swimming at the cove, Harry enters an underwater cave where an icy hand touches her. The following morning, three mysterious men appear on the beach. Their leader introduces himself as Ovid and presents his brothers, the identical twins Hadfield and Felix. The three, supposedly distant members of the Carnival clan, gradually insinuate themselves into the household. Harry, with her psychic powers, is the only one to realize that Ovid is really the ghost of Teddy Carnival and that the twins are separate facets of his personality, Hadfield representing evil and Felix good.

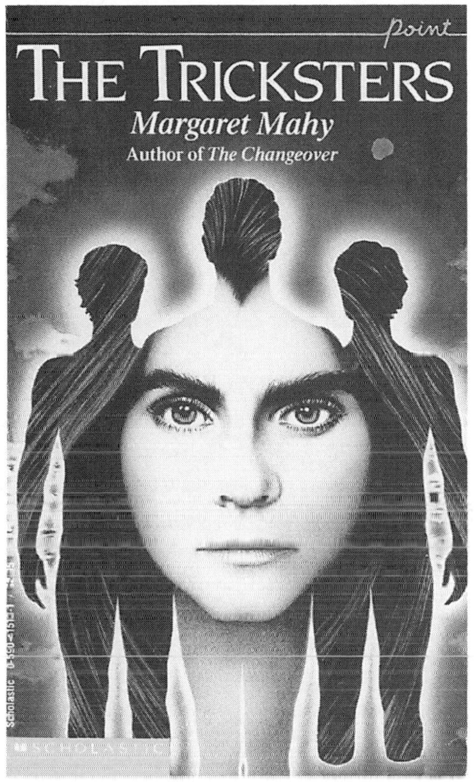

When the ghost of Teddy Carnival appears as three separate men, only a young girl with psychic powers is able to see their true identity.

Complex personal and emotional relationships evolve in the short holiday season, culminating in Harry having a love affair with Felix; in a fit of jealousy, Ovid, and particularly Hadfield, unleash evil influences to disrupt the family's harmony. They succeed. Family confidences are broken and divulged, Christo makes fun of Harry's book, not knowing it is written by her sister, and it is revealed that Jack is actually the father of Tibby. The family disperses, bruised and divided, and the Carnivals disappear. Harry burns her book on the beach and in the flames sees a face that is a combination of Ovid, Hadfield, and Felix reunited. Gradually, the family, strengthened and renewed by the ordeal caused by the tricksters, gets back together. In a gesture of reconciliation, Christobel gives Harry a blank book, and Harry begins to write again, "Once upon a time. . . ."

CHARACTERS: The middle daughter of the Hamiltons, shy, reclusive, bookish **Harry** (a variation of **Ariadne**) is the novel's central character. Attractive, with long, reddish-brown hair, she is a dreamer with a wild, romantic imagination that has an outlet in the secret writing of a medieval romance about good versus evil. She is a keen observer of people and shows astute insights into human nature. Harry gives the impression of being self-possessed and detached, but actually she is sensitive and vulnerable. Naive, sentimental, and longing for love and adventure, Harry surrenders herself in her first sexual experience to Felix, the man she feels understands, respects, and needs her. Harry does not comprehend her amazing psychic abilities, though she is actually something of an enchantress. Her remarkable powers of concentration and her preoccupation with good and evil inadvertently cause the ghost of Teddy Carnival to materialize as three separate people. She alone is able to fathom their otherworldly, supernatural existence and defy their powers. Though outwardly a docile, obedient daughter, Harry feels trapped within the household, particularly because she is overshadowed by her domineering, selfish older sister Christo. She is tired of being "good old Harry," and longs to be the "difficult, brilliant one instead." Harry believes in honesty. When Christo mistakenly pokes fun at Harry's novel not knowing she wrote it, Harry lashes out and reveals the family secret concerning Jack's dalliance with Emma. Later, she is guilt-ridden and miserable. However, the family realizes that her openness and straightforward honesty have brought the family closer together.

Harry's older sister, the difficult **Christobel**, or **Christo** for short, is a restless, domineering dynamo who accurately confesses, "I bully people." Talkative, clever, and witty, no one is spared from her barbed remarks and acid asides. Bossy and demanding, Christo exudes a charismatic charm that makes her the center of attention. She enjoys making men blush with her outrageous remarks and having them compete for her attentions. Somewhat jaded, she is particularly attracted to Ovid because, like him, she "likes things unexpected and unpredictable" and "wants life to be exciting every minute of the day." She is so incredibly beautiful and glamorous that people tolerate her controlling, competitive ways. Occasionally there are flashes of compassion in her nature. For example, she says that she is sorry for losers. Perhaps the act of contrition of giving Harry a new book is an indication that Christo is becoming more emotionally mature.

Harry's parents are Jack and Naomi Hamilton. **Jack Hamilton**, a handsome university professor in his late forties, is an amiable man who is worshipped by his family, particularly Christo. Sophisticated and erudite, he impresses all with his charm and magnetism. Easygoing and witty, Jack showers love and attention on his children, who call him by his first name. Afraid of losing his youth and appeal, he once had a secret affair with Emma that resulted in a baby, Tibby. When this is divulged by Harry, the family solidarity is temporarily shaken, and Christo succumbs to a period of disillusionment, but in time the amazing power of love that suffuses this family reunites them. In **Naomi Hamilton**, Jack has an ideal wife. With her freckles, beak-like nose, uproarious laugh, and perpetual smile, she radiates cheer and animation. As well as being a great housekeeper, Naomi is a constant source of compassion, comfort, and inspiration for her husband and children. Although she longs for a few minutes to herself, she unselfishly makes herself available to whomever needs her advice or attention. Wise and discerning, she understands why Jack was unfaithful and has long since forgiven him and tries to forget.

Their youngest daughter is **Serena**, described as "rotund and romantic." Precocious and intelligent, Serena seems mature beyond her years. She is particularly impressed with her oldest sister, Christo, whom she tries to emulate by being clever and amusing. Serena is an outspoken but pleasant girl who has a particularly close relationship with her younger brother, **Benny**, who is seven. Benny, a thin, tiny, near-sighted boy with red hair, has average interests for his age but above average discernment and intellect. Amusing and agreeable, Benny enlivens conversations with his astute, humorous remarks.

The older son, **Charlie**, is also pleasant and friendly. Trying to grow a presentable beard, his main interest is sailing, which he does on every opportunity with his friend, **Robert Huxley**. Robert is in love with and dominated by Christobel. A handsome, gracious young man, he is well liked by all, though Christo, in her characteristically blunt way, says he is "a bit thick." Like Charlie, Robert seems to live for sailing. When Christo flirts with Ovid, Robert justifiably becomes annoyed and turns his attentions to the more sympathetic, understanding **Emma Forbes**, "a small, kittenish girl with soft, brown hair, soft brown eyes and a strong sense of survival." Quiet and unpretentious, she is a patient, dependable person who makes her living cleaning offices. Hard-working and undemanding, Emma has a kindly, compassionate nature. Now a frequent guest of the Hamiltons, she has never revealed the full name of her daughter, Tibby.

The Hamiltons' other guest is the quiet, retiring English forester, **Anthony Heskett**. Supposedly in New Zealand to study Edward Carnival's forestry pamphlets, he presents a mysterious, almost enigmatic exterior. With his well-mannered, low-key demeanor and good looks, he is readily accepted by the Hamiltons. Gradually, however, his true identity is revealed. He is the great grandson of Minerva Carnival, who before her death confessed that her father, a martinet, had killed his wild, licentious son during a violent quarrel and pretended it was a drowning. Anthony has used the opportunity to forget a broken romance in England to come to New Zealand to investigate this story.

The ghost of **Teddy Carnival** appears as three people with fictitious names. Teddy himself is **Ovid**, and his two alter egos are **Hadfield** and **Felix**. As Ovid says, "I'm the head, Felix is the heart and Hadfield's the simple predator." Behind Ovid's charm and amusing banter is a cunning, shrewd operator who delights with Hadfield in producing havoc and confusion. Fair-haired with long curls and unusual, almost Mongolian, features, his intriguing non sequiturs and mysterious behavior fascinate others, particularly Christo.

The cruel, heartless side of Teddy's character is represented by tall, handsome Hadfield Carnival, who is the mirror image of his identical twin, Felix. Thus, Hadfield is left-handed and dextrocariac (the structure of his heart is reversed). He derides the wholesome attitudes of the Hamiltons and tries to destroy their family structure. He becomes particularly demonic after he fears that the strength of Felix's love for Harry will weaken his side of Ovid's character.

Felix is the wholesome, loving side of Teddy's character. When Felix begins to feels genuine love for the innocent, trusting Harry, he honorably tries to tell her the truth so that she will not be hurt. As their love grows, he defies the domination of his brothers to free himself of their power, but when Ovid and Hadfield's schemes bring disorder and division to the formerly happy family, Felix realizes that he can't win. During one violent family argument, the gentle Felix throws his arms around his brothers, causing all three to disappear.

Further Reading

Authors and Artists for Young Adults. Vol. 8. Detroit: Gale Research, 1992.

Berger, Laura Standley, ed. *Twentieth-Century Young Adult Writers.* 1st ed. Detroit: St. James, 1994.

Chevalier, Tracy, ed. *Twentieth-Century Children's Writers.* 3rd ed. Chicago: St. James, 1989.

Children's Literature Review. Vol. 7. Detroit: Gale Research, 1984.

De Montreville, Doris, and Elizabeth D. Crawford, eds. *Fourth Book of Junior Authors and Illustrators.* New York: H. W. Wilson, 1978.

Mahy, Margaret. "Mahy Hill Arbuthnot Lecture: A Dissolving Ghost." *Journal of Youth Services in Libraries* (summer 1989): 313-19.

Ward, Martha, ed. *Authors of Books for Young People.* 3rd ed. Metuchen, NJ: Scarecrow, 1990.

Harry Mazer

1925-, American young adult novelist

Snow Bound

(young adult novel, 1973)

PLOT: Most everyone thinks Tony Laporte and his three sisters are spoiled. Even though their parents don't have a lot of money, they work hard so their children can have all the advantages they never did. Tony, who is fifteen, knows he can get away with a lot, but when he befriends a stray dog and decides to adopt him, his parents draw the line.

When his father takes the dog away, Tony shows his anger by stealing his mother's old Plymouth so he can drive to his uncle's house, even though he doesn't have a license. Foolishly leaving during the middle of a snow storm, Tony ignores the possible dangers of such a trip in his attempt to get back at his parents. In addition to the storm, things become complicated when Tony decides to pick up a hitchhiker. At first thinking the lonely figure in the road is a young boy, he soon regrets stopping to pick up Cindy Reichert. The girl, who lives with her aloof father, seems to Tony to be a pain in the neck, and the two teenagers quickly grow to dislike each other. When Tony can't resist trying to show off his driving skills to Cindy, he ends up wrecking the car and stranding them both. Tony and Cindy find themselves in the middle of a January blizzard in rural New York.

Thus begins an eleven-day odyssey of survival. Tony and Cindy endure hunger, frostbite, numbing cold, fear of death, a pack of wild dogs, a severely sprained ankle (Tony's), and their own selfishness before they are able to save themselves by a painful trek through the wilderness to the out-of-the-way home of a woman named Mrs. Littlejohn. Luckily, they survive and end up recuperating in a hospital. But although they have avoided serious physical harm, both Tony and Cindy realize they will never be the same after their experiences. They have matured and are no longer the selfish teens they once were.

CHARACTERS: Tony Laporte is a typical rebellious teenager. A moody boy, he dreams of high adventure and of escaping the humdrum world of school and home. He knows his parents spoil him and his sisters, but he takes advantage of it just the same. When he finds the stray dog that he names King Arthur, he decides to see how much he can get away with by keeping the dog. When his father takes the dog away, however, Tony rebels by stealing his mother's car.

Tony shows his immaturity several times after picking up Cindy. In addition to driving recklessly and crashing the car, he selfishly eats all of the cookies Cindy had in her knapsack instead of sharing them. And when he takes off alone to find some help because Cindy's feet are too frostbitten to move, he contemplates not returning. He does return, despite almost giving up after injuring his ankle. With Cindy's help, however, Tony endures and grows up in the process. After their ordeal, he realizes he has changed. To survive the storm, he has learned to be less selfish and to cooperate with someone else. Tony demonstrates his newfound maturity when he promises to replace his mother's car. Even though his parents don't demand he do this, Tony feels it is important for him to start being responsible for his own actions.

Cindy Reichert, the hitchhiker Tony picks up, also matures during the course of the story. She had once considered herself to be like her father: calm, cool, and independent. She and her father have lived together since Cindy's mother died when she was just three years old. Somewhat rebellious, Cindy has taken up hitchhiking, even though she is sure her father wouldn't like it if he found out what she was doing. She convinces herself that she will be fine if she is careful, and she does show caution when she gets out of a car driven by a young man whose behavior seems suspicious. Left out in the snow, she is at first glad to be picked up by Tony. When Tony wrecks the car, Cindy is the first one to recognize the gravity of their situation. Trying to be practical, which only annoys Tony, she sorts out her cookies for rationing and is justifiably incensed when Tony eats them all. When Tony leaves her in the car while he goes to look for help, Cindy begins to despair, thinking he won't return. But she does not give up. She builds a fire inside the car to keep herself from freezing to death. When Tony at last returns for her, Cindy realizes how much she has changed in those three days and that she does need other people in her life.

Tony's father, **Fred Laporte**, is well aware that his son gets away with too much. Although he would like to blame his wife for spoiling their son and daughters, he must share the blame because he gives in too often. Like his wife, Fred wants his children to enjoy some of the comforts in life that he never had. Pampering his son leads to Tony's bad attitude, however, and father and son often argue. When Tony brings home the stray dog, his father decides to put his foot down once and for all. Tony's mother, **Bev Laporte**, is less resistent to the idea of a dog underfoot than is her husband. A woman with good intentions and who loves her family, she has a hard time taking care of her husband and children while holding down a full-time job. She decides to give in to her son's request at first because it is the easiest thing to do. However, when the animal's barking disturbs everyone, even Tony's mother reaches the limit of her endurance.

Further Reading

Authors and Artists for Young Adults. Vol. 5. Detroit: Gale Research, 1991.

Berger, Laura Standley, ed. *Twentieth-Century Young Adult Writers.* 1st ed. Detroit: St. James, 1994.

Holtz, Sally Holmes, ed. *Fifth Book of Junior Authors and Illustrators.* New York: H. W. Wilson, 1983.

Something about the Author. Vol. 31. Detroit: Gale Research, 1985.

Something about the Author Autobiography Series. Vol. 11. Detroit: Gale Research, 1991.

Harry Mazer

1925-, American young adult novelist

Norma Fox Mazer

1931-, American young adult novelist

The Solid Gold Kid

(young adult novel, 1977)

PLOT: Co-written by this husband-and-wife team, *The Solid Gold Kid* is a realistic novel about a wealthy teenager who is kidnapped and held for ransom. Due to a strange, last-minute accident, he is kidnapped along with four other adolescents, and in their struggle to survive the ordeal the five of them forge close bonds of friendship, which are eventually broken when they return to their old lives.

Derek Chapman is the "Solid Gold Kid," the only son of self-made millionaire Jimmy Neal Chapman. At age sixteen, Derek leads a planned but contented life. He does what his father wants him to do—attending Payne Boarding School, vacationing at Long Island Sound, going to summer camp, and occasionally visiting his father, who is always traveling on business. But Derek's life changes drastically one rainy Saturday morning while he's waiting for a bus. Impatient because the bus is late, he accepts a ride from a couple in a gray van and jokingly invites the four strangers, who are also at the bus stop, to join him. Pam Barbushek, Jeff Wyatt, Wendy Manheim, and Ed Hill step into the van before the people driving it can stop them. It turns out that the drivers of the van are a couple named Pearl and Bogie, who have offered Derek a ride in order to kidnap him. Although they hadn't planned to do so, they kidnap the others as well.

For the next six days, the five teens wait for the ransom money from Derek's father. The kidnappers are rough and vicious people who are armed and willing to use their weapons. For the first time, Derek has to make decisions on his own without someone else telling him what to do. In their struggle to survive, these five young people form a close bond. By the end of the story, Jeff, Wendy, and Pam have all been shot and wounded. Although they will recover, the psychological scars will last a very long time. Ed is perhaps the most severely traumatized of them all, having been left bound and helpless for more than three days without food or water.

After the kidnappers are caught and all of the teenagers are rescued, Derek's father sends him off to school in Paris to avoid the publicity. But he will never forget his four friends or the memories of the terrible ordeal they shared. On a return trip, he visits Pam, for whom he has developed a special friendship. Although they promise to stay in touch, Derek knows that their different worlds will keep them apart.

CHARACTERS: Derek Chapman is a likeable young man who somewhat placidly lives the life his father has planned for him. He accepts the fact that his father rarely has time for him, that he has a mistress, and that his mother is a very private person. During his six-day ordeal, for the first time he makes his own decisions and is responsible for himself and others. Derek realizes that until then he has simply been going through the motions of his life. When the ordeal is over, he worries a great deal about his newfound friends. He is stunned and hurt, for instance, when he visits Ed in the hospital and the boy's mother tells him to go because he has caused enough trouble already. But Derek comes to the realistic conclusion that he cannot go through life apologizing for his father's money. As he leaves Pam on their last visit and boards the airplane to return to school, he vows they will never grow apart and immediately begins a letter to her, but the words do not come easily. As he stares out the window at the horizon, the plane is taking him away from Pam and the others, back into his world of wealth and privilege.

Derek's father, **Jimmy Neal Chapman**, is a self-made millionaire who expects the world to act according to his wishes, and it usually does. He loves his son and cooperates with the kidnappers to get him back. He seems genuinely proud to learn that Derek survived on his own and has changed during his ordeal. But life for Derek soon reverts to the old ways, and his father continues to make decisions for him.

Pam Barbushek is an outgoing, middle-class, seventeen-year-old. She keeps a tight rein on her emotions and refuses to give in to fear. Pam is the first of the hostages to try to escape, and she is shot in the attempt. Derek and the others believe she is dead until they are rescued and discover that she was found by an old recluse who aided her until he could get help. Pam and Derek are attracted to each other, but she is more realistic about their different worlds than he is. When they part at the airport, she tells Derek that being rich is just one of the miserable facts of life he will have to learn to live with. "Think of me sometimes," she tells him as she walks away, limping from her wounds, as perhaps she always will.

Derek forms the closest bond to Pam, but he also becomes friends with the other three hostages. **Jeff Wyatt** is the same age as Pam. He remains optimistic and caring about his friends throughout the ordeal, despite the damage he suffers to his eye while trying to escape with **Wendy Manheim**. Fifteen-year-old Wendy credits Jeff with helping her survive their three nights of terror after their escape. "He was so brave," she tells Derek later. Then she adds, "We were all brave, weren't we?" The most psychologically damaged of the group is fifteen-year-old **Ed Hill**. He was left alone, bound, and helpless for more than three days. By the time he is rescued, he is in shock. Nevertheless, he proves to be an unselfish character when Derek visits him in the hospital, for Ed's first question is about Wendy's condition.

The two kidnappers are **Pearl**, whose name is actually **Sally Miles**, and **Bogie**, whose real name is **Frederick Hartmann**. She is a twenty-two-year-old high school dropout; he is a twenty-six-year-old hoodlum who has been in trouble all his life. Pearl dies of her wounds after they are captured, but Bogie survives to stand trial.

Further Reading

Authors and Artists for Young Adults. Vol. 67. Detroit: Gale Research, 1990.

Berger, Laura Standley, ed. *Twentieth-Century Young Adult Writers.* 1st ed. Detroit: St. James, 1994.

Children's Literature Review. Vol. 16. Detroit: Gale Research, 1989.

Collier, Laurie, and Joyce Nakamura, eds. *Major Authors and Illustrators for Children and Young Adults.* Detroit: Gale Research, 1993.

Donelson, Ken. "Searches and Doers: Heroes in Five Harry Mazer Novels." *Voice of Youth Advocates* 5 (February 1983).

Gallo, Donald R. *Speaking for Ourselves: Autobiographical Sketches by Notable Authors of Books for Young Adults.* Urbana, IL: National Council of Teachers of English, 1990.

Something about the Author. Vol. 67. Detroit: Gale Research, 1992.

Something about the Author Autobiography Series. Vol. 11. Detroit: Gale Research, 1991.

Wilkin, Binnie Tate. *Survival Themes in Fiction for Children and Young People.* Metuchen, NJ: Scarecrow, 1978.

Norma Fox Mazer

1931-, American young adult novelist

Silver

(young adult novel, 1988)

PLOT: This novel sensitively explores the nature of class differences and the subject of sexual abuse. As Sarabeth Silver is about to enter junior high school, her mother, Janie, discovers that the dividing line for the local school districts cuts right through their trailer park. By moving their small trailer across the park, Sarabeth becomes eligible to attend the Drumline schools, where students are mostly upper middle class. Sarabeth and her mother are anything but upper middle class: Janie, a single parent, cleans houses for a living and buys their clothes from local thrift shops, but their small family, which includes Tobias the cat and Janie's boyfriend, Leo, is close and loving.

At her new school, Sarabeth becomes friendly with Grant Varrow, a wealthy and beautiful young girl. At a dance, she also meets Mark Emelsky, who attends a nearby private school. When he calls her, Sarabeth is so pleased that she kisses her pillow, pretending it is him. Later, she tells Grant, along with Grant's friends, Asa Goronkian, Jennifer Rosen, and Patty Lewis, that Mark kissed her. Then she is too embarrassed to admit it was only a pillow. However, at a pajama party with her new friends, who call her Silver, Sarabeth confesses the truth. She also senses that Patty, who is given to dark changes of mood, is having trouble at home. Patty and her divorced mother live in the house of her mother's brother, wealthy Uncle Paul.

During intermission at a concert some time later, Patty breaks down and cries, admitting to Sarabeth that her uncle is sexually abusing her. She has told her mother, who refuses to believe such a terrible accusation about her own brother. Besides, if it were true, they would have to leave the house. Patty's mother is going to school; she has no job and without Paul's support they would have no money. Sarabeth and Grant are shocked and vow to help her, trying to make sure that Patty is not left alone with her uncle. But when she is abused again, Patty no longer wants to return home, so Sarabeth takes her to the trailer. Janie calls Patty's mother, who arrives still refusing to believe her daughter. But she realizes Patty is telling the truth when her daughter jumps out the trailer window and breaks her foot.

At last, Patty's mother has to acknowledge what her brother has been doing. Janie offers their home to Patty while her mother finds a job and a new home for them both. Conditions in the trailer are very cramped for three people and a large cat who often brings in the animals he has killed that day. During this time, Patty has recurring bouts of depression. However, she steadfastly insists that she doesn't want to tell anyone at all about what has happened and that she does not want her uncle put in jail. Sarabeth strongly disagrees with that decision; finally, Asa tells her own father, who is not only a judge but a close friend of Patty's uncle. Charges are brought against him, but Sarabeth knows that Patty will be a long time recovering.

At long last, Sarabeth has a real date and a real kiss from Mark. But when she realizes he is more attracted to someone else, her dreams about Mark do not seem quite as important as they once did. Sarabeth has her mother to count on, and she is more grateful than ever for that. She has new friends and she is also more self-reliant now. She knows there will be other boys to meet.

CHARACTERS: **Sarabeth Silver** is an outgoing young teenager with a close relationship to her mother. When she attends her new school and becomes friendly with Grant and her wealthy, sophisticated friends, Sarabeth can't believe her good fortune and asks herself why they would want to be her friends. As she spends more time with them, Sarabeth begins to see that wealth and social position are really not important and that they certainly do not bring happiness. After Patty's confession, Sarabeth realizes how important friendship and trust are. She is fortunate not only to have a close and secure relationship with her mother, who really cares about her, but to have made friends with others who care, too.

Janie Silver, Sarabeth's mother, was sixteen when she became pregnant and married Sarabeth's father. Their happy marriage ended in tragedy when he was killed a few years later. Since then, Janie has been raising her daughter alone. Hard-working and cheerful, she has a close relationship with her offbeat but likeable boyfriend, **Leo**, a chimney sweep. Leo is a friendly man who slicks back his hair and sometimes wears a pearl earring. He drives a car covered with hood ornaments, which he has nicknamed the Goldmobile. He is younger than Janie, which seems to bother her but not him.

It is the love for her daughter that keeps Janie going, however. Life is not always easy, and at one point their finances become so tight that Janie has to borrow from friends in the trailer park. Sarabeth finds out and secretly takes a job cleaning trailers to help her mother. When Janie learns of this, she becomes so angry that she slaps Sarabeth. Though they make up, it is difficult for Sarabeth to understand that her mother's anger arose from her need to protect and care for her daughter herself.

Though money is a nagging problem for her and her mother, Sarabeth learns from her contact with **Patty Lewis** that it can't solve all problems. Patty is moody and hiding a crippling secret. When Sarabeth learns the dreadful truth behind Patty's strange, unpredictable behavior, she realizes how vulnerable it has made her. Patty can no longer be outgoing and trusting with her friends. When she acts bored and careless with them, as she often does, Sarabeth realizes that it is because Patty has been wounded and does not want to be hurt more by reaching out.

A good friend of Patty's abusive uncle is **Asa Goronkian**'s father, who is a judge. After Patty and her mother have left her uncle's home, Patty wants to conceal everything that has happened. But Asa pleads with her, insisting that he should be punished. When Patty demands, "Would you put your father in jail, someone from your own family?" Asa answers, "Yes. If he did something like that, yes, I would." She then tells her father about what has happened, which begins the process of bringing Patty's uncle to justice.

Some of Sarabeth's other friends include **Grant Varrow** and **Jennifer Rosen**. Grant is a young girl of obvious wealth, and Sarabeth can hardly believe her good fortune to be her friend. Her envy of Grant quickly dies, however, when she learns that for eight years Grant has not even heard from her own father. She tells Sarabeth that she wishes he had died. When Sarabeth protests, Grant says that it is one thing to be sad about someone who has died, as Sarabeth's father did, but "it's better to be sad than to feel the way I do." Unlike Grant, Jennifer Rosen is an outgoing redhead who is friendly and funny. She likes Sarabeth and often contrasts her with Patty. Jennifer says she likes the fact that Sarabeth doesn't keep things to herself. "You mean I'm a blabbermouth," says Sarabeth. "That's one way of putting it," says Jennifer.

Further Reading

Authors and Artists for Young Adults. Vol. 5. Detroit: Gale Research, 1991.

Berger, Laura Standley, ed. *Twentieth-Century Young Adult Writers.* Detroit: St. James, 1994.

Children's Literature Review. Vol. 23. Detroit: Gale Research, 1991.

Collier, Laurie, and Joyce Nakamura, eds. *Major Authors and Illustrators for Children and Young Adults.* Detroit: Gale Research, 1993.

Contemporary Literary Criticism. Vol. 26. Detroit: Gale Research, 1983.

Gallo, Donald R. *Speaking for Ourselves: Autobiographical Sketches by Notable Authors of Books for Young Adults.* Urbana, IL: National Council of Teachers of English, 1990.

Holtze, Sally Holmes. *Presenting Norma Fox Mazer.* Boston: Twayne, 1987.

Something about the Author. Vol. 67. Detroit: Gale Research, 1992.

Something about the Author Autobiography Series. Vol. 1. Detroit: Gale Research, 1986.

Anne McCaffrey

1926-, American science fiction novelist

Dragonsong

(science fiction, 1976)

PLOT: One of McCaffrey's many books set on the planet Pern, *Dragonsong* features a young adult protagonist, whereas most of the other Pern heroes and heroines are adults. Fourteen-year-old Menolly lives in a large community called Half Circle Sea Hold on the remote eastern coast of Pern's single large continent. Life is primitive here, for the people of Pern have forgotten the technology of their star-travelling ancestors. Half Circle is essentially a huge cave with a great meeting hall and surrounding living quarters. Menolly's parents are Yanus, the community's leader, who is known as the Sea Holder, and Mavi. Yanus and Mavi are stern parents who treat their children harshly. Among Menolly's siblings are her brother, Alemi, and her ill-tempered sister, Sella. Menolly likes Alemi best, but he is often away from home.

Menolly finds a retreat from family life by taking music lessons from the Harper of Sea Hold, Petiron. Harpers are highly respected members of the community, and Petiron is very impressed with Menolly's talent for music. He sends some of her compositions to Robinton, the Masterharper of Pern. When Petiron dies suddenly, Menolly wonders whether the Harper, who had become so forgetful, had remembered to send her pieces to the Masterharper. Menolly is allowed to teach music to the younger children, but she is forbidden by her father to play her own songs. When she disobeys unintentionally, he beats her unmercifully.

One day while gutting fish, Menolly injures her hand. Discouraged because she feels she will no longer be able to play music, she runs away to a cave where she has discovered some fire lizards. Fire lizards are foot-long intelligent creatures that are nearly extinct on the planet. Menolly is able to save some of their eggs from being destroyed by high tides, and when the eggs hatch, she inadvertently becomes the mother to nine of the little dragons. When she discovers that they can be taught to sing, Menolly finds a new purpose and challenge in her life.

While Menolly is in the cave, the planet experiences an attack of Threads, deadly silvery strands that are emitted by a rogue planet called Red Star. Threads eat anything organic in their way, and they are the reason why so much of life on Pern is spent underground. Menolly's family thinks she has been killed by the Threads. When she is nearly caught in an another attack, she is saved by a dragonrider and taken to the lower caverns of Benden Weyr to be cared for by Manora, Mirrim, and others. Unused to the kindness they show her, Menolly begs not to be sent back to her family. Instead, she is visited by her pet fire lizards, including her favorite, Beauty, and returns to playing her music.

Meanwhile, the new Harper who succeeds Petiron, Elgion, has been looking for the writer of the music that was sent to the Masterharper. Menolly's father tells him a man wrote it, but Elgion discovers that Menolly is the real composer and invites her to Harperhall, the great music conservatory on Pern. Menolly is happy to accept her new life as a Harper.

There are over a dozen books set on the world of Pern, including Dragonflight *(1968),* Dragonquest *(1971),* Dragonsinger *(1977),* Dragondrums *(1979),* Dragonsdawn *(1988), and* Renegades of Pern *(1989).*

CHARACTERS: Menolly is a musically gifted young girl who unfortunately lives in a male-dominated society and is the daughter of two harsh parents. Menolly tries to endure her parents' cruelty, but life with them is so restrictive—especially when she is forbidden to play her music—that it becomes almost intolerable. When she runs away after injuring her hand, she is given the chance to find herself. With the fire lizards, she is able to express her loving nature by becoming the "mother" to nine baby dragons. And when she is sheltered by the friendly women of the lower caverns, Menolly feels loved and cared for for the first time in her life. Her true love, however, will always be music, so she reluctantly leaves Manora and Mirrim to become a Harper.

The harsh and cruel **Yanus** is displeased with Menolly, his youngest child, and ashamed of her musical talent because being a musician is a man's profession. After the death of the Harper Petiron, Yanus tells Menolly that she will be allowed to teach music to the youngsters, but she is prohibited from playing her own compositions. When she disobeys him, he beats her harder than he ever has before. Yanus later shows his contempt for his daughter again when he lies to Elgion by telling him a man composed the pieces Menolly wrote. **Mavi**, Menolly's mother, is equally strict and unloving toward her daughter. She is completely unsympathetic to Menolly after Yanus beats her, and when Menolly injures her hand and loses a lot of blood from the wound, she just tells her daughter to drink something and go to bed. Although **Petiron** the Harper knows full well that a woman can't be a musician on Pern, he admires Menolly's great musical ability and sends two of her songs to the Masterharper. Menolly is heartbroken over the death of Petiron, who was her greatest friend. She watches in deep sadness as his body, wrapped in Harper blue, is buried at sea.

The new Harper is the tall and handsome **Elgion**. Soon he wishes to know the composer of the tunes sent to the Masterharper, and, despite Yanus's deception, eventually learns it is Menolly. It is Elgion who helps Menolly go to Harperhall. **Robinton** the Masterharper is greatly impressed by Menolly's talent. When he tells her that he wants her to go to Harperhall with him, she resists, saying that she can't play because of her injury and because she is a girl. Robinton replies, "Don't you *want* to be a Harper?" When Menolly breathlessly replies that she does, Robinton squeezes her hand and, with kindness in his eyes, leads her to her new future.

After the Thread attack, Menolly finds safety and friendship in the women of Benden Weyr. **Manora**, who is the headwoman, treats Menolly with firmness, love, and kindness. Also caring for her is **Mirrim**, a girl of about Menolly's age, who Menolly is astounded to discover once lived in the Southern Weyr. From the beginning, the two girls form a close friendship. Menolly soon learns that children reared at Benden are much happier, more curious, and more active than those reared at Circle Sea Hold. It is a revelation that changes Menolly's sense of her own family and destiny.

Crystal Singer

(science fiction, 1982)

PLOT: On the planet Fuerte, Killashandra Ree has just been told that ten long and grueling years of musical training have all been for nothing. Maestro Esmond Valdi says she is not good enough to be a top-rank concert singer. Killashandra is crushed. Packing her lute, she decides to leave the planet. Her life is changed when she meets Carrik of the Heptite Guild of the planet Ballybran, where the fabled Black Crystal (a mineral used for interstellar communication) is found. When Carrik finds out that Killashandra has perfect pitch, he tells her of the Crystal Singers. Their unique vocal abilities allow them to mine the fabulous Black Crystal, but it is a dangerous job. Few who go to Ballybran ever return. There are many dangers, such as the mach storms that have damaged people's brains, leaving them mental vegetables. On the other hand, the Guild will provide her with a job, security, and a chance for wealth.

Killashandra decides to apply for the Crystal Singers. She soon learns that what appears to be a wonderful opportunity indeed has many drawbacks. For one thing, once a Singer becomes acclimated to Ballybran, he or she becomes sterile. Also, the symbiont (a Singer who has adjusted to the silicon-based ecology of the planet) can't ever leave Ballybran for long periods of time. Singers who do so suffer horrible deaths because their bodies can't survive outside of their adopted environment. Killashandra learns of this firsthand when Carrik is unable to return to Ballybran in time and dies. However, becoming a symbiont also has the side effect of increasing a Singer's life span.

Passing every test in her training to become a Singer, Killashandra becomes one of the few to adjust perfectly to the strange environment of Ballybran and the life of a Crystal Singer. She proves to be one of the unique few to become a perfect symbiont. Not only does she accomplish this, but she soon achieves an even more fantastic feat when she establishes a communication link with distant Trundimoux, the first Crystal Singer in the entire interstellar system to do so. Killashandra laughs when she remembers her music maestro telling her that she would never be a good singer.

Killashandra *(1985) is a sequel.*

CHARACTERS: Killashandra Ree is not a woman to settle for second best. After she is told she will never be a top concert singer, she becomes determined to be a superior Crystal Singer. Portrayed as a woman without any family or romantic ties, Killashandra is independent, high-spirited, and seemingly without fear. She is supremely confident of her own musical ability and is undaunted by the obvious dangers of singing crystal on Ballybran. Often abrupt in her dealings with others, she nonetheless forms romantic attachments, such as her meeting with the unfortunate Carrik and, later, her love for Lanzecki. However, Killashandra also displays a somewhat reckless streak. Danger, to her, is relative. She exhibits a tendency to rely on her own feelings until someone can show her a better way and is not afraid to question the judgment of others. All these traits combined help Killashandra become the ideal Crystal Singer.

A chance meeting on Fuerte with **Carrik** of the Heptite Guild on Ballybran sets Killashandra on a course toward becoming a Crystal Singer. A tall, arrogant man, Carrik is intriguing to Killashandra, who finds his stories about Ballybran fascinating. After a romantic interlude with Carrik, however, Killashandra witnesses Carrik's health deteriorate until he dies because he has been away from Ballybran too long.

The Guild master, **Lanzecki,** is also an intriguing figure to Killashandra. Stern and exacting, he directs the lives and fate of the Crystal Singers with assurance and certainty. Although Killashandra has an affair with him, it is not until her return from her mission on Trundimoux that she learns the extent of his interest in her. Quietly, he has been guiding her career as a Crystal Singer, so that she could master the most difficult accomplishment of singing black crystal. When Killashandra asks why he has taken such an interest in her, Lanzecki confesses that it was for more than professional reasons.

At first, maestro **Esmond Valdi** seems insensitive when he tells Killashandra she is not good enough to become a top-rank concert singer. But he shows that he actually does care when he tries to dissuade her from her dangerous plan to become a Crystal Singer.

Further Reading

Authors and Artists for Young Adults. Vol. 6. Detroit: Gale Research, 1991.

Berger, Laura Standley, ed. *Twentieth-Century Young Adult Writers.* 1st ed. Detroit: St. James, 1994.

Brizzi, Mary T. *Anne McCaffrey.* Mercer Island, WA: Starmont, 1986.

Contemporary Literary Criticism. Vol. 17. Detroit: Gale Research, 1981.

Cowart, David, and Thomas L. Wymer, eds. *Twentieth-Century American Science-Fiction Writers.* Vol. 8 of *Dictionary of Literary Biography.* Detroit: Gale Research, 1981.

Fonstad, Karen Wynn. *The Atlas of Pern.* New York: Ballantine, 1984.

Hassler, Donald M., ed. *Patterns of the Fantastic.* Mercer Island, WA: Starmont, 1983.

Something about the Author. Vols. 8, 70. Detroit: Gale Research, 1976, 1993.

Something about the Author Autobiography Series. Vol. 11. Detroit: Gale Research, 1991.

Watson, Noelle, ed. *Twentieth-Century Science Fiction Writers.* 3rd ed. Chicago: St. James, 1991.

Robin McKinley

1952-, American novelist

Beauty: A Retelling of the Story of Beauty and the Beast

(fantasy, 1978)

PLOT: Beauty's family, which includes her father and two sisters, Hope and Grace, once lived in wealthy surroundings, but their lives changed drastically when Father's merchant ships were lost, leaving them penniless. Hoping to save money, they moved into the countryside to a simple farmhouse near a dark and mysterious forest.

On the way home one day, Father takes a shortcut through the forest and discovers the castle in which the Beast lives. It turns out to be a remarkable place of enchantment where doors open by themselves and the furniture can move and talk. A chair bids him to sit at the table, and a couch made into a bed invites him to sleep. However, Father sees no sign of his host. When he leaves, he decides to take one rose from the garden for Beauty. Immediately, he is accosted by a loud roar that belongs to a dreadful-looking creature. The Beast demands one of his daughters as payment for the rose or else Father will pay with his life. He has one month to send a daughter to the Beast's castle.

Beauty, against her father's wishes, agrees to go to the castle to live. Thus begins the first of many months of Beauty's life in the castle, where she learns to see beyond the frightening exterior of the Beast. As she begins to understand his gentle and loving nature, Beauty begins to care for the Beast. But Beauty rejects the gentlemanly Beast's many offers of marriage. He eventually allows her to go home after she promises to return. When Beauty doesn't come back at the time she said she would, the Beast falls gravely ill. Finding him near death, Beauty realizes her true feelings and declares her love for him. The Beast is magically restored to his human form, and Beauty and the Beast, now a handsome gentleman, decide to marry.

CHARACTERS: Beauty's nickname (her real name is **Honour**) is ironic because she is actually quite plain—even boyish—looking. She is not envious of her other sisters, however, even though they are more attractive. She remains, instead, a likeable young woman who has a generous spirit and is considerate of others. Her agreement to live in the Beast's castle in order to save her father's life indicates this inner strength. Throughout the story, Beauty shows her love of both roses and books, symbolizing her inner beauty and sensitivity.

These qualities allow Beauty to see past the Beast's outer ugliness and see the goodness and gentleness within him. Because she is a very independent woman, however, she rejects his offers of marriage at first. But she realizes, when he is apparently dying, that she truly loves the Beast. Her declaration of love transforms him back to his human shape, breaking the wicked enchantment. When this happens, Beauty looks in the mirror and she is transformed, too. Her eyes, which she had thought to be muddy hazel, are actually amber with flecks of green; her hair is a pale coppery red, not the drab color that she remembers.

The **Beast** has a frightening appearance that conceals his inner dignity and kind spirit. He remains a gentleman at all times with Beauty in his castle, treating her as an honored guest in his home; exhibiting a most appealing personality despite his fearsome exterior, he is intelligent and cultured. When the enchantment is broken by Beauty's love, the Beast is revealed to be a handsome gentleman with brown eyes and curly brown hair streaked with gray. As he explains, he is not as young as he once was because enchantments are not a perfect protection against time. He tells Beauty that his enchantment was an old family curse placed by a local magician who grew tired of his forebears' holier-than-thou attitude and cursed them. But the inept magician couldn't make the curse stick at first, so he had to wait for another chance. The next opportunity came along when he saw the young man, who then became the Beast. When Beauty and the Beast go out into the courtyard to see her family, she asks his name. He replies that he no longer has one, so Beauty will have to name him.

Beauty's family is the source of her good qualities. Throughout the novel, the family's integrity shows through in their decisions to live up to the bargains they have made. **Father** is a kind and honest man, sincerely troubled by his financial misfortunes and concerned about providing for his daughters' welfare. When he leaves the castle of his unknown host, he desires only to return with one flower for his beloved Beauty, who so appreciates the loveliness of nature. When he is confronted by the Beast, he must promise to send one of his daughters to the castle. He does not want to make any of them go, but Beauty insists she be the one. Sister **Grace** also shows integrity by waiting faithfully for her fiance, Robbie, a promising sea captain who sailed away when she was nineteen years old. Though he has been missing at sea for six years, she promised she would wait twenty, and so she does. Sister **Hope**'s dreams of helping the family are realized when she is engaged to marry Ger the blacksmith. He is an industrious, honest man whose success in his trade will help to raise the family's fortunes.

The Hero and the Crown

(fantasy, 1984)

PLOT: Young Aerin, daughter of King Arlbeth, is not fully accepted at court because of her deceased mother's background: she was a witch from the North country who died shortly after Aerin was born. However, both Aerin's father and her older cousin, Tor, who is being groomed as the king's successor, love Aerin dearly. So does Aerin's caring maidservant, Teka. Aerin's two enemies in court are her cousin Galanna, who is jealous of Aerin's position, and Galanna's husband, Perlith.

Goaded by Galanna, the fifteen-year-old Aerin eats a surka plant, which is supposed to give a person superhuman strength. Instead, Aerin develops nightmares and convulsions from which she takes a long time to recuperate while under the watchful eye of Teka. During her convalescence, she begins to ride the king's lame horse, Talat. Also, Tor, who is beginning to take more than a friendly interest in his maturing, red-haired cousin, teaches her to be an expert with the sword.

When she is eighteen, Aerin discovers a recipe for kenet, an ointment that protects against dragon fire. When she hears of a village being frightened by a small dragon, she covers herself with kenet and rides Talat to the village, where she kills the dragon. Later, when King Arlbeth and Tor leave the castle because of trouble up North, Aerin decides to battle the awesome Black Dragon, who has been destroying many villages. She and Talat attack the savage dragon, but Aerin is badly burned. When she awakens, she finds that she has killed the dragon, known as Maur, and in its place she finds a glowing red stone that was the last drop of blood from Maur's heart.

In a dream, a tall, blonde man appears to Aerin and promises to help her. Soon Aerin meets the man, a soothsayer named Luthe, who is able to heal her wounds. He tells her she has still one mission to fulfill. The evil power that controls the Hero's Crown, a magic talisman, and has unleashed dragons such as Maur on the world is none other than Aerin's uncle, the wizard Agsded. Only one of his own blood can destroy him. With the aid of a magical blue sword given to her by Luthe, Aerin slays Agsded, saves the kingdom, and takes the Hero's Crown. Although she loves Luthe, she leaves him to return to her father and Tor. When the king dies,

Aerin marries Tor, and together they rule over a happy, peaceful land.

CHARACTERS: Aerin is a high-spirited young girl who desires to take her place among the kingdom's great dragon slayers. She is unaware of her cousin Galanna's hatred for her and is easily goaded into eating the surka leaves that almost kill her. Although she knows that she is the king's rightful heir, she is also aware that the kingdom does not favor her because of her mother's mysterious background. To prove herself worthy of her rightful place as the king's daughter, Aerin trains diligently on the lame horse Talat and works hard at the sword lessons given to her by an increasingly adoring Tor. Aerin becomes a tall, gangly teenager and then matures into a lovely, vivacious, and courageous woman who catches the eye of her cousin Tor. Strong and daring, she proves to be brave beyond her years as she sets out to claim her rightful place in the kingdom and win the respect of her father's people.

Aerin's cousin, **Galanna**, is used to being the petted darling of the kingdom, for she was just seven when Aerin was born. Galanna was exceedingly unhappy about Aerin's birth because Aerin, as the king's daughter, would always be placed above her, unless, of course, Galanna married Tor. But Tor cares only for Aerin, and so Galanna marries Perlith. Because she hates her cousin, Galanna entices her into eating the leaves of the surka, hoping to get rid of Aerin. Instead, Aerin only becomes ill for several weeks.

Another of Aerin's cousins, **Tor**, is the successor to the Damarian throne. Tor grows ever more fascinated and charmed by his headstrong cousin, who fears nothing. Although Tor is strong and brave and would give his life for the kingdom, it is Aerin who uncovers the Hero's Crown. Tor is consequently the first new king in many generations to wear the Hero's Crown at his coronation.

Though she loves Tor, Aerin also has feelings for the blonde soothsayer, **Luthe**, who tells her she must find the Hero's Crown and who gives her the magical sword, Gonturan. Aerin and Tor know, however, that it is Aerin's destiny to help rule the kingdom. With great sadness, the lovers part as Aerin goes to take her place as queen.

When Aerin meets her uncle, the evil wizard **Agsded**, who is also the man who murdered her mother, he merely laughs at this child who has come to slay him. With the help of Gonturan, however, Aerin kills Agsded, thus ridding the kingdom of the wizard who had unleashed the evil dragons upon the world and horded the Hero's Crown.

King Arlbeth, Aerin's father, is a kindly man who loves his only daughter but can't shield her from the people who mistrust her because of his wife's mysterious background. Although he fears for Aerin's safety, he is justly proud of her strength of purpose and courage.

Further Reading

Authors and Artists for Young Adults. Vol. 4. Detroit: Gale Research, 1990.

Berger, Laura Standley, ed. *Twentieth-Century Young Adult Writers.* 1st ed. Detroit: St. James, 1994.

Children's Literature Review. Vol. 10. Detroit: Gale Research, 1986.

Estes, Glenn E., ed. *American Writers for Children since 1960: Fiction.* Vol. 52 of *Dictionary of Literary Biography.* Detroit: Gale Research, 1986.

Holtze, Sally Holmes, ed. *Fifth Book of Junior Authors and Illustrators.* New York: H. W. Wilson, 1989.

Something about the Author. Vols. 32, 50. Detroit: Gale Research, 1983, 1988.

Margaret Mitchell

1900-1949, American novelist

Gone with the Wind

(historical novel, 1936)

PLOT: One of the most famous and widely read of all American novels, *Gone with the Wind* takes place in Georgia before, during, and after the Civil War, with much of the action occurring at the fictional O'Hara plantation called Tara. Raised in Atlanta and steeped in the lore of the Civil War, Margaret

Clark Gable and Vivien Leigh as Rhett Butler and Scarlet O'Hara in the classic 1939 film version of Mitchell's **Gone with the Wind.**

Mitchell began the book in 1926 but did not complete it until 1935. During the first year of publication, it sold almost one-and-a-half million copies, and it won Mitchell the Pulitzer Prize in 1937.

The story begins in 1861 when talk of war between the states annoys sixteen-year-old Scarlett, the spoiled and selfish daughter of wealthy plantation owner Gerald O'Hara. Discussions about war divert the attention of the southern gentlemen who gather at Tara around the willful, daring Scarlett. The young men of Georgia look upon the impending fight as a chance to prove their bravery, but the young women regard it more as an intrusion, rather like a rough-and-tumble game they must endure until their suitors wash up and return to dances and Saturday night suppers.

Scarlett becomes more upset when she learns that blond and aloof Ashley Wilkes of Twelve Oakes Plantation, whom she has always adored, is going to marry his cousin, plain Melanie Hamilton of Atlanta. At a ball that night, she confronts Ashley, who admits he has feelings for Scarlett but also tells her he could never stand up to her tempestuous nature. Also at the ball is a handsome and charming scoundrel, Rhett Butler. When he laughs at Scarlett's feelings for Ashley, she lashes back by lavishing attention on Melanie's ineffectual brother, Charles Hamilton. Charles is instantly overwhelmed by Scarlett, and within two weeks they marry. When the war begins, Charles and Ashley leave for the fighting; two months later, Scarlett is a widow, but she does not mourn her husband.

Sent to stay with an aunt of the Hamiltons in Atlanta "to recover," she once again meets Rhett Butler, who is now a captain and a blockade runner. When Atlanta is about to be taken by advancing Union troops, Scarlett insists on returning to Tara. With Melanie, who is sick and weak from giving birth to Ashley's son, and with a former slave named Prissy, she makes the dangerous journey home. There she finds her mother dead, her father mentally incompetent, her two sisters helpless, and the plantation in ruins. With Melanie too weak to help, the only person she can really count on is Mammy, a former slave and the caretaker of the household. Scarlett makes two vows—to rebuild Tara and to never be hungry again. When the war ends and taxes threaten the plantation, Scarlett entices her sister's prosperous fiancé, Frank Kennedy, into marrying her instead.

Ashley comes home from the war a broken man. Kennedy is killed in a skirmish with the Ku Klux Klan, and Scarlett then marries Rhett Butler, even though she tells him she doesn't love him. She claims she married him in part for his money, which he spends lavishly on her. Eventually they have a daughter, Bonnie, whom Rhett adores. Scarlett and Rhett have a difficult marriage, and it is made worse by Bonnie's death in a fall from a horse. When Melanie dies after a miscarriage and Scarlett goes to comfort Ashley, she realizes after all these years that he does not love her and that she has been chasing a dream. But when she returns to tell Rhett what she has learned about herself, it is too late. He leaves her. Scarlett is devastated until she tells herself that she will return to Tara to renew her strength. Then, tomorrow, she will think of some way to get him back.

CHARACTERS: Beautiful, intelligent, ruthless, unrepentant, and thoroughly fascinating, **Scarlett O'Hara** is one of the best-known heroines in American fiction. Raised the spoiled darling of a wealthy plantation owner, she is little more than this when the story opens. The coming Civil War is for her simply a nuisance, a disruption of her pampered way of life. Although Mitchell makes no excuses for Scarlett's faults, the novel shows this spoiled southern belle growing to maturity. Scarlett does seduce her sister's fiancé, and she does so without remorse, but it is also Scarlett's strength and persistence that pull the entire family through the miseries of the war's aftermath, and it is only Scarlett who is able to save the family's beloved Tara. At one point, she even finds the strength to kill an invading Union soldier. When Melanie has a difficult time giving birth, it is Scarlett who saves her and the baby; when Scarlett loses Rhett Butler at the end of the novel, she determinedly sets herself the task of winning him back. Mitchell was constantly asked after the book's publication whether Scarlett was ever reunited with Rhett, to which she always replied that she didn't know. Yet one is left with the impression that if Scarlett really puts her mind to something there is nothing she can't achieve.

Rhett Butler is a heroic figure. Handsome and arrogant, strong and self-assured, he is amused by human frailties, but he is also honorable, sensitive, and faithful to his principles. As attracted as he is to Scarlett O'Hara, he does not overlook her faults. However, her strength and determination impress him as he watches her rebuild her beloved Tara almost singlehandedly. He is perfectly aware of why she has seduced her sister's fiancé, and though he can't approve of her methods, he knows that he himself would do as much for a cause in which he believed. But Scarlett's pursuit of Ashley betrays Rhett's feelings for her, and when she goes to comfort Ashley after Melanie's death and then returns to tell Rhett of her change of heart, it is too late to save their relationship. Here, the depth of Rhett's feelings for Scarlett is vividly portrayed. To cover the final wound she has dealt him, he matches her own stubbornness and leaves. As he does so, he delivers one of the most famous parting lines in literature. In reply to Scarlett's plaintive question, "What shall I do?" he replies, "My dear, I don't give a damn."

The man whom Scarlett thinks she loves, **Ashley Wilkes**, is the epitome of an Old South aristocrat. Elegantly mannered, quiet, and considerate, he lives by a gentleman's code of honor. In contrast to the dashing and spirited Rhett Butler whom he admires, however, Ashley seems lifeless. He admits his feelings for Scarlett early in the novel but also says he is incapable of standing up to her. It is more important to Ashley to have peace and tradition in his life than it is to have happiness with someone like Scarlett. Ashley's code of honor is admirable and his near breakdown after the war is easy to sympathize with—at least initially—but he proves himself too weak to face the realities of life in the rapidly changing South. Whereas Scarlett knows she must change to survive, Ashley can't. At the novel's end, when Melanie dies, even Scarlett is amazed to discover the depth of Ashley's helplessness.

Melanie Hamilton Wilkes, whom Scarlett regards as spineless and plain, proves her quiet, enduring strength by the novel's end. Melanie recognizes the pride and goodness in Scarlett and is the only one to defend her when she scandalizes the town by marrying her sister's fiancé. Melanie also recognizes the qualities beneath the rough exterior of Rhett Butler and understands the extent of his love for Scarlett. Aware of Scarlett's feelings for Ashley, Melanie nonetheless remains her friend and champion.

Other, more minor characters in the novel include **Gerald O'Hara**, Scarlett's father, a typical southern plantation owner of the antebellum South. A staunch Confederate, he cannot conceive of any outcome but victory for the South. When the Union Army overruns Tara on its march through Georgia, his will and his mind are completely destroyed, and he must lean on the strength of his adored, willful daughter.

Scarlett's husband after her brief first marriage to **Charles Hamilton** is **Frank Kennedy**, a decent, plodding man whom she steals away from her sister. Frank falls completely under Scarlett's spell, never fully realizing why she married him. The two prominent slaves in the story are **Mammy** and **Prissy**. Mammy is a stout woman who runs the household at Tara like an army compound. She loves Scarlett deeply, but she recognizes her willingness to use any means to get what she wants and tries to be her conscience. At first offended by the outspoken Rhett, Mammy comes to regard him with affection and admiration. Prissy is almost a caricature of an illiterate and somewhat lazy domestic slave. Prissy tells Scarlett that she knows everything about "birthin' babies" and will be helpful when Melanie's time comes. In reality, Prissy knows nothing at all, and Scarlett is forced to take over.

Further Reading

Edwards, Anne. *Road to Tara: The Life of Margaret Mitchell.* New York: Ticknor & Fields, 1983.

Farr, Finis. *Margaret Mitchell of Atlanta: The Author of "Gone with the Wind."* New York: Morrow, 1965.

Hanson, Elizabeth. *Margaret Mitchell.* Boston: Twayne, 1990.

Harwell, Richard, ed. *"Gone with the Wind" as Book and Film.* Columbia, SC: University of South Carolina Press, 1983.

Martine, James J., ed. *American Novelists, 1910-1945.* Vol. 9 of *Dictionary of Literary Biography.* Detroit: Gale Research, 1981.

Mitchell, Margaret. *Margaret Mitchell's "Gone with the Wind" Letters.* New York: Macmillan, 1976.

Pratt, William. *Scarlett Fever.* New York: Macmillan, 1977.

Pyron, Darden A. *Southern Daughter: The Life of Margaret Mitchell.* New York: Harper, 1992.

Ryan, Bryan, ed. *Major Twentieth-Century Writers: A Selection of Sketches from Contemporary Authors.* Detroit: Gale Research, 1991.

Twentieth-Century Literary Criticism. Vol. 1. Detroit: Gale Research, 1978.

Vinson, James, ed. *Twentieth-Century Romance and Gothic Writers.* Detroit: Gale Research, 1982.

Toni Morrison

1931-, American novelist

The Bluest Eye

(novel, 1970)

PLOT: This work established Toni Morrison as a serious and important American novelist. Set in 1941 in a world that values blue-eyed, blonde little girls, the novel asks what chance an African-American child has of achieving her dreams. Eleven-year-old Pecola Breedlove looks out the windows of her old, cold apartment and longs for beautiful things—a world where flowers grow and the grass is green. Meanwhile, Pecola's mother, Mrs. Breedlove, and father, Cholly Breedlove, fight all the time. Her father drinks as well, and her brother, Sammy, runs away from home. As Pecola dreams of a more beautiful life, her longing turns to a desire for blue eyes. Little white girls with blonde hair have blue eyes. Perhaps if Pecola had blue eyes, she thinks, her world would be beautiful, too. Perhaps her father would stop drinking, and her parents would stop fighting. If only she could be more attractive then maybe someone would look at her and love her.

This fantasy world comes to a painful end for Pecola one Saturday afternoon, when her father comes home drunk and finds her alone in the kitchen. Cholly looks at his daughter and is caught in a swell of conflicting emotions—guilt, pity, and love. He wonders why Pecola is not happy, feels guilty about his own inability to give his child a better life, and then becomes angry with her for making him feel guilty and worthless. He grabs her bare foot, knocking her to the floor. Overcome with the excitement of the forbidden, Cholly rapes his daughter on the kitchen floor. For Pecola, the act mercifully renders her unconscious. Later, she awakens in physical pain with her mother standing over her.

The story soon travels around town that Pecola's father has made her pregnant, and Cholly runs off. Her mother beats Pecola so fiercely that her life is threatened; she manages to survive, however, though her baby dies at birth. After that, family life is never the same for Pecola. The years pass, and Cholly dies in a workhouse. Pecola and her mother move to a little brown house at the edge of town. In the end, Pecola slips over the edge into a kind of madness, which serves to protect her from the horror of the past as well as the present. In her insanity, she comes to believe that her eyes are the bluest blue of all.

CHARACTERS: No one notices **Pecola Breedlove**, but she yearns for beautiful things like the blue skies she can see from the windows of her cold room. In reality, Pecola's world is anything but beautiful. She stuffs rags in the windows when it gets too cold in her tiny bedroom, but still Pecola's chest is tight with phlegm. With large and rough hands, her mother swabs her chest with vapor rub and wraps hot flannel around her neck. If there is love in these ministrations, Pecola does not know it.

The Breedlove family lives in a squalid storefront apartment. They are poor and black, and their poverty makes them believe they are ugly. That is the world that Pecola, especially, sees. When she closes her eyes, however, her world is different. Her teeth are good and her nose is not bad, so she comes to believe that the problem must be with her eyes. If she had beautiful blue eyes like she sees on blonde-haired girls and dolls, she decides, people would notice her. But when Pecola looks around, instead of blue eyes and pretty things, she sees only the squalor of her neighborhood. She hears only the fighting of her parents or the conversations of the three prostitutes who live above their apartment.

The fantasy life that had sustained Pecola comes crashing down after she is raped by her father. The neighborhood finally notices her, but only as the object of vicious gossip. Eventually, she and her mother move to a little brown house on the edge of town. People see her now and again, but Pecola has slipped over into a kind of madness that protects her from people who try to see her ugliness.

The ugliness of **Cholly Breedlove**'s life manifests itself in despair and violence, which he directs at those who are too weak to stand up to him, such as his family. He and his wife have a tacit understanding that they will not kill each other, but they fight constantly. Cholly is a man beaten by circumstances who does not quite understand his life and what has happened to him. He remembers meeting his wife once long ago in Kentucky. She was hanging over a fence with a broken foot, and she charmed him and brought him joy. He does not understand where that joy has gone and does not know how to get it back. When he drinks, which is often, he can forget about his painful existence.

Most of all, Cholly does not understand the concept of fatherhood. Never having been raised by a parent, he has no idea what his role should be. He does not understand what his children want or what he should teach them. He feels frustrated that they depend upon him and look to him for guidance when he has no idea of what to do himself. Cholly reacts to his guilt and anger the only way he knows how—with violence.

Mrs. Breedlove, like Pecola, accepts the fact that her appearances don't meet the standards of white society and that she is never going to have a prosperous life. She sees her perceived ugliness every waking moment, but handles it like a martyr, taking her frustrations out on her husband and children. At first Mrs. Breedlove had loved her husband. They agreed to marry and go north looking for a better life. But with Cholly at work and no friends to talk to, she became lonely and less dependent on her husband, which he began to resent. They began to have less and less to say to each other and to quarrel more and more. When the children were still young, she went back to work. Little by little, she became the breadwinner in the family. All her life's meaning was poured into her work and her church. Intent on instilling a sense of responsibility in her children, she instead inspired fear. She taught them to be afraid of losing God's love, of becoming like their shiftless father, of being clumsy and ugly. Sammy reacted by running away, while Pecola reacted by being afraid of life.

Sammy Breedlove believes that he is ugly, too, but he reacts to this differently. He uses this sense of his own worthlessness as an excuse to cause others pain. At one point during a particularly violent fight between his parents, he watches in silence and then begins to strike his father. When his mother regains the advantage and knocks Cholly senseless, Sammy yells, "Kill him! Kill him!" He runs away often, and in the end, after the rape and his father's disappearance, Sammy leaves town and his family for good.

Tar Baby

(novel, 1981)

PLOT: *Tar Baby* does not have a well-defined plot, but is rather a lyrical novel of emotions and relationships which moves slowly through the interplay between whites and blacks, employer and servants, parents and children, friends and lovers. Touching upon the realities of the American South and the wealthy sophistication of Manhattan, most of the events take place in the Caribbean on the luxurious estate of a white millionaire. Valerian Street has retired to his breathtaking island home, and although he promises to leave it periodically for the city up north, he never does. This distresses his wife, Margaret, and somewhat amuses his servant and lifelong friend, Sydney. Sydney manages the estate along with his wife, Ondine. The other member of the household is Jade, or Jadine, a beautiful black model who lives submersed in a white culture and is regarded more like a family member. The Streets are her patrons, and Sydney and Ondine are her only family.

It is nearing the Christmas holidays, and Margaret has decided that if Valerian will not leave the estate, their son, Michael, should come down to the island to join them. She is positive he will come, and Valerian is just as positive that he will not. Annoyed at her husband's refusal to budge, Margaret says that she may go north for a while to live near Michael. Valerian is also certain the young man will not be pleased with that decision. Into this situation drops an unknown black man called Son. At first the family regards him as a thief. Son says he swam off a boat in the harbor. Inevitably, Son and Jade meet. The beautiful model both fears and desires this strange black man from a background so alien to her own world. Their affair is a torrid one.

During a fight in the household that begins over apples, Ondine and Margaret become involved in a physical battle. Hysterical, Ondine calls Margaret a baby killer, saying that she burned Michael when he was just a baby. Margaret calmly replies that she has always loved her son. Meanwhile, Jade and Son go to New York for a new life. The four people left on the island must find their own ways to deal with the terrible secret that Margaret and Ondine knew for so many years and that Valerian and Sydney have only just learned.

In the end, the worlds of Jade and Son prove to be too far apart. What she wants for him, and how she wants him to better himself, will not work. Jadine returns to the island but only as a stopover on her way to France. She tells Ondine that she will not marry Son, but it will be hard to forget him. As for Son, he returns to the island to find her, but Jade is gone. She has forgotten her ancient properties, and he must leave to find his own personal freedom.

CHARACTERS: **Jade** is a beautiful young black model who works for Margaret Street and is regarded almost as a member of the family, since Valerian and Margaret are her patrons. They educated her and paid for all her schooling, travel, lodging, and clothes. She is an orphan and Sydney and Ondine have become her only family. Jade has become socialized within the white culture, so much so that she is afraid of her powerful attraction to the raw blackness of the man called Son. Their love is passionate and total. However, when they return to New York the differences between their worlds become all too clear. After Son resists all of Jade's attempts to educate him in her ways, Jade acknowledges the gulf between them and knows she must return to her own world without him. She leaves for France knowing how difficult forgetting him will be.

Jade's lover, **Son**, is caught between his own world and the world of the white culture that Jade knows. The gulf between them is wide. They can't bridge the gap between their worlds, no matter how strong their passion and love. Son feels he must follow Jade to Paris and find her, even if she is with another man. But in the end he knows that, like Jade, he must choose his own freedom.

Valerian Street is an elderly millionaire who treasures his placid, luxurious existence. He wants nothing more out of life than to be allowed to grow hydrangeas and dahlias in his greenhouse. But his life is shattered by the revelation of his wife's treatment of their son. He later asks his wife why their son did not tell him of what she had done. "But why does he love you?" Valerian asks. "Because I love him," Margaret replies. Then Margaret asks Valerian to hit her so that in some way she will be punished for what she has done, but Valerian can't bring himself to do it. "Tomorrow," he says, "perhaps tomorrow." Besides coping with his sorrow, Valerian knows that he must live out his life with the knowledge that he had watched his son grow up and yet knew nothing about him.

A troubled woman with a lifelong secret, **Margaret Street**'s serene world crashes down around her when the abuse of her infant son is revealed. Later, she confronts Ondine. "I knew you knew," she says to the older woman. "I always knew you knew." Margaret admits that after a time, as the boy grew older, she stopped tormenting him. She says she wishes that Ondine had cared enough about her to try to stop her, but Ondine replies that it was not her job to do so. When Margaret asks for forgiveness, Ondine tells her she must forgive herself.

Sydney and **Ondine** are faithful friends and longtime servants of the Street family. Even Sydney did not know the terrible secret of Margaret's sickness, which Ondine carried around with her for so many years. At first, Ondine thought that if she told her husband and he told Valerian, they would lose their jobs, and she did not want to leave the young child in that household all by himself. Then, later, having kept the secret for so long made it difficult to reveal even when it no longer posed a danger to Michael.

Further Reading

Atwood, Margaret. "Haunted by Their Nightmares." *New York Times Book Review* (September 13, 1986).

Bishop, John. "Morrison's *The Bluest Eye*," *Explicator* 51 (summer 1993).

Bjork, Patrick Brice. *The Novels of Toni Morrison: The Search for Self and Place within the Community.* New York: Peter Lang, 1994.

Bloom, Harold. *Toni Morrison.* New York: Chelsea House, 1991.

———. *Twentieth-Century American Literature.* Vol. 5. New York: Chelsea House, 1986.

Charmean, Karen. *Toni Morrison's Work of Fiction.* Troy, NY: Whitson, 1993.

Century, Douglas. *Toni Morrison: Author.* New York: Chelsea House, 1994.

Colby, Veneta, ed. *World Authors 1975-1980.* New York: H. W. Wilson, 1985.

Contemporary Literary Criticism. Vols. 4, 10, 22, 55. Detroit: Gale Research, 1975, 1979, 1982, 1989.

Davis, Thadious M., and Trudier Harris, eds. *Afro-American Fiction Writers after 1955.* Vol. 33 of *Dictionary of Literary Biography.* Detroit: Gale Research, 1984.

Dowling, Colette. "The Song of Toni Morrison." *New York Times Magazine* (May 20, 1979).

Gates, Henry L., Jr., and K. A. Appiah. *Toni Morrison, Critical Perspectives Past and Present.* Washington, D.C.: Amistad, 1993.

Giles, James R., and Wanda H. Giles. *American Novelists since World War II, Third Series.* Vol. 143 of *Dictionary of Literary Biography.* Detroit: Gale Research, 1994.

Harris, Trudier. *Fiction and Folklore: The Novels of Toni Morrison.* Knoxville: University of Tennessee, 1993.

Henderson, Lesley, ed. *Contemporary Novelists.* 5th ed. Detroit: St. James, 1991.

Kibler, James E. Jr., ed. *American Novelists since World War II, Second Series.* Vol. 6 of *Dictionary of Literary Biography.* Detroit: Gale Research, 1980.

Kuenz, Jane. "*The Bluest Eye:* Notes on History, Community and Black Female Subjectivity." *African-American Review* 27 (fall 1993).

McKay, Nellie Y. *Critical Essays on Toni Morrison.* Boston: Hall, 1988.

Morrison, Toni. "Unspeakable Things Unspoken: The Afro-American Presence in American Literature." *Michigan Quarterly Review* 28 (winter 1989).

Naylor, Gloria. "Toni Morrison." *Southern Review* 21 (summer 1985).

Rigney, Barbara. *The Voices of Toni Morrison.* Columbus: Ohio State University, 1991.

Rood, Karen L., Jean W. Ross, and Richard Ziegfeld, eds. *Dictionary of Literary Biography Yearbook 1981.* Detroit: Gale Research, 1982.

Samuels, Wilfred D., and Clenora Hudson. *Toni Morrison.* New York: Macmillan, 1990.

Taylor-Guthrie, Danielle K., ed. *Conversations with Toni Morrison.* Jackson: University Press of Mississippi, 1994.

Walter Dean Myers

1937-, American novelist

Hoops

(young adult novel, 1981)

PLOT: Seventeen-year-old Lonnie Jackson lives for basketball, not only because he excels at the game but also because it might deliver him from the unhappiness of his Harlem home and into college and the big leagues. The game is a release from the tensions and frustrations of his everyday life, including a father who abandoned the family long ago, and a mother who nags him constantly. Now in his last year of school, Lonnie works part-time at Grant's Hotel, where he is responsible for general cleanup.

Excelling in basketball could mean an escape from Harlem for Lonnie Jackson in Myers's 1981 book.

His employer, Jimmy Harrison, is not a particularly nice character, but he lets Lonnie use one of the rooms on those nights when he can't face going home. Lonnie is lucky in that he has two good friends: his sixteen-year-old girlfriend, Mary-Ann, who works part-time in an after-hours bar for a shady character called Tyrone, and Mary-Ann's brother, Paul, who is a good ball player like Lonnie.

News spreads of an upcoming citywide Tournament of Champions that basketball scouts from all over the country will be attending. Lonnie, Paul, and other friends—Breeze, Jo-Jo, and Ox—have organized themselves into a makeshift team and decide to enter. They are assigned to coach Cal Jones, whom Lonnie recognizes as a wino he once tripped over in the park. Although at first he refuses to play for this man, Lonnie is finally won over by Cal's obvious skills and knowledge of the game. It is evident to

Lonnie that Cal has problems, but the older man shows an interest in Lonnie's talent.

Some time later, Cal confesses to Lonnie that he is separated from Allie, the wife he still loves. He also confesses that he was once a professional basketball player but was caught gambling, got a suspended sentence, and was expelled from the game. All these difficulties are compounded by the fact that, as Lonnie later learns from Allie, Cal was indirectly responsible for the death of their young child. Another complication to the story comes when Paul begins behaving strangely, spending more money on girls than he can afford. When Mary-Ann questions him, he strikes her. Later, she sees an envelope on Tyrone's desk with her brother's name on it. Voicing her suspicions to Lonnie, they break into Tyrone's office one night and find that the envelope contains stolen welfare checks. Paul confesses to his sister and Lonnie that he stole the checks, and now Tyrone is blackmailing him.

Lonnie's team wins the first game in the tournament. Then Cal disappears, and Lonnie suspects a game-fixing racket is at work. When Cal is found to be in prison for fighting, Lonnie learns that the coach was actually beaten up so that his team would lose the tournament. To secure Cal's release, Mary-Ann steals money from Tyrone, who finds out and injects her with drugs. Lonnie, who realizes how dangerous Tyrone really is, fears that under threats and the offer of big money Cal might agree to sell them out and lose the game. On the night of the big game, it looks as though Cal has given in. Lonnie is not allowed to play and Cal keeps giving signals to two men in the crowd. But after halftime, when all bets are in, the situation changes. Lonnie is brought into play, and he leads his team to victory. But by the time Lonnie gets to the locker room, Cal has been fatally stabbed. Lonnie has made one step toward a better future, but he has lost a good friend.

CHARACTERS: As in Myers's other novels, the characters in *Hoops* are resilient and realistic. They live in a tough Harlem neighborhood, but their problems are universal, and so are their hopes and dreams for the future, for love, for friendship, and for success. **Lonnie Jackson** regards the game of basketball as far more than a diversion from the tensions and frustrations of a nagging mother and an absent father. It is his ticket out of the ghetto—if only he is good enough to make it to the big leagues. Although Lonnie is disgusted with his father for deserting his family, he can't dismiss his feelings of betrayal, even after so long a time. He understands his mother's frustration, but there are times when her nagging drives him away. It is only through the friendship and love of Mary-Ann and Paul that he is able to keep his life together and his eyes fixed on his goal.

Mary-Ann is a sixteen-year-old girl, wise beyond her years from a lifetime spent in the Harlem ghetto. She is devoted to Lonnie and truly loves him, just as she cares deeply about her brother Paul. To help the boys, she opens the envelope on Tyrone's desk and, with Lonnie, steals into his office in an effort to save her brother from harm. Like Lonnie, Mary-Ann realizes that Tyrone is an evil man and must be stopped, but they have no means to do so. Her brother, **Paul**, is a good friend to Lonnie, but the young man succumbs to the lure of money and the good life to impress some wealthy girls he meets. To keep up his image with them, he steals welfare checks from mailboxes. He later admits to Lonnie and his sister that Tyrone found out about his crime and is now blackmailing him.

Cal Jones is the most pitiable character in the novel. A decent and talented man, he too was corrupted by financial temptation. After starting on what promised to be an illustrious career in professional basketball, he fell under the spell of big-time gambling. In an effort to make more money, he became involved in a point-shaving scandal that lost him his beloved wife. His indirect involvement in the death of his three-year-old child sends him over the brink into abject alcoholism. It is not unreasonable for Lonnie to think that Cal, under the threat of violence and renewed financial temptation, might succumb to the pressure and throw the game. Yet

Cal was far more devoted to the young man than Lonnie knew, and in a sense Cal sacrifices his life to give Lonnie a brighter future.

Scorpions

(young adult novel, 1988)

PLOT: Twelve years old and struggling through the seventh grade, Jamal Hicks has his share of problems. The class bully, Dwayne Parsons, never stops needling him. Jamal worries about Mama, who works hard doing cleaning for white folks to keep the family together. Jamal, Mama, and his eight-year-old sister, Sassy, of the big mouth, live in a tiny walk-up apartment in Harlem. Jamal's father, Jevon, is a shiftless man given to heavy drinking and stern lessons about having a sense of responsibility—which Jamal finds rather ironic—whenever he drops in to see his wife and children. The other missing family member is eighteen-year-old Randy, who is in jail upstate for an armed robbery in which a man was killed. Randy was sentenced to fifteen to twenty years. No one has the two thousand dollars necessary for an appeal, which is also why Mama is working so hard. Jamal cares about only three people in the world—Mama, Sassy, and his best friend, Tito Cruz. Tito admires Jamal's drawings and argues with him about who will have the biggest boat when they are rich.

One day Mama comes back from the prison and says that Randy wants Jamal to go see Mack, who was in on the robbery but was released on parole. Mack is a crackhead and a loser, but Jamal goes to see him anyway, taking Tito with him to Mack's hangout. According to Mack, Randy wants Jamal to become the leader of the Scorpions, a gang of young teenage dropouts who run drugs for Harlem narcotics bosses. Randy used to be the leader of the gang, but if Jamal takes over he can make money for Randy's appeal. Jamal is not happy with the idea, but two days later Mack gives him a gun to gain confidence. The younger boy is torn between a wish to help his brother and reluctance to get involved with the gang and with drug running. Mack is persistent, so Jamal and Tito meet the gang at the abandoned firehouse they use as headquarters. Two of the gang members, Angel and Indian, are opposed to Jamal taking over. He shows them the gun, however, and for the moment they are silent. After a visit from his father, Jamal takes the gun to school. When bully Dwayne challenges him, Jamal shows him the gun and Dwayne flees. But Jamal knows that if Dwayne tells the principal, he will be expelled. He gives the gun to Tito for safekeeping. Dwayne does tell, but since it's Jamal's word against his, the case is dismissed. More bad news soon arrives that Randy has been knifed in a prison fight. Then Tito's grandmother finds the gun he is keeping for Jamal. She throws him out of the house, but Jamal smoothes things over and takes back the gun. Soon afterwards, the two boys find a quiet moment, and Jamal draws a beautiful likeness of Tito.

Jamal plans to meet Angel and Indian one night to tell them that he wants to take over the gang and why. He gives the gun to Tito and tells him to hide in the bushes nearby in case of trouble. But Angel and Indian are not interested in talk. High on liquor, they attack Jamal, and Angel pulls out a knife. With that, Tito comes to the rescue, shooting the two boys. Jamal and Tito throw away the gun and run. Indian will recover, but Angel dies. Surprisingly, Mack takes responsibility for the shooting. Tito is in the clear, but he feels so guilty that he tells his grandmother, who calls the police. Charges are dismissed, but Tito is sent to Puerto Rico.

At the end of the novel, Jamal and Tito's lives are in tatters. At their last meeting, Jamal gives Tito the drawing he made of him.

CHARACTERS: *Scorpions* is the sad and troubling story of a teenaged boy who is burdened with problems and responsibilities that very few adults could cope with. Though troubled, **Jamal Hicks** is not a bad youngster. He has real problems with his school work, and he knows it. The only time he is happy in school is when he is drawing, and he's very good at it. He hates to admit that he is afraid of the bully **Dwayne**, but Dwayne makes him feel small.

Although he loves Mama and Sassy, Jamal relies on Tito, who is the only one who understands him. The boys argue and insult each other, but what is more important is that they can talk.

Jamal is aware that his brother, as the leader of the Scorpions, was involved with running drugs. He knows that was how Randy used to make money, and he knows he can make a lot of money himself by running crack. But he also knows the dangers of the drug trade. So his dilemma is real when he is confronted with Randy's request that he take over the leadership of the Scorpions to help raise money for the appeal. Without a father or older adult to turn to, Jamal must make decisions for himself. When Randy is knifed in a prison fight, the choice to get rid of the gun and lead a clean life becomes harder and harder to make. Finally, Jamal makes the only decision that he feels is open to him. He and his friend Tito pay a terrible price, as do the two other gang members, Angel and Indian. In the end, they all lose. When Tito leaves, Jamal is changed and hardened. He knows that he should have gotten rid of the gun long before it was used. Tito had asked him to get rid of it, but carrying that gun had made Jamal feel just a little less small, a little less afraid.

Tito Cruz is a likable youngster and a loyal friend. He loves Jamal and would do anything for him. In fact, Tito even saves his friend's life. But his loyalty exacts a devastating price, and he can't live with his guilt. In the end, no matter what the cost, he is compelled to confess to his grandmother. He is charged with juvenile delinquency and sent to Puerto Rico to live with his father. When the two boys meet for the last time, Tito is crying. He tells Jamal that he wishes Angel and Indian had beat him up instead of Jamal. Jamal understands. "Me too," he says.

Besides Tito, the most important people in Jamal's life are his mother and sister. **Mama** is a hard worker and, in a way, a dreamer. She wants to believe that she will get the money for Randy and that her son will be released from jail. Jamal realizes that it will never happen, but Mama won't listen. It hurts Jamal to see her working so hard for a dream that will never come true. **Sassy** is a typical kid sister with a big mouth. Jamal loves her, although, like a typical brother, he doesn't like to admit it. There is little redeeming about Jamal's father, **Jevon**, a loser who tries to obscure his own lack of morality by lecturing his family on the importance of responsibility. Jamal feels the same way about his father as he does about his brother, **Randy**. Both of them are gone, and he can't forgive them for taking with them a little piece of Mama, which will never be given back.

Fallen Angels

(young adult novel, 1988)

PLOT: Richie Perry, a seventeen-year-old private in the U.S. Army, is on a flight headed for Vietnam in September, 1967. He was born and raised in Harlem, along with a younger brother, Kenny, who still lives with their mother. Their father has left the household. Richie is not particularly anxious because he is convinced that he is being sent to Vietnam by a mistake that will soon be sorted out. The rest of his company has been sent to Germany, and besides Richie has a bad knee that, supposedly, will keep him out of combat duty. On the flight, Richie becomes friendly with another black soldier, wisecracking Harry ("Peewee") Gates from Chicago, and with Judy Duncan, a nurse from Texas.

But his assignment is not changed, and all too soon Richie gets his first taste of war. His platoon is led by Lieutenant Carroll, a decent man, and the squad leader, Sergeant Simpson, a longtime vet who will soon be going home. Other platoon members are Jenkins, a frightened young soldier; Monaco, who is of Italian ancestry; another African American named Johnson; the crude Corporal Brunner; pimply-faced Walowick; Lobel from Hollywood; and Brewster, a very religious young man. During a routine operation, Jenkins steps on a land mine and is killed. The sight of the tragedy terrifies and sickens Richie. Soon afterward he is cornered by a young VietCong. When his attacker's gun jams, Richie kills him—an experience made all the more terrifying because the VietCong soldier reminded him of his brother.

The killing goes on, and Richie is particularly horrified by a skirmish in which the Americans fire on their own men through a ghastly technical error. Then Lieutenant Carroll is killed. His replacement, Lieutenant Gearhart, accidentally sets off a flare at night, which results in the wounding of two members of the squad. The next to die is Brewster, and then Richie himself is wounded in the legs. After a hospital stay during which he sees Judy again, Richie dreads the return to his outfit, but he has no choice. He and Peewee are off on another patrol. Separated from the rest of the squad, they are cut off behind enemy lines. They take refuge in a hole in the side of a hill until morning. To save their lives, Richie kills another enemy soldier.

A helicopter arrives to rescue them, but both Peewee and Richie are wounded in trying to reach it. Nevertheless, they manage to get into the chopper and are flown to safety. Both will be returned to the United States, Peewee because his wounds are so severe and Richie because his "trick knee" transfer has come through. Before they board the C47 that will take them home, they learn that Judy Duncan was killed in a bombing of the field hospital where she worked. Richie watches a line of silver caskets being loaded into the plane for the last trip home and reflects on the barbaric waste and inhumanity that he has witnessed. He knows he will never forget his dead comrades or the senseless suffering he has seen.

CHARACTERS: Richie Perry is typical of many of the teenaged youngsters who went off to fight in Vietnam. He saw no way out of serving, and he realized that army duty would at least contribute to the income of his mother and younger brother back in Harlem. Richie has no real conception of the horrors of war, but he learns quickly. As he later writes to Kenny, "I had thought that this war was right, but it was only right from a distance ... but when this killing started there was no right or wrong except in the way you did your job, except in the way you were part of the killing." When Richie witnesses Jenkins's death, he is terrified by the experience. But much worse is the experience of having to kill someone himself. When he realizes what he has done, he breaks down, vomiting and sobbing uncontrollably until Peewee comes to comfort him. The novel is careful to point out that Richie is not a coward: in his struggle to survive he shows extraordinary courage and inner strength.

Peewee Gates is a wisecracking smart kid from Chicago who thinks he has the world and the army by the tail. Like Richie, however, Peewee is stunned by the carnage and brutality around him, and he exhibits extraordinary strength of character in the face of the terrible destruction that confronts him at every turn. The tough and imperturbable Peewee shows a compassionate side on the night after Richie kills the VietCong and sobs in his bunk. Peewee goes to his friend and cradles him in his arms to comfort him through his sorrow and terror.

Another comforting figure in the story is **Judy Duncan**, a likable, dedicated young nurse, who, as so many during the years in Vietnam did, braved extreme danger on the firing line to tend to those who were wounded. The tragedy of her self-sacrifice is highlighted by the fact that her involvement in the war was only to alleviate the suffering of others.

The minor characters display a range of personalities and reactions to the experience of war. **Sergeant Simpson**, for instance, only dreams of his upcoming release, when he will leave Vietnam and go, as the soldiers say, to "the World"—which is any place other than Vietnam. **Lieutenant Carroll**, who loses his life, is a well-liked leader and acts as a mediator in the petty arguments that break out when the soldiers are under stress. When the frightened and innocent young Jenkins is killed, Carroll recites a quiet prayer that says, "Let us feel pity for Private Jenkins and sorrow for ourselves and all the angel warriors that fall." When Carroll himself is killed, Monaco recites the same prayer over his body.

One of the novel's minor themes is the growing camaraderie among the soldiers under the pressures of war. Early on, **Walowick** and **Johnson** get into a fight over a supposed racial slur. But later, when the fighting and the killing start, they overcome their differences as racial and religious antagonisms lose their significance in the struggle for survival. Social differences are erased as the soldiers need to rely on each other for courage and life.

Further Reading

Authors and Artists for Young Adults. Vol. 4. Detroit: Gale, 1990.

Berger, Laura Standley, ed. *Twentieth-Century Young Adult Writers.* 1st ed. Detroit: St. James, 1994.

Children's Literature Review. Vols. 4, 16. Detroit: Gale Research, 1982, 1989.

Contemporary Literary Criticism. Vol. 35. Detroit: Gale Research, 1985.

Holtze, Sally Holmes, ed. *Fifth Book of Junior Authors and Illustrators.* New York: H. W. Wilson, 1983.

Something about the Author. Vols. 27, 41, 71. Detroit: Gale Research, 1982, 1985, 1993.

Something about the Author Autobiography Series. Vol. 2. Detroit: Gale Research, 1986.

Phyllis Reynolds Naylor

1933-, American novelist

The Keeper

(young adult novel, 1986)

PLOT: For Nick Karpinsky life seems pretty good. He lives in an apartment in Chicago with this father, Jacob, and mother, Wanda. In his last year of junior high, Nick has taken a girl to the movies for the first time, and he and his best friend, Danny, get along just fine. In fact, everything would be just about perfect, except for the problems with his father, who has been acting somewhat strange lately. More and more, he avoids his job at the post office, staying home because he can't bear to face the workplace. Nick and his mother have gotten used to his father's frequent job changes. At first, each change appeared to be for the best, but now the situation has worsened until Nick's father can't hold a job at all. Part of the reason, Jacob claims, is that the communists are after him.

Although they both try to deny it, Nick and his mother slowly begin to realize that Jacob is mentally ill. They try in various ways to get help for him, enlisting advice from the local priest, from Jacob's brother, Thad, and from their doctor. But Jacob resists seeking treatment, and without his cooperation they can't commit him to the VA hospital.

As his father's condition worsens, Nick gets a job after school to help the family and tries to shield their situation from Danny and Lois, whom Nick has begun to date, and from Karen, his friend who lives in the same apartment building. Finally, when Jacob comes home with a rifle he has bought to protect himself from his imagined enemies, Nick convinces his mother that something must be done.

Out in the car with his father and mother, Nick attracts attention by pressing on the horn. But when the police arrive, Jacob acts perfectly normal and they are reluctant to do anything. Finally, Nick calls the school nurse, Miss Etting, to whom he has confided his problems. She convinces the authorities of the seriousness of Jacob's condition and he is admitted to the VA hospital.

The doctors can give Nick and his mother no assurances that his father will ever recover fully, but they hope he will improve enough to return home eventually. Nick grieves for the father he will never have again but understands that he and his mother must build a new life for themselves.

CHARACTERS: Nick Karpinsky is a likeable, level-headed teenager in his last year of junior high. Life has taken on an exciting new meaning for him as he begins to date girls. Like his mother, he does not want to face the fact that his father is becoming mentally unstable. Denial becomes a part of Nick's everyday existence. He prefers to think more about his friends and school than about his home life. However, Jacob Karpinsky's behavior continues to deteriorate. For Nick, it is as though a stranger has moved into his home. His father, always a neat, meticulous man, now leaves clothes and newspapers strewn about the apartment. When Nick's grandparents drive in from Indiana on Christmas Day, his father has to be reminded to come to the dinner table, and even then he is silent and withdrawn. Nick is pictured as a normal, somewhat shy teenager who is faced with a terrible and serious problem, not the least of which is getting an adult to believe the truth of the situation. But he proves himself to be courageous when faced with what he knows must be done, not only to save his father but to save his family as well.

Nick's mother, **Wanda Karpinsky**, also refuses to face her husband's problems. For example, when Nick says his father is mentally ill, his mother replies that her husband is "mentally disturbed. There's a difference." She insists on being optimistic about the situation, declaring that if they *expect* improvement surely it will happen. Even when her husband brings home a gun, Nick's mother can't accept the reality that the man she loves is really mentally ill. It takes his admittance into the VA hospital to make her face the reality of her loss. However, Wanda Karpinsky shows her own mental toughness when, after hearing the doctor's report about what improvement might be expected, she tells her son that she has been reading newspaper want ads and feels an enormous need to get back into the real world again. A former music teacher, she says she noticed an ad for a music teacher at a school not far from their home. Nick is much encouraged by this change in attitude.

Jacob Karpinsky is a man succumbing to the horrors of mental deterioration. Without realizing it, he has been slipping into mental disorder for years. His family has long overlooked his constant job changes, because for a time each change seemed to be for the better, a step up for the family. But it becomes no longer possible to view his behavior in that light. Eventually staying home all the time, he grows more and more wary of everyone's actions, more fearful that he is being spied upon, and more certain that communists are out to kill him. Each new paranoid action draws him deeper into serious mental illness. Although with his son's help and determination, Jacob Karpinsky finally gets the medical attention he needs, the future does not look bright for him. The doctor tells Nick that his father will receive medication and that his condition will improve, but that is all that can be promised. Nick grieves for the man who was his father, a man he will never see in quite the same way again.

Nick hopes that his uncle, **Thaddeus Karpinsky**, will come to the aid of his father when his condition begins to deteriorate. But Uncle Thad is reluctant not only to interfere but even to believe that his brother is mentally deteriorating. Nick tells his uncle that his father tried to kill himself, but he knows that Thad does not really believe him. Thad says that Nick's mother is in the best position to judge the mental condition of her husband. "If she needs me," says Thad, "all she has to do is call." Nick knows that his mother, in denial herself, will not make that call.

The school nurse, **Miss Etting**, comes to Nick's rescue when the doctors at the VA hospital are reluctant to admit Nick's father. For some time, Nick has been telling Miss Etting about his home situation, pretending that he has been talking about some other teenager. But, of course, she has always known the truth, and she convinces the doctors at the hospital that what Nick and his mother are claiming is indeed the truth about his father.

Karen Zimmerman lives in the same apartment house as Nick and his family. Although they have long been friends and Nick really likes her, it is his friend **Danny** who dates Karen while Nick asks out **Lois**. But when Lois discovers the rumors about Nick's father, she declines to go to the dance with him. When Nick knocks on Karen's door and asks her out for a walk, she accepts. When they see that it is raining, Nick suggests they go back to his apartment, and Karen accepts.

Further Reading

Authors and Artists for Young Adults. Vol. 4. Detroit: Gale Research, 1990.

Berger, Laura Standley, ed. *Twentieth-Century Children's Writers.* 4th ed. Detroit: St. James, 1995.

———. *Twentieth-Century Young Adult Writers.* 1st ed. Detroit: St. James, 1994.

Chevalier, Tracy, ed. *Twentieth-Century Children's Writers.* 3rd ed. Chicago: St. James, 1989.

Children's Literature Review. Vol. 17. Detroit: Gale Research, 1989.

Holtze, Sally Holmes, ed. *Fifth Book of Junior Authors and Illustrators.* New York: H. W. Wilson, 1983.

Something about the Author. Vols. 12, 66. Detroit: Gale Research, 1977, 1992.

Something about the Author Autobiography Series. Vol. 10. Detroit: Gale Research, 1990.

Ward, Susan M., ed. *Authors of Books for Young People.* 3rd ed. Metuchen, NJ: Scarecrow, 1990.

John Neufeld

1938-, American novelist

Lisa, Bright and Dark

(young adult novel, 1969)

PLOT: The narrator of this story is high school junior, Betsy Goodman, who lives in an upper-middle-class neighborhood on Long Island. Her friends include M. N. (short for Mary Nell) Fickett, who is described as an all-American girl, the beautiful Elizabeth Frazer, moody Lisa Shilling, and Lisa's boyfriend, heartthrob Brian Morris. When Lisa's mood swings become more violent and erratic, her friends join together to help her. One day they find her crouching under a teacher's desk sticking pins into her wrists. Appeals to their ineffective guidance counselor, Mr. Bernstein, and to Lisa's indifferent parents result only in Lisa being sent to Florida for a brief rest when she really needs professional care. She returns more neurotic than before. Her bouts of depression become violent and more frequent. During an outdoor barbecue, Lisa tries to push Elizabeth into a fire, and on another occasion must be sent to the hospital after jumping into a glass door. Betsy's father tries to intervene and contacts the Shillings, who once again refuse to believe that their daughter is having mental problems. Because of Lisa's dangerous behavior, the girls are now forbidden to see her. Elizabeth contacts a "friend," psychiatrist Neil Donovan, and in confidence tells Betsy that Dr. Donovan had been her psychiatrist four years before. Elizabeth's father consents to pay for Lisa's treatment with Dr. Donovan if the Shillings agree. They consent after Lisa once again tries to take her life and is sent back to the hospital. There, Lisa is visited by the girls and Dr. Donovan, who wonder if the promise of treatment has come too late. At first Lisa's response at seeing her friends is only a blank stare, but when Dr. Donovan is introduced and Lisa is told that he will help her, she begins to sob. Her cry for help has finally been heard.

CHARACTERS: Fifteen-year-old **Betsy Goodman**, the novel's narrator, is very modest about herself, claiming that she is average in every way, including height and looks. Still in the throws of adolescence, Betsy is not part of the "in" crowd. Somewhat unsure of herself and still lacking the confidence and maturity that will come with time, she is given to wild crushes (often on famous people, such as actor Paul Newman) and fantasies in which she is a sophisticated femme fatale. Actually, Betsy is a sweet, innocent young girl who has a natural charm and a sensitive, sympathetic nature that endears her to all. She is honest and straightforward with others and filled with the compassion and loyalty that makes for a good friend. Betsy is amazed when Lisa comes to her for help and ignores her other friends. Elizabeth explains that Betsy has "a warmth, a naturalness, a simplicity" that the others lack and says "It's about the best therapy Lisa could ever have." Good-natured, observant, and considerate, Betsy is generous with her time and concern in helping her friend.

Betsy's closest friend is **M. N. Fickett** (M. N. is short for Mary Nell). A born leader, M. N. dreams of becoming a justice on the Supreme Court. She is a brilliant student, has a great laugh, is very popular with the boys, and looks like actress Shirley MacLaine. The daughter of an extremely liberal and popular minister, M. N. is considered an all-American girl.

Always cheery and helpful, she is known for her optimism and altruism. When she realizes that Lisa needs help, she steps in by contacting the Shillings and organizing her friends into a therapy group. Saving Lisa becomes M. N.'s crusade. Immersing herself in books on abnormal psychology, she displays misplaced benevolence that sometimes creates more havoc than good, however. Determined and dedicated, she has aspirations and dedication that are admirable, even though she can't grasp the limitations of her lack of knowledge and experience. Lisa good-naturedly often misleads M. N. during their therapy sessions by inventing vivid Freudian fantasies which Mary Nell totally believes.

The role of Princess in their group goes to **Elizabeth Frazer.** Betsy claims that Elizabeth is "like Grace Kelly used to be: regal, cool, far off, blonde, slim, with clothes you wouldn't believe, and intelligence." Aloof and distant, Elizabeth attracts boys but intimidates them with her wealth, intellect, and maturity. She is self-possessed, confident, and the envy of others. Betsy is in awe of Elizabeth's insights and shrewdness regarding Lisa and later discovers that Elizabeth had also experienced mental problems from which she is still recovering. This vulnerability partially explains her difficulty in relating to others. In spite of these difficulties, Elizabeth is a caring, unselfish person who arranges professional help for Lisa. Helping Lisa also benefits Elizabeth. Through her friendship and openness, particularly with Betsy, she becomes a more trusting, outgoing, and less remote person.

Sixteen-year-old **Lisa Shilling** is popular with the "in" group because of her intelligence, maturity, reserved behavior, and mean sense of humor. Gradually, as she sinks further into madness, her behavior becomes more erratic. Lisa has good and bad days. On her bright days she is her old self, confident, clever, and open with everyone, but on her dark days she wears black and speaks to no one. During moments of clarity, Lisa tells the girls about the dreadful abyss into which she is sinking, but these moments become fewer and her bouts of depression and withdrawal more vicious and destructive. Her self-destructive behavior is a last cry for help. Lisa shows great courage and persistence in her struggle to hang on to her dwindling sanity.

Lisa's parents, **Mr.** and **Mrs. Shilling**, are ostrich-like in their refusal to acknowledge Lisa's mental problems. Mr. Shilling is a handsome, extremely successful businessman who spends a great deal of time away from home. Betsy says that "he tries too hard to be clever, too hard to be quick and too hard at everything except at being himself." Detached and sarcastic, he refuses to believe that anyone as fortunate as his daughter could have mental problems. He considers such an accusation as a reflection of his fitness as a parent and therefore denies it, claiming it is her choice of behavior and a phase that will pass. Only after a suicide attempt does this stubborn, selfish man realize that he is in danger of losing his daughter permanently. Mrs. Shilling is more concerned with her social position than with her daughter's well-being. "Rich and snooty," she has developed an affected accent known locally as "Locust Valley lockjaw." Indifferent and impervious to Lisa's problems, she considers her outbursts simple breaches of good taste. Self-centered and superficial, she refuses to acknowledge the depth of Lisa's difficulties. She blames Lisa's friends for promoting these tantrums and claims that Lisa is only "a spoiled, selfish girl who is showing off for some reason." Pathologically concerned about her social status and with keeping up appearances, Mrs. Shilling feels such humiliation when Lisa is finally sent to a mental hospital that she refuses to appear in public.

Betsy's male counterpart in popularity is **Brian Morris**. Captain of the hockey team, president of the Student Council, and incredibly handsome, he is Lisa's faithful boyfriend. Tolerant and understanding, Brian tries to understand and sympathize with Lisa's violent mood swings, but in time, when she repeatedly embarrasses him publicly, he gives up and reluctantly stops seeing her.

The school counselor and psychologist is **Jeremy Bernstein**, a short, well-meaning man whose insecurity and timidity have made him both ineffective and pathetic. Afraid of getting involved in Lisa's case and possibly causing a disturbance, he chooses to ignore her symptoms and downplay their importance. Cowardly and indecisive, he openly admits to Betsy that he is weak and can be of little help. Later she thinks he should have been a computer technician so that he wouldn't have to meet or deal with people. Elizabeth's former doctor is the psychiatrist **Neil Donovan.** Six feet tall and amazingly handsome, he is so attractive that Betsy forgets her allegiance to Paul Newman. He is also a brilliant doctor, kind, compassionate, and understanding. He instantly wins the confidence and trust of those around Lisa and inspires hope for her recovery.

Further Reading

Authors and Artists for Young Adults. Vol. 11. Detroit: Gale Research, 1993.

Berger, Laura Standley, ed. *Twentieth-Century Young Adult Writers.* 1st ed. Detroit: St. James, 1994.

Contemporary Literary Criticism. Vol. 17. Detroit: Gale Research, 1981.

Something about the Author. Vols. 6, 81. Detroit: Gale Research, 1974, 1995.

Ward, Martha, ed. *Authors of Books for Young People.* 3rd ed. Metuchen, NJ: Scarecrow, 1990.

Joan Lowery Nixon

1927-, American young adult novelist

The Kidnapping of Christina Lattimore

(young adult novel, 1979)

PLOT: Christina Lattimore is a teenager living in a wealthy but less-than-loving family. Her grandmother, who prefers that Christina call her Cristabel, is a hard-nosed businesswoman who controls the family fortune; her father, who enjoys the pleasures of money and prestige, wants only to rest on his laurels as a respected religious man and vice president of the family business; and her mother is a weak woman who bends to the will of Christina's father. Christina finds it hard to respect her father, knowing that he does little to earn his salary and that the biblical quotes he recites "from memory" are actually given to him by his secretary.

To get away from her family, Christina pleads with her father and grandmother to be allowed to go on a European tour with her class for the summer. Soon after they turn her down, Christina is kidnapped by the unsavory Zack and his wife, Loretta. Zack works at the local hamburger joint that Christina and her best friend, Lorna, visit every Friday after class. The kidnappers want Christina's wealthy grandmother to pay ransom money. During her imprisonment, Christina overhears enough of her captor's conversation to learn that a third person is involved in the kidnapping scheme.

Christina is rescued before she is harmed or the money is paid, but her troubles aren't over yet. Zack and Loretta tell Christina's family that the kidnapping was partly Christina's idea as a way to get back at her father and grandmother for not letting her go to Europe. Not willing to trust Christina, her family believes the kidnappers. With no help from her family and little more than sympathy from the police, Christina and her newfound friend Kelly, a college student, try to prove her innocence. The trail leads to the son of Della, the woman who works in the Lattimore household. He had met Zack when the two were in jail and they concocted the scheme.

Although Christina's innocence is proven, there is little satisfaction in this. Kelly turns out to be not a friend but an opportunist who hopes that solving the case will improve his chances of getting a job in television news. Christina is also bitterly hurt by the lack of caring shown by her family, so she decides it is time to stand on her own two feet. She tells her mother that she will not be accepting Grandmother Cristabel's trust fund for her college education because it has too many strings attached. Instead, she will get a part-time job and work her way through college. Her mother is aghast, but for the first time in a long time, Christina feels good about herself.

CHARACTERS: Wealthy **Christina Lattimore** is not a happy teenager. Although she is wealthy, she receives little affection from her family. Christina loves her mother, but wishes she would show more backbone and face up to her husband and mother-in-law; she has little respect for her father, who she suspects is far more worried about his public image as a religious man than he is about practicing what he preaches; she admires her grandmother, but is unable to get close to her.

Christina nevertheless proves herself to be a courageous and resourceful young woman. When she is kidnapped by Zack and his wife, she does not panic. Instead, she tries to remain calm so she can listen to her kidnappers' conversations. In this way, she learns that she is being held by Zack and Loretta and that there is also a third person involved in the plot. After she is rescued, she resolves to identify the third person in order to prove her innocence. By the end of the story, Christina has matured considerably. Realizing she will never get the trust and emotional support she needs from her family, she rejects their financial help, too, and decides to put herself through college by finding a job.

Christina's wealthy grandmother, **Cristabel Lattimore**, is something of a legend in Houston, Texas. Besides being involved in politics and social causes, she took over her husband's oil business after he died and doubled its profits. Cristabel is a no-nonsense, efficient, intelligent woman with little time for showing affection for her granddaughter. Christabel doesn't tolerate people arguing against her decisions. When Christina visits her office to discuss the possibility of going to Europe with the rest of her class, Cristabel coldly turns her down, telling her granddaughter that she, and no one else, will dictate the course of her education. Later, when Christina pleads with her grandmother to hire a detective to prove her innocence, Cristabel refuses, afraid the scandal will taint the family name and business. Instead, she tells her granddaughter that "in time" people will forget all about the kidnapping.

After Christina is rescued from kidnappers, she has to convince her unsympathetic family that it wasn't all her idea.

Christina has little respect for her **father.** When she was a child, she adored him and sat on his lap while he told her fantastic stories. But now her father is a vice president in her grandmother's company, collects an excellent salary for doing practically nothing as far as the business is concerned, and spends his time quoting the Bible and being a highly respected lay preacher. Christina knows, however, that he is a fraud. His secretary, **Rosella**, is actually the one who looks up all the Bible verses and writes all of his memorable speeches.

Christina's **mother** tries to show affection toward her daughter, but she is no match for the energy and authoritativeness of both her husband and her mother-in-law. Indeed, when Christina announces her decision to put herself through college, her mother's reaction is to worry about what Cristabel's reaction will be. The family image is constantly on Christina's mother's mind, taking precedence over any feelings she might have for her daughter's welfare.

Christina's kidnappers are Zack and Loretta. **Zack** is tall, stoop-shouldered, skinny, and has blonde hair that always looks dirty. He tends the counter at a hamburger restaurant. It is Zack's association with Della's son when they were in jail that leads to the kidnapping scheme. Zack's wife, **Loretta**, is a plump woman with a bad complexion who is easily coerced into revealing information when Christina questions her in an effort to uncover the name of the third kidnapper. **Della**, whose son is the other conspirator, works in the Lattimore household. She is a heavyset woman who maintains that she is a beauty when she dresses up to go out on Friday nights.

Christina is attracted to **Kelly**, a tall young man with freckles and red hair, who is a college student majoring in communications. Kelly appears genuinely interested in Christina's dilemma and helps her find the third kidnapping conspirator, but Christina is disappointed to learn that Kelly only did it for the sake of his future career. She calls him an opportunist, but Kelly sees nothing wrong with what he did and can't quite understand why Christina doesn't wish him luck.

On occasion, Christina wishes she were more like her best friend, **Lorna**, whom she has known since the first grade. Lorna is ultra-proper and would certainly please Cristabel Lattimore.

Further Reading

Authors and Artists for Young Adults. Vol. 12. Detroit: Gale Research, 1994.

Berger, Laura Standley, ed. *Twentieth-Century Young Adult Writers.* 1st ed. Detroit: St. James, 1994.

Chevalier, Tracy, ed. *Twentieth-Century Children's Writers.* 3rd ed. Chicago: St. James, 1989.

Children's Literature Review. Vol. 24. Detroit: Gale Research, 1991.

Holtze, Sally Holmes, ed. *Fifth Book of Junior Authors and Illustrators.* New York: H. W. Wilson, 1983.

Something about the Author. Vols. 8, 44, 78. Detroit: Gale Research, 1976, 1986, 1994.

Something about the Author Autobiography Series. Vol. 9. Detroit: Gale Research, 1990.

Robert C. O'Brien

(pen name for Robert Leslie Conly)

1918-1973, American novelist

Z for Zachariah

(science fiction, 1975)

PLOT: After an atomic holocaust, the family of teenager Ann Burden leaves a sheltered valley close to the Amish country in the northeastern United States to hunt for survivors. They never return. For the next year Ann lives alone, subsisting on food from her garden and the family's livestock, as well as supplies from the settlement's deserted general store. She believes that she is the only survivor of the war, until one day when a stranger appears. He is wearing an unusual plastic suit that has protected him from radiation. Fearful of this intruder, Ann leaves her home and retreats to a cave, where she can hide but still spy on the stranger through her binoculars. She sees him carelessly take a bath in a polluted stream. Soon he becomes visibly sick. Concerned for his health, Ann emerges from hiding and takes him to the house, where she nurses him through his terrible illness.

The stranger's name is John R. Loomis, a thirty-two-year-old chemist from Cornell University. During his delirium, he reveals that, immediately before the terrible war, he and his colleagues had perfected a material impervious to radiation. As the bombs were dropping, only Loomis and a co-worker, Edward, survived. When Edward, who wanted to search for his family, tried to leave wearing the only safe suit made of the material, Loomis shot him. Ann sees that the suit contains three tiny patches that cover the bullet holes.

While Loomis begins a painful road to recovery, he begins behaving strangely. He is increasingly brusque and overbearing. One night, he tries to assault Ann sexually. Terrified, she runs away and takes shelter in her secret cave. Soon there begins a desperate cat and mouse game in which Loomis tries to terrorize Ann into submission. First he wounds her superficially in the foot with his shotgun, then he cuts off all of her food sources. Ann realizes she must either kill Loomis or get the safe suit and leave the valley. Unable to commit murder, she tricks him into leaving the house unguarded. In the safe suit, she confronts Loomis and tells him that he will have to kill her as he did Edward to stop her from leaving. Shaken by this reminder of his guilt, Loomis allows her to go. Ann sets out alone, hoping to find another valley where there are survivors.

CHARACTERS: There are only two characters in this novel. During the three months that transpire from Loomis's arrival in the valley to her departure, **Ann Burden** celebrates her sixteenth birthday, but her horrifying experience causes her to mature well beyond her years. Ann is a wholesome, honest girl who has shown great ingenuity and courage in surviving the loss of her family and friends. She cultivates the family garden, cares for the cows and chickens, learns to fish in the one unpolluted stream in the valley, and maintains the family homestead. Through all this hard work and deprivation, she never loses faith or succumbs to despair or depression. She learns through often painful experiences to survive and become self-sufficient, while never abandoning hope for the future.

This strength of character and pride in her accomplishments lead Ann to be cautious and suspicious when the stranger in an unusual outfit appears in her valley. However, when she sees that he is suffering from radiation illness, her selflessness and humanity triumph over apprehension. Ann sacrifices her own health and well-being to nurse Loomis. She tries everything from home medicines to prayers and bedside readings to help speed his recovery. Her childlike trust and faith in human nature are shattered when her patient turns against her and sadistically tries to rape her.

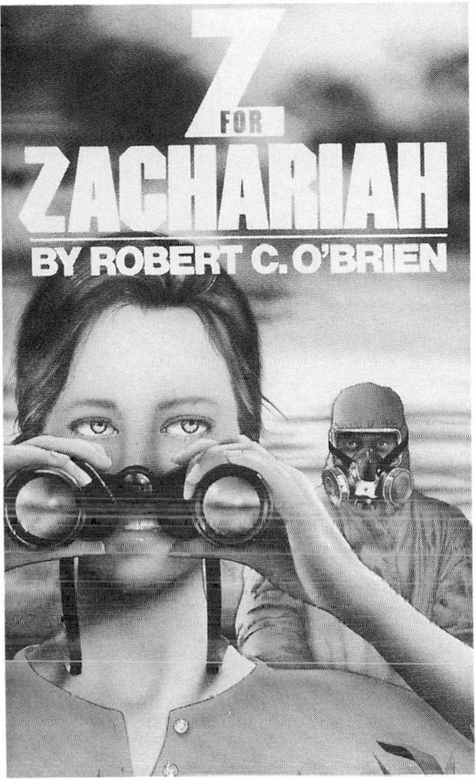

In this post-nuclear war novel, young Ann Burden finds herself in a cat-and-mouse chase with a radiation-poisoned scientist.

Forced once more to forage for food, Ann again shows her intelligence, ingenuity, and resourcefulness, refusing to sacrifice her ideals and integrity to save herself. Her compassion and high principles never leave her, even though her life is endangered. For example, she can't bring herself to shoot the family dog, even though he can be used by Loomis to track her down. Though she is faced with death, her courage and sense of decency never leave Ann. She could kill Loomis or, at least, leave the valley in the suit without his knowledge. Instead, she fearlessly confronts him. Though she sacrifices her security and well-being, Ann's wholesomeness, honesty, and old-fashioned ethics triumph over Loomis's depravity.

At one point in the novel, Ann remembers a childhood Bible ABC book that she owned. In it, A was for Adam and Z for Zachariah. From this she gathered that if Adam was the first man on earth,

Zachariah must be the last. Ann's Zachariah and eventual nemesis is **John R. Loomis**, a former research chemist from Cornell University. When he takes off his safe suit, Ann sees through her binoculars that he has a long, narrow, attractive face with a big nose. He has a tense look which Ann at first thinks is poetic and intriguing. A sullen, morose individual, he doesn't reveal his true character until he is stricken with radiation sickness. Then, in his delirium, Loomis unwittingly reveals that he has murdered a colleague to save himself. His feelings of guilt obviously torment him but have not produced contrition or remorse.

During his recovery, his selfishness and calculating nature emerge. Without any feelings of gratitude or appreciation for Ann's care and sacrifice, Loomis ruthlessly orders her about, forcing her to accept new responsibilities and extending her already long working hours. Loomis's mechanical aptitude is shown in his suggestions for improvements about the house, but he continuously belittles and disparages Ann's many accomplishments. When she rejects his sexual advances and runs away, the fine balance between bizarre behavior and insanity is tipped. Loomis can't bear being thwarted, particularly by a teenager. He sadistically tracks her down, deliberately wounds her, and cuts off her food supply to starve her into submission. Loomis's madness ends, however, at committing another murder. When Ann tells him that to stop her from leaving he will have to shoot her as he did Edward, he relents and pathetically begs her not to leave him alone. When she refuses, he shows, for the first time, a tiny bit of compassion and humanity by indicating to her the direction she should take in her search for other survivors.

Further Reading

Authors and Artists for Young Adults. Vol. 6. Detroit: Gale Research, 1991.

Berger, Laura Standley, ed. *Twentieth-Century Children's Writers.* 4th ed. Detroit: St. James, 1994.

Children's Literature Review. Vol. 2. Detroit: Gale Research, 1976.

De Montreville, Doris, and Crawford, Elizabeth D., eds. *Fourth Book of Junior Authors and Illustrators.* New York: H. W. Wilson, 1978.

Kirkpatrick, D. L., ed. *Twentieth-Century Children's Writers.* 2nd ed. New York: St. Martin's, 1983.

Something about the Author. Vol. 23. Detroit: Gale Research, 1981.

Ward, Martha, ed. *Authors of Books for Young People.* 3rd ed. Metuchen, NJ: Scarecrow, 1990.

Scott O'Dell

1903-1994, American young adult novelist

Island of the Blue Dolphins

(historical novel, 1961)

PLOT: *Island of the Blue Dolphins* is a story of survival, set in the early 1830s and based on the few known facts about an historical figure called the Lost Woman of San Nicholas. At the opening of the novel, twelve-year-old Karana, her older sister, Ulape, and younger brother, Ramo, live on an island in the Pacific Ocean, southwest of what is now the city of Los Angeles. Their mother has died, and the children live with their father, Chowig, the village chief. Food and water are plentiful on the Island of the Blue Dolphins, and occasionally an Aleut ship arrives to pay for the privilege of hunting otters for their valuable pelts. But after one such party prepares to leave without paying the promised fee, a fight erupts. The natives are no match against the ship's firepower, and many of them, including Chowig, are killed. The new chief, Kimki, decides that the few survivors must move to another island. But when the ship sails, Karana discovers that Ramo is still on the shore; she sees him running along the beach. Matasaip, who is in charge of guiding the ship away from the dangerous rocky shore, tells her they will return later for the boy. But Karana cannot leave her brother alone, and she leaps overboard to be with him.

Unafraid, the children are content with the understanding that the ship will return, and they settle in to wait. They have enough food and water, but when Ramo is killed by wild dogs Karana is left alone. There she stays for nearly twenty years. She survives by learning to do things such as making a bow and arrows, killing a huge sea elephant, and building a home. At one point, she decides to follow the villagers in a canoe, but when she sets sail the canoe starts to leak. Blue dolphins appear and guide her back to the island. Later, she rescues a wounded dog that probably belonged to the Aleuts, and only then does she realize how much she has craved companionship. She names the dog Rontu, which means "fox eyes."

After a few years, a ship arrives, but it is an Aleut vessel. Karana hides for fear the men will capture her. The ship leaves and she passes the years in isolation. When old Rontu dies, Karana's loneliness returns, until she captures a young dog with yellow eyes. She thinks he is Rontu's son and she names him Rontu-Aru, son of Rontu. After she has been alone on the island for almost twenty years, a ship finally arrives that is not Aleut, and Karana emerges from her hiding place. She is taken to Mission Santa Barbara, where she is tended to by Father Gonzales, who tells her that the boat carrying her village people sank in the ocean, which is why no one ever returned for her. Karana spends her remaining years at the mission speaking in sign language, for no one there is able to understand her strange speech.

Zia (1976) is a sequel.

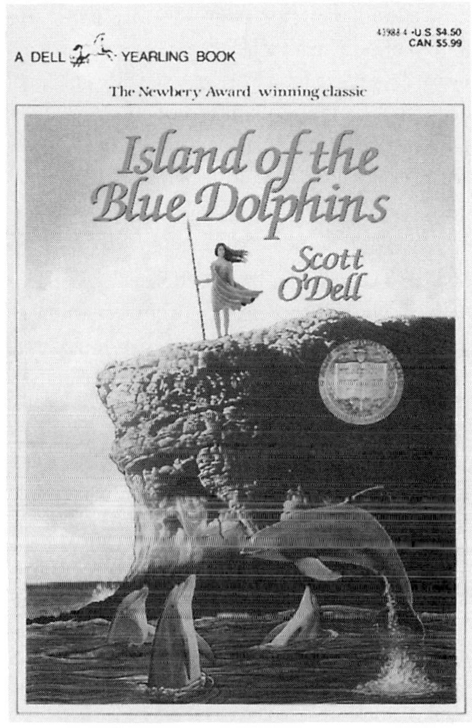

This Newbery Award winner is based on the true survival story of the Lost Woman of San Nicholas.

CHARACTERS: The historical figure called the Lost Woman of San Nicholas was also named Karana, and she is believed to have lived alone on the Pacific island of San Nicholas from 1835 to 1853. San Nicholas, here called the Island of the Blue Dolphins, is shaped somewhat like a big fish with its tail pointing eastward. In *Island of the Blue Dolphins,* **Karana** is a stoic and resourceful young girl. When Ramo is killed and she must depend only upon herself, she struggles to remember the skills she learned from her father and the other members of her village. Although she is often frightened, especially by the wild dogs, she keeps her composure and reasons her way out of danger. Perhaps the most telling indication of her loneliness is her joy in nursing the dog Rontu back to health. Woven throughout the book is the recognition of the important role that animal and plant life play in human existence. For all of Karana's resourcefulness, there is lingering sadness as the years pass and she lives her life without human companionship. And yet, after she is rescued and taken to the mission, Karana is even sadder because she now lives in a world that she does not understand and that does not understand her.

Karana's father, **Chowig**, is a kind but stern man; he is not only a benevolent chief but a brave one. He is unafraid when confronted with the trickery of the Aleuts and refuses to back down, even though this confrontation ends in his death and the near destruction of his village. **Ramo**, Karana's brother, is a typical six-year-old who has little fear of anything. Even after he and Karana are left stranded on the island, he is unafraid. He reasons that the ship will return, and until then he and Karana have nothing to do but play on their beautiful island.

Father Gonzales is the kindly priest who tries to bring Karana into the modern world. He is largely unsuccessful, however, primarily because he is unable to understand her language. The Indians of her own village had all disappeared when their ship went down and he is unable to find any Indians at the mission who can understand her speech, so he and Karana communicate only in sign language.

Rontu and **Rontu-Aru** are the main animal characters of the story. Since Rontu, with thick fur and large yellow eyes, looks so unlike the wild dogs of the island, Karana reasons that he must have been left behind when the Aleut ship hastily departed after killing so many men from the village. Skittish about accepting human kindness at first, Rontu, and later Rontu-Aru, prove to be intelligent, kind, and protective companions.

The Black Pearl

(young adult novel, 1967)

PLOT: This is a somber novel about truth and legend and the difficulty of telling them apart. At age sixteen, Ramon Salazar joins his father, Blas Salazar, in the family business of buying and selling pearls. All his life, Ramon has heard two legends about the sea. One tells of the Pearl of Heaven, a magnificent black gem; the other speaks of a monster fish called Manta Diablo, a manta ray larger than the largest ship in the harbor of their town, La Paz.

Ramon secretly asks an old Indian named Luzon to teach him to dive for pearls. After much practice and a long search, Ramon manages to find the Pearl of Heaven. But Luzon begs him to leave it, saying it belongs to Manta Diablo. Ramon scoffs at the old Indian's superstitions and becomes a hero at home, incurring the intense jealousy of Gaspar Ruiz, known as Sevillano, the best pearl diver in La Paz. But Ramon's father, Blas, cannot get the price he asks for the pearl, so he stubbornly refuses to sell it and instead gives it to Father Gallardo. It is placed in the hands of the statue of the Madonna, who watches over the fishing fleet in the harbor.

Some time later, Blas and the entire fleet, except for Sevillano, are lost in a terrible storm. Ramon believes this is his fault because he took the Pearl of Heaven. He retrieves the pearl and sails back to the island where he found it. But Sevillano follows him and forces the boy to row him to the city of Guaymas, where he intends to sell the pearl. On the way, Sevillano tells Ramon that returning the gem will not atone for his father's death. Manta Diablo is not responsible, Sevillano says. Blas Salazar died because he thought that donating the pearl to the Madonna would bring him good luck. He relied on that luck instead of his own sailing skills, and that was why he perished in the storm.

Before they reach Guaymas, a huge manta ray starts following their boat. Ramon knows it is Manta Diablo. In the attack that follows, Sevillano mortally wounds the giant ray but drowns in the sea as it dies. Ramon returns to La Paz with the Pearl of Heaven. He places it again with the statue of the Madonna, this time as a gift of love rather than defiance.

CHARACTERS: Ramon Salazar is a bright young man who is small for his age. He is acutely conscious of his size because his father, a big man, is always telling him to "pull down your cuffs" to hide his scrawny frame. The boy wants very much to please his father, especially now that he is sixteen and a partner in the family business. It is after he is insulted by Gaspar Ruiz, known as Sevillano, that Ramon begins looking for the Pearl of Heaven. He wants to outdo Sevillano as well as please his father. Although Ramon does not really believe the legend of the giant ray, Manta Diablo, he is still apprehensive when Luzon warns him about the trouble taking the magnificent gem will cause. However, watching his father show off the pearl to the villagers, Ramon forgets about the Indian's warning and is very proud of his accomplishment.

After his father is lost with the rest of the fleet at sea, Ramon begins to consider the truth in Luzon's warning. He hopes somehow to atone for his deed by returning the pearl to Manta Diablo. But when the great fish appears and Sevillano prepares to kill it, Ramon, despite his hatred for Sevillano, is ready to help him. Even before Sevillano and the great fish die, Ramon knows that he must return the pearl to the statue of the Madonna. This time he places it there as a gift of love, with prayers both for Sevillano and for the Manta Diablo. And on this day, as Ramon prepares to go home to his mother and tell her what has happened, he knows that he has reached manhood.

Blas Salazar is strong, hard-working, honorable, sensitive to insult, and proud. He loves his son Ramon, yet he is also somewhat ashamed of his size. He does not want anyone to think that Blas Salazar, himself a big man, has a puny son. When Ramon complains that Sevillano taunted him, his father replies that Sevillano is a troublemaker but asks why should Ramon care—Sevillano is the best pearl gatherer they have. Business is what counts for Blas. But when he can't get the price he wants for the Pearl of Heaven, he stubbornly refuses to sell it at all and donates it to the church. Ramon's mother is angry at this because she sees the pearl was given for the wrong reasons.

In the end, the gift and the motives for giving it may be what caused Blas's death. **Luzon**, the wise old Indian who believes in the superstitions about the giant ray, warned of coming trouble to the fleet, but, as Sevillano explains, Blas really died because he made a bad decision while at sea. As experienced a seaman as Blas was, he should have sought shelter at the first signs of the storm. Blas did not because he thought his gift to the Madonna was enough to keep him from harm; he thought he no longer had to help himself.

Gaspar Ruiz, or **Sevillano**, the finest pearl diver in the fleet, is a braggart. Older and stronger than Ramon, he constantly taunts the boy with stories of his great exploits. Although Sevillano is indeed as strong and skillful as he claims, it is this very pride that brings about his death. He cannot let the Manta Diablo escape, and much like Ahab with the White Whale at the end of *Moby Dick*, Sevillano goes to his death with his enemy.

Further Reading

Berger, Laura Standley, ed. *Twentieth-Century Young Adult Writers.* 1st ed. Detroit: St. James, 1994.

Children's Literature Review. Vol. 1. Detroit: Gale Research, 1976.

Collier, Laurie, and Joyce Nakamura, eds. *Major Authors and Illustrators for Children and Young Adults.* Detroit: Gale Research, 1993.

Contemporary Literary Criticism. Vol. 30. Detroit: Gale Research, 1984.

Estes, Glenn E., ed. *American Writers for Children since 1960: Fiction.* Vol. 52 of *Dictionary of Literary Biography.* Detroit: Gale Research, 1986.

Gallo, Donald R. *Speaking for Ourselves: Autobiographical Sketches by Notable Authors of Books for Young Adults.* Urbana, IL: National Council of Teachers of English, 1990.

Lovelace, Maud Hart. "Scott O'Dell." In *Newbery and Caldecott Medal Books: 1956-1965.* Boston: Horn Book, 1965.

Something about the Author. Vol. 60. Detroit: Gale Research, 1990.

Townsend, John Rowe. *A Sense of Story: Essays on Contemporary Writers for Children.* Philadelphia: Lippincott, 1971.

Windle, Justin, ed. "Scott O'Dell." In *The Pied Pipers.* New York: Paddington Press, 1975.

George Orwell

1903-1950, English novelist

Animal Farm

(political allegory, 1945)

PLOT: This classic political novel is an allegory of what Orwell saw to be flaws in the communist system. The story traces the revolt of the Manor Farm animals on a British farm in the 1940s. Their oppressor, Mr. Jones, is a mean farmer. One day the oldest pig, called Major, gathers the animals together to expound his theory of revolution, which includes blaming humans as the source of all animal misery. Major dies peacefully after speaking his mind, and from his theories a new social system called "Animalism" develops. The most intelligent of the barnyard animals, the pigs, are the leaders of this new order.

With the farmer and his wife chased off the farm, Animalism and its Seven Commandments take over. Dogs, sheep, and horses are kept in line by the pigs, who justify their power with misleading rhetoric. When Snowball assumes leadership and sets up a plan for the construction of a windmill that will give the farm electrical power, he is overthrown by the pig Napoleon with the help of some dogs he has trained. Napoleon revises the Seven Commandments in order to give greater privileges to the pigs. Pretty soon, the pigs are much like the humans they despised in the first place. The allegory ends with the maxim that "all animals are equal, but some animals are more equal than others." With the revolution betrayed, a dictatorship develops, a bright vision dims, and the pressure of the status quo represses any new ideas that threaten to change it.

CHARACTERS: A thinly disguised attack on the tyranny and hypocrisy of the Soviet Union's government, *Animal Farm* was written during World War II, but it wasn't published until the war ended for fear it would offend the Soviets, who were England's allies against the Nazis. Though the Soviet Union has since collapsed, political oppression still exists, making *Animal Farm* as relevant today as it was in 1945.

The wise old pig **Major** is said to represent Karl Marx and his doctrine of socialism. He is the only character that escapes Orwell's indictment. A twelve-year-old prize white boar, Major is a visionary who believes in the possibility of a better society than the one in which the animals now live, and the animals respect him enough to listen to him. Major expounds upon his vision that the animals would be better off and in better health without humans, who are essentially unproductive. He feels the animals would have more dignity and be more productive themselves if they lived on their own without being ordered about by humans. There is a beauty and simplicity in Major's vision. The animals will avoid the vices of humans and without having to give living space and food to humans they will live in more comfort, dignity, and honor.

Naturally, this vision captures the attention of the other animals. It is somewhat ironic, however, in that it comes from Major, surely the most pampered of all the animals on the farm. As a show pig, he has lived all his life in relative ease. While the other animals on the farm have had to work for their keep, Major has had the freedom and time to sit around pondering his vision. Even so, Major does provide the group with a goal toward which to work and direct their lives. Although he does not provide the details of his vision, he gives the other animals the incentive to begin to make changes. Unfortunately, Major's idea is flawed in that he assumes that all the animals will be kind and just to one another. He does not see that each individual animal may have a separate motive for making the plan succeed. But, of course, such details are not in the scope of a visionary. Three days after delivering his great oratory, Major dies.

Two of the pigs take charge of putting Major's vision into reality. One is **Snowball**, who is in tune with the Major's beliefs. With the other leader pig, Napoleon, Snowball takes charge of sorting out the details of Major's vision. He is the perfect complement to Major because he is able to organize and put the plan into practical operation. He sets up classes so that the animals can learn to read and write; he wants them all to be informed so that they will be better able to manage their lives after the revolution. Snowball sets up committees to plan the rebellion against Farmer Jones, and he plans a windmill that will be constructed in order to ease the work of the farm animals. He may be likened to Leon Trotsky, who was a major force behind the Russian Revolution.

Snowball is not merely a good strategist and organizer, however; he follows through with his words by putting them into action. When the revolution takes place, he is in the forefront of the battle against the humans. However, his downfall is that he shares Major's main weakness: he can't perceive that some of the animals have less than desirable traits and goals and misguidedly believes that all will work for the common goal. In the end, this flaw forces him to flee Animal Farm.

Napoleon is a mean-looking boar who doesn't talk much. His quiet manner makes the other animals think he has great depth, which he does not, and that Snowball, because he talks too much, is shallow. That, also, is untrue. Like Snowball, however, Napoleon does share Major's vision and plan and is willing to work to see the revolution succeed. The main difference is that Napoleon has his own agenda for a successful revolution. Whereas Snowball wants good for all, Napoleon concentrates on the advantages he can gain for himself; and whereas Snowball plans activities out in the open, Napoleon plots secretly, as when he covertly trains the dogs.

Napoleon may be likened to Stalin, the former despotic ruler of the Soviet Union. He is ruthless in carrying out his plans for his own betterment. Greed is his overall characteristic, a motive that never changes throughout the novel. Napoleon becomes better and better at satisfying his own goals and needs and in duping the other animals into believing that he is doing it all for them. Each new project that takes all their energy keeps them from questioning whether their lives are truly improved. Napoleon is a master of propaganda, as was Stalin. And like Stalin, Napoleon uses ruthless tactics to gain his objectives.

Napoleon's right-hand pig, so to speak, is **Squealer**. Although there is no one figure of the Russian Revolution who is comparable to Squealer, every revolution, dictatorship, or government of any kind must have someone that can be relied on to carry out the aims and wishes of the leader. Small, fat Squealer with his fine voice is the propagandist of the revolution. Whatever Napoleon wants, Squealer will do. He even revises the Seven Commandments when it suits Napoleon's aims. As Napoleon's official spokespig, Squealer is so persuasive that he can cleverly turn ideas and thoughts inside out until the other animals are no longer sure of what is right or even what has happened. Although Squealer presents a merry posture, he is an argumentative, vindictive pig. One does not threaten his authority. If one of the animals objects to something Squealer has said, he merely brings up the threat of Farmer Jones's return.

Boxer represents the working class in the Marxist theory of revolution. He is a strong and tall horse who works constantly for others while gaining little for himself from his labors. He has little education or intelligence and can't fully comprehend the workings of the revolution. He is, however, totally willing to follow the dictates of others and volunteer for extra work if it needs to be done. He does not quite understand some of the things that are happening on the farm or the reasons for them. But, above all, Boxer is loyal to the revolution's leaders. In human terms, a revolution needs the working class to follow, even blindly, the dictates of those who lead. Boxer's reward for a life of hard service is to be sent to the glue factory.

The survivor and oldest animal on the farm is **Benjamin** the donkey, whose main fault is his steadfast loyalty to Boxer. Benjamin learns to read as well as the pigs. He works hard but will do nothing more than necessary. Benjamin is skeptical, believing nothing good will come from this revolution, or anything else for that matter. He has a bad temper and will not take sides on issues simply because he doesn't think anything is better than anything else. Whatever happens is going to be bad, according to Benjamin, so why bother?

Other animal characters on the farm include **Moses**, the raven who tells stories to the animals, **Clover**, the mare who cares for all the animals (especially Boxer), and the frivolous and vain mare, **Mollie**, who leaves the farm to work in a pub. As for the humans, the most important character is **Mr. Jones**, the farmer who is forced off his land by the animals. Two neighboring farmers, **Mr. Pilkington**, who is a poor farmer, and **Mr. Frederick**, an efficient farmer, also make minor appearances.

Nineteen Eighty-Four

(science fiction, 1949)

PLOT: This novel, regarded as a masterpiece of modern science fiction, is set in a future country called Oceania. The people in this totalitarian state are led by Big Brother, head of the mysterious Inner Party that controls everything and everyone. To keep the people in line there are the Thought Police, who monitor two-way telescreens, public executions, and group hate sessions. Adherence to the party is assured by the constant rewriting of history.

Thirty-nine-year-old Winston Smith is a writer for the Ministry of Truth, one of four large ministries in London, which is the capital city of Airstrip One, a province of Oceania. The Ministry of Truth deals with news, education, and entertainment. The other ministries include: the Ministry of Peace, which concerns itself with war; the Ministry of Love, the province of the secret police; and the Ministry of Plenty, which is responsible for the sorely depleted economy. In his minor job, Winston has access to historical and revised records. He begins a private journal in which he records his growing anti-party, anti-Big Brother thoughts. He also begins a romantic relationship with Julia, who belongs to the Anti-Sex League. They often meet in a small bedroom rented to them by kindly Mr. Charrington, who owns the antique shop below. There, Winston and Julia share their growing understanding and affection for one another.

One day Winston discovers that his colleague, O'Brien, shares his views, too, and so he and Julia meet at O'Brien's apartment. They learn that there is an underground conspiracy to overthrow the party that is led by a man named Emmanuel Goldstein. Later, while reading Goldstein's views and plans in their rented apartment, Winston and Julia are captured by guards and arrested.

Winston is brainwashed and tortured but eventually released. He learns that Mr. Charrington is actually one of the Thought Police and that O'Brien is a member of the Inner Party. O'Brien explains that the Party invented the story of Goldstein's planned revolt for the express purpose of flushing out people like Winston who might breed opposition to the party line.

When Julia and Winston are reunited, there is little for them to say to each other. Both have been forever changed by physical torture and brainwashing. The brief glimmer of the revolt that Winston planned is over. His conditioned mind has been rewired so that he now loves Big Brother and is completely devoted to the Party. No longer posing a threat, he will be allowed to live despite his past transgressions. Winston becomes a shining example of the power of the Party.

CHARACTERS: The only character of consequence in this powerful novel, and the only one that is more than two-dimensional, is **Winston Smith**. There is some irony in the naming of this frail, thirty-nine-year-old, undernourished man who suffers from an ulcer on his ankle. His last name is one of the most common in English society, while his first name recalls that of Winston Churchill, England's great World War II leader and statesman. But Winston, unlike his namesake, is thoroughly intimidated by the society in which he lives. He fears not only Big Brother, but almost anyone else who could possibly denounce him. Winston is a member of the Outer Party, which is an offshoot of the elite ruling Inner Party. As such, he should have some special privileges. In reality, however, he only has the right to be watched for any infringement or infraction of the strict laws of the government.

Winston's revolt is brief and his fall complete. Throughout the book, he has dreams that involve his mother and sister. It is thought that the author intended them as a key to Winston's subconscious as he struggles under the repressions of his life. When he succumbs to the Party line, their control over him is absolute and permanent. He is now their model citizen.

Julia is not given a last name and is more two-dimensional than Winston. Although she, too, rebels against the system, she is less concerned with its ideologies than Winston and less terrified by its restrictions and brutality. Although she is intelligent, she is not as involved with the intellectual aspects of society. She is more concerned with its physical limitations. Part of this may be explained by the fact that she is several years younger than Winston. When she is captured by the Thought Police, Julia immediately gives in and confesses to everything. She has no inner strength and no real convictions.

Katherine, Winston's lovely but brainless wife, does not actually appear in the novel. Contrasted with Julia, she is an example of what this society has been able to do to the minds of so-called normal people. So utterly brainwashed by party teachings, Katherine is such a human automaton that Winston has seriously considered murdering her.

Big Brother is not a real person but only a picture of a handsome, rugged man with a heavy black moustache. Although he may exist only in the minds of the people, he is a powerful symbol of the government and thus helps to keep its citizens in line. **Emmanuel Goldstein** is also a government fabrication, though he is the converse of Big Brother. Created by the party to serve as a focus for its hatred against proposed enemies, real and imagined, the character of Goldstein is similar to that of Leon Trotsky, the communist leader who was exiled from the Soviet Union and later murdered. Goldstein is against Big Brother and the system of Oceania.

Winston's colleague, **O'Brien**, is one of the oligarchy of Oceania and a member of the ruling Inner Party. His job in the Ministry of Truth, working with Winston, is not identified in the novel. He is an intellectual, far more educated than Winston, about forty-five years old, and powerfully built. O'Brien is not merely a fanatic who believes in the system, he *is* the system. What is especially frightening to Winston is that O'Brien has apparently been watching and studying him for many years. He is able to bend Winston's will so that he accepts the absurd dictates of the ruling party.

The kindly, elderly widower, **Mr. Charrington**, is in reality a member of the dreaded Thought Police. When Julia and Winston are arrested in the furnished room he rents to them, Charrington's disguise drops away and reveals him to actually be a cold, devious man of about thirty-five.

The **Proles** are the faceless masses of citizens of Oceania who make up most of the population. The Party regards them as subhuman and almost encourages their corrupt moral status simply because it makes them easier to handle. In direct contrast to the Marxist theory of revolution in which the "Proletariat" (or Proles) will become the dictators, in this novel the revolution has resulted in the worst kind of tyranny against the people. When Winston Smith attempts his small, personal revolution, he believes that the Proles hold the key to any future hope for society. But in the end O'Brien sets him straight, explaining that the Proles will not revolt until they gain self-awareness. But they will not gain self-awareness until they revolt. So, as Winston learns and comes to accept, nothing will ever change.

Further Reading

Authors and Artists for Young Adults. Vol. 15. Detroit: Gale Research, 1995.

Berger, Laura Standley, ed. *Twentieth-Century Young Adult Writers.* 1st ed. Detroit: St. James, 1995.

Beum, Robert, ed. *Modern British Essayists, First Series.* Vol. 98 of *Dictionary of Literary Biography.* Detroit: Gale Research, 1990.

Bloom, Harold, ed. *George Orwell's* Nineteen Eighty-Four. New York: Chelsea House, 1987.

Brander, Laurence. *George Orwell.* New York: Longmans, 1973.

Crick, Bernard R. *George Orwell: A Life.* Boston: Little, Brown, 1980.

Critical Survey of Long Fiction. Vol. 4. Englewood Cliffs, NJ: Prentice-Hall, 1983.

Fyvel, T. R. *George Orwell: A Personal Memoir.* New York: Macmillan, 1982.

Gardner, Averil. *George Orwell.* New York: Twayne, 1987.

Gross, Miriam, ed. *The World of George Orwell.* New York: Simon & Schuster, 1972.

Hammond, J. R. *George Orwell Companion: A Guide to the Novels, Documentaries, and Essays.* New York: St. Martin's, 1982.

Howe, Irving, ed. *Orwell's* Nineteen Eighty-Four: *Text, Sources, Criticism.* New York: Harcourt, 1982.

———. 1984 *Revisited: Totalitarianism in Our Century.* New York: Harper, 1983.

Jensen, Ejner J., ed. *The Future of* Nineteen Eighty-Four. Ann Arbor: University of Michigan Press, 1983.

Kalechofsky, Roberta. *George Orwell.* New York: Ungar, 1973.

Kubal, David L. *Outside the Whale: George Orwell's Art and Politics.* Notre Dame, IN: University of Notre Dame Press, 1972.

Kuppig, C. J., ed. Nineteen Eighty-Four *to 1984: A Companion to Orwell's Classic Novel.* Washington, DC: Library of Congress, 1985.

Lee, Robert A. *Orwell's Fiction.* Notre Dame, IN: University of Notre Dame Press, 1969.

Meyers, Jeffrey, ed. *George Orwell: The Critical Heritage.* London: Routledge, 1975.

Oldsey, Bernard, ed. *British Novelists, 1930-1959.* Vol. 15 of *Dictionary of Literary Biography.* Detroit: Gale Research, 1983.

Reilly, Patrick. Nineteen Eighty-Four: *Past, Present, and Future.* New York: Twayne, 1989.

Savage, Robert L., ed. *The Orwellian Moment: Hindsight and Foresight in the Post-1984 World.* Fayetteville: University of Arkansas Press, 1989.

Shelden, Michael. *Orwell: The Authorized Biography.* New York: Harper, 1991.

Stansky, Peter, ed. *On* Nineteen Eighty-Four. New York: Freeman, 1983.

———. *Orwell the Transformation.* New York: Knopf, 1980.

Twentieth-Century British Literature. Vol. 4 of the *Chelsea House Library of Literary Criticism.* New York: Chelsea House, 1987.

Twentieth-Century Literary Criticism. Vols. 2, 6, 15, 31, 51. Detroit: Gale Research, 1979, 1982, 1985, 1989, 1994.

Watson, Noell, ed. *Twentieth-Century Science Fiction Writers.* 3rd ed. Chicago: St. James, 1991.

Wemyss, Courtney T. *George Orwell.* Westport, CT: Greenwood, 1987.

Woodcock, George. *The Crystal Spirit: A Study of George Orwell.* Boston: Little, Brown, 1988.

Katherine Paterson

1932-, American young adult novelist

Jacob Have I Loved

(young adult novel, 1980)

PLOT: The title of this novel comes from the Bible, Romans 9:13, in which the Lord says, "Jacob have I loved, but Esau have I hated." The Bradshaw twins, Louise and Caroline, are very different. Given the nickname Wheeze by her minutes-younger twin, Louise is plain and withdrawn and considers herself the ugly duckling. Caroline, on the other hand, is pretty, blonde, and always the center of attention. Musically talented, Caroline is sent every week for lessons across Chesapeake Bay from their home on Rass Island. The twins' father, Truitt, is a fisherman who combs the bay for crabs and oysters; the mother, Susan, is a former schoolteacher. Also living with the family is the girls' mean-spirited grandmother, who favors Caroline.

After World War II breaks out in 1942, elderly Hiram Wallace arrives on the island to take up residence in the old deserted Wallace place, which he had left some forty years earlier. Louise and her friend Call become friends with the old man, whom they call Captain Wallace. They are soon joined in their visits by Caroline, to Louise's displeasure. As the war drags on, Call leaves to join the navy and Caroline leaves to study voice up north. Louise drops out of school in her mid-teens to help her father on the boat, while her mother tutors her at home. When the war ends, Call returns home after visiting Caroline in New York City. He tells Louise that he and Caroline are going to be married. Louise is filled with resentment about the news. Louise becomes more and more bitter with her life, until she realizes that she must become her own master. She enters college on the mainland, and when she leaves home, she asks her mother if she will miss her as much as Caroline. She is overjoyed when her mother replies, "More."

As the years pass, Louise graduates, becomes a nurse midwife in Appalachia, and marries a widower, Joseph Wojtkiewicz, who has three small children. She is attracted to him because, like her father, she thinks he is a man who can "sing to oysters," meaning he has a deep love for the sea. When both her father and grandmother die, Louise returns to her island home to bring her mother back to live with her and her family.

CHARACTERS: Louise Bradshaw spends much of her youth in the shadow of her twin, Caroline. Everyone pampers the lovely, spoiled Caroline, while Louise retreats into the recesses of tiny Chesapeake Bay Island, where she learns the ways of the watermen and the secrets of the island. One by one, Louise feels her dreams and hopes snatched from her. It is Caroline who is given the money to go away to school, and Caroline who will marry Louise's childhood friend and companion, Call. She wonders whether anything will be left for her. Growing more alone and unsure of herself (at times even hating her twin), Louise must discover who she is, someone who does not need to be compared to Caroline. She is able to do this when the county supervisor recommends her for a scholarship to the University of Maryland. She leaves the island for a new life, does well in school, and once again is challenged when, with all the veterans returning after World War II, there is no chance of her entering a medical school. Gone are her hopes of becoming a doctor. Instead, she transfers to the University of Kentucky, taking a course in midwifery. This leads her to Appalachia, where she finds a rewarding existence in the help she can give to others and where she finds personal fulfillment in meeting Joseph, whom she marries.

Caroline Bradshaw is light and golden, her twin Louise thinks. She is also selfish, spoiled, and seemingly loved by everyone. Things come easy for Caroline, and everyone is anxious to help her through anything. She not only looks like a dream, but she sings like one, too. It seems perfectly natural to Caroline, although staggering news to Louise, when Captain Wallace announces that the money he inherited from his late wife will go to Caroline so that she can study music at the famed Julliard school in New York City.

Louise's friend, **Call**, is pudgy, bespectacled, and totally unsentimental. While they are teens on the island, Louise feels completely at home with him, as if they were two parts of a well-oiled machine. When Call returns on leave from the navy, he is a grown man, tall and broad-shouldered. She is so happy to see him that she is even able to comment favorably about Caroline's good fortune to study music at Julliard in New York City. Her heart sinks when Call tells her he is engaged to Caroline. Feeling she has lost out again to her sister, Louise is crushed when Call says he feels Caroline needs him to take care of her. Louise later marries **Joseph Wojtkiewicz** because she becomes aware that he looks like the kind of man who would "sing to the oysters." A widower with three children, he is a kind and gentle man. Before long, he and Louise have a child of their own to welcome into the family.

Captain Wallace becomes an important part of Louise's life on the island. She enjoys many happy hours with the Captain and Call, until Caroline once again becomes the center of attention in the group. Louise is inconsolable when the Captain announces that there will be money to send the gifted Caroline away to music school.

Louise's mother, **Susan**, understands the hurt that Louise is experiencing. She tries to reach out but is often shunned because Louise feels her mother only likes Caroline. Louise is pleased, however, when her mother tells her she will be missed even more than Caroline.

Lyddie

(historical novel, 1991)

PLOT: Set during the 1840s, this novel tells about young Lyddie Worthen, who, along with her brother, Charlie, is hired out by her mother to help pay off the family's debts on their Vermont farm. Charlie is sent to work in a mill and is taken in by a family who will care for him, but Lyddie is sent to work in a tavern, where she is treated no better than a slave. She therefore leaves and travels to Lowell, Massachusetts, to be with Charlie. She begins to work in the same mill as Charlie and hopes that one day she will be able to care for herself and her brother.

The pay is small and the working conditions are deplorable, but at least Lyddie feels she is free. She becomes friendly with Diana, who encourages the mill girls to sign a petition for better working conditions. Lyddie does not sign, but at Diana's urging she does improve her reading and writing skills. When Diana becomes pregnant and leaves Lowell, Lyddie befriends young Brigid. One evening she rescues Brigid from an attack by the mill supervisor, Mr. Marsden, by hitting him with a bucket. Lyddie is fired, but before she leaves Lowell she tells Marsden that if he molests or fires Brigid, Lyddie will inform his wife of what goes on at the mill between him and the young workers.

Lyddie travels to Boston to see Diana and then to Vermont for one last look at her beloved farm. There she sees Luke Stevens, the young Quaker lad who wrote Lyddie a letter asking her to return and marry him. When Luke asks about her plans, she replies that she is going to Ohio to enter college. Lyddie knows it will be a long time before she returns, but she hopes that the gentle Luke will wait for her.

CHARACTERS: Lyddie Worthen is uneducated, but she has spirit and determination. Though she works hard to keep the family farm going, she is disappointed by her mother's decision to hire her out to work at a tavern. Lyddie, however, refuses to tolerate the slavelike conditions she endures there, and so she leaves to go to the mill in Lowell where her brother works. Shocked by the poor working conditions she yet again finds, Lyddie nevertheless stays for a time because of her new friend, Diana. At this point, Lyddie still lacks some courage, which is shown by her unwillingness to sign a petition for better working conditions, but Diana helps change that. Diana builds up Lyddie's self-confidence and encourages her to learn to read and write. After Diana leaves, Lyddie shows some pluck by defending Brigid against the mill manager's advances.

Lyddie does not become truly independent, though, until after her visit with Diana in Boston. After seeing that Diana has made a life for herself, Lyddie resolves to do the same. And when she meets young Luke Stevens again back in Vermont, she realizes what she must do. She is not ready to marry yet, even though she likes Luke. Instead, she plans to attend college in Ohio. She will become educated and independent so that she can live life on her own terms.

Lyddie's friend at the mill is the radical **Diana**, who not only teaches her about the job but encourages the uneducated Lyddie to better herself by learning to read and write. Diana courageously tries to get signatures on a petition for improved working conditions, and shows kindness in taking Lyddie under her wing, but she has flaws, too. She becomes pregnant with the mill doctor's child even though he is married. Still, Diana does not let this defeat her. Instead, she moves to Boston to build a new life for herself and her baby.

After Diana leaves to have her baby, Lyddie finds a new friend in **Brigid**. Just as Diana had taken Lyddie under her wing, so does Lyddie take it upon herself to encourage Brigid. Lyddie later saves Brigid from Mr. Marsden's attack. **Mr. Marsden**, the mill overseer, is a shady character who uses his power over the young workers to force his attentions upon them. When Lyddie stops his attack on the defenseless Brigid, Marsden wreaks his revenge by firing Lyddie. But Lyddie retaliates and threatens Marsden by saying she will tell his wife about his behavior if he fires Brigid.

Lyddie's brother, **Charlie Worthen**, moves in with the Phinney family in Lowell, Massachusetts, and works at the mill there. Because the Phinneys have no children, they treat Charlie as if he were their son. It is Charlie who gives Lyddie the letter from **Luke Stevens**, the Quaker boy who asks for Lyddie's hand in marriage. Luke is a gentle young man. Lyddie sees in him a person she could love and marry, and she hopes he loves her enough to wait.

Lyddie's mother, **Mattie M. Worthen**, loses her spirit and will to survive when her husband leaves her with Lyddie, Charlie, and two other children in search of what she calls "vain riches." She becomes so desperate to leave the Virginia farm and move in with her sister, Clarissa, that she resorts to hiring Lyddie and Charlie out to work jobs. She shows her insensitivity by deserting her children, leaving them only a note of explanation.

Further Reading

Authors and Artists for Young Adults. Vol. 1. Detroit: Gale Research, 1989.

Berger, Laura Standley, ed. *Twentieth-Century Children's Writers.* 4th ed. Detroit: St. James, 1995

———, ed. *Twentieth-Century Young Adult Writers.* 1st ed. Detroit: St. James, 1994.

Children's Literature Review. Vol. 7. Detroit: Gale Research, 1984.

Estes, Glenn E. *American Writers for Children since 1960: Fiction.* Vol. 52 of *Dictionary of Literary Biography.* Detroit: Gale Research, 1986.

Holtze, Sally Holmes, ed. *Twentieth-Century Children's Writers.* 2nd ed. New York: St. Martin's, 1983.

Something about the Author. Vols. 13, 53. Detroit: Gale Research, 1978, 1988.

Ward, Martha, ed. *Authors of Books for Young People.* 3rd ed. Metuchen, NJ: Scarecrow, 1990.

Gary Paulsen

1939-, American young adult novelist

Dogsong

(young adult novel, 1985)

PLOT: *Dogsong* is a mythical tale of tribute to the magnificent sled dogs of the north country and the strength and perseverance of those who raise, train, and drive them. It is also the story of how a young boy rediscovers the ancient ways of his people as he treks through northern Alaska. Russel Susskit is fascinated by the sled dogs belonging to blind, old Oogruk. These are the only dogs left in their village, for now the men use snowmobiles to hunt seal and caribou. Fourteen-year-old Russel hates the snowmobiles and almost everything else that is modern. His father recognizes his discontent and suggests that the boy talk to wise Oogruk for "his songs are always true."

Oogruk lives as the ancient Eskimos did. Russel soon moves in with the old man and begins to learn the ways of his ancestors. Oogruk allows him to make practice runs with the dogsled. Under Oogruk's instruction and using his old weapons, Russel begins hunting for food with the dogs. On one occasion, after bagging a deer, he becomes lost on the ice for days but returns safely. Soon, the boy begins to "hear his song"—which, for an Eskimo, means finding one's identity. One morning when Russel goes out to hunt for seal, old Oogruk says he will accompany him. Realizing his death is near, Oogruk tells Russel to head north alone with the dogs to find himself and his song. Russel starts his journey, but when he returns he finds the old man sitting on the ice, dead, though his face is frozen in a peaceful smile.

Russel's search for his identity takes him across tundra, mountains, and ice fields. During his trek, he has a series of dreams—involving a woman, two small children, and a hunter—in which he sees himself as an early ancestor. Russel immediately understands that the man, who has slain a mammoth, is himself. His dreams recur in greater detail as he struggles to survive—aided by an old stone lamp he has unearthed—in the harsh, frigid climate. After surviving a two-day storm, he dreams that the hunter's family is starving. Then he finds Nancy, a young pregnant girl, near death in the snow. While he waits for her to regain consciousness in his tent, Russel has a final dream in which he realizes he is an extension of the hunter. Nancy survives and explains that after the missionaries rejected her because of her pregnancy, she went out on the tundra to die.

When starvation appears imminent, Russel becomes the hunter in his dream and kills a great bear. Soon after, Nancy's child is stillborn, and when she does not fully regain her health, Russel knows they must seek medical attention in a coastal village. As they leave the tundra, Russel is satisfied that he has found his song. He has saved both Nancy and himself; through his actions, he has rediscovered the old ways and has survived life in the unforgiving Arctic.

CHARACTERS: The author, who has run the famed Iditarod, the 1,049-mile dogsled race across Alaska, writes with profound respect and love for the far north. The Eskimo practice of assigning a "song" is similar to finding one's identity. *Dogsong* was named a Newbery Honor Book in 1986.

Russel Susskit is a fourteen-year-old Alaskan boy drawn to the ways of his ancestors. He hates the "conveniences" of modern life: the snowmobiles that the hunters ride, the oil that fuels the snowmobiles, the standard government house in which he and his father live (his mother having run off with a trapper years ago), and the cigarettes that make his father cough. He looks with longing at the sled dogs, growing fat from inactivity, that belong to old Oogruk. Russel wishes he could take them out across the ice fields, leading them as hunters of old once did. Under Oogruk's guidance, Russel does begin to hunt with the dogs. Oogruk takes him back in time to the old ways, and he learns. His dissatisfaction and unhappiness disappear as Russel moves in with Oogruk and finds his song. He learns to be a leader of sled dogs, and when Oogruk insists that the boy leave him on the tundra, he does so sadly. "I will remember you," Russel says. Oogruk's teachings remain with Russel, enabling him to interpret his dreams on the tundra and accept his own song, his own identity.

Oogruk, ancient and blind, follows the ways of his ancestors. He tells Russel of the days when the hunters had a song for everything, even for the dogs. Now, he relates, no one knows the songs any more. Oogruk understands Russel's growing love for the primitive ways of the north, and when he realizes his death is near, he sends the boy off alone, confident that ancient teachings and the boy's strength of purpose will protect him, leading him to safety and maturity.

On his journey of self-discovery, Russel meets **Nancy**, a young Eskimo girl who is wise beyond her years. Pregnant and alone, she accepts the rejection of the missionaries who cared for her and resigns herself to death. When her child is born dead, she screams at Russel to take away the lifeless body before she sees it. Nancy says little to Russel about his help and protection through their journey, yet as they near the coastal village, her despair lessens, and she looks ahead with hope.

Hatchet

(young adult novel, 1987)

PLOT: Thirteen-year-old Brian Robeson is angry because his mother divorced his father. He is also upset because he has just seen her sitting in a station wagon kissing a strange man. Getting ready to spend the entire summer in the Canadian north woods where his father, an engineer, is working in the oil fields, Brian can't wait to tell his dad "The Secret" about his mother. Just before he leaves, his mother gives him a hatchet for his scout belt as a vacation gift, but Brian thinks it's a stupid, useless present.

Flying north from New York state, Brian is the only passenger in the Cessna. He enjoys the trip, especially when the pilot lets him take the controls. The fun ends abruptly, however, when the pilot has a heart attack and dies. The plane crashes into a lake and sinks, yet Brian survives. Forced to leave the plane, he is completely alone in the wilderness with nothing but the clothes on his back and his hatchet. He has no idea of where he is, although he surmises that the plane veered off course during its last moments of descent, meaning searchers will not be looking in his current location.

For nearly two months, Brian must use all his intelligence and will to survive. Untrained in any outdoor activities, the boy learns by trial and error. His mother's hatchet becomes very valuable, aiding him in building a shelter, finding food, and defending himself from wild animals. But when a tornado whips across the lake, Brian very nearly gives up in despair, until he notices that the winds have pushed the tail of the plane out of the water. Although he dreads returning to the plane where the pilot is still strapped into the seat, Brian remembers that a survival kit was part of the plane's equipment. The kit includes a transmitter that does not seem to work. He fiddles with it awhile and then lays it aside, unaware that he has inadvertently activated the homing signal.

Soon after, a rescue plane lands on the lake. Brian is rescued, but he is no longer the same boy. Tougher, wiser, and older, he still hopes his parents will resolve their differences, but he decides not to tell his father about "The Secret."

CHARACTERS: This is a basic story of survival, showing great love and respect for the outdoors and nature. **Brian Robeson** is an average, likeable thirteen-year-old who is understandably upset and angry about his parents' recent divorce. When he sees his mother in a car kissing a strange man, he becomes even more furious. Rather than confront her with his feelings, he vows silent revenge by telling his father when he arrives at the oil fields.

When the plane crashes and Brian is left alone, he is terrified and almost paralyzed with fear. Little by little, however, Brian's instinct for survival surfaces. Although officially untrained in wilderness survival techniques, he finds his mother's hatchet gift very valuable. Through various experiences, such as getting sick on wild berries and running into a wild porcupine, Brian learns to survive on his own. When a storm pushes the tail of the plane above the lake's surface, Brian steels himself to enter the craft for the survival kit, even though he knows he must crawl over the pilot's corpse to do so.

At the end of fifty-four days in the wilderness, the rescued Brian is much different from the young boy who went north to tell his father "The Secret." In his place is a taller and tougher teenager, more thoughtful, more confident, and much wiser than before.

Mr. and **Mrs. Robeson** are average, likeable parents who, despite their own personal troubles, are deeply involved with their son and are overjoyed when he is found alive. Their intense happiness over his return convinces Brian that a reconciliation will follow. Although it is still his dearest wish, Brian soon realizes that his parents will not re-marry and that telling his father "The Secret" would be immature and hurtful to all.

The Haymeadow

(young adult novel, 1992)

PLOT: Fourteen-year-old John Barron comes from a long line of John Barrons. His great-grandfather, the original John Barron, has become a legend in his family's history, journeying west and launching a sheep ranching operation in the Wyoming mountains. A six-shooter still at his side when he died at the age of 92, he ruled his ranching wilderness with uncompromising toughness. Ever since, the men of the Barron clan have been tending the sheep. John's father, John Barron Sr., takes after the family tradition; he speaks little and shuns people, living only for his ranching work since John's mother died many years before.

This year young John must take the sheep on the annual three-day trek to a Wyoming mountain meadow and remain with them for the summer. Although one of the hired ranch hands usually performs this solitary duty, neither Tink nor Horace Cawley can go this year (circumstances at the ranch prevent any of the available adults from making the trip). Because young John is a Barron and it is expected of him, he must go, even though the prospect fills him with unspeakable dread.

Horace Cawley leads John, a horse, four Border collies, and six thousand sheep to the haymeadow. Like John's father, Cawley doesn't talk much. Since John doesn't ask many questions, he feels unprepared for life alone after Cawley heads back to the ranch. John's next human contact will be in six weeks, when someone will return with provisions.

John's troubles begin almost immediately: he kills a rattlesnake that has attacked a lamb; a skunk sprays him; one of the dogs injures a paw; a bobcat causes a stampede, scattering the supplies; and a mountain storm causes a flood that overturns the trailer in which John is living, but he recovers most of his equipment, with the exception of his rifle. When a pack of coyotes appears, John knows his rifle may make the difference between survival and a brutal death, both for himself and the herd. Eventually, he finds the gun and keeps the coyotes away. Throughout his ordeals, John begins to enjoy the beauty and serenity of the meadow, until a black bear attacks the sheep. The bear claws John on the shoulder and wounds one of the dogs. John loses sixteen sheep but saves the dog and nurses her back to health despite his own severe wound.

On the forty-seventh day, John's father arrives. He is soon amazed and proud, learning of his son's triumph over his life-threatening experiences. His concern and relief at John's survival allows him to respond emotionally. He tells John how much of a bully his great-grandfather really was and how much he loved and misses John's mother. John and his father establish a new relationship, which they hope to strengthen when his father decides to remain with him in the haymeadow for the rest of the summer.

CHARACTERS: This is an exciting story of survival and coming of age. John is torn between hero worship for his father and his ancestors and self-doubt about his own ability to measure up. The complex relationship between father and son is well drawn and satisfying in its conclusion.

John Barron understandably suffers from a lack of confidence in his ability to be as tough as his long line of noble ancestors. He respects his father, but they have not had a close relationship. A sensitive boy, John wishes to fulfill his father's expectations but constantly believes that he can't. Even the paralyzing fear he feels at spending the summer alone in the haymeadow is not enough to make him share his doubts with his father. In the haymeadow, however, confronted with situations that threaten the sheep and even his own life, John faces his responsibilities with determination and strength of purpose. He finds courage and maturity within himself, not in the stories of heroic ancestors.

John's father, **John Barron, Sr.**, is in a sense much like his son. Suffering for years in silence over the loss of his wife, he has retreated inward. He has allowed the great legend of his ancestors to live on, although he knows that his grandfather was in actuality a ruthless bully. Only when he sees the courage with which his son faces adversity alone does he allow his true feelings to show.

Further Reading

Authors and Artists for Young Adults. Vol. 2. Detroit: Gale Research, 1989.

Berger, Laura Standley, ed. *Twentieth-Century Young Adult Writers.* 1st ed. Detroit: St. James, 1994.

Collier, Laurie, and Joyce Nakamura, eds. *Major Authors and Illustrators for Children & Young Adults.* Detroit: Gale Research, 1993.

Gallo, Donald R. *Speaking for Ourselves: Autobiographical Sketches by Notable Authors of Books for Young Adults.* Urbana, IL: National Council of Teachers of English, 1990.

Handy, Alice Evans. "An Interview with Gary Paulsen." *Book Report* 10 (May/June 1991).

Something about the Author. Vol. 54. Detroit: Gale Research, 1989.

Weidt, Maryann N. "Gary Paulsen: A Sentry for Peace." *Voice of Youth Advocates* 9 (August/October 1986).

Richard Peck

1934-, American novelist

Are You in the House Alone?

(young adult novel, 1976)

PLOT: Gail Osburne is a capable, level-headed, junior attending high school in Oldfield Village, a western Connecticut town within commuting distance of New York City. One day, without warning, her comfortable life changes. She becomes aware that she is being followed, begins receiving breathy phone calls when she is alone, and is threatened with sexual abuse by obscene notes left in her school locker. Gail is confused as to where she can turn for help, particularly after she accidently discovers that her father has been fired from his job and her parents are too preoccupied with this problem, she thinks, to talk to her. Along with her friend, Alison Bremer, Gail goes to her school counselor, but she gets no real support. Mentally, she reviews all her acquaintances who might be suspects, including Alison's boyfriend, Phil Lawver, the spoiled scion of the town's wealthiest and most influential family.

One night while Gail is babysitting for her neighbor Mrs. Montgomery, someone rings the doorbell. It is Phil Lawver, who demands sex from her. She tries to elude him but, after a struggle, she is knocked unconscious and raped. Recovering in the hospital, Gail is unable to get sufficient support to press charges, and the police chief believes she was really the seducer. Gail's mother wants to bury the incident, and the family lawyer feels she has insufficient evidence to win a case. With the help of others, including her drama teacher, the flamboyant Dovina Malevich, Gail returns to school. She remains silent about her trauma, not wanting to tell her boyfriend, Steve Pastorini, about it because she doesn't want him to seek revenge. But she does talk to Madam Malevich and Alison, whom Gail feels she must warn about Phil. Alison rebuffs her, but within weeks there is another tragic incident involving another student, Sonia Slanek, who is also beaten up and raped. Though the incident is again hushed up, it seems that this time there is substantial evidence against Phil, who suddenly disappears. A shroud of silence settles over the town. Sonia and her parents move away, and Gail, though scarred and troubled by her trauma, realizes she must continue with her life.

CHARACTERS: Gail Osburne is the narrator and protagonist of this novel which explores the nightmare of rape and its aftermath. Gail is a sensible, intelligent girl who is independent in her thinking and actions. Although always alert to other people's feelings, she realizes that she must assume responsibility for her own welfare, and therefore she has begun practicing birth control when she has sex with her boyfriend, Steve Pastorini. She has also become somewhat financially independent by regularly babysitting for **Mrs. Montgomery**, a kindly neighbor with two children, who enjoys the community center dances every Saturday night. Gail exhibits unusual self-sufficiency and maturity for her age. She always tries to be an obedient and respectful daughter, but when her mother makes unfair and incorrect decisions, such as objecting to her liaison with Steve and, after the rape, suggesting that she leave town, Gail has sufficient strength and wisdom to stand up for herself. Her practical, sensible nature is shown when, for example, she accepts the lawyer's decision not to prosecute Phil. Later she exhibits uncommon courage and endurance in returning to school after her attack and facing her classmates without being able to tell the truth. She is a loyal friend who, in spite of rebuffs and cruel taunts from Alison, continues to warn her friend about Phil. Though scarred and sickened by her experiences, she never resorts to self-pity or bitterness. Gail is a survivor, an admirable, decent girl who deserves respect.

Gail's boyfriend, **Steve Pastorini**, is the school's "bustass," an overachiever who always leads his class academically. Steve's family has been in the plumbing business for years, which places him several rungs below Gail on the social ladder. But, like his family, Steve is respectable, a hard worker, and well liked. He is a serious, articulate scholar whose interests include classical music and fine literature. Though attentive to Gail and a dependable friend, his school work and obligations to his family come first. Steve is oblivious to the fact that his relationship with Gail is deteriorating, although Gail has sensed this. Because of this situation and the desire not to place Steve in the unlikely role of avenger, Gail does not reveal to him the identity of her assailant.

Lydia and **Otis Lawver** represent the pinnacle of society in Oldfield Village. They and the generations of Lawvers before them have wielded great influence in town matters and have been the arbiters of taste. **Phil Lawver**, their son, is handsome, athletic and overindulged. Tall, blond, and self-satisfied, he conceals a sick, perverted mind obsessed with sex. Because he and Alison have not slept together, he regards her as pure and untouchable, but, having discovered by spying on them that Gail and Steve have sex, he believes in his twisted and distorted way that Gail is promiscuous and a suitable target for his advances. He is so psychologically disturbed that when confronted by Gail after her return to school he shows no remorse or understanding of the enormity of his crime. It is hinted at the conclusion of the novel that Phil is receiving long-overdue psychological help.

Gail's parents, Mr. and Mrs. Osburne, are a study in contrasts. **Neal Osburne**, a New York architect, has recently lost his job, but he doesn't tell Gail for fear of worrying her unduly. Though somewhat preoccupied with his own problems, he shows remarkable understanding and compassion toward his daughter. He respects Gail's decision not to seek revenge on the Lawvers and supplies the support and security that helps Gail survive her ordeal. On the other hand, **Mrs. Osburne** is a snob who sometimes seems more intent on maintaining her social position than helping her daughter. She objects to Steve solely because his father is a plumber and, after the attack, tries to avoid confrontation and possible embarrassment by suggesting that Gail visit a relative. Though bound by superficial middle-class values, she shows some initiative by entering the real estate business to help the family's sagging finances.

Gail's best friend is **Alison Bremer**, a flighty, insecure girl who is so flattered at being wealthy Phil Lawver's girlfriend that she refuses to acknowledge any of his faults and savagely turns against Gail when she is told the truth. A fair-weather friend, she fails to support Gail during any of her crises. At the end of the book, their friendship comes to an end.

Other characters include the flamboyant, unconventional student, **Sonia Slanek**, a loner who dresses in gaudy clothes, wears heavy makeup, and seems to live in a world of her own. She emulates her iconoclastic, bohemian father, who is a sculptor. Her uninhibited, carefree behavior targets her as Phil's second victim. **Dovina Malevich** is the seemingly ageless drama teacher at Gail's school. Through Sonia's sleuthing, it is revealed that Madam Malevich was once a celebrated silent screen vamp. Her unexpected compassion and understanding help Gail accept the reality of her situation after the rape.

When he visits Gail while she is in the hospital, the town's unnamed **Police Chief** exhibits the infuriating, macho attitude that girls lead boys on and get what they deserve. His misleading, insinuating questions trap Gail, and she realizes that, in his eyes, she is the guilty one and not the victim. When she names Phil Lawver as her attacker, his response is "Honey, you're just asking for trouble."

Father Figure

(young adult novel, 1978)

PLOT: Jim Atwater was nine years old when his parents' marriage ended and his father left for Florida. Jim, along with his mother, older sister, Lorraine, and baby brother, Byron, moved in with Grandmother Livingston, an aristocratic, crusty dowager who owns a large house in Brooklyn Heights, a fashionable section of New York City. In time, Lorraine married and moved to Germany. Eight years after the divorce, Jim suffers another loss. Unable to bear any longer the dreadful pain of her terminal cancer, his mother commits suicide. At the funeral, Jim and Byron, now eight, see a stranger among the mourners—their father.

After Byron is mugged on the street and his collarbone is broken, Grandmother decides to send Jim and Byron to Miami to spend the summer with their father, Howard Atwater. On the plane, Jim meets attractive, wealthy Adele Parker and later has a disappointing visit to her home in Coral Gables (he discovers she is too much of a snob for him). Jim's father lives in a tiny two-bedroom bungalow close to the huge apartment building in which he works selling condominiums. Jim bears a deep resentment for his father's supposed desertion and therefore relations between the two are tense and unsure at first. But the tension is eased by the presence of Marietta, an outgoing, cheerful waitress in the local diner with whom Howard appears to have a special relationship.

When Byron begins to shift allegiances from his brother to his father, Jim becomes jealous and tempers flare. Later, Jim, with adolescent fervor, misinterprets Marietta's thoughtfulness and concern and falls passionately in love with her. He is firmly but compassionately rebuffed. Slowly and painfully, Jim comes to terms with himself and his father. At the end of the summer, Jim accedes to Byron's wish to stay on with his father, while Jim makes plans to return to Brooklyn for his senior year in school. At the airport, after Marietta kisses him a tender goodbye, Jim recalls the parting with his father for whom he now feels a tentative friendship.

CHARACTERS: The narrator is **Jim Atwater**, a seventeen-year-old, attractive young man who is bright, observant, and articulate. Jim is a popular and well-liked junior at a private academy for boys in the Bronx. He is extremely sensitive to others' feelings and is so anxious to become the man of the house and assume more than his share of responsibilities that he often denies himself time to have fun. He admires the genuine, sincere qualities in people and dislikes the phony, artificial values personified by many of his Grandmother's friends and later by Adele Parker. A decent, caring person, he donates his time to help others, including doing volunteer coaching after school. Not understanding all the particulars of his parents' divorce, he blames his father and holds a burning resentment and bitterness toward this man whom he feels has deserted and betrayed his family. Jim feels particularly responsible for his younger brother, Byron, a lonely, sensitive child whom he protects and for whom he tries to be a substitute father. Only slowly is he able to let go of his brother without resentment and allow a small place in his heart for his father. During his path toward maturity, Jim experiences the pangs of unrequited puppy love, learns about the corrosive power of jealousy, and begins to understand the many-sided nature of truth.

Jim's brother, the precocious **Byron Atwater**, is an eight-year-old marvel. Intelligent, independent, and imaginative, he has learned to hide his feelings and often escapes into his own private world. Overly sensitive and impressionable, he rarely allows his emotional vulnerability and inner turmoil to show. When it does, as in a bed-wetting episode after his mother's death, he feels ashamed and guilty. Byron is a courageous and adaptable youngster who showers the love and attention denied him in his family situation onto the pets that he befriends, including his cat, Nub. Byron endures suffering and disappointments with a maturity beyond his years and tolerates the pain and discomfort of a broken collarbone without complaint. Showing his ingenuity and resourcefulness, he learns to use his left hand when his right is in a cast. Byron adapts to Florida much better than Jim and becomes fascinated with the flora and fauna around him. When he wisely allows Nub his freedom, though he knows he is losing his pet, he foreshadows the decision that Jim will have to make concerning Byron's own independence. Jim says of his remarkable brother that "anything interests him" and that he regards his life and problems "with unbelievable detachment."

The boys' father, **Howard Atwater,** was once a struggling business executive, who, since the collapse of his marriage, has given up the corporate life for a job in real estate and a more laid-back existence in Florida. Now forty-six, he is described as "a stocky guy, with blondish hair going a little white at the temples." Howard is an honest, straightforward man who consents to having his two sons visit him with an understandable amount of hesitancy and apprehension. Accommodating and unselfish by nature, he makes sacrifices so his sons can be comfortable and feel wanted. He displays remarkable wisdom and insight in his interpersonal relations, knowing instinctively the needs, problems, and feelings of both his sons. His tolerance and patience regarding Jim's often confrontational behavior are admirable. Howard is a realist who makes no apologies for his modest life and lack of achievement, but his maturity, common sense, and integrity make him a memorable father figure.

Grace Livingston, the boys' grandmother, is a stolid, seemingly unperturbable pillar of old Brooklyn Heights society who lives in a century-old building that reflects her own out-of-date lifestyle. Crusty and dignified in manner, she believes in keeping up appearances at all costs. A distant, independent person used to servants and the society of a disappearing gentility, she prefers the company of her aged cronies to that of her grandsons. Though not unkind toward her charges, she is unable to give them the attention and love that they desperately need. This, combined with her inaccessibility and preoccupation with protocol and outdated social conventions, creates a communication gap that is irreparable. Always aware of propriety and correctness, she has become a stoic who stifles her emotions and hides her inner feelings for fear of being considered vulgar and unrefined. She neither comforts her grandsons nor shows any public grief after her daughter's death. Her snobbishness, class consciousness, and stubborn demeanor helped ruin her daughter's marriage and separate the boys from their father. Although tough, sarcastic, and domineering, she is sincere in trying to fulfill her familial responsibilities properly.

Both Jim and his father are in love with **Marietta**, the earthy, unaffected waitress/manager of the local diner. With her beautiful, heart-shaped face, black hair, and slim body, she presents an attractive, youthful appearance. Cheerful, witty, and outgoing, she is always attentive and responsive to Howard and his family. The ninth child from a poor family in Dothan, Alabama, Marietta is a hard worker who realizes the importance of kindness and understanding in relationships. She shows remarkable insight into human nature as well as an unfailing capability to help others. A great cook and ardent nature lover, Marietta hopes one day to achieve independence, security, and a patch of land to grow her own garden. Uncomplicated, sincere, and generous, Marietta is also a realist who respects herself and values her independence and self-sufficiency. As Jim's father says about her, "She's the most naive person I've ever met, and yet full of wisdom."

Adele Parker is the attractive girl ("a true knockout") that Jim meets on the plane to Miami. The same age as Jim, she attends a very fashionable girls' school in New York that admits only "the right people." Snobbish and spoiled, she emphasizes wealth and social position when judging friends. After their first date, both realize that they are not suited for one another. Jim unconsciously compares Adele's superficial, shallow attitudes to the honest, meaningful ones of Marietta.

Remembering the Good Times

(young adult novel, 1985)

PLOT: This novel of love, loss, and remembrance is narrated by Buck Mendenhall and tells of his friendship with two classmates: the independent Kate Lucas, who is living with her great-grandmother, outspoken Polly Prior, and often-absent mother, Janis, and, secondly, Trav Kirby, a sensitive, highly intelligent boy from a well-to-do family. Buck first meets Kate one summer when he is visiting his divorced father, a construction worker who lives in a trailer in suburban Slocum County. Two years later, when Buck has moved in permanently with his dad, he enters the eighth grade and once again encounters Kate. Both are impressed with Trav Kirby, a fellow classmate, when he uses psychology to quiet the rampaging class bully, Skeeter Calhoun. The three become close friends and hang out at Kate's farmhouse, often playing card games with Polly. They rarely see Trav's parents, a wealthy couple of overachievers who seem to have little communication with their son. In ninth grade, Trav and Kate rescue Buck from the clutches of a wisecracking cheerleader, Rusty Hazenfield. Trav's worrying nature and continuous state of anxiety send out warning signals that his friends underestimate and simply attribute to the growing-up process, so they are dumbfounded when Trav is caught shoplifting and sent away to spend the summer on a farm. Upon his return, Trav learns of several disturbing events, including Polly's decision to sell the farm he had considered his second home. Although trying to hide his feelings, he becomes more troubled and anxious. One day, he gives Kate and Buck his prized possessions; shortly afterwards, he commits suicide by hanging himself in Polly's orchard. The community is stunned by his death. At a public meeting to determine the cause, Polly Prior speaks of her love for Trav. Her gentle words release the pent-up grief inside Buck and Kate and they weep openly. In time, wounds heal and the two friends are able to speak of their dear friend and remember fondly the good times they shared.

CHARACTERS: The narrator, **Buck Mendenhall**, is an outgoing, perceptive, average youngster who tends to underestimate his own abilities and qualities. Although his parents' divorce has left scars,

Buck manages to weather these problems and others with his cheery, realistic attitude. He is sensitive to the feelings of others and appreciates the kindnesses and consideration shown him by his adored friends and loving father. He is self-effacing to the point of not appreciating his own worth. Being a typical teenager filled with doubts and questions, he often feels inferior to the brainy Trav and mature Kate, sometimes incorrectly thinking he is not wanted. Being unaware of his own attractiveness and winning personality, Buck is easily seduced by the attention of people like Rusty. He is a decent, high-minded, honorable youngster who believes in fair play, honesty, and showing compassion toward others. Buck is also not afraid to fight for his principles, even when he knows he will be beaten up, as when he must retrieve his father's construction hat from Skeeter. Like many teenaged boys, Buck is interested in football, girls, and getting a driver's license. His greatest leap toward maturity occurs when he accepts Trav's death and recognizes that loss is a natural part of life.

Buck's friend, **Kate Lucas**, is a spunky, outspoken girl who is mature far beyond her years. Before reaching her teens, she had already assumed the responsibility of looking after her great-grandmother and taking care of the house. Kate is an astute and insightful observer of people who does not judge others harshly. For example, she tolerates the loud, embarrassing behavior of her mother without bitterness or hostility. However, she is impatient with superficial behavior. An attractive girl and loyal friend who has many talents, including acting, Kate, like Buck, is conscientious, hardworking, and willing to fight for her principles. A believer in justice, she enjoys seeing Skeeter punished for his misdeeds. Though at first Kate refuses to accept Trav's death, she eventually realizes that she can do nothing to change it.

Buck and Kate's best friend is the scholarly, bespectacled, deeply troubled **Trav Kirby**. Trav is a highly intelligent, sensitive fifteen-year-old who is a perfectionist and compulsive worrier. At one point Buck says, "Trav worries about stuff that hasn't happened. He worries about things he can't do anything about." Though a straight-"A" student in the ninth grade, he begins fretting about his SATs and is deeply troubled by his class schedule, the lack of challenging courses, and his less-than-inspiring teachers. The future and its uncertainties terrify him, as do change and disorder. Trav pathetically clings to the security of the past by retaining his collection of toys from his childhood. Though once diagnosed as being hyperactive, he has refused to take any medication and instead has suppressed his feelings and emotions. Trav is careful about his appearance and always dresses in tailored pants and button-down shirts. He hates violence and injustice, avoids confrontations, and is highly competitive. Gentle, loyal, and trustworthy, Trav considers his friendship with Buck and Kate to be very important and dear to him. When he is caught shoplifting, Kate wisely realizes that "he just wanted to shift the burden [of being himself], to stop having to be responsible." Unfortunately, his cries for help are not heeded, and he hangs himself.

When Kate's great-grandmother, **Polly Prior**, introduces herself to Buck, she says, "I'm the third oldest woman in Slocum Township. But when it comes to meanness I'm Number One. I'm too mean to die." Though outspoken, blunt, and abrupt, she is far from the crotchety, disagreeable grouch she pretends to be. Wheelchair-bound, she retains her youthful attitude by associating with Kate and her friends, whom she secretly adores. Though sometimes eccentric, and not above cheating outrageously at cards, she has an understanding heart and a generous, sharing nature, even though she would be the last to admit it. Polly Prior's golden hour is when she addresses the public meeting after Trav's death and straightforwardly tells people not to be filled with hatred and recriminations but, instead, remember the wonderful young man Trav was.

Kate's mother and Buck's dad are studies in contrast. **Mr. Mendenhall** is a hardworking, conscientious construction worker who is always concerned about Buck's welfare, schooling, and happiness. He is a good provider, an understanding father, and, in Kate's eyes, a good-looking hunk. Kate's mother, **Janis**, on the other hand, is an embarrassment. Loud, vulgar, and garish, she is more interested in having a good time than in taking care of Kate and Polly.

Trav's father and mother are as driven and stressed-out as their son. **Mr. Kirby**, a prominent lawyer, is a workaholic intent on making money. Though a newcomer to the community, he soon becomes president of the school board through his intelligence, drive, handsome appearance, and polished manners. **Mrs. Kirby** is equally refined, gracious, and attractive. Neither realizes the pressure to achieve that they have placed on their son, and, at the public hearing after Trav's death, Mr. Kirby blames the confused school environment and unchallenging courses for his son's death.

Rusty Hagenfield is a flashy, wisecracking, selfish, but very attractive newcomer to Buck's school. Recently arrived from California, where she has become "practically burned out" on guys, she adopts a superior, overly confident, and scornful attitude that attracts the naive Buck. Equally obnoxious is the three friends' chief adversary, gorilla-like **Skeeter Calhoun**. He is the class bully who loves to terrorize everyone, including weak teachers. Skeeter shamelessly steals and vandalizes property and, at one point, punches Buck into unconsciousness. Kate engineers a plot that teaches Skeeter a much needed lesson.

Further Reading

Authors and Artists for Young Adults. Vol. 1. Gale Research, 1989.

Berger, Laura Standley, ed. *Twentieth-Century Young Adult Writers.* 1st ed. Detroit: St. James, 1995.

Chevalier, Tracy, ed. *Twentieth-Century Children's Writers.* 3rd ed. Detroit: St. James, 1989.

Contemporary Literary Criticism. Vol. 21. Detroit: Gale Research, 1982.

Gallo, Donald. *Presenting Richard Peck.* Boston: Twayne, 1989.

Holtze, Sally Holmes, ed. *Fifth Book of Junior Authors and Illustrators.* New York: H. W. Wilson, 1983.

Peck, Richard. "Love Is Not Enough." In *Journal of Youth Services in Libraries* 4 (fall 1990): 35-39.

Something about the Author. Vols. 18, 53. Detroit: Gale Research, 1980, 1988.

Sutton, Roger. "A Conversation with Richard Peck." In *School Library Journal* 36 (June 1990): 36-40.

Robert Newton Peck

1928-, American novelist

A Day No Pigs Would Die

(young adult novel, 1972)

PLOT: Thirteen-year-old Robert Peck is the only living son of a Vermont Shaker family in the early years of the nineteenth century. His grown sisters are scattered about the state, and he lives on the family farm with his mother and father and his mother's sister, Aunt Carrie. Rob's father slaughters pigs for a living.

One day, Rob runs away from school because Edward Thatcher makes fun of his clothes during recess break. He climbs the ridge and comes upon Apron, the big Holstein cow that belongs to their neighbor, Ben Tanner. Apron is in distress, having trouble delivering her calf. Not only does Rob help in this process, but he also yanks a goiter out of Apron's throat to save her. Apron, however, is anything but happy over this. She bites Rob's arm and runs down the ridge dragging him along. When Rob regains consciousness, Tanner is carrying him to the Peck farm. Rob's arm is so torn up that it requires his mother to sew some stitches into it. In gratitude for his help, and the fact that Apron delivered two strong bull calves, Tanner gives the boy a baby pig, the first animal he has ever owned. He names her Pinky.

With his father's help, Rob builds a pen for Pinky and delights in caring for her, envisioning the wonderful brood of piglets she will produce for him. When it is time for Tanner to show off his prize bull calves at the big fair in Rutland, he asks permission to take Rob with him. The boy will help Tanner with the work at the fair, but he can also show his own pig, Pinky. Rob has the time of his life at the fair, and Pinky wins a ribbon for the best behaved pig.

But as time goes on, it is clear that Pinky will not produce the great brood of piglets that Rob envisioned. His father fears that Pinky is barren, as she indeed turns out to be. This is a death sentence on a working farm, where there is little money or anything else to waste. Pinky will cost too much just to keep as a pet. Rob is heartbroken when his father decides to kill Pinky, but he knows it must be done, and he knows his father will be quick and merciful. When it is over, Rob kisses his father's bloody hand to show that even though it hurts him, he understands why his father had to kill Pinky.

This tragedy is soon followed by another when Rob's father dies and, at the age of thirteen, the boy assumes the role of man of the family. Some months before his father's untimely death, the boy learns of his father's illness and that he doesn't have long to live. Rob immediately says that he will quit school and take care of the farm, but his father is adamant. Rob is to "get all the teaching he can hold." Then his father warns him that he must become the man of the family even if he is only thirteen years old. He must care for the farm and see to the welfare of his mother and Aunt Carrie. At his father's funeral, Rob delivers a short eulogy. When Tanner—who asks that Rob call him Ben now that they are two men who are good friends—says he sounds sort of like his father, Rob replies, "I aim to, Ben."

CHARACTERS: Earnest, hard-working, and compassionate, **Rob Peck** is an endearing lad. He loves and respects his parents, especially his hard-working, quiet father, whom Rob tries to emulate. Although he understands that his Shaker household is a world without frills, he is nearly overcome with joy when neighbor Tanner gives him the baby pig for his own. It is the first thing he ever really wanted and owned. When the terrible realization comes that Pinky must be killed because she can't earn her keep on their working farm, Rob's grief is almost overwhelming. But he forces himself to aid his father in the slaughter, and then he breaks down and cries. His father tells him that being a man means doing what has to be done, and for the first and only time in his life, Rob sees his father shed tears. At the age of thirteen Rob must become the man of the family. This new role is one that Rob Peck does not want, but with a new dignity he accepts it and quietly takes over the leadership of the household.

In his own tart and proud way, Rob's father, **Haven Peck**, is a loving man. He cares deeply about his family and his work. The closeness, love, and respect between father and son are evident throughout the novel. Rob's father wants his son to be a good family man and to get as much education as he can. When Haven Peck becomes ill and Rob offers to quit school to take care of the farm, he insists that Rob stay in school. Especially poignant is an incident that shows Rob's coming maturity and the father's willingness to admit to a mistake. One day, Rob's father and neighbor Ira Long try to "weasel" Long's little dog, Hussy. To "weasel" means to teach her to hate weasels so that she will keep the farm clear of them and they won't raid the hen house. But the forced fight between Hussy and the weasel seriously injures the dog. Rob's father ends up having to shoot Hussy. After this, he says, "I swear by the Book of Shaker and all that's holy, I will never again weasel a dog. Even if I lose every chicken I own."

Ben Tanner is a typical "good neighbor" of rural Vermont during the early years of the century. A man of few words, he keeps to himself and respects others' privacy. But when Rob saves Tanner's cow, Apron, he repays that deed with the piglet that Rob names Pinky. Because he likes the boy's character, Tanner offers to take him to the fair where he can show Pinky off and compete for a ribbon. After Haven Peck's death, Tanner treats thirteen-year-old Rob with the same respect and friendship that one man gives to another who is his equal.

Mama Peck and **Aunt Carrie** are background characters in this story of the bond between father and son. When Rob is hurt saving Tanner's cow, Mama tends his arm with loving firmness. Aunt Carrie is fretful over the loss of the boy's trousers, which got ruined in the tussle with Apron. After the death of Haven Peck, both women silently recognize the maturity of young Rob. They hold themselves with pride and dignity, accepting their loss and the new shift in responsibility.

Further Reading

Authors and Artists for Young Adults. Vol. 3. Detroit: Gale Research, 1990.

Berger, Laura Standley, ed. *Twentieth-Century Children's Writers.* 4th ed. Detroit: St. James, 1994.

Contemporary Literary Criticism. Vol. 17. Detroit: Gale Research, 1981.

Holtze, Sally Holmes, ed. *Fifth Book of Junior Authors and Illustrators.* New York: H. W. Wilson, 1983.

Something about the Author. Vols. 21, 62. Detroit: Gale Research, 1980, 1991.

Something about the Author Autobiography Series. Vol. 1. Detroit: Gale Research, 1984.

Ward, Martha, ed. *Authors of Books for Young People.* 3rd ed. Metuchen, NJ: Scarecrow, 1990.

Meredith Ann Pierce

1958-, American young adult novelist

The Darkangel

(fantasy, 1982)

PLOT: This novel for young adult readers is based on a description of a dream from psychologist Carl Jung's book *Memories, Dreams, Reflections.* The hero in this world of mythical creatures and fantasy is Aeriel. A clumsy, unattractive girl who is very humble, Aeriel is a slave devoted to her mistress, Eoduin, who is just a few years older than she. They live on the Moon, which was settled long ago by Earth people and then largely abandoned. While there, the settlers created an atmosphere so that they could breathe on the Moon's surface. They also left behind a race of people and other creatures and plants. Those now living on the Moon refer to humans as the Old Ones; no one can remember just why the Earth people departed. In this strange world, the Earth, called Oceanus, shines down upon the Moon; the sun, called Solstar, shines from far away, and time is measured in day-months. A month of darkness follows a month of light.

The action of the novel takes place in the castle of a vampire called the Darkangel and the desert that surrounds it. The dark, dreary, and lifeless castle is inhabited by the Darkangel and his wives, the wraiths, and it is protected by gargoyles. The only bright spot in this drab environment are Aeriel's friends, Talb the duarough and Pendarlon the lion, as well as helpful people like the nomadic Ma'ambai tribe.

The Darkangel tells the story of Aeriel's growth and maturity. Eoduin, her mistress, becomes a wraith, one of the thirteen brides of the Darkangel. Aeriel accompanies Eoduin to the castle and, made helpless by the magic in the lead vials the vampire wears around his neck, she is made virtually a prisoner there. Despite herself, Aeriel is drawn to the evil vampire. As Eoduin loses her independence, however, Aeriel gains hers. She learns that if the Darkangel acquires a fourteenth bride, he will rule the world and destroy it.

In order to save herself and her world, Aeriel must cross the harsh and forbidding desert in search of the hoof of the starhorse, which can break the vampire's spell. When she has returned, Aeriel has matured and learned to trust her own abilities and skills. She has also become more physically attractive and graceful. Using the hoof, Aeriel breaks the spell, revealing the Darkangel to actually be a young prince. Aeriel and the prince fall in love and discover a new, happy life together.

The Darkangel *is the first novel in a trilogy that continues with* A Gathering of Gargoyles *(1984) and* The Pearl of the Soul of the World *(1990).*

CHARACTERS: As the novel begins, the slave girl **Aeriel** is both clumsy and unattractive. She is completely devoted and subservient to her mistress, Eoduin, but as Eoduin becomes more and more dominated by the Darkangel, so Aeriel becomes more independent. Aeriel assumes responsibility for her own life and actions as she realizes her own abilities and potential. Even her once cowering attitude toward the Darkangel changes. This change in Aeriel does not go unnoticed by the evil vampire, who, in turn, begins to look at her in a new way when she returns from her trek across the desert. As in many tales of increasing maturity and inward growth, Aeriel passes many difficult trials as she crosses the desert. Upon her return, she has improved both physically and mentally.

Throughout the story, Aeriel's attraction to the vampire increases, despite the fact that he has no redeeming qualities except physical beauty. Some critics have been disturbed by this aspect of the story. However, Aeriel is honest with herself about her fascination with the vampire, and her internal struggle between her physical desire for the Darkangel and her revulsion toward his evil ways is honestly portrayed as an all-too-human reaction.

The Darkangel, a vampire, is a person of both great physical beauty and inner evil. He is capable of senseless acts of cruelty, as when he breaks the wings of a small bat simply for the pleasure of it. His black wings and pale skin make him physically attractive to the young Aeriel, and when she becomes more independent, the Darkangel begins to find her desirable, too. After Aeriel frees him from the spell, he is able to truly love her.

Eoduin, Aeriel's mistress, comes from an aristocratic family. Often temperamental and sometimes foolish in her actions, she sets the story in motion when she insists that she and Aeriel climb ever higher into the mountains, which causes them to fall under the Darkangel's power. As Eoduin becomes a wraith, she grows more and more dependent on Aeriel. By the story's conclusion, she has become a mere shadow of her former self.

The lion **Pendarlon** teaches Aeriel about being kind to oneself and to others. He is one of the guardians that the Old Ones left behind when they departed the Moon. Pendarlon exhibits wisdom, power, and strength, teaching Aeriel about self-sacrifice and its value. Aeriel learns that she can count on Pendarlon, that he will extend help to all creatures, even the weakest of the realm. Pendarlon is a compassionate character who gives words of advice to Aeriel, which she never questions.

Talb is the only warm and Earthlike element in the cold, evil atmosphere of the vampire's castle. Aeriel trusts him immediately for his solidity and goodness. Like Pendarlon, Talb teaches Aeriel to be kind to others as well as to herself. His own careful attention to his physical needs, a trait he passes along to Aeriel, helps her to survive when she crosses the harsh desert. Talb is a duarough, a dwarf from Scandinavian myth. Duaroughs once lived underground and were closely associated with the earth. Talb helps to explain the rigid structure of the society on the Moon. Duaroughs, for example, "are miners and scholars, not spinners," Talb asserts, indicating that the role of each person in this society depends upon his or her race.

Further Reading

Authors and Artists for Young Adults. Vol. 13. Detroit: Gale Research, 1994.

Berger, Laura Standley, ed. *Twentieth-Century Young Adult Writers.* 1st ed. Detroit: St. James, 1994.

Children's Literature Review. Vol. 20. Detroit: Gale Research, 1990.

Holtze, Sally Holmes, ed. *Sixth Book of Junior Authors and Illustrators.* New York: H. W. Wilson, 1989.

Something about the Author. Vol. 67. Detroit: Gale Research, 1992.

Sylvia Plath

1932-1963, American poet and novelist

The Bell Jar

(novel, 1971)

PLOT: This largely autobiographical first-person narrative covers six traumatic months in the life of emotionally unstable nineteen-year-old Esther Greenwood. With eleven other college students, Esther has been chosen to be a guest editor of the college issue of *Ladies' Day,* which involves a month-long, expenses-paid stay in New York City during the summer between her junior and senior years. Esther is a budding poet whose work has already gained some notice. After deciding to dump Buddy Willard, her boyfriend of several years, Esther resolves to live a freer, less conventional life while in New York. She meets a number of interesting people, including fellow winner Doreen, the magazine's editor, Jay Cee, and two almost-seducers, Constantin and Marco.

Returning home to live with her mother in suburban Boston, Esther gradually loses her grip on reality and begins to feel that she is living a suffocating existence, as if she were imprisoned in a bell jar. She attempts suicide many times and is placed under the care of an unfeeling psychiatrist, Dr. Gordon. When she fails to respond to his treatments, she again tries to kill herself by overdosing on sleeping pills. Through the help of a successful writer who is interested in her work, Esther is sent to a private sanitorium, where she is placed under the care of an understanding female psychiatrist, Dr. Nolan. She also becomes reacquainted with a childhood friend, Joan Gilling, a fellow patient. After many bouts of shock therapy, Esther appears to respond to treatment and regain a grasp on reality. She is allowed outside privileges, and during these outings she has a disastrous affair with a young mathematics professor named Irwin. Esther continues to progress mentally. At the same time that she appears before the medical board of the hospital to gain a release, Esther is told that Joan has committed suicide.

CHARACTERS: The narrator is the gifted, ambitious aspiring poet, **Esther Greenwood**. Hard-working and conscientious, Esther looks back on her school career as "fifteen years of straight A's." She has devoted her life to studying, reading, and writing. Though from a poor family, she now attends a prestigious, expensive college on a full scholarship. As she says, "The one thing I was good at was winning scholarships and prizes." Her uncompromising values are put to the test in New York, where she finds frustration and disillusionment. Bored by her boyfriend Buddy's sanctimonious ways and feeling betrayed by his pretense of sexual innocence, she decides to dump him and try other men. Eager for love and compassion, she finds that each new relationship is a disaster and eventually flees the limiting male-dominated world around her. Disenchanted by the superficial, artificial life in New York, she returns home, but feels at loose ends and is unable to channel her talents constructively.

Without emotional resources, Esther experiences a sense of isolation and loneliness and enters a fantasy world where life becomes meaningless and futile. She is fixated on the absurdity of existence and is unable to relate to people and their problems. Her descent into madness and self-destruction is symbolized by the feeling of being enclosed in a stifling bell jar that isolates her from life. Feelings of inadequacy, loneliness, and detachment culminate in a nervous breakdown, a series of suicide attempts, and treatment in mental institutions. Esther's return to sanity is a tentative one. Even she doubts whether she can return to college and function independently. Overly sensitive, precociously intelligent, and emotionally fragile, Esther's future seems precarious.

Esther has a number of unsatisfying experiences with men. At first, her boyfriend, **Buddy Willard**, seems ideal. Blonde, blue-eyed, and bright, Buddy is a medical student at Yale. Esther basks in his attention but later realizes he is a controlling, unimaginative person who neither understands nor appreciates her talent. Smug and self-satisfied, he seeks a conventional, ordered life of security and orthodoxy. Esther's chief complaint concerning Buddy is his hypocrisy. He feigns innocence and virginity, when he has actually had a summer-long affair with a waitress. Esther later rebels against Buddy's constricting, domineering nature and decides that her identity is worth more than the security and physical comfort that Buddy can give her.

In New York, Esther meets **Constantin**, a simultaneous interpreter at the United Nations. Handsome, with light brown hair, dark blue eyes, and a lively, sensitive nature, he is attractive to Esther. She hopes to be seduced, but when he does not respond, she has a blind date with **Marco**, a Peruvian who appears suave and sophisticated but is inwardly sadistic and vicious. To retrieve a diamond stick pin he has been pressured into giving Esther, he abuses her physically and, before she can escape, throws her onto some muddy ground and attempts to rape her.

Determined to lose her virginity and experience physical love, Esther cultivates a friendship with **Irwin**, a young mathematician whom she meets while on an outside pass from the asylum. He is described as "a tall young man with a rather ugly and bespectacled, but intelligent face." Again, this encounter ends disastrously. After intercourse, Esther begins hemorrhaging and is taken to a hospital emergency room. Later, she is further humiliated when she must contact Irwin, who has neglected to pay the hospital bills.

Two of Esther's friends in New York are Doreen and Jay Cee. **Doreen** is beautiful, reckless, and unconventional. Amusing and daring, she is using her month in New York to have a good time. A southern belle, she attracts men easily and loves the high life. She tries to liberate Esther from her staid, serious outlook by arranging dates for her, all of which end catastrophically. Esther's boss is the editor of *Ladies' Day*, **Jay Cee**. She has brains and "plug-ugly" looks. A shrewd businesswoman, she also is a discerning literary critic and a friend to many important writers. She tries to give Esther more direction and purpose in her life. Esther pretends to comply but does so only to please Jay Cee, whom she likes and admires.

Although she tries to be supportive, Esther's **mother** neither understands nor appreciates her daughter's talents or problems. Since her husband's death some years before, she has maintained her family by teaching shorthand and typing. She is a resentful and bitter woman but has become resigned to a life of sacrifice and drudgery. She can't comprehend Esther's troubles and feels that she can end her depression with discipline and willpower. She does little to help Esther and feels disgraced at having a daughter in an asylum.

Esther's first psychiatrist is **Dr. Gordon**. Insensitive and self-satisfied, he soon alienates Esther by his unsympathetic, indifferent attitude. More interested in himself than Esther, he callously prescribes shock treatment without preparing her sufficiently. After another suicide attempt, Esther is moved to a different hospital and placed under the care of the sympathetic, nurturing **Dr. Nolan**, who is genuinely fond of Esther and anxious for her recovery. Esther says she is a "cross between Myrna Loy and my mother." Unlike Dr. Gordon, Dr. Nolan shows real understanding and trust towards Esther without any hint of condescension. Her honesty and belief in Esther help produce the confidence and strength that allows Esther to endure an extended period of shock treatment.

A less fortunate patient at the asylum is Esther's friend, **Joan Gilling**. A former girlfriend of Buddy's, she was a "big wheel" at college, president of her class, physics major, and hockey champion. Another overachiever and worrier, Joan also sank into moods of depression and was finally institutionalized. In the hospital, she has lesbian relationships and, unfortunately, does not have a doctor as caring or sympathetic as Dr. Nolan. Although she gives the impression of improving and regaining her sanity, she hangs herself after she has begun living away from the hospital.

Further Reading

Aird, Eileen. *Sylvia Plath: Her Life and Work*. New York: Harper, 1973.

Alexander, Paul. *Rough Magic: A Biography of Sylvia Plath*. New York: Viking, 1991.

Authors and Artists for Young Adults. Vol. 13. Detroit: Gale Research, 1994.

Barnard, Caroline King. *Sylvia Plath*. Boston: Twayne, 1978.

Berger, Laura Standley, ed. *Twentieth-Century Young Adult Writers*. 1st ed. Detroit: St. James, 1994.

Contemporary Literary Criticism. Vols. 1, 2, 3, 5, 9, 11, 14, 17, 50, 51, 62. Detroit: Gale Research, 1973, 1974, 1975, 1976, 1978, 1979, 1980, 1981, 1988, 1989, 1991.

Greiner, Donald J., ed. *American Poets since World War II*. Vol. 5 of *Dictionary of Literary Biography*. Detroit: Gale Research, 1980.

Hayman, Ronald. *The Death and Life of Sylvia Plath*. Secaucus, NJ: Carol, 1991.

Kibler, James E., Jr., ed. *American Novelists since World War II*. Vol 6 of *Dictionary of Literary Biography*. Detroit: Gale Research, 1980.

Macpherson, Pat. *Reflecting on* The Bell Jar. New York: Routledge, 1991.

Malcolm, Janet. *The Silent Woman*. New York: Knopf, 1994.

Rose, Jacqueline. *The Haunting of Sylvia Plath*. Cambridge: Harvard University Press, 1991.

Wagner-Martin, Linda. The Bell Jar: *A Novel of the Fifties*. New York: Twayne, 1992.

———. *Sylvia Plath: A Biography*. New York: Simon & Schuster, 1987.

World Literature Criticism. Vol. 4. Detroit: Gale Research, 1992.

Edgar Allan Poe

1809-1849, American short story writer, novelist, poet, critic, and essayist

The Masque of the Red Death

(horror short story, 1842)

PLOT: In another country, in another time, a plague known as the Red Death is wiping out the population. The narrator describes the horror of pain and profuse bleeding that kills the victim within thirty minutes of becoming infected. As if to defy this deadly plague, Prince Prospero invites a thousand of his "lighthearted friends" to a masked ball. Within his high-walled castle and in the seven rooms where the ball will take place, they will be safe from the Red Death. The narrator describes the seven rooms, all in different colors, with windows that look out onto an interior hall rather than the outside world. The first room is all in blue, casting a bluish tint even to the windows; the last room is all in black.

A stranger arrives at the ball dressed as the Red Death. Prince Prospero orders him removed, but no one dares touch him. With drawn dagger, the prince chases the stranger through six of the ballrooms. The masked stranger falls dead upon the carpet in the black room. When the guests remove his mask and costume, they find nothing there. One by one, the prince and his "lighthearted" friends all die, victims of the Red Death.

CHARACTERS: For this simple story, Poe carefully chooses his words to paint a picture of unrelieved fear, suspense, and dread. Like the ancient morality plays, *The Masque of the Red Death* presents the age-old theme of death and its inevitability. The closed castle setting, the characters who are foolish enough to think stone walls will keep away the plague, and the author's carefully molded descriptions of the merriment of the ball while the Red Death rages outside all combine to create the united effect of portending horror.

The name of **Prince Prospero** suggests a happy, prosperous person, as his actions reveal when he attempts to ward off the Red Death with the frivolity of a masked ball. The prince may be said to represent all those who try to escape death. His anger at the intrusion of the stranger is, in reality, fear caused by the realization that, despite his castle walls, he cannot thwart death.

The masked stranger, dressed as the **Red Death**, represents the futility of trying to control the inevitable. The reaction of the guests to the mask of the stranger, which shows telltale spatters of blood from the plague, illustrates the universal fear of death and the unknown.

The Purloined Letter

(detective short story, 1845)

PLOT: An unidentified narrator relates how C. Auguste Dupin, an eccentric and brilliant detective, is visited by Monsieur G— of the Paris police, who explains that a government official, Minister D—, is blackmailing another official with a stolen letter. The police have searched the Minister's home in vain for the document. Dupin tells Monsieur G— to search again and return to see him in a month. When Monsieur G—'s second investigation yields no results, he offers Dupin payment for a solution. Dupin accepts the check and, using his sharp intellect, quickly finds the letter in question.

The second half of the story explains Dupin's success. Dupin solves the crime by applying psychological deduction with which he reasons that Minister D— has fooled the police and frustrated their detailed search of his home by hiding the letter in plain sight. Dupin visits Monsieur G—'s home, sees the letter as he suspected—disguised but in plain view—and deliberately "forgets" his snuffbox upon his departure. Returning to the residence on the pretense of recovering his snuffbox, Dupin confiscates the document, substitutes a duplicated letter for the original, and leaves. Without the original, there is no blackmail, and the mystery is solved.

CHARACTERS: Poe invented the word "ratiocination" for this type of short story. The term means that the reader, along with the fictional detective, must apply logic and reasoning to solve the crime. *The Purloined Letter* is generally considered Poe's best of this type. The story establishes the method of psychological deduction and introduces the formula of the "obvious place." **C. Auguste Dupin**, the detective, is brilliant, eccentric, and somewhat enigmatic. He says little but listens carefully to the information given him and then reflects for a time. He is a private man, but he has an interest in and an understanding of people and their motivations.

Monsieur G— of the Paris police is the opposite of Dupin. G— talks a lot and is vastly concerned with all manner of physical evidence and crime details. If he can't categorize a piece of information, he dismisses it as unimportant. He sincerely tries his best, but he does not possess the brilliant deductive powers of Dupin. The **narrator** of the story is unnamed and is used to guide the reader through Dupin's reasoning. The narrator explains the information as he receives it, thus making the reader a participant in the investigation. However, the narrator, like G—, lacks Dupin's cleverness, so he sometimes makes incorrect assumptions about the information he receives. In this way, Poe allows the reader to feel superior.

The Fall of the House of Usher

(gothic short story, 1845)

PLOT: The narrator is urgently called to the home of his distraught friend, Roderick Usher, who lives in a decaying castle near a dark mountain lake. Usher, who looks ghastly, explains that neither he nor his twin sister, Lady Madeline, has left the castle for years. Usher states that the Lady Madeline has long been ill and in a "cataleptical" state. After some days, he announces that she has died. Usher and the narrator bury her in a deep underground vault. Soon, the narrator begins to hear peculiar sounds at night. A terrified Usher hears them too and believes they somehow come from Lady Madeline: "We have put her living in the tomb!" He hears the coffin being opened, the sound of chains, and her footsteps on the stairs. The heavy door is flung open, and Lady Madeline appears in bloody white robes. She falls upon her brother, and he dies. The narrator flees the castle and looks back to see the House of Usher collapse and fall into the dark lake.

This wood etching by Fritz Eichenberg illustrates a scene from Poe's horror classic, **The Masque of the Red Death.**

CHARACTERS: Gothic literature emphasizes the mysterious, grotesque, and horrible. The setting, generally in a remote place, is often a decaying, fearsome castle with cobwebs, bats, and secret corridors, contributing to an eerie and ghostly atmosphere. The main characters may be abnormal, with strange powers of communication not possessed by most humans. Physical properties may be suspended and often mysteriously transmuted, as when apparently dead bodies return to life.

Roderick Usher is a tortured, overly sensitive man who appears to be suffering from some ghastly disease. Some say his paleness stems from the fact that his twin is a vampire and has been sucking his blood. A weak, delicate man, he harbors an unknown terror that may stem from an extra-sensory relationship with his sister. **Lady Madeline** possesses more fortitude than her brother. With superhuman strength, she overcomes being buried alive and escapes from her tomb. She finds her twin and in the last embrace of death, they are joined once more.

The Cask of Amontillado

(horror short story, 1846)

PLOT: Set in an unspecified foreign land, the story is narrated by Montresor. For some time he has endured repeated insults against himself and his family's honor from a man named Fortunato. Now it is carnival time, and Montresor has conceived a diabolical revenge. With all the servants celebrating at the carnival, Montresor lures Fortunato down into his wine vaults to sample a fine sherry known as Amontillado.

Dressed in a carnival costume with bells on his cap, Fortunato willingly follows Montresor. Plied with wine, the inebriated Fortunato casts more slurs on his companion's family. When they reach a small niche in the wall, Montresor quickly manacles Fortunato and begins to seal the only escape route. As Montresor mortars the last stone into place, he hears the jingling of Fortunato's bells. The narrator reveals that the entombing took place fifty years ago, implying that Montresor has committed the perfect revenge.

CHARACTERS: This is generally regarded as one of Poe's best short stories. Every sentence contributes to the menacing mood of the simple plot. The gaiety of the carnival contrasts sharply with the horror of Fortunato's gruesome interment. **Montresor** is an old man by the time he relates this fifty-year-old crime, possibly as a confession before death. From an ancient and noble family, he has executed the perfect crime through a combination of careful planning and fortuitous circumstances. He never faces criminal punishment for his evil actions.

The character of **Fortunato** abounds in irony. His name means "the fortunate one," belying his ultimate fate. He is gaily dressed as he walks drunkenly to his macabre death. Despite the grim nature of his situation, he keeps flinging insults almost until the last stone entombs him, appearing not to realize the role his derision played all along in his final, sinister interment.

Further Reading

Anderson, Madelyn K. *Edgar Allan Poe: A Mystery.* New York: F. Watts, 1993.

Bloom, Harold, ed. *Edgar Allan Poe.* New York: Chelsea House, 1985.

Carlson, Eric W., ed. *The Recognition of Edgar Allan Poe: Selected Criticism since 1829.* Ann Arbor: University of Michigan Press, 1970.

Bruccoli, Matthew J., and Richard Layman, eds. *Colonization to the American Renaissance: 1640-1865.* Vol. 1 of *Concise Dictionary of American Literary Biography.* Detroit: Gale Research, 1987.

Buranelli, Vincent. *Edgar Allan Poe.* Boston: Twayne, 1977.

Kesterton, David B., ed. *Critics on Poe.* Coral Gables, FL: University of Miami Press, 1973.

Knapp, Bettina L. *Edgar Allan Poe.* New York: Ungar, 1984.

Meyers, Jeffrey. *Edgar Allan Poe: Life & Legacy.* New York: Scribner's, 1992.

Nineteenth-Century Literature Criticism. Vols. 1, 16. Detroit: Gale Research, 1981, 1987.

Short Story Criticism. Vol. 1. Detroit: Gale, 1988.

Something about the Author. Vol. 23. Detroit: Gale, 1981.

Symons, Julian. *The Tell-Tale Heart: The Life and Works of Edgar Allan Poe.* New York: Harper, 1978.

Charles Portis

1933-, American novelist

True Grit

(western, 1968)

PLOT: This wild adventure story takes places in the western frontier in the late 1870s, but is told in retrospect some fifty years later by the indomitable Mattie Ross. Fourteen-year-old Mattie learns that her father has been shot and robbed by the family's newly hired hand, Tom Chaney, while the two were on a horse buying expedition. She leaves her grieving mother and two younger siblings to travel seventy miles to Fort Smith, Arkansas, to claim the body. Mattie's hidden purpose, however, is to find a way to avenge her father's murder. After some tough trading, she manages to sell back her father's horses to the reluctant auctioneer, Mr. Stonehill, and find lodging at Mrs. Floyd's boarding house. She learns that Tom Chaney has fled into the Oklahoma Territory and hires a weather-beaten, dissolute federal marshal from the territory named Rooster Cogburn (whom she hears has "true grit") to hunt down Chaney.

At the boarding house, Mattie meets Sergeant LeBoeuf of the Texas Rangers. He is also hunting Chaney, who, under the name of Theron Chelmsford, shot a senator in Texas. A reluctant LeBoeuf and Rooster let Mattie join them. They learn that Chaney has joined a gang of train robbers led by Lucky Ned Pepper and including a Mexican named Greaser Bob. The gallant trio have several violent encounters with the gang, with the body count rising after each escapade.

In crisis after crisis, all three show amazing fortitude and spunk. In the last encounter with the outlaws, Mattie is captured, placed under the surveillance of Chaney and, during an escape attempt, falls into a pit of rattlesnakes and breaks her arm. All of the gang members, including Chaney, are eventually killed by Rooster and LeBoeuf, but Mattie sustains a life-threatening snake bite before she is rescued from the pit. Rooster saves her life by taking her on a breakneck ride to Fort Smith for medical help, while LeBoeuf returns to Texas with Chaney's body to collect the reward money. Mattie's arm must be amputated and she is sent home. Twenty-five years later and after many attempts, she is able to locate Rooster, who has become a star sharpshooter in a carnival. But she reaches him too late. Rooster has died only days before. Mattie takes his body home and buries him next to her father.

CHARACTERS: The narrator is the stubborn, indomitable, and engaging **Mattie Ross**. A short, slight, bony girl, she is far from pretty. One character's assessment of her is, "You look like somebody has worked you over with the ugly stick," and another comments, "I thought you was a walking hat." Though unimpressive physically, Mattie draws undivided attention, respect, and sometimes hostility with her assertive, blunt, inflexible speech and behavior and her firm beliefs in justice and fair play. She has sworn to avenge her father's death, and, regardless of the obstacles, she is determined to fulfil that goal without delay or compromise. Persistent, bright, determined, and shrewd, she can astonish and then intimidate people into complete acquiescence. "Take me as I am" is Mattie's philosophy.

Mattie instinctively knows how to handle people and is an astute judge of character. In spite of her aggressive, outspoken ways, Mattie can also be polite and proper, unless someone crosses her. Equipped with outstanding common sense and a matter-of-fact, no-nonsense view of life, she drives hard bargains and uses bold, sometimes outrageous tactics to get her own way. Though she often utilizes threats and coaxing to achieve her ends, Mattie never resorts to asking for pity or special attention because she is a girl. She is neither dismayed nor frightened by hardships or misfortunes. As she says, "I have never been one to flinch or crawfish when faced with an unpleasant task." She is frugal, sometimes stingy, but always willing to pay an honest price for goods and services if they are indeed worth it. Mattie has an opinion about everything and everybody; many reflect her narrow experiences and

In the 1969 movie True Grit, *John Wayne plays Rooster Cogburn, the aging gunfighter whose life is turned around by young Mattie (Kim Darby).*

her backwoods upbringing. Some of her views are absurdly crazy but marvelously funny, such as her belief that all Slovaks "love candles and beads." A dedicated Presbyterian, she tolerates other religions but is positive that she has found the true Christian denomination. Mattie is fearless and shows the extraordinary courage and grit that she demands in others. Her headstrong, pushy ways, though comic and delightful to many, can be an ordeal to others. As a family friend says, "Mattie, you are a pearl of great price, but there are times when you are a mighty trial to those who love you."

Mattie's reluctant and tarnished Galahad is **Rooster Cogburn**, an out-of-shape, forty-year-old gunfighter who reminds Mattie of President Cleveland because of his figure and large mustache. One of Rooster's eyes is almost completely shut with a tiny crescent of white showing at the bottom. Weather-beaten and clad in a dusty black suit of clothes, Rooster is said by the local sheriff to be the meanest marshal around: he is "a pitiless man, double-tough, and fear don't enter into his thinking." Mattie later learns that Rooster is also a killer, unschooled, filthy, and capable of taking bribes. Yet with all these faults, she finds that he is also capable of rare loyalty, courage, and devotion. Wily and shrewd, he lives in a squalid, rat-infested single room and is filthy (Mattie says, "If I smelled as bad as you I would not live in a city.")

Initially, Rooster is repelled by Mattie's bossy ways, but in time he grows to love and respect her and later risks his own life to save her. When Rooster tells Mattie about his past experiences, she realizes that until he became a marshal he was most frequently on the wrong side of the law. A confessed renegade and multiple murderer (always with good cause, he claims), Mattie wonders whether at times he is "stretching the blanket" (i.e., exaggerating). Tough as nails, Rooster, as cocky as his name, is able to withstand pain and suffering much more than he can competition or rivalry. A macho man, he bristles when LeBoeuf questions his exploits and prowess. Though his former wife tells Rooster that "a love of decency does not abide in you," he remains a strong, colorful man of great courage and basic decency.

Mattie's other hesitant ally is **Sergeant LeBoeuf** of the Texas Rangers. A good-looking man of about thirty, he appears to Mattie to be "a man of good family," but she adds that "he had a smug grin that made you nervous." Conceited and opinionated, he immediately locks horns with self-willed Mattie and refuses to take her along on his hunt for Tom Chaney. Later, when she persists and he is impressed with her spunk, he reluctantly gives in. LeBoeuf angers easily, is hot-tempered, and has a huge ego that is easily offended. His conceit does not allow him to admit his mistakes readily, and his pride and vanity cause several flare-ups with both Mattie and Rooster. LeBoeuf ultimately shows that he is a man of rare courage, sacrifice, and endurance.

Mattie's father, **Frank Ross**, is a handsome, decent man who has both instilled love in his family and taught them proper values and ethics. He reminds his daughter of "a gallant knight of old." His murderer is **Tom Chaney**, a short man of about twenty-five, with cruel-looking features and a permanent black smudge on his face from powder burns. Abusing the Ross's trust, he killed Frank while drunk and fled into the Oklahoma territory. A born loser, he is scorned by fellow gang members and eventually is killed by Rooster.

In Fort Smith, Mattie takes refuge in the Monarch boardinghouse run by **Mrs. Floyd**, a stingy woman and big talker who is noted for serving skimpy dinner portions and providing uncomfortable lodgings. One lodger correctly comments that looking for the chicken in her chicken and dumplings will result in eye strain. Unable to keep secrets, she innocently blabs her clients' confidences. Though cheap, she is honest and kind, nursing Mattie with meals in bed when she becomes sick.

Colonel Stonehill, a prissy, bald-headed man with eyeglasses, is the auctioneer who has cared for the horses Frank Ross bought in Fort Smith before his death. A pompous man who uses flowery elocutions like calling criminals "felonious intruders," he is a wheeler-dealer accustomed to bargaining with clients. Though he uses every trick in his repertoire, he is no match for Mattie, who outwits him every time. Out of his element on the frontier, he longs to return to the safety and civilization back east. For all his coldness and disenchantment with his lot, however, he shows increasing kindness toward Mattie, whom he refers to as "an unnatural child."

The leader of the robber gang is **Lucky Ned Pepper**, a short, feisty fellow with a scarred lip and an excitable, high-strung personality. A ruthless murderer without a conscience or scruples, he is scornful of a young gang member who has sacrificed his life to save him. Lucky's luck finally runs out when he is killed by Rooster in a shootout. The gang's second-in-command is a Mexican gambler from Fort Worth named the **Original Greaser Bob**. Well dressed in a linen suit and a bearskin coat, Greaser Bob impresses Mattie with his elegance. He, too, is a merciless killer who meets his end by Rooster's gun.

Further Reading

Contemporary Authors New Revision Series. Vol. 1. Detroit: Gale Research, 1981.

Kibler, James E. Jr., ed. *American Novelists since World War II, Second Series.* Vol. 6 of *Dictionary of Literary Biography.* Detroit: Gale Research, 1980

Chaim Potok

1929-, American novelist

The Chosen

(novel, 1967)

PLOT: Set in Brooklyn, New York, during World War II, *The Chosen* is a story about friendship, religion, and tradition. Danny Saunders and Reuven Malter, both fifteen when the story opens, come from very different family backgrounds. Though they are both Jewish, Danny comes from an orthodox Russian family that belongs to a Hasidic sect led by his father, the sect's tzaddik. Reuven, although orthodox, lives in a far more liberal environment. His relationship with his father, a rabbi, is loving and close, while Danny and his father are much more formal and do not speak much to each other.

The two boys first meet while playing baseball on opposite teams. During the game, Danny accidentally injures Reuven's eye severely. Reuven has to go to the hospital, and when Danny visits him, Reuven rejects the boy's apology at first. On his father's advice, however, Reuven forgives Danny and the two begin a long-lasting friendship.

Danny confides to Reuven that he doesn't want to take his father's place as tzaddik. Instead, he wants to become a doctor and let his younger brother take his father's place. Although he applies to a number of universities for his medical education, he is terrified to confront his father with his decision. Eventually, with Reuven's help, the two boys face the elder Saunders and tell him what he has already long suspected. Danny's father tries to explain his silences and the strained relationship with his son. He felt it was duty to have his son follow in the tradition of his sect, but he accepts Danny's decision.

The Promise *(1969) is a sequel.*

CHARACTERS: Reuven Malter is a typical teenage boy growing up in an orthodox Jewish family in World War II America. He has a close relationship with his father, who helps Reuven to understand the turmoil that surrounds his friend Danny, a boy with a truly brilliant mind who is torn between two worlds. At first hating Danny's father for his cold treatment of his son, Reuven seeks advice from his own father, who encourages him to remain Danny's friend and offer his support. Although Reuven can't fully appreciate Danny's problem, he sticks by him until Danny is able to confront his father.

Reuven's friend, **Danny Saunders**, is caught between the world of the strict teachings of the Hasidic sect and his own ambition to satisfy his inquisitive mind and study to become a doctor. A tall, lanky boy with blue eyes and dark hair, he wears the beard and earlocks of the Hasidic sect. His growing friendship with Reuven becomes increasingly important to him as a buffer between him and his father's strict dictates. Danny confides in Reuven about his secret trips to the forbidden public library, about his growing desire not to follow in his father's footsteps to lead the flock, about his rebellion against the planned marriage that is destined for him, and, finally, about his decision to stand up to his father.

Danny's father, **Reb Saunders**, rules his flock with zealousness and a profound respect for Jewish law. His relationship with his son grows ever more tense and bitter as the boy matures and begins to rebel. When Danny finally works up the courage to tell him he doesn't want to be the tzaddik, Reb Saunders explains why he has been so hard on Danny. He says that he wanted Danny to have a soul as well as a mind, and to do that he had to teach his son about the pain that exists in life. In this way, he hoped Danny would develop compassion for others. He admits that his methods were cruel, but he knew no other way. Reb Saunders has known for some time that Danny would not succeed him, but now he can accept his son's decision because, in his heart, Danny will always be a tzaddik. The boy may shave his beard and his earlocks, but he will always observe the Commandments. Danny's father asks for his son's forgiveness for raising him this way.

Reuven's father, **Rabbi Malter**, has little love for the Hasidic sect and its teachings. Malter explains to his son the traditions of the Hasidim and their great leaders. He tells Reuven that Danny's father, who has a reputation for brilliance and compassion, inherited his position as tzaddik from his father and must pass it on to his son. Malter is a Zionist and believes in the creation of the nation of Israel, a position that Danny's father rejects because the creation of such a state is not stipulated in the Torah.

Further Reading

Abramson, Edward A. *Chaim Potok.* Boston: Twayne, 1986.

Authors and Artists for Young Adults. Vol. 15. Detroit: Gale Research, 1995.

Berger, Laura Standley, ed. *Twentieth-Century Young Adult Writers.* 1st ed. Detroit: St. James, 1994.

Contemporary Literary Criticism. Vols. 2, 7, 14, 26. Detroit: Gale Research, 1974, 1977, 1980, 1983.

Dictionary of Literary Biography Yearbook: 1984. Detroit: Gale Research, 1985.

Something about the Author. Vol. 33. Detroit: Gale Research, 1983.

Walden, Daniel. *The World of Chaim Potok.* Albany, NY: State University of New York Press, 1985.

Philip Pullman

1946-, English novelist

The Ruby in the Smoke

(historical novel, 1985)

PLOT: In London, during October, 1872, sixteen-year-old Sally Lockhart receives a belated cryptic message from her deceased father, Matthew Lockhart, warning her to beware the Seven Blessings and to seek help from a Major George Marchbanks. Since her father's death three months ago in the South China Sea while investigating stories of corruption in his shipping firm of Lockhart and Selby, Sally has moved to London and is living with a vicious, distant relative, Aunt Caroline Rees. While investigating the contents of the letter, Sally meets her father's partner, the unhelpful Mr. Selby, and his saucy office boy, Jim Taylor. She also tracks down Marchbanks in his coastal home, where he gives her some mysterious papers concerning the whereabouts of a fabulously costly ruby that rightfully belongs to her. On this excursion, Sally meets a young photographer named Fred Garland and immediately feels she can trust him.

Meanwhile, in a combination opium den and rooming house run by a wicked crone, Mrs. Holland, a drugged sailor, Matthew Bedwell, raves in his delirium about the Seven Blessings and the fact that Mr. Selby has been embezzling money from Lockhart's firm. Mrs. Holland begins blackmailing Mr. Selby and, through a previous connection with Marchbanks, hears about the ruby and begins her own search for

Set in the London of 1872, this novel is about Sally Lockhart's quest to find a valuable ruby that she has inherited.

the precious gem. These incidents lead to complications that result in romance, several murders, breakneck chases, and general mayhem. Involved are Mrs. Holland, her enforcer, Mr. Berry, and their pathetic serving girl, Adelaide, as well as Matthew Bedwell and his twin brother, Reverend Nicholas Bedwell, and the family with whom Sally later lives, including Fred Garland, his sister, Rosa, and their helper, Trembler. By the last chapter, Marchbanks, Selby, and Matthew Bedwell have been murdered, Mrs. Holland and Mr. Berry meet grisly ends, Sally has thrown the ruby into the Thames where it will cause no further harm, and she and Fred have fallen in love. Sally also has a confrontation with the mastermind behind much of this dirty dealing: Henrik van Eeden, alias Ah Ling, leader of the international gang of pirates and smugglers known as the Seven Blessings. She mistakenly believes she has killed her arch enemy but discovers otherwise in the sequels, *The Shadow in the North* and *The Tiger in the Well.*

CHARACTERS: The heroine of the novel, **Sally Lockhart**, is very different from the stereotypical helpless Victorian damsel in distress. She is bold, high-spirited, and independent. Accustomed to being self-reliant, she never allows anyone to take risks on her behalf. Instead, she prides herself on fighting her own battles and overcoming problems through her skill and stamina. As a result, she confronts her two deadly foes, Mrs. Holland and Mr. van Eeden, alone and overcomes both through her boundless courage.

Sally is an uncommonly pretty girl. Slender and pale, she has dark-brown eyes and long, blond hair. Instead of going to a regular school, Sally has been taught by her businessman father, Mr. Lockhart, and therefore has not received much education in the humanities. Instead, she knows a great deal about military tactics (Mr. Lockhart served in India), Hindustani, shipping, horsemanship, rifles and pistols, and book-keeping. Today, Sally would be called an entrepreneur. She brings order to the Garland photography enterprise, counsels them on new ways of making money, and puts their business on a sound financial foundation. She is also bright, clever, and pleasant. Friendly and loyal, Sally is well liked by others. She is also uncommonly resourceful and mature beyond her sixteen years.

By contrast, twenty-one-year-old **Fred Garland** is a happy-go-lucky, impractical romantic. Though a genius at photography, he knows nothing (and couldn't care less) about everyday concerns and, as a result, has made a shambles of his business. Essentially an artist and born Bohemian, he scorns the inconvenience of making a living and tending to mundane financial matters. Witty and cheerful, Fred is also a courageous and loyal friend who risks his life to fight wrong-doing. He shows uncommon bravery in challenging the gargantuan Mr. Berry and, though bloody and beaten up, continues to hold him at bay in one incident until Berry knocks him senseless. Fred is described as possessing a humorous face, stiff and tousled straw-colored hair, and having an alert and intelligent expression. Fred's sister, **Rosa Garland**, is also lively and high-spirited. A beautiful young woman of eighteen, she has long red hair and a fiery temperament to match. Often exasperated by her brother's impracticalities, she welcomes Sally into the mismanaged household to bring order out of their chaos. An aspiring actress, she possesses both the disposition and the passion for the profession. Rosa, a loving sister and a dependable friend, is willing to forfeit her well-being and safety to help others, including Sally, whom she scarcely knows.

The Garlands' helper in the photography shop is **Trembler**, whose real name is **Theophilus Molloy**. A small, wizened man, he gained his nickname because, when agitated, his body shakes uncontrollably. Fred explains how Trembler came into their lives: "He's an unsuccessful pickpocket. I met him when he tried to pick mine. He was so relieved when I stopped him that he practically wept with gratitude and he's been with us ever since." Trembler is a caring, dependable ally who is a steadying influence on Fred and a devoted friend to Sally.

The cockney office boy at Lockhart and Selby's is the impudent, clever, and courageous **Jim Taylor**. Addicted to reading and trading "penny dreadfuls," he possesses a quick mind and an easygoing perspective on life. Through his sharp, intuitive thinking, he is able to decode a cryptic message and locate the missing ruby, and though he is just a boy he is a fearless fighter. Jim is street-wise and attuned to London's underworld. A staunch friend, he is always ready to help Sally and her friends when asked.

The twin brothers **Matthew** and **Nicholas Bedwell** are also Sally's allies. Matthew, a seaman who sailed on the ship where Sally's father was killed, has succumbed to an opium addiction and has fallen into the hands of the unscrupulous Mrs. Holland. He is rescued with the help of his brother, Nicholas, a former boxer turned minister, but he is murdered by van Eeden to prevent him from going to the police. Both brothers are dependable and affable, ready to help in the fight for justice.

Major George Marchbanks served with Mr. Lockhart in India, where he gained possession of the ruby. Now in his sixties, he is a sallow, broken man, troubled by guilt and memories of years of dissipation. While in the army, he became addicted to opium, and to pay his mounting debts traded Sally, then a baby, to Mr. Lockhart for possession of the ruby. Thus began his life of deceit and duplicity. Before he can clear his conscience completely and reveal all his secrets to Sally, he is murdered by **Mrs. Holland**, the woman who reminds Fred of one of the witches in *Macbeth*. A squat, dumpy woman, she has a wrinkled, hideous face with sunken cheeks and pinched lips made all the more ugly when she removes her teeth. Mrs. Holland is completely unscrupulous and warped, plotting evil against the innocent and murders without conscience. The operator of an opium den, she manipulates everyone around her to achieve her sinister goals. Mrs. Holland is known and feared by the entire London underground. Wicked and unprincipled, she is driven to madness by her pursuit of the fabulous ruby. She is killed when she tries to retrieve the jewel by jumping into the Thames. Her henchman, **Mr. Berry**, is equally depraved and fiendish but lacks Mrs. Holland's cunning. A thief, mugger, and murderer, he self-righteously refuses to drink alcohol, claiming ironically, "I got me principles." Berry is killed when he falls off a wharf while persuing Jim Taylor and Fred Garland. Their maidservant is the pathetic nine-year-old **Adelaide**. Terrorized by Mrs. Holland and living in constant fear of being murdered, she is a forlorn, piteous waif until rescued and brought to live with the Garlands.

Mr. Lockhart's corrupt partner is **Mr. Selby**, a short, portly man with high, rosy cheeks. He has been stealing from the firm and making fraudulent deals involving the shipping company. Blackmailed by Mrs. Holland, he is later murdered by the master criminal **Henrik van Eeden** so that he won't talk. Van Eeden is described as a stout fellow, clean-shaven, with fair hair and sunburned complexion. Beneath this ordinary-looking facade there is a fiendishly clever outlaw also known as the diabolical pirate chief, **Ah Ling**. Killing without conscience, he has gained international notoriety because of his ingenious plotting and ruthless conduct. He is responsible for the deaths of many people, including Mr. Lockhart, Selby, and Matthew Bedwell. In a final confrontation during which he tries to kidnap Sally, she shoots him, but he escapes into the night.

Further Reading

Authors and Artists for Young Adults. Vol. 15. Detroit: Gale Research, 1995.

Berger, Laura Standley, ed. *Twentieth-Century Young Adult Writers*. 1st ed. Chicago: St. James, 1994.

Children's Literature Review. Vol. 20. Detroit: Gale Research, 1990.

Holtze, Sally Holmes, ed. *Sixth Book of Junior Authors and Illustrators*. New York: H. W. Wilson, 1989.

Something about the Author. Vols. 65. Detroit: Gale Research, 1991.

Something about the Author Autobiography Series. Vol. 17. Detroit: Gale Research, 1994.

Ayn Rand

1905-1982, Russian-born American novelist

The Fountainhead

(novel, 1943)

PLOT: Howard Roark is expelled from the Stanton Institute of Technology just before Commencement Day, 1922. A brilliant and idealistic architectural student, he has declined to complete an exercise in historical styles because he refuses to imitate or copy the work of others. His classmate, Peter Keating, possessing only average talent, graduates with honors, and joins the prestigious architectural firm run by Guy Francon. Roark has difficulty finding employment because no one likes his attitude or understands his unique designs. Yet Roark resists compromising his architectural ideals and integrity. Eventually, Henry Cameron, an old maverick among architects whom Roark has always admired, hires him. When Keating is given the opportunity to design a skyscraper, which he lacks the proficiency to complete, he asks Roark's opinion and then steals his ideas. When Keating is subsequently awarded the commission, Roark keeps silent. Later, Roark receives a rare commission to design a house for Austen Heller. Upon its completion, Heller adores it, while the public considers it unusual. Ellsworth Toohey, an influential journalist who writes an architectural column for the New York *Banner*, owned by newspaper magnate Gail Wynand, pointedly ignores it.

Roark meets Dominique Francon, daughter of Guy Francon, and they fall instantly and passionately in love. However, Dominique, who has grown cynical and withdrawn by the hypocrisy of the world surrounding her, cannot bear to see Roark's genius degraded and destroyed as she knows it must be, so she sets out to destroy him herself in order to at least protect him from the rejection of society. In part, she accomplishes Roark's humiliation by denying their great love through her marriages to Peter Keating and then Gail Wynand, two men whom she despises.

Toohey, who controls people with the power of his words, also sets out to destroy Roark, although for reasons different from Dominique's. With ulterior motives, he is influential in getting Roark a commission to build the Stoddard Temple. When it is completed, Toohey publicly ridicules it in his column, and his many public supporters follow his lead. Stoddard sues Roark and wins.

Years later, Roark, now thirty-seven, is asked by Keating to design Cortlandt Homes, a housing project. Keating realizes he is incapable of the job, as he has always inwardly known, but without Cortlandt his career will be ruined. Roark agrees to help, with conditions: he will design the project under Keating's name, but *only* if Keating swears it will be built exactly as Roark draws it, with no compromises or modifications. Keating promises. The design of Cortlandt is magnificent, innovative, ground-breaking, perfect. Yet despite Keating's guarantee, he is too weak to prevent the changes made to Roark's plans. When Cortlandt Homes is completed in accordance with its altered design, Roark reacts by dynamiting the entire structure. He stands trial for his actions, which manifest his strong belief in the integrity of his work.

Wynand, for the first time fighting for something he believes in, backs Roark with his paper and incurs the wrath of Toohey, whom Wynand fires. At his trial, Roark states: "I recognize no obligations toward men except one: to respect their freedom and to take no part in a slave society. To my country, I wish to give the ten years which I will spend in jail if my country exists no longer. I will spend them in memory and in gratitude for what my country has been. It will be my act of loyalty, my refusal to live or work in what has taken place."

Howard Roark is acquitted, and Gail Wynand is forced to rehire Toohey. He does so and then shuts down the *Banner*, forever silencing Toohey's abusive voice. Roark is now free to open his own firm and to do his own work. Dominique divorces Wynand, and she and Roark marry.

CHARACTERS: Russian-born American novelist and philosopher Ayn Rand described this best-selling work as only a "prologue to *Atlas Shrugged*." In both novels, she presents her philosophy of objectivism, which holds that all true human achievement is the product of individual ability and effort, that a capitalist society best allows the free exercise of talent, and toward that end, altruism becomes a vice and selfishness a virtue.

Howard Roark represents the creative man, the person of self-sufficient ego whose values and convictions are those of his own mind, not those directed by others. He is an architect, a builder of the skyscrapers that signify America's great industrial achievements. Some have suggested that Rand modeled the character of Roark on architect Frank Lloyd Wright, but Rand, who admired Wright, denied this connection. Roark's strength of character and his insistence on his own terms has jeopardized both his professional reputation and public opinion. He agrees to design Cortlandt Homes anonymously only because he realizes he will never have a chance to build this project under his own name. His reward, however, will be its completion as he designed it. But when Roark views the unauthorized alterations to the finished building, he destroys it rather than allow a substandard design to exist. Roark's subsequent acquittal on all charges represents the author's assertion that the independent mind has the right to exist purely for its own sake. Says Roark at his trial, "I came here to say that I do not recognize anyone's right to one minute of my life. Nor to any part of my energy. . . . I wished to come here and say that I am a man who does not exist for others."

Dominique Francon is a complex woman and, according to many critics, the novel's most unsatisfactory figure. She cannot bear to face the cynicism, phoniness, and deceit rampant in society. She loves Roark, but because she cannot stand to see his idealism slowly destroy him, she decides to deliberately ruin him herself. She accomplishes her objective in part by marrying two men whom she despises—Peter Keating and Gail Wynand—to make Roark suffer. At the novel's end, when Dominique realizes that the power of Roark's genius and convictions triumphs over social artifice and mediocrity, she is able to return to him and acknowledge that their love is possible, even in this world.

Peter Keating signifies the spiritual parasite, the opposite of Howard Roark. Keating is directed—and indeed shaped—by others. He possesses morals, judgments, and convictions only because he looks to others for decisions and guidance. Keating, like all followers, moves without being internally directed because he has no sense of purpose. Only once, in trying to save Cortlandt from architectural ruin according to his promise to Roark, does Keating show some mettle. But he fails in his effort, resulting in both professional disaster and the realization of his own inferiority.

Ellsworth Toohey, the architectural critic, is the story's villain. He uplifts himself by robbing others of their self-esteem and honor through a constant theme of extolling noble self-sacrifice. With this philosophy, he turns others into willing victims. The difference between Keating and Toohey is that, while both are less than ideal men, only Toohey actually comprehends his true nature. When Wynand's newspaper closes, Toohey realizes his years of scheming have only led to his defeat.

Gail Wynand, a brilliant newspaper publisher, lacks great stature, mainly because his overriding aim in life is to have power over others. He seeks this power through his newspaper, by publishing not what he believes in but what he believes others want to hear. Critics claim he was modeled after newspaper magnate William Randolph Hearst, which Rand acknowledged in part. With Roark's legal difficulties, Wynand for the first time uses his newspaper to fight for a cause in which he believes, only to see the public turn against him. He ultimately realizes that the public had been directing him all along, and he had been *their* puppet.

Henry Cameron is an architect and man for whom Roark has profound respect. Frank Lloyd Wright, who bears some resemblance to the character of Howard Roark, greatly admired and worked for an older architect with ideas somewhat similar to his own. That man was Louis H. Sullivan (1856-1924), regarded as the father of modernism in architecture. Among his designs are the Transportation Building for the World's Columbian exhibition (1893) and the Stock Exchange Building, both in Chicago.

Further Reading

Baker, James T. *Ayn Rand.* Boston: Twayne, 1987.

Branden, Barbara. *The Passion of Ayn Rand.* New York: Doubleday, 1987.

Branden, Nathaniel. *Who Is Ayn Rand?: An Analysis of the Novels of Ayn Rand.* New York: Random House, 1962.

Collier, Laurie, and Joyce Nakamura, eds. *Major Twentieth-Century Writers: A Selection of Sketches from Contemporary Authors.* Detroit: Gale, 1991.

Contemporary Literary Criticism. Vols. 3, 30, 44. Detroit: Gale Research, 1975, 1984, 1987.

Gilder, George. "Ayn Rand: Sex, Money, and Philosophy." *Chicago Tribune Book World* (19 June 1986): 1, 10.

Gladstein, Mimi Reisel. *The Ayn Rand Companion.* Westport, CT: Greenwood, 1984.

Gordon, Philip. "Extroflective Hero: A Look at Ayn Rand." *Journal of Popular Culture* X (spring 1977): 701-10.

McGann, Kevin. "Ayn Rand in the Stockyard of the Spirit." In *The Modern American Novel and the Movies.* New York: Ungar, 1978.

Erich Maria Remarque

1898-1970, German novelist

All Quiet on the Western Front

(novel, 1928; published in Germany as Im Westen nichts Neues*)*

PLOT: This staunchly anti-war novel is set principally in the trenches of the German Army during World War I. It is told in the first person by Paul Bäumer, a sensitive, sympathetic nineteen-year-old recruit. While his outfit is stationed behind the German front lines, Paul recalls the exhortations of his domineering school master, Kantorek, who had coerced his entire class into enlisting in the army through his shameless appeals to their patriotism. Now several are already dead, including Josef Behm, the boy most reluctant to join. Three of Paul's former classmates, Müller, Albert Kropp, and Leer, are in his outfit, which also includes Tjaden, a former locksmith, Haie Westhus, a peat digger, and Detering, a peasant farmer. They are all only nineteen years old, except for their acknowledged leader, Stanislaus Katczinsky—Kat for short—a shrewd forty-year-old cobbler, whom they all respect and admire. During their ten weeks of training, most of the group had suffered under sadistic Corporal Himmelstoss, but they recall having had their revenge before being sent to the front. Covering him with a blanket to avoid detection, they beat him mercilessly.

Paul and his friends visit another former classmate, Kemmerich, in the hospital and witness his tragic death from a leg amputation. Later, while laying barbed wire at the front, the unit sees action, and during a fierce barrage they are trapped in a graveyard filled with broken coffins and upended corpses. The horror mounts, and the death toll increases. Back behind the lines, the group often discusses the effects of war. Kropp sums up their experiences by saying, "The war has ruined everything for us." There is more trench warfare, and only thirty-two men of the original 150 in Paul's company survive. Haie Westhus is among the dead.

In a field depot behind enemy lines, Paul and his friends find diversion with some French girls, and later Paul is granted a two-week leave to visit his family. His war experiences have changed him so much that he finds he can no longer communicate with his mother and father. While at home he gains some satisfaction in learning that Kantorek has been conscripted as a reservist.

Back in action with his unit, Paul is trapped in a shell hole and stabs a French soldier who has jumped in with him. For an entire day, before he can crawl back to safety, Paul helplessly witnesses the horror of the young man's agony as he slowly dies. In a later attack, both Paul and his friend Albert Kropp are wounded. Feigning a high temperature to remain with his friend, Paul stays in the hospital, while Albert has a leg amputated and is sent home. After recovering, Paul is sent back to the front, and, as the months drag on and the carnage increases, he loses his beloved comrades one by one, including Detering, Leer, and Müller. Kat sustains a leg wound, and, while being carried to safety by Paul, he is hit in the head with a shrapnel splinter and dies. Paul is devastated.

The war drags on. At the novel's end, it is October, 1918, and rumors of an armistice are circulating. But Paul does not live to see peace. He is killed on a day when there is so little military activity, official reports state, "All quiet on the Western Front."

CHARACTERS: The protagonist and narrator is a young German soldier, **Paul Bäumer**. At school, he is portrayed as an ambitious, idealistic young man,

eager to learn and anxious to succeed. An aspiring writer, an intellectual, and something of a dreamer, he is an easy target for Kantorek's chauvinistic myths about Iron Youth and German Destiny. A compassionate man, he is always helpful to others. He ministers to Kemmerich in his final hours and visits his dead comrade's mother, telling her lies to ease the pain of her son's death. His loyalty to his friends is shown frequently. Paul refuses to leave Albert Kropp when his buddy is wounded; he risks his life to save Kat on the battlefield; and he shares his belongings and gifts with others and helps young recruits who are assigned to his outfit. Paul clings to a belief in the dignity and worth of the individual, even giving possessions to the half-starved Russian prisoners of war he encounters.

In his fight for justice and fairness, Paul challenges the sadistic Corporal Himmelstoss, even though this results in severe physical punishment. Noble in spirit, as well as understanding, and sympathetic toward others, this innocent young man loses his

Richard Thomas plays young German soldier Paul Bäumer in the 1979 film adaptation of **All Quiet on the Western Front.**

hopes and ideals under the unrelenting horror and waste of war. A profound sense of loss takes their place. He retreats inwardly and becomes completely disillusioned. The war shatters his sensitivity, intelligence, and integrity. Devoid of emotions and thought, he continues to fight for his survival during the stress of battle, even though the war has so emptied him internally that he knows that he has no future. In death, "his face had an expression of calm, as though almost glad the end had come."

Stanislaus Katczinsky, or **Kat**, the unofficial leader of the group, is Paul's best friend and mentor. A simple cobbler by trade, he is twice as old as the others. This difference in age shows in his experience, wisdom, and shrewdness. Kat is described as cunning and hard-bitten, "with a face of the soil, bent shoulders, and a remarkable nose for dirty weather, good food and soft jobs." Although lacking in the book knowledge that Paul and his friends have, he has better survival skills, being able to locate food and creature comforts that elude the others. Self-reliant and inventive, he is also good-natured and genuinely fond of Paul. The war occasionally turns him into a thief, but he is essentially a good person. When discussing the war, he demonstrates his common sense and practical nature, rightfully blaming the power-hungry world leaders for their misery. His imaginative, ingenious way of solving problems and his warm and caring attitude make his death the final and greatest blow that Paul sustains.

Franz Kemmerich is one of Paul's former classmates. He is particularly youthful for his years and even more innocent and childlike than his friends. Though approaching death after a botched amputation, he pathetically talks of his possessions, including a missing watch, and clings to a waning hope of survival. He fears death and, when it occurs, this tragedy deeply affects Paul and emphasizes the waste and inhumanity of war. Paul later visits Franz's mother and lies about the circumstances of his death to comfort the distraught woman.

Paul's other classmates in the unit are Müller, Leer, and Albert Kropp. Of these, only **Albert Kropp** survives the war. He has a reputation for being the brightest and cleverest of Paul's classmates. Paul comments wryly that Albert has only become a lance corporal because he is too smart to be an officer. Albert exhibits his wit on several occasions. For example, at one point he suggests that the war should really be handled as a gladiatorial combat in which the politicians and generals fight while the common people act as spectators. Uncompromising in his beliefs and standards, Albert is practical and wise beyond his years, and a true friend to Paul.

In many ways, **Müller** acts as if he were still in the classroom. Though at the front, he carries his textbooks with him, dreams of exams, and ponders over theories in physics. But he is also a realist, managing to inherit Kemmerich's fine boots after his death. Although Albert considers this to be grossly callous, it is only part of Müller's pragmatic, scientific way of viewing life. He dies of a point-blank shot in the stomach. **Leer**, the best mathematician at Paul's school, is the same age as his classmates but more mature in his actions and appearance. (He is the first to sport a beard and have sex with a woman.) After Leer is killed by a flying piece of shrapnel, Paul cynically remarks that his mathematical prowess meant nothing in battle.

Other members of Paul's unit are Haie Westhus, Tjaden, and Detering. **Haie Westhus** is a muscular former peat digger who is Kat's accomplice and enforcer on foraging expeditions. Of the group, he is the least unhappy about being in the army and confesses that after the war he would willingly stay in the military for the security and comfort it provides. **Tjaden** is a skinny locksmith with a voracious appetite. He has small, mousy features and is noted for being stingy and cunning. However, he gallantly stands up to the tyranny of Himmelstoss and is later imprisoned for his actions. Though completely uneducated and little interested in intellectual pursuits, he makes some direct and discerning comments on the origins of war. **Detering** is a peasant who thinks of nothing but his farm and his wife. His love of animals is shown in his deep concern when some horses are wounded and in terrible pain. A simple, peace-loving farmer, he finally cracks, not under the strain of battle, but at the sight of a blossoming cherry tree that reminds him of home. Detering deserts, but he is captured and eventually court-martialed.

Corporal Himmelstoss is the sadistic corporal who leads Paul and his friends in basic training. Without humanity or character, he cruelly debases his victims, turning respectable men into animals. A little man who typifies all that is inhuman in the Prussian military mentality, he compensates for his small stature by his unnatural desire for power. In a wonderful act of revenge, he is thrashed by his oppressed trainees. Later, Himmelstoss matures somewhat under the fire of battle.

Paul's schoolmaster, **Kantorek**, is a strict disciplinarian. By his hectoring and cajoling, he convinces his senior class that their patriotic duty is to enlist en masse. Blinded by feelings of German superiority and the supposed chivalry of warfare, he seduces and betrays the generation that looked up to him for guidance. Later, he is forced to become a reservist and suffers some of the indignities and outrages that he caused others to suffer. In his outlandish uniform, he is a ridiculous, humiliated person who, under other circumstances, would be an object of pity. Probably the most unfortunate of his pupils was plump, homely **Josef Behm**, who was the most fearful of enlisting. He is killed early in the war.

Further Reading

Barker, Christine R., and R. W. Last. *Erich Maria Remarque.* London: Wolff, 1979.

Contemporary Literary Criticism, Vol. 21. Detroit: Gale Research, 1982.

Domandl, Agnes Korner. *Modern German Literature.* New York: Ungar, 1972.

Eksteins, Modris. "*All Quiet of the Western Front* and the Fate of a War." *Journal of Contemporary History* 15 (April, 1980).

Encyclopedia of World Literature in the Twentieth Century. New York: Ungar, 1984.

Firda, Richard. All Quiet on the Western Front: *Literary Analysis and Cultural Context.* New York: Twayne, 1993.

———. *Erich Maria Remarque: A Thematic Analysis of His Novels.* New York: Peter Land, 1988.

Hardin, James, ed. *German Fiction Writers.* Vol. 56 of *Dictionary of Literary Biography.* Detroit: Gale Research, 1987.

Kunitz, Stanley, and Howard Haycraft. *Twentieth Century Authors.* New York: H. W. Wilson, 1942.

Wagener, Hans. *Understanding Erich Maria Remarque.* Columbia: University of South Carolina Press, 1991.

Mary Renault

(pen name for Mary Challans)

1905-1983, English novelist

The King Must Die

(novel, 1958)

PLOT: The narrator of this historical novel based on Greek myths is Theseus, grandson of Pittheus, King of Troizen on the Isle of Pelops. When Theseus is seventeen, his mother, Aithra, reveals that his father is Aigeus, the king of nearby Athens. Theseus decides to travel north to meet his father, but on the way he is forced by circumstance to kill the king of Eleusis, Kerkyon, and take his place in the royal palace. Eleusis is a matriarchal society in which the men are treated as vassals and the Queen reigns supreme. Theseus gains great power, particularly after he rids the area of robbers. This incurs the jealousy of both his lover, the Queen, and her brother, Xanthos. Theseus uncovers a plot against him, and after slaying Xanthos, the ringleader, and forcing the Queen into exile, he is declared the sole monarch of Eleusis.

Continuing his journey to Athens, Theseus meets his father, King Aigeus, and ousts the reigning priestess, the evil Medea. When the Cretan ships come to Athens's harbor to collect tribute, Theseus gallantly volunteers to be part of the fourteen young men and women conscripted to be bull dancers at the labyrinthine palace of King Minos of Crete. (Bull dancing is a deadly balletic exercise in which participants must jump over a bull's horns.) Among his colleagues are the boys Amyntor, Iros, and Hippon, and the girls Chryse, Helike, and Nephele. Theseus manages to shape his inexperienced band into a crack team called the Cranes and arouse the reluctant admiration of the king's evil son, their patron, Asterion.

From afar Theseus admires the high priestess, or Goddess-on-Earth, Ariadne, King Minos's young daughter. This attraction is reciprocated, and soon, by following a network of thread fashioned by Ariadne, he begins spending nights with her in the goddess's chambers. When a series of earthquakes destroys the palace, Theseus is able to escape with his Cranes and Ariadne to the island of Naxos. Once there, he realizes that Ariadne, with her strange religious beliefs and rituals, belongs with her Cretan people. One evening, Theseus and his band of followers steal off to their boat and sail for Athens, leaving Ariadne behind.

CHARACTERS: The narrator and hero of this adventurous tale is **Theseus**, the bold, courageous young prince of Troizen. While still a youngster, Theseus realizes an affinity with the god Poseidon, ruler of the ocean and creator of earthquakes. Theseus develops telepathic communications with the god, whom he considers to be his spiritual father. Because of this relationship, Theseus devotes his life to serving this deity. A believer in the importance of physical strength, Theseus endures incredible hardships and trials to produce a powerful, muscular body that is stronger and more robust than his modest height and weight would suggest. He is fearless and daring in battle, performing feats of courage that amaze and inspire both friend and foe. A strong believer in principles, he is a loyal, trustworthy friend and staunch ally.

Though born into royalty, he won't receive preferential treatment because of his station in life, but instead insists that he be sent to Crete, along with commoners his age, knowing that no one has emerged from the Bull Court alive. He is a man of honor and integrity who will fight for justice and truth regardless of the odds. Theseus also possesses a rare intelligence and powers of discernment. A born leader, he knows how to motivate and reward his associates, always fulfilling his duty regardless of how abhorrent the task. Through his iron will, tenacity, and determination, he develops into the best runner in the Bull Court. He is physically handsome and is not above using his good looks to attract women. Though still only eighteen at the close of the novel, he has accomplished more daring feats, experienced more amazing exploits, and bedded more women, than could be expected in the average lifetime.

Theseus's grandfather is **King Pittheus**, the ruler of Troizen. A wise and valiant leader, he takes great pains to indoctrinate young Theseus, his only legitimate grandson, into the mysteries of their religion and the responsibilities that he must shoulder. Realizing that the boy is growing up without a father, he assumes many of these functions, instilling in the boy the concepts of duty, honor, and sacrifice. Theseus venerates and loves his grandfather. Theseus's mother, **Aithra**, was still in her teens when she gave birth to her son. A priestess, she had bravely obeyed her father's orders and sacrificed her body and virginity without complaint in order to appease the gods. Since then, she has remained chaste and interested only in raising her son properly. A modest, accepting woman, she is always ready to comfort and support Theseus, acting as a buffer between the harsh realities of their primitive customs and the sensitive nature of her son. She is described as being astonishingly beautiful—"her forehead was broad, her gray eyes widely set, with soft brows nearly meeting above her proud nose." Theseus adores her, heeds her wishes, and tries to bring honor to her name.

Aigeus, Theseus's father, is unaware that the one sexual encounter he agreed to in Troizen had produced a son. When Theseus first sees him, he finds that he is handsome but old before his time. His "brown hair was streaked with grey and he was indeed a man whom trouble had set his mark on." Believing that he is without an heir and beset with political worries, Aigeus has become reclusive, weary, and overly reliant on his priestess, Lady Medea. With the appearance of Theseus, Aigeus's life regains meaning. He embarks on a successful war against his enemies in Attica and rejoices in the friendship and love that his son has brought him. A decent, responsible man, he shows many of the admirable qualities concerning honor and bravery that Theseus possesses. The depth and intensity of his love for Theseus is shown when he commits suicide after mistakenly believing that his son is dead.

The **Queen of Eleusis** is a scheming, wily woman who is intent solely on maintaining her control over her matriarchal kingdom. She is described as being a stately woman with fiery red hair who wears an impressive diadem of purple stitched with gold. She annually revels in the ritual of having her husband killed and embracing a new king. Treacherous and unfaithful, the Queen will deceive and even murder to keep her throne. Through her seductive, enticing ways, she makes Theseus her love slave while concurrently conniving with her brother, Xanthos, to kill him should he become too powerful. Theseus, who enjoys their lovemaking immensely, believes that she possesses some genuinely warm feelings for him. Later he realizes the enormity of her wickedness but charitably allows her to escape without punishment. Through this experience, Theseus learns the painful lesson of misguided love. The queen's brother, **Xanthos**, has both the same red hair and evil disposition as his sibling. He acts as her enforcer and executioner. Theseus uncovers Xanthos's plot to have him killed and slays him without mercy.

Also known as the **Cunning One** and the **Scythian Witch**, the priestess **Medea** is the powerful, sinister force behind King Aigeus in Athens. Ruthless and ambitious, she plans to marry the king and make her sons his successors. When Theseus appears, she tries to poison him and is banished from the kingdom when her depravity is discovered.

Of the thirteen other members of the Cranes, several play important roles in the story. **Nephele** is an overly demure, immature girl who often ruffles Theseus's usually calm exterior. She reacts childishly to every misfortune, is prone to fits of screaming and sobbing, and is generally disliked by the group. By contrast, the shy **Chryse**, though child-like, evokes sympathy and support from the group because of her timid, sensitive ways. **Helike** is a born athlete and acrobat who shines early as a bull jumper. However, her silent, independent ways mark her as a loner and ultimately she does not live up to her promise in the bull ring.

Theseus's best friend and the member of the Cranes he trusts most is the tall, fiery believer in justice, **Amyntor**. With the courage and endurance of a lion, he is noted for his maturity and good judgement. The oldest and tallest of the group, he is too slow for bull leaping but ideal for catching. Before his experience in Crete, he was considered rash and impetuous, but the anxiety and constant pressure of bull running transform him into a mature, prudent colleague. Lastly, **Iros** and **Hippon** are two somewhat giddy but likable members of the troupe. Their effeminate natures are so pronounced that Theseus can disguise them as girls and smuggle them into the women's quarters to set the women free on the night of the earthquake.

Asterion is the bastard son of King Minos. With his thick neck, blue-black beard, and coarse, oily hair, he has a beast-like face and "eyes that told nothing." His domineering, tyrannical ways make him despised by others. Theseus, a fine judge of character, refers to him as an "insolent swine." Secretly he has been plotting to turn the native Cretans against the ruling Hellenes to gain control of the throne from **King Minos**, an old, infirm monarch who has become increasingly reclusive. In his rare appearances, Minos always wears long robes and covers his head with a large bull mask. When the fame of Theseus spreads through the palace, Minos takes him into his confidence and reveals that Asterion has infected him with leprosy and, to hide the disease, he covers all parts of his body. Sick both physically and mentally, this noble man begs Theseus to kill him and lead an uprising against Asterion before his pain becomes too great to endure. Theseus obeys him and, later, the wrath of his father god, Poseidon, causes an earthquake that destroys Asterion and the palace.

Theseus's greatest love is the shy, timid **Ariadne**, who is also known as the **Holy One** and **Goddess-on-Earth**. When Theseus first sees her in the robes of a priestess, he says that "she stood like a gilded image, stiff and still; even when she lifted her hands, she hardly seemed made of flesh." Transformed by the power of love and fearful that she will have to marry her half-brother, Ariadne reveals hidden strength and fortitude. Though barely sixteen, she breaks her vows of virginity and delights in her passionate love for Theseus. She also courageously risks her life to thwart Asterion's evil plans. However, on Naxos, when she engages in frenzied religious rituals that involve sexual promiscuity, Theseus decides he must leave her behind.

Further Reading

Authors and Artists for Young Adults. Vol. 10. Detroit: Gale Research, 1993.

Berger, Laura Standley, ed. *Twentieth-Century Young Adult Writers.* 1st ed. Detroit: St. James, 1995.

Bruccoli, Mary, and Jean W. Ross, eds. *Dictionary of Literary Biography Yearbook: 1983.* Detroit: Gale Research, 1984.

Chevalier, Tracy, ed. *Twentieth-Century Children's Writers.* 3rd ed. Detroit: St. James, 1989.

Children's Literature Review. Vol. 15. Detroit: Gale Research, 1988.

Contemporary Authors. Vols. 81-84, 111. Detroit: Gale Research, 1979, 1984.

Contemporary Literary Criticism. Vols. 3, 11, 17. Detroit: Gale Research, 1975, 1979, 1981.

Gallo, Donald R. ed. *Speaking for Ourselves, Too: More Autobiographic Sketches by Notable Authors for Young Adults.* Champaign-Urbana, IL: National Council of Teachers of English, 1993.

Holtze, Sally Holmes, ed. *Sixth Book of Junior Authors and Illustrators.* New York: H. W. Wilson, 1989.

Something about the Author. Vols. 23, 36. Detroit: Gale Research, 1981, 1984.

Anne Rice

1941-, American novelist

Interview with the Vampire

(gothic horror, 1976)

PLOT: The themes of good versus evil, the opposing forces in human nature, the struggle for one's identity, and the loneliness of alienation are all explored in this modern novel that blends contemporary concerns with the classic horror story of gothic richness. The central character is Louis, a young man who became a vampire in the year 1791 at the age of twenty-five. Throughout one long night, he recounts his life to a young interviewer who tapes Louis's story. After the death of his brother, for which he feels responsible, Louis was initiated into vampire life by the older and charismatic vampire Lestat. A child named Claudia is Louis's first victim, and after he has bitten her, Claudia is forever trapped in the body of a five-year-old.

More than half a century later, both Louis and Claudia remain under Lestat's control. To escape his power, Claudia kills the elder vampire. But Lestat is able to come back to life and he attacks them both. In fear for their lives, Louis and Claudia flee to Europe. Intent on finding out all they can about the nature and origin of vampires, Louis and Claudia end up in Paris. At the city's Theatre des Vampires, they meet an entire group of kindred souls. In time, both of them form relationships. Claudia meets an adult woman named Madeleine, and Louis forms an attachment with Armand, who is much older than he and extremely knowledgeable in the ways of vampirehood.

In the end, however, neither Claudia nor Louis can escape the power of Lestat. He suddenly appears in Paris and kills both Claudia and Madeleine when the theatre burns down. Louis is able to flee from both Armand and Lestat, but he is determined to devote his life in a quest to find and destroy Lestat.

Other books in Rice's "Vampire Chronicles" series are The Vampire Lestat *(1985),* The Queen of the Damned *(1988),* The Tale of the Body Thief *(1992), and* Memnoch the Devil *(1995).*

CHARACTERS: As portrayed in this novel, **Louis** is not the typical vampire of the gothic genre. Unlike typical vampires, he feels sorrow, even guilt over his murderous nature and his deeds. When his brother, Paul, was alive, Louis often scoffed at his religious leanings. Only after Paul falls down a flight of stairs and breaks his neck (Louis feels somehow responsible for this because he failed to hear his brother's last words before the accident) does Louis regret not following his brother's inclinations. Also unlike vampires, who usually abhor the church and all its outward symbols of devotion, especially the crucifix, Louis is actually drawn to the church, hoping to find an answer to his life of loneliness and despair.

But there are no answers for him. Louis is doomed to follow his vampire instincts and live a life of alienation. All the while he loathes and condemns his actions and behavior, he is irresistibly compelled to follow the dictates of his desires. Louis knows there is no escape from this life, but he is so remorseful that he agrees to give the long overnight interview to a young journalist in the hope that his own experience, guilt, and sadness will warn others away from such a terrible existence. If this is the price of perpetual life, Louis intimates, no one should seek it.

Louis speaks plainly and gently as he tells the interviewer of his first two hundred years as a vampire. Born into a cultured life as the heir to a great Louisiana plantation in the year 1791, he leaves human life after coming under the influence of the vampire Lestat. Now he is an ageless man, his skin white and smooth as if sculpted from bleached bone, his green, searing eyes intent as he recounts his fascinating story.

Devastated by the death of his brother, he leaves the plantation and wanders the streets of New Orleans like a man who desires only death. Instead, he is attacked by a vampire who sucks his blood and initiates Louis's wanderings on the earth. In plain, almost shockingly mild terms, he describes his "endless life." Under the instruction of the sinister Lestat, he begins his vampire days by sucking the blood of rats in the New Orleans streets, then, of course, moving on to the blood of humans. Yet when he finds the exquisite lost child Claudia, the last vestige of human feeling that is in him wants to save her from his own fate. However, Claudia, too, is soon lost.

Louis recounts his travels with Claudia across Austria and Transylvania and finally to Paris and the Theatre des Vampires, where, through their meeting with Armand, they are introduced to a decadent but brilliant vampire society that fills them with fascination and terror.

Louis fails in his attempt to keep others from his own fate. At the novel's end, the interviewer expresses his desire to become a vampire himself. He asks Louis to initiate him into the mysteries of vampirehood. As Louis ends his tale in despair, he is astounded to hear the journalist demand, "Make me a vampire now!" Louis gasps, "This is what you want? This . . . after all I've told you . . . is what you ask for?" Then, just before the vampire's long, silky lips recede to reveal two long fangs that come down into the interviewer's flesh, Louis says, "I've failed. I have completely failed. . . ."

Beyond the fact that the **interviewer** is a young man, the reader knows little. Throughout the long night of Louis's story, he asks question after question, prodding the vampire into more details and growing ever more fascinated with the frightening tale. Finally, at the end, rather than being revolted he begs to join the dreadful brotherhood. Once the deed is done, he sinks into unconsciousness. In the

***Tom Cruise is the vampire Louis in the 1994 film version of Rice's gothic horror story,* Interview with the Vampire.**

morning, he presses his hand to the place where Louis had drawn blood. Then he picks up his tape recorder and presses on to see Lestat.

The vampire **Lestat** is Louis's evil, dangerous, and spellbinding teacher. Louis explains how Lestat drained him of his blood so that he was at the very threshold of death. It is only Louis's own will that keeps him alive. At that moment, he becomes a vampire. Yet as much as Louis desires it, he can't escape Lestat. Although he flees from him with Claudia and loses himself in Paris, Lestat pursues him.

Louis had thought at first that Lestat died when the Theatre des Vampires burned, but Armand informs him that is not so. Instead, he had fled to the cemetery in Montmartre. Louis encounters his mentor once again in New Orleans. When he leaves Lestat, he sees him hovering at the window as if he were afraid to go out. Louis realizes that perhaps the vampire will never go out again. The great power that Lestat holds over Louis is his ability to blur the distinction between good and evil, so much so that Louis finds it difficult to distinguish between the two. Louis recounts to the interviewer his last meeting with Lestat, saying he has lost all desire for revenge because Lestat is dying, just as humans die, of fear and rigidity.

Perhaps the most tragic figure in the novel is the female vampire **Claudia**, who gains perpetual life as a vampire at a price that dooms her to live forever in the body of a five-year-old. This sets up a dramatic confrontation within herself—the innocent-looking body of a child surrounds the bloodthirsty longings of her vampire nature. Because of her frustration and anger over her predicament, Claudia attempts unsuccessfully to kill Lestat.

The ancient **Armand**, whom Louis meets at the Theatre des Vampires, is very knowledgeable in the ways of vampires. Extremely cynical, Armand becomes Louis's mentor, and Louis develops not only admiration but also a deep love—both physical and spiritual—for this vampire, who denies the existence of both God and the devil. For Armand, the self is the absolute power, and therefore there is no reason to suffer from guilt over one's evil acts. Louis's relationship with Armand emphasizes the futility of finding love or meaning in this life.

Claudia may be seeking a surrogate mother in the dollmaker **Madeleine**, a woman driven insane by the death of her daughter. Louis is convinced by Claudia to turn Madeleine into a vampire, perhaps as a possible companion for himself. Both Claudia and Madeleine die in Paris at the hands of Lestat, when the Theatre des Vampires burns to the ground.

Further Reading

Authors and Artists for Young Adults. Vol. 9. Detroit: Gale Research, 1992.

Berger, Laura Standley, ed. *Twentieth-Century Young Adult Writers.* 1st ed. Detroit: St. James, 1995.

Contemporary Literary Criticism. Vol. 41. Detroit: Gale Research, 1987.

Ferraro, Susan. "Novels You Can Sink Your Teeth Into." *New York Times Magazine* (October 14, 1990): 26-28.

King, Maureen. "Contemporary Women Writers and the 'New Evil': The Vampires of Anne Rice." *Journal of the Fantastic in the Arts* 5:3 (1993): 75-84.

Ramsland, Katherine. *Prison of the Night: A Biography of Anne Rice.* New York: Dutton, 1992.

Roberts, Bette B. *Anne Rice.* New York: Twayne, 1994.

Ann Rinaldi

1934-, American young adult novelist

Wolf by the Ears

(historical novel, 1991)

PLOT: The main character of this novel, Harriet Hemings, is the mulatto child of Sally Hemings and Thomas Jefferson, who is retired from his term as third President of the United States when this story begins in 1820. Harriet, with her light skin, freckled face, and red hair, could pass for a young white woman, but she and her mother are actually slaves owned by Jefferson, working in his home at Monticello. Sally Hemings, however, has gotten Jefferson to agree to grant his children their freedom when they reach the age of twenty-one. Already, Harriet's brother Tom has left Monticello, never to return. Tom, Harriet later learns, has entered white society, breaking all ties with his family and his black heritage. As Harriet's twenty-first birthday nears, she feels that she can't bear to leave Monticello and her mother and family. If she goes and obtains her freedom, she must leave the state and can never return. On the other hand, if she stays she will undoubtedly be married to one of the other black slaves on the plantation and spend the rest of her life in servitude.

Remaining at Monticello means accepting a life of limited opportunity, even as one of President Jefferson's children. For example, when Harriet's brother Beverly asks Jefferson if he can attend the University of Virginia, an institution Jefferson himself founded, his father tells him he is unable to do that. When Beverly complains to Harriet about it, though, she refuses to hear anything derogatory about Jefferson, whom she loves and calls Master.

One day, Charles Bankhead, who is married to Jefferson's granddaughter, Anne, drunkenly attacks Harriet. She is rescued by Thurston, a slave and Harriet's friend and admirer, and also by Thomas Randolph, Jefferson's son-in-law who is the Governor of Virginia. Randolph talks to Harriet about accepting her freedom and leaving Monticello. He asks Harriet if she would be willing to meet with a young white man who much admires her. This could be Harriet's chance for a better life, but it would also mean she would have to pretend she was a white woman. Harriet is horrified by this prospect and refuses. When she meets the young man, Thaddeus, she is nevertheless very taken with him. Thad offers Harriet a home with his sister until that day when they might marry.

After some soul-searching and a long talk with her mother, Harriet decides to leave the only world she has ever known and become a white woman, assuming the name Elizabeth Lackland. Before she leaves Monticello, she speaks with Jefferson, hoping he will at last acknowledge that he is her father. But he does not. For the first and last time, Harriet calls him "Mister Jefferson" instead of Master. When she departs Monticello, she sees the tears in Jefferson's eyes.

CHARACTERS: Tall, intelligent, light-skinned, and red haired **Harriet Hemings** has long heard the rumors that Thomas Jefferson, former President of the United States and owner of Monticello, is her father. Such a relationship is, of course, never acknowledged by Jefferson or by Harriet's mother, Sally. Harriet adores Jefferson, calls him Master, and doubts that she will leave Monticello when she is twenty-one, even though Jefferson has promised to grant her her freedom then. The price of this freedom is leaving Virginia forever and moving north, a price Harriet is reluctant to pay. She doesn't want to leave her family or spend her life pretending she is white to gain acceptance into society. She only begins to think seriously about leaving when Charles Bankhead attacks her. Then, when she meets Thad and is unable to get her own father to acknowledge his paternity, she decides it is best for her to depart Monticello after all.

Harriet's mother, **Sally Hemings**, is portrayed as a woman obsessed with the word "freedom." She accepts her own life as Jefferson's mistress, taking pride in her work running the plantation, but she exacts a promise from Jefferson that her children

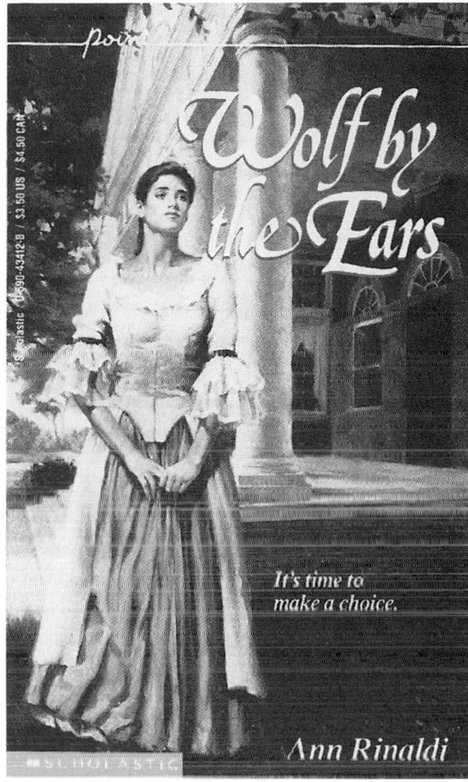

As the daughter of Thomas Jefferson, young slave Harriet Hemings can receive her freedom, but she wants her father to acknowledge her even more.

will be given the option of their freedom when they reach the age of twenty-one. When Harriet objects to leaving behind everything she has known, Sally urges her to reconsider.

The master of Monticello and retired third President of the United States, **Thomas Jefferson**, is portrayed as an intelligent, gentle man caught between the restrictions of the time and his own beliefs. On the subject of slavery, he says: "we have the wolf by the ears, and we can neither hold him, nor safely let him go. Justice is in one scale, and self-preservation in the other." In the end, however, he can't bring himself to break the conventions of the time and acknowledge his own children as his.

Thomas Randolph, Governor of Virginia and Jefferson's son-in-law, is often regarded to be peculiar for his ideas on justice and freedom. He plants in Harriet's mind thoughts of freedom for herself, even at the cost of never returning to Monticello. He tells her that an imperfect world awaits her even when passing as a white woman, but that she can't deny herself the opportunity. He therefore proposes that Harriet meet **Thaddeus** (also called **Thad**), a tall, young, white man with a ruddy face and laugh lines around his eyes. Harriet can tell at once that he is a kind man, and he is also very outspoken against slavery. Consequently, he condemns Thomas Jefferson for keeping slaves. He assures Harriet that if they marry she would not be substituting one white master for another.

Unlike Harriet, her brother **Beverly** is not held back by his fears. An intelligent young man, he is much favored by Jefferson, with whom he has a close relationship. But he is frustrated when Jefferson tells him that he won't help his son go to a university. Before he leaves to find freedom and his own way in the world, Beverly discovers and discloses to Harriet that Jefferson has kept a list of all his slaves. Beverly, Harriet, and Sally are all on that list, so no one will ever know their true relationship to Jefferson.

Further Reading

Authors and Artists for Young Adults. Vol. 15. Detroit: Gale Research, 1995.

Berger, Laura Standley, ed. *Twentieth-Century Children's Writers.* 4th ed. Detroit: St. James, 1995.

Something about the Author. Vols. 51, 78. Detroit: Gale Research, 1988, 1994.

Cynthia Rylant

1954-, American young adult novelist

A Fine White Dust

(young adult novel, 1986)

PLOT: Thirteen-year-old Pete Cassidy has a growing interest in attending church, which he attends by himself in his small home town in North Carolina. Mother and Pop have never cared about formal religion and don't even like to talk about it, so they are mildly surprised when Pete shows an interest, though they do nothing to interfere. Then one day in the town drugstore Pete sees the Man. Right away, he knows this is no ordinary stranger; he has light blue eyes and a special kind of look. At first, Pete wonders if he isn't some kind of crazy strangler. In fact, Pete is kind of glad that his best friend, Rufus the confirmed atheist, comes in at that point and gets him away from the Man's stare.

Later, Pete is astonished to discover that the Man is a preacher. When Pete goes to the revival meeting one hot, steamy night, the Man puts his hands on Pete's head and tells him he has been born again. Pete faints, and when he wakes up he knows he has been saved. All this causes some trouble with his parents because Pete becomes more critical of their irreligious attitudes. It also causes a conflict between him and Rufus that ends in a falling out. But it doesn't matter to Pete, who is certain he is in the right.

Pretty soon, going "his own way" means running away with the Man, who offers him the opportunity to travel, see the world, spread the word, and save people. Pete is spellbound. Willing to leave his home and go with the Man, he agrees to meet the preacher after a prayer meeting. He leaves a note for his parents and goes to the appointed spot, but the Man never shows up. Rufus appears instead and tells Pete to go home. The Man, it seems, has already left town with a girl named Darlene Cook. Apparently, he forgot all about Pete Cassidy.

Pete is stunned, and it take some time before he is able to straighten out his emotions. He doesn't hate the Man for leaving, however, figuring the preacher just wanted to find someone to ease his loneliness. In the meantime, Pete has learned to appreciate the life he has. He has a mother and father who care about him; he has a best friend, too. Rufus may be a hard-nosed atheist, but Pete figures he's a good, honest person and a fine friend. After his experiences with the Man, Pete keeps his religion more to himself. He knows he needs God, but he just doesn't need the church quite as much as he once did. Symbolically, at the end of the story he throws out the broken ceramic pieces in the bottom of his drawer that used to be parts of a cross that belonged to the Man. To Pete they're now just pieces of fine white dust.

CHARACTERS: Pete Cassidy is an unusual young boy who has a serious mind, especially when it comes to religion. At first, he takes this interest in stride. It is just something he's felt a need for since that time in the second grade when he invited himself to go to church with the folks next door because his parents showed no interest. By the fourth grade, Pete began going by himself. But his encounter with the Man changes all that. From the very first meeting at the beginning of the summer, when he sees the hitchhiker with the light-blue eyes, Pete is spellbound. Restless and confused by his feelings, he gets into a mild argument with his parents over religion, which prompts him to attend the revival meeting, where he sees the Man again and is saved. From then on, Pete is drawn ever closer into the magnetic spell of the preacher, and ever more apart from his parents and his best friend, Rufus. Pete begins to feel that if his parents were more religious, they'd be a real family, and he also begins to resist Rufus's flippant attitude about religion.

Finally, with some misgivings, Pete makes the decision to leave his family and go with the Man. He knows how much he will be hurting them, but he feels he has no other choice. Yet, when he is bitterly disappointed because the Man doesn't show up at the appointed hour, Pete begins to come to some understanding about his own religious feelings and about the needs of others. He sees the Man as someone with a gift, but someone who, perhaps, does not know how to cope with his own loneliness. He sees his parents as two loving, responsible people who reserve the right to their own religious opinions just as they allow their son his, and he sees Rufus for the strong, kind, and steadfast friend that he is, no matter what his beliefs. Pete Cassidy learns that religion is a private decision, something that will

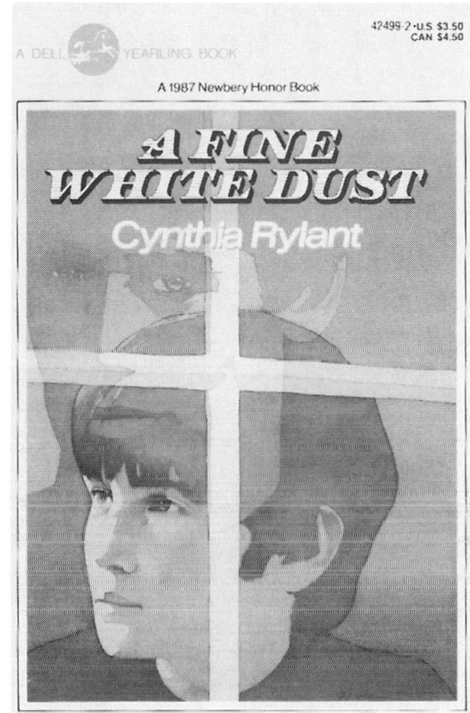

When Pete Cassidy falls under the spell of a smooth-talking preacher, he has to decide whether to accept an invitation to leave his family forever.

continue to grow and be a part of him. The Man is behind him now, but for Pete, God is still there.

James W. Carson is the **Man**, the preacher with the astonishingly blue eyes and the charismatic stare and wondrous voice. Although at first Pete wonders if Carson is an ax murderer, he is soon drawn into the almost hypnotic spell of the preacher man, who saves souls with his promise of a new life. He offers Pete the chance to travel with him by speaking of his own life, the friends he has lost, and the loneliness he has felt. Jesus Christ was fortunate, the Man tells Pete, because he had companions, someone to talk to. He offers that chance to Pete. He tells the boy that he sees the preacher inside him, too. And when he whispers, "Will you come?" Pete can only answer yes. In the end, James W. Carson appears as a man with a gift but also as a lonely soul whose need for companionship overshadows the hurt he might inflict on others. Pete reasons that the Man probably did not mean to hurt him by running off with Darlene Cook and likely never even thought any more about it.

Pete's friend, **Rufus**, calls himself a confirmed atheist, but he is also a confirmed friend. When he sees that there is no way to talk his friend out of running away with the Man, it is Rufus who waits in the shadows to see if the Man will come to get Pete. When he doesn't, Rufus appears to walk the dejected boy back home. Rufus is hurt by Pete's rejection, but he seems to understand Pete's pain, too.

Mother and **Pop** are portrayed as gentle, loving, kind parents who are secure enough in their own convictions to allow their son to follow his inclinations toward religion without apologizing for their own beliefs. After the Man leaves town, they try to talk to Pete about it, but he isn't ready. When he refuses, his mother does not push but says only, "We love you, Pete." In time, Pete comes to understand how strong their love is.

The girl who leaves town with the Man, **Darlene Cook**, returns after about three weeks. She refuses to say a word about where she has been. She says not one word about the preacher either, good or bad.

Missing May

(young adult novel, 1992)

PLOT: Since she was six years old, motherless Summer has lived with Aunt May and Uncle Ob in West Virginia. Now twelve, she dearly loves this elderly couple who adopted her and took her into their rusty old trailer home on a mountainside and into their loving hearts. May constantly tells Summer what a gift she has been to them in their declining years. Aunt May spends most of her time with her garden; Uncle Ob, a disabled war veteran who isn't quite as verbal as his wife, spends his time making whirligigs, pieces of delicate sculpture.

Summer recognizes not only how deeply they love her, but also how much her aunt and uncle love each another. And so it is devastating to both Summer and Uncle Ob when Aunt May dies suddenly while working in her garden. Both of them retire into their separate grief, neither able to help the other. Ob actually seems to retreat into a trance-like existence.

After a few months, a classmate of Summer's, the eccentric Cletus Underwood, appears. He is an oddball whose hobby is saving collections of almost anything that comes to hand. When he begins to search for old newspapers outside the trailer, Uncle Ob invites him in. Summer isn't pleased because Cletus is a rather strange boy. But after his initial appearance, Cletus becomes a frequent visitor, and his company seems to keep Uncle Ob's mind off his grief.

One day Uncle Ob announces that he felt May's presence in the garden. It was so real to him that Cletus becomes interested. Cletus says that he once had an amazing out-of-body experience. With Summer and Cletus, Ob tries once again to bring May's presence back into the garden, but nothing happens this time. After this failure, Uncle Ob withdraws further into himself. Finally, his grief becomes so great that the elderly man no longer bothers to dress in the morning; he just wanders around in his pajamas.

This sad development inspires another idea from Cletus. He has heard about a medium named Reverend Miriam B. Conklin, who lives about three hours away in Glen Meadow. They go to visit Miriam, who calls herself a Small Medium at Large, to get help contacting Aunt May. Summer is dubious but will do almost anything to help Uncle Ob out of his depression. The three drive to Glen Meadow after Cletus gets permission from his parents. To their great disappointment, the three learn that Reverend Conklin has died. Ob insists they return home immediately, which they do in dejected silence. But, suddenly, near the Charleston exit, Uncle Ob announces that they are going to tour the capital city. He has finally accepted the death of his beloved wife and is ready to once again embrace the love of both Summer and Cletus.

When they return to the old trailer, it is Summer's turn to grieve for her beloved aunt, which she does by breaking down into tears. Uncle Ob holds her tenderly. Then the two of them take Uncle Ob's whirligigs out into Aunt May's garden.

CHARACTERS: Summer never knew the love and caring of a family until she was taken in by the elderly Aunt May and Uncle Ob. Until that time, she was cared for by indifferent relatives around the state of Ohio. But since living with her aunt and uncle she has known only love and joy and kindness. She is also witness to a special kind of love between her two caretakers. Their love seems so complete that Summer often wonders to herself how they have any left to spare for her. But she is constantly reminded by her aunt what a special gift she is to them and how she has brightened and blessed their later years. Summer grows to love their life in rural West Virginia, which, though not luxurious, has all the benefits of a close and loving family.

Summer is therefore crushed when her aunt dies so unexpectedly. Although she is grief-stricken herself, Summer is shocked by the actions of her uncle, who seems to retreat into a trance. This becomes worse after the funeral when the two of them must return home to the empty trailer.

Although Summer is at first annoyed at the appearance of the oddball Cletus, she grows fond of this eccentric boy with his sensitive feelings toward others. She is most impressed when she meets his parents in order to secure their permission for the trip to see the medium. His mother and father are so obviously proud of their son that she grows even more fond of him herself.

The miracle Summer never expected occurs on the trip home from Glen Meadow when Uncle Ob is able to accept his wife's death. When they return to the trailer, Summer is at last able to release her own grief. Together, they will keep the memory and the joy of Aunt May alive with the sparkling whirligigs in her garden.

A disabled war veteran, **Uncle Ob** is a loving man who doesn't talk much. He spends most of his time creating the lovely sparkling and spinning sculptures that line the shelves of the trailer. His love for his wife was so complete that even the presence of Summer, whom he deeply loves, can't stop his retreat into loneliness and despair. Uncle Ob will grab at any straw in an attempt to ease his grief and in some sense bring back the wife he so desperately misses. He is crushed when they reach Glen Meadow only to discover that the medium he had convinced himself could help has died. But after this disappointment, Ob is finally able to break through his depression and accept both his deep loss and Summer's love. In that moment he comes to terms with his grief, reawakens his love for Summer, and comes back to life.

Aunt May is a loving and caring woman who is utterly devoted to her husband yet has more than enough love left over for Summer. For Aunt May, the young girl is a precious gift to be cherished and cared for. A giving person, May finds joy in the simple pleasures of her garden and the love of her family.

Most of Summer's classmates, and Summer herself, regard **Cletus Underwood** as eccentric, to say the least. One reason is his predilection for collecting just about anything, starting with potato chip bags. At first finding Cletus mildly amusing, Summer grows fond of this young boy whose compassion and sensitivity is mature for his years. When Uncle Ob first declares that he feels Aunt May's presence in the garden, Cletus is perfectly understanding and willing to help summon her. When that fails and Uncle Ob retreats further into himself, Cletus comes up with the idea of seeing a medium. Rather than reject him or try to cover the fact that their child is considered odd by his peers, Cletus's parents are genuinely proud of his unusual gifts. In his own way, Cletus helps both Summer and Uncle Ob accept the pain of their loss and rejoice in the memory of so much love.

Further Reading

Antonucci, Ron. "Rylant on Writing: A Talk with 1993 Newbery Medalist Cynthia Rylant." In *School Library Journal* 39 (May 1993): 26-29.

Authors and Artists for Young Adults. Vol. 10. Detroit: Gale Research, 1993.

Berger, Laura Standley, ed. *Twentieth-Century Young Adult Writers.* 1st ed. Detroit: St. James, 1995.

Chevalier, Tracy, ed. *Twentieth-Century Children's Writers.* 3rd ed. Detroit: St. James, 1989.

Children's Literature Review. Vol. 15. Detroit: Gale Research, 1988.

Cooper, Ilene. "The Booklist Interview: Cynthia Rylant." *Booklist* 89 (June 1993): 1840-41.

Gallo, Donald R. *Speaking for Ourselves, Too: More Auto-Biographical Sketches by Notable Authors for Young Adults.* Champaign-Urbana, IL: National Council of Teachers of English, 1993.

Holtze, Sally, ed. *Sixth Book of Junior Authors and Illustrators.* New York: H. W. Wilson, 1989.

Rylant, Cynthia. *But I'll Be Back Again: An Album.* New York: Orchard, 1989.

———. *Best Wishes.* New York: Owen, 1992.

———. "Appalachia: The Voices of Sleeping Birds." *Horn Book* 68 (January/February 1992): 31.

Silvey, Anita. "An Interview with Cynthia Rylant." *Horn Book* 63 (November/December 1987): 695-702.

Something about the Author. Vols. 50, 76. Detroit: Gale Research, 1988, 1994.

Something about the Author Autobiography Series. Vol 22. Detroit: Gale Research, 1996.

Ward, Diane. "Cynthia Rylant." *Horn Book* 69 (July/August 1993): 420-23.

Ward, Martha, ed. *Authors of Books for Young People.* 3rd ed. Metuchen, NJ: Scarecrow, 1990.

J. D. Salinger

1919-, American novelist

The Catcher in the Rye

(novel, 1951)

PLOT: In this first-person narrative, Holden Caulfield is a sixteen-year-old, emotionally disturbed boy. In a mental hospital in California, he provides a sort of confession or oral statement to his psychoanalyst. The novel itself is a flashback, introducing many individuals of more or less importance and revealing insights into Holden's character and disturbances. Most of the action in these flashbacks takes place in New York City. Although the time span covered in the book is about four days, the flashbacks are of different times, depending upon the significant event that Holden is recalling. The actual events in this novel are of far less importance than the nuances of detail and language.

In the opening chapter, Holden recalls his days at Pencey Prep, a boy's school in Pennsylvania, from which he has just been expelled. This is not the first time Holden has been in trouble. After a fight with Ward Stradlater, Holden's roommate, who has just returned from a date with a girl Holden likes, Holden leaves school and takes a train to New York City. He checks into a hotel and has some experiences in the city, meeting several characters at different locations. Back at the hotel, he accepts the elevator operator's offer of "a girl." This adventure with a prostitute does not turn out well, resulting only in Holden's frustration and embarrassment.

The next day, Holden has a date with Sally Hayes at the theater and Radio City, but they have an argument and Sally goes home. Next, he meets Carl Luce, a student at Whooton, at the Wicker Bar, and they have a long conversation that is mostly about sex. He gets drunk and decides he'd better go home to the apartment where his family lives. Not knowing that he was in town, his sister Phoebe is at first delighted to see him, but then she realizes he has been expelled again and refuses to talk to him. This is Holden's most serious disappointment.

When Phoebe finally does talk to him and asks why he has failed again, he tries unsuccessfully to explain. Phoebe asks him to name something he likes to do or would like to be. He answers, "the catcher in the rye," which comes from his erroneous reading of a line from a Burns poem, "If a body catch a body coming through the rye." When his parents return, Holden hides from them. He goes to see Mr. Antolini, his former English teacher, remembering that the man was someone he could talk to. Holden, who is exhausted and goes to sleep at the teacher's home, awakens to find Mr. Antolini patting his head. Holden interprets this to be a perverted act, so he flees.

On Monday, Holden goes back to Grand Central Station where he meets Phoebe. She offers to run away with him, but he refuses. They end up at the carousel, where Holden experiences a feeling of perfect freedom. He is happy, even though he is quite sick. In the last chapter, back at the mental hospital in California, Holden expresses the feeling that he will be out soon and will be able to return to school.

CHARACTERS: Although many people appear in this novel, the main—and in a sense only—character of any importance is **Holden Caulfield**. In one way, his story is the story of any boy reeling toward manhood. Like many other literary characters his age, Holden is concerned with the problems of adolescence. But Holden Caulfield is a new kind of hero, a modern hero, Salinger's hero. He is a victim of his society, in the same sense that Willie Loman is in Arthur Miller's *Death of a Salesman*. The modern hero is also found in works by Eugene O'Neill, Tennessee Williams, Carson McCullers, and many others. These people do not fail because there is some flaw in their character—say, jealously or overambition—but rather because the overwhelming force of modern society crushes them. As a result, they are the depressed victims of something they can't overcome or control.

During the four-day journey recounted in this novel, Caulfield is looking for a way to "return home" to a place where he will not be crushed or depressed by the pressures around him. He wants to become involved with people, but they invariably fail or disillusion him. He is, of course, hypersensitive to the people and places around him, so that he often overreacts. Everything and everyone in Holden's world is "phony."

Holden Caulfield is constantly beset by the injustices he sees around him. He has a highly overdeveloped sense of morality and justice. He wants to see things in a moral light, but he is constantly swept into depression by the actions of those people with whom he has personal contact. Everyone fails Holden in a sense, especially his parents. The experience with his English teacher, Mr. Antolini, is also a failure in his view. This is an especially important moment for Holden, who has always looked up to his English teacher as a model of morality. When Mr. Antolini does something that Holden perceives as perverted, Holden flees in horror. In fact, Holden is quite drunk when he goes to see his teacher and could not possibly fully understand what is being said to him or what the teacher intends.

The entire novel is a flashback of Holden Caulfield's experiences and character development. The action is secondary to what is going on in Holden's head as he reveals his thoughts and feelings in a sort of "oral statement" to a psychoanalyst. It is obvious that the young man is emotionally disturbed. He has not learned how to live with the evils of the world that everyone encounters, and he allows it to oppress and depress him. In his inability to cope, Holden remains a child, incapable of being mature enough to deal with anything troubling. Although Holden is confident he will return to school soon, it is clear by the end of the book that he still has not controlled his mental and emotional instabilities.

There are many minor characters in this novel, but they all serve as a backdrop to highlight Holden's reactions and feelings. **Phoebe** is Holden's ten-year-old sister. When he returns to their apartment in New York, he tries to explain to her how he got expelled again. Her disappointment makes Holden feel rejected, and when he tries to tell her how he feels she confronts him with the fact that he doesn't seem to be able to deal with anything that happens to him.

Holden once again feels rejection when he arrives at **Mr. Antolini**'s apartment. His respected English teacher is married to a woman he obviously does not love. This, of course, depresses Holden, who at the time is too drunk to judge anything accurately. The teacher's advice to Holden is good, but the boy is in no condition or frame of mind to receive it. When he falls asleep and awakens to feel Mr. Antolini's hand on his hair, Holden interprets this as a perverted act and leaves, feeling revulsion and disappointment once again. Yet, Holden is changed somewhat by the encounter, for although he condemns his teacher when he flees the apartment, he later reconsiders and changes his mind.

Holden has a date with **Sally** during his New York trip. He says to himself at this time that he must be crazy because although he didn't even like Sally very much, he all of a sudden feels he is in love with her. He gets annoyed during the date when Sally meets a boy she knows. Later, when he tries to tell her of his troubles, she does not show interest and wants him to change the subject. When Holden tells her that she is depressing him, she understandably leaves in a huff.

Further Reading

Authors and Artists for Young Adults. Vol. 2. Detroit: Gale Research, 1989.

Belcher, William Francis, ed. *J. D. Salinger and the Critics.* Belmont, CA: Wadsworth, 1962.

Berger, Laura Standley, ed. *Twentieth-Century Young Adult Writers.* 1st ed. Detroit: St. James, 1994.

Bloom, Harold, ed. *Twentieth-Century American Literature.* Vol. 6 of the *Chelsea House Library of Literary Criticism.* New York: Chelsea House, 1987.

———, ed. *Holden Caulfield.* New York: Chelsea House, 1990.

Children's Literature Review. Vol. 18. Detroit: Gale Research, 1989.

Contemporary Literary Criticism. Vols. 1, 3, 8, 55, 56. Detroit: Gale Research, 1973, 1975, 1978, 1989, 1989.

Critical Essays on Salinger's Catcher in the Rye. Boston: Hall, 1989.

Critical Survey of Long Fiction. Vol. 6. Englewood Cliffs, NJ: Prentice-Hall, 1983.

Daughtry, Vivian F. "A Novel Worth Teaching: Salinger's *The Catcher in the Rye.*" In *Virginia English Bulletin* 36: 2 (winter 1986): 88-94.

French, Warren G. *J. D. Salinger.* Boston: Twayne, 1976.

Grunwald, Henry A., ed. *Salinger: A Critical and Personal Portrait.* New York: Pocket Books, 1962.

Gwynn, Frederick L. *The Fiction of J. D. Salinger.* Pittsburgh: University of Pittsburgh Press, 1958.

Hamilton, Ian. *In Search of J. D. Salinger.* New York: Random House, 1988.

Hamilton, Kenneth. *J. D. Salinger: A Critical Essay.* Grand Rapids, MI: Eerdmans, 1967.

Hassan, Ihab. "J.D. Salinger: Rare Quixotic Gestures." In *Radical Innocence: Studies in the Contemporary American Novel.* Princeton: Princeton University Press, 1961.

Helterman, Jeffrey, and Richard Layman, eds. *American Novelists since World War II.* Vol. 2 of *Dictionary of Literary Biography.* Detroit: Gale Research, 1978.

Kimbel, Bobby Ellen, ed. *American Short-Story Writers, 1910-1945, Second Series.* Vol. 102 of *Dictionary of Literary Biography.* Detroit: Gale Research, 1991.

Lundquist, James. *J. D. Salinger.* New York: Ungar, 1979.

Marsden, Malcolm M. *If You Really Want to Know: A Catcher Casebook.* Chicago: Scott, Foresman, 1963.

Miller, James E. *J. D. Salinger.* Minneapolis: University of Minnesota Press, 1965.

New Essays on Catcher in the Rye. Cambridge: Cambridge University Press, 1992.

Pinsker, Sanford. The Catcher in the Rye: *Innocence under Pressure.* New York: Twayne, 1993.

Salzman, Jack, ed. *New Essays on* The Catcher in the Rye. New York: Cambridge University Press, 1991.

Simonson, Harold Peter, ed. *Salinger's "Catcher in the Rye": Clamor vs. Criticism.* Boston: Heath, 1963.

Something about the Author. Vol. 67. Detroit: Gale Research, 1992.

Ouida Sebestyen

1924-, American young adult novelist

Words by Heart

(young adult novel, 1968)

PLOT: The Sills family, including Lena, her papa, Ben Sills, her stepmother, Claudie, and the younger kids, Roy, Armilla, and the baby, have moved to Bethel Springs, where they are the only black family around. It is the dawn of the twentieth century, and Papa hopes to find better opportunities for his family out west, where he prays the lingering effects of racial prejudice will not be as strong as they were in the south.

Not long after the Sills settle in, however, they become the target of resentment. For example, when Mr. Haney, a sharecropper on Mrs. Chism's land, is fired for drinking on the job, Lena's papa is hired in his place. Naturally, that doesn't sit well with the Haneys, including the nearly grown Tater Haney. The Starnes family isn't too pleased with the Sills either, especially Lena, who won the scripture reciting contest at school when everyone was convinced that the winner would be Winslow Starnes. When the Sills return from the contest they find a huge butcher knife stabbed into a fresh loaf of bread Claudie baked. It is clearly a threat. Still, Papa assures Lena that they just have to have patience with people. Lena isn't so certain things will work out for her family, though.

Lena gets a job after school helping the cranky, demanding Mrs. Chism. The old lady has many books, and Lena "borrows" a few to read at home without telling Mrs. Chism. Even though Lena returns them, Papa tells her that what she did was stealing and makes her confess to Mrs. Chism. To ease the woman's wrath, Papa agrees to do some fence mending for her for a few days. While he is gone, a drunken Mr. Haney tries to break into the Sills house but is frightened away. When Papa doesn't return, Lena bravely goes after him. She finds him dying of a gunshot wound from Tater Haney, who is also hurt. Knowing he is near death, Papa nevertheless makes Lena promise not to reveal who shot him.

With Papa gone, Lena wonders how they will survive. She tells her stepmother that she will go back east if it will help, but Claudie says Papa wanted them to build a life out west. Claudie agrees to work for Mrs. Chism, as long as she is treated with respect. When Lena sees Mr. Haney picking the last of the cotton in the Sills field for them, she believes there might be hope for the future after all.

CHARACTERS: Papa calls his daughter, **Lena Sills**, a "magic mind" because she is so smart in school and loves to read. But Lena by no means tries to flaunt her intelligence. When she wins the scripture reciting contest, beating the white boy who was expected to win, her goal was only to make her

Lena Sills and her family must struggle to find acceptance in an all-white community in this 1968 novel.

father proud. She hoped that skin color would not matter in their new home, yet Lena is determined to be judged by her own worth. She fights back against her young schoolmates' injustices, proudly standing her ground. Lena faces her biggest challenge when her father is shot by Tater. At first, she refuses to help the wounded Tater as her father has asked her to, but her father convinces her that if she can do this she will have the courage to face almost anything for the rest of her life.

Lena does not understand **Papa**'s tolerant attitude toward the white people of the town. **Ben Sills** tries to explain to her that violence only begets violence. He tells her about how they moved to Kansas to find freedom, then back south when they were still faced with prejudice, and finally out west to seek another chance. Ever optimistic that one day things will get better, Papa says all these moves constitute a "hoping time." A man of incredible compassion, he forgives Tater for shooting him and even tells Lena to help the boy.

Claudie, Lena's stepmother, is a practical woman, less of a dreamer than her husband. When he dies, she stands up to the difficult Mrs. Chism, declaring that she will work for the old lady, but only on her terms. A woman of great determination and courage, she vows to raise her sons to be like her husband and stand up to racism with pride and compassion for all.

Mrs. Chism is a rich resident of the community. Jowly, sharp-eyed, and sharp-tongued, Mrs. Chism strikes fear into almost everyone, Lena included. Lena is awed by Mrs. Chism's home but loves her books most of all. When Lena "borrows" some without telling her, she fires the girl. Although Mrs. Chism's character does not soften, even with the death of Lena's father, she displays a sense of fairness as she resolves the issues of how the Sills family can continue to live and work on her land.

Mr. Haney and his son **Tater** are portrayed as typical whites of the time who are filled with racial hatred, frightened that blacks will take their jobs. When the elder Haney is fired for drinking at work, he blames Ben Sills for taking over his position. Tater does, too, which leads him to shoot Ben. When Lena does not get Tater thrown in jail for his crime, however, Mr. Haney is big enough to show his gratitude by helping the Sills in their cotton field.

Another white character who changes his racist ways is **Winslow Starnes**. Winslow was taught not to trust blacks, and he is resentful when he loses the scripture recital contest to Lena, but after the tragedy of Lena's father, Winslow appears at the Sills home. His father orders him back to school, but young Winslow stands his ground for once. "I'm going to stay here," he says firmly. "in case there's anything else I can do."

Further Reading

Authors and Artists for Young Adults. Vol.8. Detroit: Gale Research, 1992.

Berger, Laura Standley, ed. *Twentieth-Century Young Adult Writers.* 1st ed. Detroit: St. James, 1994.

Children's Literature Review. Vol. 17. Detroit: Gale Research, 1989.

Contemporary Literary Criticism. Vol. 30. Detroit: Gale Research, 1984.

Holtze, Sally Holmes, ed. *Fifth Book of Junior Authors and Illustrators.* New York: H. W. Wilson, 1983.

Something about the Author. Vol. 39. Detroit: Gale Research, 1985.

Something about the Author Autobiography Series. Vol. 10. Detroit: Gale Research, 1990.

Mary Wollstonecraft Shelley

1797-1851, English novelist

Frankenstein; or, The Modern Prometheus

(horror novel, 1818)

PLOT: The novel is narrated by Robert Walton, an English explorer. Walton writes to his sister about embarking on a journey to the arctic. When his expedition becomes stranded by huge blocks of ice, Walton and the ship's company are astonished to see what appears to be a huge figure on a dogsled in the distance. The following day, they discover an emaciated man adrift near their ship. They take him aboard, and when he is able to talk he relates an incredible story.

The man introduces himself as Victor Frankenstein, a scientist from a distinguished Geneva family. Victor relates to his rescuers the fantastic story of his experiences. Educated at the University of Ingolstadt, Victor developed an interest in science and became especially fascinated with the possibilities of overcoming death. After many years of intense study and unconventional experiments, he was able to fashion an eight-foot monster from body parts he collected from dissecting rooms and butcher shops. Putting his research to the test, he endowed the creature with life but was horrified by the results. For the next two years, Victor knew nothing of the whereabouts of the monster and was bedridden with brain fever. His friend, Henry Clerval, came to nurse him, but Victor did not tell him of the experiment. Victor's condition began to improve

Boris Karloff played Frankenstein's monster in the classic 1931 movie version of Shelley's horror novel.

after receiving news from Elizabeth, an orphan whom his parents adopted when Victor was a child. (In Shelley's original concept of the novel, the letter from Elizabeth was to be the starting point. When she was persuaded to lengthen the story, however, Shelley described the monster's creation in far more detail than she originally intended.)

Terrible news arrives from Geneva in a letter from Victor's father, Alphonse. His young brother, William, has been strangled. Alphonse asks Victor to return to Geneva after his six-year absence. It is at this point in the novel that the reader begins to see the effect that the monster has had on Victor's life. Victor realizes that his monster is responsible for the death, but he says nothing as Justine Moritz, another orphan adopted by the family, is charged with the murder. Both Victor and Elizabeth believe her to be innocent, but she is hanged for the crime. Now Victor feels responsible for two deaths.

Soon afterward, when Victor is out alone in the countryside, the monster appears. He explains that since Victor deserted him he has been without companionship; all who see him run away in terror. This has filled his heart with bitterness and fury, which made him strangle young William. The monster demands that Victor make him a mate so that he will no longer be lonely. If Victor creates him a companion, the monster promises, he and his mate will go to the wilds of South America and never be seen again. Reluctantly, Victor agrees and begins work in a remote part of Scotland. But in the middle of the process, he changes his mind because he fears his monsters will spawn a new race. The creature sees Victor destroy what was to have been his mate and threatens vengeance.

Soon after, Henry Clerval is murdered. Although Victor is suspected for a time, he is released and he returns to Geneva. He and Elizabeth decide to marry, despite the monster's warnings that a terrible punishment will befall him on his wedding night. Keeping his word, the monster strangles Elizabeth in the nuptial chamber. Victor vows that he will find the monster and destroy him for this. His travels take him to the arctic, where Walton finds him. After telling his story, the weakened Frankenstein dies. The monster appears and tells Walton that it was Frankenstein who committed the greater crime, having created a being without a soul, without love, and without a friend. Telling Walton that he plans to make a gigantic funeral fire and throw himself on it, the monster disappears over the ice fields.

CHARACTERS: Frankenstein's monster is one of the most fascinating characters of this type in literature. He is commonly referred to by the name of the man who created him, but critics argue that the misnomer is not really a mistake, since the monster is really Victor's other self. At the outset, the monster is gentle and intelligent. He is a kind of noble savage, unschooled and unlettered and dropped into a world he does not understand. Once he is subjected to the cruelty of the real world, rejected and abhorred, he turns bitter, rebellious, and brutal. Not only does his isolation serve to illustrate the cruelty of humanity, but his existence warns of the dangers of science gone unchecked. Although Shelley's work is not unanimously considered great literature, the monster and his story have stirred readers for decades.

Described by Shelley herself as a modern Prometheus—a figure in Greek mythology who tried to wrest power from the gods and was dealt a terrible punishment—**Victor Frankenstein** is portrayed as a young scientist with romantic qualities. He rebels against society by creating his monster, but that act results in his isolation and terrible guilt. Some critics argue that Frankenstein's true tragedy is that he doesn't take responsibility for his own creation. He is also seen as a character filled with such overambition that it leads to his downfall. Once Frankenstein realizes what a terrible mistake he has made, instead of destroying the monster, he runs away from it, both physically and mentally. Although Victor is initially portrayed in a positive light, his deepening moral cowardice ultimately alienates the sympathies of the reader.

Elizabeth Lavenza, adopted by Victor's parents and raised as if she were his real sister, is an innocent victim of Frankenstein's creation. She is murdered on her wedding night because of her husband's unwillingness to fulfill his promise of creating a mate for his monster. Elizabeth, like **Justine Moritz** and young **William Frankenstein**, represents purity and innocence. The fates of Elizabeth and Justine parallel each other: both are orphans adopted by the Frankenstein family and they both come to a terrible end. They represent the good and the innocent who are destroyed by the evils of humankind.

Another innocent victim of the monster is **Henry Clerval**, Victor's close friend. Henry is a romantic and chivalrous person who functions as a foil to the scientific, often tormented Frankenstein. During the period when Victor suffers from confusion and despair after creating the monster, he impulsively begs his friend to save him. But Henry, who is somewhat short on imagination, interprets the outburst as an attack of brain fever, and it is not mentioned again. During Victor's long recuperation, Henry alone attends him, and the true cause of Victor's suffering is not discussed.

Minor characters include **Alphonse Frankenstein**, Victor's father, who is portrayed as a noble humanitarian, accepting those less fortunate into his household and caring for them. Arctic explorer **Robert Walton**, the narrator of the novel, relates the particulars of Frankenstein's tale in a practical way, befitting a man of science. He also provides a dramatic opening and closing for the story.

Further Reading

Bann, Stephen. *Frankenstein, Creation and Monstrosity.* Seattle: University of Washington Press, 1955.

Bennett, Betty T., and Charles E. Robinson. *Mary Shelley Reader.* New York: Oxford, 1990.

Bleiler, E. F., ed. *Science Fiction Writers.* New York: Scribner's, 1982.

Bloom, Harold, ed. *Mary Wollstonecraft Shelley.* New York: Chelsea House, 1986.

Botting, Fred. *Making Monstrous: Frankenstein, Criticism, Theory.* New York: St. Martin's, 1991.

Critical Survey of Long Fiction. Vol. 6. Englewood Cliffs, NJ: Salem Press, 1983.

Greenfield, John R., ed. *British Romantic Prose Writers, 1789-1832, Second Series.* Vol. 110 of *Dictionary of Literary Biography.* Detroit: Gale Research, 1991.

Hindle, Maurice. *Mary Shelley:* Frankenstein. New York: Penguin, 1995.

Levine, George, and U. C. Knoepflmacher, eds. *The Endurance of* Frankenstein: *Essays on Mary Shelley's Novel.* Berkeley: University of California Press, 1979.

Nineteenth Century Literary Criticism. Vol. 14. Detroit: Gale Research, 1987.

Phy, Allene S. *Mary Shelley.* San Bernardino: Borgo, 1988.

Spark, Muriel. *Mary Shelley.* New York: Dutton, 1987.

Sunstein, Emily. *Mary Shelley: Romance and Reality.* Boston: Little, Brown, 1989.

Veeder, William. *Mary Shelley and Frankenstein: The Fate of Androgyny.* Chicago: University of Chicago Press, 1986.

Walling, William A. *Mary Shelley.* New York: Twayne, 1972.

William Sleator

1945-, American novelist

House of Stairs

(young adult novel, 1974)

PLOT: In this novel set sometime in the future, five sixteen-year-old orphans are taken from their various institutional residences, blindfolded, and transported to a strange environment where there are no walls or windows—only endless flights of stairs broken by an occasional landing. The first to arrive are the fearful, shy Peter and the brash, outspoken Lola. Soon they are joined by fat and vindictive Blossom, the impressionable Abigail, and the handsome Oliver, an overly confident boy who enjoys being the center of attention. Blossom is the first to discover the food machine, which disgorges food seemingly erratically when activated by various movements, including dancing, by the young people. On another landing they find water and toilet facilities.

Soon their lives become a constant battle to trigger the food machine. The stress caused by their surroundings and the struggle for food gradually takes its toll. The teens reveal weaknesses and strengths as they battle constant hunger. After weeks of confinement it becomes apparent to the group that the machine is conditioning them to hate and distrust; it rewards them with food for attacking and brutalizing one another. Lola refuses to accept these conditions for living and persuades Peter to leave the others with her. They move to a distant landing.

After several days of isolation they visit their former friends and find they are receiving nourishment only because they perform acts of mental and physical violence upon each other. Horrified, Lola and Peter return to their perch. As death from starvation approaches, Lola's survival instincts compel her to seek food, regardless of the consequences. Reluctantly, Peter agrees to accompany her back to the machine, but elevators mysteriously appear and take all five friends away.

After recuperating from their ordeal, they are debriefed by the officious Dr. Lawrence, who explains that they have been part of a conditioning experiment designed to produce unquestioning, dispassionate automatons to form part of an elite presidential corps. The doctor states that the procedure was only partly successful because only three of the subjects are ready for further conditioning. The other two, Peter and Lola, are sent to the outside world as "misfits"; the doctor never realizes how close he came to complete success.

CHARACTERS: In addition to their fast-paced plots, Sleator's novels contain serious elements involving personal development, interpersonal relationships, and ethical choices. The anti-behaviorist message in *House of Stairs* explores the inhumanity of subjecting people to conditioning tests. The first youngster introduced is **Peter**, a pathetically shy, withdrawn boy, frail and unattractive, with a pale face and whitish-blonde hair. He is overly-cautious, fearful, and impressionable. Since his parents' death, he has been shunted from one institution to another for "not adjusting." In one placement, he formed a deep attachment to a boy named Jason who had protected and shielded him, but since the most recent move, Peter has become more withdrawn and distant. On first meeting him, Lola correctly assesses him as a "shy, sensitive creep. The kind who never wants to have any fun because he is always afraid of getting caught." His soft voice and quiet, mumbling speech coupled with his compliant disposition allows him to be virtually invisible to others. When the fight for food becomes more violent, he lapses further into himself and his own illusory perceptions to escape the harsh reality of their situation. He is portrayed as unambitious and unresourceful, easily swayed, and lacking a sense of self-worth. When he and Lola defy the others and resist the dehumanizing conditioning of the food machine, a transformation takes places in which Peter suddenly finds a previously unknown inner strength. He discovers a purpose in life—a reason for being—and a cause for which he can sacrifice his life if necessary. He has never before experienced these feelings of independence or identity, and they give him courage and stamina. Only his loyalty towards Lola convinces him to momentarily abandon his newfound convictions. Peter emerges from this ordeal a mature, confident, and secure person.

Lola is a "tough cookie." With her dark hair, olive skin, and brassy demeanor, she presents the picture of an aggressive, outspoken, sensible girl who has been hardened and shaped by adversity. She is fearless, confident, and assertive. A born leader, she enjoys adventure, trickery, and defying authority. Always positive in her outlook, the bright and resourceful Lola refuses to accept defeat. Beyond her rugged exterior, she has compassion for others less fortunate. Although she despises human weakness, Lola realizes that Peter deserves her concern and protection because of his helplessness. Lola abhors phony behavior or male chauvinism, and this intolerance causes frequent conflicts with Blossom and Oliver. Although experience has made her an independent loner, she is willing to compromise for the benefit of the group. A logical thinker, Lola frequently suggests solutions to the group's dilemmas. Though she has not had the nurturing benefit of positive familial or social relationships, Lola's ingrained belief in human dignity and worth causes her to face starvation rather than to submit to the inherently unjust conditioning of the food machine. However, when faced squarely with the possibility of her own death, her love of life and desire to live overcome her aversion to the food machine's methods. Saved from jeopardizing her ideals when the experiment ends, Lola emerges as a strong and admirable young woman, a born survivor.

Overweight, disagreeable **Blossom Pilkington** is snobbish about her apparently privileged background. She claims, without proof, that her family is wealthy and influential and that her parents were killed only one month before. Cow-like with large golden curls and dressed in an unattractive ruffled dress, she appears more like an overgrown child than a teenager. Her behavior—spoiled, petulant, and devious—matches her appearance. When thwarted, she indulges in temper tantrums, foot stomping, and shrieking. In addition to her emotional immaturity, she exhibits deceitful behavior, deriving satisfaction from turning people against each other. She resents Lola's self-assurance and leadership, telling lies about her to Oliver and Abigail. Perhaps due to her own appearance and bodily shortcomings, she dislikes beauty, either physical or psychological, in others. Conscious of her obesity and unpopularity, she has developed a sly, vindictive personality, delighting in destroying friendships and goodwill to compensate for her own loneliness and unhappiness. This divisive behavior leads to constant tension within the group. Because she craves attention and affection, she often shows mock concern and phony congeniality to attract attention. Blossom is a cunning and selfish youngster who knows how to take advantage of human vulnerabilities. She has channeled much of her thwarted needs and negative energy into eating; she has a voracious appetite and will fight fiercely to protect her food supply. Her mean, selfish ways guarantee at least one "successful subject" in the experiment to dehumanize the teenagers.

The naive and innocent **Abigail** is a sweet, unassuming girl whose institutional days have been spent in a sheltered, protected environment lacking contact with both boys and any of life's cruelties. Her beautiful appearance (slender and tall, with shining blonde hair) reflects a serene disposition; she radiates an attractive purity and gentleness. She is accepting of others, sympathetic, and always anxious to please. Despite her open and placid temperament, however, she is unsure of herself, unable to accept responsibilities or make decisions. Others take advantage of her easily because she lacks assertiveness and self-confidence. Impressionable, innocent, and trusting, she presents the perfect target for the advances of Oliver and the deceit of Abigail. Easily led, she initially becomes confused by the behavioral conditioning and in time loses all traces of human feelings.

The fifth member of the group is **Oliver**, a handsome, self-assured young man with curly, dark-blonde hair, intense blue-grey eyes, and a muscular, athletic body. He exudes charm and confidence. With his chiseled features and puckish good humor, he is popular with all. However, behind this forced cheerfulness and congeniality resides a massive ego that thrives on attention and adulation. He must be the center of attention in a group, the primary person who wields the power and makes the decisions. When confronted by a rival, such as Lola, he retreats and becomes moody and petulant. He takes advantage of the innocent Abigail but lacks the assurance to consummate their union. Beneath this arrogant self-confidence and conceit, Oliver is actually unsure of himself and of his real worth. These internal conflicts and weaknesses identify him as an easy mark for behavior modification.

Dr. Lawrence is the diabolical and corrupt power behind the experiments. In his coldly scientific way, he never acknowledges that his actions have been monstrous or inhumane. Sensitive to criticism, he bridles at any questions posed by Lola concerning the cruel and barbarous nature of the experiments or the unethical thinking behind them. Dr. Lawrence believes that the value of scientific theories and research supersedes concerns about human values, ideals, and morality. He simplistically maintains that the ends justify the means; in this case, his goal of creating heartless, savage robots for the purpose of military or government applications rationalizes his mistreatment of the teens.

Interstellar Pig

(science fiction novel, 1984)

PLOT: Sixteen-year-old Barney and his parents are spending their two-week summer vacation in a cottage on Cape Cod owned and cared for by Ted Martin. Barney learns that, more than one hundred years earlier, a sea captain named Latham had imprisoned his brother in Barney's room after the young man killed a stranger they had rescued during one of their voyages. Shortly after Barney hears about the history of the house, three attractive college-age people—Zena, Joe, and Manny—arrive next door and befriend him. They exhibit somewhat unusual behavior, including a fanatical interest in the room where Barney sleeps and a tendency to speak English as if they had only recently learned it.

They introduce Barney to a board game called "Interstellar Pig," in which each player becomes a creature from outer space trying to get possession of a card marked "Piggy." At the end of the game, the player who owns the Piggy wins, and all the other players and their planets are destroyed. Barney presently discovers that his neighbors own a copy of Latham's diary and that scratch marks made by the prisoner a century earlier on his bedroom walls intersect on the windowpane in line with a huge boulder at the tip of a neighboring island. When his new friends insist on exploring this island, Barney tags along. Eluding his companions for a few moments, Barney uncovers a small box buried close to the rock and hides it. Back on the mainland, he opens the box and finds a repellent carved figure—the real Piggy. Barney now realizes that the three visitors are actually extraterrestrials in disguise intent on surviving the end of a gigantic galactic game of Interstellar Pig by gaining possession of this figure.

Concluding that the Piggy was lost when one of their number had fallen to Earth with it in his possession, Barney believes that, after being saved by Latham's brother, the creature momentarily assumed its real appearance and so frightened the young man that he killed it, stole the talisman, and buried it on the island. Subsequent to his discovery, during an unpredicted violent storm one night, Barney's three neighbors come over to play another game with him while he is alone in the house. Because they now know that Barney has recovered the real Piggy, they play in deadly earnest, with each of them assuming their true identity. Zena becomes Zulma, an arachnoid monster, Manny becomes Moyna, a female octopus-like creature, and Joe is Jrlb, a gill-man.

The game develops into a life or death struggle with each player attempting in various ways to gain possession of the Piggy and, if necessary, to kill Barney. The unexpected arrival of more game players, man-eating lichen from outer space—which also intend to secure the Piggy—saves Barney from certain death. When the lichen prevail and escape into space with the figurine, the three other aliens follow, each in a separate spacecraft. One final question remains: Having lost the Piggy, will Barney and his planet, Earth, be destroyed at the end of the game?

CHARACTERS: The extremely likable hero and narrator of this thriller is sixteen-year-old **Barney**, who prefers reading science fiction over spending a boring afternoon at the beach. Unhappy at being isolated for two weeks without companions his own age in a remote cottage far from his big-city interests, he can't even enjoy time outdoors, as sun exposure produces painful burns on his fair skin. Zena exploits his photosensitivity by deliberately engineering an agonizing sunburn in a vain attempt to immobilize Barney while she and her friends explore the island. Like other boys his age, Barney is curious, inquisitive, and anxious to explore the unknown and the bizarre. Restless and eager for adventure, he is especially susceptible to the attentions of the three strangers, particularly the alluring Zena. Fearful of endangering this new-found friendship and intrigued by their sophisticated ways and disarming mannerisms, Barney tries to please them by acquiescing to their requests, such as their peculiar desire to search his house and bedroom. But Barney's superior intelligence and keen perception soon surface, prompting him to question their bizarre behavior. His creative imagination and sharp insights lead him to conclusions that would escape others his age. He shows remarkable resourcefulness and great courage in combating his enemies; he also displays previously unrealized powers of endurance. Barney is also a dutiful, obedient son who, at the height of the battle with the three alien monsters, worries as much about ruining the living room rug as about the impending destruction of the planet Earth.

Barney's parents, known only as **Mom** and **Dad**, appear to be typically middle-aged and middle-class. Both are concerned about their son's welfare. His mother tends to be overly solicitous, particularly about keeping the cottage neat and clean. A social climber who is impressed by wealth and position more than character, she is normally suspicious of strangers, yet when the three new arrivals seem both refined and affluent, she accepts them immediately. She especially tries to impress the two young men, actually becoming jealous that her son has been accepted by them before she has. She also exhibits a vain side, placing suntanning above regular household concerns. Her husband is a less prominent character. Quiet and unassuming, he tends to pale in comparison with his more dominant wife.

Ted Martin is the owner and caretaker both of the house where Barney's family are staying and of the ugly cinderblock cottage rented by the three strangers. The second house was built by the Martin family solely as a rental income property. Ted shares his wealth of information about local history with Barney, telling him about the house, Captain Latham, and the unusual markings around the bedroom window.

The first of the inhuman trio to insinuate itself into Barney's life is **Zena**, later known as **Zulma**. In her human form she is ravishingly beautiful, with "a figure as flawless as a movie star's." With her long, slender neck, wide mouth, and piercing eyes, she immediately captivates Barney. Like her companions, she is about college age and radiates charm and good breeding. At first, she appears demure and kittenish, but in times of tension, her appearance alters; Barney notices that she becomes suddenly heavy, brusque, controlling, and abusive—her true, ruthlessly cruel nature emerges. She is cunning and determined to secure the Piggy at any price. Though all three act together in the game, only one can finally secure the figurine and ultimately survive. Therefore, in the absence of her companions, she attempts to bribe Barney to produce the talisman by offering him an intelligence booster which supposedly will guarantee him power and success. (As the most intelligent of the group, her Interstellar Relative Sapience Code is 10, a very high rating.) When she reveals her true identity, she transforms into Zulma, an arachnoid nymph from Vavoosh characterized as "brilliant and marvelously sneaky." This hairy spider woman who speaks with a hoarse, guttural chirping and weaves a deadly web about her victims, is four feet high and so fat that she must move sideways through doorways. Her leg joints ride higher than her body, and she has huge insect eyes. Ugly and vindictive, her only regret in leaving Earth in pursuit of the Piggy is that she did not kill Barney.

Joe, who later becomes **Jrlb**, is introduced as a handsome, powerfully built, athletic type sporting a brown mustache. He, too, befriends Barney to further his own ends. Acting alone, he attempts to secure the Piggy from Barney by offering him travel in hyperspace. Barney first becomes suspicious of Joe when he notices his wide, bumpy, calloused feet with purple stains under his toenails. Joe's real name is Jrlb, a water-breathing gill man from Thrilb, who resembles a swordfish with rudimentary arms and legs. This fish man with a long, razor-sharp horn protruding from his head emits a powerful briny reek and has a smooth, oily grey hide. His scaly webbed hands and feet contrast with his noseless, earless face with its lipless mouth slit. The fact that Jrlb can live only a short time out of water helps Barney escape his clutches.

The third member of the trio is **Manny**, who becomes **Moyna**. Like the others he is physically attractive, well-built, and handsome in his human form. He is somewhat more vain than the other two and is accused by Zena of bleaching his well-trimmed blond beard. In addition to his veneer of charm, he too employs flamboyant speech, flatters Barney, and exhibits reluctance to reveal details about his past. Of the three, he appears to show the most genuine interest in Barney, but, in his attempt to gain possession of the Piggy, he also resorts to bribery, tempting Barney with eternal youth as an inducement (he confesses to be 138 years old!). Manny often displays a feminine side to his character through frequent giggles and prissy attitudes. This effeminate aspect of his nature naturally reflects his true identity, Moyna, a female octopus gas bag creature from the planet Flaeioub. She is a fearsome sight with talons at the end of each tentacle and a soft, pulsating head covered with a slimy, mucous-like membrane. She has bulbous eyes and a mouth shaped like the end of a balloon which emits a fetid, sour breath.

The object of the aliens' quest is the **Piggy**, a small, round, lightweight, garish-pink figurine. Its face contains only a mouth with a mocking smile and a single deformed open eye. This repulsive creature speaks in enigmas to Barney, who even after surrendering it to the lichen, is mystified about its real significance: Is it a cosmic hoax or a real threat to the Earth's future?

Singularity

(science fiction novel, 1985)

PLOT: With their parents' consent, identical twins Harry and Barry Krasner leave their Boston home to take care of a house in Sushon, Illinois, which their mother has just inherited from an eccentric uncle, Ambrose Kittery. Though physically alike, the sixteen-year-old boys have very different personalities. Harry's quiet passivity contrasts with Barry's overbearing aggressiveness. These differences often result in situations in which Harry must either retreat or become the scapegoat for Barry. After obtaining the keys to their deceased uncle's strange, forbidding house from the lawyer Mr. Crane, they begin to explore the property and meet attractive Lucy Coolidge, the daughter of their new neighbors. She tells them about their quirky uncle and how, before Ambrose built an outbuilding called the playhouse on his property, unusual circumstances often beset the Coolidge farm animals: sometimes after wandering onto Kittery property they would return looking ancient and haggard, or, in some cases, they would disappear completely.

The three find keys to the playhouse and discover that it contains the furniture and belongings of a studio apartment plus a large supply of stored food. Through a series of mysterious occurrences, including the death of Harry's dog Fred, they deduce that the playhouse conceals an awesome phenomenon: it is built on the entrance to another universe where time proceeds at a different pace than on earth, so that an hour in the playhouse equals one second outside. This hidden universe reveals material before it appears on Earth by a reflection in the water of the washbasin. When the reflection shows a monster with gigantic rows of teeth, all three are terrified.

Harry votes to throw away the keys and notify the police, but Barry disagrees. When the two quarrel, Barry takes possession of the keys. Harry, hurt and resentful, devises a daring plan of action which will sever his unique relationship with Barry. He will spend a night—the equivalent of one year—alone in the playhouse; he will emerge no longer a twin, but an older brother. That night he gathers up extra clothes, books, and provisions, steals the keys, and begins his lonely, solitary vigil in the playhouse. Twice, at several months' intervals, which really constitute only a little over an hour each in earth-time, he allows himself a fifteen minute respite on the outside. When he leaves the playhouse in the morning, he has matured in many ways, including adding three inches to his height. During the reconciliation with Barry, a loud explosion signals that the monster has broken through. Fortunately, it devours its own tail with such ferocity that it consumes itself. The force of its entry into this world cracks and destroys the interdimensional portal under the playhouse, leaving Harry to decide how he will explain his physical and emotional transformation to his parents when they arrive in a week's time.

CHARACTERS: The identical twins provide a study in contrasts. The narrator is **Harry Krasner**, an introspective, timid, and cautious youngster who enjoys reading science fiction more than participating in athletics. He is fearful and apprehensive about embarking on new ventures. Initially, he dislikes the idea of traveling with his brother to take care of Uncle Ambrose's house; only loyalty to his brother and the fear of being seen as a coward make him consent to the trip. When they first glimpse the imposing Victorian structure, Barry can scarcely contain his excitement, whereas Harry's thoughts center on practical matters, including wondering if the electricity is on and if the telephones are still connected. Harry is basically afraid of his brother and tries whenever possible to placate him and avoid scenes. Although he resents always being denigrated and ridiculed by his brother, he lacks both the courage and fortitude to object. It is easier for him to accept his brother's domination and abuse rather than to assert his own wishes. He therefore often must extricate himself from predicaments that Barry has caused.

Though he frequently shows a lack of courage, Harry rallies to Barry's aid whenever he thinks his brother might be in danger. Harry's level-headed practicality allows him to use powers of deduction and logical thinking. He often displays a brilliant analytic reasoning. At school, he is a better student than Barry, particularly in math and science. He also recognizes the value of hard work; he does the cooking and cleaning while Barry socializes with Lucy. Lacking the support and affection one would expect from a brother, Harry has turned to his dog Fred for companionship. The boy's sensitive nature is decimated by the news that Fred has accidentally aged and perished in the playhouse due to Barry's carelessness. Unlike his brother, Harry exhibits good common sense when, for example, he tries to convince Barry to lock the playhouse and bring in the police.

The major difference between Harry and Barry, however, is that Harry genuinely and sincerely loves his brother in spite of Barry's meanness and ill temper. When he realizes that his brother would like to break their bond as identical twins, Harry exhibits a heretofore hidden side of his character. He conquers his fear and embarks on an endeavor that requires immense willpower, endurance, and personal sacrifice. In a feat of great self-discipline and determination, he lives for a year in solitude in another dimension inside the playhouse. Determined not to give in to his anxieties, Harry undertakes a spartan regime that involves physical exercise, rationing of food, and planned daily activities. Throughout his sojourn he displays incredible stamina, courage, and endurance, emerging a more mature individual, both physically and mentally. When the twins are reunited, Harry now admits that although he still loves his brother, "he no longer matters at all."

Harry's twin, **Barry Krasner**, is more outgoing, athletic, and aggressive than his brother. The popular Barry exhibits a brash, confident exterior, capable of charming others, including Lucy. Persuasive and shrewd, Barry always needs to get his own way, even if he must resort to begging, pleading, sulking, and throwing temper tantrums. Spoiled by his parents, he regularly attracts more attention because of his bold, engaging behavior. Barry resents being an identical twin. He sees Harry as a negative mirror, magnifying and reflecting his own flaws. He feels trapped by Harry's physical representation of everything he hates about himself and can't change. These feelings of frustration provoke deeds of both physical and mental abuse towards his brother. He pounces on every weakness his brother exhibits. Scathing in his sarcasm and lazy about household chores and maintenance, Barry repeatedly belittles Harry, constantly tormenting and teasing him. When, on one occasion, he thinks that Harry has deliberately locked him in the playhouse, he becomes both verbally and physically abusive, though when he is indirectly responsible for Fred's death he shows neither remorse nor sympathy. He hates to be contradicted and resents Harry's theoretical insights regarding the playhouse singularity. When Harry emerges from the playhouse changed and more mature, Barry at last realizes that he truly loved his brother as he was, and that this relationship is now lost forever. At first he can't believe that Harry had the inner strength and resolution to execute this daring, dangerous plan. Now, in a reversal of roles, he admires and respects Harry, acknowledging the magnitude of his undertaking.

In Illinois, the boys' new neighbor is **Lucy Coolidge**, the daughter of the farmer whose home and pastures abut the Kittery property. Brought up in a humble, rural environment, she uses many provincial expressions, such as "Well, I never," and appears ignorant of the basic rules of grammar. Ironically, she considers the boys' proper Bostonian English odd. She is the athletic, outdoors type, straightforward and honest in her dealings with the boys, sparing no details of the way the locals felt about their uncle. She prefers the active, outgoing Barry to the bookish and reserved Harry. Lucy demonstrates an adventurous spirit in exploring the playhouse and its mysteries with the twins and also displays good midwestern common sense when she questions Harry's theories about the possibility of differing realities and time shifts.

Though never present, **Uncle Ambrose Kittery** is important in the unfolding of the plot. Once a wealthy man, he lost millions overnight in the great stock market crash of 1929. The twins' mother, his niece, remembers that he had a glass eye which held people in a fixed stare while the other eye roamed. Ambrose's amazing discovery—that his property contained a singularity, an opening to another dimension, a universe with an altered speed of time—led to his characterization as an eccentric. His papers and artifacts reveal that he was scientifically studying this phenomenon. The boys find a letter proving that he had contacted scientists for help but had been rebuffed as a crackpot. To safeguard this profound power so that it could be carefully studied and analyzed, he constructed the playhouse on his property where Harry later gained personal courage and maturity.

Further Reading

Authors and Artists for Young Adults. Vol. 5. Detroit: Gale Research, 1991.

Berger, Laura Standley, ed. *Twentieth-Century Young Adult Writers.* 1st ed. Detroit: St. James, 1994.

Children's Literature Review. Vol. 29. Detroit: Gale Research, 1993.

Daggett, Margaret L. "Recommended: William Sleator." *English Journal* 76 (1987).

Davis, James, and Hazel Davis. *Presenting William Sleator.* New York: Twayne, 1991.

Holtze, Sally Holmes, ed. *Fifth Book of Junior Authors and Illustrators.* New York: H. W. Wilson, 1983.

Roginski, Jim, ed. *Behind the Covers.* Englewood, CO: Libraries Unlimited, 1985.

Something about the Author. Vols. 3, 68. Detroit: Gale Research, 1972, 1992.

Betty Smith

1904-1972, American novelist

A Tree Grows in Brooklyn

(young adult novel, 1943)

PLOT: It is the summer of 1912, and a tree is growing in the Williamsburg section of Brooklyn, New York. There is only one tree in Francie Nolan's backyard, and every Saturday afternoon, the eleven-year-old girl sits on the fire escape and imagines that she is living in a tree. *A Tree Grows in Brooklyn* is a quiet, colorful chronicle of a young girl's journey into womanhood, of a family's broken dreams, and struggles for a better tomorrow.

Francie loves her family. She adores her father, the handsome Johnny Nolan, a man who never realized his dreams and now feels he is doomed to live in quiet desperation. Francie loves him despite the nights he comes home staggering up the stairs after having too much to drink. She knows the pain her mother feels, and recognizes her steely strength as well.

When Francie is fourteen, her father begins to stay out late more often and hardly speaks to anyone. His hands tremble and he looks very old. One night he is thrown out of the Waiters' Union because they do not believe him when he says he hasn't touched a drop of liquor for a long time. Faced with the certainty that he will never get another waiter's job, he dies three days later of pneumonia. His wife, Katie, is pregnant at the time of his death, and, months later, Annie Laurie Nolan is born.

Both Francie and her brother, Neeley, go to work while attending school. When they graduate from elementary school, there is the question about high school. Francie desperately wants to go, but Neeley doesn't. Their mother says there is money enough for only one of them to continue. The other must work full time to support the family. Neeley is selected to go to school because he is a boy and more likely to get a better job, which means there isn't enough money for Francie to do so. Francie protests in vain. In the end, she agrees to go to work so that Neeley can continue school, but both women know that nothing will be right between them again.

Later, Francie has the idea that perhaps she can take courses at college if she attends without working for a diploma or grades. In this way, she registers for college classes. Not only is she successful for two summers, but in time she passes the regents' college exam. She also has a brief romance with a young soldier, with whom she falls in love immediately, only to be disappointed. In college, she meets Ben. She likes him very much and wishes they could find love together.

By the end of the novel, Francie has many possibilities in her life and is successfully attending the University of Michigan at Ann Arbor. With her mother about to remarry, Francie has a last look at her Brooklyn home and the tree that grows there before she starts her brand new life.

CHARACTERS: Francie Nolan is the center of this story of growing up in Brooklyn, New York, in the early years of the twentieth century. She has inherited the traits of both sides of her family. She has some of the toughness of the Rommely family, but not as much as her mother and her aunts. Like her Aunt Sissy, she loves life; like her grandfather, she has a cruel will; like her grandmother, she is a teller of tales and a dreamer. She is not good looking like her father, but she has his sentimentality and she has all of her mother's sympathetic ways.

Katie Rommely Nolan, Francie's mother, is the heart and soul of the household. She makes sure that each night Francie and Neeley read a page from the Bible and a page from Shakespeare before they go to bed. Katie married when she was seventeen and worked in the Castle Braid Factory. From the first time she saw Johnny Nolan, she decided that she wanted nothing more than to look at him for the rest of her life. They were married four months later, and her father never forgave her. By the time her second child, Neeley, is born and her husband is drinking heavily, Katie is not so sure she made the right choice, but she is a survivor. Although there are many ups and downs in her marriage, many different homes, and many nights when her husband comes home drunk, Katie forges ahead. The best of all their homes, in Francie's opinion, is where they are now—mostly because of the tree.

Francie's brother, **Neeley**, helps her collect junk on Saturdays. They spend half of what they make reselling it; the other half goes into their bank account. Neeley agrees that Francie should be the one to continue school. He doesn't want to go, but his mother insists and he obeys. Neeley grows up with the charm and good looks of his father, but, as Francie observes, with more strength in his face than Papa had.

Johnny Nolan is Francie's father. He's a waiter with a sweet voice and everybody loves him, including Francie. He loves his wife and children, but he never makes quite enough money to support them, which makes him feel guilty. With increasing frequency, he spends his nights in bars and staggers home drunk, to the despair of his wife and the shame of his daughter. Often he thinks of winning it big on the horses, but Johnny will never win it big on anything. He married too young, and he feels fate has kept him from reaching his full potential. Johnny is a dreamer, but now he has become a useless dreamer, unlike his wife, who has a fierce yearning for survival.

Francie's favorite aunt is **Aunt Sissy**, her mother's sister. By age thirty-five, Sissy has been married three times and has given birth to ten children, all of

Set in 1912, this sensitive novel traces a young girl's journey toward womanhood

whom died soon after birth. Aunt Sissy has black eyes and curly hair and works in a rubber factory. She makes Mama laugh and she makes everything around her seem glamorous—at least, that's how it looks to Francie. But there are rumors around the neighborhood that Sissy knows too many men, that she is in fact a "bad girl." Francie loves her all the same, just like she loves **Aunt Evy**, who also married young. Her husband wasn't exactly a bum, but he was close to it. Evy was the refined sister. She was determined that her children would have the advantages she didn't, including a musical education, even though not one of her three children was interested in music.

Francie has another aunt, too, although she doesn't see her very much (only once, in fact). **Aunt Eliza** is now **Sister Ursula**, who entered a strict convent at age sixteen. Francie's grandmother decided that one of her daughters should enter the church, and she picked Eliza. One time she came out of the convent to attend her father's funeral. Francie was very excited about meeting her, but when she saw that Sister Ursula had a mustache, she was turned off to the idea of becoming a nun.

Further Reading

Contemporary Literary Criticism. Vol. 19. Detroit: Gale Research, 1981.

Ross, Jean W., and Lynne C. Zeigler, eds. *Dictionary of Literary Biography Yearbook: 1982.* Detroit: Gale Research, 1982.

Something about the Author. Vol. 6. Detroit: Gale Research, 1974.

Squier, Susal Merrill, ed. *Women Writers and the City: Essays in Feminist Literary Criticism.* Knoxville: University of Tennessee Press, 1984.

Elizabeth George Speare

1908-, American novelist

The Witch of Blackbird Pond

(historical novel, 1958)

PLOT: In mid-April, 1687, sixteen-year-old Kit Tyler sees the coast of Connecticut for the first time from the deck of the brigantine *Dolphin* that has transported her from her former home in Barbados. She has been forced to leave her native land after the death of her grandfather, a former plantation owner who had cared for Kit since her parents died in a boating accident years before. Kit is headed to the town of Wethersfield on the Connecticut River close to Hartford, where she will live with her aunt Rachel Wood and her family. Kit is somewhat attracted to the captain's son and first mate, the young and appealing Nathaniel Eaton.

At the coastal town of Sayville, the boat takes on other passengers bound for Wethersfield: a young divinity student named John Holbrook and the dour Cruff family, including Goodwife Cruff, her docile husband, and their sickly daughter, Prudence. High-spirited Kit has problems fitting into the joyless, puritanical Wood household, which consists of Aunt Rachel, her gruff, dominating husband, Matthew, and two daughters, Judith, who is Kit's age, and the slightly older Mercy, a withdrawn cripple. At Sabbath meeting, Kit is introduced to Mistress Ashley and her son, William, the most eligible bachelor in town. William begins to visit Kit regularly. Soon the Woods have another regular visitor in John Holbrook, who is studying with the town's Reverend Bulkeley and appears to be courting Judith.

One day in the Great Meadow close to Blackbird Pond outside town, Kit meets the town's outcast, Hannah Tupper, an aged Quaker woman who has been branded a witch because her religious beliefs are different. Although forbidden by Matthew to go to Hannah's home, Kit secretly visits this kind, understanding woman and finds that Nat Eaton is also a friend of Hannah's and visits her whenever his ship is in the area. Prudence Cruff also begins calling on Hannah, and soon Kit is able to teach this hapless waif how to read and write.

When a mysterious disease strikes Wethersfield, many of the young people, including Mercy and Judith, become dangerously ill. The townspeople blame Hannah's witchcraft and try to take her prisoner. Nat and Kit elude her pursuers and smuggle Hannah to safety on the *Dolphin*. But the wrath of the townspeople turns against Kit because of her association with Hannah. She is brought to trial for witchcraft by the Cruffs, who have discovered that Prudence has been visiting Hannah's home. At her trial, Nat appears with Prudence and proves that Kit's only crime has been to try to educate Prudence. His testimony gets Kit exonerated. When Kit decides she can't marry the stuffy, narrow-minded William, he turns his attention to Judith, who welcomes him as a suitor. Soon there are two weddings in town: Judith and William's and John and Mercy's. After Nat learns that Kit is free of William, he returns to Wethersfield to ask her to be his bride.

CHARACTERS: High-spirited, outspoken **Kit Tyler**, the heroine of the novel, has problems adjusting to the oppressive, cheerless, puritanical life in

Wethersfield. Accustomed to having many servants, fancy dresses, and complete freedom and independence, Kit finds the austerity and regimen of the Puritans difficult to endure. She is a straightforward, honest girl who is accustomed to speaking her mind and getting her own way. Although she has a temper that is sometimes difficult to control, Kit is thoughtful toward others, anxious to please, and willing to adapt. At first she feels like a charity case in the Wood household, but she gradually learns simple household skills and earns the respect of all when she shows incredible endurance and selflessness in nursing the family during the epidemic. Kit is bold, enterprising, and courageous. She admires honesty, openness, and compassion in others and tries to practice these qualities herself. Over the course of the story, Kit learns to control her pride and dislike of the bigotry she sees around her without sacrificing her ideals and desire to be kind. She hates prejudice and ignorance and defies the community by visiting Hannah and teaching the forlorn Prudence. With her thin, plain features, Kit is not a great beauty, but she gains admirers easily because of her charming, animated ways and her lovely, warm smile.

There are three young men in Kit's life. The most important is the first mate of the *Dolphin* and her future husband, **Nathaniel (Nat) Eaton.** Described as an attractive young man with a wiry body and sandy, sun-bleached hair, he often mystifies Kit with his alternating moods. At times he is caring, but he is also sometimes aloof and distant. Kit never knows what to expect of him next and describes him as a "contradictory person." Actually Nat shows many New England traits: caution, independence, wariness, and pride. Inwardly, he has a kindly, compassionate nature and shares Kit's abhorrence of prejudice and narrow-mindedness. He cares for the outcast Hannah, risks life and limb to rescue her, and courageously confronts the town bigots to save Kit; he is hard-working, ambitious, and self-assured.

In contrast to Nat's dash and energy, there is the quiet, bookish divinity student, **John Holbrook**, a young man with a pale, narrow face and shoulder-length fair hair. Coming from a poor family and unable to afford college, John has become a student of Wethersfield's leading cleric, Reverend Bulkeley. The young man has a solemn, austere demeanor but at times reveals an inner gentle nature, and sometimes he displays a disarming smile. John slavishly parrots his teacher's narrow-minded pronouncements, appearing to have no mind of his own. Even Matthew calls him "a young toady." John denies himself any pleasure or recreation and his sole diversions are visiting the Woods and reading dull, obscure religious tracts. Through adversity, including the time he spent as a captive of the Indians, John matures and gains strength, certainty, and confidence. Suddenly he becomes an individual, a believable entity who is able to assert himself. Still a gentle, sensitive man, he looks forward to leading his own church and marriage with Mercy.

Kit's most persistent suitor is nineteen-year-old **William Ashley**, scion of the town's richest family. A handsome young man who is keenly aware of his privileged position, William is a dull, wooden individual who is shrewd and calculating in planning his future. Quiet and with an implacable gaze, he is determined to win Kit and sequester her in the best house in town which is now under construction. Kit finds his constricted views of life and condescending attitude toward her unacceptable and gladly relinquishes him to Judith.

The patriarch of the Wood family is **Matthew Wood**. A tall man with angular features, bony fingers, thin, stern lips, and dark, glowering eyes, he epitomizes the strict, severe Puritan. Always formal, he is a gruff, silent man who denies himself and his family any luxuries because he considers such pleasures ungodly and sinful. Hard-working and harsh, he believes life involves only labor and sacrifice. Embittered at the death of his two sons, Matthew has become increasingly severe and disciplined. But although he is stubborn, Matthew is a highly principled man who occasionally shows a warmer, more human side best illustrated when he defends Kit against charges of witchcraft. Matthew's wife and Kit's aunt, **Rachel Wood**, was once a beautiful English girl who disobeyed her parents and ran away to the Colonies with Matthew. Now a thin, grey-haired woman bent by years of sacrifice and drudgery, she is completely dominated by him. This gentle, sensitive woman has become a kitchen slave and household drudge to pacify her demanding husband.

The Woods have two daughters. The older of the two is the saintly, well-named **Mercy**. Disabled by a crippling disease, she has a kind, considerate nature and always thinks of others before herself. She is accomplished in many crafts and, because of her patient, loving disposition, is an excellent teacher at the dame school she has organized. Her industry, ingenuity, and understanding have made her the pivotal influence in the household. Mercy coaxes her father out of bitter moods, gives support to her mother, and acts as a gentle restraint on sister **Judith**, who at times can be difficult. Judith, a beauty, is somewhat spoiled and stubborn. At first resentful of Kit, she often displays a proud, unfriendly disposition and makes sharp, sarcastic remarks. Gradually, Judith changes and matures. When she falls in love and feels wanted and secure, she develops a new sweetness and a more tolerant attitude towards others.

Hannah Tupper, a lonely figure dressed in a ragged dress and tattered shawl, is considered the witch of Blackbird Pond. Persecuted and branded because of her Quaker beliefs, she and her now-deceased husband were driven out of the Massachusetts colony. She now lives a solitary existence with her cat, eking out a living from her garden and her weaving. Far from embittered, however, she remains a gentle, loving person who graciously shares her few possessions and her wisdom with a grateful Kit. After being rescued from the townspeople by Kit and Nat, Hannah is taken in by Nat's caring family in Sayville, where she finds security and peace.

Kit's archenemy, **Goodwife Cruff**, is a shrewish, mean-spirited, superstitious woman who hates Kit and her supposedly heathen ways. Dour-looking and spiteful, she dominates her unfortunate husband, the spineless, cowardly **Goodman Cruff**. When he learns that Kit's only crime was to make his daughter Prudence literate, Goodman Gruff unexpectedly gains courage and gumption and silences his wife in court with a firm and satisfying, "Hold your tongue, woman." **Prudence** is their pathetic wisp of a child. Intimidated and dominated by her despotic mother, the young girl has become a withdrawn, woebegone creature, but under the guidance and friendship of Kit and Hannah, she blossoms. Gradually she opens up and is able to face her mother unafraid.

The Bronze Bow

(historical novel, 1961)

PLOT: Since his parents died as a result of Roman cruelty, Daniel bar Jamin, an eighteen-year-old Galilean, has lived in the hills with an outlaw band led by Rosh, who is conducting guerrilla warfare against the occupying Roman forces. One day, while on a scouting expedition, Daniel sees two former acquaintances from his village: Joel bar Hezron, the studious son of the town scribe, Hezron, and Joel's twin sister, Malthace, who is also called Thace or Thacia. While his two friends watch, Daniel participates in a raid on a caravan during which a gargantuan slave named Samson is freed and joins Rosh's gang. Later, Daniel is sent on a mission to Capernaum, where Hezron and his family live, and there becomes more attached to Joel and his sister. The three swear an oath to help liberate their homeland from the Romans, using the sign of the bronze bow from one of David's Songs, as their symbol of might. Daniel also encounters his old friend Simon the Zealot, a blacksmith who has become a follower of a gentle, kindly preacher named Jesus. Daniel is impressed, though somewhat mystified, by this man who preaches love and forgiveness.

When Daniel's grandmother dies, he is forced to leave Rosh and return to his village, where he cares for his emotionally withdrawn sister, Leah, and manages Simon's blacksmith shop. Joel is given a dangerous espionage assignment by Rosh. He completes it successfully, but eventually he is apprehended by the Romans and sentenced to deportation. When Rosh refuses to help Joel, Daniel organizes the local youths and, with Samson's help, effects a daring rescue operation.

Although Daniel is excited by Jesus's teachings, he is still so filled with hatred towards the Romans that he threatens to kill a young Roman soldier, Marcus, after he finds him talking to Leah about his eminent departure for Corinth. When the young girl becomes critically ill with a fever, Daniel thinks of Jesus and sends a message to Simon. After three days, Jesus appears at Daniel's house. He enters and gazes at Leah. She opens her eyes and is suddenly well. After Jesus leaves, Daniel again sees Marcus in the area and, this time, invites him into his home to say farewell. Daniel has learned by Jesus's example that love has the strength to bend the bow of bronze.

CHARACTERS: The story is told from the viewpoint of **Daniel bar Jamin**, a bitter, sullen eighteen-year-old boy who is slowly transformed by the power of Jesus's teachings from a hostile, resentful youth to one who will allow love and compassion to enter his heart. While still a youngster, he witnessed his father and uncle being crucified by the Romans for a minor infraction and later saw his mother die of grief. For five years, he has lived a fugitive life in the mountain camp of the bandit Rosh, whose life is dedicated to harassing the Romans and their collaborators. These influences have turned Daniel into a cold, morose person who bears a fanatical hatred for the Roman occupiers and who has dedicated his life to their downfall. Without friends, he has become a loner, unable to feel compassion or pity. Courageous to the point of being foolhardy, his unswerving belief in his cause leads him to commit impulsive acts of violence and to deny any feelings of charity and tenderness. This all-consuming bitterness has turned him into a scowling and unapproachable person who, in Thacia's words "doesn't know how to smile." Daniel, however, has many admirable characteristics; he is loyal, dependable, and willing to sacrifice his future to care for his pathetic sister. Fiercely dedicated to his friends, he risks his life to save his friend Joel. Daniel is also bright and quick-thinking; he is a born leader who is able to invent ingenious, often audacious, solutions to problems. During the course of story, Daniel changes and matures. He realizes the value of fellowship and personal relationships, experiences the pangs of first love, accepts responsibilities, and

Daniel bar Jamin learns from the teachings of Jesus to set aside his hatred of the Romans in this historical novel.

grows to realize the futility of force and violence as a method of achieving goals.

Daniel's dearest friends are **Joel bar Hezron** and his twin sister, **Malthace**, also called **Thace** or **Thacia**. Joel is a sensitive, intellectual youngster who would like to devote his life to learning. Unlike Daniel, Joel is a congenial, outgoing person and an idealist who passionately believes in freedom and justice. After his encounter with Daniel, he decides that he must, like their idol, Rosh, devote all his energies to fighting tyranny and the Roman occupation. An emotional, excitable young man, he is thrilled to be chosen by Rosh for the secret mission which he accomplishes in a bold, courageous manner. He is a devoted friend and a considerate, dutiful son. Joel is understandably adored by his sister, sixteen-year-old Thacia, the young girl with whom Daniel eventually falls in love. Thacia is a beautiful girl, "like a brilliant scarlet lily, glowing and proud."

She is also intelligent, caring, and more independent and self-reliant than other girls her age. Though she dislikes violence, Thacia, like Joel, dedicates herself to fighting tyranny, and, in fulfilling this purpose, shows as much courage, intelligence, and endurance as her male counterparts. She possesses a kind and loving nature that is shown in her relations with family and friends and the many hours she spends with Leah to bring her a sense of security and worth.

Joel and Thacia's father, **Hezron**, a tall, distinguished-looking scholar, is the town scribe. A quiet, peace-loving man, he preaches patience and pacifism in dealing with the Romans. He firmly believes in the Jewish Law. A fatalist, Hezron knows that in time God's wishes will prevail and justice will triumph. Although not an active collaborator, he does not want his children to become involved in the resistance movement.

Daniel met **Simon the Zealot** when they were both apprenticed to the cruel town blacksmith. Simon, who is six years older than Daniel, had established his own blacksmith shop when he fell under the spell of the preacher, Jesus. Though once an advocate of violence, he is now a believer in the conquering power of love and compassion. Simon introduces Daniel to the teachings of Jesus and brings him to Jesus's meetings. Later, this gentle, generous man lives up to his ideals by giving his business to Daniel.

Daniel, and later Joel, both idolize the ruthless, dedicated guerilla fighter, **Rosh**. A gruff, demanding disciplinarian, Rosh regards any act of compassion or kindness as a sign of weakness. He is a powerfully built man with a squat, thick body, short muscular neck, and a grizzled beard. With his weather-pitted face and fierce black eyes, he instills fear and devotion in his followers. Rosh is a pitiless, exacting leader who demands complete obedience. He places the cause of robbing the rich and attacking Romans above all else and will sacrifice men to fulfil his dreams. When he refuses to help rescue Joel, Daniel becomes disillusioned with Rosh and realizes that many of the bandit's actions are motivated by self-interest and a desire for personal glory.

On one of Rosh's forays, a gargantuan black slave is captured. Described as having lash-ridged shoulders and ugly scars, he looks like a beast carved out of stone. Because of his size, he becomes known as **Samson**. Unable to speak and seemingly deaf, Samson becomes the workhorse of Rosh's gang. However, he responds to Daniel's kindness and treats him like a master. Always a faithful servant and loyal friend to Daniel, he deserts Rosh's camp to help Daniel rescue Joel. During this struggle, Samson is mortally wounded.

Daniel's wretched, pitiable sister, **Leah**, has been scarred by the experience of losing her parents. Traumatized when she witnessed the death of her father, this oversensitive child has withdrawn from life to the point of catatonia. She is so terrified of life outside the family hut that she never ventures outside and, except when she is weaving fabrics, usually cowers silently in a corner. After her grandmother's death, Leah is cared for by Daniel. His concern for her and the love shown to her by Thacia affect some changes, but she still remains pathetically timid and frightened. She is intrigued by Daniel's stories about the teachings of Jesus, and when she is close to death she responds to his healing powers.

The Roman soldier **Marcus** is a blonde, sixteen-year-old German who has been conscripted into the Roman army. Homesick, he finds that Leah reminds him of his sisters. He enjoys innocently watching her at her work. Naive and blameless, he can't understand Daniel's anger over his simple display of friendliness.

Jesus is portrayed in the novel as a gentle, peace-loving man who is not afraid of the possible consequences for preaching a doctrine of acceptance and love. He is described as a vigorous, confident, and happy man who dresses simply in a white robe. Through his words and actions, he is able to inspire an amazing devotion and altruism in others.

Further Reading

Berger, Laura Standley, ed. *Twentieth-Century Young Adult Writers.* 1st ed. Detroit: St. James, 1994.

Children's Literature Review. Vol. 8. Detroit: Gale Research, 1985.

Fuller, Muriel, ed. *More Junior Authors.* New York: H. W. Wilson, 1963.

Something about the Author. Vols. 5, 62. Detroit: Gale Research, 1973, 1991.

Ward, Martha, ed. *Authors of Books for Young People.* 3rd ed. Metuchen, NJ: Scarecrow, 1990.

Jerry Spinelli

1941-, American young adult novelist

Maniac Magee

(young adult novel, 1990)

PLOT: Jeffrey Lionel Magee—known as Maniac—has been an orphan since the age of three, when a trolley car carrying his parents went off the tracks and into the Schuylkill River. When the story opens, Maniac, now twelve, is aimlessly walking down the streets of Two Mills, a small town in Pennsylvania. He has run away from the unhappy home of his guardians, Aunt Dot and Uncle Dan, where he lived for eight years. His aunt and uncle hate each other but won't get a divorce because they're Catholic. For the past year, he has been on his own. Maniac has never seen Two Mills before and is unaware of the town's rigid racism. Innocently, he walks back and forth across Hector Street, not knowing that it is the dividing line between blacks and whites: blacks live in the East End, whites in the West End.

The first person Maniac meets is Amanda Beale, who lives in the black neighborhood. He likes this spirited young girl and is pleased when she lends him one of her valued reading books. But on the other side of town, Maniac becomes famous and earns his nickname for his incredible feats. Maniac accomplishes many amazing deeds, but none so fine as his performance at a Little League game. Before Maniac, the town hero was John McNab, an unbeatable pitcher. Not only does Maniac hit several home runs off this hero but he even bunts successfully when McNab scornfully throws him a frog instead of a ball. Although McNab is at first Maniac's enemy, the two boys eventually become friends and Maniac even lives with the McNab family for a while.

Maniac is still wandering about town without a home when one day, while in the black neighborhood, he is challenged by a bully named Mars Bar Thompson. But he is saved by Amanda, who takes him home, where the Beale family welcomes him warmly into their brood. But for all Maniac's amazing talents, his naivete blinds him to other people's hatred and bigotry. It therefore doesn't occur to him that although the Beales want him in their home, others may not. So, one hot night while Maniac and the other kids are cooling off at a kind of block party, he hears a strange, unfriendly voice calling him "Whitey." The man tells him to move on. "You pick up your gear and move on out. Time to go home now." When Maniac replies that he is home, the man threateningly tells him to go back to his own kind. Just when it seems that Maniac has found a home at last, he learns that black extremists don't want him in their neighborhood, so he returns to the zoo where he had been sleeping before.

Maniac's friendship with the elderly Grayson leads him to a place to stay in the equipment room behind the bandstand. Grayson has lots of stories to tell about his days in the minor leagues, and he and Maniac become such good friends that Grayson moves into the equipment room as well. The two outcasts settle into a warm relationship. Grayson has many wonderful baseball stories to tell Maniac, and, in exchange, Maniac begins to teach the old man to read. But when Grayson dies Maniac is homeless again. After some more hair-raising exploits, Maniac goes back to the zoo, where he remains until Amanda finds him and insists he return to the Beale home. Maniac is secretly thrilled that someone cares about him and returns home with her.

CHARACTERS: Maniac Magee is a legend in his own time. He can untie any knot, run faster than the wind, hit the longest home run. Orphaned at the age of three and shipped off to his aunt and uncle in western Pennsylvania, he ran away when he was twelve because his guardians despised each other so much that he couldn't stand to be with them any more. Maniac is an interesting study in contrasts. He is a natural athlete and is incapable of prejudice or hatred of other people; on the other hand, he has an inability to deal with crises. In addition to running away from his home in Pennsylvania, he later runs away again in another incident. When he and Mars Bar see one of the young McNab brothers stranded on the track where Maniac's parents were killed, Maniac doesn't have the nerve to stay and help. Despite this failure, Mars Bar still offers his friendship to Maniac. Maniac, however, eventually decides to stay with the Beales.

The first person who speaks to Maniac when he arrives in Two Mills is **Amanda Beale**. She is suspicious of this white stranger who is in the wrong part of town. However, she is also naturally friendly, so she lends him one of her books anyway. This causes Amanda to be late for school for the first and only time in her life. Although she fully realizes the problems with having Maniac Magee in the Beale home, she also understands what Maniac needs most. "You are coming home with me," she says. "And you are going to sleep there tonight and tomorrow night and the night after that."

John McNab is involved with one of Maniac's greatest exploits. McNab is a giant: five-feet-eight-inches tall and more than 170 pounds at the tender age of twelve. He is a pitcher of renown with just one pitch: a fastball. But McNab meets his match in the bat prowess of the great Manic Magee, who even manages to score with a bunt when McNab pitches him a frog instead of a baseball. Later on, however, Maniac learns of McNab's problems with a redneck father filled with racial hate. Maniac also learns that McNab has two younger brothers and that their father is not very concerned about keeping them in school.

Besides McNab, Maniac has problems with a big bully named **Mars Bar Thompson**. Maniac is rescued from their first encounter by Amanda, but later on the boys meet again and engage in a road race to settle their differences. Maniac isn't sure how to run this race. Naturally, he wants to win, but somehow he feels that there are other considerations on account of his opponent. Maniac does win the race, and the onlookers go wild—absolutely bananas—because he runs the race backwards. Then Maniac realizes that perhaps that wasn't a smart thing to do because Mars Bar no longer hates just a white kid, he hates Maniac personally. It takes some time, but the two boys eventually become friends, which is what they wanted in the first place.

One day, Maniac and Mars Bar wander out to the trestle where Maniac's parents were killed. They see one of McNab's younger brothers stranded out on the track. Maniac is so traumatized by being so close to this site of the disaster that he runs away and leaves Mars Bar to rescue the boy. Even so, Mars Bar offers Maniac his friendship and his home, but Maniac chooses the Beale family and their warm and comforting love.

Old man **Grayson** shelters Maniac for part of the story and becomes his friend. He regales the boy with stories of his days in the minor leagues, while always insisting that "I ain't got no stories." His very best story recounts the time that he pitched to the great Willie Mays, the Say Hey Kid, just before he joined the New York Giants and became a baseball immortal. Grayson struck out the great Mays with just three pitches. In return for all these wonderful stories, Grayson requests that Maniac teach him to read, which the boy does gladly.

Further Reading

Authors and Artists for Young Adults. Vol. 11. Detroit: Gale Research, 1993.

Berger, Laura Standley, ed. *Twentieth-Century Young Adult Writers.* 1st ed. Detroit: St. James, 1995.

Children's Literature Review. Vol. 26. Detroit: Gale Research, 1992.

Holtze, Sally Holmes, ed. *Sixth Book of Junior Authors and Illustrators.* New York: H. W. Wilson, 1989.

Something about the Author. Vols. 39, 71. Detroit: Gale Research, 1985, 1993.

Spinelli, Jerry. "Maniac Magee: Homer on George Street." *Horn Book* 67 (January/February 1991): 40-41.

John Steinbeck

1902-1968, American novelist

The Grapes of Wrath

(novel, 1939)

PLOT: Called a novel of protest and a social document, *The Grapes of Wrath* is the story of the Joad family of Oklahoma. Tom Joad is hitchhiking back to his family's farm after serving four years of a seven-year sentence for homicide. On the way he meets Jim Casy, an itinerant preacher who accompanies him to the Joad farm. It is the 1930s, and, with little rain and the crops dying, the once fertile lands of the plains are turning into a giant dust bowl. When Tom reaches the farm, the family is gone and the neighboring farms also seem to be deserted. Neighbor Muley Graves tells Joad that his folks are at his Uncle John's, where he and Jim go the next day.

Tom and Jim catch up with the rest of the Joad family, which consists of Pa and Ma, Grampa and Granma, sons Noah, Al, and Winfield, daughters Rose of Sharon and Ruthie, and son-in-law Connie Rivers. They are getting ready to leave for California, having sold all their belongings for the grand total of eighteen dollars. Times are too hard in Oklahoma, and supposedly there is work to be had out west. Casy decides to join in the migration, but Grampa Joad doesn't want to leave. In fact, the family has to drug him to make him come along. On the first night of their trip, the old man has a stroke and dies. The Joads borrow a quilt from fellow migrants Ivy and Sairy Wilson to bury Grampa, and then the two families, after having fixed the Wilsons' broken-down car, head for California together. When they get there, Mrs. Wilson is too ill to travel farther, and the families part. The Joads cross the California desert at night, and Granma Joad, who has also become ill, is the next to die. Without money for a funeral, the Joads must leave the old woman to be buried as a pauper.

The family reaches a filthy migrant camp, where they stop, but the men can't find work. When a fight breaks out among the migrants, the sheriff threatens to burn down the camp, and so the Joads move on. Eventually, they reach a peach orchard where they immediately get to work picking fruit. Later that night, Tom learns from Jim Casy that the men are striking because the orchard owners have cut their wages in half. Casy is killed shortly afterwards by some men who are against the strike, and Tom is so angered that he kills one of them, getting his nose broken during the fight. The Joads leave for a cotton farm, and Tom hides his disfigured face. When one of the younger Joads brags that Tom killed a man, Ma tells Tom to leave. He does, determined to carry on Jim Casy's work for the migrants. The rest of the family continues to pick cotton until the rains come and they must leave. However, during the rainstorm, Rose of Sharon gives birth and the baby dies. The Joads must live in a boxcar for two days, waiting for the rains to subside. On the road again, the Joads, without money or food, search for a dry place to rest. They find a barn with dry hay. Inside is a man who is dying from starvation. At Ma's suggestion, Rose of Sharon revives the dying man with her breast milk.

CHARACTERS: The main protagonist of the novel is **Tom Joad**, who feels no guilt over killing a man who knifed him. He is intelligent, independent-minded, and quick to anger. When he leaves prison, his only thoughts are for his own personal comforts. But he is the character in the novel who develops most. Stubborn and obstinate at the outset, he turns more and more toward violence as circumstances force him into desperate situations.

But there is also a decency and kindness in Tom, and he has a strong sense of morals. As he witnesses the injustices to the migrant workers, his compassion grows despite himself. Jim Casy becomes his teacher, setting an example of looking out for others without regard to one's own needs. When Tom is hiding out in the woods after Casy's death and after having killed a second time, he reconsiders Casy's words and actions. He realizes that strength among people lies in their unity, not in their separateness. Tom decides that he will carry on Casy's work. He will leave his own family because he must, but the entire world will now become his family. Society still regards him as outside the law at the novel's end, but Tom is a changed man, fighting for a better way of life for all people. He tells Ma that perhaps Casy was too much of an idealist, too much of a talker. Tom Joad will find a more practical way to deal with the world and carry out Casy's philosophy.

Ex-preacher **Jim Casy**, who serves as a model for Tom to follow, is a Christ-like figure who sees good in all people. At the beginning of the novel, however, he has not quite figured out his views. After spending some time in prison for his involvement in a strike, he realizes that he does not believe in the old hell-fire religion anymore. Instead, he emerges with a calling to lead and comfort people, in the end laying down his life for Tom Joad. He feels a kinship for all people because he believes that all have come from the same essential source and will return there. After his death, his message becomes clear to Tom.

Tom's family members also serve as important influences for him. **Ma Joad** is a tower of strength. Through all the adversities of her life, she remains calm and imperturbable. She knows that to do otherwise would be to have the entire family collapse around her. She fights to keep the family together because she realizes that is the only source of strength left to them. Yet she knows that a breakup is inevitable. She is the unassuming figure of love throughout the novel, the ultimate maternal figure. A kind, gentle woman with a sense of humor, she thoroughly understands the weaknesses and strengths of the family members, goading or cajoling them into the actions necessary to keep the family together to survive. Ma is willing to extend a helping hand to others, such as the Wilsons, but it is her concern for her family that drives her. She knows that as long as some part of the family stays together, they will survive. They are the only ones who can help each other. Ma Joad is the living embodiment of Casy's belief that all is holy and all action is a holy action. She is a woman of insight and intuition, and her son Tom is her unconscious disciple.

Although the titular head of the family, **Pa Joad** looks to Ma for guidance and strength. He is a man beaten by circumstances and forces beyond his control. He does not understand the reasons for his failure because he is not a lazy man and has worked for his family all his life. He is more defeated than Ma by the novel's end. **Grampa** and **Granma Joad** are wonderful, larger-than-life characters. He is cranky and loud, vulgar and antireligious, a man who takes delight in his constant quarreling with his wife. Granma is his equal in whatever they are doing, but her strength seems only to have come from her relationship with her husband. After he dies, she does not live much longer.

The rest of the Joad family is made up of more minor characters. From an accident at birth, **Noah Joad** is left slightly feeble-minded. He moves and talks slowly, and when the family is ready to cross the California desert his decision to "remain by the river and fish" seems natural enough. **Rose of Sharon** is a dreamer, constantly looking for the beauty in life that is denied her. She is also a whiner, especially after her husband, **Connie**, deserts her. Petulant and overbearing throughout the novel, Rose of Sharon comes into her own at the end, when she gives her dead baby's breast milk to a dying man. It is her first unselfish act. The behavior of **Al, Ruthie**, and **Winfield Joad** is typical for their ages. Al, at sixteen, is concerned only with cars and girls. Ruthie, who is twelve, is suspended between girlhood and womanhood, and Winfield is an awkward, pesky ten-year-old.

Several other characters outside the Joad family also appear in the novel. **Ivy** and **Sairy Wilson** are the sad young couple from Kansas who meet up with the Joads on their first night west. By the novel's conclusion, it is clear that Sairy is too weak and ill to endure the rigors of migrant life in California. The Joads realize that she will soon die, but they have no choice but to leave the Wilsons and continue their search for survival. **Muley Graves**, the Joads' neighbor, is the melancholy figure left behind in Oklahoma. He is another of the "Okies" that fortune forgot. Not strong enough to brave the trail to California, he is left forlorn in the dry, deserted dust bowl.

The Pearl

(novel, 1947)

PLOT: *The Pearl* is based on the Native American legend "The Pearl of the World." It is the story of a young Indian of South America, Kino, his discovery of a pearl, and the effects it has on his life until he returns it to the sea three days later. As dawn begins a new day, Kino and his wife, Juana, tend to their respective chores. The calm of the morning is broken when a scorpion strikes their infant son, Coyotito. Kino kills the scorpion, and Juana tries to draw out the poisoned blood, but it is soon obvious that the child is dying. Juana tells her husband to get the doctor. However, the town doctor has never come to the village, having nothing but contempt for the native people. In desperation, Kino takes the baby into town to the doctor's home, while the entire village follows. The doctor, who is relaxing inside over a sumptuous meal and dreaming of Paris, tells his servant that he will not see Coyotito unless Kino can pay. Kino gives the servant a few seed pearls, which are refused. In anger, Kino strikes his fist against the gate and injures himself.

Kino and Juana, with their gravely ill son, go out in their canoe so that Kino can dive for oysters. Juana has applied a homemade poultice to the baby's infected shoulder. Kino brings up an unusually huge oyster that contains a pearl as large as a seagull's egg. Juana suddenly sees that the baby's shoulder is now healed, and Kino howls for joy. The other men rush toward their canoe.

Oblivious to the jealousy caused by his discovery of so large a gem, Kino makes plans for the future, which include sending his son to school. The priest pays a visit to Kino and Juana, reminding them to give thanks for the pearl. The doctor arrives and tricks Kino into letting him minister to the child, even though the infant is now well. The doctor deliberately makes the child ill so that his medical services will be needed again. Kino is suspicious but can say nothing. He tells the doctor that he will sell the pearl to help pay the bill. When the doctor offers to keep the pearl in a safe place until it is sold, Kino refuses but inadvertently glances toward the pearl's hiding place. The doctor leaves. That night someone tries unsuccessfully to steal the pearl, and Kino is injured by a blow on the head.

Kino goes to town to sell the pearl. His brother, Juan Tomas, warns him not to be cheated by the pearl buyers. Kino refuses all offers. Although he is terrified to go to the capital to sell the pearl, he realizes he must if he is to realize his dream. Once again, he is attacked, but the pearl remains safe. Juana asks him to get rid of the evil pearl, but Kino can't let go of his vision of a new future.

That night, Juana attempts to get rid of the pearl herself, but Kino awakens and stops her by striking her in the face. More and more, he is turning into an animal. Later, he is once again assaulted by an unknown attacker. He is knocked unconscious and awakens to find the attacker dead. Juana, who still has the pearl, tells him they must leave the village, because no one will believe his story of self-defense. However, Kino discovers a hole in his precious canoe. They return to their home only to find it in flames. With the baby, they hide in the home of Kino's brother. Juan Tomas lets the villagers think that they have escaped. Kino's home and canoe have been destroyed, and his family is on the verge of breaking up, yet the pearl has become part of his soul, and he can't bring himself to part with it.

Kino and Juana leave the village to find a new life, but they are followed. They head for the high mountains to escape, but Kino knows that the three trackers will never stop until they have the pearl. He must kill them. Becoming almost a vicious animal himself, Kino is able to kill all three, but before expiring one of them fires his rifle and kills Coyotito. Carrying the lifeless bundle of their child, Kino and Juana return to the town. They look at no one but march to the sea where Kino, after first offering the option to his wife, which she refuses, tosses the evil pearl into the water.

CHARACTERS: Kino is the pristine innocent, the "noble savage," at harmony with his simple life and perfectly in tune with his environment. He is devoted to his wife and son and respectful of the traditions of his village. Even when his canoe is destroyed, closing off his family's means of escape, he does not think of stealing one of his neighbors' canoes. And when he dreams of the fortunes the pearl can bring him, they are riches that will benefit his family: he will become a better provider with a new rifle, and his son will go to school. He is unaware how his people are exploited by the doctor and others in the town. It is only when tragedy threatens his son, when the doctor refuses to treat him, that Kino first revolts against circumstance.

The incidents that follow the discovery of the pearl tax Kino's capacity to function as one with his environment. Suddenly, he is in an alien and hostile world. His reaction to finding the pearl and to the events that follow set him apart from his former simple existence. The hopes he now harbors for his son's future would never have entered his consciousness but for the pearl, but, once they are there, he can't rid himself of them until it is too late, until he loses the very reason for his hopes: his infant son.

If Kino is the "noble savage," **Juana** is his female equivalent, the prototype of the primitive native wife, a helpmate to her husband in all things. She is patient, obedient, dependable, and loyal. Uncomplaining and hardworking, she seems completely subservient to Kino, but she is not. When the baby is injured and Kino kills the scorpion in an almost helpless fury, it is Juana who decides on a course of action that takes them to the doctor in town, an unprecedented move. In her own way, she is as atypical in her responses to their situation as is her husband. She efficiently takes control in a crisis, and when called upon she can be assertive and determined. That is why she can go against her husband's wishes and attempt to destroy the pearl when she feels it threatens the safety of her family. When Juana and Kino return to the village, they walk side by side. This symbolizes the new equality in their relationship that their experience has given them. Yet when Kino offers her the opportunity to return the pearl to the sea, she refuses, granting him the right to destroy what killed their son and nearly Kino as well.

Another character who supports Kino is his older brother, **Juan Tomas**. He loves Kino, although he does not understand his refusal to relinquish the pearl. Juan Tomas accepts his life and his environment, neither condemning nor praising them. Even though his aid to his brother puts him and his family at some risk, he would not think to do otherwise because Kino is his brother and he loves him.

Cynical, dishonest, avaricious, and hypocritical are all words that describe the **doctor**, the story's villain who has no other name in this novel. He is so devoid of human sympathy that he seems more a caricature than a character. He is totally heartless and has no redeeming qualities whatsoever. It is obvious that he cares for no one and has only contempt for people of Kino's socio-economic status. It is also obvious that he deliberately makes the baby ill in order to find some way to discover the pearl's whereabouts.

Further Reading

Authors and Artists for Young Adults. Vol. 12. Detroit: Gale Research, 1994.

Benson, Jackson J. *The True Adventures of John Steinbeck.* New York: Viking, 1984.

Bloom, Harold. *John Steinbeck.* New York: Chelsea House, 1987.

———. *John Steinbeck's* The Grapes of Wrath. New York: Chelsea House, 1988.

———. *Twentieth-Century American Literature.* Vol. 6 of *The Chelsea House of Literary Criticism.* New York: Chelsea House, 1986.

Bruccoli, Matthew J., and Richard Layman, eds. *The Age of Maturity 1929-1941.* Volume 5 of *Concise Dictionary of American Literary Biography.* Detroit: Gale Research, 1989.

Critical Survey of Long Fiction. Vol. 6. Englewood Cliffs, NJ: Salem, 1986.

Contemporary Literary Criticism. Vols. 1, 5, 9, 13, 21, 34, 45. Detroit: Gale Research, 1973, 1976, 1978, 1980, 1982, 1985, 1987.

Ditsky, John. *Critical Essays on Steinbeck's* The Grapes of Wrath. Boston: G. K. Hall, 1989.

Fensch, Thomas, ed. *Conversations with John Steinbeck.* Jackson: University Press of Mississippi, 1988.

Fontenrose, Joseph. *John Steinbeck: An Introduction and Interpretation.* New York: Barnes & Noble, 1963.

French, Warren. *Companion to* The Grapes of Wrath. Seaman, OH: Kelley, 1972.

———. *John Steinbeck.* New York: Macmillan, 1975.

———. *John Steinbeck's Fiction Revisited.* New York: Twayne, 1994.

Gannett, Lewis. *John Steinbeck.* New York: Haskell, 1979.

Hayashi, Tetsumaro, ed. *Steinbeck's Literary Dimension.* Metuchen, NJ: Scarecrow, 1973.

Levant, Howard. *The Novels of John Steinbeck: A Critical Survey.* Columbia: University of Missouri Press, 1974.

Lisca, Peter. *John Steinbeck: Nature and Myth.* New York: Crowell, 1978.

———. *Steinbeck: The Man and His Work.* Corvallis: Oregon State University Press, 1971.

———. *The Wide World of John Steinbeck.* New Brunswick, NJ: Rutgers University Press, 1958.

MacNicholas, John, ed. *Twentieth-Century American Dramatists.* Vol. 7 of *Dictionary of Literary Biography.* Detroit: Gale Research, 1981.

Martine, James J., ed. *American Novelists, 1910-1945.* Vol. 9 of *Dictionary of Literary Biography.* Detroit: Gale Research, 1981.

McCarthy, Paul. *John Steinbeck.* New York: Ungar, 1979.

Moore, Harry T. *The Novels of John Steinbeck.* Philadelphia: R. West, 1976.

Owens, Louis D. *The Grapes of Wrath: Trouble in the Promised Land.* New York: Macmillan, 1989.

Parini, John. *Steinbeck: A Biography.* New York: Holt, 1995.

Reef, Catherine. *John Steinbeck.* New York: Clarion, 1995.

Steinbeck, John. *A Life in Letters.* New York: Viking, 1975.

Tedlock, E. W., and C. V. Wicker, eds. *Steinbeck and His Critics: A Record of Twenty-Five Years.* Albuquerque: University of New Mexico Press, 1957.

Timmerman, John H. *John Steinbeck's Fiction: The Aesthetics of the Road Taken.* Norman: University of Oklahoma Press, 1986.

Van Antwerp, Margaret A., ed. *Dictionary of Literary Biography Documentary Series.* Vol. 2. Detroit: Gale Research, 1982.

Watt, F. W. *John Steinbeck.* New York: Grove, 1962.

World Literature Criticism. Vol. 5. Detroit: Gale Research, 1992.

Robert Louis Stevenson

1850-1894, English novelist

Treasure Island

(novel, 1883)

PLOT: During the 1740s, young Jim Hawkins and his mother and father are the proprietors of the "Admiral Benbow," an inn situated in a secluded part of Devon, England. One day, their peaceful lives are interrupted with the arrival of a new customer, an old, disreputable seafarer named Bill Bones, who spends his time drinking, swearing, singing old sea songs, and anxiously watching for the arrival of unwanted visitors from his unsavory past. The first to arrive is an old sailor, Black Dog, whom Bones drives off, but the second, who comes shortly after the death of Jim's father, is a sightless sailor named Blind Pew, who presents Bones with the Black Spot, a death sentence for pirates. Bill Bones is so terrified by this ominous sign that he has a stroke and dies. Jim and his mother manage to open the old man's sea chest and take the money owed them plus a packet of papers. They escape before a gang of men arrive intent on confiscating Bill Bones's personal effects. In the ensuing melee, Pew is killed by charging horses.

Jim delivers the packet to two of the town's most respected men, Dr. David Livesey and Squire John Trelawney, who discover the packet contains the map of an island where the treasure of the dreaded pirate, Captain Flint, is hidden. They decide to outfit the schooner *Hispaniola* in Bristol and sail for the treasure. The captain is stern, honest Alexander Smollett, and the leader of the crew and ship's cook is an apparently affable, outgoing, one-legged salt named Long John Silver.

Before landing on the island, Jim, while hiding in an apple barrel, overhears plans for a mutiny led by Silver, who, as a former member of Flint's crew, is intent on collecting the treasure for himself. Upon landing, Smollett, Livesey, Trelawney, and the other loyal members of the crew manage to take over a deserted stockade and successfully withstand an attack by the mutineers, who outnumber them two to one. Jim, an adventurous lad, sets out on his own on two expeditions. On the first he meets a deranged castaway, Ben Gunn, who has lived alone on the island for three years; and on the second he manages to get control of the *Hispaniola* by killing Israel Hands, the pirate left in charge of the ship after the crew goes ashore. Eventually, Jim's side triumphs, and the pirates are either killed or captured. The treasure is loaded aboard the ship and Long John Silver, with an apparent change of heart, decides to return with Jim and his friends to face the consequences of his actions. However, in a West Indies port, Silver escapes with a bag of coins. The other voyagers sail back to England, where the survivors, including Jim, divide the remaining treasure equally.

CHARACTERS: *Treasure Island,* one of the best-loved adventure stories of all time, is unique in the history of children's literature in two respects. First, it represents a departure from the didactic, moralizing novels that preceded it. In *Treasure Island,* all of the characters are motivated by greed—the desire to obtain a treasure that is not rightfully theirs. Second, the villain, Long John Silver, emerges at the end of the story neither repentant nor punished, a ground-breaking development in stories for young people.

The central character and chief narrator is **Jim Hawkins**, the high-spirited, courageous boy whose life changes radically from a mundane existence at his parent's quiet inn to swashbuckling adventures amid bloodthirsty pirates. Devoted to the care of his mother, he signs on as cabin boy on the *Hispaniola,* in part hoping to gain financial security for her. His initial naivete and immaturity lead him to be overly trusting of others; as a result, he is easily taken in by Long John Silver's smooth talk. His feelings of outrage and betrayal when he discovers Silver's true intentions provide a hard-learned lesson in understanding human nature. Heroism and bravery result from Jim's newfound maturity, but his actions often border on the foolhardy. Twice he leaves his companions to pursue highly dangerous missions. In each case, largely by chance, his daring brings fortuitous results, although he rashly places his own life in danger. Bright and resourceful, he rescues the *Hispaniola* single-handedly from the pirates. In the climatic scene between Jim and Israel Hands, he demonstrates an unusual degree of physical courage when, in spite of being pinned to the mast by a dagger, he summons enough strength to shoot his adversary. Jim's gallantry, audacity, and fearlessness emerge throughout the novel. At one point, he faces his enemies and says, "I no more fear you than I fear a fly. Kill me, if you please, or spare me." Though still a boy at the novel's close, by his valiant actions, inner strength, and noble sentiments, Jim proves himself a true hero.

Perhaps the most interesting character in *Treasure Island* is the one-legged villainous ruffian, **Long John Silver.** Stevenson was so intrigued with this character that he initially named the novel *The Sea-Cook.* Silver is a fifty-year-old, tall, strong, ham-faced study in contrasts. At first, he is presented as a helpful, obedient, somewhat obsequious member of the crew fondly nicknamed "Barbecue." Always cheerful and smiling, he takes a particular interest in Jim, and through flattery, colorful tales, and his parrot Captain Flint (whose favorite expression is "pieces of eight"), wins the boy's confidence. Although many of these admirable characteristics, such as his exuberance and occasional kindnesses, persist through the novel, his darker side eventually dominates.

Silver emerges as a devious, cruel manipulator whose intellect and courage have made him a natural leader. He deceives with ease and, through his uncanny intelligence and knowledge of human nature, fools both friends and enemies alike. He often exhibits ruthlessness and audacity. Without compunction, he plans the cold-blooded murder of Jim's friends and later is responsible for the deaths of several uncooperative crew members. Through smooth talking, sheer temerity, and the ability to control others, he engineers the mutinous plot that at first seems bound to succeed. His physical handicap in no way inhibits his actions, although he is not above using it as an excuse for help. When his fortunes turn and the mutineers refuse to obey him, Silver reveals a pragmatic side to his character. He saves Jim's life by bravely standing up to the mutineers, but one wonders whether this was a genuine act of friendship or a way to regain the confidence of Jim's allies. At the close of the novel, Silver once again assumes the role of the charming servant to bargain safe passage back to England. These complexities and contradictions make Long John Silver a memorable, well-rounded character.

Jim's two mentors are **Dr. Livesey** and **Squire Trelawney**, the former sometimes serving as narrator, recounting the events at the stockade in Jim's absence. Dr. Livesey is a dignified, courageous man whose medical practice has taken him far afield, where he has faced death and learned the ways of human nature. The depth of Long John Silver's villainy, however, initially exceeds his experience. With his bright black eyes, calm attitude, and pleasant manner, Livesey displays an ability to organize the opposition to the mutineers. He is a man of principle and dignity, who, true to his medical oath, always treats the wounded, whether they be his allies or members of the mutinous pirate gang. Squire Trelawney, a man of considerable economic means, finances the expedition. Over six feet tall, he possesses many fine attributes, such as honesty and benevolence, typical of an English gentleman. Unfortunately, he is also high-tempered, rash, gullible, and unable to keep a secret. His inability to judge character results in his hiring Long John Silver and his fellow conspirators as crew members, and his impetuous nature and feelings of self-importance sometimes interfere with his honest, well-meaning nature.

Trelawney's flaws also create an early hostility toward the honest **Captain Smollett**, who from the beginning disapproved of the hiring of the ruffian crew. Smollett is a realistic, no-nonsense sailor. Even Silver grudgingly acknowledges him as "a first-rate seaman." The captain is the first to detect trouble with the crew and is fearful of a mutiny. Unlike Trelawney, he is dour and taciturn, but quickly assesses situations, proposes workable solutions, and effectively organizes the opposition to the pirates.

Stevenson presents a colorful cast of secondary pirates in his story. The first pirate Jim meets is **Bill Bones**, a weather-beaten old seaman with a tarry pigtail, a ragged body, and the scar of a saber wound on his face. Formerly Captain Flint's first mate, he is a lonely, fearful, malicious man who, having taken refuge at the "Admiral Benbow," obsessively guards the secret of the old pirate's treasure. Prone to excessive drinking, he becomes so unhinged when angered that he dies of a stroke after Blind Pew's visit. A former member of Captain Flint's crew, blind **Pew** presents a dreadful appearance with his large green eyeshade and huge hooded sea cloak. He is a suitable deliverer of the Black Spot, Bill Bones's death warrant.

Other unsavory characters include **Black Dog**, a pale, tattered figure whose fawning, sneering exterior hides a cunning and cruel personality. It is he who discovers Bones's hideout. Equally disagreeable is the coxswain of the *Hispaniola*, **Israel Hands**, a wily old sailor with thirty years experience whose cynical philosophy is summed up in his statement: "I never seen good come o' goodness yet." This treacherous, drunken seaman, who is the second in command among the pirates, almost murders Jim before succumbing to his own watery grave. Off the ship, Jim also meets **Ben Gunn**. After being abandoned by his shipmates three years before, Gunn has now become a babbling, half demented resident of Treasure Island. He survives by eating goats, berries, and oysters. In his solitude, however, he has learned to be gentle and pious. Dressed in tattered clothing that gives him a wild, unkempt look, he at first presents a frightening appearance to Jim.

Although he doesn't appear in the novel, the spirit of the dead pirate, **Captain Flint**, is present throughout. When he was alive, the name of this bloodthirsty buccaneer struck fear in everyone's hearts. It is the search for his treasure that produces the framework of this novel.

Kidnapped

(novel, 1886)

PLOT: This rousing adventure story takes place in Scotland during a two-month period in 1751, only five years after the Whigs, the supporters of King George II, defeated an uprising of the Jacobites, Catholic Highlanders intent on placing a member of the royal Stuart family—Bonnie Prince Charlie—on the throne of Scotland.

With the death of his schoolmaster father, seventeen-year-old David Balfour finds that his inheritance consists of a letter to his uncle, Ebenezer

Balfour of Shaw. With the blessing of the local minister, Mr. Campbell, David travels to his uncle's home, a gloomy, ill-kept mansion now partly in ruins. His uncle proves to be an obsessive miser, who, David suspects, has cheated his father of his rightful inheritance. After a failed attempt on his life, David forces Ebenezer to make an appointment with the family lawyer, Mr. Rankeillor, some miles away. Before reaching their destination, however, David is kidnapped and forced into servitude on the *Covenant*, a ship commanded by Captain Hoseason that is bound for the Carolinas. When the cabin boy, Ransome, is beaten to death by the drunken first mate, Mr. Shaun, David replaces him and becomes friendly with several crew members, including the second mate, Mr. Riach.

While at sea, the *Covenant* collides with a smaller boat and causes it to sink. Alan Breck, who was on the other boat but managed to survive, is brought aboard. He is a dashing adventurer, a Highland Jacobite with a price on his head who is bound for France and the court of his leader, Bonnie Prince Charlie (referred to as Ardsheil in the novel). Though different in age, background, and political beliefs, David and Alan become fast friends. David warns Alan of a plot by the captain and his men to seize Alan and claim a reward. The two withstand attacks by the crew on their hiding place, the roundhouse, but they are separated when, during a severe storm, the ship breaks up on a reef and both are cast into the ocean.

Making his way back to land, David wanders alone through the barren Highlands. There he encounters a group of soldiers led by the dreaded king's factor, Colin Roy, the Black Campbell of Glenure. When Colin is shot by an unknown assailant, David flees into the woods, fearful that he will be considered an accomplice, and is reunited with Alan Breck. They decide to escape to the Lowlands where David can contact Mr. Rankeillor and secure money for Alan's passage to France. The journey through rugged, unfriendly Scottish territory is a nightmare, particularly for David who is unprepared for such hardships. Along the way, they receive aid from several of Alan's outlaw patriot friends, including James Stewart, half brother of Prince Charles, and Cluny Macpherson, a Jacobite clan leader who is also a fugitive from justice.

At last they reach Mr. Rankeillor, who explains that David's father gave the family inheritance to his younger brother, Ebenezer, as a consolation prize for when the woman they both loved chose David's father as her husband. Ebenezer tries to eliminate David because he realizes that David is now the rightful heir to the Balfour fortune. In a confrontational scene, Ebenezer is frightened into giving two-thirds of his income to his nephew. David arranges safe passage for Alan to France, and the two bid each other a tender farewell.

CHARACTERS: In addition to being a tale of high adventure, this is the touching story of a deep and abiding friendship that gradually develops between two men of different backgrounds and beliefs. The hero is **David Balfour**, a Lowlander and Protestant who is a Whig, supporting the English King George II. At the beginning of the novel, David is a somewhat callow, good-natured but narrow-minded young man who is ill-equipped to face the calamities that befall him. Through his trials and encounters with a variety of people, many of whom subscribe to opposing political and religious beliefs, David gains maturity and the ability to see different points of view. In this journey to self-discovery, he learns to tolerate and respect differences in people and their convictions. In moments of crisis, he summons untapped resources of courage and loyalty. Although naturally cautious, he learns to defend his own rights and those of others. He exhibits his growing belief in justice and fair play when he endangers his own life to warn Alan of the plot against him.

David also possesses a sensitive nature. He sobs with uncontrollable remorse after he has killed crew members during the attack on the roundhouse, and at the final parting with Alan, he weeps like a baby. He sometimes displays a stubborn, somewhat petulant side to his character. When he thinks Alan has behaved insensitively towards him during their flight to the Lowlands, he responds with fits of pouting and silence until he realizes that he is behaving immaturely and effects a reconciliation. For David, the experiences that led to claiming his rightful inheritance have also been a journey to adulthood from which he has learned to accept responsibility, respect differences between people, and realize the importance and complexity of maintaining loving friendships.

The Jacobite **Alan Breck** is a small, wiry man of unusual physical strength and commanding appearance. His innate vanity is shown in the elegance of his clothes and his flamboyant behavior. A dashing, impetuous romantic with a sense of bravado, he also demonstrates skills in both music and writing poetry. Though a condemned man with a price on his head, he still maintains his self-assured, impulsive behavior; his impetuous nature causes him to take offense easily, leading to numerous quarrels. He courageously and loyally defends his beliefs. Through his fight for the rights of the Jacobites, he represents the gallantry of the Scottish people and their struggle for independence and justice.

In times of trial, Alan is enterprising and resourceful. He knows the ways of high society, as well as the skills that allow him to endure great physical hardships. David discovers that Alan is also an accurate shot, a good angler, an excellent fencer, and a bad gambler. A faithful friend capable of sacrifice for those he loves, he at one point tells David, "I love ye like a brother." The bond of love and respect that grows between Alan and David forms the basic theme of the novel.

David's miserly and cowardly uncle, **Ebenezer Balfour**, is described as "mean, stooped, narrow-shouldered, and clay-faced." His greed so consumes him that he would willingly sacrifice the life of his only nephew to retain the family fortune. He is avaricious to the point of self-deprivation, existing only on the meanest and most ordinary food possible—porridge. He neither maintains and repairs the family home nor spends money on any of life's comforts. He is a malicious schemer whose plotting against David sets into motion the rest of the story. At the end of the novel, Mr. Rankeillor provides an explanation for Ebenezer's pathological behavior: he was once a gallant, attractive, and somewhat debonair young man whose loss of his true love so embittered him that he avoided all social contact and became obsessed with the accumulation of money.

On board the *Covenant,* David encounters several interesting characters. **Captain Hoseason**, a rough, fierce, unscrupulous man, noted for his brutal, tyrannical behavior while at sea, is supposedly a kind, considerate person on land. This stiff, dour, and studious person occasionally displays genuine feelings of compassion toward David. Though motivated by a consuming greed, he refuses to commit murder to increase his fortunes. The captain is wounded in the battle of the roundhouse. **Ransome** is the half-witted pathetic cabin boy who feigns high spirits but is actually the victim of cruel physical and mental abuse. He is fed liquor by the crew to perform for their amusement, and eventually this pitiful, mistreated waif is murdered by a drunken **Mr. Shaun**, the ship's second mate. Gentle and pleasant when sober, Mr. Shaun transforms into a raging madman when drunk. Though he suffers from remorse for his actions, he remains an unsympathetic figure who is later killed by Alan Breck. By contrast, the first mate, **Mr. Riach**, a lord's son, is sullen and unkind when sober but pleasant and understanding when inebriated. During his drinking bouts, he tries to help David and makes several attempts to cheer him up.

The honest, kindly lawyer who helps David secure his inheritance is **Mr. Rankeillor**. A proper gentleman who has a sharp sense of humor and courtly appearance, he is so cautious and fearful of being involved in any Jacobite activities that he refuses to acknowledge Alan Breck's true identity and refers to him always as "Mr. Thomson." His often pompous conversation frequently includes Latin phrases. However, Mr. Rankeillor is otherwise well-meaning, helpful, and trustworthy.

Another minor character is **Mr. Campbell**, the caring minister of David's church. He is a simple, religious person who helps and encourages David on his first trip to his uncle's home. During their journey through the Highlands, David and Alan encounter several historical figures who actually lived during this period. Red-headed **Colin Roy**, also known as the **Red Fox**, was a King's factor and ardent royalist supporter intent on driving innocent Highlanders from their homes to crush their support of Bonnie Prince Charlie. In the book, he also attempts to capture Alan and bring him to justice. David witnesses Roy's murder by **James Stewart** of the Glens, the half brother of Prince Charles, who was a tall, handsome man who lead the Highlanders against the British. Though he and his followers are in hiding, in the novel he provides Alan and David with weapons, clothes, and provisions to aid in their flight south. Eventually, he is hanged for the murder of the Red Fox. Another fugitive leader is **Cluny Macpherson**, who, though stripped of his legal powers, still exercises patriarchal power over his clan. He supplies the two runaways with hospitality, and after winning Alan's money at gambling, he returns it at David's request, so the two can continue their journey.

Further Reading

Bevan, Bryan. *Robert Louis Stevenson: Poet and Teller of Tales.* New York: St. Martin's, 1993.

Bruccoli, Matthew J., and Richard Layman, eds. *Late Victorian and Edwardian Writers, 1890-1914.* Vol. 5 of *Concise Dictionary of British Literary Biography.* Detroit: Gale Research, 1992.

Fredeman, William E., and Ira B. Nadel, eds. *Victorian Writers after 1885.* Vol. 18 of *Dictionary of Literary Biography.* Detroit: Gale Research, 1983.

Magill, Frank N. *Critical Survey of Long Fiction: English-Language Series: Authors.* Vol. 6. Englewood Cliffs, NJ: Prentice-Hall, 1983.

Maixner, Paul. "Robert Louis Stevenson." In *The Critical Heritage.* London: Routledge & Kegan Paul, 1981.

Nineteenth-Century Literary Criticism. Vols. 5, 14. Detroit: Gale Research, 1984, 1987.

Rankin, Nicholas. *Dead Man's Chest: Travels after Robert Louis Stevenson.* London: Faber, 1987.

Sabin, Francene. *Robert Louis Stevenson: Young Storyteller.* Mahwah, NJ: Troll, 1992.

Spaosnik, Irving S. *Robert Louis Stevenson.* Boston: Twayne, 1974.

Thesing, William B., ed. *Victorian Prose Writers after 1867.* Vol. 57 of *Dictionary of Literary Biography.* Detroit: Gale Research, 1987.

Yesterday's Authors of Books for Children. Vol. 2. Detroit: Gale Research, 1978.

Bram Stoker

1847-1912, Irish novelist

Dracula

(horror novel, 1897)

PLOT: This original vampire horror tale, *Dracula,* set in the late-nineteenth century, is told in a series of journal entries. Jonathan Harker, a young English lawyer, travels to the castle of Count Dracula in Transylvania on a real estate matter. The strange behavior of the gaunt, pale Count accentuates the dark, foreboding nature of the castle. The castle of Count Dracula, set in the sparsely populated and thoroughly mysterious countryside of Transylvania, is a great ruined building of iron-studded stone doors, clanking chains, and rounded arches. Howling wolves surround the grounds and horses are afraid to approach. After Jonathan cuts himself shaving and is subsequently attacked by the Count, the young man realizes that Dracula is a vampire who survives by drinking human blood. Imprisoned and assaulted by three female vampires, Jonathan is left, weak and sick, in the castle. The Count leaves for England transporting fifty boxes of earth, which he takes because vampires need to sleep in their native soil every day.

In England some time later, Jonathan's fiancée, Mina Murray, and her friend, Lucy Westenra, witness a shipwreck. Unknown to the women, the ship's cargo contains Dracula's boxes of earth. Soon after, Mina discovers that Lucy, who is engaged to Arthur Holmwood, has returned to her old habit of sleepwalking. On successive nights, Mina finds Lucy wandering about or standing in front of her bedroom window; sometimes a large bat is nearby. Mina notices two small red marks on Lucy's neck, but Lucy remembers nothing of her nightly wanderings. Lucy's health inexplicably declines, and she is examined by ex-suitor, Dr. John Seward, who, along with another ex-suitor, American Quincey Morris, is visiting Holmwood. Perplexed over Lucy's condition, Seward calls in his mentor, Dr. Abraham Van Helsing. Meanwhile, Mina hears from the ailing Jonathan, who has escaped from Castle Dracula (although the reader never learns how) and leaves to nurse him.

Neither blood transfusions nor anti-vampire remedies such as garlic draped about her neck can save the now mortally ill Lucy. As she dies, she attempts to attack Holmwood, but he is saved by Van Helsing. Mina and Jonathan, now married, return to England. After seeing Jonathan's journal, which describes the strange behavior of Count Dracula, Van Helsing explains that Lucy has become a vampire. To save her soul and rescue her remains from living death, they must open her coffin, drive a stake through her heart, cut off her head, and stuff it with garlic—all of which they successfully accomplish.

A search begins for Count Dracula and the fifty boxes of earth. When Mina begins to act strangely, Van Helsing and Seward suspect the Count's presence. They break into her room to find Jonathan unconscious and Mina sucking blood from a cut on Dracula's chest. The Count escapes with one box of earth. Mina and Jonathan, now recovered, along with Van Helsing, Seward, and Morris, follow the vampire to Transylvania where they find the last box in the possession of gypsies. A fight ensues, and Morris is wounded. The opened box reveals the body of Count Dracula. Jonathan cuts off his head, and Morris manages to drive a knife into his heart. Dracula crumbles into dust, and Morris dies from his wound. The novel ends with a note from Jonathan, some seven years later, revealing that he and Mina have had a son, whom they have named Quincey after the deceased Morris.

CHARACTERS: From his appearance in the first vampire novel in literature, **Count Dracula** of Transylvania has become the prototype of all vampires. "Un-dead" for several hundred years, he sucks blood from live victims in order to maintain his vitality. Although he actually appears in relatively few scenes in this novel, his presence constantly pervades the reader's mind and permeates all action. Just as Dracula is the prototype for all vampires, so his home has become the prototype for all forbidding, dark, and mysterious castles in horror fiction.

Stoker describes the Count as old, clean-shaven, except for a long white moustache, and always dressed in black. Although his manner to Jonathan Harker is cordial upon their first meeting, the young lawyer senses peculiarities about his host, including the startling coldness of his handshake. Extremely thin, with pale, pointed ears and sharp, unusually long teeth, Stoker's Count is bushy haired with shaggy white eyebrows.

Jonathan Harker's journal entries provide much of the essential facts concerning Dracula and his castle. The young lawyer is portrayed as rational, organized, and logical. His straightforward descriptions of the horrors that befall him and others makes the chilling events of the story all the more shocking and believable. The reader reacts so strongly to the contrast between Harker's observations and Count Dracula's actions largely because Harker records them so rationally and earnestly. Much of the plot is also related through the journals of Jonathan's fiancée, **Mina Murray**, a young assistant schoolmistress. An orphan, she is innocent and very naive about almost all manner of worldly things, and this innocence stands in sharp contrast to the total horror of vampirism.

Mina's friend, nineteen-year-old **Lucy Westenra**, is similarly naive and unsophisticated. Her sleepwalking provides the reader with the first glimpse into the actual creation of a vampire. In a letter to Mina sent before the young women witness the shipwreck, she confesses her elation at having received three marriage proposals in one day—from Dr. Seward and Quincey Morris, both of whom she turned down, and from Arthur Holmwood, whom she accepted. **Arthur Holmwood** is the lively, twenty-nine-year-old son of Lord Godalming and will later inherit his title. After being forced to drive a stake through the heart of his beloved fiancée, he seeks revenge against the vampire Dracula. **Quincey P. Morris** is a wealthy Texan whose money pays for many of the expenses incurred in the journey to find and slay Count Dracula.

The third suitor to Lucy is **Dr. John Seward**, the director of a lunatic asylum. He is an intelligent man who summons his old mentor Van Helsing when he cannot determine the cause of Lucy's mysterious malady. **Dr. Abraham Van Helsing**, who is also a lawyer, is a kind and caring father figure. His extensive knowledge of the occult and folklore sets him on the trail of vampirism and allows him to persuade the others to perform the terrible acts needed to save Lucy's soul. He leads the plan to track down Dracula.

Further Reading

Bruccoli, Matthew J., and Richard Layman, eds. *Late Victorian and Edwardian Writers, 1890-1914*. Vol. 5 of *Concise Dictionary of British Literary Biography*. Detroit: Gale Research, 1991.

Farson, Daniel. *The Man Who Wrote Dracula*. New York: St. Martin's, 1975.

McCormack, W. J. *The Novel to 1900*. New York: St. Martin's, 1980.

Mitchell, Sally. *Victorian Britain*. Hamden, CT: Garland, 1988.

Roth, Phyllis A. *Bram Stoker*. Boston: Twayne, 1982.

Something about the Author. Vol. 29. Detroit: Gale Research, 1982.

Staley, Thomas F., ed. *British Novelists, 1890-1929: Modernists*. Vol. 36 of *Dictionary of Literary Biography*. Detroit: Gale Research, 1985.

Twentieth-Century Literary Criticism. Vol. 8. Detroit: Gale Research, 1982.

Wolf, Leonard, ed. *The Annotated Dracula*. New York: Ballantine, 1975.

Harriet Beecher Stowe

1811-1896, American novelist

Uncle Tom's Cabin; or, Life among the Lowly

(novel, 1852)

PLOT: In pre-Civil War Kentucky, plantation owner Arthur Shelby must sell some of his slaves to pay off his debts. Haley, an evil slave trader from New Orleans, selects both Uncle Tom, Shelby's most loyal slave, and talented five-year-old Harry as partial payment. Shelby is upset with the choice but can't refuse, due to his financial difficulties. When Harry's mother, Eliza, hears of the sale, she steals away in the night with the boy, stopping at Uncle Tom's cabin. She implores Uncle Tom to travel north with them via the "Underground Railroad" to freedom. However, Uncle Tom feels he must be loyal to Shelby.

Eliza and Harry flee north, pursued by Haley. At the Ohio River, she escapes by jumping from ice floe to ice floe with her son in her arms. On the other side, she is befriended by Mr. Symmes, who hates slave traders and conveys them to the home of Senator and Mrs. Bird. From there, they go to the Halliday household in a kindly Quaker community, where Eliza is reunited with her husband, George Harris. Although Haley and two vicious slave hunters, Loker and Marks, nearly capture them, the family eludes their captors by boarding a ship bound for Canada. Frustrated, Haley returns to take Uncle Tom to New Orleans. Shelby's son, George, gives Uncle Tom a dollar and promises he will buy him back one day.

On the steamboat trip south, Uncle Tom saves the life of frail young Eva St. Clare. In gratitude, her father, Augustine, buys him, and Uncle Tom enjoys life as head coachman on the St. Clare plantation. The spoiled Eva, although fragile and delicate, wins the heart of both Topsy, a clever little slave girl, and Eva's aunt, Miss Ophelia, who has come from Vermont to manage the mansion due to the poor health of Eva's mother. Before the ailing Eva's death, she makes her father promise to free all the slaves. Although he does give Topsy to Miss Ophelia, he doesn't manage to free the other slaves before he is killed trying to settle a brawl. Marie St. Clare, Augustine's wife, has no intention of freeing the slaves and puts Tom up for auction.

Tom is bought by the villainous Simon Legree, a brutal drunkard who beats his slaves until they drop. However, Legree does fear one slave, Cassy, who threatens the superstitious miscreant with voodoo. Cassy and another slave, Emmeline, escape and hide in the garret. Legree beats Tom unmercifully to learn their whereabouts. George Shelby then arrives to buy back Tom as he had earlier promised. After Legree mocks him, Shelby knocks him down. Unfortunately, George has arrived too late to help Tom, who dies from injuries sustained from Legree's beating. He is buried in a peaceful, shady spot.

George encounters Cassy and Emmeline on a steamboat headed for Kentucky. They all meet Madame de Thoux, George Harris's sister, and learn that Cassy is really Eliza's mother. The former slaves are reunited in Canada, and eventually the family goes to Liberia. Topsy travels to Vermont to live with Miss Ophelia, while George Shelby returns to the plantation in Kentucky and frees his slaves in the name of Uncle Tom.

CHARACTERS: Although the character traits of **Uncle Tom** have come to popularly symbolize a lackey or toady, Stowe's original intention was to portray a Christ-figure, a man of basic goodness and intelligence. Tom exhibits love for all people and always strives to better himself. He is loyal to his master and almost childlike in his determination to avoid confrontation or retaliation for the injustices he suffers. Although Tom stoically accepts his fate instead of fighting against prejudice and racial inequities, Stowe intended his death as a strong indictment of the evil institution of slavery. Interjecting her religious beliefs, Stowe believed it impossible to be a Christian *and* a slave owner. Today, some see Tom's "turning the other cheek" as reminiscent of the teachings of Gandhi and Martin Luther King, Jr.

Uncle Tom's owner, **Arthur Shelby**, is portrayed as a kind man who is generous to his slaves. Despite these positive qualities, however, Stowe utilized the character of Shelby to illustrate that even prominent and upstanding men regarded other races as innately inferior to whites. When financial misfortune jeopardizes his continued well-being, Shelby sells even his most beloved slave. His son, **George**, however, sincerely loves Uncle Tom, although he arrives too late to honor his promise to buy him back.

Eva St. Clare, like Uncle Tom, is an allegorical figure. She is the classic angel with her golden hair and beatific face, always dressed in white, always spotless. Goodness and love both radiate from and surround her, even though she often plays the spoiled imp. Although her implausible dying scene is affected and sensational by today's standards, it illustrates the mid-nineteenth-century passion for melodrama. Eva's devotion to Uncle Tom demonstrates Stowe's belief that only love can surmount the insufferable wickedness of slavery. The slave **Topsy** provides a perfect foil for the angelic Eva. A high-spirited young girl who sings and dances, she doesn't care whether anyone likes her or not. Ignorant of her origins and ancestry, she has not known love and doesn't care to. When Topsy finally accepts that Eva truly does love her, she cries in a rare display of profound emotion. **Miss Ophelia**, Eva's aunt, personifies the pious New England personality and Puritan consciousness. She is righteous in her opposition to slavery but repulsed by the slaves themselves. Her confrontation with the equally stubborn Topsy is both humorous and endearing. **Augustine St. Clare**, Eva's father, is an agreeable but weak man whose failure to fulfill his promise to his daughter leads to Uncle Tom's eventual death. His wife, **Marie St. Clare**, is a bored, self-centered southern aristocrat who cares nothing for the slaves

Illustrations from early editions of Uncle Tom's Cabin, *such as this one by James Daugherty published in 1929, are clearly unflattering by today's standards.*

on the plantation and who has no intention of freeing them if she could sell them instead for profit.

Besides Uncle Tom, **Eliza** serves as an important vehicle for Stowe's message, fighting valiantly to save her five-year-old son, Harry, from a life of slavery. Best characterized by her intense family love and her undaunting courage, Eliza demonstrates her resourcefulness through her successful escape over the ice floes on the Ohio River. While critics initially derided the plausibility of this maneuver, Stowe later provided proof that it had actually taken place. Eliza is pictured as light-skinned, a device often used in fiction of the time to appeal to white readers. **George Harris** is Eliza's intelligent and sensitive husband who bitterly resents his slavery.

Arguably the most infamous villain in American literature, **Simon Legree** has no redeeming qualities whatsoever. Like Uncle Tom, the name "Simon Legree" has also become part of English vernacular, symbolizing a brutal taskmaster, a tyrant. He lives in squalor, incites violence at every encounter, and drinks himself senseless. A Yankee living in the South, he demonstrates that southerners alone were not responsible for the institution and perpetuation of slavery. Other reprehensible characters include **Haley**, a cruel slave trader who considers himself to be a humanitarian, and slave catchers **Marks** and **Loker**, two of literature's most inhumane characters.

There are a number of minor but still important characters that add to the fulfillment of the tale. Proud and defiant **Cassy** proves a formidable opponent for Simon Legree even though she belongs to him. **Emmeline** illustrates the often degrading relationship between masters and slave women. **Senator** and **Mrs. Bird** and the **Hallidays** are sympathetic characters who detest the evils of slavery and help slaves escape north to freedom.

Further Reading

Adams, F. C. *Uncle Tom at Home.* Philadelphia: Ayer, 1977.

Adams, John R. *Harriet Beecher Stowe.* New York: Twayne, 1963.

Ammons, Elizabeth. *Critical Essays on Harriet Beecher Stowe.* Boston: Hall, 1980.

Bland, Celia. *Harriet Beecher Stowe: Anti-Slavery Author.* New York: Chelsea House, 1993.

Coil, Suzanne M. *Harriet Beecher Stowe.* New York: F. Watts, 1993.

Critical Survey of Long Fiction. Vol. 6. Englewood Cliffs, NJ: Salem, 1983.

Crozier, Alice. *The Novels of Harriet Beecher Stowe.* New York: Oxford, 1969.

Donovan, Josephine. Uncle Tom's Cabin: *Evil, Affliction, and Redemptive Love.* New York: Macmillan, 1991.

Estes, Glenn E., ed. *American Writers for Children before 1900.* Vol. 42 of *Dictionary of Literary Biography.* Detroit: Gale Research, 1985.

Fritz, Jean. *Harriet Beecher Stowe and the Beecher Preachers.* New York: Putnam, 1994.

Harbert, Earl N., and Donal Pizer, eds. *American Realists and Naturalists.* Vol. 12 of *Dictionary of Literary Biography.* Detroit: Gale Research, 1982.

Hedrick, Joan D. *Harriet Beecher Stowe: A Life.* New York: Oxford, 1995.

Kimbel, Bobby Ellen, ed. *American Short-Story Writers before 1880.* Vol. 74 of *Dictionary of Literary Biography.* Detroit: Gale Research, 1988.

Myerson, Joel, ed. *The American Renaissance in New England.* Vol. 1 of *Dictionary of Literary Biography.* Detroit: Gale Research, 1978.

Nineteenth-Century Literature Criticism. Vol. 3. Detroit: Gale Research, 1983.

Sundquist, Eric J. *New Essays on "Uncle Tom's Cabin."* New York: Cambridge, 1986.

Wilson, Edmund. *Patriotic Gore: Studies in the Literature of the American Civil War.* New York: Oxford University Press, 1962.

Wilson, Robert F. *Crusader in Crinoline: The Life of Harriet Beecher Stowe.* Westport, CT: Greenwood, 1972.

Rosemary Sutcliff

1920-1992, English novelist

The Eagle of the Ninth

(historical novel, 1954)

PLOT: In Roman Britain, 117 A.D., the Ninth Roman Legion (named Hispana) disappears after marching into barbarian territory north of Hadrian's Wall.

Ten years later, the son of the commander of the ill-fated Ninth, the youthful centurion Marcus Flavius Aquila, is sent from Italy to Britain on his first assignment to be the Cohort Commander of the Second Legion. At the frontier post at Isca Dumnoniorum (Exeter) in the southwest of present-day England, Marcus distinguishes himself in battle during a barbarian revolt in which Cradoc, a barbarian whom Marcus had trusted, is revealed to be one of the leaders of the insurrection. Seriously wounded, Marcus is released from duty and goes to live with his Uncle Aquila, a retired army officer who has decided to remain in Britain. There, Marcus saves the life of a gallant slave named Esca, who has been condemned to death after losing a gladiatorial combat. Marcus also meets the willful, high-spirited Cattia, daughter of his neighbors, Kaeso and Valaria.

When Marcus learns from his uncle's friend, the respected Legate Claudius, that the lost eagle standard of the Ninth has been seen in the hands of barbarians, Marcus sets out with Esca on a perilous journey to retrieve this symbol of the legion's—and his father's—honor. In the hostile Highlands north of Hadrian's Wall they are given directions by a hunter, Guern, who has assumed the identity of a barbarian after deserting the Ninth during battle.

In the territory of Chieftain Dergdian and his brother, Liathan, Marcus and Esca witness sacred rites in which the Eagle of the Ninth is revealed. Marcus discovers that his father died gallantly with the remnants of his legion after being attacked repeatedly by hordes of barbarians. Marcus devises a bold plan to steal the Eagle. After many narrow escapes and near-fatal adventures, he and Esca successfully bring the standard back to Roman territory. Esca is rewarded by being granted full Roman citizenship, and Marcus is given a large tract of land, where he plans to settle down with his new bride, Cattia.

CHARACTERS: Though still in his early twenties, **Marcus Flavius Aquila** displays a remarkable maturity in both the decisions he makes and in the way he commands his troops. Through his quick thinking and use of keen powers of observation, he is able to assess situations astutely to determine the best course of action. For example, Marcus saves a patrol from slaughter by the barbarians during their attack on Isca Dumnoniorum. Though his gallantry and courage in leading the charge during this battle cost him his army career because of debilitating wounds, he accepts his fate without rancor or self-pity.

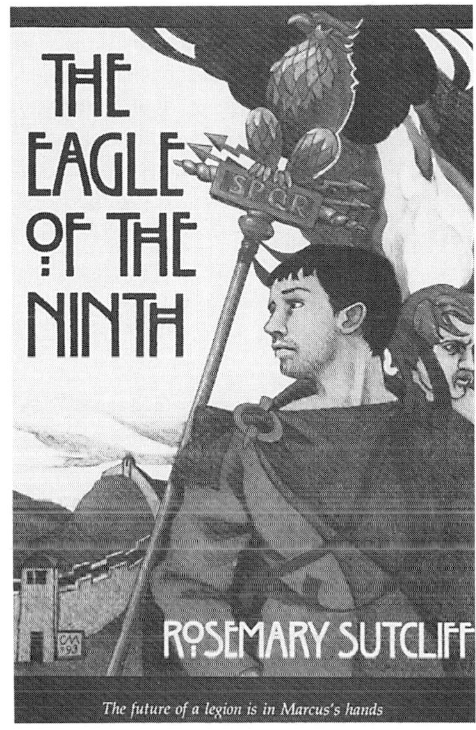

A young Roman soldier named Marcus journeys to distant Britain to restore his father's honor in this historical novel.

Marcus respects the integrity and dignity of others, even though they may be the enemy. While an army officer, he never uses his power to debase or take advantage of others. He evaluates people on their merits, not on their social position. This ability to empathize with others has made him a compassionate and understanding person, unwilling to exploit or manipulate others. For example, to ensure that Esca's decision will be free of coercion, he grants his slave freedom before asking him to accompany him into barbarian country. Marcus is a great lover of justice and fair play. He deplores the misuse of authority to further personal ambition, believing instead that it is the obligation of a Roman citizen to sacrifice and endure hardship, if necessary, to maintain the honor of family and country. Marcus is a man of rare courage and endurance. He suffers great pain without complaint and often sacrifices his own safety to help others. Though admired by others, Marcus remains a modest man. Grateful for the success of his mission, he looks forward to marriage and a life of peace.

Marcus's slave and steadfast follower is **Esca MacCunoval**, a native Briton from the Brigantes tribe. A short, powerfully built man, he is in his early twenties. The son of a clan chieftain, Esca was captured in battle and sold into slavery. He is fiercely proud of his heritage and, unable to accept the yolk of slavery and loss of his freedom, has become sullen and morose. Defeated in an unfair gladiatorial combat, he prefers death to begging for mercy but is saved against his will through Marcus's intervention. The two nevertheless form a touching friendship built on mutual love, trust, and respect. Though naturally silent and withdrawn, Esca opens up to Marcus and reveals his sensitive nature. He is fiercely loyal and dedicated to Marcus, willing to sacrifice his life to ensure the safety of his master and the success of his mission. Despite having been freed, Esca's feelings of devotion and affection towards Marcus and admiration for his crusade compel him to accompany Marcus, though it may result in his own death. Esca is granted full Roman citizenship for his heroism in rescuing the Eagle of the Ninth, but he decides to remain with Marcus in his new life as a landlord.

Marcus's only relative in Britain is his crusty, brusque **Uncle Aquila**. Twenty years older than Marcus's father, he has had little connection with his younger brother or his family, yet he welcomes Marcus into his household without hesitation. Aquila is outwardly curt and grumpy, sparing no one from his gruff, contrary nature. Yet in spite of this, he is inwardly proud of his nephew and his accomplishments and worried about his well-being. After trying unsuccessfully to dissuade Marcus from his quest to recapture the eagle of the Ninth, he lends his wholehearted support. This tough old bird is described as a huge, bald man whose "authority hangs on him in easy and accustomed folds, like his toga."

Aquila's dear friend is the wise, highly respected legate, **Claudius.** This kindly, generous man, an Egyptian, served with Aquila in various parts of the Empire and is now an esteemed representative in the Roman Senate. He reveals to Marcus the rumor about the whereabouts of the Eagle and later is responsible for passing legislation granting land to Marcus and citizenship to Esca.

The Magistrate **Kaeso** and his wife, the overbearing **Valaria**, are Aquila's neighbors. Kaeso is a fat, good-natured man who is dominated by his wife, who is described as having "a fair and rather foolish face, prinked out in what had been the height of fashion in Rome two years before." Both are born Britons but have acclimated themselves to Roman society and have made their way up its social ladder. Valaria, in particular, wishes to forget her roots and become Romanized. To this end she even changes her daughter's name from **Cattia** to Camilla. Cattia, however, rejects her mother's affectations. She is an honest, opinionated girl of about thirteen who hates taking orders from others and is noted for her high spirits and bold, somewhat brazen nature. Cattia is a tall, thin girl with a pointed face that reminds Marcus of a vixen. Beneath her wide, impetuous exterior, however, she has a compassionate disposition. She hates cruelty towards animals and admires Marcus for his courage and endurance. When he returns from his mission, Marcus finds that Cattia has matured. Though still outspoken and independent, she is now ready for marriage.

During their Highland adventures, Marcus and Esca encounter many interesting people. Among them is **Guern the Hunter**, a lean, powerful, middle-aged man who graciously shares his home and provisions with Marcus and Esca. Through clever detection, Marcus discovers that Guern once served in the Ninth Legion. The hunter confesses that after he was severely wounded in battle and was no longer able to fight, he deserted and assumed the identity of a native Briton. Though ashamed and contrite, he refuses Marcus's offer of a pardon and decides to remain in his adopted land. Guern is a good-natured, upstanding man whose basic honesty and decency are shown when he risks his life to help Marcus. **Dergdian** is the chief of the Epidaii, the Highland clan that has captured the Eagle. He is a firm, strict leader who is a sworn enemy of the Roman invaders. Nevertheless, he abides by the customs of his tribe and generously offers hospitality and friendship to Marcus and Esca, who have disguised themselves as an oculist and his assistant. **Liathan** is Dergdian's fierce, daring brother. When he is taken prisoner by Marcus and Esca during their escape with the Eagle, he displays an understanding and respect for their sense of honor and justice and nobly returns to Marcus a ring that had belonged to his father.

Marcus has his first close encounter with native Britons when he meets **Cradoc**, his guide and companion at Isca Dumnoniorum. Marcus learns to respect and admire this bold, independent man and to honor his self-assurance and dexterity. Marcus realizes that freedom means more than friendship to Cradoc when he discovers that Cradoc is one of the leaders of the insurrection during which Marcus is badly wounded and Cradoc is killed.

Further Reading

Authors and Artists for Young Adults. Vol. 10. Detroit: Gale Research, 1993.

Berger, Laura Standley, ed. *Twentieth-Century Young Adult Writers.* 1st ed. Chicago: St. James, 1994.

Children's Literature Review. Vols. 1, 37. Detroit: Gale Research, 1976, 1996.

Contemporary Literary Criticism. Vol. 26. Detroit: Gale Research, 1983.

Crouch, Marcus. *Treasure Seekers and Borrowers.* Chicago: American Library Association, 1962.

Fuller, Muriel, ed. *More Junior Authors.* New York: H. W. Wilson, 1963.

Meek, Margaret. *Rosemary Sutcliff.* New York: Walck, 1962.

Sutcliff, Rosemary. *Blue Remembered Hills: A Recollection.* New York: Morrow, 1984.

Townsend, John Rowe. *A Sense of Story.* New York: Lippincott, 1971.

Something about the Author. Vols. 6, 44, 78. Detroit: Gale Research, 1974, 1986, 1994.

Ward, Martha, ed. *Authors of Books for Young People.* 3rd ed. Metuchen, NJ: Scarecrow, 1990, p. 683.

Glendon Swarthout

1918-1992, American novelist

Bless the Beasts and Children

(young adult novel, 1970)

PLOT: The Bedwetters are considered the lowest of the low at Box Canyon Boys Camp. These six young men—Lawrence Teft III, Sammy Shecker, Gerald Goodenow, William Lally, and Stephen Lally, Jr., and their leader, John Cotton—are the offspring of well-to-do parents who are too busy going on safari, or divorcing, or making money to have time for them and their problems. Their parents send them to the boys camp, which the boys all hate since nobody likes them there either.

With a week to go, the Bedwetters make plans for one last shot at glory before they leave the camp. After borrowing some horses from the corral, they ride into town, where to their surprise and delight Teft is able to hot-wire a truck. Stopping for some food at an all-night eatery, they run into trouble with some smart-alecky locals who chase them when the Bedwetters drive away. Teft gets rid of the locals with a BB gun, but the boys know the law will soon be after them. They decide to head back to camp, until they see the sign for a buffalo preserve. Unwilling to pass up this chance, they run into a so-called hunt in which people are given the opportunity to shoot captive, helpless buffalos.

The boys know what they have to do. Without a definite plan in mind, they set out to free the remaining buffalo from the pen before they can be slaughtered the next morning. It takes some doing, but the boys—with the help of some well-placed bales of hay—lead the animals out of the slaughter bin. Thrilled with their accomplishment, they don't

Troubled teens find friendship in each other at a summer camp in **Bless the Beasts and Children,** *which was adapted for the screen in 1971.*

even care when a dozen men with big hats and boots hop out of their jeeps and pickups and chase after them.

CHARACTERS: Lawrence Teft III, is a fourteen-year-old New Yorker who doesn't like authority. An expert at opening locks and hot-wiring cars, he has had to be bailed out of trouble many times by his father. Once Teft took his father's luxury car for a joy ride; another time he stole his mother's purse; and, of course, he's already stolen a few cars of his own. He doesn't worry about the consequences of his actions; his father, who works for a Wall Street firm, pays for any damages that result from his son's high jinks. Teft is sent to camp because the headmaster at his exclusive prep school recommended discipline for the boy. Although Teft is fascinated by the West, when sent to the camp he has to be put aboard the plane as a virtual prisoner. During the flight, he makes himself as much of a nuisance as possible, ripping out an oxygen mask and attempting to open an emergency exit.

Sammy Shecker has a father, **Sid**, who is a big-time comic. Sid drops his son off at camp on his way to a month-long engagement at Vegas and Tahoe. Sammy, an overweight boy, remembers his big-affair bar mitzvah and how livid his father was when he flubbed his lines. To cover himself, Sammy went right into one of his father's old jokes, but nobody laughed. Sammy is so overindulged by a parent who doesn't have time for him that he is rapidly becoming as obnoxious as his father. He remembers the night his father was showing off for his friends and bet that his son could eat a dozen pieces of pie in four minutes, but Sammy could only manage ten. Sammy was particularly obnoxious when he first arrived at the camp, but after a fight with Cotton he straightened out and became almost human.

At fourteen, **Gerald Goodenow** still wets the bed and is a sissy. When he arrived at the camp he was homesick, and all he did was cry and make a mess out of everything, until Cotton stood up for him and promised he would not let anyone laugh at him. Gerald has undergone treatment for emotional problems that began when his father died. He slept in his mother's bed for the next several years until she married again. His stepfather doesn't care about him. In fact, he gave Gerald's mother an ultimatum: either she would send her son to camp or she could find a new husband. One night when Cotton caught Gerald trying to telephone his mother, which was against the rules, Gerald threatened suicide. He even tried to hang himself in the barn, but Cotton found him. Cotton wonders if Gerald really would have gone through with it.

Stephen Lally, Jr. and **William (Billy) Lally** are fourteen and twelve, respectively. Back home in Illinois, they live in a sixteen room house in which they are often left alone with the servants while their parents are busy divorcing, or making up, or skiing somewhere. Billy finds the house lonely at those times, so he takes his pillow down to the sauna his father built and sleeps there. He is the youngest boy at camp. Usually only boys between thirteen and sixteen are accepted, but his parents couldn't have gone off to Kenya without someplace to put him, so they paid the camp enough money to make an exception. Billy is a loner, and when he can't cope, he simply draws into a world of fantasy populated by the Ooms, little people who live under the rocks and who are his friends. He has also learned that the more he acts like a baby, the greater advantage he has over his older brother. The boys have always competed for the sparse attention of their parents. Billy does so by sucking his thumb, wetting the bed, and having bad dreams; Stephen has temper tantrums, expressing his frustration by taking his anger out on others, usually his brother. For example, he kills Billy's pets after Cotton tears up a letter Stephen had written to his parents because they never would have received it.

John Cotton (no one dares call him by his first name) is the unofficial but powerful leader of the small group. He keeps all these misfits together and he is willing to fight anyone to keep it that way. His mother, a lonely, frightened woman, has been married and divorced three times. Cotton's favorite father was her second husband, who was rich and grandfatherly. When his stepfather suggested, before the divorce, that perhaps his mother would sell Cotton to him, the boy believed she might. Cotton tells her that on his seventeenth birthday he plans to join the marines. She says she won't sign the necessary papers, but he tells her she will probably be too drunk to notice what she is signing.

Further Reading

Berger, Laura Standley, ed. *Twentieth-Century Young Adult Writers.* 1st ed. Detroit: St. James, 1995.

Contemporary Literary Criticism. Vol. 35. Detroit: Gale Research, 1985.

Karolides, Nicholas J., ed. *Censored Books: Critical Viewpoints.* Metuchen, NJ: Scarecrow, 1993.

Something about the Author. Vol. 26. Detroit: Gale Research, 1982.

Amy Tan

1952-, American novelist

The Joy Luck Club

(novel, 1989)

PLOT: This story concerns four women who are Chinese immigrants and their four American-born daughters. The action takes place in modern San Francisco and in pre-World War II China. Each of the book's eight characters narrates a portion of the novel. The Joy Luck Club has been meeting since 1949. It was started by Suyuan Woo and has three other members: An-mei Hsu, Lindo Jong, and Ying-Ying St. Clair. They meet to play mah-jong, share stories, and eat good food. As the story opens, Suyuan Woo has died of a cerebral aneurysm, and her daughter, Jing-mei "June" Woo, has been asked by her father to take her mother's place at the next Joy Luck Club meeting. When she does, June is told by her three "aunts" that they have collected enough money to send her to China where she will meet her two half-sisters. June's mother had to abandon them in China when the Japanese invaded, and she died not knowing that the twin girls had survived. June agrees to the trip.

The cast of the film version of* The Joy Luck Club*, a sensitive multigenerational story about Chinese immigrants and their daughters.

The story shifts to various parts of China to relate the stories of the other mothers. One chapter tells of An-Mei Hsu, who grew up with her aunt and uncle because her mother was in disgrace after becoming a rich man's concubine. Her mother commits suicide. In another, Lindo Jong, who was betrothed at the age of two and married at sixteen, convinces her husband's family that he should divorce her. Eventually, Lindo Jong is able to come to the United States, where she works in a cookie factory until she marries a Chinese boy. Ying-Ying St. Clair's story involves her wealthy family and her trips on a luxurious barge to see the performance of the mysterious Moon Lady. She also tells of her marriage to a brutal man and, finally, a second marriage to an American.

Again the story shifts to focus on the lives of the daughters, who are now grown. Waverly Jong was a child chess prodigy and is now an attorney and in love with a caucasian, whom she is afraid her mother will not accept. Lena St. Clair is married to a man who takes advantage of her passiveness. Rose Hsu Jordan is getting a divorce from her husband. In the last chapter, Jing-Mei Woo travels to China to meet her half-sisters.

CHARACTERS: The main focus of the book is on the ties between mothers and daughters, blending the lives of China-born women and their customs and traditions with those of their American-born daughters. With all their differences, both generations must struggle to overcome their inborn passivity. The four mothers of *The Joy Luck Club* feel that they can enrich the lives of their daughters by sharing the secrets of their past.

An-Mei Hsu remembers a life of shame in which she was forced to live with an aunt and uncle because her own mother was the third concubine, and eventually fourth wife, of a rich man. When An-Mei's grandmother was dying, her mother returned briefly and added a small piece of her own flesh to the soup in an effort to save her. This action forever dramatized to An-Mei the strong bond between mother and daughter, and she wishes to translate this bond into a way to help her own daughter's life. The passivity of An-Mei's daughter, **Rose Hsu Jordan**, who is now in the midst of a divorce from her husband, Ted, worries her mother. An-Mei tells

Rose that she too easily bends to the will of others. Rose herself realizes the truth in this and admits that she was attracted to Ted at first because her parents disapproved of her relationship with him. However, Rose finds the courage in the end to stand up for herself. Ted demands that she sign the divorce papers, leaving the house to him. She tells her husband that he will get his divorce, but she will under no circumstances give him the house.

As for **Ying-Ying St. Clair**, she too worries about her troubled daughter. Ying-Ying's own sense of low self-esteem is the result of her being abandoned in China by her first husband. After her abortion, she lived with poor relatives for a number of years. Finally, she met Clifford St. Clair and moved to the United States. Although she loved her husband, Ying-Ying never felt secure or happy. Her emotional instability draws her into a depression that troubles her daughter, **Lena St. Clair**. Lena seems to have inherited her mother's deep fears and emotional instability. She endures an unhappy marriage with Harold, who constantly takes advantage of her passive nature. Her mother sees that Lena and Harold are only going through the motions of their marriage, but Lena seems unable to leave him. Although she can live without Harold's love, she apparently can't live without his attention.

Lindo Jong lived for many years in the home of her betrothed before the marriage. She was treated like a servant and eventually was married to an immature boy. The marriage was never consummated. Desperately unhappy, Lindo cleverly convinces the family that she has had a dream foretelling that her husband is destined to marry someone else. She is granted a divorce and through her own devices eventually makes her way to America, where she marries a Chinese boy. Despite the accomplishment, Lindo's adult life is spent in trying to balance obedience to her husband with a sense of self-worth.

A chess prodigy as a child, **Waverly Jong**, who is named after the San Francisco street where her parents lived, also has problems trying to balance her own sense of independence with her need to have her mother's approval. Waverly has always had trouble in her relationship with her mother. She quit playing chess, even though she had gained national recognition, just to spite her. Now Waverly is an attorney with a young daughter of her own from a failed marriage. She is worried because she feels that Lindo will not approve of her fiance, Rich Shields, because he is caucasian. In the end, Lindo surprises her daughter by not objecting. Waverly has been imagining problems where none existed.

The knowledge that would make **Suyuan Woo**'s life happy comes too late. After her death, the existence of her twin daughters, whom she was forced to leave in China many years ago, is confirmed. Knowing the Japanese would soon capture her, Suyuan had left the infants by the side of a road with a note asking someone to take care of them. She never saw them again. After the death of her first husband, she remarried and moved to the United States, where she founded the Joy Luck Club in San Francisco. Her daughter, **Jing-Mei (June) Woo**, is often considered the voice of the author in this novel. June is unlike her mother in that she has never believed in herself or felt she could become anything she wanted. As a result, she is bored with her life and indifferent about its outcome. She recalls her childhood and the attempts of her mother to make her into a child prodigy in the wake of Waverly Jong. The result was a piano recital that turned into a profound embarrassment. Before her mother died, however, she gave Jing-Mei a jade pendant, which seems to convey Suyuan's steadfast belief in the worth of her child. June's journey to China for a touching reunion with her half-sisters marks the beginning of a profound change in her life. It provides a bridge not only with her deceased mother but also with her Chinese heritage.

Further Reading

Authors and Artists for Young Adults. Vol. 9. Detroit: Gale Research, 1992.

Berger, Laura Standley, ed. *Twentieth-Century Young Adult Writers.* 1st ed. Detroit: St. James, 1994.

Brown, Anne E. *International Women's Writing: New Landscapes of Identity.* Westport, CT: Greenwood, 1995.

Contemporary Literature Criticism. Vol. 59. Detroit: Gale Research, 1990.

Something about the Author. Vol. 75. Detroit: Gale Research, 1994.

Mildred D. Taylor

1943-, American novelist

Roll of Thunder, Hear My Cry

(historical novel, 1976)

PLOT: This story, set in Mississippi from the fall of 1933 through the summer of 1934, centers on the Logan family. Poor land-owning blacks who suffer incredible discrimination and poverty, the Logans nevertheless retain their dignity and strength. The family consists of Grandmother (called Big Ma), Mary and David Logan, and their four children, Stacey, who is almost thirteen, Cassie, the nine-year-old narrator, seven-year-old Christopher-John, and the baby, six-year-old Little Man. One day, Mr. Logan, who is often absent while working on the railroad, brings home a giant of a man, Mr. Morrison. Mr. Morrison's job is to work for them and protect them when the father is away. The family is also occasionally visited by Uncle Hammer, who works in Chicago and often helps them financially.

The children must walk to their run-down segregated school where their mother teaches, while the white children ride in buses. Most of the share-croppers in the area live on land owned by Harlan Granger, who would also like to own the Logan land, part of which is still mortgaged. With the help of a liberal white lawyer named Mr. Jamison, the Logans organize the poor blacks so they can buy their food and supplies in Vicksburg rather than pay the high interest rates at the local store run by the Wallace family, who are toadies of Harlan Granger.

T. J. Avery, one of Mrs. Logan's seventh-grade pupils, is caught cheating and, for revenge, badmouths her to the whites at Wallace's store. Granger uses her "bad teaching methods" as an excuse to have her fired and to intimidate the Logans into ending their boycott of the store. When this doesn't work, night riders attack the Logan's wagon bringing supplies from Vicksburg and Mr. Logan's leg is broken, preventing him from working on the railroad.

In the meantime, Cassie fights her own battle and forces an apology from a snooty white girl, Lillian Jean Simms, who has humiliated her with racial slurs. Lillian has a gentle, younger brother, Jeremy, and two older ones, ruffians R. W. and Melvin. T. J. begins associating with the trashy older brothers, and the three stage a robbery in which the store owner is killed. The Simms brothers frame T. J., and soon after a lynch mob arrives at the Averys' home. To save T. J. and divert the angry crowd, Mr. Logan sets fire to his own cotton fields. As the fire spreads, the men rush off to fight it, and T. J. is whisked off to jail. With a quarter of their cotton crop destroyed, the Logans face even tougher financial times.

See below for character descriptions.

Let the Circle Be Unbroken

(historical novel, 1981)

PLOT: Four months have elapsed since events in *Roll of Thunder, Hear My Cry,* and news arrives that T. J.'s trial date is scheduled with Mr. Jamison as his lawyer. In spite of parental opposition, on the day of the trial the Logan children and other youngsters skip school, borrow a horse and wagon, and head for town. The trial is a mockery, with an all-white jury and a red-neck judge finding T. J. guilty of murder in spite of evidence to the contrary. The teenager is sentenced to death. When union leaders come to the district to organize both the white and the black sharecroppers, trouble begins as crooked landlords like Harlan Granger use any methods necessary to thwart the workers from organizing. Uncle Hammer pays one of his visits, and soon the Logans have another guest. It is Mama's cousin, Bud Rankin, who has married a white woman in New York and has a fifteen-year-old daughter, Suzella. He is having marriage problems and asks the Logans to take in Suzella until things are straightened out between him and his wife. Suzella arrives and captures everyone's hearts and attention. Cassie, however, is jealous of having her place in the household taken over by this attractive girl who could pass as white.

One day, some white boys try to date Suzella. Mama, in a rare show of anger, tells Suzella that, like it or not, she is colored. While Mr. Logan is at work on the railroad, Stacey, who has grown to young manhood, runs away with his friend Moe Turner to seek work. The family is devastated. Papa is sent for and a search for Stacey begins. Bud returns to say his marriage has ended, and he takes Suzella back to New York. When the time to go comes, even Cassie admits she will miss Suzella.

Mrs. Lee Annie Lees, the grandmother of Wordell Lees, Cassie's friend, decides at age sixty-five that she wants to vote. No other blacks in the district have registered because they fear the consequences from their landlords. Under Cassie's tutelage, Lee Annie studies American government. On registration day, however, she is made to fail the test and ordered off her land by an angry Granger. A union rally is dispersed and its leaders arrested for disturbing the peace. But encouraging news arrives that two black boys, who have escaped from a sugar plantation, are in a nearby town. In Uncle Hammer's car, the family drives through the night and is reunited with Stacey and Moe. The Logans are together again.

CHARACTERS: Taylor's inspiration to write about Cassie Logan came from her father, who often told her about the hardships blacks faced in trying to establish themselves as landowners after the Civil War. The young heroine and narrator of both books is **Cassie Logan**, a courageous, spunky fourth-grader. She resents being treated like an inferior by whites and being discriminated against solely because of her skin color. As a result, she often finds herself in scrapes impossible to resolve satisfactorily because of existing social conditions. Cassie is an inventive and resourceful young girl, able to find solutions that will not endanger her family. For example, when she is publicly humiliated by being unjustly forced to apologize for an imagined slight to Mr. Simms's spiteful daughter, Lillian Jean, Cassie craftily gains the girl's confidence. Learning Lillian Jean's secrets, Cassie gains an apology by threatening to reveal the secrets to everyone. Cassie finds that revenge is sweet when it is deserved. She fights racism and injustice, whether it comes from her mealy-mouthed, Uncle Tom black teacher or such avowed white bigots as the Simms family.

Cassie is an obedient, dutiful daughter who loves and respects her parents and elders. She is an astute, bright girl who is able to judge people accurately (for example, she distrusts T. J. and warns others to avoid him) and assess situations and reach mature conclusions easily. However, when T. J. is sentenced her heart is filled with sorrow and pity and she has recurring nightmares about this sad youngster. Cassie is outspoken, candid, and truthful no matter what the consequences might be. When Suzella arrives and gets all the attention and notice that Cassie once received, she resents her presence and continually finds fault with her. Big Ma tells her she has "a bad case of the jealous." Gradually, Cassie realizes her grandmother is right. In a display of growing maturity, she accepts and eventually becomes fond of her cousin.

Cassie's elder brother is **Stacey Logan**, a thoughtful, sincere young teenager who, like Cassie, resents and fights discrimination. For example, Stacey gets revenge on the white kids' school bus driver, who likes to splash the black children with mud. Stacey digs a huge trench in the road and covers it with water so that the bus sinks into it and is disabled with a broken axle. Stacey is an honorable, sensitive boy who is susceptible to being manipulated. In one instance, T. J. tricks him out of his new wool coat by maintaining he looks funny wearing it. Stacey is rapidly reaching manhood and anxious to assume the duties of being the head of the household when his father is away. He therefore at first resents the presence of Mr. Morrison, until he realizes that he is an honorable man who does not interfere in family matters. With each added responsibility, Stacey gains maturity and knowledge. He is a trustworthy, obedient son and fiercely protective and supportive of his younger siblings. He is a loyal friend who stands by T. J. and disobeys his father to attend the trial. During the throes of adolescence, Stacey grows both in stature and character. He becomes more of a loner and feels the need to contribute to the family's finances. Stacey runs away to find work, but instead he finds hardship and cruelty. When the family arrives to take him home, he sobs with gratitude.

Cassie's two younger brothers are Christopher-John and Little Man. **Christopher-John Logan**, age seven, is short and pudgy. Always agreeable and cheerful, he avoids trouble at all costs. He is quiet, tactful, unadventurous, and timid. Basically a docile, compliant child, Christopher-John becomes fearful and apprehensive when crises occur. The opposite is true of **Little Man** (whose real name is Clayton Chester). Though only six and usually a perfect little gentleman, he already bristles at his first encounters with prejudice and actively opposes them. Forthright and direct, he refuses to use a tattered, filthy textbook rejected by white students and is whipped for his disobedience. Each encounter with discrimination brings the response "It ain't fair" and tears of frustration. Little Man is meticulously neat and tidy. He is a loving, caring son who complies with his parents' wishes and showers them with affection.

Their father, **David Logan**, is a hard-working, responsible, loving family man. Tall, powerfully built, and with square, high cheekbones, he presents a figure of dignity and might. Proud of his racial heritage and that he owns his own land, he fights courageously but cautiously for justice and equity for his family and friends. For example, he has instilled in his family a sense of morality and truth. Though strict and not above using a switch as a punishment, he is adored by his children. David Logan bravely takes the initiative to organize the sharecroppers into a cooperative buying venture, and, when things look impossibly bleak, he never loses hope or faith in his ideals. He encourages his children to fulfil their potential and develop their aptitudes. Even though he is bowed by work, sacrifice, and obligations, Papa is always a tower of strength and inspiration. Slow to anger, he is a thoughtful, dutiful father. Through bitter experience, he has grown to distrust whites and avoids them whenever possible.

His wife, **Mary Logan**, called **Mama** by her family, shares her husband's admirable characteristics. Born in the Delta, she is a sharecropper's daughter. Hard-working and proud of herself and her family, she, too, tries to fight the prejudice she sees around her. She resents the Uncle Tom-ism of her fellow teachers and tries to instill in her pupils some pride in their heritage. A strong, thin, sinewy woman, she is a wonderful housekeeper and mother. She is also a strict teacher with high standards who never shows favoritism, even if the pupil is her own child. A caring, devoted mother, she tries to protect her family from many of life's harsh realities and instills in them a proper sense of values and morals. Mama teaches them to accept things they can't change while fighting for those they can. Though discretion is sometimes the better part of valor, she maintains that one must still fight for what is right and just. As she says to Cassie, "We have no choice of what color we're born or who our parents are or whether we're rich or poor. What we do have is some choice over what we make of our lives once we're here." Frugal, sacrificing, and strict, she is a wonderful role model for her children.

Cassie's **Uncle Hammer** has left Mississippi to seek his fortune in the more liberal Chicago. Unselfish and outgoing, he has learned to fight openly for his rights and privileges. He is remarkably generous in helping the Logans with mortgage money, though they are often too embarrassed to ask for help. An impulsive, unpredictable man with a fiery temper, Uncle Hammer is often kept in the dark about local inequities because the Logans fear that his revenge will cause reprisals. Uncle Hammer, a bachelor who is two years older than his brother David, is a tall, handsome man who dresses with style and prides himself on his elegance and polish. Like his brother, he is a disciplined man of high moral principles who expects the same from the Logan children, whom he adores. A fierce separatist, he distrusts whites. Contemptuous of Bud and his mixed marriage, he warns Cassie never to mix with whites. He is touchy and sometimes difficult, but his instincts are honorable and altruistic.

The mother of Papa and Uncle Hammer is **Big Ma (Caroline Logan)** who is now in her mid-sixties, yet she still works in the fields like a young woman of twenty. Tall and strong, she has learned resiliency and fortitude from the hard life she has led. Though proud and tenacious, she has been taught to bow to the white man's wishes rather than cause trouble. This annoys Cassie, who is a born fighter. Big Ma is the matriarch of the family and receives the respect and deference her position deserves. Her knowledge of folk medicine using herbs and home remedies is still called upon by members of the community.

Mr. L. T. Morrison is Mr. Logan's co-worker and friend who is brought to the Logan home to work after Morrison loses his job. Cassie describes him as "the most formidable-looking man we had ever encountered.... The long trunk of his massive body bulged with muscles, and his skin, of the deepest ebony, was partially scarred upon his face and neck." The family later learns that he was scarred as a child by a fire started during a raid by white night riders, which also caused the death of his parents and sisters. With his deep quiet voice, gentlemanly manners, and imposing figure, Mr. Morrison commands respect. In time, this gentle, solitary man also gains the family's love and devotion.

Stacey's sometime friend is the unfortunate **T. J. Avery**. A tall, emaciated-looking fourteen-year-old, T. J. tries to hide his lack of brains and character by indulging in underhanded, devious schemes to enhance his sagging ego. Basically harmless and pathetic, T. J. talks too much and works too little. He cheats on tests rather than studying and ends up repeating the seventh grade. T. J. blames others, like Mrs. Logan, for his lack of success. A liar and double-dealer, he dupes Stacey into giving him his coat, and is also responsible for Mrs. Logan being fired. When ostracized by his black buddies for his actions, T. J. is exploited by two cynical boys who use him and flatter him into thinking they are his friends. T. J. is framed for the murder of a storekeeper, and this pitiable, forlorn youngster is sentenced to death in another case of miscarriage of justice. Cassie will never forget his wan smile and tears as he sees the Logans while being led from the courtroom.

T. J.'s two manipulators belong to the white Simms family, which also includes Lillian Jean and her younger brother, Jeremy Simms. **Lillian Jean Simms** is a pesky, spoiled youngster who has learned to behave in a condescending, superior way toward blacks. She publicly humiliates Cassie and in her spiteful, vindictive way continues to torment the powerless Cassie until the tables are turned. **Jeremy Simms** is a sensitive, pale, towheaded boy who longs to make friends with the Logan children. A lonely, withdrawn boy who tends to daydream, he has no friends. In spite of whippings from his unfeeling father who forbids such visits, Jeremy continues to reach out to the Logans. Although they would like to make friends with Jeremy, they are forced to rebuff his gifts and attention because of existing racial barriers.

The district's greedy landlord is **Harlan Granger**, who arrogantly drives around his domain in a sleek, silver Packard. Although he feigns gentlemanly manners, he is a rapacious, unprincipled, heartless man who will stop at nothing to protect his empire. In his smug, superior way, he resents the fact that the Logans own land that was once in his family and is determined to acquire it regardless of what it takes. When he learns of Lee Annie's attempt to register to vote, he callously throws the aged woman off his property.

The white liberal lawyer **Wade W. Jamison** realizes that the treatment of blacks in the south is monstrous and cruel. He becomes dedicated, regardless of the consequences, to fighting these injustices. A tall, thin man in his mid-fifties, he warns the Logans about challenging the power of Harlan Granger but generously offers to underwrite a credit note so that they will not lose their property. Though his home is burned and his dog poisoned, he continues to defend T. J. at his trial. A noble, gallant man, Jamison is accused by his enemies of being "a nigger with a white skin."

Mrs. Logan's cousin, **Bud Rankin**, is an outgoing, cheerful, handsome man with a winsome smile and a sweet, gentle disposition. Though his mixed marriage with the white woman he adores is unable to withstand social pressure, he continues to be a loving father and tries to provide the right environment for his daughter, Suzella. The Logans like this lighthearted, lively man who entertains them with his beautiful voice, but they can't accept his violation of the rules of segregation.

His daughter, fifteen-year-old **Suzella Rankin**, is a charming, beautiful girl who has long, wavy, auburn hair and an engaging smile. With her gracious, refined ways and fetching personality, she enchants everyone she meets, except the jealous Cassie. Suzella is modest, eager to fit in, and generous. A talented girl who knows how to design and sew clothes, she unselfishly volunteers her abilities to help the Logans. Able to pass as white, she is confused about her racial identity and hates the stigma of being considered black. When she leaves the Logans to live with her mother in New York, she will presumably adopt a white identity.

Though sixty-five, **Mrs. Lee Annie Lees** says one day, "I thinks I wants to vote." Although she knows that this could bring disaster and perhaps death, she gallantly sticks to her resolve. Heavy-set and with fine bones and skin the color of honey, she is, according to Cassie, "one of the most beautiful women ever seen." Determined and intrepid, her resolve brings terrible consequences. She and the neighbors who have supported her are ordered off their land by Harlan Granger. Lee Annie's grandson is the shy, withdrawn **Wordell Lees**. Always alone and silent, Wordell appears stupid but actually lives in a world all his own where he shares a unique bond with nature and its creatures. Given to unpredictable moods, Wordell can also show unusual sensitivity and gentleness. A shy, pensive boy who plays the harmonica skillfully, he eventually comes out of his shell and responds to Cassie's special kindness.

Stacey's buddy is **Moe Turner**, a sensitive, decent young man whose family is dirt poor. With six siblings and economic disaster upon the family, Moe decides to leave with Stacey and seek work. He is conscientious and eager but unprepared for the terrible working conditions he and Stacey find on the plantations. Like his friend, Moe is indebted to the Logans for rescuing him.

Further Reading

Authors and Artists for Young Adults. Vol. 10. Detroit: Gale Research, 1993.

Berger, Laura Standley, ed. *Twentieth-Century Children's Writers.* 4th ed. Detroit: St. James, 1994.

Contemporary Literary Criticism. Vol. 21. Detroit: Gale Research, 1982.

Estes, Glenn E., ed. *American Writers for Children since 1960: Fiction.* Vol. 52 of *Dictionary of Literary Biography.* Detroit: Gale Research, 1986.

Holtze, Sally Holmes, ed. *Fifth Book of Junior Authors and Illustrators.* New York: H. W. Wilson, 1983.

Kirkpatrick, D. L., ed. *Twentieth-Century Children's Writers.* 2nd ed. New York: St. Martin's, 1983.

Something about the Author. Vols. 15, 70. Detroit: Gale Research, 1979, 1993.

Ward, Martha, ed. *Authors of Books for Young People.* 3rd ed. Metuchen, NJ: Scarecrow, 1990.

Theodore Taylor

1921-, American novelist

The Cay

(young adult adventure novel, 1969)

PLOT: Phillip Enright is an eleven-year-old boy living in the Netherlands Antilles with his father, an American engineer working for the oil refineries, and his homesick mother. The story is set in the year 1942, and Phillip's mother is worried about World War II. She longs to return to the quiet and safety of Virginia, but her husband's job keeps them on the island. Phillip's mother nags him to stop talking to the black men who work down at the docks, where he and his friend Henrik van Boven like to hang out. Her prejudices against blacks unfortunately influence Phillip.

When German U-boats attack tankers and an oil refinery nearby, Phillip's father reluctantly books passage for his wife and son on a Dutch freighter, the *S.S. Hato,* to take them to Miami, Florida. But after a stop in Panama, the old freighter is sunk by a German submarine. Phillip is knocked unconscious and separated from his mother. He awakens to find himself on a raft with a member of the ship's crew named Timothy and the ship cook's cat, Stew. Although Timothy cares for Phillip and reassures him that they will be rescued, Phillip does not trust him because he is black.

After four days, they land on a small cay, where Timothy builds a fire so that they might be spotted by a passing ship. Phillip has become blind from his head injury. Timothy assures him the blindness is probably temporary, but Phillip will not be consoled and refuses to help Timothy in any way. His disdain for Timothy grows when he learns that Timothy can't read or write and needs assistance to spell the word "help" in stones on the sand.

Timothy later comes down with tropical fever and, delirious, rushes into the ocean. Phillip is able to save him, but Timothy remains weak. Realizing he might die, he teaches Phillip all the survival skills he knows. When a hurricane strikes, Phillip loses consciousness and wakens to find Stew gone and Timothy near death after sheltering the boy from the storm with his body. Timothy soon dies, leaving Phillip to fend for himself. Stew returns, and Phillip, who has learned Timothy's lessons well, keeps them both alive.

Many weeks later, Phillip hears the sound of explosions somewhere out at sea. He lights a signal fire and draws the attention of a small boat, which lands on the cay. It contains sailors from an American destroyer. Phillip, along with Stew, returns to his parents and eventually goes to New York City, where an operation restores his sight. When he has recovered, he studies nautical maps and locates the cay—Devil's Mouth—where he and Timothy were shipwrecked. Phillip knows that someday he will return there to visit the gravesite of his protector and friend.

Timothy of the Cay *(1995) is a sequel.*

Phillip is cured of racial prejudice when he finds true friendship with a black man in this survival story.

CHARACTERS: Eleven-year-old **Phillip Enright** has learned from his mother to look down on black people. When he finds himself stranded on the cay with a black man, he resents the fact that his life is in the hands of the uneducated Timothy. Despite their perilous circumstances, Phillip refuses to cooperate with Timothy in his efforts to save them both. However, little by little, and despite himself, Phillip begins to learn the survival lessons that Timothy so patiently teaches, and he even begins to appreciate and like Timothy. One day he quietly tells Timothy that he wants to be his friend, and the black man replies that he was always Phillip's friend.

When the ordeal has ended and Phillip is rescued, leaving Timothy behind forever in a grave on Devil's Mouth, he is a changed boy. He has learned the invaluable lesson of friendship and love. Phillip knows that one day he will charter a schooner out of Panama and set sail for Devil's Mouth. He will find the little island and stand before the grave of his dear friend.

Timothy, an experienced black sailor, is described by Phillip as extremely old yet powerful. He speaks in the singsong lilt of the West Indies. Even in the face of Phillip's obvious resentment and uncooperative demeanor, Timothy remains patient, friendly, and, above all, reassuring. He slowly teaches Phillip the things he must know to survive, even blind and alone. When the hurricane comes and Phillip survives, he realizes that Timothy has given him the greatest gift he had to give: his own life. He so protected the boy during the terrible storm that Timothy's back is cut to ribbons and there is little the boy can do to stop the bleeding. Timothy dies, leaving Phillip alone, but not unprotected. Indeed, Timothy's lessons enable to the boy to endure and stay alive until he and Stew cat are rescued.

Mrs. Enright has planted the seeds of prejudice in her young son Phillip so that he resents Timothy from the start. The author makes it clear that it is Phillip's mother who instills this attitude in Phillip at first, because when Phillip and his friend Henrik play near the schooners down at the bay, they are friendly with the black people who work there. But Phillip's mother teaches him that these people are different, inferior, and not to be trusted.

All during the war, she has longed to leave the islands and return to Virginia "where it is safe." That meant, in essence, where there was no smell of gas or oil, where no one spoke Dutch, and where there weren't so many black people. However, her ordeal at sea and the presumed loss of her son for so many months have a profound effect on Mrs. Enright. After Phillip is reported missing, she returns to be with her husband, and when Phillip is rescued, she no longer feels the need to leave the islands.

Phillip's father, **Mr. Enright**, is a busy man with little time to spend with his family. Even when nearby refineries are bombed, he is reluctant to have his wife and son leave, but Mrs. Enright is insistent. He therefore gives in and secures passage on the *S.S. Hato*, a small Dutch freighter, which he wrongly believes will be safe from German attack.

Phillip's friend, **Henrik van Boven**, is a chubby lad with red cheeks and straw-colored hair. He is very serious about everything, especially about the fact that the Germans have conquered his native Netherlands. When Phillip says goodbye to him as he gets ready to sail with his mother to the safety of America, Phillip has a premonition that it will be a long time before he will see Henrik again.

Further Reading

Authors and Artists for Young Adults. Vol. 2. Detroit: Gale Research, 1989.

Berger, Laura Standley, ed. *Twentieth-Century Children's Writers.* 4th ed. Detroit: St. James, 1995.

De Montreville, Doris, and Elizabeth D. Crawford, eds. *Fourth Book of Junior Authors and Illustrators.* New York: H. W. Wilson, 1978.

Kirkpatrick, D. L., ed. *Twentieth-Century Children's Writers.* 2nd ed. New York: St. Martin's, 1983.

Something about the Author Autobiography Series. Vol. 4. Detroit: Gale Research, 1987.

Ward, Martha, ed. *Authors of Books for Young People.* 3rd ed. Metuchen, NJ: Scarecrow, 1990.

J. R. R. Tolkien

1892-1973, English academic and author

The Hobbit; or, There and Back Again

(fantasy, 1937)

PLOT: This prelude to *The Lord of the Rings* introduces the reader to the fantasy land of Middle Earth and the hobbit Bilbo Baggins. Hobbits are smaller than dwarves and have large, furry feet. One fateful day, Bilbo is persuaded by the wizard Gandalf to join thirteen dwarves on a dangerous mission to Lonely Mountain to retrieve the lost treasure of the dwarves now guarded by the wicked dragon Smaug. The dwarves are led by Thorin and include fat Bombur, the ancient Balin, Dori, the youngest members, Kili and Fili, and Bifur, Bofur, Dwalin, Nori, Ori, Oin, and Gloin. Their journey is filled with adventure and narrow escapes, including being captured by giant goblins called orcs, whom they manage to escape through Gandalf's intervention and the killing of the Great Goblin. At one point, Bilbo becomes lost in a cave and finds a magic ring that will turn its wearer invisible. But Gollum, a slimy pathetic creature who lives in the cave where he survives on raw fish, claims the ring is his and challenges Bilbo to a battle of wits, the winner of which will keep the ring. Bilbo wins the game, but has to escape the enraged Gollum by using the ring.

After Bilbo rejoins the group, they are attacked by a pack of evil wolves called Wargs but are rescued by a band of eagles led by the Lord of the Eagles. After Bilbo saves the dwarves from being eaten by giant spiders, they are taken prisoner by the Elfenking and his throng of wood elves. Again through Bilbo's ingenuity, a daring escape is effected and the group floats downriver to freedom by hiding in empty wine barrels.

Two pleasant respites occur when they visit the hospitable Elrond and, later, Beorn, a gruff woodsman who has the power to change himself into a bear. Their last stop before Lonely Mountain is Esgaroth, a lake town inhabited by men who offer them shelter and supplies. Now within the territory of Smaug, the travelers find a secret entrance into the mountain but can't recapture the treasure because the fire-breathing dragon keeps a constant vigil over it. When the dragon learns that the people of Esgaroth have helped the intruders, he destroys the town but is killed by an enchanted arrow shot from the bow of Bard, a gallant warrior.

With the liberation of the treasure, greed and avarice take over and a great battle takes places in which the armies of the Lake People, the Wood Elves, an army of eagles, a neighboring colony of dwarves, and Thorin's group join forces to repel an attack by the goblins and Wargs. Thorin is killed in the battle and a truce is arranged among the other parties. Bilbo Baggins returns to his quiet hobbit hole in Hobbiton to live in peace and quiet.

CHARACTERS: The hero of this adventure fantasy is the unassuming, modest hobbit **Bilbo Baggins** (see also *The Lord of the Rings* below). Though initially reluctant to participate in the dwarves' expedition, he wishes to help the others and therefore feels obliged to accept the wizard Gandalf's invitation to join the quest. Bilbo is basically a homebody, proud of his tidy, comfortable home and, like other hobbits, gentle and peace loving. He is fond of both good food and the pleasure that giving and receiving presents brings. His adventures with the dwarves create a transformation in Bilbo, however, causing him to become more courageous. Through adversity he learns to be resourceful and brave while still remaining good natured and humble. Bilbo is always loyal and devoted to the dwarves in spite of their frequent derision and lack of gratitude. Through his boldness and heroism, he saves his comrades from death or imprisonment on several occasions and gradually learns how to be a leader and devise his own plans and ideas. Bilbo possesses a keen intelligence and cleverness that are shown, for example, when he matches Gollum riddle for riddle in an amazing battle of wits. His sincere belief in justice and fair play leads him to act as a mediator between the rival factions who each want part of the dwarves' treasure. When his efforts fail, he is unable to understand how people can be so motivated by greed and selfishness. Bilbo hates war and violence and watches the climactic battle with horror and incredulity. When he weeps over the death of Thorin, he reveals his sensitive, compassionate nature. Bilbo is a generous and unselfish person who willingly gives away his share of the treasure to help others. Even Thorin, who only grudgingly gives compliments, says Mr. Baggins "has proved himself a good companion and a hobbit full of courage and resource far exceeding his size."

Gandalf (see also *The Lord of the Rings* below) is a wandering wizard noted among the hobbits for his wisdom, kindness, and the wonderful stories he tells. The possessor of magical powers, he uses them only to help correct injustices and fight evil, which is one of the reasons why he has thrown his weight into the struggle to return the dwarves' treasure. A fighter for all that is good and true, he tries to inspire independence in those he helps but, when situations become dire, he will intervene, as when he saves the dwarves from the goblins by killing their king. Gandalf is a fine judge of character, and he realizes Bilbo's potential, knowing that the hobbit has the inner strength to meet the challenges of the quest.

The dwarves' leader is **Thorin Oakenshield**, grandson of Thror who, with his people, was driven out of Lonely Mountain by Smaug. Thorin is filled with his own importance and is inclined to be pompous and overbearing. Stubborn and jealous of his position, he also tends to be domineering and dictatorial. At first he is suspicious and condescending toward Bilbo, but he later grows to respect the hobbit's bravery and ingenuity. Although Thorin is generally a good and wise leader capable of bravery and making wise decisions, his obsession with regaining and keeping the treasure later affects his judgement and sense of justice. This greed and selfishness are flaws that result in his death and are almost fatal to his comrades, who begin to feel some shame over their leader's actions. Though stubborn and misguided, Thorin evokes a devotion and respect in others and his death is cause for genuine grief.

Others of the twelve dwarves on the expedition include **Bombur**, a lazy, fat complainer who loves both food and sleep and objects to being considered different because he is so heavy and clumsy, and **Balin**, an ancient elder who often acts as their lookout. Balin is one of the first to accept Bilbo into the group. **Dori** is the strongest dwarf and is described as "a decent fellow." He frequently helps Bilbo by carrying him to safety. **Kili** and **Fili** are the youngest members of the band, each sporting yellow—instead of the usual white—beards. Because of their fine eyesight, they are used as scouts. Brave and courageous fighters, they are both killed in the final battle.

Elrond (also see *The Lord of the Rings* below) is a half-elf human who lives in the Last Homely House in Rivendell. He is described as wise, strong, noble, venerable, and kind. This gracious man cordially welcomes the travelers into his house and gives them help, including deciphering an ancient map to guide them on their journey. Although gruff and impolite, **Beorn** also shows the travelers hospitality. He is a "skin-changer," that is, he appears as either the strong man with huge arms and a great beard that greets the wayfarers, or as a huge black bear that roams the wilds. A vegetarian, he talks to animals and keeps hives to provide him with honey. Not used to visitors, Beorn displays a rough, fierce exterior, but inwardly he is a lover of justice who is interested not in material goods but only in living in harmony with nature. He, too, gives the dwarves excellent advice.

Gollum (also see *The Lord of the Rings* below) is a miserable, wicked creature who lives on a slimy rock island in the middle of an underground lake. Living in isolation, he talks to himself in the third person and refers to the ring he once owned as "my precious." A clever riddler, he attempts to outwit poor Bilbo, who is almost eaten by this malevolent, odious creature. Gollum weeps uncontrollably at the loss of his magic ring which can make a person invisible.

Another evil being is the huge, greedy dragon **Smaug**, who looks like an "immeasurable bat" with a "long, pale belly crusted with gems and fragments of gold" from lying on his treasure. Clever, vindictive, and vengeful, his overriding conceit and vanity accidentally make him reveal the small vulnerable patch of skin on his underside, and this leads to his destruction at the hands of the master archer, **Bard** of Esgaroth. Bard is an honorable, honest man who believes in fairness and integrity. When Bard, a gallant fighter, is offered a crown by his people, this modest, unassuming man refuses the honor, fearful that being king will upset the democratic traditions of his city. Because the dragon's attack has left many of his people homeless and in misery, he petitions Thorin for a small part of the treasure to rebuild his ruined city. When he is refused, Bard's sense of justice and fairness are aroused to the point where he threatens war against the dwarves. Fortunately, with Thorin's death, his wishes are granted and this noble man now has the resources to rebuild Esgaroth.

Two other important characters in this fantasy are the Elfenking and the Great Goblin. The **Elfenking** is an ethical monarch who rules his subjects wisely. However, when the dwarves are found wandering in his realm without permission and refuse to give any information about their mission, he imprisons them, although they later escape in empty wine barrels. When the town of Esgaroth is destroyed by Smaug, the Elfenking brings his army at Bard's request to help the beleaguered city. Like all the goblins, the **Great Goblin** is cruel and wicked and has dirty, disorderly habits. His subjects never make anything useful, spending their time producing weapons of destruction. Intent on devouring the dwarves, the Great Goblin is killed by Gandalf's magic sword.

The Lord of the Rings

(fantasy trilogy, 1954-1956)

PLOT: The trilogy opens with ***The Fellowship of the Ring*** (1954). Sixty years have passed since Bilbo Baggins returned triumphantly to Hobbiton with the treasure that he acquired after defeating the evil dragon, Smaug, as well as the enchanted ring, which can make its wearer invisible. On his 111th birthday, which coincides with the thirty-third birthday of his beloved adopted son, the orphaned Frodo Baggins (who is also Bilbo's cousin), Bilbo decides he will again journey into Middle Earth alone. But before leaving, he bequeaths his fortune and the ring to Frodo. The wizard Gandalf tells Frodo that the ring contains a wicked enchantment and is sought by Sauron, the Dark Lord of Mordor, who will stop at nothing to possess its evil power. Sauron has a powerful ally in the defrocked wizard Saruman, who also has an insatiable desire for power.

Aware of the danger that now surrounds him, Frodo flees his home in the company of three other hobbits: his faithful servant Sam (Samwise Gamgee) and his second cousins, Pippin (Peregrine Took) and Merry (Meriodac Brandybuck). Pursued by Sauron's agents, the Black Riders, Frodo and company find shelter, first at the home of Farmer Maggot, then with Tom Bombadil and his wife Goldberry, and later at Barliman Butterbur's inn, The Prancing Pony, where they are joined by another fighter against evil, a human named Aragorn, who is also known as Strider. With the additional help of the elf Glorfindel, the band reaches safety at the home of Elrond, the lord of the elves at Rivendell. There, a great Council is convened and it is decided that the ring must be destroyed in the fires of Mount Doom (Orodruin) in Mordor, where it was forged ages ago, along with the lesser magical rings it dominates: three elfin rings, seven rings for the dwarf race, and nine rings for mankind. To accomplish this mission, a fellowship of the ring is established consisting of nine people: Frodo, who will be the Ring-bearer, his fellow hobbits Sam, Pippin, and Merry, Gandalf, Aragorn, the elf Legolas, a dwarf named Gimli, and another human, the nobleman Boromir. During their journey through the vast underground mines of Moria, the companions repulse an attack of orcs. Gandalf loses his footing after fighting the monstrous Balrog and falls into an abyss. Later, the band receives shelter and help at another elfin colony, Lorien, ruled by Celeborn and his wife Galadriel. Again on the road and still harassed by attacking orcs, the fellowship must decide whether to seek aid at the town of Minas Tirith or press on to Mordor. Overcome by the evil power of the ring, Boromir tries unsuccessfully to seize it from Frodo. Beset by a massive orc attack, Boromir is killed and Frodo, shaken by Boromir's betrayal and not wishing to inflict more danger on the now disintegrating group, steals off with Sam and the ring to begin a solitary journey to Mordor.

In ***The Two Towers*** (1955), a repentant Boromir is killed during the attack of the orcs who take Merry and Pippin prisoner and set off for their headquarters in Isengard, where their leader, the evil wizard Saruman, rules. On their way, the orcs are surrounded and destroyed by the valiant Riders of Rohan led by Eomer the Marshall. Eomer and his sister Eowyn are the nephew and niece of the childless King Theoden of Rohan. In the confusion of the battle, the two hobbits escape and wander into the forest of Fangorn where they encounter Treebeard, the kindly chief of the Ents, a tree-like people that live in the forest. Aroused to action by the destruction of forests by the orcs, the Ents, along with Merry and Pippin, march to Isengard to wage war against Saruman. In the meantime, Aragorn, Gimli, and Legolas set out to find their hobbit friends. They encounter a mysterious wizard clothed all in white who reveals himself to be their old friend and mentor, Gandalf, who has escaped from the mines of Moria and risen from the rank of grey to white wizard. The three companions seek help from the ancient King Theoden of Rohan, whom Gandalf restores to health and rescues from the domination of his evil councilor, Grima Wormtongue, a secret agent of Saruman. The forces of Rohan, led by Theoden and Eomer, along with Gandalf and company, are victorious in a fierce battle with the orcs at Hormburg, and when they arrive at Isengard they find that the courageous Ents have destroyed the fortress and made prisoners of Saruman and Wormtongue in their black tower. Gandalf's superior power conquers the will of an unrepentant Saruman whose staff, the symbol of his strength, is broken. Gandalf also takes possession of one of the palantiri (magical seeing stones) and gives it to Aragorn. The wizard and Pippin ride off to the friendly city of Minas Tirith to seek further help for the imminent final war with Sauron.

Meanwhile, Frodo and Sam, lost in the approaches to Mordor, capture Gollum, who is intent on reclaiming his ring. Temporarily obedient, Gollum promises to help escort the two travelers into Mordor.

On the way they are helped by a scouting band of the Men of Gondor led by Faramir, but later are betrayed by the treacherous Gollum to the monstrous spider-like creature, Shelob. Frodo, in a coma from the spider's venom, is captured by the orcs, and Sam, now in possession of the ring and invisible, follows as his master is carried by his captors into their tower.

The trilogy concludes with ***The Return of the King*** (1956). At Minas Tirith, Gandalf and Pippin meet the father of Boromir and Faramir, Denethor, the chief Steward of Gondor, a wise but increasingly unstable leader. When the army of orcs besiege his city, Denethor decides it is nobler to die by suicide than in battle and creates a funeral pyre for himself and his surviving son, Faramir. Gandalf is unable to prevent his death but manages to save Faramir. Outside the city walls, the fierce Battle of Pelennor Fields takes place with the assembled forces of King Theoden and Aragorn against the power of Mordor. Eowyn, Eomer's sister, disguised as a man, enters the battle. When she is attacked by the Lord of the Nazguls, Merry stabs the Nazgul from behind and Eowyn finishes him off. Although the forces of good are victorious, it is not without a price. Eowyn and Merry are badly wounded and King Theoden lies dead. Eomer is named Theoden's successor, Aragorn reclaims his family birthright as King of Gondor, and Faramir and Eowyn fall in love and marry. Rested after the terrible battle, Gandalf, Aragorn, and Eomer set out with their forces to the land of Mordor to find the two lost hobbits.

In the meantime, Sam rescues Frodo from the orcs and the two set out once again to reach Mount Doom. At their destination, they are again accosted by Gollum. Gollum grabs the ring from Frodo, who has become overwhelmed by the seductive powers of the ring, and plunges to his death in the flames of the giant volcano. The destruction of the ring means the destruction of Mordor and the power of Lord Sauron. All the allies are reunited, and one by one they return victorious to their respective lands. The hobbits, however, find their land plundered by a band of intruders led by a vengeful Saruman. The ruffians are expelled and Saruman is murdered by his henchman Wormtongue. His mission completed, Frodo, along with Bilbo, Gandalf, and others, sails off, thus opening up Middle Earth to the new Age of Mankind.

CHARACTERS: Like his illustrious adoptive father, Bilbo, **Frodo Baggins** evolves throughout these novels from an average, somewhat naive and carefree hobbit to a creature of wisdom and heroic stature. Although he maintains that he is "not made for perilous quests," Frodo summons previously unrealized inner resources and capabilities to conquer seemingly insurmountable dangers and temptations. Unimpressed with the vast power that the ring offers him, he modestly and unselfishly sacrifices his own well-being in the quest to ensure a better, purer world. He is devoted to his fellow companions to the point of leaving them and embarking on the quest alone with Sam, rather than having them exposed to further dangers. As well as embodying the concepts of brotherly love and service, Frodo is able to instill in his companions a sense of meaning and purpose. He is sensitive to the feelings of others and, unlike Gandalf, rarely critical. Throughout these novels, he demonstrates great courage, resourcefulness, and good judgment. In spite of inner doubts and misgivings, he finds within himself unsuspected fortitude, stamina, and wisdom. Frodo often displays an innocent and unsophisticated sense of wonder and awe at the mysteries and marvels of nature. He also develops a mystical power to experience sweeping visions that foretell future events or clarify struggles and perceptions. With his trusting nature, Frodo sometimes gets taken advantage of, such as when Gollum betrays him to Shelob. Gandalf describes Frodo as "a stout little fellow with red cheeks, taller than some and fairer than most, and he has a cleft in his chin: a perky chap with a bright eye." Although he appears to be an unlikely candidate to save his companions, Frodo is an amazing person who contrasts refreshingly with the traditional epic hero while emerging as equally admirable. When he realizes his mission is over and it is time for the Age of Man, he leaves Middle Earth on his final voyage.

There are eight other members of the Fellowship of the Ring. **Gandalf** (see also *The Hobbit*), also known by his elfin name, **Mithrandir**, is first presented as a stereotypical wizard with a bag of magic tricks who has particular skill with "fire, smokes and lights." "His long white hair, his sweeping silver beard, and his broad shoulders, made him look like some wise king of ancient legend. In his aged face under great snowy brows his dark eyes were set like coals that could leap suddenly into fire." He soon becomes a moving force in directing the plan to destroy the ring, and he initiates the strategy to fight the evil forces of Sauron and Saruman. Gandalf is a vast source of information about ancient lore and a tireless fighter against the forces of evil. Impatient with stupidity and recklessness, he admires the steady, solid virtues that Frodo displays and continually shows him his support. He commands respect from others who admire not only his magical powers but also his wisdom, erudition, and insights. A discerning judge of character who is able to make judicious decisions, Gandalf is courageous and capable of great bravery, sacrificing his own safety to save his companions during the struggle in the mines of Moria. Though originally known as Gandalf the Grey, he becomes Gandalf the White or the **White Rider** after his fight with the Balrog. To make way for the new age after the fall of Sauron, Gandalf, with his friends, leaves Middle Earth.

The character closest to the purity of an Arthuri an knight is **Aragorn**. He is first introduced as **Strider**, a Ranger who is a guest at The Prancing Pony inn. Aragorn is a man of mystery, "a strange-looking, weather-beaten man" who "wore a hood that overshadowed his face." Later "he threw back his hood, showing a shaggy head of dark hair flecked with grey, and in a pale stern face a pair of keen grey eyes." He is actually the son of King Arathorn, a victim of Sauron's evil. Raised in the court of Elrond, Aragorn later went out into the world to join the fight against his family's enemy. For seventy years he has scoured the countryside and has gained great knowledge of the land and its people. According to a prophecy, he will one day be restored to the throne of Gondor. Aragorn has endured many hardships and sacrifices, including escaping from the captivity of Gollum, in fulfilling his sworn duty to reestablish the kingdom. He embodies the virtues of courage, goodness, strength, and wisdom and possesses unusual talents in healing and in conversing with animals and birds. After Gandalf's disappearance in the mines of Moria, Aragorn becomes the group's leader, acting fairly and judiciously towards all. He is both protective and wise and exhibits a purity of mind and spirit that embodies the knightly virtues of chivalry. Aragorn renounces the wooing of Elrond's fair daughter, Arwen, whom he chastely loves, for his commitment to the cause of justice and freedom. Later, after his mission is completed, he marries her. In his many displays of understanding, grace, and compassion, Aragorn emerges as a father figure whose courage and honesty show the mark of sound leadership. After the fall of Sauron, Aragorn fulfills the prophecy and becomes King of Gondor.

Boromir, a human like Aragorn, is described as "a tall man with a fair and noble face, dark-haired and grey-eyed, proud and stern of glance." Unlike Aragorn, he is neither wise nor interested in learning but, instead, is a dedicated warrior who delights in battle and trial by arms. A courageous and fearless warrior, he is honored to become part of the Fellowship, excelling in feats of daring and bravery for the group. However, he tends to be reckless, impulsive and immoderate in his behavior. Unfortunately, Boromir becomes possessed by the evil influence of the ring and, in a bid for power, attempts to gain ownership by physical force. Frodo escapes him, and Boromir later repents and begs for forgiveness. He dies defending himself and his friends during an orc attack.

The dwarves are represented in the Fellowship by **Gimli**, son of Gloin, one of the original dwarves who accompanied Bilbo in *The Hobbit*. Outspoken, courageous, and independent, he is a fierce fighter who can wield an ax with deadly precision. His knowledge of fellow creatures amuses and instructs his traveling companions. Gimli gradually loses his instinctive dislike of elves through his friendship with Legolas. While in Lorien he develops a great and pure love for the Lady Galadriel, and later considers himself her champion.

Elrond's choice to represent the elves in the Fellowship is **Legolas**. Though not known for any unusual power, Legolas is a brave, trustworthy companion who does his duty without complaint. With his keen eyes, he is both an outstanding scout and exceptional archer. Courageous and fearless, he forms a lasting and touching friendship with the dwarf Gimli.

Three hobbits make up the remaining members of the fellowship. The first is **Sam (Samwise) Gamgee**, Frodo's trusting and dedicated servant. He is a gardener who has become attached to the Baggins household. Sam has a touching loyalty and devotion to his master, Frodo, and vows that he will accompany him and protect him wherever his quest should lead. Through the many trials and hardships he endures, he never complains or falters. Sam's sacrifice and loyalty give Frodo the support and strength necessary to complete his mission. His character develops as a result of his experiences: from a fearful, timid young man, he changes into a confident, fearless champion of right who risks his life to save his master and the cause he believes in. The nobility and depth of his attachment to Frodo is moving. Sam weeps when his master is wounded, springs to his defense whenever necessary, saves his life on many occasions, and shares Frodo's feelings and experiences. As a reward, Sam is considered, like his master, to be a Ring-bearer. After his numerous adventures, this modest hero returns to Hobbiton, marries, and raises a family. **Merry**, whose full name is **Meriodac Brandybuck**, is a longtime friend of Frodo. As his name suggests, he is a carefree, lighthearted hobbit who enjoys youthful adventure and good times. Merry is a bright and knowledgeable lad who cheerfully agrees to accompany Frodo without any real idea of the nature or seriousness of the quest. He is not an unusual hobbit in his love of comfort and good times and his fear of the unknown. Merry rises above the hardships he endures and grows into a more responsible, mature young man. At first, he only performs commonplace duties for the Fellowship, including serving meals and tending the ponies, but later he assumes greater responsibilities and proves himself a gallant and noble warrior who risks his own life to save the beautiful Eowyn. Merry was a particular favorite of Theoden. Merry's cousin, **Pippin**, or **Peregrine Took**, is similar to Merry in many ways, although not as mature. He is also naturally exuberant and animated; however, his foolish, childish ways often get him into trouble and initially incur the displeasure of Gandalf, who sometimes becomes impatient with Pippin's constant prattle and foolishness. But Pippin is a good-natured and resilient youngster who later influences many great events beyond his understanding. During the course of events, Pippin also matures until he becomes a favorite of both Gandalf and Denethor, both of whom grow to admire and respect this outspoken, daring young hero.

In *The Fellowship of the Ring,* Frodo meets many minor characters. While fleeing the Black Riders, the hobbits are helped by **Farmer Maggot**, a mushroom grower who years before had caught Frodo stealing his mushrooms. Old grudges are forgotten, however, and the farmer not only gives Frodo and his hobbit friends shelter but also good advice on how to avoid the infamous Black Riders. The encounter with the normal, simple Maggot family is the last touch of ordinary life that the hobbits will experience on the journey.

While traveling through the old forest, the hobbits are saved from being enveloped by a huge willow by the "master of wood, water and hill," **Tom Bombadil**, an unusual creature who dresses in a huge battered hat, giant yellow boots, and a blue coat. He has "a long, brown beard; his eyes were blue and bright, and his face was red as a ripe apple, but creased into a hundred wrinkles of laughter." A jolly, outgoing man, he lives as one with nature and is so unfettered by care or worldly concerns that he is impervious to the ring's strength. Tom possesses unusual, benevolent powers that have made him master and steward of the forest. This ageless, picturesque figure exudes cheer and generosity. His wife, **Goldberry**, is also a child of nature, a water sprite whose serene, tranquil nature contrasts interestingly with that of her ebullient husband.

The innkeeper at the Prancing Pony in Bree is **Barliman Butterbur**, a bald-headed, red-faced man who is often flustered and forgetful. He does, however, supply shelter and sustenance to the traveling hobbits, and helps them escape the Black Riders. At first the travelers are suspicious of him, but he supplies a vital link between the hobbits and Gandalf and proves to be a valuable, albeit inefficient ally.

At Rivendell, Frodo and his companions meet **Elrond**, the Lord of the great Elven kingdom (see also *The Hobbit*). His palace, known as the Last Homely House, lives up to its name by supplying sustenance, safety, and song to the weary hobbits. Elrond's home is not a fortress but a place of learning, jollity, and peace, where, at least temporarily, there is power enough to withstand Sauron. The ambience of Elrond's home reflects the nature of the elf king, a benevolent, wise ruler who is a Solomon-like figure. "The face of Elrond was ageless, neither old nor young, though in it was written the memory of many things both glad and sorrowful. Venerable he seemed as a king crowned with many winters, and yet hale as a tried warrior in the fullness of his strength." Elrond possesses remarkable insights and knowledge and unusual powers of healing. He is the head of the Council, to whom he imparts the ancient lore about the ring. Under his guidance, the Fellowship of the Ring is formed and the nature of their quest determined. Second in command at Rivendell and Elrond's chief counselor is **Glorfindel**, a dauntless warrior who helped save the hobbits from the Black Riders and led them to the safety of Rivendell. Dressed in white and riding a white horse, this blonde, dashing champion at first appears otherworldly.

In the kingdom of Lorien, the members of the Fellowship meet another group of friendly elves ruled by **Celeborn** and his wife, **Galadriel**. Celeborn is a peace-loving, humane king who openly offers his lands and hospitality to the travelers. Galadriel is even more generous. She allows Frodo to look into a magic mirror and lavishes presents on them before their departure, including a life-giving vial to Frodo and ringlets of her hair to the dwarf Gimli. Throughout her encounters with the Fellowship she exudes beauty, gentleness, and love.

Bilbo Baggins (also see *The Hobbit*), the fearless hobbit who gained control of the ring from Gollum, makes several brief appearances in *The Lord of the Rings*. At the beginning, he initiates the action in the trilogy by giving the ring to Frodo before disappearing to relive his journey of sixty years ago. He reappears at Elrond's house, where he nurses Frodo back to health after Frodo is wounded by the orcs. During the Council meetings, Bilbo supplies valuable information to the participants, as well as sound advise to Frodo. A very old hobbit, he joins Frodo and Gandalf on their final journey from the Grey Havens. There are many evil characters in *The Lord of the Rings*. Overriding all is **Sauron**, also known as the **Dark Lord** or the **Lord of Mordor**. In these novels he is also sometimes called the Black Hand, the Eye, the Great Eye, and Red Eye. The self-styled ruler of Middle Earth and declared enemy of the Free Peoples, his one desire is to gain complete dominance over the entire land, which leads to an obsession to steal the One Ring from Frodo. Sauron represents all the evil, greed, and lust in the world, and he uses terror, treachery, and deceit as weapons to maintain his tyrannical grip over others. Though he never appears in the ring cycle, his monstrous presence pervades all of the action. Sauron's main servants of evil are the **Black Riders**, or **Ringwraiths**, the nine horsemen clad in black who ride black horses and roam the countryside as his sinister agents. They exist in an otherworldly dimension and, through the use of the Black Breath, can produce a coma-like state in their victims. Once common men, they were transformed by Sauron, who enslaved them with the nine Rings of Power. Also referred to as the **Nazguls**, their leader is killed by Merry during the Battle of Pelennor Fields.

Like Lucifer who fell from heaven, the white wizard **Saruman** represents goodness turned to evil by the pursuit of power. Saruman was once a great and respected wizard who was head of the White Council of wizards which withstood the power of Sauron. But as his pride and power grew, Saruman became corrupt, jealous of his authority, and, in time, fell under Sauron's control. When Gandalf resisted his corruption and exposed Saruman for what he was, he was dismissed from the order of wizards. In his pursuit of evil, he has changed from Saruman the White to Saruman the Many Colored, having changed his white robe (signifying purity) for one of bright colors (symbolizing corruption.) Still unrepentant, his power is taken from him by Gandalf after his capture at Isengard, but he continues in his spiteful, evil ways until he is murdered by his henchman, Wormtongue. The despicable servants of Sauron and Saruman are the **orcs**, large, evil goblins. Continually stalking and harassing the Fellowship, they are fierce, ugly creature with fangs, squat legs, and squinty eyes who avoid the day and thrive in darkness.

Gollum (see also *The Hobbit*) was originally called **Smeagol** and came from a family of Stoors, a lowly hobbit species. While a young man, he killed his best friend to gain possession of the One Ring, was ostracized from his community, and became transformed through the evil power of the ring into a slimy, contemptible creature that slithers about gazing through huge, heavy-lidded eyes and, because of his years of isolation, talks incessantly to himself, usually about repossessing "my precious." Obsessed with his mission, this misshapen, evil-minded creature feigns obedience to gain the confidence of Frodo and later betrays him. His self-serving treachery, however, is often oddly mixed with a genuine devotion to Frodo. His life ends ironically when he loses his footing and plunges into the flames of Mount Doom, taking the ring with him.

Among the most enduring and interesting creatures in the trilogy are the **Ents**, the guardian genii of old trees who, through time, have become tree-like themselves. Their leader is the ancient, fourteen-foot-tall **Treebeard**, or **Fangorn**, a gentle, benevolent creature who cares for Pippin and Merry when they stray into his domain. Though usually docile and peaceful, when aroused Treebeard and the Ents reveal a nature as tough as their bark-like skin. Incensed by the wanton destruction of the orcs, they march without fear against Isengard and conquer Saruman.

The King of Rohan is **Theoden**, who is first described as "a man so bent with age that he seemed almost a dwarf, but his white hair was long and thick and fell in great braids from beneath a thin golden circlet upon his brow." A kindly, noble man, Theoden became so despondent at the death of his sister that he fell prey to the evil influences of **Grima**, also known as **Wormtongue**, a mean-spirited person who was secretly betraying his country and in the employ of Saruman. Gandalf is able to restore King Theoden's health and confidence and has Wormtongue expelled from the country. The wretched man flees to Isengard, where he is captured by Treebeard. King Theoden later undertakes a number of heroic campaigns during the War of the Ring. He dies gallantly at the Battle of Pelennor Fields, naming his nephew Eomer as his successor. Of Theoden, Aragorn says, "he was a gentle heart and a great king and kept his oaths."

Eomer, the new king, is also a valiant, honorable warrior who fights fiercely on the side of right and justice. Though sometimes headstrong and unyielding, Eomer is a staunch ally and later a mighty king. His sister is the fair **Eowyn**. High-spirited and daring, she disguises herself as the warrior **Dernhelm** to fight beside her kinsmen in the Battle of Pelennor Fields. Though wounded, she continues to fight. Independent and self-willed, she later falls under the spell of Faramir, whom she marries.

While trying to gain access to Mordor, Frodo and Sam are captured by the friendly scouting-force of the Men of Gondor, lead by **Faramir**, younger brother of Boromir. Like his brother, Faramir takes pleasure in battles and valorous deeds, but he also is a man of culture and grace who enjoys music and folklore. A strong believer in punishing evil, it is only through the intervention of Frodo that Faramir is prevented from killing the loathsome Gollum. Because he is more thoughtful and less impetuous than his brother, Faramir is not as highly regarded by his father, Denethor. This becomes a source of pain and humiliation for Faramir, who adores and seeks only to obey his father.

Denethor, the Steward of Gondor, is a proud, shrewd man who is jealous of his power and authority. He often engages in verbal combat and obvious rivalry with Gandalf. When he realizes that his days of authority are over whether or not Sauron wins (because Aragorn is the true heir to the throne), this arrogant but honorable man loses his reason and tries to kill both himself and his surviving son.

The guardian of the pass through the Mountains of Shadow is **Shelob**, a huge, spider-like creature that feeds on strangers who invade her lair. This odious monster stings Frodo with her venom, placing him in a death-like coma, but she is partially blinded by Sam while he courageously tries to save his master.

Further Reading

Authors and Artists for Young Adults. Vol. 10. Detroit: Gale Research, 1993.

Berger, Laura Standley, ed. *Twentieth-Century Young Adult Writers.* 1st ed. Detroit: St. James, 1994.

Carpenter, Humphrey. *J. R. R. Tolkien: A Biography.* Boston: Houghton Mifflin, 1977.

Carter, Lin. *Tolkien: A Look behind The Lord of the Rings.* Boston: Houghton Mifflin, 1969.

Chance, J. Lord of the Rings: *The Mythology of Power.* New York: Twayne, 1992.

Contemporary Literary Criticism. Vols. 1, 2, 3, 8, 12, 38. Detroit: Gale Research, 1973, 1974, 1975, 1978, 1980, 1986.

Crabbe, Katharyn F. *J. R. R. Tolkien.* New York: Ungar, 1981.

Critical Survey of Long Fiction. Vol. 7. Englewood Cliffs, NJ: Prentice-Hall, 1983.

Day, David. *A Tolkien Bestiary.* New York: Ballantine, 1979.

Ellwood, Gracia F. *Good News from Tolkien's Middle Earth: Two Essays on the Applicability of* The Lord of the Rings. Grand Rapids, MI: Eerdmans, 1970.

Fonstad, Karen Wynn. *The Atlas of Middle Earth.* Boston: Houghton Mifflin, 1981.

Foster, Robert. *The Complete Guide to Middle Earth.* New York: Ballantine, 1978.

Giddings, Robert, ed. *J. R. R. Tolkien: This Far Land.* Totowa, NJ: Barnes & Noble, 1983.

Green, William. The Hobbit: *A Journey to Maturity.* New York: Twayne, 1994.

Helms, Randel. *Tolkien's World.* Boston: Houghton Mifflin, 1974.

Isaacs, Neil D., and Rose A. Zimbardo, eds. *Tolkien: New Critical Perspectives.* Lexington: University Press of Kentucky, 1981.

———. *Tolkien and the Critics.* Notre Dame, IN: Notre Dame University Press, 1968.

Johnson, Judith Anne. *J. R. R. Tolkien: Six Decades of Criticism.* Westport, CT: Greenwood, 1986.

Kocher, Paul. *Master of the Middle Earth.* Boston: Houghton Mifflin, 1972.

Lobdell, Jared, ed. *England and Always: Tolkien's World of the Rings.* Grand Rapids, MI: Eerdmans, 1981.

———. *A Tolkien Compass.* LaSalle, IL: Open Court, 1975.

Oldsey, Brian, ed. *British Novelists, 1930-1959.* Vol. 15 of *Dictionary of Literary Biography.* Detroit: Gale Research, 1983.

Purtill, Richard L. *Lord of the Elves and Eldils: Fantasy and Philosophy in C. S. Lewis and J. R. R. Tolkien.* Grand Rapids, MI: Zondervan, 1974.

Ready, William B. *The Tolkien Relation: A Personal Inquiry.* Washington, DC: Regnery, 1968.

Rogers, Deborah W. *J. R. R. Tolkien.* Boston: Twayne, 1980.

Sale, Roger. *Modern Heroism: Essays on D. H. Lawrence, William Empson, & J. R. R. Tolkien.* Berkeley: University of California Press, 1973.

Shippey, T. A. *The Road to Middle Earth.* Boston: Houghton Mifflin, 1983.

Something about the Author, Vols. 3, 32. Detroit: Gale Research, 1972, 1983.

Stimpson, Catherine R. *J. R. R. Tolkien.* New York: Columbia University Press, 1969.

Twentieth-Century British Literature. Vol. 5 of *Chelsea House Library of Literary Criticism.* New York: Chelsea House, 1987.

West, Richard C. *Tolkien Criticism: An Annotated Checklist.* Kent, OH: Kent State University Press, 1970.

Mark Twain

(pen name for Samuel Langhorne Clemens)

1835-1910, American novelist, short story writer, and journalist

The Adventures of Tom Sawyer

(novel, 1876)

PLOT: Set in antebellum America, this novel features Tom Sawyer, an independent, imaginative adolescent who lives in the small Mississippi River town of St. Petersburg with his half-brother Sid, cousin Mary, and Aunt Polly, the sister of Tom's deceased mother. While trying to avoid school, church, and work, Tom shares innocent adventures with his best friend, Joe Harper, and the town's "bad boy," Huckleberry Finn, son of a drunken father and absent mother. The book is episodic, relating stories of how Tom avoids Aunt Polly's attempts at punishment for his misdeeds and tries, when possible, to repay Sid for his often deceitful ways. One well-known episode tells how Tom, who is wise in his knowledge of human nature, convinces his schoolmates that whitewashing Aunt Polly's fence is an honor. Their subsequent eagerness to complete the job frees him from the long, boring task. In another incident, Tom is awarded a Bible in Sunday school by the minister, Mr. Sprague, and superintendent, Mr. Walters, through amassing illegal tickets that represent memorization of Bible verses.

For all his clever resourcefulness, Tom also shares the problems of every typical boy—fighting with the new boy in town, Alfred Temple, and shamelessly flirting with lovely, blue-eyed Becky Thatcher, daughter of the respected Judge and Mrs. Thatcher. His courting suffers a temporary setback when he inadvertently mentions Amy Lawrence, his former girlfriend, in front of Becky.

One day, after failing to escape the wrath of his schoolmaster, Mr. Dobbins, Tom meets Huck at midnight in the graveyard to practice a sure-fire cure for warts. While there, they witness a grave robbery involving the town drunk, Muff Potter, the villainous Injun Joe, and Dr. Robinson. The boys overhear a quarrel and watch as Potter is knocked unconscious and Injun Joe stabs Dr. Robinson to death. In fear for their own safety, Tom and Huck vow never to tell what they have seen. When Muff is accused of the murder, Tom and Huck, along with Joe Harper, escape to neighboring Jackson's Island to lay low and play pirate. When they discover that the townspeople think that, due to their absence, they have drowned, Tom sneaks back to leave a comforting note to Aunt Polly; later, the conscience-stricken boys return in time to interrupt their "funeral." Tom then gallantly breaks his oath and testifies on behalf of Muff Potter at his trial, but unfortunately Injun Joe escapes.

Afterward, during a picnic, Tom and Becky become lost in McDougal's cave. During their wanderings, Tom catches sight of Injun Joe hiding in the cave. After three days of fear and loneliness, during which Tom displays great courage, the two youngsters find their way out. The children inform the authorities of Joe's whereabouts, and after the townspeople explore the cave and discover Joe's emaciated body, Tom and Huck return and discover his hidden treasure.

Both boys are now rich, and Huck reluctantly is persuaded to live with the Widow Douglas, who agrees to refine his manners. In the meantime, energetic Tom is planning to organize a gang of young robbers who will become the Robin Hoods of their neighborhood.

See below for character descriptions.

The Adventures of Huckleberry Finn

(novel, 1884)

PLOT: This novel, narrated entirely in slangy vernacular by Huckleberry Finn, begins where *Tom Sawyer* ends. Huck and Tom Sawyer are each six thousand dollars richer from collecting Injun Joe's treasure. Huck is gradually adjusting to indoor life—which involves such niceties as sleeping on a bed, going to school, and giving up smoking and swearing—with the Widow Douglas and her sister Miss Watson. Soon, Huck's villainous, drunken father appears and kidnaps him, forcing him to live out of town in an abandoned shack where the boy is periodically beaten and half starved. Cleverly staging his own "murder," Huck escapes to Jackson's Island where he finds another escapee, Jim, Miss Watson's slave who has run away when he learns that she plans to sell him for eight hundred dollars. The two form an unlikely alliance and head down the Mississippi River on a raft, hoping to deliver Jim into free territory.

One night after the raft collides with a large boat, the two become separated. On shore, Huck is taken in by a friendly aristocratic family, the Grangerfords, and is later reunited with Jim, who is hiding in the woods. When the long-standing feud between the Grangerfords and the Shepherdsons re-erupts, Huck and Jim take off again on their raft, where they meet two grafting carpetbaggers who call themselves the Duke and the King. Clever con artists who specialize in schemes involving swindling and deception, the cheaters are no match for the cleverness of Huck, who foils their plot to defraud three helpless orphans, the Wilks sisters, of their inheritance. Finally, the two rascals are tarred and feathered, but not before they turn in Jim for a reward.

Huck discovers Jim's new owners are the Reverend and Mrs. Sally Phelps. Arriving at their farm, Huck is mistaken for their nephew, Tom Sawyer, who is expected for a visit. When Tom does appear, he pretends to be his own half-brother, Sid. With Huck's help, Tom hatches a complicated escape plot to free Jim. Although the plot goes awry and Tom sustains a leg wound, the novel ends happily when Tom reveals that Miss Watson, now deceased, has given Jim his freedom in her will and that Huck's vindictive father has also died. Aunt Polly arrives to clear up the problems in identity, and Huck, remembering his experiences with the Widow Douglas, refuses the kind invitation of Aunt Sally Phelps to live with her family.

CHARACTERS: Although both novels were inspired by Mark Twain's actual experiences, *Tom Sawyer* is decidedly more autobiographical. A setting used in both is St. Petersburg, a thinly disguised version of the author's home town of Hannibal, Missouri, which is a few miles north of St. Louis. In a brief preface to *Tom Sawyer*, Twain states that the characters are based on real people and that some of the events actually occurred. According to Twain, in both books **Tom Sawyer** "is a combination of the characteristics of three boys whom I know." Certainly one must have been the author himself, who played hooky as a child; he also played tricks on his mother, the prototype for Aunt Polly.

Capable of both extreme mischief and deviltry, Tom also demonstrates instances of great nobility and courage. He is torn between two influences: the conventional puritanism of Aunt Polly and the freedom and adventure represented by Huck Finn. His nature embodies the spirit of nineteenth-century America, which respected the Old World traditions while exploring the challenges of the coming Industrial Age. He is also a typical early adolescent, showing off to impress his new girlfriend, Becky. While rebelling against dull, constraining routines imposed by church and school, he still enjoys childish games such as Robin Hood. He is becoming aware of his own individuality and fights his rivals

***Huck hides from Miss Watson for fear of being civilized in this illustration by Steven Kellogg from* Huckleberry Finn.**

for position and territorial rights. The mysteries of the world intrigue Tom, and he tends to believe in the occult and places some stock in superstitions, although not as strongly as his friend Huck. Like other adolescents, he has persecution daydreams of the "perfect revenge" variety and is reluctant to show tender emotions, such as compassion and affection, toward adults, including Aunt Polly.

Tom's intelligence makes him a born leader who has an instinctive knowledge of human nature. He outwits Aunt Polly easily and in true entrepreneurial fashion convinces his friends to paint his fence and horse-trades his way into winning a Bible at Sunday school. He also displays a rich, fertile imagination, enabling him to transport himself to distant places and situations. His plan to free Jim in *Huckleberry Finn* (in which he plays only a minor part) encompasses myriad and elaborately unnecessary complexities.

Tom possesses courage and a rare idealism that emerges in moments of great stress. Unlike Huck, he places his own life in danger to free the innocent

Muff Potter. Similarly, in the cave he risks his life to save Becky. Reveling in his youth, Tom is all boy, sorting through his emotions and attitudes on his way to attaining maturity.

Tom's dear friend, **Huckleberry Finn**, is described as "the juvenile pariah of the village." About the fourteen-year-old, free-spirited loner, Twain writes in his *Autobiography*, "In Huckleberry Finn I have drawn Tom Blankenship [a childhood friend] exactly as he was. He was ignorant, unwashed, insufficiently fed: but he had as good a heart as any boy had. His liberties were totally unrestricted.... [He] was tranquilly and continuously happy, and was envied by all the rest of us." Because he is idle, lawless, and vulgar, Huck is both a hero to the children and a threat to their parents. He is the son of the town drunk and a mother whom he scarcely remembers. When readers first meet him, he dresses in cast-off clothes, does not attend school, sleeps in any convenient shelter, hunts and fishes when hungry, and engages in any activities, legal or otherwise, that he fancies at the moment. He often rationalizes stealing as simply borrowing. Although temporarily "civilized" by the Widow Douglas, he reverts quickly to his former life when kidnapped by his father.

A master of survival skills, Huck also possesses an uncanny knowledge of human nature. His cleverness and intelligence belie a strong belief in superstitions, and he readily discerns the schemes of such ruffians as the Duke and the King. Although more realistic than Tom, he has his own set of ethics based on fair play and justice. Huck decides to help Jim in his escape attempt, even knowing the "criminal" nature of his actions, because of his profound friendship and respect for Jim. His decision means he must risk his own well-being for Jim's welfare.

The growth in his sense of morality and integrity occurs gradually in the two books. In *Tom Sawyer* he remains silent during the trial of Muff Potter, but in *Huckleberry Finn* he risks his life saving the Wilks' fortune and helping Jim in his escape plans. His honest, straightforward nature is revealed in his shrewd, no-nonsense comments on human nature. Ever present in his character is the mischievous imp who delights in exposing the phoniness and pomposity in others. At times, he exhibits extreme resourcefulness and trustworthiness. In all respects, Huck Finn is a true American original.

In both books, Tom's kind, simple-hearted guardian, **Aunt Polly**, is based on the author's mother, Jane Clemens. In a perpetual quandary about how she should treat Tom, Aunt Polly explains, "He's my own dead sister's boy, poor thing, and I ain't got the heart to lash him, somehow. Every time I let him go, my conscience hurts me and every time I hit him my old heart most breaks." Realizing his aunt's dilemma, Tom often takes advantage of her uncertainty. Aunt Polly is not nearly as quick-witted or clever as Tom, who is usually able to outsmart her. Her gullibility and eagerness to believe Tom are also associated with a need for love. She tolerates his pranks, as long as she knows he cares about her. Her naive character and trusting nature extends to believing in fake health publications and quack medicines. She is a God-fearing woman who attends church regularly and supplies Tom with the traditional values of society—the values that he eventually demonstrates and that outshine his faults. Her teachings help make him the town hero and a nephew of whom she is proud.

There are two other members in Aunt Polly's household. Tom's half-brother, **Sidney** (*Tom Sawyer*), a quiet and submissive goody-goody who enjoys the things Tom hates (such as going to school), has a contrasting facet to his personality: he is a sly snitch who delights in getting Tom into trouble. The motivation behind Sid's priggish, cunning behavior is never explained, but perhaps he envies the love and attention Aunt Polly showers on Tom. In *Huckleberry Finn*, Tom impersonates Sid to fool Aunt Sally. Cousin **Mary** (*Tom Sawyer*), is also passive and obedient, but unlike Sidney, she lacks deceitfulness and guile. She is a gentle, kindly friend who tries to help Tom stay out of trouble.

In the two books, Huck's father, **Mr. Finn**, is a man of no redeeming virtues. With his ragged clothes, long tangled hair, and pasty white skin, he presents a frightening appearance that matches the meanness of his spirit. He abuses Huck unmercifully, both physically and mentally, and in an attempt to steal his son's newly acquired fortune, kidnaps him and holds him captive in a hut where he continues to beat him and starve him. His drunkenness has reached such proportions that he experiences delirium tremens. He is a bitter, self-pitying man who blames the "govment" for his own failures. His intolerance and violent racism are revealed in tirades against blacks. He prevents Huck from going to school to improve himself and upbraids him for his "uppity" ways. His death goes unmourned both by Huck and the reader.

Tom's bosom friend, **Joe Harper** (*Tom Sawyer*), is a pale copy of Tom. Although similar to Tom in background and interests, he lacks Tom's leadership qualities and depends more on the security of his home and mother. Motivated by conscience and the possible consequences of his actions rather than the desire for action and adventure, he is a true and loyal friend. Two other minor acquaintances of Tom's include his former girlfriend, **Amy Lawrence**, and **Alfred Temple** (both *Tom Sawyer*), the new boy in town with whom Tom picks a fight.

Tom's girlfriend is **Becky Thatcher** (*Tom Sawyer*), daughter of **Judge Thatcher** (both books), an honest and respected resident of St. Petersburg, who later helps Tom and Huck manage the money gained from the treasure. Becky is "a lovely blue-eyed creature with yellow hair." A flirt, she is aware of her breathtaking beauty. However, she is sincere in her romantic feelings toward Tom. When she discovers that he has another girlfriend, she responds by being hurt, angry, and jealous. She resorts to conventional wiles to increase Tom's discomfort and assuage her wounded feelings. When she and Tom get lost in the cave, however, she reacts gallantly and maturely. She does not blame Tom for their predicament, and, although she sobs at the hopelessness of their situation, she faces the possibility of death with courage and resignation.

In *Tom Sawyer,* Huck correctly refers to **Injun Joe** as "that murderin' half-breed." He is a thieving liar who betrays his friend Muff by incriminating him falsely in a murder that Injun Joe actually committed. He is completely ruthless, and others fear him. Both wily and clever, his audacity and daring know no bounds. He even volunteers to help remove from the graveyard the body of Dr. Robinson, the man he has just murdered. His fearlessness and ingenuity also help make him one of the most imposing renegades in literature. The weak, gullible drunk, **Muff Potter** (*Tom Sawyer*), is a pitiable character. A fearful, haggard man, he is caught in a hopeless situation; only the honesty of Tom saves him.

The **Widow Douglas** (both books) is "fair, smart and forty, a generous soul and well-to-do." Along with her sister **Miss Watson** (*Huckleberry Finn*), they try unsuccessfully to reform Huck. Whereas the Widow always displays a kindly, understanding nature, her overly strict sister nags Huck incessantly. Although supposedly a woman of great religious principles, Miss Watson owns a slave, Jim, and her greed leads her to contemplate selling him for a profit.

Some other adult authority figures in *Tom Sawyer* include Tom's minister, **Mr. Sprague**, who is given to lengthy, boring prayers and sermons; the Sunday school superintendent, **Mr. Walters**, an unctuous, sanctimonious man who practices his religion only on Sundays; and **Mr. Dobbins**, the schoolmaster of Tom's one-room school, who rules his small domain with an iron hand and a ready whip. Mr. Dobbins's wig is the object of derision by his pupils.

Besides Huck Finn, the other central character in *Huckleberry Finn* is **Jim**. He is referred to as "Miss Watson's big nigger"—"nigger" being employed by Twain as a descriptive, rather than pejorative, term that is authentic for the time period. Jim speaks with a heavy black dialect and, like Huck, believes in superstitions and voodoo. Because of his upbringing, he lacks Huck's survival skills, but because he believes in liberty and his own worth, he sets out on a perilous, perhaps fatal, attempt to find freedom for himself and, eventually, for his wife and children. A simple soul who grows to love Huck, Jim exhibits the kindness, concern, and loyalty that Huck never received from his father. Jim is brave and resourceful to the point of risking his own freedom by coming out of hiding to help the doctor save Tom after the boy is wounded. Although Jim never complains about his lot in life, his dignity and compassion acquaint the reader with Twain's opinion of the wickedness of slavery.

The two scoundrels whom Huck and Jim meet on their travels are the **Duke** and the **King** (*Huckleberry Finn*). The former is so named because he claims to be the Duke of Bridgewater and the latter because he maintains that he is really the Dauphin of France. Both are unscrupulous impostors who help contribute to the unsavory reputations of carpetbaggers. The King is a bald-headed, gray-haired man in his seventies. As an unprincipled charlatan, he bilks people by pretending to be a preacher who, hypocritically, gives sermons on the evils of drink. Although a little more compassionate and less crafty than his companion, the Duke is also dishonest. He is a failed printer and actor who makes a living giving theatrical performances and selling fraudulent medicines. While they provide some comic relief, the Duke and King reveal the extent of their subterfuge by deceiving innocent townspeople, attempting to swindle a fortune from the three gullible Wilks sisters and turning Jim in for the reward. When they are eventually caught, tarred, and feathered, it is a just punishment.

Three of the targets for the Duke and King are the **Wilks sisters** (*Huckleberry Finn*): attractive, red-headed **Mary Jane**, age nineteen, **Susan**, age fifteen, and **Joanna**, age fourteen. After the death of their father, they await a visit from two English uncles. The Duke and the King assume these identities and systematically try to swindle the innocent teens out of their fortune. Fearlessly, Huck hatches a clever scheme to thwart these plans without revealing his part in the proceedings.

Huck and Jim meet a number of other interesting people on their voyage down the Mississippi. **Colonel Saul** and **Rachel Grangerford** (*Huckleberry Finn*) and their family provide shelter for Huck when he is forced to swim to shore after the destruction of his raft. They are a genteel family, kind and generous in some respects, while adhering to the fading traditions of the aristocratic South. Bound to a misperceived code of honor, they senselessly murder members of the Shepherdson family because of a thirty-year-old feud whose origins are long forgotten. When their daughter, Charlotte, elopes with young Harney Shepherdson, the killing begins again.

The home of the **Reverend Silas Phelps** and his wife, **Aunt Sally** (*Huckleberry Finn*) is the last stop on Huck and Jim's odyssey. The Phelps own a small cotton plantation and have purchased Jim as their new slave. Huck pretends to be their nephew, Tom Sawyer, to gain access to their house. They are well-intentioned people who, like others of their day, see no harm in slavery. Sally, a kindly woman, tries to adopt Huck—an offer he tactfully refuses.

Further Reading

Bruccoli, Matthew J., and Richard Layman, eds. *Realism, Naturalism, and Local Color: 1865-1917.* Vol. 2 of *Concise Dictionary of American Literary Biography.* Detroit: Gale, 1987.

Collier, Laurie, and Joyce Nakamura, eds. *Major Authors and Illustrators for Children and Young Adults.* Detroit: Gale Research, 1993.

Emerson, Everett. *The Authentic Mark Twain: A Literary Biography of Samuel L. Clemens.* Philadelphia: University of Pennsylvania Press, 1984.

Fiedler, Leslie A. "Come Back to the Taft Ag'in, Huck Honey!" In *The Collected Essays of Leslie Fiedler.* Vol. 1. Briarcliff Manor, NY: Stein & Day, 1971.

Furnas, J. C. "The Crowded Raft: 'Huckleberry Finn' and Its Critics." *American Scholar* 54 (autumn 1985): 517-24.

Gerber, John C. *Mark Twain.* Boston: Twayne, 1988.

Hargrove, Jim. *Mark Twain: The Story of Samuel Clemens.* Chicago: Children's Press, 1984.

Lyttle, Richard B. *Mark Twain: The Man and the Adventure.* New York: Atheneum, 1994.

Magill, Frank N. *Critical Survey of Long Fiction: English Language Series: Authors.* Vol. 7. Englewood Cliffs, NJ: Salem Press, 1983.

Press, Skip. *Mark Twain.* San Diego: Lucent Books, 1994.

Sabin, Louis. *Young Mark Twain.* Mahwah, NJ: Troll, 1990.

Seelye, John. "What's in a Name: Sounding the Depths of Tom Sawyer." *Sewanee Review* XC (summer 1982).

Trilling, Lionel. "Huckleberry Finn." In *The Liberal Imagination: Essays in Literature and Society.* New York: Viking, 1950.

Twentieth-Century Literary Criticism. Vols. 6, 12, 19, 36, 48. Detroit: Gale Research, 1982, 1984, 1986, 1990, 1993.

Warren, Robert Penn. "Mark Twain." *Southern Review* VIII (summer 1972): 459-92.

Yesterday's Authors of Books for Children. Vol. 2. Detroit: Gale Research, 1978.

Jules Verne

1828-1905, French novelist

Twenty Thousand Leagues under the Sea

(science fiction, 1870; published in France as Vingt mille lieues sous les mers*)*

PLOT: In the year 1866, ships begin sighting a huge sea monster so powerful that it has attacked and sunk several ships. Professor Pierre Aronnax, the famous French scientist whose specialization is aquatic flora and fauna, along with his faithful servant, Conseil, join an expedition on the American frigate *Abraham Lincoln,* led by Captain Farragut, to pursue and destroy this marine menace. After three months cruising the waters of the north Pacific, their quarry is sighted. A sudden explosion rocks the ship, and Aronnax, Conseil, and the ship's harpooner, a Canadian named Ned Land, are thrown overboard. They are rescued and taken aboard the monster, which proves to be a two-hundred-foot-long, cigar-shaped submarine. The trio meets the vessel's commander, Captain Nemo, and his first mate and are made comfortable. They tour the submarine and are given details on how it was constructed, its power source, and its components, but they never learn any particulars about the background or intentions of the enigmatic Captain Nemo. Although Aronnax and Conseil adjust to this life of captivity, Ned Land longs for a chance to escape.

During the eight months they spend as virtual prisoners on the *Nautilus,* they travel around the world underwater and experience a series of amazing adventures. They engage in hunting expeditions underground, run aground in the Torres Strait, where they are attacked by hostile Papuan Indians, and enter the Mediterranean Sea via a secret tunnel through the Suez. Off the coast of Spain, they visit the sunken land of Atlantis and later travel under the polar ice cap to visit the South Pole. There are also many nearly fatal adventures, including being trapped beneath two giant icebergs with a dwindling supply of air and repulsing an attack by giant squids.

When Nemo is responsible for the sinking of a ship and the loss of many innocent lives, Aronnax realizes that he must acquiesce to Ned's plans and try to escape. One night, when the craft surfaces off the coast of Norway, the three sneak out to the outside platform, intending to swim to shore. Without warning the submarine is sucked into a maelstrom. Miraculously, Aronnax, Conseil and Ned survive, but no one ever learns what happened to Nemo and his *Nautilus.*

CHARACTERS: One of the most interesting and enigmatic characters in all fiction is the mysterious **Captain Nemo.** An accomplished organist and linguist who has mastered several languages and invented his own for the men of the *Nautilus,* he is also the engineering genius who designed the submarine and supervised its clandestine construction on a desert island. A master navigator, he possesses an encyclopedic knowledge of marine life and underwater geography. A born scientist, he has an interest in every aspect of the natural world and human experience. Nemo continually impresses Aronnax and his companions with the amazing breadth of his learning. He is a born leader who commands respect and obedience through his wisdom and towering presence. He is also a man of great courage who, without hesitation, will risk his own life to save others, including, at one point, that of his enemy, Ned Land. Capable of making difficult decisions with prudence and speed, he is responsible and accountable for every aspect of life on the submarine.

In spite of this considerable intelligence and great talent, however, Captain Nemo is a tormented man. Though outwardly calm and composed, he is a solitary and sullen figure who in unguarded moments betrays his inner torment and turmoil. Terrible events in his past have turned Nemo against humanity and given him a desire to seek revenge upon others. As he says, "I am not a civilized man." He destroys human lives without hesitation, yet he refuses to kill any animal except for food and exhibits a touching paternalism toward every member of his crew. When one of his men dies in an accident, Nemo weeps openly and needlessly accepts the blame. The cause of his monstrous hatred of mankind is hinted at when he mentions the agony of needlessly losing one's family and he is found sobbing in front of a portrait of a woman with two children. There is also a suggestion that he uses part of his massive wealth (obtained from collecting sunken treasures) to help oppressed people.

Nemo is a stern authoritarian and insists that everyone must adhere to his wishes and commands. He inflicts the same self-control and constraints on his own life. Aronnax describes Nemo as "the most remarkable man I have ever seen." Tall with an imposing physique, he has a broad forehead, straight nose, and piercing eyes. From a study of his features and manners, Aronnax immediately realizes this is a man filled with self-assurance, composure, courage, and pride. Even though he later realizes that Nemo is a man possessed, in retrospect Aronnax says, "Captain Nemo stood out like a colossus. His qualities assumed superhuman proportions. He was king of the water, the genie of the seas!" Yet, like his name, which means "no one," Nemo remains a man of mystery by the novel's end.

The narrator of the novel is the distinguished marine biologist, the forty-year-old Honorable **Pierre Aronnax**, a professor at the Museum of Paris. One of the world's foremost authorities on all forms of sea life, he is the author of the highly regarded *The Mysteries of the Ocean Depths.* A dedicated scientist, he willingly sacrifices his freedom for the opportunity to study marine life on board the *Nautilus.* Aronnax is a patient man, who tries to understand Captain Nemo and find good in his obsessions. An adventurous man, he often risks life and limb to further his scientific pursuits and accumulate new knowledge on his chosen subject. His vast knowledge encompasses more than science, however, and he shows a keen interest in all aspects of the world around him. A serene, tolerant man, Aronnax respects others and is a faithful, dependable friend who elicits loyalty from those close to him.

If Professor Aronnax is the epitome of the perfect French gentleman, **Conseil** embodies the concept of the faithful servant. With a name that translates as "advice" or "council," this thirty-year-old Flemish man is both his master's attendant and confidante. He has been in Monsieur Aronnax's employ for ten years, traveling whenever and wherever the scientist goes and "never once had he complained of the length or hardship of the journey." A man of strength and "good muscle," his devotion to his master is boundless to the point of endangering his own life to insure Aronnax's safety. Ethical and uncomplaining, he also exhibits intelligence and aptitude in many areas. He is a self-taught marine biologist whose knowledge rivals that of his master. Conseil has an accepting, patient nature and a caring disposition. Without family or responsibility, Conseil has allowed himself to be completely engulfed in Aronnax's life and concerns. His only flaw, according to his master, is that he is excessively formal to the point of continually addressing Aronnax in the third person.

Ned Land, the prince of harpooners, is also called **the Canadian** because he originally comes from Quebec. Usually quiet and reserved, he displays a hot, fiery temper when crossed. Ned is about forty years old, tall, and very strong. Aronnax says, "The best way of describing him would be to liken him to a powerful telescope that could double as a cannon and was always ready for action. He possessed the qualities of skill, coolness, daring and cunning to a higher degree than most." Fiercely independent, Ned objects to the forced confinement on the *Nautilus* and becomes increasingly belligerent and violent. Uninterested in marine biology and bored by the monotony of submarine life, he craves a return to his former active, outdoor life. This becomes such an obsession that in time he becomes excessively emotional and begins behaving irrationally. This impulsive, impetuous behavior disturbs Aronnax, who fears that Ned will commit suicide. In spite of this fixation, Ned is capable of heroic self-sacrifice. He saves Nemo's life, even though he regards the captain as his jailor, and forfeits some of his dwindling air supply to keep Aronnax alive. His evaluation of others shows his astute, practical nature. He is the first to perceive that Nemo is a dangerous man, and he eventually convinces Aronnax the captain is mentally deranged and that escape from the submarine is imperative.

There are two minor characters of note in the novel. **Captain Farragut** is the captain of the frigate *Abraham Lincoln.* Described as "a good-looking officer" and "a fine sailor," he is dedicated to his mission of tracking down the mysterious sea monster that is first believed to be a huge narwhal. He is courageous, affable, and gracious. The **first mate** on the Nautilus is Nemo's version of Conseil. Described as short and muscular with a thick black mustache, he is a trustworthy, loyal assistant.

Around the World in Eighty Days

(novel, 1872; published in France as Le tour du monde en quatre-vingts jours*)*

PLOT: Members of the exclusive Reform Club in London, which includes Andrew Stuart and the reclusive, quiet Phileas Fogg, are positively buzzing about the latest news concerning a daring bank robbery and an item in the paper stating that it is now possible to travel around the world in eighty days. When several members doubt that such a trip is possible, Fogg wagers half his fortune—twenty thousand pounds—that he will be able to accomplish such a feat and appear at the club in exactly eighty days, at 8:45 p.m. on December 21, 1872. He leaves immediately, accompanied only by his newly hired servant, Passepartout. In Suez, a British detective named Mr. Fix, mistakenly believing that Fogg is the escaped bank robber, begins tailing him.

Crossing India by railroad, the travelers are forced to travel by elephant to cover a fifty-mile stretch that has no railroads. During this safari they rescue Aouda, a young Indian girl who is about to be burned alive with her dead husband in a rite known as a suttee. She travels with them and shares their many adventures, which include missed connections and several unforeseen delays often caused by Fix, who is trying to delay them until the arrival of a warrant for Fogg's arrest. Fortunately for the travelers, he is unsuccessful.

The ever punctual Phileas Fogg from **Around the World in Eighty Days**, *as illustrated by Barry Moser*

In San Francisco, Fogg and company run afoul of the unruly mob leader, Colonel Stamp Proctor, during a heated political rally and, on the train crossing the great plains, barely survive an attack by Sioux Indians. Having narrowly missed their ship in New York, Fogg hires the trading vessel *Henrietta* from its captain, Andrew Speedy, to accomplish the trans-Atlantic crossing. When fuel runs low, Fogg buys the vessel and begins stripping it of all its wood furnishings to feed the furnaces.

Arriving in England supposedly on time, the travelers are stopped by Fix, who now is in possession of the arrest warrant. Hours later Fogg is cleared of charges, but too late to win the bet. The next day brings some consolation for Fogg when Aouda agrees to marry him. But, while out shopping, Passepartout makes a marvelous discovery. Because the travelers had passed the international date line and not changed their calendars, it is now the eightieth day since their departure. Promptly at 8:45 that evening, Phileas Fogg enters the Reform Club to claim his winnings.

CHARACTERS: Outwardly the model of the stereotypical, upper-class, imperturbable Englishman, **Phileas Fogg** is considered an odd duck, even by the staid, ultraconservative members of the Reform Club. A man in his forties, he is a slave to punctuality and loves silence, routine, reading his newspapers, and playing whist. He is described as being tall, well-shaped, and possessing fine, handsome features. Precise, placid, and self-assured, he is without wife or children. Living alone in a house on fashionable Saville Row, Fogg has become increasingly eccentric and bound to a fixed routine that never varies from day to day. The servant before Passepartout was dismissed for bringing him shaving-water at eighty-four degrees Fahrenheit rather than the usual eighty-six degrees. Each item in his tasteful, conservative wardrobe is labeled to indicate the time of year when each is to be worn. Fogg lives modestly but is not stingy, giving frequently to charities, often anonymously. A quiet person, he talks little and is noted for being "the least communicative of men."

This aura of confidence and placidity is demonstrated as he plans the trip. Precise and methodical, Fogg is aware of every detail when he designs the methods of transportation and anticipates the possibility of emergencies. Tranquil and seemingly emotionless, in the face of each setback he believes completely in his dictum, "The unforeseen does not exist." During the trip, he remains objective and detached, neither aware nor impressed by the scenery and culture around him and showing only a "majestic and unconscious indifference." Fogg is also, however, a man of honor and integrity. Though obsessed with winning the bet, he decides to delay the expedition to save Aouda, and he later loses time rescuing Passepartout when he is captured by Indians. His sense of justice, honor, and propriety bring him to propose a duel with the crude Stamp Proctor, and his bravery and loyalty to his friends are shown on many occasions, though always in a quiet, unassuming way. When he believes he has lost the bet, Fogg, always the perfectly reserved gentleman, never shows any outward sign of disappointment or despondency. A man of great learning and many talents, he demonstrates such skills as expertise in seamanship and dueling only in emergencies. In spite of his fastidious, exacting exterior, Fogg reveals a hidden sensitivity and tenderness in his love for Aouda and his concern for Passepartout.

Fogg's new servant, **Passepartout**, supplies a perfect contrast to his master. Emotional, good-natured, and outgoing, he is the antithesis of gentility and tranquility. A true Parisian, he is described as "honest, with a pleasant face, good, round head, and tumbled brown hair." He possesses a muscular body and fully developed physical prowess. Something of a vagrant as a youth, he has been an itinerant singer, a circus-rider, a professor of gymnastics, and a fireman. Now seeking a quiet life, Passepartout has turned to domestic service. In French his name means "master key" or "skeleton key," and he supplies that function for Fogg by finding many ingenious solutions to their problems, such as masquerading as Aouda's dead husband to effect an escape. He is a man of great courage and fierce loyalty to his master. He risks his life to stop the train when it is attacked by Indians and frequently sacrifices his well-being to protect Fogg. Passepartout has a sympathetic, compassionate nature and is easily moved to tears. In his naivete and innocence, Passepartout can also be easily victimized and exploited, particularly by the unscrupulous Fix. Though he is uneducated (at one point he asks, "In what country is Bombay?"), he possesses remarkable native intelligence and wisdom and is determined that his master will win the bet regardless of the sacrifices he must make. Thus, when circumstances call for it, he behaves audaciously and with great daring. Fogg aptly describes him as "a worthy fellow."

Fogg's nemesis is **Mr. Fix**. As a detective, Fix is clever, unscrupulous, relentless, tenacious, and always one hundred percent wrong. He misinterprets facts, misunderstands signals, and misconstrues conversations. Yet in other respects he is a model investigator. Fix is persistent and determined in fulfilling his mission to bring the bank robber to justice. To do this, he endures hardship, humiliation, and many indignities, yet he is stubborn and dogged in his determination. He stops at nothing, including drugging the hapless Passepartout, to capture Fogg—a man he grows to admire in time. In moments of danger, such as the Indian attack, Fix shows rare courage and bravery. Described as a small, slight-built person with an intelligent face, bright eyes, nervous habits, and twitching eyebrows, Fix lends both intrigue and humor to the story.

The novel's damsel in distress is **Aouda**, a young, exceedingly beautiful maiden with eyes "clear as the sacred lakes of the Himalaya." Educated in England, she has returned to India to a forced marriage that ends with her narrowly escaping death by suttee (the custom of burning a woman at her husband's funeral pyre as a sign of her devotion to him). She is charming, gracious, and endearingly grateful to her liberators. Aouda has a tender, compassionate nature and shows genuine concern for the well-being of both Fogg and Passepartout. She is loyal to her friends and will not leave them in spite of danger and adversity. A less submissive side of her nature is revealed when she picks up a revolver and joins the others during the Indian attack. Her charm and beauty prove to be irresistible to the otherwise implacable Fogg.

There are several minor characters of note in the novel. One of the mainstays of the Reform Club is the engineer, **Andrew Stuart**. He thinks that circling the globe in eighty days is an absurd idea and instigates the wager against it. He continues to be the chief doubter until Fogg returns triumphantly to the club. The English army general, **Sir Francis Cromarty**, is a tall, fair-skinned man of fifty who is on his way to join his regiment in Benares. A distinguished soldier and fine whist player, he has an extensive knowledge of Indian customs and culture. He unselfishly and gallantly helps in the rescue of Aouda. **Colonel Stamp Proctor** is a blustering ruffian described as "a big brawny figure, with a red beard, flushed face, and broad shoulders." A rabble-rouser who is always eager for a fight, he is a brawling Yankee who dislikes Englishmen, particularly Fogg. After their first violent encounter in San Francisco, they meet again aboard the transcontinental train, where anger and dislike again surface, culminating in a duel that is interrupted by the Indian attack. Proctor fights in his usual fearless, reckless manner during the attack and is seriously wounded. The captain of the ship *Henrietta,* which Fogg hires in New York to go to England, is **Andrew Speedy**. A fine sailor, he is determined to follow his planned course to Bordeaux causing Fogg to lock him in a stateroom and take command. Later, when the ship is low on fuel, Speedy accepts Fogg's generous offer to buy the boat so that it can be stripped and used to power the engine.

Further Reading

Allott, Kenneth. *Jules Verne.* London: Cresset, 1940.

Authors and Artists for Young Adults. Vol. 16. Detroit: Gale Research, 1996.

Brosman, Catharine Savage, ed. *Nineteenth-Century French Fiction Writers: Naturalism and Beyond, 1860-1900.* Vol. 123 of *Dictionary of Literary Biography.* Detroit: Gale Research, 1992.

Butcher, William. *Verne's Journey to the Centre of the Self: Space and Time in the Voyages Extraordinaires.* New York: St. Martin's, 1991.

Costello, Peter. *Jules Verne: Inventor of Science Fiction.* New York: Scribner's, 1978.

Evans, Arthur B. *Jules Verne and His Work.* New York: Twayne, 1966.

———. *Jules Verne Rediscovered: Didacticism and the Scientific Novel.* New York: Greenwood, 1988.

———. "The 'New' Jules Verne." In *Science Fiction Studies* 22:1 (March 1995): 35-46.

Gallagher, Edward J. *Jules Verne: A Primary and Secondary Bibliography.* Boston: Hall, 1980.

Jules-Verne, Jean. *Jules Verne: A Biography.* New York: Taplinger, 1976.

Levi, Anthony. *Guide to French Literature: 1789 to the Present.* Detroit: St. James, 1992.

Lynch, Lawrence W. *Jules Verne.* New York: Twayne, 1992.

Martin, Andrew. *The Mask of the Prophet: The Extraordinary Fictions of Jules Verne.* Oxford: Oxford University Press, 1990.

Seed, David, ed. *Anticipations: Essays on Early Science Fiction and Its Precursors.* Syracuse: Syracuse University Press, 1995.

Something about the Author. Vol. 21. Detroit: Gale Research, 1980.

Twentieth-Century Literary Criticism. Vols. 6, 52. Detroit: Gale Research, 1982, 1994.

Cynthia Voigt

1942-, American young adult novelist

Dicey's Song

(young adult novel, 1982)

PLOT: Dicey Tillerman, sister Maybeth, and brothers James and Sammy have moved in with their grandmother, whom they have never met before. Gram lives in Chesapeake Bay country in the house in which Dicey's mother grew up. Now Dicey's mother lies in an asylum, no longer recognizing or caring about her children, which is why the Tillermans have come to Gram's. For some time since their mother abandoned them and before she was traced to the asylum, Dicey has been in charge of her siblings, and she takes her responsibilities seriously. With Gram to help, though, she feels it is time for her to be a little selfish. She has plans to earn some spending money of her own and also refinish an old sailboat that she finds in Gram's barn.

Yet the change from caretaker to independent teenager is not as easy as Dicey had imagined. The old problems and the old worries about her mother do not go away, nor can Dicey stop worrying about the welfare of her younger brothers and sister, even though Gram is now in charge. Adjusting to Gram is not easy either, for she is a feisty and somewhat eccentric woman who knows her own mind. Gram often talks of reaching out and letting go. Dicey is not sure what she means, but she soon learns the hard way about letting go when she and Gram travel to Boston to see Dicey's mother. When Dicey enters the room, she knows why Gram wanted to rush up there: Momma is dying. Both Dicey and Gram agree that they will take Momma home with them.

But the promise can never be kept because Dicey's mother dies in the hospital, and though they want to ship her body to Maryland for burial, they can't afford it. They agree on cremation, but the burial urns don't seem right either. When Dicey spots a box made from different kinds of wood in a store in Boston, she knows this is what she is looking for, and she and Gram are persuaded by a kind young man in the shop to accept it as a gift. They bury Momma near the house in which she lived beneath the old paper mulberry tree. Grieving but keeping Momma in their hearts, they know now they must go on with their lives.

Other books featuring the Tillerman family are Homecoming *(1981),* A Solitary Blue *(1983),* The Runner *(1985),* Come a Stranger *(1986),* Sons from Afar *(1987), and* Seventeen against the Dealer *(1989).*

CHARACTERS: Cynthia Voigt is best known for her "Tillerman" novels, of which *Dicey's Song* is the second. Though the first of these books, *Homecoming,* contains more narrative action and suspense, *Dicey's Song* is more thoughtful and illustrative of the process of personal growth and developing values.

If she thinks about it, **Dicey Tillerman** would conclude that she has been worrying all her life. Now, at age thirteen, she worries more than ever. She is the oldest of the four Tillerman children, and since Momma disappeared and left them alone all summer her worries have increased a thousandfold. Even with Gram's help, Dicey can't seem to ease her concerns. It isn't that Dicey wants to worry. Actually, she feels that she's due a little free time to herself. But James doesn't talk much, Maybeth may be retarded as some people suspect, and Sammy gets so angry that sometimes he hits people. Dicey has a rough time giving up responsibility for them, especially when it means letting her grandmother take over. It isn't until her mother dies in a Boston asylum that Dicey begins to understand what Gram means when she talks about letting go. "You told me to reach out, to hold on, but you also tell me to let go. How can I do all those things together?" she asks.

Gram's answer is to tell her that no one ever knows what is truly the right thing to do. If it feels right, that is about all anyone has to go by. But what is most important, Gram tells her, is to keep trying. It's not a happy answer, but it's one Dicey can begin to understand.

Gram Tillerman is a feisty, independent eccentric. It is just as difficult an adjustment for her as it is for Dicey when the children move in. But Gram loves her grandchildren and is willing to take on the additional burden. As she says to Dicey when her presence is needed to resolve a problem with Maybeth at school, "You're not the only one responsible, girl. You've been responsible for a long time and done a good job. Take a rest now." She also teaches Dicey about handling the death of a loved one when Momma dies. Later, after the burial back home in Chesapeake Bay country, Gram gathers the children together to look at some old photographs of Momma as a child with her brothers. In this way, Gram brings the family closer together by teaching the children how to love and remember their mother and accept her death.

Dicey's brother, **James**, is the smart one, almost too smart to keep up with. Tending to keep to himself, he does not always say what is on his mind. As their life at Gram's becomes more secure, Dicey begins to appreciate her brother more and to try to understand him. She is able to talk to him about how their brother, **Sammy**, gets so angry at times that he gets into fights. Dicey learns that at least one fight was over the fact that some people in town consider Gram a little weird. But Dicey's biggest worry is **Maybeth**, who just doesn't learn as quickly as the others. Some people think she is retarded, but when Dicey talks about Maybeth with James, he has an idea. He says his sister isn't learning to read because she doesn't quickly make the connection between the words she sees with her eyes and what they mean in her brain, so they come up with another way of teaching Maybeth. Maybeth proves she is not stupid, just a little slower than other children.

Despite the worries over her siblings, Dicey is beginning to adjust to her new life and make new friends. One of them is **Mina**, who is tall for her age, black, and smart. She figures out that one of Sammy's fights is over the fact that someone called Gram weird. Mina is popular in school and the only one who stands up for Dicey in science class when she is accused of cheating. Mina is able to prove that Dicey didn't cheat because they had worked on the project together. Dicey gets an apology from the teacher and consequently becomes sort of a celebrity in school. Another new friend is **Jeff**, who plays guitar. When Jeff starts coming around to the farm, he meets some opposition from Sammy at first, but his playing delights Maybeth, who is also musically talented.

Izzy, Willy Nilly

(young adult novel, 1986)

PLOT: Once a happy, popular cheerleader, fifteen-year-old Isobel "Izzy" Lingard has her life turned upside down when one of her legs is amputated. It all started with a date with Marco, a senior and notorious flirt. Izzy was only a tenth-grader at the time, and even though there were other seniors she liked more than Marco, she couldn't resist being the first of her crowd to be asked for a date by a senior, so she accepted. But Marco had too much to drink, and as he drove her home they had an accident. Now crippled by the crash, Izzy is an entirely different person. Her parents are very caring and supportive and try to help her adjust, but they find it difficult to comfort Izzy. The simplest tasks she used to do with ease are now very hard for her, and she has become depressed.

Then Rosamunde Webber steps into her life. Before the accident, Rosamunde was a girl Izzy never bothered with. But things are different now, and it is Rosamunde, the girl Izzy always felt could use a hair stylist and makeup artist, who begins to put her world back together again. Rosamunde begins to help Izzy view her new life as it is, not without pain or adjustment but with the sense that there is still something worthwhile inside her. Though not the life Izzy was used to, it is one in which she can begin to feel less sorry for herself. It is Rosamunde who coaxes her back to school, to the swimming pool, and to that first basketball game where she isn't a cheerleader.

Izzy knows it will take time. There will be the long slides into depression, there will be the tears she will shed for the perfect girl she will never be again. But slowly and painfully Izzy has begun the journey into finding the person she really is inside.

CHARACTERS: At fifteen, **Isobel Lingard** (nicknamed **Izzy**) has everything going for her. Pretty and popular, she is a cheerleader with loving parents who always deal with their problems in the most practical way. After the accident, and the operation that leaves her an amputee, they are supportive and anxious to help her adjust. But Izzy is not ready for the adjustment and doesn't think she ever will be. Even her brother Joel, who never had a kind word to say to her before, now says she always was a pretty kid. That makes Izzy feel worse than before. Her other brother, Jack, doesn't help either. He can't face her at all. Izzy can understand that. Before the accident, she didn't bother with people who were ugly or disabled either. Even her little sister Francie has a hard time adjusting.

Izzy's plan to deal with her disability is to hide or to be understanding of everyone's possible aversion to her. It is a long, slow, and painful adjustment for her as, with Rosamunde's help, she begins to face the reality of her situation and come to terms with it. When Izzy can do that, when she can stop looking at herself with a stiff upper lip and laugh at her mistakes, she is on the road back to being a whole person.

Izzy's new friend, **Rosamunde**, is not much to look at and, in fact, Izzy wouldn't have looked at her before. But in her own special way Rosamunde begins to bring Izzy out of her self-constructed shell, making her look her new life square in the eye for what it is and what it can be. When Izzy takes a nasty sprawl on her crutches in the school hallway right in front of everyone, it is Rosamunde who says, "She's fine, she's just doing this for attention," and she doesn't reach out a hand to help her. Rosamunde already realizes what Izzy has yet to learn: that she can be a worthwhile person standing on one foot and that beauty does not make one person better than another.

Izzy's mother, **Mrs. Lingard**, is determined that her daughter will adjust to her disability, yet she has very little understanding of what Izzy is going through or how important Rosamunde really is to her recovery. She tells her daughter that she is afraid Rosamunde is a "clinger," and that a girl like Rosamunde will cut Izzy off from the type of friends she usually spends time with. At the same time, Izzy's mother sometimes wants to hug Rosamunde for caring about her daughter. Izzy wonders whether her mother thinks pity is the only reason Rosamunde hangs around. In their determination to "make things right," Mrs. Lingard and her husband suggest building a pool for Izzy to exercise in, though the whole family could enjoy it, too. Izzy's reaction is to be bitter. She thinks that the high fence her parents are planning to build around the pool is meant to prevent her family's embarrassment.

Izzy's young sister, **Francie**, is jealous because of the special attention Izzy receives. When the subject of the pool comes up, she insists that she should have a special time to use it just as Izzy does. Francie's reaction, although childish, is far more sympathetic than that of the parents, who are uncomfortable with Izzy's handicap and try to resume a "normal" life rather than deal directly with their daughter's emotional suffering.

Marco is portrayed as a selfish, reckless young man whose main concern after the accident is that Izzy might tell the police he had too much to drink. Izzy, of course, realizes that if she were to do such a thing, not only Marco but all the other young people at the party would be in trouble, too. When Izzy returns to school, she and Marco avoid each other.

Further Reading

Authors and Artists for Young Adults. Vol. 3. Detroit: Gale Research, 1990.

Berger, Laura Standley, ed. *Twentieth-Century Young Adult Writers.* 1st ed. Detroit: St. James, 1995.

Chevalier, Tracy, ed. *Twentieth-Century Children's Writers.* 3rd ed. Chicago: St. James, 1989.

Children's Literature Review. Vol. 13. Detroit: Gale Research, 1987.

Contemporary Literary Criticism. Vol. 30. Detroit: Gale Research, 1984.

Holtze, Sally Holmes, ed. *Fifth Book of Junior Authors and Illustrators.* New York: H. W. Wilson, 1983.

Reid, Suzanne. *Presenting Cynthia Voigt.* New York: Twayne, 1995.

Sutton, Roger. "A Solitary View: Talking with Cynthia Voigt." *School Library Journal* 41, no. 6 (June 1995): 28-32.

Kurt Vonnegut, Jr.

1922-, American science fiction novelist

Cat's Cradle

(science fiction, 1963)

PLOT: This surrealistic fantasy about the end of the world takes place on the island of San Lorenzo in the Caribbean. It deals mainly with religion and science as opposite means of solidifying human knowledge. Religion, according to Vonnegut, is based on satisfying lies, and science on horrifying truths. Told in episodes, the novel investigates the nature of good and evil and searches for meaning in life.

The chief protagonist is the narrator, Jonah, or John. While researching a book called *The Day the World Ended,* which concerns what happened to important Americans after the atomic bomb was dropped on Hiroshima in 1945, the narrator's interest focuses on Dr. Felix Hoenikker, a scientist who is regarded as the father of the atomic bomb. Those who knew him describe him as a peculiar person who never seemed to need or desire human companionship. The only time anyone remembers seeing him interact with someone else was when he tried to play the child's string game called "cat's cradle" with his midget son, Newton, who was six years old at the time. Now twenty, Newt has horrid memories of that incident because he was unable to visualize the imagined cat's cradle made of string that his father insisted was there.

From Dr. Asa Breed, who worked with Hoenikker, Jonah learns that his last scientific project involved developing ice-nine, a substance that can instantly solidify water. Jonah believes that Hoenikker succeeded and gave each one of his children, Newton, Frank, and Angela, a sliver of this deadly substance. Jonah goes to the island of San Lorenzo to see Frank Hoenikker. On the plane he also meets Newt and Angela, who are going to visit their brother. By the time Jonah arrives, he has learned of Dr. Julian Castle, who, with his partner, Dr. Schlichter von Koenigswald, has set up a hospital called the House of Hope and Mercy in the Jungle.

Jonah also learns of the island's religion, Bokononism, to which he becomes a convert. Bokononism is a "pack of lies" invented by Lionel Boyd Johnson, a black so-called holy man who was marooned on the island after his boat capsized. The god of Bokononism is totally indifferent to people and does not care about the planet at all; humans were created solely for the purpose of admiring the rest of creation.

Each chapter of the novel tells a separate incident or relates a conversation. Jonah learns that the Hoenikkers did have slivers of ice-nine but gave them away. Frank gave his to the island's dictator, Papa Monzano. The fatally ill Monzano decides to end his life by swallowing the sliver and is immediately frozen to death. Unfortunately, his body falls into the sea and the end of the world begins as the oceans freeze. Newt, Frank, and Jonah are among the last survivors.

CHARACTERS: **Jonah**, the narrator, whose real name is **John**, plays the role of detached observer as the world comes to an end. Like the biblical Jonah, Vonnegut's character seems to be working God's will without understanding why. His main purpose is to complete a book entitled *The Day the World Ended,* and, ironically, he witnesses the world's actual destruction. As he freezes to death, he thumbs his nose at God, referred to as "You Know Who," in a meaningless gesture of defiance.

While conducting research for his book, Jonah becomes interested in **Dr. Felix Hoenikker**, the scientist who was doing research on the atomic bomb and on "ice-nine," which has a melting point of 114.4 degrees Fahrenheit. The late Hoenikker was apparently a most peculiar man without need or desire for human contact. The most brilliant scientist of his time, he had no social graces whatsoever. Like a person with arrested development, he regarded his scientific research as mere play, losing interest in it when it no longer amused him. He has no concept of moral or social importance regarding his work.

Therefore, he would not feel guilt over deaths caused by the atomic bomb or responsibility for the end of the world because of ice-nine. Hoenikker serves as Vonnegut's example of the dangers of amoral scientific research.

The incident in which Hoenikker tries to pester his midget son **Newton** into seeing the supposed "cat's cradle" he has constructed out of string is important to the novel because it establishes the recurring theme of illusion versus reality. It would take a great deal of imagination to see a connection with a real "cat's cradle" and the string concoction put together by Hoenikker. When Newt can't make the connection, his father tries to badger him into seeing it. Newt later develops psychological problems from this frightening experience because he can't see reality in another person's illusion. As he says, there is "no damn cat, and no damn cradle."

The self-proclaimed holy man and inventor of the island's religion, Bokononism, is **Lionel Boyd Johnson**, a black man who turned up on the island with a deserter, **Earl McCabe** of the U.S. Marines, after their boat was wrecked. Finding the island in chaos because no one thought it was worth the trouble to govern, the two men invented a game to take the people's minds off their misery. The game soon became reality, however. McCabe became the cruel city dictator; Johnson was the holy man in the jungle. When McCabe outlawed Bokononism, the issue became a division between good and evil. Even though Johnson insisted his religion was nothing but a pack of lies, it continued to thrive because it gave the islanders something hopeful to focus on.

Like all religions, Bokononism, no matter how absurd, does offer love, even if it is in ridiculous forms such as the ritual of putting feet together—called boko-maru—as an expression of love, or the "intermingling of souls." Boko-maru is not meant to be monogamous but is extended to everyone, as the lovely **Mona Aamons Monzano** says after she refuses the sexual advances of the narrator. True love is to be shared by all, not given to one individual alone. Although Vonnegut's satire of religion seems harsh, by the end of the novel religion becomes a more attractive alternative than science simply because it is more humane. Neither religion nor science, however, is an accurate description of reality on Earth.

A medical scientist on San Lorenzo is **Dr. Julian Castle** who, along with his partner, has set up a hospital called the House of Hope and Mercy in the Jungle. These doctors, however, are not truly interested in aiding the lives of people; they are only going through the motions. Castle was once a millionaire playboy who is trying to redeem his useless life by an equally useless fight against death and disease in the squalid jungle conditions on the island. Yet Castle seems to live by no moral code at all. Although his deeds are admirable, he is a cynical man. He is sacrificing himself for no cause at all and acting out of no principles whatsoever.

Even more strange and absurd is Castle's partner, **Dr. Schlichter von Koenigswald**. Once a physician at Auschwitz, he is doing penance for all the lives he destroyed in the Holocaust. He, too, professes no moral beliefs whatsoever and is only working off his "penance," which he figures will be repaid by about the year 3010. His virtue, therefore, is meaningless because it lacks sincerity.

Slaughterhouse-Five

(science fiction, 1969)

PLOT: This novel, perhaps Vonnegut's most famous, combines the grim reality of war with the escapism of science fiction. It is the story of Billy Pilgrim, who has come "unstuck in time." Although it tells the chronological story of his capture during World War II and the bombing of Dresden, Germany, while Billy was a prisoner there, interspersed are events of his life before and after the war. Most fantastic among these are Billy's voyages to the planet Tralfamadore, where he is kept in a zoo and mates with a movie star named Montana Wildhack.

Slaughterhouse-Five begins with Billy's account of his near-fatal plane crash in which his wife is killed; it ends with the bombing of Dresden, even though many of the events actually occur later in the novel. The bombing is contrasted with the scene on

Tralfamadore where Montana is nursing her and Billy's child, thus showing that life goes on amid the destruction.

In Vonnegut's portrayal of World War II, nothing functions as it should, and there is no justice. A soldier is shot, for example, because he stole a teapot, but the diamond Billy stowed in the lining of his coat goes undetected. There is especially no justice in the bombing of Dresden, which had been designated a free city. But it was bombed by the Allies to induce the Germans to surrender, just as the atomic bomb was dropped on Hiroshima as a way of getting the Japanese to surrender quickly.

Before the war, Billy's life was quite mundane; after the war, he marries, fathers two children, and becomes a fairly successful optometrist. Although his time-tripping begins in 1944, Billy does not understand what is happening to him until the Tralfamadorians explain it all on his trip there in 1966. Like most human beings, Billy lives each moment separately, whereas Tralfamadorians live all moments at the same time. For them, there are no distinctions between past, present, and future. Because of this, they know how the universe will end, but they also recognize that there is nothing that can be done to avoid the Apocalypse (which, they admit, will be caused by a Tralfamadorian). The aliens teach Billy to accept this inevitability and to live for the good things in life, rather than concentrating on the ill. Embracing this philosophy, Billy goes on to become a lecturer, spreading the news to mankind that life endures and that time is irrelevant.

CHARACTERS: Although **Billy Pilgrim**'s ramblings sound like those of a senile man, he knows his story will one day be accepted because he has the ability to travel back and forth in time. Although he moves from event to event in his life, he occasionally finds himself on the planet Tralfamadore, where he lives as a kind of zoo specimen. Billy has no control over his time travel. One minute he is discussing literature with the Tralfamadorians, the next he is in the German camp where English prisoners are staging a satire of Cinderella.

After the war, Billy becomes an optometrist and leads a boring, mundane life. His wartime experience, however, is quite different. As a soldier, Billy is totally inadequate. He lacks self-confidence and is cast about by the whims of chance. He is out of place in the army, becoming a victim, rather than a soldier who sees a responsibility to fulfill. Becoming lost behind German lines, he loses some of his clothing and equipment. When he is captured, his appearance is so ludicrous that the Germans use Billy in propaganda films to show how pathetic the American army has become. In the midst of the tragedy of war, Billy becomes a ridiculous clown.

His life as a peacetime dentist also stands in contrast to his time-travel experiences on Tralfamadore. His inability to control his journeys to that planet is similar to his impotence during the war. However, Billy's time-tripping changes his outlook on life. Unlike humans, Tralfamadorians live all moments at the same time. There is no past, present, or future for them, only one eternal moment, a concept that Billy has trouble comprehending. This Tralfamadorian belief, which they teach to Billy, leads to the concept that everything that happens *must* happen and that nothing can be done to change events. This, in turn, leads to Billy's new belief in a sort of resigned stoicism: if it is true that one can't change the future, then one must learn to accept it. Tralfamadorians, for example, admit to Billy that they are responsible for a technological accident that will (or, rather, has already) destroyed the universe. After Billy adopts the Tralfamadorian philosophy, he gives lectures about it back on Earth. His new philosophy transforms Billy into a man at peace with himself.

Behind German lines, Billy is picked up by two scouts and an anti-tank gunner named **Roland Weary**. The scouts, who are good men, are killed; Weary, who delights in torturing Billy while claiming to save his life, is captured along with Billy. Weary is another war misfit, a stupid young man who had an unhappy childhood. Tired of being ditched by people who never wanted him around, including his parents, he tries to find someone more unpopular than himself to torment. Under the pretext of friendship, he gets close to his targets until he finds some way of hurting them. In Billy's case, Weary claims he is trying to save Billy's life; in reality, he delights in torturing him. Ironically, Billy's escape from the hands of Weary comes at the expense of his capture by the Germans. Billy and Weary survive the war, while others more worthy perish. In this topsy-turvy world, according to Vonnegut, that is just as it should be.

Movie star **Montana Wildhack**, with whom Billy has an affair and a child on Tralfamadore, wears a locket that captures one of the themes of the novel. It is inscribed with the words: "God grant me the serenity to accept the things I cannot change, courage to change the things I can, and wisdom always to tell the difference." A tender scene in which she is nursing the baby contrasts sharply with the climax of the novel—the bombing of Dresden—which illustrates man's inhumanity to man. The mother-and-child scene suggests that life, in the end, goes on despite the world's suffering.

Kurt Vonnegut appears in several places in his own novel. He tells the story he is writing and the events that led up to it in the first and last chapters of the book. He also appears in some of the prison camp scenes.

Further Reading

Allen, William Rodney. *Understanding Kurt Vonnegut.* Columbia, SC: University of South Carolina Press, 1991.

Authors and Artists for Young Adults. Vol. 6. Detroit: Gale Research, 1991.

Berger, Laura Standley, ed. *Twentieth-Century Young Adult Writers.* 1st ed. Chicago: St. James, 1994.

Bleiler, E. F. *Science Fiction Writers.* New York: Scribner's, 1982.

Contemporary Literary Criticism. Vols. 1, 2, 3, 4, 5, 8, 12, 22, 40, 60. Detroit: Gale Research, 1973, 1974, 1975, 1975, 1976, 1978, 1980, 1982, 1986, 1990.

Cowart, David, and Thomas L. Wymer, eds. *Twentieth-Century American Science-Fiction Writers.* Vol. 8 of *Dictionary of Literary Biography.* Detroit: Gale Research, 1981.

Giannone, Richard. *Vonnegut: A Preface to His Novels.* Port Washington, NY: Kennikat, 1977.

Giles, James, and Wanda Giles, eds. *American Novelists since World War II, Fourth Series.* Vol. 152 of *Dictionary of Literary Biography.* Detroit: Gale Research, 1995.

Goldsmith, David H. *Kurt Vonnegut: Fantasist of Fire and Ice.* Bowling Green, OH: Bowling Green University, 1972.

Helterman, Jeffrey, and Richard Layman, eds. *American Novelists since World War II.* Vol. 2 of *Dictionary of Literary Biography.* Detroit: Gale Research, 1978.

Klinkowitz, Jerome. *Kurt Vonnegut.* New York: Methuen, 1982.

———, and Donald L. Lawler, eds. *Vonnegut in America: An Introduction to the Life and Work of Kurt Vonnegut.* New York: Delacorte, 1977.

Lunquist, James. *Kurt Vonnegut.* New York: Ungar, 1970.

Mayo, Clark. *Kurt Vonnegut: The Gospel from Outer Space.* San Bernardino, CA: Borgo, 1977.

Merrill, Robert. *Critical Essays on Kurt Vonnegut.* Columbia, SC: University of South Carolina Press, 1991.

Schatt, Stanley. *Kurt Vonnegut, Jr.* Boston: Twayne, 1976.

Vonnegut, Kurt. *Fates Worse than Death.* New York: Putnam, 1982. Watson, Noelle, ed. *Twentieth-Century Science Fiction Writers.* 3rd ed. Detroit: St. James, 1991.

Alice Walker

1944-, American novelist

The Color Purple

(novel, 1982)

PLOT: This novel is written in a series of undated letters that span about forty years. In Celie's opening letter to God, we learn that she is a fourteen-year-old, nearly illiterate black girl living in rural Georgia. She bears two harsh burdens: she must care for her siblings because of her mother's ill health, and she is pregnant, having been raped by Fonso, her father. This is her second pregnancy by him, and she believes that Fonso killed the first child. After the second birth, Celie thinks that Fonso sells the boy; she feels happy that he will have a good home.

Celie's mother subsequently dies. When Celie is about twenty, Fonso marries her off to Albert, a cruel, weak man whose mistress is the beautiful and flashy blues singer, Shug Avery. Celie is once more abused and virtually enslaved. Nettie, Celie's younger sister whom she deeply loves, runs away from

Whoopi Goldberg (left) and Margaret Avery play Celie and Shug in the 1985 screen version of **The Color Purple.**

home to escape Fonso's brutality. Nettie has a burning passion both to be educated and to teach, and she urges Celie to be strong and to fight for her rights. Nettie leaves, promising to write, but Celie never receives any letters. She eventually believes her sister to be dead.

A few years pass and Harpo, Albert's loutish but weak-willed son, marries the strong and daring Sofia, who is different from any black woman Celie has ever known. Like Nettie, Sofia advises Celie to fight against injustice. But when Sofia stands up to a white man, she is thrown in jail; Harpo's mistress, Squeak, secures her release.

Celie falls under the spell of the glamorous Shug Avery. She is the first beautiful element in Celie's life. When Shug falls ill, Celie tends her and learns the meaning of love. With Shug's help, she becomes aware of her own sensuality. She learns that rough sex does not necessarily indicate love and that making love can be pure, natural, and tender.

Celie continues to endure Albert's cruelty for years, until she quite unexpectedly discovers a letter from Nettie. When she finds further proof that Albert has been hiding her sister's letters all these years, she finally revolts. Cursing her husband, she leaves him to go to Memphis with Shug. She rejoices at the exhilarating news that Nettie is alive, a missionary in Africa. Celie learns that Nettie has Celie's two children by Fonso, Olivia and Adam, with her. They had been adopted by a missionary couple, and they all come home before another year passes.

Nettie's letters bring more happiness to Celie, for Nettie has discovered that Fonso is not actually their father, but rather their stepfather—which means that Celie's children are not the result of incest. And when Fonso dies, Celie and Nettie inherit the house and land. The two sisters will spend the rest of their lives there together.

With her newfound strength, Celie has become a whole woman. She forgives Albert for his cruelty, and they become friends. She knows Shug will always have lovers, male or female, yet she will always love Shug, and Shug will always be family. Celie has endured and triumphed over unspeakable cruelty and oppression. Nurtured by love, she has grown into a modern, strong, twentieth-century woman.

CHARACTERS: Although the unusual style of this novel—often cryptic letters written to God—tells little about the setting or motivation of the characters, *The Color Purple* is extraordinary for the depth of emotion it generates. All of the women in this novel are strong characters. They have all been abused by men in some way, but they have all survived. The story, however, focuses not on mere survival but on growth, strength, and the enduring power of love. For her work, Walker earned the Pulitzer Prize for Literature.

The survival and maturation of **Celie** are the book's central and most pervasive themes. At the novel's beginning, she is a young illiterate creature almost totally without a sense of self-worth. It is painful to watch her endure overwhelming degradation time and again, passively accepting unending misery as her lot in life. Despite enduring unspeakable cruelty, Celie does not break. She suffers physical and emotional torment by the men who enter her life, until Shug Avery teaches her about love. Shug urges her to become strong in mind and spirit, while Sofia encourages her to stand up determinedly against injustice.

Once Celie learns that Albert has intentionally kept Nettie's letters from her for so many years, she finally rebels. Celie vows never again to be anyone's slave. As Celie learns to fight and stand up for herself, she grows. By the end of the novel, she has matured into a self-confident woman with a strong sense of her own worth. Out of the horrors of sexism and racism, Celie now knows love, family, friendship, strength, and loyalty.

Shug Avery, the flashy blues singer who is Albert's mistress, is a free spirit. A beautiful, uninhibited, self-centered, and superficial woman, she is also bisexual. While she enjoys being with men, she refuses to allow them to control her. A painfully honest person, the first words Shug says when she meets Celie are "You sure *is* ugly." But Shug later becomes Celie's true friend, teaching her the wonders of love and awakening her first feelings of self-worth. In return, Celie's adoration brings out in Shug a generosity of spirit not previously evident. For all of her life, Shug has been preoccupied with her own needs and wants. Growing up without affection in her life, she has offered none to others. In fact, she and her lover Albert have three children, none of whom she rears or cares for. When she falls ill, not even Albert shows concern, but Celie nurses her with joy and eagerness. For the first time, the glamorous, jazzy Shug Avery responds to the love offered by another person. Shug will continue taking love where and when she finds it, but she is positively affected by Celie, just as Celie is profoundly changed by her.

In sharp contrast to timid Celie, **Sofia**, who is married to Albert's son, Harpo, is a fighter. She will not be oppressed despite the prejudiced society of the 1930s South in which they all live. This refusal to accede to authority very nearly leads to her downfall. When she slugs the white mayor for patronizing her, she is put in jail for twelve years. Incarcerated, Sofia's spirit falters. Her release is conditional upon her employment in a white woman's home as a maid, which Sofia finds more difficult to bear than prison. But Sofia does survive and even learns to compromise. Refusing to be ruled by her husband, they develop a workable relationship by the novel's end. Harpo does the housework, and she works outside the home. Sofia, as a symbol of those who fight against overwhelming odds, is responsible, along with Shug Avery, for instilling in Celie a newfound strength.

Another person who tries to teach Celie to be more daring and independent is her sister, **Nettie**, with whom Celie shares a quiet bond of love. When she leaves as a young girl, Nettie urges Celie to become stronger, to fight. Later, through her letters, Nettie shares her experiences as a missionary in Africa. At the novel's end, the two sisters spend the rest of their lives together.

The two most prominent male figures in the novel are Albert and Harpo. **Albert** is a cowardly and weak bully. He loves Shug Avery, but because he can't dominate her he unleashes his rage through abominable cruelty to Celie. Because Nettie would not accept his advances before she ran away, Albert retaliates by hiding her letters to Celie over the years. However, when Celie leaves him, Albert begins to change. He sees that his own character has cost him the love of both Celie and Shug. By the novel's end, Albert is reformed enough to have become Celie and Shug's friend; they accept him as family.

Harpo, Albert's son, is weak like his father. Unfortunately, his father is his only role model for being a husband. Harpo marries Sofia and also keeps a mistress, constantly bemoaning the fact that he can't control his wife. He wants to grow big and strong so that he can physically overpower Sofia, but he only grows fat. However, Harpo does have one redeeming quality: he really loves his wife, and in the end they are able to compromise in their marriage. Harpo's mistress, **Squeak**, is mouse-like with milky skin. She is chosen to intercede with the white prison warden on Sofia's behalf. In the process, he rapes Squeak, who is, in fact, his niece. The warden finds nothing wrong with this incestuous coupling since Squeak is black. When she returns, Squeak tells Harpo that she has earned the right to be called by her true name, Mary Agnes.

Unlike Albert and Harpo, who at least retain a redeeming quality or two, **Fonso** is completely without appealing attributes. He is an unthinking brute who not only feels no remorse about raping a young girl but then sells Celie's child without a second thought. Uneducated and unintelligent, he knows no other life but his own pathetic existence. Fonso takes what he can get by physical force and is little more than an animal.

Further Reading

Barthelme, Elizabeth. "Victory Over Bitterness." *Commonweal* 110 (February 11, 1983): 93-94.

Bloom, Harold. *Alice Walker.* New York: Chelsea House, 1990.

Bruccoli, Matthew J., and Richard Layman, eds. *Broadening Views, 1968-1988.* Vol. 6 of *Concise Dictionary of American Literary Biography.* Detroit: Gale Research, 1988.

Contemporary Literary Criticism. Vols. 5, 6, 9, 19, 27. Detroit: Gale Research, 1976, 1976, 1978, 1981, 1984.

Davis, Thadious M., and Trudier Harris, eds. *Afro-American Fiction Writers after 1955.* Vol. 33 of *Dictionary of Literary Biography.* Detroit: Gale Research, 1984.

Early, Gerald. "*The Color Purple* as Everybody's Protest Art." *Antioch Review* 44 (summer 1986).

Gentry, Tony. *Alice Walker.* New York: Chelsea House, 1983.

Kibler, James E., Jr., ed. *American Novelists since World War II, Second Series.* Vol. 6 of *Dictionary of Literary Biography.* Detroit: Gale Research, 1980.

Ryan, Bryan, ed. *Major Twentieth-Century Writers: A Selection of Sketches from Contemporary Authors.* Detroit: Gale Research, 1991.

Smith, Valerie. *African American Writers.* New York: Scribner's, 1991.

Tucker, Lindsey. "Alice Walker's *The Color Purple:* Emergent Women, Emergent Text." *Black American Literature Forum* 22 (spring 1976).

Washington, Mary Helen. "An Essay on Alice Walker." In *Sturdy Black Bridges.* New York: Anchor, 1979.

Winchell, Donna H. *Alice Walker.* Boston: Twayne, 1992.

H. G. Wells

1866-1946, English novelist

The Time Machine

(science fiction, 1895)

PLOT: The central character of this novel is a late nineteenth-century English inventor—identified only as the Time Traveler—who has developed a revolutionary theory of geometry. The story begins with a dinner party at the inventor's home one evening, during which he attempts to explain his theory to his guests. It involves the idea that time is merely another dimension of space. To demonstrate this, he shows off a small model of his time machine which makes it possible for a person to visit both the past and the future. His guests are skeptical, including the story's narrator, who is quickly proven wrong when the Time Traveler pushes a lever and the machine disappears along with its passenger.

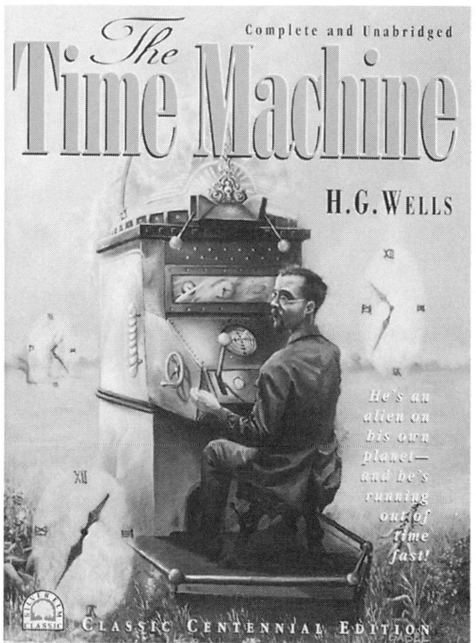

The Time Traveler voyages into the distant future in Wells's classic science fiction story.

A week later, the guests return. This time, however, their host arrives late and appears disheveled. His guests are astonished with his tale of time travel. He regales them with his eight-day adventure to the England of 802,701 A.D. There he has met people called the Eloi, a rather simple folk who are loving, playful vegetarians who also have a great fear of darkness. The Time Traveler meets an Eloi woman named Weena, and he soon understands her people's fears when they meet the Morlocks. Although descended from humans, the Morlocks look like big spiders and fear light. Weena is killed by the Morlocks that evening, and the Time Traveler escapes the Morlocks by accidentally setting the forest on fire. Fleeing from his pursuers, he finds his Time Machine, which had previously disappeared. But in his haste to escape, he mistakenly thrusts the levers forward. Instead of returning to his own time, he journeys farther into the future.

Finally able to slow his furious pace, the Time Traveler ends up thirty million years in the future. The sun is dying, and the earth has come to rest with one side toward the dull red of the sun. There are no ocean currents, no wind, no waves upon the shore. The Time Traveler is terrified by the sight of what appears to be a giant rock moving toward him. It is actually a giant crab covered with slime and it seems intent on eating him. The Time Traveler finds it difficult to breathe in the icy cold of this future beach. Terrified that he will die there, he quickly pushes back the levers of his Time Machine and returns to his own age.

The narrator returns to the inventor's home the day after the dinner party. The Time Traveler is getting ready for another journey. He assures the narrator that this time he will bring a camera as proof of his fantastic adventures and bids the narrator to wait outside the laboratory while he makes some necessary preparations. But when the narrator finally reenters the lab, the Time Traveler is gone. And that, reveals the narrator, was three years ago. There has been no sign of the Time Traveler nor his Time Machine since that day.

CHARACTERS: Wells's novel incorporates many of the philosophical and scientific ideas that were popular in late nineteenth-century England. Theories about evolution, struggles between the social classes, and the decline in the total energy of the universe consequently form the background for this book.

The only significant characters in *The Time Machine* are the Time Traveler and the narrator. The **Time Traveler** is presented as a whimsical, intelligent, and clever man. He tells his amazing stories of time travel with enough details and credibility that his guests, although skeptical, are nonetheless fascinated by his amazing exploits.

At the initial dinner party, the Time Traveler discusses his theories on the Fourth Dimension, or time. When one guest, a psychologist, observes that people can't move about in time like they do through space, the Traveler disagrees, declaring that his marvelous invention uses the force of gravity to do just that. His guests are merely amused, but the Time Traveler is intent upon proving his theories. To do so, he brings out his marvelous invention, the Time Machine. As impressive as it is and as seriously as he details its workings, his guests give each other knowing winks. The Time Traveler obviously must prove his theories to them. When the guests return some days later and the Time Traveler appears disheveled and bruised, he relates to them his incredible adventures of traveling to the future.

When the Time Traveler meets the gentle, child-like Eloi, he speculates on how humanity has developed. These peculiar little people live serenely and without fear, but they seem to have the intelligence of five-year-olds. The Time Traveler decides that because they have overcome their environment and their needs are so perfectly fulfilled, they have lost the vigor and intelligence of their ancestors. When he meets the Morlocks, the Time Traveler surmises that humanity has evolved into two distinct species: the happy, playful folk above ground and the subhuman night creatures who live below. In an evolutionary exaggeration of the Haves versus the Have-nots, there is no utopian paradise in this future.

The Time Traveler realizes how incredible his story must sound and vows to take another journey and bring back proof. In his quest, the Time Traveler symbolizes the insatiable curiosity of the human mind. He becomes a wandering pilgrim, seeking the answers to human evolution. But in the end, says the narrator, it does not matter whether the Time Traveler returns, for the journey is what is important. We do not know how the future will evolve, or whether humans will become Eloi or Morlock or something better or worse. Even if the truth lies in that scene upon the beach when a slimy crab walks under a dying sun, humanity must still strive to improve itself.

The **narrator** serves as the voice of humanity. He waits for the return of the Time Traveler, reflecting on his vision and his adventures, his questing spirit and bravery. Like the other guests at the dinner party, the narrator is skeptical and bemused by the Time Traveler's stories, but he is, perhaps, more intrigued than the others, more inquiring. Returning the following morning after the second dinner party, he is there when the Time Traveler disappears and is left to wonder and wait.

The War of the Worlds

(science fiction, 1898)

PLOT: The novel begins with the earth's citizens blissfully unaware that the world is about to change forever. The narrator, who is preoccupied with the problems of learning to ride a bicycle, is also ignorant of the impending invasion from Martians far more intelligent and deadly than humans. Although scientists had speculated about possible intelligent life on Mars, they did not know that the Martians have long been observing Earth. Being a much older planet, Mars is cooling down, just as the earth will someday. The Martians, aware of the coming disaster and possessing superior intellects and resources, have decided to avoid extinction by searching for a new home, and the green and fertile Earth is the obvious candidate.

In 1894, the narrator explains, a brilliant light was observed coming from the planet Mars. The narrator speculates that this was the flash from the great gun that hurled space projectiles at earth. He is in his study when the first such projectile lands. Among other people, the narrator goes to investigate the strange cylinder, which is immediately assumed to have come from Mars because of the earlier observed flashes of light.

A creature with tentacles emerges from the cylinder, sending panic through the crowd. This is followed by another grotesque limb, and then a truly repulsive, huge mass emerges, glistening like wet leather. A type of heat ray is emitted, killing several spectators. Although the narrator runs away with the rest of the crowd, he eventually calms down and decides to join his wife. They resolve to go to the home of a cousin, but once there the narrator goes back, caught up in the war fever that is spreading throughout the region. He teams up with a passing soldier who is on his way to rejoin his battery in London. By this time, the fighting between Martians and humans has begun in earnest. At one point, the narrator meets a curate, whose reaction to the invasion is total fear and selfishness.

The Martians devour all available food. The pit where they landed is empty now, but a carpet of red weeds has grown everywhere. It creeps over everything, even clogging up the rivers. With all supplies of food gone, it seems to the narrator that humanity is doomed. Full of despair, he once again runs into the soldier, and they greet each other warmly.

In the meantime, the reader also learns of how Londoners are reacting to the landing of the Martians through the experiences of the narrator's brother, who tries to leave the city in a calm and rational manner in the face of this terrifying situation. He also tries to aid the Elphinstones, two women who have very different reactions to the impending disaster.

When the once-vibrant Martian weeds begin to deteriorate it proves to be a sign of the end of the Martians themselves. Like the red plants, they are succumbing to a common Earth bacteria. Eventually, the invasion fails, ironically because these superintelligent creatures were woefully susceptible to an invisible bacteria. But the narrator is aware that this does not mean the world is safe from invasion. He realizes, too, that there may come a time when humans will have the need to travel to other planets.

CHARACTERS: The **narrator** is the central and only true character in this science fiction classic. A capable and intelligent human, he nonetheless possesses human frailties. Although he never completely panics or loses self-control, he does become frightened by the threat of the Martian attack and at times acts unwisely. Near the end of the novel, when all seems lost, he gives in to despair, but this may be just as much an indication of exhaustion as of character weakness. Most of the time, he acts in a courageous, self-composed manner, in contrast to most of the populace which flees in utter panic.

At the beginning of the novel, the narrator, although busy with his own pursuits, prophetically establishes a sense that time is running out for Earth. Like the others in the crowd observing the Martian craft, the narrator is frightened and disgusted by the sight of these loathsome creatures emerging from the cylinder, but he manages to keep his wits about him until the death ray strikes. Exhaustion stops his headlong dash away from this horror and he is able to get a grip on himself, becoming a reliable reporter of the terrifying events he witnesses. He reaches his home and tells his wife about the invasion, assuring her that the Martians will never be able to get out of the pit because of the earth's gravity. With that flimsy assurance, they sit down to a meal.

But, of course, another ship lands, and the War of the Worlds commences. The narrator and his wife decide to go to her cousin's home in Leatherhead, but the narrator, caught up in the war fever that has overtaken the whole region, later returns to his home. The fighting continues in earnest as more Martians land, and the narrator, now in the company of the curate, tries to rejoin his wife. He is disgusted by the actions of the selfish curate, who whimpers pitifully every time they face danger. Despite the terror of the situation around him, the narrator is fascinated by the incredible technology of the Martian war machines, as well as by the mysterious red weed that has sprung up everywhere. He can't help but be impressed by the intelligence and ingenuity of these creatures, while still being terrified by the impending doom they portend. He feels weak, as if the stature of humanity has been humbled in the face of such a superior civilization. He begins to feel as if he is one of the few people left upon the earth.

When the narrator meets the soldier the second time, they greet each other like old friends, and the narrator is impressed by the soldier's plans for the survival of the human race in the face of destruction. But when he realizes that the soldier is in reality only a dreamer and not a doer, he leaves him and presses on once more toward London. Back in London and prepared to die, the narrator is astonished at the sight of dead Martians. An invisible bacteria spells the downfall of these superintelligent aliens. The human race has won, but it is a strange victory for human ingenuity has played no part in the Martians' defeat.

With this lesson in humility, the narrator returns to find that his wife, as well as her cousin, have survived. Never again can he be so complacent about life or the well-being of the human race. But, for now, the narrator is merely glad to be able to hold the hand of the woman he thought was lost to him forever.

The **soldier**, or artilleryman, at first appears to be capable of stemming the invasion with his resourcefulness and will to survive. With intelligence and scientific knowledge, he is confident Earth will win. But the soldier is incapable of putting his brave and encouraging words into action. He seems to be the antithesis of the cowardly curate, but in reality they are both merely frail and flawed humans.

The response of the **curate** to the Martian invasion is one of fear, instability, cowardice, and, finally, insanity. He can't face the reality of the situation, nor can he deal with his fear for his own safety. Instead of standing up to the problem confronting him, he retreats into impotence, claiming that this misfortune is the will of God. People are being punished for their sins, he believes; therefore, there is no reason to try to do anything. Just as the narrator finally sees the soldier for the dreamer that he is, he is revolted by the simpering curate. For all his proclaimed faith, the curate is indeed a weak man.

Three other minor characters are worth noting. **Miss Elphinstone** reacts with courage and dignity in the face of disaster. She is the opposite of her sister-in-law, **Mrs. Elphinstone**, who is incapable of rational thought in a crisis and must be directed if she is to survive at all. The narrator's **brother** is much like the narrator. He remains self-composed despite the terror of the invasion.

Further Reading

Benstock, Bernard, and Thomas F. Staley, eds. *British Mystery Writers, 1860-1919.* Vol. 70 of *Dictionary of Literary Biography.* Detroit: Gale Research, 1988.

Berger, Laura Standley, ed. *Twentieth-Century Young Adult Writers.* 1st ed. Detroit: St. James, 1995.

Bergonzi, Bernard. *The Early H. G. Wells: A Study of the Scientific Romances.* Toronto: University of Toronto Press, 1961.

———, ed. *H. G. Wells: A Collection of Critical Essays.* Englewood Cliffs, NJ: Prentice-Hall, 1976.

Bloom, Robert. *Anatomies of Egotism: A Reading of the Last Words of H. G. Wells.* Lincoln: University of Nebraska Press, 1977.

Borrello, Alfred. *H. G. Wells: Author in Agony.* Carbondale: Southern Illinois University Press, 1972.

Brooks, Van Wyck. *The World of H. G. Wells.* St. Claire Shores, MI: Scholarly Press, 1970.

Coren, Michael. *The Invisible Man: The Life and Liberties of H. G. Wells.* New York: Atheneum, 1993.

Foot, Michael. *H. G.: The History of Mr. Wells.* Washington, DC: Counterpoint, 1995.

Hammond, J. R. *H. G. Wells and the Modern Novel.* New York: St. Martin's, 1988.

Hillegas, Mark. R. *The Future as Nightmare: H. G. Wells and the Anti-Utopians.* New York: Oxford University Press, 1967.

Huntington, John. *Critical Essays on H. G. Wells.* New York: Macmillan, 1991.

McConnell, Frank. *The Science Fiction of H. G. Wells.* New York: Oxford University Press, 1981.

Smith, David C. *H. G. Wells: Desperately Mortal.* New Haven, CT: Yale University Press, 1986.

Something about the Author. Vol. 20. Detroit: Gale Research, 1980.

Staley, Thomas F., ed. *British Novelists, 1890-1929: Traditionalists.* Vol. 34 of *Dictionary of Literary Biography.* Detroit: Gale Research, 1985.

Suvin, Darko, and Robert M. Philmus, eds. *H. G. Wells and Modern Science Fiction.* Lewisburg, PA: Bucknell University Press, 1977.

Twentieth-Century Literary Criticism. Vols. 6, 12, 19. Detroit: Gale Research, 1982, 1984, 1986.

Wells, H. G. *Experiment in Autobiography: Discoveries and Conclusions of a Very Ordinary Person.* New York: Macmillan, 1934.

West, Anthony. *H. G. Wells: Aspects of a Life.* New York: Random House, 1984.

Williamson, Jack. *H. G. Wells: Critic of Progress.* Baltimore: Mirage, 1973.

Barbara Wersba

1932-, American novelist

Run Softly, Go Fast

(young adult novel, 1970)

PLOT: Nineteen-year-old David Marks looks back on the tangled relationship with his father, Leo, who has recently died. Angry, resentful, guilty, and hurt, he must face the knowledge that old problems will never be resolved. He can't understand the mixed feelings he is experiencing when he thinks about his father. David recalls the years with his father that began so well and ended so poorly. He remembers summers at the lake when he thought his father was the most wonderful man in the world and he wanted only to be like him and to make him proud. He also remembers the day he fell overboard, how his father dove into the water to save him, and how his father comforted him from the nightmares that followed.

Trying to find the source of their rift, David sifts through the years of his childhood, watching his father change as he becomes more obsessed with success and making money. David marks the change in his father as being the day he became partners with Shulman and started being dissatisfied with his place in the world. Money and success seemed to be the only things that mattered to him. Little by little, David begins to resent his father's preoccupation with "fitting in" with the wealthy Protestant world. More and more, he begins to respect his quiet Uncle Ben. Uncle Ben is a man interested in poetry, gentleness, and spending time at the Library of Jewish Studies. He is constantly criticized by David's father.

The rift widens when David discovers that his father is being unfaithful to his mother. He resents his mother for quietly putting up with such a situation, and in desperation he runs to Uncle Ben for advice. He is shocked and dismayed when he learns that Ben does not want to cause a confrontation. It is a bitter lesson that turns David away from both men.

The more that David's father harps on his education at a prestigious eastern college, the more the boy rebels. Then, while still in high school, David meets Rick. Because Rick is against the Vietnam war, David's father immediately dislikes Rick. One night when he walks in on the two boys, who are engaged in some foolish roughhousing, Leo misinterprets their actions as being homosexual and throws Rick out of the house. This prompts David to leave as well. He moves to the Village in lower New York City, where he begins to paint. At first, David has visions of sharing an apartment in the Village with Rick and leading a bohemian life. He is crushed to learn that, after Rick's visit to his own parents, he gives in to the insistence on "conforming." Despite his feelings about Vietnam, Rick joins the army and is later killed.

In his despair, David goes on a binge of drugs and alcohol. He shares an apartment with Maggie, who in her gentle way encourages him to paint and to find himself, especially with regard to his feelings about his father. But David blames his father for everything and is adamantly against any reconciliation. He does not budge from this stance, even when he learns that Leo is in the hospital with cancer. Finally, at his mother's stubborn insistence, David goes to visit his father. It is an awkward meeting, and the two end up at opposite ends once again. His father stays in the hospital for weeks and David stubbornly refuses to go back, despite his family and Maggie's urgings.

Then one day, David trims his long hair as his father wishes, irons his summer suit, and puts on a tie. He goes to the hospital, where he hardly recognizes the shrunken man who is his father. After that, David goes to the hospital every day. Sometimes his father does not even know him. When Leo Marks dies, David is left with his unresolved feelings. He wishes they could start over, but he knows that even if they did their relationship would probably have turned out the same way.

CHARACTERS: David Marks is a teenager in turmoil. A young man growing up in the time of Vietnam, he is trying to find his way between manhood and childhood. He loves his father and wants desperately to make him proud. At the same time, however, he grows to resent what his father has become: a man obsessed by the need to amass wealth, as though it will buy respect and honor. David is as selfish and spoiled as his mother accuses him of being. For all the pain that David suffers in his estrangement with his father, he is slowly maturing, although in a sad and haunting way. He knows that he does not hate his father, that perhaps he never hated his father. He has not found the answers that he seeks, but it doesn't seem so important anymore to do so. At nineteen, David is a sad young man. Though he wants to be a better person, he doesn't know how to change, how to keep from repeating the old patterns that brought him to where he is today. He can only thank his father for the gift of life and wish him peace.

Typical of many men who grew up with nothing and turned their work into material wealth, **Leo Marks** is a man who desperately needs to succeed. He feels he must prove to the world that he has risen out of poverty and by his own sweat and brains can enter the world of the successful. Even if this means denying his own Jewishness, cheating on his wife, or ignoring the dreams and needs of his son, he is resolved to stay on his course. He wants David to conform because that, too, would be a mark of Leo's success. But Leo Marks also has some good qualities David does not see. David's mother knows that her husband has guts and goodness. He makes mistakes, but he tries to do what is best for his family.

David's **mother** is pictured as a quiet woman dominated by her successful husband. When David learns of his father's unfaithfulness, he blames his mother somewhat for her seeming acceptance of the situation. But when his father is in the hospital, David sees a new side to his mother. She berates her son for his treatment of his father. Calling him spoiled and selfish, she says he lacks the capacity to forgive. She tells David that she has known about the other women and the fact that Leo is ashamed of being a Jew. She knows he is far from perfect, but she forgives him. She understands that because he did not have enough to eat as a child, he is desperate to make a better life for his family, no matter what the cost.

David is devastated when he confronts his **Uncle Ben** with the fact of his father's unfaithfulness only to realize that Ben wants no part of any unpleasantness and turmoil. David believed that his uncle was concerned only with the finer things in life, but he realizes in that moment that Ben has actually withdrawn from life. In that moment, David's love for his uncle dies.

David's friends also play important roles in the novel. **Rick Heaton**, a relative of David's, is a boy from a well-to-do family. He has the courage to stand up to his parents to protest the war in Vietnam. But David is disillusioned when Rick gives in to his family's pressure and joins the army and dies in the war. For all her own rebellion, **Maggie** is a young girl wise beyond her years. Sharing an apartment with David, she comes to understand David's turmoil over his father and gently tries to help him confront his anger and fears.

Further Reading

Authors and Artists for Young Adults. Vol. 2. Detroit: Gale Research, 1989.

Berger, Laura Standley, ed. *Twentieth-Century Young Adult Writers.* 4th ed. Detroit: St. James, 1994.

Chevalier, Tracy, ed. *Twentieth-Century Children's Writers.* 3rd ed. Chicago: St. James, 1989.

Contemporary Literary Criticism. Vol. 30. Detroit: Gale Research, 1984.

De Montreville, Doris, and Donna Hill, eds. *Third Book of Junior Authors.* New York: H. W. Wilson, 1972.

Estes, Glenn E., ed. *American Writers for Children since 1960: Fiction.* Vol. 52 of *Dictionary of Literary Biography.* Detroit: Gale Research, 1986.

Ward, Martha, ed. *Authors of Books for Young People.* 3rd ed. Metuchen, NJ: Scarecrow, 1990.

Robert Westall

1929-1993, English young adult novelist

The Machine Gunners

(young adult historical novel, 1976)

PLOT: The year is 1941 and Chas McGill of Garmouth, England, has grown used to the German planes overhead and to nights spent trying to sleep in an air raid shelter. One day after a shelling, the fourteen-year-old spots a German plane shot down in a wooded area. The pilot is dead, but Chas finds a machine gun still in its pinnings and intact. What a treasure to add to his souvenir collection! But before he can retrieve it, he must avoid the watchful eye of Fatty Hardy, the local policeman who has chased Chas away from wrecked building sites many times before. Chas solves that problem by telling the policeman that his mother has found a deep hole in the garden with ticking coming from it. Having lured Fatty away, Chas enlists the aid of Cemetery Jones in freeing the machine gun.

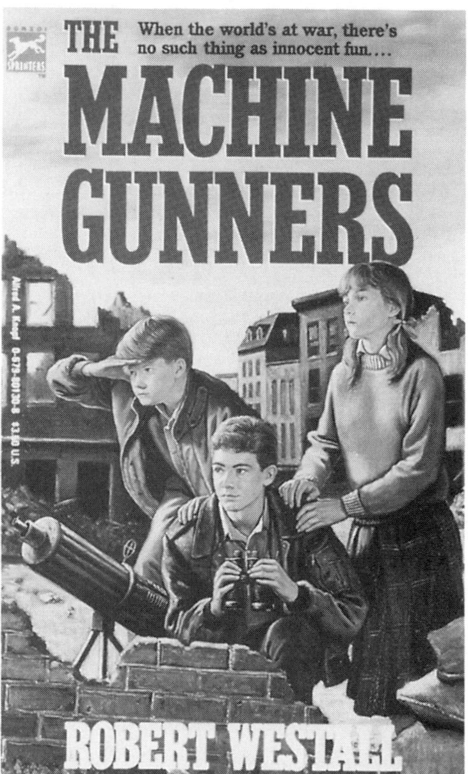

In England during World War II, a group of boys arm themselves with a machine gun that almost causes more harm than good.

When the bomb squad arrives, they immediately perceive that someone has taken the gun. Although they suspect that it might be children, there is no proof. In the meantime, Chas decides not to turn the gun in for money but to keep it to fight the enemy. (There have been repeated rumors of a German invasion.) He and his friends, who include Cemetery Jones and Audry Parton, build a secret encampment for the gun in the garden of one of their schoolmates named Sicky Nicky. Since nobody likes Sicky, they feel it's safe that no one will go there and find the gun.

Sometime later, the boys actually fire the gun at a German Messerschmitt. The plane is hit, although not by the boys, and goes down. The rear gunner, Sergeant Rudi Gerlath, parachutes into a garden where he lands safely with only a sprained ankle. When he leaves the area in search of food, he stumbles into the abandoned garden where he surprises the boys and discovers the gun. Chas and his friends feed the German soldier and slowly try to communicate with him. The soldier learns that the gun has been damaged and agrees to repair it if, in return, the children will find a boat for him so that he can escape. They agree and are able to convince Nicky to let them have his father's boat.

Soon the whole town is abuzz with news of the coming invasion. Rudi escapes in the boat and heads out to meet his comrades, but he realizes that there is to be no invasion and heads back to the garden encampment. Before Rudi returns, everyone except the children knows that the invasion has been a false rumor. Seeing a group of foreign soldiers marching toward them and thinking the invasion has come, the children fire the gun. Luckily, no one is hurt. Rudi surrenders to the British and the missing machine gun is turned over to the authorities. The boys get a stern punishment from their parents, but they promise to write to Rudi if they are able to.

CHARACTERS: Chas McGill is a resourceful, cheerful, typical teenaged boy living in London during World War II. He has occasional problems with his parents, who are busy with their own war responsibilities, as well as trying to keep the family safe and together in dangerous times. As much as they warn their son about being careful during his forays for souvenirs, Chas forges ahead, often without being very careful. After all, his collection of war souvenirs is second in Garmouth only to Boddser Brown's, and he has to try and outdo his competition. Chas therefore can't believe his good luck when he sees the downed German plane, which he recognizes as a Heinkel He III. For a moment, he imagines himself on the nine o'clock news with the report of this great find. And then he sees the still-intact machine gun, hanging from the turret. To one-up Boddser, he decides he must have the gun.

Chas is a very resourceful lad. First, he is able to trick **Fatty Hardy**, the policeman, into leaving his post by the German plane so that Chas can retrieve the machine gun. Then he comes up with the perfect plan to hide the gun by putting it in Nicky's garden where no one will ever look. The most tragic part of Chas's ingenuity is his plan to turn a hobby of collecting war souvenirs into a scheme to actually fire the gun at invading Germans. By the end of this escapade, however, Chas has come to understand the realities of war a little better, as well as the consequences of acting irresponsibly.

To move the heavy machine gun, Chas enlists the aid of **Cemetery Jones**, who is named after his father, the keeper of the Garmouth graveyard. Cemetery has yellow teeth because he never brushes them. He claims the dentist told him they would never rot and he's testing the theory. Another friend is **Audry Parton**. Though she tends to be bossy, she is the only girl that Chas ever talks to. She is also the only girl he knows who always has bandages on her knees. Chas's mother likes her because her family is "posh" and owns a car. Chas and Cem decide to let Audry in on their find.

The downed German gunner is **Rudi Gerlath**. When his plane is shot down, he is lucky to escape with only an ankle injury. He contemplates giving himself up after a few days, but he does not relish the thought of becoming a prisoner. What is even worse, however, is to find himself a prisoner of children. In time, and despite himself, Rudi grows to depend on these English youngsters who are so unlike the swaggering "little pigs of Hitler's youth." When Rudi is finally captured, wounded this time by a bullet, the children ask if they can have permission to write to him.

Nicky is somewhat amazed to find himself the center of attention when the children decide to hide the machine gun in his family's garden. For the first time after the adventure begins, Chas really looks at this boy they call Sicky Nicky. He is a pale, good-looking lad with an operation scar on the side of his neck. Chas thinks that every kid has something strange about him. Chas himself has thick lips, so he doesn't know why people pick on Nicky. For the first time in his young life, Nicky is part of a group. Another minor character is **Boddser Brown**. With his cropped hair and round spectacles, Boddser is a bully and Chas hates him, though mostly because he has a better war souvenir collection. That aside, Chas still considers Boddser to be a stupid arm-twister.

Further Reading

Authors and Artists for Young Adults. Vol. 12. Detroit: Gale Research, 1994.

Berger, Laura Standley, ed. *Twentieth-Century Young Adult Writers.* 1st ed. Detroit: St. James, 1995.

Chevalier, Tracy, ed. *Twentieth-Century Children's Writers.* 3rd ed. Detroit: St. James, 1989.

Contemporary Literary Criticism. Vol. 17. Detroit: Gale Research, 1981.

Estes, Glenn E., ed. *American Writers for Children since 1960: Fiction.* Vol. 52 of *Dictionary of Literary Biography.* Detroit: Gale Research, 1986.

Holtze, Sally Holmes, ed. *Fifth Book of Junior Authors and Illustrators.* New York: H. W. Wilson, 1983.

Newsinger, John. "Futuretracks: The Juvenile Science Fiction of Robert Westall." *Foundations* 63 (1995): 61-67.

Something about the Author. Vols. 23, 69. Detroit: Gale Research, 1981, 1992.

Something about the Author Autobiography Series. Vol. 2. Detroit: Gale Research, 1986.

T. H. White

1906-1963, English novelist

The Once and Future King

(fantasy tetralogy, 1958)

PLOT: In these four books, originally published separately, White retells the legend of King Arthur from the legendary king's boyhood to his death. ***The Sword in the Stone*** (originally published in 1938) is a combination of fantasy, adventure story, and humorous satire that traces Arthur's boyhood, when the future king goes by the name Wart. Wart, a corruption of the name Art, lives in the Castle of the Forest Sauvage with his guardian, Sir Ector, and Ector's son, the often peevish Kay. One day, while lost in the woods, Wart encounters a bumbling knight, King Pellinore, whose crusade is the pursuit of the Questing Beast. Later, he meets a wise but absent-minded magician named Merlyn who volunteers his services as tutor at Sir Ector's castle. Wart is fascinated by Merlyn and his pet owl, Archimedes.

While Kay is busy training to become a knight (a position denied Wart because of his humble birth), Merlyn concentrates on Wart's education. Through a series of physical transformations, Wart gains knowledge and wisdom as he converses with falcons, fish, and a scholarly badger, flies with a flock of geese, and joins an ant colony. With Kay, he helps Robin Hood (who maintains his real name is Robin Wood) and Maid Marion rescue some unfortunates from the hands of the enchantress Morgan le Fay; and, later, he accompanies the king's huntsman, William Twyti, on a boar hunt. The absurdities of chivalry are exposed when Wart witnesses a hilarious jousting tournament between King Pellinore and the equally inept Sir Grummore Grummurson.

After Merlyn's seventh year at the castle, news arrives that the king, Uther Pendragon, is dead and that his successor will be the person who removes the sword Excalibur from a stone in a London churchyard. The family travels to London, where Kay is to fight in his first tournament. Utilizing all the advice and truths taught him by Merlyn, Wart draws out the sword. Sir Ector reveals that Wart is really Uther Pendragon's son, and the crowd proclaims the young man King Arthur.

In ***The Queen of Air and Darkness*** (originally published as *The Witch in the Wood,* 1939) young Arthur's ascendancy is threatened by an alliance of Saxon warriors intent on settling old scores with the deceased Pendragon. Their leader is King Lot of Orkney. While the rebel forces are massing in the plain of Bedegraine, Arthur has a series of conferences with Merlyn before the magician's intended departure. Plans are conceived for Arthur's reign which will bring peace and prosperity to his land. A new breed of knights—the youngest, bravest and most idealistic—are to be brought to Camelot where they will be assured equality and fairness by taking their seats at a round table. Arthur's aim is to insure safety and security for all his subjects in a land where Right will take precedence over Might.

Meanwhile, in King Lot's fiefdom in the Out Isles, his wife, Queen Morgause, and his four young, mischievous sons, Gawaine, Agravaine, Gaheris, and Gareth, cope with his absence. On one adventure the boys use an innocent kitchen maid as bait to capture a unicorn. In spite of protests, the brutal, overly zealous Agravaine kills the beautiful beast, and the boys drag home the head as a souvenir only to be whipped by their unimpressed mother.

Morgause, who, like her sister, Morgan le Fay, is an authority in necromancy and witchcraft, nurtures a special hatred for Arthur. Years ago, her mother, Igraine, was raped by Arthur's father, Uther Pendragon. Arthur was the result of this union. An unexpected diversion in the Out Isles occurs when a ship arrives bearing King Pellinore, Sir Grummore, and a third knight, the Saracen Palomides. Pellinore is suffering a double loss: the absence of the Questing Beast and losing contact with his true love, a princess of Flanders known as Piggy. To soothe Pellinore, Grummore and Palomides build a large costume in the likeness of the Beast, but when they wear it outdoors the real Beast appears and falls madly in love with their creation. Fortunately, Piggy arrives and Pellinore becomes involved in wedding plans.

Through a series of clever strategies and maneuvers, Arthur is victorious against King Lot, who swears allegiance to Arthur, but Morgause still plans her own vengeance. Before Merlyn can tell him that Igraine is his mother and Morgause his sister, she has already used her charms to bewitch and confuse the young monarch. He sleeps with her, and in nine months a son, Mordred, is born. The seeds of Arthur's eventual destruction have been planted.

The Ill-Made Knight (originally published in 1940) introduces the character of Lancelot Dulac. In the castle of Benwick in France, Lancelot, the ugly fifteen-year-old son of King Ban, is undergoing harsh physical training with his mentor, Uncle Dap, so that one day he may join the fabled knights of the Round Table and serve the man he loves, King Arthur. Three years later the young Lancelot leaves for England, where, through his prowess and courage, he gains the title of the greatest knight in Europe. Pure in heart and body, he becomes so distressed over his growing love for Arthur's wife, Queen Guenever, that he leaves the court to pursue a number of seemingly impossible quests, each of which ends in success and glory for Lancelot. On one such quest, he rescues Elaine, the daughter of

King Pellas, from a spell placed on her by Morgan le Fay. Elaine falls in love with Lancelot and, with the help of some alcohol and subterfuge, seduces him. The knight, filled with anger and guilt, refuses to marry this woman he doesn't love and returns to Camelot, where he consummates his love with Guenever. Later, Elaine bears a son she names Galahad, Lancelot's boyhood nickname.

While Arthur is away at war, Guenever and Lancelot continue their affair. But when Arthur returns and Elaine appears with her child, Guenever turns on the hapless knight, forcing him once more into exile. Driven mad with anguish and despair, Lancelot turns feral and roams the countryside until found by King Pellas and nursed back to health by Elaine. Again Lancelot returns to Camelot and resumes the love triangle that once more produces anguish and divided loyalties. In search of salvation, he leaves to seek the Holy Grail. Lancelot is joined by several other knights, including Galahad and the sons of Morgause: Gawaine, Agravaine, Gaheris, and Gareth. Their half-brother Mordred, who has also gravitated to Arthur's court, remains at Camelot. The priggish Galahad succeeds in the quest and dies from ecstasy when he sees the Grail.

During the next years there are changes in the circle around Arthur. Agravaine kills his mother, Morgause, when he finds her with a lover; the families of Pellinore and Morgause engage in a bitter blood feud ended only through Arthur's intervention; and Elaine commits suicide when, after years of hoping, she realizes she will never possess Lancelot, who continues to defend Guenever's honor even though he is a partner in her adulterous affair. Though convinced of his worthlessness and damnation, proof at last comes to Lancelot that he is actually one of the blessed when, through touch alone, he heals the open wounds of a knight who has come to ask for his succor.

White brings the tetralogy to a conclusion in ***The Candle in the Wind*** (first published with the tetralogy in 1958). Driven by intense jealousy and hatred of Arthur, Agravaine and Mordred hatch a plot to make public the affair between Lancelot and Guenever and force Arthur to punish them both by death, as proscribed by law. Agravaine's brothers, Gawaine, Gaheris, and the noble Gareth, refuse to be part of the conspiracy. While Arthur is on a hunting trip, Lancelot steals into Guenever's bedchamber. Soon there is a pounding on the door and, only after killing the thirteen knights that were laying in wait for him, including Agravaine, Lancelot escapes. (The noble knight spares Mordred's life out of a sense of fealty to Arthur.) Guenever is then condemned to death by burning in the castle square. Certain that Lancelot will attempt to free her, Arthur half-heartedly organizes a security guard. Lancelot successfully rescues Guenever, but in the melee the unarmed Gaheris and Gareth are slain.

Lancelot takes Guenever to his castle, Joyous Gard, and Arthur, along with Gawaine, now Lancelot's sworn enemy because of the death of his brothers, lays siege to it. Through the intervention of the clergy, a truce is declared. Guenever returns to Arthur and Lancelot is banished to the continent. Anxious to see justice prevail, Arthur and Gawaine follow Lancelot and lay siege to his castle there. During their absence, Mordred falsely announces the death of Arthur, proclaims himself King of England, and reveals plans to marry the "widow" Guenever. Arthur swiftly returns to England with his army. On the eve of the last and decisive battle, he ponders why his dream of peace and justice never materialized. He asks a young page to remember the glory of Camelot and to tell others about it so that his aspirations will not be forgotten. Before drifting off to sleep, Arthur gets a glimpse of the future: Guenever enters a convent, Lancelot joins a monastery, Mordred is killed in the battle, and Arthur, mortally wounded, is transported to the enchanted land of Avilion from which one day he may return to create another Camelot.

The Book of Merlyn: The Unpublished Conclusion to The Once and Future King *was published posthumously in 1977.*

CHARACTERS: King Arthur, who is called **Wart** as a boy, is a high-spirited, honest person as a youth, reveling in fun and adventure but also respectful and considerate of others. Bright and eager to learn, he is in a precarious social position as a foster son of

Sir Ector, which has taught him both humility and compassion. However, when confronted with a worthy challenge he becomes a bold and fearless crusader in the name of justice. Through Merlyn's tutelage, Arthur is able to curb his childish high spirits and temper them with wisdom and knowledge.

Arthur discovers two aspects of the world of chivalry. From King Pellinore's example, he finds that it can represent a ridiculous, pompous set of conventions that are meaningless and wasteful of time and energy, but from the falcons he discovers a code of courage and honor to which humans should aspire. The ants and geese teach him how different societies are organized and thrive. He learns about the origins of life from a snake and the secret of the relationship between humans and nature from a badger, who also counsels him that the true end of philosophy is "to dig and love your home." Arthur also learns that people should seek to live in peace and harmony with each other and the world around them.

While preparing for the battle of Bedegraine, Arthur has an opportunity to explore intellectually with Merlyn the relationship of Might versus Right and its ramifications for rulers. During this time he solidifies his ideas of creating a benevolent monarchy that is considerate of all its subjects, not just the ruling class. From these discussions, Arthur also develops his sense of mission, and his concepts of knighthood and true chivalry. His conduct during the battle reveals that he is a brilliant tactician and a fearless leader. After victory and the consolidation of his power, Arthur has difficulty teaching chivalry to a seemingly untrainable group of knights who are intent on fighting and killing. He therefore devises the scheme of the search for the Holy Grail as a noble diversion for them, hoping that it will impress on them the need for ideals and a mission in life.

King Arthur, who is described as lacking "malice, vanity, suspicion, cruelty or selfishness," inwardly knows that Guenever is being unfaithful with his most beloved knight, yet he denies this knowledge because of his great love for both his wife and Lancelot. When Mordred makes Arthur choose between his vows regarding justice and this love, the king's sense of duty prevails and, placing the law above his own feelings, he condemns both of them. The last glimpse of Arthur is as a broken, disillusioned old man, who is left to wonder why his high aspirations came to nothing.

Arthur's foster brother, Sir Ector's only son, **Kay**, is two years older than Arthur. Spoiled and indulged by his father and the castle staff, Kay is inclined to petulance and ill humor. He is a poor loser and becomes angry and moody when surpassed by Wart in games. He frequently reminds Wart of his inferior position, orders him around, and often pulls rank to get his own way. Merlyn calls him "a proud and ill-tongued speaker." As he grows older, Kay loses his temper more frequently and challenges nearly everybody to fights in which he is invariably beaten. In spite of these flaws, Kay has several virtues. He is courageous and fearless, though somewhat foolhardy. During his adventures with Robin Hood, he shows that he is a reliable, dauntless fighter willing to take risks and endanger his life for others. The fact that beneath his bravado and bluster there is an insightful, understanding young man is shown when Kay bows before Arthur, acknowledging him as his king after the sword has been taken from the stone. After the coronation, Kay remains a faithful follower.

Kay's father, **Sir Ector**, is the blustering, somewhat ineffective lord of the Castle of the Forest Sauvage. A kindly man, he is generous and benevolent in his treatment of Wart and is good-natured and tolerant of the boys and their whims and misdemeanors. Though he loves his independence, and hates to have his routine disturbed by others, he shows hospitality and charity towards others. Two of his occasional guests are **Sir Grummore Grummurson**, a stuffy, well-meaning noble filled with his own self-importance, and **King Pellinore**, a ludicrous, bungling knight who has spent the past seventeen years pursuing the illusive **Glatisant**, the **Questing Beast**. On his huge white horse and clad in outsized armor, he frequently catches his thick, horn-rimmed spectacles in his visor, loses his balance and falls, or gets tangled in the rope attached to his hound dog. Though Pellinore longs for a feather bed instead of the hard ground, after he accepts Ector's hospitality for a few days the Questing Beast becomes so upset at not being chased that he returns to remind Pellinore of his mission. The antics of Pellinore and Grummurson represent a gentle spoof of the affected, silly protocol connected with medieval chivalry.

In a later episode in the Out Isles, Pellinore and Grummore are joined by a learned Saracen, a man named **Sir Palomides.** It is he who devises the ruse of dressing up in a costume resembling the Questing Beast to dissipate Pellinore's melancholy. Pellinore's malaise is later cured with the arrival of his true love, **Piggy**, the Queen of Flanders' daughter. Described as a stout, middle-aged lady with a red, horselike face, booming voice, and hair coifed in a bun, she is proof that love can be blind.

William Twyti, the king's hunter, is an annual guest of Sir Ector, who tolerates these visits to placate and pay homage to his king, Uther Pendragon. Twyti, a shrivelled, harassed man, dislikes his job of killing wild boars to supply the king's table but fearlessly pursues his occupation with great skill and courage. His tender nature is shown when he openly sobs at the death of one of his hounds.

Wart's teacher is the incredible **Merlyn the Magician**. Though absent minded and sometimes woolly-headed, Merlyn has mastered and commands the collective knowledge and wisdom of the world and skillfully arranges a series of experiences for Wart to further his learning and help him gain insights. Merlyn has a long, white beard and moustaches, wears spectacles, and is clad in a flowing gown covered with the signs of the zodiac and a pointed hat in which birds frequently nest, causing the gown to be spattered with droppings. Merlyn is living time backwards, and he therefore has a perfect knowledge of what will happen in the future. Content to be left to his musings with his owl-assistant **Archimedes**, Merlyn is nevertheless conscientious in his mission to educate Wart. He shows love and tenderness towards his charge but also can be impatient and peevish when Wart fails to grasp concepts and abstractions. Though forgetful and often distracted, Merlyn is Arthur's most staunch ally. Unfortunately, his forgetfulness in not telling Arthur about his mother's identity has profound consequences. Merlyn later falls under the enchantment of a young sorceress, **Nimue**, who keeps him imprisoned in a cave under her spell.

During one his adventures, Wart meets **Robin Hood**, who maintains that his real name is really **Robin Wood**, and **Maid Marion**. Robin is a tall, sinewy fellow of about thirty, dresses in green and is gnarled like the roots of a tree. Marion is a beautiful girl with a waterfall of shining brown hair. Both Robin and Marion impress Wart with their courage, their knowledge of forest lore and weaponry, their skills in strategic planning and fighting, and their devotion to the cause of justice and right.

The wicked enchantress and queen of the fairies, **Morgan le Fay**, is their archenemy. Equipped with knowledge and power that dates back to the ancient Gaels, she rules her kingdom from Castle Chariot. A fat, dowdy, middle-aged woman with black hair and a slight moustache, she represents the power of witchcraft and superstition. Morgan's mother, Igraine, the Queen of Cornwall, had another daughter, **Morgause**, who married Lot, King of Orkney, and settled in the Out Isles, where she bore him four sons. Like her sister Morgan, Morgause is a mistress of the occult arts. A neglectful mother, she prefers magic and flirting with other men over caring for her children, whom she only tolerates and treats as playthings. Eager for revenge because Uther Pendragon raped her mother, Morgause successfully uses her sorcery to disgrace Arthur by bewitching him into committing the ultimate sin of incest. Her unbridled sexual appetite and craving for younger men results in her murder at age seventy by her son Agravaine.

Morgause's four sons are first introduced when they are youngsters, ranging in age from ten to fourteen. The youngest is **Gareth**, an inquisitive, precocious lad who is daring, generous, and has a sensitive nature. A lover of beauty and defender of the weak and powerless, he is disgusted when his brother Agravaine kills a unicorn. As an adult, this likable, trustworthy young man becomes one of Arthur's most beloved knights. Handsome, high-principled, and loyal, Gareth is loved by everyone. Next is **Gaheris**. Stolid, dull, and unimaginative, Gaheris is a born follower. Both Gareth and Gaheris are killed unintentionally by Lancelot during his attempt to rescue Guenever from immolation. The bully of the family is **Agravaine**. Shifty-eyed, "inclined to cry and frightened of pain," he has a good imagination and intellect. However, he loses his temper easily, is inclined to be boastful and defensive, and behaves irresponsibly when provoked. He has an unusually strong, almost unhealthy attachment to his mother. After his father's death, he finds his mother in bed with a young lover, and in a fit of rage and jealousy he kills her. Agravaine becomes one of the malcontents at Camelot and, envious of Lancelot's power and goodness, allies himself with Mordred. Middle-aged and a dissipated drunkard, he rashly plots with Mordred to surprise Lancelot in Guenever's bedchamber. He quarrels fiercely with his brothers because they don't support the scheme and is killed by Lancelot during the brawl. The oldest brother is **Gawaine**, a high-spirited lad of sound ideals and insights. He feels shame and indignation when Agravaine senselessly kills the beautiful, defenseless unicorn. Gawaine is proud of his heritage and fiercely loyal to his family. An independent person, he is a fine leader who longs to avenge his grandmother Igraine's rape and save the family honor. Later, when he becomes a knight at Camelot, this brawny, red-haired warrior often causes problems because of his impulsive, rash behavior, but he always remains loyal to Arthur. He turns against Lancelot when the knight inadvertently kills Gareth and Gaheris, but later absolves him when Lancelot pleads for forgiveness. Gawaine is killed serving his king in the first battle against Mordred.

Arthur's favorite knight is the melancholy, self-doubting **Lancelot Dulac**, son of King Ban of Benwick, one of Arthur's supporters at Bedegraine. In love with Arthur and passionately wanting to please him and be part of his entourage, Lancelot endures spartan training until he is eighteen, when he feels confident enough to venture forth and swear allegiance to Arthur. A fearless fighter and expert warrior, he soon becomes invincible in all forms of combat. His strength and fortitude are matched by his capacity for mercy and forgiveness. He refrains from killing his opponents, even though he knows many deserve death. Lancelot is a sullen, moody person obsessed with pleasing and being worthy of Arthur. From early childhood, Lancelot has mistakenly felt inferior, believing that he has serious flaws and is somehow incomplete. For this reason he calls himself Chevalier Mal Fet, or the Ill-Made Knight. Though he is the best knight in the world, he can't believe he is good or respectable. When he realizes that he loves Guenever, his shame and self-loathing increase. The conflict between his firm Christian beliefs in duty and truth and this secret passion produce a turmoil that leads to a mental breakdown.

Lancelot's sensitive, impressionable nature stands in sharp contrast to his physical features. With an ape-like, twisted face, protruding ears, and large body, he is repugnant to others until they recognize his inner beauty and purity. Obsessed with the concepts of chastity and goodness and believing in a vengeful God, Lancelot continually feels unhealthy and unclean. Even his many honorable quests and innumerable good deeds fail to assuage his debilitating sense of shame and lack of confidence. However, when he is the only knight that is able to heal the unhealed wounds of a sick knight, he at last believes that he is accepted by God and forgiven for his sins. Lancelot's loyalty and steadfastness begin to unravel when his adulterous affair is made public. Forced to fight the king he served and adored, his lofty ideals and scruples are tested. Weighed down by his feelings of being both inadequate and immoral, he retreats to a monastery.

Lancelot's mentor is the strict but fair **Uncle Dap**. Dap's real name is **Gwenenbors**, and he is a genuine maestro of the art of chivalry. An expert in all forms and variations of armor, combat, and gallantly, he is also the only person at court who takes his nephew seriously. They form an unbeatable combination. With his long, white moustaches, extravagant gestures, and wagging eyebrows, Uncle Dap presents a passionate exterior that fills the young boy with excitement and intensity. He demonstrates a genuine love and concern for his solitary, troubled charge and accompanies him to the court of King Arthur, where he continues to give advice and guidance.

Lancelot is loved by the naive, obtuse **Elaine**, daughter of King Pellas, whom he saves from the spell of Morgan le Fay. Not clever and lacking social skills, Elaine, who does not realize Lancelot already loves Guenever, hopes that her simple virtues of compassion and tenderness will win him over. When she tricks Lancelot into losing his chastity, he feels unclean and rejects her. Elaine believes that her patience, faith, and restraint will eventually prevail, even though Lancelot has given her no hope of a lasting union. After years of waiting, she becomes so disillusioned and disheartened that, unable to face a future of loneliness and rejection, she commits suicide, adding to Lancelot's guilt.

Lancelot and Elaine's son is **Galahad**. Raised by his mother, he has grown into a pious, priggish individual, so self-satisfied with his sanctimonious way of life that he is rude, distant, and disliked by all. Totally without manners, he exhibits insufferable self-confidence and otherworldliness. A vegetarian and teetotaller, his piety and spirituality are eventually rewarded: he is the only knight to defeat Lancelot in a tournament and, later, is granted the honor of seeing the Holy Grail. He is overcome by this experience and dies.

The object of love of both Lancelot and Arthur is the enigmatic **Guenever**, who is known affectionately as **Jenny**. She is described as having "hair so black that it was startling, and her blue eyes, deep and clear, had a sort of fearlessness which was startling too." Unlike Lancelot, Guenever does not feel the pangs of guilt that wrack her lover about their illicit affair. She feels that it is perfectly natural to love two men at the same time. Her love for Arthur is absolute and undisputed. She is faithful (in her fashion), dependable, and supportive. Always helpful and understanding, she is characterized as a loyal, dedicated wife and inspiring companion. Although her love for Lancelot is more glamorous because of the secrecy and intrigue that surrounds it, she also genuinely loves Lancelot in spite of his gargoyle-like looks. When deprived of his presence, she becomes jealous, cruel, and unreasonable, and she is scornful of his quest for the Grail. When crossed, she has extreme mood swings that make her difficult to live with. But when she is satisfied by the companionship of her two men, she is renowned for her courage, honesty, generosity, and sympathy. Part of Guenever's flouting of conventions is caused by the disappointment and bitterness she feels at not giving Arthur the heir he wants. When her infidelity is discovered, Guenever accepts her lot stoically. Clear-headed and intelligent, she faces the future realistically. When the world of Camelot ends, she retreats to a convent with her memories.

Arthur's son from an incestuous affair with Morgause is **Mordred**. Rejected by his father, who actively tried to have him killed while he was still a baby, Mordred is driven by anger and a desire for revenge. People think of him as "a cold wimp of a man." He presents an unusual physical picture: "a thin wisp of a fellow, so fair-haired that he was almost an albino; his bright eyes were so blue that you could see into them. The colour had been washed out of him it seemed." One of his shoulders is higher than the other, giving Mordred the appearance of a hunchback, and so he wears exaggerated, gaudy clothes to hide his this flaw. Inwardly, Mordred is barbarous, cunning, and defiant, willing to sacrifice close members of his family to achieve his ends. Remorseless and without pity, he uses people shamelessly but, in spite of his weak body, exhibits a strange type of courage and defiance based on desperation and malevolence. Shrewd and crafty, he carefully plots each of his villainous maneuvers and uses his persuasive, forceful way with words to secure confederates, like Agravaine, to commit violent acts and even murder in the name of justice. Mordred's ultimate goal is to cause the death of Arthur and secure the throne he believes is rightfully his. Goodness triumphs when he is killed in battle before ascending the throne.

Further Reading

Berger, Laura Standley, ed. *Twentieth-Century Children's Writers.* 4th ed. Detroit: St. James, 1994.

Contemporary Literary Criticism. Vol. 30. Detroit: Gale Research, 1984.

Crane, John Kenny. *T. H. White.* New York: Twayne, 1974.

Hettinga, Donald R., and Gary D. Schmidt, eds. *British Children's Writers, 1914-1960.* Vol. 160 of *Dictionary of Literary Biography.* Detroit: Gale Research, 1996.

Kellman, Martin. *T. H. White and the Matter of Britain: A Literary Overview.* Lewiston, NY: Edwin Mellen, 1988.

Something about the Author. Vol. 12. Detroit: Gale Research, 1977.

Warner, Sylvia Townsend. *T. H. White.* New York: Viking, 1967.

White, T. H. *Letters to a Friend.* New York: Putnam, 1982.

Patricia C. Wrede

1953-, American novelist

Dealing with Dragons

(fantasy, 1990)

PLOT: Cimerone, seventh and youngest princess of the king and queen of Linderwall, is not at all what her parents expect a princess to be. She is too tall, her hair is not golden, she is very strong-willed, and she hates embroidery, dancing, and etiquette lessons. Cimerone was quite interested in fencing, however, until her parents found out and were shocked at this improper behavior. Fated to marry Prince Therandil, Cimerone is not at all happy with the prospect and wants to find her Prince Charming on her own.

Taking some advice from a well-intentioned frog, Cimerone leaves her idyllic kingdom and finds herself in the home of some dragons. Although they first debate about whether or not to eat her, more logical heads prevail and Cimerone takes a position as princess to a powerful, fascinating, and very exacting dragon named Kazul. Kazul is quite fond of cherries jubilee, a dish that happens to be a specialty of Cimerone's. But almost as soon as Cimerone has settled down to her new life, princes, including Therandil, begin to arrive with the earnest intent of rescuing her. Cimerone, of course, doesn't want to be rescued and has a hard time getting rid of her would-be saviors, especially Therandil, who returns repeatedly until he becomes a complete nuisance. Besides the pesky prince, Cimerone is visited by some other princesses, such as Princess Keredwel of Raxwel, Princess Hallanna of Poranbuth, and Princess Alianora of the Duchy of Toure-on-Marsh. They are all captive princesses and behave quite differently than Cimerone. They can't believe that Cimerone actually volunteered for the job of dragon's princess.

Before long, Cimerone learns that life is not exactly idyllic with the dragons either, for some very oily and disreputable wizards, especially one called Zemenar, are out to thwart the naming of a new king of the dragons. Kazul explains that the dragons use the Colin's Stone to name a new king. The dragon who is able to move this small but magical stone to the Vanishing Mountain will be the next king. Cimerone uncovers some evidence that in the end proves that the dragon Woraug was consorting with the evil wizards to make himself the next dragon king. With the help of the great witch Morwen, Cimerone and Kazul save the day and Kazul is pronounced the new king. Although this makes Cimerone happy, she is worried about her own position. Surely, she thinks, the new king of the dragons doesn't need a princess. But Kazul, who is actually a female dragon, convinces Cimerone she does need her—especially for making her delightful cherries jubilee.

CHARACTERS: Cimerone does not seem cut out for the life of a princess in an idyllic kingdom. All her sisters are blonde and beautiful, while she is dark-haired, tall, and rather ungainly. Life is just unbearably dull in the kingdom as far as Cimerone is concerned. She hates her lessons in dancing, embroidery, and etiquette, preferring fencing, magic, cooking, and economics. But none of these activities, according to her very proper parents, are suitable for a princess. Life takes an unexpected turn for Cimerone, however, when she meets Kazul, a female dragon who is not only powerful, but fascinating to be with. Cimerone finds that she actually likes polishing swords and making cherries jubilee for Kazul, as well as reading Latin scrolls and organizing the dragon's rather messy library. After discouraging the persistent Therandil, whom Cimerone finds too boring, and all the other knights who come to her "rescue," she helps thwart the evil wizards who want to disrupt the selection of a new dragon king, and helps place Kazul on the throne.

Kazul is a powerful, no-nonsense sort of dragon with grey-green scales and three horns on her head. Startled when she learns that Cimerone is much smarter than the typical bubble-headed princesses she has encountered before, Kazul ignores the other dragons' suggestion that they eat the girl. Instead, Kazul hires her to be the dragon's princess, especially because Cimerone can make cherries jubilee and conjugate Latin verbs. Kazul, being rather lazy, also wants Cimerone to catalog her library. Later, when Kazul has been installed as King of the Dragons (gender has no bearing on the title in this case), she declares that she still will always need Cimerone's services, much to the princess's delight.

Morwen the witch is a long-time friend of Kazul's. She becomes Cimerone's friend almost immediately when she offers the distraught princess some advice on how to get rid of all the princes who keep showing up to rescue her. For example, Morwen suggests putting up signs that say "Road Washed Out" or "Alternate Route." But Morwen proves even more helpful when she aids Kazul and Cimerone by uncovering the diabolical plot of the evil wizards to make Woraug king instead of Kazul.

The three princesses who are also captives among the dragons serve as contrasts to the unconventional Cimerone. **Princess Keredwel** of the Kingdom of Raxwel, who wears a gold crown, is the captive of the dragon Gornul. When Cimerone asks why she doesn't try to escape, Keredwell is shocked, replying that a princess simply doesn't escape, she must be rescued. **Princess Hallanna** of the Kingdom of Poranbuth is held captive by the dragon Zareth and wears a silver crown. She is afraid to run away from her dragon because she might be eaten by a troll or other beast. Her simpering cowardice only disgusts Cimerone. **Princess Alianora** comes from the Duchy of Toure-on-Marsh, wears a pearl circlet, and is the captive of the dreaded dragon, Woraug, who later schemes to become king.

The wizard **Zemenar** is an evil sort. A tall man, he has a hard, bright look to his eyes, and although he is not old, he has a grey beard that hangs nearly down to his waist. Cimerone decides on their first meeting that she does not like him. Her instinct proves correct when Zemenar's plot against Kazul is revealed.

Further Reading

Berger, Laura Standley, ed. *Twentieth-Century Young Adult Writers.* 1st ed. Detroit: St. James, 1994.

Collier, Laurie. *Authors and Artists for Young Adults.* Vol. 8. Detroit: Gale Research, 1992.

Something about the Author. Vol. 67. Detroit: Gale Research, 1992.

Richard Wright

1908-1960, American novelist

Black Boy: A Record of Childhood and Youth

(autobiography, 1937)

PLOT: This chronicle of the author's early life begins with remembrances from when he is four years old and ends when he leaves the South to seek his fortune in Chicago at age nineteen. Richard's early life is one of brutal beatings, starvation, and deprivation. Two of his most vivid early memories involve an experiment with fire that almost destroyed the family shack and the time he hanged a stray kitten out of spite and frustration. After the family moves to Memphis, Richard's father abandons them, and his mother becomes a cook to support herself, Richard, and his younger brother. Later they move to Arkansas to live with Aunt Maggie and Uncle Hoskins, a saloon owner. But after Uncle Hoskins is murdered by whites who resent his modest prosperity, they move again.

When a series of paralyzing strokes incapacitates Mama, she and her two boys are forced to live with neurotic, fanatical Granny, a Seventh Day Adventist, Grandpa, a reclusive Civil War veteran, and other hostile relatives in Jackson, Mississippi. Here, Richard again endures hunger, beatings, and hardship. His younger brother is sent to live with Aunt Maggie in the North, and Richard is temporarily housed with Uncle Clark and Aunt Jody in a nearby town. However, his fear of sleeping alone in a room where a boy his age has just died produces such trauma that he returns to his granny's, where Mama remains bedridden. He is sent to a religious school taught by another relative, Aunt Addie, who also lives at home. Her deranged behavior leads to more confrontations, and Richard moves to a public school. In spite of Granny's hysterical protests about employment on Saturday, her Sabbath, Richard works a series of menial jobs for white folks and for the first time experiences the degradation of racism, being treated like a subhuman creature incapable of feeling or intelligent thought. With the help of Griggs, a friend, he sells newspapers and later secures a job with Mr. Crane, an optician. Here, two white workers, Pease and Reynolds, force him to resign due to their racial hatred. Further problems arise at home when Grandpa dies. More relatives, including his overbearing Uncle Tom, move in to help with expenses.

Through all this hardship, Richard matures and gains self-knowledge. In the eighth grade he publishes his first story in a local black newspaper. By both legal and illegal means, he saves enough money to move alone to Memphis, the first stop on his way north. On Beale Street, he rents a room from Mrs. Moss, who is anxious to have this attractive seventeen-year-old marry her daughter, Bess. Richard gets a job in another optometrist's lab, and there, through a series of duplicitous machinations, a white worker, Mr. Olin, conspires to make Richard believe that another black worker, Harrison, plans to kill him. Realizing the manipulative nature of Mr. Olin's deception, the two boys are forced to punch and slug one another to satisfy their white co-worker's sadism and prejudice. Richard begins an active campaign of self-improvement after he persuades Mr. Falk, another white co-worker, to allow him the use of his library card, a privilege denied blacks. He also enjoys the company of many black friends, including the elevator operator, Shorty. Soon, his mother, brother, and Aunt Maggie join him in Memphis, and the family plans to move farther north, with Richard and Aunt Maggie leaving first. As he boards the train, Richard hopes that he will find a new life of freedom and opportunity in Chicago.

CHARACTERS: In spite of the unbelievable hardships and ordeals he describes, **Richard Wright** emerges as a dignified, admirable young man whose inner strength and integrity triumph over unending adversity. Though forced to live under humiliating physical and mental conditions, he never compromises his fierce honesty and his fight for justice. He stands up for his own rights and those of others, even though his principles might alienate his family or endanger his life. Intelligent, adventurous, and sensitive, he is curious to learn and anxious to succeed. Richard makes sacrifices to gain advantages and, in spite of rejection and indifference from his family and others, continues to believe in himself and his potential. Sublimating his true feelings in front of whites fills him with self-loathing, and he vows to regain his dignity. His relationship with his mother shows him to be a compassionate and forgiving man, and he agonizes over the times when his need for honesty and truth results in hurt feelings. Even though his own well-being and safety may be in peril, he continually refuses to abandon his belief in fairness and decency. This stubborn adherence to principles sometimes produces feelings of alienation and loneliness, but Richard refuses to compromise his ethical convictions. Though young and vulnerable, he resists indulging in self-pity and, in spite of temptation, he maintains his sense of honor and self-respect. Richard's story illustrates both triumph over a bleak environment and the salvation of a creative, independent mind.

Richard's mother, **Mrs. Wright (Mama)**, is outwardly a cruel, harsh martinet, who rigidly believes in the value of corporal punishment. For the slightest error in action or speech, she beats Richard unmercifully. Many of these violent episodes, however, teach Richard street survival skills and protect him from evil influences. She is a right-minded, religious woman who has been so brutalized by adversity that, in time, she has become the oppressor. Abandoned by her husband and forced to work slavishly to feed her family, she becomes less threatening with age, particularly when stricken with a debilitating illness. As he matures, Richard views his mother as a pathetic figure and tries to help her. Richard's unnamed brother is both younger and more docile than Richard. He is a tolerant, obedient child who is accepted more readily by family members, including Aunt Maggie, who adopts him and takes him north.

Mr. Wright, Richard's father, is a shadowy stranger who deserts his family when Richard is still a child. A night porter in a drugstore, he is portrayed as a harsh, selfish, bloated man who brutalizes his children and, though faced with legal action in court, refuses to provide child support. (When Richard is thirty, he sees him again. His father has become a defeated man, a gnarled, toothless sharecropper, far from the menacing man Richard knew as a child.)

Richard's **Granny** is a religious fanatic obsessed with ferreting out and destroying the devil's work. Her religion is not based on love but rather centers on hatred, repression, and fear. She frequently initiates all-night prayer sessions, and, through her intimidating tactics, forces Richard into a pretence of worship. She is a cruel, spiteful woman, who also brutally beats Richard and slaps him for the slightest—often imagined—offense. A forceful, domineering woman, she has instilled the same vicious and spiteful attitudes in her children, particularly **Aunt Addie**, the church's secretary and day-school teacher. Aunt Addie demands slavish obedience from Richard, both at home and at school, and, at the slightest provocation, engages in screaming tirades and physical violence. When she unjustly accuses the boy of a minor transgression, he stands up for his rights and, in a tense confrontational scene in which she tries to thrash him, Richard threatens her with a knife. An uneasy truce results, and afterwards she and Richard rarely speak. **Uncle Tom** is another hate-filled member of the household. After he accuses Richard of a minor slight, the innocent boy refuses his beating and again draws a knife to save himself. Uncle Tom's increasing hatred now consumes him, and he systematically turns other members of the household against Richard.

When Richard's mama becomes ill, **Uncle Clark**, a contracting carpenter, and his wife, **Aunt Jody**, a reserved, stern woman, offer him a home. Though well-intentioned, their rigid manners and inability to understand Richard's fears and insecurities lead to a crisis, and the boy returns to Granny's home. Richard's most sympathetic relative is **Aunt Maggie**, who is married to **Uncle Hoskins**, a successful saloon owner who is murdered by jealous white neighbors. Maggie is a spunky, courageous woman who is able to survive tragedy and move forward. She often exhibits kindness and generosity toward the impoverished Wright family, including giving Richard's brother a home.

Richard's **Grandpa** is an ancient Civil War veteran—a tall, skinny, silent man who keeps to himself, although at one time he too was a strict disciplinarian and child-beater. Through a bureaucratic error or perhaps governmental retribution for his participation in the struggle for voting rights for blacks, he has been denied his pension, resulting in perpetual poverty for his family.

In Memphis, Richard rooms with **Mrs. Moss**, a trusting, ebullient, kindly woman who shamelessly tries to match Richard up with her not-too-bright, sex-crazed daughter, **Ella**. When Richard politely declines the repeated offer and retreats nightly to his room, relations cool between the Mosses and their boarder.

One of Richard's many black friends in his office building is **Shorty**, the yellow, fat elevator operator. Like Richard's friend **Griggs** in Jackson, Shorty has learned to play the white man's game by debasing himself and acting the part of the jovial, dumb, and always subservient "nigger." Filled with a consuming hatred for the despicable whites who humiliate him, he justifies his servile actions for economic reasons, stating that "my ass is tough and quarters is scarce."

The whites Richard encounters are less than admirable. **Mr. Crane**, a seemingly understanding employer, lacks the backbone to counter the prejudice of his two workers, **Mr. Pease** and **Mr. Reynolds**, when they lie to teach "that uppity nigger" Richard a lesson, forcing his resignation. **Mr. Olin**, a malicious worker at Richard's other job in optometry, sadistically delights in promoting unwarranted hatred between Richard and another black youth, **Harrison**, so that he can instigate and witness a violent fight. Fearful of the consequences if they don't cooperate, the two are forced to fight tenaciously to satisfy the white man's blood lust. Timid and fearful **Mr. Falk**, another co-worker, makes one kindly gesture toward Richard. With trepidation, he allows the young man to use his library card, though he is terrified that his "transgression" will be discovered.

Native Son

(novel, 1940)

PLOT: In the late 1930s, a twenty-year-old black man, Bigger Thomas, is living with his mother and younger brother and sister, Buddy and Vera, in a squalid one-room apartment in a Chicago South Side black ghetto. Already saddled with a police record and having spent time in a reform school, Bigger continues his helpless, hopeless existence, often hanging out with friends Gus, G. H., and Jack at Doc's local pool hall. Under Bigger's direction, the four friends plan a robbery that is later aborted because of Bigger's violent behavior toward Gus, whom he accuses of cowardice. In reality, his attack on Gus masks Bigger's own fears. At his mother's insistence, Bigger follows a job lead from a relief agency and becomes a chauffeur for the Daltons, a wealthy, liberal white family. On his first evening working, he secretly escorts their twenty-three-year-old daughter, Mary, to a meeting of the Labor Defenders, a Communist-front organization to which she belongs despite the objections of her parents.

Afterwards, he spends an uncomfortable interval driving around and drinking with Mary and her boyfriend, Jan Erlone, both of whom are believers in social equality and try to befriend the suspicious Bigger. Mary gets drunk, and Bigger is forced to carry her to her bedroom. When Mrs. Dalton, who is blind, enters the room, he fears detection and, to prevent Mary from crying out and revealing his presence, places a pillow over her face. After Mrs. Dalton leaves, Bigger discovers that Mary has suffocated. Panicking, he cremates the body in the basement furnace, cutting off the head to make all the parts fit. Under questioning, he places the blame for Mary's disappearance on Jan and the Communists.

The Daltons hire an investigator named Britten, but Bigger, emboldened by the apparent success of his lies, concocts a kidnapping story to collect ransom money. Bigger's girlfriend and mistress, Bessie Mears, cooperates with his plan only because of her love for him. While newspapermen are present in the Dalton's basement, human bones and an earring are unexpectedly recovered from ashes in the furnace. Bigger flees, hiding in a deserted building with Bessie. Realizing that she will hinder his escape, he murders her in desperation and throws her body down an elevator shaft. He is eventually captured after a chase across the rooftops of other derelict buildings.

A forgiving Jan later visits him in jail to introduce him to Boris A. Max, a Communist lawyer from the Labor Defenders Office, who has agreed to defend Bigger without charge. Max is a wise, understanding man who maintains that social attitudes have contributed to Bigger's guilt. The state's attorney, David A. Buckley, is a racist who knows that a conviction will improve his chances for re-election. Under Max's guidance, Bigger pleads guilty, and Buckley, fearful of an insanity plea, presents a parade of witnesses to prove that Bigger was aware of his actions and their consequences. In turn, Max's defense is an indictment of a society that permits and even encourages the dehumanization of blacks and forces them to strike out senselessly for survival. Despite Max's eloquence, the court sentences Bigger to death. Before facing the electric chair, Bigger has many conversations with Max, during which he begins to know himself and better understand his motivations. He reaches the point where he can forgive his enemies because they are unaware of their own crimes of social injustice. He faces death with dignity and acceptance.

CHARACTERS: Although told in the third person, the novel is seen entirely through the perspective of **Bigger Thomas**, a complex young black man who deeply resents the opportunities denied him by a society that judges his worth solely on the color of his skin. About whites, Bigger says, "They don't let us do nothing," and "They kill you before you die." Inwardly, he seethes with anger, yet outwardly he must adopt a subservient, compliant attitude in the presence of whites. Physically attractive and graceful, Bigger has a muscular body and a very dark complexion. Poverty and the death of his father have forced him to leave school after the eighth grade when his family moved north from Mississippi. As a young adult, three basic emotions dominate Bigger's life: anger, fear, and shame. His socially-instilled sense of worthlessness often produces bouts of violently uncontrollable anger and rage. This destructive impulse is demonstrated in his vicious assault on his friend Gus while planning the robbery. Aggression toward others also hides his basic fear and despair about the life of crime that seems to be the ultimate destination of his debilitating environment. His inability to help himself and his family, plus the sense of inferiority instilled into blacks by whites, have produced a sense of shame and resentment that he directs toward himself, his family, and his race.

Bigger's bitterness about white privilege and his disillusionment over the graft and corruption around him leads him to search for any escape possible, including retreats into the magical world of movies and occasional fantasies about a utopian future. Although he commits horrifying crimes, he is not sadistic or intentionally cruel; he simply lacks positive influences and an understanding of acceptable solutions. Confusion forces him to resort to the only retaliation he knows—violence. In a rare insight, he confesses to Max that killing Mary Dalton produced a relief of tension, a feeling of release and a sense of equality. Through his growing respect and affection for Max, Bigger is able, for the first time, to articulate his feelings and gain self-understanding. With this new knowledge comes an awareness of emotions that his corrosive environment have suppressed, such as love and compassion for others. He begins to love his family anew and to show charity toward his persecutors. He realizes that they, too, are living lives of fear. With this insight, Bigger at last finds a meaning to his life and his death.

Bigger's mother, **Mrs. Thomas**, loves her family and, in spite of a life of hardship and drudgery, still maintains hope for their future. Though tired, discouraged, and without a husband to help her, she maintains an unshakable religious faith and a belief in common decencies, such as having her boys turn their heads when she and Vera are dressing. She nags her children, not out of irritation or displeasure, but rather from a desire for them to advance socially and seek higher goals. She is old-fashioned in her acceptance of the inferior position of blacks in society, leading to the moving scene in which she grovels shamelessly in front of the Daltons to plead for Bigger's life. In essence, Mrs. Thomas represents the humble, self-sacrificing, accepting black mother whose faith and love of family are the only things that sustain her.

Bigger's young sister, **Vera Thomas**, is a somewhat timid adolescent who helps her mother, loves her brothers, and hopes eventually to advance within the existing social structure through hard work and honesty. Principled and believing in the importance of proper manners, witnessing her brother's ordeals tests Vera's convictions. **Buddy Thomas**, Bigger's young brother, is more aggressive than his sister. He adores his older brother and is fiercely loyal to him. His character is still developing and malleable, raising the question of whether or not he will learn from his brother's death.

Bessie Mears, Bigger's girlfriend, is a pathetic product of a racist society. She works long hours—seven days a week in a white family's kitchen—and hopes that marriage to Bigger will bring her some security and relief from this drudgery. She drinks too much and trusts blindly in Bigger, hoping that through his love she can achieve some fulfillment in life. Ironically, the man she regards as her savior becomes her killer.

Henry Dalton, a multimillionaire, symbolizes the well-intentioned white crusader who, in spite of noble aims and altruistic motives, does not really wish to change society but simply to supply some benevolent therapy. He has given five million dollars to help black causes, yet still practices the discriminatory policies in his real estate company that produce racial segregation, exploitation, and inequality. In spite of his short-sightedness, he is basically a kind man whose conscience, good breeding, and wealth have led him to adopt a paternalistic and somewhat condescending racial attitude. His wife, **Mrs. Dalton**, shares her husband's opinions about blacks. A former schoolteacher who has been blind for ten years, her ghostly white face and hair inspires a certain fear in Bigger. Like Mama Thomas, she is religious and accepting, though somewhat more rigid and aloof. Charitable toward blacks, she, like her husband, displays no real understanding of their problems. (For example, she addresses Bigger as "boy.") Both Mr. and Mrs. Dalton adore their daughter and, though devastated by her death, maintain their composure and dignity. **Mary Dalton** is an attractive twenty-three-year-old, who is rebelling against parental authority by adopting unconventional, defiant behavior, including excessive drinking and flirting with communism. She is well-intentioned but undisciplined and naive. Though she accuses her parents of insensitivity and misconceptions concerning blacks, she often displays these same attitudes herself.

Jan Erlone, Mary's boyfriend, is a highly principled, idealistic worker for the Communist Party. A good-looking blonde man with a gentle manner and pleasant disposition, he believes in the innate goodness of people and detests racial prejudice. Though framed by Bigger, he is compassionate, forgiving, and helpful. This absence of hatred and anger help convert Bigger's belligerence into trust and ultimately love. Jan demonstrates his unselfish dedication to Bigger by enlisting the aid of **Boris A. Max**, the tall, silver-haired Jewish lawyer. Max, a prominent Communist, agrees to defend Bigger without remuneration. Through his uncanny insight into human emotions, Max breaks down Bigger's distrust and helps the young man understand his true feelings. Max is a master lawyer, brilliantly eloquent, and confident in his strategies and maneuvers. He is sickened by the intolerance, greed, and inhumanity that have led to the cruel social conditions that have permeated all aspects of Bigger Thomas's life. He genuinely believes that love and understanding can eradicate hate and violence. His insight and empathy produce in Bigger a belief in himself and instill in him the courage to face his death.

Max's courtroom adversary is the state's attorney **David A. Buckley**, an evil opportunist who takes advantage of human fears and prejudices. He resorts to intimidation and racial insults to wrest a confession from Bigger and uses bombast, phony piety, and racial anxieties to gain a conviction. This despicable, unprincipled man also exploits the Bigger Thomas case to insure his reelection to public office.

Minor characters include Bigger's three friends—**Gus, G. H.**, and **Jack**—and the private investigator, **Britten**. Bigger's friends have turned to petty crime but lack Bigger's determination and motivation. Gus is more practical and accepting of social conditions than Bigger. His unusual insight into Bigger's fears makes Bigger feel so uncomfortable and vulnerable that he strikes out against this dear friend. Hired by the Daltons, Britten exhibits contempt for blacks and employs the same harassing and domineering approach as Buckley.

Further Reading

Abcarian, Richard. *Richard Wright's Native Son: A Critical Handbook.* Belmont: Wadsworth, 1970.

Bakish, David. *Richard Wright.* New York: Ungar, 1978.

Baldwin, James. *Notes of a Native Son.* Boston: Beacon, 1955.

Bloom, Harold. *Bigger Thomas.* New York: Chelsea House, 1990.

———. *Richard Wright.* New York: Chelsea House, 1987.

———. *Richard Wright's Native Son.* New York: Chelsea House, 1988.

———. *Twentieth-Century American Literature.* Vol. 6 of *The Chelsea House Library of Literary Criticism.* New York: Chelsea House, 1987.

Brignano, Russell C. *Richard Wright: An Introduction to the Man and His Works.* Pittsburgh: University of Pittsburgh, 1970.

Contemporary Literary Criticism. Vols. 1, 3, 4, 9, 14, 21, 48. Detroit: Gale Research, 1973, 1975, 1975, 1978, 1980, 1982, 1988.

Critical Survey of Long Fiction. Vol. 7. Englewood Cliffs, NJ: Salem, 1983.

Fabre, Michel. *The World of Richard Wright.* Jackson: University of Mississippi, 1985.

Felgar, Robert. *Richard Wright.* New York: Macmillan, 1980.

Gates, Henry L., and K. A. Appiah. *Richard Wright: Critical Perspectives Past and Present.* Washington, DC: Amistad, 1993.

Gayle, Addison. *Richard Wright: Ordeal of a Native Son.* Magnolia, MS: Peter Smith, 1983.

Harris, Trudier, ed. *Afro-American Writers, 1940-1955.* Vol. 76 of *Dictionary of Literary Biography.* Detroit: Gale Research, 1988.

Howe, Irving. *A World More Attractive.* New York: Horizon, 1963.

Kinnamon, Keneth, and Michel Fabre, eds. *Conversations with Richard Wright.* Jackson: University Press of Mississippi, 1993.

———. *New Essays on "Native Son."* New York: Cambridge, 1990.

Margolies, Edward. *Native Sons: A Critical Study of Twentieth-Century Negro American Authors.* New York: Lippincott, 1968.

Rampersad, Arnold, ed. *Richard Wright: A Collection of Critical Essays.* Englewood Cliffs, NJ: Prentice-Hall, 1994.

Ray, David, and Robert M. Farnsworth, eds. *Richard Wright: Impressions and Perspectives.* Ann Arbor: University of Michigan, 1973.

Smith, Valerie. *African American Writers.* New York: Scribner's, 1991.

Urban, Joan. *Richard Wright.* New York: Chelsea House, 1989.

Van Antwerp, Margaret A., ed. *Dictionary of Literary Biography Documentary Series.* Vol. 2. Detroit: Gale Research, 1982.

Laurence Yep

1948-, American novelist

Dragonwings

(historical novel, 1975)

PLOT: Based on an actual incident in which a Chinese immigrant constructed a flying machine and flew it on September 22, 1909, this novel recreates a fascinating period in San Francisco history (from 1903 to 1910), as well as describing the customs and culture of early Chinese Americans. Moon Shadow Lee is only eight when he leaves his mother and grandmother in China to join his father, Windrider, whom he has never known. Moon Shadow's escort to San Francisco is Hand Clap, part owner of the laundry where Windrider works. In America, the boy meets Lefty, a laundry worker, and the other owners, White Deer, a master chef, and Uncle Bright Star whose son, Black Dog, is a vicious opium addict.

After Black Dog robs and beats Moon Shadow, Windrider seeks revenge. In the ensuing fight, a man is killed and, fearing reprisals, father and son flee the Tang community (Chinatown) to seeks their fortune with the white people, whom the Chinese call "demons." They live in a stable behind kindly Miss Whitlaw's boarding house. Windrider becomes a janitor and general repair man and Moon Shadow his helper and housekeeper. All of Windrider's spare time is spent building and flying gliders, models for the full-scale plane he plans to build. Meanwhile, Miss Whitlaw and her young niece, Robin, teach Moon Shadow English and help him write a letter to the Wright brothers who, in time, send plans to help Windrider construct his own flying machine.

During the earthquake of 1906, both the boarding house and the laundry are destroyed. Windrider and Moon Shadow help save victims from the wreckage. Windrider then decides to devote his life to building an airplane, *Dragonwings,* to fulfill a vision he once had in which the Dragon King granted him wings. After three years of obsessive work, he takes his plane on its maiden flight. In a triumph of spirit and determination, Windrider flies his creation over the hills of San Francisco for several minutes before crashing. Fortunately, he escapes with only a broken arm. His brief success is enough, however, and, having achieved his dream, Windrider resolves to devote the rest of his life to his family. He accepts a partnership in the laundry and the next summer goes to China to bring back Moon Shadow's mother.

CHARACTERS: The novel describes the eventful years in the life of narrator **Moon Shadow Lee** as he ages from a boy of eight to a young man of fifteen. Even as a child, Moon Shadow reveals a strong, independent nature that enables him to sustain hardship and affliction with courage and incredible endurance. He is a spunky youngster who is not afraid to speak out for fairness and honesty. Though by nature a gentle, sensitive boy who avoids violence, when necessary Moon Shadow is prepared to fight for his rights, showing great courage in a confrontation with a neighborhood bully and in trying to fight off Black Dog's attacks. In his relations with others, Moon Shadow reveals a compassionate, understanding temperament. For example, he is unfailingly loving and courteous towards the "demoness" Miss Whitlaw and responds to her every act of kindness. He is also unselfish and generous, always willing to share his few possessions with others. Moon Shadow often shows unusual inventiveness and ingenuity, as when, for example, he decides to contact the Wright brothers for help in building an aeroplane. Moon Shadow's most salient quality, however, is his adoration and devotion to his father, Windrider. He idolizes and venerates this man who represents to Moon Shadow all that is noble and virtuous in mankind. Without complaint, he endures incredible hardships and sacrifices to help make his father's dream come true and delights in his triumph.

Moon Shadow's father, **Windrider Lee**, is a rare individual. Hard working and resourceful, he could easily pursue a successful, secure career at the laundry. Instead, his vision and intelligence lead him to explore the mysteries of flight and the construction of one of the earliest airplanes. A self-taught mechanical genius, he is able to repair all sorts of machines from clocks to automobile engines. Windrider is an idealist and visionary who believes in the innate nobility of mankind and the importance of believing in higher goals and pursuing worthy causes. He also shares many of his son's characteristics. Though showing reverence for his elders and superiors, he is an intensely independent man who endures incredible suffering and adversity to pursue the goals he believes in. He courageously fights for justice and fair play, endangering his own life to avenge Black Dog's cowardly attack on his son. He is also a loving and honorable man. Though surrounded by white "demons" and their prejudice, insults, and threats, he unselfishly helps those trapped in the earthquake. He develops a touching, caring relationship with his son in which he gently counsels and sustains him through childhood troubles. In time, Moon Shadow regards his father as both guide and friend. Windrider also displays unusual wisdom and maturity. Once he has attained his goal of flight, he is content to move on to more practical matters: attaining financial security and bringing his wife from China to provide a real home for his son.

When he comes to America, Moon Shadow leaves behind his loving **mother**. Uncomplaining, this woman works longs hours doing hard physical labor to maintain the family's small farm. A noble person, she has instilled in her son the traditional values and beliefs of her people and endures their separation stoically. Though she finds it difficult to believe in her husband's seemingly foolhardy quest, in her letters she supports him and, through instructions to her son, gives her husband encouragement and reassurance.

The three owners of the laundry are an unusual lot. **Hand Clap** is a good-natured, honest man given to practical jokes and exaggeration. A loyal friend and conscientious worker, Hand Clap acts as a surrogate father to Moon Shadow when he generously accompanies the boy to America. **White Deer** is a sixty-year-old man who is also friendly and supportive of Windrider and his son. An unselfish, affable man, he is considered one of the finest cooks in the area, though being a devout Buddhist he eats no meat. The eldest of the group is Windrider's **Uncle Bright Star**, a man in his eighties whom Windrider respects and obeys not only because of his position in the Lee family but also because of his age. Outwardly, Uncle Bright Star is cantankerous and stubborn, given to gruff pronouncements and dictatorial commands. This harsh exterior, however, masks a caring nature that emerges in time of crisis.

Seemingly scornful of Windrider's mad scheme to build an aeroplane, he ultimately rallies the others to help and lend support. As Moon Shadow states, "In true hardship, he could be a source of immense strength." One reason for Uncle Bright Star's bitterness and grumpiness is his disappointment in his only son, **Black Dog**, who has become an incurable opium addict. Black Dog is a strange, brooding man in his late forties who resents leaving the luxury of his life in China to do drudge work for his father in San Francisco. He has turned to opium for release and, to feed his habit, commits terrible crimes, including robbing and beating up the helpless Moon Shadow. Forced to flee because of his crimes, he is later robbed and murdered. **Lefty** is another worker in the laundry. Like Black Dog, he has an all-consuming vice: gambling, which he has taken up to fill his lonely, empty hours. One time during a dice game he lost his ticket back to China and was so disgusted with himself that he cut off his right hand. Still struggling to control his vice, Lefty is a cheerful, conscientious worker and a faithful friend to Windrider and his son.

After leaving the Chinese community, Windrider rents a stable behind a boarding house operated by **Miss Whitlaw**. Never patronizing or smug, this kindly, generous woman tries to help both Moon Shadow and Windrider whenever possible. She extends her hospitality and friendship to both them and their friends without prejudice, condescension, or thought of reward. Miss Whitlaw takes a genuine interest in their culture and troubles and extends herself to teach Moon Shadow in his few free hours. Even Uncle Bright Star is won over by her warmth and outgoing thoughtfulness. A believer in justice, Miss Whitlaw combats prejudice and intolerance, particularly when it affects her Chinese friends. She also shows remarkable wisdom, maturity, and resilience. Though she loses her home in the earthquake, she salvages a few treasured possessions and, without complaint or self-pity, begins a new life as a housekeeper. Windrider aptly sums up her qualities when he calls her, "a superior woman."

Miss Whitlaw's orphaned niece, **Robin**, is a feisty dynamo whom Moon Shadow refers to as a "fox demoness" because of her bright-red hair. Outspoken and direct, what she lacks in the social graces she makes up for by being amiable and well-intentioned. Like her aunt, she grows to love and respect Windrider and his son. In addition to teaching Moon Shadow English, she instructs him on many practical matters about life in America, including how to confront and defeat a neighborhood bully who has tormented the usually timid boy.

Child of the Owl

(young adult novel, 1977)

PLOT: Twelve-year-old Casey Young, a motherless Chinese American, has been living a pillar-to-post existence with her shiftless, gambling-addicted father, Barney, whom she adores. When Barney goes to the hospital in Stockton, California, after being injured in a mugging incident during which he was robbed, Casey is sent across the bay to San Francisco in the year 1964 to live with her middle-class lawyer uncle, Phil, his wife, Ethel, and their two daughters, Pam Pam and Annette. Casey's unconventional behavior and independent ways lead to conflicts and result in her being sent to her maternal grandmother, Paw-Paw Low, in the city's Chinatown.

Gradually, Casey learns to love the somewhat eccentric old lady who teaches the young girl about her Chinese heritage, tells her a folktale about the owl (the family good-luck symbol), and shows Casey her only valuable possession, a beautiful jade carving of an owl. Casey learns about her family background and about her gentle, loving mother, Jeanie. She also makes several new acquaintances including Mr. Jeh, an ancient family friend; his nephew Sherman, an art dealer; Sheridan, a childhood friend of Barney's; and Sheridan's son, a would-be hood named Gilbert. Their landlord's daughter, Tallulah Chew, whose nickname is Booger, immediately becomes Casey's closest friend.

After his release from the hospital, Barney decides to try his luck on the road, so Casey's stay with her grandmother stretches into months. One night after returning home from a movie, Casey and Paw-Paw interrupt a robbery. Paw-Paw is thrown to the floor and breaks her leg; the assailant escapes with the jade charm. Through some clever detective work by Casey and friends, however, the robber is identified and the charm returned. The culprit is Barney, who, after returning to San Francisco, had entered Paw-Paw's apartment and panicked when he was caught rifling through her drawers. Casey is completely disillusioned and refuses to forgive her father, but when he promises to mend his ways and Paw-Paw, in a gesture of forgiveness, sells her charm to a museum to pay Barney's gambling debts, Casey relents and gives him another chance.

CHARACTERS: The narrator, Chinese American **Casey Young**, is an intelligent, imaginative street-smart youngster who, though only twelve, has learned to cope with adversity and hardship. A hard worker who already has taken odd jobs to help her father, she has developed into a tough, independent individual who dislikes phoniness. She worships her father and his unconventional ways, defending him even though his continual losses at gambling bring them only suffering and poverty. Her honest, candid opinions and straightforward behavior result in conflicts with her button-down Uncle Phil and his family, but are viewed as admirable characteristics by her grandmother. Casey is sensitive to other people's feelings and is responsive to their problems. For example, when she learns that her friend Booger hates her nickname, she immediately begins calling her Talia, the name she prefers. Though outwardly self-assured, Casey is actually a lonely child, anxious for security and eager to put down roots. Paw-Paw and Chinatown help her in her search for identity and self-confidence. She learns to appreciate her Chinese culture and gain strength from it. Overcoming the disillusionment caused by her father's disgraceful behavior helps mold her into a more mature person who has learned the meanings of understanding, forgiveness, and acceptance. Now proud of her heritage and secure in her beliefs and her grandmother's love, Casey can face the future with confidence and assurance.

Casey's father, **Barney Young**, is a born loser. As a youngster, he was gentle, sensitive, and eager to get ahead, but after serving in World War II he returned to civilian life to find that job opportunities were denied him because of his race. Easily discouraged, he turned to gambling and get-rich-quick schemes to make a fast buck. Once hooked, however, there was no turning back. Lacking the inner strength of character to reform and make a new start, Barney sank further into debt, particularly after the death of his wife. Although many call him shiftless and irresponsible, he is actually a kind, loving but weak man who lives in a fantasy world and believes that one day he will suddenly become rich. Slowly, Casey realizes that he is a pathetic, tragic character who is unable to face reality. Though genuinely devoted to his daughter, Barney's addiction leads him to commit acts that hurt and alienate the one person he loves. When he swears to mend his ways and to join Gamblers Anonymous, Casey wonders if he can change. Though skeptical, she decides to forgive him and give him another chance.

Casey's grandmother is the amazing **Paw-Paw Low**. Her son calls her "eccentric" and granddaughter Annette says she is "as superstitious and impossible to live with as anybody can be," but actually she is, like Casey, simply direct, unpretentious and unwilling to accept the false, artificial values of her middle-class son. Though set in her ways, she is nevertheless willing to assimilate some western culture if it appears to be worthy enough. For example, she has become an avid Beatles fan. However, she remains basically un-Americanized, rarely venturing outside of Chinatown and still clinging to the beliefs and traditions of her Chinese ancestors. A part-time dressmaker who is addicted to card games, Paw-Paw lives a modest life in a tiny apartment some would call squalid. Never complaining, she has accepted her life of poverty and its simple pleasures. Her wise, understanding nature fascinates Casey, who soon grows to love her grandmother. Paw-Paw tells Casey about her Chinese heritage and gives her a new perspective on life and a sense of being part of a rich culture worthy of preserving. Described as a tiny, pleasant, round-faced woman, she has bright-red cheeks and frizzy gray hair. Paw-Paw is loyal and loving toward both family and friends. Her trusting nature and faith in the goodness of others is shown particularly when she refuses to turn Barney over to the police, instead selling her precious jade charm to help rehabilitate him.

Paw-Paw's son, **Phil Low**, known to Casey as Phil the Pill, is "a hotshot lawyer with a fancy house." Short, fat, and afflicted with dandruff, Phil has abandoned his cultural birthright in favor of solid, dull, American middle-class values. A smug, self-satisfied conformist, he is proud of his accomplishments, scornful of those, like Barney, less fortunate than himself, and almost ashamed of his ethnic background. Casey astutely sums up his character: "There was nothing he valued inside of himself; it was only the things outside—like he could make up for being empty inside by having a lot of stuff outside." Phil's family also reflects his values and materialism. Wife Ethel maintains a well-ordered, modern household that, she hopes, is the envy of others; eldest daughter **Annette Low**, a junior at Berkeley, is president of her sorority and preoccupied with her looks and status; and younger daughter **Pam Pam Low**, short for Pamela, is a goody-goody snob who looks down on Casey and her common ways.

Casey's friends in Chinatown include **Mr. Jeh**, a dignified, elderly man who, though destitute, maintains a formal appearance and courtly manners. He befriends Casey, acquaints her with some of the history and cultural traditions of Chinatown, and elicits the help of his nephew, **Sherman**, a fat, avaricious antique dealer, to help locate Paw-Paw's stolen charm.

Casey's best friend, the landlord's daughter, has problems with her first name. Christened **Tallulah Bankhead Chew**, she would like to be called **Talia** but is best known as **Booger**, because of a nose-picking habit she once had. A quiet, lonely, overweight girl, she conceals an amazing artistic talent, particularly in dress design. Under Casey's tender care and guidance, Talia gains confidence and the two become fast friends.

In trying to reconstruct her parents' past, Casey locates her father's childhood friend, **Sheridan**, who is still only an insignificant clerk at an Orange Julius snack bar. Like Barney, he encountered discrimination and disappointments in the job market, but, always a realist, he has settled for menial work and a life of honesty rather than escape into a life of crime or gambling like Barney. His son, **Gilbert**, is a flashy dresser and amateur hood who models his behavior on the current Hollywood star, James Dean. Dressed in leather and feigning a slouching swagger, he is the chauffeur for a professional gambler. Behind the tough exterior, however, Gilbert is a caring, sympathetic man who anonymously tries to help others, including Casey, with small gifts of money. He risks his life to retrieve Paw-Paw's missing charm and, like Barney, promises at the end of the story to reform and lead a straight life.

Further Reading

Authors and Artists for Young Adults. Vol. 5. Detroit: Gale Research, 1990.

Berger, Laura Standley, ed. *Twentieth Century Young Adult Writers.* 1st ed. Chicago: St. James, 1994.

Children's Literature Review. Vol. 17. Detroit: Gale Research, 1989.

Contemporary Literary Criticism. Vol. 35. Detroit: Gale Research, 1985.

Estes, Glenn E., ed. *American Writers for Children since 1960: Fiction.* Vol. 52 of *Dictionary of Literary Biography.* Detroit: Gale Research, 1986.

Holtze, Sally Holmes, ed. *Fifth Book of Junior Authors and Illustrators.* New York: H. W. Wilson, 1983.

Something about the Author. Vols. 7, 69. Detroit: Gale Research, 1975, 1992.

Jane Yolen

1938-, American young adult novelist

Dragon's Blood

(science fiction, 1982)

PLOT: On the planet Austar IV, thirteen-foot-long dragons are raised to fight in gaming pits. One of the breeding farms employs fifteen-year-old Jakkin, whose job it is to clean the stables and take care of the male dragons. He and his friends Slakk and Errikkin work for the cruel Likkarn, who is usually under the influence of the mind-altering drug known as blisterweed. Although Jakkin was born into the Master caste, and therefore should be free, after his father died he was sold into slavery as a Bonder.

Like most Bonders, Jakkin wants to buy back his freedom. His plan is to steal a fertile egg and raise a fighting dragon on a small secret patch of land where he is growing blisterweed and burnwort for the dragons to eat. But when the eggs hatch at the farm and are counted, Jakkin is in the hospital recovering from an attack by one of the dragons. When he recovers with the help of an attractive nurse named Akki, he finds that the eggs of one of the dragons has not been counted. He takes the egg to his patch of land. When he gets back, narrowly missing detection, he reports that he saw a feared bird called a drakk. With his help the drakk is killed and Jakkin is a hero.

One day, Jakkin and his dragon are attacked by another drakk. The boy is wounded but is once more attended by Akki, who has discovered his hiding place. Jakkin begins to train his dragon, which he names Jakkin's Red, to fight. Akki helps him to obtain the necessary registration papers. At the first fight, Jakkin is worried when he learns that his dragon must fight a veteran called Bottle O'Rum. He is also upset because Master Sarkkhan, who owns the breeding farm where the boy works, is going to be at the fight.

After a fierce battle, Red wins in an upset. Jakkin then learns that Sarkkhan deliberately planted the extra dragon egg a year ago, hoping the boy would steal it to obtain his freedom just as Sarkkhan had once done. Sarkkhan has been monitoring Jakkin's actions all year with the help of his daughter, Akki. Jakkin can now buy his freedom and renames his dragon Heart's Blood. He wants to marry Akki, but she leaves the nursery. However, Jakkin plans to wait for her to come back to him.

CHARACTERS: Jakkin is a young Bonder who longs to buy his freedom. He sees that his only chance to do so is to steal a dragon egg so that he can raise a fighting dragon, but he is hampered by the fact that his experience has only been with grown dragons. His father never had time to teach Jakkin the skills that would allow him to sense a living dragon within the shell, which would make stealing an egg much easier. Jakkin's father had been killed by a dragon long ago, and his mother had had to sell herself and her young son into slavery as a result.

Jakkin single-mindedly throws himself into the task of training his dragon so that he can earn enough money to buy back his freedom. But training a dragon is no easy job, and Jakkin must show patience, courage, and intelligence to accomplish his goal. He becomes so involved with this that he forgets to get the necessary registration papers. Fortunately, Akki obtains them for him. when Jakkin's Red wins his first match, Jakkin earns his freedom. He is surprised to learn that he has Sarkkhan to thank for it.

Lithe, black-haired **Akki** becomes Jakkin's ally in his quest for freedom. When he is injured, she tends his wounds and nurses him back to health. Jakkin does not know for some time that Akki is actually Sarkkhan's daughter. When Jakkin is able to buy his freedom, he wishes to marry Akki, but she proves to be a more independent spirit. When Jakkin tells her that her father said she needed Jakkin to be her master and take care of her, Akki laughs and calls them both foolish children. She leaves, but Jakkin hopes she will return someday.

Jakkin is a bond servant in **Master Sarkkhan**'s dragon barns on Austar IV. He learns that Sarkkhan deliberately planted the extra dragon egg in the hope that the boy would steal it to earn his freedom, just as he once did. When Jakkin accuses Sarkkhan of merely tormenting or playing with him, the master replies that stealing the egg was a kind of test for Jakkin. Some people are meant to be bonders, he tells the boy, and some to be masters. Jakkin had to prove himself worthy of being a master. Sarkkhan grants Jakkin his freedom and promises to sponsor the boy in return for the first hatching after Jakkin's dragon has mated.

Two minor characters are **Slakk** and **Errikkin**, Jakkin's two bondmates. Although the three boys are close, Jakkin does not confide to them his secret ambition to steal a dragon's egg.

The Devil's Arithmetic

(young adult novel, 1988)

PLOT: Twelve-year-old Hannah Stern finds the Jewish holidays boring. She is tired of listening to the same stories about the Holocaust over and over again because it all happened before she was born and has nothing to do with her, she thinks. Whenever Grandpa Will goes into one of his strange fits, showing the tattoo on his left arm from a concentration camp and shouting in English and Yiddish, she doesn't want to listen.

During the Passover Seder, however, something very unusual happens. Her younger brother, Aaron, calls to her to open the door to let in the prophet Elijah. When she does so, Hannah finds herself back in the 1940s in a Polish shtetl, a Jewish village where everyone seems to think that her name is Chaya, Hannah's Hebrew name given her to honor her Aunt Eva's dead friend. Hannah can't understand what is happening to her, but she soon begins to forget about her former life.

As Chaya, Hannah becomes very popular in the village. The young people there are entranced with the stories she recalls from movies like *Star Wars, Fiddler on the Roof,* and *Yentl.* Then, one day, Nazi soldiers arrive in the village to take the Jews to concentration camps. With her new friends, including Gitl, Shmuel, Yitzchak, and Rivka, Hannah is herded into a boxcar for the trip. For four days, they travel in deplorable conditions. The real horror begins, however, after they arrive at the camp and no one knows who will be the next chosen to die. Hannah learns that the "devil's arithmetic" involves counting the days that she survives.

Finally, the day comes when Hannah's friend, Rivka, is chosen to be exterminated, but Hannah takes her place instead. Determined that the story of the Holocaust will never be forgotten, she goes through the door repeating the tale of a little girl from New Rochelle named Hannah Stern. When she turns to look back, she is once more at the Seder table with her family. For the first time, Hannah is no longer bored with the stories of the Holocaust. When she asks her Aunt Eva to tell her about the past, Eva begins: "In my village, in the camp . . . in the past, I was called Rivka."

Hannah Stern doesn't appreciate the history of the Holocaust until she is transported back in time and meets her aunt in a concentration camp.

CHARACTERS: Hannah Stern is a typical teenager growing up in a middle-class Jewish American family. She finds the old traditions boring and grows tired of hearing the stories about concentration camps repeated over and over again. Hannah does not understand her family's preoccupation with the past, especially Grandpa Will's obsession. Her lack of comprehension is illustrated by an incident in which she tries to please him by writing a string of numbers on her left arm just like her grandfather's tattoo. He becomes terribly upset, and Hannah never quite forgives him or even understands what had so upset him.

However, once Hannah steps back into the world of the Holocaust and becomes immersed in the strange and terrifying world of concentration camps, she learns firsthand why the experience was so important to her family. Making friends with the people from the shtetl and suffering with them in the camp, she grows to love them so much that she is willing to sacrifice herself for the young Rivka. When Hannah returns to the present and learns that Rivka and her Aunt Eva are one and the same, a powerful connection is made between the generations.

At the beginning of the novel, Hannah has a hard time understanding her elders. **Grandpa Will** spends a good deal of his time shouting at the television set and raising his left arm, the one with the tattoo numbers he received at a concentration camp. He is also given to strange fits, during which he thinks he is back in the camp and begins screaming in English and Yiddish. **Aunt Eva**, on the other hand, does not express herself so angrily. When Hannah was a young child, she was fascinated with Aunt Eva, who seemed magical to her. Now that Hannah is older, the magic seems to have disappeared, although sometimes, when Aunt Eva lights the candles and says prayers, she seems almost pretty to her young niece. In an odd way, Hannah feels she shares some unnamed bond with her aunt. Later, when she returns to the present world from her strange journey into the past, she learns that Aunt Eva was called **Rivka** back in Poland, the name of the young girl whose life Hannah saved. Rivka is a plain young girl who protects Hannah and the others in the camp by showing them how to survive. Without her guidance, many of the prisoners would have died. Hannah repays that kindness by taking Rivka's place as one of the "chosen" to die.

In the past, Hannah also meets **Shmuel** and his sister, **Gitl**. Apparently, they are her uncle and aunt, although Hannah had no prior knowledge of them. Shmuel is a big, bearded, happy man who smells of horses. Along with **Yitzchak**, he becomes part of a plan to escape from the camp, but the plan fails and he suffers a horrible death. According to Eva's story, Yitzchak survived and moved to Israel, where he remained friends with Gitl all his life. He became a politician and finally a member of Israel's senate, the Knesset. Gitl also survived the camp, although she weighed only seventy-three pounds at the time of her rescue by the Allies in 1945. She emigrated to Israel, never married, but lived well into her seventies. Gitl organized a rescue mission to help survivors of the camps to reunite with family members. The mission later became an adoption agency, which she named after her niece, Chaya, who died a hero in the camp.

Further Reading

Berger, Laura Standley, ed. *Twentieth-Century Children's Writers.* 4th ed. Detroit: St. James, 1995.

———, ed. *Twentieth-Century Young Adult Writers.* 1st ed. Detroit: St. James, 1994.

Chevalier, Tracy, ed. *Twentieth-Century Children's Writers.* 3rd ed. New York: St. James, 1989.

Estes, Glenn E., ed. *American Writers for Children since 1960: Fiction.* Vol. 52 of *Dictionary of Literary Biography.* Detroit: Gale Research, 1986.

Something about the Author. Vols. 4, 40, 75. Detroit: Gale Research, 1973, 1985, 1994.

Ward, Martha, ed. *Authors of Books for Young People.* 3rd ed. Metuchen, NJ: Scarecrow, 1990.

Yolen, J. H. *Touch Magic: Fantasy, Faerie and Folklore in the Literature of Childhood.* New York: Philomel, 1981.

Paul Zindel

1936-, American young adult novelist and playwright

The Pigman Books

(young adult novels, 1968, 1980)

PLOT: ***The Pigman*** (1968) introduces readers to high school sophomores Lorraine Jensen and John Conlan. Rebelling against a society they don't understand and families they can't respect, Lorraine and John find comfort in their offbeat friendship. One of their amusements is to pick a name from the phone book and try to engage the stranger in a long conversation. Lorraine picks "Pignati, Angelo," which begins their strange friendship with the Pigman. Despite themselves, Lorraine and John become caught up in the life of this cheerful but lonely person, who refuses to face the reality of his beloved wife's death. When the teenagers discover his extensive collection of figurine pigs, they nickname him the Pigman and begin to meet regularly at his little house. They are confused by their own fascination but touched by his innocent sharing of love and his generous, undemanding nature. After he suffers a heart attack, Lorraine and John use his home as a private place while they wait for his return. Unfortunately, John decides to stage a party for schoolmates, which gets out of hand, and he becomes very drunk. The house is damaged and, worse, so is the Pigman's beloved figurine collection. The old man returns in the midst of the carnage and, overwhelmed by what has happened, he dies. Lorraine and John are left with feelings of great loss and guilt, aware that with the death of the Pigman, their childhood has also come to an end. It is no longer possible to blame others for their actions, only themselves. The Pigman had taught them that.

The Pigman's Legacy (1980) continues the story of Lorraine and John, who discover that the Pigman's former house is inhabited by a squatter, Colonel Parker Glenville, a once famous subway designer and now a suspicious, angry, and ailing man. Lorraine and John once again become caught up in the life of an older person. When the Colonel becomes ill, they enlist the aid of Dolly Racinski, a cleaning woman at their school. At the Colonel's urging, the four head for Atlantic City, where the old man intends to spend his hoard of silver dollars. They win a good deal of money and then quickly lose it, for which John feels responsible. The Colonel, however, tells them that the happiness they have shared more than makes up for any loss. Upon their return, the Colonel ends up in the hospital, where he marries Dolly on his deathbed. But instead of being sad, Lorraine and John slowly become aware of their true feelings for each other. They realize that this old man has given them a priceless gift, a gift that started with the Pigman. The legacy is love.

The Pigman's Legacy is a young adult novel of transition. Although John and Lorraine are far from mature individuals in the second book, there are obvious signs that they are growing and maturing in their understanding of themselves and others.

Lorraine and John take a step toward adulthood in their relationship with a lonely widower they nickname the Pigman.

CHARACTERS: John Conlan, described as six feet tall with longish brown hair and gigantic blue eyes, doesn't so much hate school as he just hates everything. John lives in a society with which he is often at odds. He knows he smokes and drinks too much, which is part of the reason he does it. He is rebellious against his family; most of this rebellion is directed against a father who lives for his work, admires an older son who has joined the business, and finds John's dream of being an actor incomprehensible. John is openly contemptuous of the fact that he can so easily "snow" his parents, but it is obvious that he wants to be shown that they really notice and love him. Yet John often seems unaware of how his own attitude and character contribute to his rocky relations with his parents and other adults. In truth, he is a difficult youngster, who regularly shows his immaturity despite his bravado and condescending attitude. Much more than Lorraine, he is apt to act before he thinks and then suffer the consequences of his carelessness, although in *The Pigman's Legacy* the beginnings of maturity and a sense of responsibility begin to show.

Lorraine Jensen, like John, is a lonely teenager who feels alienated from society. However, she is more in tune with her own feelings, admitted or not, than John is. She is more apt to think about the consequences of her actions, even if she often goes ahead with John's plans anyway. Sometimes annoyed and disgusted by what he does, she nevertheless admires his strength and daring as much as she is drawn to his good looks. Lorraine is also a little more compassionate and realizes that John secretly harbors a similar empathy for others that comes to light during their short involvement with the Pigman. Very much like John, Lorraine does not feel respect for her family, which, in her case, is her mother. Lorraine actually tries hard to get along with her mother, but, as with John's parents, her mother can't seem to see past her own fears, insecurities, and unhappiness to understand how her daughter feels. Although Lorraine's mother constantly harps about where her daughter spends her time, she doesn't make a genuine effort to get involved in her daughter's life and lets her do as she pleases. Deep down, Lorraine wishes it were not quite so easy to "get away." She would like her mother to care, to take the time to find out what she is doing with her time. Lorraine is a short step ahead of John on the road to maturity and adult understanding. Both she and John become painfully aware of the end of childhood and irresponsibility as they accept their actions in the fate of their friend, the Pigman.

Angelo Pignati (*The Pigman*) is jokingly named **the Pigman** by John and Lorraine because of his incredible pig figurine collection. He is a lonely, cheery, almost childlike old man, who lives in a world of his own making. In this world, he can refuse to accept the reality of his beloved wife's death and can find happiness in his communication with his closet friend, the baboon from the zoo. The Pigman has retreated into his fantasy world as an escape, a place where he can maintain the friendship he so desperately needs. Mr. Pignati and the Colonel in *The Pigman's Legacy*, are people that Zindel feels every young person should find. It is people like the Pigman who teach that experience is wonderful, that being different is wonderful. The Pigman teaches you to recognize your mistakes so that you know what you're doing when you repeat them.

If the Pigman is gullible—even amusing—in his innocence, he makes a great change in the lives of two young people. At his death, Mr. Pignati leaves two lonely, confused teenagers with a valuable lesson about the end of childhood. As he opens their eyes, he lets them see for the first time that caring is what living is about, but that caring brings with it a certain responsibility.

Other minor characters are John's mother and father and Lorraine's mother. All three fit into stereotypes. As they see it, they express concern and caring for their children but are too caught up in their own fears and worries to actually see them as the confused, lonely, and needy young people they are. All three parents are really unaware of John and Lorraine's feelings and, indeed, are oblivious to almost anything concerning the true natures of their children.

Colonel Parker Glenville (*The Pigman's Legacy*) is a sick, suspicious, and angry old man, who, like the original Pigman, helps two lonely and misfit teenagers discover themselves. His retreat into a fantasy world may not be so profound as the Pigman's, but he teaches Lorraine and John the same important lessons of being oneself, valuing people's differences, and understanding and accepting responsibility for one's mistakes. When the Colonel acknowledges that the teenagers and Dolly Racinski have filled his last hours with friendship and joy and restored dignity to his life, he completes the Pigman's legacy of love. As John and Lorraine realize their feelings for one another, this, too, is the gift of the Pigman and the Colonel.

Dolly Racinski (*The Pigman's Legacy*), a high school cafeteria cleaning woman, is a no-nonsense person who takes life, love, and happiness, as they come. She accepts the love of Colonel Parker, short-lived as it is, and will carry on with her life, finding comfort in the Colonel's dog, Gus. She is the better for having shared this feeling with the elderly man.

My Darling, My Hamburger

(young adult novel, 1969)

PLOT: This novel of teenage sexual awakening and emotional maturity deals with the consequences of premarital sex and the trauma of abortion. It points out the fact that when life presents challenges, decisions must be made, and some of them are tough. But, once made, one must learn to live with the consequences.

It is senior year for four high school kids in the 1960s. Liz Carstensen, Maggie Tobin, Sean Collins, and Dennis Holowitz live in an unspecified waterfront community, and their lives revolve around the happenings during their last year in high school. The expectations of their teachers and of their parents all add to the pressures they feel. Liz and Sean come from middle-class backgrounds, whereas the families of Maggie and Dennis are less well established.

All four teenagers have problems. Liz can't talk to her mother and gets constant verbal abuse from her stepfather, whose interest in her sexual activity arouses suspicions about his own motives. Maggie is overweight and has little self-confidence. To her, Liz is the perfect teenager and exactly what Maggie wants to be. Sean has difficulty with his macho father, who can't understand how his own son can prefer creative writing to football. At times, Sean has contemplated suicide. His buddy, Dennis, also is unable to communicate with his parents. He is shy and self-conscious about his looks. Maggie describes him as "an undernourished zucchini."

Maturity comes slowly to these four during their senior year, and Maggie and Dennis begin to date. She loses weight and starts to like herself a little more. Dennis gains weight and resembles a thin vegetable less and less. His growing relationship with Maggie adds to his self-confidence as well. Encouraged by Maggie and Dennis, Liz and Sean also begin to date, but they soon run into the problem of premarital sex. Sean asserts that it is natural because they care about each other, but Liz refuses. Although Liz's mother encourages her daughter to break off with Sean because he is not good enough for her, Liz deliberately throws herself at handsome Rod to make Sean jealous. After Sean rescues Liz from a near rape, the two young people make love.

Shortly before graduation, Liz discovers that she is pregnant. Although Sean admits responsibility and says he loves her, he is soon dismayed by the thought that a child will ruin his chances for college. Pretending to be asking about someone else, Sean talks to his father about the situation and is given one word of advice: abortion. Because Liz is unable to confide in her parents, the illegal abortion is arranged for her by Rod.

Liz develops complications following the abortion, forcing Maggie to confide in Liz's parents. This in turn makes Liz feel that Maggie has betrayed her. Their friendship is destroyed, and that same night Maggie loses Dennis as well. He feels rejected because Maggie broke an important date with him to be with Liz. The two get together again at graduation and talk it out, but they both realize they have changed and their relationship will never be the same. Neither will life be the same for Sean and Liz. The knowledge of what has happened, what Liz has gone through, and the consequences of their thoughtless sexual act will be with him forever. But, of course, it is Liz who suffers the most, both physically and emotionally. She draws into a shell and does not attend graduation. She has paid a high price for her mistake.

CHARACTERS: Liz Carstensen is an attractive and confident teenager when the story opens. She is, however, troubled by her relationships at home. She has little or no rapport with her mother, who Liz feels constantly submerges her own personality to get along with her second husband, who disgusts Liz. His constant verbal abuse and preoccupation with his stepdaughter's sex life arouse her suspicions that he has an unnatural interest in her. Although her troubles stem in part from her parents, some of the blame falls on her as well because she abandons a sense of responsibility for her own actions and therefore suffers real and terrible consequences. This experience has forever changed the articulate, loving young teenager, and her silence after the abortion becomes a sign of her retreat into herself.

Like Liz, **Sean Collins** has difficulty relating to his home life and, also like Liz, he abandons personal responsibility in a time of crisis. He is alienated from his father and from others around him, except for Liz. Although he attempts to "do the right thing" by proposing marriage to Liz, his life is forever changed when he begins to realize the true consequences of what they have done. Sean is unable to explain the depth of his confusion and pain over the abortion that Liz endures, but it is evident in small, almost veiled ways as he struggles to come to terms with the consequences of his actions.

Maggie Tobin makes difficult, costly decisions, too, such as when her friendship and feelings for Liz lead to the end of her relationship with Dennis. Although Maggie's decision to tell the truth to Liz's parents has cost her Liz's friendship, the decision was the right one for Maggie, and she accepts the consequences, becoming a more mature and thoughtful person in the process.

Shy and self-conscious **Dennis Holowitz** blossoms in his relationship with Maggie, but what he sees as her rejection of him leaves him with the old feelings of hurt and abandonment. His reunion with Maggie illustrates his emotional growth during the year, even though it means that their relationship has changed and they will go their separate ways.

Handsome **Rod**, whom Liz uses to make Sean jealous, has already gone through one abortion experience: he walked out on another girl who was pregnant with his child. A cynical good-for-nothing, Rod finds amusement in arranging the illegal abortion.

The minor characters in the novel are important to the motivations for the four central characters. Although Dennis's parents and Maggie's mother are portrayed in a positive light, the others are not. **Mrs. Carstensen** sacrifices her relationship with her daughter by submerging her own personality to live in peace with her husband. **Mr. Carstensen** is a brutish, troubled man whose interest in his stepdaughter's sexuality takes on ominous undertones. Sean's father, **Mr. Collins**, is a macho male stereotype who so alienates his son that Sean is basically unable to show affection for anyone except Liz.

I Never Loved Your Mind

(young adult novel, 1970)

PLOT: Dewey Daniels is not your typical seventeen-year-old. Having dropped out of school, he works at the Richmond Valley Hospital, directly under the supervision of Mr. Donaldson, whose physique reminds Dewey of an egg. Mr. Donaldson wants to know why Dewey quit school, to which Dewey answers that he wasn't learning anything. He likes to write, but he doesn't see why he needs to go to school for that. Hospital work is a cinch, even though Dewey passes out the first time he sees a tracheotomy performed. With time, he gets a little better acclimated to hospital work, although it can involve such unpleasant tasks as having to listen to the very bad poetry of elderly patient Irene.

Yvette Goethals works at Richmond Valley also. Dewey almost immediately notices that she is stealing supplies from the hospital. Yvette makes no excuses, even when he confronts her with the thefts. Nevertheless, Dewey is intrigued by Yvette, who doesn't seem particularly turned on by him. They do have one thing in common, however, in that they are both dropouts. But that is about all they have in common. Yvette won't eat meat, lives with a bunch of rock musicians, and is tuned in to her inner bodily rhythms; Dewey smokes too much and gorges on cheeseburgers. Despite Yvette's discouragement, Dewey is persistent. He writes her notes, sends flowers, and talks to her a lot. She tries to ignore him, but in the end she finally gives in and accepts his request for a date. They end up at the raunchy Bridge Cafe, where Yvette tells him that she sleeps with the drummer of the band, but not sexually.

When Dewey drops by the house where Yvette lives with the rock musicians, he finds her cleaning house in the nude. They have a romantic interlude, and Dewey notices that the word "THANKSGIVING" is printed in big letters on the bedroom wall. He is in love. But when he returns to Yvette's house, he learns that she and the rock musicians have been thrown out. Afterwards, she doesn't report for work for a few days. When she does, Dewey finds out that Yvette is moving on. She doesn't want him, and he can't understand why. Her last words to him are: "I never loved your mind, Dewey Daniels! I never loved your mind!"

Later, one of the girls at the hospital gets a card from Yvette from New Mexico. Dewey thinks she just wanted to let him know where she was and suspects she is just testing him to see whether he is worthy of her. At the story's conclusion, Dewey isn't sure just what he is going to do, but he eventually admits to himself that Yvette really didn't care for him. The idea floats into his mind that maybe he should go back to school and maybe even pursue a medical career.

CHARACTERS: Dewey Daniels is a likeable seventeen-year-old who thinks he has the world by the tail. He has mostly contempt for the adult world around him. Though he won't admit it, he is actually inexperienced and naive, a fact that is demonstrated when he passes out at his first sight of blood at the hospital. Yet through his veneer of bravado he is sympathetic and sensitive to the needs of the patients in the hospital where he works, especially Irene, who looks to be eighty years old and writes dreadful poetry. As he says, "If someone ever told me I'd meet a wrinkled eighty-year-old sunken skull that looked cute, I'd tell them they were crazy. But she was."

Dewey meets his match in **Yvette Goethals**. He is immediately intrigued with this far-out girl with a chalk-white face and dark hair that hangs straight down like No. 10 vermicelli. She tells him that she left school because she hated it, that she is in tune with her body—she offers him a broccoli sandwich—and that he is a pathological flesh-eater. She's eighteen years old and accuses Dewey of acting as though he were twelve. Yvette is systematically stealing from the hospital—facial tissue, bandages, paper towels, anything she can get her hands on. She explains that she ran away from home some five months ago because her parents were lousy to her.

When she allows Dewey to take her out, she persuades him to give her the five dollars he would have spent on a movie for her because she needs the money for other things. After their romantic evening, Dewey is sure he is in love. But she tells him that they are too different. She is leaving with her friends and she doesn't want him. When he asks why, she tells him that he's too much like most people. He's at such a "primitive level of consciousness that he doesn't even see the hate in him."

After Yvette sends the postcard, Dewey at first thinks that it is some sort of message, some sort of test for him to follow. Then he tells himself what he already knows: Yvette doesn't really want him in her life, and there is no use in kidding himself into believing otherwise. He hasn't made any decision by the novel's end, but something is happening. He starts wondering about elderly Irene and why she has to be suffering in the hospital; he starts thinking about a lot of things. Maybe it's time to get on with some direction in his life after all. A very important person has crossed his life and has gone away, but she made a difference.

Another person who has made a difference in Dewey's life is **Irene**. Despite himself, Dewey begins to care about the elderly woman with her sunken eyes and wrinkled face who he knows will never leave the hospital. Irene insists that she must read her poetry to him. It is dreadful, but the old lady begins to matter to Dewey, and that helps make him a more caring person. Another character at the hospital is **Mr. Donaldson**, Dewey's boss. He looks like a forty-five-year-old Easter egg. He never quite understands the young people he has working for him and is very concerned about his pet's performance in the local dog show.

Confessions of a Teenage Baboon

(young adult novel, 1977)

PLOT: Chris Boyd is a scruffy and depressed teenage nerd and knows it. Living on Staten Island with his mother, whom he calls Helen, he was abandoned by his father, who left a long time ago and has since died. Chris has recollections of him and owns the overcoat his father wore, which he is waiting to grow into. Chris's family life is erratic. Helen works as a live-in nurse, which means that they have to move around a lot, and Chris lives in whatever home Helen is working in at the time. The particular job she has at the novel's beginning is for elderly Mrs. Carmelita Dipardi. Mrs. Dipardi has recently returned from the hospital to her Staten Island house, which she shares with her son, Lloyd. Lloyd drinks and Chris thinks he is weird because, for one thing, kids are always hanging around him. One of the kids is named Harold, a youngster who is far more often at the Dipardi home than he is at his own.

Right away Lloyd is on Chris's case. He gets after him for his scruffy appearance, his out-of-shape body, and his poor eating habits. When he's sober, Lloyd goads Chris, as well as Harold, into getting some exercise in his well-equipped gym. Lloyd also has a running battle with Helen, whom he discovers stealing cans of food and other items from the house. She also has the habit of handing Chris a milk bottle to use at night instead of using the bathroom of the house they are tending at the time. Lloyd finds this out and tells Chris to throw the bottle away, stand up to his mother, and be a man. Eventually, he does. Lloyd also finds out that Chris is carrying around his father's old Chesterfield coat and tells him he should be his own man rather than trying to fit into someone else's clothes. But Chris keeps the coat anyway.

Chris also meets Rosemary, a high school junior who is a frequent visitor to the Dipardi home, too. She tells Chris that, despite the way he acts, Lloyd really cares about his mother. He pays all of her bills, but now that she is dying, he's given up on her and himself. She also tells Chris about what Lloyd's mother did to him. When Lloyd was very young, she found him "playing doctor" with a toy bear. In her anger, she dragged him to the stove and told him she was going to burn him for his sinful act. Lloyd was never the same after that. Now he spends his time with kids in an attempt to prove what a man he really is. After hearing this, Chris begins to feel pity for the gruff Lloyd, as well as love for Rosemary.

Disgusted with the crazy goings-on at the Dipardi house, Helen leaves before her nursing obligations are done, taking Chris with her. But Chris forgets his father's coat and returns. To his surprise, he finds Rosemary with a young man. When Chris confronts her, Rosemary says that, although she cares about Chris, she cares about other people, too. Chris also loses someone else that night: in his despair, Lloyd shoots and kills himself. Before he does, he tells Chris that the reason he has been so mean to him is that Chris reminds him so much of himself a long time ago.

Chris walks outside and finds Rosemary sitting on a bench. "I tried to tell him all the things he had to live for," she says, "all the good things that he did for kids and how we really needed him and liked him, but he was so depressed he wouldn't believe me." Chris holds her hand and says, "Now that I'm ready to learn, he's not here anymore." He remembers that he left his father's coat behind, but now it doesn't matter.

CHARACTERS: All **Chris Boyd** lives for is the day he will fit into his father's coat. He hates his life and detests his mother, though he obeys her, even when he is reduced to urinating in a milk bottle at night so he won't have to use the bathroom of the homes in which they stay. A self-confessed nerd, he shows no interest in improving himself until confronted by the belligerent Lloyd. Grudgingly, Chris begins to listen to the older man and starts to take some small pride in his appearance, while at the same time growing up a little in his relationship with his domineering, disturbed mother. Chris genuinely begins to care for Rosemary and is dismayed to discover that his feelings are not returned in kind. But at the end, sitting on a bench with Rosemary's hand in his, Chris begins to feel like less of a misfit. Life is a mystery, to be sure, but perhaps he can change some of the things about his life, just like Lloyd said. Perhaps he deserves a change.

Life has beaten down Chris's mother, **Helen Boyd**. Having lost her husband, she takes no guff from anyone and has no time for sensitivity and love in her hard life. She steals things from her employers regularly and is seemingly unaware of how she degrades her teenage son. Chris's need for a father figure in his life is partly filled by **Lloyd Dipardi**, a sad and sensitive character. Emotionally scarred in childhood by his mother's actions against the natural sexual curiosity of an innocent three-year-old, he lives for his booze and his interaction with young people. In his own gruff way, Lloyd reaches out to help the young who are misfits just as he is, teaching them, as he does with Harold and Chris, to stand on their own feet and be worthy of themselves and their dreams. His mother, sickly **Carmelita Dipardi**, lives her life oblivious to the great harm she has caused her son. Now in the last days of her life, she remains feisty as always, which Chris discovers when he tries to turn her over in bed one day and she bites him.

Two of Lloyd's hangers-on are described in some detail. **Rosemary** is an honest, caring young woman who understands Lloyd's pain, although she can't help him. She tries to show Chris that it is possible to care about him and also about someone else, which Chris is not yet ready to hear. **Harold** is a precocious youngster whose parents don't want him. His mother is a bartender and his father is a shoeshine man on a ferryboat. They like Harold to spend time at Lloyd's rather than with them.

Further Reading

Angelotti, Michael. "The Effect of Gamma Rays on Man and the Writer Zindel: *The Pigman* Plus Twenty and Counting." *ALAN Review* 16 (fall 1989).

———. "Zindel on Writing and the Writing Process: An Interview." *ALAN Review* 18 (summer 1991).

Authors and Artists for Young Adults. Vol. 2. Detroit: Gale Research, 1989.

Children's Literature Review. Vol. 3. Detroit: Gale Research, 1978.

Collier, Laurie, and Joyce Nakamura, eds. *Major Authors and Illustrators for Children & Young Adults.* Detroit: Gale Research, 1993.

Contemporary Literary Criticism. Vols. 6, 26. Detroit: Gale Research, 1976, 1983.

Estes, Glenn E., ed. *American Writers for Children since 1960: Fiction.* Vol. 52 of *Dictionary of Literary Biography.* Detroit: Gale Research, 1986.

Forman, Jack Jacob. "Father and Mothers, Boys and Girls: Gender Treatment in Paul Zindel's Young Adult Novels." *Journal of Youth Services in Libraries.* 2 (spring 1988).

———. *Presenting Paul Zindel.* Boston, Twayne, 1988.

Gallo, Donald R., ed. *Speaking for Ourselves: Autobiographical Sketches of Notable Authors of Books for Young Adults.* Urbana, IL: National Council of Teachers of English, 1990.

Hansen, Kim. "Something Wonderful Something Beautiful: Adolescent Relationships through the Eyes of Paul Zindel." *Alan Review* 18 (summer 1991).

Something about the Author. Vol. 58. Detroit: Gale Research, 1990.

Top of the News 34 (summer 1978).

Zindel, Paul. *The Pigman and Me.* New York: Harper, 1991.

Character and Title Index

This index includes references to both *Characters in Children's Literature* (*CCL*) and *Characters in Young Adult Literature* (*CYAL*)

A

B

C

D

E

F

G

H

I

J

K

L

M

N

O

Q

R

S

T

U

V

W

X-Y

Z